Chile
& Easter Island

Carolyn McCarthy
Greg Benchwick, Jean-Bernard Carillet,
Victoria Patience, Kevin Raub

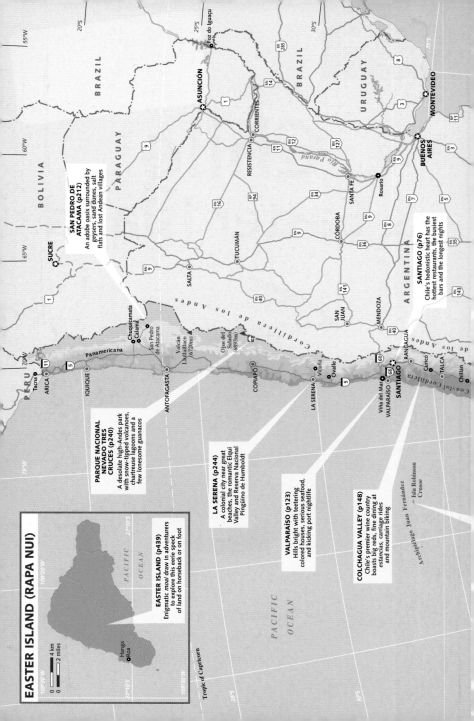

EASTER ISLAND (RAPA NUI)

0 4 km
0 2 miles

PACIFIC
OCEAN

Hanga
Roa

EASTER ISLAND (p439)
Enigmatic *moai* draw in adventurers
to explore this eerie speck
of land on horseback or on foot

SAN PEDRO DE ATACAMA (p212)
An adobe oasis surrounded by
geysers, sand dunes, salt
flats and lost Andean villages

SANTIAGO (p76)
Chile's hedonistic heart has the
hottest restaurants, the busiest
bars and the longest nights

PARQUE NACIONAL NEVADO TRES CRUCES (p240)
A desolate high-Andes park
with snow-tipped volcanoes,
chartreuse lagoons and a
few lonesome guanacos

LA SERENA (p244)
A colonial city near great
beaches, the romantic Elqui
Valley and Reserva Nacional
Pingüino de Humboldt

VALPARAÍSO (p123)
Hills bright with teetering
colored houses, serious seafood,
and kicking port nightlife

COLCHAGUA VALLEY (p148)
Chile's premier wine country
boasts big reds, fine dining at
estancias, carriage rides
and mountain biking

Tropic of Capricorn

PACIFIC

OCEAN

Archipiélago Juan Fernández

Isla Robinson
Crusoe

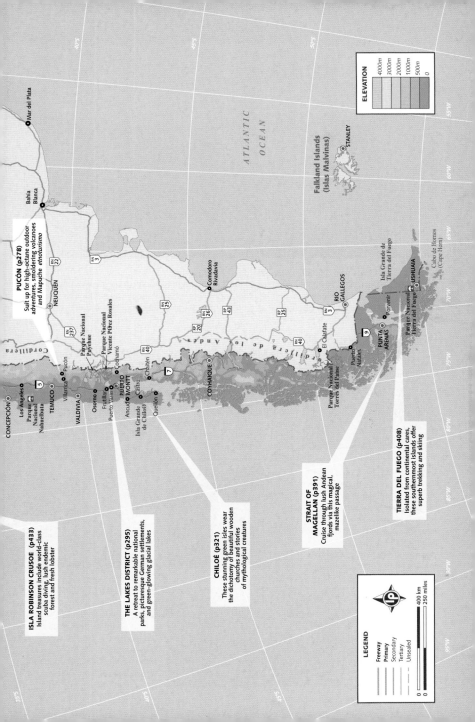

ISLA ROBINSON CRUSOE (p433)
Island treasures include world-class scuba diving, lush endemic forest and fresh lobster

THE LAKES DISTRICT (p295)
A retreat to remarkable national parks, picturesque German settlements, and green-glowing glacial lakes

CHILOÉ (p321)
These stunning green isles wear the dichotomy of beautiful wooden churches and stories of mythological creatures

STRAIT OF MAGELLAN (p391)
Cruise through lush Andean fjords via this magical, mazelike passage

TIERRA DEL FUEGO (p408)
Isolated from continental cares, these southernmost islands offer superb trekking and skiing

PUCÓN (p278)
Suit up for high-octane outdoor adventures, smoldering volcanoes and Mapuche *etnoturismo*

ELEVATION
4000m
3000m
2000m
1000m
500m
0

ATLANTIC OCEAN

Falkland Islands
(Islas Malvinas)

STANLEY

Cabo de Hornos
(Cape Horn)

LEGEND
Freeway
Primary
Secondary
Tertiary
Unsealed

0   400 km
0   250 miles

CONCEPCIÓN
Los Ángeles
Parque Nacional Nahuelbuta
TEMUCO
Pucón
Villarrica
VALDIVIA
Osorno
Frutillar
Puerto Varas
PUERTO MONTT
Ancud
Castro
Isla Grande de Chiloé
Quellón
Codramó
Chaitén
Parque Nacional Puyehue
Parque Nacional Vicente Pérez Rosales
Cordillera de los Andes
COYHAIQUE
Parque Nacional Torres del Paine
Puerto Natales
El Calafate
PUNTA ARENAS
Porvenir
Isla Grande de Tierra del Fuego
USHUAIA
Parque Nacional Tierra del Fuego
RÍO GALLEGOS
Comodoro Rivadavia
Bahía Blanca
Mar del Plata
NEUQUÉN

On the Road

CAROLYN McCARTHY COORDINATING AUTHOR

Mirador de Selkirk (p437), Isla Robinson Crusoe, is where the real Robinson Crusoe searched the horizon for ships. My search brought up murta berries – a yummy windfall – at eye level. The hike takes some two hours of huffing straight up a steep hillside but I'd say the views are worth it, whether you're shipwrecked or not.

KEVIN RAUB Climbing Volcán Villarrica (p284) is no cakewalk. We donned crampons for a fairly technical and precarious glacier segment. On reaching the summit, Villarrica was roaring – its gaseous fumes were a menacing reminder that this is one volcano not to be messed with!

VICTORIA PATIENCE Valparaíso (p123) is my favorite place to get lost. Scrambling up impossibly steep cobbled streets I'd turn a corner onto a full-on view of the bay or find graffiti even more colorful than the paint-chart-worthy hues of Valpo's houses: this tag said it all.

GREG BENCHWICK Here I am in Pisagua (p193), above a grave where 20 political prisoners executed by the Pinochet regime were secretly buried. So why the look of elation? I was fortunate enough to talk with two men who survived the prison camp, and I learned from them that life is too short not to smile.

JEAN-BERNARD CARILLET
Horseback riding is the perfect way to explore Easter Island. I couldn't resist the temptation to clip-clop to the top of Maunga Terevaka (p455), the island's highest point. I was rewarded by a sensational panoramic view – and sore buttocks.

For full author biographies see p506.

BEST OF CHILE

Spindly Chile stretches over half the continent, from the driest desert in the world to massive glacial fields. Its slenderness makes it a snap to explore its boggling diversity of volcanoes, geysers, beaches, lakes, rivers, steppe and countless islands. So, what's on offer? Everything. With easy infrastructure, spectacular sights and the most hospitable hosts around, the hardest part of a visit to Chile is planning your day.

Santiago

All roads lead to Santiago. Scout out the urban edge of this once-conformist capital at design shops and chic clubs or soak up some classic Latin culture at lively café debates and Sunday dinners that stretch all day. Once your urban fix is filled, stroll the parks or take refuge in the Andean peaks just beyond the city skyline.

① Cerro San Cristóbal & Parque Metropolitano

With its 880m summit, steep funicular, and 5km of cable car, this enormous city park (p87) offers stunning vistas of the city. If smog hides the view, there's a zoo, botanical gardens and swimming pools to keep you busy.

② Barrio Lastarria & Barrio Bellas Artes

Don your chunky black spectacles and turtleneck, then strike a pose amongst the designers and writers: with two great museums, a string of bijoux bars and cafés and dinky design stores, these two central hoods (p86) are the heart of Santiago's art scene.

③ Mercado Central & La Vega Central

See some of Santiago's best food *before* it makes it onto your plate at the city's best markets. The Mercado Central (p83) is a shining silver-mine of seafood while La Vega Central (p89) is the mother lode for fruit and vegetables.

④ Maipo Valley Wineries

Sample big-bodied reds at top wineries (p118) without leaving town. From chichi boutique set-ups like Viña Aquitania to vinicultural behemoths like Viña Cousiño Macul or Viña Concha y Toro, some of Chile's finest wine is only a bus- or subway-ride away.

⑤ Barrio Bellavista

Pablo Neruda was as skilled with the cocktail shaker as he was with the pen, so it's fitting that one of his houses (p87) now watches over the bar-lined cobbled streets of Bellavista (p87) where Chile's most kicking *carrete* (partying) goes down.

⑥ Museo Chileno de Arte Precolombino

Ceramics, metalwork, textiles and stone carvings from all over Latin America chart the continent's rich history and culture before the European invasion. Mummies and trippy shamanic accessories make for more offbeat finds (p83).

⑦ Cajón del Maipo

Ditch the traffic and the smog and head for the hills: you can hike, ride and raft your way along the steep-sided canyon of the Río Maipo (p116), just two hours from Santiago.

⑧ La Piojera

It's riotously loud, reeks of sour booze and cat pee, and the name translates as 'the louse-pit.' Yet with its dangerously potent drink mixes, aging barmen and rowdy, guitar-strumming regulars, this 90-year-old bar (p105) is a local institution.

Middle Chile

Step out of the capital and you step into the middle of a vineyard, onto the craggy, surf-sculpted coast or into the powdery snow bowl of an Andean ski resort. Most travelers skip Chile's agricultural heartland, but that's all the more for you to savor. Stunning parks and scintillating surf are just beyond the city limits.

Author Tip
Would-be wine growers can refine their grape-picking skills on harvest tours or play winemaker or blender for the day in special programs (p141); however, we have never heard of anybody getting a permanent job).

① Pichilemu
The water's icy and the sand's black, but with waves this good, who's complaining? Certainly not the scores of surfers that storm this sleepy seaside resort (p149) all year.

② Valparaíso
Unlike many great beauties, Valpo (p123) wears time and gravity lightly. Teetering impossibly atop its achingly steep hills is an array of corrugated-iron-clad houses painted in all the colors of the spectrum.

③ Nevados de Chillán & Valle Las Trancas
The longest ski run, the most snow, the wildest après-ski, the best off-piste offerings – amazingly, they're not exaggerating when they describe this ski resort (p161). Off-season, the views and tranquility here are equally superlative.

④ Parque Nacional Laguna del Laja
Condors circle overhead and an icy lake glitters below, but only your crunching footsteps break the eerie silence of the barren black lava flows of Laguna del Laja (p169). The volcano casts a menacing eye on things – it might be quiet, but it's still active.

⑤ Quintay
As the sun sets over the Pacific, the craggy rocks protecting this tiny fishing cove (p140) are stained a rich pink. Once your eyes have drunk their fill, retreat to dine on seafood stew to the sound of crashing waves.

⑥ Colchagua Valley Wineries
'Explosions of blackberries.' 'Leather and a hint of spice.' At Chile's best vineyards (p148), it only takes a few rounds of the swirl-see-sniff-swill routine to bring out the wine buff in all of us.

⑦ El Enladrillado, Reserva Nacional Altos de Lircay
Some people ooh and aah. Most just pant in exhilarated relief as they take in the panoramas from this 2300m basalt plateau (p156). UFOs are said to land here – if we were little green men, we'd want to, too.

⑧ Buchupureo
Best not to tell anyone you're coming. This sleepy rural beach town (p163), contained by steep green hills and accessible only by dirt road, is the kind of place you want as much to yourself as possible.

The North

Norte Chico's balmy coast of sunbathers and surfers shifts to cactus scrub plains and copper mountains. This is Norte Grande and its granddaddy feature is the Atacama Desert, the driest in the world. Its alien terrain offers plenty to explore, from bubbling geysers and sculpted moonscapes to geoglyphs with the stamp of ancient cultures.

1 Elqui Valley
Find God or some other deity on a pilgrimage to Nobel Laureate Gabriela Mistral's birthplace (p252). From there, it's a simple jaunt or bike tour to the rustic towns of Pisco Elqui (pictured; p257) and Cochiguaz (p256).

2 Around San Pedro de Atacama
Chill out at the stratospheric El Tatio geysers (pictured; p221), climb dunes in the ethereal Valle de la Luna (p220) or have an otherworldly experience listening to the wind howl across the Salar de Atacama salt flat (p220).

3 Parque Nacional Lauca
Head up to ear-popping altitudes in Norte Grande's famous Parque Nacional Lauca (p189), stopping to visit traditional Andean villages along the way.

4 Iquique
Paraglide off a towering sand dune in Iquique (p197), or simply hang out with the dudes on the beach, catching some of the north's best waves.

5 Coquimbo & Reserva Nacional Pingüino de Humboldt
Spirit yourself from the colonial comforts of Norte Chico's La Serena (p244), heading out for day trips to up-and-coming Coquimbo (p251) and to the penguin stronghold of Reserva Nacional Pingüino de Humboldt (p243).

6 Bahía Inglesa
Get too much sun as you lay out for a day of relaxation in Norte Chico's best beach town (p235) or scoot north to the desolate, beachfront Parque Nacional Pan de Azúcar (p233).

7 Parque Nacional Nevado Tres Cruces
Devil dust your way up to this vast and austere national park (p240), stopping to snap photos of guanaco, vicuña and other high-plain drifters.

8 Nitrate Towns
Go back in time to the El Dorado days when nitrate towns like Pisagua (p193), Humberstone (p201) and Chacabuco (p207) reigned supreme. History truly lies just beneath the surface in this arching land of sea and sand.

The South

The further south you go, the greener it gets, until you find snow-bound volcanoes that tower over verdant hills and lakes. This bucolic region makes a great escape to a slower pace. Hospitality is *sureños'* (southerners') strong suit, so take time to enjoy it. Adventurers recharge by going rafting, hiking, riding or hot-springs hopping.

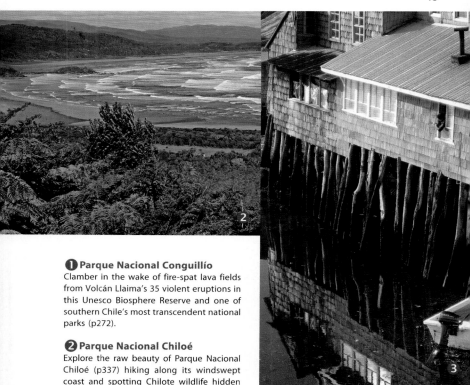

1 Parque Nacional Conguillío

Clamber in the wake of fire-spat lava fields from Volcán Llaima's 35 violent eruptions in this Unesco Biosphere Reserve and one of southern Chile's most transcendent national parks (p272).

2 Parque Nacional Chiloé

Explore the raw beauty of Parque Nacional Chiloé (p337) hiking along its windswept coast and spotting Chilote wildlife hidden deep within the evergreen forest.

3 Isla Mechuque

Wander the idyllic streets of this tiny isle (p328), taking in all of Chiloé's highlights – *palafitos* (waterside houses on stilts), alerce-shingled homes, and tasty *curanto al hoyo* (p326) – on a small island lost in time.

4 Reserva Nacional Malalcahuello-Nalcas

Blink twice and take in the burnt desertscape of ash and sand in this otherworldly national park (p274) under the nose of three stunning volcanoes: Volcán Lonquimay, Volcán Tolhuaca and Volcán Callaqui.

5 Chepu

Kayak the misty Río Puntra through sunken forest in Chepu (p327), the northern and less explored gateway to Parque Nacional Chiloé, where you'll also find Ahueco, a more stunning and accessible penguin colony than nearby Pingüinera Puñihuil.

6 Río Cochamó Valley

Hike off the beaten path through the Río Cochamó Valley (p311), home to a wonder of granite domes, lush rainforest, massive alerce trees and that ever-elusive feeling of discovery.

7 Llanada Grande

Mingle with gauchos while gnawing on traditional lamb *asado* (barbecue) during the cross-Andean trek into Argentina via Llanada Grande (p312), sleeping in pioneer homes and B&Bs along the way.

8 Termas Geométricas

Spend a day romancing your significant other in the stunning Termas Geométricas (p286), an Asian-inspired, red-planked maze of 17 beautiful slate hot springs set deep into a verdant canyon outside Pucón.

Patagonia & Tierra del Fuego

'*Quien se apura en la Patagonia pierde el tiempo,*' locals say (he who hurries loses his time). Weather decides all in this great wilderness so don't rush. Missed flights, delayed ferries and floods are routine; take the wait as locals would – another opportunity to heat the kettle and strike up some slow talk.

Author Tip
Some nationalities chain smoke, Patagonians sip *maté*, bitter tea drunk from a metal straw in a gourd. In the ritual (no, it's not illegal) the gourd travels clockwise among guests. Saying 'thank you' means you've had enough.

❶ Parque Pumalín
Get back to nature in a sublime setting of thundering waterfalls, fern-choked trails and ancient forests (p345). It's hard not to worship Mother Earth at this ultimate outdoor cathedral.

❷ Parque Nacional Torres del Paine
One wilderness rite of passage never loses its appeal, so strap on that heavy pack and hike through howling steppe and winding forests to behold these holiest-of-mountain-holy granite spires (p393).

❸ Beagle Channel
Follow in Darwin's wake by cruising this mythical southern passage in a sailboat (p414) or in a kayak (p420), jeered by the cross winds and sea lions.

❹ Carretera Austral
Every wanderer's dream, this dusty washboard road to nowhere (p345) didn't even exist when you were born. Find out what adventures wait on this 1240km romp through Andean backcountry dotted with parks and pioneer homesteads.

❺ Palena
Aspiring Clint Eastwoods should sample Patagonia's cowboy country – leave the sharp-shooter at home and ride the meandering mountain trails, ford icy rivers and find bonfire barbecues at the day's end (p353).

❻ Caleta Tortel
If you ever wanted to get lost, this tiny village (p370) on the sound awaits. Isolated and ice-field bound, there are no streets; instead, you have to navigate a fun maze of cypress boardwalks.

❼ Isla Navarino
Explore the Americas' southernmost outpost (p413) where colts roam Main Street, yachties trade round-the-world tales and wilderness looms larger than life.

❽ Laguna San Rafael
Its crumbling contours and icy-blue hues are nothing short of awe-inspiring. Setting your sights on this magnificent glacier (p364) – a million years in the making and melting steadily – will make you want to reconcile those inconvenient truths.

Easter Island

Few areas in the world possess a more mystical pull than this tiny speck of land. Look at the enigmatic *moai* (anthropomorphic statues), and you'll see why. Restless? Easter Island is also a great place for a few days' strenuous activity, with a startling variety of adventure options. And for beach bums, a couple of blonde beaches beckon.

1 Tapati Rapa Nui Festival

February's Tapati Rapa Nui (p449) is the island's premier festival. Attend the Haka Pei, when a dozen young males shoot down the grassy flanks of an extinct volcano on a makeshift sled. Awesome!

2 Ahu Tongariki

The monumental Ahu Tongariki (p456), the largest one ever built, has plenty to set your camera clicking. Come here at sunrise, when the silhouetted statues are washed in a golden light – unforgettable.

3 Rano Kau & Orongo Ceremonial Village

Standing on the rim of the sublime Rano Kau (p455), an extinct volcano whose crater is filled by a lake, you'll never forget the dizzying panorama. Built on the edge of the crater wall, the ancient Orongo Ceremonial Village is scenic to boot.

4 Anakena Beach

Who said that Easter Island was only for culture buffs and outdoorsy types? Sun worshippers will be mesmerized by the postcard-perfect, white-sand Anakena Beach (p459), with two major archaeological sites as a backdrop.

Contents

On the Road   4

Best of Chile   5

Destination Chile & Easter Island   20

Getting Started   21

Itineraries   25

History   30

The Culture   44

Food & Drink   53

Environment   62

Outdoors   70

Santiago   76
History   77
Orientation   77
Information   77
Dangers & Annoyances   82
Sights   82
Activities   92
Walking Tour   93
Courses   94
Santiago for Children   94
Tours   94
Festivals & Events   95
Sleeping   95
Eating   98
Drinking   104
Entertainment   107
Shopping   110
Getting There & Away   112
Getting Around   113
AROUND SANTIAGO   115

Pomaire   115
Cajón del Maipo   116
Ski Centers   119

Middle Chile   121
VALPARAÍSO & THE CENTRAL COAST   123
Valparaíso   123
Viña del Mar   134
North of Viña del Mar   138
South of Valparaíso   140
Parque Nacional La Campana   141
ACONCAGUA VALLEY   142
Los Andes   142
Portillo   143
SOUTHERN HEARTLAND   144
Rancagua   144
Around Rancagua   146
Santa Cruz   147
Pichilemu   149
Curicó   151
Reserva Nacional Radal Siete Tazas   152
Talca   153
Around Talca   156
Reserva Nacional Altos de Lircay   156
Chillán   158
Around Chillán   161
Concepción   163
Around Concepción   167
Cañete   168
Salto del Laja   168
Parque Nacional Laguna del Laja   169
Los Angeles   170
Angol   171
Parque Nacional Nahuelbuta   172

Norte Grande   174
Arica   177
Around Arica   185
Chile 11 Highway   185
Parque Nacional Lauca   189
South of Parque Nacional Lauca   192
Pisagua   193
Iquique   194
East of Iquique   201

Destination Chile & Easter Island

Meet a land of extremes. Preposterously thin and unreasonably long, Chile stretches 4300km from the belly of South America to its foot, from the driest desert on earth to vast glacial fields. On its way, it unfurls into an incredible landscape of polychrome diversity, with parched plains, fertile valleys, vineyards, volcanoes, ancient forests, lakes, fjords and those massive glaciers. Bookended by the Andes and the Pacific, it averages just 175km wide. Chile's close borders foster intimacy: no matter where you find yourself, it feels a little like a backyard. You start seeing the same faces. Stay one or two days too long and it may feel like home.

Those who come here would be foolish not to take advantage of the outdoors. When in Mother Nature's playground, play. The options are innumerable. You can seek out sweeping desert solitude, craggy Andean summits or the lush forests of the south. Surf, paddle or sail your way up or down the seemingly endless coast. But you don't have to sweat it. You can also explore Easter Island's mysteries, stargaze, soak in bubbling hot springs or watch glaciers calve. Or simply uncork a bottle of Carmenere to fuel some leisurely café conversation.

Chile is so laid-back that you might get the impression that not much is happening here. But it is. On the heels of whirlwind change, this is a country facing up to its violent past and blossoming into a respected regional force. Its economy has been thriving, cultural barriers are falling and Chileans have rediscovered their voice after a long period of inhibition. In 2006, the same year that Michelle Bachelet was elected the first female president, former dictator General Augusto Pinochet passed away and the nation made a collective push to move on.

Moving on, however, means entering a dialogue about Chile's complex issues. After widespread student protests, the quality of public education has come under serious scrutiny. Income gaps are widening and inflation is quickly rising. The elite have profited far more than the poor from the recent economic good times. Chile's wealth also comes at no small environmental cost, as the country forges ahead with environmentally damaging mining, salmon farming and hydroelectricity projects.

Yet, today's Chile as a whole is more self aware than ever and the younger generation is far more determined than previous ones to have its say in shaping the future. There is a lot at stake. Chile may not be rich in natural resources, but its extraordinary landscapes and vast wilderness amount to immeasurable wealth. And the word is out. Despite the global economic slump, 2008 has seen a 22% increase in tourism and the numbers just keep growing. So all in all it would be a good decision to make your trip now!

FAST FACTS

Population: 16.6 million

Percentage of population below poverty line: 18%

Unemployment rate: 8%

Population growth rate: 0.9%

Adult literacy: 95.7%

Inflation (2007): 2.9%

Growth rate (2007): 5%

GDP: $163 billion

Pisco consumed annually: 47 million liters

Produces 35% of world copper (55% of national exports)

Getting Started

Fun, frugal destinations, a dizzying array of choices – Chile has everything a traveler could hope for. But take a minute to juggle a map of its absurd string-bean design and you'll realize that a trip here takes careful planning. Not only are traveling distances exaggerated by the country's length, but climate and seasonal differences are vast. After all, this is a country with one foot in the tropics and the other touching Antarctica.

Travel here can be as hard-core or as pampered as you please. There are accommodations and transport options to suit most budgets, and tourist infrastructure is fairly well developed, if narrowly focused on certain hot spots. Vast areas of wilderness still beckon to free spirits while luxurious resorts lay in wait for serious relaxation time.

WHEN TO GO

Chile always has a region ripe for exploration whatever the season. But if your heart is set on one part of the country, pick your dates carefully.

Chile's southern charms, including Torres del Paine and the Lakes District, are best visited in summer (December through March) as some are all but impenetrable in winter (June through September). The summer's long days boost outdoor fun, though the spring months of November and December and fall months of March and April can be nearly as good.

Meanwhile Chile in the winter can be a wonderland for skiers; the country's resorts attract hordes from July through September. Middle Chile is best in the verdant spring (September through November) or during the fall harvest (late February into April).

The Atacama Desert can be explored all year, but summer days sizzle and nights are bitterly cold at higher altitudes throughout the year. In the northern altiplano, summer is the rainy season, which usually means an afternoon downpour. Easter Island and the Juan Fernández archipelago are cooler and quieter outside summer; March is an ideal time to visit.

High season is December through March.

See Climate Charts (p464) for more information.

COSTS & MONEY

Chile is not cheap by South American standards, but is more economical than Europe or North America. Prices can double during the late-December to mid-March high season, but travel just before or after the official season and you'll most likely score bargain accommodations. Increased competition in internal flights means that there are good deals to be found (see p480).

Shoestring travelers should budget around CH$20,000 per day for food and lodging, though with determination – camping or staying in hostels, eating in markets – you could cut that to below CH$15,000. Surprisingly cheap and ridiculously filling set lunch menus are served by most restaurants and seafood is served at bargain prices.

From about CH$50,000 per day you can wine and dine well and sleep in cozy accommodations. Families can enjoy excellent deals in fully equipped cabins wherever Chileans like to spend their summers. Spend more than CH$50,000 per day and you can enjoy luxuries that would commonly cost you double that in North America or Europe.

HOW MUCH?

Local call per minute CH$180

A 100km bus fare CH$3000

Bottle of red wine CH$3000

Set lunch CH$3500

Internet per hour CH$500

See also Lonely Planet Index, inside front cover

TRAVELING RESPONSIBLY

At its best, travel is a form of altruism. Each decision we make on the road can have positive and negative impacts on the place we are visiting.

Choosing more sustainable forms of travel, using resources wisely and becoming informed about the options is important.

Government and nonprofit initiatives are giving remote communities a leg up by training locals as trekking and horseback guides and turning rural homes into B&Bs in Patagonia (p353) and around San Pedro de Atacama (p217). These encounters can provide excellent off-the-beaten-path experiences. Look for them in other regions – local tourist offices often have information on *turismo rural*.

Also, look for market restaurants run by women's collectives – who really do know how to simmer seafood – in Chaitén (p350) and other coastal areas.

In extremely popular destinations, such as San Pedro de Atacama, and Torres del Paine, keep in mind that attitudes make an impact too. Using Spanish and adjusting to local customs goes a long way toward maintaining paradise.

Chile's energy resource shortcomings mean that the country has few attractive alternatives (including coal and wood burning, using expensive imported gas and the prospect of widespread damming) to keep the heat on. While visiting, try to keep your energy use to a minimum. At present, recycling is still in its early stages but you can help by traveling with a water bottle that you can refill instead of purchasing bottled drinks.

Lastly, when purchasing souvenirs, choose locally made sustainable goods over valuable hardwoods or mass-made products. Santiago has a good selection of fair-trade crafts (p110).

For a list of sustainable businesses in Chile that we have checked out, consult p524.

TRAVEL LITERATURE

Charles Darwin's time-honored *Voyage of the Beagle* is a perfect companion for trips around Chile, with descriptions as fresh as if he'd just disembarked the Navimag ferry.

Ariel Dorfman's *Desert Memories* is an evocative trawl through Chile's thirsty north, touching on its most ancient and recent past, written by one of Chile's top literary figures. Fans of verse should grab a copy

---

DON'T LEAVE HOME WITHOUT...

- Warm waterproof gear – indispensable year-round in Patagonia
- Bomber sunblock, lip block and sun hat for high altitudes and the southerly ozone hole
- Polarized dark sunglasses for glaciers, desert and the altiplano
- Foldaway umbrella for Santiago and the south from May through September
- A cozy sleeping bag in winter, even if you're not camping
- Camping gear – it's available but expensive, so best bring it from home
- Essentials such as a Swiss Army knife
- Earplugs to combat onboard bus videos and noisy hotels
- Extra memory cards for digital snaps – they're hard to find outside cities
- Toilet paper, since public bathrooms may lack it
- Zoom lens or binoculars to capture Chile's more bashful wildlife
- Medical items – see p488

TOP 10

ADRENALINE RUSHES

In a country ringed by Andean steeps and Pacific breaks, you can pretty much pick your poison when it comes to adventure. Start with these picks and see the Outdoors chapter for more options.

1 Ski your choice of pristine Andean peaks (p72)

2 Burn bicycle rubber in La Araucanía (p280)

3 Hike the 'W' in Parque Nacional Torres del Paine (p395)

4 River-run with the pros on Patagonia's Futaleufú (p351), Petrohué (p309) or Río Trancura (p280)

5 Canter with *huasos* (Chilean cowboys) pretty much anywhere (p73)

6 Paraglide along Iquique's coastal cliffs (p197)

7 Surf Arica's towering breaks (p180)

8 Pack your crampons for Volcán Ojos del Salado (p240) or tackle the less technical Volcán Villarrica (p284)

9 Dive deep off Easter Island (p446) or Archipiélago Juan Fernández (p435)

10 Sand-board dunes near San Pedro de Atacama (p216)

NATIONAL PARKS

Seekers of spectacular scenery, nature and tranquility are positively spoiled for choice. See p65 for more information.

1 Parque Nacional Torres del Paine (p393)

2 Parque Nacional Rapa Nui (p454)

3 Parque Nacional Lauca (p189)

4 Parque Nacional Vicente Pérez Rosales (p308)

5 Parque Pumalín (p345)

6 Reserva Nacional Los Flamencos (p220)

7 Parque Nacional Nevado Tres Cruces (p240)

8 Parque Nacional Conguillío (p272)

9 Parque Nacional Chiloé (p337)

10 Parque Nacional Juan Fernández (p436)

FESTIVALS & EVENTS

Book your digs in advance for these hot-ticket events. More information is at p467. The following will get your toes tapping:

1 New Year's Eve (p129), Valparaíso

2 Encuentro Folklórico de las Islas del Archip iélago (p331), first week in February, Chiloé

3 Campeonato Nacional de Rodeo (p145), late March, Rancagua

4 Semana Musical (p301), late January to February, Frutillar

5 Fiesta de Candelaria (p238), early February, Copiapó

6 Festival Internacional de la Canción (p135), February, Viña del Mar

7 Carnaval (p188), February, Putre

8 Fiesta de San Pedro y San Pablo (p216), June 29, San Pedro de Atacama

9 Festival de la Virgen del Carmen (p203), mid-July, La Tirana

10 Carnaval de Invierno (p379), late July, Punta Arenas

of *The Essential Neruda: Selected Poems by Pablo Neruda* edited by Mark Eisner.

The most famous (some say infamous) Patagonian travelogue is Bruce Chatwin's classic *In Patagonia* (see p392), an inspirational and enigmatic Cubist synthesis of Patagonian characters and landscape.

Against the Wall by Simon Yates (of *Touching the Void* fame) is a ripping yarn for armchair mountaineers about a punishing expedition to climb the world's largest vertical rock face.

Sara Wheeler's *Travels in a Thin Country* is a fun meander through the country from tip to tail, without delving too deeply.

'The young Che Guevara's iconic *Motorcycle Diaries* charts his laddish romp through Chile and beyond in the 1950s; to bring the story up to date, try Patrick Symmes' *Chasing Che*.

Part travelogue, part autobiography, *Full Circle: A South American Journey* is a provocative journey through Chile by Luis Sepúlveda, who was exiled for many years. His other works, including *Patagonia Express* are also well worth reading.

The Last Cowboys at the End of the World: The Story of the Gauchos of Patagonia, by Nick Reding, is a fascinating account of the oft-overlooked culture of Chile's southern gauchos.

For more Chilean literature, see p48.

> 'The young Che Guevara's iconic *Motorcycle Diaries* charts his laddish romp through Chile and beyond in the 1950s'

INTERNET RESOURCES

Chile Information Project (www.chip.cl) Umbrella for English-language *Santiago Times;* discusses everything from human rights to souvenirs.

Chiloé (www.chiloeweb.com, in Spanish) Terrific information on the island of Chiloé.

Go Chile (www.gochile.cl) General tourist information.

Interpatagonia (www.interpatagonia.com) All things touristy in Patagonia.

Latin American Network Information Center (www.lanic.utexas.edu/la/chile) Links to Chilean government, politics, culture, environment and more.

Lonely Planet (www.lonelyplanet.com) Has travel news and tips, and you can interrogate fellow travelers on the Thorn Tree bulletin board.

Sernatur (www.visitchile.org or www.sernatur.cl) The national tourism organization in French, Spanish or English.

Itineraries
CLASSIC ROUTES

THE ULTIMATE TASTER
Four Weeks / Santiago to Easter Island

One month in Chile provides a full introduction to its boggling diversity. From **Santiago** (p76), launch into boho capital **Valparaíso** (p123), a great place to wander and feed your creative yen. In winter you can cash in on nearby powder stashes at Andean ski resorts such as **Portillo** (p143). Then turn up the dial with desert heat. Fly or bus to the tiny highland village of **San Pedro de Atacama** (p212). Altiplano ambiance needs several days to absorb; do so visiting the moonlike **Valle de la Luna** (p220), the steaming and strange **El Tatio geysers** (p221) and the stark **Reserva Nacional Los Flamencos** (p220). Back in the village, bonfires and star-stocked skies wind up busy days of hiking, horseback riding or volcano climbing.

Switch gears to rainforest retreat in **Pucón** (p278), where rafting, hiking and hot springs fill up your Lakes District dance card. From **Puerto Montt** (p313), detour to explore the old island culture of **Chiloé** (p321); or steam ahead on a four-day ferry ride through Patagonian fjords and ice fields to **Puerto Natales** (p386). By now you are probably in top shape for **Parque Nacional Torres del Paine** (p393). Give yourself up to a week to tread the trails of this world-famous hiking destination. Then barrel back to Santiago and hop on a plane to **Easter Island** (p439) to puzzle over its archaeological treasures for a week.

Even with four weeks you'll need your skates on to cover all this ground. Remember you'll lose whole days in traveling so it pays to be selective and to take advantage of speedy internal flights. If you have less than three weeks, concentrate on one or two regions to avoid frantic transfers.

HEAD TO TAIL
Two Months / Arica to Patagonia

Shoot south through this string-bean-shaped country to experience one climatic extreme to another. Start in the Atacama, the driest desert in the world, at seaside **Arica** (p177) and venture into **Parque Nacional Lauca** (p189) to see llamas, snowcapped peaks and springy grasslands. Further south, the area around **Iquique** (p194) is famed for its forgotten ghost towns. You can even climb inside the gargantuan copper mine of **Chuquicamata** (p210) for perspective. Cool adobe **San Pedro de Atacama** (p212) awaits, with its weird and wonderful desert landscapes – including the steamy **El Tatio geysers** (p221). Sun, surf and sand make **La Serena** (p244) a place to linger. Stop at New Age haven **Elqui Valley** (p252) for a taste of pisco vineyards before joining the central valley.

The pace picks up in the central valley. Don't bypass the gorgeous tumbledown city of **Valparaíso** (p123) in your rush to wine and dine in pulsing **Santiago** (p76). You can dip into vineyards around **Talca** (p153) or ski the snow at **Chillán** (p158) on your way further south.

Volcano ascents, fat-tire descents and hot thermal baths define the rainforest resort of **Pucón** (p278); or groove to the student beat at waterfront university town **Valdivia** (p289). You can lake-hop across the Andes to Argentinean **Bariloche** (p308), or ferry to the fabled isle of **Chiloé** (p321) for rural relaxation.

Regional hub **Puerto Montt** (p313) can link you to the heart of Patagonia, where you can paddle the famed **Futaleufú** (p351) or trek under the towering canopy of **Parque Pumalín** (p345). Next stop, hike around turquoise lagoons with sawtooth spires exploring **Parque Nacional Torres del Paine** (p393), then detour to Argentina's awe-inspiring **Glaciar Perito Moreno** (p404). Plug even further south to **Tierra del Fuego** (p408) and Isla Navarino to soak up the end-of-the-world ambiance of **Puerto Williams** (p413).

Chile is 4300km from head to toe. This trip can be completed in six weeks, but it's more rewarding to linger along the way. Consider a long-term car rental, or a purchase, to give you more freedom to explore off the beaten track. Arriving in Chile from Peru can also be advantageous.

ROAD LESS TRAVELED

PIONEER PATAGONIA   Four Weeks / Carretera Austral Loop

If you wish to travel only back roads, if you desire getting dirty, almost lost and awe-inspired, look no further than this four-week plan. Following the **Carretera Austral**, this route criss-crosses its little-known offshoots and gives you plenty of time on the hoof. Leave **Puerto Montt** (p313) or Puerto Varas for the **Río Puelo Valley** (p312), where you can hike or horseback ride, staying at remote homesteads. From Puerto Montt, ferry to **Parque Pumalín** (p345), an ancient forest with boardwalk trails to booming waterfalls. Next stop, **La Junta** (p353), where a farmstay and river run will put you in the Huck Finn mode. Check out the hot springs options near **Puyuhuapi** (p354) or if you're not ready to come clean, camp under the hanging glacier at **Parque Nacional Queulat** (p355).

    Coyhaique (p357) is the next major hub. After making connections to **Chile Chico** (p365) on the great Lago General Carrera, hop the border to Los Antiguos and travel Argentina's classic Ruta 40 to **El Chaltén** (p405) for hiking around the amazing Cerro Fitzroy or to **El Calafate** (p400), to see the great glacier **Perito Moreno** (p404) in the Parque Nacional Los Glaciares. From El Calafate it's an easy bus connection to **Parque Nacional Torres del Paine** (p393) via Punta Arenas and Puerto Natales. By now you're in prime hiking shape – enjoy passing the other hacks on the trail, then head back to Puerto Montt via the **Navimag ferry** (p319).

    An alternative route would be to skip Chile Chico and follow the Carretera Austral to its southern terminus – **Villa O'Higgins** (p371). From here, a rugged boat-hike combination can get you across the border to El Chaltén, where you can rejoin the itinerary.

You can discover the wilds of Patagonia in just two weeks, but it's best to allow yourself more time to cover this nearly 3500km route in order to appreciate the remoteness and local pace, and to protect yourself against fickle weather and ferry schedules.

DESERT SOLITAIRE
Seven to 10 days / Iquique Loop North

How about a few weeks sleeping under star-crazy skies, following condor shadows through desert contours? You'll need a 4WD and plenty of food, water and extra gas. Start with a surfboard in **Iquique** (p194) to sample the swells of Playa Cavancha and Playa Huaiquique. The first stop is nitrate ghost town **Humberstone** (p201), where you can poke around and explore the crumbling grandeur. Head north, stopping in the isolated coastal village of **Pisagua** (p193) where algae gatherers work alongside the ruins of busted mansions. In **Arica** (p177) there's plenty of sun and surf as well as a wild crafts market on the edge of town. Your new *charango* (small lute) in hand, head inland to **Parque Nacional Lauca** (p189) via Hwy 11, passing geoglyphs, colonial chapels and mountain villages. Take in the perfect cone of Volcán Parinacota and awesome wildlife in this Unesco Biosphere Reserve. Further south, the remote **Reserva Nacional Las Vicuñas** (p192) shelters thousands of these flighty creatures and few interlopers to spook them, so go easy. Heading south on tough terrain, your reward is reaching the ultra-removed **Parque Nacional Volcán Isluga** (p202), looping back to Iquique.

After hitting northern Chile's coastal highlights, venture into the most raw and remote terrain you've ever seen. Take along extra water and filled gas jugs for this 10-day desert sojourn – probably not the best place to test that bare-bones rental car.

TAILORED TRIPS

SWIRL, SWIG & SMILE

Chile's wineries embrace independent travelers with open arms and flowing casks, so what could be a better excursion into the countryside? Big-bodied reds are crafted in Santiago's outskirts; sample from both a commercial heavy hitter, such as **Viña Concha y Toro** (p118) and a boutique winemaker – our fave is **Viña Aquitania** (p118). You can sip Chile's signature whites in the **Casablanca Valley** (p141), where aspiring grape pickers can join Casas del Bosque's March harvest tour.

Explore the de facto capital of Chilean wine on a **Colchagua Valley wine tour** (p148) at Santa Cruz. Highlights include a carriage ride through Viu Manent's vineyards, the organic, biodynamic wines at Emiliana and the haute hand-picked approach of Casa Apostolle Clos Apalta. Half the fun is getting there – the Santa Cruz steam engine **Tren del Vino** (p147) offers doorstop delivery (with shuttles) as well as on-board wine tasting for over-eager tasters.

Other acclaimed tours take in **Talca** (p157), where lovers of a fine vintage get a varied experience; at Viña Gillmore you can even get wine therapy at the spa. (And you thought you were already getting it!)

CHASING CHE

Follow in the tire tracks of revolutionary icon Ernesto 'Che' Guevara through the route laid out in the cult movie *Motorcycle Diaries*. The youthful Che – then a medical student bumming around South America with his buddy Alberto Granado – crossed into Chile by lake-hopping from Argentina through what is now **Parque Nacional Vicente Pérez Rosales** (p308). This route is now popular with tourists so you won't have to operate the bilge pumps like Che did. Arriving in **Petrohué** (p309), take the road skirting the enormous Lago Llanquihue and past the huge **Volcán Osorno** (p308) – a prime destination for mountain climbers and skiers. From there the adventurers revved their way to the lively, handsome port of **Valdivia** (p289), then courted press publicity and paid homage to Pablo Neruda in his native **Temuco** (p266). As their ancient motorbike sighed its last before reaching **Santiago** (p76), Che and Alberto rode a truck to the beautiful colonial city of **Valparaíso** (p123). You could also shoot up north to see the awesome copper mine of **Chuquicamata** (p210), and poke your nose into a few nitrate ghost towns around the laid-back city of **Iquique** (p194), some of which were still functioning when Che visited. Then round off the Chilean leg of the journey beachside at **Arica** (p177).

History

BEGINNINGS

It doesn't sound like much: a small child's footprint left in a marshy field. However, it took just one little *huella* found in Chile's Monte Verde, near Puerto Montt, to rock the foundations of archaeology in the Americas during the 1980s. The footprint was estimated to be 12,500 years old, and other evidence of human habitation in Chile dated back still further – perhaps as far as 33,000 years.

These highly controversial dates pooh-poohed the long-accepted Clovis paradigm, which stated that the Americas were first populated via the Bering land bridge some 11,500 years ago, after which the Clovis people scattered southwards. This footprint suddenly opened the way for a wave of new theories suggesting multiple entries, different routes, or coastal landings by the first peoples. Following a landmark 1998 convention, the Monte Verde site was acknowledged as the oldest inhabited site in the Americas, although more recent discoveries, notably in New Mexico, are now thought to date back as far as 40,000 years.

The Chinchorro culture began mummifying their dead some 2000 years before the Egyptians. The oldest known mummy dates from around 5050 BC.

EARLY CULTURES

Most pre-Columbian remains have been recovered in the north of Chile, preserved by the extreme desert aridity. Most famous is the nomadic Chinchorro culture, which left behind the oldest known intentionally preserved mummies (see p185 and p83).

OLD POTATOES

The fight is, shall we say, simmering. Peru and Chile, whose cultures overlapped in pre-Columbian times, are at odds over which country grew potatoes first. Like wrestling siblings in the backseat, Peru and Chile have already fought over borders and the bragging rights to pisco. Peruvians say the spud comes from an area near Lake Titicaca. But researchers at Chile's Austral University have evidence showing human potato consumption as far back as 14,000 years ago in southern Chile. That fries Peru's claims – at least for now.

Today, 99% of all European potato varieties can be traced back to Chilean origin, specifically, the island of Chiloé. In recent years, the island has been actively trying to rescue its some 200 indigenous spud varieties. At Castro's annual Feria de Biodiversidad, held each February, local farmers participate in a seed exchange. It seems that diversity went south when the whole world narrowed their taste to *solanum tuberosum tuberosum*. However, the gourmet value and distinct flavours of narrow yellows, nutty purples and stubby blues are encouraging tradition to take root once more.

TIMELINE

12,500 BC	1520	1535
A footprint discovered outside modern Puerto Montt in Monte Verde – the oldest inhabited site in South America – shows evidence of human habitation in Chile long before the supposed migration from the Bering land bridge.	On a voyage where his fleet had already faced mutiny and shipwreck, Ferdinand Magellan, is the first European to sight Chilean territory on November 1, 1520 while sailing the strait now named for him.	Diego de Almagro attempts to conquer Chile with 500 men, 100 African slaves and 10,000 Yanacona Indian porters. Many freeze to death crossing harsh terrain and 4000m passes. Finding no riches, Almagro abandons the claim.

In the canyons of the north desert, sedentary Aymara farmers cultivated maize, grew potatoes and tended llama and alpaca; their descendants still practice similar agricultural techniques around Parque Nacional Lauca. Another important civilization in Chile's northern reaches was the Atacameño culture. It too left remarkably well-preserved remains, from mummies to ornate tablets that were used in the preparation of hallucinogenic substances. The El Molle and Tiwanaku were among other important cultures that left enormous geoglyphs, rock etchings and ceramics, still visible in Chile's northern reaches. Meanwhile, Chango fisherfolk occupied northern coastal areas, and Diaguita peoples inhabited the inland river valleys.

The invasive Inka culture enjoyed a brief ascendancy in northern Chile, but its rule barely touched the central valley and the forests of the south, where the sedentary farmers (Picunche) and shifting cultivators (Mapuche) fiercely resisted any incursions. Meanwhile the Cunco fished and farmed on the island of Chiloé and along the shores of the gulfs of Reloncaví and Ancud.

INVASION

In 1495, unbeknownst to the indigenous peoples of the Americas, their land was already being earmarked by two superpowers of the day – Spain and Portugal. Thousands of miles away, the papal Treaty of Tordesillas was signed and sealed, delivering all the territory west of Brazil to Spain. By the mid-16th century, the Spaniards dominated most of the area from Florida and Mexico to central Chile. Though few in number, the conquerors were determined and ruthless, exploiting factionalism among indigenous groups and frightening native peoples with their horses and firearms. But their greatest ally was infectious disease, to which the natives lacked immunity.

The Spaniards' first ill-fated foray into northern Chile was led over frozen Andean passes in 1535 by Diego de Almagro. He chose the harshest of routes, and many men and horses froze to death during the expedition. However, his subsequent retreat north laid the groundwork for an expedition by Pedro de Valdivia in 1540. Valdivia and his men trawled south through the parched desert, reaching Chile's fertile Mapocho Valley in 1541. There they subdued local indigenous groups and founded the city of Santiago on February 12. Only six months later, the indigenous peoples struck back, razing the town and all but wiping out the settlers' supplies. But the Spaniards clung on, and the population burgeoned. By the time of his death in 1553, at the hands of Mapuche forces led by the famous *caciques* (chiefs) Caupolicán and Lautaro, Valdivia had founded numerous settlements and laid the groundwork for a new society.

So, you don't say…the ancients did drugs? Ancient Atacameños had a hallucinogenic habit, but all that remains are the accessories: mini spatulas, snuff boards, tubes, little boxes and woolen bags.

1535–1880	1540	1541
The Arauco War marks the Mapuches' 300-year resistance. Most meet Chile's revolt from the Spanish crown with indifference. The area south of the Río Biobío remains their stronghold.	After crossing the Atacama Desert and facing its blistering extremes, Pedro de Valdiva and a group of 150 Spaniards start a colony on the banks of the Río Mapocho.	Santiago is officially founded on September 11, despite fierce resistance by indigenous Araucanian people, who number around 500,000 at the time. The presence of colonists brings disease and death to the indigenous Arucanians.

Isabel Allende's historical
novel *Inés of My Soul* is
based on facts from the
real-life *conquistadora*
and former seamstress
who fatefully trailed
Pedro de Valdivia to the
future Chile.

COLONIAL CHILE

Lust for gold and silver was always high on the Spaniards' agenda, but they
soon realized that the true wealth of the New World consisted of the large
indigenous populations. Disdaining physical labor themselves, they exploited
indigenous peoples through the *encomienda* system, by which the Crown
granted individual Spaniards rights to indigenous labor and tribute. This
system was established in northern Chile (then part of Peru). The indigenous population in this northern region was easily controlled, ironically
because they were highly organized and more accustomed to similar forms
of exploitation.

The Spaniards also established dominance in central Chile, but the semi-
sedentary and nomadic peoples of the south mounted vigorous resistance
and even into the late 19th century the area remained unsafe for white
settlers. Crossing the Andes, the Mapuche had tamed the feral horses that
had multiplied rapidly on the fine pastures of the Argentine pampas; they
soon became expert riders, which increased their mobility and enhanced
their ability to strike.

Caupolicán led the
Mapuches in their first
uprising against the
Spanish *conquistadores*.
It's believed he became
a *toqui* (military leader)
by holding a tree trunk
for three days and
nights and improvising a
poetical speech to incite
Mapuches to defense.

Despite the Crown's distant disapproval Valdivia began rewarding his followers with enormous land grants, resembling the feudal estates of his Spanish
homeland of Extremadura. Such estates *(latifundios)*, many intact as late as
the 1960s, became an enduring feature of Chilean agriculture and society.

Mestizo children of mixed Spanish and indigenous parentage soon out-
numbered the indigenous population as many died through epidemics,
forced-labor abuses and warfare. Chile's neo-aristocracy encouraged the
landless *mestizo* population to attach themselves as *inquilinos* (tenant farmers) to large rural estates.

REVOLUTION

Independence movements that sparked into life between 1808 and 1810
were born from the emergence of the *criollo* (creole) class – American-born
Spaniards who increasingly longed for self-government. To facilitate tax
collection, Madrid decreed that all trade to the mother country must pass
overland through Panama rather than directly by ship. This cumbersome
system hampered commerce and eventually cost Spain its empire.

Chile may seem
homogenous but black
culture dates back to
early Arica where a black
mayor was elected in
1620 (the viceroy of Peru
later annulled the
victory). Today
Foundación Oro Negro
preserves black cultural
heritage.

During colonial times, Chile was judged a subdivision of the ponderous
Viceroyalty of Peru, which was based in Lima. This subdivision, called the
Audiencia de Chile, had jurisdiction from present-day Chañaral south to
Puerto Aisén, in addition to the present-day Argentinean provinces of
Mendoza, San Juan and San Luis. But, despite formally being under the
thumb of Lima, in practice Chile developed in near isolation from Peru,
creating an identity that is distinct from its northern neighbor.

Independence movements ignited throughout South America to expel
Spain by the 1820s. From Venezuela, a *criollo* army under Simón Bolívar

1548	1553	1818
Wine comes to Chile via mission-aries and conquistadores. Jesuit priests cultivated early vine-yards; today Chile has more than 70 wineries and international distribution.	Conquistador Pedro de Valdivia is captured in the Battle of Tucapel, when 6000 Mapuche warriors, led by *toqui* (war chief) Caupolicán and vice *toqui* Lautaro, attack Spanish forts in the south. Valdivia is bound to a tree and beheaded.	With independence movements sweeping the continent, Argen-tine José de San Martín liberates Santiago. Under his tutelage, Chilean Bernardo O'Higgins, the illegitimate son of an Irishman, becomes 'supreme director' of the Chilean republic.

fought its way west and south toward Peru. The Argentine liberator José de San Martín marched over the Andes into Chile, occupied Santiago and sailed north to Lima.

San Martín appointed Bernardo O'Higgins second-in-command of his forces. O'Higgins, the illegitimate son of an Irishman who had served the Spaniards as Viceroy of Peru, became supreme director of the new Chilean republic. San Martín helped drive Spain from Peru, transporting his army in ships either seized from the Spaniards or purchased from Britons or North Americans who knew that the Spaniards' loss could mean their commercial gain. Thus it was that Scotsman Thomas Cochrane, a colorful former Royal Navy officer, founded and commanded Chile's navy.

THE EARLY REPUBLIC

Battered, bruised, but buoyed up by their newborn independence, South American republics began to shape themselves in line with the old Spanish administrative divisions. Chile was but a fraction of its present size, consisting of the *intendencias* (administrative units of the Spanish Empire) of Santiago and Concepción, and sharing ambiguous boundaries with Bolivia, Argentina, and the hostile Mapuche nation south of the Río Biobío.

Chile managed to wriggle free of the economic black hole suffered by many Latin American countries during this period. It achieved relative political stability, and set about rapid development of agriculture, mining, industry and commerce.

O'Higgins dominated Chilean politics for five years after formal independence in 1818, but the landowning elite that first supported him soon objected to increased taxes, abolition of titles and limitations on inheritance. O'Higgins was forced to resign in 1823, and went into exile in Peru where he died in 1842.

The embodiment of landowning interests was Diego Portales, interior minister and de facto dictator until his execution following an uprising in 1837. His custom-drawn constitution centralized power in Santiago, limited suffrage to the propertied and established indirect elections for the presidency and senate. Portales' constitution lasted, with piecemeal changes, until 1925.

Robert Harvey's extremely readable *Liberators: South America's Struggle for Independence* (2002) tells the epic history of colonial Latin America through larger-than-life heroes and swashbucklers such as O'Higgins, San Martín and Lord Cochrane.

If you read Spanish, check out the detailed biographies of early Chilean heroes such as O'Higgins and Cochrane on the Chilean Navy website, www.armada.cl. If not, Wikipedia also does a fine job.

COLD HARD FACTS

Little is known about the Selk'nam (Ona) people who once inhabited present-day Magallanes, but it is well documented that they withstood extreme temperatures wearing little or no clothing. On the **Chilean Cultural Heritage site** (www.nuestro.cl), anthropologist Francisco Mena recounts, 'An investigator of the 19th century writes that he once met a naked man, and asked him how come he felt no cold. And the Selk'nam answered: My whole body has become face.'

1834–35	1860	1865
HMS *Beagle* sails along Chile's coast with Charles Darwin on board; the planned two-year expedition actually lasts five, giving Darwin fodder for his later-developed theory of evolution.	French adventurer Orelie-Antoine de Tounens befriends Mapuche leaders and assumes the title King of Araucania and Patagonia. This seemingly protective act ends in his confinement to an insane asylum.	Sheep from the Falkland Islands are introduced into Patagonia, starting a prosperous new era for big landowners in the Magallanes region.

EXPANSION & MINERAL WEALTH

A pivotal boost to the country's fortunes came with the War of the Pacific (1879–84), in which Chile annexed vast areas of land from Peru and Bolivia. The battles began after Bolivia prohibited a Chilean company from exploiting the nitrate deposits in Atacama, then owned by Bolivia. Chile retaliated by seizing the Bolivian port of Antofagasta and wresting the Tacna and Arica provinces from Peru; thus they robbed the Bolivians of all access to the Pacific. This fiercely fought campaign is still celebrated by Chileans with as much gusto as it is bitterly resented by Peruvians and Bolivians.

Santiago's intervention proved a bonanza. The nitrate boom brought great prosperity to Chile, or at least to certain sectors of Chilean society. British, North American and German investors supplied most of the capital. Railroads revolutionized Chile's infrastructure, and the economy boomed. Later, when the nitrate bubble burst, this land would again provide Chile with a get-out-of-jail-free card: copper is still the power behind the Chilean economy. The development of northern ports such as Iquique and Antofagasta also added to Chile's success.

In this era of shifting boundaries, treaties with the Mapuche (1881) also brought temperate southern territories under Chilean authority. At much the same time, Chile had to abandon much of Patagonia to Argentina but sought a broader Pacific presence, and annexed the tiny remote Easter Island (Isla de Pascua, also known as Rapa Nui) in 1888.

Naturally occurring nitrate or 'saltpeter' created an early-20th-century boom. Today, the Atacama Desert is home to 170 nitrate ghost towns, only one, María Elena, remains open.

CIVIL WAR

Mining expansion created a new working class, as well as a class of nouveaux riches, both of which challenged the political power of the landowning oligarchy. The first political figure to tackle the dilemma of Chile's badly distributed wealth was President José Manuel Balmaceda, elected in 1886. Balmaceda's administration undertook major public-works projects, revolutionizing infrastructure and improving hospitals and schools. However, he met resistance from a conservative Congress, which in 1890 voted to depose him. Naval Commander Jorge Montt was elected to head a provisional government.

More than 10,000 Chileans died in the ensuing civil war, in which Montt's navy controlled the country's ports and eventually defeated the government, despite army support for Balmaceda. After several months' asylum in the Argentine embassy, Balmaceda shot himself.

Although they weakened the presidential system, Balmaceda's immediate successors continued many of his public-works projects and also opened Congress to popular rather than indirect elections. Major reform, though, wouldn't come until after WWII.

Watch the intense movie *Sub Terra* (2003) for a savage indictment of the exploitation that used to go on in Chile's mining industry, often at the hands of gringos.

1879–84	1881	1885–1900
Chile's active development of nitrate deposits in Peruvian and Bolivian territories leads to the War of the Pacific; the country increases its territory by one-third after defeating both countries.	While expanding northward, Chile signs a treaty with Argentina conceding all of eastern Patagonia but retaining sovereignty over the Strait of Magellan.	British, North American and German capital turn the Atacama into a bonanza, as nitrates bring some prosperity, create an urban middle class and fund the government.

20TH CENTURY

The Chilean economy soon suffered for its crippling dependence on nitrate revenue. New petroleum-based fertilizers were developed, making mineral nitrates all but obsolete. To add to the country's misery the opening of the Panama Canal in 1914 nearly eliminated traffic around Cape Horn, which had been so important to ports such as Punta Arenas, Valparaíso, Antofagasta and Iquique.

Despite economic hardship, the election of President Arturo Alessandri Palma seemed a hopeful sign for Chile's working class. To reduce landowners' power, he proposed greater political autonomy for the provinces, and taxes to finance better working conditions, health, education and welfare. However, conservatives obstructed the reforms and army opposition forced Alessandri's resignation in 1924.

The dictatorial General Carlos Ibáñez del Campo held power for a few years, but his poor economic policies (exacerbated by global depression) led to widespread opposition, forcing him into Argentine exile in 1931.

After Ibáñez was ousted, political parties realigned. Several leftist groups briefly imposed a socialist republic and merged to form the Socialist Party. Splits between Stalinists and Trotskyites divided the Communist Party, while splinter groups from radical and reformist parties created a bewildering mix of new political organizations. For most of the 1930s and '40s the democratic left dominated Chilean politics, and government intervention in the economy through Corfo, the state development corporation, became increasingly important.

Meanwhile, the early 20th century saw North American companies gain control of the copper mines, the cornerstone – then and now – of the Chilean economy. WWII augmented the demand for Chilean copper, promoting economic growth even as Chile remained neutral.

LAND REFORM

A revealing set of statistics from the 1920s state that around 75% of Chile's rural population still depended on haciendas (large rural landholdings), which controlled 80% of the prime agricultural land. *Inquilinos* (tenant farmers) remained at the mercy of landowners for access to housing, soil and subsistence. Their votes belonged to landowners, who naturally used them to maintain the status quo. Haciendas had little incentive to modernize, and production stagnated – a situation that changed little until the 1960s.

Former dictator Ibáñez del Campo started land reform when he returned from exile and won the presidency back democratically in 1952; he tried to reduce landowners' control over the votes of their tenants and laborers. He also revoked an earlier law banning the Communist Party, before his government faltered and fell.

In 1915, the British Royal Navy took down the German SMS *Dresden* in the harbor of Isla Robinson Crusoe. The infamous war cruiser had successfully slipped detection throughout WWI, only to be discovered because its sailors had joined a soccer match on shore.

In the Santiago's poor urban neighborhood of La Victoria, the protest murals by the BRP (Brigada Ramona Parra) have appeared since the 1940s, stirring up subversive thought. View them along Avenida 30 de Mayo.

1888–1960s	1890–91	1927
Chile annexes Easter Island and confines the Rapa Nui people to Hanga Roa while the rest of the island is run as a sheep ranch until 1953; it reopens to its own citizens in the 1960s.	Tackling unequally distributed wealth and power with reforms, President José Manuel Balmaceda ignites congressional rebellion in 1890; it results in a civil war with 10,000 deaths and Balmaceda's suicide.	General Carlos Ibáñez del Campo establishes a de facto dictatorship, which will prove to be one of the longest lasting of ten governments in the unstable decade.

The subsequent jostling over power brought several important figures into the spotlight. In 1958 socialist Salvador Allende headed a new leftist coalition known as FRAP (Frente de Acción Popular, or Popular Action Front). Meanwhile Eduardo Frei Montalva represented the newly formed Democracia Cristiana (Christian Democrats), another left-leaning reformist party with a philosophical basis in Catholic humanism.

The old order feared these new leftists, and the conservative and liberal parties decided to join forces as a result. They chose Jorge Alessandri, son of former president Arturo Alessandri, to head a coalition between the two parties.

Alessandri scraped through the election with less than 32% of the vote, while Allende managed 29% and Frei 21%. An opposition Congress forced Alessandri to accept modest land-reform legislation, beginning a decade-long battle with the haciendas.

CHRISTIAN DEMOCRATIC PERIOD

The 1964 presidential election was a choice between Allende and Frei, who drew support from conservative groups who detested the leftist physician. During the campaign, both parties promised agrarian reform, supported rural unionization and promised an end to the hacienda system. Allende was undermined by leftist factionalism and Frei won comfortably.

Genuinely committed to social transformation, the Christian Democrats attempted to control inflation, balance imports and exports, implement agrarian reform and improve public health, education and social services. However, their policies threatened both the traditional elite's privileges and the radical left's working-class support.

The Christian Democrats had other difficulties. The country's economy had declined under Jorge Alessandri's presidency, and limited opportunities in the countryside drove the dispossessed to the cities, where spontaneous squatter settlements, known as *callampas* (mushrooms), sprang up almost overnight. Attacks increased on the export sector, then dominated by US interests. President Frei advocated 'Chileanization' of the copper industry (getting rid of foreign investors in favor of Chileans), while Allende and his backers supported the industry's nationalization (placing the industry under state control).

The Christian Democrats also faced challenges from violent groups such as the Movimiento de Izquierda Revolucionario (MIR; Leftist Revolutionary Movement), which began among upper-middle-class students in Concepción. The MIR's activism appealed to many urban laborers, who formed the allied Frente de Trabajadores Revolucionarios (Revolutionary Workers Front). Activism also caught on with peasants who longed for land reform. Other leftist groups supported strikes and land seizures by Mapuche Indians and rural laborers.

The strongest earthquake *ever* recorded, on May 22, 1960, measured between 8.6 and 9.5 on the Richter scale and rattled from Concepción to southern Chiloé. The resulting tsunami wreaked havoc 10,000km away in Hawaii and Japan.

Norwegian Thor Heyerdahl explored Easter Island while crossing the Pacific in the 1950s; it became the centerpiece of his theories about the South American origins of Polynesian civilization. For more details, read *Aku Aku* and *Kon Tiki*.

1938–46	1945	1952
Communists, socialists and radicals form the Popular Front coalition, rapidly becoming popular with the unionized working class and playing a leading role in the Chilean labor movement.	Poet, teacher and foreign consul Gabriela Mistral becomes the first Latin American and fifth woman to win the Nobel Prize (for literature).	Ibáñez returns to power, this time as an elected president promising to sweep out corruption. He revokes the ban on the Communist Party but sweeps himself out with plans for an auto-coup.

Frei's reforms were too slow to appease leftists and too fast for the conservative National Party. Despite better living conditions for many rural workers and good gains in education and public health, the country was plagued by inflation, dependence on foreign markets and capital, and inequitable income distribution. The Christian Democrats could not satisfy rising expectations in Chile's increasingly militant and polarized society.

ALLENDE'S RISE TO POWER

In this discomforting political climate, a new leftist coalition was gathering its forces. With Allende at its head, the Unidad Popular (UP) was shaping a radical program that included the nationalization of mines, banks and insurance, plus the expropriation and redistribution of large landholdings.

The 1970 election saw one of Chile's closest ever results. Allende squeezed 36% of the vote, against the National Party's 35%. Under the constitution, if no candidate obtained an absolute majority, Congress had to confirm the result. Christian Democrats weighed in behind Allende, and thus he became the world's first democratically elected Marxist president.

But the country – and for that matter Allende's own coalition – was far from united. The UP consisted of socialist, communist and radical parties that disagreed on their objectives. Lacking any real electoral mandate, Allende faced an opposition Congress, a suspicious US government, and right-wing extremists who even advocated his overthrow by violent means.

Allende's economic program, accomplished by evading rather than confronting Congress, included the state takeover of many private enterprises and massive income redistribution. By increasing government spending, the new president expected to bring the country out of recession. This worked briefly, but apprehensive businesspeople and landowners, worried about expropriation and nationalization, sold off stock, machinery and livestock. Industrial production nose-dived, leading to shortages, hyperinflation and black marketeering.

Peasants, frustrated with an agrarian reform, seized land and agricultural production fell. The government had to use scarce foreign currency to import food.

Chilean politics grew increasingly polarized and confrontational, as many of Allende's supporters resented his indirect approach to reform. The MIR intensified its guerrilla activities, and stories circulated in Santiago's factories about the creation of armed communist organizations.

Expropriation of US-controlled copper mines and other enterprises, plus conspicuously friendly relations with Cuba, provoked US hostility. Later, hearings in the US Congress indicated that President Nixon and Secretary

Chilean Director Andrés Wood's hit *Machuca* (2004) chronicles the bittersweet coming-of-age of two very different boys during the class-conscious and volatile Santiago of 1973.

1948–58	1960	1964
The Communist Party is banned due to spreading local fears that its electoral base is getting too strong amid the growing conservative climate of the Cold War.	The strongest earthquake ever recorded takes place in southern Chile. It flattens coastal towns between Concepción and Chiloé and creates a tsunami that hits Hawaii and Japan.	On Easter Island, the Rapa Nui (native islanders) are granted full Chilean citizenship and the right to vote.

of State Kissinger had actively undercut Allende by discouraging credit from international finance organizations and supporting his opponents. Meanwhile, according to the memoirs of a Soviet defector published in 2005, the KGB withdrew support for Allende because of his refusal to use force against his opponents.

Faced with such difficulties, the Chilean government tried to forestall conflict by proposing clearly defined limits on nationalization. Unfortunately, neither extreme leftists, who believed that only force could achieve socialism, nor their rightist counterparts, who believed only force could prevent it, were open to compromise.

RIGHTIST BACKLASH

In 1972 Chile was paralyzed by a widespread truckers' strike, supported by the Christian Democrats and the National Party. As the government's authority crumbled, a desperate Allende invited constitutionalist army commander General Carlos Prats to occupy the critical post of interior minister, and he included an admiral and an air-force general in his cabinet. Despite the economic crisis, results of the March 1973 congressional elections demonstrated that Allende's support had actually increased since 1970 – but the unified opposition nevertheless strengthened its control of Congress, underscoring the polarization of Chilean politics. In June 1973 there was an unsuccessful military coup.

The epic documentary, *La Batalla de Chile*, brilliantly chronicles the year leading up to the military coup of 1973. Filmed partly in secret on stock sent from abroad, the footage had to be smuggled out of Chile and was eventually edited in Cuba.

The next month, truckers and other rightists once again went on strike, supported by the entire opposition. Having lost military support, General Prats resigned, to be replaced by the relatively obscure General Augusto Pinochet Ugarte, whom both Prats and Allende thought loyal to constitutional government.

On September 11, 1973 Pinochet unleashed a brutal *golpe de estado* (coup d'état) that overthrew the UP government and resulted in Allende's death (an apparent suicide) and the death of thousands of Allende supporters. Police and the military apprehended thousands of leftists, suspected leftists and sympathizers. Many were herded into Santiago's National Stadium, where they suffered beatings, torture and even execution. Hundreds of thousands went into exile.

September 11 is as of much significance to Chileans as North Americans. The date of the 1973 coup, it's commemorated with a major avenue in Santiago.

The military argued that force was necessary to remove Allende because his government had fomented political and economic chaos and because – so they claimed – he himself was planning to overthrow the constitutional order by force. Certainly, inept policies brought about this 'economic chaos,' but reactionary sectors, encouraged and abetted from abroad, exacerbated scarcities, producing a black market that further undercut order. Allende had demonstrated commitment to democracy, but his inability or unwillingness to control factions to his left terrified the middle class as well as the oligarchy. His powerful last words, part of a radio address just before

mid-1960s–70s	1970	1973
Musical movement La Nueva Canción Chileana revitalizes folk by pairing Aymara and Quechua music with activist lyrics; it's driven underground during the dictatorship.	Salvador Allende becomes world's first democratically elected Marxist president; radical social reform follows, with state control of many private enterprises alongside massive income redistribution.	A military coup on September 11, 1973 overthrows the UP government, resulting in Allende's death (an apparent suicide) and the death of thousands of his supporters.

the attacks on the government palace, La Moneda, expressed his ideals but underlined his failure:

> My words are not spoken in bitterness, but in disappointment. There will be a moral judgment on those who have betrayed the oath they took as soldiers of Chile…They have the might and they can enslave us, but they cannot halt the world's social processes, not with crimes, nor with guns…May you go forward in the knowledge that, sooner rather than later, the great avenues will open once again, along which free citizens will march in order to build a better society. Long live Chile! Long live the people! Long live the workers! These are my last words, and I am sure that this sacrifice will constitute a moral lesson that will punish cowardice, perfidy and treason.

March Cooper, Allende's translator before the coup, takes an insightful and poignant look at Chile's politics and society from the coup to today's cynical consumer society in *Pinochet and Me: A Chilean Anti-Memoir* (2002).

MILITARY DICTATORSHIP

Many opposition leaders, some of whom had encouraged the coup, expected a quick return to civilian government, but General Pinochet had other ideas. From 1973 to 1989, he headed a durable junta that dissolved Congress, banned leftist parties and suspended all others, prohibited nearly all political activity and ruled by decree. Assuming the presidency in 1974, Pinochet sought to reorder the country's political and economic culture through repression, torture and murder. The Caravan of Death, a group of military that traveled by helicopter from town to town, mainly in northern Chile, killed many political opponents, many of whom had voluntarily turned themselves in. Detainees came from all sectors of society, from peasants to professors. Around 35,000 were tortured and 3000 were 'disappeared' during the 17-year regime.

The CNI (Centro Nacional de Informaciones, or National Information Center) and its predecessor DINA (Directoria de Inteligencia Nacional, or National Intelligence Directorate) were the most notorious practitioners of state terrorism. International assassinations were not unusual – a car bomb killed General Prats in Buenos Aires a year after the coup, and Christian Democrat leader Bernardo Leighton barely survived a shooting in Rome in 1975. Perhaps the most notorious case was the 1976 murder of Allende's foreign minister, Orlando Letelier, by a car bomb in Washington, DC.

By 1977 even air force general Gustavo Leigh, a member of the junta, thought the campaign against 'subversion' so successful that he proposed a return to civilian rule, but Pinochet forced Leigh's resignation, ensuring the army's dominance and perpetuating himself in power. By 1980 Pinochet felt confident enough to submit a new, customized constitution to the electorate and wagered his own political future on it. In a plebiscite with narrow options, about two-thirds of the voters approved the constitution and ratified Pinochet's presidency until 1989, though many voters abstained in protest.

1973–89	1978	1980
General Augusto Pinochet heads a durable junta that dissolves Congress, bans leftist parties and suspends all others, prohibiting nearly all political activity and ruling by decree.	Chile and Argentina almost go to war over three small islands in the Beagle Channel. The Beagle Conflict is finally settled by Papal mediation in 1979.	Pinochet submits a new, customized constitution to the electorate which ratifies his presidency until 1989. It passes though many voters abstain in protest.

RETURN TO DEMOCRACY

The cracks in the regime began to appear around 1983, when leftist groups dared to stage demonstrations and militant opposition groups began to form in the shantytowns. Political parties also started to regroup, although they only began to function openly again in 1987. In late 1988, trying to extend his presidency until 1997, Pinochet held another plebiscite, but this time voters rejected him. In multiparty elections in 1989, Christian Democrat Patricio Aylwin, compromise candidate of a coalition of opposition parties known as the Concertación para la Democracia (Concertación for short), defeated Pinochet protégé Hernán Büchi, a conservative economist.

Consolidating the rebirth of democracy, Aylwin's relatively uneventful four-year term expired in 1994. His elected successor was Eduardo Frei Ruiz-Tagle, son of the late president Eduardo Frei Montalva, for a six-year term. The Concertación maintained Pinochet's free-market reforms, while struggling with a limiting constitution in which the military still held considerable power. Pinochet's military senate appointees could still block reform, and he assumed a senate seat upon retirement from the army in 1997 – at least in part because it conferred immunity from prosecution in Chile. This constitutional hangover from the dictatorship was finally swept away in July 2005 when the president was granted the right to fire armed forces commanders and abolish unelected senators.

THE PINOCHET SAGA

The September 1998 arrest of General Pinochet in London at the request of Spanish judge Báltazar Garzón, who was investigating deaths and disappearances of Spanish citizens in the aftermath of the 1973 coup, caused an international uproar.

The Pinochet File by Peter Kornbluh (2003) is a surprising and revealing look at US involvement in Chilean politics in the run-up to the military dictatorship of 1973 to 1989.

Following the arrest, US president Bill Clinton released files showing 30 years of US government covert aid to undermine Allende and set the stage for the coup d'état. Pinochet was put under house arrest, and for four years lawyers argued whether or not he was able to stand trial for crimes committed by the Caravan of Death, based on his health and mental condition. Both the Court of Appeals (in 2000) and the Supreme Court (2002) ruled him unfit to stand trial. As a consequence of the court's decision – that he suffered from dementia – Pinochet stepped down from his post as lifetime senator.

It seemed the end of judicial efforts to hold him accountable for human rights abuses. But in 2004 Pinochet gave a TV interview in which he appeared wholly lucid. A string of court decisions subsequently stripped Pinochet of his immunity from prosecution as a former head of state. One of the key human rights charges subsequently brought against him revolved around his alleged role in Operation Condor, a coordinated campaign by several South American regimes in the 1970s and 1980s to eliminate their leftist opponents.

1989	1994–95	1998
The Concertación para la Democracia (Consensus for Democracy) is formed of 17 parties and its candidate, Christian Democrat Patricio Aylwin, ousts Pinochet in the first free elections since 1970.	The new president, Christian Democrat Eduardo Frei, reduces the military's influence in government.	Pinochet arrested in UK on murder charges relating to his time in power; the nearly unprecedented action is one of the first arrests of a dictator based on universal jurisdiction. Seven years of legal battles ensue.

Chileans then witnessed a string of yo-yoing court decisions that first stripped his immunity, subsequently reversed the ruling, then again decided that he could stand trial. Revelations made in early 2005 about Pinochet's secret foreign bank accounts – in which he squirreled away more than US$27 million – added to the charges against him and implicated his wife and son. It was also revealed that the judge investigating the former dictator's bank accounts had received death threats.

Despite the intense legal activity, Pinochet never reached trial. He died on December 10, 2006 at the age of 91. In Santiago's Plaza Italia, 6000 demonstrators gathered to celebrate, tossing confetti into the air and drinking champagne, but there were also violent riots. Tens of thousands of Pinochet supporters attended his funeral and honored him as a patriot who gave Chile a strong economic future. President Bachelet was noticeably absent. There was no state funeral.

THE RISE OF THE LEFT

The Concertación narrowly scraped through the 2000 elections for its third term in office. Its candidate, the moderate leftist Ricardo Lagos, joined a growing breed of left-leaning governments elected across South America, all seeking to put a little or a lot more space between themselves and Washington. Lagos became an important figure in this shift in 2003 when he was one of the most determined members of the UN Security Council to oppose war in Iraq. It was a move that won him much approval with Chileans, and quieter respect from other world leaders. Predictably, however, it earned him no points with Washington.

Proof that a more united South America was increasingly banding together to contest US hegemony came when Chile's socialist interior minister José Miguel Insulza was elected to lead the 34-member OAS (Organization of American States) in 2005. The US had initially thrown its weight behind candidates from El Salvador and Mexico. However, when it became apparent that Chile's candidate would win, the US made a speedy show of backing him. Face-saving maneuvers aside, Insulza's election marked the first time since the OAS was founded in 1948 that the US-backed nominee had not won.

Chilean alliances with other South American countries are warming up (in spite of Bachelet's on-camera shudder when he was embraced by populist Venezuelan president Hugo Chávez). A landmark 2008 defense agreement opened the door to warmer relations with Bolivia, a landlocked nation still very much missing the ocean access it lost in the 1876 War of the Pacific. (President Ricardo Lagos once deemed poor relations with Bolivia a 'great failure' of his presidency).

However, relations with neighboring Peru remain fragile. Spats with the northern neighbor have included the alleged sale of arms by Chile to Ecuador and the battle over pisco rights (see the boxed text, p253).

'Despite the intense legal activity, Pinochet never reached trial'

2000	2002	2002
Beating a former aide to Pinochet, moderate leftist Ricardo Lagos is elected president, joining a growing breed of left-leaning governments elected across South America.	Chile loosens up – over 3000 eager citizens volunteer for artist Spencer Tunick's call for naked bodies for a now infamous Santiago photo shoot.	Portraying Chile's disaffected urban youth, young novelist Alberto Fuget lands the cover of *Newsweek*; he claims the era of Latin American magic realism dead.

BRAVE NEW WORLD

In the last decade Chile has become Latin America's brightest economic star – boosted by record prices for its key export, copper. Public and foreign debt is low, foreign investment is up, and government wrists are sore from signing free-trade agreements, notably with the EU and North America; Chile was the first South American state to go free trade with the US. China is another crucial trading partner, boosting the price of copper thanks to its rapid industrialization. As hard as Chile tries to diversify, copper still accounts for a whopping 55% of exports.

Chile is now ranked as the world's 40th most developed country; its health-care has improved, life expectancy is up and poverty rates have decreased to become among the lowest in Latin America.

Socially Chile is rapidly shedding much of its traditional conservatism. The death penalty was abolished in 2001 and a divorce law was finally passed in 2004 (although the morning-after pill still provokes decisive controversy). The arts and free press are once again flourishing and women's rights are being increasingly recognized in law.

The 2005 election of Michelle Bachelet, former Minister of Defense under Lagos, was a watershed event. Not only because she is a woman, but because as an agnostic, socialist single mother she represents everything that Chile superficially is not. Her father was an Air Force general who died under the hands of Pinochet's forces; she was also detained and tortured but released, and lived in exile abroad. She's a former doctor, and her skill as a consensus builder has helped her heal old wounds with the military and the public. For voters, she represented a continuum of the policies of Lagos, moving forward Chile's already strong economy.

Pinochet's death may have closed the chapter on Chile's dictatorship – certainly many Chileans are tired of digging up the past – but the question remains as to whether reconciliation has actually been achieved. Chile has already changed enormously, developing international influence, expanding economically and casting off conservative shackles socially. But that's not the end of the story.

RESETTING THE COMPASS

Soon after Michelle Bachelet took the presidency, divisions within her coalition (La Concertacion Democratica) made pushing through reforms difficult. She also was tested by emerging crises with no easy answer.

First was the introduction of Transantiago, the ambitious new transportation system poised to replace Santiago's rickety, polluting dinosaur-era buses. The sudden transition was a disaster. Transportation routes were slashed from one day to the next, leaving commuters with additional bus transfers and long waiting periods between buses. Filling the gap, the metro has since been packed to the gills. Although Transantiago was masterminded by the

'The 2005 election of Michelle Bachelet was a water-shed event because she represents everything that Chile superficially is not'

2003	2004	2005
Its economy booming, Chile, in a controversial move, becomes the first South American country to sign a free-trade deal with the USA.	In a break with ultra-conservative Catholic tradition, Chile establishes the rights of its citizens to divorce; the courts are flooded with cases and proceedings backlog.	Senate approves more than 50 constitutional reforms to fully restore the democracy, allowing the president to dismiss non-elected senators (known as 'senators for life') and military commanders.

Lagos administration, the fallout cost the new administration its initially strong approval ratings.

The student protests of 2006–07 had a similar effect. Protesting the dismal quality of state schooling, over 600,000 students nationwide – nicknamed *pinguinos* (penguins) for their uniforms – staged marches, sit-ins and protests, often with teacher support. Violence marred some protests yet they eventually succeeded in shaming the government into a long-overdue education overhaul. Inequity drove the issue: on a national test, private-school fourth-graders were outperforming their public-school counterparts by 50%. Reform, in the form of state grants and a new quality agency for monitoring, is on the way, although some question whether weaker municipalities are equipped to implement it.

At the root of the problem is Chile's remarkably high income inequality. The number of millionaires doubled in the early 2000s, yet close to 500,000 residents live in extreme poverty. While the poverty has declined by a third since 2003, critics argue that the national poverty line is just too low to give an accurate picture. In 2008, runaway inflation had hit Chile's poor the hardest –the cost of bread had doubled from 2007 and the prices of staple goods was steadily on the rise.

In January 2008, the police killing of an unarmed Mapuche youth sparked massive demonstrations and vandalism. The youth had been symbolically occupying a privately owned farm near Temuco with over thirty activists. The death came in the wake of a 2005 police killing of a 17-year-old Mapuche that went unprosecuted. With a history of conflict, tensions are again mounting between the state and the Mapuche indigenous community, who today number around one million.

Chile's seemingly incorruptible image may have been brought down a notch. The state railway company, EFE, went bankrupt, despite an infusion of US$1 billion in state funds, and proposed regional sports complexes similarly tanked when national funding disappeared. Chile's environmental record might also face scrutiny: the administration has acted in support of extensive mining operations and a number of hydroelectric proposals meant to alleviate growing energy needs that could be extremely destructive to the environment.

Heading toward presidential elections in late 2009, pundits expect more cooperation between political parties although the government's hesitancy to rock the boat means that few advances are expected. Capitalizing on the gaffes of the current administration, the center-right Alianza por Chile is well positioned to grab power. Popularity polls show Bachelet's former presidential race opponent, billionaire businessman Sebastian Piñera, more popular than ever.

Navigating its way through financial highs and domestic woes, Chile may have to reset its north to find its way through mounting social, ecological and economic issues; it's complicated, but par for the course of progress.

'Protesting the dismal quality of state schooling, over 600,000 students nationwide staged marches. Inequity drove the issue'

2006	**2006**	**2007**
Michelle Bachelet is elected the first female president of Chile and faces key crises: massive student protests seeking education reform and Santiago's traffic paralysis during transportation reform.	At the age of 91, General Augusto Pinochet dies, having never reached trial. He is denied a state funeral.	Santiago's youth get radical, from a penchant to protest to the emergence of Pokemones – Goth-inspired youth who embrace kissing parties.

The Culture

In this former 'island' between the Andes and the sea, isolation may have nurtured Chilenos for decades, but in recent times they've received a tsunami of outside influence. The internet, shopping malls, and Direct TV have radically recalibrated the tastes and social norms in even the most rural outposts of this once super-conservative society. There's a duality to this: while innovations and creativity are keeping the culture abuzz, there's also that consumer hangover to deal with. But there is still much to be said for the sacred backyard barbecue, and Sundays continue to be reserved for family, all generations included. One thing is for sure: while Chile sits at a cultural crossroads, it leaves the visitor with much to see, enjoy, debate and process.

THE NATIONAL PSYCHE

Centuries with little exposure to other countries, accompanied by an especially influential Roman Catholic church, fostered a high degree of cultural conformity and conservatism in Chile. This isolation was, if anything, compounded during the Pinochet years of repression and censorship. Perhaps for this reason outsiders often comment on how Chileans appear more restrained than other Latin American nationalities: they seem a less verbal, more heads-down and hard-working people.

But the national psyche is now at its most fluid, as Chile undergoes radical social change. The Roman Catholic church is losing ground after years hunkering down during a brutal dictatorship and slowly overcoming it. Society is becoming more and more open, embracing its new freedom, introducing liberal laws, and challenging conservative values. Nowhere is this trend more evident than with the urban youth.

Chileans are known for compliance and passive political attitudes, yet this tendency is shifting. Many see new social changes as a Generation Y and Z impetus; they are the first generation to grow up without the censorship, curfew or restrictions of the Pinochet dictatorship. As a result, they are far more questioning and less discouraged by theoretical consequences. Authorities may perceive it as a threat, but Chile's youth is poised to stand up for what's theirs in a way their predecessors would not have.

The most lasting impression you'll take away of Chileans is undoubtedly of their renowned hospitality, helpfulness, genuine curiosity and heartfelt eagerness to make travelers feel at home.

Want to go local? The book *Chilenismos: A Dictionary and Phrasebook for Chilean Spanish* (2005) by Daniel Joelson will make you fluent in street talk.

LIFESTYLE

Travelers crossing over from Peru or Bolivia may wonder where the stereotypical 'South America' went. Superficially at least, Chilean lifestyle has many similarities to Europe. Dress is conservative, leaning towards business

---

A NEW URBAN TRIBE

Santiago's teens are a whole new breed, addicted to *flogeando* (fotologging), chat and cult styles. A 2007 *Newsweek* article portrayed the culture of Pokemones, teens with an androgynous Goth style, as involving public oral-sex orgies. The reality turns out to be a little less lurid – Pokemones say anonymous kissing is more the name of the game, but they do partner up with the same sex. In any case, it's a radical change for Chile. Some see it as a rebuke to the ultra-preppy elite Pelolais, the so-called 'straight-haired' youth. But at its core it's a backlash against ultra-conservative upbringings.

formal; the exception being the scantily clad coffee-bar waitresses and teenage fashion slaves. And while most Chileans are proud of their traditional heritage, there's a palpable lack of investment in it.

The average Chilean focuses energy on family, home and work. They are very kid-oriented although don't have huge families. Children live with their families until they marry; they're not encouraged to grow up too quickly, and families spend a great deal of time together. Independence isn't nearly as valued as family unity and togetherness. Regardless, single motherhood is not uncommon. Though divorce is now legal, its absence in previous decades did not so much keep spouses together as increase the acceptance of couples living together and having children out of wedlock. While not aggressively anti-gay, Chile offers little public support for alternate lifestyles.

There is a yawning gulf between highest and lowest incomes in Chile, and therefore a dramatic gap between living standards and an exaggerated class consciousness. Lifestyles are lavish for Santiago's *cuicos* (upper-class yuppies), with swish apartment blocks and a couple of maids, while at the other end of the scale some of Chile's poorest coastal families eke out a living fishing, while Aymara raise llama and alpaca on the altiplano, and Mapuche scrape together a living from agriculture and handicrafts. That said, poverty has been halved in the last 15 years, while housing and social programs have eased the burden on Chile's poorest.

> Get your fix on Chilean news (in English) at www.santiagotimes.cl.

Chileans have a strong work ethic, and often work six days a week, but are always eager for a good *carrete* (party). Military service is obligatory for males (though university students can get out of it), but there is growing sentiment towards eliminating conscription. Chile's excellent 96% literacy rate is thanks to elementary school being both free and compulsory, and three out of four children now finish secondary school (up from 50% in 1990).

A lack of ethnic and religious diversity in Chile makes racism a relatively minor problem, although some distinctions do exist: the Mapuche still complain of prejudice and marginalization, and formidable class barriers are as strong as ever. Prejudice against foreigners is generally not common but it does exist, especially towards young backpackers from Israel whose uninhibited traveling styles can clash with Chile's social codes.

ECONOMY

With the highest nominal GDP per capita in Latin America, Chile has enjoyed a robust economy since Pinochet introduced economic reform. The democratic governments that followed have stayed the course, encouraging privatization of state-owned industries and a high level of foreign trade. This approach has taken Chile down a different path than its neighbors and has been a distinct source of national pride. However, income distribution is extremely poor – Chile's richest top 10% hold 47% of the country's wealth.

> For an inside scoop on Mapuche culture and issues, check out the five-language Mapuche international site (www.mapuche-nation.org), created with foreign collaboration.

The US is Chile's biggest trading partner, receiving 17% of its exports and providing 18.5% of its imports. Chile is aggressively seeking to expand its trade partners, however, and newer agreements with China and Japan have potential to change the future trade dynamic. Copper has been a windfall for the country, accounting for over half of its total exports. Nonmineral exports include forestry and wood products, fresh fruit, fishmeal and seafood and manufactured products.

The country's willingness to become an investment platform for foreign multinationals means that these companies, with huge mining and energy interests, might have a bigger say in Chile's future than its own people do and has definite repercussions for the environment.

DOS AND DON'TS

- Keep your behavior circumspect around indigenous peoples, especially in the altiplano of Arica, around San Pedro de Atacama and in the Mapuche south. Aggressive photo-taking and rowdiness can be particularly offensive.

- Upon greeting and leaving, cheek kisses are exchanged between men and women and between women. Both parties gently touch cheek to cheek and send the kiss to the air. Between men, the kissing is replaced with a hearty handshake.

- Chileans can be weary to discuss their dictatorship past, which has undergone intense examination in the media. In discussion, at least start with a focus on more contemporary issues.

POPULATION

While the vast majority of the population is of Spanish ancestry mixed with indigenous groups, several moderate waves of immigrants have also settled here – particularly British, Irish, French, Italians, Croatians (especially to Magallanes and Tierra del Fuego) and Palestinians. Germans also began immigrating in 1848 and left their stamp on the Lakes District.

The northern Andes is home to around 69,200 indigenous Aymara and Atacameño peoples. Almost 10 times that amount (around 620,000 people) are Mapuche, many of whom consider the south (La Araucanía) their home. Their name stems from the words *mapu* (land) and *che* (people). About 3800 Rapanuians, of Polynesian ancestry, live on Easter Island.

About 75% of Chile's population occupies just 20% of its total area, in the main agricultural region of Middle Chile. This region includes Gran Santiago (the capital and its suburbs), where over a third of the country's estimated 16 million people reside. More than 85% of Chileans live in cities. In Patagonia, the person-per-square-kilometer ratio in Aisén is just 1:1 – in the Región Metropolitana that ratio is closer to 400:1.

SPORTS

Explore everything from tripe stew to tongue-twisters at www.folklore .cl, in Spanish, a website aiming to rescue folkloric traditions.

The most popular spectator sport may still be *fútbol* (soccer), but tennis is Chile's recent sporting success story. Marcelo (Chino) Ríos showed the way when he became world number one in 1998. Nicolás Massú and Fernando Gonzáles followed his lead, winning Chile its first ever gold medal (in men's doubles) at the 2004 Athens Olympics. The occasion brought thousands of Chileans into the streets to celebrate. To add icing on the cake, Massú went on to win gold in the men's singles while Gonzáles took bronze. Chile added to its medal chest at the 2008 Beijing Olympics when Gonzáles took silver after losing to Spain's Rafael Nadal in men's singles.

Meanwhile, *fútbol* rules the hearts of all Chileans. In rural Patagonia teams will travel a full day on horseback to play a Sunday match. Soccer games are infused with cultural flavor, singing, colored smoke and fireworks, although Chilean football has recently suffered financial woes and disturbing crowd violence. The main teams are Santiago-based Colo Colo, Universidad de Chile and the more elitist Universidad Católica. Followers of Colo Colo are dubbed *garras blancas* (white claws), while Universidad de Chile fans are called *los de abajo* (the underdogs). The season is from March to November, though play-offs run into December.

Given that they have the perfect natural environment for it, most young Chileans who can afford it go big on individual sports like surfing, skiing and windsurfing. Adventure racing is also gaining popularity. Other sports followed keenly are volleyball, basketball, boxing, horse racing and hockey, but great fun can also be had watching local sports. Chilean rodeos see teams of flamboyantly dressed *huasos* (cowboys) traveling from village to village. Also watch out for *chueca,* a traditional team game played with a small rubber ball and curved sticks.

RELIGION

The church is still one of Chile's most influential institutions, and about 90% of Chileans are Roman Catholic. But, as evidenced by sweeping reforms in the last few years, the church's iron grip over Chilean culture is loosening as the country becomes increasingly liberal.

It was the church's influence that kept Chile the only democratic country in the world without a divorce law until 2004. It continued battling against the law until the last, wielding its heavy influence through radio and TV. It is interesting to note that, while Chile's leading TV network didn't broadcast the church's anti-divorce-law TV adverts, the second- and third-biggest channels ran them for free as a 'community service.'

The government has found it difficult to institute critically important sex-education programs and distribute contraception due to ecclesiastical opposition, although this too is now changing despite an impassioned advertising campaign on the church-run TV Channel 13.

However, high church attendance speaks eloquently of the continuing importance of religion, especially in rural areas. Countless roadside shrines, some of them extraordinary examples of folk art, also testify to the pervasiveness of religion.

WOMEN IN CHILE

These are exciting times for Chilena (Chilean women). After years of taking a back seat, especially during the dictatorship, they are back in prominent positions in government, political parties and corporations. The legal status of women has also been transformed in recent years: key changes have been laws against sexual harassment and allowing divorce, and heavier sentencing for domestic violence. There have been gains with maternity leave, and refuges are being opened for victims of rape.

A high percentage of children in Chile are born outside marriage. Until recently men were free to simply leave their girlfriends holding the baby, but mid-2005 saw a crucial new law to force fathers to recognize children born outside wedlock and take DNA tests if necessary. After much controversy, legislators are pushing to allow for the free distribution of the morning-after pill.

Generally, the famous Latin American *machismo* (chauvinism) is subtle in Chile and there's a great deal of respect for women. However, this doesn't mean that it's exactly liberal. In Chile, traditional roles still rule. At present, the government is addressing income inequity: Chilenas still make 31% less than their male counterparts. Domestic abuse is a major issue, with a poll of women in Santiago revealing that half had been victims of physical or emotional violence.

While the picture is less than rosy, the willingness of the government and public to address these issues has never been greater.

ARTS

The military dictatorship in Chile discouraged any 'subversive' activities or education and prompted an artistic exodus. But these days Chile is making up for lost time with a fresh burst of creativity and eager exercising of its new freedom. Proof positive of this artistic reawakening and shedding of inhibitions came on a bitterly cold morning in 2002 when artist Spencer

Get a grip on Chilean culture with the dynamic website www.nuestro.cl, from the Chilean Cultural Heritage Corporation. You'll find everything from artist interviews to rich stories and profiles.

Tunick advertised for 400 souls to pose naked for a photo shoot, and more than 3000 showed up.

Literature & Poetry

Twentieth-century Chile has produced many of Latin America's most celebrated writers, and two names stand head and shoulders above the rest: Nobel Prize–winning poets Pablo Neruda (see the boxed text, opposite) and Gabriela Mistral are both giants of world literature. Mistral (born Lucila Godoy Alcayaga; 1889–1957) was a shy young rural schoolmistress who won great acclaim for her compassionate, reflective and mystical poetry. When Mistral taught in Temuco, the young Neruda worshipped her. She became South America's first Nobel Prize winner for literature in 1945. Her work is not as easily translated as Neruda's but try US poet Langston Hughes' *Selected Poems of Gabriela Mistral*, or find out more in Margot Arce de Vásquez's *Gabriela Mistral, the Poet and Her Work*. Many still pay Mistral homage in her native Elqui Valley.

Nicanor Parra (b 1914), part of the famous Parra musical dynasty, drew Nobel Prize attention for his hugely influential and colloquial 'antipoetry.' *De Hojas de Parra* (From the Pages of Parra) and *Poemas y antipoemas* (Poems and Antipoems) are his most well known. Jorge Teillier (1935–96), a bohemian character quick to the bottle, wrote poetry of teenage angst and solitude, which has been translated into English.

Chile's fragile social facades were explored by José Donoso (1924–96). His celebrated novel *Curfew* offers a portrait of life under the dictatorship through the eyes of a returned exile, while *Coronación* (Coronation), made into a hit film, follows the fall of a dynasty.

Chile's most famous contemporary literary export is Isabel Allende (b 1942), niece of the late president Salvador Allende. She wove 'magical realism' into captivating – and best-selling – stories with Chilean historic references, such as *House of the Spirits*, *Of Love and Shadows*, *Eva Luna*, *Daughter of Fortune* and *Portrait in Sepia*. *My Invented Country* (2004) gives insight into perceptions of Chile and Allende herself.

Arial Dorfman (b 1942), who divides his time between Chile and the US, is another huge presence on the literary scene: critic, novelist, playwright, travel writer and human-rights activist. His play *La Negra Ester* (Black Ester), an adaptation of a poem by Chilean musician and writer Roberto Parra Sandoval, is one of the country's most beloved plays, while *Death and the Maiden*, set after the fall of a South American dictator, was made into an internationally successful movie.

Novelist Antonio Skármeta (b 1940) became famous for *Ardiente Paciencia* (Burning Patience), inspired by Neruda and adapted into the award-winning film *Il Postino* (The Postman).

Luis Sepúlveda (b 1949) is one of Chile's most prolific writers, with such books as *Nombre de Torero* (The Name of the Bullfighter), a tough stylish noir set in Germany and Chile with loads of political intrigue involving Nazi gold and interesting perspectives on exile; and the novella *Un Viejo que Leía Novelas de Amor* (The Old Man Who Read Love Stories), a fictional account of life and society on Ecuador's Amazonian frontier. For a lighter romp through Chile, Roberto Ampuero (b 1953) writes mystery novels, such as *El Alemán de Atacama* (The German of Atacama), whose main character is a Valparaíso-based Cuban detective.

The work of Roberto Bolaño (1955–2005) is enjoying a renaissance of sorts; the posthumous publication of encyclopedic *2666* (set to be released in waves) seals his cult-hero status, but it's also worth checking out his other works.

THE POET-POLITICIAN: PABLO NERUDA

Understand the life and work of Neftalí Ricardo Reyes Basoalto, better known by his adopted name Pablo Neruda (1904–73), and you're well on the way to understanding Chile. His often combative, frequently sentimental, sometimes surreal and always provocative poetry offers a path straight into his country's soul, while his own life story has played an intimate part in Chile's recent history.

Born in a provincial town in Maule and schooled in Temuco, he devised his famous alias fearing that his blue-collar family would mock his ambition. He was soon awarded a diplomatic post after enjoying early literary success, and his subsequent travels brought him international celebrity. Despite his leftist beliefs the poet led a flamboyant life and developed a taste for the ostentatious; he built gloriously outlandish homes in Santiago, Valparaíso and Isla Negra, each decorated with ever more quirky belongings. He named his most famous house, La Chascona (see p87), after his third wife Matilde Urrutia's perpetually tangled shock of hair.

Neruda always wore his political opinions on his sleeve. He helped political refugees flee after the Spanish Civil War and officially joined the Communist Party once back in Chile, where he was elected senator for Tarapacá and Antofagasta. After Neruda helped Gabriel González Videla secure the presidency in 1946, the capricious president promptly outlawed the Communist Party. Neruda was driven into exile, forced to escape on foot and horseback over the southern Andes to Argentina.

Neruda resumed his political career once González Videla had stepped down, all the while continuing to churn out his poetry. A presidential candidate in 1969, he pulled out of the race in support of Salvador Allende. He became Allende's ambassador to France for two years, and it was during this time that he received his Nobel Prize, becoming only the third Latin American writer to win the award.

Soon afterward he returned to Chile with failing health. But he enjoyed no quiet retirement as pressure mounted on Allende's presidency. Mere days after the 1973 coup, Neruda died of cancer and a broken heart. His will left everything to the Chilean people through a foundation.

The power of Neruda's political poems was feared by Pinochet's regime, which set about trying to wipe out his memory. His homes were sacked and vandalized. However, his widow Matilde lovingly restored them, and they are now open to the public.

Much of Neruda's own work, such as *Heights of Macchu Picchu*, *Canto General* and *Passions and Impressions*, is available in English translation.

Bestselling author Marcela Serrano (b 1951) tackles women's issues in books such as *Antigua Vida Mia* (My Life Before: A Novel) and others. Homosexuality, transgender issues and other controversial subjects are treated with top-notch shock value by Pedro Lemebel (b 1950). His novel *Tengo Miedo Torero* (My Tender Matador) was selected as Chile's 'novel of the year' for 2001.

Younger writers developing a style far from the 'magical realism' that brought Latin literature to the international scene include Alberto Fuguet (b 1964), whose novella *Sobredosis* (Overdose) and tale of drug addiction *Mala Onda* (Bad Vibes) have earned acclaim and scowls; the latter has been translated to English. There are scores of other contemporary talents, but keep a special eye out for the erotic narratives of Andrea Maturana, up-and-coming novelist Carlos Franz and Gonzalo Contreras.

Sex, drugs, and poetry recitation drive *Los Detectives Salvajes* (The Savage Detectives), late literary bad boy Roberto Bolaño's greatest novel. Like him, the main character is a Chilean poet exiled in Mexico and Spain.

Cinema

Before the 1973 coup Chilean cinema was among the most experimental in Latin America and it is now returning to reclaim some of this status. Alejandro Jodorowsky's kooky *El Topo* (The Mole; 1971), an underground cult classic that dabbled with mixing genres long before Tarantino ever did, is still available internationally on DVD.

There was little film production in Chile during the Pinochet years, but outside Chile exiled directors were busily shooting. Miguel Littín's *Alsino y el Condor* (Alsino and the Condor; 1983) was nominated for an Academy Award. Documentary-maker Patricio Guzmán was earning considerable respect in Europe, where he still lives. His recent movies include *Chile, La Memoria Obstinante* (Chile, Obstinate Memory; 1998) and an intimate portrait of *Salvador Allende* (2004). Paris-based Raúl Ruiz, another exile, has been prolific in his adopted country and has released English-language movies, including the psychological thriller *Shattered Image* (1998).

Following the dictatorship Chile's weakened film industry was understandably preoccupied with its after-effects. Ricardo Larrain's *La Frontera* (The Borderland; 1991) explored the issues of internal exile and Gonzalo Justiniano's *Amnesia* (1994) used the story of a Chilean soldier forced to shoot prisoners to challenge Chileans not to forget past atrocities.

The mood lightened somewhat in later years. The most successful Chilean movie to date is *El Chacotero Sentimental* (The Sentimental Teaser; 1999), which won 18 national and international awards. The movie, which is directed by Cristian Galaz, tracks the true story of a frank radio host whose listeners start to reveal on the airwaves all sorts of complicated and passionate love stories. Another acclaimed movie soon followed about the fall of a family dynasty, by Silvio Caiozzi, one of Chile's most respected veteran directors. It was adapted from José Donoso's novel *Coronación* (Coronation; 2000). *Taxi Para Tres* (Taxi for Three; 2001), by Orlando Lubbert, is a sharp comedy about bandits and their heisted taxi.

Chile's film industry has worked through the country's traumatic past in a kind of celluloid therapy. This is true of three of the most internationally successful Chilean films of recent decades. *Machuca* (2004), directed by Andrés Wood, follows the story of two little boys during the 1973 Pinochet coup. *Sub Terra* (2003) dramatizes the exploitation that used to go on in Chile's mines. *Mi Mejor Enemigo* (My Best Enemy; 2004), a collaboration with Argentina and Spain, is set in Patagonia during the Beagle conflict (a 1978 territorial dispute between Argentina and Chile over three islands in the Beagle channel).

It's not all war, torture and politics though. Diego Izquierdo's *Sexo con Amor* (Sex with Love; 2002) is an entertaining insight into the sexual habits of Chileans. And a new breed of teen flicks influenced by global culture is also emerging: young director Nicolás López has taken the youth market by storm with films full of comic-book culture, teen angst, dark humor, horror and gore. Check out his coming-of-age schoolroom comedy *Promedio Rojo* (loosely translated as Flunking Grades; 2005). Another young filmmaker to watch for is Alicia Scherson, whose offbeat trawl through Santiago in *Play* (2005) won Best Latin American Film at the Montreal World Film Festival.

Further proof of fast-diversifying genres is found in Chile's fledgling animation industry, with children's movie *Ogú y Mampato en Rapanui* (2002) and black comedy *Cesante* (Unemployed; 2003). Chile's fabulous scenery makes it a dream location for foreign movies too; contemporary films to have been shot here include *The Motorcycle Diaries* (2004) and the James Bond movie *Quantam of Solace* (2008), which drew sharp criticism from Chileans since it is really supposed to be Bolivia.

Music

Chile's contemporary music spans from the revolutionary tunes of the 1960s and '70s to Andean folklore to today's one-hit-wonder sexy crooners and hip-hoppers.

Hit foreign movies based on the work of Chilean writers include award-winning Il Postino *(The Postman), inspired by Skármeta, Roman Polanski's adaptation of Dorfman's* Death and the Maiden *and a star-studded* House of the Spirits.

Filmed partly in secret and smuggled out of Chile, Patricio Guzmán's epic documentary, La Batalla de Chile, *chronicles the year leading up to the military coup of 1973.*

Chile's most famous TV export is the portly Mario Kreuzberger, aka 'Don Francisco,' host of the cheesy variety show Sábado Gigante, *watched throughout Latin America and on Spanish-language channels in the US.*

La Nueva Canción Chilena (New Chilean Song Movement) revitalized the songs and instruments of Chile's folk singers, and lyricized the social hopes and political issues of the time. Its most legendary figure is Violeta Parra, known for her enduring theme *Gracias a la Vida* (Thanks to Life). Her children, Isabel and Angel, established Peña de los Parra, the first of many *peñas* (musical and cultural clubs often showcasing unapologetically political material) in Santiago in the mid-1960s. The movement spurred on stars such as Victor Jara, and international groups Quilapayún and Inti-Illimani. Jara in particular used song to attack political corruption, and songs like *Preguntas por Puerto Montt* were full-blooded accusations of atrocities.

Immediately after the coup, many Nueva Canción musicians were imprisoned. Victor Jara was brutally murdered in the National Stadium. Quilapayún and Inti-Illimani stayed exiled in Europe, where they happened to be touring at the time, building international reputations for both their music and politics.

Other groups (mainly rock) also went into exile and opposed the regime from afar. Los Prisioneros was the most influential, with energetic tunes and controversial lyrics. Paris-based Los Jaivas was another popular band in exile; they were fond of stunts like playing a grand piano on Machu Picchu and singing lyrics by Neruda. The lead singer 'El Gato' died in 2003 and days of national mourning followed.

Among Chile's biggest rock-pop bands is La Ley (based in Mexico). Although they have a love-hate relationship with the Chilean public, you'll still hear their sugary but catchy tunes played continually throughout Latin America. They won a Grammy for Best Alternative Rock Group, and their MTV *Unplugged* album was a huge hit.

Sweden-based DJ Mendez enjoys more fame in Europe than in his home country. Spunky young singer Nicole has caused a few waves and 15 years of Alberto Plaza's croonings have made him a national treasure. Los Tres was a major band in the '90s but they have disbanded and their lead singer now plays with new band the Pettinellis. Joe Vasconcellos is a favorite for energetic Latin fusion.

Contemporary bands that have grabbed domestic and international attention include La Ley, Lucybell, Tiro de Gracia, Los Bunkers, Javiera y los Imposibles and Mamma Soul. Look for the Strokes-like Teleradio Donoso and Chico Trujillio, whose *cumbia chilombiana* has a bit of Manu Chao and Mano Negra.

Bars are the staging grounds for Chile's new bands. Summer cultural festivals also feature everything from folk and jazz to rock. Radio play generally sticks to international pop standards, while the pelvic-thrusting rhythms of *reggaeton* dominate the nightlife. To dial into the Chilean music scene, check out www.musical.cl.

Architecture

Earthquakes have repeatedly robbed Chile of much of its architectural treasures from the colonial era, although compelling architectural gems do exist: not least the delightful colonial adobe churches of the Norte Grande; Santiago's Catedral Metropolitana and colonial Iglesia San Francisco; the gorgeous World Heritage–listed mansions of Valparaíso; and shingled chapels of Chiloé. You can also get an eyeful of Eiffel (of tower fame) architecture in the northern city of Arica. Sadly, Santiago's predilection for apartment blocks is savaging views for everyone except those who live in them. However, design is finding an increasingly important role in Chile and visitors will notice that the well heeled have developed a taste for innovative and modern design.

Chile's answer to *National Geographic*, the award-winning Canal 13 TV program *Tierra Adentro* (www.tierra-adentro .cl, in Spanish) explores the country's nooks and crannies.

Santiago sound is yours at www.santiagoradio.cl, the city's only all-English radio with updates on local concerts.

To learn more about Easter Island, click on www.islandheritage.org.

Painting & Sculpture

A leading light in Latin American surrealism, Chile's best-known painter was Paris-based Roberto Matta (1911–2002). Jesuit-educated in Chile, he went to France in 1934 to study architecture with Le Corbusier, but he also lived in New York and Mexico City. His famous abstracts are accompanied by work in sculpture and engraving.

The contemporary Chilean art scene loves to analyze its post-dictatorship identity, and puzzle over what makes its nation tick; you'll likely see a range of art and photographic exhibits on these themes. Sculptor Ivan Navarro's modernist work deals with themes of fear, exile and consumerism.

Alongside its literary heavyweights, one of Chile's most famous literary exports is *Condorito*, a comic-book character with the head of a condor.

Theater & Dance

Chile's national dance is *La Cueca:* dancers twirl a bandana above their heads then hide it behind their backs and prance around each other, in a sort of fight or flirt provocation. Chileans themselves say they aren't much into dancing, at least not like their northern and eastern neighbors, but still there's plenty of nightlife to go round.

Santiago has a thriving – if underfunded – performing arts scene, talented playwrights and a whole range of ambitious theater groups that survive on a shoestring budget. Keep an eye open for posters in the streets and adverts in newspapers such as *La Tercera* and *El Mercurio*. Outside Santiago you'll find theater and dance groups in university cities, especially Valdivia. Folkloric dance shows are often held during town festivals in January and February.

Food & Drink

Chile's best offerings are its raw materials: in the market you can get anything from goat cheese to avocados, pomegranates, good yogurt, fresh herbs and a fantastic variety of seafood. What Chilean cuisine lacks in spice and variety it makes up for in abundance. Wine is dutifully present, sometimes in box form, even at the most modest table. Chile produces over 700 million liters of it annually – don't miss out on your share. In particular, Chile's signature variety Carmenere is well worth a try. Although it is more an eat-in country, Santiago boasts its fare share of sophisticated restaurants and creative cuisine is catching on in tourist destinations as well. You'll pick out clues to Chile's cultural heritage through its cuisine, and not just in indigenous-influenced or Spanish dishes: there's a dash of German strudel here and a splash of British-style tea there, not to mention Chinese *chifas* (restaurants) and US-style fast-food chains.

What's that ugly bumpy green fruit? It's called chirimoya and it's sublime; the texture is creamy and the taste offers a hint of pineapple – locals drizzle it with orange juice but it's just fine on its own.

STAPLES & SPECIALTIES

Coastal folk eat almost anything that swims, crawls or slithers its way along Chile's lengthy Pacific coastline: octopus, sea barnacles, rays, urchins, clams, crabs, abalone, salmon, hake, oysters, scallops…the list goes on and on. One of the most common ways to eat seafood is in soups such as *caldillos* – usually made with congrio (conger eel) and potato chunks, and spiced up with lemon, cilantro and garlic. *Chupe* is a seafood casserole, cooked in clay bowls with a rich, gooey sauce of butter, breadcrumbs, cheese and spices. *Paila marina* is a delicious fish and shellfish chowder. In Chiloé, *curanto* combines shellfish, meat, chicken and sausages and steams it underground in nalca leaves before it is served in heaping bowls. Another exquisite dish when it is properly prepared, though stomach churning when it is not, is *ceviche* – raw fish or shellfish marinated in lemon juice, served cold. Many restaurants over-fry fish, but on request will prepare it *al vapor* (steamed) or *a la plancha* (grilled).

Paltry portions are never a problem here. Some of the most gargantuan and best for splitting are *chorillana, curanto, paila marina* (a seafood stew) and *tablas*.

Despite Chile's aquatic abundance, it's meat that fires up most Chileans. The most common dish is *lomo a lo pobre* (literally 'poor man's steak'), which is not particularly cheap. It consists of an enormous slab of beef topped with

---

TASTY TRAVEL

While Peruanos and Chilenos will dispute its origin to a stalemate, the pisco sour is an Andean masterpiece. With one of these before dinner your Spanish suddenly gets a whole lot better (but we can't account for the effects of two…). Visitors to the Araucanía can take their meals with a spicy dash of *merquen* – ground smoked chilies used in traditional Mapuche cooking. Another treat for the taste buds is Chiloé's unique cuisine that focuses on seafood and potatoes; try a just-made *chapalele* (potato bread) or *milcao* (twice-cooked potato dumplings).

We Dare You

- *charqui* – any kind of dried meat (we're partial to the llama jerky from the northern altiplano); a real workout for jaw muscles
- *carne de castor* – love 'em or loathe 'em, furry tree-felling beavers are fair game in Tierra del Fuego
- *pico roco* – this sea creature tastes much better than it looks, which is like a barnacle with tentacles
- *calzones rotos* – with a name like 'busted underwear' you might think twice, but this sugary, deep fried bread resembles a donut (gone anatomically awry)

greasy fried eggs and buried in salty fries. The equally meaty *chorrillana*, a platter of fried steak strips, potatoes, eggs and grilled onions, can easily feed two. To really splurge, Chileans love to indulge in a heart-stopping *parrillada*, a huge plate overflowing with different cuts of grilled beef. A common accompaniment to meat is *chancho en piedra* – their version of tomato salsa, with vinegar and cilantro.

Corn-based dishes are common during the summer maize harvest in central and northern Chile. They include *pastel de choclo*, a maize casserole that sometimes contains chicken or beef, and *humitas*, steamed corn tamales that usually come wrapped in corn husks. In the south, lamb (*cordero*) is a staple dish, served in stews (*estofados*) year-round and barbecued whole on a spit in summer.

The most prolific snack is the humble empanada – a large pastry turnover that is either fried or *al horno* (oven baked). Fillings are rich and gloopy: cheese and *pino* (ground beef with a taste of hard-boiled egg and olive) are especially popular, but sometimes you can get a seafood or veggie version. Sandwiches are equally ubiquitous. A cold ham-and-cheese sandwich is an *aliado*, which, when melted, is a more appetizing *Barros Jarpa* (named after a Chilean painter who practically lived on them). Steak with melted cheese is a *Barros Luco*, while beefsteak with tomato and green beans is a *chacarero*. A *completo* is a hot dog toppled with avocado, tomato and mayo.

Snackers will doubtless discover *sopaipilla* (deep-fried batter bread made from squash and flour); perfect post-drinks food and a real Chilean specialty. It goes well with the typical sauce called *pebre*, made from tomatoes, onion, garlic, chilies, cilantro, oil and lemon.

As for dessert, German influence in the south provides a variety of mouth-watering strudels, küchens (German-style cakes) and cheesecakes.

Meals

A simple affair, breakfast (*desayuno*) usually comprises white rolls with butter and jam, and tea or instant coffee. Some places offer eggs. In the Lakes District, breakfasts tend to be heartier with a slice of küchen and bread.

For lunch (*almuerzo* or *colación*) Chilean restaurants offer down-home cooking in super-size portions. Cheap set meals (*comida corrida*, *almuerzo del día* or *menú del día*) are routinely proffered; though less often for dinner (*la comida* or *cena*). The first course is usually a soupy stew called *cazuela*, with rice, a half ear of corn and some meat. This is followed by a main fish or meat dish, some veggies and a simple dessert. Lunch is the biggest meal.

Despite its name, the Chilean tradition of *onces* (elevenses) is not like the British tea and crumpet at 11am, but afternoon tea taken around 5pm. There are various entertaining theories as to how it was named, including one that it was the men's codeword to nip outside for a gulp of *aguardiente* liquor, which has 11 letters.

Tasting Chile: A Celebration of Authentic Chilean Foods and Wines, by Daniel Joelson, is a good place to start if you're looking to reproduce dishes you've tried on your travels.

When you've enjoyed Chilean food a little too much, try an *aguita*, a digestive tea made from native herbs.

THE BEST BARS IN CHILE

- With live jazz and signature pisco sours, Años Luz (p335) rocks Castro, Chiloé.
- Soak up the sailor ambiance in Club de Yates Micalvi (p415) in Puerto Williams.
- Quaff cocktails with a cutting edge in Bar Yellow (p106) in Santiago.
- Backstreet boho rocks Almendra Bar (p166) in Chile's university hub.
- With its own beer sommelier and 400 varieties to choose from, Eurohappy (p106) makes us just that.

DRINKS

Chile's ambrosial juices *(jugos)* – freshly squeezed, sweetened and thick enough to stand your straw upright – deserve a chapter of their own. Freshly squeezed orange juice is *jugo de naranja exprimido*. Other choices are *pomelo* (grapefruit), *damasco* (apricot), *piña* (pineapple), *mora* (blackberry), *maracuyá* (passion fruit) and *sandía* (watermelon). The distinctively Andean *mote con huesillo* is a traditional thirst quencher with rehydrated peaches in nectar and barley kernels. *Licuados* are milk-blended juices; unless you like yours *very* sweet, ask them to hold the sugar *(sin azúcar, por favor)*.

Sweet-toothed Chileans also guzzle prodigious amounts of soft drinks, from international brands to their super-sweet local counterparts such as Bilz and the unfortunately named Pap. Mineral water, both carbonated *(con gas)* and plain *(sin gas)*, is widely available, but tap water is generally potable.

Decent coffee is like gold dust in Chile. Gut-wrenching instant coffee is the norm in most households and at budget restaurants. *Café con leche* is literally milk with coffee – instant coffee dissolved in hot milk. *Café solo* or *café negro* is coffee with hot water alone. Most upmarket restaurants and hotels have espressos. A *cortado* is a shot with a splash of hot milk.

Tea is normally black and avalanched in sugar. If you'd like a splash of milk, an idea most Chileans find bizarre, ask for *un poquito de leche*. Asking for *té con leche* (tea with milk) brings a tea bag submerged in warm milk. *Yerba maté* (a tea typical in Argentina, consumed in a gourd with a metal straw) is a household staple in Patagonia. *Aguitas* (herbal teas) such as *manzanilla* (chamomile), *rosa mosqueta* (rose hip) and *cedrón* (lemon verbena) are often ordered after a meal.

Turistel's Guia de Vinos de Chile by Sara and Francisca Sánchez is the best bottle-by-bottle wine guide. It comes out yearly and is available in English.

Alcoholic Drinks

Chile's superb wines may grab the limelight, but there are plenty more tipples to try. Pisco is a top contender for the nation's favorite drink. This potent brandy is made from distilled grapes with a high sugar content, grown in the dry soils of the Copiapó and Elquí Valleys in Norte Chico. Chileans often quaff a pisco sour cocktail before eating. Premixed sours are available, but the best are shaken by bartenders until the ice melts and the sugar dissolves. Barhoppers order piscola, a mix of pisco and cola (and hence alcohol, caffeine and sugar) to keep them on the dance floor all night. Pisco also mixes well with ginger ale or vermouth, respectively named *chilcano* and *capitán*. Popular brands are Capel, Tres Erres and Los Artesanos del Cochiguaz. Higher-end brands are Mistral and Monte Fraile.

Need a primer on Chilean wine? Start at www .winesofchile.org, where you will find everything from special events and production information to vineyard maps. Wine enthusiasts pour forth on vintages and valley tours at www.chileanwines .survino.com.

Escudo and Cristal are the most popular beers, and it's hard to tell the difference between them. Becker is another decent choice, but Kunstmann, started by German colonists in Valdivia, is by far the best, making both ale and lager. Draft beer goes by its German name, *schop*; it's cheaper and often better than the bottled options.

Other Chilean concoctions include southern *gol*, a translucent mixture of butter, sugar and milk, left to ferment for two weeks. It's drunk mostly at home and is not readily available in restaurants. *Licor de oro*, found in Chiloé, also uses fermented milk but has other secret ingredients. *Guinda* is a sour cherry that is

---

HOW TO MAKE PISCO SOURS

This puckery cocktail is a frothy mix of three parts pisco (grape brandy) and one part límon de pica (a miniature lime). It requires serious elbow grease to squeeze all those little limes, but the end result is well worth the effort. Shake it together and add powdered sugar to taste.

CHILE: A WINEMAKER'S PARADISE

Why a paradise? Firstly, Chile is the only country in the world free of the two most destructive grapevine pests – downy mildew and the infamous root louse, phylloxera. The next major factor is the climate – in all of the major grape-growing regions it is virtually unheard of for it to rain during harvest time (from mid February until mid May), in stark contrast to more marginal climates such as France or New Zealand. Add to this moderate summer temperatures due to the cooling influence of the Pacific Ocean and snowcapped Andes, unprecedented amounts of sunshine (more than 250 days per year), a willingness to adopt new winemaking technology and very low labor costs, and it is not surprising that Chilean wine has been taking the world by storm.

Although Chile initially made its name internationally with cheap, drinkable reds, it is now becoming increasingly recognized for its super-premium wines increasingly grown on low-yielding hillside vineyards. The other plus for the traveler is that Chilean wineries are now catching on to the potential for wine tourism, finally making wine touring an option.

History: A Tale of Boom & Bust

As in many parts of the new world it was Christianity that originally brought the grapevine to Chile. The first recorded plantings in the country were made in 1548 by the catholic priest Francisco de Carabantes, who brought a selection of vines with him from Spain. However, quality wine production only began during the last half of the 19th century with the introduction of noble French vines such as Cabernet Sauvignon and Merlot. This was soon followed by the sudden arrival of technical know-how in the form of desperate French winemakers willing to travel to Chile in order to find work after phylloxera had left so many of Europe's vineyards decimated.

By 1877 winegrowing had become the most prosperous agricultural activity and Chilean wineries were already exporting to Europe. In the following 20 years production doubled and by 1900 Chile had 400 sq km of vineyards producing some 275 million liters. At this point, Chile's annual wine consumption had reached a historical high of 100L per capita sending alcoholism spiraling. To combat this, the government introduced an aggressive alcohol tax in 1902, which was followed by a second law in 1938 prohibiting the planting of new vineyards, leading to more than 30 years of stagnation.

In 1974, under Pinochet's free-market reforms, new vineyards were finally permitted. However, this sudden freedom resulted in a planting boom that lead to overproduction at the start of the '80s – the end result of which was a collapse in wine prices. By 1986 almost half of the country's vineyards had been uprooted and many of the most famous wineries were on the verge of bankruptcy.

Chile's fortunes turned, however, with the arrival of foreign companies such as Miguel Torres of Spain and Baron Rothschild of Bordeaux. These companies brought not only technical expertise but also modern winemaking equipment – notably temperature-controlled stainless-steel tanks and imported oak barrels – and the result was a rapid improvement in wine quality. Seeing the potential to exploit new export markets, traditional Chilean producers soon followed suit.

By the mid-1990s good fortune was once again smiling on Chile and exports were booming. Between 1998 and 2008 grape plantations increased more than 80% to a total of 1250 sq km with Chile currently producing about 5% of all wine globally. Chile currently exports over 70% of its total wine production with its biggest export market being the UK followed by the USA.

Wine Regions

Wine grapes are grown throughout much of the country from near La Serena in the north to near Temuco in the south, a total distance of about 1200km. The principal wine regions are all located in valleys (for the most part named after the main river running through them on its journey from the snow-capped Andes to the Pacific Ocean). From north to south they are the valleys of Elqui, Limari, Aconcagua, Casablanca, San Antonio/Leyda, Maipo, Cachapoal, Colchagua, Curicó, Maule and Biobío.

Fortunately for the tourist, three of the most important valleys in terms of quality are also three of the most accessible: Maipo Valley (boxed text, p118), immediately south of Santiago; Casablanca Valley (boxed text, p141), on the main road from Santiago to Valparaiso; and Colchagua Valley (boxed text, p148), the hub of which is the town of Santa Cruz. In addition, the Maule Valley (boxed text, p157) also has a well-organized wine route, although it's further from Santiago and has somewhat more variable wine quality.

Chilean Specialties

Ever since Alexander Payne's 2005 hit film *Sideways*, Pinot noir has become a worldwide phenomenon. Nowhere has this been more apparent than in Chile, where amid a frenzy of vineyard planting demand continues to considerably outstrip supply. Despite this Chile arguably remains the only country in the world currently producing good honest Pinot at a reasonable price. The best values are produced by Casas del Bosque (Gran Reserva, CH$10,690) and Cono Sur (Vision, CH$7130); the latter is currently the largest producer of Pinot noir in the world. But for something really top notch try Garces Silva (Amayna, CH$19,600), or the superb Casa Marin (Lo Abarca Hills, CH$42,175).

But if you are only going to try only one bottle of wine while in Chile, the one to try is a Carmenere. This little-known grape variety is originally from the Bordeaux region of France, and was widely planted there prior to the devastation wreaked by the phylloxera plague that occurred in the last half of the 19th century. Its tendency to ripen late combined with Bordeaux's decidedly cool, rainy climate made it unpopular there, and it was not replanted when the Bordelaise reestablished their vineyards. However, shortly before phylloxera hit, cuttings of the vine were brought to Chile and, mistaken for Merlot, it was subsequently widely planted. It was not until 1994 that it was identified as a separate grape variety and thanks to Chile's hot, sunny climate, it has proven itself to be capable of producing exceptional wines. A good Carmenere should be deeply colored with ripe, round tannins and a rich bouquet of plum, cassis and a slight hint of bell pepper accompanied by flavors of tobacco, cedar, black tea and spice. As it's a Chilean specialty there is a plethora of great Carmeneres to choose from; for something really outstanding, try the De Martino Legado (CH$8315) or Single Vineyard (CH$16,630).

In spite of the up-and-coming Carmenere, Cabernet Sauvignon remains the most widely planted grape in Chile and is a safe bet – especially those from the Maipo and Colchagua Valleys. Good examples are produced by Los Vascos (Grande Reserve, CH$8315), De Martino (Legado, CH$8315) and Tabalí (Reserva, CH$7720).

Syrah too has proven itself at home in Chile and is perhaps the most consistent red around. Try Tabalí (Reserva, CH$10,690), Loma Larga (BL-BK, CH$20,195) or, for something really stunning, the Matetic (EQ, CH$29,700).

Although Chile is most famous for its reds, it also produces some exceptional white wines, especially Sauvignon Blanc and Chardonnay from the cooler coastal valleys of Casablanca and San Antonio along with the up-and-coming Limari region. The following Sauvignons are all top notch: Casas del Bosque (Reserva, CH$5940), Los Vascos (CH$7130) and Casa Marin (Los Cipreses, CH$19,000). For Chardonnay try Errazuriz (Max Reserva, CH$8910), De Martino (Single Vineyard, CH$13,660) and Garces Silva (Amayna, CH$14,255).

And for those for whom money is no object the following super-premium wines are simply stunning and guaranteed to impress the palate: Domus Aurea (CH$47,520), Clos Apalta (CH$83,160) and Almaviva (CH$92,070).

Grant Phelps, Chief Winemaker, Viña Viu Manent

CHILE'S TOP EATS

- Seafood classics are piled high at any *cocinas custombristas*, informal dining featuring regional food, often found near marketplaces.
- Underground restaurant Los Deportistas (p132) serves up the best steaks.
- Diners go Nativo (p242) with exotic pizzas; try the charqui de burro.
- Gourmet goodness reigns at the posh Astrid y Gastón (p103).
- Mapuche fare is mouthwatering at Currarrehue's Cocinería La Ñaña (p287).

---

the basis of *guindado*, along with brandy, cinnamon, and cloves. *Murtillado* is a similar concept, with the blueberrylike *murtilla*. *Chicha* is fermented apple cider common in rural areas. A popular Christmas and holiday drink with added kick is the powerful but sweet liqueur *cola de mono* (literally 'tail of the monkey'), which consists of milk, *aguardiente*, coffee, cloves and vanilla.

CELEBRATIONS

The Chilean Kitchen, written by Belgian expat Ruth Van Waerebeek-Gonzalez, not only has recipes but also explores the customs surrounding food in Chile.

Food and family go hand in hand in Chile so important fiestas are often celebrated with family *asados* (barbecues) and *fondas* (fairs with plentiful food tents serving typical Chilean snacks and drinks). Christmas, New Year's Eve and the Fiestas Patrias are some of the biggest such celebrations. In the north of Chile, carnival celebrations set about filling bellies fit to bust before the fasting of Lent. Chiloé's festivals, which mostly take place in January and February, are terrific occasions to sample a wide variety of the island's distinctive dishes. On New Year's Eve, some Chileans eat a spoonful of lentils for good luck.

WHERE TO EAT & DRINK

Usually the main meal of the day, lunch is typically served between 1pm and 3pm. Dinner tends to be a lighter version of lunch and is eaten around 8pm or it is skipped altogether in favor of a late *once*. Lunch specials are a popular choice but if you don't like what's on offer, there is usually a more formal menu *(carta)*, although offerings are practically uniform throughout Chile.

When it comes to dining, Chileans tend to be homebodies. Spots that draw lunch crowds include *casino de bomberos*, literally the fire-station restaurant, great for cheap set lunches. Larger cities have a *fuente de soda* – a budget greasy-spoon café serving sandwiches, juices and drinks. Other popular cheapies include *pollerías*, recognizable for the rotisserie hens in the window.

Quinoa, a 'supergrain' grown in Chile's northern altiplano, contains more protein than any other grain with levels comparable to meat.

When browsing the *mercado* (market), you might happen upon tiny kitchens or cheap restaurants called *cocinerías* or *comedores*. The quality of these varies but it's generally a good sign if they are clean and packed with patrons. In Patagonia and Chiloé, some towns have renovated *cocinerías costumbristas* that offer quality home-style cooking.

Chile is notoriously conservative when it comes to ethnic fare but Chinese restaurants called *chifas* are ubiquitous, some even serving a few Chilean dishes. Regional fare is showcased at a *restaurante turístico*, popular for weekend outings, and sometimes including a music or dance performance. Ever-popular *parrillas* (grill restaurants) range from informal to fancy. All specialize in meat, though you won't find as much diversity in their offerings as you will in their Argentine counterparts. For white-linen service, a *club de unión* restaurant may be good, though sometimes they're a little stuffy and staid. In the south, where German heritage is prevalent, the local *club Aleman* is the spot to fill up on sausages and sauerkraut. A *schopería* is usually a downmarket bar serving draft beer and snacks.

Quick Eats

Nothing about eating out in Chile is quick. If you find service particularly slow, it's ok to walk up to the register and settle your bill there. But if you want food on the go, try a *panadería* – these bakeries have fresh bread, pastries, dairy products and savory empanadas. Street food includes roasted peanuts or hot dogs – known as *completos,* probably because they come heaped with everything but the kitchen sink, including fresh avocado and tomato. Vendors often board long-distance buses at stops to offer coffee, ice cream and homemade snacks. Fast-food chains are ubiquitous but if you're short on time, your best bet may be making a trip to the market or grocery store for picnic supplies.

VEGETARIANS & VEGANS

For strict herbivores, menus are limited. Most restaurants have side dishes of veggies that you can order as a main dish. When explaining that you don't eat meat it's helpful to say it is due to an allergy *(alergia)*, and re-member when ordering salads that it's not enough to ask if it has any *carne* (meat) because chicken and fish are in a separate linguistic class. Many of the white-bread rolls served at restaurants and *hospedajes* are made with lard. In popular tourist haunts there are always vegetarian pizzas, pasta and omelets available. *Porotos granados,* spiced beans with corn and pumpkin, is a good traditional option. In the north, *quinoa* is a tasty alternative to rice or pasta. Larger cities have better options, with dedicated vegetarian restaurants.

Southern Chile's answer to the peanut, *piñones* are much larger than other varieties of pine nut. They come from the araucaria (monkey-puzzle tree) and are usually roasted and served warm.

EATING WITH KIDS

Chileans are very family-oriented and your kids will be welcomed, even fussed over, in most restaurants. Children's menus are not common but Chilean cuisine is generally bland despite the occasional hot sauce. Lunch portions are of such whopping proportions that you can easily split your meal with your kids, something that few establishments will mind.

HABITS & CUSTOMS

Eating here is as much social as it is nutritional. Long-lingering lunches and afternoon teas with friends are de rigueur. Waiters tend to give Chileans space to enjoy a long, sociable coffee after their meal, so make an effort to call for their attention if you want the bill. Dinners are for families to spend quality time together, so lunchtime is the time to eat in restaurants if you're looking for a lively atmosphere. Table manners are more or less the same as those in North America or Europe.

DOS & DON'TS

- It is customary – and expected – to leave a 10% tip.
- Wish your fellow diners *buen provecho* (bon appetit) before tucking in.
- When drinking say *salud* (good health).
- When raising your glasses to each other in a toast, it's customary to meet your companion's eyes.

EAT YOUR WORDS

Order *locos* (crazy people) in Chile and you'll be served with chewy abalone. Ask for *onces* at 11 o'clock and you'll be looked at as if *you're* the *loco*. Navigate the Chilean cuisine scene by getting to know the language.

Useful Phrases

I'm a vegetarian.
  soy ve-he-tah-*rya*-no/a   Soy vegetariano/a.
Do you have any vegetarian dishes?
  tieh-nen al-*goon pla*-toh ve-he-tah-*rya*-no?   ¿Tienen algún plato vegetariano?
I don't eat meat, chicken or fish.
  no *ko*-moh *kar*-ne nee *po*-yo nee pes-*ka*-doh   No como carne, ni pollo ni pescado.
I'm allergic to peanuts/wheat/eggs.
  soy ah-*ler*-he-ko/a al mah-*nee/tri*-go/whe-vo   Soy alérgico/a al maní/trigo/huevo.
Do you have a menu (in English)?
  ai *oo*-na *kar*-ta (en een-*gles*)?   ¿Hay una carta (en Inglés)?
Does that come with salad/fries?
  Ve-*eh*-ne con *pa*-pas *free*-tas?   ¿Viene con ensalada/papas fritas?
What do you recommend?
  Keh meh reh-coh-mee-*en*-dah?   ¿Qué me recomienda?
I didn't order this.
  No peh-*dee es*-toh   No pedí esto.
The bill, please.
  lah *cwen*-tah, por fah-*vohr*   La cuenta, por favor.
Thanks, that was delicious.
  Grah-see-ahs, es-*tah*-bah sah-*bro*-soh   Gracias, estaba sabroso.

With flavors like chocolate basil and *miel de ulmo* (wild honey), Santiago's own Emporio La Rosa churns out some of the best ice cream on the continent.

Food Glossary

ajiaco	ah-hee-*ah*-coh	spiced beef stew
almejas ahl-*meh*-hahs	clams	
arroz	a-*roz*	rice
ave or *pollo*	ah-veh, po-yo	chicken
azúcar	a-*zoo*-kar	sugar
bebida	beh-*bee*-dah	drink
calamares	cah-lah-*mah*-rehs	squid
caldo	*cahl*-doh	soup
camarones	cah-mah-*roh*-nes	shrimp
cangrejo or *jaiba*	kan-*gre*-hoh, *hai*-bah	crab
carne	*kar*-neh	meat
cazuela	cah-*zueh*-lah	potato or maize stew with beef or chicken
centolla	cehn-*toh*-yah	king crab
cholgas	*chohl*-gahs	mussels
churrasco	choo-*rrahz*-coh	steak
comida	coh-*mee*-dah	food
ensalada	en-sah-*lah*-dah	salad
erizos	eh-*ree*-zohs	sea urchins
fruta	*froo*-tah	fruit
jamón	hah-*mon*	ham
helado	eh-*lah*-doh	ice cream
hielo	ee-*eh*-loh	ice
huevo	*wheh*-voh	egg

legumbres	leh-*goom*-bres	vegetables
locos	*loh*-cohs	abalone
machas	*mah*-chahs	razor clams
maíz	ma-*eez*	corn, maize
mantequilla	man-teh-*kee*-ya	butter
mariscos	mah-*rees*-cohs	shellfish
mermelada	mer-meh-*lah*-dah	jam
ostiones	os-*tioh*-nes	scallops
ostras	*ohs*-trahs	oysters
palta	*pal*-tah	avocado
pan	pan	bread
papas fritas	*pa*-pas *free*-tas	fries
pastel	pas-*tel*	pastry
pescado	pes-*cah*-doh	fish
picoroco	pee-coh-*roh*-coh	giant barnacle
pimienta	pee-mee-*en*-tah	pepper
postre	*pos*-treh	dessert
pulpo	*pool*-poh	octopus
queso	*keh*-so	cheese
sopa	*so*-pah	soup
trigo	*tree*-goh	wheat

Environment

Nature can't help but prevail in visitors' impressions of Chile, where even the Santiago skyline is dominated by the high Andes. Geography students could cover almost their entire syllabus in this slinky country: some 4300km long and 200km wide, Chile is hemmed in by the Pacific Ocean on one side and the Andes on the other. Stunning in variety, it features the driest desert in the world, temperate rainforest and an ice-capped south, all linked by 50 active volcanoes and woven together by rivers, lakes and farmland. In recent years, mining, salmon farming and hydroelectric proposals have put many parts of this once-pristine environment under imminent threat.

For information about traveling responsibly, see p21.

Did you know that Chile contains approximately 10% of all the world's active volcanoes?

THE LAND

The Andes, which form Chile's rugged spine, began forming about 60 million years ago. While southern Chile was engulfed by glaciers, northern Chile was submerged below the ocean: hence today the barren north is plastered with pastel salt flats and the south is scored by deep glacially carved lakes, curvaceous moraine hills, and awesome glacial valleys.

Still young in geological terms, the Chilean Andes repeatedly top 6000m and thrust as high as 6893m at Ojos del Salado, the second-highest peak in South America and the highest active volcano in the world.

Much like a lanky totem pole, Chile can be split into easily caricatured horizontal chunks. Straddling the Tropic of Capricorn, the Norte Grande (Big North) is dominated by the Atacama Desert, supposedly the driest in the world with areas where rainfall has never been recorded. The climate is moderated by the cool Humboldt Current which parallels the coast. High humidity conjures up a thick blanket of fog known as *camanchaca,* which condenses on coastal ranges. Coastal cities here hoard scant water from river valleys, subterranean sources and distant stream diversions. The canyons of the precordillera (foothills) lead eastwards to the altiplano (high steppe) and to high, snow-sprinkled mountain passes.

Copper accounts for roughly one-third of Chile's exports today, and the world's top-producing copper mine, the massive Mina Escondida, is found in Chile.

CHILE'S UNESCO SITES

- Juan Fernández Biosphere Reserve (p429)
- Parque Nacional Rapa Nui (p454)
- Churches of Chiloé (p334)
- Historic quarter of Valparaíso (p123)
- Torres del Paine Biosphere Reserve (p393)
- Humberstone and Santa Laura saltpeter works (p201)
- Fray Jorge Biosphere Reserve (p261)
- Laguna San Rafael Biosphere Reserve (p364)
- Lauca Biosphere Reserve (p189)
- Cabo de Hornos Biosphere Reserve (p416)
- La Campana-Peñuelas Biosphere Reserve (p141)
- Parque Nacional Conguillío (p272)

Further south, the Norte Chico (Little North) sees the desert give way to scrub and pockets of forest. Several green river valleys streak from east to west, allowing agriculture. In those rare years of heavy rainfall, the landscape blossoms with masses of wildflowers.

South of the Río Aconcagua begins the fertile heartland of Middle Chile, carpeted with vineyards and abundant agriculture. It is also home to the capital, Santiago (with at least a third of the country's population), vital ports, and the bulk of the country's industry and employment.

Descending south another rung, the Lakes District undulates with green pastureland, temperate rainforest and foothill lakes, watched over by snow-capped volcanoes. The region is drenched by high rainfall, most of which dumps between May and September, but no month is excluded. The warm but strong easterly winds here are known as *puelches*. Winters are snowy, making good skiing but border passage difficult.

The country's largest island, Isla Grande de Chiloé, hangs off the continent here, battered by Pacific winds and storms. The smaller islands on its eastern flank make up the archipelago, but there's no escaping the rain: the archipelago gets up to 150 wet days per year.

The Aisén region is an intoxicating mix of fjords, raging rivers, impenetrable forests and high peaks. The Andes here jog west to meet the Pacific and the vast Campo de Hielo Norte (Northern Ice Field), where 19 major glaciers coalesce, nourished by heavy rain and snow. To the east, mountainous rainforest gives way to barren Patagonia steppe. Here South America's deepest lake, the enormous Lago General Carrera, is shared with Argentina.

At the foot of the country, the Campo de Hielo Sur (Southern Ice Field) separates the mainland from sprawling Magallanes and Tierra del Fuego. The weather is exceedingly changeable (expect four seasons in a day), and winds are brutal. Tapering into the wet foot of the continent, pearly-blue glaciers, crinkled fjords, vast ice fields and mountains join in a marvelous jumble before reaching the Magellan Strait and Tierra del Fuego. The barren eastern pampas stretch through northern Tierra del Fuego, abruptly halting by the Cordillera Darwin.

For a detailed breakdown of climatic conditions, see p464.

WILDLIFE

A bonus to Chile's glorious scenery is its abundant and fascinating wildlife. Bounded by ocean, desert and mountain, the country is home to a unique environment that developed much on its own, creating a number of endemic species.

Animals

Chile's comical domestic camelids and their slimmer wild cousins get much of the attention in the northern altiplano (see the boxed text, p64). Equally unusual are creatures such as the gangly-legged ostrich-like rhea (called ñandú in Spanish), which struts about the northern altiplano and southern steppe, and the plump, scraggly-tailed viscacha (a wild relative of the chinchilla) that hides amid the rocks at high altitude.

The puma still prowls widely through the Andes, although it's rarely seen. The rare and diminutive deer, pudú, hides out in thick forests throughout the south. Still rarer is the huemul deer (see the boxed text, p65), an endangered species endemic to Patagonia.

Chile's long coastline features many marine mammals, including many raucous colonies of sea lions, slippery sea otters as well as fur seals in the south. Playful dolphin pods and whales (see p68) can be glimpsed, while seafood platters evidence that fish and shellfish are abundant.

In Inka times there were millions of vicuña that ranged throughout the Andes. Today in Chile, there are only 25,000.

COOL CAMELIDS

For millennia, Andean peoples have relied on the New World camels – the wild guanaco and vicuña; the domesticated llama and alpaca – for food and fiber.

The delicate guanaco, a slim creature with stick-thin legs and long, elegant neck, can be found in the far north and south, at elevations from sea level up to 4000m or more. It is most highly concentrated in the plains of Patagonia, including Parque Nacional Torres del Paine. It is less common and flightier in the north where you're most likely to get photos of guanaco behinds as they high-tail it to a safe distance.

The leggy vicuña is the smallest camelid, with a swan neck and minuscule head. It lives only above 4000m in the puna and altiplano, from south-central Peru to northwestern Argentina. Its fine golden wool was once the exclusive property of Inka kings, but after the Spanish invasion it was hunted mercilessly. However, conservation programs came to the rescue. In Parque Nacional Lauca and surrounds, vicuña have sprung back from barely a thousand in 1973 to about 25,000 today.

Many highland communities in northern Chile still depend on domestic llamas and alpacas for their livelihood. The taller, rangier and hardier llama is a pack animal whose relatively coarse wool serves for blankets, ropes and other household goods, and its meat makes good *charqui* (jerky). It can survive – even thrive – on poor, dry pastures.

The slightly smaller but far shaggier alpaca looks like an overgrown poodle with tiny little legs poking from the bottom. The alpaca is not a pack animal and requires well-watered grasslands to produce its fine wool; you'll see stalls overflowing with alpaca woolens in the north.

Bird-watchers will also be well satisfied. The northern altiplano contains all manner of interesting bird life, from Andean gulls to giant coots. But the star of the show is, of course, the flamboyant flamingo, large nesting colonies of which speckle highland lakes pink, from the far north down to Torres del Paine. There are three species of flamingo here, including the rare James variety (in Spanish parina chica; *Phoenicoparrus jamesi*). Colonies of endangered Humboldt and Magellanic penguins scattered along Chile's long coastline are another crowd-pleaser; they are a particular hit at Parque Nacional Pingüino de Humboldt, off the northwestern coast of Chiloé and near Punta Arenas.

For an easy-to-use field guide to Chile's feathered friends, seek out the highly illustrated *Birds of Chile*, by A Jaramillo et al.

If you really hit the jackpot you may also spy the legendary Andean condor circling on high mountain updrafts. Meanwhile the awkward-looking ibis, which makes a loud knocking call, is commonly seen in pastures. The queltehue, with black, white and grey markings, has a loud call used to protect its ground nests: if there's a bird that will wake you up at any hour, it's this one.

Plants

When heading into the wild, grab a great field guide like *Birds of Patagonia, Tierra del Fuego & Antarctic Peninsula* (2003) and *Flora Patagonia* (2008), published by Fantástico Sur (www.fantastico sur.com).

Chile boasts a wealth of interesting and unique plant life. While few plants can eke out an existence in its northern desert, those that manage do so by extraordinary means. More than 20 different types of cacti and succulents survive on moisture absorbed from the ocean fog. One of the most impressive varieties is the endangered candelabra cactus (*Browningia candelaris*), which looks as it sounds and reaches heights up to 5m.

The high altiplano is characterized by patchy grassland, spiky scrub stands of queñoa (*Polylepis tarapacana*) and weird ground-hugging species like the lime-green llareta (*Laretia compacta*), a dense shrub resembling a large lumpy cushion. The native tamarugo (*Prosopis tamarugo*) tree once covered large areas of Chile's northern desert; this scraggly-looking tree determinedly digs roots down as far as 15m to find water.

However the desert's biggest surprise of all comes in years of sudden rainfall in Norte Chico. Delicate wildflowers break through the barren desert

---

CAN SCIENCE SAVE A NATIONAL SYMBOL?

In 2005 scientists at the Universidad de Chile in Santiago announced that they were working to clone Chile's national symbol, the huemul deer, to save it from extinction. While the public is still waiting to meet Bambi II and Bambi III, efforts to preserve those already in the wild are becoming more urgent. The docile huemul is the world's fifth-most endangered species of deer and could disappear from mainland Chile in the next few years if radical steps are not taken to protect it.

Deforestation, hunting and habitat destruction for pasture have been the main causes of the decreasing numbers in central Chile, where only a few dozen are thought to remain, and in southern Aisén, where there are only a few hundred. After several reintroductions into Parque Nacional Torres del Paine, the population there is still considered low. Your best bet to see a wild huemul is in Reserva Nacional Tamango (see p369), though chances even there are slim.

---

crust in a glorious phenomenon called the *desierto florido*, which showcases rare and endemic species (see the boxed text, p242).

From Norte Chico through most of Middle Chile, the native flora consists mostly of shrubs whose glossy leaves conserve water during the long, dry season. However, pockets of southern beech (the *Nothofagus* species) cling to the coastal range nourished by the thick ocean fog. Few stands of the grand old endemic Chilean palm *(Jubaea chilensis)* exist nowadays, but you can still see it in Parque Nacional La Campana.

Southern Chile boasts one of the largest temperate rainforests in the world. Its northern reaches are classified as Valdivian rainforest, a maze of evergreens, hugged by vines and its roots lost under impenetrable thickets of bamboo-like plants. Further south, the Magellanic rainforest has less diversity but hosts several more important species. Equally breathtaking is the araucaria forest, home to the araucaria *(Araucaria araucana)* – a grand old species of pine that can age up to 1000 years. The English name became 'monkey puzzle,' since its forbidding foliage and jigsaw-like bark would surely stump a monkey.

Meanwhile in the southern lakes region, the 'sequoia of South America,' commonly known as the alerce *(Fitzroya cupressoides)*, is one of the longest-living trees in the world, growing for up to 4000 years. You can admire them from Lago Llanquihue south to Chaitén, especially in Parque Nacional Alerce Andino and Parque Pumalín. Also see the boxed text, p346.

On Chiloé and in Aisén, the rhubarb-like nalca is the world's largest herbaceous plant, with enormous leaves that grow from a single stalk; the juicy stalk of younger plants is edible.

Meanwhile, the Juan Fernández archipelago is a major storehouse of biological diversity: of 140 native plant species found on the islands, 101 are endemic (see p432).

La Tragedia del Bosque Chileno (1999), edited by Adriana Hoffman, is a powerful condemnation of how commercial interests are devastating Chile's natural forests. Available in Spanish only.

PROTECTED AREAS

Nineteen percent of Chile is preserved as national parks, national monuments and nature reserves. These stunning parks are one of the country's top international attractions, and visitor numbers have snowballed since the first park was inaugurated in the 1920s. Visits to national parks and reserves have almost doubled in the last ten years. In 2007 alone, there were around 1.7 million visitors, 40% of whom were foreign. But while scene-stealing parks such as Torres del Paine are annually inundated, the majority of Chile's protected areas remain underutilized, wild and begging to be explored. Hikers have their pick of trails, and solitude is easily found, especially if you avoid the summer high season of January and February.

CHILE'S NATIONAL PARKS

Protected Area	Features	Activities	Best Time to Visit
Parque Nacional Alerce Andino	mountainous alerce forest; pumas, pudú, condors,	hiking kingfishers, waterfowl	Dec-Mar
Parque Nacional Bernardo O'Higgins (p392)	remote ice fields, glaciers, waterfalls; cormorants, condors	boat trips	Dec-Mar
Parque Nacional Chiloé (p337)	coastal dunes, lagoons & folklore-rich forest; rich bird life, pudú, sea lions	hiking, wildlife, kayaking, horse-trekking	Dec-Mar
Parque Nacional Conguillío (p272)	mountainous araucaria forests, lakes, canyons, active volcano	hiking, climbing, skiing, boating, hiking Dec-Mar, skiing	Jun-Oct
Parque Nacional Fray Jorge (p261)	cloud forest in dry desert coastline	hiking, flora	year-round
Parque Nacional Juan Fernández (p436)	remote archipelago, ecological treasure trove of endemic plants	hiking, boat trips, diving, flora	Dec-Mar
Parque Nacional Huerquehue (p286)	forest, lakes, waterfalls & outstanding views	hiking	Dec-Mar
Parque Nacional La Campana (p141)	coastal cordillera: oak forests & Chilean palms	hiking, flora	Nov-Feb
Parque Nacional Laguna del Laja (p169)	Andean foothills, waterfalls, lakes, rare trees; condors	hiking	Dec-Mar
Parque Nacional Laguna San Rafael (p364)	glaciers reach the sea at this stunning ice field	boat trips, flights, hiking, climbing	Sep-Mar
Parque Nacional Lauca (p189)	altiplano volcanoes, lakes, steppe; abundant bird life & vicuñas	hiking, wildlife, traditional villages, hot springs	year-round
Parque Nacional Llanos de Challe (p242)	coastal plains; 'flowering desert' occurs after heavy rains; guanaco	flora & fauna	Jul-Sep in rainy years
Parque Nacional Nahuelbuta (p172)	high coastal range of araucaria forests, wildflowers; pumas, pudú, rare woodpeckers	hiking	Nov-Apr
Parque Nacional Nevado Tres Cruces (p240)	volcano Ojos del Salado; flamingos, vicuñas, guanacos	climbing, hiking, wildlife	Dec-Feb

National parks and reserves are administered by **Conaf** (www.conaf.cl). Before leaving Santiago, visit their central **information office** (☎ 02-390-0282; Av Bulnes 265, Centro; ⏱ 9:30am-5:30pm Mon-Fri) for basic maps and brochures.

Chile's 95 protected areas are divided into three different categories: *parques nacionales* (national parks); *reservas nacionales* (national reserves), which are open to limited economic exploitation; and *monumentos naturales* (natural monuments), which are smaller but strictly protected areas or features. Combined, these protected areas cover around 19% of the country.

Conaf is underfunded and many parks are inadequately protected. However, other government-financed projects are showing a commitment to ecotourism, including the mega-long **Sendero de Chile** (www.senderodechile.cl, in Spanish), a 8000km trail from Chile's top to its bottom nearing completion (see the boxed text, p72).

Private Protected Areas

Chilean law permits private nature reserves: *áreas de protección turística* (tourist protection areas) and *santuarios de la naturaleza* (nature sanctuaries). Private parks started making Chilean headlines when American businessman Douglas Tompkins (see the boxed text, p347) purchased an area the

Ancient Forest International's *Chile's Native Forests: A Conservation Legacy*, by Ken Wilcox, provides an accessible overview of the history and description of Chile's forests and the environmental issues affecting them.

Protected Area	Features	Activities	Best Time to Visit
Parque Nacional Pan de Azúcar (p233)	coastal desert; penguins, otters, sea lions, guanacos & cacti	boat trips, wildlife, swimming, hiking	year-round
Parque Nacional Puyehue (p299)	volcanic dunes, lava rivers, forest	hiking, skiing, hot springs, biking, lake canoeing	hiking Dec-Mar, skiing Jun-Oct
Parque Nacional Rapa Nui (p454)	isolated Polynesian island with enigmatic archaeological treasures	archaeology, diving, hiking, horseback riding	year-round
Parque Nacional Torres del Paine (p393)	Chile's showpiece park of spectacular peaks, forest, glaciers; guanacos, condors, ñandú, flamingos	trekking, wildlife, climbing, glacier trekking, kayaking, horseback riding	Dec-Mar
Parque Nacional Vicente Pérez Rosales (p308)	hiking, climbing, skiing, boat trips, rafting, kayaking, canyoning	Chile's oldest national park crowded with lakes & volcanoes hiking Dec-Mar, skiing	Jun-Oct
Parque Nacional Villarrica (p284)	smoking volcanic cone overlooking lakes & resorts	trekking, climbing, skiing	hiking Dec-Mar, skiing Jun-Oct
Parque Nacional Volcán Isluga (p202)	remote altiplano, volcanoes, geysers, unique pastoral culture; rich bird life	villages, hiking, bird-watching, hot springs	year-round
Reserva Nacional Altos de Lircay (p156)	Andean forests, plateaus; native parrots, other bird life	trekking, horseback riding	Dec-May
Reserva Nacional Los Flamencos (p220)	desert altiplano, salt flat, eerie land forms; flamingos,	hiking, biking, horseback riding, sand-boarding, wildlife, archaeology, hot springs	year-round
Reserva Nacional Pingüino de Humboldt (p243)	islands; Humboldt penguins, otters & sea lions	boat trips, wildlife	year-round
Reserva Nacional Radal Siete Tazas (p152)	precordillera forest & scrubland, stunning waterfalls	hiking	Nov-Apr
Reserva Nacional Tamango (p369)	transitional area to Patagonian steppe; huemul deer	hiking	Dec-Feb

size of Rhode Island to create Parque Pumalín. Concerns were raised about national security and ulterior money-making motives, but in August 2005 Pumalín was donated to a Chilean foundation (Fundación Pumalín) and became a bona fide nature reserve. Tompkins may have ignited a great debate about land ownership and use, but he has also inspired others, including Kris Tompkins, his wife, to preserve Patagonia's Valle Chacabuco (p369), and ex-presidential candidate Sebastián Piñera to create Chiloé's Parque Tantauco (see boxed text, p340).

In all, Chile has around 133 privately protected areas, reaching a total of almost 4000 sq km. Codeff (p69) maintains a database of the properties, all of which have joined together to create Red de Areas Protegidas Privadas (RAPP; Network of Private Protected Areas).

Information on Chile's myriad national parks and reserves can be found on Conaf's website www.conaf.cl.

ENVIRONMENTAL ISSUES

Chile is considered to be one of the least sustainable countries in the world, indiscriminately using its natural resources to improve economic growth, and often allowing foreign companies to do all the exploiting. However, many Chileans, not to mention international foundations, are becoming more aware of the environmental issues and the government's lack of foresight.

Along with Mexico City and Sao Paolo, Santiago is one of the Americas' most polluted cities. The smog blanket is at times so severe that people sport surgical facemasks, school children are ordered not to participate in physical education, and the elderly are advised to stay indoors. There have been significant recent efforts to reduce pollution, including a major overhaul of the city's bus system and the creation of no-drive days for private vehicles (see p485), but there is still room for improvement.

Chile's forests continue to lose ground to plantations of fast-growing exotics, such as eucalyptus and Monterey pine. Caught in a tug-of-war between their economic and ecological value, native tree species have also declined precipitously to logging. The alerce is supposedly protected by laws prohibiting its export and the felling of live trees. But loggers and traffickers of the tree continue undaunted, finding ways around the laws or ignoring them.

Canadian beavers, first introduced for their fur, are busily felling trees, causing floods and spreading disease across Tierra del Fuego and surrounding islands (see the boxed text, p416). A plague of introduced mink has also forced the government to take action in southern Chile.

Water and air pollution caused by the mining industry has long been a concern. Some mining towns have suffered such severe contamination that they have been relocated. The industry also demands huge energy and water supplies, and mining locations can interfere with water basins. In 2006, the Chilean government approved a proposal by Canadian mining company Barrick Gold to begin extraction. The plan is part of a 2004 mining agreement between Chile and Argentina called the Pascua Lama treaty. Farmers and environmental groups are opposed to the operation, which was also initially rejected by the Regional Environmental Commission.

Water and energy are key components of Chile's race toward modernization. The country has often had to deal with energy shortages, so successive governments have promoted hydroelectricity. Heavy spring snowmelt in the high Andes feeds raging rivers that pass through narrow canyons, making ideal sites for dams. However these projects also have major social and environmental drawbacks. High-profile battles are underway over dams on the Río Baker and Pascua, among ten other Patagonian rivers (see the boxed text, p359). The Bachelet government has come out in favor of the dams, although officially, approval pends upon the results of environmental impact studies. Recent reports have also suggested that Chile is toying with the idea of building nuclear power stations.

Spanish-language picture book *Patagonia Chile ¡Sin Represas!*, edited by Chilean environmentalist Juan Pablo Orrego, uses before and after images to illustrate the impact of proposed hydroelectric projects in Patagonia.

IN DEFENSE OF THE BIG GUYS

The largest animal in the world came perilously close to extinction just a few decades ago. So it was with great excitement in 2003 that what seems to be a blue whale 'nursery' was discovered in sheltered fjords just southeast of Chiloé in the Golfo de Corcovado. More than 100 whales gathered here to feed, including 11 mothers with their young. Since then, calls for Chile's government to create Area Marina y Costera de Multiples Usos de Chiloé-Corcovado-Chonos, a protected area, have been intensifying. It's hoped that this area could eventually become a world-class ecotourism destination. Moving toward this effort, Chile banned whale hunting off the entire length of its coast in September 2008. For news and detailed conservation information, try **Centro Ballena Azul** (www.ballenazul.org, in Spanish) and the **Whale and Dolphin Conservation Society** (www.wdcs.org).

Whale-watching is increasingly popular in Patagonia. A variety of species can be spotted, including fin, humpback, killer and sperm whales. Current hubs for Patagonian whale-watching trips include Punta Arenas, and in Argentina Puerto Madryn.

Another issue is the intensive use of agricultural chemicals and pesticides to promote Chile's flourishing fruit exports, which during the southern summer furnish the northern hemisphere with fresh produce. Likewise industrial waste is a huge problem. A Celco paper-pulping plant near Valdivia is a much-publicized example; its emissions killed thousands of swans in a nearby nature sanctuary. After being temporarily shut, the plant soon reopened with plans to direct its arsenic-heavy waste out to sea – simply trading river life for ocean life.

The apparently inexorable expansion of southern Chile's salmon farms is polluting water, devastating underwater ecology, and depleting other fish stocks (see the boxed text, p315). Some areas, such as the Lakes Region Seno de Reloncaví, have become too polluted for sustainable production; sadly, farming operations are just skirting further south to Aisén. However, a 2007 *New York Times* report revealing widespread virus outbreaks in Chilean salmon and questioning aquaculture practices has rocked the industry and inspired tighter government controls and monitoring. Salmon is a $2.2 billion-dollar industry in Chile, the world's second-largest producer of farmed salmon.

Forest fire continues to damage many of Chile's national parks. Most famously, Torres del Paine was ignited accidentally by a careless tourist in 2005. Be ultra careful with camping stoves (or any open flame) and avoid areas with dry grass.

The growing hole in the ozone layer over Antarctica has become such an issue that medical authorities recommend wearing protective clothing and heavy sunblock to avoid cancer-causing ultraviolet radiation, especially in Patagonia (see the boxed text, p398).

Global warming is also having a significant impact on Chile. No where is it more apparent than with the melting of glaciers (see boxed text, p405). Scientists have documented many glaciers doubling their thinning rates in recent years while the northern and southern ice fields continue retreat. In particular, the Northern Patagonian Ice Field is contributing to rising ocean levels at a rate one-quarter higher than formerly believed. In fact, reports say that glaciers are thinning more rapidly than can be explained by warmer air temperatures and decreased precipitation. While tour operators and real estate hawks in the rainy south may be reaping the short-term benefit of a warmer and drier climate, the change also stands to impact plant and animal life, water levels in lakes and rivers, and overall sustainability.

> Erosion is the major environmental threat in Easter Island but reforestation programs are in the process of bringing all that loose land under control.

> Navigate the Chilean roads and parks via the detailed maps and information (in Spanish) found on Turistel's website www.turistel.cl.

Environmental Organizations

Ancient Forest International (AFI; ☎ 707-923-4475; www.ancientforests.org) US-based organization with close links to Chilean forest-conservation groups.

Codeff (Comité Pro Defensa de la Fauna y Flora; off Map pp90-1; ☎ 02-777-2534; www.codeff.cl, in Spanish; Ernesto Reyes 035, Providencia, Santiago) Campaigns to protect the country's flora and fauna, especially endangered species. Trips, seminars and work projects are organized for volunteers.

Defensores del Bosque Chileno (Map pp80-1; ☎ 02-204-1914; www.elbosquechileno.cl, in Spanish; Diagonal Oriente 1413, Ñuñoa) Defending the native forests through education, lobbying, promoting the planting of native species over exotics, and taking legal action against logging interests.

Greenpeace Chile (Map pp80-1; ☎ 02-634-2120; www.greenpeace.cl, in Spanish; Agromedo 50, Centro, Santiago) Focuses on forest conservation, ocean ecology and dealing with toxic waste.

Patagonia Sin Represas (Patagonia Without Dams; www.patagoniasinrepresas.cl) A coalition of Chilean environmental groups supporting the anti-dam movement in Patagonia.

Terram (Map pp80-1; ☎ 02-269-4499; www.terram.cl; Bustamante 24, Providencia, Santiago) One of the biggest-hitting pressure groups at the moment.

WWF (☎ 063-244-590; www.wwf.cl; Carlos Andtwander 624, Casa 4, Valdivia) Involved with the preservation of the temperate rainforests around Valdivia, conservation in southern Patagonia, and protection of the native wildlife.

> You can catch up with the latest conservation headlines through English-language news portal the *Santiago Times*, www.santiagotimes.cl, by selecting its Environmental News header.

Outdoors

Get ready for the real deal: Chile has abundant wilderness prime for exploration. It starts in the desert north, travels through the high Andes and lush rainforest to the glacier-studded south. You can get wet surfing the Pacific breaks, kayaking fjords, rafting white-water rivers, or soaking in sublime hot springs. You can get vertical burning down volcanoes on a mountain bike, skiing in the Andes or hiking in the footsteps of explorers. The crazes of kite-surfing, sand-boarding, heliskiing and waterfall rappelling have all made it here too. Don't limit a trip to the spring and summer: winter in the Andes has its own special kind of magic.

HIKING & TREKKING

The number one reason to come to Chile is to get off the roads and into nature – on foot. Some of the most inspirational and iconic hiking trails in the world are here, passing through scenery of such exquisite beauty that all thoughts of heavy packs and aching legs will be forgotten. What follows barely touches the extent of the possibilities but should tantalize you enough to pack those heavy boots.

The sublime Torres del Paine (p395), in the heart of the Patagonia wilds, is one of the continent's most beloved hiking destinations, graced by glaciers, gemstone lakes and the world-famous granite spires. The park has decent transportation links, *refugios* and campsites that allow for day hikes and multiday circuit treks. However, its popularity has led to overcrowding in summer months. For awe-inspiring isolation, Tierra del Fuego's Dientes de Navarino (p414) hiking circuit is equally stunning but much harder to get to; once there, you won't find any infrastructure either.

Within the northern corner of Patagonia, the Río Cochamó valley (p311), though not protected as a park, has enticing treks through the 'Yosemite of the south,' while further afield, the Puelo Valley offers treks through gorgeous mountain farmland. Pumalín (p346) has some great day and multiday hikes on offer.

The Lakes District abounds with trails and tantalizing terrain, but hikes through Conguillío (p272), along the Valdivian coast, and around Volcán Puyehue (p299) – with out-of-place and out-of-this-world landscapes, hot springs and geyser fields – are highlights.

The citybound can escape above Santiago's smogline with jaunts to nearby El Morado (p119) or Parque Nacional La Campana (p141). Altos de Lircay (p156), in Chile's middle, has a great backcountry circuit. In the north, desert oasis San Pedro de Atacama (p212) has a number of intriguing hikes, as does Parque Nacional Lauca (p189).

Hiking in Parque Nacional Juan Fernández (p436) is a highlight for anyone who makes it there, with a system of independent and guided hikes through steep terrain filled with endemic plants and birds. The magic Easter Island (p447) lures some travelers to trek its circumference.

Most national parks and reserves have at least a few decent trail networks, although there are not many in comparison to the amount of protected land; Conaf's insufficient funding means that for years they've had to focus more on maintaining what they already have rather than developing the trail systems. But opportunities are not limited to the national parks: check out the Sendero de Chile (see p72) and opportunities for rural community tourism in the south. Private reserves, such as Chiloé's newly inaugurated Parque Tantauco (boxed text, p340) and El Mirador de Chepú (p327), as well

Trekkers can go further afield with Lonely Planet's *Trekking in the Patagonian Andes*, where you will find detailed descriptions and maps of extensive walks in Chile, plus others across the border in Argentina.

RESPONSIBLE TREKKING

To help preserve Chile's pristine wilderness, consider the following tips.

■ Take the utmost care not to cook or smoke near dried grass or other combustible materials, especially in the windy Patagonian steppe. In 2005, a tragic fire swept Torres del Paine when a trekker used his camp stove in windy conditions outside a campground; it destroyed 150 sq km of forest.

■ Don't depend on open fires for cooking. Cook on a lightweight camp stove and dispose of butane cartridges responsibly.

■ Carry out all rubbish. Don't overlook easily forgotten items such as silver paper, orange peel, cigarette butts and plastic wrappers.

■ Contamination of water sources by human waste can lead to the transmission of all sorts of nasties. Where there is a toilet, please use it. Where there is none, bury your feces. Dig a small hole 15cm deep and at least 100m from any watercourse. Cover the waste with soil and a rock. Pack out toilet paper.

■ For washing, use biodegradable soap and a water container at least 50m away from any watercourses. Disperse the waste water widely to allow the soil to filter it fully.

■ Do not feed the wildlife as this can lead to animals becoming dependent on hand-outs, to unbalanced populations and to diseases.

■ Some trails pass through private property. It's polite to ask residents before crossing their property and leave all livestock gates as you found them.

---

as Valle Chacabuco (p369) near Cochrane and others are building model parks preserving top-notch destinations.

Some regional **Conaf** (Corporación Nacional Forestal; Map pp84–5; ☎ 02-663-0000; www .conaf.cl, in Spanish; Av Bulnes 285, Centro, Santiago; ⦿ 9:30am-5:30pm Mon-Thu, 9:30am-4:30pm Fri) offices have reasonable trail maps, and the JLM maps also have trail indicators on the more specific tourist-oriented maps (see p469).

Hikers and trekkers visiting the southern hemisphere for the first time should look for a compensated needle compass such as the Recta DP 10; northern hemisphere compasses can be deceptive as an indicator of direction in far southern latitudes.

MOUNTAINEERING & CLIMBING

Chile is prime mountaineering and ice-climbing territory. There are hundreds of peaks to choose from, including 50 active volcanoes. They range from the picture-perfect cone of dormant Parinacota (p190) in the northern altiplano, which has a twin just across the Bolivian border, to the challenging active volcano Ojos del Salado (p240), the height of which just falls short of Aconcagua, the highest mountain on the continent just over the border in Argentina.

A charm bracelet of lower volcanic cones also rises through La Araucanía and the Lakes District and Torres del Paine. The most popular climbs here are Volcán Osorno (p308), which has summit ice caves, and Volcán Villarrica (p284), which still smolders ominously. Meanwhile ice-climbers can look into the Loma Larga and Plomo massifs, just a few hours' drive from Santiago.

Climbers intending to scale border peaks like the Pallachatas or Ojos del Salado must have permission from Chile's **Dirección de Fronteras y Límites** (Difrol; Map pp84–5; ☎ 02-671-4110; www.difrol.cl, in Spanish; Bandera 52, 4th fl, Santiago). It's possible to request permission prior to arriving in Chile; a request form can be accessed on the agency's website.

For detailed stats, route descriptions and inspirational photos of mountaineering, volcaneering and ice-climbing throughout Chile, visit www .escalando.cl.

THE ULTIMATE TRAIL: TOP TO BOTTOM CHILE

Conceived as a cross-country adventure as great as the Appalachian Trail or Pacific Crest Trail, Chile's **Sendero de Chile** (www.senderodechile.cl, in Spanish) aims to create one of the longest pathways in the world, approximately 8000km, designated for hiking, mountain biking and horse riding. Starting in the desert north at Visviri and ending at the tip of Cape Horn, it would pass through around 40 watershed systems and encourage a necklace of ecotourism projects along its path. However, not all is rosy with this mega project. Funding appears to be running out, infrastructure is lacking and some stretches follow gravel road instead of beautiful trails – in short, research the part that you will undertake. There are updates and maps on the website and in Chile's guidebook series, Turistel.

For more information, contact the **Federación de Andinismo** (Map pp84-5; ☎ 02-222-9140; www.feach.cl, in Spanish; Almirante Simpson 77, Providencia, Santiago).

SKIING & SNOWBOARDING

Powder junkies rejoice. World-class resorts in the Chilean Andes offer myriad possibilities for skiing, snowboarding, and even heliskiing for the daredevils. Don't expect too many bargains though; many resorts have prices to match their quality.

Most resorts are within an hour's drive of Santiago, including a wide variety of runs at family-oriented La Parva (p120), all-levels El Colorado (p120) and Valle Nevado (p120), which is renowned for its heliskiing. Legendary Portillo (p143), the site of several downhill speed records and summer training base for many of the northern hemisphere's top skiers, is northeast of Santiago near the Argentine border crossing to Mendoza. Termas de Chillán (p161), just east of Chillán, is a more laid-back spot with several beginners' slopes, while Parque Nacional Villarrica (p284), near the resort town of Pucón, has the added thrill of skiing on a smoking volcano. Volcanoes Osorno and Antillanca (p300), east of Osorno, have open terrain with incredible views and a down home atmosphere. Those last four have the added bonus of being close to hot springs, great to soak in after a hard day of descents.

A newly revamped site offers skiing on Volcán Osorno (p308), also popular for randonee skiing. Coyhaique (p360) has its own small resort, while Punta Arenas can lay claim to having one of the few places where one can ski with an ocean view. 'First descents' of Chilean Patagonia's numerous mountains is a growing (but limited) trend. Ski novices can also find suitable terrain and cheaper prices at Volcán Lonquimay, while well-kept secret Chapa Verde (p146) near Rancagua is another low-key, cheap alternative with a variety of slopes.

Ski season runs from June to October. Santiago has some rental shops; otherwise resorts rent full packages.

CYCLING & MOUNTAIN BIKING

Whether you are looking to slowly pedal your way around tranquil lakeside trails or bomb down still-smoking volcanoes, there's plenty of opportunity to get around on two wheels. A favorite mountain-biking destination in the north is San Pedro de Atacama (p212), while bikers can enjoy any number of fabulous trips in the Lakes District, accessing pristine areas that have limited public transportation. The unspoiled trails around Lago Llanquihue are very popular, as is the Ojos de Caburgua (p280) loop near Pucón. The long, challenging, but extremely rewarding Carretera Austral (p345) also attracts many cycling groups, and is well worth the effort.

A good website to gather general information on Chile and Argentina's big ski resorts is www.andesweb.com, with photo essays, reviews and trail maps.

Detailed – if slightly dated – information on cycling in South America can be found in Walter Sienko's *Cycling in Latin America*.

More and more bikers are taking on the ultimate challenge: to cycle Chile's entire length. Most large towns have bike-repair shops and sell basic parts, but packing a comprehensive repair kit is essential. See p481 for more details of cycling through Chile, renting bikes and transporting them.

HORSEBACK RIDING

Saddling up and following in the path of Chile's *huasos* (cowboys) is a fun and easy way to experience the wilderness. Chilean horses are compact and sturdy, with amazing skill fording rivers and climbing Andean steeps. Now more than ever, multiday horseback-riding trips explore cool circuits, sometimes crossing the Andes to Argentina, on terrain that would be inaccessible otherwise. Except in the far north, opportunities can be found just about everywhere.

With strong initiatives for community-based rural tourism in the south, guided horseback riding and trekking with packhorses is a great way to discover remote areas. Rural guides charge affordable rates, provide family lodging in their own homes and offer invaluable cultural insight. Check out offerings in Río Cochamó (p311), Palena (p353) and Coyhaique (p360).

Adventure outfitters offer multilingual guides and a more elaborate range of services. Most places offer first-time riders preliminary lessons before taking to the trails. Favorites for single- or multiday treks are: Pucón (p280), Cochamó (p311), Puyehue (p299), Valle Elqui (p252), Hurtado (p260), San Pedro de Atacama (p216) and around Torres del Paine (p397). The island of Chiloé (p321) is also popular.

The highest active volcano in the world is Ojos del Salado at 6893m on the Chilean-Argentinean border east of Copiapó.

RAFTING & KAYAKING

The wealth of scenic rivers, lakes, fjords and inlets in southern Chile make it a water-lover's dream destination. And white-water junkies agree that Chile's rivers, raging through narrow canyons from the Andes, are world class. While hydroelectric projects are mercilessly taming many excellent rivers, the Futaleufú River (p351) still offers world-class runs with plenty of Class IV and V water to get the blood racing. Other popular runs include those along the Liucura and Trancura (p280) outside Pucón and the beautiful Petrohué (p309), which flows through Valdivian rainforest and past volcanoes near Puerto Varas in the Lakes District. Also worth investigating are Río Simpson (p363) and Río Baker (p368) in the Aisén region. Even near Santiago, the Cajón del Maipo (p118) offers a gentle but enjoyable run.

Agencies in Santiago, Pucón, Puerto Varas and elsewhere offer trips for different levels; equipment is usually of high quality. Several US outfitters also operate here in summer.

Meanwhile the southern fjords and bays of southern Chile are a sea-kayaker's paradise. Popular spots include the fjords in Parque Pumalín (p347) and around the sheltered bays of Chiloé (p337), though more intrepid kayakers have been known to paddle their way around Cape Horn. Lake kayaking is also terrific throughout the Lakes District.

Paddlers bound for the Futaleufú should check out this excellent online guide (www.exchile.com/KayakChile_futaleufu_river_guidebook.html) by Expediciones Chile with interactive maps and the scoop on other great Patagonian rivers.

SURFING & KITESURFING

With breaks lining the long Pacific Coast, Chile nurtures some serious surf culture. Developed surf scenes, however, are best found along the coast of middle and northern Chile. Iquique (p197) has a shallow reef break; bring booties to spare yourself from the sea urchins. Coastal Ruta 1 is lined with surfing beaches and, unfortunately, mountains of trash from careless campers. With big breaks and long left-handers, surf capital Pichilemu (p149) hosts the national surfing championship.

Only at Arica (p180) is the water comfortably warm, so wetsuits are imperative. The biggest breaks are seen in July. Rough surf and rip currents also

---

THAT'S THE BREAKS: CHILE'S TOP FIVE SURF SPOTS

■ The Classic Wave: pilgrims crowd Pichilemu's 'Punta de Lobos,' a perfect left break.

■ One with the Surf: pitch a tent in view of Puertecillo's gnarly curlers. This wilderness surf paradise isn't signposted; ask a Pichilemu local to tag along.

■ The Urban Surf Myth: Iquique's shallow reef break jumps unsuspecting newcomers. Booties will spare your feet from the sea urchins.

■ The Serious Wave: Arica's 'El Gringo' is shallow, top-heavy and unfriendly to its namesakes.

■ The Bunny-slope of Surf: beginners head to La Puntilla in Pichilemu. Seek out a surf school and a nice, thick wetsuit.

---

make some areas inadvisable, and it's best not to surf alone anywhere. You can buy or hire boards and track down lessons in all these surfing hotspots.

Chile also has opportunities for kite surfing, although equipment and lessons are harder to come by: try Pichilemu and Iquique. Spanish-speakers can find more information on www.kitesurf.cl.

CANYONING & CANOPYING

Canyoning and rappel outfitters take advantage of southern Chile's wet and wild stream canyons to take you up (or down) a maze of natural features, through clear pools and under gushing waterfalls. It's a cool way to take in the Jurassic scenery of overgrown ferns and nalca plants. Necessary gear includes a helmet, sticky-soled shoes and a wetsuit for the icy waters. Hotspots near Petrohué are easily reached from Puerto Varas (p304) and others are found around Pucón (p280), further north.

Canopy involves zip-line travel through the treetops with a by-product of a full adrenaline rush with little physical exertion. The activity has exploded in popularity, particularly in the Lakes District and La Araucanía. Go with well-recommended tour operators. Minimal gear is a secure harness with two straps that attach to the cable (one is a safety strap), a hard hat and gloves.

Spanning 16,800 sq km, the Hielo Continental Sur (southern ice field) is the world's third biggest extension of continental ice after Antarctica and Greenland. Its first north–south crossing was accomplished by a Chilean team in 1998 and took a total of 98 days.

PARAGLIDING & LANDSAILING

For a truly uplifting experience, sail off the windy coastal cliffs of northern Chile. Paragliders adore Iquique (p197) for its steep coastal escarpment, rising air currents and soft, extensive dunes – it ranks among the continent's top spots for paragliding. Study up at www.parapenteiquique.cl, in Spanish. Tandem beginners' flights, rental for experts and long courses are all available. For something more down to earth, ask the same agencies about desert landsailing and kitebuggying.

SAND-BOARDING

This infinitely warmer and softer alternative to snowboarding is catching on in Chile's northern desert; San Pedro de Atacama (p216), and to a lesser extent Iquique (p197), are the best towns to hire guides and gear. Be prepared to get sand in places you never imagined possible.

DIVING

Some exciting dive sites can be found on the Juan Fernández archipelago (p435) and around Easter Island (p446). The Chilean mainland is not known for diving or snorkeling, since even the tropical segments of its long coastline experience cold currents. There are limited opportunities, however, notably off the coast of Norte Chico.

SWIMMING

Chile's almost endless coastline offers plenty of opportunity for swimming in summer, but be warned – while sandy beaches abound, the Humboldt Current makes most of Chile's waters cold (except in the far north, around Arica). Another important thing to remember is that strong rip currents make some beaches unsuitable for swimming. Look for signs saying *Playa Apta* (beach safe for swimming) or *Playa No Apta* (beach not safe for swimming).

FLY FISHING

The Lakes District is a prime destination for anglers who want to reel in monster trout (brown and rainbow) and Atlantic salmon (a non-native species). The season generally runs from November to May although there are a few variations. A number of high-end lodges cater exclusively to fly-fishers but it's also possible to contract freelance guides in Puerto Varas (p304), Ensenada (p307) and Coyhaique (p359). Licenses are required and can be obtained from the local municipality.

Whatever activity you pick, you want to keep an eye on the weather forecast, so check www .meteochile.cl, in Spanish, and click on *Pronóstico General.*

Santiago

There's definitely something in the air here. But like its infamous cloud of smog, Santiago's charm is hard to pin down. When people make comparisons, Santiago always seems to come up short. Less cultural than Buenos Aires. Less colonial than Lima. Less Latin American than Mexico City. Less exciting than Rio. But it's also less chaotic, less run down, less insular, less dangerous and less damn large. If Latin America's cities are a family of hotheads and outrageous flirts, then Santiago's the cool, well-balanced sibling who knows what's what and just gets on with it.

The rest of Chile does a roaring trade in life-changing views and earth-shattering experiences. In the capital, pleasures are more measured. Think diverse dining, walks in parks, kicking nightlife, low-key hiking and skiing on its outskirts, and an independent cultural scene that's slowly blossoming. And for all Santiago's differences with its Latino neighbors, it still has its fair share of fin-de-siècle townhouses and colonial mansions, hectic food markets, steaming street-side snack stands, mass demonstrations and hordes of fanatical *fútbol* fans, all overlooked by the stark peaks of the Andes.

Glance at any road map of Chile and it's clear that all roads lead to Santiago. Chances are your trip will come through here, so take a couple of days to see the city. Forget the put-downs: whether you're running errands, shopping for dinner or planning a night on the tiles, this is the place to give out-and-out touring a break and live a little more like a local.

HIGHLIGHTS

- Get a different perspective on Santiago – and the mountains behind it – from the top of **Cerro San Cristóbal** (p87)

- People-watch over coffee and cake in the **cafés** (p104) of Barrio Bellas Artes or Barrio Lastarria, Santiago's hippest 'hoods

- Dine, drink, then dance your way to dawn in **Bellavista** (p106), *carrete* (party) central

- Trace the roots of Chilean culture through the preconquest art of the **Museo Chileno de Arte Precolombino** (p83)

- Tear up the slopes at **Valle Nevado** (p120), Chile's top ski resort

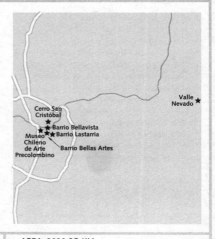

Valle Nevado ★

Cerro San Cristóbal ★

★★ Barrio Bellavista
★★ Barrio Lastarria

Museo Chileno de Arte Precolombino

Barrio Bellas Artes

- POPULATION: 4,946,345

- ELEVATION: 543M

- AREA: 2030 SQ KM

- TELEPHONE CODE: ☎ 02

HISTORY

Nomadic hunter-gatherers wandered here as early as 10,000 BC, but only in 800 BC did Mapuche-related peoples settle here. Not longer after the Inka made the area a major hub on their road network, Spanish soldier Pedro de Valdivia arrived and founded the city of Santiago de la Nueva Extremadura on February 12, 1541, then marched off to attack the Mapuche to the south.

Mapuche living nearby weren't happy and attacked: Valdivia's girlfriend, Inés de Suárez, turned out to be as bloodthirsty as he was, and led the defense of the city, personally decapitating at least one Mapuche chief. Despite ongoing attacks, floods and earthquakes, the conquistadores didn't budge and eventually Santiago began to grow.

Santiago was the backdrop for Chile's declaration of independence from Spain in 1810 and the final battle that overthrew the colonial powers in 1818. As the population grew, public-works projects transformed the city, which became the hub of Chile's growing rail network before displacing Valparaíso as Chile's financial capital in the early 20th century.

Not everyone prospered, however. Impoverished farmers flocked to the city and the upper classes migrated to the eastern suburbs. Rapid post-WWII industrialization created urban jobs, but never enough to satisfy demand, resulting in scores of squatter settlements known as *callampas* ('mushrooms', so-called because they sprang up virtually overnight).

Santiago was at the center of the 1973 coup that deposed Salvador Allende. During the dark years that followed, thousands of political prisoners were executed, and torture centers and clandestine prisons were scattered throughout Santiago. Despite this, military commander-in-chief General Augusto Pinochet was Chile's president until 1990.

Smog set in and the gap between rich and poor widened in the '90s. Authorities are trying to resolve the city's problems, but social inequality – though less pronounced than in other Latin American cities – looks set to linger for some time at least.

ORIENTATION

Greater Santiago is wedged between two mountain ranges, the Andes and the coastal cordillera. Although it's made up of some 32 *comunas* (districts), most sights and activities are concentrated in a few central neighborhoods.

East–west thoroughfare Av O'Higgins (better known as the Alameda) is the city's main axis; east of Plaza Italia it becomes Av Providencia and then Av Apoquindo. Metro Línea 1 runs under it for much of its length. Flowing roughly parallel to the north is the highly polluted Río Mapocho, which effectively acts as the border between downtown and the northern suburbs.

Two hills punctuate the otherwise flat cityscape: Cerro San Cristóbal, a major recreational park, and the smaller Cerro Santa Lucía. Efficient, regular bus services connect Santiago with Arturo Merino Benítez airport, just west of the city (see p112) and the four main long-distance bus stations all lie along Línea 1 of the metro (see p114).

Maps

Tourist offices distribute an ever-changing collection of free (ie sponsored) maps of the Centro and Providencia, but many lack entire streets or sights. The searchable map at **Map City** (www.mapcity.com, in Spanish) is one reliable online resource.

For trekking and mountaineering information, as well as inexpensive maps and other national park publications (mostly in Spanish), visit **Conaf** (Corporación Nacional Forestal; Map pp84-5; ☎ 390-0125; www.conaf.cl, in Spanish; Bulnes 285, Centro; ☺ 9:30am-5:30pm Mon-Thu, 9:30am-4:30pm Fri). For more detailed topographical maps, go to the **Instituto Geográfico Militar** (IGM; Map pp84-5; ☎ 460-6800; Dieciocho 369, Centro; ☺ 9am-5:30pm Mon-Fri). The road maps in the Spanish-language Turistel guides are invaluable when driving in the areas around Santiago, but have no city plan.

INFORMATION
Bookstores

Books in Chile are seriously expensive, especially books in English – new English-language guidebooks start at around CH$25,000, for example. Foreign newspapers and magazines are available at kiosks at the junction of Ahumada and Huérfanos.

Books Secondhand (Map pp90-1; ☎ 235-1205; Av Providencia 1652, Galería del Patio Local 5, Providencia; ☺ 11am-2pm & 4-8pm Mon-Fri, 11am-3pm Sat; Ⓜ Pedro de Valdivia) The best range of quality English-language paperbacks in town, including some guidebooks.

Contrapunto (www.contrapunto.cl; ☺ 10:30am-8pm Mon-Fri, 10:30am-2pm Sat) Centro (Map pp84-5; ☎ 481-9776; Huérfanos 665, Local 1, Centro; Ⓜ Universidad de Chile); Providencia (Map pp90-1; ☎ 231-2947; Av

SANTIAGO

SANTIAGO IN...

Two days

Start your day in the heart of town, at the bustling **Plaza de Armas** (p82). Visit the **Museo Chileno de Arte Precolombino** (p83) and stroll around **Palacio de la Moneda** (p83), the presidential palace. Grab a seafood lunch at the **Mercado Central** (p83) then hotfoot it up **Cerro Santa Lucía** (p86) to see the city from above. Coffee, cake and people-watching at a **Barrio Bellas Artes café** (p104) are your rewards. Head to Bellavista for a slap-up Chilean dinner at **El Caramaño** (p101), then get down at **Bar Constitución** (p107). Get inspiration for your second day at Pablo Neruda's house, **La Chascona** (p87), then take in more great views atop **Cerro San Cristóbal** (p87). After lunch at **Patagonia** (p100), check out the **Museo de Artes Visuales** (p87) or browse crafts at **Ona** (p100). Later, splurge on dinner at **Astrid y Gastón** (p103) in Providencia, then wander down the road for cool cocktails at **Bar Yellow** (p106).

Four Days

On your third day visit the **Cajón del Maipo** (p116) or a **winery** (boxed text, p118) or two. In winter, you could head for the snow at **Tres Valles** (p119). Spend your fourth day wandering **Barrio Brasil** (p89) and **Parque Quinta Normal** (p91) or shopping in **Providencia** (p110). Wind things up with dinner and drinks at **Ébano** (p104) in Ñuñoa.

Providencia 2124, Galería Drugstore, Local 010-011e, Providencia; Ⓜ Pedro de Valdivia) Art, architecture, photography, design: if it'll look good on your coffee table, Contrapunto sells it.

Feria Chilena del Libro (Map pp84-5; ☎ 345-8315; www.feriachilenadellibro.cl; Huérfanos 623, Centro; Ⓥ 8:30am-6pm Mon-Fri, 10am-1pm Sat; Ⓜ Universidad de Chile) Solid selection of Spanish-language literature and a few dusty English-language paperbacks.

Gaia Centro de Difusión Ecológica (Map pp90-1; ☎ 252-0243; Orrego Luco 054, Providencia; Ⓥ 11am-8pm Mon-Fri, noon-5pm Sat; Ⓜ Pedro de Valdivia) Books on flora and fauna, and indigenous and spiritual issues.

Librería Australis (Map pp90-1; ☎ 236-8054; Av Providencia 1670, Galería del Patio Local 5A, Providencia; Ⓥ 9:30am-8pm Mon-Fri & 10:30am-3pm Sat Dec-Mar, 10am-7pm Mon-Fri & 10:30am-3pm Sat Apr-Nov; Ⓜ Pedro de Valdivia) Specializes in guidebooks (including Lonely Planet and Turistel), maps, Chilean flora and fauna guides and coffee-table books.

Metales Pesados (Map pp84-5; ☎ 638-7597; www.metalespesados.cl; JM de la Barra 460, Centro; Ⓥ 10am-8pm Mon-Fri, 11am-2:30pm & 4:30-8pm Sat, 4-8pm Sun; Ⓜ Bellas Artes) Super-savvy selection of Chilean and Latin American literature (in Spanish).

Paisajes de Chile (Map p88; 762-1322; www.paisajesdechile.cl; Constitución 50, Patio Bellavista Local 29-30, Bellavista; Ⓥ 10am-10pm Sun-Wed, 10am-11pm Thu-Sat; Ⓜ Baquedano) Sells Lonely Planet guides in English and Spanish, maps, wildlife guides, Turistels and photography books.

Cultural Centers

Centro Cultural Matucana 100 (Map p89; ☎ 682-4502; www.m100.cl; Av Portales 3530; Ⓜ Quinta Normal & Estación Central) Hosts provocative or political photography exhibitions, gigs, concerts and plays.

Centro de Extensión de la Universidad Católica (Map pp84-5; ☎ 354-6599; www.puc.cl/extension, in Spanish; Alameda 390, Centro; Ⓜ Universidad Católica) University-run cultural center that organizes musical recitals, exhibitions and art-house and documentary film cycles.

Estación Mapocho (Map pp84-5; ☎ 787-0000; www.estacionmapocho.cl, in Spanish; Plaza de la Cultura s/n, Centro; Ⓜ Puente Cal y Canto) Santiago's main cultural center (see p83) hosts plays, concerts, exhibitions and trade expos. Look out for the exuberant Dieciocho (National Independence Day) celebrations on September 18.

Instituto Chileno-Británico (Map pp84-5; ☎ 638-2156; www.britanico.cl, in Spanish; Miraflores 123, Centro; Ⓜ Santa Lucía) Qualified English teachers may find work at this language school, which also has a library with some English-language newspapers and periodicals.

Instituto Chileno-Norteamericano de Cultura (Map pp84-5; ☎ 800-200-863; www.norteamericano.cl, in Spanish; Moneda 1467, Centro; Ⓜ La Moneda) Has an English-language library, and organizes art exhibitions and American art-house film cycles.

Emergency

Ambulance (☎ 131)
Fire department (☎ 132)
Police (☎ 133)
Prefectura de Carabineros (main police station; ☎ 922-3660; Alameda 280, Centro)

Internet Access & Telephones

Most hostels and hotels in Santiago have a
guest computer and wi-fi. Cybercafés are also
everywhere: prices range from CH$300 to
CH$800 per hour. Many are part of a *centro
de llamados* (public telephone center) where
you can make local and long-distance calls.
There are plenty of pay phones in Santiago
(most metro stations have one or two), but
you need coins to use them.

Centro de Llamados Merced (Map pp84-5; Merced
16, Centro; per hr CH$700; ☎ 10am-10pm Mon-Fri,
10am-9pm Sat & Sun; Ⓜ Baquedano) Moneda (Map
pp84-5; Moneda 1118, Centro; per hr CH$450; ☎ 9:30am-
10:30pm Mon-Fri, 10am-8pm Sat & Sun; Ⓜ Universidad
de Chile) Fast internet and cheap international calls.

Ciberplaza Express (Map p89; Compañía 2143, Barrio
Brasil; per hr CH$400; ☎ 9am-11pm Mon-Fri, 9am-10pm
Sat; Ⓜ Cumming) A quiet basement full of new computers.

Tecomp (Map pp90-1; ☎ 333-0316; Holley 2334,
Providencia; per hr CH$500; ☎ 9:30am-midnight Mon-
Thu, 9:30am-1am Fri & Sat; Ⓜ Los Leones) Internet and
cheap international calls.

Laundry

Nearly all hotels and hostels offer laundry
service. Note that self-service launderettes
are uncommon in Chile.

EasyWash (Map pp84-5; ☎ 638-5813; Londres 68,
Centro; per load CH$3500; Ⓜ Universidad de Chile)

Lavandería Autoservicio (Map pp84-5; ☎ 632-1772;
Monjitas 507, Centro; per load CH$4000; Ⓜ Bellas Artes)

Lavandería del Barrio (Map p89; ☎ 673-3575; Huérfanos 1980, Barrio Brasil; per load CH$2500; Ⓜ Cumming)

Lavaseco Astra (Map pp90-1; ☎ 264-1946; Av Providencia 1604, Providencia; per load CH$4000; Ⓜ Manuel Montt)

Libraries

Biblioteca Nacional (Map pp84-5; ☎ 360-5232; www
.dibam.cl, in Spanish; Alameda 651, Centro; ☎ 9am-6:45pm
Mon-Fri, 9:10am-2pm Sat; Ⓜ Santa Lucía) You can consult –
but not borrow – works at the country's largest library and
research facility. You need your passport to sign in.

Media

Santiago Times (www.santiagotimes.cl) Respected
English-language daily.

Medical Services

Consultations are cheap at Santiago's public hospitals but long waits are common and
English may not be spoken. For immediate
medical or dental assistance, go to a *clínica* (private clinic), but expect hefty fees – insurance
is practically a must.

Clínica Alemana (off Map p80-1; ☎ 210-1111; www
.alemana.cl; Av Vitacura 5951, Vitacura) One of the best –
and most expensive – private hospitals in town.

Clínica Las Condes (off Map p99; ☎ 210-4000; www
.clinicalascondes.cl, in Spanish; Lo Fontecilla 441, Las Condes)

Clínica Universidad Católica (Map pp84-5; ☎ 384-
6000; www.clinicauc.cl, in Spanish; Lira 40, Centro;
Ⓜ Universidad Católica)

Farmacia Ahumada (Map pp84-5; ☎ 631-3005; Av
Portugal 155, Centro; Ⓜ Universidad Católica) A 24-hour
pharmacy.

Hospital de Urgencia Asistencia Pública (Map
pp84-5; ☎ 436-3800; Av Portugal 125, Centro; ☎ 24hr;
Ⓜ Universidad Católica) Santiago's main emergency room.

Hospital San Juan de Dios (Map p89; ☎ 574-2091;
www.hospitalsanjuandedios.cl, in Spanish; Huérfanos
3255; Ⓜ Quinta Normal) Major public hospital.

Money

You're never far from an ATM in Santiago.
Supermarkets, pharmacies, gas stations,
and plain old street corners are all likely
locations: look for the burgundy-and-white
'Redbanc' sign.

Cambios Afex (www.afex.cl; ☎ 9am-6pm Mon-Fri,
10am-2pm Sat) Centro (Map pp84-5; ☎ 688-1143;
Agustinas 1050, Centro; Ⓜ Universidad de Chile);
Providencia (Map pp90-1; ☎ 333-2097; Av Pedro de
Valdivia 12, Providencia; Ⓜ Pedro de Valdivia) Reliable
exchange office with branches around town.

Post

FedEx (Map pp90-1; ☎ 301-6000; Av Providencia 1951,
Providencia; ☎ 9am-1:30pm & 2:30-7pm; Ⓜ Pedro de
Valdivia)

Post Office (☎ 800-267-736; www.correos.cl) Centro
(Map pp84-5; Catedral 987, Plaza de Armas, Centro;
☎ 8am-7pm Mon-Fri, 9am-2pm Sat; Ⓜ Plaza de
Armas); Providencia (Map pp90-1; Av Providencia 1466,
Providencia; ☎ 9am-6pm Mon-Fri, 10am-2pm Sat;
Ⓜ Manuel Montt); República (Map p89; Alameda 2352,
Barrio Brasil; ☎ 9am-6pm; Ⓜ República)

Tourist Information

Municipal tourist office (www.municipalidadde
santiago.cl, in Spanish; ☎ 10am-6pm Mon-Thu, 10am-
5pm Fri) Casa Colorada (Map pp84-5; ☎ 632-7783; www
.ciudad.cl, in Spanish; Merced 860, Centro; Ⓜ Plaza de
Armas); Terraza Neptuno (Map pp84-5; ☎ 664-4216;
Cerro Santa Lucía, Centro; Ⓜ Santa Lucía) Well-meaning
but under-resourced staff provide basic maps and
information. The Terraza Neptuno office, in the yellow
building up the stairs to the left of the fountain in Cerro
Santa Lucía, organizes guided tours of the park in Spanish
and English on Thursdays at 11am.

SANTIAGO

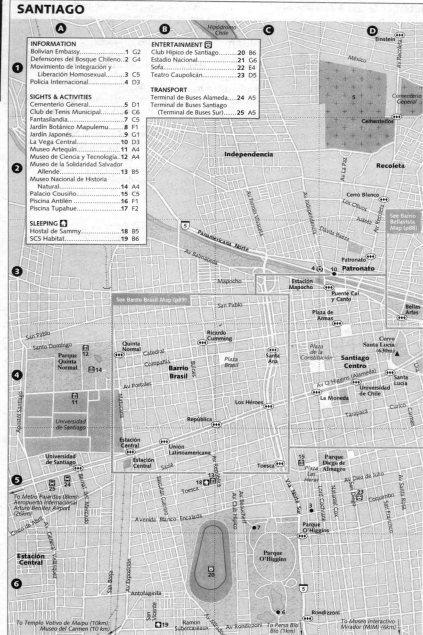

INFORMATION
Bolivian Embassy	1	G2
Defensores del Bosque Chileno	2	G4
Movimiento de Integración y Liberación Homosexual	3	C5
Policia Internacional	4	D3

SIGHTS & ACTIVITIES
Cementerio General	5	D1
Club de Tenis Municipal	6	C6
Fantasilandia	7	C5
Jardín Botánico Mapulemu	8	F1
Jardín Japonés	9	G1
La Vega Central	10	D3
Museo Artequin	11	A4
Museo de Ciencia y Tecnología	12	A4
Museo de la Solidaridad Salvador Allende	13	B5
Museo Nacional de Historia Natural	14	A4
Palacio Cousiño	15	C5
Piscina Antilén	16	F1
Piscina Tupahue	17	F2

SLEEPING
Hostal de Sammy	18	B5
SCS Habitat	19	B6

ENTERTAINMENT
Club Hípico de Santiago	20	B6
Estadio Nacional	21	G6
Sofa	22	E4
Teatro Caupolicán	23	D5

TRANSPORT
Terminal de Buses Alameda	24	A5
Terminal de Buses Santiago (Terminal de Buses Sur)	25	A5

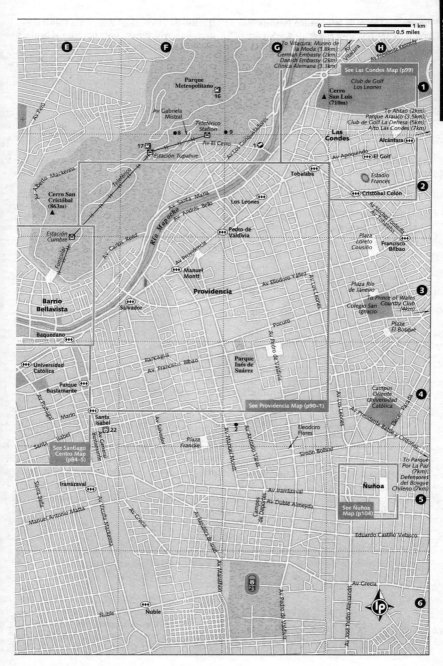

0 _____ 1 km
0 _____ 0.5 miles

To Vitacura; Museo de
la Moda (1.8km);
German Embassy (2km);
Danish Embassy (2km);
Clínica Alemana (3.3km)

See Las Condes Map (p99)

Club de Golf
Los Leones

Cerro
San Luis
(710m)

To Ahtao (2km);
Parque Arauco (3.5km);
Club de Golf La Dehesa (5km);
Alto Las Condes (7km)

Las
Condes

Alcántara

Parque
Metropolitano

Av Gabriela Mistral

Teleférico
Station

Av El Cerro

Estación Tupahue

Av Apoquindo   El Golf

Tobalaba

Estadio
Francés

Cristóbal Colón

Cerro San
Cristóbal
(863m)

Av Santa María

Los Leones

Río Mapocho

Av Andrés Bello

Pedro de
Valdivia

Plaza
Loreto
Cousiño

Francisco
Bilbao

Estación
Cumbre

Av Carlos Reed

Av Providencia

Manuel
Montt

Providencia

Av Eliodoro Yáñez

Plaza Río
de Janeiro

To Prince of Wales
Country Club
(4km)

Barrio
Bellavista

Salvador

Colegio San
Ignacio

Plaza
El Bosque

Baquedano

Pocuro

Av Pedro de Valdivia

Universidad
Católica

Rancagua

Av Francisco Bilbao

Parque
Inés de
Suárez

Campus
Oriente
Universidad
Católica

Parque
Bustamante

Marín

Santa
Isabel

Av Salvador

Plaza
Francke

Eleodoro
Flores

See Providencia Map (p90–1)

See Santiago
Centro Map
(p84–5)

Santa
Isabel

Av Manuel Montt

Av Antonio Varas

Simón Bolívar

To Parque
Por La Paz
(7km);
Defensores
del Bosque
Chileno (7km)

Irarrázaval

Ñuñoa

See Ñuñoa
Map (p104)

Av Irarrázaval

Av Grecia

Manuel Antonio Matta

Av Vicuña Mackenna

Av Grecia

Campos
de Deportes

Av Duble Almeyda

Eduardo Castillo Velasco

Ñuble

Av Matahambre

Av Pedro de Valdivia

Av Grecia

Providencia Centro de Información Turística (Map pp90-1; ☎ 374-2744; www.providencia.cl, in Spanish; Providencia 2359, Providencia; ☽ 10am-6pm Mon-Thu; Ⓜ Los Leones) Young staff distribute maps and limited information about Providencia.

Sernatur (www.sernatur.cl) Airport (☎ 601-9320; Aeropuerto Arturo Merino Benítez at Pudahuel; ☽ 8:15am-9:30pm); Providencia (Map pp90-1; ☎ 731-8310; Av Providencia 1550, Providencia; ☽ 8:45am-6:30pm Mon-Fri, 9am-2pm Sat, to 7pm or 8pm in summer; Ⓜ Manual Montt) Gives out maps, brochures and advice; reserves winery visits.

Travel Agencies

Sertur Student Flight Center (Map pp90-1; ☎ 411-2000; www.sertur.cl, in Spanish; Av Hernando de Aguirre 201, Oficina 401, Providencia; Ⓜ Tobalaba) Sells reasonably priced air tickets.

DANGERS & ANNOYANCES

Violent crime is relatively rare in Santiago. Pickpocketing and bag-snatching, however, are on the rise, and tourists are often targets. Keep your eyes open and bags close to you around the Plaza de Armas, Mercado Central, Cerro Santa Lucía and Cerro San Cristóbal in particular. Look around you before whipping out a digital camera and avoid large, flashy jewelry. Organized groups of pickpockets sometimes target drinkers along Pío Nono in Bellavista, and Barrio Brasil's smaller streets can be dodgy after dark. As in any big city, women are wiser to go out at night in a group. All the same, Santiago remains one of South America's safest cities. Exercise a little common sense and the chances of any problems are slim.

SIGHTS

True, Santiago has its share of decent museums, parks and old buildings, mostly clustered in a few central neighborhoods. We'll be honest, though: Paris it ain't. So once you've chosen some museums in El Centro or Barrio Bellas Artes, checked in on Neruda and gone up Cerro San Cristóbal in Bellavista, take some time out just to wander. Food markets, residential streets, café tables and even tacky shopping strips are sometimes the best places to see the strange mix of distinctly Latin American hustle-and-bustle and more Old World reticence that defines Santiago.

Centro

The wedge-shaped Centro is the oldest part of Santiago, and the busiest. It's hemmed in by three fiendishly hard-to-cross borders:

the Río Mapocho and Autopista Central expressway, which have only occasional bridges over them, and the Alameda, where the central railing puts your vaulting skills to the test. Architecturally, the Centro is exuberant rather than elegant: haphazardly maintained 19th-century buildings sit alongside '80s eyesores and the odd glittering high-rise, and its crowded *paseos* (pedestrian precincts) are lined with cheesy clothing stores and fast-food joints. Government offices, the presidential palace and the banking district are here, making it the center of civic life. A few standout sights (and plenty of tick-the-box ones) mean it's the center of tourist life, too.

Since the city's founding in 1541, the **Plaza de Armas** (Map pp84-5; Ⓜ Plaza de Armas) has been its symbolic heart. In colonial times a gallows was the square's grisly centerpiece; today it's a fountain celebrating *libertador* (liberator) Simón Bolívar, shaded by more than a hundred Chilean palm trees. Parallel pedestrian precincts Paseo Ahumada and Paseo Estado disgorge scores of strolling Santiaguinos onto the square on weekends and sunny weekday afternoons: clowns, helium-balloon sellers and snack stands keep them entertained.

Overlooking the Plaza de Armas is the neoclassical **Catedral Metropolitana** (Map pp84-5; Plaza de Armas, Centro; ☽ 9am-7pm Mon-Sat, 9am-noon Sun; Ⓜ Plaza de Armas), built between 1748 and 1800. Bishops celebrating mass on the lavish main altar may feel uneasy: beneath them is the crypt where their predecessors are buried.

Colonial furniture, weapons, paintings, historical objects and models chart Chile's colonial and republican history at the **Museo Histórico Nacional** (National History Museum; Map pp84-5; ☎ 411-7000; www.museohistoriconacional.cl, in Spanish; Plaza de Armas 951, Centro; adult/child CH$600/300, free Sun; ☽ 10am-5:30pm Tue-Sun; Ⓜ Plaza de Armas). After a perfunctory nod to pre-Colombian culture, the ground floor covers the conquest and colony. Upstairs goes from independence through Chile's industrial revolution right up to the 1973 military coup but no further – Allende's broken glasses are the chilling final exhibit. The Spanish-only explanations are only helpful if you've taken Chilean History 101, but English versions of the texts sell for CH$100 at the ticket counter.

Few colonial houses are still standing in Santiago, but the simple, oxblood-colored **Casa Colorada** (Red House; Map pp84-5; Merced 860, Centro) is a happy exception, although only the front half of the original 18th-century building has survived. It contains a small, under-resourced branch of the municipal tourist office and the sweetly amateurish **Museo de Santiago** (Map pp84-5; ☎ 633-0723; Merced 860, Centro; adult/child CH$500/400, free Sun; ☼ 10am-6pm Tue-Fri, 10am-5pm Sat, 11am-2pm Sun; Ⓜ Plaza de Armas). Maps, scale models and dynamic pint-sized dioramas illustrate highlights of Santiago's history.

Exquisite pottery from most major pre-Colombian cultures is the backbone of Santiago's best museum, the **Museo Chileno de Arte Precolombino** (Chilean Museum of Pre-Colombian Art; Map pp84-5; ☎ 688-7348; www.precolombino.cl, in Spanish; Bandera 361, Centro; adult/child CH$3000/free, free Sun; ☼ 10am-6pm Tue-Sat, 10am-2pm Sun; Ⓜ Plaza de Armas). As well as dozens of intricately molded anthropomorphic vessels, star exhibits include hefty Mayan stone stele and a fascinating Andean textile display. More unusual are the wooden vomit spatulas used by Amazonian shamans before taking psychoactive powders. Note that though Sunday admission is free, groups of two or more are pressed into a 'voluntary' contribution.

Gleaming piles of fresh fish and crustaceans atop mounds of sparkling ice thrill foodies, fishers and photographers alike at the **Mercado Central** (Central Market; Map pp84-5; bordered by 21 de Mayo, San Pablo, Paseo Puente & Valdés Vergara, Centro; ☼ 7am-5pm Mon-Sat, 7am-3pm Sun; Ⓜ Puente Cal y Canto). Fishmongers compete noisily for customers in one half of the market, while touts for its many seafood restaurants make an equal racket in the other.

Rail services north once left from **Estación Mapocho** (Mapocho Station; Map pp84-5; ☎ 787-0000; www.estacionmapocho.cl, in Spanish; Plaza de la Cultura s/n, Centro; Ⓜ Puente Cal y Canto). Earthquake damage and the decay of the rail system led to its closure, but it's been reincarnated as a cultural center which hosts art exhibitions, major concerts and trade expos. The soaring cast-iron structure of the main hall was built in France then assembled in Santiago behind its golden beaux arts–style stone facade.

Chile's presidential offices are in the **Palacio de la Moneda** (Map pp84-5; ☎ 690-4000; Morandé 130, Centro; admission free; ☼ 10am-6pm; Ⓜ La Moneda). The ornate neoclassical building was designed by Italian architect Joaquín Toesca in the late 18th century, and was originally the official mint – its name means 'the coin.' The north facade was badly damaged by air-force missile attacks during the 1973 military coup when President Salvador Allende – who refused to leave – was overthrown here. A monument honoring Allende now stands opposite in **Plaza de la Constitución.** Shiny-booted *carabineros* (police) stamp through a brief changing-of-the-guard ceremony every other day at 10am.

Underground art takes on a new meaning in Santiago's newest cultural space: the **Centro Cultural Palacio La Moneda** (Map pp84-5; ☎ 355-6500; www.ccplm.cl; Plaza de la Ciudadanía 26, Centro; adult/child & student CH$600/CH$300; ☼ 10am-7:30pm; Ⓜ La Moneda) is beneath **Plaza de la Ciudadanía**. A glass-slab roof floods the vaultlike space with natural light, and ramps wind down through the central atrium past the Cineteca Nacional, a state-run art-house movie theater, to two large temporary exhibition spaces. The uppermost level contains a fair-trade crafts shop, a café and a gallery celebrating Chilean folk singer, artist and activist Violeta Parra.

When you need a breather from the Centro's busy streets, drop by the **Museo La Merced** (Map pp84-5; ☎ 664-9819; www.museolamerced.cl, in Spanish; MacIver 341, Centro; adult/child CH$1000/500, free Sun; ☼ 10am-1pm & 3-6pm Mon-Sat, 10am-2pm Sun; Ⓜ Bellas Artes). Most people skip the main collection (it documents the history of the Merced religious order in Chile) in favor of the Easter Island collection, which includes a Rongorongo tablet, and the shady, plant-filled courtyard.

The first stone of the austere **Iglesia de San Francisco** (Map pp84-5; Alameda 834, Centro; ☼ 11am-6pm Mon-Sat, 10am-1pm Sun; Ⓜ Universidad de Chile) was laid in 1586, making it Santiago's oldest surviving colonial building. Its sturdy walls have weathered some powerful earthquakes, although the current clock tower, finished in 1857, is the fourth. On the main altar look for the carving of the Virgen del Socorro (Our Lady of Perpetual Help), which Santiago's founder Pedro de Valdivia brought to Chile on his 1540 conquistador mission to protect him from attacks.

Alongside the church is the **Museo Colonial de San Francisco** (Map pp84-5; ☎ 639-8737; www.museosanfrancisco.cl; Londres 4, Centro; adult/child CH$1000/500; ☼ 10am-1pm & 3-6pm Tue-Sat, 10am-2pm Sun; Ⓜ Universidad de Chile). The dark and dusty rooms contain 17th-century colonial ecclesiastical art, as well as a creepy collection of whips and scourges used for penitential self-flagellation. A small room is rather randomly dedicated to poet Gabriela Mistral and includes correspondence and a replica of her Nobel medal. What the staff are most proud of, however, is their pet chicken, Martín, who patrols the palm- and creeper-filled courtyard.

SANTIAGO

SANTIAGO CENTRO

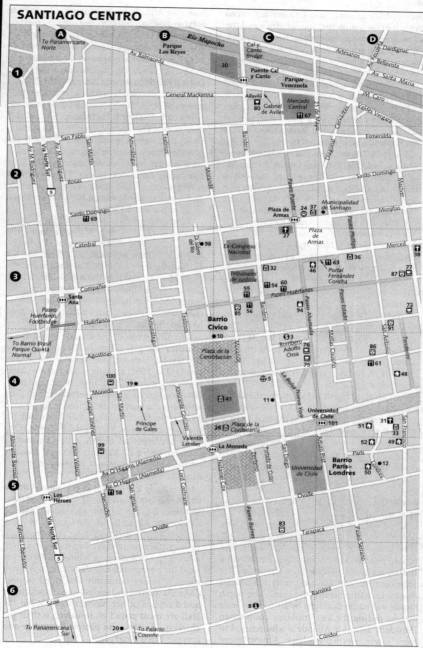

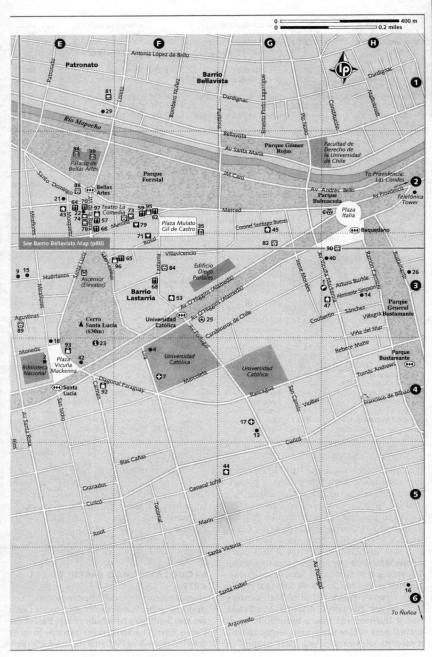

INFORMATION
Argentinian Embassy...............1 H3
Biblioteca Nacional...................2 E4
Cambios Afex..........................3 C4
Centro de Extensión de la
 Universidad Católica.............4 F4
Centro de Llamados..................5 C4
Centro de Llamados..................6 H2
Clínica Universidad Católica....7 F4
Conaf.....................................8 C6
Contrapunto...........................9 E3
Departamento de
 Extranjería.........................10 C4
Dirección de Fronteras y
 Límites..............................11 C4
EasyWash..............................12 D5
Estación Mapocho info.........(see 30)
Farmacia Ahumada................13 G4
Federación de Andinismo.......14 H3
Feria Chilena del Libro............15 E3
Greenpeace...........................16 H6
Hospital de Urgencia Asistencia
 Pública..............................17 G4
Instituto Chileno-Británico.....18 E4
Instituto Chileno-Norteamericano
 de Cultura..........................19 B4
Instituto Geográfico Militar
 (IGM)................................20 B6
Lavandería Autoservicio..........21 E2
Metales Pesados....................22 E2
Municipal Tourist Office Casa
 Colorada........................(see 36)
Municipal Tourist Office Terraza
 Neptuno.............................23 E4
Post Office............................24 C2
Prefectura de Carabineros.......25 F3
Terram.................................26 H3

SIGHTS & ACTIVITIES
Casa Colorada....................(see 36)
Catedral Metropolitana...........27 C3
Centro Cultural Palacio La
 Moneda.............................28 C4
Chip Travel...........................29 E1
Estación Mapocho.................30 C1
Iglesia de San Francisco..........31 D4
La Bicicleta Verde.................(see 29)

Museo Arqueológico de
 Santiago..........................(see 35)
Museo Chileno de Arte
 Precolombino.....................32 C3
Museo Colonial de San
 Francisco...........................33 D4
Museo de Arte Contemporáneo
 (MAC)...............................34 E2
Museo de Artes Visuales.........35 F2
Museo de Santiago................36 D3
Museo Histórico Nacional.......37 C2
Museo la Merced...................38 D3
Museo Nacional de Bellas
 Artes................................39 E2
Natalis Language Center.........40 H3
Palacio de la Moneda.............41 C4
Terraza Neptuno....................42 E4

SLEEPING
Andes Hostel.........................43 E2
Ecohostel..............................44 G5
Hostal Forestal......................45 D2
Hostal Plaza de Armas............46 C3
Hostal Río Amazonas.............47 H3
Hotel Galerías.......................48 D4
Hotel París 813......................49 D5
Hotel Plaza Londres...............50 D5
Hotel Plaza San Francisco.......51 D4
Hotel Vegas..........................52 D5
Lastarria 43...........................53 F3

EATING
Bar Nacional.........................54 C3
Bar Nacional 2.......................55 C3
Bravíssimo Gelatería..............56 C3
Café Bistro de la Barra............57 E2
Confitería Torres....................58 B5
Don Pepe.........................(see 63)
El Bombón Oriental................59 C3
El Naturista..........................60 C3
El Naturista..........................61 D4
Emporio La Rosa....................62 F2
Fast-food restaurants.............63 D3
Kintaro................................64 D2
Ona....................................65 F3
Opera.................................66 E2
Pailas Denisse.......................67 C1
Patagonia.............................68 F3

Restaurant Majestic...............69 A2
Verace.................................70 E2

DRINKING
Bar Berri..............................71 F3
Baron Rojo............................72 D3
Café Abarzúa........................73 F2
Café Brainworks....................74 E2
Café Caribe...........................75 C4
Café Haiti..............................76 C4
Café Ikabarú.........................77 D3
Café Tomodashi Chillout.........78 E2
Catedral..........................(see 66)
El Diablito............................79 F2
La Piojera.............................80 C1
La Signoria...........................81 E1

ENTERTAINMENT
Cine Arte Alameda.................82 G3
Cine Arte Normandie..............83 C5
Cine El Biógrafo....................84 F3
Cine Gran Palace...................85 C3
Cine Hoyts...........................86 D4
Cine Hoyts...........................87 D3
Cineteca Nacional..............(see 28)
El Tunel...............................88 E2
La Berenjena.........................89 E3
Teatro de la Universidad de
 Chile................................90 H3
Teatro Municipal....................91 D3

SHOPPING
Centro Artesanal Santa Lucía....92 E4
Centro de Exposición de Arte
 Indígena............................93 E4
Feria del Disco......................94 C3
Ocho Fortuna........................95 F2
Ona....................................96 F3
The Clinic.............................97 E2

TRANSPORT
EFE Ticket Office..............(see 101)
La Bicicleta Verde trans.......(see 29)
Manzur Expediciones.............98 B3
Terminal Los Héroes..............99 A5
Tur-Bus Aeropuerto..............100 B4
Universidad de Chile metro
 station.............................101 D4

Immediately south of the Iglesia San Francisco is the **Barrio París-Londres**, a pocket-sized neighborhood made up of two intersecting cobbled streets called – yes, you guessed it – París and Londres. They're lined by graceful European-style townhouses built in the 1920s, some of which now contain run-down hotels.

Rising out of the eastern side of the Centro is **Cerro Santa Lucía** (Map pp84-5; entrances at cnr Alameda & Santa Lucía, & cnr Santa Lucía & Subercaseaux; 9am-7pm Mar-Sep, 9am-8pm Oct-Feb; Santa Lucía or Bellas Artes). It was a rocky hill until 19th-century city mayor Benjamín Vicuña Mackenna had it transformed into a beautifully landscaped park where the grassy verges are still a favorite with canoodling local couples. A

web of trails and steep stone stairs leads you up through terraces to the Torre Mirador at the top. Charles Darwin proclaimed the view from here 'certainly most striking' in 1833 – the smog-and-skyscraper-filled 21st-century version may have changed a little but it's still well worth the climb. You need to sign in with your passport details when you enter.

BARRIO LASTARRIA & BARRIO BELLAS ARTES

Home to three of the city's best museums, these dinky neighborhoods near Cerro Santa Lucía are also Santiago's twin hubs of hip. East of the Cerro, Barrio Lastarria takes its name from its cobbled main drag JV Lastarria, lined with arty bars and restaurants. The intersecting street, Merced, adds a few funky shops and some cafés to the mix. The real center of Santiago café culture, however, is over at Barrio Bellas Artes, as the few blocks north of Cerro Santa Lucía are now known. JM de la Barra is the main axis.

Exposed concrete, stripped wood and glass are the materials local architect Cristián Undurraga chose for the stunningly simple **Museo de Artes Visuales** (MAVI, Visual Arts Museum; Map pp84-5; ☎ 638-3502; www.mavi.cl, in Spanish; Lastarria 307, Plaza Mulato Gil de Castro, Centro; adult/child CH$1000/free, free Sun; 🕙 10:30am-6:30pm Tue-Sun, closed Feb; Ⓜ Bellas Artes). The contents of the four open-plan galleries are as winsome as the building: top-notch modern engravings, sculptures, paintings and photography form the regularly changing temporary exhibitions. Admission includes the **Museo Arqueológico de Santiago** (MAS, Santiago Archeological Museum), tucked away on the top floor. The low-lighted room with dark stone walls and floors makes an atmospheric backdrop for a small but quality collection of Diaguita, San Pedro and Molle ceramics, Mapuche jewelry and Easter Island carvings.

On weekend afternoons, the temperature rises in **Parque Forestal**, a narrow green space wedged between Río Mapocho and Merced. This is when hordes of the highly pierced, disaffected Santiaguino teenagers who call themselves Pokemones gather for *ponceo* – a word they've coined for making out with lots of different people. The rest of the week it's more about joggers and power walkers.

In the park's center is the stately neoclassical **Palacio de Bellas Artes** (Palace of Fine Arts; Map pp84-5), built as part of Chile's centenary celebrations in 1910. Two of Santiago's art museums share the premises. An excellent permanent collection of Chilean art fills the **Museo Nacional de Bellas Artes** (National Museum of Fine Art; Map pp84-5; ☎ 633-0655; www.mnba.cl, in Spanish; Parque Forestal s/n; adult/child CH$600/300; 🕙 10am-6:50pm Tue-Sun; Ⓜ Bellas Artes), on the eastern side. Look out for works by Luis Vargas Rosas, erstwhile director of the museum and a member of the Abstraction Creation group, along with fellow Chilean Roberto Matta, whose work is also well represented.

Temporary exhibitions showcasing contemporary photography, design, sculpture, installations and web art are often held at the neighboring **Museo de Arte Contemporáneo** (MAC, Contemporary Art Museum; ☎ 977-1741; www.mac.uchile.cl, in Spanish; adult/child CH$600/300; 🕙 11am-7pm Tue-Sat, 11am-6pm Sun; Ⓜ Bellas Artes). Its pristine

galleries are the result of extensive restoration work to reverse fire and earthquake damage. Twentieth-century Chilean painting forms the bulk of the permanent collection.

North of the Centro
BELLAVISTA

Mention Bellavista to locals, and one word is bound to come up: *carrete* (nightlife). Partying to the wee hours makes Bellavista's colorful streets and cobbled squares deliciously sleepy by day. Toss your map aside: the leafy residential streets east of Constitución are perfect for aimless wandering, while the graffitied blocks west of it are a tagspotter's paradise.

When poet Pablo Neruda needed a secret hideaway to spend time with his mistress Matilde Urrutia, he built **La Chascona** (Map p88; ☎ 777-8741; www.fundacionneruda.org; Márquez de La Plata 0192, Bellavista; admission by tour only, adult/child in Spanish CH$2500/1000, in English CH$3500; 🕙 10am-7pm Tue-Sun Jan & Feb, 10am-6pm Tue-Sun Mar-Dec; Ⓜ Baquedano), which he named for her unruly hair. Neruda loved the sea (but disliked sailing) so the dining room is modeled on a ship's cabin and the living room on a lighthouse. Guided tours walk you through the history of the building and the collection of colored glass, shells, furniture and artworks by famous friends that fills it – sadly much more was lost when the house was ransacked during the dictatorship. The Fundación Neruda, which maintains Neruda's houses, has its headquarters here and runs a swank gift shop and lovely café.

Upmarket eateries and posh souvenir shops ranged around a huge courtyard make up **Patio Bellavista** (Map p88; ☎ 777-4582; www.patiobellavista.cl; Pío Nono 71, Bellavista; 🕙 10am-2am Sun-Wed, 10am-4am Thu-Sat; Ⓜ Baquedano), a clear attempt by developers to spruce up the barrio's tattered charm. True, it's very 'for export,' but they've kept things classy enough to make it worth a wander.

Smog permitting, the best views over Santiago are from the peaks and viewpoints of the **Parque Metropolitano**, better known as **Cerro San Cristóbal** (Map p88; ☎ 730-1331; www.parquemet.cl, in Spanish) Bellavista entrance (Pío Nono 450, Barrio Bellavista; Ⓜ Baquedano); Providencia entrance (Av Pedro de Valdivia & El Cerro, Providencia; Ⓜ Pedro de Valdivia). At 722 ha, the park is Santiago's biggest green space, but it's still decidedly urban: cable cars and a funicular carry you between different landscaped sections, and roads through it are aimed at cars rather than hikers. The park lies north of Bellavista and Providencia and has entrances in both

BARRIO BELLAVISTA

INFORMATION
Codeff...1 D3
Paisajes de Chile...........................2 C3

SIGHTS & ACTIVITIES
Escuela de Idiomas Tandem/Violeta
Parra..3 C2
Funicular..4 C2
La Chascona...................................5 C2
Santuario de la Inmaculada
Concepción..................................6 D1
Teleférico......................................7 D1
Terraza Bellavista...........................8 D1
Urbanightour..................................9 D3
Virgen de la Inmaculada
Concepción..........................(see 6)
Zoológico Nacional.......................10 D2

SLEEPING
Bellavista Hostel...........................11 D3
Hotel del Patio..............................12 C3
La Chimba.....................................13 C3

EATING
Ali Baba..14 C2
Azul Profundo................................15 D3
El Caramaño...................................16 C2
El Mesón Nerudiano........................17 C2
El Toro..18 B3
Empanatodos.................................19 C3
Fast-food stands............................20 C4
Galindo..21 C3
Il Siciliano.....................................22 D3
Zhi Dong.......................................23 A3

DRINKING
Amor del Bueno.............................24 C2
Bar Dos Gardenias..........................25 C3
Dublin...26 C3
Mundo de Papel.............................27 C3
Vox Populi.....................................28 C2

ENTERTAINMENT
Bar Constitución............................29 D3
Bokhara..30 C2
Bunker..31 B3
Centro Cultural Teatro del
Puente.......................................32 C4
El Clan..33 B2
El Perseguidor Jazz Club.................34 D3
La Casa en el Aire..........................35 D3
La Feria...36 C2

SHOPPING
Joyas Lapizlazuli............................37 D3

TRANSPORT
Chilean...38 D3

neighborhoods: the cheapest and most logical way to visit is to buy a joint cable car and funicular ticket (adult/child one way CH$2500/1500) to start on one side and finish on the other.

A snowy white 14m-high statue of the **Virgen de la Inmaculada Concepción** (Map p88) towers atop the *cumbre* (summit) at the Bellavista end of the park. The benches at its feet are the outdoor church where Pope John Paul II said mass in 1984.

The quickest way up is the **funicular** (Map p88; adult/child round trip CH$1400/800; ⏰ 1-8pm Mon, 10am-8pm Tue-Sun), which climbs 284m from Plaza Caupolicán at the north end of Pío Nono. It stops halfway up at the dinky **Zoológico Nacional** (National Zoo; Map p88; ☎ 730-1334; Parque Metropolitano, Bellavista; funicular & zoo adult/child CH$2500/1500; ⏰ 10am-6pm Tue-Sun; Ⓜ Baquedano), which houses an aging bunch of neglected animals. It is, however, probably the only place in Chile where you are assured a glimpse of the dinky pudú deer, Chile's national animal. Near the top of the funicular is the **Terraza Bellavista** (Map p88) where there are extraordinary views across the city.

A 2000m-long **teleférico** (cable car; Map p88; adult/child round trip CH$1600/900; ⏰ 2:30-6:30pm Mon, noon-6:30pm Tue-Fri, 10:30am-7:30pm Sat & Sun) runs east from Estación Cumbre. The first stop is Estación Tupahue, around which are clustered the **Jardín Botánico Mapulemu** (Map pp80–1), a botanical garden, as well as two huge public swimming pools, the Piscina Tupahue and Piscina Antilén (see p93). The cable car continues to Estación Oasis, at the north end of Av Pedro de Valdivia in Providencia (about 10 minutes' walk from Pedro de Valdivia metro station). The small but perfectly landscaped **Jardín Japonés** (Japanese Garden, Map pp80-1) is 400m east. There are snack stands near the cable-car stations, but Cerro San Cristóbal is also a prime picnicking spot.

OTHER

Raspberries, quinces, figs, peaches, persimmons, custard apples… if it grows in Chile, you'll find it at **La Vega Central** (Food Market; Map pp80-1; bordered by Dávila Baeza, Nueva Rengifo, López de Bello & Salas; ☼ 6am-6pm Mon-Sat, 6am-3pm Sun; Ⓜ Patronato). Go early to see the hollering vendors in full swing.

More than just a graveyard, Santiago's **Cementerio General** (Map pp80-1; ☎ 737-9469; www.cementerio general.cl; Av Profesor Alberto Zañartu 951; ☼ 8:30am-6pm;

Ⓜ Cementerios) is a veritable city of tombs, many adorned with works by famous local sculptors. The names above the crypts read like a who's who of Chilean history: its most tumultuous moments are attested to by Salvador Allende's tomb and the **Memorial del Detenido Desaparecido y del Ejecutado Político**, a memorial to the 'disappeared' of Pinochet's dictatorship. To reach the memorial from the main entrance, walk down Av Lima, turning right into Horvitz for another 200m; it's over the bridge to the right.

West of the Centro
BARRIO BRASIL

Locals are often baffled by Barrio Brasil's popularity with foreigners: it's short on sites and has a dodgy reputation after dark. Yet there's a

BARRIO BRASIL

INFORMATION		EATING 🍴		DRINKING 🍷	
Ciberplaza Express..................1 C2		2008...........................12 C2		Baires..........................19 C2	
Hospital San Juan de Diós........2 A2		Las Vacas Gordas................13 C2		Eurohappy....................20 C1	
Lavandería del Barrio..............3 C2		Ocean Pacific's.................14 C2			
Post Office.............................4 B4		Ostras Azócar..................15 C3		ENTERTAINMENT 🎭	
		Ostras Squella.................16 C3		Blondie.........................21 B4	
SIGHTS & ACTIVITIES		Platipus.........................17 C3		Centro Cultural Gran Circo	
Centro Cultural Matucana 100..5 A3		Plaza Garibaldi................18 C3		Teatro...................22 C4	
Instituto Chileno de la Lengua....6 D2				Cine Hoyts....................23 A4	
Museo de Arte Contemporáneo				Galpón Víctor Jara.........24 C4	
Espacio Quinta Normal.........7 A2					
SLEEPING 🛏					
Happy House Hostel.................8 C1					
Hostelling International Hostel....9 D2					
La Casa Roja..........................10 C2					
Luz Azul................................11 D3					

TRANSPORT	
Buses Centropuerto.................25 D3	
Terminal San Borja..................26 A4	

PROVIDENCIA

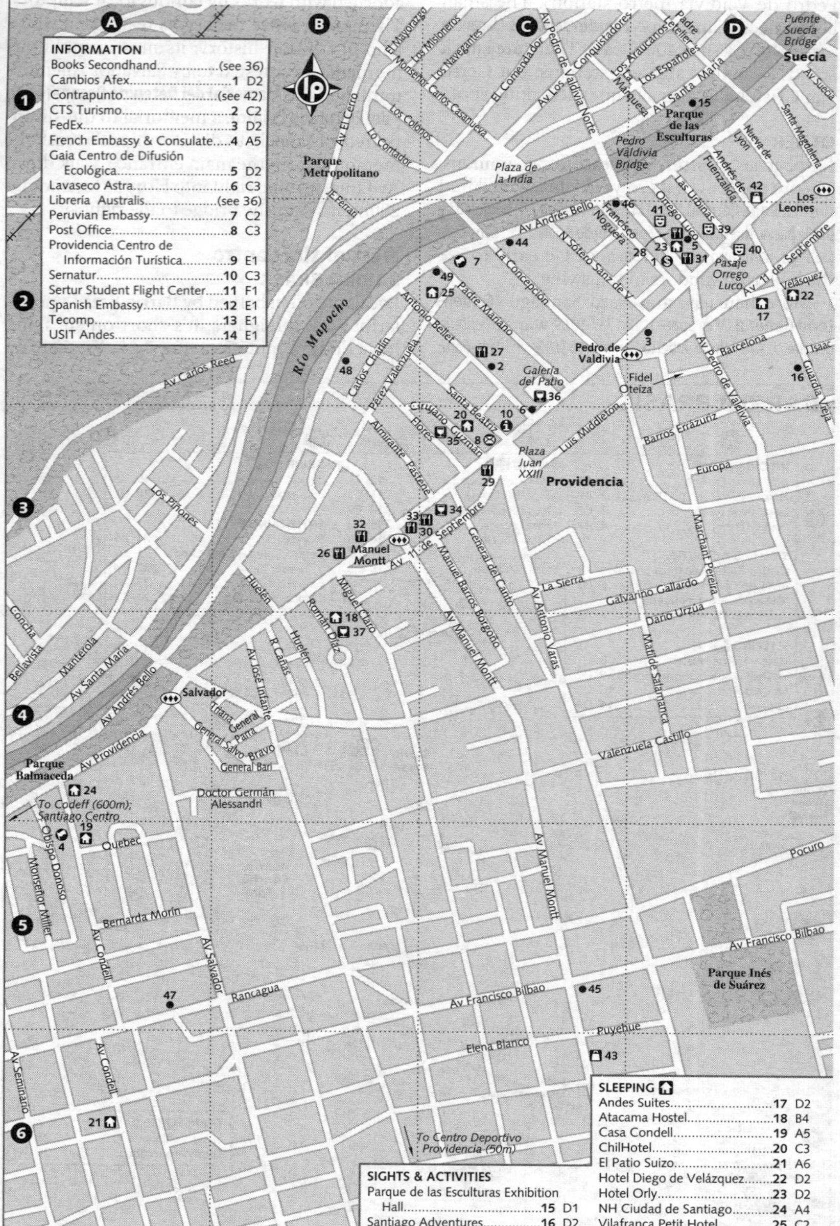

INFORMATION

Books Secondhand	(see 36)
Cambios Afex	**1** D2
Contrapunto	(see 42)
CTS Turismo	**2** C2
FedEx	**3** D2
French Embassy & Consulate	**4** A5
Gaia Centro de Difusión Ecológica	**5** D2
Lavaseco Astra	**6** C3
Librería Australis	(see 36)
Peruvian Embassy	**7** C2
Post Office	**8** C3
Providencia Centro de Información Turística	**9** E1
Sernatur	**10** C3
Sertur Student Flight Center	**11** F1
Spanish Embassy	**12** E1
Tecomp	**13** E1
USIT Andes	**14** E1

SIGHTS & ACTIVITIES

Parque de las Esculturas Exhibition Hall	**15** D1
Santiago Adventures	**16** D2

SLEEPING

Andes Suites	**17** D2
Atacama Hostel	**18** B4
Casa Condell	**19** A5
ChilHotel	**20** C3
El Patio Suizo	**21** A6
Hotel Diego de Velázquez	**22** D2
Hotel Orly	**23** D2
NH Ciudad de Santiago	**24** A4
Vilafranca Petit Hotel	**25** C2

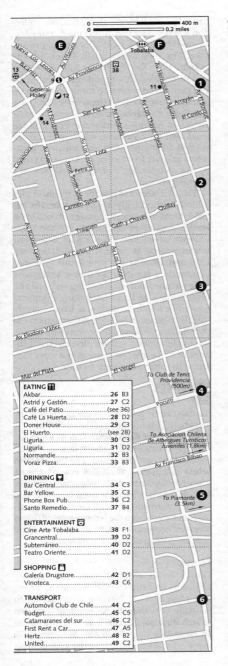

EATING 🍴
Akbar..................................26 B3
Astrid y Gastón....................27 C2
Café del Patio................(see 36)
Café La Huerta.....................28 D2
Doner House.........................29 C3
El Huerto........................(see 28)
Liguria...............................30 C3
Liguria...............................31 D2
Normandie..........................32 B3
Voraz Pizza.........................33 B3

DRINKING 🍷
Bar Central.........................34 C3
Bar Yellow..........................35 C3
Phone Box Pub....................36 C2
Santo Remedio....................37 B4

ENTERTAINMENT 🎭
Cine Arte Tobalaba...............38 F1
Grancentral.........................39 D2
Subterráneo........................40 D2
Teatro Oriente.....................41 D2

SHOPPING 🛍
Galería Drugstore.................42 D1
Vinoteca............................43 C6

TRANSPORT
Automóvil Club de Chile.........44 C2
Budget...............................45 C5
Catamaranes del sur.............46 C2
First Rent a Car....................47 A5
Hertz.................................48 B2
United................................49 C2

crumbling charm to its run-down old townhouses and the slightly sleepy streets are a welcome respite from the hectic Centro. A spindly monkey-puzzle tree shades **Plaza Brasil**, the green heart of the 'hood. A wave of urban renovation is slowly sweeping the surrounding streets, where more and more bars and hip hostels are mushrooming. Incongruous among the carparts shops between here and the Alameda is pint-sized **Barrio Concha y Toro**, a gorgeous little square fed by cobblestone streets and overlooked by art deco and beaux arts mansions.

PARQUE QUINTA NORMAL

Strolls, picnics, pedal-boating, soccer kickabouts and soapbox rants are all popular activities at the 40-hectare **Parque Quinta Normal** (Map pp80-1; Ⓜ Quinta Normal), west of Barrio Brasil. Several museums are also here, though sadly it's a question of quantity over quality. For information on the child-oriented Museo Nacional de Historia Natural and Museo Artequín, see p94.

The best of a bad lot is the **Museo de Arte Contemporáneo Espacio Quinta Normal** (Museum of Contemporary Art, Quinta Normal Branch; Map p89; ☎ 977-1741; www.mac.uchile.cl; Matucana 464; adult/child CH$600/400, free Sun; ⏲ 11am-7pm Tue-Sat, 11am-6pm Sun; Ⓜ Quinta Normal), a branch of the downtown Museo de Arte Contemporáneo (see p87) which specializes in intriguing, off-beat or experimental exhibitions.

Halfway between Parque Quinta Normal and the Alameda lies one of Santiago's hippest alternative arts venues. The huge red-brick **Centro Cultural Matucana 100** (Map p89; ☎ 682-4502; www.m100.cl; Av Portales 3530; admission free; ⏲ 11am-1pm & 2-9pm; Ⓜ Quinta Normal & Estación Central) gets its gritty industrial look from its previous incarnation as government warehouses. Renovated as part of Chile's bicentennial project, it now contains a hangarlike gallery and a theater for art-house film cycles, concerts and fringe productions.

East of the Centro
PROVIDENCIA

Head east from the Centro, and Santiago's neighborhoods slowly get swisher. First up: Providencia, a traditionally upper-middle-class area that's short on sights but very long indeed on drinking and dining possibilities. The '70s and '80s tower blocks along the area's main artery, Av Providencia, are an eyesore, but the more residential side streets contain some lovely early-20th-century buildings.

On the north side of the Río Mapocho lies a rare triumph in city landscaping: the **Parque de las Esculturas** (Sculpture Park; Map pp90–1; ☎ 340-7303; Av Santa María 2201, Providencia; admission free), a green stretch along the river decorated with sculptures by noted Chilean artists. Trees muffle the sounds of the Costner Norte freeway, which runs through a tunnel beneath the park.

VITACURA

Santiago's plushest neighborhood is home to the über-rich, the seriously expensive restaurants and bars they frequent, and Santiago's most exclusive shopping street, Av Alonso de Córdova. Appropriately, it's also home to the **Museo de la Moda** (Museum of Fashion; off Map pp80–1; ☎ 219-3623; www.museodelamoda.cl; Av Vitacura 4562, Vitacura; admission CH$3000; ❦ 10am-6pm Wed-Sun; Ⓜ Escuela Militar). The slick set-up comprises an exquisite permanent collection of western clothing – 20th-century designers are particularly well represented – and, more unusually, tennis wear. From Escuela Militar metro, take bus 305 from the west side of Américo Vespucio (you need a Bip! card) and get off at the intersection with Av Vitacura.

OTHER

During Chile's last dictatorship some 4500 political prisoners were tortured and 266 were executed at Villa Grimaldi by the now-disbanded DINA (National Intelligence Directorate). The compound was razed to conceal evidence in the last days of Pinochet's dictatorship, but since the return of democracy it has been turned into a powerful memorial park known as **Parque por la Paz** (off Map pp80–1; ☎ 292-5229; www.villagrimaldicorp cl; Av Arrieta 8401; ❦ 10am-2pm & 3-6pm). Each element of the park symbolizes one aspect of the atrocities that went on there and visits here are fascinating but harrowing – be sensitive about taking pictures as other visitors may be former detainees or family members. Take the yellow bus D09 (you need a Bip! card) from right outside the Av Vespucio exit of Plaza Egaña metro station; it drops you opposite.

South of the Centro

Picasso, Miró, Tápies and Matta are some of the artistic heavyweights who gave works to the **Museo de la Solidaridad Salvador Allende** (Map pp80–1; ☎ 689-8761; www.museodelasolidaridad.cl; Av República 475; adult/child & student CH$600/300; ❦ 10am-5pm Tue-Sun; Ⓜ República). Begun as a populist art initiative during Allende's presidency – and

named in his honor – the incredible collection was taken abroad during the dictatorship, where it became a symbol of Chilean resistance. The 2000 works finally found a home in 2006, when the Fundación Allende bought and remodeled this grand old townhouse. The permanent collection sometimes goes on tour and is replaced by temporary exhibitions, and there's a darkened room with an eerie display of Allende's personal effects. Guided tours visit the basement, where you can see tangled telephone wires and torture instruments left over from when the house was used by the dictatorship's notorious DINA as a listening station.

'Flaunt it' seems to have been the main idea behind the shockingly lavish **Palacio Cousiño** (Map pp80–1; ☎ 698-5063; www.palaciocousino.co.cl; Dieciocho 438; admission on guided tour only CH$2100; ❦ 9:30am-1:30pm & 2:30-5pm Tue-Fri, 9:30am-1:30pm Sat & Sun, last tours leave an hr before closing; Ⓜ Toesca). It was built between 1870 and 1878 by the prominent Cousiño-Goyenechea family after they'd amassed a huge fortune from wine-making and coal and silver mining, and it's a fascinating glimpse of how Chile's 19th-century elite lived. Carrara marble columns, a half-ton Bohemian crystal chandelier, Chinese cherrywood furniture, solid gold cutlery, and the first electrical fittings in Chile are just some of the ways they found to fritter away their fortune.

ACTIVITIES
Golf

Santiago's best golf courses are in the wealthy neighborhoods northeast of the city center. The 18-hole **Prince of Wales Country Club** (off Map pp80–1; ☎ 757-5700; www.pwcc.cl, in Spanish; Las Arañas 1901, La Reina) has the best reputation. The **Club de Golf La Dehesa** (off Map pp80–1; ☎ 216-6816; www.golfladehesa.cl, in Spanish; Camino Club de Golf 2501, Lo Barnechea) is another 18-hole course with wide open fairways. You can get information on golf courses, competitions and shops from the **Federación de Golf Chilena** (Chilean Golf Federation; Map p99; ☎ 208-7080; www.chilegolf .cl, in Spanish; Málaga 665, Las Condes; Ⓜ Alcántara).

Tennis

Tennis is an abiding passion for many Chileans, and the country has many excellent players. The cheapest court rental in Santiago is at the city government–run **Club de Tenis Municipal** (Map pp80–1; ☎ 555-6761; Rondizzoni s/n, Parque O'Higgins; per hr CH$2500; Ⓜ Rondizzoni). A more upmarket option is the **Club de Tenis**

Providencia (Map pp90-1; ☎ 223-7500; www.tenisclub providencia.cl, in Spanish; El Vergel 2855, Providencia; per hr CH$7500-10,000; Ⓜ Cristóbal Colón).

Swimming

There are fabulous views from the two huge, open-air pools atop Cerro San Cristóbal, **Piscina Tupahue** (Map pp80-1; ☎ 732-0998; adult/child CH$5000/3500; 10am-7pm Tue-Sat Nov-Mar) and **Piscina Antilén** (Map pp80-1; ☎ 732-0998; adult/child CH$6000/3500; 10am-7pm Nov-Mar). Both are more for splashing about that serious training. You can do your lengths year-round at the 25m indoor pool of the **Centro Deportivo Providencia** (off Map pp90-1; ☎ 341-4790; www.cdprovidencia.cl; Santa Isabel 0830; monthly membership CH$26,000).

Walking, Running & Cycling

From about mid-May through September, the fumes that hang over Santiago make outdoor exercise tough going. Outside those months, locals run, walk and cycle along the Río Mapocho (especially through the Parque Forestal), in Parque Quinta Normal (p91), and along the steep roads of Cerro San Cristóbal (p87). You can rent bikes and helmets from **La Bicicleta Verde** (Map pp84-5; ☎ 570-9338; www.labici cletaverde.cl; Santa María 227, Oficina 12, Bellavista; per hr CH$3000, per day CH$10,000-13,000; Ⓜ Bellas Artes).

WALKING TOUR

Start around noon at the square outside Puente Cal y Canto metro station. Take in the facade of **Estación Mapocho** (**1**; p83), once a railway station and now a cultural center, then prefuel with a *terremoto* (cheap wine with a dollop of ice cream) at **La Piojera** (**2**; p105), just over the road; it's sure to get you into the mood. A block east along Av Balmaceda is the **Mercado Central** (**3**, p83), a bustling seafood market. After you've cruised and perused, take off south down Paseo Puente till you reach the **Plaza de Armas** (**4**; p82), which

WALK FACTS

Start Puente Cal y Canto metro station
Finish Parque Forestal
Distance 4km
Duration From two hours

SANTIAGO WALKING TOUR

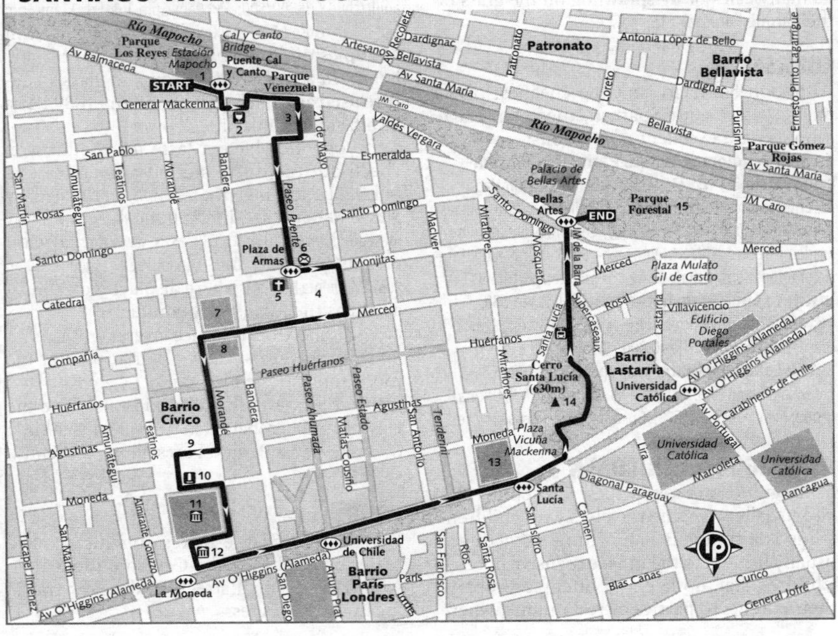

is flanked by colonial and neoclassical buildings. These include the **Catedral Metropolitana** (**5**; p82) and the **main post office** (**6**) that was built in 1882 over the site of the city's first house, which belonged to Pedro de Valdivia. Take a turn round the square then walk west along Compañía, which runs between two neoclassical public buildings: the cream-colored **Ex-Congreso Nacional** (**7**) and Santiago's main law courts, the steely gray **Tribunales de Justicia** (**8**). Turn left into Morandé and walk a block to the landscaped **Plaza de la Constitución** (**9**; p83), which includes a **statue** (**10**) that commemorates President Salvador Allende. He died during the 1973 coup inside the presidential palace, **Palacio de la Moneda** (**11**; p83), on the south side of the square. Pass through another vast square on the south side of the palace, the **Plaza de la Ciudadanía** (**12**; p83), and strike out east along the chaotic Alameda, central Santiago's main artery. Seven blocks later you pass the monumental **Biblioteca Nacional** (**13**), which has a beautiful classical facade, and arrive at the Terraza Neptuno entrance to **Cerro Santa Lucía** (**14**; p86), from the very top of which are great views over the Centro. Leave from the northern exit and wander down JM de la Barra and reward your efforts at one of its many cafés or by sprawling on the grass of the **Parque Forestal** (**15**; p87).

COURSES

Although Santiago isn't the cheapest place to kick-start your Spanish, these language schools have excellent reputations:

Escuela de Idiomas Violeta Parra/Tandem Santiago (Map p88; ☎ 735-8211; www.tandemsantiago .cl; Ernesto Pinto Lagarrigue 362-A, Bellavista; 35hr courses from CH$131,000; Ⓜ Baquedano) Combines outstanding academic record with a friendly vibe and cultural activities. Accommodations include shared or private apartments.

Instituto Chileno de la Lengua (ICHIL; Map p89; ☎ 697-2728; www.ichil.cl; Riquelme 226, 2nd fl, Barrio Brasil; courses from CH$240,000; Ⓜ Santa Ana)

Natalis Language Center (Map pp84-5; ☎ 222-8685; www.natalislang.com; Av Vicuña Mackenna 6, 7th fl, Oficina 4, Centro; per week CH$77,500). Great for quick, intense courses.

SANTIAGO FOR CHILDREN

Santiaguinos are very much into family life and usually welcome travelers with children. (This is a boon, as babysitting services are usually limited to the most expensive hotels.) Children stay up late and often accompany their parents to parties or restaurants, where they order from the regular menu rather than one for children. That said, most kiddy-oriented activities here are helpful distractions rather than standout sights.

Give them their dose of adrenaline and cotton candy at **Fantasilandia** (Map pp80-1; ☎ 476-8600; www.fantasilandia.cl; Av Beaucheff 938; admission Mon-Fri CH$5800, Sat & Sun CH$6500, children under 90cm free; ☉ noon-9pm daily Jan–mid-Feb, noon-7pm daily mid-Feb–Mar, noon-7pm Sat & Sun Apr-Jun; Ⓜ Parque O'Higgins).

Your one-stop shop for good clean fun is the Parque Metropolitano (p87), which combines a modest zoo, two great outdoor swimming pools and a well-maintained playground with interesting transport – a creaky cable car and a funicular. Toffee-apple vendors and fee-charging, photogenic llamas crowd the Bellavista entrance on weekends.

The stimulus is more intellectual – but still fun – at the **Museo Interactivo Mirador** (MIM, Mirador Interactive Museum; off Map pp80-1; ☎ 280-7800; www .mim.cl, in Spanish; Punta Arenas 6711, La Granja; adult/child CH$4500/3500; ☉ 9:30am-1:30pm Mon, 9:30am-6:30pm Tue-Sun; Ⓜ Mirador). Forget 'do not touch': you can handle, push, lie on, and even get inside most of the exhibits. Education and entertainment also come together at the **Museo Artequín** (Map pp80-1; ☎ 681-8656; www.artequin.cl; Av Portales 3530; adult/child CH$800/500; ☉ 9am-5pm Tue-Fri, 11am-6pm Sat & Sun, closed Feb; Ⓜ Quinta Normal), a museum of copies of famous artworks hung at kiddy height in a striking cast iron and glass structure used as Chile's pavilion in the 1889 Paris Exhibition (think Eiffel Tower).

If your kids have a taste for the bizarre, check out the dusty stuffed animals (we're talking taxidermy, not teddies) in the nearby **Museo Nacional de Historia Natural** (Natural History Museum; Map pp80-1; ☎ 680-4615; www.mnhn.cl; adult/child CH$600/300; ☉ 10am-5:30pm Tue-Sat, noon-5:30pm Sun; Ⓜ Quinta Normal), where displays look almost as old as the fossils they contain.

For bribery or treats, ice creams from cheap 'n' cheerful Bravíssimo Gelatería (p99) or the more sophisticated Emporio La Rosa (p100) usually do the trick. Local kids also love the clowns and acrobats that appear in the Plaza de Armas and Parque Forestal on weekends.

TOURS

For basic, tick-the-boxes touring, you're better off exploring the Centro on foot than with a tour: small streets and heavy traffic mean slow progress.

Chip Travel (Map pp84-5; ☎ 737-5649; www.chip travel.cl; Av Santa María 227, Oficina 11; Ⓜ Bellas Artes) Runs a human rights–oriented tour combining Parque por la Paz, a memorial for victims of the last dictatorship (see p92), with a stop at the Fundación Pinochet.

La Bicicleta Verde (Map pp84-5; ☎ 570-9338; www .labicicletaverde.cl; Santa María 227, Oficina 12, Bellavista; half-day tours CH$15,000; Ⓜ Bellas Artes) Two-wheel town tours with a cultural bent: one takes in the fruit and veg market, for example, while another passes political sights.

Santiago Adventures (Map pp90-1; ☎ 244-2750; www.santiagoadventures.com; Guardia Vieja 255, Oficina 403, Providencia; Ⓜ Los Leones) Savvy English-speaking guides lead personalized city, food and wine tours, and day trips to the coast.

Turistik (☎ 800-471-174; www.turistik.cl; day pass adult/child CH$15,000/5000; ⏰ 9:30am-6pm). Hop-on hop-off double-decker bus tours run between the Centro and Parque Arauco mall.

Urbanightour (Map p88; ☎ 735-0679; www .urbanightour.blogspot.com; Dardignac 0157, Oficina 3, Bellavista; tours CH$10,000; Ⓜ Baquedano). Biking, buildings and bar-hopping led by architecture students.

FESTIVALS & EVENTS

Santiago a Mil (www.stgoamil.cl) This major theater festival draws experimental companies from around the world to Santiago's stages in January.

Festival del Barrio Brasil Exhibitions, theater, dance and music bring even more life to Plaza Brasil each January.

Festival Nacional del Folklore (www.sanbernardo.cl/ festivalnacionaldelfolklore) In the southern suburb of San Bernardo, this five-day festival in late January celebrates traditional Chilean music, culture, dance and food.

Feria Internacional del Aire y del Espacio (www .fidae.cl) The latest commercial and military airplanes attract an odd combination of arms merchants, pilots and plane-spotters at this major international air show, held every two years in late March.

Rodeo season (www.rodeochileno.cl, in Spanish) In Chile, March is all about *huasos* (cowboys) and bucking broncos. The focus of the action is Rancagua, 145km south of Santiago, but events also take place in Santiago.

Santiago Festival Internacional de Cine (SANFIC; www.sanfic.cl) Each August, the city's week-long film festival showcases choice independent cinema in several movie theaters.

Festival de Jazz de Ñuñoa (www.ccn.cl) Free jazz and blues concerts from some of Chile's top musicians take place at the Teatro Municipal de Ñuñoa over a weekend in August.

Feria Internacional de Artesanía Talented crafts-people show off their creations each November in Parque Bustamante, Providencia.

Feria Internacional del Libro (www.camlibro.cl) Scores of publishing houses and authors from throughout the Spanish-speaking world move into Estación Mapocho in the last week of November. New and antiquarian books are also sold.

SLEEPING

Never before have there been so many places in Santiago to lay your head. Indeed, budget accommodations are booming so much you'd be forgiven for thinking that opening a hostel is the latest Santiaguino fashion. But be warned: value for money varies vastly at all price points, so do your homework.

For longer stays, renting a furnished apartment can save you loads. **Contact Chile** (☎ 264-1719; www.contactchile.cl) and **Lastarria 43** (Map pp84-5; ☎ 639-3132; www.apartmentssantiago.cl; Lastarria 43, Centro) are two reliable rental services.

Centro
BUDGET
Hostel Plaza de Armas (Map pp84-5; ☎ 671-4436; www .plazadearmashostel.com; Compañía 960, Apt 607, Plaza de Armas; dm CH$5500-7500, d incl breakfast CH$16,500-23,000; 🖳; Ⓜ Plaza de Armas) A funky renovation made a hostel out of a large apartment with great views over the Plaza de Armas. Dorms are so tight that the lockers are in the hall, but the hot-pink and orange bedspreads are cheery. Best of all are the self-contained doubles in another apartment down the hall.

Hotel París 813 (Map pp84-5; ☎ 664-0921; carbott@ latinmail.com; París 813; incl breakfast s CH$12,000-14,000, d CH$14,000-18,000; 🖳; Ⓜ Universidad de Chile) Heavily beamed ceilings and dark mismatched furniture lend an air of elegant gloom to the clean upstairs rooms. Beds sag and quarters are tight downstairs in the budget section – but with prices this low, it's hard to complain. Rates include wi-fi and cable TV.

MIDRANGE
Hotel Plaza Londres (Map pp84-5; ☎ 633-3320; www.hotel plazalondres.cl; Londres 77; incl breakfast s/d without bathroom CH$10,000/20,000, s/d/q CH$18,500/30,000/45,000; 🖳; Ⓜ Universidad de Chile) Behind the grand facade lurks a bewildering maze of accommodations (there's also an overflow branch at Londres 35). Rooms with private bathroom are hit-and-miss: some have original wood paneling and high ceilings but no windows, others are light and airy but with flaking bathrooms. The musty hostel-style accommodation is best skipped.

Hostal Río Amazonas (Map pp84-5; ☎ 635-1631; www.hostalrioamazonas.cl; Av Vicuña Mackenna 47; s/d/q incl breakfast CH$19,000/25,000/43,000; 🖳 ; Ⓜ Baquedano) Families and couples make up most of the guests at this mock-Tudor mansion painted a warm orangey-yellow. Rooms are plain but bright and have lovely parquet floors; double-glazing keeps the sounds of the avenue at bay.

Hotel Vegas (Map p84-5; ☎ 632-2498; info@hotelvegas .net; Londres 49; s/d incl breakfast CH$26,900/32,500, 2-bed apt CH$25,000-29,000; Ⓟ 🖂 🖳 ; Ⓜ Universidad de Chile) Despite the classy Barrio París-Londres setting, the '70s are alive and well in Hotel Vegas' wood-paneled rooms and beiger-than-thou bathrooms. Though clean and functional, they're not quite up to the price. The spanking new apartments (in another building down the road) are excellent value, but there's a three-day minimum stay.

TOP END

Hotel Galerías (Map pp84-5; ☎ 470-7400; www.hotel galerias.cl; San Antonio 65; s/d incl breakfast CH$57,200/70,400; 🖂 🖳 🕿 ; Ⓜ Santa Lucía) This hotel is certainly proud to be Chilean: Mock *moai* (Easter Island statues) guard the entrance, the gift shop sells gourmet local food, and staff are dressed like upscale *huasos* (Chilean cowboys). In the well-appointed rooms, traditional weavings offset the clean neutrals and simple hardwood furniture.

Hotel Plaza San Francisco (Map pp84-5; ☎ 639-3832; www.plazasanfrancisco.cl; Alameda 816; s/d incl breakfast CH$83,200/87,500; 🖂 🖳 🕿 ; Ⓜ Universidad de Chile) An oak-paneled reception, hunting prints and sober maroon and mustard furnishings in the rooms: this hotel is angling for the English drawing-room look. The impeccably mannered staff are a match for any butler, though the muzak and scuffed furniture somewhat let the side down.

Barrio Lastarria & Barrio Bellas Artes

Hostal Forestal (Map pp84-5; ☎ 638-1347; www.hostalfor estal.cl; Coronel Santiago Bueras 120; dm/s without bathroom CH$7000/12,000, d CH$22,000; 🖳 ; Ⓜ Baquedano) With its basement bar and pool table, party-go-lucky staff and a reputation for all-nighters, Forestal is clearly more about celebrating than sleeping. That's just as well: the neon strip lights, basic bathrooms and scuffed walls aren't exactly homey.

Andes Hostel (Map pp84-5; ☎ 633-1976; www.andes hostel.com; Monjitas 506; dm CH$8500, s/d without bathroom CH$16,000/20,000, s/d CH$23,000/27,000; 🖳 ; Ⓜ Bellas ▸tes) Pistachio-colored walls, a zebra-print

rug, mismatched retro sofas and a mosaic-tiled bar are some of the poptastic charms of the Andes Hostel's communal areas. Sleek wooden bunks and individual reading lights carry the style over to the dorms (though they can be a bit airless), whereas doubles are surprisingly bland, like the service.

Bellavista
BUDGET

La Chimba (Map p88; ☎ 735-8978; www.lachimba.com; Ernesto Pinto Lagarrigue 262; incl breakfast dm CH$5500-7000, r CH$18,000; 🖳 ; Ⓜ Baquedano) Extra-wide bunks with well-sprung mattresses and feather quilts practically guarantee sweet dreams at this small hostel (though the beats from nearby clubs can filter in on weekends). The red-painted living room is cozy and the kitchen small but well equipped: if only they'd put the same effort into the bread-and-marge breakfast or leaking showers… Still, the friendly staff bend over backwards to help.

Bellavista Hostel (Map p88; ☎ 732-8737; www.bella vistahostel.com; Dardignac 0184; incl breakfast dm CH$7000-8000, s/d CH$15,000/20,000; 🖳 ; Ⓜ Baquedano) Brightly painted walls crammed with colorful paintings and graffiti announce this hostel's relaxed, arty vibe. The city's best bars and clubs are on your doorstep and so, sometimes, are their clients – peaceful slumbers are not the main aim here, though rooms in the annex are quieter. A vast TV-and-pool room distracts from the brief breakfasts and faulty showers.

TOP END

Hotel del Patio (Map p88; ☎ 732-7571; www.hotel delpatio.cl; Pío Nono 61; s/d/tr incl breakfast CH$50,000/ 60,000/75,000; 🖳 ; Ⓜ Baquedano) Cerulean and emerald or pistachio and chocolate are some of the chi-chi color combos used to dolly up a rambling 19th-century house. Breakfasts are abundant and staff ultrafriendly, but 'boutique' is only skin-deep here: despite cute mosaic tiles the bathrooms are boxlike and thin walls let in the noise from the adjoining Patio Bellavista.

Barrio Brasil
BUDGET

La Casa Roja (Map p89; ☎ 696-4241; www.lacasaroja .cl; Agustinas 2113; dm CH$6500, d with/without bathroom CH$20,000/16,800; 🖳 ; Ⓜ Cumming) With its swimming pool, airy patios, outdoor bar, garden and a huge, well-designed kitchen, it's easy to see why this Aussie-owned outfit is backpacker central. Serious socializing isn't the only appeal: with its sweeping staircases and sky-high molded ceilings, the lovingly restored 19th-century mansion oozes character. Especially great value are the doubles, fitted with stylish retro furniture and bijoux bathrooms.

Hostelling International Hostel (Map p89; ☎ 671-8532; www.hisantiago.cl; Cienfuegos 151; dm/d without bathroom CH$7000/26,000, d CH$30,000; ☐; Ⓜ Los Héroes) Brightly colored walls and quilts add a touch of cheer to this spotless but rather institutional-looking hostel. Despite skimpy breakfasts, dorms are reasonable value, and though you might baulk at the prices of doubles, they've had an IKEA-look makeover and some even have flat-screen TVs.

Luz Azul (Map p89; ☎ 698-4856; www.luzazulhostel .cl; Santa Mónica 1924; dm CH$7150-9500, d CH$23,800; ☐; Ⓜ Los Héroes) Stripped pine floors and walls painted mocha and pistachio give Luz Azul a pleasantly un-hostellike look. But they've privileged prettiness over practicalities: they're short on showers, dorms lack lockers and beds are half-enclosed in strange boxes. The open-plan kitchen, dinky roof terrace and squishy-but-stylish sofas all make great meeting places.

MIDRANGE

Happy House Hostel (Map p89; ☎ 688-4849; www.happy househostel.cl; Catedral 2207, Barrio Brasil; dm/s/d/tr incl breakfast CH$11,000/25,000/33,000/45,000; ☐; Ⓜ Cumming) It's all about design at Happy House, a converted old townhouse where hand-carved wooden furnishings and rich colors like olive green and ochre predominate. Bathrooms, however, are cramped and iffy-smelling and though the ultraspacious dorms have wide bunks and cute throws it's not enough to justify the prices.

Providencia

BUDGET

Atacama Hostel (Map pp90-1; ☎ 264-2012; www.ata camahostel.cl; Román Díaz 130; dm CH$7200, d with/without bathroom CH$24,000/19,000; ☐; Ⓜ Salvador) Bright mosaics adorn the entrance of this big old house, and the cramped rooms are painted cheerful candy colors. Equally warming is the lovely sunny patio where the hostel's young, well-traveled owners organize barbecues and meals.

Casa Condell (Map pp90-1; ☎ 717-8592; www.casacondell .com; Av Condell 114; s/d without bathroom CH$10,000/20,000; Ⓜ Salvador) Grown-up backpackers who've

tired of in-house partying can still sleep cheap at this small guesthouse. Gleaming floors and butter-yellow walls greet you in reception, but rooms are drab and the bathrooms damp. There's no guest kitchen, but the tented roof terrace is great for swapping road tales.

MIDRANGE

El Patio Suizo (Map pp90-1; ☎ 474-0634; www.patiosuizo .com; Av Condell 847, Providencia; incl breakfast s/d without bathroom CH$15,000/20,000, s/d CH$22,000/30,000; ☐; Ⓜ Parque Bustamante) This B&B's pristine rooms overlook a deliciously green patio, complete with a barbecue and hammock – lounging here or in the snug living room is positively encouraged. The Swiss owners are knowledgeable though sometimes a little indifferent.

ChilHotel (Map pp90-1; ☎ 264-0643; www.chilhotel .cl; Cirujano Guzmán 103; incl breakfast s CH$26,000-31,000, d CH$27,700-32,700; ☐; Ⓜ Manuel Montt) Don't be put off by the worn reception and squeaky-floored corridors – rooms are cozy and bright, with simple wooden furniture and springy white-covered beds. Rates include cable TV and wi-fi.

our pick Vilafranca Petit Hotel (Map pp90-1; ☎ 235-1413; www.vilafranca.cl; Pérez Valenzuela 1650; incl breakfast s CH$30,000, d CH$36,000-40,000; ☐; Ⓜ Pedro de Valdivia) Why can't all B&Bs be this good? Squishy sofas in the living room and wooden steamer chairs in a plant-filled patio invite you to make yourself at home. The rooms feel deliciously Merchant Ivory: think sage-colored walls hung with dried flowers, time-worn parquet and artfully mismatched antique furniture.

TOP END

Hotel Orly (Map pp90-1; ☎ 231-8947; www.orlyhotel.com; Av Pedro de Valdivia 027; s/d incl breakfast CH$45,600/52,800; ☒ ☐; Ⓜ Pedro de Valdivia) Dark wood furniture, crisp white linens and heavy maroon drapes mean rooms here are classic but cozy. They're big on details: the renovated bathrooms have big marble sinks, the windows contain soundproof glass, and there's coffee, tea and cake on hand all day in the breakfast room. Cable TV and wi-fi are included.

Hotel Diego de Velázquez (Map pp90-1; ☎ 234-4400; www.hoteldiegodevelazquez.com; Guardia Vieja 150; s/d incl breakfast CH$52,800/60,000; ☒ ☐; Ⓜ Pedro de Valdivia) Friendly staff, reasonable value and the location a block south of Av Providencia make this long-running hotel a solid choice. Despite the very '70s stucco-and-tinted-glass lobby, the newly renovated standard rooms have clean-lined modern furniture, cable TV and parquet floors, and are bright and airy.

NH Ciudad de Santiago (Map pp90-1; ☎ 341-7575; www.nh-hoteles.com; Av Condell 40; ste incl breakfast CH$53,760-105,600; ❄ ▢ ; Ⓜ Salvador) It's home suite home at this Spanish-owned hotel: the seriously spacious rooms all have king-sized beds, living rooms with tea- and coffee-makers, two cable TVs, and walk-in closets with an iron inside. Most guests are business travelers but the location – halfway between Providencia and the Centro – is perfect for touring, too.

Andes Suites (Map pp90-1; ☎ 761-7070; www.andes-suite.cl; Diego de Velázquez 2071; 1-/2-bedroom apt incl breakfast CH$60,000/67,200; ❄ 🛗 ; Ⓜ Pedro de Valdivia) Hotel Diego de Velázquez runs these furnished apartments, so you get the best of both worlds: the independence of your own living room and kitchen, but with daily maid service and breakfast. Indulgent details include king-sized beds, huge closets and a gorgeous rooftop pool with views over the Andes.

Las Condes

Ritz-Carlton (Map p99; ☎ 470-8500, www.ritzcarlton.com/hotels/santiago; El Alcalde 15; r US$220; ▢ 🛗 ; Ⓜ El Golf) A glittering symbol of Chile's soaring economy, the Ritz is the luxury choice in Santiago. Detail is what it does best: the king-sized beds have Egyptian cotton sheets and deliciously comfortable mattresses, and there's even a menu of bath treatments. The jewel in the crown is the top-floor health club and pool, with a vaulted glass roof that means you can swim beneath the stars. If you prefer liquid treats that come in a glass, the bar's novelty pisco sours are legendary.

Grand Hyatt Santiago (off Map p99; ☎ 950-1234; http://santiago.grand.hyatt.com/; Av Kennedy 4601; ▢ 🛗) This shiny tower in Las Condes gleams in the shadow of the Andes. Rooms are huge and so are the cushion-covered beds – from them, and from the small living areas, there are spectacular views of Santiago and the mountains. Landscaped gardens contain a gorgeous pool complete with waterfalls, and a jogging track and tennis courts. Its Thai, Japanese and Italian restaurants all have excellent reputations. Check online for prices, which change daily.

South of the Centro

SCS Habitat (Map pp80-1; ☎ 683-3732; scshabitat@yahoo.com; San Vicente 1798; dm CH$3000-4000, d without bathroom

CH$8000; Ⓜ Estación Central) The cheapest digs in town are a little out of the way, but at these prices, who's kvetching? Dorms have skinny three-tier bunks, but there's a large, well-equipped kitchen complete with a recycling system. Owner Scott is a mine of information and even allows camping in the garden. To get there from Estación Central, take a taxi or bus 109 (you need a Bip! card) 17 blocks down Exposición, then walk left (east) three blocks to San Vicente; SCS is the green house on the corner.

Hostal de Sammy (Map pp80-1; ☎ 689-8772; www.hostalsammy.com; Toesca 2335; dm CH$5000-6000, s/d without bathroom CH$8500/14,000; ▢ ; Ⓜ Toesca) Guests have been known to get fanatical about this hostel: could the Foosball, pool table, Playstation, big-screen TV and movie collection, free bikes, and five computers have something to do with it? The rest is low-frills, with ultraplain doubles and tight-packed, curtainless dorms.

Ecohostel (Map pp84-5; ☎ 222-6833; www.ecohostel.cl; General Jofré 349B; dm/d without bathroom CH$6000/18,000; ▢ ; Ⓜ Universidad Católica) Backpackers and families looking to chill love this hostel's friendly, personalized service, cozy couches and sunny patio (complete with hammock). Dorms in the converted old house can be dark, but bunks and lockers are both big and there are plenty of well-divided bathrooms. Trash gets separated here, hence the name.

EATING

Eating is definitely one of the best ways to spend your time in Santiago. In the last few years, the arrival of creative restaurateurs from Peru, Argentina, Europe and the Antipodes has added extra oomph to the city's already excellent restaurant scene. Traditional Chilean food, especially seafood, is still top of the list here, but modern Peruvian and Japanese are also on the up, as is sophisticated café fare.

Cheap Chilean fast food abounds – the places we've mentioned are worth stopping at if you're hungry and nearby, but don't make a cross-town trip for them. The best higher-end restaurants are concentrated in Lastarria, Bellavista and Providencia – you can sample many of them for less by going for midweek set lunch menus. Most have at least one vegetarian dish, and fishetarians are spoilt for choice.

Centro

From local office workers lunching on the clock to tourists needing a bite between sights, downtown diners are mainly inter-

LAS CONDES

0 — 300 m
0 — 0.2 miles

INFORMATION
Australian Embassy...................1 C2
British Embassy........................2 B3
Canadian Embassy & Consulate..3 A3
Irish Embassy...........................4 C2
Israeli Embassy.........................5 B3
La Parva Ski Office....................6 B2
Netherlands Embassy................7 C3
New Zealand Embassy...............8 D3
US Embassy & Consulate...........9 A2

SIGHTS & ACTIVITIES
Navimag..................................10 A2

SLEEPING
Ritz Carlton.............................11 C3

EATING
Akarana...................................12 C3
Café Melba..............................13 B3
Fast Good................................14 B2
Liguria.....................................15 A3
Pinpilinpausha.........................16 B2
Tiramisú..................................17 C2

DRINKING
Flannery's Irish Geo Pub..........18 B3

SHOPPING
Andesgear...............................19 A3
El Mundo del Vino....................20 B2
Vinoteca.................................21 B2

---

ested in getting their food fast. Many restaurants churn out set-price lunch menus on weekdays, so it's not all junk-food combos, either. At night you're best looking elsewhere for quality dining.

BUDGET
The cheapest meals in town come from the string of food stands and *fuentes de soda* (diners) that line the Portal Fernández Concha, the arcade along the north side of Plaza de Armas. Supersized empanadas, *completos* (hot dogs), slice pizza and fried chicken are the staples here, day and night. The pick of the bunch is **Don Pepe** (Map pp84-5; Portal Fernández Concha; fast-food combos CH$990-1380; **M** Plaza de Armas), which has several packed branches in the arcade.

Bravíssimo Gelateria (Map pp84-5; Paseo Huérfanos 1162; ice cream CH$790-1600; **M** Plaza de Armas) The ice cream at this popular chain comes in colors as lurid as its sign, but it still goes down a treat on a hot day.

Mercado Central (Central Market; Map pp84-5; bordered by 21 de Mayo, San Pablo, Paseo Puente & Valdés Vergara; food stands & restaurants 9am-5pm Mon-Fri, 7am-3.30pm Sat & Sun; **M** Puente Cal y Canto) Santiago's wrought-iron fish market is a classic for long lunches (or hangover-curing fish-stew breakfasts). Skip the overpriced tourist traps in the middle, and make for one of the tiny, low-key stalls around the edge, such as the cheap and friendly Pailas Denisse (672-2926) at Local 16, where you can pick up tasty meals (CH$2500 to CH$3500).

El Naturista (mains CH$2600-3300; set lunch CH$3500; ☻9am-8pm Mon-Fri, 10am-3:20pm Sat; **V**) Huérfanos (Map pp84-5; Huérfanos 1048; **M** Plaza de Armas); Moneda (Map pp84-5; ☎ 390-5940; Moneda 846; **M** Santa Lucía) If you thought meat was a must on Chilean menus, think again. El Naturista's feasts are flesh-free, but don't expect haute veg – this definitely subscribes to the spinach-and-lentils school of cooking.

MIDRANGE

Bar Nacional (Map pp84-5; ☎ 695-3368; Bandera 317; mains CH$3400-4500; ☻7am-11pm Mon-Sat; **M** Plaza de Armas) From the chrome counter to the waitstaff of old timers, this *fuente de soda* is as vintage as they come. It has been churning out Chilean specialties like *pastel de jaiva* (crab pie) and *lomo a lo pobre* (steak and fries topped with fried egg) for years. There's a second branch, Bar Nacional 2 (☎ 696-5986), at Paseo Huérfanos 1151.

Kintaro (Map pp84-5; ☎ 638-2448; Monjitas 460; sushi CH$3900-6200, mains CH$3900-4700; ☻12:30-3pm & 7:30-11pm Mon-Fri, 7:30pm-midnight Sat; **M** Bellas Artes) This unassuming restaurant has been doing seriously authentic sushi since long before there were sushi bars on every Santiago street. Big steaming bowls of ramen and yakisoba are on hand if you're all rolled out.

Restaurant Majestic (Map pp84-5; ☎ 695-8366; Santo Domingo 1526; mains CH$3900-6200; ☻12:30-3:30pm & 7:30pm-midnight; **M** Santa Ana; **V**) The chef at Santiago's only Indian restaurant is Bangladeshi and the menu revolves around rich northern dishes like Rogan Josh, tandoori meats and breads. There's a good selection of vegetarian curries, but let them know if you like yours hot. Predictably decorated with elephant statues and batik tablecloths, it's inside the Majestic Hotel.

Confitería Torres (Map pp84-5; ☎ 688-0751; Alameda 1570; mains CH$6200-7200; ☻9am-midnight Mon-Sat; **M** Los Héroes) One of Santiago's oldest cafés wears its history on its sleeve. Golden oldies play on the radio, aging waiters attend with aplomb, and the green-and-white floor tiles are worn from use. Former president Barros Luco always ordered a steak and melted cheese sandwich here – the dish now bears his name throughout Chile.

Barrio Lastarria & Barrio Bellas Artes

In the last few years, these two neighborhoods' stars haven't stopped rising. Restaurateurs from overseas are behind some of the hip new eateries that are giving the barrios' well-established classics a run for their money.

BUDGET

El Bombón Oriental (Map pp84-5; ☎ 633-8563; Merced 353; empanadas & falafels CH$800-1500; ☻10am-10pm; **M** Bellas Artes) You'll need all the paper napkins you can find: from the shawarma, empanadas and falafel to the baklava, everything this tiny Middle Eastern café serves is divinely drippy.

Emporio La Rosa (Map pp84-5; ☎ 638-9257; Merced 291; ice cream CH$900-1800, salads & sandwiches CH$2500-3900; ☻8am-9pm Mon-Wed, 8am-10pm Thu & Fri, 9am-10pm Sat & Sun; **M** Bellas Artes; **V**) Chocochilli, strawberry and black pepper, and rose petal are some of the fabulous flavors of this extra-creamy handmade ice cream, which has been known to cause addiction. Flaky pains-au-chocolat and squishy focaccia sandwiches are two more reasons to plonk yourself at the chrome tables.

Ona (Map pp84-5; ☎ 664-8224; Rosal 386; salads & sandwiches CH$1750-2750, set menu CH$3150; ☻9am-8:30pm; **M** Bellas Artes & Universidad de Chile; **V**) At this handkerchief-sized deli, wholemeal empanadas, stuffed breads and sandwiches are served on handmade plates at sidewalk tables, or in paper bags to take away (prime picnic spot Cerro Santa Lucía is right next door).

Verace (Map pp84-5; ☎ 633-3014; JM de la Barra 486; pizzas CH$3000-5000, slice & drink CH$1500; ☻11am-11pm Mon-Sat; **M** Bellas Artes; **V**) It's a tough call as to who's quicker: the chefs whipping up these amazing thin-crust pizzas or the enraptured diners guzzling them down. Either way, turnover is high at Verace's four or five chrome tables.

MIDRANGE

Café Bistro de la Barra (Map pp84-5; ☎ 664-5505; JM de la Barra 455; sandwiches CH$4000-7000; ☻9am-9:30pm Mon-Fri, 10am-9.30pm Sat & Sun; **M** Bellas Artes; **V**) Worn old floor tiles, a velvet sofa, 1940s swing and light fittings made from cups and teapots make a quirky-but-pretty backdrop for some of the best brunches and *onces* in town. The rich sandwiches include salmon-filled croissants or Parma ham and arugula on flaky green olive bread, but make sure you save room for the perfectly firm, berry-drenched cheesecake.

Patagonia (Map pp84-5; ☎ 664-3830; Lastarria 96; mains CH$4000-7000; ☻9am-1am; **M** Bellas Artes) No prizes for working out where the star ingredients at this cozy wood-lined restaurant come from. Harder to predict are the combinations the Argentine chefs cook them into: Patagonian lamb comes in a *calafate* (berry) sauce, rainbow trout is dressed in smoked goat cheese, and the brownies come with a Cabernet coulis. Wild boar and venison are also on the cards, but there's also a plain old *parrillada* (mixed grill) if you're not feeling, um, game.

TOP END
Opera (Map pp84-5; ☎ 664-3048; Merced 395; mains CH$8200-9800; ☽ 1-3:30pm & 8-11pm Mon-Fri, 8pm-midnight Sat; Ⓜ Bellas Artes) From the first mouthful of foie gras to the last smear of crème brulée, the food at Opera bears the mark of classic French cooking, but it's made with the best Chilean ingredients. Hefty mains include lamb shank in a Cabernet reduction or the perfectly pink veal ribchop in a buttery béarnaise. The upstairs sister bar, Catedral (p106), does simpler but equally excellent food.

Bellavista
Restaurants in Bellavista divide into two basic categories. New posh restaurants open all the time along Constitución and Dardignac, while on Pío Nono the specialty is rough-and-ready staples to sustain you through a night of drinking, including *completo* stands near the bridge.

BUDGET
Empanatodos (Map p88; ☎ 783-2709; Pío Nono 153; empanadas CH$800; ☽ 11:30am-midnight Sun-Thu, 11:30am-6am Fri & Sat; Ⓜ Baquedano) The perfect pit stop for a boozy night out in Bellavista, this two-chair eatery churns out an inventive range of hot, flaky empanadas.

Zhi Dong (Map p88; ☎ 732-3599; Loreto 150; mains CH$1900; ☽ noon-midnight; Ⓜ Bellas Artes) Frills are sparse, but servings are anything but stingy in this exceptionally cheap Chinese restaurant.

MIDRANGE
Galindo (Map p88; ☎ 777-0116; Dardignac 098; mains CH$2900-5500; ☽ 12:30pm-2am Sun-Thu, 12:30pm-4am Fri & Sat; Ⓜ Baquedano) Retro neon signs adorn the wood-backed bar at this long-running local favorite, which is usually packed with noisy but appreciative crowds. It's easy to see why: unlike the precious restaurants around it, Galindo's all about sizzling *parrilladas* (mixed grills), burgers and fries, and hearty

Chilean staples washed down with freshly pulled pints.

El Caramaño (Map p88; ☎ 737-7043; Purísima 257; mains CH$2990-5790; ☽ 1pm-midnight; Ⓜ Baquedano) Good-value Chilean classics like *machas a la parmesana* (gratinée razor clams), *merluza a la trauca* (hake baked in chorizo and tomato sauce) and *oreganato* (melted oregano-dusted goat cheese) keep local families coming back here year after year.

Ali Baba (Map p88; ☎ 732-7036; Santa Filomena 102; mains CH$2990-6990; ☽ 1-4pm & 7:30pm-1am Tue-Sun; Ⓜ Baquedano; Ⓥ) The tented ceiling, Persian carpets and minaret-shaped mirrors tick all the right boxes in tasteful Middle Eastern restaurant decor. The really authentic part is the food, which goes from classics like falafel and Moroccan-style chicken to more intriguing fare like stuffed lamb intestines.

El Toro (Map p88; ☎ 737-5937, 737-0589; Loreto 33; mains CH$5700-7200; ☽ noon-midnight Mon-Sat; Ⓜ Bellas Artes) This restaurant has transformed the western end of Bellavista from backwater to hip hangout – spend a lunchtime here to spot the soap stars. Sandwiches, quiches and salads complement filling Chilean classics, but it's the cocktail menu most people are interested in.

Il Siciliano (Map p88; ☎ 737-2265; Dardignac 0102; mains CH$5900-6900; ☽ 1pm-1am Sun-Thu, 1pm-2am Fri & Sat; Ⓜ Baquedano) Seafood is the favorite filling for the *pansotti*, lasagna and other filled pastas that Il Siciliano specializes in – there's usually plenty of cheese involved, too, so the results are very rich. With its plain wooden tables and exposed brick walls, it's smart but not stuffy, and usually packed at weekends.

TOP END
Azul Profundo (Map p88; ☎ 738-0288; Constitución 111; mains CH$7500-9900; ☽ 12:45-4:30pm daily, 7:30pm-12:30am Sun-Thu, 7:30pm-1:30am Fri & Sat; Ⓜ Baquedano) Even the best Chilean seafood restaurants feel obliged to publicize their specialty by going all-out on the maritime decor. But overlook Azul Profundo's humdrum nets and telescopes and focus on its fabulously inventive food, like grilled grouper with laurel ice cream, or shellfish served on maizemeal and *merquén*-infused butter.

El Mesón Nerudiano (Map p88; ☎ 737-1542; www.elmesonnerudiano.cl; Dominica 35; mains CH$7900-11,500; ☽ noon-4pm & 7pm-2am Mon-Sat; Ⓜ Baquedano) The menu here takes inspiration from Neruda's favorite dishes, including the *caldillo de*

SANTIAGO

congrio (fish stew) he immortalized in an ode. The rough stone walls and close, candle-lit tables definitely make for romance.

Barrio Brasil
MIDRANGE

Platipus (Map p89; ☎ 672-2762; Agustinas 2099, Barrio Brasil; sushi CH$2900-4000, 2-person combos CH$6900-9800; ☯ 1-4pm & 6-11pm Mon-Fri, 7-11pm Sat; Ⓜ Cumming) Candles cast a warm glow on the exposed brick walls of this laidback sushi spot. Don't come here in a hurry, but both the sushi and the *tablas* (boards of finger food) are worth the wait.

Plaza Garibaldi (Map p89; ☎ 699-4278; Moneda 2319; mains CH$3800-5800; ☯ noon-4pm & 7pm-midnight Mon-Sat; Ⓜ Cumming) From the bright walls and saloon-style doors to the tacos, quesadillas and *chimichangas* (fried burritos), Plaza Garibaldi wears its Mexican heart on its sleeve. The food's too bland to be really authentic, but it's tasty and filling and service is friendly.

2008 (Map p89; ☎ 671-4230; Av Brasil 84; large pizzas CH$4000-6000; ☯ noon-midnight Mon-Sat, 8-11pm Sun; Ⓜ Los Héroes; Ⓥ) The deliciously gooey thin-crust pizzas here look big, but they disappear damn quickly. Add cheap beer and pisco sours, rough-and-ready wooden tables and classic rock 'n' roll, and you've got the perfect budget dinner.

Las Vacas Gordas (Map p89; ☎ 697-1066; Cienfuegos 280, Barrio Brasil; mains CH$4000-6000; ☯ noon-4pm & 7pm-midnight Mon-Sat, noon-4pm Sun; Ⓜ Cumming or Santa Ana) The name means 'fat cows' and cow-print paint plasters the outside walls and pavement: if it once said 'moo', it's on the menu and in hefty portions, too. Your steak sizzles on the giant grill at the front of the clattering main dining area, then dead-pan old-school waiters cart it over to your table. It's usually packed, so reserve or get there very early.

Ostras Azócar (Map p89; ☎ 682-2203; General Bulnes 37, Barrio Brasil; mains CH$5900-7900; ☯ 12:30-4:30pm & 7:30-11:30pm Mon-Sat, 12:30-4:30pm Sun; Ⓜ Republica) A beautifully preserved old townhouse contains Barrio Brasil's classic seafood restaurant. Candlelight, stiff white tablecloths and perfect platters of oysters (the house specialty) all point to it being ideal for a date night.

Ocean Pacific's (Map p89; ☎ 697-2413; www.oprestaurant.cl; Av Ricardo Cumming 221; mains CH$6000-8000; ☯ noon-11pm Sun-Thu, noon-midnight Fri & Sat; Ⓜ Cumming) From glass-rimmed portholes to fish tanks and a massive fiberglass whale skeleton, they've gone all out on under-the-sea decor

here. The menu should come as no surprise then, not least because they've illustrated it with photos of each fishy dish. The kitsch factor is reason enough to come, but the massive seafood platters and traditional fish stews are surprisingly good, too.

TOP END

Ostras Squella (Map p89; ☎ 699-3059; Av Ricardo Cumming 94; mains CH$8200-9000; ☯ 7pm-midnight Mon-Sat; Ⓜ Cumming) A suitably salty smell fills this minimal white restaurant: that's because your dinner is still swimming or crouching in the bubbling pools that line one side of it. The oysters are what have kept diners coming back for over 30 years, though the ceviches are also pretty fabulous.

Providencia
BUDGET

Doner House (Map pp90-1; ☎ 264-3200; Av Providencia 1457, Providencia; shawarma CH$2500; ☯ 12:30-10pm Mon-Sat; Ⓜ Manuel Montt) The doner maestro carves up a killer shawarma at this tiny eatery. Falafels and stuffed vine leaves are some of the other quick bites on hand.

Voraz Pizza (Map pp90-1; ☎ 235-6477; Av Providencia 1321, Providencia; pizzas CH$2500-3500; ☯ 1-11pm Mon-Wed, 1pm-midnight Thu-Sat; Ⓜ Manuel Montt; Ⓥ) This hole-in-the-wall pizzeria serves great-value thin-crust pizzas and artisanal beers at sidewalk tables, or will deliver to your hostel. If you're really in a hurry, you can wolf down a slice or two at the bar.

Akbar (Map pp90-1; ☎ 596-8500; Av Providencia 1130, Providencia; sushi CH$2500-3500, lunch menus CH$3500; ☯ noon-midnight Mon-Thu, 7:30pm-2am Fri & Sat; Ⓜ Manuel Montt) Bare concrete and dark wood panels are the functional but cool backdrop for well-priced, reasonably authentic sushi. Dinner stretches well into the wee hours on weekends, when live DJs and powerful cocktails make the perfect dessert for your *maki*.

MIDRANGE

Café del Patio (Map pp90-1; ☎ 236-1251; www.cafedelpatio.cl, in Spanish; Av Providencia 1670, Local 8A; mains CH$4000-5500; ☯ noon-1:30am Mon-Sat; Ⓜ Manuel Montt; Ⓥ) Locals rave about the superfresh vegetarian specialties at this cute eatery, where the best tables are clustered in a brightly painted courtyard. As well as tofu- and seitan-based stir-fries, there are salads, sandwiches and a few fish options.

Normandie (Map pp90–1; ☎ 236-3011; Av Providencia 1234; mains CH$4200-6200; ☻ 9am–1am Mon–Thu, 9am–3am Fri & Sat; Ⓜ Manuel Montt) With its varnished wood paneling and deadpan waiters, Normandie strives hard to look like a typical French café. The food is equally Gallic: think well-executed classics like *lapin en gibelotte* (rabbit in red wine) or duck à l'orange.

El Huerto (Map pp90–1; ☎ 233-2690; Orrego Luco 054; mains CH$4700-5900; ☻ 12:30-3:30pm & 7:30-11pm; Ⓜ Pedro de Valdivia; Ⓥ) This earthy restaurant's changing vegetarian fare is a big hit with both hip young things and ladies who lunch. Some dishes err on the stodgy side, but most are fresh and tasty. Next door, smaller Café La Huerta does salads and sandwiches on weekdays.

Liguria (www.liguria.cl, in Spanish; mains CH$5200-7500; ☻ noon–1am Mon–Sat) Av Pedro de Valdivia Norte (Map pp90–1; ☎ 334-4346; Av Pedro de Valdivia 047, Providencia; Ⓜ Pedro de Valdivia); Av Providencia (Map pp90–1; ☎ 235-7914; Av Providencia 1373, Providencia; Ⓜ Manuel Montt); Las Condes (Map p99; ☎ 231-1393; Luis Thayer Ojeda 019, Las Condes; Ⓜ Tobalaba) A legend on the Santiago restaurant circuit, Liguria mixes equal measures of bar and bistro perfectly. Stewed rabbit or silverside in batter are chalked up on a blackboard, then dapper old-school waiters place them on the red-checked tablecloths with aplomb. Vintage adverts, Chilean memorabilia and old bottles decorate the wood-paneled inside, but it's the sidewalk tables that diners really fight over – even on weeknights you should book ahead.

TOP END

our pick **Astrid y Gastón** (Map pp90–1; ☎ 650-9125; Antonio Bellet 201; mains CH$7800-11,800; ☻ 1-3:30pm & 8pm–midnight Mon–Fri, dinner only Sat; Ⓜ Pedro de Valdivia) The seasonally changing menu of Peruvian haute cuisine has made this one of Santiago's most critically acclaimed restaurants. The warm but expert waitstaff happily talk you through the chef's subtle, modern take on traditional ceviches, *chupes* (fish stews) and *chochinillo* (suckling pig), all beautifully presented. The barman deserves an ovation for his complex cocktails: Peruvian pisco comes with physalis juice in the Aquaymanto, for example.

Las Condes

Glittering skyscrapers, security-heavy apartment blocks, spanking-new malls, and five-star hotels: Las Condos is determined to be the international face of Chile's phenomenal economic growth. Brash, bustling, and far from beautiful, it's worth visiting for its fine restaurants.

MIDRANGE

Fast Good (Map p99; ☎ 326-2604; Isidora Goyenechea 2890; mains CH$2700-3800; ☻ noon–midnight Mon–Fri; Ⓜ El Golf; Ⓥ) The name says it all: the beef, tuna and veggie burgers here are as fresh as they are quick, and come with sides like fries cooked in extra-virgin olive oil. The small, ultraminimal space is painted bright green, just like the large fiberglass horse outside (best not to ask). Food god Ferràn Adrià is behind this chain – this is the first branch outside of his native Spain.

Café Melba (Map p99; ☎ 232-4546; Don Carlos 2898; sandwiches CH$2900, mains CH$6000; ☻ 7:30am–8pm Mon–Fri, 8am–8pm Sat; Ⓜ Tobalaba; Ⓥ) Eggs and bacon, muffins, bagels and hotcakes are some of the moreish all-day breakfast offerings at this New Zealand–owned café. Well-stuffed sandwiches and heartier dishes like green fish curry or pork medallions are popular with lunching local finance workers and the steady stream of gringos it draws.

Tiramisú (Map p99; ☎ 519-4900; pizzas $3400-4900; Isidora Goyenechea 3141; ☻ 12:45-4pm & 7:15pm–midnight; Ⓜ Tobalaba; Ⓥ) Bright murals, rough-hewn tables and cheerful red-checked cloths set the tone at this busy pizzeria. You'll spend more time choosing one of the myriad thin-crust pizzas than wolfing it down – consider the *gamberetti*, which combines buffalo mozzarella and prawns.

TOP END

Pinpilinpausha (Map p99; ☎ 232-5800; Isidora Goyenechea 2900; mains CH$6900-9900; ☻ 12:30-11:30pm Mon–Sat, 12:30-4pm Sun; Ⓜ El Golf) There's a friendly, family feel to this Basque restaurant. The trademark fish dishes typically involve heavy sauces – try the *merluza austral* (hake in creamy artichoke) or *corvina a la Donostiarra* (a peppery sea bass). Add fuel to the fire by ordering a rich *crema catalana* (Spanish-style crème brulée) for dessert.

Akarana (Map p99; ☎ 231-9667; Reyes Lavalle 3310; mains CH$7800-10,500, set lunch menu CH$7900; ☻ noon–midnight; Ⓜ El Golf; Ⓥ) Orange-infused water and hunks of homemade bread with peppery olive oil keep you busy while you wait for the creative but unpretentious fare that have made this bright New Zealand–run restaurant one of Santiago's best. Even the dishes' names are inventive: Bambi on the Grill is venison in a redcurrant glaze. Potted olive trees decorate the huge, inviting terrace, which is shaded by canvas umbrellas in the day and lit by oil lamps at night.

Ñuñoa

A low-profile but happening food and bar scene makes Ñuñoa a favorite night out for urbane Santiaguinos. East of the Centro but well south of Providencia, it's far from the metro, but don't let that put you off: bus 505 runs along Merced and Salvador to Plaza Ñuñoa, the heart of all the action. A taxi here from the Centro will cost around CH$4000.

BUDGET

Fuente Suiza (Map p104; ☎ 204-7199; Av Irarrázaval 3361; sandwiches CH$2400-3400; ☯ 10:30am-midnight Mon-Sat) Dripping *lomo* (pork) sandwiches and flaky deep-fried empanadas make this simple family-run restaurant the perfect place to prepare for (or recover from) a long night of drinking.

MIDRANGE

Ébano (Map p104; ☎ 453-4665; Jorge Washington 176; sandwiches CH$2500, mains CH$6000; ☯ 7pm-2am Mon-Sat) Unusual ingredient combinations are at the heart of Ébano's small menu: there's a bean and strawberry salad, for example, or grilled pork chops with mango and wild rice risotto. Equally inventive cocktails are popular with an arty older crowd who love the understated concrete walls and slick music.

El Amor Nunca Muere (Map p104; ☎ 274-9432; Trucco 43; mains CH$4800-6200; ☯ 6pm-2am Sun-Thu, 6pm-4am Fri & Sat) Subtle lighting, soft mood music and simple bistro-style fare draw couples from across the city here. Crêpes are the house specialty, but the omelets and fondue are just as tempting. Dinner merges into long nights of drinking on the terrace during the summer.

DRINKING
Cafés

Santiago's booming café culture centers on JM de la Barra, a short stretch of street between Cerro Santa Lucía and the river. By nightfall, the tables of the hip cafés that line it are packed with drinkers of both java and stronger brews.

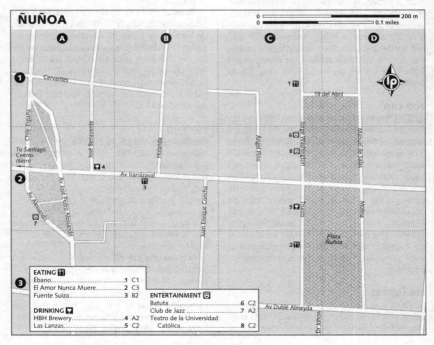

ÑUÑOA

0 ——————— 200 m
0 ——————— 0.1 miles

EATING 🍴
Ébano...1 C1
El Amor Nunca Muere.............2 C3
Fuente Suiza..............................3 B2

DRINKING 🍸
HBH Brewery..............................4 A2
Las Lanzas..................................5 C2

ENTERTAINMENT 🎭
Batuta..6 C2
Club de Jazz...............................7 A2
Teatro de la Universidad
  Católica.....................................8 C2

COFFEE WITH LEGS

Skinny lattes and mochaccinos are relatively new to Santiago, but a very different sort of café culture has long been part of local life: *cafés con piernas*, or 'coffee with legs.' Forget hip baristas, here the female-only servers wear string bikinis to bring your espresso. The customers, in contrast, are usually businessmen in suits and ties. Despite the lurid air created by blacked-out windows and neon lights, the popular chains serve nothing stronger than cheap espresso and are only open Monday to Friday during the day. And though customers might be discussing mergers and acquisitions, coffee here is cheap and other kinds of financial transactions with the waitresses are generally (but not always) discouraged. Many Chileans look on *cafés con piernas* as a harmless – if sometimes ridiculous – part of life; for others, they're a measure of just how far gender equality in Chile still has to come. Perhaps the best way to make up your mind on the issue is to have a chat with the waitresses yourself. Although most clients are men, women are also welcome.

Micro-mini dresses are the almost matronly attire of servers at **Café Haití** (Map pp84-5; Paseo Ahumada 140) and **Café Caribe** (Map pp84-5; Paseo Ahumada 120). Ultra-high-leg '80s bikinis have given **Baron Rojo** (Map pp84-5; Agustinas 717) and **Café Ikabarú** (Map pp84-5; Huérfanos 709, Local 2) a decidedly racy reputation. Most of these cafés have numerous other branches about town.

Café Tomodashi Chillout (Map pp84-5; ☎ 638-4700; JM de la Barra 432; ⏰ 8:30am-11pm Mon-Fri, 10am-11pm Sat & Sun; Ⓜ Bellas Artes) One of the best on the street, this has sofas so comfortable you'll never want to stand up.

Café Brainworks (Map pp84-5; ☎ 633-9218; JM de la Barra 454; ⏰ 10am-8pm Mon-Fri, 10am-7pm Sat & Sun; Ⓜ Bellas Artes) There's no booze at this neighboring spot but its retro plastic chairs deserve the street's design prize, and the smoothies are divine, too.

Café Abarzúa (Map pp84-5; ☎ 638-7256; Merced 337, Centro; ⏰ 8am-11pm; Ⓜ Bellas Artes) A scaffolded mezzanine lends an industrial look to things here. The coffee, tea and cakes are the main attractions, but the temporary exhibitions by local art students might also catch your eye.

La Signoria (Map pp84-5; ☎ 813-6591; Bellavista 211, Centro; ⏰ 9am-9pm; Ⓜ Bellas Artes) Squidgy cakes, juices and espressos make crossing to the north side of the river worth your while.

Mundo de Papel (Map p88; ☎ 735-0411; Constitución 166, Bellavista; ⏰ 11am-8pm; Ⓜ Baquedano) The cluttered shelves and tables of this independent bookshop and café provide literary inspiration as you write your postcards – or your novel – over a late breakfast combo or a juice and sandwich.

Pubs & Bars

Boy do Santiaguinos love to drink. And we're talking all-out, under-the-table boozing that rivals their international counterparts. Even on weeknights, by 8pm or 9pm many bars are packed with after-work or after-school gatherings, their tables cheerfully heaving under empty bottles and beer jugs. From rowdy pubs to snug bars, wherever you stay, the chances are you'll have a great drinking venue just around the corner.

CENTRO

La Piojera (Map pp84-5; ☎ 698-1682; Aillavilú 1030, Centro; ⏰ noon-midnight Mon-Sat; Ⓜ Plaza de Armas) Saved from developers by protests from its loyal clientele – including presidents and poets – this bare-bones drinking den is the real deal. Noisy regulars pack the sticky tables, which are crammed with glass tumblers of the two house specialties: *chicha*, sweet Chilean cider, and the earth-moving (or gut-wrenching) *terremoto*, a potent mix of wine and ice cream. Sawdust strewn on the cement floor soaks up spillage.

BARRIO LASTARRIA & BARRIO BELLAS ARTES

El Diablito (Map pp84-5; ☎ 638-3512; Merced 336, Centro; ⏰ 9:30am-3am Mon-Sat, 6:30pm-1am Sun; Ⓜ Bellas Artes) Old photos and vintage household items clutter the already dark walls of this smoky den. After dark, the tiny candlelit tables seem to invite you to huddle conspiratorially into the small hours; great value *schop* (draft beer) and pisco sours are two more reasons to stay.

Bar Berri (Map pp84-5; ☎ 632-3190; Rosal 321, Centro; ⏰ 7pm-3am Mon-Thu, 8pm-4am Fri & Sat; Ⓜ Bellas Artes) Forget what's hot and what's not: with its close mishmash of antique furniture and classic rock 'n' roll, Berri is totally timeless.

Well-pulled *schop* keeps the crowd of toe-tapping 30-somethings – many of them expats – happy.

Catedral (Map pp84-5; ☎ 664-3048; JM de la Barra & Merced; 12:30pm-3am Mon-Thu, 12:30pm-5am Fri & Sat; Ⓜ Bellas Artes) With accomplished dishes like lamb and beer stew or violet crème brulée, Catedral's menu goes way beyond bar snacks. A poised crew of professionals in their 20s and 30s love the minimal two-tone couches and smooth tunes here.

BELLAVISTA

In Santiago, the life and soul of the *carrete* is Barrio Bellavista. By 10pm tables inside and outside of its many bars are filled with rowdy groups of Santiaguinos giving their all to the *previa* (preclub drinking). Many of the restaurants and clubs in Bellavista also double as drinking spots.

The identical watering holes along Pío Nono are seedy but ultracheap – pitchers of watery beer are the standard order. Both the drinks and the crowds are a bit more sophisticated along Constitución and Antonia López de Bello, which are peppered with arty spots. Further west, Bombero Núñez is home to a handful of more underground bars and clubs, including some of Santiago's best gay nightlife (see the boxed text, p109).

Although the bars and cafés inside **Patio Bellavista** (Map p88; ☎ 777-4582; www.patiobella vista.cl; Pío Nono 73; Ⓜ Baquedano) are a bit bland, they're just about the only places open on Sunday nights.

Bar Dos Gardenias (Map p88; ☎ 474-4534; www .bardosgardenias.cl, in Spanish; Antonia López de Bello 0199, Bellavista; ☿ 7pm-2am; Ⓜ Baquedano) A portrait of Che surveys the revelers in this relaxed little enclave with low lighting and high spirits, one of several similar places in this block. Son and other Cuban sounds are often played, and there are live folk or tango performances.

Dublin (Map p88; ☎ 730-0526; Constitución 58, Bellavista; ☿ noon-midnight Sun-Thu, noon-4am Fri & Sat; Ⓜ Baquedano) As at all the best fake-Irish pubs, they've been generous with the green paint here. A growing backpacker clientele proves that on-tap Kross and well-chosen rock go a long way towards redemption.

BARRIO BRASIL

Baires (Map p89; ☎ 697-4430; Brasil 255, Barrio Brasil; ☿ 1pm-midnight Sun-Thu, from 1pm Fri & Sat; Ⓜ Cumming) The slick orange-and-white decor is as self-consciously cool as the waitstaff is snooty. But the terrace tables fill up quickly even on weeknights, and DJs get going upstairs on weekends.

Eurohappy (Map p89; ☎ 672-1016; Maturana 516, Barrio Brasil; ☿ 7pm-midnight Sun-Thu, 7pm till late Fri & Sat; Ⓜ Cumming) Over 400 types of beer – including local artisanal and microbrewery options – are expertly poured by Santiago's only beer sommelier. Sip your selection out on the pavement or head for the candlelit vermillion-and-white interior to strike a pose on 1950s furniture.

PROVIDENCIA

Bar Yellow (Map pp90-1; ☎ 946-5063; General Flores 47, Providencia; ☿ 6pm-1am Mon-Wed, 6pm-3am Thu-Sat; Ⓜ Manuel Montt) Truly magic mixology has made this small but achingly cool bar the hands-down favorite among cocktail quaffers. Give yourself a wake-up call with a Breakfast Martini (marmalade is involved) or let loose with a Golden Shower (we'll let you find out what's in it).

Bar Central (Map pp90-1; ☎ 264-2236; Av Providencia 1391, Providencia; ☿ 11am-2am Mon-Sat, 8pm-1am Sun; Ⓜ Manuel Montt) A linchpin of Providencia nightlife, self-consciously cool Bar Central attracts hip media types with its sleek chrome furnishings and well-mixed pisco sours.

Phone Box Pub (Map pp90-1; ☎ 235-9972; Av Providencia 1670, Providencia; ☿ 1am-3am Mon-Sat; Ⓜ Manuel Montt) Plonking a bright-red British phone box outside is hardly the most subtle attempt to appeal to the expat community, granted, but the combination of well-pulled pints and classic pub grub works perfectly.

Santo Remedio (Map pp90-1; ☎ 235-0984; Román Díaz 152, Providencia; ☿ from 7:30pm Mon-Sat, from 8pm Sun; Ⓜ Manuel Montt) Strictly speaking, this low-lighted, high-ceilinged old house is a restaurant, and an aphrodisiac one at that. But it's the bar action people really come for: powerful, well-mixed cocktails and regular live DJs keep the 30-something crowds happy.

LAS CONDES

Flannery's Irish Geo Pub (Map p99; ☎ 233-6675; Encomenderos 83, Las Condes; ☿ noon-2am Mon-Fri, 6pm-3am Sat, 6pm-1am Sun; Ⓜ Tobalaba) Guinness and Kilkenny imports help make this a popular – if somewhat cheesy – gringo watering hole. Your favorite team's playing back at home? This is the best bet for catching the action on TV.

ÑUÑOA

Las Lanzas (Map p104; ☎ 225-5589; Trucco 25, Ñuñoa; ☼ noon-2am Mon-Sat) Neon lighting and no-frills furniture that hasn't changed much since the '70s are part of the charm of this Ñuñoa mainstay. Rock-bottom prices mean it's usually full right up to closing, especially in the summer, when revelers spill out onto the sidewalk terrace.

HBH Brewery (Map p104; ☎ 209-9614; Av Irarrázaval 3176, Ñuñoa; ☼ 7pm-2am Mon-Sat) Beer buffs and students rave about this laid-back microbrewery. As well as its own stout and lager, it stocks near a hundred bottled brews.

ENTERTAINMENT

Whether you get your kicks on the dance floor or at the soccer stadium, and whether you'd rather clap in time to strumming folksingers or at the end of three-hour operas, Santiago has plenty to keep you entertained. National dailies *El Mercurio* and *La Tercera* carry cinema, theater and classical music listings. Information and tickets for many major performances and sporting events are available through **Ticketmaster** (☎ 689-2000; www.ticketmaster .cl), which also has sales points in Falabella department stores and Hoyts cinemas, and **FeriaTicket** (☎ 592-8500; www.feriaticket.cl), which operates in Feria del Disco music stores. For the latest on clubbing, live music and nightlife check out the searchable listings on **Saborizante** (www.saborizante.com) or go straight to the source by visiting the websites or blogs of the clubs and bars themselves: those listed here update theirs regularly.

Live Music

Chile hasn't got the musical reputation other Latin American countries do. But there are some seriously good bands here, and a gaggle of Santiago bars are usually the best places to catch them. Save the salsa and tango for the countries that do them best: instead, your best bets in Santiago will be folksy singer-songwriters, Chilean or Argentinian indie groups, *rock nacional* (Chilean rock) upstarts, and purveyors of the most Latin of local beats, *cumbia chilombiana*. International greats also visit Chile regularly, and tickets are usually much cheaper than at home.

our pick **Bar Constitución** (Map p88; ☎ 244-4569; www.barconstitucion.cl, in Spanish; Constitución 61, Bellavista; ☼ 8pm-5am Mon-Sat; Ⓜ Baquedano) The coolest nightspot of the moment has no sign outside:

find a huge gray sliding door with a long queue of trendies and you're in the right place. Live bands and DJs play nightly – the bar's eclectic (but infallible) tastes include electroclash, garage, nu-folk, house and more, so check the website to see if the night's program suits.

Batuta (Map p104; ☎ 274-7096; www.batuta.cl, in Spanish; Jorge Washington 52, Ñuñoa; ☼ 10pm-3am Wed-Sat) Enthusiastic crowds jump to ska, *patchanka* (think: Manu Chau) and *cumbia chilombiana*; rockabilly and surf; tribute bands and goth rock… at Batuta, just about anything alternative goes.

Galpón Víctor Jara (Map p89; ☎ 657-9455; www .galponvictorjara.cl, in Spanish; Huérfanos 2146, Barrio Brasil; Ⓜ Cumming) Named in memory of disappeared singer-songwriter and activist Víctor Jara, this warehouselike space hosts gigs from hot alternative local bands like Teleradio Donoso and Chico Trujillo.

Teatro Caupolicán (Map pp80-1; ☎ 699-1556; www .teatrocaupolican.cl, in Spanish; San Diego 850; Ⓜ Parque O'Higgins) From Jarvis Cocker and Brett Anderson to the Hives, the choicest international gigs happen here. Latin American rockers who've trod the boards include far-out Mexicans Café Tacuba, and Oscar-winning Uruguayan Jorge Drexler.

Teatro Oriente (Map pp90-1; ☎ 335-0023; www.tea troriente.cl, in Spanish; Av Pedro de Valdivia 099, Providencia; Ⓜ Pedro de Valdivia) International indie artists like Benjamin Biolay and Jane Birkin have played this Providencia venue, which also hosts visiting Latin American folk musicians and choice classical performances.

Club de Jazz (Map p104; ☎ 326-5065; www.clubdejazz .cl, in Spanish; Av Alessandri 85, Ñuñoa; ☼ 10:30pm-3am Thu-Sat) One of Latin America's most established jazz venues – Louis Armstrong and Herbie Hancock are just two of the greats to have played here – this large wooden building hosts local and international jazz, blues and big band performers.

El Perseguidor Jazz Club (Map p88; ☎ 777-6763; www.elperseguidor.cl, in Spanish; Antonia López de Bello 0126, Bellavista; cover CH$1000-3000; ☼ from 7pm Mon-Sat; Ⓜ Baquedano) Established local jazz, funk and soul groups perform nightly to enthusiastic crowds here – arrive early or book on weekends if you want a table. There's a small dinner menu as well as drinks and tapas.

La Casa en el Aire (Map p88; ☎ 735-6680; www .lacasaenelaire.cl, in Spanish; Antonia López de Bello 0125, Bellavista; ☼ 8pm-late Mon-Sun; Ⓜ Baquedano) Latin-American folk music, storytelling gatherings, film cycles and poetry readings are some of the arty events that take place nightly in this low-key old house turned bar.

Nightclubs

Don't even think about showing up at any of these places before midnight: in Santiago, if it's not all night it's not a night out. Most clubs close at about 4 or 5am, at which point those still on their feet adjourn to an after-hours to wind things up.

La Feria (Map p88; ☎ 735-8433; www.clublaferia.cl; Constitución 275, Bellavista; cover CH$3000-5000; ☙ from 11pm Thu-Sat; Ⓜ Baquedano) Euphoric house and techno, an up-for-it crowd and banging DJs mean this is still the place to go for a fix of electronic music.

El Clan (Map p88; ☎ 735-3655; www.barelclan .cl; Bombero Núñez 363, Bellavista; cover CH$2000-5000; ☙ from 11pm Tue-Sat; Ⓜ Baquedano) The name's short for 'El Clandestino,' a throwback from this small club's undercover days (there's still no sign outside). A small crew of resident DJs keep the 20-something crowds going – expect anything from '80s to house, R&B, funk or techno. Cheap beer and pisco is your fuel.

Sofa (Map pp80-1; ☎ 249-8175; www.sofa.cl; Santa Isabel 0151, Providencia; cover CH$1000-4000; ☙ from 9pm Tue-Thu, from midnight Fri & Sat; Ⓜ Santa Isabel) Yes, there are plenty of sunken couches to slump into. But that's not all: at this effortlessly cool club you stand your drinks – chilled in an old bathtub – on retro cabinets and then groove to funk, soul, hip-hop, R&B or breakbeats.

Blondie (Map p89; ☎ 681-7793; www.blondie.cl, in Spanish; Alameda 2879, Barrio Brasil; cover CH$3000-5000; ☙ from 11pm Thu-Sat) The '80s still rule at least one floor of Blondie, while the other could have anything from goth rock and techno to Britpop or Chilean indie. A favorite with both Santiago's student and gay communities, it's usually packed.

La Berenjena (Map pp84-5; ☎ 664-2855; www.laberen jena.cl; Agustinas 676, Centro; cover CH$4000; ☙ from midnight Fri & Sat; Ⓜ Santa Lucía) Indie hits from the '80s and '90s usually please the youngish crowds on one of this club's two floors. The DJ on the other could be spinning jungle and drum'n'bass or techno, usually encouraged by plenty of followers.

Grancentral (Map pp90-1; ☎ 234-2726; www.grancentral .cl; Las Urbinas 44, Providencia; ☙ from 10pm Wed-Sat) A slick, low-lighted bar where the night begins, Grancentral heats up to club temperature sometime after midnight. DJs vary, but dub,

freestyle and house are often on the menu. There's a huge roof terrace to cool off on.

El Tunel (Map pp84-5; ☎ 639-4914; www.bareltunel.cl; Santo Domingo 439, Centro; cover CH$2000-3000; ☙ 10pm-4am Wed-Sat; Ⓜ Bellas Artes) Teenyboppers of the world unite: if you missed the '70s and '80s the first time round, this is the place to show the world your best John Travolta moves. The decor is dingy and the vibe is cheesy but cheap drinks mean everyone emerges perspiring but happy.

Subterráneo (Map pp90-1; ☎ 335-0951; www.subter raneo.cl; Pasaje Orrego Luco 46, Providencia; ☙ from 10pm Tue-Sat) Each night, different beats pull in a particular tribe of young groovers – Wednesdays and Thursdays are more about dub, hip-hop and R&B, while weekends are trashier and often packed.

Theater, Dance & Classical Music

Although much of Chilean theater revolves around the besequined, tassel-toting showgirls that star in so-called *comedias musicales*, Santiago is also home to some excellent stage and ballet companies, orchestras and choirs.

Teatro Municipal (Map pp84-5; ☎ 463-1000; www .municipal.cl, in Spanish; Agustinas 794, Centro; ☙ box office 10am-7pm Mon-Fri, 10am-2pm Sat & Sun; Ⓜ Santa Lucía) This exquisite neoclassical building is the most prestigious performing-arts venue in the city. It's home to the Ballet de Santiago and also hosts world-class opera, tango and classical music performances.

Teatro Universidad de Chile (Map pp84-5; ☎ 634-5295; http://teatro.uchile.cl, in Spanish; Providencia 043, Centro; Ⓜ Baquedano) The Orquesta Sinfónica de Chile and Ballet Nacional de Chile are two high-profile companies based at this excellent theater. There is a fall season of ballet, choral, orchestral and chamber music, as well as the occasional rock gig.

Teatro de la Universidad Católica (Map p104; ☎ 205-5652; www.teuc.cl, in Spanish; Jorge Washington 26, Ñuñoa) Collective performances, new Chilean plays, and off-beat stagings of classics have made this theater in Ñuñoa a focal point of Santiago's drama scene.

Centro Cultural Teatro del Puente (Map p88; ☎ 732-4883; www.teatrodelpuente.cl; Parque Forestal s/n, Centro; Ⓜ Baquedano) Experimental theater companies and the occasional Chilean indie band perform in this space between Pío Nono and Purísima bridges.

Centro Cultural Gran Circo Teatro (Map p89; gran circoteatro@hotmail.com; Av República 301; Ⓜ República)

Santiago's best-known street theater troupe was given this run-down house by the government in 2008. Avant-garde theater and circus performances are the group's specialty – it was behind *La Negra Ester*, one of Chile's most famous plays.

Cinemas
New releases take a long, long time getting to Santiago, where most big cinemas show the same few Hollywood blockbusters. Tickets are often discounted Monday through Wednesday and for the first show or two of the day.

Cine Hoyts (☎ 600-5000-400; www.cinehoyts.cl, in Spanish) Estación Central (Map p89; Exposición 155; Ⓜ Estación Central); Huérfanos (Map pp84-5; Paseo Huérfanos 735, Centro; Ⓜ Santa Lucía); San Agustín (Map pp84-5; Moneda 835, Centro; Ⓜ Santa Lucía) Modern multiplexes showing mainstream movies.

Cine Gran Palace (Map pp84-5; ☎ 696-0082; www.cinemundo.cl, in Spanish; Paseo Huérfanos 1176, Centro; Ⓜ Plaza de Armas) This four-screen complex shows mainstream fare at reasonable prices.

Cineteca Nacional (Map pp84-5; ☎ 355-6500; www.ccplm.cl/cinetecanacional.php, in Spanish; Plaza de la Ciudadanía 26, Centro; Ⓜ La Moneda) Inside the Centro Cultural Palacio La Moneda, this state-funded microcinema organizes film cycles and retrospectives.

Centro Arte Alameda (Map pp84-5; ☎ 664-8821; www.centroartealameda.cl; Alameda 139, Centro; Ⓜ Baquedano) International art-house flicks are shown alongside the latest Chilean releases at this excellent cinema, which also has a bar and exhibition space.

Cine Arte Normandie (Map pp84-5; ☎ 697-2979; www.normandie.cl, in Spanish; Tarapacá 1181, Barrio Cívico; Ⓜ Moneda) Cycles of work by local directors alternate with international indie flicks at

---

GAY & LESBIAN SANTIAGO
Although Santiago is still not on the Latin American gaydar in the same way as Buenos Aires or Rio, the scene's surprisingly good for a country that's still ultra-Catholic and very socially conservative.

Every June, thousands of people now take part in the **Marcha del Orgullo Gay** (Gay Pride Parade), organized by the **Movimiento de Integración y Liberación Homosexual** (Movilh; Map pp80-1; ☎ 671-4855; www.movilh.org, in Spanish; Coquimbo 1410, Centro). The website has links to social events. There's another annual parade in late November, the **Open Mind Fest** (☎ 671-4855; www.gayparade.cl, in Spanish), which is one big electronic street party. **Sitiosgay** (www.sitiosgay.cl, in Spanish) has listings of Chilean gay and gay-friendly organizations, hotels, pubs and bars, clubs, salons and more.

The heart of the nightlife action is Bellavista, home to the bar-lined street Bombero Núñez as well as several other bars and clubs. In addition to the places mentioned below, clubs Blondie (opposite) and La Feria (opposite) draw reasonably large gay crowds.

Amor del Bueno (Map p88; ☎ 735-9270; www.amordelbueno.cl, in Spanish; Ernesto Pinto Lagarrigue 257, Bellavista; ☽ 6pm-4am Mon-Thu, from 7pm Fri & Sat; Ⓜ Baquedano) Hands down the best girl bar in town, warm and friendly Amor del Bueno hosts film cycles and workshops early in the evening, then shifts into bar mode later on. There's a small snack menu and live music performances on weekends.

Bokhara (Map p88; www.bokhara.cl, in Spanish; Pío Nono 430, Bellavista; ☽ 10pm-4am Mon-Sun; Ⓜ Baquedano) Although local connoisseurs think it slightly passé, Bokhara is still the automatic choice for midweek clubbing. House and techno are the main beats on its two floors; there are rather tired live shows on weekends.

Bunker (Map p88; www.bunker.cl, in Spanish; Bombero Núñez 159, Bellavista; cover CH$5000; ☽ from 11pm Fri & Sat; Ⓜ Baquedano) The hippest gay club night in town draws a mix of well-dressed locals (including minor celebs) and visitors who love the high-octane music. Its sister bar next door, Femme, isn't nearly as cool.

Vox Populi (Map p88; ☎ 738-0562; Ernesto Pinto Lagarrigue 364, Bellavista; ☽ from 9pm Tue-Sat; Ⓜ Baquedano) An old house filled with mismatched furniture is the setting for this relaxed bar, popular with an arty crowd, both gay and straight. In summer, you can sip your cocktails on a plant-filled patio, and work by local artists is often on the walls inside. The volume gets turned up on weekends.

this small cinema, where low ticket prices attract arty students.

Cine El Biógrafo (Map pp84-5; ☎ 633-4435; www.trans europafilms.cl, in Spanish; Lastarria 181, Centro; Ⓜ Universidad Católica) Surrounded by Barrio Lastarria's best bars and cafés, this great little arthouse cinema shows infrequently changing European films.

Cine Arte Tobalaba (Map pp90-1; ☎ 231-6630; www .showtime.cl, in Spanish; Av Providencia 2563, Providencia; Ⓜ Tobalaba) New European movies are mainly shown here.

Spectator Sports
SOCCER

On the whole, Chileans are a pretty calm lot – until they step foot in a soccer stadium, that is. Mad screaming and dancing (or cursing, weeping and hair-tearing) accompanies international games, the most dramatic of which are against local rivals like Peru or Argentina, when 'Chi-Chi-Chi-Lay-Lay-Lay' reverberates through the **Estadio Nacional** (National Stadium; Map pp80-1; ☎ 238-8102; Av Grecia 2001, Ñuñoa). Tickets can be bought at the stadium or from the Feria del Disco (opposite). Equally impassioned are the *hinchas* (fans) of Santiago's first-division soccer teams, of which Colo Colo, Universidad de Chile and Universidad Católica are the most popular.

HORSE RACING

If museums and churches are boring you brainless, consider seeing a faster side of Santiago by spending the afternoon at the races. The main racetrack is the grand **Club Hípico de Santiago** (Map pp80-1; ☎ 693-9600; www.club hipico.cl, in Spanish; Av Blanco Encalada 2540; Ⓜ Parque O'Higgins), where views of the Andes compete for your attention with the action on the turf. It was once the preserve of Chile's elite, but the CH\$200 minimum bet means it's now very egalitarian indeed. Races take place here every Friday and on alternate Mondays.

SHOPPING

Santiago may not be a world-class shopping destination, but you can still pick up interesting craft pieces and unusual clothing or houseware by young local designers. The Centro's busiest – and tackiest – shopping streets are pedestrianized Ahumada and Huérfanos, which are lined with cheap clothing, shoe and department stores. For seriously cheap clothes, head to the Korean and

Palestinian immigrant area of Patronato, west of Bellavista between Patronato and Manzano. Secondhand clothes stores abound in the city (often flagged by signs saying 'Ropa Europea/ Americana'). Many have gathered around Providencia's Manuel Montt metro station.

Camping Gear

Andesgear (Map p99; ☎ 245-7076; Helvecia 210, Las Condes; ☾ 10am-8pm Mon-Fri, 10:30am-2pm Sat; Ⓜ Tobolaba) Climbing and high-altitude camping gear – much of it imported – makes up the bulk of the stock here.

Crafts

The top-quality Chilean crafts you can find in Santiago include hand-woven alpaca shawls, Mapuche silver jewelry, wood and leatherwork and, occasionally, copperware. Santiago's lapis lazuli trade centers on a handful of stores on Av Bellavista east of Pío Nono – shop around and compare prices.

Ona (Map pp84-5; ☎ 632-1859; Victoria Subercaseaux 295, Centro; ☾ 9am-8:30pm; Ⓜ Bellas Artes or Universidad de Chile) Exquisite, fairly traded traditional crafts – Chiloé knitwear, hand-carved bowls and naturally dyed alpaca shawls – sit alongside tableware and jewelry by local designers.

Artesanías de Chile (off Map p88; ☎ 777-8643; Bellavista 0357, Bellavista; ☾ 10:30am-7pm Mon-Sat; Ⓜ Baquedano) Not only do this foundation's jewelry, carvings, ceramics and woolen goods sell at reasonable prices, most of what you pay goes to the artisan that made them (their names are on each piece).

Centro de Exposición de Arte Indígena (Map pp84-5; ☎ 632-3668; Alameda 499, Centro; ☾ 10am-6pm Mon-Sat) Indigenous craftspeople sell a small selection of wares at these stalls next to the Terraza Neptuno entrance to Cerro Santa Lucía; goods include silver jewelry, postcards, instruments and Mapuche dictionaries.

Patio Bellavista (Map p88; ☎ 777-4582; Pío Nono 73, Bellavista; ☾ 10am-9pm Sun-Wed, 10am-10pm Thu-Sat; Ⓜ Baquedano) Posh contemporary and traditional crafts sell at premium prices in the 40 or so stalls inside this courtyard shopping center. Leather goods, weavings and jewelry feature heavily.

Centro Artesanal Santa Lucía (Map pp84-5; cnr Carmen & Diagonal Paraguay, Centro; ☾ 10am-7pm; Ⓜ Santa Lucía) It's a stretch to call this market's mass-produced weavings and leather goods 'crafts,' but it's certainly a good place to go for cheap souvenirs. Panpipes, silver jewelry and

Andean-style sweaters are some of the been-there-bought-that products available.

Joyas Lapislazuli (Map p88; ☎ 737-0466; Bellavista 0290, Bellavista; ☻ 10:30am-8pm Mon-Fri, 10:30am-1pm Sat; Ⓜ Baquedano) Lapis lazuli comes mostly in contemporary silver settings here; it's one of scores of stores selling the stone along this stretch of Bellavista.

Pueblito Los Dominicos (off Map p99; ☎ 220-0180; Av Apoquindo 9085, Las Condes; ☻ 11am-7:30pm Tue-Sun; Ⓜ Escuela Militar) Next to the twin white domes of Los Dominicos church in Las Condes, this small market sells a mix of quality crafts made onsite and brought in from throughout Chile. From Escuela Militar metro station take orange bus 401 or 407 (they leave from stop 4) along Av Apoquindo.

Chilean Design

Galería Drugstore (Map pp90-1; ☎ 490-1241; Av Providencia 2124, Providencia; ☻ 10:30am-8pm Mon-Sat; Ⓜ Los Leones) Head to this retro-cool four-storey arcade for clothes no one back home will have – 0it's home to the boutiques of several tiny, up-and-coming designers, arty bookstores and cafés.

Ocho Fortuna (Map pp84-5; ☎ 638-5429; Merced 307, Bellas Artes, Centro; ☻ noon-9:30pm Mon-Fri, noon-9pm Sat & Sun; Ⓜ Bellas Artes) Sweet but sarcastic messages of hope adorn colorful shopping bags, old-school exercise books and travel-size notebooks here. Ultra-Latino fridge magnets make cool souvenirs.

The Clinic (Map pp84-5; ☎ 632-0736; José Miguel de la Barra 459, Centro; ☻ 11am-8pm Mon-Fri, noon-8pm Sat & Sun; Ⓜ Bellas Artes) T-shirts bearing ironic slogans, neat little notebooks and kooky tableware are some of the hipper-than-thou offerings at this spin-off shop of the satirical local newspaper of the same name.

Food & Wine

Emporio Nacional (off Map p88; ☎ 481-3820; www.emporionacional.com; Bellavista 0360, Bellavista; ☻ 11am-8pm Mon-Fri, 11am-4pm Sat; Ⓜ Baquedano) Room after wooden-shelved room is stacked high with delectable goodies from all over Chile. Weigh your suitcase (or yourself) down with ostrich pâté, pickled walnuts, *merquén* (a smoky local spice mix), bottled seafood, and more jams than you knew existed.

El Mundo del Vino (Map p99; ☎ 244-8888; www.elmundodelvino.cl, in Spanish; Isidora Goyenechea 2931, Las Condes; ☻ 10am-9pm Mon-Sat, 11am-6pm Sun; Ⓜ Tobalaba) South America's only master sommelier,

Héctor Vergara, oversees the huge selection at this large-scale wine store, which always has something open for tasting.

Vinoteca (www.lavinoteca.cl, in Spanish) Las Condes (Map p99; ☎ 334-1987; Isidora Goyenechea 2966, Las Condes; ☻ 10am-8pm Mon-Fri, 10am-9pm Sat; Ⓜ Tobalaba); Providencia (Map pp90-1; ☎ 343-3607; Manuel Montt 1452, Providencia; ☻ 9am-9pm Mon-Fri, 9am-3pm Sat; Ⓜ Manuel Montt) A staff of friendly, unpretentious sommeliers guide you through this small store's choice selection of wines from lesser-known vineyards.

Malls

Oh, how Chileans love their malls: Santiago's biggest are incredibly similar to the standard North American shopping centers they're modeled on. As clothes aren't especially cheap here, the main appeal is finding Chilean brands that don't exist back home. Free orange shuttle buses take you from Escuela Militar metro station to these two.

Alto Las Condes (Map pp80-1; ☎ 299-6999; www.altolascondes.cl, in Spanish; Av Kennedy 9001, Las Condes; ☻ 10am-10pm) As well as top-end Chilean and Argentine clothing brands, this has a branch of department store Falabella and a cinema complex.

Parque Arauco (Map pp80-1; ☎ 299-0500; www.parquearauco.cl, in Spanish; Av Kennedy 5413, Las Condes; ☻ 10am-9pm) A huge range of local and international clothing stores make this the fashionista mall of choice. There's also a cinema, bowling alley and skating rink.

Markets

Persa Bío Bío (Franklin Market; Map pp80-1; ☻ 9am-7pm Sat & Sun; Ⓜ Franklin) Antiques, collectibles and fascinating old junk fill the cluttered stalls at this market between Bío Bío and Franklin. The origins of some items – like secondhand bikes – may be a little sketchy, but sifting through it all is loads of fun.

Music

Kind of Blue (Map pp84-5; ☎ 664-4322; www.kindofblue.cl, in Spanish; Merced 323; ☻ 10am-10pm Sun-Thu, 10am-11pm Fri & Sat; Ⓜ Bellas Artes) At the best music shop in town, savvy multilingual staff happily talk you through local sounds and artists, and can get hard-to-find imports in a matter of days.

Feria del Disco (Map pp84-5; ☎ 471-3253; www.feriadeldisco.cl, in Spanish; Paseo Ahumada 286, Centro; ☻ 9:30am-9pm Mon-Sat; Ⓜ Plaza de Armas) This bland superstore has well-stocked shelves and also sells tickets to live music and sporting events at a slightly marked-up price.

GETTING THERE & AWAY

Air

Chile's main air hub for both national and domestic flights is **Aeropuerto Internacional Arturo Merino Benítez** (Pudahuel; Map p117; ☎ 690-1752, lost property 690-1707; www.aeropuertosantiago.cl). It's 26km west of central Santiago.

Lan (☎ 600-526-2000; www.lan.com), **Aerolíneas Argentinas** (☎ 800-610-200; www.aerolineas.com.ar) and low-cost airline **Gol** (☎ 1-888-0042-0090; www.voegol .com.br) run regular domestic and regional services from here. Major international airlines that fly to Chile have offices or representatives in Santiago: see p475 for a complete list. For a list of Lan's Santiago offices and sample one-way domestic airfares from Santiago, see p481.

Bus

A bewildering number of bus companies connect Santiago to the rest of Chile, Argentina and Peru. To add to the confusion, services leave from four different terminals and ticket prices fluctuate wildly at busy times of year, and often double for *cama* (sleeper) services. The following sample *clásico* or *semi-cama* (standard) fares (approximate only) and journey times are for major destinations that are served by a variety of companies – discounts often apply so shop around. For fares to smaller destinations, see the listings under each terminal.

Destination	Cost (CH$)	Duration (hr)
Antofagasta	26,700	19
Arica	34,400	30
Buenos Aires (Argentina)	28,000	22
Chillán	7200	5
Concepción	8800	6½
Copiapó	15,500	12
Iquique	31,200	25
La Serena	14,000	7
Mendoza (Argentina)	9000	8
Osorno	15,500	12
Pucón	13,300	11
Puerto Montt	16,700	12
San Pedro de Atacama	32,700	23
Talca	4400	3½
Temuco	11,100	9½
Valdivia	14,400	10–11
Valparaíso	3800	2
Viña del Mar	3800	2¼

TERMINAL DE BUSES ALAMEDA

Tur Bus (☎ 600-660-6600; www.turbus.cl) and **Pullman Bus** (☎ 600-320-3200; www.pullman.cl) operate from this **terminal** (Map pp80-1; ☎ 270-7500; Alameda 3750;

Ⓜ Universidad de Santiago), next door to Terminal de Buses Santiago. The two companies run comfortable, punctual services to destinations all over Chile, including every 15 minutes to Valparaíso and Viña del Mar.

TERMINAL DE BUSES SANTIAGO

Santiago's largest **terminal** (Map pp80-1; ☎ 376-1750; Alameda 3850; Ⓜ Universidad de Santiago) is also known as Terminal Sur, and is usually manically busy. The companies operating from the large, semi-covered ticket area mainly serve destinations south of Santiago, including the central coast, the Lakes District and Chiloé. A few companies also operate northbound buses.

Bus Norte (☎ 779-5433; www.busnorte.cl) runs excellent-value services to Puerto Montt and Valparaíso. The modern, well-appointed buses operated by **Línea Azul** (☎ 481-8862; www.buseslinea azul.cl) connect Santiago with southern destinations, as do **JAC** (☎ 481-1678; www.jac.cl) and **Andimar** (☎ 779-3810; www.andimar.cl). **Inter** (☎ 270-7508; www.busesinter.cl) has routes all over Chile.

Nilahué (☎ 778-5222; www.busesnilahue.cl) goes to Cobquecura (CH$10,000, seven hours, once daily), Termas de Chillán ski resort (CH$10,000, seven hours, once daily), Santa Cruz (CH$4000, four hours, two hourly) and Pichilemu (CH$6000, seven hours, hourly). **Pullman del Sur** (☎ 776-2424; www.pdel sur.cl) has similar services to Santa Cruz and Pichilemu, but is slightly more comfortable. **Condor** (☎ 680-6900; www.condorbus.cl) goes to Con Con and Quintero (CH$3600, 2½ hours, three hourly) and to major southern cities.

International tickets are sold from booths inside the terminal. **Cata Internacional** (☎ 779-3660; www.catainternacional.com) has four daily services to Mendoza and Buenos Aires. **El Rápido** (☎ 779-0310; www.elrapidoint.com.ar) has similar but slightly cheaper services, as does **Tas Choapa** (☎ 490-7561, www.taschoapa.cl), which also goes to **Lima** (CH$70,000, 60 hours, two weekly).

TERMINAL LOS HÉROES

Also known as Terrapuerto, this small but central **terminal** (Map pp84-5; ☎ 420-0099; Tucapel Jiménez 21; Ⓜ Los Héroes) is the base for a handful of companies. **Libac** (☎ 698-5974) runs two daily northbound services whereas **Cruz del Sur** (☎ 696-9324) has three going south, and also sells connecting tickets to Bariloche in Argentina via Osorno (CH$26,000, 24 hours, one daily). **Ahumada International** (☎ 784-2512; www.busesahumada.cl) goes three times daily to

Mendoza; some services continue to Buenos Aires.

TERMINAL SAN BORJA
Services to the area around Santiago depart from this **terminal** (Map p89; ☎ 776-0645; www .terminalsanborja.cl, in Spanish; San Borja 184; Ⓜ Estación Central). At the time of research, it was being completely rebuilt and bus companies were operating from temporary booths. The new two-storey set-up is due to open in late 2008 and will still be at the end of the shopping mall behind the main railway station. Ticket booths will be on the 2nd floor, divided by region. The most useful services from here are **Ahumada** (☎ 684-2516; www.busesahumada.cl) and **Pullman Bus** (☎ 764-5060; www.pullman.cl), which offer similar services to Los Andes (CH$2800, two hours, hourly). Buses to Pomaire leave from here: see p115.

TERMINAL PAJARITOS
Buses from Santiago to the airport and Valparaíso and Viña call in at this small **terminal** (Map pp80–1; ☎ 250-3464; General Bonilla 5600; Ⓜ Pajaritos). It's on Metro Línea 1, so by getting on buses here you avoid downtown traffic.

Car
Intense rush-hour traffic and high parking fees mean there's little point hiring a car to use in Santiago. However, having your own wheels is invaluable for visiting the Casablanca Valley (boxed text, p141) and places of natural beauty like Cerro la Campana (see p141).

Chilean rental-car companies tend to be cheaper than big international ones, but note that they often have sky-high deductibles. Cars must have an electronic windshield sensor, known as a TAG, to circulate within Santiago: some companies charge extra for this. Most rental companies have their own roadside assistance; alternatively the **Automóvil Club de Chile** (Acchi; Map pp90–1; ☎ 431-1000; www.automovilclub .cl; Av Andrés Bello 1863) provides reciprocal assistance to members of the American Automobile Association and some other associations, but you need to stop by the office to register. Some of the companies listed below also have airport offices at Pudahuel.

Budget (Map pp90–1; ☎ 362-3605; www.budget.cl; Av Francisco Bilbao 1439, Providencia) Incredibly helpful staff and no deductible.

Chilean (Map p88; ☎ 737-9650; www.chileanrentacar .cl; Bellavista 0183, Bellavista) High deductibles and add-ons.

First Rent a Car (Map pp90–1; ☎ 225-6328; www .firstrentacar.cl; Rancagua 0514, Providencia)

Hertz (Map pp90–1; ☎ 496-1000; www.hertz.com; Av Andrés Bello 1469, Providencia) No deductible.

Piamonte (off Map pp90–1; ☎ 225-2623; www.pia monte.cl; Irarrázaval 4110, Providencia) Rock-bottom rates.

United (Map pp90–1; ☎ 236-1483; www.united-chile .com; Padre Mariano 430, Providencia) Reasonable rates and low deductibles.

Train
Chile's recently revamped train system, **Empresa de Ferrocarriles del Estado** (EFE; ☎ 600-585-5000; www.efe.cl, in Spanish), operates out of **Estación Central** (Alameda 3170; Ⓜ Estación Central). You can also buy tickets inside **Universidad de Chile metro station** (Map pp84–5; ☺ 9am-8pm Mon-Fri, 9am-2pm Sat). Train travel is generally slightly slower and more expensive than going by bus, but wagons are well maintained and services are generally punctual.

The TerraSur rail service connects Santiago three to five times daily with Rancagua (CH$5000, one hour), San Fernando (CH$5500, 1½ hours), Curicó (CH$6000, 2¼ hours), Talca (CH$6500, three hours) and Chillán (CH$10,500, 5½ hours), from where there's a connecting bus to Concepción (from Santiago CH$12,500, 6½ hours). There's a 10% discount if you book online; first-class tickets cost about 20% more.

GETTING AROUND
To/From the Airport
Two cheap, efficient bus services connect the airport with the city center: **Buses Centropuerto** (Map p89; ☎ 601-9883; Plazoleta Los Héroes; one way/round trip CH$1300/2350; ☺ every 15min 6am-11:30pm) and **Tur Bus Aeropuerto** (Map pp84–5; ☎ 607-9573; www.turbus .cl; Moneda 1523, Centro; one way/round trip CH$1500/2500; ☺ every 20min 5:30am-midnight). Both leave from right outside the arrivals hall, and you can buy tickets on board or from the ticket desks inside the terminal. All but the earliest buses stop at metro station Pajaritos on Line 1 – you avoid downtown traffic by transferring to the metro here. The total trip takes about 40 minutes.

A pushy mafia of 'official' taxi drivers tout their services in the arrivals hall. Although the ride to the city center should cost CH$11,000, drivers are famous for ripping tourists off. A safer bet for private transfers is to approach the desks of **Transvip** (☎ 677-3000; www.transvip.net) or **TurBus Aeropuerto** (☎ 607-9573; www.turbus.cl), which offer fixed-price taxis (from CH$11,000) and eight-seater minibuses (from CH$17,000) to the Centro. Trips to Providencia and Las Condes cost slightly more.

Bicycle

Santiago is flat and compact enough to get around by bike and the climate is ideal for it – even if the smog isn't. Although the city still isn't particularly bike-friendly, it does have a small network of *ciclovías* (bike lanes). You can download a map of these from **Ciclosantiago** (www.ciclosantiago.cl, in Spanish), which promotes urban biking. Another linchpin of the local cyclist movement is **Movimiento Furiosos Ciclistas** (www.furiosos.cl, in Spanish), which organizes a Critical Mass–style bike rally the first Tuesday of each month. You can rent bikes and helmets from tour operator **La Bicicleta Verde** (Map pp84-5; ☎ 570-9338; www.labicicletaverde .cl; Santa María 227, Oficina 12, Bellavista; per hr CH$3000, per day CH$10,000-13,000; Ⓜ Bellas Artes).

Car & Motorcycle

To drive on any of the expressways within Santiago proper, your car must have an electronic sensor known as a TAG in the windshield – all rental cars have them. Alternatively, you can get a one-off *Pase Diario Único* (day pass) from **Servipag** (www .servipag.cl; day pass CH$4400). On-street parking is banned in some parts of central Santiago and metered (often by a person) in others; costs range from CH$600 to CH$1200 per hour depending on the area. Private parking lots cost CH$800 to CH$2000 per hour.

Colectivo

Taxi colectivos are basically four-passenger buses on fixed routes with flat fares (usually displayed in the window). They are quicker than buses and not much more expensive – about CH$500 within Santiago city limits. They're more common in the suburbs or residential neighborhoods than in the town center.

Taxi

Santiago has abundant metered taxis, all black with yellow roofs. Flagfall costs CH$200, then it's CH$80 per 200m (or minute of waiting time). For longer rides – from the city center out to the airport, for example – you can sometimes negotiate flat fares. It's generally safe to hail cabs in the street, though hotels and restaurants will happily call you one, too.

Most Santiago taxi drivers are honest, courteous and helpful, but a few will take roundabout routes, so try to know where you're going.

Transantiago

In 2006, sleek extra-long buses replaced the city's many competing private services when the bus and metro were united as **Transantiago** (☎ 800-730-073; www.transantiago.cl), a government-run public transportation system. The transition has been bumpy: many buses now feed into the metro, leading to chronic overcrowding, and many locals find the new bus routes hard to grasp. Protests aside, the system is actually quick, cheap and efficient for getting around central Santiago. The Transantiago website has downloadable route maps and a point-to-point journey planner.

You can buy one-off tickets to use the metro, or get a tarjeta Bip! (a contact-free card you wave over sensors). Buses only accept Bip! cards. You pay a nonrefundable CH$1200 for a card, and then 'charge' it with as much money as you want. Two people can share a card. Transantiago operates a flat fare of CH$420 during rush hour (7am to 9am and 6pm to 8pm) and CH$380 the rest of the time. However, if you pay using Bip!, you can take up to four bus journeys (or one metro and three bus journeys) within two hours of your start time for the same price.

BUS

Transantiago buses are a cheap and convenient way of getting around town, especially when the metro shuts down at night. Green-and-white buses operate in central Santiago or connect two areas of town. Each suburb has its own color-coded local buses and an identifying letter that precedes routes numbers (for example, routes in Las Condes and Vitacura start with a C and vehicles are painted orange). Buses generally follow major roads or avenues; stops are spaced far apart and tend to coincide with metro stations. There are route maps at many stops and consulting them (or asking bus drivers) is usually more reliable than asking locals, who are still confused by new routes. You can only pay for bus rides using a Bip! card.

METRO

Now part of Transantiago, the city's ever-expanding **metro** (www.metrosantiago.cl; ☢ 6am-11pm Mon-Fri, 6:30am-10:30pm Sat, 8am-10:30pm Sun) is

SANTIAGO METRO

a clean and efficient way of getting about. Services on its five interlinking lines are frequent, but often painfully crowded.

AROUND SANTIAGO

Just because you're staying in Santiago, it doesn't mean you have to deal with smog, traffic and crowds. National parks, sleepy villages, and (in winter) snowy slopes all make easy escapes from the city.

POMAIRE

In this small, dusty village 68km southwest of Santiago, skilled potters make beautifully simple brown and black earthenware ceram-

ics. A trip here makes a pleasant half-day out, especially as the town is also celebrated for its traditional Chilean food. Grilled meats make up most of the menu at ever-popular **La Greda** (☎ 831-1166; Manuel Rodriguez 251; mains CH$3000-5800; ☺ 10am-midnight). The name means 'clay,' and indeed, the hearty casseroles are cooked in locally made dishes. Pomaire is packed with day-trippers on weekends but is practically deserted on Monday when the potters have a day off.

Autobuses Melipilla (☎ 776-2060) runs one direct Pomaire service daily from Santiago's San Borja terminal (CH$1000, 1½ hours), leaving at 9:30am and returning to Santiago at 6pm. Alternatively, take one of the regular services to Melipilla (CH$1300, 30 minutes, four hourly) and get off at the Pomaire *cruce* (crossroads), where *colectivos* and *liebres* (minibuses) take you into town (CH$300). **Buses Jiménez** (☎ 776-5786) also goes to Melipilla (CH$1500, 50 minutes, six hourly).

CAJÓN DEL MAIPO

Rich greenery lines the steep, rocky walls of this stunning gorge that the Río Maipo flows through. Starting only 25km southeast of Santiago, it's popular on weekends with Santiaguinos, who come here to camp, hike, climb, cycle, raft and ski. Plenty of traditional restaurants and teahouses, and a big winery, mean that overindulgence is also on the menu.

Two roads wind up the Cajón on either side of the river, and join at El Melocotón, 7km before San Alfonso. The numberless road on the southern side goes through Pirque, whereas the G-25 runs along the north side past San José de Maipo and San Alfonso to Baños Morales and the Monumento Nacional el Morado.

The river itself is made up of a series of mostly Class III rapids with very few calm areas – indeed, rafters are often tossed into the water. Still, it's less hazardous than when the first kayakers descended in the 1970s and found themselves facing automatic weapons as they passed the grounds of General Pinochet's estate at El Melocotón (the narrow bedrock chute here, one of the river's more entertaining rapids, is now known as 'El Pinocho,' the ex-dictator's nickname).

November through March is rafting season; ski bums and bunnies flock here June through September; and walking, horseback riding and lunching are popular year-round. Make sure you take your documents with you if you are going beyond San Gabriel (the end of the paved road and the turnoff to Baños Morales): the closeness of the Argentine border means the police run regular checks here.

GETTING THERE & AWAY
Metrobus 74 (CH$400, 1½ hours, four hourly) goes to Pirque and El Principal, 4km before the entrance to RN Río Clarillo (some services continue to the park entrance). You get to San Alfonso on Metrobus 73 (CH$600, two hours, two hourly). The bus continues to Baños Morales from September to March, and there's one service a day there from April

to October at 7am on weekends, returning at 5pm. Note that all other Metrobus 73 services only go as far as San José de Maipo (CH$400, 1½ hours, four hourly). From San José, you may be able to catch a *colectivo* to San Alfonso, but services are infrequent. Both Metrobus lines start at Conexión Intermodal platform C at Bellavista La Florida metro station (Línea 5) and also stop on Av Vicuña Mackenna Poniente outside Las Mercedes metro station (Línea 5).

There is no public transportation to Termas Valle de Colina. However, private vans run by **Manzur Expediciones** (☎ 777-4284) go to the baths from Plaza Italia, usually on Wednesday, Saturday and Sunday. Call to confirm times. The 93km drive from central Santiago to Baños Morales takes about two hours, and is usually doable in a regular car. Count on another 20 minutes to reach Termas Valle de Colina; depending on the state of the last stretch of road, you may need a 4WD here.

Pirque
Although it's only just outside Santiago, Pirque has a very small-town feel to it. There's nothing small-scale or low-key about its main attraction, however: **Viña Concha y Toro**, Chile's largest and most industrial winery (boxed text, p118). The main road leads east from Concha y Toro up the south side of the Cajón towards San Alfonso. About 3km along it is a string of restaurants: the long-running local favorite is **La Vaquita Echá** (☎ 854-6025; Ramón Subercaseaux 3355, Pirque; mains CH$5200-7600; ☒ noon-midnight). It's rightly famed for its grill – steaks, ribs, fish and even wild boar all sizzle over the coals.

Reserva Nacional Río Clarillo
A mix of Andean forest and scrubland make up this hilly, 100-sq-km nature reserve (adult/child CH$2500/700; ☒ 8:30am-6pm) in a scenic tributary canyon of the Cajón del Maipo, 18km southeast of Pirque. It's home to abundant bird species, foxes and rodents, and the endangered Chilean iguana. Two short, clearly labeled trails start near the Conaf rangers' office, about 300m after the entrance: Quebrada Jorquera takes about half an hour, and Aliwen Mahuida takes 1½ hours. The rangers give advice on longer hikes along the river, but plan on starting early as camping is not allowed here. There are several picnic areas with tables and barbecue pits, though.

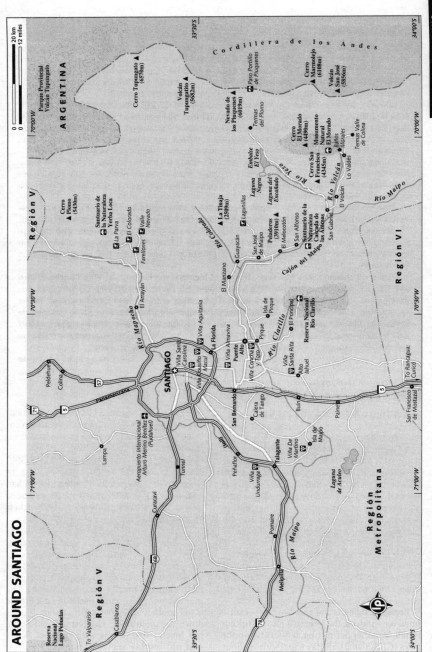

AROUND SANTIAGO

Región V

**Reserva Nacional
Lago Peñuelas**

To Valparaíso

Casablanca

Curacaví

Tunnel

Lampa

Pomaire

**Región
Metropolitana**

Laguna
de Aculeo

Melipilla

Peldehue

Colina

Aeropuerto Internacional
Arturo Merino Benítez
(Pudahuel)

SANTIAGO

Peñaflor

Talagante

Viña
Undurraga

Isla de
Maipo

Viña De
Martino

San Bernardo

Calera
de Tango

Buin

Paine

San Francisco
de Mostazal

To Rancagua;
Curicó

Río Maipo

Viña Santa
Carolina

Viña Cousiño
Macul

Viña Aquitania

Viña Amaviva

La Florida

Puente
Alto

Viña Concha
y Toro

Pirque

Isla de
Pirque

Viña
Santa Rita

Alto
Jahuel

El Principal

**Reserva Nacional
Río Clarillo**

Río Clarillo

Región VI

El Manzano

Guayacán

San José
de Maipo

▲ La Tinaja
(2509m)

Lagunillas

Peladeros
(3910m)

San Alfonso

El Melocotón

Santuario de la
Naturaleza
Cascada de
las Ánimas

San Gabriel

Cajón del Maipo

Cerro San
Francisco
(4345m) ▲

El Volcán

Lo Valdés

Baños
Morales

▲ El Morado

Termas Valle
de Colina

Cerro
El Morado
(490m) ▲

Monumento
Natural

Laguna del
Encañado

Laguna
Negra

Embalse
El Yeso

Río Yeso

Río Volcán

Río Maipo

Río Maipo

Río Mapocho

El Arrayán

Cerro
Plomo
(5430m) ▲

Santuario de
la Naturaleza
Yerba Loca

La Parva

Farellones

El Colorado

Valle
Nevado

Río Colorado

Termas
del Plomo

Nevado de
los Piuquenes
(6019m)

Paso Portillo
de Piuquenes

Cerro
Marmolejo
(6108m) ▲

Volcán
San José
(5856m) ▲

Cordillera de los Andes

ARGENTINA

Parque Provincial
Volcán Tupungato

Cerro Tupungato ▲
(6570m)

Volcán
Tupungatito ▲
(5682m)

Región V

0   20 km
0   12 miles

VIÑAS SANTIAGUINAS

When you've had your fill of museums and plazas, head south of the city center to check out its more intoxicating sights: the wineries of the Maipo Valley, one of Chile's major wine regions. Big-bodied reds are what the valley is all about: Cabernet Sauvignon, Merlot, Carmenere and Syrah. Notes of eucalyptus or mint are a typical trait. Wine tours aren't really necessary here – the wineries below are within 1½ hours of the city center on public transport.

Santiago's most central winery, **Viña Santa Carolina** (☎ 450-3000; www.santacarolina.com; Rodrigo de Araya 1431, Macul; standard tours incl 2 reservas CH$7000, icon tours incl 2 premium & 1 icon CH$15,000; standard tours 10am in Spanish & 12:30pm in English Mon-Sat, icon tours 4:30pm Mon-Fri; **M** Rodrigo de Araya), dates from 1875. The vines themselves have long since moved out of town, but the historical main house and cellars are still here. Also within the urban sprawl is **Viña Cousiño Macul** (☎ 351-4175; www.cousinomacul.cl; Av Quilín 7100, Peñalolén; tours incl 1 varietal & 1 reserva CH$5000; tours 11am & 3pm Mon-Fri in Spanish & English, 11am Sat in Spanish; **M** Quilín). Most of the vineyards are now at Buin, but tours take in the production process and underground bodega, built in 1872. It's a 2¼km walk or taxi ride from the metro.

Only 2km away is Santiago's most interesting winery: **Viña Aquitania** (☎ 791-4500; www.aquitania.cl; Av Consistorial 5090, Peñalolén; standard tours incl 2 reserva CH$5000, premium tours incl 3 premium CH$13,000; 9am-5pm Mon-Fri by appointment only; **M** Grecia), which works with tiny quantities and sky-high quality. From Grecia metro station (Línea 4), take bus D07 south from bus stop 6 and get off at the intersection of Av Los Presidentes and Consistorial (you need a Bip! card). Aquitania is 150m south.

To see winemaking on a vast scale, do one of the mass-market tours at **Viña Concha y Toro** (☎ 476-5269; www.conchaytoro.com; Virginia Subercaseaux 210, Pirque; tours CH$6000; 10am-5pm). For information on getting to Pirque, see p116. At the other extreme from Concha y Toro on the winemaking spectrum is the boutique vineyard it runs in partnership with Baron Philippe de Rothschild, **Viña Almaviva** (☎ 852-9300; Av Santa Rosa 821, Paradero 45, Puente Alto; www.almavivawinery .com; tours incl 1 pour CH$15,000; 9am-5pm Mon-Fri by appointment only). Bus 207 from Estación Mapocho runs past the entrance (you need a Bip! card), 1km from the winery building.

Other worthy Maipo set-ups include **Viña Santa Rita** (☎ 362-2594; www.santarita.cl), **Viña de Martino** (☎ 819-2959; www.demartino.cl) and **Viña Undurraga** (☎ 372-2900; www.undurraga.cl). For approximate locations of wineries near Santiago, see map p117.

San Alfonso & Cascada de las Animas

Halfway up the Cajón del Maipo, a cluster of houses and tea rooms make up San Alfonso. It's home to the beautiful private nature reserve **Santuario de la Naturaleza Cascada de las Animas** (☎ 861-1303; www.cascadadelasanimas .cl; Camino al Volcán 31087), which is set up like a natural, outdoorsy theme park. Organized activities are the only way to visit it: hiking, horseback riding, rafting, and zip-lining are among the options, which you need to book in advance.

The reserve takes its name from a stunning waterfall reached by the shortest walk offered (CH$4000); there are also guided half-day hikes into the hills (CH$10,000) which include use of the pool when you get back. **Horseback riding** is the real house specialty, however – indeed, the reserve is also a working ranch. Weather permitting, it offers two-hour rides (CH$20,000), all-day trips (with/without transport from Santiago CH$114,000/60,000) and overnighters (CH$160,000). Most adventurous of all are the two-week pack expeditions across the Andes (US$2730).

The three-hour **rafting trips** (CH$17,500) descend Class III or IV rapids, taking in some lovely gorges before ending up in San José de Maipo. They're led by experienced guides, and helmets, wetsuits and life jackets are provided.

You can stay well inside Cascada de las Animas in well-appointed **wood cabins** (CH$44,000-88,000) with log fires and well-equipped kitchens, or smaller **guest rooms** (d/q CH$25,000/35,000). Alternatively, pitch your tent in the shady **campsite** (per person CH$6000). The management also runs **Hostal La Casa Grande** (d incl breakfast CH$23,000-28,000), three blocks down the main road. The restored old house has lovely, airy rooms with parquet floors and old-worldly metal bedsteads, but you don't get the same peace and quiet as in the reserve itself.

Baños Morales & Monumento Natural El Morado

The G-25 continues uphill from San Alfonso – there's about 10km of tarmac, then 20km of rutted, unpaved dirt before you reach the small thermal springs of Baños Morales. You can camp here, or stay in one of the simple, wood-clad rooms at **Refugio Lo Valdés** (Refugio Alemán; ☎ 099-220-8525; www.refugiolovaldes.com; Ruta G-25 Km77; dm/d incl breakfast CH$8000/16,000), across the Río Volcán from Baños Morales. Popular at weekends, it has a stunning view over the Cajón. The onsite restaurant is renowned for its hearty meals and *onces* (afternoon tea).

Also at Baños Morales is the entrance to **Monumento Natural El Morado** (adult/child CH$1500/500; ☒ Oct-Apr), a small national park. Inside, from the banks of sparkling Laguna El Morado, there are fabulous views of the San Francisco glacier and the 5000m summit of Cerro El Morado. It takes about two hours to reach the lake on the well-marked 8km trail from the Conaf post. In summer, motivated hikers can continue to the base of Glaciar El Morado, on the lower slopes of the mountain; there are free campsites around the lake.

Termas Valle de Colina

About 16km after the turn-off to Baños Morales, the G-25 (now a basic dirt track best negotiated in a 4WD) reaches the thermal springs of **Termas Valle de Colina** (Baños Colina; ☎ 239-6797; www.termasvalledecolina.cl; entrance to springs & camping CH$5000; ☒ Oct-Feb), where rather murky hot pools overlook the valley. There's a well-organized camping ground, but be sure to bring plenty of food supplies. The administration also offers guided hikes and one- to three-day horseback-riding expeditions.

SKI CENTERS

Several of Chile's best ski resorts are within day-tripping (or two-day tripping) distance from Santiago. Aim to go midweek, if you can: snow-happy Santiaguinos crowd both the pistes and the roads up to the resorts on weekends.

GETTING THERE & AWAY

There is no public transport to Santiago's ski resorts. The following private companies run regular shuttle services to the Tres Valles and

Lagunillas during ski season as well as private taxis or minibuses and equipment rental.

KL Adventures (Map p99; ☎ 217-9101; www.kladventure.com; Augusto Mira Fernández 14248, Las Condes; round trip to Tres Valles CH$8000-9000, with hotel pick-up CH$18,000) The shuttle leaves at 8am and returns at 5pm.

Manzur Expediciones (Map pp84-5; ☎ 777-4284; Dr Sótero del Rio 475, Oficina 507, Centro; round trip to Tres Valles CH$7500-8500, to Lagunillas CH$8500, with hotel pick-up CH$12,000-13,000). Leaves from Plaza Italia (Baquedano metro station) and also rents gear.

Ski Ahorro (Map p99; ☎ 229-4532; www.skiahorro.cl, in Spanish; Av Las Condes 9143, Las Condes; round trip to Tres Valles CH$8500-9000, with hotel pick-up CH$16,000) The shuttle leaves at 8:30am and returns at 5:30pm.

SkiTotal (Map p99; ☎ 246-0156; www.skitotal.cl; Av Apoquindo 4900, Local 39-42, Las Condes, Santiago; round trip to Tres Valles CH$9000-9500, with hotel pick-up CH$16,000) The shuttle leaves at 8am and returns at 5pm.

You can also reach Lagunillas by taking a bus to San José de Maipo (see p116) and getting a taxi for the remaining 20km.

Lagunillas

The cheapest skiing to be had near Santiago is at **Lagunillas** (☎ 638-0497; www.skilagunillas.cl, in Spanish; day ski pass adult/child CH$16,000/10,000), a small resort 67km southeast of Santiago via San José de Maipo. Run by the Club Andino de Chile, it has four lifts and 13 runs; note that though the scenery is stunning, the snow here is generally not as good as at Santiago's more exclusive resorts. The Club Andino runs a few small cabins here, but it's an easy day trip from Santiago.

Cajón de Mapocho – Tres Valles

Santiago's four most popular ski centers – Farellones/El Colorado, La Parva and Valle Nevado – are clustered in three valleys in the Mapocho river canyon, hence their collective name, Tres Valles. Although they're only 30km to 40km northeast of Santiago, the traffic-clogged road up can be slow going. All prices given here are for weekends and high season (usually early July to mid-August). Outside that time, there are hefty midweek discounts on both ski passes and hotels. Well-marked off-piste runs connect the three valleys, and you can buy combination ski passes, known as an **interconectado** (Valle Nevado & La Parva or Farellones/El Colorado adult/child CH$38,000/25,000, Tres Valles CH$60,000). The predominance of drag lifts means that lines get long during the winter holidays, but otherwise crowds here are bearable.

FARELLONES & EL COLORADO

Just 32km from Santiago, these two **resorts** (☎ 398-8080; www.elcolorado.cl; Apoquindo 4900, Oficina 48, Santiago) are close enough together to be considered a single destination.

The cheaper of the two is the village of **Farellones** (day ski pass adult/child CH$8000/6000), Chile's first ski resort. At about 2500m, it's lower than El Colorado and its handful of runs tend to attract mainly beginner skiers, as well as tubing fans. There's more choice further up the mountain at **El Colorado** (day ski pass adult/child CH$28,000/19,000). The 22 runs range from beginner to expert and the highest of its 18 lifts takes you 3333m above sea level.

The eating and after-ski scenes are scanty here, so locals tend just to come up for the day. However, you can ski right up to the door of **Refugio Aleman** (☎ 227-2605; www.refugioaleman .cl; Camino Los Cóndores 1451, Farellones; dm/d incl breakfast & dinner CH$24,000/54,000). Its clean dorms, two big living rooms and friendly multilingual staff make it the best budget option.

Clapboard walls and crisp quilts give the rooms at **Hotel Posada de Farellones** (☎ 248-7672; www.skifarellones.com; s/d incl breakfast & dinner US$258/300) a Swiss-chalet feel. Although not particularly luxurious, it's the most upmarket place on these slopes.

LA PARVA

The most exclusive of Santiago's ski resorts, **La Parva** (Map p99; ☎ in Santiago 339-8482, in La Parva 220-9530; www.skilaparva.cl; Av El Bosque Norte 0177, 2nd fl, Las Condes, Santiago; day ski pass adult/child CH$28,000/20,000) is definitely oriented towards posh families rather than the powder-and-party pack. Private cottages and condos make up ski base Villa La Parva, from where 14 lifts take you to its 30 runs, the highest of which starts at 3630m above sea level. Snow permitting, there's plenty of off-piste skiing here, too. The ski between La Parva and Valle Nevado or Farellones (via Valle Olímpico) is also a favorite among more experienced skiers.

The only accommodation options here are the self-catering apartments run by the resort itself. The two-bedroom **Departamentos Standard** (6-person apt per week US$1700) are the cheapest, but levels of both luxury and basic maintenance are highly unpredictable. Eating at home is definitely the fashion in La Parva, but be sure to bring plenty of supplies as groceries are limited and overpriced. The favorite of the resort's six restaurants, **La Marmita** (☎ 321-1083; mains CH$5000-9900; ⏰ noon-4pm & 7-11pm), is known for its delicious fondues. It's only open during the ski season.

VALLE NEVADO

About 12km of unpaved road takes you from Farellones to **Valle Nevado** (☎ 477-7700; www.valle nevado.com; Av Vitacura 5250, Oficina 304, Santiago; day ski pass adult/child CH$29,500/20,000). Modeled on European setups, it's the best-maintained of Santiago's resorts and has the most challenging runs. A magic carpet and ample beginner runs make it good for kids, too. Seven drag lifts and four chairs take you to the 27 pistes' high-altitude start points, which range from 2860m to 3670m. Adrenaline levels also run high here: there's a snow park, good off-piste action, and heli-skiing.

Valle Nevado's three hotels are all expensive, yet the quality of both accommodations and service is usually woefully lacking. Rates at all include a ski pass and half-board. You can ski right onto your balcony at **Hotel Valle Nevado** (s/d incl breakfast & dinner US$847/900; 🖳 🐾). The best-appointed option, it has a heated outdoor pool, spa, and piano bar with a huge open fire. Dinner at the hotel's Fourchette D'or restaurant goes some way to offsetting the rates. The 'budget' option skimps on luxury but not on prices: at **Hotel Tres Puntas** (dm/ s/d/t incl breakfast & dinner US$228/504/576/741) there's a mix of regular and dorm-style rooms, all of which are cramped but functional.

The most distinguished of the resort's six restaurants is **La Fourchette D'or** (☎ 698-0103; Hotel Valle Nevado; mains CH$12,000-16,000; ⏰ 8-11pm Mon-Fri, 12:30-3:30pm & 8-11pm Sat & Sun). There are two fast-food joints up the mountain.

Middle Chile

It's ironic: the easiest part of the country to get to is also the least explored. Travelers blitz through here on their way north, south or east in search of extreme outdoor experiences, never guessing that the central foothills of the Andes contain some searingly beautiful national parks which have the advantages of being open for more months of the year and receiving less visitors. Pucón? Torres del Paine? Everyone's been there. But Altos de Lircay and Laguna del Laja? Now there's something different.

Parks and reserves aren't the only thing the Andes have to offer: some of South America's best ski resorts nestle high on the slopes here. A different kind of hill – or rather, 42 different kinds of hill – bedecked in a crazy quilt of colorful houses are what characterize another of Chile's star attractions, the port city of Valparaíso. North and south along the coast are some intensely varied beaches – swimming and suntanning probably won't be on the cards, but these places are perfect for melancholic mooching and windy winter walks as well as year-round surfing.

Indulgence is also an option: the central valleys are where most of Chile's wine is produced. The booming wine-tourism industry has spearheaded a cultish interest in food and drink, and chefs in Valparaíso and the wine valleys are beginning to give Santiaguino gourmets a run for their money.

MIDDLE CHILE

HIGHLIGHTS

- Get lost in the steep maze of streets that wind around the hills of **Valparaíso** (p123)

- Survey the vines then savor the wines at a **Colchagua Valley vineyard** (p148) around Santa Cruz

- Thrill at the 360-degree views from atop El Enladrillado in the **Reserva Nacional Altos de Lircay** (p156)

- Stroll at sunset along the quiet sands of **Buchupureo** (p163)

- Ski through the trees on the 13km piste Las Tres Marías at **Nevados de Chillán** (p161)

- ★ Valparaíso
- ★ Colchagua Valley
- ★ Reserva Nacional Altos de Lircay
- ★ Buchupureo
- ★ Nevados de Chillán

| POPULATION: 5,364,762 | AREA: 100,141 SQ KM | ELEVATION: 0–6500M |

MIDDLE CHILE

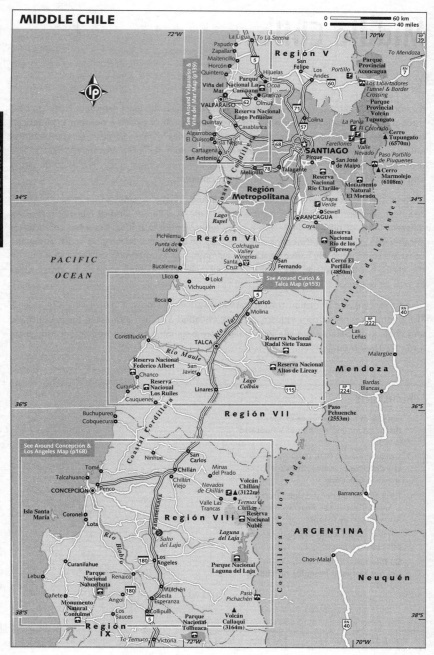

MIDDLE CHILE

0 _____ 60 km
0 _____ 40 miles

History

After 7000 relatively undisturbed years, central Chile's Mapuche communities were invaded twice in quick succession, first by the Inka and then by the Spanish. Earthquakes and constant Mapuche sieges meant that early Spanish colonial cities floundered almost as often as they were founded. Eventually the Mapuche retreated south of the Río Biobío, and colonial central Chile grew, becoming a linchpin in the struggle for independence. Political change gave way to economic growth: massive irrigation projects transformed the central valleys into fertile agricultural land, and major natural resources were discovered and exploited – coal mines near Concepción, copper at Rancagua and an oil field in Concón. The area was a focus of repression during the dictatorship, but since the return to democracy has been the backdrop for vociferous strikes by students and workers.

Today over half Chile's population live in the middle swathe of the country (including Santiago), making this Chile's center socially, politically and economically speaking, as well as merely geographically.

Climate

Chile's central valley has a pleasant Mediterranean climate. Golden sunshine bathes the region from about mid-September until mid-May, whereas June and July are often quite wet. The area's ski resorts tend to open between mid-June and late September, although Chillán sometimes has snowfalls in mid-May and can open earlier. Along the coast thick morning fogs often float between you and the ocean view, and the area is prone to more rain. Winter temperatures average around 10°C to 15°C, while in the summer they can rise to around 30°C. See the climate charts on p464.

Getting There & Away

The Panamericana runs through or near to most of the areas covered in this chapter, all of which are less than an overnight journey from Santiago. The excellent long-distance bus services that travel up and down this highway are the quickest and cheapest way to arrive, whether you're coming from the Lakes District to the south, from Santiago or the north, or internationally via Mendoza in Argentina.

Getting Around

Frequent local and long-distance buses connect all the major towns in Middle Chile to each other and to Santiago, which sits in the center of the region. Trains are also an option for travel between cities on the Panamericana between Santiago and Chillán – journeys take as long as on a bus, and are markedly more expensive, so train travel is probably only worth doing for the novelty value.

Getting to national parks and smaller towns can be trickier: snow closes some areas in winter, in others public transportation reduces to a trickle outside summer, and a few have no public transportation at all.

Having a car is invaluable for quick trips to far-flung parks and for touring wineries.

MIDDLE CHILE

VALPARAÍSO & THE CENTRAL COAST

Only 120km northwest of Santiago lies Chile's second-most-important city, distinctive Valparaíso: cultural capital, seat of congress and a vital port. North of the city is Viña del Mar and the string of coastal towns where Santiaguinos love to holiday. A major wine region (the Casablanca Valley) and a little-known national park (La Campana) are between the coast and Santiago.

VALPARAÍSO

☎ 032 / pop 295,821

Pablo Neruda said it best: 'Valparaíso,/how absurd/you are…you haven't/combed your hair,/you've never/had/time to get dressed,/life/has always/surprised you.' But Neruda wasn't the only artist to fall for Valparaíso's unexpected charms. Poets, painters and would-be philosophers have long been drawn to Chile's – no, Latin America's – most unusual city. Along with the ever-shifting port population of sailors, dockworkers and prostitutes, they've endowed gritty and gloriously spontaneous Valparaíso with an edgy air of 'anything goes.' Add to this the spectacular faded beauty of its chaotic *cerros* (hills), a maze of steep, sinuous streets, alleys and *escaleras* (stairways) piled high with crumbling mansions, and it's clear why some visitors are spending more time here than in Santiago.

History

The sea has always defined Valparaíso's history. Fishing sustained the area's first inhabitants, the Chango, and no sooner had the Spanish conquistadores arrived than Valparaíso became a stop-off point for boats taking gold and other Latin American products to Spain. More seafaring looters soon followed: English and Dutch pirates, including Sir Francis Drake, who repeatedly sacked Valparaíso for gold.

The city grew slowly at first, but boomed with the huge demand for Chilean wheat prompted by the California gold rush. The first major port of call for ships coming round Cape Horn, Valparaíso became a commercial center for the entire Pacific coast and the hub of Chile's nascent banking industry.

The 20th century was not so rosy. The 1906 earthquake destroyed most of Valparaíso's buildings, then the opening of the Panama Canal had an equally cataclysmic effect on the city's economy. Only the Chilean navy remained a constant presence.

Today Valparaíso is back on the nautical charts as a cruise-ship stop-off, and Chile's growing fruit exports have also boosted the port. More significantly, the city has been Chile's legislative capital since 1990 and was voted the cultural capital in 2003. Unesco sealed the deal by giving it World Heritage status, prompting tourism to soar.

Orientation

Valparaíso is a city of two parts: El Plan, the congested, flat commercial district closest to the sea; and the 42 *cerros* (hills) that rise up steeply behind it. Most major thoroughfares in El Plan run east–west, parallel to the shoreline: the closest is Av Errázuriz, which merges with Av España and leads to Viña del Mar. The oldest part of town, Barrio El Puerto (the port neighborhood), is in the west of El Plan. The two main streets in the east are Independencia and Av Pedro Montt, where you'll find the bus station.

Valparaíso's hills defy even determined cartographers. Av Almirante Montt and Urriola lead from El Plan to Cerros Concepción and Alegre. From Plaza Aníbal Pinto, Cumming takes you to Cerro Cárcel; from nearby Av Ecuador, Yerbas Buenas winds up Cerro Bellavista, accessible from the other side by Ferrari. Av Alemania winds along the top of the more central cerros.

Valparaíso Map (www.valparaisomap.cl) is by far the best map of this notoriously hard-to-navigate city. Hotels and tourist information kiosks often have copies.

Information

BOOKSTORES

Cummings 1 (☎ 099-8606-1605; www.cummings1.cl; Subida Cummings 1, Plaza Aníbal Pinto, El Plan; ☺ noon-9pm Mon, 11:30am-2pm & 4:30-9pm Tue-Sat) Used social science texts and Latin American literature in Spanish, English, French and German.

INTERNET ACCESS & TELEPHONE

Many lodgings have free internet or wi-fi.
Centro de Llamados (☎ 259-5002; Condell 1332, El Plan; per hr CH$600; ☺ 8am-9:30pm) One of several along this street.
Cerro@legre (☎ 276-9440; Urriola 678, Cerro Alegre; per hr CH$500; ☺ 9am-9pm Mon-Sat, 10am-8pm Sun) Popular cybercafé.

LAUNDRY

Lavanda Café (Av Almirante Montt 454, Cerro Alegre; per load CH$6800; ☺ 9:30am-7pm Mon-Fri, 10am-2pm Sat)

MEDIA

El Mercurio de Valparaíso (www.mercuriovalpo.cl, in Spanish) The city's main newspaper.
Valparaíso Times (www.valparaisotimes.cl) Online English-language newspaper run by the same people as the *Santiago Times*.

MEDICAL SERVICES

Clínica Valparaíso (☎ 226-8108; www.clinicavalpa raiso.cl; Av Brasil 2350, El Plan) Private clinic.
Hospital Carlos Van Buren (☎ 220-4000; Av Colón 2454, El Plan) Public hospital on the corner of San Ignacio.

MONEY

Banco Santander (☎ 220-7940; Prat 882, El Plan) One of many banks with ATMs along Prat.
Inter Cambio (☎ 215-6290; Plaza Sotomayor 11, El Plan; ☺ 9am-6pm Mon-Fri, 10am-1pm Sat)

POST

Post office (Prat 856, El Plan; ☺ 9am-6pm Mon-Fri, 10am-1pm Sat)

TOURIST INFORMATION

Tourist information kiosks (☎ 800-322-032; www .municipalidaddevalparaiso.cl/depturismo; ☺ 10am-2pm & 3-6pm Mon-Sat) Muelle Prat (opposite Plaza Sotomayor, El Plan) Plaza Aníbal Pinto (cnr O'Higgins & Plaza Aníbal Pinto, El Plan) At these two small and under-resourced information stands, students hand out free city maps but have little useful advice.

Dangers & Annoyances

Petty street crime and muggings are often reported in the old port area, so keep a close watch on your belongings, especially cameras and other electronics. Dark alleys intersect the main streets here, so women should come here in groups at night. The rest of Valparaíso is fairly safe, but stick to main streets at night and avoid sketchy *escaleras*.

Sights

Don't take it from us, take it from Unesco: the whole of Valparaíso is a sight worth seeing. Beautiful buildings and a handful of museums, these Valpo has; but the most exciting thing to do here is just walking the city streets. Extra adrenaline shots come courtesy of the 15 rattling *ascensores* (funiculars) built between 1883 and 1916 that crank you up into the hills and meandering back alleys. Wherever you wander, have your camera at the ready: Valpo brings out the photographer in most people.

CERROS CONCEPCIÓN & ALEGRE

Sighing on every corner quickly becomes a habit on these two hills, whose steep cobbled streets are lined with traditional 19th-century houses with painted corrugated-iron facades that form a vivid patchwork of colors. Some of the city's best cafés and restaurants are here (though not clubs, as late-night music is banned) and new hotels and hostels open up here all the time. Lower Cerro Concepción is more touristy, whereas Cerro Alegre still has an arty air to it.

The city's oldest elevator, **Ascensor Concepción** (CH$250; ☉ 7am-10pm) takes you to Paseo Gervasoni, at the lower end of Cerro Concepción. Built in 1883, it originally ran on steam power.

Local cartoonist Lukas had a sharp eye for the idiosyncrasies of Valparaíso. You need to speak Spanish to understand his sardonic political strips in the **Museo Lukas** (☎ 222-1344; Paseo Gervasoni 448, Cerro Concepción; adult/child CH$1000/500; ☉ 11am-6pm Tue-Sun) but the ink drawings of Valpo buildings speak for themselves.

The rambling art nouveau building at the western end of Cerro Alegre is **Palacio Baburizza** (Paseo Yugoslavo s/n, Cerro Alegre); it houses the **Museo de Bellas Artes** (Fine Arts Museum) but was closed for renovation at this writing. **Ascensor El Peral** (CH$100; ☉ 7am-8pm) runs here from just off Plaza Sotomayor. A quick way up to the eastern side of Cerro Alegre is the **Ascensor Reina Victoria** (CH$250; ☉ 7am-11pm), which connects Av Elias to Paseo Dimalow.

CERRO CÁRCEL

The prison that gave this hill its name was closed in 1999, but the crumbling remains of cellblocks and exercise yards are still standing – or they were at this writing. Decorated with huge graffiti, the space has functioned since 2000 as a grass-roots cultural center known as the **Parque Cultural Ex-Cárcel** (Former Prison Cultural Park; ☎ 225-8567; Castro s/n, Cerro Cárcel; admission free; ☉ 9am-7pm Mon-Fri, 11am-7pm Sat & Sun), but seven unexplained fires and a government eviction order have all but emptied it. The official plan is a massive arts center designed by Brazilian Oscar Niemeyer although protests have slowed the process. Reach it by walking up Subida Cumming.

CERRO PANTEÓN

The city's most illustrious, influential and infamous residents love the afterlife style of Valpo's **Cementerio 1** (Dinamarca s/n; ☉ 8am-dusk), where tombs are actually ornate mini palaces. Adjoining it is the back-up option, **Cementerio 2**, and the **Cementerio de Disidentes**, or 'dissident cemetery' – despite the name, it's the final resting place of Protestants rather than rabble-rousers.

CERRO BELLAVISTA

Artists and writers have long favored this quiet residential hill, but the steady stream of hotels and hostels opening here signal that Cerro Bellavista may well be Valpo's next big thing. Some 20 colorful, if rather flaky, murals are dotted through its lower streets, forming the **Museo a Cielo Abierto** (Open-Air Museum; www.pucv.cl/site/pags/museo; admission free), created between 1969 and 1973 by students from the Universidad Católica's Instituto de Arte. The **Ascensor Espíritu Santo** (CH$250; ☉ 7am-8:30pm) takes you from behind Plaza Victoria to the heart of this art.

Bellavista's most famous resident artist was Pablo Neruda, who made a point of watching Valparaíso's annual New Year's fireworks from his house at the top of the hill, **La Sebastiana** (☎ 225-6606; www.fundacionneruda .org; Ferrari 692, Cerro Bellavista; adult/child CH$2500/1500; ☉ 10:30am-6:50pm Tue-Sun Jan & Feb, 10:10am-6pm Tue-Sun Mar-Dec). Getting here involves a hefty uphill

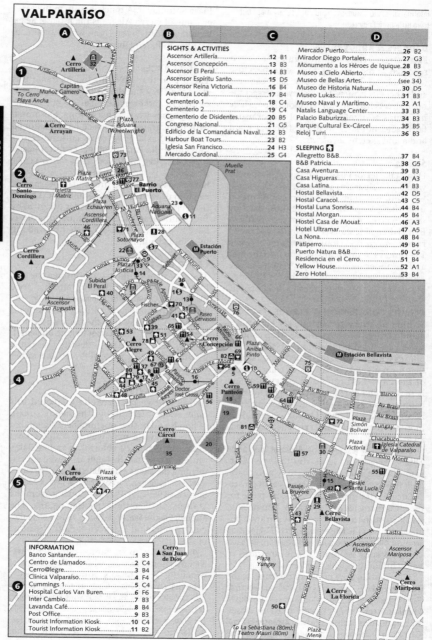

VALPARAÍSO

SIGHTS & ACTIVITIES

Ascensor Artillería	**12** B1
Ascensor Concepción	**13** B3
Ascensor El Peral	**14** B3
Ascensor Espíritu Santo	**15** D5
Ascensor Reina Victoria	**16** B4
Aventura Local	**17** B4
Cementerio 1	**18** C4
Cementerio 2	**19** C4
Cementerio de Disidentes	**20** B5
Congreso Nacional	**21** G5
Edificio de la Comandancia Naval	**22** B3
Harbour Boat Tours	**23** B2
Iglesia San Francisco	**24** H3
Mercado Cardonal	**25** G4

Mercado Puerto	**26** B2
Mirador Diego Portales	**27** G3
Monumento a los Héroes de Iquique	**28** B3
Museo a Cielo Abierto	**29** C5
Museo de Bellas Artes	(see 34)
Museo de Historia Natural	**30** D5
Museo Lukas	**31** B3
Museo Naval y Marítimo	**32** A1
Natalis Language Center	**33** B3
Palacio Baburizza	**34** B3
Parque Cultural Ex-Cárcel	**35** B5
Reloj Turri	**36** B3

SLEEPING

Allegretto B&B	**37** B4
B&B Patricia	**38** G5
Casa Aventura	**39** B3
Casa Higueras	**40** A3
Casa Latina	**41** B3
Hostal Bellavista	**42** D5
Hostal Caracol	**43** C5
Hostal Luna Sonrisa	**44** B4
Hostal Morgan	**45** B4
Hostel Casa de Mouat	**46** A3
Hotel Ultramar	**47** A5
La Nona	**48** B4
Patiperro	**49** B4
Puerto Natura B&B	**50** C6
Residencia en el Cerro	**51** B4
Yellow House	**52** A1
Zero Hotel	**53** B4

INFORMATION

Banco Santander	**1** B3
Centro de Llamados	**2** C4
Cerro@alegre	**3** B4
Clínica Valparaíso	**4** F4
Cummings 1	**5** C4
Hospital Carlos Van Buren	**6** F6
Inter Cambio	**7** B3
Lavanda Café	**8** B4
Post Office	**9** B3
Tourist Information Kiosk	**10** C4
Tourist Information Kiosk	**11** B2

MIDDLE CHILE

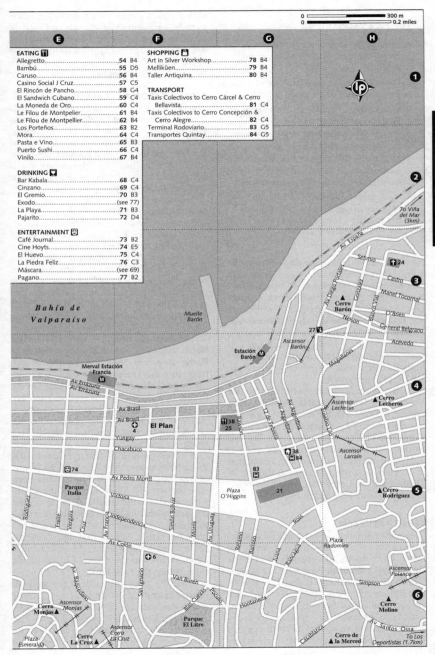

MIDDLE CHILE

EATING 🍴
Allegretto...............................**54** B4
Bambú...............................**55** D5
Caruso...............................**56** B4
Casino Social J Cruz...............................**57** C5
El Rincón de Pancho...............................**58** G4
El Sandwich Cubano...............................**59** C4
La Moneda de Oro...............................**60** C4
Le Filou de Montpelier...............................**61** B4
Le Filou de Montpellier...............................**62** B4
Los Porteños...............................**63** B2
Mora...............................**64** C4
Pasta e Vino...............................**65** B3
Puerto Sushi...............................**66** C4
Vinilo...............................**67** B4

DRINKING 🍷
Bar Kabala...............................**68** C4
Cinzano...............................**69** C4
El Gremio...............................**70** B3
Exodo...............................(see 77)
La Playa...............................**71** B3
Pajarito...............................**72** D4

ENTERTAINMENT 🎭
Café Journal...............................**73** B2
Cine Hoyts...............................**74** E5
El Huevo...............................**75** C4
La Piedra Feliz...............................**76** C3
Máscara...............................(see 69)
Pagano...............................**77** B2

SHOPPING 🛍
Art in Silver Workshop...............................**78** B4
Melliküen...............................**79** B4
Taller Antiquina...............................**80** B4

TRANSPORT
Taxis Colectivos to Cerro Cárcel & Cerro
  Bellavista...............................**81** C4
Taxis Colectivos to Cerro Concepción &
  Cerro Alegre...............................**82** C4
Terminal Rodoviario...............................**83** G5
Transportes Quintay...............................**84** G5

Bahía de Valparaíso

To Viña del Mar (3km)

Muelle Barón

Estación Barón

Merval Estación Francia

Ascensor Barón

Cerro Barón

Setimio
Castro
Manel Tocornal
O'Brien
General Belgrano
Acevedo
Magallanes

Av España
Av Diego Portales
González
Blanco Viel
Nelson

Av Errázuriz
Av Errázuriz

Av Brasil
Av Brasil
El Plan
Yungay
Chacabuco

Cerro Lecheros
Ascensor Lecheros

Ascensor Larraín

Av Argentina
12 de Febrero
Eusebio Lillo

Parque Italia

Av Pedro Montt
Victoria
Independencia
Simón Bolívar
Morris
Av Uruguay
Rawson
Rioseco
Juana
Plaza O'Higgins
Plaza Radomiro
Ross

Cerro Rodríguez

Av Colón

Rodríguez
Freire
Vergara
Cruz
Av Francia

Van Buren
San Ignacio

Blas Cuevas
Pocito
Hontaneda

Parque El Litre

Ascensor Polanco
Simpson

Cerro Molino

Cerro Monjas
Ascensor Monjas

Plaza Esmeralda
Cerro La Cruz
Ascensor Cerro La Cruz

Casablanca
Cerro de la Merced

Av Santos Ossa
To Los Deportistas (1.7km)

TOP FIVE VALPO VIEWS

- Paseo 21 de Mayo on Cerro Artillería to survey the cranes and containers of the port.
- Plaza Bismark on Cerro Cárcel for a panoramic take of the bay.
- Mirador Diego Portales on Cerro Barón for a sweeping perspective of Valpo's colorful house-cluttered central views.
- The viewpoint at the end of Calle Merlet on Cerro Cordillera to see the rusting roofs of Barrio El Puerto and the civic buildings of Plaza Sotomayor from above.
- Paseo Atkinson on Cerro Concepción for views of typical Valpo houses during the day, and a twinkling sea of lights on the hills at night.

hike, and the climbing continues inside the house – you're rewarded on each floor with ever more heart-stopping views over the harbor. The best of all are from Neruda's crow's nest study. Unlike at Neruda's other houses, you can wander around La Sebastiana at will, lingering over the chaotic collection of ship's figureheads, glass, 1950s furniture and artworks by his famous friends. Just don't go behind the bright pink bar, which was reserved for Don Pablo himself.

Alongside the house, the Fundación Neruda has built the **Centro Cultural La Sebastiana**, containing a small exhibition space, café and souvenir shop. To get here, walk 800m uphill along Héctor Calvo from Ascensor Espíritu Santo. Alternatively, take green bus O (CH$440) on Serrano near Plaza Sotomayor in El Plan, or from the plaza at the top of Templeman on Cerro Alegre and get off at the 6900 block of Av Alemania.

CERRO ARTILLERÍA

Clear views out over the sea made this southwestern hill a strategic defense spot, hence the name. Cannons still stand ready outside the **Museo Naval y Marítimo** (Naval & Maritime Museum; ☎ 243-7651; www.museonaval.cl; Paseo 21 de Mayo 45, Cerro Artillería; adult/child CH$500/200; ☟ 10am-5:30pm Tue-Sun). The contents suggest they'd rather like to fire them at Peru – much space is devoted to Chile's victory in the 19th-century War of the Pacific. Other exhibits include his-

torical paintings, uniforms, ship's furniture, swords, navigating instruments and medals, all neatly displayed in exhibition rooms along one side of a large courtyard. Rattling **Ascensor Artillería** (CH$250; ☟ 7am-10pm) brings you here from Plaza Wheelwright.

CERROS BARÓN & LECHEROS

You can see all of central Valpo's colorful hills from the **Mirador Diego Portales** (cnr Av Diego Portales & Castelar, Cerro Barón) in the east of town. Nearby, the bell tower of the ornate, red-brick **Iglesia San Francisco** (cnr Blanco Viel & Zañartu, Cerro Barón) served as a landmark for approaching mariners, who gave the city its common nickname 'Pancho' (a diminutive of Francisco).

EL PLAN & EL PUERTO

Valparaíso's flat commercial zone isn't as atmospheric as the hills that rise above it, but it contains a fair few monuments.

In the west of El Plan, **Barrio El Puerto** (the port neighborhood) has the twin honors of being the oldest part of Valparaíso and the most run-down. Crumbling stone facades hint of times gone by – such as the **Mercado Puerto** (cnr Cochrane & San Martín, Puerto), a defunct food market now home to a pack of street cats.

The historic heart of the city is **Plaza Matriz**, which is watched over by **Iglesia La Matriz**. Begun in 1837, it's the fifth church to occupy this site since the construction of the original chapel in 1559. In nearby streets, luridly lit 'cabarets' (read: brothels) and liquor stores testify that port life in Valpo is still very much alive. The prime point for crane- and container-spotting is **Muelle Prat**, along the seafront.

A severer strain of seafarers dominates Plaza Sotomayor: the Chilean navy, whose petrol-blue **Edificio de la Comandancia Naval** (Naval Command Bldg) looms large on the southwestern side. In the middle of the square lies the **Monumento a los Héroes de Iquique**, a tribute to Chile's naval martyrs, who are buried in a crypt beneath it. Where Prat and Cochrane converge to become Esmeralda, the Edificio Turri narrows to the width of its namesake clock tower, the **Reloj Turri**.

What the security guards at the **Museo de Historia Natural** (☎ 254-4840; www.mhnv.cl; Condell 1546, El Plan; adult/child CH$600/300; ☟ 10am-1pm & 2-6pm Tue-Fri, 10am-2pm Sat & Sun) most love to show visitors is the two-headed human baby (in formaldehyde) that was born in the city in

---

SENDERO BICENTENARIO

To really get to the bottom – or rather, the top – of Valparaíso, explore part of the **Sendero Bicentenario**, a 30km cultural and historical route designed by local not-for-profit organization **Fundación Valparaíso**. The trail is divided into 15 themed sections and takes in parts of the port, El Plan and many of the city's lesser-known hills. From the excellent **website** (www.sendero bicentenario.cl) you can download maps and English-language instructions for each section, which include all sorts of juicy details about the streets and buildings you pass.

1915. Yes, really. Ask nicely and you may be allowed to pet the taxidermized viscacha, too. The museum is closed for renovations until July 2009.

One of Valpo's only modern landmarks is the controversial **Congreso Nacional** (Av Pedro Montt s/n, El Plan), in the east of El Plan. Its roots lie in Pinochet's presidency both literally and legislatively: it was built on one of his boyhood homes, mandated by his 1980 constitution (which moved the legislature away from Santiago).

As colorful as Valparaíso's trademark houses – and built almost as high – are the fruit and vegetable displays in the **Mercado Cardonal** (🕒 6am-5pm), bordered by Yungay, Av Brasil, Uruguay and Rawson. Ground-floor stalls spill out onto the street, while upstairs is taken up by cheap seafood restaurants (see p131). Whole families of cats are on constant leftover-fish patrol.

Courses
COOKING COURSES
Aventura Local (☎ 259-3918; www.aventuralocal .cl; San Enrique 555-B, Cerro Alegre; 5hr course per person CH$35,000) The culinary geniuses behind Caruso (see p131) help you shop for ingredients at the local market, taste local wine, then cook (and eat) a seafood dish.
Gonzalo Lara (☎ 223-0665; gonzalolarachef@yahoo .es; 6hr course per person CH$50,000) After an introduction to traditional Chilean ingredients you're into the kitchen creating a three-course meal (complete with pisco sours), guided by the madcap chef of Vinilo (see p131).

LANGUAGE SCHOOLS
Natalis Language Center (☎ 246-9936; www.nata lislang.com; Plaza Justicia 45, 6th fl, Oficina 602, El Plan;

courses per week from CH$77,500, 3-day crash courses CH$99,000, 1-day survival Spanish CH$33,000) Has a good reputation for quick results.

Tours
Aventura Local (☎ 259-3918; www.aventuralocal.cl; San Enrique 555-B, Cerro Alegre; 3hr walking tours from CH$11,000) A geologist and anthropologist deliver a mix of hard facts and colorful local insight.
Harbor boat tours (from Muelle Prat; 20min tour per person CH$1000, 1hr tour on private boat CH$10,000; 🕒 9:30am-6:30pm) Pass alongside giant cruise vessels or naval battleships, or spot sea lions frolicking in the harbor.
Ruta Bellavista (www.rutabellavista.cl; Teatro Mauri, Av Alemania 6985, Cerro Bellavista; 🕒 noon Sat) Free walking tours of Cerro Bellavista, departing from Teatro Mauri, led by an enthusiastic local not-for-profit organization.

Many companies run whistle-stop day tours from Santiago, but most leave little time for the aimless wandering that's central to experiencing Valparaíso. **Santiago Adventures** (☎ 02-244-2750; www.santiagoadventures.com; Guardia Vieja 255, Oficina 403, Providencia, Santiago; per person CH$50,000-110,000) operates good, customizable tours from Santiago.

Festivals & Events
Año Nuevo (New Year's) Fantastic fireworks displays over the harbor draw hundreds of thousands of spectators to the city each December 31. Book accommodation well in advance.

Sleeping
BUDGET
Casa Aventura (☎ 275-5963; www.casaventura.cl; Pasaje Gálvez 11, Cerro Concepción; dm/s/d without bathroom incl breakfast CH$7000/9000/17,000) Airy, pastel-painted dorms and doubles come with sky-high ceilings and their original wooden floors in the ramshackle old house that contains one of Valpo's oldest hostels. Bathrooms, conversely, are small and dingy, and the kitchen and eating area are a bit scuffed, but breakfasts include fruit and cheese. The location is excellent.

Hostal Bellavista (☎ 212-1544; www.hostalbellavista .biz; Pasaje Santa Lucía 5, Cerro Bellavista; dm/s/d without bathroom incl breakfast CH$7000/12,000/20,000; 🖳) The quirky tile mosaics that line the steep staircase to this new hostel are entirely in keeping with its location on artsy Cerro Bellavista. Rooms are decorated equally creatively with bright turquoise walls and large Valparaíso-themed murals, and include thoughtful details such as feather comforters, tables and chairs, and wi-fi and cable TV. The singles, though small, are cozy and good value.

our pick **Hostal Caracol** (☎ 239-5817; www.hostal caracol.cl; Hector Calvo 371, Cerro Bellavista; dm/d incl break-fast CH$8000/20,000; 🖥) There's no skimping on details here: a wood-burning stove keeps the living room warm, breakfasts include homemade jam and cereal, and dorm beds come with feather comforters, well-sprung mattresses and reading lights. Walls painted crimson, ultramarine or vermillion accentuate each of the private rooms, and the crisp cotton bedclothes coordinate. Staying longer than you planned is a common issue.

Allegretto B&B (☎ 296-8517; www.allegretto.cl; Lautaro Rosas 540, Cerro Alegre; dm/d CH$8000/25,000) Like many properties along this iconic Cerro Alegre street, the tall house containing this B&B has been totally renovated. They've struck a nice balance between past and present by mixing old furniture with trendy wall colors such as pistachio, olive-green or arctic blue.

Also recommended:

Hostel Casa de Mouat (☎ 225-9309; Víctor Hugo 89, Cerro Cordillera; s/d CH$5000/10,000) The cheapest accommodation in Valpo and the most genuinely bohemian.

B&B Patricia (☎ 222-0290; www.hostalpatricia.cl; 12 de Febrero 315, El Plan; dm/s/d without bathroom incl breakfast CH$5000/7000/12,000) Cheap and clean but far from Valpo's hills.

Patiperro (☎ 317-3153; www.patiperrohostel.cl; Templeman 657, Cerro Alegro; dm CH$7000; 🖥) Bright, ultrasimple dorms.

Residencia en el Cerro (☎ 249-5298; pierreloti51@ gmail.com; Pasaje Pierre Loti 51, Cerro Concepción; dm/d without bathroom incl breakfast CH$7000/20,000; 🖥) Friendly, family-run B&B with passable doubles but an over-crowded, windowless dorm.

Hostal Luna Sonrisa (☎ 273-4117; www.lunasonrisa.cl; Templeman 833, Cerro Alegre; dm/d without bathroom incl breakfast CH$7000/22,000) Quiet and close to Cerro Alegre's restaurants and bars, though dorms could do with freshening.

MIDRANGE

La Nona (☎ 249-5706; www.bblanona.com; Galos 660, Cerro Alegre; s/d incl breakfast CH$11,000/22,000; 🖥) The English-speaking owners of this B&B are mad about Valpo, and love sharing insider tips with their guests. The pastel-painted rooms could do with freshening up, but the bright pink living room is a step in the right direction, and there's a kitchen and free wi-fi.

Casa Latina (☎ 249-4622; www.casalatina.com, in Spanish; Papudo 462, Cerro Concepción; s/d incl breakfast

CH$18,000/30,000; 🖥) The traditional Valparaíso facade of this tiny B&B belies the contemporary interior: three large rooms have maroon-stained floors, boxy modern furniture and wood-clad bathrooms with big bowl sinks.

Hostal Morgan (☎ 211-4931; www.hostalmorgan .cl; Capilla 784, Cerro Alegre; d incl breakfast CH$40,000, dm/d without bathroom CH$15,000/36,000; 🖥) The old-fashioned iron and wooden bedsteads, springy mattresses and crisp white sheets at this deliciously homey old house are perfect for long lie-ins. Do try to get up for breakfast, though, which is served on country-style pine tables in a light-filled dining room. Wi-fi is included.

Yellow House (☎ 239-9435; www.theyellowhouse .cl; Capitán Muñoz Gamero 91, Cerro Artillería; d incl breakfast CH$26,000-33,000, s/d without bathroom CH$18,000/24,000; 🖥) Oh-my-god views over the old port and the hills really set this quiet B&B apart, and so does the friendly care lavished on guests by the Australian-Chilean couple that owns it. The cozy, pastel-painted rooms come with kettles and heaters; add the big breakfasts, kitchen, laundry, wi-fi and peaceful location on Cerro Artillería, and it's clear why the Yellow House is so popular with older travelers.

TOP END

Puerto Natura B&B (☎ 222-4405; www.puertonatura .cl; Héctor Calvo 850, Cerro Bellavista; s/d without bathroom incl breakfast CH$27,900/50,000; 🖥) The fluffy beds and spotless, individually decorated rooms in this 1935 castle make it like staying at a very well-appointed relative's – but so do the shared bathrooms. The owners are actually natural therapists: reiki, massages, yoga and Turkish baths are available on-site. A terraced garden filled with fruit trees is tucked away behind the house.

Hotel Ultramar (☎ 221-0000; www.hotelultramar.cl; Pérez 173, Cerro Cárcel; s/d incl breakfast CH$52,500/70,500; 🖥) Unparalleled views over the bay justify the trek to sleek Ultramar, high on Cerro Cárcel. Behind the drab brown-brick front it's very mod, with soaring red and white walls, black banisters and checkered floor tiles. The rooms are just as colorful but their shoddy furniture falls a bit short of the price, as do the tiny bathrooms.

Zero Hotel (☎ 211-3113; www.zerohotel.com; Lautaro Rosas 343, Cerro Alegre; d overlooking street/sea incl breakfast CH$90,000/140,000; 🖥) Sprawl under soaring ceilings on your over-sized bed then make the hardest choice of the day: where to take in the views from – the bay windows of the living room, the pool or the three-tier garden bursting with bougainvillea. Wi-fi is included.

Casa Higueras (☎ 249-7900; www.hotelcasahigueras .cl; Higuera 133, Cerro Alegre; r CH$106,700-143,700; 🏊) Rich Santiaguinos always preferred weekending in Viña to Valpo but they've been won over by slick rooms with dark-wood furniture and huge beds, mosaic-tiled bathrooms with big bowl sinks and the quiet living room filled with Asian sculptures and low beige sofas. Like the swimming pool, it has views out over the bay (less inspiring are the vistas of nearby hills, artfully strewn with garbage).

Eating
BUDGET
Mora (☎ 098- 8393-6446; Brasil 1388, El Plan; quiche or salad CH$1000; 🕙 9am-9pm Mon-Sat; **V**) Meat might be murder, but healthy lunchers are considerably less ethical about table-snitching at this earthy hole-in-the-wall. We can't blame them: you get super-fresh salads, soups, sandwiches and cookies at great prices.

El Sandwich Cubano (☎ 223-8247; O'Higgins 1224, Local 16, El Plan; sandwiches CH$1590-1700; noon-10pm Mon-Sat) Barely bigger than Fidel's handkerchief, this churns out son, salsa and over-stuffed sandwiches. Don't get revolutionary: go for the classic *ropa vieja* (literally, 'old clothes,' a shredded beef sandwich).

Casino Social J Cruz (☎ 221-1225; Condell 1466, El Plan; 2-person meals CH$4500; 🕙 10pm-1am Sun-Thu, 10am-4am Fri & Sat) Liquid paper graffiti covers the tabletops and windows at this tiny café, tucked away down a narrow passageway in El Plan. Forget about menus, there are two options here: *chorrillana* (a mountain of French fries under a blanket of fried pork, onions and egg) and *desmechada* (stewed beef) – one dish serves two. Folk singers serenade you into the wee hours on weekends.

La Moneda de Oro (☎ 225-1733; O'Higgins 1252, El Plan; set lunches CH$1700, mains CH$2200-4200; 🕙 10am-midnight Mon-Thu, 10am-1:30am Fri & Sat) Dripping hunks of grilled meat is what this dark 'n' dusty *parrilla* does best – what it lacks in frills it definitely makes up for in serving size. Football flags and port paraphernalia festoon the bottle-packed bar.

Also recommended:

Puerto Sushi (☎ 223-9017; Esmeralda 1138, El Plan; sushi CH$1300-2900, 2-person combos CH$4900; 🕙 1-4pm & 6-11pm Mon-Thu, 1-4pm & 6pm-1am Fri, 6pm-1am Sat) Good-value sushi platters.

Bambú (☎ 223-4216; Independencia 1790, 2nd fl, El Plan; set lunch CH$1800; 🕙 10:30am-5:30pm Mon-Sat Mar-Dec, 10am-7pm Jan & Feb; **V**) Ultrahealthy tofu dishes, salads and wholemeal pizza and pasta.

MIDRANGE
El Rincón de Pancho (☎ 222-8531; Mercado Cardonal, 2nd fl, Local 164, El Plan; mains CH$3000-5000; 🕙 11am-6pm) The best-known of many seafood places in the main food market, Pancho does good-value fried-fish combos which come heaped with chips or salads. Have a coin or two ready for the troupe of aging troubadours who stagger through periodically to belt out the same two boleros.

Los Porteños (☎ 225-2511; Valdivia 169, Puerto; set lunch CH$2200, mains CH$4200-5200; 🕙 10am-8pm) Something about this place is very fishy – in fact, everything is. Nets, buoys and anchors are draped across the flaking walls almost as lovingly as the battered and fried hake or sea bass is laid across your cheap glass plate.

Allegretto (☎ 296-8839; www.allegretto.cl; Pilcomayo 529, Cerro Concepción; large pizzas CH$4600-5800; 🕙 1-3:30pm & 7-11pm Mon-Thu, 1-3:30pm & 7pm-midnight Fri & Sat, 1-4:30pm & 7-11pm Sun; **V**) Big, deliciously crispy pizzas come with very creative toppings here. Things get rowdy round the upstairs Foosball table, which is surrounded by a mural of screaming fans.

Caruso (☎ 259-4039; www.caruso.cl; Av Cumming 201, Cerro Cárcel; mains CH$5000-6700; 🕙 1-4pm Tue & Wed, 1-4pm & 8:30pm-midnight Thu-Sat) Locally caught rock- and shellfish get fresh, unpretentious treatment at Caruso. Start with the flaky filo seafood empanadas, then move on to the spicy Peruvian ceviche. Corn ice cream makes a teeth-stickingly good finish.

Vinilo (☎ 223-0665; Almirante Montt 448, Cerro Alegre; snacks & sandwiches CH$4000, mains CH$6900; 🕙 9am-midnight Mon-Thu, 9am-3am Fri & Sat, 10am-midnight Sun) From bakers to butchers to effortlessly hip resto-bar: the mismatched tile floor tells the story of the many incarnations of this Cerro Alegre institution. Sandwiches and chocolate-and-raspberry cake seduce during the day. Later, quirky Chilean fare takes center stage. As the last plates are licked, the namesake vinyl gets turned up and things slips into bar mode.

Le Filou de Montpellier (☎ 222-4663; Av Almirante Montt 382, Cerro Alegre; weekday set lunch CH$3600, weekend set lunch CH$6400, mains CH$5600; 🕙 1-4pm Tue-Thu & Sun, 1-4pm & 8pm-midnight Fri & Sat) The three-course lunches at this cluttered bistro are worth staying on an extra day for – rabbit stew, beef bourguignon and sauce-laced fish are mainstays, but always, always leave room for whatever chocolate-based dessert is on the menu. There's a posher branch up the hill at Lautaro Rosas 510.

our pick Los Deportistas (☎ 237-5159; Colo-Colo 1217, Barrio O'Higgins; set menu CH$8500; ⏰ 12:30-3:30pm & 8-11:30pm Wed-Sat, 12:30-3:30pm Sun-Tue) No sign outside, no menu inside, but don't worry: for 45 years, Valpo's biggest feasts have been happening here. Watch and weep as the owner plonks down bowl after bowl of salads and cigar-sized French fries with your grilled salmon, tongue in walnut sauce or bloody steak. The thimbleful of local digestif Araucano seems an ironic gesture. To get here, catch a *colectivo* or bus from along Condell or Av Pedro Montt to San Roque or Ramaditas and ask to be let off at the 'cancha del Barrio O'Higgins,' a neighborhood soccer ground: Los Deportistas is round behind it.

TOP-END

Pasta e Vino (☎ 249-6187; Templeman 352, Cerro Alegre; mains CH$6900-8900; ⏰ 12:30-4pm & 8pm-midnight Wed-Sat, noon-3:30pm Sun) The word on Pasta e Vino – credited with starting Valpo's gastro revival – has gone from 'fabulous' to 'overrated' and back to 'fabulous' again. Your prize for bagging a table (at this writing, it was first-come, first-served) is watching the chefs make whatever the inventive pasta of the day is, and then eating it. Expect unusual combinations – bean with orange or duck with plum, for example.

Drinking

Pajarito (☎ 225-8910; Salvador Donoso 1433, El Plan; ⏰ 11am-2am Mon-Thu, 11am-late Fri & Sat) Artsy *porteños* in their 20s and 30s cram the formica tables at this laid-back, old-school bar to talk poetry and politics over beer and piscola.

Cinzano (☎ 221-3043; www.barcinzano.cl; Plaza Aníbal Pinto 1182, El Plan; ⏰ 10am-2am Mon-Sat) Drinkers, sailors and crooners have been propping themselves up on the cluttered bar here since 1896. It's now a favorite with tourists, too, who come to see tuneful old-timers knocking out tangos and boleros like there's no tomorrow.

Bar Kabala (☎ 229-940; Almirante Montt 16, El Plan; ⏰ noon-1am Sun-Thu, noon-3am Fri & Sat) With its low-lit wooden tables and exposed brick walls, Kabala is perfect for quiet drinking week-round – locally brewed Cerveza del Puerto is the obvious choice.

La Playa (☎ 259-4262; www.barlaplaya.cl; Serrano 567, Puerto; ⏰ 10am-late) It might be nearly 80 years

old, but this traditional wood-paneled bar shows no signs of slowing down. On weekend nights, cheap pitchers of beer, powerful pisco and a friendly but rowdy atmosphere draws such crowds a cover (CH$2000) is charged.

El Gremio (☎ 222-8394; Pasaje Gálvez 173, Cerro Concepción; ⏰ 7pm-midnight Tue & Wed, 7pm-1:30am Thu, 7pm-3am Fri & Sat) With its crimson walls, sofas and low tables, there's something pleasingly intimate about this bar, which is half-hidden down a narrow alley. The huge cocktail list ranges from creative martinis to girly concoctions such as vanilla daiquiris.

Exodo (☎ 223-1118; www.paganoindustry.cl/exodo; Blanco 298, Puerto; ⏰ 9:30pm-3:30am Wed & Thu, 10pm-4:30am Fri & Sat) Bar staff here dress like wannabe members of Scissor Sisters and scare you into submission with dirty looks (or maybe it's just the eyeliner). A cornerstone of the Valpo gay scene, Exodo's good-value cocktails keep both gay and straight regulars returning.

Entertainment

El Huevo (www.elhuevo.cl; Blanco 1386, El Plan; cover CH$1000-3000; ⏰ 11pm-late Wed-Sat) Ask any heavily made-up 20-year-old where they're going on a Saturday night and this behemoth of a building will be their answer. For some, its shaking floors are a meat market; for others, they're dance heaven.

Máscara (☎ 221-9841; www.mascara.cl; Plaza Aníbal Pinto 1178, El Plan; cover CH$2500-3000; ⏰ 11pm-late Tue-Sat) Music-savvy clubbers in their 20s and 30s love Máscara: the beer's cheap, there's plenty of room to move and hardly any teenyboppers.

Pagano (☎ 223-1118; www.paganoindustry.cl; Blanco 236, Puerto; cover free Sun-Wed, CH$2000-3000 Thu-Sat; ⏰ 10pm-late) Die-hard clubbers both gay and straight can dance all week on Pagano's packed, sweaty floor.

Café Journal (☎ 259-6760; Cochrane 81-87, Puerto; ⏰ 10pm-late Wed-Sat) In one of the unlikeliest quick-change routines since Superman, Café Journal goes from traditional seafood restaurant by day (complete with nets and anchors on the wall) to kicking electronic club by night.

La Piedra Feliz (☎ 225-6788; www.lapiedrafeliz.cl; Av Errázuriz 1054; admission from CH$3000) Jazz, blues, tango, son, salsa, rock, drinking, dining, cinema: is there anything this massive house along the waterfront doesn't do? You can even rent a room by the hour if you can't wait to get your date home…

Cine Hoyts (☎ 594-709; Av Pedro Montt 2111) This five-screen cinema shows the latest releases.

Shopping

Young clothing designers, craftspeople and artists abound in Valparaíso. So do easy-come easy-go shops selling their wares, most of which are concentrated on Cerros Concepción and Alegre: wander for a couple of hours and you'll have seen them all. Painters, photographers and fridge-magnet makers often set up stands on Pasaje Atkins.

Taller Antiquina (☎ 099-9378-1006; San Enrique 510, Cerro Alegre; ☘ 11am-8pm) Beautifully worked leather bags, belts and wallets are lovingly made on-site here.

Art in Silver Workshop (☎ 222-2963; Pasaje Templeman 8, Cerro Concepción; ☘ 10am-7:30pm) Silver and lapis lazuli come together in unusual designs at this small, cluttered workshop, where you can sometimes see their creator, silversmith Victor Hugo, at work.

Melliküen (☎ 212-6686; San Enrique 546, Cerro Alegre; ☘ 10am-8pm) Silver jewelry by local craftspeople and soft woven ponchos from the south of Chile are the main offerings here.

Getting There & Away

BUS

All major intercity services arrive and depart from the **Terminal Rodoviario** (☎ 293-9695; Av Pedro Montt 2800, El Plan), about 20 blocks east of the town center.

Services to Santiago leave every 15 to 20 minutes with **Tur Bus** (☎ 221-2028; www.turbus .cl) and **Condor Bus** (☎ 221-2927; www.condorbus.cl), which both also go south to Puerto Montt (three each daily), Osorno (two each daily) and Temuco (two each daily). In addition, Tur Bus goes to Pucón (four daily) and Concepción (five daily), and Condor serves Chillán (once daily). **Bus Norte** (☎ 225-8322; www .busnorte.cl) has comfortable services to Osorno and Puerto Montt (two daily).

Tur Bus also operates to the northern cities of Arica and Iquique (once daily), Calama (twice daily), and Antofagasta and La Serena (four daily). **Romani** (☎ 222-0662; www.romani.cl) has less frequent services on the same routes.

You can reach Mendoza in Argentina with Tur Bus, **Cata Internacional** (☎ 225-7587; www .catainternacional.com), **El Rápido** (☎ 225-8322; www .elrapidoint.com.ar) and **Ahumada** (☎ 221-6663; www.busesahumada.cl). The latter two continue to Buenos Aires. **Pullman Bus San Felipe de los Andes** (☎ 225-3125) and **Buses JM** (☎ 225-2106; www.busesjm.cl) each have two hourly services to Los Andes.

Pullman Bus Lago Peñuela (☎ 222-4025) leaves to Isla Negra every 10 to 15 minutes. From 12 de Febrero, just outside the terminal, **Transportes Quintay** (☎ 236-2669) runs *taxi colectivos* every 15 minutes to Quintay.

The city transport network, **Transporte Metropolitano Valparaíso** (TMV; www.tmv.cl), has services to the beach towns north of Valparaíso and Viña del Mar. For Reñaca, take green 201, blue 405 or the orange 607, 601 or 605. The 601 and 605 continue to Concón. All run along Condell then Yungay. **Sol del Pacífico** (☎ 275-2030) has buses to the beach towns Horcón (CH$1100) and Maitencillo (CH$1200) every 20 minutes, and to Cachagua (CH$1300), Zapallar (CH$1500) and Papudo (CH$1600) roughly every 40 minutes. They run along Av Errázuriz and call in at Viña del Mar on their way.

Note that fares may increase considerably during school holidays or long weekends.

Destination	Cost (CH$)	Duration (hr)
Antofagasta	18,900	15
Arica	25,000	24
Buenos Aires	33,000	19
Calama	20,200	23
Chillán	12,000	8
Concepción	10,000	9
Iquique	22,800	20
Isla Negra	2600	1½
La Serena	5900	7½
Los Andes	4200	7
Mendoza	9000	8
Osorno	13,800	14
Pucón	13,000	12
Puerto Montt	14,800	16
Quintay	1400	1
Santiago	3700	1½
Temuco	11,900	11

CAR

Valparaíso's steep hills and traffic-clogged streets make driving here a nightmare. However, a car is indispensable for exploring the Casablanca Valley wineries, and useful for getting to Cerro La Campana. The closest car rental agencies to Valparaíso are in Viña del Mar (p138) – if you book in advance, some will bring cars to your hotel.

Getting Around

Walking is the best way to get about central Valparaíso and explore its cerros – you can cheat on the way up by taking an *ascensor* or a *taxi colectivo* (CH$400). *Colectivos* to Cerros Concepción and Alegre line up at the bottom of Almirante Montt, while those to Cerros Cárcel and Bellavista leave from Av Ecuador.

Countless local buses run by **TMV** (one way within El Plan CH$330, El Plan to Cerro CH$400) run along Condell and Av Pedro Montt, Av Brasil and Yungay, connecting one end of El Plan with the other. A few climb different cerros and continue to Viña (CH$460) or along the northern coast; destinations are displayed in the windshield. The city's most famous line is the 801, which uses the oldest working trolleybuses in the world. The curvy cars date to 1947 and have been declared a national monument.

The **Metro Regional de Valparaíso** (Merval; ☎ 252-7633; www.merval.cl) operates commuter trains every 6 to 12 minutes from Valparaíso's **Estación Puerto** (cnr Errázuriz & Urriola) and **Estación Bellavista** (cnr Errázuriz & Bellavista) to Viña del Mar (CH$432). The catch is that you need to buy a nonrefundable contactless card (CH$2000) to use the trains.

Taxis are much more expensive in Valparaíso than other Chilean cities. High-speed driving round hairpin bends on steep roads makes them more alarming, too.

VIÑA DEL MAR

☎ 032 / pop 318,218

Clean, orderly Viña del Mar is a sharp contrast to the jumble of neighboring Valparaíso. Manicured boulevards lined with palm trees and beautiful expansive parks have earned it the nickname of *Ciudad Jardín* (Garden City). Its official name, which means 'vineyard by the sea,' stems from the area's colonial origins as the hacienda of the Carrera family.

Viña remains a popular weekend and summer destination for well-to-do Santiaguinos, despite the fact that its beaches get seriously packed and the Humboldt Current causes waters chilly enough to put off most would-be swimmers. Although Chileans rave about the city, visitors tend to find it rather bland and lacking in things to do: if you're short on time, consider just making it a day trip from Valparaíso.

Orientation

The heavily polluted Río Marga Marga effectively divides Viña in half. Immediately south is the main commercial district, which hinges around Av Valparaíso and Plaza Vergara, the main square. Several bridges cross the Marga Marga into the newer residential area to the north, where the two main drags are Av San Martín, which runs parallel to the sea, and Av Libertad. In this part of town, most streets are identified by a number and direction, either Norte (north), Oriente (east) or Poniente (west). Av Libertad separates Ponientes from Orientes. These streets are usually written as a numeral, but are sometimes spelled out, so that 1 Norte may also appear as Uno Norte.

Viña's white-sand beaches stretch northward from the northern bank of the Estero Marga Marga to the suburbs of Reñaca and Concón.

Information

Afex (☎ 268-8102; Av Arlegui 690; 9am-6:30pm Mon-Fri, 9am-2pm Sat) Change cash and traveler's checks here.

Banco Santander (☎ 226-6917; Plaza Vergara 108) One of several banks with ATMs on the main square.

Conaf (☎ 232-0210; 3 Norte 541; 8:30am-5:30pm Mon-Fri) Provides information on nearby parks, including Parque Nacional La Campana.

Hospital Gustavo Fricke (☎ 265-2200; Alvares 1532) Viña's main public hospital, located east of downtown.

Lavarápido (☎ 290-6263; Av Arlegui 440; per load CH$3700; 10am-9pm Mon-Sat)

Municipal tourist office (www.visitevinadelmar.cl) Plaza Vergara (☎ 226-9330; Av Arlegui 715; 9am-2pm & 3-7pm Mon-Fri, 10am-2pm & 3-7pm Sat & Sun) Rodoviario (☎ 275-2000; Av Valparaíso 1055; 9am-7pm) Distributes an adequate city map and a monthly events calendar, but little else.

Post office (Plaza Latorre 32; 9am-7pm Mon-Fri, 10am-1pm Sat)

Tecomp (Av Valparaíso 684; 9am-midnight Mon-Sat, 11am-9pm Sun) One of many phone centers along the street offering cheap international calls and internet access.

Tera Cyber (☎ 276-8091; Quinta 219; per hr CH$500; 9am-12:30am) The 50 well-maintained machines at this internet café all have flat-screen monitors and headsets.

Dangers & Annoyances

Summer brings pickpockets as well as tourists so watch your belongings, especially on the beach.

Sights

The original *moai* (Easter Island statues) standing guard outside the **Museo de Arqueología e Historia Francisco Fonck** (☎ 268-6753; www.museo fonck.cl; 4 Norte 784; adult/child CH$1500/200; ❂ 10am-6pm Tue-Fri, 10am-2pm Sat & Sun) are just a teaser of the beautifully displayed archaeological finds from Easter Island within, along with Mapuche silverwork and anthropomorphic Moche ceramics. Upstairs are old-school insect cases and a lively explanation of how head shrinking works (finished examples are included).

Nowhere is Viña's nickname of 'the garden city' better justified than at the magnificently landscaped **Parque Quinta Vergara** (❂ 7am-6pm); the entrance is on Errázuriz at the south end of Libertad. It once belonged to one of the city's most illustrious families, the Alvares-Vergaras, but when they fell on hard times they sold it to the city council. Their residence was the Venetian neo-Gothic–style Palacio Vergara, which houses the **Museo Municipal de Bellas Artes** (☎ 273-8762; adult/child CH$600/300; ❂ 10am-1:30pm & 3-5:30pm Tue-Sun). The interesting collection of 17th- to 19th-century European and Chilean art includes works by Murillo, Modigliani, Rubens and Sorolla y Bastida. Major concerts and the celebrated Festival Internacional de la Canción (below) are held in the striking concrete amphitheater in the grounds.

Squat-looking **Castillo Wulff** (☎ 226-9728; Av Marina s/n; admission free; ❂ 10am-1:30pm & 3-5:30pm Tue-Sun) hangs half over the sea: skip through the art exhibitions to the tower at the back, where you can peer through the thick glass floor at the rocks and waves below.

There are over 3000 plant species in the 61 hectares of parkland that comprise Chile's **Jardín Botánico Nacional** (National Botanical Garden; ☎ 267-2566; www.jardin-botanico.cl, in Spanish; Camino El Olivar s/n; adult/child CH$900/300; ❂ 10am-6:30pm). It's 8km southeast of the city center; catch bus 203 from Viana east to the end of the line (CH$440), then cross the bridge and walk about 1km north up Camino El Olivar.

Festivals & Events

Festival Internacional de la Canción (International Song Festival; www.festivaldevina.cl) At Chile's biggest music festival, Latin American pop, rock and folk stars have been drawing huge crowds since 1960.

Sleeping

Viña's hotels have a reputation for high prices but indifferent quality, despite the fact that outside summer supply really exceeds demand.

Che Lagarto Hostel (☎ 262-5759; www.chela garto.com; Av Diego Portales 131; dm/d incl breakfast CH$6950/23,540; ▣) The huge long garden in front of Viña's only real hostel means you don't have to limit your open-air lounging to the beach. The right-on vibe stops at the door: clean but bare dorms mean inside feels like a characterless university residence.

Hotel Monaldi (☎ 288-1484; www.hotelmonaldi .cl; Av Arlegui 172; s/d incl breakfast CH$15,000/25,000, s without bathroom CH$9000; ▣) Five old houses have been knocked together to form this labyrinthine hotel. Knickknacks and photos clutter the walls and surfaces of the two living rooms - one has big sofas and a DVD player - and you can use the kitchen, too. Try to get yourself one of the bigger, brighter upstairs rooms.

Vista Hermosa 26 (☎ 266-6820; www.vistahermosa26 .cl; Vista Hermosa 26; s/d incl breakfast CH$23,000/26,000; ▣) Polished wooden floors and a big fireplace lend stately charm to the lounge of this quiet but friendly hotel on the edge of Cerro Castillo. You get plenty of space (and plenty of towels) in the simple rooms, which have small but new bathrooms.

Residencia Offenbacher-hof (☎ 262-1483; www .offenbacher-hof.cl; Balmaceda 102; s incl breakfast CH$25,000, d CH$30,000-38,000; ▣) There are fabulous views over the sea and the city from this commanding chestnut-and-yellow clapboard house atop quiet Cerro Castillo. Sea views, newly renovated bathrooms and antique furnishings make the spacious superior rooms worth the extra.

Hotel Monterilla (☎ 297-6950; www.monterilla.cl; 2 Norte 65; s/d CH$49,700/62,200; ▣) The dead-plain facade is deceiving: bright artworks and engravings offset the white walls and boxy sofas in this hotel's light-filled lobby and restaurant. The tiled floors and sparse furnishings look refreshing in hot weather but might leave you longing for some color in winter. Doubles in the quieter annex at the back have king-size beds, and there are flat-screen TVs and wi-fi throughout.

Hotel Cap Ducal (☎ 262-6655; Av Marina 51; r incl breakfast CH$55,200-64,400; ❂ ▣) Waves batter the foundations of this iconic art deco

VIÑA DEL MAR

INFORMATION	
Afex	**1** F3
Banco Santander	**2** F3
Conaf	**3** F2
Hospital Gustavo Fricke	**4** H4
Lavarápido	**5** E2
Municipal Tourist Office	**6** F3
Municipal Tourist Office	(see 35)
Post Office	**7** F2
Tecomp	**8** F3
Tera Cyber	**9** E3

SIGHTS & ACTIVITIES	
Castillo Wulff	**10** C1
Museo de Arqueología e Historia	
Francisco Fonck	**11** F1
Museo Muncipal de Bellas	
Artes	**12** E4
Parque Quinta Vergara	**13** E4

SLEEPING ⚑	
Che Lagarto	**14** C3
Hotel Cap Ducal	**15** C1
Hotel del Mar	**16** D1
Hotel Monaldi	**17** D2
Hotel Monterilla	**18** D2
Residencia Offenbacher-hof	**19** C2
Vista Hermosa 26	**20** C3

EATING 🍴	
Arena Bistro	**21** D1
Divino Pecado	**22** D1
Enjoy Café	**23** D1
Enjoy del Mar	**24** D1
Entremasas	**25** E1
Panzoni	**26** E3
Portal Alamos	**27** E3
Samoiedo	**28** E3
Schawerma	**29** D3

DRINKING 🍷	
Barlovento	**30** D2

ENTERTAINMENT 🎭	
Café Journal	**31** C3
Casino Municipal	**32** D1
Cine Arte	**33** F3

TRANSPORT	
Budget	**34** G1
Rodoviario Viña del Mar	**35** G3
Sol de Pacífico bus stop	**36** F3

building, which was built to resemble a ship.
Spiral staircases and narrow corridors lead
to irregular-shaped rooms with big squishy
beds and cruise-liner-worthy sea views
(those on the 3rd floor have balconies, too).
The seafood restaurant here is a classy Viña
classic.

Hotel del Mar (☎ 250-0800; cnr Av Perú & Los Héroes;
r incl breakfast CH\$209,250-262,200; 🖳 🏊) The view
from the sleek, glass-fronted lobby of Viña's
top hotel is a taster of what awaits upstairs –
on many floors you can see the sea from your
bed and even the indoor pool seems to merge
with the waves beyond the window. The welcome bottle of champagne and chocolates and
a few free chips for the adjoining casino win
over most guests.

Eating

Most of Viña's cheap eats are clustered on
and around busy Av Valparaíso in the town
center. These include the string of samey
schop-and-sandwich joints that fill the
open-fronted 2nd floor of **Portal Álamos** (Av
Valparaíso 553; meals CH\$2200), a downtown shop-
ping arcade.

Entremasas (☎ 297-1821; 5 Norte 377; empanadas
CH\$900; 🕑 10:30am-9:30pm) Prawn and mush-
room in a cheese-cilantro sauce; ground beef
and bacon seasoned with merquén; chorizo
and goat's cheese…Who knew empanadas
got this interesting?

Schawerma (☎ 233-6835; Ecuador 225; kebabs &
falafels CH\$1600-2500; 🕑 11:30am-9:30pm Mon-Sat; 🅥)
Everything comes on flimsy plastic plates

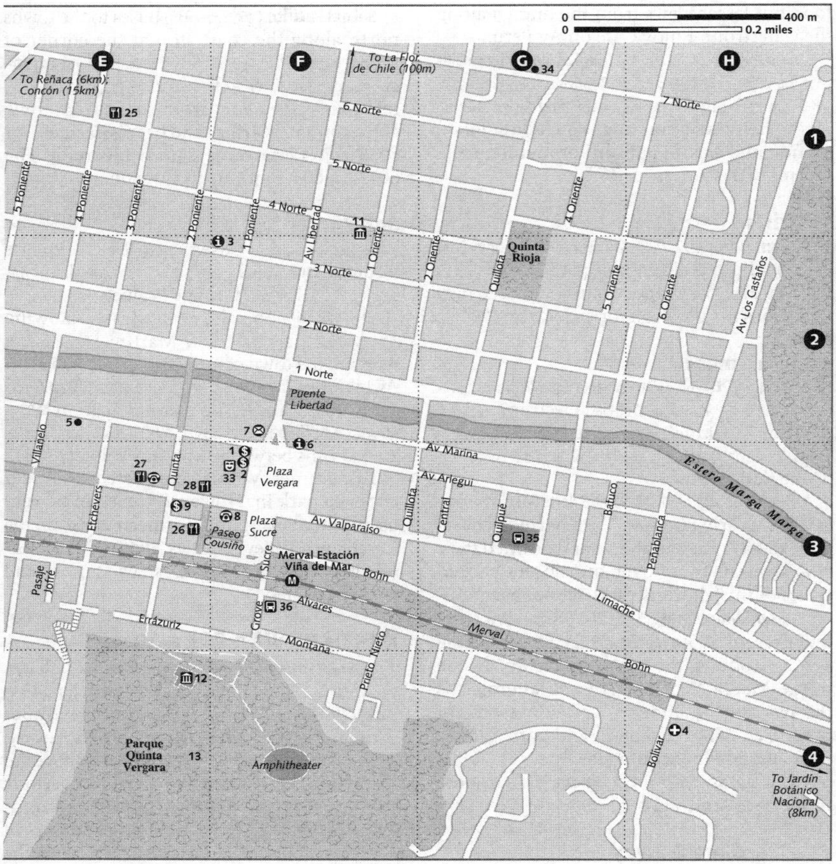

and there's not so much as a straw between you and your drink bottle. Who cares? The shawarma here's so damn tasty we'd eat it off the floor if we had to.

Panzoni (☎ 268-2134; Paseo Cousiño 12-B; mains CH$3000-3500; ⌚ noon-4pm & 8pm-midnight Mon-Sat) One of the best-value eateries in central Viña, Panzoni's uncomplicated Italian food and friendly service reel in the lunchtime diners. Pastas make up most of the offerings – the favorite filling is pork and plum.

Arena Bistro (☎ 273-6250; Av San Martín 304; mains CH$3600-5900; ⌚ 9am-1:30am Sun-Thu, 9am-4am Fri & Sat; Ⓥ) Arena bridges the gap between the posh restaurants and fast-food chains around it: pizzas, sandwiches, empanadas and wraps fill the menu, but they're made with interesting combinations of fresh ingredients. Later on, cocktails clutter the pale wood tables and the music gets turned up.

Samoiedo (☎ 268-1382; Valparaíso 637; set lunch menu CH$4000-6500, sandwiches CH$2200-2800; ⌚ 12:30-11pm Mon-Sat) For half a century the old boys have been meeting at this traditional *confitería* (tearoom) for lunchtime feasts of steak and fries or well-stuffed sandwiches.

Enjoy del Mar (☎ 250-0788; Av Perú s/n; sandwiches & sushi CH$3500-4500, mains CH$7500-10,500; ⌚ 9am-midnight) A sunset drink here should be on everyone's Viña to-do list – there are panoramic views of the Pacific from its terrace above the mouth of the Marga Marga. The ice-cream bar includes kooky flavors such as pisco sour and Coca-Cola. You get cheaper food but lesser views from the branch along the waterfront, Enjoy Café on Av Perú.

Divino Pecado (☎ 297-5790; Av San Martín 180; mains CH$6300-7900; ⏱ 12:30-3pm & 8-11pm Mon-Sat, 12:30-4pm & 8-11pm Sun) The short but surprising menu at this Italian restaurant might include smoked salmon and wasabi pansotti or merquén fettuccini with lamb ragu.

Drinking

Barlovento (☎ 297-7472; 2 Norte 195; ⏱ 6pm-3am Mon-Sat) Hipster headquarters in Viña is this industrial-looking concrete-and-steel bar, which has a reputation for spot-on cocktails.

Entertainment

Café Journal (☎ 266-6654; cnr Santa Agua & Alvares; cover free-CH$3000; ⏱ 10pm-late Wed-Sat) Electronic music is the order of the evening at this boomingly popular club, which now has three heaving dance floors.

La Flor de Chile (☎ 268-9554; 8 Norte 601; ⏱ 10pm-late) For nearly 80 years Viñamarinos young and old have chewed the fat and downed their *schops* (draft beer) over the closely packed tables of this gloriously old-school bar.

Casino Municipal (☎ 250-0700; www.casino devinadelmar.cl; Av San Martín 199; ⏱ 6pm-early morning) Overlooking the beach on the north side of the Marga Marga, this local landmark is the place to squander your savings on slot machines, bingo, roulette and card games. Formal attire is encouraged.

Cine Arte (☎ 288-2798; Plaza Vergara 142) Arthouse movies are screened here.

Getting There & Away

All long-distance services operate from the **Rodoviario Viña del Mar** (☎ 275-2000; www.rodoviario .cl; Valparaíso 1055), four long blocks east of Plaza Vergara. Nearly all long-distance buses to and from Valparaíso stop here; see p133 for details of services.

Sol del Pacífico (☎ 275-2030) buses to the towns north along the coast stop at the corner of Grove and Álvares – for prices and frequencies see p133. Local buses also go to Reñaca, including green 201 (from Av España), blue 405 (from Av Marina) and orange 607, 601 or 605 (from Plaza Vergara or Av Libertad). The 601 and 605 continue to Concón.

Getting Around

Frequent local buses run by **Transporte Metropolitano Valparaíso** (TMV; www.tmv.cl; one way CH$460) connect Viña and Valparaíso. Some routes run along the waterfront following Av Marina and Av San Martín; others run through the town center along Av España and Av Libertad. Destinations are usually displayed in the windshield. The commuter train **Metro Regional de Valparaíso** (Merval; ☎ 252-7633; www.merval .cl) also runs between Viña and Valpo (p134).

In summer Viña is congested and very tricky to park in. However, a car can be very useful for touring the northern coast or the Casablanca Valley wineries. **Budget** (☎ 268-3420; www.budget.cl; 7 Norte 1023) has stellar service and no deductibles.

NORTH OF VIÑA DEL MAR

The road snakes along the coast north of Viña, passing through a string of beach towns that hum with holidaying Chileans December through February. There's plenty of variety: the beaches range from small, rocky coves to wide open sands. Towering condos overlook some of them; others contain rough-and-ready cabins or the huge summer houses of Chile's rich and famous. Even off-season, the drive along the coast is beautiful. Note that though buses run here from Viña, Valpo and Santiago, services to the further beaches are infrequent and they don't always take you right up to the sands: if you want to hit several towns in a day, consider renting a car.

DETOUR TO RITOQUE

Vast rolling dunes hide **Ritoque**, one of the best and most undiscovered beaches on this part of the coast. A small group of houses (some of them built from recycled materials) is clustered around the northern end of the 10km stretch of sands. Surfing, horseback riding and sea-kayaking are all popular here – **Ritoque Expediciones** (☎ 032-281-6344; www.ritoqueexpediciones.cl) runs full- and half-day riding trips through the dunes, and there's a night ride each full moon. You can stay in Ritoque, or come on a day trip from Valpo or Viña. To get here catch a **Sol del Pacífico** (☎ 032-275-2030) bus from Av Errázuriz in Valparaíso or Av Libertad in Viña to Quintero (CH$1000, every 20 minutes). From there, it's a CH$2000 taxi ride to Ritoque.

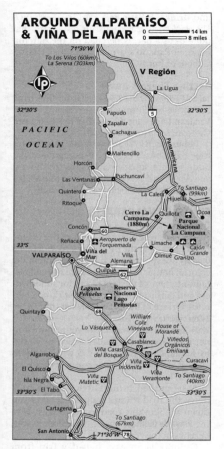

AROUND VALPARAÍSO & VIÑA DEL MAR

0 — 14 km
0 — 8 miles

71°30'W
To Los Vilos (60km);
La Serena (303km)

V Región

32°30'S — 32°30'S

PACIFIC OCEAN

33°S

33°30'S — 33°30'S

71°30'W

La Ligua
Papudo
Zapallar
Cachagua
Maitencillo
Horcón
Las Ventanas
Puchuncaví
Quintero
La Calera
To Santiago (99km)
Ritoque
Hijuelas
Cerro La Campana (1880m)
Quillota
Ocoa
Concón
Parque Nacional La Campana
Reñaca
Aeropuerto de Torquemada
Limache
Cajón Grande
VALPARAÍSO
Viña del Mar
Villa Alemana
Olmué Granizo
Quilpué
Laguna Peñuelas
Reserva Nacional Lago Peñuelas
Quintay
William Cole Vineyards
House of Morandé
Lo Vásquez
Viñedos Orgánicos Emiliana
Casablanca
Viña Casas del Bosque
Algarrobo
Viña Indómita
Curacaví
El Quisco
Viña Veramonte
To Santiago (40km)
Isla Negra
Viña Matetic
El Tabo
Cartagena
To Santiago (67km)
San Antonio
78

Reñaca & Concón

Viña's high-rises merge into the multitiered apartments of Reñaca, a northern suburb with a wide, pleasant beach. Concón, just north of Reñaca, also has reasonable sands. Informal seafood restaurants line the coast road: prices and quality are fairly consistent, but locals usually agree that the empanadas at **Las Deliciosas** (☎ 032-290-3665; Av Borgoño 25370; empanadas CH$850; ⏰ noon-11pm) are hard to beat. Crab and cheese is the classic.

Horcón

Chile's hippie movement began at the small fishing town of Horcón, on a small curving peninsula that juts out into the Pacific 28km north of Concón. These days peace, love and communal living are gone, but brightly painted, rather run-down buildings clutter the steep main road down to its small, rocky beach where fishing boats come and go. It's overlooked by a smattering of samey seafood restaurants doing cheap set menus, *pailas* (seafood stews) and empanadas. Regulars rave about the *machas a la parmesana* at **Las Brisas de Horcón** (☎ 032-279-6771; Av Costanera s/n; mains CH$2200-4900; ⏰ 9am-11pm).

In summer, the sands at **Caleta Horcón** (the main beach) heave with vacationers, but there are usually fewer people on nearby **Playa Cau-Cau**, which used to be one of Chile's few nudist beaches (taking your kit off is now optional). A signposted sand road leads off Horcón's main drag to a car park where a rickety walkway plunges down to the beach. Mellow tunes and fresh fish await you at the beachside tables of **Caballo del Mar** (☎ 032-279-6138; Playa Cau-Cau; mains CH$5500-6200; ⏰ noon-10pm Nov-Easter, noon-9pm Sat & Sun Easter-Oct). Try the ceviche, which comes served in a seashell.

Maitencillo

About 21km north of Horcón, Maintencillo's long, sandy beaches stretch for several kilometers along the coast and attract many visitors. Although the town's packed with holiday homes, it retains a pleasant low-key vibe.

Cabins and rental houses line the seafront, but the loveliest by far are the earthy wooden **Cabañas Hermansen** (☎ 032-771-028; www.hermansen .cl; Av del Mar 592; 2-/3-/4-person cabins CH$32,000/ 40,000/45,000). The complex is set back from the coast road, but you can always hear the waves and, in several cabins, look out over them, too. The all-wood vibe spills over into the restaurant and bar, **La Canasta** (☎ 032-771-028; set menu CH$5000, mains CH$5600-6200; ⏰ noon-3:30pm & 6pm-late Tue-Sun). Wood-baked pizzas and – of course – fresh fish are the house specialties. A DJ gets a crowd going on weekend nights in high season.

Cachagua

This small, laid-back town 13km north of Maitencillo sits on the northern tip of a long crescent beach. Just across the water is the **Monumento Nacional Isla de Cachagua**, a guano-stained rocky outcrop that's home to more than 2000 Humboldt penguins, as well as a colony of sea lions. Conservationists are concerned that overdevelopment of the coastline is causing numbers to dwindle.

Zapallar

Santiago's elite wouldn't dream of taking their beach holidays anywhere but here, the most exclusive of Chile's coastal resorts, 2km north of Cachagua. Instead of high-rises, multimillion-dollar mansions (many of them historic) cover the wooded hillsides leading up from the beach, which is a small but unspoiled arc of yellow sand in a sheltered cove. **La Caleta de Pescadores**, a tiny wet-market where fishermen sell their catch, is near the large rock at the southwestern end of the beach. A short walk around the promontory leads to the **Plaza del Mar Bravo** view point, where waves crash onto shoreline rocks.

Zapallar is oriented toward those with summer houses – if you can't swing an invite, make it a day trip. Everyone who's anyone in Zapallar makes a point of lunch at **El Chiringuito** (☎ 033-741-024; Caleta de Pescadores; mains CH$8100-10,300; ⏰ noon-6pm Mon-Thu, noon-midnight Fri-Sun), where terrace tables look out over the rocks and hungry pelicans fishing for their dinner. Yours is almost as fresh: locally caught king-klip, sea bass and sole are what it does best, dressed in whatever sauce you choose.

Papudo

The northernmost town on this stretch of coast is known for its down-to-earth vibe and long, straight beach, **Playa Grande**. Papudo falls well short of paradisiacal, however: 1980s high-rises crowd the shore and the tiny town center is dusty and run-down. The coast road, Av Irarrázaval, first passes sheltered Playa Chica and then runs on to Playa Grande.

Time seems to have stood still in most of **Hotel Restaurant La Abeja** (☎ 033-791-116; Chorrillos 36; r incl breakfast CH$20,000-25,000), a pleasantly worn old house where vintage textured wallpaper and linoleum still reign supreme. Angle for a repainted room out the back with bright bedspreads (but tiny bathrooms). The motley crew of facilities includes a fridge, table tennis table and plant-filled patio. Ships' wheels and nets decorate the restaurant, which is famous for its empanadas (CH$900).

The huge ultramarine dining room at **Gran Azul** (☎ 033-791-584; Irarrázaval 86; mains CH$4500-5900; ⏰ noon-midnight Sep 18-Easter, 8pm-late Fri, noon-4pm & 7-11pm Sat & Sun Easter-Sep 18) fills up quickly in summer – classic Chilean seafood is the attraction. On the sand below, the same owners operate a cheaper, outdoor bar called **Banana** (snacks CH$950) which does empanadas, burgers

and drinks. **El Barco Rojo** (☎ 033-791-488; ⏰ 7-11:30pm Mon-Sat), a French-run restaurant that doubles as a bar, is perched on the outcrop between Papudo's two beaches in a crimson clapboard house.

Getting There & Away

Sol del Pacífico (☎ 032-275-2030) has services to all the above beach towns from Valparaíso and Viña, and TMV local buses run to Reñaca and Concón; see p133 for details.

Turbus (☎ 033-791-377; www.turbus.cl) operates four daily buses between Santiago and Papudo's main square (CH$5200, 2¾ hours) and Av Olegario Ovalle in Zapallar (CH$5200, three hours), six blocks from the beach.

SOUTH OF VALPARAÍSO
Quintay

As the sun sets over the Pacific, the craggy rocks protecting the tiny fishing cove of **Caleta Quintay** are stained a rich pink. Several of the colorful houses clustered here are seafood restaurants. One of the best places for sundowners and garlic prawns or *centolla* (king crab) is the terrace of **Restaurant Miramar** (☎ 032-236-2406; Costanera s/n; CH$5900-7900; ⏰ 10am-4pm Mon-Thu, 10am-10pm Fri & Sat). You can see your future dinner up-close on the guided scuba dives run by **Austral Divers** (☎ 02-492-7975; www.australdivers.cl), a PADI-certified dive company with an outpost here.

A signposted turnoff about 1.2km back down the road toward Valparaíso takes you down a 1.5km dirt road to the long, sweeping **Playa de Quintay**, one of the most unspoilt beaches in the region.

Quintay is an easy half-day trip from Valparaíso, but you can also stay up the road in Quintay proper at **Cabañas Bosquemar** (☎ 032-236-2093; www.bosquemarquintay.com; Jorge Montt 187; 2-person cabins CH$23,000). The small, basic cabins are and are kitted out with run-down furniture and foam mattresses and have no views, but they're an OK base for visiting the area.

Tranportes Quintay (☎ 032-236-2669) operates *taxi colectivos* between just outside Valparaíso's bus terminal and Quintay's main street (CH$1400, one hour), 500m from Caleta Quintay and 2.5km from Playa de Quintay. If you're coming by car, take Ruta 68 from Valparaíso or Viña toward Santiago; the turnoff is 18km south of Valpo, then it's another 23km to Quintay.

MIDDLE CHILE

CASABLANCA VALLEY WINERIES

A cool climate and temperatures that vary greatly from day to night have made this valley halfway between Santiago and Valparaíso one of Chile's best regions for fruity Chardonnays, Sauvignon Blancs and Pinots. Its well-organized wineries take food and wine tourism seriously, and many have on-site restaurants. There's no public transport to any of the wineries, but in a rental car you can easily blitz four or five of them in a day – most are on or around Ruta 68. Alternatively, contact the **Ruta del Vino de Casablanca** (☎ 032-274-3755; www.casablancavalley.cl; Punta Arenas 46, Casablanca) for tours. Note that servings at tastings tend to be generous – you can save money and sobriety by sharing them between two people.

The tours at **Viña Veramonte** (☎ 032-232-9924; www.veramonte.cl; Ruta 68 Km66; tours incl 3 pours CH$3500, tasting only CH$2000; ⊗ 9am-5pm Mon-Fri, 9am-2pm Sat & Sun) include plenty of background on wine production in the Casablanca Valley.

Tastings at **Viñedos Orgánicos Emiliana** (☎ 099-9327-4019; www.emiliana.cl; Ruta 68 Km61.5; tasting incl 4 pours CH$6500; ⊗ 10am-5pm) take place in a gorgeous slate-and-wood building looking out over the vines, grown organically using biodynamic principles.

The wines are indifferent, but there's no beating the views from **Viña Indómita** (☎ 032-275-4400; www.indomita.cl; Ruta 68 Km6; tour incl 3 pours CH$3000; ⊗ 11am-5pm), whose Hollywood-style sign on the hillside is easily spottable from afar.

Stop for early lunch at **House of Morandé** (☎ 032-275-4701; www.morande.cl; 4-step tasting menus CH$7000-22,000; ⊗ 10:30am-4pm Tue-Thu, Sat & Sun), which does unusual four-course tasting menus with wine pairings, but you need to order before 1pm.

The real show-stopper is **Viña Matetic** (☎ 032-232-3134; www.matetic.com; Fundo Rosario, Lagunillas; tours incl 2 reservas/1 reserva & 1 premium/4 reservas CH$7000/10,000/14,000; ⊗ 11am-3:30pm Tue-Sun), off highway F-962G, whose glass, wood and steel gravity-flow winery has attracted almost as much attention as the wines. Reservations several days in advance are essential.

Fabulous wines and peaceful surroundings come together at **Viña Casas del Bosque** (☎ 02-480-6900; www.casasdelbosque.cl; tours CH$6000, tastings incl 2/3 pours CH$4000/5000; ⊗ tours 10:30am, 12:30pm, 2:30pm & 4pm). The restaurant is open from 12:30pm to 5:30pm Tuesday to Sunday, and there's a harvest tour in late March and April.

Other Casablanca wineries open to the public include **William Cole Vineyards** (☎ 032-275-4444; www.williamcolevineyards.cl), **Catrala** (www.catrala.cl) and **Viña Mar** (☎ 032-275-4300; www.vinamar.cl).

Isla Negra

The spectacular setting on a windswept ocean headland makes it easy to understand why **Isla Negra** (☎ 035-461-284; www.fundacionneruda.org; Poeta Neruda s/n; admission by guided tour only in English/Spanish CH$3500/3000; ⊗ 10am-6pm Tue-Sun) was Pablo Neruda's favorite house. Built by the poet when he became rich in the 1950s, it was stormed by soldiers just days after the 1973 military coup when Neruda was dying of cancer. Overenthusiastic commercialization gives a definite Disney-Neruda vibe to visits here: indifferent guides quick-march you through the house, and they'd rather you lingered in the gift shop than over the extraordinary collections of shells, ships in bottles, nautical instruments, colored glass and books. Despite this, the seemingly endless house (Neruda kept adding to it) and its contents are still awe-inspiring. There's no one to stop you taking your time on the terrace outside, however,

where Neruda's tomb and that of his third wife, Matilde, overlook the sea. Reservations are essential in high season.

Isla Negra is an easy half-day trip from Valparaíso: **Pullman Bus Lago Peñuela** (☎ 032-222-4025) leaves from Valparaíso's bus terminal every 10 to 15 minutes (CH$2600, 1½ hours). **Pullman Bus** (☎ 600-320-3200; www.pullman.cl) comes here direct from Santiago's Terminal de Buses Alameda (CH$6000, 1½ hours, every 30 minutes).

PARQUE NACIONAL LA CAMPANA

Looming large within this **national park** (☎ 033-441-342; adult/child CH$1500/500; ⊗ 9am-5:30pm Sat-Thu, 9am-4:30pm Fri) are two of the highest mountains in the coastal range, **Cerro El Roble** (2200m) and **Cerro La Campana** (1880m), which Charles Darwin climbed in 1834. Visitor numbers have risen since then, but

La Campana remains relatively uncrowded despite its closeness to Santiago. It's subdivided into two main sectors: Conaf's main administration station is at **Granizo**, near Olmué, 1.5km before the southwest entrance side of the park; and there are sometimes rangers at **Ocoa**, in the north of the park.

In geological structure and vegetation, most of the park's 80 sq km resemble the dry, jagged scrubland of the mountains of Southern California. The park protects stands of the deciduous roble de Santiago (*Nothofagus obliqua*) and is known for its 20 sq km grove of Chilean palms (*Jubaea chilensis*). There's excellent hiking to be had here: profuse wildflowers and a reliable water supply make spring the best time for a visit. Paved access roads lead to the two entrances, but there are no roads within the park.

Sights & Activities

Most people come to make like Darwin and ascend Cerro La Campana: on clear days its summit affords spectacular views stretching from the Pacific to the Andean summit of Aconcagua. From the Granizo park entrance (373m above sea level), the **Sendero Andinista** climbs 1455m in only 7km – mercifully, most of the hike is in shade, and there are three water sources en route. Prior to the final vertiginous ascent you pass a granite wall with a plaque commemorating Darwin's climb. Figure at least four hours to the top and three hours back down.

The 5.5km **Sendero Los Peumos** connects the Granizo entrance to the **Sendero Amasijo**, which winds for another 7km through a palm-studded canyon to Ocoa. The whole hike takes five hours, one way. The southern part of Sendero Amasijo plunges down into Cajón Grande, a canyon with deciduous forests of southern beech. From Ocoa, **Sendero La Cascada** leads 6km to **Salto de la Cortadera**, an attractive 30m waterfall that is best during the spring runoff.

Sleeping

Conaf runs two basic 23-tent **campsites** (CH$6000) with toilets, barbecue areas and cold-water showers at Granizo and Cajón Grande, further south. Backcountry camping is not permitted. In really dry weather, only a handful of campers are permitted at a time to reduce the risk of fires. You need to bring all food – and,

depending on the weather, drinking water – supplies with you.

Getting There & Away

Ranger presence is sporadic at Ocoa, so it makes more sense to go through the Granizo entrance. Buses go regularly from Errázuriz in Valparaíso to Limache (CH$800), from where local buses and *colectivos* continue to Olmué, and some to Granizo. Talca-based **El Caminante** (☎ 071-197-0096; www.trekkingchile.com) operates guided hiking trips to the park.

The park is accessible by car from Santiago (160km) and Viña del Mar/Valparaíso (60km). Head north from Santiago on the Panamericana (CH-5), take the turnoff to Tiltil and continue to Olmué, 4km from Granizo. From Viña and Valparaíso take the Autopista Troncal Sur (CH-62) past Quilpué and Villa Alemana to Limache, where you head east to Olmué.

ACONCAGUA VALLEY

If you arrive in Chile overland from Mendoza, the fertile Valle de Aconcagua is the first scenery you see. It's watered by the Río Aconcagua, which flows west from the highest mountain in the Americas, Cerro Aconcagua (6959m), just over the Argentine border. Scenic highway CH-60 runs the length of the valley and across the Andes to Mendoza.

LOS ANDES
☎ 034 / pop 61,627

They couldn't have chosen a better name: the mountains loom large and lovely over this foothill town. Indeed, most of Los Andes' visitors are on their way to ski the slopes at the Portillo resort near the Argentine border. But skiers aren't the only ones the Andes have inspired. Two of Chile's most famous daughters lived here: Nobel Prize–winning poet Gabriela Mistral, who taught at the school; and Saint Teresa de los Andes, who became a nun and died here. The town is a pleasant stop-off but there's not enough here to justify a visit in itself.

Orientation & Information

The highway to the Argentine border (CH-60, the Carretera Internacional) runs across the north of Los Andes, where it's called Av Argentina. The bus station lies north of it, eight blocks from the town center. Esmeralda, the main commercial street, runs along the south side of the Plaza de Armas.

Banco Santander (☎ 421-061; O'Higgins 348; ☒ 9am-2pm)

Hospital San Juan de Diós (☎ 490-300; www.hosla .cl; Av Argentina 315 & Hermanos Clark) Public hospital.

Municipal tourist office (☎ 902-525; Av Santa Teresa 333; ☒ 10am-6pm Tue-Sun) Helpful tourist office near the archaeological museum.

Post office (☎ 800-267-736; Av Esmeralda 387; ☒ 9am-2pm & 3:30-6pm Mon-Fri, 10am-1pm Sat)

Telecabinas (☎ 405-738; Maipú 283; per hr CH$400; ☒ 9am-10pm Mon-Sat) Fast internet and cheap international calls.

Sights & Activities

Aside from the views, Los Andes is short on sights. Its small **Museo Arqueológico** (☎ 420-115; Av Santa Teresa 398; admission CH$1000; ☒ 10am-8pm Tue-Sat) contains some interesting pre-Columbian pottery displayed in dusty exhibit cases.

The award for the most unintentionally bizarre museum displays in Middle Chile goes to the **Museo Antiguo Monasterio del Espíritu Santo** (☎ 421-304; Av Santa Teresa 389; ☒ 9am-1pm & 3-6pm Mon-Fri, 10am-6pm Sat & Sun). Mannequins in nuns' habits re-create scenes from Santa Teresa's life: she took her vows in this ex-convent then died of typhus, aged 19. Also celebrated is folk saint and preteen rebel Laura Vicuña, who willed herself to die because her widowed mother took a married lover.

Sleeping & Eating

Hotel Don Ambrosio (☎ 425-496; Freire 472; s/d incl breakfast CH$16,000/22,000; ☐) The cheapest rooms in town are dark and a bit poky, but they're clean, perfectly serviceable and come with cable TV and free wi-fi. It's on a quiet street two blocks from the Plaza de Armas.

Hotel Plaza (☎ 421-929; www.hotelplazalosandes.cl, in Spanish; Rodríguez 368; s/d CH$25,520/29,040) With its beige bedspreads and varnished wood furnishings, there's something very 1970s about Los Andes's upmarket option (a very relative claim to fame). Rooms look out onto the car park but they're big, airy and light-filled, and have heating and cable TV. The on-site restaurant has good-value set lunch menus.

La Toscana (☎ 429-000; O'Higgins 289; set lunch CH$1900, large pizzas CH$4900-6500; ☒ noon-4pm & 7-10pm Mon-Sat) Chrome tables and pale formica floors give this little pizza joint a bright, modern

look. Locals hungry for its thin-crust pizzas keep the waiter on his toes at night.

Donde El Guatón (☎ 423-596; Av Santa Teresa 240; mains CH$2850-4900; ☒ noon-1am Mon-Sun) Los Andes' most popular parrilla gets pretty hectic on weekends when local families pile into its close-packed dining room hungry for the mixed grills, *plateada* (stewed beef) and *pasteles* (mashed-potato-topped pies) it does so well.

La Table de France (☎ 406-319; Camino Internacional Km3, El Sauce; mains CH$4800-8900; ☒ 1-4pm & 8-11pm Tue-Sat, 1-6pm Sun) Rolling countryside is the only thing between the Andes and the sweeping terrace of this French-run restaurant on a hill 3km out of town. Duck, rabbit, wild boar and even ostrich satisfy creative carnivores, while dishes such as goat's cheese gnocchi or kingklip in Carmenere mean vege- and fishetarians aren't neglected.

Getting There & Away

Los Andes is the last (or first) Chilean town on the route between Santiago and Mendoza in Argentina – buses pass through its **Rodoviario Internacional** (☎ 408-188; Av Carlos Díaz 111), eight blocks northwest of the Plaza de Armas on the northern extension of Av Santa Teresa.

Ahumada (☎ 421-227; www.busesahumada.cl) and **Pullman Bus** (☎ 425-973; www.pullman.cl) have regular services to Santiago's terminal San Borja (CH$2800, two hours, hourly). **Buses Tas Choapa** (☎ 438-238) stops at Portillo ski resort en route to Mendoza (CH$9000, six hours, four daily). Other companies serving Mendoza include **El Rápido** (☎ 779-0310; www.elrapidoint.com.ar).

PORTILLO

Set around the spectacular alpine lake of Laguna del Inca on the Argentine border, **Portillo** (☎ 02-263-0606; www.skiportillo.com; daily ski pass adult/child CH$28,500/18,000) is one of Chile's favorite ski resorts. It's not just amateurs who love its ultrasteep slopes: the US, Austrian and Italian national teams use it as a base for their summer training and the 200km/h speed barrier was first broken here. Some of its terrain is apt for novices but it's hard-core powder junkies that really thrive. Altitudes range from 2590m to 3310m on its 19 runs, the longest of which measures 3.2km. The slopes are prepared daily, apart from expert runs like Cóndor, La Garganta and Roca Jack, which are left with their natural ice pack.

MIDDLE CHILE

Accommodation in Portillo is geared around week-long stays, and much cheaper choices are available 69km west in Los Andes. Portillo's most luxurious option is the **Hotel Portillo** (r per person per week full board US$2690-3200), which has smallish doubles with views of the lake or valley. Bunk-bed accommodation is available at the resort's other two lodging options. The **Octagon Lodge** (r per person per week full board US$1390) has four-bunk rooms with bathrooms and draws a slightly older crowd, while the **Inca Lodge** (r per person per week full board US$700) has a bit more of a backpacker vibe to it. You can pay extra to have rooms to yourself at the Octagon and Inca lodges and regardless of where you stay you can use the heated outdoor swimming pool, gym, yoga classes, skating rink, games room, small cinema and babysitting services for free. Shops, an internet café and a bar and disco are also on-site.

Driving to Portillo takes one to two hours, depending on road conditions.

Getting There & Away

The Santiago–Mendoza services run by **Buses Tas Choapa** (☎ 02-438-238) stop at Portillo – if there are seats you can catch them to Los Andes, Santiago or Mendoza. An alternative is provided by private ski transfers (they usually rent gear, too).

Manzur Expediciones (Map pp84-5; ☎ 02-777-4284; Dr Sótero del Rio 475, Oficina 507, Centro; round-trip to Portillo CH$25,000, with hotel pick-up CH$30,000). Leaves from Plaza Italia (Baquedano metro station) and also rents gear.

Ski Ahorro (Map p99; ☎ 02-229-4532; www.skiahorro .cl, in Spanish; Av Las Condes 9143, Las Condes; round-trip to Portillo minimum 5 passengers CH$16,000).

SOUTHERN HEARTLAND

South of Santiago, squeezed between the Andes and the coastal cordillera, the central valley is Chile's fruit bowl, with a Mediterranean climate and endless orchards and vineyards – this region produces most of Chile's wine. The Andes in this sector are spectacular, with deciduous beech forests climbing their slopes and broad gravel-bedded rivers descending into the valley. Most of the large settlements here are unattractive agricultural service towns that make good bases for excursions to the hinterland.

RANCAGUA
☎ 072 / pop 231,945

Copper and cowboys might be an unlikely combination, but sprawling industrial Rancagua is synonymous with both. The nearby El Teniente copper mine has driven the city's economic success, but it's the rip-roaring antics of the annual rodeo season that people get more excited. Late March and early April is the time for bucking broncos; the rest of the year there's little to do in Rancagua itself, though it makes a useful base for visiting the Reserva Nacional Río de los Cipreses, the fascinating deserted mine at Sewell and Chapa Verde ski resort. Rancagua's standard grid centers on Plaza de los Héroes, which is intersected by Estado and Independencia.

Information

Afex (☎ 227-003; Mall del Centro, cnr Cuevas & Campos, Local 009; ◷ 10am-9pm Mon-Sat, 11am-9pm Sun) Currency-exchange office.

BancoEstado (☎ 745-200; Independencia 666; ◷ 9am-2pm) One of several banks with ATMs along Independencia.

Conaf (☎ 204-645; www.conaf.cl; Cuevas 480, 1st fl; ◷ 8:30am-5:30pm Mon-Fri) Advice on getting to nearby national parks.

Entel (☎ 320-006; Independencia 486; ◷ 8:30am-9pm Mon-Fri, 9am-6:30pm Sat) Long-distance calls.

Hospital Regional (☎ 338-000; www.hospitalranca gua.cl; O'Higgins 611) Public hospital.

Lava Express (☎ 241-738; Av San Martín 270; per kg CH$1400; ◷ 9:30am-1pm & 3:30-8pm Mon-Sat)

Plaza Online (☎ 320-944; Edificio Plaza Oriente 390, Plaza de los Héroes; per hr CH$500; ◷ 9am-11pm Mon-Sat, 10am-10pm Sun) Fast internet.

Post office (☎ 800-267-736; Campos 322; ◷ 9am-6:45pm Mon-Fri, 10am-1pm Sat)

Sernatur (☎ 230-413; Germán Riesco 277, 1st fl; ◷ 8:30am-6pm Mon-Fri) Helpful staff run this office one block east of Plaza de los Héroes.

Sights

The austere white **Iglesia de la Merced** (cnr Estado & Cuevas) was built of adobe in 1743. Chile's liberator Bernardo O'Higgins used the bell tower as a lookout during the 1814 Battle of Rancagua. Another religious landmark, the peach-and-white **Iglesia Catedral** (cnr Estado & Plaza de los Héroes) overlooks the Plaza de los Héroes.

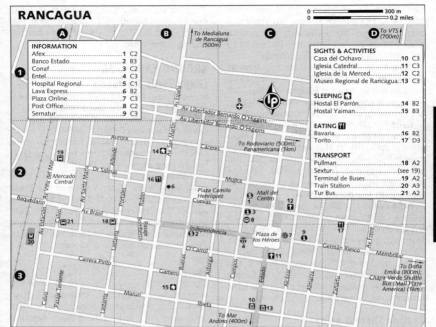

RANCAGUA

0 ———— 300 m
0 ———— 0.2 miles

INFORMATION
Afex.................................1 C2
Banco Estado.....................2 B3
Conaf................................3 C2
Entel.................................4 C3
Hospital Regional...............5 C1
Lava Express......................6 B2
Plaza Online......................7 C2
Post Office.........................8 C2
Sernatur............................9 C3

SIGHTS & ACTIVITIES
Casa del Ochavo...............10 C3
Iglesia Catedral.................11 C3
Iglesia de la Merced..........12 C2
Museo Regional de Rancagua..13 C3

SLEEPING 🏠
Hostal El Parrón................14 B2
Hostal Yaiman...................15 B3

EATING 🍴
Bavaria.............................16 B2
Torito...............................17 D3

TRANSPORT
Pullman............................18 A2
Sextur...........................(see 19)
Terminal de Buses.............19 A2
Train Station.....................20 A3
Tur Bus............................21 A2

MIDDLE CHILE

The centerpiece of the plaza is a tired-looking statue dedicated to O'Higgins.

From the plaza the quiet pedestrian street Estado leads south past well-maintained colonial dwellings to the two-building **Museo Regional de Rancagua** (☎ 221-524; www.museo rancagua.cl; Estado 685; CH$600, free Tue, Sat & Sun; ✆ 10am-6pm Tue-Fri, 9am-1pm Sat & Sun). Head up the courtyard stairs in the main house for small but thoughtfully displayed exhibits on local archaeological finds, indigenous culture, traditional instruments and the copper industry, ingots and all. Temporary art exhibitions go on downstairs. Over the road in the **Casa del Ochavo** they've tried to re-create an 18th-century Chilean home.

Festivals & Events
From late March to early April, the **Campeonato Nacional de Rodeo** (National Rodeo Championship; ☎ 221-286; www.rodeochileno.cl; Medialuna de Rancagua, cnr Av España & Germán Ibarra; admission CH$75,000-12,000) takes place. At night, traditional Chilean *cueca* dances are held and a market of regional foods and crafts is set up in the Plaza de los Héroes. Make hotel reservations early if you want to

stay in Rancagua at this time; otherwise, it's an easy day trip from Santiago.

Sleeping & Eating
You get notoriously little bang for your buck at Rancagua's hotels, mainly because of the guaranteed trade generated by the nearby copper mine.

Hostal Yaiman (☎ 641-773; Bueras 655; s/d incl breakfast CH$13,500/27,000, without bathroom CH$10,500/21,000) A regular clientele of traveling workers and salespeople mean this converted family house is often full. Its clean but drab rooms have strangely carpeted walls and cable TV.

Hostal El Parrón (☎ 758-550; www.hostalelparron .cl; San Martín 135; s/d incl breakfast CH$18,0000/24,000) With their butter-yellow walls, springy beds and big windows, rooms in this new hotel are bright but homey. The only downside is the location: an uninspiring avenue close to the bus station.

Mar Andino (☎ 645-400; www.hotelmarandino.cl; Bulnes 370; s/d CH$36,740/60,400; ✆ 🖥 🏊) Hats off to the person who realized that Rancagua needed a decent hotel. Rooms are spacious with rustic-looking wooden beds topped with moss-green throws, gleaming bathrooms and cable TV. The garden is bare but the small pool is a boon. So is the slick restaurant, which saves you walking the 10 blocks to the city center along Av Cachapoal.

Bavaria (☎ 241-241; Av San Martín 255; sandwiches CH$1500-3200, mains CH$3600-5000; ◷ 9:30am-4pm & 7-11:30pm Mon-Sat, noon-4pm & 7-10pm Sun) You can wash down fries and a steak with a cold *schop* at the local branch of this national chain.

Torito (☎ 222-704; Zañartu 323; mains CH$4500-5900; ◷ 11am-1am) Mixed grills and generous steaks are the specialty at this enormous family-oriented parrilla, but there's also salmon and sea bass, steamed, fried or grilled. The live music on weekends can be as cheesy as the topping on the *paila marina*.

Doña Emilia (☎ 239-483; Diego de Almagro 440; set lunch CH$5900, mains CH$5500-7900; ◷ noon-4pm & 8pm-midnight Mon-Fri, 8pm-midnight Sat) A far cry from the home-style cooking of downtown Rancagua (both geographically and conceptually), the beautifully presented French and Spanish fare here has turned Doña Emilia into a local foodie landmark. Book a table on the terrace overlooking the garden.

Getting There & Away
BUS
Rancagua has a confusing number of bus terminals: there's the big **Rodoviario** (O'Higgins 0484), northeast of the town center; the downtown **Terminal de Buses** (☎ 225-425; Dr Salinas 1165); and central, individual terminals used by each company. You need a taxi to get from the Rodoviario but the others are within walking distance of the town center.

From their terminals in the west of town, **Tur Bus** (☎ 230-341; www.turbus.cl; O'Carrol 1175) and **Pullman** (☎ 227-756; www.pullman.cl; cnr Av Brasil & Lastarria) have at least one hourly service to Santiago (CH$2200, 1¼ hours) and several daily services to cities further south, including Curicó (CH$2100, 1¾ hours), Talca (CH$3400, 3½ hours), Chillán (CH$6200, 4½ hours) and Puerto Montt (CH$15,700, 13 hours).

From the main Terminal de Buses, **Sextur** (☎ 231-342) leaves for Pichilemu (CH$3000, three hours) daily at 6:40am.

TRAIN
From the EFE **train station** (☎ 600-585-5000; cnr Av Estación & Carrera Pinto) there are seven daily

Terrasur trains north to Santiago (CH$5000, one hour) and south to Talca (CH$6000, two hours) and Chillán (CH$9500, 3½ hours), among other stops.

AROUND RANCAGUA
Chapa Verde Ski Resort
Some 50km northeast of Rancagua via a mostly paved highway, **Chapa Verde** (☎ 072-294-255; www.chapaverde.cl; Av Miguel Ramírez 665, Rancagua; daily ski pass adult/child CH$16,000/9000) is a low-key ski resort originally created for employees of Codelco (the national copper company). It has 22 long runs served by 10 lifts.

Shuttle buses (CH$5000, one hour) leave from outside the Líder Vecino at the Plaza America mall (Av Miguel Ramírez 665), 2km east of the center of Rancagua, from 9am to 9:30am on weekdays or 8am to 9:30am on weekends. Return buses leave at 5pm. Private vehicles are not allowed.

Sewell
Up to 15,000 people once lived at **Sewell** (www.sewell.cl, in Spanish), an atmospheric ghost town 55km northeast of Rancagua. Between 1904 and 1975 it housed mining families from El Teniente, the world's largest subsurface copper mine, and has been preserved as a monument to the copper workers and their way of life. Built on a steep slope at 2600m, its distinctive, brightly colored houses are connected by stairways rather than roads.

You can only visit the town and El Teniente on organized tours run by **VTS** (off Map p145; ☎ 072-210-290; www.vts.cl; Manuel Montt 192, Rancagua; tour in Spanish of mine & town incl transport from Rancagua adult/child CH$20,000/15,000; ◷ 10am Fri-Sun). Tours leave from both Santiago and Rancagua, and include a trip down into the still-functioning mine, a tour of the town itself and a visit to the Museo de la Gran Minería de Cobre, a museum housed in a beautiful 1940s modernist building.

Reserva Nacional Río de los Cipreses
Set in the Andean foothills 40km east of Rancagua, this little-visited 370 sq km **park** (☎ 072-297-505; adult/child CH$2000/1000; ◷ 8:30am-8pm Tue-Sun) contains a variety of volcanic landforms, hanging glacial valleys, waterfalls and fluvial landscapes. The park ranges in altitude from 900m to the 4900m summit of **Volcán El Palomo**.

As its name suggests, the park is home to forests of fragrant cypress, olivillo (*Aextoxicon punctatum*) and other native tree species. Among the animals living here are pumas, guanacos, two fox species, viscachas, condors and tricahues, Chile's largest native parrots. Indigenous peoples first settled here between 6000 and 3500 BC; rock drawings from this time remain in several sites in the upper canyon. You need to register with Conaf rangers to visit them.

The park entrance and Conaf rangers' office is at the north end of the reserve, along a dirt road. About 6km on, and accessible by car, is **Ranchillos campsite** (7-person campsites CH$5000), which has drinkable water, toilets and cold showers. Bring all food supplies with you.

A track just beyond Ranchillos continues 6km to **Maitenes**, the trailhead for the 20km hike to **Urriola**, which passes through cypress forests and gives you great views of some of the mountains in the park. Count on at least six hours to get there from Ranchillos; there's a basic refuge at Urriola where you can spend the night.

There's no public transport direct to the reserve. To get here, catch a *taxi colectivo* from Rancagua's Rodoviario to Coya (CH$5000), from where you can get a taxi to the park entrance or to the campsite itself (CH$7000). To drive here from Rancagua, take the Carretera El Cobre toward Coya and Pangal, cross the Perales bridge over the Río Cachapoal and continue 12km along the dirt road toward Puente Chacayes.

SANTA CRUZ
☎ 072 / pop 31,391

You're a major arms dealer and you love the Napa Valley wine scene. You can't leave Chile because the US Customs Service has put a half-million-dollar reward on your head for dodgy dealings with Iraq. So what do you do? Why, pour your own millions into Chile's top wine region and give Napa a run for its money – or at least that's what local bad boy Carlos Cardoen has in mind. His home town of Santa Cruz is now the epicenter of Chile's winemaking and wine-touring scenes. Aside from a pretty main square, the town itself is unremarkable, although a major casino being built at the time of research might move Santa Cruz into the fast lane. The valley surrounding it, however, has a spectacular Mediterranean-style beauty to it, with low hills lined with row

upon row of vines interrupted occasionally by traditional finca houses.

Orientation & Information

The highway between San Fernando and Bucalemu runs east–west through Santa Cruz, forming its main street, Rafael Casanova, which borders the south side of the Plaza de Armas. Parallel streets Nicolás Palacios and Besoain run along the east and west of the plaza, and eventually merge to form the highway leading north to Pichilemu.

BancoEstado (☎ 745-874; Besoain 24; 🕑 9am-2pm Mon-Fri) Has an ATM and changes dollars.

Cibermanía (☎ 821-527; Av Errázuriz 559; per hr CH$500; 🕑 11am-10pm) One of several internet cafés on the main avenue.

Post office (☎ 800-267-736; Besoain 96; 🕑 9am-2pm & 3-6pm Mon-Fri, 10am-1pm Sat)

Sights & Activities

Most people come to Santa Cruz to visit the surrounding **Colchagua Valley vineyards** (see boxed text, p148), which you can do independently or on organized wine tours.

Along with dealing arms, Carlos Cardoen has made a name for himself as a hardcore collector. The fruit of his passion is the incredible **Museo de Colchagua** (☎ 821-050; www.museocolchagua.cl; Errázuriz 145; adult/child CH$3000/1000; 🕑 10am-6pm), the largest private museum in Chile. The collection includes pre-Columbian anthropomorphic ceramics from all over Latin America; weapons, religious artifacts and Mapuche silver; and a whole room of *huasos* cowboy gear. Steam-driven machinery, winemaking equipment and a re-creation of Colchagua's original train station fill the huge courtyard, and adjoining display rooms showcase old carriages and vintage cars.

The most novel way to try the local wine is aboard the **Tren del Vino** (☎ 02-470-7403; www.trendelvino.cl; incl transport to & from Santiago CH$62,000; 🕑 8am Sat), a steam-train tour that leaves every Saturday from San Fernando station. You start the wine tasting on board, visit a vineyard and have lunch there, then wind up at the Colchagua museum before returning to Santiago by bus.

Festivals & Events

Santa Cruz celebrates the grape harvest each March with the lively **Fiesta de la Vendimia**. Local wineries set up stands in the Plaza

MIDDLE CHILE

MIDDLE CHILE

COLCHAGUA VALLEY'S RUTA DEL VINO

With around 20 wineries open to the public, the Colchagua Valley is Chile's biggest and best established wine region. Its deep loamy soils, abundant water, dry air, bright sunshine and cool nights have given rise to some of the country's best reds: Cabernet Sauvignon, Merlot and Carmenere make up most of the grapes, but top-notch Malbecs are also appearing.

Several vineyards are a short taxi ride from Santa Cruz, the region's hub, but it makes sense to hire a car to get to the further-flung ones. Alternatively, you can take a tour with the **Ruta del Vino** (☎ 823-199; www.rutadelvino.cl; Plaza de Armas 298, Santa Cruz), though prices are high and you have to do a full tour at each winery.

At third-generation family-owned vineyard **Viu Manent** (☎ 072-858-751; www.viumanent.cl; Carretera del Vino Km37; tours incl 3 pours CH$10,000, premium tours incl 5 pours CH$20,000, 3-pour tasting CH$5000; ☯ tours 10:30am, noon, 3pm & 4:30pm Tue-Sun), tours involve a carriage ride through 80-year-old vineyards and an insightful visit to the winery.

The most exclusive setup in Colchagua is **Casa Apostolle Clos Apalta Winery** (☎ 072-321-803; www.closapalta.cl; tour incl 2 pours CH$20,000), which produces a single premium wine from hand-picked, hand-separated grapes. Open by reservation only.

As well as wine tours, **MontGras** (☎ 072-823-242; www.montgras.cl; Camino Isla de Yáquil s/n, Palmilla; tours incl 2 pours CH$8000, 2/4/6 reservas tastings CH$5000/10,000/15,000; ☯ tastings 10:30am-6pm Mon-Fri, 10:30am-4:30pm Sat, tours 11am, 12:30pm, 3:30pm & 5pm Mon-Fri, 11am, 12:30pm & 3:30pm Sat) offers horseback riding, hiking, zip lining and mountain biking, all on the vineyard.

Biodynamic growing techniques involving insects and even ground cow horn are explained at organic vineyard **Emiliana** (☎ 099-9225-5679; www.emiliana.cl; Camino Lo Moscoso s/n, Placilla; tours incl 4 pours CH$8400, tastings per pour CH$1000-2350; ☯ tours 10:30am, noon, 3:30pm & 4:30pm).

Other noteworthy wineries:

Estampa (☎ 02-202-7000; www.estampa.com)
Montes (☎ 072-825-417; www.monteswines.com)
Viña Bisquertt (☎ 072-821-792; www.bisquertt.cl)
Viña Casa Silva (☎ 072-710-204; www.casasilva.cl)
Viña Santa Laura (☎ 072-823-179; www.laurahartwig.cl)

---

de Armas, a harvest queen is crowned, and there is singing and folk dancing all round.

Sleeping & Eating

Hostal del Valle (☎ 821-297; www.valledecolchagua.cl/hostaldelvalle; 21 de Mayo 0317; d incl breakfast CH$35,000, s/d without bathroom CH$15,000/27,000; 💻) Peach-colored walls and feather comforters warm up the otherwise plain rooms at this small hotel a couple of blocks east of the Plaza de Armas, on the corner of Av Las Toscas. Cable TV and wi-fi are included.

Hostal D'Vid (☎ 821-269; www.dvid.cl; Alberto Edwards 205; d incl breakfast CH$18,000, s without bathroom CH$18,000; 🅿 💻) At this spanking new hostel, crisp cotton bedclothes embroidered with geometric designs coordinate perfectly with the lime-green walls. Beds are well sprung, bathrooms are big and there's cable TV, wi-fi and a lovely garden around a pool. Best of all, however, is the friendly, down-to-earth help you get from the owners.

Casa Silva (☎ 710-204; www.casasilva.cl; Hijuela Norte s/n, San Fernando; d incl breakfast CH$108,650-137,800) Maple trees shade the stone-tiled courtyard, complete with fountain, at the heart of this 100-year-old house on the edge of a vineyard, near Ruta 5 Km132. The sumptuous rooms ooze old-world style with their padded fabric wall-coverings, old prints, and antique wardrobes and bedsteads (many are four-posters).

Café Domo (☎ 824-950; General del Canto 56; ☯ 9am-7pm) Whether you're getting over the wine tastings of the day before or caffeining yourself up for the ones ahead, the huge flavored coffees here are sure to give you a buzz.

Sushi Restaurant (☎ 822-059; General de Canto 5; rolls CH$2400-3900; ☯ noon-4pm & 7:30pm-midnight Mon-Fri, 7:30pm-midnight Sat) With its pale, stripped-wood bar and stools, this tiny Japanese restaurant on the corner of the Plaza de Armas looks surprisingly authentic. The sushi, though nothing special, is fresh and well made.

Alma Campesina (☎ 823-882; Ramón Sanfurgo 148; mains CH$3600-5000; ⏱ noon-3:30pm & 7:30-11pm Mon-Sat, noon-4pm Sun) A classy take on country is the idea at this cavernous restaurant, where simple steaks, ribs and grilled fish are served at rustic wooden tables. It's above a shop of the same name – the stairs are round the side of the building.

La Casita de Barreales (☎ 824-468; Barreales s/n; mains CH$4600-6100; ⏱ 12:30-3pm & 8-11pm Tue-Sat, 12:30-3:30pm Sun) Local foodies are unanimous: the subtle Peruvian ceviches and *chaufas* (a Peruvian take on Chinese-style fried rice) here are the most exciting thing to arrive on Santa Cruz's tables in years. The secret is definitely out – the warmly lit adobe house fills up quickly on weekends so try to book.

La Cava de Don Miguel (☎ 858-751; www.viu manent.cl; Carretera del Vino Km37; mains CH$6900-8900; ⏱ noon-6pm Tue-Sun) A century-old family recipe book inspired the menu at this hushed, candlelit restaurant in the old *estancia* house at Viu Manent winery. Outside, a sizzling grill provides the hunks of barbecued beef and chicken served at tables on the shaded terrace.

Getting There & Away

At the time of writing, all long-distance buses operated from the open-air **Terminal de Buses Santa Cruz** (Rafael Casanova 478), about four blocks west of the Plaza de Armas, but there were plans to build a new terminal nearby. **Buses Nilahué** (☎ 825-582; www.busesnila hue.com) connects Santa Cruz with Pichilemu (CH$2000, two hours, two hourly), as well as San Fernando (CH$1000, 30 minutes, two hourly) and Santiago (CH$4000, four hours, two hourly). **Buses Jet-Sur** (☎ 02-778-7080) go to Bucalemu (CH$2000, four hours, hourly). To get to Lolol (CH$800, 30 minutes), take one of the local buses from opposite the bus station.

DETOUR TO LOLOL

Beautifully preserved colonial houses make sleepy **Lolol**, 23km southeast of Santa Cruz, a picture-perfect side trip. The main two or three streets are fronted by long galleries supported by wooden columns and overhung by terracotta roofs. Once you've had a wander, you can take time out with a book in the quiet Plaza de Armas.

PICHILEMU

☎ 072 / pop 12,847

Wave gods and goddesses brave the icy waters of Chile's unofficial surf capital year-round, while mere beach-going mortals fill its long black sands December through March. All but the major streets here are still unpaved, which lends a dusty, ramshackle air to the town. Its wealthy early-20th-century founder, Agustín Ross Edwards, had quite a different image in mind: an upmarket beach resort based around a now crumbling (but soon-to-be-restored) casino on an outcrop overlooking the sands.

The westernmost part of Pichi juts out into the sea, forming **La Puntilla**, the closest surfing spot to town. Fronting the town center to the northeast is calm **Playa Principal** (main beach), while south is the longer and rougher **Infiernillo**, known for its more dangerous waves and fast tow. The best surfing in the area is at **Punta de Lobos**, 6km south of Pichi proper, which you need to drive or hitchhike to.

Although Pichilemu itself isn't particularly attractive, the laid-back vibe, great waves and surprisingly energetic summer nightlife make it easy to see why it's so popular with visiting board-riders.

Orientation & Information

On the map, Pichilemu opens butterfly-like into two rough parts: the town center, to the east, and the sector along Infiernillo, to the west. Road I-50 from San Fernando feeds through the northeast of town, becoming Av Ross, which cuts south then west. It intersects with looping seafront Av Costanera. Comercio leads south off Av Ross to Punta de Lobos and Bucalemu.

BancoEstado (☎ 745-650; Errázuriz 397; ⏱ 9am-2pm Mon-Fri) ATM and currency exchange.

Oficina de Información Turística (☎ 841-017; www .pichilemu.cl; Municipalidad, Angel Gaete 365; ⏱ 9am-6pm) Basic information about accommodations and events is available from this office within the main municipal building.

Post office (☎ 800-267-736; Av Ortúzar 568; ⏱ 9:30am-4pm Mon-Fri, 9:30-noon Sat)

Surfnet (☎ 841-324; Aníbal Pinto 105; per hr CH$400; ⏱ 9am-11:30pm Mon-Sun) Cheap phone calls and internet access.

Activities

Surfing (see p74) is what most people come here for – you can hire boards, wetsuits (a must) and take classes with internationally certified instructors at **Lobos del Pacífico** (☎ 098- 461-3634; www.lobosdelpacific.cl; Av Costanera 720; full-day board hire CH$4000-5000, 2hr classes CH$5000), at Infiernillo. It's also tipped to be the best board repair shop in Pichi. Another reliable surf school is **Escuela de Surf Manzana 54** (☎ 099-574-5984; www.manzana54.cl; Av Costanera s/n; half-/full-day board & gear hire CH$3500/6000, 2hr classes CH$10,000) on La Puntilla beach, where conditions are good for beginners.

Sleeping & Eating

Book well ahead at the following places during summer, and enquire about discounts during winter and fall.

Hotel Chile España (☎ 841-270; www.chileespana .cl, in Spanish; Av Ortúzar 255; s/d/tr incl breakfast CH$11,000/22,000/33,000; ▯) Once a popular surfer hangout, this central budget hotel now mainly caters to Chilean pensioners on package getaways. Rooms, if you can get one, are clean but cramped because of the new bathrooms they've squeezed into corners, and they open onto a long, plant-filled patio.

Pichilemu Surf Hostal (☎ 842-350; www.pichile musurfhostal.com; Eugenio D Lyra 167; s/d/tr/q CH$15,000/ 24,000/30,000/34,000) Attic-style lookouts with incredible sea views top all the rooms at this unusually designed clapboard hostel opposite Infiernillo beach. Each has firm beds, pale linens and huge framed photos of the nearby waves. You get expert wave advice from the windsurfing Dutch owner, Marcel, and a proper eggs-and-toast or muesli-and-yoghurt brekkie at his restaurant over the road.

Posada Punta de Lobos (☎ 099-8154-1106; www .posadapuntadelobos.cl; d/tr/q incl breakfast CH$48,000/ 54,000/60,000, 4-/10-person cabins CH$60,000/90,000) Pines and eucalypti surround the boxy, modular structures of this self-styled surf lodge, set 1km from the turnoff to Punta de Lobos. Rooms are earthy – think pine-paneled

walls and slate-tiled bathrooms – but not entirely tranquil, due to thin partitions. You can have all your meals in the lodge's restaurant for an extra CH$8000 per day.

Eating & Drinking

Restaurant Los Colchaguinos (☎ 841-243; Aníbal Pinto 298; empanadas & pailas CH$900-1500; ☷ noon-3pm & 7:30-11pm Mon-Sat, noon-3pm Sun) Big, dripping empanadas are the star attraction at this small, family-run hole-in-the-wall, which also makes rich, homey seafood *pailas*.

Donde Pinpón (☎ 842-820; Av Ross 9; mains CH$3000; ☷ 12:30-3:30pm & 7:30-11pm Mon-Sat, 12:30-3:30pm Sun) The menu runs to steak, fried fish and seafood stews, but that's more than enough to keep local families returning to this friendly, low-key restaurant whose long windowed front looks out onto the main drag.

El Puente Holandés (☎ 842-350; Costanera Eugenio Díaz Lira 167; mains CH$3500-4900; ☷ 9am-11pm) An arching wooden bridge leads from the Costanera into this high-ceilinged bar and restaurant on Infiernillo beach. It does simple seafood dishes well – grilled sea bass or clam and prawn ravioli, for example – or you can nurse a beer and some empanadas on the terrace out the front.

Xel-ha (☎ 843-042; Av Ortúzar 275; ☷ 6pm-midnight Mon-Thu, 6pm-late Fri & Sat Mar-Nov, 6pm-late Dec-Feb) Simpsons murals overlook the pool tables and reggae and hip-hop pulse in the background of this popular pub. Young staff pull pints of artisanal lager, ale and stout, which you can accompany with enchiladas, quesadillas or plain old burgers.

Disco 127 (Av Angel Gaete 217; ☷ 10pm-late Thu-Sat Mar-Dec, 10pm-late daily Jan & Feb) Most travelers' stories of derring-do in Pichilemu feature at least one 'and then I collapsed on the dancefloor' moment at this rowdy club.

DETOUR TO BUCALEMU

If you prefer your beaches quiet, rocky and windswept, try wandering to **Bucalemu**, a sleepy fishing village 37km south of Pichilemu. Small, crumbling hotels such as **Hotel Rocha** (☎ 072-825-923; Av Celedonio Pastene s/n; r incl breakfast CH$16,000) seem to cultivate a David Lynch vibe with their damp, mismatched rooms. Local fishermen may well have caught the merluza (hake) they fry at the small seafood restaurants along the beachfront. Hiking south for two or three days along the beach (camping on the way) takes you to the seaside village of **Llico**, a popular windsurfing spot. **Buses Jet-Sur** (☎ 02-778-7080) has several services a day to Bucalemu (CH$2000, four hours) from Santa Cruz, all of which pass through Pichilemu.

Getting There & Away

The **Terminal de Buses** (☎ 841-709; cnr Av Millaco & Los Alerces) is in the southwestern section of Pichilemu – the closest stop to the town center is the corner of Santa María and Ortúzar. From the terminal there are frequent services to Santa Cruz (CH$2500, three hours, hourly), San Fernando (CH$3000, 3½ hours, hourly) and Santiago (CH$6000, seven hours, hourly) with **Buses Nilahué** (☎ 842-138; www.busesnilahue.cl; Aníbal Pinto 301) and **Pullman del Sur** (☎ 843-008; wwwpdelsur .cl; Aníbal Pinto 213, Local A) – you can buy tickets at the downtown offices. Change at San Fernando for buses or trains south.

CURICÓ

☎ 075 / pop 123,875

'Nice plaza' is about as much as most locals have to say about Curicó. They're right: some 60 towering palm trees ring the square, while the inside is decorated with cedars, monkey puzzles, a striking early-20th-century wrought-iron bandstand and a wooden statue of the Mapuche chief Toqui Lautaro. On the west side, the restored 18th-century facade of the **Iglesia Matriz** belies its contemporary interior: the 1939 earthquake destroyed much of the original building. But beyond taking a turn around the square, the only real reason to visit Curicó is to use it as a base for exploring the stunning, relatively undiscovered Reserva Nacional Radal Siete Tazas (p152). Although it's very sleepy most of the year, Curicó bursts into life for the **Festival de la Vendimia** (Wine Harvest Festival), which lasts three days in early fall.

Orientation & Information

The main square, Plaza de Armas, is bordered by Merced, Estado, Carmen and Yungay, which is one of the main commercial drags along with intersecting street Prat.

Banco Santander (☎ 311-585; Estado 356; ☯ 9am-2pm Mon-Fri) One of many banks with ATMs around the Plaza de Armas.
Centro de Llamados (☎ 314-426; Prat 588; ☯ 9am-9pm Mon-Sat, 10am-2pm Sun)
Post office (☎ 800-277-736; Carmen 556; ☯ 9am-6pm Mon-Fri, 9am-12:30pm Sat)
Tourist office (☎ 543-027; www.curico.cl; Yungay 620)
World Service Internet (☎ 311-433; Prat 369; per hr CH$400; ☯ 9am-10pm)

Sleeping & Eating

Hotel Prat (☎ 311-069; Peña 427; hotelpratcurico@yahoo .es; s/d incl breakfast CH$15,000/20,000, s without bathroom CH$7500; 🖳) A rambling old building painted in acid colors houses Curicó's cheapest digs. The kitchen, in-room cable TV and free wifi make it popular with exchange students, but beware that there's no heating and most rooms open straight onto the patio.

Hostal Viñedos (☎ 222-083; www.hostalvinedos.cl; Chacabuco 645; s/d/tr incl breakfast CH$17,900/23,800/29,900, s/d without bathroom CH$15,000/20,000) Rooms at this modern, wine-themed B&B are named after different grapes – the ones at the front are lighter. Whether you've been drinking or not, the huge bouncy beds are a godsend.

Hotel Turismo (☎ 310-823; www.hotelturismo curico.cl; Carmen 727; s/d incl breakfast CH$40,800/47,800) Businesspeople in the wine industry usually stay here. Service is indifferent and corridors damp, but rooms are stylish with beige and red linens, modern furniture and cable TV.

Pizzería A Casa Tua (☎ 099-839-4761; Prat 395; pizzas CH$3500-5500; ☯ noon-11pm Mon-Sat) Ice-cold beer and a good selection of tasty thin-crust and deep-pan pizzas make this small pizzeria popular with young Curicanos.

La Parrilla del Abastero (☎ 318-536; Argomedo 330; mains CH$4000; ☯ noon-midnight) Why bother with a menu when everyone in town knows you specialize in two things: *lomo* (fillet steak) and *parrilladas* (mixed grills). Old road signs adorn the walls, the smell of steak fills the air and crowds of hungry friends pack the plastic-clothed tables.

Club de la Unión (☎ 310-026; www.rubentapia .cl; Merced 341; set lunch CH$3500, mains CH$3000-4000; ☯ 10am-11:30pm) It's set in a time-honored social club, yet this restaurant is known for adventurous dishes like pork tenderloin in orange sauce or roast duck in a red wine reduction.

Mistiko (☎ 310-868; Prat 21; mains CH$4500-6300; ☯ 12:30-3:30pm & 8-11:30pm Mon-Fri, 8pm-1am Sat) If you thought 'cool' and 'Curicó' couldn't go together, think again. This old house is painted in rich colors such as raspberry and lavender and has a regularly changing menu of Peruvian-fusion fare – pork and coconut milk empanadas, for example.

Getting There & Away
BUS

Most Curicó buses arrive and leave from the **Terminal de Buses** (cnr Prat & Maipú), near the train station five blocks west of the Plaza de Armas.

MIDDLE CHILE

From here **Andimar** (☎ 312-000; www.andimar.cl) and **Pullman del Sur** (☎ 328-090; www.pdelsur.cl) have frequent services to Santiago (CH$2000 to CH$3000, 2½ hours, every 30 minutes). **Talmocur** (☎ 311-360) goes to Talca (CH$1300, 1¼ hours, every 15 minutes).

To get to Parque Nacional Las Siete Tazas, catch a bus to Molina (CH$400, 35 minutes, every five minutes) with **Aquelarre** (☎ 314-307) from the Terminal de Buses Rurales, opposite the main bus terminal. From Molina there are frequent services to the park in January and February, and one daily service to Radal, 9km before the park proper, the rest of the year. For more information, see right.

Tur Bus (☎ 312-115; www.turbus.cl; Av Manso de Velasco 0106) has its own terminal southeast of town. From here, services leave to Santiago (CH$3500, 2½ hours, three daily) and Valparaíso (CH$8000, 4½ hours, one daily), and also south to Osorno (CH$19,500, 10 hours, four daily), Puerto Montt (CH$20,500, 12 hours, two daily) and Valdivia (CH$18,800, 11 hours, two daily).

TRAIN
EFE passenger trains between Santiago and Chillán stop at Curicós **train station** (☎ 600-585-5000; Maipú 657), five blocks west along Prat from the Plaza de Armas, near the bus station. There are seven trains a day to Santiago (CH$6000, 2¼ hours) and Chillán (CH$7000, 2½ hours), with connections from there to Concepción.

RESERVA NACIONAL RADAL SIETE TAZAS
The upper basin of the Río Claro marks the beginning of the ecological transition between the drought-tolerant Mediterranean vegetation to the north and the moist evergreen forests to the south. Here, 78km southeast of Curicó along a narrow gravel road, lies the **Reserva Nacional Radal Siete Tazas** (☎ 071-209-542; admission adult/child CH$3.000/500; ☼ 9am–5:30pm Mar-Nov, 9am–8:30pm Dec-Feb).

Conaf's main post is at the **Parque Inglés** sector, 9km beyond the park entrance at Radal, but there are two interesting stop-offs between the two points. The **Velo de la Novia** (literally, 'the bridal veil') is a 40m waterfall which you can see from a small roadside viewing point 2.6km from Radal. Another 4.4km on is the car park and Conaf ranger hut (usually only used in summer) that mark the access point

for the 400m trail to the **Siete Tazas** (literally, 'seven cups'), a breathtaking series of seven waterfalls and pools carved out of black basalt rock by the Río Claro. From here, another short trail leads to a viewpoint for the **Salto la Leona**, a waterfall that drops more than 50m from a narrow gorge to the main channel of the Río Claro.

Two well-marked hiking trails loop from Camping Los Robles at Parque Inglés: the 1km **Sendero el Coigüe** and 7km **Sendero Los Chiquillanes**, which has great views of the Valle del Indio (plan on about four hours in total). The first segment of this trail is part of the **Sendero de Chile** (www.senderodechile.cl), which continues to El Bolsón, where there is a refuge, and Valle del Indio. From here you can trek across the drainage of the Río Claro to Reserva Nacional Altos del Lircay (p156), taking about two days: the route is unsigned and crosses private land, so either do it with a guide or get detailed information from Conaf and carry a topographical map, compass and adequate supplies.

Sleeping & Eating
Conaf runs two cold-water **campsites** (☎ 075-228-029; campsites per person CH$1500) at the Parque Inglés: Camping Rocas Basálticas and Camping Parque Inglés. Both get very busy during summer.

Camping Los Robles (☎ 075-228-029; 6-person campsites CH$8000). There's hot water and barbecue areas at this privately run campsite. Bring food supplies with you – there's a big supermarket opposite the bus station in Molina.

Hostería Flor de la Canela (☎ 075-491-613; 4-person r with/without bathroom CH$26,000/20,000) This *hostería* (guesthouse) has basic but clean wooden rooms with creaking bunks. Main meals here cost CH$6000.

Getting There & Away
During January and February **Buses Hernández** operates frequent services from Molina (Maipú 1735) to the Parque Inglés sector of the park (CH$1500, 2½ hours, eight daily). From March to December there is one daily bus to Radal (CH$1500, two hours, daily at 5pm), 9km down the hill from Parque Inglés.

To drive to Radal Siete Tazas, take the Panamericana south of Curicó then turn off to Molina. Leave Molina to the south on paved road K-25 toward Cumpeo, 25km

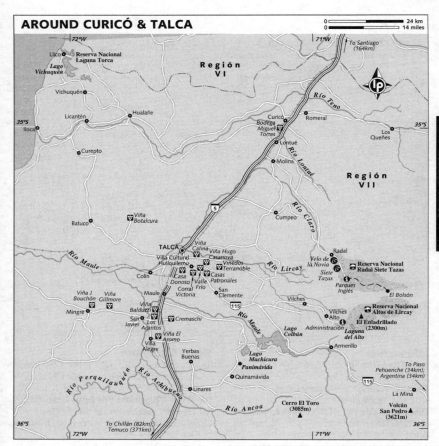

AROUND CURICÓ & TALCA

further on, where the road turns to gravel. From here, it's a bumpy 39km more to Radal, and another 9km to Parque Inglés.

El Caminante (☎ 071-197-0097; www.trekkingchile .com) offers one-day guided excursions to Siete Tazas from Talca.

TALCA
☎ 071 / pop 198,757

'Talca, París y Londres.' Signs behind receptions, souvenir plates and proud locals all repeat this mantra with a mystifying lack of irony. Architectural beauty and cultural life clearly have nothing to do with it, so what are they on about? Perhaps Paris is an oblique allusion to the reasonable food and wine scene. Or maybe it's a liberté-

egalité thing – Chile's 1818 declaration of independence was signed here. Perhaps Talquinos just have a weird sense of humor. Either way, it might not be a muse for poets and painters but Talca is a good base for exploring the gorgeous Reserva Nacional Altos de Lircay (p156) and the Maule Valley wineries (p157).

Orientation

Talca is contained to the east by the Panamericana and to the west by the shallow Río Claro. Talca follows a strict grid pattern, and streets have cardinal points (Norte, Oriente, Sur and Poniente) and numbers – the Plaza de Armas is the zero point.

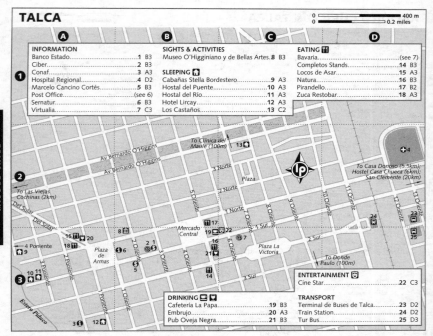

TALCA

INFORMATION		
Banco Estado	.1	B3
Ciber	.2	B3
Conaf	.3	A3
Hospital Regional	.4	D2
Marcelo Cancino Cortés	.5	B3
Post Office	(see 6)	
Sernatur	.6	B3
Virtualia	.7	C3

SIGHTS & ACTIVITIES		
Museo O'Higginiano y de Bellas Artes.	.8	B3

SLEEPING		
Cabañas Stella Bordestero	.9	A3
Hostal del Puente	.10	A3
Hostal del Río	.11	A3
Hotel Lircay	.12	A3
Los Castaños	.13	C2

EATING		
Bavaria	(see 7)	
Completos Stands	.14	B3
Locos de Asar	.15	A3
Natura	.16	B3
Pirandello	.17	B2
Zuca Restobar	.18	A3

ENTERTAINMENT		
Cine Star	.22	C3

DRINKING		
Cafetería La Papa	.19	B3
Embrujo	.20	A3
Pub Oveja Negra	.21	B3

TRANSPORT		
Terminal de Buses de Talca	.23	D2
Train Station	.24	D2
Tur Bus	.25	D3

Information

BancoEstado (☎ 345-201; 1 Sur 971; ◷ 9am-2pm)
One of many ATMs along 1 Sur.

Ciber (☎ 232-961; 1 Sur 975; per hr CH$500;
◷ 8:30am-9pm Mon-Fri)

Clínica del Maule (☎ 201-800; www.clinicadelmaule
.cl; 4 Norte 1640) Private clinic.

Conaf (☎ 228-029; 3 Sur 564; ◷ 9am-1pm &
2-5:30pm Mon-Fri) Limited information about nearby
national parks.

Hospital Regional (☎ 242-406; www.hospitalregional
detalca; 1 Norte) Busy public hospital on the corner of 13
Oriente.

Marcelo Cancino Cortés (☎ 226-748; 1 Sur 898,
Oficina 15; ◷ 9am-7pm Mon-Sat) Currency exchange.

Post office (☎ 800-267-736; 1 Oriente 1150; ◷ 9am-
6pm Mon-Fri, 9am-noon Sat) Inside a large building off
Plaza de Armas.

Sernatur (☎ 233-669; 1 Oriente 1150; ◷ 8:30am-
5:30pm Mon-Fri) An exceptionally helpful, English-
speaking staff offer travelers clued-up advice on
accommodations, activities as well as money-saving tips
in Talca.

Virtualia (☎ 343-203; 1 Sur 1330, Local 3; per hr
CH$400; ◷ 9am-11pm Mon-Sat) New computers and
cheap IP phone calls.

Sights & Activities

Talca's one and only sight is the 1762 house
where Bernardo O'Higgins signed Chile's declaration of independence in 1818. Known as
the **Museo O'Higginiano y de Bellas Artes** (☎ 227-
330; 1 Norte 875; admission free); at this writing it was
closed for a total overhaul and isn't due to
reopen until late 2009.

One interesting outing from Talca is to
take the early-morning **train** to the port of
Constitución (CH$800, three hours), depart-
ing at 7:50am daily and 4:30pm on weekdays.
The journey is the destination: the slow old
train runs alongside the Río Maule with amazing views out over the valley. The return train
doesn't leave until 4:15pm, and there's not
much to do in Constitución, so you might
want to get a bus back. You buy tickets from
the train station.

Sleeping

Los Castaños (☎ 684-531; loscastanostalca@gmail
.com; 8 Oriente 1481; s/d without bathroom incl breakfast
CH$9000/16,000) The cheapest digs in Talca are run
by a friendly English-speaking owner who's
tuned-in to traveler needs. Add big breakfasts

and small but cozy rooms with cable TV and you've got a place that's so popular they're thinking of expanding next door.

Hostal Casa Chueca (☎ 197-0096, 099-419-0625; www.trekkingchile.com/Casachueca; Viña Andrea s/n, Sector Alto Lircay; dm incl breakfast CH$8000-10,000, d CH$32,000; ⓧ closed Jun-Aug; ⓡ) Gardens looking over the Río Lircay surround the rustic cabins at Casa Chueca, whose knowledgeable German owners also run famed hiking company El Caminante (see p157). It's in the countryside outside Talca, but has become a destination in its own right for fans of the great outdoors. Call first from Talca terminal, then take the Taxutal 'A' micro toward San Valentín to the last stop, where you'll be picked up.

Hostal del Río (☎ 510-218; www.hostaldelrio.cl; 1 Sur 411; s/d/tr/q incl breakfast CH$12,000/19,000/22,000/ 27,000; ⓠ) Despite indifferent service, rooms are warm and clean, if very cramped. Be careful with your valuables in case keys are left in the door after cleaning.

Hostal del Puente (☎ 220-930; www.hostaldelpuente .cl; 1 Sur 407; s/d/tr/q incl breakfast CH$14,900/24,990/ 29,600/36,000) Go for the airy renovated rooms at the back, which are around a galleried outdoor patio, but avoid the dingy singles toward the front.

Hotel Lircay (☎ 682-141; www.hotelerallircay.cl; 1 Poniente 865; s/d/tr CH$16,500/24,500/34,500; ⓠ) This new hotel two blocks south of the Plaza de Armas has big bright rooms with simple wooden furniture, cable TV and wi-fi, but no heating. A few rooms aimed at families have extra beds on a mezzanine.

Cabañas Stella Bordestero (☎ 235-545; www .turismostella.cl; 4 Poniente 1183; s/d/tr/q CH$18,000/ 25,000/36,000/42,000; ⓧ ⓠ ⓡ) Four blocks from the Plaza de Armas but a world apart, these clapboard cabins are surrounded by a leafy garden with a swimming pool, deck chairs and swings. They've been just as thorough inside: the nicely kept wood-paneled rooms have firm beds, wi-fi, cable TV, air-conditioning and small decks.

Casa Donoso (☎ 341-400; www.casadonoso.cl; Fundo La Oriental, Camino a Palmira Km3.5; d CH$140,000) Talca's ultimate in indulgence, this boutique guesthouse is in a 160-year-old homestead on the grounds of a working vineyard (see boxed text, p157). The wooden-floored rooms are huge and so are the beds, which have jewel-colored silk covers (and electric blankets in winter). Heavy antique wardrobes, wallpaper made of old wine labels and sinks set in wine barrels add to the atmosphere. Across the garden is a micro-cinema, and horseback riding and massages are also available.

Eating

Locals swear by the *completo* (hot dog) stands on 5 Oriente at 2 Sur – a hot dog with the works costs around CH$800.

Donde Paulo (☎ 712-843; 9 Oriente 894; mains CH$2500; ⓧ noon-11:30pm) A plain brick house with only a small sign outside feels like Talca's best-kept secret as you enter. But the packed tables inside let you know that word long got out about the rich, homey *plateada*, chicken stew and fried fish served here.

Las Viejas Cochinas (☎ 221-749; Rivera Poniente; mains CH$4000-6000; ⓧ noon-midnight) Talca's best-known restaurant is a huge, clattering, low-roofed canteen out of town alongside the Río Claro. Dour waiters take forever to bring out the house specialty, *pollo mariscal* (chicken in a brandy and seafood sauce), but it's worth the wait. Fresh fried fish is a quicker, and equally tasty, option.

Zuca Restobar (☎ 236-124; Isidoro del Solar 5; mains CH$4900-5900; ⓧ 7pm-midnight Mon-Sat) The hippest of the many restaurants on this street, Zuca's small but intriguing menu includes squid-ink fettuccini with razor clams and squid or grilled fish on mashed potatoes infused with *merkén* (a Mapuche spice mix made of smoked chilli and coriander seeds). Pastel stucco walls and old movie posters strike just the right side of kitsch.

Locos de Asar (☎ 213-851; Isidoro del Solar 56; mains CH$5900-6700; ⓧ 12:30-3:30pm & 7:30-11:30pm Mon-Sat) Don't bother with salad: limp lettuce leaves are the chef's way of telling you to focus on the meat. He's right: as well as perfectly grilled Temuco rib-eyes, there are intriguing starters such as sweetbreads in port and creamy *criadillas* (um…mountain oysters).

Also recommended:

Pirandello (☎ 511-051; 5 Oriente 1186; set lunch CH$1600, large pizzas CH$5000; ⓧ 10am-midnight Mon-Sat) Cheap meals, cheap pisco sours, cheap everything.

Bavaria (☎ 211-061; 1 Sur 1330, Local 21-26; sandwiches CH$1500-3200, set-lunch CH$3600; ⓧ 10am-11:30pm Mon-Sat, noon-10pm Sun) Glazed pork sandwiches are this German-inspired chain's trademark.

Natura (☎ 212-214; 5 Oriente 1058; salads CH$1890-2190; ⓧ noon-3pm & 5:30-9:30pm) Fresh, natural ingredients are creatively combined into salads or simple grilled fish and chicken dishes.

Drinking & Entertainment

Cafetería La Papa (☎ 216-238; 1 Sur 1271; espresso CH$800; ☷ 9:30am-8:30pm Mon-Sat, 11am-8pm Sun) Strong espressos and squishy cakes prove the perfect pick-me-up if you overindulged in the local vintage the night before, although you usually have to deal with a long wait first.

Pub Oveja Negra (5 Oriente 1054; ☷ 8pm-late Mon-Sat) Hip students and older rockers love this laid-back bar, where live bands often perform on weekends.

Embrujo (☎ 970-707; Isidoro del Solar 38; ☷ 7:30pm-3:30am Tue-Fri, 10pm-3:30am Sat) This candlelit bar is popular with Talquinos in their 20s and 30s. The empanadas, pizzas and french fries are nothing special (CH$2290 to CH$4690), but they're half-price during happy hour (7:30pm to 10pm weeknights).

Cine Star (☎ 211-763; cnr 1 Sur & 6 Oriente) An old two-screen cinema in the Galería Zaror shopping arcade.

Getting There & Away
BUS

Most companies use the **Terminal de Buses de Talca** (☎ 243-366; 2 Sur 1920, cnr 12 Oriente), 11 blocks east of the Plaza de Armas. **Talca, París y Londres** (☎ 261-000) has hourly buses to Santiago. So does **Buses Linatal** (☎ 242-759), which also has 11 southbound buses daily. **Buses Línea Azul** (☎ 613-670; www.lineaazul.cl) has hourly buses south to Chillán. **Buses Vilches** (☎ 235-327) has four daily buses to Vilches Alto, gateway to the Reserva Nacional Altos de Lircay. To get to Villa Cultural Huilquilemu (right), take a bus to San Clemente and ask to be let off at Ruta del Vino (CH$500, 10 minutes).

Tur Bus (☎ 265-715; www.turbus.cl; 3 Sur 1960) uses a separate terminal south of the main terminal, with hourly buses to Santiago and six buses south to Puerto Montt, stopping at Chillán, Los Angeles, Temuco, Osorno and other cities on the Panamericana. Other companies operating from here with similar services include **Pullman del Sur** (☎ 264-787; www.pdelsur.cl) and **Pullman Bus** (☎ 244-039; www.pullman.cl).

Destination	Cost (CH$)	Duration (hr)
Chillán	2700	3
Osorno	10,500	11
Puerto Montt	10,900	12
Santiago	4000	3
Temuco	6300	6
Valparaíso/Viña del Mar	7000	6
Vilches	1600	1½

TRAIN

From the EFE **train station** (☎ 226-254; 11 Oriente 1000) there are seven trains a day to Santiago (CH$6500, 2¾ hours) and south to Chillán (CH$6000, two hours). See p154 for information on the train to Constitución.

AROUND TALCA
Villa Cultural Huilquilemu

Once an important *fundo* (farm), this complex of restored 19th-century buildings 7km east of Talca houses the headquarters of the Ruta del Vino (see opposite) and **museum** (☎ 071-242-474; adult/child CH$500/200; ☷ 9am-1pm & 3-6:30pm Tue-Fri, noon-6pm Sat & Sun). As well as dusty religious tableaux and folk art, it contains the basin where local hero Bernardo O'Higgins was baptized. Sequoias, araucarias, magnolias, palms and oaks fill the adjoining garden. All buses to San Clemente from Talca's bus station pass Huilquilemu.

RESERVA NACIONAL ALTOS DE LIRCAY

The great range of challenging hikes at this well-organized, easily accessible **national park** (admission 1st day/subsequent days CH$3000/1500; ☷ 8:30am-7pm) will leave you as short of breath as the fabulous views. Its 121 sq km are made up of a mix high-Andean steppes and deciduous forest – notably seven species of *Nothofagus* (southern beech) and *Austrocedrus chilensis*, a native conifer – which is home to a large population of tricahues and other native parrots. Pudú deer, Patagonian foxes and Pampas cats also live here, though sightings are uncommon.

About 2km before the park entrance, Conaf runs the **Centro de Información Ambiental**, which has displays on local natural and cultural history (the area has seen four sequential indigenous occupations). You pay admission and register for camping and trekking at the **Admnistración**, about 500m after the entrance.

Activities
HIKING

The helpful team of Conaf rangers who run the park give detailed advice about hiking and camping within it, and distribute photocopied maps of the area. Arguably the best hike in the whole of Middle Chile, the **Sendero Enladrillado** takes you the top of a 2300m basalt plateau. The trail starts with a two-hour

MAULE VALLEY WINERIES

The Maule Valley is a hugely significant wine-producing region for Chile, and is responsible for much of the country's export wine. You can visit many of its vineyards independently or through one of the tours run by the **Ruta del Vino** (☎ 071-246-460; www.valledelmaule.cl; Villa Cultural Huilquilemu; 8:30am-1pm & 2:30-6:30pm Mon-Fri, noon-6:30pm Sat & Sun Nov-Mar, 8:30am-1pm & 2:30-6:30pm Mon-Fri Apr-Oct). Fifteen wineries are associated with the Ruta del Vino, including the following standouts (see Map p153 for locations).

Casa Donoso (☎ 071-341-400; www.casadonoso.cl; Fundo La Oriental, Camino a Palmira Km3.5; tours incl 2 pours CH$5000-7000 8am- 6pm Mon-Fri) A traditionally run vineyard set around a colonial homestead.

Viña Balduzzi (☎ 073-322-138; www.balduzziwines.com; Av Balmaceda 1189, San Javier; tours CH$5000 9am-6pm Mon-Sat) A fourth-generation winery surrounded by spacious gardens and well-kept colonial buildings near San Javier.

Viña Gillmore (☎ 073-197-5539; www.gillmore.cl; Camino Constitución Km20; 9am-5pm Mon-Sat) A winery and agro-tourism resort – wine therapy is the favorite treatment at the spa.

Viña Hugo Casanova (☎ 071-266-540; www.casanova.cl; Fundo Purísima, Camino Las Rastras Km8; tours incl 2 pours CH$5000, tastings CH$3000; 9am-noon & 3:30-5pm Mon-Fri) A traditional vineyard with beautiful colonial buildings near Talca – reserve in advance.

stretch east along the Sendero de Chile, then a signposted right-hand fork climbs steeply through dense forest for about an hour before leveling off. You eventually emerge onto the dead-flat platform of **El Enladrillado** – many people think it's a UFO-landing ground. To the west you can see the flat-topped crater of the **Volcán Descabezado** (literally, 'headless volcano') and next to it the sharp peak of **Cerro Azul**. The 10km trek takes about four hours up and three down. There are two or three potable springs before the trail emerges above the treeline, but carry as much water as possible.

The **Sendero Laguna** also follows the Sendero de Chile for an hour before forking right into a steep, three-hour uphill stretch to the gorgeous **Laguna del Alto**, a mountain-ringed lake at 2000m above sea level. Plan on three hours there and back, or you can continue for two hours on a trail leading northwest to El Enladrillado – the round-trip takes eight hours.

A gentler three-hour hike along the Sendero de Chile takes you from the Administración to the **Mirador del Valle Venado**, which has views over the Volcán Descabezado and the Río Claro Valley. A trail continues southeast from here (still along the Sendero de Chile) through a long gorge, before arriving at Río Claro, 15km (six hours) from the Administración, where there's a small refuge. Another 5km (three hours) further on is Valle del Venado, where camping is permitted. It's a two-day trip.

Longer hikes in and around the park include the seven-day **Circuito de los Cóndores**, for which it's advisable to carry topographic maps or hire a guide. Another such offering is the loop across the drainage of the Río Claro to exit at Reserva Nacional Radal Siete Tazas (p152).

Respected hiking guides and operators in the area:

El Caminante (☎ 071-197-0096; www.trekkingchile .com) Run by expert German hiker Franz Schubert of Talca's Hostal Casa Chueca (p155).

Leonardo Cáceres (☎ 099-641-5582) Infectiously enthusiastic Conaf ranger.

Maule Expediciones (☎ 099-861-7159) Reliable, well-priced trekking guides.

HORSEBACK RIDING

If you want a taste of the wilderness without getting chafed feet, you could always let a beast of burden take the strain. Several Vilches residents rent horses from near the park entrance (horse/guide per day CH$10,000/12,000).

Sleeping

Conaf runs the excellent **Camping Antahuara** (campsites per person CH$2500 & one-off site fee CH$8000) about 500m beyond the Adminstración, next to Río Lircay. It's accessible by car and has electricity, hot water, flush toilets and garbage collection. There are two *campings primitivos* (designated camping areas with no facilities) which are respectively one-hour and 2½-hour hikes east

MIDDLE CHILE

from the Administración along the Sendero de Chile.

You can stay just outside the park but keep the back-to-nature vibe at **Biota Maule** (☎ 099-569-4436; www.biotamaule.blogspot.com; Vilches Alto Km67; dm/d CH$5000/15,000), a hostel and ecological foundation run by biologists who lead hiking and riding expeditions. Rooms in the huge, all-wood, wheelchair-accessible house are simple but light-filled, and you can use the kitchen and even the lab if you want. They compost, separate garbage and treat waste water with a worm filter. They've got another cabin just down the road, but try to book ahead as both are popular with researchers and students.

Getting There & Away

Buses Vilches goes from the **Terminal de Buses de Talca** (☎ 071-243-366; 2 Sur 1920, Talca) to Vilches Alto (CH$1400, two hours), a scattering of houses about 3km below the Centro de Información Ambiental and 5km from the Administración of the Reserva Nacional Altos de Lircay. Buses leave Talca daily at 7:15am, noon, 1pm and 4:50pm from March to December, and there are 10 services daily in January and February.

It takes about 1½ hours to drive to the reserve from Talca. Take road 115 through San Clemente; 38km from Talca is the left-hand turnoff to Vilches, another 25km further on. At this writing, the last 15km were unpaved but paving work was in progress.

CHILLÁN

☎ 042 / pop 180,197

Earthquakes have battered Chillán throughout its turbulent history, so most of its colonial buildings were bulldozed away decades ago and replaced with the sweeping concrete shopping precincts that characterize the city center. One of the city's previous incarnations, Chillán Viejo, is now a southwestern suburb of Chillán proper – despite the name it's as modern-looking as the rest of Chillán. But though Chillán itself is neither particularly beautiful nor especially interesting, it is the gateway to some of the loveliest landscapes in Middle Chile.

Orientation

The heart of the city is the Plaza Bernardo O'Higgins (also known as the Plaza de Armas), which is bounded by Av Libertad, 18 de Septiembre, Constitución and Arauco, which is a pedestrian-only shopping street for a few blocks south of the square. Av O'Higgins leads north to the Panamericana (which passes northwest of the city) and south to the suburb of Chillán Viejo. Av Argentina flanks the easternmost side of the city center and leads south to the road to the Termas de Chillán.

Information

A&S Internet (☎ 435-005; Arauco 628, 2nd fl; per hr CH$400; ⌚ 8:30am-11pm Mon-Fri, 10:30am-8:30pm Sat) One of several internet cafés nearby.

BancoEstado (☎ 455-291; Constitución 500; ⌚ 9am-2pm Mon-Fri) One of many ATMs on this street.

Clínica Los Andes (☎ 433-000; Pedro Aguirre Cerda 35) Private clinic.

Hospital Herminda Martín (☎ 208-221; Francisco Ramírez 10) Public hospital on the corner of Av Argentina.

Lavaseco Marcela (☎ 262-868; Arauco 707; per load CH$3500; ⌚ 9am-1pm & 3:30-7:30pm Mon-Fri, 9am-2pm Sat) Laundrette.

Post office (☎ 800-267-736; Av Libertad 501; ⌚ 8:30am-6:30pm Mon-Fri, 9am-12:45 Sat)

Schüller Cambio (☎ 238-688; Constitución 550, Local 10; ⌚ 10am-2pm & 4-6pm Mon-Fri, 11am-2pm Sat) Changes traveler's checks and cash.

Sernatur (☎ 223-272; 18 de Septiembre 455; ⌚ 8:30am-1:30pm & 3-6pm Mon-Fri) Friendly staff provide city maps and information on accommodations and transport.

Telefónica (☎ 214-918; Arauco 601; ⌚ 9am-7pm Mon-Sat) On the corner of Constitución.

Sights

On the northeast corner of Chillán's main square stands the stark, modernist **Catedral de Chillán** (cnr Av Libertad & Arauco; ⌚ 10am-6pm Mon-Sat, 10am-2pm Sun). Built in 1941, its soaring semi-ovaloid form is made of a series of earthquake-resistant giant arches. The 36m-high cross next to it commemorates the thousands of Chillán residents who died in the 1939 earthquake.

In response to the devastation that the quake caused, the Mexican government of President Lázaro Cárdenas donated the **Escuela México** (O'Higgins 250; donations welcome; ⌚ 10am-1:30pm & 2-6pm Mon-Fri, 10am-6pm Sat & Sun) to Chillan. At Pablo Neruda's request, Mexican muralists David Alfaro Siqueiros and Xavier Guerrero decorated the school's library and stairwell, respectively, with fiercely symbolic murals, now set within an

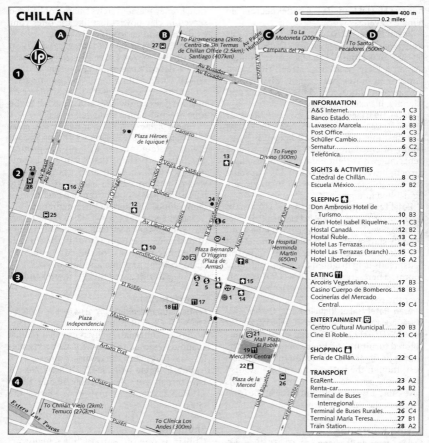

CHILLÁN

0 ————— 400 m
0 ————— 0.2 miles

INFORMATION
A&S Internet.............................1 C3
Banco Estado............................2 B3
Lavaseco Marcela......................3 B3
Post Office................................4 B3
Schüller Cambio........................5 B3
Sernatur..................................6 C3
Telefónica................................7 C3

SIGHTS & ACTIVITIES
Catedral de Chillán....................8 C3
Escuela México.........................9 B2

SLEEPING
Don Ambrosio Hotel de
  Turismo................................10 B3
Gran Hotel Isabel Riquelme.....11 C3
Hostal Canadá..........................12 B2
Hostal Ñuble...........................13 C2
Hotel Las Terrazas...................14 C3
Hotel Las Terrazas (branch)....15 C3
Hotel Libertador......................16 A2

EATING
Arcoiris Vegetariano................17 B3
Casino Cuerpo de Bomberos....18 B3
Cocinerías del Mercado
  Central................................19 C4

ENTERTAINMENT
Centro Cultural Municipal.......20 B3
Cine El Roble..........................21 C4

SHOPPING
Feria de Chillán.......................22 C4

TRANSPORT
EcaRent..................................23 A2
Renta-car...............................24 B2
Terminal de Buses
  Interregional.........................25 A2
Terminal de Buses Rurales......26 C4
Terminal María Teresa............27 B1
Train Station..........................28 A2

MIDDLE CHILE

otherwise normal working school. At the time of writing, the works were due to be restored in 2009.

The city's **main market** (☉ 9am-6pm) is split into two sections on either side of Maipón between Isabel Riquelme and 5 de Abril. On the north side is a covered section known as the **Mercado Central**, which contains cheap eateries (see p160) and butchers stands festooned with strings of the *longaniza* (a spicy salami-type sausage) that Chillán is famous for throughout Chile. The open-air stalls on Plaza de la Merced form **La Feria de Chillán** and are taken up with a mix of fresh produce and local arts and crafts. Simple ceramics, leather *huaso* (cowboy) gear and wickerware are good-value buys.

Sleeping

Chillán's hotels fill up very rapidly during the ski season so try to book ahead.

Don Ambrosio Hotel de Turismo (☎ 099-8614-1093; Constitución 337; s/d incl breakfast CH$5000/10,000) Rooms at Chillán's cheapest hotel are dingy but have large, if slightly sagging, beds, cable TV and small private bathrooms. The Plaza de Armas is a block away.

Hostal Canadá (☎ 234-515; hostalcanada269chile@gmail.com; Av Libertad 269; s/d CH$6000/12,000) A night at this friendly mother-and-daughter setup is a bit like staying with family – fraying floral sheets, worn carpets, lumpy pillows and all. Other budget places line the same block, but are more like men's boarding houses: Hostal Canadá is a better bet for solo female travelers.

Hostal Ñuble (☎ 321-813; 18 de Septiembre 240; conaver@gmail.com; s/d without bathroom incl breakfast CH$7500/16,000) Housed in a lilac-painted building on a leafy residential street, this small family-run hotel has bright, airy rooms with parquet floors and cable TV. Quiet and friendly, it's excellent value.

Hotel Libertador (☎ 223-255; www.hlbo.cl; Av Libertad 85; s/d/tr incl breakfast CH$17,000/25,000/33,000; 🖳) Bustling, matronly staff keep this large, family-oriented motel spick and span. Rooms here come with bright floral bedspreads, thick carpets, heavy drapes and cable TV – upstairs ones are bigger. There's wi-fi in the lovely light-filled lounge.

Hotel Las Terrazas Express (☎ 437-000; www.las terrazas.cl; Constitución 663; s/d incl breakfast CH$31,650/34,500/45,850; 🖳) An airy light-filled lobby and friendly staff greet you at this small hotel half a block from the Plaza de Armas. Crimson bedspreads help brighten the slightly gloomy rooms. There are hefty mid-week discounts both here and at the business-oriented branch over the road.

Gran Hotel Isabel Riquelme (☎ 434-400; www .hotelisabelriquelme.cl; Constitución 576; s/d/tr incl breakfast CH$39,500/47,900/62,200; 🖳) Clean-lined chestnut-colored furniture and linens in tasteful earthy shades justify this hotel's claim to be Chillán's best, though the bathrooms and standoffish staff could both do with a revamp. All rooms have cable TV and wi-fi, and those at the front overlook the Plaza de Armas.

Eating & Drinking

Casino Cuerpo de Bomberos (☎ 222-233; El Roble 490; set lunch CH$1300; ⏱ 12:30-2:30pm & 6:30-11pm Mon-Sat) Families, office workers and groups of friends head to this basic restaurant on the 1st floor of the local fire station for *colaciones* (set lunches) at, well, fire-station prices.

Cocinerías del Mercado Central (Maipón btwn 5 de Abril & Isabel Riquelme; set lunches CH$1800-2500; ⏱ 8am-6pm Mon-Sat) The dinky eateries at the market specialize in local classics such as *chupe* (a rich fish stew) or *paila marina*. The *longaniza* (spicy salami) adorning the surrounding butchers' stalls also appears regularly in the grease-slicked but filling fare.

La Motoneta (☎ 276-693; Av Padre Alberto Hurtado 242; mains CH$2000-3100; ⏱ noon-3pm & 8-11pm Mon-Sat) Locals are unanimous: this is the best *picada* (cheap 'n' cheerful restaurant) in town. Think

rich, homey pies and stews (many cooked and served in clay bowls) just like the ones your Chilean grandma would have made.

Arcoiris Vegetariano (☎ 227-549; El Roble 525; set lunch CH$2500; ⏱ 9am-6:30pm Mon-Sat; Ⓥ) Praise be – a decent vegetarian restaurant in provincial Chile. Filling lentil-and-bulgur-style set lunches are served at the back, while a café upfront does sandwiches and cakes, all to the tune of wind-chime and whale music.

Fuego Divino (☎ 430-988; Gamero 680; mains CH$5500-6800; ⏱ 12:30-3:30pm & 8-11:30pm Mon-Sat) Stylish restaurants are thin on the ground in Chillán – perhaps that's why the gleaming black tables here are always booked up at weekends. Or maybe it's because the expertly barbecued prime cuts of Temuco beef taste so damn good. The perfect posh night out.

Santos Pecadores (☎ 430-443; Av Vicente Méndez 275; ⏱ 8:30pm-late Tue-Sat) Chillanejos with plenty of dash and cash pour into this chi-chi red-walled bar northeast of the city center for sushi, ceviche and lots and lots of cocktails. DJs keep things going till late at weekends.

Entertainment

Centro Cultural Municipal (☎ 433-459; 18 de Septiembre 590, 3rd fl) Chillán has a fine classical music pedigree – internationally renowned pianist Claudio Arrau came from here. Concerts, ballets and plays keep the tradition alive.

Cine El Roble (☎ 239-022; El Roble 770) A two-screen complex theater inside Plaza El Roble shopping mall that shows the latest blockbusters.

Shopping

Chillán is one of central Chile's major artisan zones, and there's a reasonable selection of crafts at the **Feria de Chillán** (Plaza de la Merced; ⏱ 9am-6pm). Especially good are ceramics from the nearby village of Quinchamalí, but you'll also see rawhide and leatherwork, basketry, weavings and the typical straw hats called *chupallas*.

Getting There & Around

BUS

Chillán has two long-distance bus stations. The most central is **Terminal de Buses Interregional** (☎ 221-014; Constitución 01), five blocks east of the Plaza de Armas on the corner of Rosas. From here, **Tur Bus** (☎ 248-327; www.turbus.cl) has services to Santiago (hourly), some of which stop in Talca and other cities along the Panamericana.

MIDDLE CHILE

Tur Bus also goes direct to Valparaíso and south to Temuco, Osorno, Valdivia and Puerto Montt (seven daily). There are similar services to Santiago with **Línea Azul** (☎ 211-192; www.buses lineaazul.cl), which also goes Los Angeles (10 daily), Angol (two daily) and Concepción (every 15 minutes).

Other long-distance carriers use the newer **Terminal María Teresa** (☎ 272-149; O'Higgins 010), just north of Av Ecuador. These include **Buses Jota Be** (☎ 423-230), which makes several journeys daily to Salto del Laja and has direct services to Los Angeles (hourly). **Pullman Bus** (☎ 272-178; www.pullmanbus.cl) has routes north to Calama, Antofagasta and Arica (five daily), and south to Puerto Montt (five daily).

Sol del Pacífico (☎ 272-177) also goes to Santiago, Viña and Valparaíso. Other companies covering the Panamericana include **Buses Jac** (☎ 273-581) and **Condor** (☎ 270-264), traveling between Temuco and Santiago.

Local and regional services leave from the **Terminal de Buses Rurales** (☎ 423-814; Maipón 890). **Rembus** (☎ 229-377) takes you to Valle Las Trancas (six to seven daily); the 7:50am and 1:20pm buses continue to Valle Hermoso on Fridays, Saturdays and Sundays. **Vía Itata** operates routes to Ninhué (10 daily) and Cobquecura (four daily), as does **Petorbus** (☎ 223-606), whose 9am and 4:30pm services continue to surf hangout Buchupureo.

Destination	Cost (CH$)	Duration (hr)
Angol	2500	2¼
Arica	35,000	28
Buchupureo	1800	3
Calama	20,000	24
Cobquecura	1400	2¾
Concepción	1000	1½
Los Angeles	1500	1½
Ninhue	800	1
Osorno	9200	8
Puerto Montt	13,000	9
Santiago	9900	6
Talca	2700	3
Temuco	4500	5
Termas de Chillán	2200	1½
Valdivia	8500	6
Valparaíso	9800	8
Valle Los Trancas	1300	1¼

CAR

Driving makes it possible to cram in lots of national park action or quick day trips up the mountain to Termas de Chillán. Local rental companies include **Renta-car** (☎ 212- 243; 18 de Septiembre 380) and **EcaRent** (☎ 229-262; Av Brasil, Oficina 3) at the train station. Rates at both start at about CH$27,000 a day. Note that if the mountain roads are slippery you may need to hire wheel chains, too.

TRAIN

The EFE TerraSur line runs from the **train station** (☎ 222-424; cnr Av Brasil & Libertad) to Santiago (CH$10,500, 4½ hours, seven daily), stopping along the way at Talca (CH$8000, 1¾ hours), Curicó (CH$7000, 3¼ hours) and Rancagua (CH$9500, 3½ hours), among other places.

AROUND CHILLÁN
Termas de Chillán & Valle Las Trancas
A winding road leads from Chillán 80km up into the mountains to Valle Las Trancas and the Termas de Chillán. Chilean powder-fiends flock to these slopes in winter, when bumper-to-bumper traffic is common at the top. The pace is less manic the rest of the year, when the valleys turn a luscious green and are perfect for hiking, climbing and horseback riding, or just lazing around and drinking in the views.

The southern slopes of the 3122m Volcán Chillán are the stunning setting of the **Nevados de Chillán ski center** (☎ 600-626-3300; www.nevados dechillan.com; day ski pass adult/child CH$25,000/15,000). Unusually for Chile's ski resorts, many of its 30 runs track through forest, and there's a good mix of options for beginner and more experienced skiers. Superlatives abound here: they've got the longest piste in South America (13km Las Tres Marías), the longest chairlift and some of the biggest and best off-piste offerings. A new company took over the concession in 2008 and has added a snow park, too. The season can start as early as mid-May and usually runs to mid-October – locals swear that great snow, empty slopes and discounted ski-passes make the beginning of October one of the best times to come.

A turnoff halfway between Valle Las Trancas and the ski center takes you to **Valle Hermoso** (admission CH$3000), a leafy recreational area. Most people come here for the **thermal springs** (☼ 9am-5pm) – sheltered inside a wooden house, they're open year-round. Zip-lines and climbing walls provide extra action in summer, when you can stay at the small **campsite** (per tent CH$15,000), the cheapest accommodations on the mountain. There's a basic minimarket and fast-food restaurant.

SLEEPING & EATING

Accommodations on the mountain divide into two camps. The posh hotels in Termas de Chillán, at the top of the road, get you closest to the slopes. Prices are much lower, however, and dining and après-ski are notably better if you stay in the cabins, hostels and lodges downhill at Valle Las Trancas. Most places have huge low-season discounts.

Chil-in Hostal & Restaurant (☎ 042-247-075; www .chil-in.com; Ruta 55, Camino Termas de Chillán Km72; dm/d without bathroom CH$8000/20,000; 🖵) The cheapest sleep on the slopes is at this wooden lodge – rooms are simple but clean, and several have mezzanines for squeezing more people in. The cozy living room has a log fire and wi-fi, while out front French owner Gregory serves up delicious thin-crust pizzas loaded down with toppings.

Hostelling International Las Trancas (☎ 042-243-211; hostellinglastrancas@gmail.com; Ruta 55, Camino Termas de Chillán Km73.5; dm/d without bathroom incl breakfast CH$10,000/20,000) A log fire keeps this pleasantly worn lodge toasty in the downstairs restaurant – beer, burgers and boasting about your ski escapades are all on the menu. Simple, clapboard-walled dorms make up most of the rooms – book way in advance to bag one of the two private rooms.

Ecobox Andino (☎ 042-423-134; www.ecoboxandino .cl; Camino a Shangri-Lá Km0.2; 4-person cabins CH$65,000; 🛒) It's hard to guess these impeccably decorated cabins were once shipping containers – bright geometric patterns cover the outside walls; inside, modern furnishings are offset by handicrafts. Wooden decks overlook the tree-filled garden through which paths wind to the pool.

M I Lodge (☎ 099-9623-0412; www.milodge.com; Camino a Shangri-Lá; s/d/tr/q incl breakfast & dinner CH$53,000/ 80,000/108,000/120,000; 🖵 🛒) Why can't everywhere you stay be this wonderful? Tasteful rustic furniture, thick carpets and springy beds with sky-blue covers mean the rooms here feel really homey and a fire crackles in the middle of the beautifully designed glass-and-wood-walled restaurant. The snowboarding French owners give expert advice on the ski scene and offer hiking and horseback riding expeditions in summer. You get unobstructed views from the deck-rimmed pool and outdoor hot tubs.

Hotel Nevados de Chillán (☎ 600-626-3300; www .nevadosdechillan.com; 3 days s/d incl breakfast & dinner CH$410,000/635,700; 🛒) Owned by the same company that has recently taken over the ski center, this hotel brings a bit of style to the slopes. Sleek modern furniture, flat-screen TVs and moss-green or chocolate-colored throw cushions are enough to overlook the aging bathrooms. Thermal waters fill the outdoor pool so you can swim surrounded by snow. Prices include ski passes and babysitting.

Snow Pub (☎ 042-213-910; Ruta 55, Camino Termas de Chillán Km71; ✆ 1pm-late) For years the après-ski in Valle Las Trancas has centered on this feel-good bar, which gets packed with revelers in high season.

GETTING THERE & AWAY

From Chillán's Terminal de Buses Rurales, **Rembus** (☎ 042-229-377) has buses to Valle Las Trancas (CH$1300, 1¼ hours) at 7:50am, 11:50am, 12:40pm, 1:20pm, 3:10pm, 3:50pm and 7:20pm from Monday to Saturday; all but the last two also run on Sundays. On Fridays and weekends the 7:50am and 1:20pm services continue to Valle Hermoso (CH$2200, 1½ hours). From Santiago's Terminal Sur there's one direct service to Valle Las Trancas (CH$10,000, seven hours, daily at 2:50pm) with **Buses Nilahué** (☎ in Santiago 02-778-5222, in Chillán 042-270-569; www.busesnilahue.cl). In winter there are shuttle buses from Valle Las Trancas up to the ski center. Hitchhiking up is also possible.

Coastal Towns

Quiet beaches come with rural surroundings in the remote coastal towns northwest of Chillán. The area's perfect for long lazy walks along the sand, and there's good, low-key surfing for those who want the waves without the parties.

COBQUECURA

A quiet little town with picturesque houses and dry walls made from local slate, Cobquecura has a long, wide beach with wild surf. The sands fill up in early February when Cobquecura hosts the Campeonato Nacional de Surf y Body Board. A deep baying sound resonates from a rock formation 50m offshore: known as the **Piedra de la Lobería**, it's home to a large colony of sunbathing sea lions. Follow the coast road 5km north and back to the beach and you reach the exquisite **Iglesia de Piedra** (Church of Stone), a massive monolith containing huge caves that open to the sea. The light inside the caves is mysterious –

Cobquecura's pre-Hispanic inhabitants held ritual gatherings inside the stone, and it now contains an image of the Virgin Mary.

From Chillán's Terminal de Buses Rurales, **Petorbus** (☎ 042-223-606) has buses to Cobquecura (CH$1400, 2½ hours) at 6:30am, 9am, 12:30pm, 1:30pm, 4:30pm and 7:20pm. **Nilahué** (☎ 02-778-5222; www.busesnilahue.cl) operates a direct bus from Santiago's Terminal Sur to Cobquecura (CH$10,000, seven hours, once daily) at 3:50pm.

BUCHUPUREO

Perhaps the most magical spot along Middle Chile's coastline, this tranquil farming village 13km north of Cobquecura along a dirt road is increasingly popular with surfers and moochers. Steep slopes covered with lush greenery surround the settlement, lending it a tropical air. Indeed, papayas are a major crop, as are potatoes, which many claim are the best in the country. Despite growing interest from tourists, the pace of life is slow here: oxen pulling carts are still a common sight. It's also a famous fishing spot – corvina (sea bass) apparently jump onto any hook dangled off the beach.

Dunes and scrubland separate the beach from the main road, which runs parallel to the shore before looping through the small town center to the beach. A couple of wooden walkways also connect the road and the sand.

Sleeping

Ayekán Aldea Turística (☎ 042-197-1756; www.turismoayekan.cl; campsites CH$15,000, 4-/6-/8-person cabins CH$50,000/60,000/70,000) In summer you can pitch your tent at one of 20 campsites in a pretty clearing at the bottom of a eucalypt-lined drive, close to the beach. A wooden barn-like building contains a restaurant serving cheap homemade food, and there's also a cabin for rent.

Cabañas Mirador de Magdalena (☎ 042-197-1890; www.miradormagdalena.com; La Boca s/n; 4-person cabin CH$35,000) Perched on stilts beside the river delta at the entrance to Buchupureo, these all-wood cabins have incredible sea views. The cabins are simple but clean, clustered around a lush garden with a walkway straight to the beach.

La Joya del Mar (☎ 042-197-1733; www.lajoyadelmar .com; 2-/4-person villas incl breakfast US$225/295; ☼) With their springy white beds, stylish bathrooms and open decks with panoramic views of the Pacific, these villas are so perfect a honeymoon spot they're worth getting married for.

Creepers and rich tropical plants overhang the terraces, and the pool seems to merge with the view of the sea. The vibe spills over into the airy, glass-fronted restaurant (mains CH$4100 to CH$6300, open from noon to 10pm), where locally grown ingredients play a big role in the creative pizzas, salads and sandwiches. Sundowners here are a must.

Getting There & Away

From Chillán's Terminal de Buses Rurales, **Petorbus** (☎ 042-223-606) has buses to Buchupureo (CH$1800, three hours) at 9am and 4:30pm.

CONCEPCIÓN

☎ 041 / pop 221,163 / 12m

Manufacturing industries, port facilities and nearby coal deposits have all conspired to make Concepción Chile's second most important city, economically speaking. It's also the most left-leaning – indeed, Chileans consider it a socialist hotbed – mainly because of the intellectual influences of the dozen or so universities scattered through town. When it comes to tourism, the story's not so exciting: Concepción is neither particularly scenic, nor is there a lot to do. But if you need to break up a long cross-Chile journey, do some shopping or change your air tickets, Conce's leafy squares, busy shopping streets and reasonable nightlife mean it's a pleasant stop-off.

History

In 1551 Pedro de Valdivia founded the original city of Concepción north of where it is today, near Penco (indeed, Conce's inhabitants are still known as Penquistas). Over the next few centuries the city was repeatedly besieged during the Spanish-Mapuche war, attacked by British and Dutch pirates and devastated by earthquakes in 1730 and 1751. But the colonizing residents stuck to their guns, and Concepción eventually became one of the Spanish empire's southernmost fortified outposts.

After independence, Concepción's isolation from Santiago, coupled with the presence of lignite (brown coal) near Lota, a coastal town south of Concepción, fomented an autonomous industrial tradition. The export of wheat for the California gold-rush market further spurred the area's economic growth.

During the early 1970s the city was a bulwark of support for Marxist President

Salvador Allende and his Unidad Popular party. As a result, it suffered more than other regions under the military dictatorship of 1973 to 1990.

Orientation

Concepción sits on the north bank of the Río Biobío, Chile's only significant navigable waterway, about 10km from the river's mouth. Hills block the city's expansion to the south and east, so Concepción's urban sprawl is moving rapidly in the opposite direction, toward Talcahuano, 15km to the northwest.

Downtown Concepción is a standard grid centered on Plaza Independencia, a bustling, wide-open square with the city's cathedral. It's bordered on the east and west by Aníbal Pinto and Caupolicán; and on the north and south by Barros Arana, a busy pedestrian street, and O'Higgins, a major east–west thoroughfare.

Information

Afex (☎ 223-9618; Barros Arana 565, Local 57; ◷ 9am-5:30pm Mon-Fri, 10am-1pm Sat) Changes traveler's checks.
BancoEstado (☎ 905-200; O'Higgins 486; ◷ 9am-2pm Mon-Fri) One of many banks with ATMs near Plaza Independencia.
Conaf (☎ 262-4000; Barros Arana 215; ◷ 8:30am-1pm & 2:30-5:30pm Mon-Fri) Limited information on nearby national parks and reserves.
Entel (☎ 225-5750; Barros Arana 541, Local 2; ◷ 9am-8pm Mon-Sat) One of several phone centers along Barros Arana.
Hospital Regional (☎ 220-8500; cnr San Martín & Av Roosevelt) Public hospital.
Laverap (☎ 223-4826; Caupolicán 334; per load CH$3600; ◷ 9:30am-8pm Mon-Fri, 9:30am-3pm Sat) Self-service and full-service.
Matrix (☎ 279-0460; Caupolicán 346; per hr CH$450; ◷ 9:30am-11pm Mon-Sat) Fast internet and cheap calls.
Post office (☎ 800-267-7736; cnr O'Higgins & Colo Colo; ◷ 8:30am-7pm Mon-Fri, 8:30am-1pm Sat)
Sanatorio Alemán (☎ 279-6000; Pedro de Valdivia 801) Efficient private clinic.
Sernatur (☎ 2741-4145; Aníbal Pinto 460; ◷ 8:30am-8pm Jan & Feb, 8:30am-1pm & 3-6pm Mon-Fri Mar-Dec) Provides brochures, but little else.

Sights

The massive, fiercely political mural *La Presencia de América Latina* is the highlight of the university art museum **La Casa del Arte** (☎ 224-2567; cnr Chacabuco & Paicaví, Barrio Universitario; admission free; ◷ 10am-6pm Tue-Fri, 10am-5pm Sat, 10am-2pm Sun). It's by Mexican artist Jorge González Camarena, a protégé of muralist legend José Clemente Orozco, and celebrates Latin America's indigenous peoples and independence from colonial and imperial powers. The museum also contains several rooms of paintings by major Chilean artists, and hosts regular temporary exhibitions.

Political correctness is clearly not a priority at the **Galería de la Historia** (☎ 285-3756; cnr Av Lamas & Lincoyán; admission free; ◷ 3-6:30pm Sun & Mon, 10am-1:30pm & 3-6:30pm Tue-Fri), where small dioramas representing local history gleefully celebrate the massacre of the Mapuche at the hands of conquistadores and pioneers. If you're able to overlook such ideological undertones, the models themselves are vivid and fun.

The museum is a few blocks south of the city center within **Parque Ecuador** (Av Lamas), a narrow stretch of well-maintained urban parkland which runs along the foot of **Cerro Caracol** – walk up one of the two access roads (continuations of Caupolicán and Tucapel) to a viewpoint with great views of Concepción.

Sleeping

Be they suited business types or lowlier employees, most of Concepción's hotel guests are here to work. The constantly high demand they create means lodgings here tend to be expensive and maintenance and service are slapdash, even at top-end hotels.

Hostal Bianca (☎ 225-2103; www.hostalbianca.cl; Salas 643-C; s/d incl breakfast CH$17,850/24,800, without bath CH$11,900/17,800; ▯) Conce's best budget hotel has bright, newly renovated – if rather small – rooms with firm beds and cable TV. Breakfast even includes scrambled eggs.

Hotel San Sebastián (☎ 295-6719; www.hotelsansebastian.cl; Rengo 463; s/d/tr CH$17,000/21,000/26,000, without bathroom CH$15,000/18,000/22,000) Plastic flowers and bright lilac walls in the hallway can't hide the fact that this hotel needs a revamp. Sagging beds and damp-stained carpets make the top-floor rooms a bit depressing, but the downstairs doubles are cleaner and brighter.

Hotel Alonso de Ercilla (☎ 222-7984; www.hotelalonsodeercilla.cl; Colo Colo 334; s/d/tr incl breakfast CH$31,000/39,200/53,500; ▯) Basic wood furnishings and beige-and-white linens mean this central hotel's compact rooms are ultraplain, but the friendly staff keep them spotless. Some rooms are nonsmoking, and there's wi-fi and cable TV in all of them.

Germania (☎ 274-7000; Aníbal Pinto 295; www.hotelgermania.cl; s/d/1-bedroom apt incl breakfast

CONCEPCIÓN

INFORMATION	
Afex	1 B1
BancoEstado	2 B2
Conaf	3 A2
Entel	4 B1
Hospital Regional	5 D1
Laverap	6 B2
Matrix	7 B2
Post Office	8 C1
Sernatur	9 B1

SIGHTS & ACTIVITIES	
Galería de la Historia	10 B3
La Casa del Arte	11 D2

SLEEPING	
Germania	12 C2
Hostal Bianca	13 A2
Hotel Alonso de Ercilla	14 C2
Hotel El Araucano	15 B1
Hotel San Sebastián	16 B2

EATING	
Chela's	17 B2
Crepería Jardín Secreto	18 B2
Fina Estampa	19 B2
Rancho de Julio	20 A2

DRINKING	
Café Rometsch	21 B1
Choripan	22 A2
Sauré Roeckel	23 B1

ENTERTAINMENT	
Cine Universidad de Concepción	24 B2
Club 592	25 A2

TRANSPORT	
EFE Ticket Office	26 A2
Hertz	27 A2
Jota Ewert ticket office	28 B2
Lan	29 B2
Rosselot	30 C2
Sky Airline	31 B2
Tur Bus Ticket Office	32 C1

CH$43,800/48,000/55,000;) They haven't stinted on the size of the rooms or of the TV sets at Germania. It's popular with business travelers, though the pine closets, olive-green walls and country prints make the vibe more homey than corporate.

Hotel El Araucano (274-0606; www.hotelarau cano.cl; Caupolicán 521; s/d incl breakfast CH$49,200/58,800;) Bizarrely, you have to walk through a shopping arcade to reach the all-marble reception of Conce's most upmarket hotel. The rooms themselves are run-of-the-mill: try to get one on floors four to seven, which have new bathrooms and flat-screen TVs.

Eating

Chela's (224-3367; Barros Arana 405; set lunch CH$1450, mains CH$2000; 8:30am-midnight Mon-Sat, noon-8pm Sun) The TV blares in this cheap, corner café, which serves up mountainous portions of *chorillana* (a pile of fries and onions with bits of sausage) and steaks that are perfect for throwing cholesterol counts to the wind.

Crepería Jardín Secreto (299-0130; O'Higgins 338; set lunch CH$2300, mains CH$2150-3450; 9am-11pm;) Crepes, pancakes, and waffles come with eggs and bacon at breakfast, topped with *manjar* (a milk caramel spread) at teatime or stuffed with Peking-style duck at dinner.

Rancho de Julio (223-9976; O'Higgins 36; mains CH$4500-6500; noon-4pm & 7pm-midnight) Cow is the name of the game at this ever-popular Argentine restaurant, which specializes in grilled-meat fests. Even the space itself smacks of the barn, both in terms of size and decoration. A few pasta dishes cater to noncarnivores.

Fina Estampa (222-1708; Angol 289; mains CH$4900-5900; 1-4pm & 8pm-midnight Mon-Sat, 1-4pm Sun) Starched tablecloths, fiercely folded napkins and deferential bow-tied waiters bring old-time elegance to this Peruvian restaurant. Ceviches, *ají de gallina* (chicken in a spicy yellow-pepper sauce) and other classics are perfectly executed, as is grilled seasonal fish.

Sublime (279-4194; Freire 1633; mains CH$4300-6900; 7pm-midnight Mon-Sat) Spidery chrome light fittings, stripped pine floors and upholstered red leatherette booths with unusual donut-shaped tables are an unusual way to kit out a traditional townhouse. But Conce's coolest eatery is all about unexpected combinations: mains could include kingklip in a hazelnut crust or steak served in pear sauce.

Drinking
CAFÉS
Penquistas have an almost religious obsession with *onces* (afternoon tea), so there's great coffee and moreish cakes and pastries to be had all over town.

Sauré Roeckel (☎ 279-9797; Barros Arana 541, Local 1; ﹁ 9am-9pm Mon-Fri, 9am-8pm Sat) Over 40 types of tea – including black, green, red, fruit, rooibusch and single-origin Chinese leaves – and a dazzling display of cream puffs make this the connoisseur's choice for afternoon indulgence.

Café Rometsch (☎ 274-7040; Barros Arana 685; ﹁ 8:30am-8:30pm) First you need to beat the hordes of stiffly coiffed fur-coat-toting old ladies to a table – your reward at this classic café is great cakes and gelato.

BARS
Concepción's nightlife has long centered on Plaza España and Arturo Prat, an area known as Barrio Estación. A new drinking and dancing scene is emerging along Av Pedro de Valdivia, 30 blocks southwest of the city center.

Club 592 (☎ 294-4497; www.592.cl; Arturo Prat 592; ﹁ 9pm-late Wed-Sat) Some of Conce's coolest club nights have been going down in this club for years: with two different dance floors, it's got something for both ravers and rockers.

Almendra Bar (☎ 246-4865; www.almendrabar .cl; Rengo 1624; ﹁ 9pm-4am Wed-Sat) Bespectacled design types lounge on the low 1950s sofas at this recycled old garage, the hippest haunt in Conce. Weekdays are about cool tunes, cocktails and sushi, but the dance floor gets going on weekends.

Madero Lounge (☎ 298-7877, Av Pedro de Valdivia; ﹁ 7pm-late Mon-Sat) One of the cluster of bars in the block, Madero attracts trendy, well-to-do Penquistas on the hunt for martinis and feel-good music.

Choripan (☎ 225-3004; Arturo Prat 542; ﹁ 7:30pm-late) A young, laid-back crowd gathers here for cocktails, pitchers of beer and lively conversation over the reggae and blues in the background.

Entertainment
Cine Universidad de Concepción (☎ 222-7193; O'Higgins 650) Shows arthouse movies every Tuesday.

Getting There & Around
AIR
Aeropuerto Carriel Sur (☎ 279-0907; Ruta Interportuaria) lies about 7km north of central Concepción. **Lan** (☎ 600-526-2000; www.lan.com; O'Higgins 648) flies here from Santiago (return from CH$40,000, one hour, four daily). **Sky Airline** (☎ 600-600-2828; www.skyairline.cl; O'Higgins 537) connects Conce with Puerto Montt.

There's no public transport directly to and from the airport, but the bright orange buses to the Universidad de las Américas (CH$500, every 20 minutes) leave you 500m south on the Ruta Interportuaria. From downtown, they run east along San Martín.

BUS
Concepción has two long-distance bus terminals. Most companies use the **Terminal de Buses Collao** (☎ 274-9000; Tegualda 860), 3km east of central Concepción. From outside the terminal, taxis and Bus 41 (CH$400, 10 minutes, four hourly) take you into town. Some companies also use the separate **Terminal Chillancito** (☎ 231-5036; Camilo Henríquez 2565), northeast along the extension of Bulnes. Unless otherwise indicated, the following companies use Terminal de Buses Collao.

There are dozens of daily services to Santiago with companies including **Eme Bus** (☎ 232-0094), **Pullman Bus** (☎ 232-0309; www.pull manbus.cl), **Nilahué** (☎ 231-0489; www.busesnilahue.cl) and **Tur Bus** (☎ 231-5555; www.turbus.cl; Tucapel 530), which also goes to Valparaíso and south to Temuco, Valdivia and Puerto Montt.

Línea Azul (☎ 286-1179; www.buseslineaazul.cl) goes to Chillán (half-hourly). **Buses Jota Be** (☎ 286-1533; www.busesjotabe.cl) connects Conce with Los Angeles (25 daily); some stop at the Salto del Laja. **Buses Biobío** (☎ 231-5554; www.busesbiobio.cl) has similar services and also goes to Angol (11 daily).

For services south along the coast, try **Jota Ewert** (☎ 285-5587; downtown ticket office at Lincoyán 557), which serves Cañete (25 buses daily). **Maga Bus** (☎ 225-6101) goes north to Cobquecura five times daily.

To get to Lota, take one of the local buses that run north along Tucapel every 10 minutes. Similar services to Talcahuano stop along O'Higgins.

MIDDLE CHILE

Destination	Cost (CH$)	Duration (hr)
Angol	3500	1½
Cañete	1000	2½
Chillán	2000	2
Cobquecura	2500	2½
Los Angeles	2000	2
Lota	500	½
Puerto Montt	10,000	7
Santiago	9000	7
Talcahuano	500	½
Temuco	5500	4
Valdivia	8000	6
Valparaíso/Viña del Mar	10,000	8

CAR

A car can be useful for exploring the national parks south of Concepción. These companies have downtown agencies.

Hertz (☎ 279-7461; www.autorentas.cl; Av Arturo Prat 248) Prices include all insurance and no deductibles.

Rosselot (☎ 273-2030; www.rosselot.cl; Chacabuco 726) Low prices with a high deductible.

TRAIN

There are no direct trains to Concepción, but you can buy combination bus–train tickets to Santiago (CH$12,500, 6¼ hours, five daily) from **EFE** (☎ 286-8008; www.efe.cl; cnr Freire & Av Padre Hurtado) in Barrio Estación. You transfer to the train at Chillán so direct buses, though they take slightly longer, are an easier (and cheaper) option.

AROUND CONCEPCIÓN
Buque Huáscar

More than a century has passed since the Guerra del Pacífico ended, but Chileans are still chuffed to have robbed the Peruvian navy in 1879 of the **Buque Huáscar** (☎ 041-274-5715; adult/child CH$1000/500; ☼ 9am-noon & 2-5:30pm Tue-Sun). Built in Birkenhead, England, in 1864, it's one of the world's earliest ironclad battleships and is now proudly moored at the naval base in Talcahuano, 13km north of Concepción. You can wander through cabins, communal areas and the engine room – all perfectly preserved, largely thanks to the never-ending spit-and-polish labor of naval conscripts – and see the spot where their idol, Arturo Prat, died in battle.

To get there take any local bus (CH$500, 30 minutes, every 10 minutes) with a 'Base Naval' sign in its windshield east along San Martín. Get off at the Apostadero Naval, beyond the Talcahuano Club de Yates on Av Villaroel.

You'll be required to leave your passport at the gate.

Lota

Concepción's exponential industrial and economic growth owes much to the huge offshore coal deposits discovered south of the city along the so-called Costa del Carbón (Coal Coast). The hilly coastal town of Lota spiraled into poverty when the mines closed in 1997, ending up with some of the most deprived shantytowns in the country. However, it has now reinvented itself as a tourist destination and makes an interesting half-day out from Concepción.

The star attraction is the **Mina Chiflón del Diablo** (Devil's Whistle Mine; ☎ 041-287-1549; www.lota sorprendente.cl; tours CH$4000; ☼ 9am-6:30pm), a naturally ventilated undersea mine that operated between 1884 and 1976. Ex-coal miners now work as guides on well-organized 45-minute tours that take you through a series of galleries and tunnels to a coal face some 50m under the sea. Before clambering into the rattling metal cage-elevator that takes you down, you're kitted out with safety gear. You can also visit the **Pueblito Minero**, painstaking re-creations of typical miners' houses built for the Chilean movie *Sub Terra* (Underground), which was filmed here.

The house where the general managers of the mine lived is now the almost-empty **Museo Histórico de Lota** (☎ 041-287-1549; www .lotasorprendente.cl; museum & botanical gardens adult/child CH$1600/1300; ☼ 9am-8pm Dec-Mar, 9am-6pm Tue-Sun Apr-Nov), about 2km further south. Skip on down the road to the entrance to a small peninsula containing the stunning 14-hectare **Parque Botánico Isidora Cousiño** (☎ 041-287-1549; www.lota sorprendente.cl; adult/child CH$1600/1300; ☼ 9am-8pm summer, 9am-6pm Apr-Oct, closed Mon). Paths wind through the mix of manicured flower beds, small ponds and wilder woodland to a lighthouse on a tip of land jutting out into the sea. To the right, an abandoned mineshaft and slag heap form stark industrial contrasts to the park's cultivated beauty.

GETTING THERE & AWAY

To reach Lota from Concepción, catch a Coronel–Lota bus (but not one to Lota-Arauco, which serves another part of town) from the corner of Tucapel and Av Los Carrera (CH$500, 30 minutes, every 15 minutes). The bus goes into Lota along Vista Hermosa, which later becomes Carlos Cousiño. For the mine, get off next to the Iglesia Parroquial and follow the signs downhill – it's a 15-minute walk, but *taxi colectivos* pass by regularly. For the park and museum, get off about 1.5km further down the road at the intersection with Av del Parque, which you walk 500m down.

CAÑETE

At Cañete, 135km south of Concepción, Mapuche resistance led to the death of Pedro de Valdivia in 1553. One of the best collections of Mapuche art and cultural artifacts in Chile is about 3km south of Cañete on Ruta 160 at the **Museo Mapuche de Cañete** (☎ 041-261-1093; www.dibam.cl; Camino Contulmo s/n; admission CH$600; ⏰ 9:30am-7pm Mon-Fri, 11am-7pm Sat & Sun Jan & Feb, 9:30am-5:50pm Mon-Fri, 11am-6pm Sat, 1:30-6:30pm Sun Mar-Dec). Inside are extensive, well-presented exhibits on Mapuche funerary customs, musical instruments, textiles and a great array of their legendary silverwork.

Jota Ewert (☎ in Cañete 041-261-1914, in Concepción 042-285-5587; Riquelme 98) operates 25 daily buses here from Concepción's Terminal de Buses Collao (CH$1000, 2½ hours).

SALTO DEL LAJA

Halfway between Los Angeles and Chillán, the Río Laja plunges nearly 50m over a steep escarpment to form a horseshoe-shaped **waterfall**. Some have dubbed the sight a miniature Iguazú Falls when it's full, but the comparison is far-fetched. Still, there are great views from where the road bridges the Río Laja. This road is the old Pan-American Hwy, but a new Ruta 5 bypass to the west means that only a few buses between Chillán and Los Angeles detour through here. A cluster of tacky souvenir stands and competing restaurants are evidence of the Salto del Laja's popularity with Chileans on road trips or outings from nearby cities.

To linger longer at Salto del Laja, check into **Los Manantiales** (☎ 043-314-275; Variante Salto del Laja Km480; s/d incl breakfast CH$15,000/21,000; ⊠), an HI-affiliated hotel whose large restaurant has spectacular views over the falls. The wood-paneled rooms are spacious and clean, and the decor of the whole complex seems gloriously unchanged since the 1970s. Regardless of what the signs at the entrance say, it's a good 15-minute walk along the winding access road.

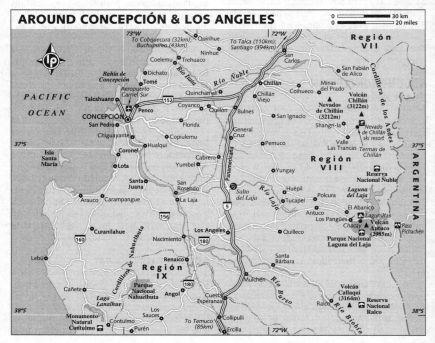

AROUND CONCEPCIÓN & LOS ANGELES

Many of the services run by **Buses Jota Be** (☎ in Concepción 041-286-1533; www.busesjotabe .cl) between Los Angeles and Concepción or Chillán stop at Salto del Laja. Times change frequently so always confirm the time of the next bus through to make sure you don't get stranded.

With its gorgeous rural setting, 15km south of Salto del Laja, the German-run **Residencial El Rincón** (☎ 099-9082-3168; www.el rinconchile.cl; s/d CH$23,000/28,000, dm/s/d without bath CH$10,000/15,000/22,000) is a destination in its own right, and the perfect place to take time out from traveling. The lodge has cozy, all-wood rooms and does fabulous homemade breakfasts and dinners. The owners also lead hiking and horseback riding excursions and in-house Spanish courses. Call in advance to arrange pick-up from Los Angeles or get off southbound buses at the Perales/Los Olivos exit of the Panamericana (Km494), also known as Cruce La Mona. Signs point the 2km to the lodge.

PARQUE NACIONAL LAGUNA DEL LAJA

Some 93km east of Los Angeles lies the 116 sq km **Parque Nacional Laguna del Laja** (adult/ child CH$1000/500; ⏱ 8:30am-7:30pm). Within the park is the **Volcán Antuco** (2985m), whose strikingly symmetrical flat-topped cone lies ahead of you on the drive up. Lava from this volcano dammed the **Río Laja**, creating the lake from which the park takes its name. The lava fields immediately around the lake form an eerie lunar landscape. Although the volcano may seem quiet, it is not extinct: volcanic activity was last recorded about 70 years ago.

The park protects the mountain cypress (*Austrocedrus chilensis*) and the monkey-puzzle tree, as well as other uncommon tree species. Mammals are rare, though puma, fox and viscacha have been sighted. Nearly 50 bird species inhabit the area, including the Andean condor.

There's a small Conaf post at **Los Pangües**, the park entrance, where you sign in. From here, a winding road takes you to the park headquarters at **Chacay**, 3km on.

Sights & Activities

Chacay is the starting point for several well-marked hiking trails. On the left-hand side of the road is the easy 1½-hour trail to two small but stunning waterfalls, the **Salto de Las Chilcas** (the point where the underground Río Laja emerges) and the **Salto del Torbellino**.

A 10km section of the Sendero de Chile leaves from the right-hand side of the road and goes to the **Laguna del Laja**. Nearby is the starting point for **Sendero Los Coigües**, a 2.5km hike to a spot with fabulous views of Volcán Antuco.

The park's star trek is the three-day **Sendero Sierra Velluda** circuit, named for the hanging glacier you pass along the way. It winds around Volcán Antuco, passing waterfalls and lava fields on the way; condors are also a common sight. Conaf rangers provide detailed instructions and information about all these hikes.

You can also drive through parts of the park: there's another 6km of uphill hairpin bends between Chacay and the start of the lava-edged Laguna del Laja. The road then winds alongside the lake for 28km until it reaches the red army hut at Los Barros, from where 4WD vehicles can continue to the Argentine border (closed April through September).

In winter the **Club de Esqui de los Angeles** (☎ 043-322-651; www.skiantuco.cl; day ski pass adult/child CH$12,000/8000) operates two drag-lifts and small restaurant on the slopes near Chacay, known as the Cancha de Ski Antuco.

Sleeping

You can camp inside the park at **Lagunillas** (campsites CH$10,000), 1km from the park entrance, where there are 22 sites with electricity, showers and toilets. At this writing a private company was renovating the four **Cabañas Lagunillas** (☎ 043-321-086; 6-person cabins CH$30,000), next to the campground. You need to bring all your own food supplies with you.

If you arrive near dark, you can stay the night at **Hostería El Bosque** (☎ 043-197-2719; Malacural 1360, El Abanico; dm/d without bathroom CH$6000/12,000, cabins CH$15,000), a simple family-run setup with clean, basic rooms.

Getting There & Away

From Los Angeles' Terminal de Buses Rurales, **Buses R-R** (☎ 043-369-563) goes through Antuco to the village of El Abanico, 8km from the entrance to Parque Nacional Laguna del Laja (CH$1400, 1½ hours, 11 daily). The last bus back to Los Angeles leaves at 8pm. It takes about 1½ hours to walk from here to the park, and another half-hour to reach the Lagunillas campsite. Hitchhiking is technically possible, but vehicles are a rare sight. The road is paved as far as El Abanico, where it switches to reasonably maintained gravel. All the same, you need a 4WD and chains to negotiate it between May and September.

LOS ANGELES

☎ 043 / pop 169,929

A useful base for visiting Parque Nacional Laguna del Laja (p169), Los Angeles is an otherwise unprepossessing agricultural and industrial service center 110km south of Chillán.

Orientation & Information

Los Angeles' Plaza de Armas is bounded by Valdivia, Caupolicán, Lautaro (which becomes Av Alemania to the east) and Colón, the city's main shopping street. The long-distance bus terminals are northeast of the city center on Av Sor Vicenta.

BancoEstado (☎ 455-450; Colón 140) Has an ATM and changes dollars.

Centro de Llamados FPL (☎ 314-829; Villagrán 401; ☑ 8:30am-9pm Mon-Sat) Cheap long-distance calls.

Ciber Plus Internet (☎ 345-710; Colo Colo 451, Local 1; per hr CH$400; ☑ 9:30am-midnight)

Clínica los Andes (☎ 210-200; www.clinicalosangeles .cl; Doctor Genaro Reyes 581) Large private hospital on the corner of Av Alemania.

Hospital Los Angeles (☎ 409-600; Ricardo Vicuña 160) Public hospital.

Lavandería Matic (☎ 348-015; Almagro 748; per kg CH$900; ☑ 9am-1pm & 3-6:30pm Mon-Sat)

Post office (800-276-7736; Caupolicán 464; ☑ 9am-7pm Mon-Fri, 9am-1pm Sat)

Sernatur (☎ 317-107, Caupolicán 450, 3rd fl, Oficina 6; ☑ 9am-5:30pm Mon-Fri)

Sights

An extraordinary collection of Mapuche silverwork is the star exhibit at the **Museo de la Alta Frontera** (☎ 408-643; Colón 121, 2nd fl, Plaza de Armas; admission free; ☑ 8:15am-2pm & 2:45-6:30pm Mon-Thu, 8:15am-2pm & 2:45-6pm Fri). Masks and headdresses, textiles and ceramics are among the other pieces on display.

Sleeping & Eating

A string of *residenciales* line Caupólican west of the Plaza de Armas. Despite appearances, they're not particularly cheap and mostly function as men's boarding houses, so women travelers might not feel comfortable there.

Hotel Antilén (☎ 322-948; Av Alemania 159; r with/without bathroom incl breakfast CH$19,000/12,000) Leatherette couches and a slate-fronted log fire lend a 1970s-chalet vibe to this budget hotel five blocks east of the Plaza de Armas. The excellent-value rooms, however, are newly renovated, clean and cozy, and have cable TV.

Hotel Dikran (☎ 230-030; www.hoteldikran.cl; Almagro 393; s/d/tr incl breakfast CH$29,000/39,000/48,000; 💻) Wicker furniture, wooden floors and ocher- or butter-colored walls give this friendly hotel a warm, homey feel. Singles are a bit cramped, but all rooms have cable TV and wi-fi.

Hotel Mariscal Alcázar (☎ 311-725; www.hotelal cazar.cl; Lautaro 385; s/d incl breakfast CH$45,530/56,118; 💻) The dour staff and sober navy-blue-and-white color scheme lets you know this is the city center's main business hotel. But if it's you and not your company paying the bill, you might balk at the peeling bathrooms, scuffed surfaces and cell-like gray doors here.

Solcito (☎ 313-499; Villagrán 300; mains CH$2700-4000; ☑ 9am-midnight Mon-Sat, noon-7pm Sun) Tables in the front half of this bright restaurant on the corner of Lautaro are scattered with newspapers, coffees and hot chocolates during the day, and icy *schops* at night. At the back, simple but flavorful grilled steaks or fish are served – soccer games on TV are the soundtrack.

Julio's Pizza (☎ 314-530; Colón 452; large pizzas CH$3600-5600, mains CH$4500-5500; ☑ 10am-midnight) Part of a small Argentine chain, this restaurant looks dim and rather past it, but its extra-cheesy pizzas and no-frills steak and fries are both tasty and filling.

Getting There & Away

BUS

Long-distance buses leave from two adjacent long-distance bus terminals on Av Sor Vicenta, the continuation of Villagrán, on the northeast outskirts of town.

Pullman Bus (☎ 363-053) and **Tur Bus** (☎ 600-660-6600; www.turbus.cl) leave from the **Tur Bus terminal** (☎ 363-136; Av Sor Vicenta 2061). Both have numerous daily departures to Santiago (CH$12,000, 6½ hours), most of which stop at Talca, Curicó and Rancagua. Over 20 daily services head south to Temuco (CH$6000, two hours), Osorno (CH$11,000, 5½ hours) and Puerto Montt (CH$14,000, seven hours).

All other services use the next-door **Terminal Santa María** (☎ 363-035; Av Sor Vicenta 2051). From here **Buses Jota Be** (☎ 533-181; www.busesjotabe .cl) runs buses to Concepción (CH$2000, two hours, every 30 minutes) and to Angol (CH$1200, 1½ hours, hourly), the gateway to Parque Nacional Nahuelbuta (p172). Some buses to Chillán (CH$1500, 1¾ hours, hourly) pass by the Salto del Laja (CH$1500, ¾ hour). **Buses Bío Bio** (☎ 534-699; www.busesbio bio.cl) operates along the same routes slightly less frequently.

Local bus routes operate out of the **Terminal de Buses Rurales** (Terminal Santa Rita; ☎ 313-232; Villagrán 501), on the corner of Rengo. To get to Parque Nacional Laguna del Laja, see p169.

CAR

As there's no public transport right up to the entrance of the Parque Nacional Laguna del Laja, a rental car can be really useful, especially for one- or two-day visits. **Rosselot** (☎ 314-487; www.rosselot.cl; Alemania 147) charges around CH$33,000 per day for a compact car and CH$58,200 for a 4WD truck.

ANGOL
☎ 045 / pop 56,204

It was seventh time lucky for Angol, which was razed to the ground on six separate occasions during the conflict between the Mapuche and the conquistadores. Despite its turbulent history, Angol is a small, sleepy town with little to do, but it provides the best access into mountainous Parque Nacional Nahuelbuta (p172), a forest reserve that protects the largest remaining coastal stands of araucaria pines, or monkey-puzzle trees.

Orientation & Information

Angol straddles the Río Vergara, an upper tributary of the Biobío formed by the confluence of the Ríos Picoiquén and Rehue. The city's older core lies west of the river and centers on an attractive Plaza de Armas (bounded by Lautaro, Prat, Bunster and Chorrillos).

BancoEstado (☎ 945-900; Chorillos 390) ATM and currency exchange.

Hospital Angol (☎ 551-048; Ilabaca 752) Public hospital.

Municipal tourist office (☎ 990-840; Glorieta Plaza de las Siete Fundaciones; ☺ 8:30am-5:20pm Mon-Fri Mar-Dec, 8am-8pm daily Jan & Feb) In the middle of the main square.

Net Cafe (☎ 714-408; Lautaro 465; ☺ 9am-11pm Mon-Sat, 9am-9:30pm Sun; per hr CH$300)

Post office (☎ 800-276-7736; Lautaro 202; ☺ 9am-1pm & 3-6:30pm Mon-Fri, 9am-12:30pm Sat)

Telefónica (☎ 711-102; Lautaro 491; ☺ 9am-9:30pm

Mon-Fri, 10am-2pm & 5-9:30pm Sat, 10:30am-2pm Sun; per hr CH$400) Long-distance calls and internet.

Sights

The centerpiece of the Plaza de Armas is a fountain adorned by four gloriously poised marble statues that represent Europe, Asia, the Americas and Africa. Huge, shady trees and well-kept flower beds make for a

Endearingly retro displays chart Angol's eventful history at the **Museo Histórico de Angol** (☎ 717-441; Sepulveda 371; adult/child CH$400/200; ☺ 10am-1:30pm & 3-7pm Mon-Fri, 10am-1pm Sat).

A plant nursery and agricultural college 5km east of town surround the **Museo Dillman Bullock** (☎ 711-142; Liceo Agrícola El Vergel; adult/child CH$500/200; ☺ 9:30am-7pm), which houses a collection of natural history specimens, archaeological artifacts and indigenous jewelry. Take *taxi colectivo* 2 from the Plaza de Armas.

Festivals & Events

Brotes de Chile One of Chile's biggest folk festivals takes place in the second week of January and includes traditional dances, food and crafts.

Sleeping & Eating

Ginna Medina (☎ 711-923; Covadonga 55; dm/s/d without bathroom incl breakfast CH$6000/6000/12,000; ☐) Some of the rooms at Angol's most popular budget lodgings are in a rather makeshift wooden cabin overlooking the back garden; others once belonged to the super-friendly owners' grown-up children. There's one basic dorm and you can camp in the garden if it's full. Use of the kitchen and wi-fi are included.

Duhatao (☎ 714-320; www.hotelduhatao.cl; Arturo Prat 420; s/d incl breakfast CH$25,500/38,500; ☐) A design hotel in Angol – who'da thunk it? The Duhatao blends clean modern lines with local crafts and colors – the springy beds have headboards made from old gate posts and handwoven throws, for example, and bathrooms have big bowl sinks. A slick restaurant and bar are on-site, and wi-fi is included.

Las Tortoras (☎ 712-275; Ilabaca 805; set menu CH$2400; ☺ 10am-midnight) Locals love the family-style cooking at Las Tortoras, where a moustachioed waiter gleefully wheels out huge portions of whatever's scrawled on the board near the door. *Plateada* or *lomo a lo pobre* (steak topped with a fried egg and served with French fries) are the house specials.

Sparlatto Pizza (☎ 716-272; Lautaro 418; large pizzas CH$5500-8000; ☺ 9:30am-1am Mon-Fri, 10:30am-3am

MIDDLE CHILE

Sat) This bustling little restaurant attracts golden oldies at teatime, then fills up with a younger crowd for pizzas and beer into the small hours.

Paraíso (☎ 719-560; Colipí 369; set lunch CH$1800, mains CH$3500-5500; ☺ 11am-8pm Mon-Fri, 6pm-1am Sat, 11am-6pm Sun; **V**) Lime-green walls and rustic tables announce the right-on vibe here. Healthy interpretations of Chilean classics and veggie enchiladas and burgers are on the menu.

Getting There & Away
Most long-distance bus services leave from Angol's **Terminal Rodoviario** (Bonilla 428), a 10-minute walk from the Plaza de Armas. To get to the center of town, turn left from the main exit and walk four blocks along José Luis Osorio to Bulevar O'Higgins, the main road, where you turn right and cross the bridge.

Several companies go north to Santiago (CH$7700 to CH$9700, eight hours), including **Pullman JC** (☎ 716-866) with four services daily, **Línea Azul** (☎ 715-867; www.buseslineaazul.cl) with two services daily and **Tur Bus** (☎ 711-655; www.turbus.cl) with seven buses daily also stopping at Chillán (CH$3200, 3¼ hours, two daily), Talca (CH$5600, five hours, two daily), Curicó (CH$9700, six hours, four daily) and Rancagua (CH$9700, seven hours, four daily). **Buses Jota Be** (☎ 712-262; www.busesjotabe.cl) has buses to Los Angeles (CH$1200, one hour, 22 daily) and also travels to Concepción (CH$2800, 2½ hours, every 30 minutes).

Leaving from its own terminal, **Buses Bio Bio** (☎ 465-387; www.busesbiobio.cl; Caupolicán 98) serves Temuco (CH$2800, two hours, 25 daily), Los Angeles (CH$1000, one hour, 11 daily) and Concepción (CH$3500, 2½ hours, 25 daily).

Buses Thiele's (☎ 711-110) extensive regional services connect Angol to Cañete (CH$2400, 2½ hours, nine daily) and Lebú (CH$3000, three hours, nine daily). Local and regional services leave from the **Terminal de Buses Rurales** (☎ 712-021; Ilabaca 422), including buses to Parque Nacional Nahuelbuta.

PARQUE NACIONAL NAHUELBUTA
Between Angol and the Pacific, the coast range rises to 1550m within the 68 sq km **Parque Nacional Nahuelbuta** (admission adult/child CH$4000/2000; ☺ 8am-8pm), one of the last non-Andean refuges of pehuenes, or monkey-puzzle trees. In summer, other interesting plant life includes 16 varieties of orchids and two carnivorous plant species. Various species of

Nothofagus (southern beech) are common here, and the Magellanic woodpeckers that typically inhabit them make for great bird-watching. Rare mammals such as pumas, Darwin's fox and the miniature Chilean deer known as the pudú also live in the park. According to some, it's a prime location for UFO spotting, too.

The dirt road between Angol and Cañete runs through the park. Conaf maintains the park headquarters and information center at **Pehuenco**, roughly halfway between the two park entrances, which are sometimes manned by rangers, too. There are no shops or restaurants within Nahuelbuta, so bring your own supplies. The park enjoys warm, dry summers, but is usually snow-covered during winter. November to April is the best time to visit.

Sights & Activities
Some 30km of roads and 15km of footpaths crisscross the park, so you can tour by car and on foot. Several marked hiking trails start at Pehuenco. The most popular is an easy 4.5km walk through pehuén forests to the 1379m granite outcrop of **Cerro Piedra del Águila** (literally, 'eagle rock'), which has fabulous views from the Andes to the Pacific. To the southeast you can see the entire string of Andean volcanoes – from Antuco, east of Chillán, to Villarrica and Lanín, east of Pucón. You can loop back to Pehuenco via the valley of the Estero Cabrería to the south: the trail starts beneath the west side of the outcrop and the whole hike takes about three

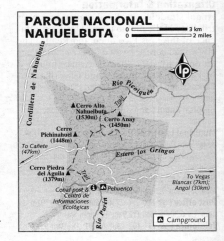

PARQUE NACIONAL NAHUELBUTA

hours. Alternatively, you can reach Piedra del Águila by walking 800m from the end of a shorter approach accessible by car. Another trail leads 5km north from Pehuenco to **Cerro Anay**, a 1450m hill with similar views. It's an easy three-hour walk there past wildflower beds and huge stands of araucarias.

Sleeping

Camping Pehuenco (6-person campsites CH$12,000) is next to the park headquarters, 5.5km from the entrance on the Angol side of the park. There are 11 campsites in shady forest clearings with picnic tables, and basic bathrooms with flush toilets and cold showers. Four rustic campsites make up **Camping Coimallín** (6-person campsites CH$12,000), 5km north of Pehuenco.

Getting There & Away

Local buses depart Angol at 6:45am and 4pm Monday to Saturday for Vegas Blanca

(CH$1200, 1½ hours), 7km from the eastern park entrance and 12.5km from the park headquarters at Pehuenco. **Buses Carrasco** (☎ 045-715-287) operates the route on Mondays, Wednesdays and Fridays; **Buses Nahuelbuta** (☎ 045-715-611) does the rest of the week. Both leave from Angol's **Terminal de Buses Rural** (cnr Ilabaca & Lautaro), and return from Vegas Blancas at 9am and 6pm. In January and February the morning service usually continues to the park entrance (CH$1400). Motorists with low-clearance vehicles may find the steep and dusty road difficult in spots, and you need a 4WD and chains June through August.

Mountain bikers generally need to dismount and walk at least part of the way up, and note that water is hard to find along the way. However, both bus services to Vegas Blancas are happy to carry bikes, so cycling from there is an alternative.

Norte Grande

Devil dusters zoom wantonly through the vast wasteland of the Atacama Desert, spinning dirt high into the air like an inverted waterfall. It's as if Pachamama, the earth goddess herself, decided to take back her creation and start anew in this sun-scorched land of dust, dirt and decay. But Chile's Norte Grande – with its undulating curves of rock and stone, Andean lagoons, snow-capped volcanoes, salt flats and sensuously perforated coastline – is here to stay.

Famous as much for its hilltop observatories as for its massive copper mines and high prices, Norte Grande is not for everyone. It holds less visceral appeal than many of the high-profile stops to the south and is quite expensive to get around. But there's just something about those vast, uninhabited spaces that seems to touch the soul and the imagination, and many travelers say there's simply no better place.

The star attraction of El Norte Grande is the tiny adobe village of San Pedro de Atacama. Ideally situated just a day trip away from the world's highest geyser field and some astounding desert formations, San Pedro has become Chile's number-one tourist draw in recent years.

But there's more to Norte Grande than San Pedro. Go for lung-bursting, jaw-dropping adventure in the high-altitude reserves of Parque Nacional Lauca and Parque Nacional Volcán Isluga, spend a week perfecting your tan on the beaches outlying old nitrate ports like Iquique and Pisagua, or make your own adventure in the lost ghost towns and hard-sprung mining centers that make this region unique.

HIGHLIGHTS

- Illuminate the past as you marvel at the expressive masks of the oldest mummies in the world at the **Museo Arqueológico San Miguel de Azapa** (p185)

- Test your lungs as you visit the Andean villages and high-altitude lagoons of **Parque Nacional Lauca** (p189)

- Charge the big breaks of **Iquique** (p194) by day, sipping pisco sours by night in this charming nitrate-era town

- Leave the tourist trail behind, visiting the rural communities around **San Pedro de Atacama** (boxed text, p217)

- Spot llama and vicuña on the way to **El Tatio** (p221), the highest geyser field in the world

Parque ★ Nacional Lauca
Museo Arqueológico ★ San Miguel de Azapa
Iquique ★
El Tatio Geysers ★
San Pedro ★ de Atacama

| POPULATION: 922,578 | AREA: 185,148 SQ KM | ELEVATION: 0-6700 M |

History

The past seems to be repeating itself in Norte Grande, playing over and over again like a heavy dub beat. It's a story of ecstatic booms and woeful busts, of resplendent pre-Columbian cultures fighting for survival in a dry, desolate land, and – like all of history – it's a tale of greed and pride, of subsistence and gluttony, of war and hard-won peace.

Despite its distance from Santiago, the region has always played a strong role in Chile's political and economic arenas, thanks mostly to the vast mineral wealth sitting just below the rocky surface. And even with its extreme desert aridity, it has sustained humans for many thousands of years.

The earliest culture to leave its mark was the Chinchorro, famous for its extraordinary burial practices (boxed text, p186). Coastal Chango peoples also fished from inflatable sealskin canoes and hunted guanaco here in pre-Columbian times. Far into the desert, irrigated agricultural practices adopted from the Tiwanku culture, which had its power center near Lake Titicaca in present-day Bolivia, sustained the Atacameño people who lived in oases near Calama and San Pedro de Atacama. These cultures – along with the Inka, who enjoyed a brief reign here from 1470 till the time of conquest – left impressive fortresses, agricultural terraces and huge stylized designs or geoglyphs on hillsides. Representations of llama trains still decorate the same valleys that served as pre-Columbian pack routes from cordillera to coast.

The indigenous populations were largely subdued during the conquest, which took place in the later part of the 16th century, with the Spaniards implementing the *encomienda* system, by which the Crown granted individual Spaniards rights to indigenous labor and tribute, and establishing ports in the coastal towns of Arica, Pisagua and Iquique. But pockets of independent Changos remained, and the area wasn't substantially resettled until large deposits of 'white gold' – nitrate (saltpeter) – brought the first boom to the region in the 1810s.

Interestingly, this part of the country was not actually Chilean until the late 19th century. It was claimed rather by Peru and Bolivia. However, that all changed with the pivotal War of the Pacific (1879–84), which was provoked by treaty disputes, the presence of thousands of Chilean workers in Bolivian mines, and Bolivian attempts to increase taxation on mineral exports. Within five years, Chile took control of the staggeringly important copper- and nitrate-rich land.

However Chileans were not the only ones to reap the benefits. Foreign prospectors had been sniffing around for some time, and moved quickly to capitalize on Chilean land gains. Beneficiaries included British speculator John Thomas North, who went on to take control of the railroads and more or less dominate the region's postwar economy.

The nitrate boom was uniquely explosive here. Nitrate *oficinas* (company towns) such as Humberstone flourished in the early 20th century and became bubbles of energy and profit in the lifeless desert. Large port cities such as Antofagasta and Iquique also began to flourish. However, the swift rise of the industry would be followed by a sharp fall. New petroleum-based fertilizers were devised in Europe and the nitrate-mining industry withered, exposing Chile's crippling dependence upon its revenue.

The nitrate bust drove the nation to near bankruptcy, and scores of creepy 19th- and 20th-century nitrate ghost towns now pockmark both sides of the Panamericana. Luckily for Chile, Norte Grande had another trump card up its sleeve – copper. Vast veins of this valuable resource sprang to the country's rescue and still keep it afloat today, especially with copper prices soaring. One of the world's largest open-pit copper mines, at Chuquicamata, is just one of many vast mines honeycombing the region. But with the boom came a slew of unique, modern problems, including environmental degradation, higher prices, overcrowding and pollution.

The region's rich pickings have at times acted as a kind of political smokescreen; the steady flow of revenue allowed Chilean politicians to postpone dealing with major social and political issues until well into the 20th century.

Militant trade unions also first developed in the north, during the late 19th and early 20th century, and introduced a powerful new factor into Chilean politics.

Climate

The Atacama is the most 'perfect' of deserts. Some coastal stations have never recorded measurable rainfall, although infrequent El Niño events can bring brief but phenomenal

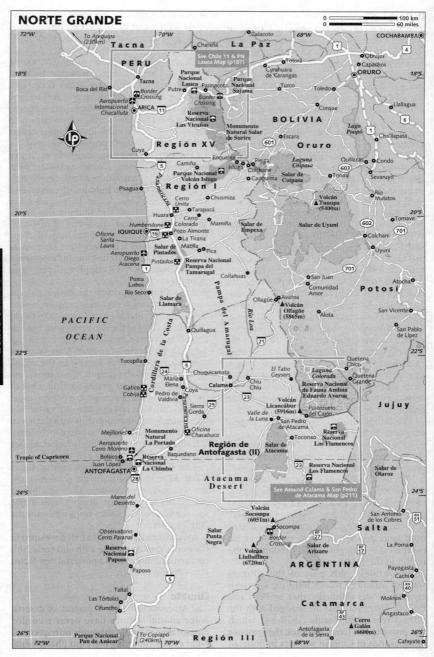

downpours in other places. Otherwise, the only precipitation comes from the convective fogs known as *camanchaca* (or *garúa*), which condense at higher elevations and support scattered vegetation on coastal hills. The meandering Río Loa is the only river here whose flow consistently reaches the Pacific.

Rainfall and vegetation increase with elevation and distance from the sea. In the precordillera (foothills) Aymara farmers still cultivate manmade terraces that have covered the hillsides for millennia. In the very high, arid Puna de Atacama, there is too little moisture to support human habitation – even the 5916m peak of Licancábur has no permanent snow cover.

Dangers & Annoyances

Northern Chile is a very safe place all in all. In the rough-and-tumble mining towns like Calama, however, women may get unwelcomed leers, hisses and whistles, and should be careful walking alone at night. Many of the low-budget hotels in the region are now full-time residences of visiting miners, which may make for an unpleasant situation for single female travelers. A general rule: if there are women and children around, you are probably safe. The currents on the beaches can be quite strong, making for good surf, but less-than-ideal swimming. Signs saying '*no apta para banarse*' (not suitable for swimming) are posted on most beaches that have strong currents. You should drive with your lights on during the day (and at night), and use caution when you see *zona de derrumbes* (rock-fall zone) signs.

Getting There & Away

If you are taking a car to Peru or Bolivia, check with the consulate about the latest required forms. The border at Chacalluta is open from 8am to midnight (Chilean time) and 24 hours from Friday to Saturday. Be sure to bring extra gas, water and antifreeze. If heading north to

Peru, you'll pass through the new Complejo Fronterizo Santa Rosa at Tacna, open 7am to 11pm (Peru time), and 24 hours Friday to Saturday.

Getting Around

The easiest way to get around Norte Grande is by rental car, which you can arrange in major cities. Buses run frequently, and offer top-notch service to nearly everywhere you'll want to go, and tour agencies run trips to the hard-to-reach national parks. While it's very expensive, you can fly to all of Norte Grande's major cities.

ARICA

☎ 058 / pop 199,877

The pace of Arica is simply delightful. It's warm and sunny year-round, there's a cool pedestrian mall to flip-flop around come sunset and decent brown-sugar beaches are just a short walk from the town center. Top this off with some kick-ass surf breaks and a cool clifftop War of the Pacific battlefield at El Morro, and you may just stay another day or two before you head up to nearby Parque Nacional Lauca or take an afternoon off from 'beach duty' to visit the Azapa Valley, home to some of the world's oldest known mummies.

History

The city's long history reveals itself unselfishly when you know where to look. Pre-Hispanic peoples have roamed this area for millennia. Arica itself was the terminus of an important trade route where coastal peoples exchanged fish, cotton and maize for the potatoes, wool and charqui from the people of the precordillera and altiplano. You can pore over their fascinating remains in the nearby Azapa Valley (p185) and marvel at their geoglyphs at several other sites, including the Lluta Valley (p186).

With the arrival of the Spanish in the early 16th century Arica became the port for the bonanza silver mine at Potosí, located in present-day Bolivia. As part of independent Peru, the city's 19th-century development lagged behind the frenzied activity in the nitrate mines further south. Following the dramatic battle over Arica's towering El Morro in the War of the Pacific, the city became de facto Chilean territory, an arrangement formalized in 1929.

The War of the Pacific left Bolivia completely landlocked. Chile has periodically

NORTE GRANDE

CALL AHEAD TO BOOK HOTELS

Many of the *residenciales* and budget hotels in Norte Grande are being used as housing for visiting miners. There are plans to build more hotels and housing in the region, but for now it's best to call ahead for reservations.

proposed territorial compensation to provide Bolivia sea access. As recently as 2005, proposals for a narrow Bolivian landing strip near the Peruvian border were being tossed around.

Orientation

Lording over the city is the dramatic headland, El Morro de Arica, a major battle site during the War of the Pacific. Beware the yeco birds that nest in the palm trees and whose droppings turn trees into ghostly silhouettes and splatter on tourists' heads.

Between El Morro and Río San José (which rarely has any surface flow), the city center is a slightly irregular grid. The main shopping street, 21 de Mayo, has a pleasant pedestrian mall running between Av Máximo Lira and Patricio Lynch.

At the foot of El Morro are the manicured gardens of Plaza Vicuña Mackenna, from which Av Comandante San Martín (not to be confused with Calle San Martín, east of downtown) snakes west and south towards the city's most popular beaches. In the other direction, Av Máximo Lira swerves sharply at sprawling Parque Brasil to become Av General Velásquez, leading to the Panamericana Norte and the Peruvian border, 20km to the north. To get to the Panamericana Sur, toward Iquique, take either 18 de Septiembre or 21 de Mayo eastbound.

MAPS

The **Automóvil Club de Chile** (☎ 252-678; 18 de Septiembre 1360; ☺ 9am-1pm & 3-7pm Mon-Fri, 9am-1pm Sat) sells highway maps, and Sernatur, the local tourist office, hands out city plans to fold into a back pocket.

Information

INTERNET ACCESS

Several internet cafés can be found on and around 21 de Mayo and Bolognesi.
Ciber Tux (Bolognesi 370; per hr CH$400; ☺ 10am-midnight)

INTERNET RESOURCES

Info Arica (www.infoarica.cl) An independent site in English and Spanish.

LAUNDRY

Lavandería La Moderna (☎ 232-006; 18 de Septiembre 457; ☺ 9:30am-9pm Mon-Fri, 9:30am-2pm Sat) Has reliable drop-off service, though it's not cheap (CH$1800 per kg).

LEFT LUGGAGE

Terminal Rodoviario de Arica (Terminal de Buses, Local 18; per half day CH$400; ☺ 8.30am-10.30pm) Leave baggage with the *custodia de equipaje*.

MEDICAL SERVICES

Farmacias Ahumada (cnr Colón & 21 de Mayo) Pharmacy.
Hospital Dr Juan Noé (☎ 232-242; 18 de Septiembre 1000) A short distance east of downtown.

MONEY

Arica enjoys good rates for changing money, and there are numerous 24-hour ATMs along the pedestrian mall (21 de Mayo).

Casas de cambio on 21 de Mayo change US dollars, Peruvian, Bolivian and Argentine currency, and euros. If you're game, try the street moneychangers at the corner of 21 de Mayo and Colón.

POST

Post office (Prat 305; ☺ 8:30am-1:30pm & 3-6:30pm Mon-Fri, 9am-12:30pm Sat) On a walkway between Pedro Montt and Prat.

TELEPHONE

There are public payphones along 21 de Mayo, and Centros de Llamadas (phone centers) throughout the city.

TOURIST INFORMATION

Conaf (☎ 201-200; tarapaca@conaf.cl; Av Vicuña Mackenna 820; ☺ 8:30am-5:15pm Mon-Fri) Has some information on Región I (Tarapacá) national parks. To get there, take *micro* 9 or *colectivos* 7, 2 or 23 from downtown (*micro* CH$300, *colectivo* CH$400).
Sernatur (☎ 252-054; infoarica@sernatur.cl; San Marcos 101; ☺ 8:30am-8pm Jan-Feb, 8:30am-5:30pm Mar-Dec) Friendly service with some brochures on Tarapacá and other Chilean regions.

Dangers & Annoyances

While Arica is a very safe city, it has a reputation for pickpockets. Be especially cautious at bus terminals and beaches.

Sights

EL MORRO DE ARICA

This imposing coffee-colored shoulder of rock looms 110m over the city. It makes a great place to get your bearings, with vulture-eye views of the city, port and Pacific Ocean. However, this lofty headland has a far greater significance to Chileans, for this

ARICA

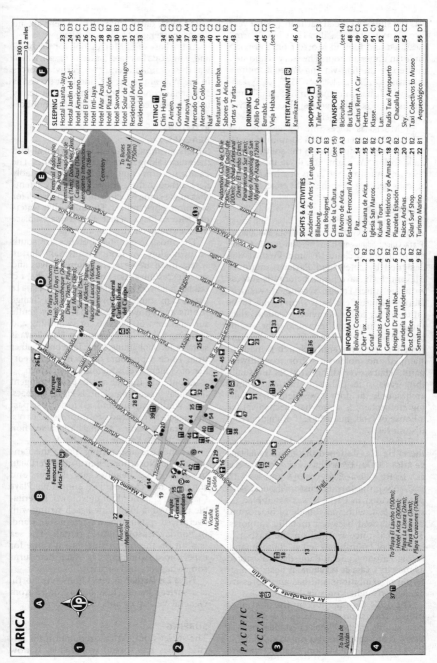

NORTE GRANDE

PACIFIC OCEAN

SLEEPING
Hostal Huanta-Jaya	23 C3
Hostal Jardín del Sol	24 D3
Hotel Americano	25 C2
Hotel El Paso	26 C1
Hotel Inti-Jaya	27 D3
Hotel Mar Azul	28 C2
Hotel Plaza Colón	29 B2
Hotel Savona	30 B3
Hotel Solar de Almagro	31 C3
Residencial Arica	32 C2
Residencial Don Luis	33 D3

EATING
Chin Huang Tao	34 C3
El Arriero	35 C2
Govinda	36 C3
Maracuyá	37 A4
Mercado Central	38 C3
Mercado Colón	39 C2
Naïf	40 C1
Restaurant La Bomba	41 C2
Sabores de Arica	42 B2
Tortas y Tartas	43 C2

DRINKING
Altillo Pub	44 C2
Barrabás	45 C2
Vieja Habana	(see 11)

ENTERTAINMENT
Kamikaze	46 A3

SHOPPING
Taller Artesanal San Marcos	47 C3

TRANSPORT
Bicircuitos	(see 14)
Bus Lluta	48 E2
Cactus Rent A Car	49 C2
Hertz	50 D1
Klasse	51 C1
Lan	52 B2
Radio Taxi Aeropuerto Chacalluta	53 C3
Sky	54 C2
Taxi Colectivos to Museo Arqueológico	55 D1

INFORMATION
Bolivian Consulate	1 C3
Ciber Tux	2 B2
Conaf	3 E2
Farmacias Ahumada	4 C2
German Consulate	5 B2
Hospital Dr Juan Noé	6 D3
Lavandería La Moderna	7 C2
Post Office	8 B2
Sernatur	9 B2

SIGHTS & ACTIVITIES
Academia de Artes y Lenguas	10 C2
Billabong	11 C2
Casa Bolognesi	12 B3
Casa de la Cultura	(see 15)
El Morro de Arica	13 A3
Estación Ferrocarril Arica-La Paz	14 B2
Ex-Aduana de Arica	15 B2
Iglesia San Marcos	16 B2
Kukuki Tours	17 C2
Museo Histórico y de Armas	18 A3
Plazoleta Estación	19 B2
Raíces Andinas	20 B2
Solari Surf Shop	21 B2
Turismo Marino	22 B1

To Playa Chinchorro (1km); Sunny Days (1km);
Soda Dipeloche (2km); Dirake (3km); Playa
Las Machas (3km); Suriaki (5km)

Tacna (40km); Parque
Nacional Lauca (160km);
Panamericana Norte

To Terminal Rodoviario
de Arica (1km);
Terminal Internacional de
Buses (1km); Doña Inés (2km);
Carolina Azul (10km);
Aeropuerto Internacional
Chacalluta (18km)

To Buses
La Paloma
(750m)

Cemetery

To Automóvil Club de Chile
(750m); Peruvian Consulate
(200m); El Tambo (2km);
Panamericana Sur (2km);
Museo Arqueológico San
Miguel de Azapa (12km)

To Playa El Laucho (100m);
Hotel Arica (300m);
Playa La Lisera (2km);
Playa Brava (3km);
Playa Corazones (10km)

To Isla de
Alacrán

Estación
Ferrocarril
Arica-Tacna

Muelle
Municipal

Parque
Brasil

Parque General
Carlos Ibáñez
del Campo

Parque
General
Baquedano

Plaza
Vicuña
Mackenna

Plaza
Colón

0   300 m
0   0.2 miles

was the site of a crucial battle in 1880, a year into the War of the Pacific. The Chilean army assaulted and took El Morro from Peruvian forces in under an hour. The story is told step by step in the flag-waving **Museo Histórico y de Armas** (☎ 229-192; adult/child CH$600/300; ⏱ 8am-8pm), which has information in Spanish and English. Look for plaques placed by ever military-minded Pinochet.

El Morro is accessible by car or taxi (CH$4000 round trip with a 30-minute wait), or by a steep footpath from the south end of Calle Colón. At night, you'll see the lighted head and outstretched arms of a huge statue of Jesus peeking over the cliff's edge.

CITY CENTER

Arica's oddest attraction is also its most admired. The Gothic-style **Iglesia San Marcos** (Plaza Colón; admission free; ⏱ 9am-2pm & 6-8pm) has a threefold claim to fame. First, it was designed by celebrated Parisian engineer Alexandre Gustave Eiffel, before his success with the Eiffel Tower. Second, it was prefabricated in Eiffel's Paris shop in the 1870s (at the order of the Peruvian president) then shipped right around the world to be assembled on site. Still more curious is the construction itself: the entire church is made of stamped and molded cast iron, coated with paint. That's everything from its unusually thin walls to its pillars, beams and pointy arches; only the door is wooden. The resulting atmosphere is somewhat mechanical for a house of God, but as a feat of engineering it's impressive.

Eiffel's legacy in Arica does not stop there. He also designed the grand **Ex-Aduana de Arica** (☎ 206-366; admission free; ⏱ 8:30am-8pm daily Jan-Feb, 8:30am-5:30pm Mon-Fri & 10am-4pm Sat & Sun Mar-Dec), the former customshouse. Also prefabricated in Paris, it was assembled on site in 1874, with walls made of blocks and bricks stacked between metallic supports. Though it once fronted on the harbor, a century of landfill has left it 200m inland, facing Parque General Baquedano. Restored as the city's **Casa de la Cultura**, it hosts a smattering of exhibitions and has an impressive 32-step wrought-iron spiral staircase.

The 1924 German locomotive that once pulled trains on the Arica–La Paz line now stands in the **Plazoleta Estación** (cnr 21 de Mayo & Pedro Montt). On the north side of the Plazoleta, the train station, **Estación Ferrocarril Arica-La Paz**, dates from 1913. There are no longer passenger trains to La Paz.

At the base of El Morro, look for the blue-and-white **Casa Bolognesi** (cnr Colón & Yungay), which was the command center for Peruvian forces in the War of the Pacific, and later served as a Peruvian consulate for a time. It is currently being renovated and is closed to the public.

Activities
BEACHES

Surfers, swimmers and sunbathers can all find their niche along Arica's plentiful beaches. The Pacific is warm enough to bathe comfortably here, although there are strong ocean currents that make some beaches more dangerous for swimming than others. The mirrorlike waters of sheltered Playa La Lisera is the safest place to take young children swimming.

The most frequented beaches are south of town, along Av Comandante San Martín, where there are several sheltered coves and seaside restaurants. The closest is **Playa El Laucho**, followed by decidedly prettier **Playa La Lisera**, 2km south of downtown, with change rooms and showers. Both have only gentle surf and are worthy spots for swimming and lounging alike. Nearby, rougher **Playa Brava** is suitable for sunbathing only. Take bus 8 either from 18 de Septiembre or the northeast corner of General Velásquez and Chacabuco.

About 7km further south, past a pungent fish-meal processing plant, is **Playa Corazones**, with wild camping and a kiosk. Just past the beach a trail leads to impressive caves, cormorant colonies, tunnels and a sea-lion colony. Hire a cab or bike it here.

Beaches are also strung along the Panamericana Norte for 19km to the Peruvian border; these beaches are longer and rougher, but cleaner. The enormous **Playa Chinchorro**, 2km north of downtown, is veritable playland: a long wide beach strung with overpriced restaurants, ice-cream shops and, in holiday seasons, jet-ski rentals. The sea is a bit on the rough side, but it's fine for experienced swimmers. The water here turns somewhat silty in February.

Playa Las Machas, a few kilometers north, is a surfer's haunt. Take bus 12 or 18 from General Velásquez and Chacabuco.

SURFING

The secret's out: Arica's reputation for terrific tubes has spread worldwide. It now hosts high-profile championships and tempts surfing film crews to the area. July sees the biggest breaks. As well as Playa Las Machas, expert surfers also hit the towering waves of El Gringo and El Buey at Isla de Alacrán, an expert point break south of Club de Yates.

Billabong (☎ 232-599; 21 de Mayo 493) sells boards, and you can get board shorts and other threads at **Solari Surf Shop** (☎ 233-773; 21 de Mayo 160).

Courses

Academia de Artes y Lenguas (☎ 258-645; www .spanishinchile.blogspot.com; 21 de Mayo 483, 3rd fl) offers Spanish courses (CH$5000 per hour or CH$135,000 for 30 hours) and occasional dance classes.

Nueva Acropolis (☎ 233-967; www.arica.nueva -acropolis.cl, in Spanish; Lastarria 1327) has a variety of courses and intellectual talks with everything from tai chi to cooking on offer.

Tours

Every other doorway on Bolognesi leads into a tour agency offering city tours or trips to the Azapa Valley, the precordillera, Parque Nacional Lauca and other altiplano destinations; some run trips themselves, while others contract out.

Kukuli Tours (☎ 255-030; kukulitours@tie.cl; Bolognesi 470) Runs day trips to Lauca (CH$15,000 per person).

Raices Andinas (☎ 233-305; www.raicesandinas.com; Paseo Thompson, Local 21) A respectable little Aymara-run outfit recommended for encouraging better understanding of the local people. Tours into the mountains last from two days (around CH$50,000) to four (around CH$145,000); prices vary according to the number of participants.

Turismo Marino (☎ 099-682-5005; turismomarinio@ gmail.com; muelle municipal) For expensive boat trips to Pisagua (CH$300,000) ask for Don Raul at the muelle municipal.

Festivals & Events

Carnaval Ginga Visitors in mid-February witness blaring brass bands and dancing by traditional *comparsas* groups. The festival draws around 15,000 spectators during a three-day weekend. Most of the action takes place on Av Comandante San Martín near El Morro, which the Municipalidad blocks off to traffic.

Concurso Nacional de Cueca A folkloric dance festival in the Azapa Valley held each June.

Semana Ariqueña Arica week is held in early June.

Sleeping

BUDGET

Taxi drivers earn commission from some *residenciales* (budget accommodations) and hotels; be firm in your decision. Free camping is possible at dark-sand, no-shade Playa Corazones, 8km south at the end of Av San Martín, with dirty, crowded sites; bring water.

Sumaki (campsites per person CH$1500), 5km north of Arica near Playa Las Machas, has a volleyball court, bathrooms and showers.

Residencial Arica (☎ 255-399; 18 de Septiembre 466; r with/without bathroom CH$5000/4000) Clean and central, this little joint is a good bet for budget hunters.

Residencial Don Luis (☎ 252-668; Sotomayor 757; r per person CH$5000) If every cent counts, this ill-lit but friendly *residencial* offers aging rooms that smell of wood polish, a communal kitchen and laundry service. Entertainment is provided by the small dogs scurrying around the parquet floor.

Doña Inés (☎ 248-108; casadehuespedes@hotmail .com; Manuel Rojas 2864; dm incl breakfast CH$5500-6500, d CH$12,000-14,000) As much a hip hang-out as a hostel, this small Hostelling International (HI) property is run by a laid-back motorbike fanatic. It has contemporary rooms, a cozy patio with hammock, Ping-Pong, and a wall that's set aside for graffiti artists. Breakfast and checkout times are flexible. It's a 20-minute walk or call ahead to arrange a free pick-up at the bus station. Paragliding tours are available.

Sunny Days (☎ 241-038; www.sunny-days-arica.cl; Tomas Aravena 161; dm CH$6000, r per person incl brekfast with/without bathroom CH$8000/7000; P ⌨) About 300m from the bus terminals in a residential area near the beach, this supremely welcoming hostel is run by a helpful Kiwi-Chilean couple. Laundry, storage, bike and boogie-board rental and a communal kitchen are all available. Rates include an 'all you can eat' breakfast.

Hostal Jardín del Sol (☎ 232-795; www.hostaljardin delsol.cl; Sotomayor 848; r per person incl breakfast CH$8000; ⌨) This is the best hostel in town. There's a relaxed atmosphere with an airy lounge room (complete with stereo), open-air mezzanine, excellent beds, fans and cable TV, bike hire and a big communal kitchen. Rooms upstairs are better quality. There's even a book exchange and wi-fi for you media-heads.

Hostal Huanta-Jaya (☎ 314-605; hostal.huanta .jaya@gmail.com; 21 de Mayo 660; r per person CH$8000) A good bet for clean freaks, the Huanta-Jaya has uber-clean rooms reached from a dark shot-gun hall. They'll bring you a fan upon request (and believe us, you'll need them). The beds are new and comfy, with nuevo-Andean covers providing a bit of style.

Hotel Mar Azul (☎ 256-272; www.hotelmarazul.cl, in Spanish; Colón 665; s/d incl breakfast CH$9000/14,000; ☎) A superb deal with a fancy-schmancy facade, the Mar Azul has an alluring little outdoor pool, cable TV, bleached bathrooms and a kaleidoscopic collection of chirruping birds to announce your arrival. A sauna and massage can be arranged, and there's wi-fi.

MIDRANGE

ourpick Hotel Inti-Jaya (☎ 230-536; www.hotelintijaya .cl; 21 de Mayo 850; s/d incl breakfast CH$13,000/CH$20,800; ☒ ▣) Release your inner Dirk Diggler in this unabashedly over-the-top hotel, jam-packed with intricate wood-carvings, over-sized mirrors, polished stone, statues, drapes and potted plants. Its 12 rooms are well equipped, and bathrooms are stocked with everything from disposable toothbrushes to shaving cream. In case you were wondering, Inti-Jaya means 'distant sun' in Aymara. They don't accept credit cards, which is unfortunate to say the least.

Hotel Solar de Almagro (☎ 224-444; hotelalmagro arica@entelchile.net; Sotomayor 490; s/d CH$18,490/21,700; ℗) An old favorite, this large, accommodating hotel offers spacious, bright rooms with irreproachable bathrooms and cable TV. While the private terraces make a nice touch, all things said, it's not the best value in the price category.

Casona Azul (☎ 216-491; casonaazul@hotmail.com; Mariscal Sucre 65, Villa Frontera; d incl breakfast CH$27,300; ☎) If you've got wheels, it's worth the 10km trip to this guesthouse in a restored railroad building. It's located in Villa Frontera, between Arica and the airport, and about 800m from the Panamericana. Rooms retain traditional English style and the large porch overlooks the grassy garden.

Hotel Plaza Colón (☎ 231-244; www.hotelplaza colon.cl, in Spanish; San Marcos 261; s/d/tr incl breakfast CH$21,000/29,000/37,500; ℗ ▣ ♿) The superb position facing Iglesia San Marcos and the towering El Morro makes up for stale and dusty rooms in this Pepto Bismal–colored hotel. Breakfast is served in the top-story salon – perhaps the best view in town.

Hotel Savona (☎ 231-000; www.hotelsavona.cl, in Spanish; Yungay 380; s incl breakfast CH$21,000-26,000, d CH$31,000; ℗ ▣ ☎) One of the best values in this category, Savona is a snowy-white hotel at the foot of El Morro, with concertina-style design and built around an attractive terrace with bougainvillea blooms and a pill-shaped pool. Rooms are also pleasantly decorated and decent value.

TOP END

Hotel El Paso (☎ 230-808; www.hotelelpaso.cl, in Spanish; Av General Velásquez 1109; incl breakfast CH$30,000-46,000, d CH$34,000-53,000; ℗ ☒ ▣ ☎) A deservedly popular hotel with single-story buildings scattered through a maze of courtyards and gardens, the Paso is a bit '70s bebop, but a solid buy for the price. It's within walking distance of the town center and the waterfront. Highly deodorized rooms are bright and well equipped, but the hotel is best known for its excellent service (overseen directly by the owner).

Hotel Arica (☎ 254-540; www.panamericanahoteles .cl; Av Comandante San Martín 599; incl breakfast s/d CH$36,680/43,500, ste CH$56,500-68,300; ℗ ☒ ▣ ☎) This large-scale resort hotel offers a variety of rooms, including cabins that overlook the crashing surf, and is hands-down the fanciest digs in town. It's located south of the city center by Playa El Laucho.

Hotel Americano (☎ 257-752; www.hotelamericano .cl; General Lagos 571; s/d incl breakfast CH$38,900/43,400; ℗ ▣) The spacious all-business rooms at this modern hotel do at least deliver comfort, but they're a bit uninspired – as the late, great J. Brown said, 'where's the soul?' Then again, the Sultan of Soul himself would be pleased by the mod-con conveniences like fridge, hairdryer, ceiling fan, and – for crashing out after a night of 'groovin' it like a sex machine' – cable TV.

Eating
BUDGET

Govinda (Blanco Encalada 200; set meals CH$800; ⊙ 12:30-3:30pm Mon-Fri; Ⓥ) Even nonvegetarians declare this diminutive Hare Krishna restaurant a winner. Hidden away in a quiet residential area, it feels much like eating in somebody's living room. Imaginative three-course lunch menus (served on a single metal platter) include fresh organic produce and cost laughably little for the quality.

Naif (☎ 258-682; Sangra 365; breakfast CH$1000-1500, set lunch CH$1600; ⊙ breakfast, lunch & dinner Mon-Sat) Tucked away on an easily missed pedestrian

---

SELF-CATERING OPTIONS

There's nothing better than making your own picnic lunch. Here's some places to buy your eats:

Mercado Central (Sotomayor 340; set menu CH$800-1500; ☺ breakfast & lunch) Cater your own takeaway beach meal or eat at the family-friendly food stalls in the old central market.

Mercado Colón (cnr Colón & Maipú; set menu CH$800-1500, fish dishes CH$1300-2000; ☺ breakfast & lunch) Small-time restaurants offer cheap and freshly fried *corvina* (sea bass), *cojinova* (Spanish hake) and other fish dishes under this bustling little covered market. For a more relaxed environment, try El Rey del Marisco, located above the market.

Sabores de Arica (☎ 259-101; www.saboresdearica.cl; Bolognesi 317; ☺ 10am-6pm Mon-Fri, 10am-2pm Sat) If you'd like to literally take home a taste of the region, this place sells neatly packaged local produce, from juicy olives and wicked Mayacuyá liquors to organic quinoa.

---

street, this is a funky little café-cum-bar with curly ironwork chairs, sharp art and occasional live music. Happy hour runs from 8pm to 11pm.

Restaurant La Bomba (☎ 255-626; Colón 357; set menu CH$2000, mains CH$1300-$2000; ☺ lunch & dinner) Pass the shiny red engine to reach this unpretentious café in the local fire station. If you can't find it, listen for its deafening siren at noon. There's nothing particularly spectacular about the food, which focuses on Chilean fare, but you can't beat the setting.

Chin Huang Tao (☎ 232-823; Patricio Lynch 224; set lunch CH$2500-3500, mains CH$2500-3000; ☺ lunch & dinner) A small atmospheric Cantonese *chifa* (Chinese restaurant), warmly lit and watched over by poker-faced goldfish. Save money by taking your set lunch with you. Hunan beef on the beach – perfect!

MIDRANGE & TOP END

Tortas y Tartas (☎ 258-538; 21 de Mayo 233; mains CH$2400-5100; ☺ 9:30am-11pm) Relax on the open-air terrace with a beer or head here for a late breakfast and some of the best coffee in town. The food is surprisingly good, featuring an eclectic mix from teriyaki chicken to a salad topped with fresh salmon.

El Arriero (☎ 232-636; 21 de Mayo 385; mains CH$4000-5200; ☺ lunch & dinner) This old-school eatery is perfect for red-blooded carnivores who don't mind waiting for an old-fashioned *parrillada* (a mixture of grilled meats). Expect gracious service and an aging steak-house atmosphere.

Maracuyá (☎ 227-600; Av Comandante San Martín 0321; mains CH$5000-10,000; ☺ noon-3pm & 8pm-1am) To treat yourself to a superb seafood meal complete with bow-tie service and sea view, head to this villa-style restaurant, down-

town next to Playa El Laucho. Enjoy the salty air mingled with scents of flowering vines and relax to a soundtrack of waves booming below.

Drinking

Take time out over a hot coffee or a chilled Escudo in one of a dozen streetside cafés strung along the 21 de Mayo pedestrian mall. Head over to 18 de Septiembre, west of Patricio Lynch, for late-night fun.

Barrabás (☎ 230-928; 18 de Septiembre 560; ☺ 6pm-late) For live music or DJs, a happy youthful crowd and deep lounge areas where you can cozy up.

Altillo Pub (☎ 231-936; 21 de Mayo 260; ☺ 6pm-late Mon-Sat) This buzzing pub has candlelit tables, a lengthy drinks and snacks menu and comfy chairs perfect for some serious 21 de Mayo people-watching. Don't eat here if you're in a hurry though.

Vieja Habana (21 de Mayo 487; ☺ 6pm-late Mon-Sat) Has salsa classes to get those gringo hips 'shaking like a polaroid picture.'

Entertainment

Kamikaze (☎ 258-136; Av Comandante San Martín 055; cover CH$1200; ☺ 7pm-3:30am Thu-Sat) A hopping seafront bar and *discoteca* (disco) with a macabre WWII theme at the foot of El Morro; although it sometimes opens early for live gigs, the action usually starts after midnight.

Some of the hippest bars and discos are strung along Playa Chinchorro, including **Soho Discotheque** (www.aricaxtreme.cl, in Spanish; Playa Chinchorro; cover CH$1500; ☺ 11pm-late Thu-Sat) and the attached pub **Drake** (cover with drink around CH$1300), both of which get a variety of DJs as well as live salsa and rock bands.

Shopping

A part-kitsch, part-crafts artisans' market is strung along Pasaje Bolognesi, a narrow passageway running from Plaza Colón.

Poblado Artesenal (☎ 222-683; Huelles 2825; ⏱ 9:30am-1:30pm & 3:30-8pm Tue-Sun) On the outskirts of Arica, near the Panamericana Sur, is this more full-on shopping experience: a mock altiplano village filled with serious craft shops and studios, selling everything from ceramic originals to finely tuned musical instruments. The village even has its own church, a replica of the one in Parinacota (see p190), complete with copies of its fascinating murals. A *peña folclórica* (folk-music and cultural club) meets here irregularly, usually on Saturday nights. *Taxi colectivos* (shared taxis) numbers 8, 13 and 18, and U pass near the entrance, as do buses 2, 3, 7, 8 and 9.

Taller Artesanal San Marcos (☎ 203-405; Sotomayor & Baquedano; ⏱ 2-5pm Mon-Sat) Operated by the Gendarmería de Chile and selling a hotchpotch of prisoners' crafts. Where else can you get a cotton bikini handmade by Chilean women prisoners? Knock on the door if the Gendarmería cabin is shut.

Getting There & Away

From Arica, travelers can head north across the Peruvian border to Tacna and Lima, south toward Santiago or east to Bolivia.

AIR

Aeropuerto Internacional Chacalluta (☎ 211-116) is 18km north of Arica, near the Peruvian border. Santiago-bound passengers should sit on the left side of the plane for awesome views of the Andes and the interminable brownness of the Atacama Desert.

Lan (☎ 600-526-2000; www.lan.com; Arturo Prat 391) has one direct daily flight to Santiago (CH$34,950) and four one-stop flights through Iquique (CH$34,950 to CH$81,450). Flights to Iquique are CH$26,900. To get to La Paz, Bolivia, you'll need to fly through Iquique (p200).

Sky (☎ 600-600-2828; www.skyairline.cl, in Spanish; 21 de Mayo 356) has less frequent flights to Santiago (around CH$87,200) and Iquique (CH$17,000).

BUS

Arica has two main bus terminals. **Terminal Rodoviario de Arica** (Terminal de Buses; ☎ 241-390; Diego Portales 948) houses most companies traveling south to other destinations in

Chile. Next door, **Terminal Internacional de Buses** (☎ 248-709; Diego Portales 1002) handles international and some regional destinations. The area is notorious for petty thievery, so be sure to keep an eye on your luggage at all times. To reach the terminals, take *colectivo* 1, 4 or 11 from Maipú or bus 8 from San Marcos.

More than a dozen companies have offices in Terminal Rodoviario de Arica, and ply destinations toward the south, from Iquique to Santiago. Some major ones:
Buses Pullman Santa Rosa (☎ 241-029)
Flota Barrios (☎ 223 587)
Pullman Bus (☎ 223-837)
Pullman Carmelita (☎ 241-591)
Pullman San Andrés (☎ 242-971)
Ramos Cholele (☎ 221-029)
Tur Bus (☎ 222-217)

A schedule board inside the terminal helps you find your bus (but it's not always accurate). Buses on Sunday run less often.

Some of the standard destinations and fares are shown here.

Destination	Cost (CH$)	Duration (hr)
Antofagasta	16,000	13
Calama	16,000	10
Copiapó	24,400	18
Iquique	7000	4½
La Paz, Bolivia	8000	9
La Serena	31,600	22
Santiago	35,000	28

Bus Lluta (cnr Chacabuco & Av Vicuña Mackenna) goes to Poconchile and Lluta six to nine times daily (CH$700 to CH$1000, one hour).

Buses La Paloma (☎ 222-710; Germán Riesco 2071) travels to the Belén precordillera villages of Socoroma on Tuesday and Saturday (CH$2500), Belén on Tuesday and Friday (CH$2800) and to Putre daily (CH$2500); all depart Arica at 7am. It's recommended you take a taxi to this area when leaving early in the morning. La Paloma also goes to the precordillera villages of Tignamar and Codpa Tuesday and Friday at 8am (CH$2600, three hours), returning at 5pm. It's possible to make a loop on public transportation, but it's not particularly convenient. You would have to walk or hitchhike (with very few vehicles on the dry and dusty road) the 13km between Belén and Tignamar. Lonely Planet does not recommend hitchhiking.

For Parinacota (CH$5000) and Parque Nacional Lauca, look for **Trans Cali Internacional** (☎ 261-068) in the international terminal. Trips depart daily at 9:30am.

To get to Tacna, Peru, **Adsubliata** (☎ 263-526) buses leave the international terminal every half-hour (CH$1000); *colectivos* charge CH$3000. No produce is allowed across the border. **Tas-Choapa** (in Santiago ☎ 02-490-7561; Terminal Internacional de Buses) has a service to Lima, Peru (CH$59,000, 20 hours) on Tuesday, but it's cheaper to take local transportation to Tacna and then buy a separate ticket to Lima, Cuzco or elsewhere in Peru.

To get to La Paz, Bolivia (around CH$7000, nine hours), the comfiest service is with **Chile Bus** (☎ 222-817), but cheaper buses are available with Trans Cali Internacional, Buses Litoral, Pullman Zuleta, **Cuevas y Gonzalez** (☎ 241-090) and **Trans Salvador** (☎ 246-064) in the international bus terminal; most have morning departures (8am to 10am). Buses on this route will drop passengers in Parque Nacional Lauca, but expect to pay full fare to La Paz.

Buses Géminis (☎ 241-647), in the main terminal, goes to Salta and Jujuy in Argentina via Calama and San Pedro de Atacama (CH$22,000, three weekly).

TRAIN
Trains to Tacna (CH$1200, 1½ hours) depart from **Estación Ferrocarril Arica-Tacna** (☎ 231-115; Av Máximo Lira 889) at 9am and 7pm, Monday to Saturday.

Getting Around
TO/FROM THE AIRPORT
Aeropuerto Internacional Chacalluta (☎ 211-116) is 18km north of Arica. Taxis charge CH$5000 to the airport. In town, call **Radio Taxi Aeropuerto Chacalluta** (☎ 254-812; Patricio Lynch 371). **Arica Service** (☎ 314-031) runs airport shuttles (CH$2500 per person).

BICYCLE
You can rent decent mountain bikes with double shock absorbers at **Bicircuitos** (Estación Ferrocarril Arica-La Paz) for CH$6000 per day or CH$2000 per hour.

BUS & TAXI
Arica is in the process of changing many of its bus routes, so check with locals before you hop on a line. Local buses (*micros*) and shared taxis (*colectivos*) connect downtown with the main bus terminal. *Taxi colectivos* are faster and more frequent, costing CH$400 per person. Destinations are clearly marked on an illuminated sign atop the cab. *Micros* run to major destinations, and cost CH$300 per person. **Radio Taxi service** (☎ 259-000) – if you don't like sharing your cab – is CH$1200.

CAR
Rental cars are available, starting at around CH$16,000 per day.
Avis (☎ 228-051; Aeropuerto Internacional Chacalluta)
Budget (☎ 258-911; Aeropuerto Internacional Chacalluta)
Cactus Rent a Car (☎ 257-430; cactusrent@latinmail .com; Baquedano 635, Local 40) Prices are cheaper than the chains.
Hertz (☎ 231-487; Baquedano 999)
Klasse (☎ 254-498; www.klasserentacar.cl; Av General Velásquez 762, Local 25) Also cheaper than the chains.

AROUND ARICA
Museo Arqueológico San Miguel de Azapa
Some of the world's oldest known mummies reside in the Azapa Valley's superb **Museo Arqueológico** (☎ 205-555; adult/child CH$1000/500; ☺ 9am-7pm Jan & Feb, 10am-6pm Mar-Dec). The museum displays a large assemblage of exhibits from 7000 BC right up to the Spanish invasion, including an outdoor 'petroglyph park' and an enormous olive press. Well-written booklets in several languages are available to carry around the museum. No photos are allowed.

The staff can point out nearby archaeological sites: ask about early geoglyphs at **Atoca**; Tiwanaku-era (AD 700–1000) fortifications at **Pukará San Lorenzo**; and the Inkaic **Cerro Sagrado** (AD 1000–1400). Some Arica tour companies include the museum and other valley sites on their itineraries.

The museum is 12km east of Arica. From Parque General Carlos Ibáñez del Campo in Arica, at the corner of Chacabuco and Patricio Lynch, *taxi colectivos* charge CH$800 (one way) to the front gate of the museum. There is also a stand outside the Terminal Internacional de Buses.

CHILE 11 HIGHWAY
About 10km north of Arica, the Panamericana intersects paved Chile 11, which ushers traffic east up the valley of the Río Lluta to Poconchile and on to Parque Nacional Lauca. The national

---

TEN STEPS TO A CHINCHORRO MUMMY

The Chinchorro mummies are the oldest known artificially preserved bodies in the world, pre-dating their Egyptian counterparts by more than two millennia. They were created by small groups that fished and hunted along the coast of southern Peru and northern Chile from around 7000 BC. The mummification process was remarkably elaborate for such a simple culture. While the order and methods evolved over the millennia, the earliest mummies were made more or less by doing the following:

- dismembering the corpse's head, limbs and skin
- removing the brain by splitting the skull or drawing it through the base
- taking out other internal organs
- drying the body with hot stones or flames
- repacking the body with sticks, reeds, clay and camelid fur
- reassembling parts, perhaps sewing them together with cactus spines
- slathering the body with thick paste made from ash
- replacing the skin, patched with sea-lion hide
- attaching a wig of human hair and clay mask
- painting the mummy with black manganese (or, in later years, red ochre)

Several hundred Chinchorro mummies have now been discovered; all ages are represented and there's no evidence to suggest that mummification was reserved for a special few. Interestingly, some mummies were repeatedly repainted, suggesting that the Chinchorro kept and possibly displayed them for long periods before eventual burial. Millennia later, the conquistadores were appalled by a similar Inka practice, in which mummified ancestors were dressed up and paraded in religious celebrations.

---

park is the area's trump card, but a succession of ancient ruins, colonial churches and mountain villages are also worthy stops.

Lluta Geoglyphs

Also known as the Gigantes de Lluta (Giants of Lluta), these pre-Columbian geoglyphs are sprinkled along an otherwise barren slope of the southern Lluta Valley. The diverse and delightful figures include a frog, an eagle, llamas and the occasional human. The geoglyphs recall the importance of pre-Columbian pack trains on the route to Tiwanaku, a traffic that only recently disappeared with the construction of good motor roads.

The geoglyphs are a short distance inland from the intersection of the Panamericana and Chile 11; markers indicate when to pull over and squint toward the hillsides.

Poconchile

Despite being one of Chile's oldest churches, Poconchile's 17th-century **Iglesia de San Gerónimo** has sadly relinquished much of its character in a succession of earthquakes.

One kilometer east of the church, near the river, is a slightly surreal Hare Krishna 'eco-town' and yoga school called **Eco-Truly** (☎ 098-976-3137; www.ecotruly-arica.org, in Spanish; Sector Linderos Km29; campsites per person CH$2000, r incl breakfast CH$6000). It's a nice spot to stop for lunch (vegetarian, CH$2500) on your way to Parinacota, or stay for a few days of simplified relaxation. There's little proselytizing going on – though residents are happy to share their religious and spiritual views – and the funky conical 'truly' rooms are made with local and recycled materials, which, they say, keeps your energy from escaping.

To get to Poconchile, 35km from Arica, take Bus Lluta (p184) to the end of the line at the police checkpoint. *Taxi colectivos* charge around CH$3000 from outside Arica's international bus terminal.

Lluta to Pukará de Copaquilla

Feast your eyes on the views back over the Lluta Valley as you zigzag up the Chile 11 highway. Also keep your eyes peeled for a scattering of the aptly named cactus candelabro ('candle-holder' cactus; *Browningia candelaris*). This spiky character grows a paltry 5mm to 7mm a

CHILE 11 & PARQUE NACIONAL LAUCA

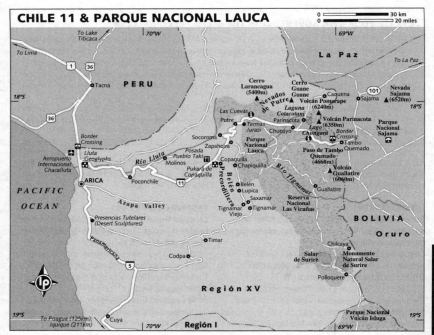

year, and flowers once a year for only 24 hours. It yields surprisingly tough wood, which highlanders use all too readily for building – the principal reason for the species' rapid decline. These cacti absorb scant moisture from the *camanchaca* that penetrates inland.

Teetering on the brink of a spectacular chasm near Copaquilla, the partially restored 12th-century fortress **Pukará de Copaquilla** (admission free) was built to protect pre-Columbian farmlands below. Peering over the canyon's edge will reward with views of the abandoned terraces.

Along the highway just west of Copaquilla the **Posada Pueblo Taki** (☎ 098-368-1143; givelifeto thedesertfoundation@gmail.com; campsites per person CH$3500) is a wind- and solar-powered roadside attraction. Stop for delicious freshly baked bread, hot drinks and a chat with its 'happy-not-hippie' resident couple. Tours are available. Any highway bus will drop you off and pick you up here.

Beyond Copaquilla, paved Chile 11 climbs steadily through the precordillera to the park entrance at Las Cuevas, where the altiplano proper begins.

Socoroma

On the colonial pack route between Arica and Potosí, Socoroma, 5km along a rough road from Chile 11, is an Aymara farming village featuring cobbled streets, the 17th-century **Iglesia de San Francisco**, other colonial remains, and terraced hills of oregano. The church was damaged by an earthquake in June 2005, but is undergoing restoration.

See information on Buses La Paloma (p184) for transportation details.

Putre
☎ 058 / pop 2468

Pocket-sized Putre is an appealing Aymara village perched precariously on a hillside in the precordillera at a dizzying elevation of 3530m. Just 150km from Arica, it serves as an ideal acclimatization stop en route to the elevated Parque Nacional Lauca on the altiplano. As such, the village now hosts a fast-multiplying number of hostels and tour agencies. Originally a 16th-century *reducción* (Spanish settlement to facilitate control of the native population), the village retains many houses with late-colonial elements. In the surrounding

---

CREATE YOUR OWN ADVENTURE IN THE BELÉN PRECORDILLERA

Take a break from the 'Lonely Planet Trail' by putting the guidebook down for a day or two and heading off on your own adventure. One great trip in the area takes you to the isolated villages reached by the gravel road that leaves Chile 11 at Zapahuira. This route passes through a necklace of traditional villages, pre-Columbian fortresses and agricultural terraces. Highlights are the *pukarás* (pre-Hispanic fortifications) of **Belén**, **Lupica** and **Saxamar**. There are also colonial churches at Belén and **Tignamar Viejo**.

This route makes an excellent day trip from Arica for travelers with vehicles, but tourist services are rare other than a few simple *hospedajes* (budget accommodations) dots. See information on Buses La Paloma (p184) for transportation details.

---

hills local farmers raise alfalfa for llamas, sheep and cattle on extensive stone-faced agricultural terraces of even greater antiquity.

INFORMATION
BancoEstado (cnr Arturo Prat & Cochrane) Putre's only bank, but it has no ATM. It changes US cash only so bring sufficient cash with you from Arica.
Centro de Llamadas (9am-1pm & 4-8pm) Call home at this phone center, opposite the tourist office.
Oficina de Información Turística (252-803, 252-744, ext 125; imputre@entelchile.net; Arturo Prat s/n; 8am-7pm) A handy resource on the plaza's southern flank, although it has no town maps.
Post office (Carrera s/n; 9am-1pm Mon-Fri, 10am-2pm Sat) A short distance from the plaza.
Quipon@t (Latorre 337; per hr US$1; 9am-1pm & 3-7pm Mon-Fri, 10am-2pm Sat) Has internet access; on the plaza's northern side.

SIGHTS
Dating from 1670, the adobe **Iglesia de Putre** (Plaza de Armas) was restored two centuries later. To visit the valuable colonial artifacts kept within, ask for the keys and leave a small donation.

TOURS
Tours from Putre usually work out cheaper than tours from Arica, and will give you more time to acclimatize to the altitude. Destinations include Parque Nacional Lauca, Salar de Surire, Parque Nacional Volcán Isluga and more.
Alto Andino Nature Tours (099-282-6195; www
.birdingaltoandino.com; Baquedano 299) Alaskan biologist Barbara Knapton offers expensive but high-quality birding and natural-history excursions in English or Spanish. Make reservations well in advance. She also has a house available to rent.
Tour Andino (099-011-0702; www.tourandino
.com, in Spanish; Baquedano s/n) A one-man show run

by warmly recommended local guide, Justino Jirón. He specializes in small groups, and is knowledgeable about local wildlife and customs.

FESTIVALS & EVENTS
Carnaval Visitors get dragged into the fun during Putre's Carnaval in February. Scores of balloon-bombs filled with flour are pelted around, not to mention clouds of *chaya* (multicolored paper dots). Two noncompetitive groups, the older *banda* and younger *tarqueada*, provide the music. The event ends with the burning of the *momo*, a figure symbolizing the frivolity of Carnaval.
Feria Regional Held in November; music and dancing are accompanied by dozens of stalls selling crafts, regional produce and tasty local dishes.

SLEEPING
Residencial La Paloma (099-197-9319; lapaloma putre@hotmail.com; Baquedano s/n; s with/without bathroom CH$5000/3000, d CH$12,000; P) Putre's most established *residencial* and restaurant slots a dozen rooms around two concrete courtyards, the first painted with cutesy animal murals. It has hot showers, spacious rooms and comfy beds, but the thin walls mean it's noisy sometimes, and the price you are probably better at the Cali.
Refugio Putre (201-225; O'Higgins s/n; dm CH$5000) Opposite the army camp, this Conaf-run spot offers comfy dorm-style lodging when space permits. There are six beds, hot showers and cooking facilities.
Pachamama (231-028; ukg@entelchile.net; r per person without bathroom CH$7800; P) Putre's most attractive hostel has a generous communal kitchen, pleasing floral courtyard dotted with rattan furniture, and young staff who are knowledgeable about the area. To get here from Baquedano, head west from the Residencial La Paloma, desending a small hill to the hostel.
Hostal Cali (098-543-8716; hostal_cali@hotmail .com; Baquedano s/n; r without bathroom CH$10,000, d/tr incl

breakfast CH$16,000/20,000; 💻) Cute and clean, this is one of the cheapest spots in Putre, and is a good bet for budget-busters. The hot gas-heated showers are a godsend, and they offer tours to Lauca.

Hotel Kukuli (☎ 099-161-4709; off Baquedano; s/d/tr incl breakfast CH$13,000/22,000/30,000; 🅿) One of Putre's newer hotels, Kukuli is comfortable, spotless and well heated, and each room has its own little terrace. Inquire about rooms in the owner's store at Baquedano 301. In case you were wondering, 'kukuli' means dove in Aymara.

Hotel Las Vicuñas (☎ 231-028; www.chileanaltiplano.cl; s/d incl breakfast CH$31,500/48,500; 🅿 💻) This large hotel sprawls by the approach to town, and was originally built for mining interests. It has more than a hundred simple yet functional bungalows. The heaters work really well: a bonus for sure at this high altitude.

EATING
Residencial La Paloma (opposite) has a decent restaurant.

Restaurant Rosamel (Cochrane s/n; set meal CH$1500; ☾ lunch & dinner) A modest restaurant serving set meals to a mixed bunch of locals and Lauca tour groups.

Kuchu-Marka (Baquedano 351; set lunch CH$2500, set dinner CH$3800; ☾ lunch & dinner) A cozy restaurant with a great ambience, the Kuchu-Marka stays open late and dishes up delicious quinoa soup, alpaca steaks, vegetarian options, drinks and atmosphere. Folk musicians also visit for tips.

GETTING THERE & AWAY
Putre is 150km east of Arica via paved Chile 11, the international highway to Bolivia. **Buses La Paloma** (☎ 099-161-4709; Germán Riesco 2071) serves Putre daily, departing Arica at 6:30am, returning at 2pm (CH$2500). Buy return tickets at Baquedano 301. Buses to Parinacota, in Parque Nacional Lauca, pass the turnoff to Putre, which is 5km from the main highway.

PARQUE NACIONAL LAUCA
It's not just the exaggerated altitude (between 3000m and 6300m above sea level) that leaves visitors to this national park breathless. Lauca is home to some breathtaking altiplano scenery, snow-sprinkled volcanoes, sparkling lakes and isolated hot springs. It also shelters pretty highland villages and a huge variety of wildlife. The nimble-footed vicuña and the rabbit-like viscacha are the star attractions, but

you're also likely to see other South American camelids and a variety of bird species.

Lauca's most spectacular feature is the glistening Lago Chungará, one of the world's highest lakes. Looming over it is the impossibly perfect cone of Volcán Parinacota, a dormant volcano with a twin brother, Volcán Pomerape, just across the border. These pristine white-capped volcanoes could almost be painted onto the landscape, but the ominous Volcán Guallatire puffs up dark fumes a short distance to the south.

Situated 160km northeast of Arica, near the Bolivian border, Parque Nacional Lauca comprises 1380 sq km of altiplano. It nuzzles close to two more protected areas, the Reserva Nacional Las Vicuñas (p192) and Monumento Natural Salar de Surire (p192). Once part of the park, they now constitute technically separate units but are still managed by Conaf. A trip that combines these parks is well worth the extra time and energy.

Rainfall and vegetation increase with altitude and distance from the coast; it can snow in the park during the summer rainy season, known as *invierno boliviano* (Bolivian winter), when heavy fog often covers the precordillera approaches to the park.

Information
The park is administered from the *refugio* (rustic shelter) at Parinacota. Otherwise, rangers at the Las Cuevas entrance (p190) and at Lago Chungará are available for consultation; posts are staffed from around 9am to 12:30am then 1pm to 5:30pm.

Dangers & Annoyances
Take it easy at first: the park's altitude is mostly well above 4000m and overexertion is a big no-no until you've had a few days to adapt. Eat and drink moderately; if you suffer anyway, try a cup of tea made from the common Aymara herbal remedy *chachacoma* or *mate de coca*. Keep water at your side, as the throat desiccates rapidly in the arid climate, and wear sunblock – tropical rays are brutal at this elevation.

Sights
TERMAS JURASI
A cluster of **thermal baths** (admission CH$1000; ☾ dawn-dusk) huddle amid rocky scenery 11km northeast of Putre. To get down and dirty,

---

VICUÑA RESURGENCE: AN ENVIRONMENTAL SUCCESS STORY

Back in Inka times vast herds of vicuña, numbering in the millions, roamed the altiplano from here all the way to southern Ecuador. But over-predation and habitat loss have sorely depleted the herds over the years, and in the 1970s barely a thousand vicuña were left in northern Chile. Today, there are more than 25,000 in the region and several hundred thousand throughout the Andes: an environmental success story that seems to only be getting better.

Unlike the alpaca or llama, the vicuña has never been domesticated. These shy fellows just don't seem to want to mate in captivity. So conservationists had to figure out a way to protect them, while still providing an economically viable trade for local Aymara who for centuries have relied on vicuña for their valuable meat and fur. Initially, species-protection measures were put in place, but even its endangered status could not save the vicuña, whose buttery wool is used to make shawls that cost hundred (if not thousands) of US dollars. In the 1990s, they started to catch the vicuña live, shear them on the spot, and then release them back in the wild. This innovative program has allowed for continued cultivation of vicuña wool, while providing a deterrent to poachers: a shorn vicuña is essentially worthless. These measures, combined with larger national parks and greater protection, mean that herds of these beautiful, elegant creatures may again trundle across the vast expanses of the high Andes.

---

there's also a red-mud bath. The gravel road branches right off Chile 11 around 8km from Putre. It's a further 3km to the site.

LAS CUEVAS

At the park's western entrance, Las Cuevas has a **ranger station** (9am-12:30pm & 1-5:30pm), a handy place to glean directions. Small rustic **thermal baths** can be accessed along a winding path where wild vicuña pay scant attention to passers-by and viscacha play hide and seek in the rocks.

Just beyond Las Cuevas is the viewing point **Mirador Pampa Chucuyo**, marked by an ugly sculpture resembling *zampoña* (panpipes) balanced on a garish staircase.

BOFEDAL DE PARINACOTA

Another 4km east, on the north side of Chile 11, domestic llama and alpaca graze on emerald-green pastures among crystalline lagoons with drifting guallatas (Andean geese) and ducks. Meanwhile viscacha peek out from rockeries above the swampy *bofedal* (the park's largest).

The *bofedal* also shelters some curious cultural relics: there's a **colonial chapel** just below Chucuyo, and another about half an hour's walk from Parinacota.

PARINACOTA

Beautiful Parinacota is a tiny Aymara village of whitewashed adobe and stone streets, 5km off the international highway or 46km from Putre. Vendors sell fluffy llama toys, model churches and a mountain of woven goods around the plaza. However, the town's undisputed gem is the 17th-century **colonial church** (admission by donation), reconstructed in 1789 (the key is kept by caretaker Sererino Morales). Inside is a glorious display of surrealistic murals, the heartfelt work of artists from the Cuzco school: think Hieronymus Bosch in a hurry. One of the quirkier features is the depiction of curly-mustachioed soldiers – looking suspiciously like Spanish conquistadores – bearing Christ to the cross.

Also look for a small table tethered down like a dog; local legend tells how this little critter once escaped, walked through town and stopped in front of someone's house; the next day, that man died.

There are several excellent hikes around Parinacota, including Laguna Cotacotani and Cerro Guane Guane. Conaf has a ranger station at Parinacota: ask here for information on surrounding hikes.

LAGUNA COTACOTANI

Now sadly shallow, but still picturesque, Laguna Cotacotani sparkles at the foot of sprawling lava flows and cinder cones. The lake has been partially drained by the national electricity company, damaging its ecological integrity. However you will still see diverse bird life along its shores and scattered groves of queñoa (*Polylepis tarapacana*), one of the world's highest-elevation trees, reaching about 5m in height. Conaf maintains tranquil walks alongside the lake; ask for directions in Parinacota.

CERRO GUANE GUANE

Jaw-dropping panoramas of the park and beyond can be seen from atop Cerro Guane Guane, which ascends to a 5096m peak immediately north of Parinacota. From the village, it's climbable along its eastern shoulder in about four hours, but the last 500m are a difficult slog through porous volcanic sand – one step forward, two steps back. Ask advice from Conaf's rangers, and do not attempt to climb in threatening weather as there is no shelter.

LAGO CHUNGARÁ

Lauca's crown jewel, the glittering Lago Chungará (4500m above sea level), is a shallow body of water formed by lava flows damming the snowmelt stream from Volcán Parinacota (6350m), a beautiful snow-capped cone that rises immediately to the north.

The lake is 192km from Arica. You can reach the west end of the lake from Parinacota on foot in about two hours, but you won't see much wildlife on this route; for that, you'll need to pass near the Conaf ranger station on Chile 11 and the Chilean customs post near the border. You may want to drive to one of these spots and then hike.

Arica's increasing consumption of hydroelectricity, and the Azapa Valley's insatiable thirst, led to an intricate system of pumps and canals that constitute a continuing menace to Lago Chungará's ecological balance. Since the lake is so shallow, any lowering of its level can dramatically reduce its overall surface area and impinge on those parts where wading birds such as the flamingo and giant coot feed and nest.

Woolens and other crafts are sold by the Conaf *refugio,* but much of it comes from Bolivia; for locally made goods, try the stores in Parinacota or Chucuyo.

The border post of Tambo Quemado lies at the east end of Lago Chungará.

WILDLIFE

Lauca is a Unesco Biosphere Reserve rich in wildlife. Along the highway and at Las Cuevas (the entrance and information center), vicuña (*Vicugna vicugna*), a fragile-looking wild relative of the llama and alpaca, are living advertisements for a major Chilean wildlife success story (see the boxed text, opposite).

Lauca also harbors slitty-eyed little viscacha (*Lagidium viscacia*), a wild Andean relative of the chinchilla that resembles a kind of prehistoric rabbit with a long scraggly tail. Bird lovers will be kept busy too: there are more than 150 bird species (including the occasional condor and fast-footed rhea). Lago Chungará is home to especially abundant and unusual bird life, including the flamboyant Chilean flamingo (*Phoenicopterus chilensis*), hardy wader tagua gigante (giant coot; *Fulica gigantea*), and the black-headed Andean gull (*Larus serranus*).

Visiting nearby Surire is a surefire way to see huge herds of roaming vicuña, pockets of viscacha, and three species of flamingo, as well the occasional ungainly ñandú (the ostrich-like rhea).

The flora here is curious: pay special attention to the ground-hugging, bright-green llareta (*Laretia compacta*), a dense shrub with a bulbous cushionlike appearance that belies the fact that it's rock hard – the Aymara need a pick or mattock to break open dead llareta, which they collect for fuel.

You're also guaranteed to spot grazing herds of domesticated woolly llamas and alpacas at every turn. The Aymara pasture their camelids on verdant *bofedales* (swampy alluvial grasslands) and the lower slopes of the surrounding mountains, and sell handicrafts woven from the animals' wool.

Tours

Many agencies offer one-day blitzes from sea-level Arica to 4515m Lago Chungará in Parque Nacional Lauca – a surefire method to get *soroche* (altitude sickness). These tours cost from CH\$15,000 (including a late lunch in Putre) and leave around 7:30am, returning about 8:30pm. Verify whether the operator carries oxygen on the bus, as many people become very sick at high altitudes. Avoid overeating, smoking and alcohol consumption the day before and while you are on your tour.

Tours lasting 1½ days (from CH\$25,000) include a night in Putre, allowing more time to acclimatize. A three-day circuit to Lauca, the Monumento Natural Salar de Surire, Parque Nacional Volcán Isluga and Iquique (around CH\$90,000) returns to Arica late the third night.

English-speaking tour guides are rare, though with extra time and money you can eventually find one. Many operators have limited departures, so a certain amount of flexibility is helpful. The Sernatur office occasionally has warnings on operators against whom they've received a lot of complaints.

See p181 for details of travel agencies.

NORTE GRANDE

Sleeping & Eating

Most people shack up in Putre, but the park has a few basic options for the hardcore. Several families in Parinacota will shelter tourists, but don't expect hot showers. Call **Conaf** (☎ 058-201-225; amjimene@conaf.cl; dm CH$5000) in advance to inquire about staying in the no-frills *refugios* at Parinacota and Lago Chungará; it also maintains free camping grounds, the larger of which is at Lago Chungará and has a superb lakefront position and low stone walls to shelter from the freezing winds. At 4500m above sea level, it gets frigid at night.

Limited supplies, including food, are available in Putre, but it's cheaper and more convenient to bring them from Arica.

Hostal Terán (☎ 058-228-761; Parinacota; per person CH$2000), opposite the church in Parinacota, has a draughty *refugio* with lots of crocheted blankets. You can use the sunken kitchen (handy to escape the night chill) or the *señora* will prepare meals.

Copihue de Oro (Chucuyo; dm CH$2000) has a basic single six-bed room and a warm shower, and serves meals. Chucuyo is situated near the junction to Parinacota.

Getting There & Away

Parque Nacional Lauca straddles Chile 11, the paved Arica–La Paz highway; the trip from Arica takes about three hours. There are several buses from Arica, mostly leaving on Tuesday and Friday. Other bus companies with daily service to La Paz, Bolivia will drop you off in the park, but you might have to pay the full fare. See p184 for details.

Agencies in Arica offer tours (see p181), though most of the time is spent in transit. Renting a car in Arica will provide access to the park's remoter sites such as Guallatire, Caquena and the Salar de Surire (the latter only with a high-clearance vehicle, since you'll ford several watercourses). Carry extra fuel in cans; most rental agencies will provide them. Do not forget warm clothing and sleeping gear, and take time to acclimatize.

SOUTH OF PARQUE NACIONAL LAUCA
Reserva Nacional Las Vicuñas

More than 20,000 wild vicuña are thought to roam the sparsely inhabited 2100 sq km of this off-the-beaten-path reserve, directly south of Lauca and surrounded by sky-hugging volcanoes. Formed to provide a protective zone for Lauca, the reserve is facing increased environmental degradation with the Vilacollo mining company winning approval in August 2007 to explore for mineral resources in the reserve.

At the base of smoking Volcán Guallatire, 60km from Parinacota via a roundabout route, the village of **Guallatire** features a 17th-century church. The town's community-run **Casa de Hospedaje Guallatire** (☎ 242-542; r per person incl breakfast CH$5000) has hot water (except when the pipes freeze) in shared bathrooms, extremely welcoming hosts and food. Also in Guallatire is Conaf's no-frills **Refugio Guallatire** (dm CH$5000). Bring a sleeping bag and don't be surprised if you sleep on the floor. There is a kitchen.

South of Guallatire, on the Surire road, are ruins of a colonial **silver mill**.

Further south, bridges cross the Río Viluvio, but the road can still be impassable during summer rains, even with a 4WD. Police at Guallatire and Chilcaya (further south) have 4WD vehicles and *may* be able to help vehicles in distress.

Monumento Natural Salar de Surire

Grazing vicuña and enclaves of cuddly viscacha are just two reasons why this isolated salt flat is a magical place to visit. Its star attraction is the flamingo; three species, including the rare James flamingo (parina chica; *Phoenicoparrus jamesi*), come to nest in the sprawling salt lake. The best time to see them is from December to April. Also keep your eyes peeled for ostrich-like ñandú (*Pterocnemia pennata*) sprinting around on their matchstick legs.

Situated 126km from Putre, the 113-sq-km reserve was formed in 1983, when the government chopped up Parque Nacional Lauca. In 1989, the outgoing dictatorship gave 45.6 sq km to mining company Quiborax.

There is no public transportation. While Lonely Planet doesn't recommend hitchhiking, it may be possible to hitchhike with trucks from the borax mine or with Conaf, whose decent **Refugio Surire** has a hot shower and a handful of beds for CH$5000; reserve with Conaf in Arica (p178). Camping is possible beside Polloquere's tempting **thermal baths**, but there are no toilet facilities and it's bitterly exposed to the elements.

Although most visitors return to Putre, it's possible to make a southerly circuit through Parque Nacional Volcán Isluga and back to Arica via Camiña or Huara. Always consult

Conaf or police first. This route is particularly iffy during the summer rainy season.

PISAGUA

☎ 057 / pop 260

The ghosts of Pisagua's past permeate every aspect of life in this isolated coastal village, located 120km north of Iquique. Not much more than a ghost town these days – locals make their living harvesting *huiro* (algae) and mariscos – Pisagua was once one of Chile's largest 19th-century nitrate ports. Eventually it became a penal colony where Pinochet cut his teeth as an army captain. The town would acquire its true notoriety shortly afterwards when it became a prison camp for Pinochet's military dictatorship (1973–89). After the return to democracy, the discovery of numerous unmarked mass graves in the local cemetery caused an international scandal.

But there is a magic and lyricism to the town that transcends the past. Crouching like a wounded tiger on a narrow shelf below a near-vertical rock face, Pisagua has numerous nitrate-era mansions, and history buffs will be greatly rewarded with tales of grand balls and woeful sorrows.

Orientation & Information

There are good free campsites and beaches at the north end of town, but be sure to plan ahead, and bring the food, money and supplies you will need for the duration of your stay as the town's hotel is often booked up, and finding food can be quite difficult. There is no bank in town.

An information kiosk sits opposite the Teatro Municipal, though it only opens sporadically. Try the public library by the theater for internet access.

Sights & Activities

Pisagua's syringe-like **Torre Reloj** (Clock Tower) sits on a hillock over the town along the 'new road,' which was closed for rehabilitation at the time of research. This national monument dates from the nitrate glory days, when the port had thousands of inhabitants.

North of the palm-shaded Plaza de Armas, the surf laps at the foundations of the **Teatro Municipal**, a once-lavish theater with a broad stage, opera-style boxes, and ceiling murals of cherubim. The building's northern half is also worth exploring, but be cautious – one 2nd-story door plunges directly into the ocean. Ask for the key at the information kiosk or the Armada de Chile, two doors from the theater.

Next to the theater is a poignant **mural** warning of the perils of ignoring the past. A half-block inland from the plaza, the **Colonia Penal Pisagua** was the old jail and one of the original (but not principal) sites used to incarcerate political prisoners after the 1973 coup.

Just beyond the police station, the **abandoned train station** recalls the time when Pisagua was the northern terminus of El Longino, the longitudinal railway that connected the nitrate mines with the ports of the Norte Grande. Just outside town and off the road to the north, the **Monolito Centenario** commemorates a battle during the War of the Pacific.

A 30-minute hike or 10-minute boat ride (CH$8000) south of town will take you to a colony of **sea lions**.

Pisagua's most sobering site is its old **cemetery** 2km north of town, spread over a lonely hillside that slips suddenly into the ocean. Here, vultures guard over a gaping pit beneath the rock face, where a notorious mass grave of victims of the Pinochet dictatorship was discovered. A poignant memorial plaque quotes Neruda, 'Although the tracks may touch this site for a thousand years, they will not cover the blood of those who fell here.' Nearby there is a monument to the people found in the mass grave.

Beyond the cemetery, the road continues to **Pisagua Vieja**, with a handful of adobe ruins, a pre-Columbian cemetery and a broad sandy beach, which looks like it has a decent **surf break**. From here a rough road (4WD vehicles only) continues up to **Hacienda Tiliviche**, a 19th-century British nitrate family's house. Summer rains can create dangerous washouts.

Sleeping & Eating

Hostal La Roca (☎ 731-502; viejopisagua2@hotmail.com; s/d/tr/q incl breakfast CH$12,000/18,000/20,000/28,000; 🖳) This rustic but clean hostel is perched on a rocky rise overlooking the ocean. It offers four rooms, each with a charming but quirky combination of mismatched wallpaper, paint and concrete – ask for a room facing the sea and call ahead as the hotel books up quickly. The *señora* speaks French and some English. Request hot water before showering.

La Picada de Don Gato (☎ 731-511; mains CH$2400-3200; ✆ breakfast, lunch & dinner) The town's only restaurant, near the turnoff to the cemetery, is a small, unhurried affair with an outdoor terrace. They often close, and may have rooms for rent.

Camping Municipal is essentially a large parking lot with free camping at Playa Seis, a small but fine sandy beach just beyond the ruins of the fish-processing factory that once incarcerated political prisoners. It has reasonably clean toilets and showers. You can also camp north of town at Playa Blanca, but there are no facilities.

Getting There & Away

Pisagua is 40km west of the Panamericana by a paved but potholed road from a turnoff 85km south of the police checkpoint at Cuya, and 47km north of Huara. The main road was under construction at research time, so you'll need to take the 'old road' 10km from town. There is no public transportation to the town, but you can have a bus leave you at the junction then hitch a ride into town. Beware, there are very few trucks or cars.

IQUIQUE

☎ 057 / pop 197,602

Barefoot surfers, paragliding pros, casino snobs and frenzied merchants all cross paths in the rather disarming city of Iquique. Located in a golden crescent of coastline, this city is fast becoming Chile's premier beach resort, with a glitzy casino, pleasant beachfront boardwalk, and more activities – from paragliding to sand-boarding – than any sane person can take on in a week. The big draw here, of course, are the arching swaths of pitch-perfect beach, which offer some of the best surfing – and sunbathing – around.

Refurbished Georgian-style architecture from the 19th-century mining boom is well preserved, and the Baquedano pedestrian mall sports charming wooden sidewalks. Iquique's main claim, however, is its duty-free status, with a chaotic duty-free shopping zone (zona franca), which takes the ominous sandy hills behind the town as an outlandish nighttime billboard.

The city, 1853km north of Santiago and 315km south of Arica, is squeezed between the ocean and the desolate brown coastal range rising abruptly behind it.

History

The lifeless pampa around Iquique is peppered with the geoglyphs of ancient indigenous groups (see p204 and p202), and the shelf where the city now lies was frequented by the coastal Chango peoples. However, the Iquique area was first put on the map during the colonial era, when the Huantajaya silver mine was discovered.

During the 19th century, narrow-gauge railways shipped minerals and nitrates through Iquique. Mining barons built opulent mansions, piped in water from the distant cordillera and imported topsoil for lavish gardens. Downtown Iquique reflects this 19th-century nitrate boom, and the corroding shells of nearby ghost towns such as Humberstone and Santa Laura whisper of the source of this wealth.

After the nitrate bust, Iquique reinvented itself primarily as a fishing port, shipping more fish meal than any other port in the world. However, it was the establishment of the zona franca in 1975 that made this one of Chile's most prosperous cities.

Orientation

Iquique sits on a narrow terrace at the foot of the coastal range, which rockets abruptly up to 600m. Blocked by these mountains, the town has sprawled north and south along the coast.

The city's focus is Plaza Prat. Av Baquedano is the main thoroughfare, and its northern section is an attractive pedestrian mall. The main beaches are south of downtown.

Information

There are many ATMs downtown and at the zona franca. There's enough internet cafés (CH$400 per hour) downtown to keep Steve Jobs in turtlenecks for the rest of his life.

Afex (Serrano 396; ✆ 8:30am-5:30pm Mon-Fri, 10am-1:30pm Sat) Changes foreign currency and traveler's checks.

Books and Bits (☎ 471-080; Ramírez 1341; ✆ 10am-2pm & 4:30-8pm Mon-Fri, 10am-2pm Sat) All-English bookstore stocking mostly children's books and classics.

Hospital Regional Dr Torres (☎ 395-555; cnr Tarapacá & Av Héroes de la Concepción) Ten blocks east of Plaza Condell.

Lavandería Vaporito (☎ 421-652; ✆ 9am-9:30pm) Plaza Condell (Bolívar 505); Mercado Centenario (Juan Martínez 832) Has drop-off service starting at CH$1000 per kg.

Post office (Bolívar 458; ✆ 8:30am-1pm & 3-7pm Mon-Fri, 9am-12:30pm Sat)

BLOOD IN THE STREETS – THE OTHER SIDE OF THE NITRATE BOOM

While history tends to focus on the ornate architecture and Bacchanalian balls of the nitrate-era belle époque, a dark, insidious monster lurks just below its surface. While many got rich from this white dust, it was only from the strong backs and spilled blood of the Chilean peasantry that this mere dust turned to gold.

The nitrate workers lived hand to mouth. Payment for heavy labor was mostly made in company store 'cash.' And, of course, the bosses were in charge of the company store. There was no way out. But by the turn of the 20th century, the workers had had enough and Chile's first modern labor movement kicked into action.

The city of Iquique witnessed one of the bloodiest events of this era of protest. In 1907, nearly 8500 strikers gathered around the Escuela Santa María to protest unfair treatment in the nitrate mines. In exasperation, police and military fired upon the unarmed strikers, killing hundreds and wounding many more. Chilean folk group Quilapayún immortalized the tragic incident with their recording *Cantata Popular Santa María de Iquique*.

Sernatur (☎ 419-241; infoiquique@sernatur.cl; Anibal Pinto 436; ⏲ 8:30am-5:30pm Mon-Fri, 9:30am-5:30pm Sat & Sun) Tourist information, free city maps and brochures.

Sights

The good ol' nitrate days are evident throughout Iquique's center. Its beautiful wood-fronted 19th-century buildings also speak eloquently of foreign influences during the nitrate boom.

The city's 19th-century swagger is especially hard to miss in Plaza Prat. Pride of place goes to the whimsical **Torre Reloj** (1877) clock tower, seemingly baked and sugar-frosted rather than built. Jumping fountains line the short walkway south to the marble-stepped **Teatro Municipal** (☎ 414-398), an ostentatious neoclassical building that has been hosting opera, theater and more since 1890; take a quick peek at the painted ceilings inside.

A handsomely restored **tram** sits outside the theater and occasionally jerks its way down Av Baquedano in the tourist high season. On the theater's opposite side is the 1913 **Sociedad Protectora de Empleados de Tarapacá** (Thompson 207), historically significant as one of the country's first labor union buildings.

Despite hot competition, however, the prize for the showiest building in Iquique goes to the Moorish-style **Casino Español** (1904) on the plaza's northeast corner. This gaudily tiled creation is now a club and restaurant, but staff are surprisingly tolerant of travelers taking a quick whirl around the fanciful interior, which features murals and paintings of Don Quixote.

South of the plaza, Av Baquedano is lined with Georgian-style balustraded buildings

dating from 1880 to 1930. Among them are the former **Tribunales de Justicia** (Law Courts; Baquedano 951), now the Museo Regional; the cream-and-lime painted **Palacio Astoreca** (☎ 425-600; Baquedano & O'Higgins; admission free; ⏲ 10am-1pm & 4-7pm), a nitrate baron's mansion that now also functions as a museum; and the **Iquique English College** (cnr Av Arturo Prat & Patricio Lynch).

About five blocks east of the Mercado Centenario, the **Iglesia San Antonio de Padua** (cnr Latorre & 21 de Mayo) is worth a visit for its twin bell towers and star-encrusted ceiling.

MUSEO REGIONAL

Iquique's former courthouse now hosts the catch-all **regional museum** (☎ 411-214; Baquedano 951; admission free; ⏲ 10am-5pm Mon-Fri), which earnestly recreates a traditional adobe altiplano village (complete with mannequins in Aymara dress). The surrounding chambers also have some attention-grabbing exhibits, from animal fetuses floating in formaldehyde to masked Chinchorro mummies and elongated Tiwanaku skulls. Interesting photographs also explore Iquique's urban beginnings, and a fascinating display dissects the nitrate industry.

PALACIO ASTORECA

Built for a nitrate tycoon, this 1904 Georgian-style mansion is now a **Centro de Cultura** (☎ 425-600; O'Higgins 350; admission free; ⏲ 10am-5pm Mon-Fri), which exhibits paintings by local artists. It has a fantastic interior of opulent rooms with elaborate woodwork and high ceilings, massive chandeliers, a gigantic billiard table and balconies.

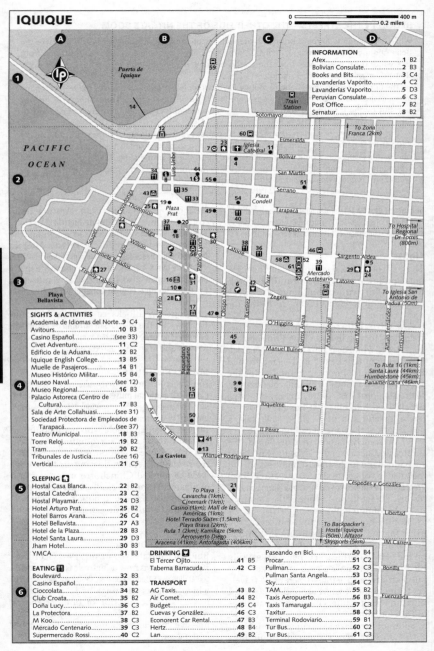

IQUIQUE

INFORMATION
Afex	1 B2
Bolivian Consulate	2 B3
Books and Bits	3 C4
Lavanderías Vaporito	4 C2
Lavanderías Vaporito	5 D3
Peruvian Consulate	6 C3
Post Office	7 B2
Sernatur	8 B2

SIGHTS & ACTIVITIES
Academia de Idiomas del Norte	9 C4
Avitours	10 B3
Casino Español	(see 33)
Civet Adventure	11 C2
Edificio de la Aduana	12 B2
Iquique English College	13 B5
Muelle de Pasajeros	14 B1
Museo Histórico Militar	15 B4
Museo Naval	(see 12)
Museo Regional	16 B3
Palacio Astoreca (Centro de Cultura)	17 B3
Sala de Arte Collahuasi	(see 31)
Sociedad Protectora de Empleados de Tarapacá	(see 37)
Teatro Municipal	18 B3
Torre Reloj	19 B2
Tram	20 B2
Tribunales de Justicia	(see 16)
Vertical	21 C5

SLEEPING
Hostal Casa Blanca	22 B2
Hostal Catedral	23 C2
Hostal Playamar	24 D3
Hotel Arturo Prat	25 B2
Hotel Barros Arana	26 C4
Hotel Bellavista	27 A3
Hotel de la Plaza	28 B3
Hotel Santa Laura	29 D3
Jham Hotel	30 B3
YMCA	31 B3

EATING
Boulevard	32 B3
Casino Español	33 B2
Cioccolata	34 B2
Club Croata	35 B2
Doña Lucy	36 C3
La Protectora	37 B2
M Koo	38 C3
Mercado Centenario	39 C3
Supermercado Rossi	40 C2

DRINKING
El Tercer Ojito	41 B5
Taberna Barracuda	42 C3

TRANSPORT
AG Taxis	43 B2
Air Comet	44 B2
Budget	45 C4
Cuevas y González	46 C3
Econorent Car Rental	47 B3
Hertz	48 B4
Lan	49 B2
Paseando en Bici	50 B4
Procar	51 C2
Pullman	52 C3
Pullman Santa Angela	53 D3
Sky	54 C2
TAM	55 B2
Taxis Aeropuerto	56 B3
Taxis Tamarugal	57 C3
Taxitur	58 C3
Terminal Rodoviario	59 B1
Tur Bus	60 C2
Tur Bus	61 C3

SALA DE ARTE COLLAHUASI
The Collahuasi mining company got it right when they built this small **art hall** (Baquedano 930; admission free; 🕒 11am-7pm Tue-Sat), with rotating installations by local artists.

EDIFICIO DE LA ADUANA & MUSEO NAVAL
Thick walls enclose this haughty colonial-style **customshouse**, built in 1871 when Iquique was still Peruvian territory. Peru incarcerated prisoners here during the War of the Pacific, and the building would later see battle in the Chilean civil war of 1891.

The Aduana houses a small **naval museum** (Esmeralda 250; adult/student CH$200/free; 🕒 10am-1pm & 4-7pm Tue-Sat) with artifacts salvaged from the sunken *Esmeralda,* a plucky little Chilean corvette that challenged ironclad Peruvian warships in the War of the Pacific.

The ship was captained by Arturo Prat (1848–79), whose name now graces a hundred street maps, plazas and institutions. In an impassioned speech aboard the *Esmeralda,* Prat swore to die in battle and challenged his officers to also 'know their duty.' Sure enough, he was promptly killed, the ship was sunk and the Battle of Iquique was lost. However Chile went on to win the war, spurred on by popularly published accounts of Prat's heroism.

MUELLE DE PASAJEROS
Iquique's 1901 passenger pier is just west of the Edificio de la Aduana. Hour-long boat **tours** (adult/child CH$3000/2000, min 10 passengers) around the harbor leave from here, passing the **Boya Conmemorativa del Combate de Iquique**, a buoy marking the spot where the *Esmeralda* sank in a confrontation with the Peruvian ironclad *Huáscar.* They also approach a colony of sea lions.

MUSEO HISTÓRICO MILITAR
Iquique's little **military museum** (☎ 431-555; Baquedano 1396; donation requested; 🕒 10am-1:15pm & 4:15-7pm Mon, Tue, Thu & Fri, 10am-1:30pm Wed) features a patriotic parade of exhibits on the War of the Pacific. The enthusiastic guard usually allows guests to wield an original cavalry sword.

Activities
BEACHES
Playa Cavancha (from Av Arturo Prat & Amunátegui) is Iquique's most popular beach. It's pleasant for swimming but is sometimes crowded. There are also some decent surf breaks along its rocky northern parts, and a playground for children.

Further south, crashing waves and rip currents at scenic **Playa Brava** make it dangerous for swimming, but there's plenty of space to sunbathe. Toward the hills, look for the massive dunes of Cerro Dragón, which looks like a set for a science-fiction movie.

Taxi colectivos run to Playa Brava from downtown – look for the destination on the sign atop the cab. There are scores of sandy beaches further south, but you'll need to rent a car or bike, or take a taxi.

SURFING & SAND-BOARDING
An army of wetsuited warriors is always to be found dripping its way along Iquique's coastal road. Surfing and body-boarding are best in winter, when swells come from the north, but they're possible year round (see the boxed text, p74). There's less competition for early-morning breaks at Playa Cavancha. **Playa Huaiquique**, on the southern outskirts of town, is also an exhilarating choice but the sea is warmer further north near Arica.

Vertical (☎ 376-031; www.verticalstore.cl, in Spanish; Av Arturo Prat & Ramírez) sells and rents equipment. Wetsuit and board will set you back CH$7000 for two hours. Lessons start at CH$12,000, and they run surf and paragliding trips outside the city.

Sand-boarding trips to Cerro Dragón cost around CH$7000. Check in at Vertical for more information.

PARAGLIDING
Go jump off a cliff…and fly! That's the message you'll get from Iquique's many paragliding *(parapente)* fanatics. The city's unique geography, with its steep coastal escarpment, rising air currents and the soft, immense dunes of Cerro Dragón, makes it one of the best places for paragliding in South America. It's theoretically possible to glide all the way to Tocopilla, 240km south – but that's not for novices. For general information try www .parapenteiquique.cl, in Spanish. Bring along a windbreaker, sunblock and guts.

Altazor Skysports (☎ 380-110; www.altazor.cl; Flight Park, Vía 6, Manzana A, Sitio 3, Bajo Molle), 500m south and 200m east of the Universidad del Mar (south of Iquique's center), offers paragliding courses (CH$65,125 per day, including equipment and transportation). An introductory tandem flight costs CH$28,200; two-week courses are also available. Rental equipment and repair is available for experienced paragliders. Owners Philip Maltry and Marlene Carrasco speak German, Spanish, English, Portuguese and French.

Courses

The Swiss-run **Academia de Idiomas del Norte** (☎ 411-827; www.languages.cl; Ramírez 1345) provides Spanish-language instruction. Classes are small (one to four students) and cost CH$225,300 to CH$280,000 per week, depending on intensity. Accommodations and meals with guest families can be arranged from CH$9500 per day.

Tours

Public transportation to many surrounding attractions is tricky, so tours are worth considering.

Traditional 12-hour excursions take in the nitrate ruins at Humberstone and geoglyph sites at Cerro Unita and Pintados, and may include trips to the oases at Pica and Matilla (CH$16,000 to CH$30,000 per person). There are three-hour city tours (CH$8500 to CH$15,000), 10-hour coastal excursions (CH$16,000 to CH$30,000), and 14-hour trips to the Gigante de Atacama and Pisagua (CH$40,000). Most trips require a four-person minimum. English-speaking guides are sometimes available for an extra charge.

Three-day jaunts into the altiplano explore the Parque Nacional Volcán Isluga, Monumento Nacional Salar de Surire, Reserva Nacional Las Vicuñas and Parque Nacional Lauca, finishing in Arica or returning late to Iquique (around CH$80,000). A one-day back-busting trip to Isluga runs around CH$35,000.

Avitours (☎ 527-692; www.avitours.cl; Baquedano 997) Offers most of the major tours.

Civet Adventure (☎ 428-483; civetcor@vtr.net; Bolívar 684) Organizes small, all-equipped 4WD or bicycle adventure tours to altiplano destinations for three or more days, as well as camping and land-sailing trips in the Atacama Desert. German and English spoken.

Sleeping

BUDGET

Taxi drivers earn commission from some *residenciales* and hotels; be firm in your decision or consider walking. Wild camping is free on the beaches north of Iquique near Pisagua and Cuya.

Hostal Playamar (☎ 421-546; Juan Martínez 852; s without bathroom CH$4000, d CH$14,000; ℗) Some of the cheapest rooms in central Iquique are available at this boxy, rather dark hostel near the market and bus offices. The shared bathrooms are relatively clean – gracias Don Limpio!

ourpick Backpacker's Hostel Iquique (☎ 320-223; www.hosteliquique.cl; Amunategui 2075; incl breakfast members dm/s/d CH$5000/7500/12,000, nonmembers CH$5500/8000/13,000; 🖳) This is the best hostel in town, sitting just steps from the beach and with a sociable 'surfer dude' vibe. There's a great lounge, shared kitchen, Ping-Pong, Foosball, laundry, internet and more. Breakfast is included.

YMCA (☎ 573-596; Baquedano 964; r per person CH$6000) They took an elegant *casona* (mansion) and wedged the works of a YMCA in the interior. Rooms have bunk beds (there will be no hanky-panky going on here – unless you are an original Village Person) and clean bathrooms. You might be able to get in on some salsa classes downstairs if you ask nicely.

Hotel de La Plaza (☎ 417-172; Baquedano 1025; s/d incl breakfast CH$11,000/18,000) One of the best deals in this category, this Georgian-style building fronts onto the pedestrian mall. The cordial señora makes sure things are clean, and there are welcomed touches such as a courtyard and Andean bedspreads.

Hostal Catedral (☎ 391-296; Obispo Labbé 253; s/d incl breakfast CH$12,000/18,000) Homey place opposite the city's main church, and handy for early or late Tur Bus connections. Has stuffy but very adequate rooms – firm beds and clean baths are a godsend – and fluorescent lights and scattered fake and real plants.

Hotel Santa Laura (☎ 474-238; hotelsantalaura@hotmail.com; Juan Martínez 849; s/d/tr CH$12,000/18,000/20,000; ℗ 🖳) An ambitious hotel on the up, Santa Laura is brightly lit and fitted to modern standards. The surrounding area is a bit rough, but you'll have no trouble inside the immaculate interior.

MIDRANGE

Hostal Casa Blanca (☎ 420-002; Gorostiaga 127; s/d incl breakfast CH$12,600/18,700) This congenial guesthouse is tucked away down a nondescript street near the plaza. It's a sedate spot with kindly service and a palette of simple pastel shades.

Hotel Bellavista (☎ 517-979; www.hotelbellavista iquique.cl, in Spanish; Freddy Taberna 106; s/d incl breakfast

CH$16,900/24,900; (P) (⌨)) Reliable but unexceptional Bellavista is a five-story pink building with comfortable accommodations. The simple breakfast is served with rooftop view to the sea.

Hotel Barros Arana (☎ 412-840; www.hotelbarros arana.cl; Barros Arana 1302; incl breakfast s CH$25,000-30,400, d CH$31,000-37,000; (P) (P) (⌨)) The wide inner courtyard and sunchair-fringed pool make this professional hotel a pleasant place to recharge batteries. Economical rooms are tidy but stingy on space and just a bit stale feeling, whereas the superior rooms are big enough to swing a giraffe without hitting any walls.

Jham Hotel (☎ 428-642; www.hoteljham.cl; Latorre 426; incl breakfast s CH$27,000-30,000, d CH$35,000; (P)) For the price you can get better digs at the Barras or Prat, but Hotel Jham is not without its charms. Ask for a room in the back of this all-business hotel.

TOP END
Hotel Arturo Prat (☎ 520-000; www.hotelprat.cl; Aníbal Pinto 695; incl breakfast s CH$39,000-52,000, d CH$41,650-55,930; (P) (⊞) (⌨) (⌨)) A traditional favorite, this hotel has prime position lording it over Plaza Prat, and is the best buy for this category. Cheaper 'classic' rooms overlook the noisy plaza but are smaller. 'Superior' rooms are larger, quieter, and have air-con.

Hotel Terrado Suites (☎ 437-878; www.terrado .cl, in Spanish; Los Rieles 126; s/d incl breakfast from CH$45,100/55,500; (P) (⊞) (⌨) (⌨)) Lording it over Playa Cavancha, this lofty five-star hotel has every luxury, including both outdoor and indoor pool, wi-fi internet, sauna and gym. Smaller rooms have city views; bigger, pricier rooms look out to sea.

Eating
BUDGET
Supermercado Rossi (Tarapacá 579; ⊙ 9am-10pm Mon-Sat, 10am-2:30pm Sun) Stock up for DIY meals at this large supermarket between Labbé and Ramírez.

Mercado Centenario (Barros Arana) This boxy market between Sargento Aldea and Latorre is the cheapest and fastest place for a no-frills set lunch. Upstairs cocinerías also offer varied seafood, and stalls offer fresh produce for self-caterers. You can buy coca leaves (CH$500 for a bag) and sex tonics in the roadside stalls. Coca leaves are great for treating altitude sickness (brew them up in

a tea), while the sex tonics don't work at all (believe us, we tried!).

M.Koo (☎ 412-532; Latorre 596; snacks from CH$500; ⊙ 8:30am-10pm Mon-Sat, 8:30am-4pm Sun) Simple corner shop famous for its crumbly *chumbeques* (sweet regional biscuits), the recipe for which is guarded zealously. It also sells neatly wrapped in-season specials, such as *humitas* (corn tamales) and *pastel de choclo* (maize casserole) to go.

Doña Lucy (☎ 314-800; Vivar 855; sandwiches CH$1000-2300, cakes CH$1300; ⊙ breakfast, lunch & dinner, closed Sun) Locals pile into this fussy little tea shop for its ambrosial cream cakes, equally creamy cappuccinos, ice cream, teas and freshly squeezed juices. The sandwiches aren't bad either. Tables spill onto the hedged courtyard behind.

Cioccolata (☎ 413-010; Aníbal Pinto 487; set menu CH$3100, sandwiches CH$2400; ⊙ 8:30am-10pm Mon-Sat, 5-10pm Sun) Proof positive that Chileans really do enjoy a decent espresso, this classy coffee shop is usually crammed with businessfolk. It also offers filling breakfasts, sandwiches, scrumptious cakes and chocolates.

Club Croata (☎ 427-412; Plaza Prat 310; set lunch CH$3000; ⊙ lunch, closed Sun) Plaza-side restaurant with arched windows and Croatian coats of arms. It has the best fixed-price lunch on the plaza.

El Tercer Ojito (☎ 426-517; Patricio Lynch 1420; CH$3200-6900, set meal CH$3500; ⊙ lunch & dinner; (V)) Recognizable by the huge lump of quartz outside, this informal New Age restaurant serves great vegetarian and carnivore-friendly dishes. Its international repertoire includes Peruvian dishes, curries and occasional sushi. Its pleasant patio sports cacti, murals and even a turtle in a bathtub.

MIDRANGE & TOPEND
La Protectora (☎ 421-923; Thompson 207; set lunch CH$2900, mains CH$2500-6200; ⊙ lunch & dinner, Sun dinner only) Old World atmosphere reigns at this civilized restaurant nestling beside the theater and fronting onto the plaza; the building, the Sociedad Protectora de Empleados de Tarapacá, hosted one of Chile's first trade unions.

Boulevard (☎ 413-695; Baquedano 790; set lunch CH$2900, mains CH$3000-7500; ⊙ lunch & dinner, Sun dinner only) Laid-back streetside café without, and smooth Gallic restaurant within, this is the place to relax and let the world traipse by. On offer are delicious fondues, pizzas, crepes and enormous salads with zesty dressings. Service is hit or miss, but the fixed lunch is definitely worth it. There's occasional live music.

Casino Español (☎ 333-911; Plaza Prat 584; mains CH$4200-8500; ⏰ lunch & dinner, closed Sun) Prepare for pattern overload: Moorish designs intertwine, compete and clash in this unabashedly decadent 1904 building. Expect tooth-bitten arches, a high dome, stained glass, checked tiles, suits of armor and…oh yeah, it has food, too, including Spanish, Italian and Chilean favorites. Service moves at a leisurely pace.

Drinking

Iquique has a fun-filled nightlife, with clubs and pubs clustering along the seafront south of town.

El Tercer Ojito (☎ 426-517; Patricio Lynch) The laid-back patio here is ideal to enjoy a drink or three after dark; happy hour is from 8pm to 10pm.

Taberna Barracuda (☎ 427-969; www.taberna barracuda.cl, in Spanish; Gorostiaga 601) English pub meets US sports bar, popular with all ages; the two-for-one happy hour (8pm to 10pm) makes expensive drinks (CH$2000) more reasonable. Food, including tapas, is also available.

Entertainment

Cinemark (☎ 600-600-2463; Mall de las Américas, Heroes de la Concepción; tickets CH$2000) A multiplex cinema showing latest releases.

Kamikaze (☎ 440-194; www.kamikaze.cl; Bajo Molle, Km7, Manzana K; cover incl drink CH$2000; ⏰ midnight-early Thu-Sat) Huge pub-club with bamboo bars and two floors playing everything from Cuban Pachanga to cheesy '90s *pop en español* (Spanish-language pop).

Shopping

Created in 1975, Iquique's **zona franca** (Zofri; ☎ 515-600; ⏰ 11am-8pm Mon-Sat) is a massive monument to uncontrolled consumption. The entire region of Tarapacá is a duty-free zone, but its nucleus is this shopping center for imported electronics, clothing, automobiles and almost anything else.

If you want to shop, take any northbound *colectivo* from downtown.

Getting There & Away
AIR

The local airport, **Aeropuerto Diego Aracena** (☎ 410-787), is 41km south of downtown via Ruta 1.

Lan (☎ 600-526-2000; www.lan.cl; Tarapacá 465; ⏰ 9am-1:30pm & 4-8pm Mon-Fri, 9:30am-1pm Sat) flies four or five times daily to Arica (CH$26,900, 40 minutes), once daily to Antofagasta (CH$24,900 to CH$39,900, 45 minutes), about seven times per day to Santiago (CH$34,950 to CH$89,450, 2½ hours), and four times a week to La Paz, Bolivia (around CH$137,000, two hours). Prices are cheaper the further ahead you book.

Sky (☎ 600-600-2828; www.skyairline.cl; Tarapacá 530) also goes to Arica (CH$22,400), Antofagasta (CH$30,300), Santiago (CH$98,300) and other destinations in the south of Chile. **Air Comet** (☎ 600-625-0000; www.aircomet.com; cnr San Martín & Patricio Lynch) also has decent rates including Antofagasta (CH$28,900 round trip) and Santiago (CH$106,000 round trip).

TAM (☎ 390-600; www.tam.com.py, in Spanish; Serrano 430) flies three times weekly to Asunción, Paraguay (CH$269,000), and offers decent deals to Miami, USA, and Paris, France.

BUS

The bus station, **Terminal Rodoviario** (☎ 416-315), is at the north end of Patricio Lynch, but it's easier to catch buses at ticket offices clustered around the Mercado Centenario. Services north and south are frequent, but most southbound services use Ruta 1, the coastal highway to Tocopilla (for connections to Calama) and Antofagasta (for Panamericana connections to Copiapó, La Serena and Santiago).

Several major bus companies travel north to Arica and south as far as Santiago:

Pullman (☎ 425-280; Barros Arana 897)
Ramos Cholele (☎ 411-144; Barros Arana 851)
Tur Bus (☎ 472-984; www.turbus.cl, in Spanish) Mercado Centenario (Barros Arana 869); Plaza Condell (Esmeralda 594)

Sample fares are as follows:

Destination	Cost (CH$)	Duration (hr)
Antofagasta	12,000	8
Arica	7000	4½
Calama	12,000	7
Copiapó	20,000	14
La Serena	23,000	18
Santiago	31,000	26

To get to Pica, try **Taxitur** (☎ 414-875; Sargento Aldea 783) with *colectivos* to Pica (about CH$4500) and Arica (about CH$6500). **Pullman Santa Angela** (☎ 423-751; Barros Arana 971) also travels to Pica for CH$2500.

Taxis Tamarugal (☎ 419-288; Barros Arana 897-B) has daily *colectivo* minibuses for Mamiña (CH$6000 round trip).

To get to La Paz, Bolivia, **Cuevas y González** (☎ 412-471; Sargento Aldea 850) leaves daily at 1:30pm (CH$15,000, 20 hours).

The easiest way to get to Peru is by going first to Arica (CH$7000), then hooking up with an international bus there.

Getting Around

As in Arica, *colectivos* are the easiest way to get around town. Destinations are clearly marked on an illuminated sign on top of the cab.

TO/FROM THE AIRPORT

Iquique's Aeropuerto Diego Aracena is 41km south on Ruta 1. Minibus transfer to your hotel costs CH$2500 with **Aerotransfer** (☎ 310-800), which has a stand in the arrivals hall. Alternatively, shared taxis charge CH$4500 per person; private cabs cost CH$9000. Try **Taxis Aeropuerto** (☎ 419-004; cnr Gorostiaga & Baquedano) just off the plaza, or **AG Taxis** (☎ 413-368; Aníbal Pinto s/n).

BICYCLE

Paseando en Bici (☎ 098-916-5706; paseandoenbici@ gmail.com; Baquedano 1440) rents bucolic bamboo bikes for CH$2000 (1½ hours) to CH$3500 (six hours). They rent 'real' bikes, too, for the same cost.

CAR

Cars cost from CH$18,000 per day. Local agencies often require an international driver's license. The following rental vehicles also have stands at the airport:

Budget (☎ 416-332; Manuel Bulnes)
Econorent Car Rental (☎ 417-091; reservas@ econorent.net; Obispo Labbé 1089)
Hertz (☎ 510-432; Aníbal Pinto 1303)
Procar (☎ 413-470; Serrano 796)

EAST OF IQUIQUE
☎ 057

Ghost towns punctuate the desert as you travel inland from Iquique; they're eerie remnants of once-flourishing mining colonies that gathered the Atacama's white gold – nitrate. Along the way you'll also pass pre-Hispanic geoglyphs, recalling the presence of humans centuries before. Further inland the barren landscape yields up several picturesque hotspring villages, while the high altiplano is home to some knockout scenery and a unique pastoral culture.

Humberstone & Santa Laura

The influence and wealth of the nitrate boom whisper through the deserted ghost town of **Humberstone** (www.museodelsalitre.cl; adult/child CH$1000/500; ☺ 9am-7pm). Established in 1872, this mining town once fizzed with an energy, culture and ingenuity that peaked in the 1940s. However, the development of synthetic nitrates forced the closure of the *oficina* by 1960; 3000 workers lost their jobs and the town dwindled to a forlorn shell of itself.

The grand theater (rumored to be haunted) that once presented international starlets; the swimming pool made of cast-iron scavenged from a shipwreck; the ballroom, where scores of young *pampinos* (those living or working in desert nitrate-mining towns) first caught the eye of their sweethearts; schools; tennis and basketball courts; a busy market; and a hotel frequented by industry big-shots: all now lie quiet and emptied of life.

Some buildings are restored, but others are crumbling; take care when exploring interiors. At the west end of town, the electrical power plant still stands, along with the remains of the narrow-gauge railway to the older Oficina Santa Laura.

Although designated a historical monument in 1970, Humberstone fell prey to vandalism and unauthorized salvage. However, the site's fortunes were boosted in 2002, when it was acquired by a nonprofit association of *pampinos* (Corporación Museo del Salitre) that set about patching up the decrepit structures. Then, in July 2005, the site was designated a Unesco World Heritage site. New plans are gaining steam, and there are hopes that the old hotel and swimming pool will eventually reopen to guests.

Admission includes a free leaflet in English or Spanish. A stand opposite the entrance has booklets and souvenirs for sale.

The skeletal remains of **Oficina Santa Laura** (admission free) are a half-hour walk southwest across the highway. It's worth the trip to snoop around the monstrous machinery, used to crush minerals, and visit the small, free museum.

GETTING THERE & AWAY

Humberstone is an easy day trip from Iquique. It sits less than 1km off the Panamericana, about 45km due east of the city. Any eastbound bus from Iquique will drop you off there, and it is easy to catch a return bus (CH$1300, 40 minutes). You can also catch a *colectivo* from the mercado central for CH$2000. Tours are available from Iquique. Take food, water and a camera, since it's easy to spend hours exploring the town. Early morning is best, although afternoon breezes often moderate the midday heat.

El Gigante de Atacama

It's the biggest archaeological representation of a human in the world – a gargantuan 86m high – and yet little is really known about the 'Giant of the Atacama.' Reclining on the isolated west slope of Cerro Unita 14km east of Huara, the geoglyph is thought to represent a powerful shaman.

Its skinny limbs are spread wide, and it clutches what seems to be an arrowhead in one hand and a medicine bag in the other. Its open mouth and owl-like head, topped by vertical rays (and horizontal lines only visible from above), give it the perpetual appearance of hair-raising shock.

Experts estimate that the giant dates from around AD 900. On one side of the slope (visible as you approach the hill) are several enormous clearings, like giant slides down the hillside. Don't climb the slope, as it damages the site.

The Huara–Colchane road, the main Iquique–Bolivia route, is paved; only the very short stretch (about 1km) from the paved road to the hill itself crosses unpaved desert. The isolated site is 80km from Iquique; the best way to visit is to rent a car or taxi, or take a tour (p198).

Tarapacá

In colonial and early republican times, tiny San Lorenzo de Tarapacá was one of Peru's most important settlements. However, the Battle of Tarapacá (1879) marked the town's eclipse. Its 18th-century **Iglesia San Lorenzo** was sadly all but flattened in the 2005 earthquake, and many other adobe buildings were destroyed. There is only a handful of remaining residents.

Tarapacá has neither accommodations nor restaurants. About 5km east of Cerro Unita a paved lateral drops into the Quebrada de Tarapacá to the valley.

Parque Nacional Volcán Isluga

If you want to get off the beaten track, this isolated national park richly rewards the effort. Dominated by the malevolently smoking Volcán Isluga, the park is dotted with tiny pastoral villages that house just a few hardy families or, at times, nobody at all. The park's namesake village, **Isluga**, is itself uninhabited. It functions as a *pueblo ritual* (ceremonial village), where scattered migrational families converge for religious events that center on its picture-perfect adobe church.

The park's highlights include **Puchuldiza** geyser, which shoots up a spear of water that freezes into an iceberglike sculpture. It is 21km off the Iquique–Colchane road; take the rough track 5km southwest of Colchane, signposted to Isluga and Enquelga. Hot springs can be found 2km from the village of **Enquelga**.

Parque Nacional Volcán Isluga's 1750 sq km contain similar flora and fauna to those of Parque Nacional Lauca, but it is far less visited. The park is 250km from Iquique and 13km west of **Colchane**, a small village on the Bolivian border.

From Isluga it's a bouncy but beautiful off-road trip to the stunning **Monumento Natural Salar de Surire** and Parque Nacional Lauca, finishing up down in Arica. Inquire about the state of the roads first, especially in the summer rainy season, and do not attempt the trip without a high-clearance vehicle, extra petrol and antifreeze. Several tour agencies in Arica (p181) and Iquique (p198) offer this trip.

SLEEPING

Chilly little Colchane, 3730m above sea level, is the easiest base for travelers.

Hostal Camino del Inca (Teniente González s/n, Colchane; dm/d/tr incl breakfast & dinner CH$5000/8000/12,000) Run by a local family with two floors of sparse but clean concrete rooms. Shared bathrooms have hot water. It gets bitterly cold, so bring a sleeping bag. A flashlight is also advisable because electricity is cut at midnight.

Refugio Enquelga (Enquelga; dm CH$5000) Try this basic eight-bed *refugio* in Enquelga, if you're in a pinch. You can book ahead in Arica's Conaf office (p178).

Camping Aguas Calientes is a no-frills site, 2km south of Enquelga. It has warm, if not steaming, thermal baths, two ill-maintained toilets and free camping.

GETTING THERE & AWAY

The road to Colchane is paved, but the park itself is crisscrossed by myriad dirt tracks. Infrequent buses go to Colchane from Iquique (CH$3200, five hours), 251km away.

At Colchane it's also possible to cross the border and catch a truck or bus to the city of Oruro, in Bolivia.

Mamiña

☎ 057 / pop 1090

Upon arrival, Mamiña appears a dusty desert village surrounded by parched precordillera. However the valley floor below is home to famously pungent hot springs, around which a small resort has shaped itself. The baths are particularly popular with local miners.

The village huddles into upper and lower sectors, the former clustered around the rocky outcrop where the church stands, while the latter lies low in the valley. There's no bank, but a public telephone office can be found opposite the church. Nights can get very chilly here.

SIGHTS & ACTIVITIES

A sandy walk 3km south will take you to the pre-Hispanic fortress **Pukará del Cerro Inca** (Cerro Ipla), still riddled with tiny pieces of pottery and defensive nooks. Near the town's entrance, **Iglesia de Nuestra Señora del Rosario** is a national historical monument dating from 1632, though it's been substantially remodeled. Its twin bell tower is unique in Andean Chile. The **Centro Cultural Kespikala** (☎ 099-364-4762) is a gathering place for Aymara artists and artisans, selling volcanic-rock sculptures and assorted textiles.

'Resort' facilities include **Barros Chinos** (☎ 751-298; ⏲ 9am-3pm Tue-Sun), 1km from the entrance, with restorative mud treatments (sit in a flimsy lawn chair and get plastered with the stuff) for CH$1500; **Baños Ipla** (⏲ 8:30am-2pm & 3:30-8:30pm), where CH$1500 buys a 20-minute soak in tiny (dirty) tubs; and **Baños Rosario**, below Refugio del Salitre.

SLEEPING & EATING

Cerro Morado (in Santiago ☎ 02-599-4760; cerro_morado @hotmail.com; campsites per person CH$2000, r per person incl full board CH$15,000) A simple spot alongside Hotel Los Cardenales, Cerro Morado has basic, slightly rundown rooms. On the plus side, the rooms are cheap, and some even have hot-springs tubs. You can camp across the

street by the bizarre cargo carrier with statues on the top. The owner says this is for good luck. The restaurant (set lunch CH$2800) is quite good, and is open to the pubic.

Hotel Los Cardenales (☎ 517-000; r per person incl full board CH$30,000; P ⚎) One of the coziest places in town, Cardenales has a large covered pool fed by spring waters, and, if you just want a bit of privacy, many of the rooms have oversized tubs that pipe in the curative (and *muy romantico*) waters. The Latvian owners are as cute as can be, and speak several languages. You'll no doubt get a chance to chat with them, as meals are served family-style in the large dining room.

Hotel Llama Inn (in Santiago ☎ 02-599-4776; www .termasdemamina.cl; Sulumpa s/n; r per person incl full board CH$35,000-40,000; P ⚎) Perched just above the valley floor, this recently renovated hotel is popular with visiting miners, so you'll need to call ahead. Rooms come with big tubs (they pipe the hot-springs water right in), and are simply designed. There's a hot-springs pool and game room, and the restaurant is reputed to be the best in town.

GETTING THERE & AWAY

Mamiña is 73km east of Pozo Almonte. Buses and *taxi colectivos* from Iquique stop in the plaza opposite the church. See p200 for details.

La Tirana

Curly-horned devils prance, a sea of short skirts swirls, a galaxy of sequins twinkles, and scores of drum-and-brass bands thump out rousing rhythms during La Tirana's **Virgin of Carmen festival**. Chile's most spectacular religious event, the fiesta takes place in mid-July. For ten days, as many as 80,000 pilgrims overrun the tiny village (permanent population 800) to pay homage to the Virgin in a Carnaval-like atmosphere of costumed dancing.

The village, 72km from Iquique at the north end of the Salar de Pintados, is famed as the final resting place of a notorious Inka princess (see the boxed text, p204), and is home to an important religious shrine.

The Santuario de La Tirana consists of a broad ceremonial plaza graced by one of the country's most unusual, even eccentric, churches.

Although several restaurants surround the plaza, there are no accommodations. Pilgrims

---

THE TYRANT PRINCESS

The village of La Tirana is named after a bloodthirsty tale from the era of the conquistadores. It's said that a feisty Inka princess was forced to accompany Diego de Almagro on his foray into Chile in 1535. The wily young miss gave him the slip at Pica, where she assembled a band of loyal Inka warriors eager for revenge. They promptly set about exterminating as many Spaniards as they could, as well as any indigenous people who had been baptized. Thus she earned the title La Tirana – The Tyrant.

However, her fearful image took a fatal blow in 1544, when her followers captured a Portuguese miner fighting for the Spanish. According to the legend, this pale-skinned soldier left the ferocious princess weak at the knees; and she provoked a major scandal (the Inka paparazzi would have had a field day) by shielding him from execution. However that was nothing compared to her followers' fury when she converted to her lover's Catholic faith: moments after her baptism, the pair was killed by a storm of arrows.

Ten years later, a traveling evangelist discovered a cross in the woods, supposedly marking the lovers' grave, and built a chapel. This structure was eventually replaced by a larger building, and the legend of La Tirana has flourished ever since.

---

camp in the open spaces east of town. Have a glance at the one-room **Museo Regional del Salitre** (admission free) on the north side of the plaza, which has a haphazard assortment of artifacts from nitrate *oficinas*.

Reserva Nacional Pampa del Tamarugal

The desolate pampas of the Atacama seems an improbable site for a forest, but the straggly roadside groves south of Pozo Almonte are no mirage. The trees are a native species, the tamarugo *(Prosopis tamarugo)*, which, though feeble in appearance, is astonishingly determined. It sprouts roots three times the length of its overground height, thus clawing its way to hidden water reserves.

This tree once covered thousands of square kilometers, but was then endangered by heavy felling in the nitrate era. Now managed by Conaf, the (largely replanted) 1080-sq-km reserve is a brief diversion on an uneventful stretch of the Panamericana.

Conaf's **Centro de Información Ambiental** (☎ 57-751-055; pampadeltamarugal@ctcinternet.cl; Panamericana Km1787; ☼ 8:30am-1pm & 2-6pm Mon-Fri) is 24km south of Pozo Almonte, with exhibits on the biology and ecology of the tamarugo and the pampas.

Opposite the Centro de Información Ambiental, Conaf maintains a dry and dusty **campground** (campsites CH$3500, dm CH$2500).

Pintados

No less than 355 geoglyphs decorate the hills like giant pre-Colombian doodles at **Pintados** (adult/child CH$1000/free; ☼ 10:30am-5:30pm), 45km south of Pozo Almonte. Geometrical designs (totaling 137) include intriguing ladders, circles and arrows, and 121 depictions of humans include vivid scenes of hunting in canoes and women giving birth. Almost 100 animal figures also roam the hillsides.

These enigmatic geoglyphs are thought to have served as signposts to nomadic peoples: marking trade routes and meeting points, indicating the presence of water, identifying ethnic groups and expressing religious meaning. Most date from between AD 500 and AD 1450.

A derelict nitrate rail yard of ruined buildings and rusting rolling stock, Pintados lies 7km west of the Panamericana via a gravel road, nearly opposite the eastward turnoff to Pica.

PICA

☎ 057 / pop 2870

The friendly and laid-back desert oasis of Pica appears as a painter's splotch of green on a lifeless brown canvas. It boasts lush fruit groves and is justly famous for its limes, a key ingredient in any decent pisco sour. Visitors come here to cool off in the attractive but overcrowded freshwater pool and to slurp on the plethora of fresh fruit drinks. An earthquake in late 2007 rumbled through the town, damaging several buildings, but the townspeople seem to be rebuilding quickly.

Spanish conquistador Diego de Almagro fell foul of indigenous groups near Pica in 1535 (see the boxed text, above), but this lush little oasis town later became a sort of 'hill station' getaway for nitrate barons. Furthermore, it acted as Iquique's water pump during the nitrate boom, as water was tunneled an impressive 119km to feed the city's growth.

A tiny **tourist office** (☎ 741-310; Almaceda s/n; ☺ 8:30am-1:30pm & 2:30-6pm Mon-Fri), just a few blocks east of the plaza, offers advice on accommodations.

Sights

Most visitors make a beeline to the fresh-water pool at **Cocha Resbaladero** (admission CH$1000; ☺ 8am-9pm), at the upper end of General Ibáñez. Encircled by cool rock, hanging vegetation and a watery cave, it makes a terrific spot to beat the desert heat – but in itself, it's not reason enough to visit Pica.

It's also worth poking your nose into Pica's 19th-century **Iglesia de San Andrés** (Plaza de Armas). Notice the out-of-place wardrobe, which contains a dozen costumes for San Andrés' doll-like statue. This saintly follower of fashion gets a new suit every year during the last two days of November, when Pica celebrates the **Fiesta de San Andrés** with dancing and fireworks. Just east of the Plaza the **Museo y Biblioteca** (Museum & Library; Balmaceda 178; ☺ 8:30am-1:30pm & 3-6:20pm Mon-Fri) has a small pre-Colombian art collection and free internet.

In the adjacent village of Matilla, 3km west, the **Iglesia de San Antonio** is a national monument built on 17th-century foundations. The bell tower was reconstructed after a 2005 earthquake did some serious damage. Around the corner, on the northwest corner of the plaza, is the **Lagar Siglo XVIII Museo de Sitio**, an on-site museum with a colonial wine press made from a hefty tree trunk. It's opened only sporadically but is visible through a side window.

Sleeping & Eating

There are numerous roadside eateries on the road to the Resbaladero. All offer decent food; pick the ambience you like best.

El Tambo (General Ibáñez 68; r per person CH$3500, cabins CH$20,000; **P**) This historic old-timer (built in 1906) is right opposite the Resbaladero pool. It has rickety, simple but characterful (that's guidebook speak for dirty) rooms with shared bathrooms. There are also *cabañas* (cabins) for four with kitchens and bathrooms out back.

ourpick **Hostal Los Emilios** (☎ 741-126; Lord Cochrane 213; s/d incl breakfast CH$8000/16,000; 🖳) Situated on a quiet side street two blocks southeast of the

---

> ### PAYING THE TAXMAN IN QUILLAGUA
>
> With the entire region of Tarapacá being a duty-free zone, it's no surprise that the taxman decided to put up a checkpoint in Quillagua. Tourists are generally allowed to bring up to CH$440,000 of tax-free goods out of the region, but if you go over you'll need to pay tax on the excess items. You'll need to get down from your car or bus in Quillagua and allow your bags to be examined before you head on down the road. Stay cool – just think what Fonzi would do – and you should have no problem.

---

plaza, this is a delightful little hostel – the best in town – with a familial atmosphere, comely blue-and-cream rooms and an attractive patio overlooking a forest of fruit trees. There's also a restaurant next door.

Hostal Café Suizo (☎ /fax 741-551; cafésuizo@latin mail.com; Ibáñez 210; s/d CH$14,000/20,000; **P**) Just 100m west of the Resbaladero, this is a great little Danish-Swiss guesthouse with a handful of sprucely kept rooms behind a white-picket-fenced facade. There's also a cool little café serving fresh cakes, pastries and natural juices. Reserve by fax.

Visit **Alfajores Rah** (Balmaceda; alfajores CH$100), opposite the church, for the best *alfajores* (crackers sandwiching sweetened condensed milk, and rolled in shredded coconut) and local honey.

Getting There & Away

Only 42km from La Tirana by paved road, Pica is served by buses and tours operating from Iquique (p200).

TOCOPILLA

☎ 055 / pop 32,209

Halfway house between Antofagasta and Iquique, Tocopilla is an ugly port for the remaining nitrate *oficinas* of Pedro de Valdivia and María Elena. Its dubious beauty is further marred by a monstrous thermoelectric plant for Chuquicamata. However, Tocopilla's smattering of wooden buildings, mostly along Prat and 21 de Mayo, give it a whiff of turn-of-the-20th-century charm. The town offers a chance to break long journeys along a desolate stretch of coast.

Ruta 1, the paved highway between Iquique and Tocopilla (Región II), has largely superseded the older Panamericana for south-bound travelers. There is spectacular coastal desert scenery, but heavy truck traffic rattles along this narrow highway, and careless campers have despoiled the beaches with trash.

While most beaches south of Iquique are too rocky for surfing, the beach near the customs post at Río Loa, on the border between Regiónes I and II, has good breaks.

Orientation

The main thoroughfare is the north–south Arturo Prat, while the main commercial street is 21 de Mayo, one block east. Most services are a few blocks from Plaza Condell.

Information

Hospital (☎ 821-839; cnr Santa Rosa & Matta) A few blocks northeast of downtown.
Post office (cnr 21 de Mayo & Aníbal Pinto)
Telefónica CTC (21 de Mayo 1721) Telephone center.
Tockonet (☎ 813-590; Bolívar 1331) Internet café.

Sights

The dinky little wooden **Torre Reloj** (Clock Tower; cnr Prat & Baquedano) was relocated intact from the nitrate *oficina* of Coya, near María Elena. **Playa El Salitre**, reached by a staircase from Calle Colón, is OK for sunbathing, but the water is too contaminated for swimming.

Sleeping & Eating

There are several restaurants of varying quality along 21 de Mayo. If the place is crowded, you are most likely onto something good.

Hotel Croacia (☎ 810-332; hotelcroatia@yahoo.com; Bolívar 1332; s/d incl breakfast CH$12,000/15,000; P) Run by Croatian immigrants, this ship-shape guesthouse has wood-style veneer on the walls and floors. Bathrooms are large and in good shape.

Hotel Atenas (☎ 613-650; 21 de Mayo 1448; s/d CH$18,000/24,000; P) With moist, springy beds, and circumspect cleanliness, this is your second choice in town.

Club de la Unión (☎ 813-198; Prat 1354; set lunch CH$2000; ☽ lunch & dinner) This civilized wooden-fronted building, opposite the clock tower, is Tocopilla's top restaurant. It has three cavernous dining halls and serves a mean pisco sour.

Getting There & Away

Buses between Iquique and Antofagasta stop here. Get outbound tickets at the **Tur-Bus office** (21 de Mayo 1497).

GATICO & COBIJA

The crumbling remains of these two coastal ghost towns lie off the coastal highway, 130km north of Antofagasta and 60km south of Tocopilla. Though it's hard to imagine today, Cobija was once a flourishing town and Bolivia's outlet to the Pacific, serving the mines of the altiplano. After an earthquake and tsunami nearly obliterated the town in 1877, Cobija's population dwindled to a few families eking out an existence fishing and collecting seaweed. Gatico is 10km further north, and features the eerie shell of an abandoned hotel looming over the ocean.

There is shelter to camp among the atmospheric adobe walls, but bring supplies with you.

MARÍA ELENA
☎ 055 / pop 12,370

Near the junction of the Panamericana and the Tocopilla-Chuquicamata highway, sleepy María Elena is one of the last functioning nitrate *oficinas*. A visit here offers a unique opportunity to see what a real living salitre town looked like. And there's something very attractive about walking among the dilapidated crumbling buildings that are still in use today: it's like walking into a somnambulist's dream. There is also a **Museo Arqueológico e Histórico** (☎ 632-935; Ignacio Carrera Pinto; admission free; ☽ 8:30am-1pm & 5-10pm) on the south side of the plaza.

CALAMA
☎ 055 / pop 147,594

How do we put this delicately? Hmm, there's just no other words for it: Calama is a shithole. But it's the shithole that happens to be the pride and joy of northern Chile, an economic powerhouse that pumps truckloads of copper money into the Chilean economy year on year. And while Calama (elevation 2250m) holds little attraction for visitors – most people will only stop here for the night (if they have to) on their way to the lala-land of San Pedro de Atacama – there is a gritty, visceral appeal to this mining town that definitely goes that extra mile in 'keeping it real.'

Everywhere are reminders of the precious metal: copper statues, copper wall-etchings and reliefs, and even a copper-plated spire on the cathedral (talk about a lightning rod!). In 2004 the city also inherited a wave of copper refugees when the entire population of polluted mining town Chuquicamata relocated here.

ANOTHER ROADSIDE ATTRACTION: EXPLORE THE PAST AT CHACABUCO & BAQUEDANO

There are dozens of nitrate ghost towns in the Antofagasta region, lining both sides of the highway between Baquedano and Calama, and along the Panamericana north of the Tocopilla–Chuquicamata highway. The best preserved is **Oficina Chacabuco** (☎ 098-314-1745; corporacion-chacabucogmail.com; admission adult/child CH$1000/500; ☿ 10am-5pm Wed-Sat, 10am-7pm Sun), 2km north of the I-5 and I-25 intersection on I-5. This national monument was closed to the public at the time of research, after a 2007 earthquake made it unsafe for visitors. Plans are in the works to re-open the site, but you should call ahead.

After its glory days, Chacabuco fell into disrepair, but if the site reopens, you can still visit the somewhat restored theater and town center. It was later used as a prisoner camp during the early years of the Pinochet regime. Keep your eyes peeled for graffiti left by the nearly 1800 political prisoners held here between 1973 and '74. You'll also want to be mindful of the landmines (on the outside of the town's walls) that are still in place. Signs give warning.

Further down route 25, on your way to the coast, is the nondescript town of **Baquedano**. It's worth taking a pit stop here to visit the open-air **Museo Ferroviario** (train museum; admission free), with a century-old locomotive and a turn station. Get here by walking about 150m south of the town's train station (which still operates freight trains); signs will lead the way.

The city's short history is inextricably tied to that of Chuquicamata (see p210). It's a measure of Calama's relative youth that it did not acquire its cathedral until 1906 – until then, it was ecclesiastically subordinate to tiny Chiu Chiu.

Orientation

Calama sits on the north bank of the Río Loa. Though the city has sprawled with the influx of laborers from Chuquicamata, its central core is still pedestrian-friendly. Calle Ramírez begins in an attractive pedestrian mall leading to the central Plaza 23 de Marzo.

Information

There are pay phones throughout the pedestrian mall.

Centro de Llamadas (☎ 314-515; cnr Sotomayor & Vivar; per hr CH$400; ☿ 9am-10pm) Cheap broadband connection and calling center.

Cybernet (☎ 347-504; Vargas 2054; per hr CH$400; ☿ 8am-11pm) Internet access.

Hospital Carlos Cisterna (☎ 342-347; Av Granaderos) Five blocks north of Plaza 23 de Marzo.

Lavexpress (☎ 313-361; Sotomayor 1887; ☿ 9am-9pm Mon-Sat) Has excellent drop-off laundry service for CH$1000 per kg.

Moon Valley Exchange (☎ 361-423; Vivar 1818) Competitive rates for money exchange.

Oficina Municipal de Información Turística (☎ 345-345; calamainfotour@entelchile.net; Latorre 1689; ☿ 8am-1pm & 2-6pm Mon-Fri) The tourist office has cordial, helpful staff.

Post office (Vicuña Mackenna 2197; ☿ 9am-1:30pm & 3:30-6:30pm Mon-Fri, 10am-12:30pm Sat)

Sights

Calle Ramírez is enlivened by a host of unlikely buskers and a suggestive copper statue of a miner, with two legs spread wide and a drill posing as his third. At the end of Calle Ramírez, shady Plaza 23 de Marzo bristles with market stalls and disorientated pigeons. You'll find the sizable pink-and-copper **Iglesia Catedral San Juan Bautista** here.

At the south end of Av O'Higgins, **Parque el Loa** (admission free; ☿ 10am-8pm) has a riverside swimming hole and a replica of Chiu Chiu's celebrated church. It's the best picnicking spot in town and a nice break from the bustle. Here also is the diminutive **Museo Arqueológico y Etnológico** (☎ 316-400; adult/child CH$200/100; ☿ 10am-1pm & 2-6pm Tue-Fri, 2-6pm Sat & Sun), with decent exhibits on the highland culture of the Atacama. Also in the park, across the river, is the **Museo de Historia Natural y Cultural del Desierto** (☎ 349-103; adult/child CH$500/200; ☿ 10am-1pm & 3-7pm). This small, well-presented museum explores the region's ecology, culture and paleontology.

Tours

A handful of travel agencies, including **Tour Aventura Valle de la Luna** (☎ 310-720; golden.eye@ctc-mundo.net; Abaroa 1620), will arrange excursions to remote parts of the desert, although trips are cheaper and more easily arranged from San Pedro de Atacama.

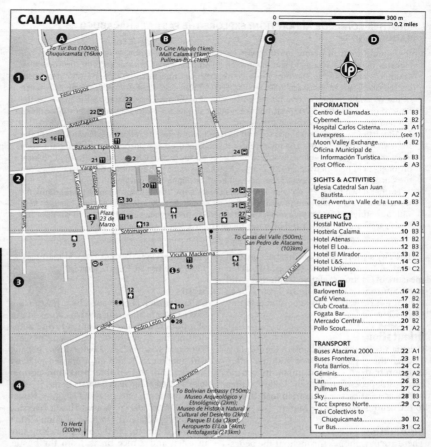

CALAMA

0 — 300 m
0 — 0.2 miles

INFORMATION
Centro de Llamadas..................1 B3
Cybernet...............................2 B2
Hospital Carlos Cisterna..........3 A1
Lavexpress...........................(see 1)
Moon Valley Exchange............4 B2
Oficina Municipal de
  Información Turística............5 B3
Post Office............................6 A3

SIGHTS & ACTIVITIES
Iglesia Catedral San Juan
  Bautista.............................7 A2
Tour Aventura Valle de la Luna..8 B3

SLEEPING
Hostal Nativo.........................9 A3
Hostería Calama...................10 B3
Hotel Atenas........................11 B2
Hotel El Loa.........................12 B3
Hotel El Mirador...................13 B2
Hotel L&S............................14 C3
Hotel Universo......................15 C2

EATING
Barlovento...........................16 A2
Café Viena...........................17 B2
Club Croata..........................18 B2
Fogata Bar...........................19 B3
Mercado Central....................20 B2
Pollo Scout..........................21 A2

TRANSPORT
Buses Atacama 2000...............22 A1
Buses Frontera......................23 B1
Flota Barrios.........................24 C2
Géminis................................25 A2
Lan......................................26 B3
Pullman Bus.........................27 C2
Sky......................................28 B3
Tacc Expreso Norte................29 C2
Taxi Colectivos to
  Chuquicamata.....................30 B2
Tur Bus................................31 C2

Festivals & Events

Calama's major holiday is March 23, when the city celebrates the arrival of Chilean troops during the War of the Pacific with fireworks and many other festivities in Parque Loa.

Sleeping

Prices are inflated in Calama, partly because most hotels cater to workers at the town's lucrative copper mine. Call ahead to ensure a reservation.

BUDGET

Casas del Valle (☎ 340-056; Francisco Bilbao 1207; campsites per person CH$4000) This well-shaded campground behind the municipal stadium, about 700m east of the train station, is a bit pricey, but you get showers, drinkable water and electricity.

Hostal Nativo (☎ 347-414; www.nativo.cl, in Spanish; Sotomayor 2215; s with/without bathroom CH$11,000/7000, d CH$14,000) The best buy in this category, this little crash pad has a sparkling tiled entryway that leads you to a handful of toxically clean rooms. The beds are a bit bowed and spongy, but still, this is probably your best bet on a budget.

Hotel El Loa (☎ 341-963; Abaroa 1617; s without bathroom CH$7000, d CH$16,000) An amiable but average spot with red curly ironwork outside and plain cell-like rooms inside. Double rooms have cable TV and above-average water pressure, and the shared bathrooms are actually rather clean.

Hotel Atenas (☎ 342-666; inmobiliariacalama@yahoo
.com; Ramírez 1961; incl breakfast s with/without bathroom
CH$12,650/7700, d CH$17,600; 💻) A dark warren
of rooms right off the pedestrian mall, the
Atenas is a bit odiferous, but with sparkling
bathrooms and a 'pimp' location, it's the sec-
ond-best value for the price.

MIDRANGE
Hotel Universo (☎ 361-640; hoteluniverso@gmail
.com; Sotomayor 1822; s/d incl breakfast CH$24,900/29,000;
ℙ 💻) It's a dark, dark universe (literally, this
place definitely could use a lighting consultation with one of those Fab Five guys), but this
little cosmic cutie does have some redeeming
qualities: big thick mattresses and gleaming
bathrooms. Alas, rooms are a bit smoky.

Hotel El Mirador (☎ 340-329; www.hotelmirador
.cl; Sotomayor 2064; s/d incl breakfast CH$29,000/39,000;
ℙ 💻) This historic hotel, fronted by a dainty
balcony and octagonal tower, is a sure bet.
Rooms have vaulted ceilings, enormous bathrooms and cheery white bed covers, though
the mashed-potato pillows could use some
fluffing (or replacing). The sun-scorched
patio is a pleasant enough spot to check your
email with the wi-fi, or you can head into the
sitting room, complete with historic photos
of Calama.

TOP END
Hostería Calama (☎ 341-511; www.hosteriacalama.cl;
Latorre 1521; s/d/tr incl breakfast CH$35,000/42,000/50,000;
ℙ 💻 🏊) It's a bit '70s bebop and a bit beige,
but the Hostería remains one of Calama's best
hotels. It's not as fancy as the L&S, but it holds
its ground by offering decently priced rooms,
and all the conveniences of a modern business
hotel, such as a gym and a games room.

Hotel L&S (☎ 361-113; www.lyshotel.cl, in Spanish;
Vicuña Mackenna 1819; s/d/tr incl breakfast CH$36,000/
45,000/60,000; ℙ 💻) This sleek stylish 'busi-
ness-lite' hotel is obsessively well polished;
when staff members are not buffing the already dazzling floors, they seem to be attack-
ing the bathrooms with a toothbrush. The
large rooms have cable TV and heating, but
can smell just a bit smoky.

Eating
Mercado Central (Latorre; set meals CH$1200-2000) For
quick, belly-filling eats, while rubbing shoulders with local workers, take advantage of the
cocinerías in this busy little market between
Ramírez and Vargas.

Café Viena (☎ 341-771; Abaroa 2023; set lunch CH$1500,
dishes CH$1000-2000; 🕑 closed Sun) A down-home
diner with a wide choice of unpretentious salads and sandwiches, as well as decent java and
fresh juices. Plates are piled generously high.

Pollo Scout (☎ 341-376; Vargas 2102; chicken from
CH$1500; 🕑 lunch & dinner, closed Sun) If you can't wait
to be fed, there is always spit-roasted chicken
and steaming *cazuela* (stew) at the ready in
this down-to-business cheapie.

Club Croata (☎ 332-850; Abaroa s/n; mains CH$2000-
5800, set lunch CH$3000; 🕑 lunch & dinner) Decorated
with the Croatian coat of arms and dog-eared
posters of the country's distant coastline, this
restaurant serves some wonderful Chilean
favorites, including *pastel de choclo* (maize
casserole). It's one of the best traditionally
styled eateries in town.

Barlovento (☎ 342-848; Av Granaderos 2030; set
lunch CH$2000, mixed grill for two CH$18,000; 🕑 breakfast,
lunch & dinner) With frequent *peña* (live folkloric performances), this little restaurant is
a nice place to go for dancing or just dinner. The meaty menu tempered by a few
vegetarian choices.

ourpick Fogata Bar (☎ 099-007-8624; Vicuña
Mackenna 1973; mains CH$2800-6000; 🕑 7pm till late Tue-
Sat) A welcome taste of San Pedro smack dap
in the middle of rough-and-tumble Calama,
this bar and restaurant serves up everything
from pizzas to tacos in two storeys of hard-
hewn earthy goodness. There's a *fogata* (outdoor fireplace) in the corner and occasional
live music.

Entertainment
Indicative of its macho mining culture,
Calama's streets are lined with seedy bars
waitressed by short-skirted eye candy. **Cine
Mundo** (☎ 349-480; Mall Calama, Balmaceda 3242; tickets
CH$2000) shows big-name movies; catch north-
bound *colectivos* signed 'Mall.'

Getting There & Away
AIR
Lan (☎ 600-526-2000; Latorre 1726) flies to
Antofagasta (CH$37,000 to CH$45,000) and
Santiago (CH$32,400 to CH$57,400) five
times daily. **Sky** (☎ 600-600-2828; Latorre 1499) has
pricy flights to Santiago (from CH$85,000).

BUS
Bus companies are scattered throughout the
town. Those with services northbound and

southbound on the Panamericana include the following:

Flota Barrios (☎ 345-883; Av Balmaceda 1852)

Géminis (☎ 341-993; Antofagasta 2239) To Salta and Arica only.

Pullman Bus (☎ 341-282) Center (cnr Av Balmaceda & Sotomayor); Mall Calama (Balmaceda 3242, Local 130)

Tacc Expreso Norte (☎ 347-250; Balmaceda 1902)

Tur Bus (☎ 313-700; Balmaceda 1852) For tickets only - departures are from Granaderos 3048.

Destination	Cost (CH$)	Duration (hr)
Antofagasta	4000	3
Arica	14,500	10
Iquique	14,000	6½
La Serena	22,800	16
Santiago	30,000	20

Tur Bus provides regular services to San Pedro de Atacama (CH$1800, one hour). **Buses Frontera** (☎ 824-269; Antofagasta 2046) also has buses to San Pedro and Toconao (CH$2200). **Buses Atacama 2000** (☎ 316-664; Abaroa 2106) serves San Pedro, Toconao and Peine for a few cents less.

A community service organized by **Richard Pérez** (☎ 343-400) runs *colectivos* to Chiu Chiu (CH$1300) and Lasana (CH$2000), and also organizes tours.

International buses are invariably full, so reserve as far in advance as possible. To get to Uyuni, Bolivia (CH$9000, 15 hours) via Ollagüe (CH$6000, six hours), ask at Frontera and Buses Atacama 2000; services go twice weekly. Service to Salta and Jujuy, Argentina, is provided by Pullman on Tuesday, Friday and Sunday mornings at 9:05am (CH$20,000, 12 hours), and more

cheaply by Géminis on Tuesday, Friday and Sunday mornings at 9am (CH$13,000, 12 hours).

Getting Around

Aeropuerto El Loa (☎ 312-348) is a short cab ride south of Calama (CH$3000). Minibus transfers cost CH$2000 per person to drop you at your hotel. Taxis (from CH$18,000) will drive tourists to San Pedro de Atacama.

Frequent *taxi colectivos* to Chuquicamata (CH$1000, 15 minutes) leave from Abaroa, just north of Plaza 23 de Marzo.

Car-rental agencies include **Hertz** (☎ 341-380; Av Granaderos 1416) and **Avis** (☎ 363-325; calama@avischile.cl; Aeropuerto El Loa). To visit the geysers at El Tatio, rent a 4WD or pickup truck; ordinary cars lack sufficient clearance for the area's rugged roads and river fords.

AROUND CALAMA
Chuquicamata

Slag heaps as big as mountains, a chasm deeper than the deepest lake in the USA, and trucks the size of houses: these are some of the mind-boggling dimensions that bring visitors to gawp into the mine of Chuquicamata (or just Chuqui). This awesome abyss, gouged from the desert earth 16km north of Calama, is one of the world's largest open-pit copper mines.

Chuqui was also, until quite recently, the world's largest single supplier of copper (a title just snatched by Mina Escondida, 170km southeast of Antofagasta), producing a startling 630,000 tons annually. It's largely thanks to Chuqui, then, that Chile is the world's greatest copper producer. In total, copper accounts for around one-third of Chilean exports. And

---

CHUQUI THROUGH THE EYES OF CHE

Over 50 years ago, when it was already a mine of monstrous proportions, Chuquicamata was visited by a youthful Ernesto 'Che' Guevara. The future revolutionary and his traveling buddy Alberto Granado were midway through their iconic trip across South America, immortalized in Che's *Motorcycle Diaries*. An encounter with a communist during his journey to Chuqui is generally acknowledged as a turning point in Che's emergent politics. So it's especially interesting to read his subsequent memories of the mine itself (then in gringo hands). In one vivid paragraph, the wandering medical student writes of such mines: '...spiced as they would be with the inevitable human lives – the lives of the poor, unsung heroes of this battle, who die miserably in one of the thousand traps set by nature to defend its treasures, when all they want is to earn their daily bread.'

In a footnote to this much-analyzed encounter, the 'blond, efficient and arrogant managers' gruffly told the travelers that Chuquicamata 'isn't a tourist town.' Well, these days it receives around 40,000 visitors per year.

with the price of copper shooting up in recent years (courtesy of huge demand in China) its importance to the Chilean economy is hard to overestimate.

The mine spews up a perpetual plume of dust visible for many miles in the cloudless desert, but then everything here dwarfs the human scale. The elliptical pit measures an incredible 8 million square meters, and is 900m deep. Most of the 'tour' is spent simply gazing into its depths and clambering around an enormous mining truck with tires more than 3m high; information is minimal, although the bilingual guide answers questions.

Chuquicamata was once integrated with a well-ordered company town, but envi-

ronmental problems and copper reserves beneath the town forced the entire population to relocate to Calama by 2004. The 'city of Chiquicamata' is not much more than a ghost town these days.

HISTORY

Prospectors first hit the jackpot at Chuquicamata in 1911. However, they were soon muscled out by the big boys, otherwise known as the US Anaconda Copper Mining Company, from Montana. In the blink of an eye, this foreign company created a fully functioning mining town, with rudimentary housing, schools, cinemas, shops and a hospital. However, Chileans began accusing the gringos of taking far more than they gave

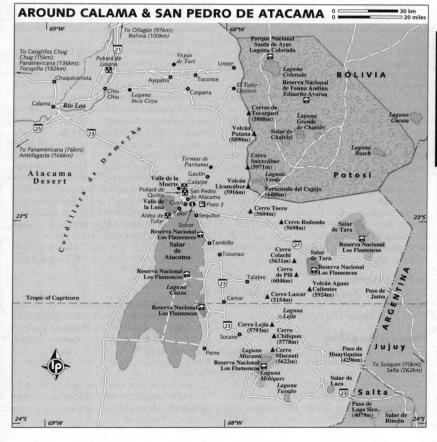

back. Labor unrest became rife and resentment toward the corporation snowballed.

By the 1960s Chile's three largest mines (all run by Anaconda) accounted for more than 80% of Chile's copper production, 60% of total exports and 80% of tax revenues. Despite coughing up elevated taxes, Anaconda was a sitting duck for the champions of nationalization.

During the government of President Eduardo Frei Montalva in the late 1960s, Chile gained a majority shareholding in the Chilean assets of Anaconda and Kennecott. Then in 1971 Congress finally approved the full nationalization of the industry. After 1973 the new military junta agreed to compensate companies for loss of assets, but retained ownership through the Corporación del Cobre de Chile (Codelco).

Some conservative legislators are urging privatization of Codelco.

TOURS
Arrange visits through **Codelco** (☎ 322-122; visitas@codelco.cl; cnr Tocopilla & JM Carrera, Calama; ☑ bookings 8:30-11:30am & 3-5pm Mon-Fri) by phone or email, or ask Calama's tourist office to make the reservation. Tours run from Monday to Friday, in both English and Spanish. Report to the Oficina Ayuda a la Infancia, at the top of Av JM Carrera, 30 minutes before your tour; bring identification and make a voluntary donation. Tours are limited to 40, but they occasionally add a second bus. Demand is high in January and February, so book several days ahead.

The 50-minute tour begins at 2pm. Wear sturdy footwear (no sandals), long pants and long sleeves. Do not arrange the tour through agencies in Calama, as they charge over the odds.

GETTING THERE & AWAY
From Calama, *taxi colectivos* (CH$1000, 15 minutes) leave from Abaroa, just north of Plaza 23 de Marzo and Ramírez.

Geoglifos Chug Chug
A mixed bag of pre-Colombian geoglyphs, one resembling an ancient surfer, are scattered across a remote hillside 35km west of Chuquicamata. Take the paved highway to Tocopilla for about 20km, then follow a dirt road north to Chug Chug. The images are mostly geometric rhomboids. Some date

from the Tiwanaku culture (AD 500–1000) from Bolivia and Peru, while others are regional (1100–1450), and the remainder Inkaic (1450–1530).

SAN PEDRO DE ATACAMA
☎ 055 / pop 3212
They say the high quantities of quartz and copper in the region gives their people positive energy, and the good vibes of northern Chile's number-one tourist draw, San Pedro de Atacama (elevation 2440m), are sky high.

The popularity of this adobe precordillera oasis stems from its position in the heart of some of northern Chile's most spectacular scenery. A short drive away lies the country's largest salt flat, its edges crinkled by volcanoes (symmetrical Licancábur, at 5916m, looms closest to the village). Here too are fields of steaming geysers, a host of otherworldly rock formations and weird layer-cake landscapes.

San Pedro itself seems hardly big enough to absorb the hordes of travelers that arrive; it's little more than a handful of picturesque adobe streets clustering around a pretty tree-lined plaza and postcard-perfect church. However, the last decade has seen a proliferation of guesthouses, restaurants, internet cafés and tour agencies wedging their way into its dusty streets, and turning the town into a kind of highland adobe-Disneyland. And sure enough, San Pedro suffers from the classic drawbacks of any tourist honey pot: high costs, irritating restaurant touts (with way too much quartz in their system to be good) and lackadaisical tour agencies. However, the town has an addictively relaxed atmosphere and an enormous array of tours that can hook travelers for weeks. And at the end of every trip, there's the comfort of a creamy cappuccino, a posh meal and a soft bed waiting in San Pedro.

History
San Pedro was once a pre-Columbian pit stop on the trading route from the highlands to the coast. It was visited by Pedro de Valdivia in 1540, and the town later became a major stop on early-20th-century cattle drives from Argentina to the nitrate *oficinas* of the desert.

Locals still practice irrigated farming in the *ayllus* (a-ee-oos; small indigenous communities). Many still farm on terraces over a thousand years old.

Orientation

San Pedro is 106km southeast of Calama via paved Chile 23. The village itself is small and compact, with almost everything of interest within easy strolling distance of the plaza.

Many buildings now have street numbers, although many still do without. The main commercial street is Caracoles, south of the Plaza de Armas.

MAPS

The excellent JLM map of San Pedro and surroundings is a worthwhile investment for exploring without tours. It's available at Azimut 360 (p216) and other agencies.

Information

INTERNET ACCESS

Half a dozen internet cafés (CH$1000 per hour) dot Caracoles, and many accommodations offer access.

MEDICAL SERVICES

Posta Médica (☎ 851-010; Toconao s/n) The local clinic, on the plaza.

MONEY

San Pedro's lack of a bank has long been a sore point with travelers, who until recently had to bus back to Calama to fill their pockets. There are now two ATMs in town, but they do not always have money, so bring a big wad of cash, just in case. Many establishments take plastic, but some prefer the real stuff.

ATM (Caracoles s/n; ☿ 9am-10pm) Takes visa. On the western side of the village.

ATM (Gustavo Le Paige; ☿ 9am-10pm) Opposite the museum. Only works with Mastercard.

Money Exchange (Toconao 492) Changes cash. Don't expect competitive rates for traveler's checks.

LAUNDRY

Viento Norte (☎ 851-329; Vilama 432-B) Has drop-off service for CH$1500 per kilogram, or CH$2500 if you need it back the same day.

POST

Post office (Caracoles s/n, in Librería Ebenezar; ☿ 9am-12:30pm & 2:30-6pm Mon-Fri) The location changes almost yearly, so ask locals if you can't find it here.

TELEPHONE

Many internet cafés now offer internet calling for cheap.

Entel (Plaza de Armas; ☿ 8:30am-10pm Mon-Fri, 9am-9pm Sat & Sun) International calling center.

Media Luna (Caracoles; ☿ 8:30am-10pm Mon-Fri, 10am-10pm Sat & Sun) Calling center near the plaza.

TOURIST INFORMATION

Conaf information center (Solcor; ☿ 10am-1pm & 2:30-4:30pm) About 2km past San Pedro's customs post on the Toconao road.

Oficina de Información Turística (☎ 851-420; sanpedrodeatacama@gmail.com; cnr Toconao & Gustavo Le Paige; ☿ 10am-1:30pm & 3-8:30pm Mon-Fri, 10am-2pm Sat) Helpful tourist office offering advice and doling out town maps.

Sights

The sugar-white **Iglesia San Pedro** (admission free; Plaza de Armas) is a delightful little colonial church built with indigenous or artisanal materials – chunky adobe walls and roof, a ceiling made from *cardón* (cactus wood) resembling shriveled tire tracks and, in lieu of nails, hefty leather straps. The church dates from the 17th century, though its present walls were built in 1745, and the bell tower was added in 1890.

On the east side of the plaza stands the restored adobe **Casa Incaica**, ostensibly built in 1540 for Valdivia, but it might be safer to say that Valdivia slept here. It's closed to the public.

MUSEO GUSTAVO LE PAIGE

Even if museums aren't your thing, make an exception for San Pedro's superb **Museo Gustavo Le Paige** (☎ 851-002; Gustavo Le Paige; adult/student CH$2000/1000; ☿ 9am-6pm Mon-Fri, 10am-6pm Sat & Sun).

The Atacama is nirvana for archeologists because of its nearly rainless environment, which preserves artifacts for millennia. And

---

RESPONSIBLE TOURISM

High season brings thousands of tourists to tiny San Pedro. Residents, especially the indigenous Atacameño peoples, are sensitive to the overwhelming presence of outsiders. Make a special effort to behave appropriately and blend in as best you can; avoid wearing highly revealing clothes in town (save those bikinis for the hot springs), remove hats while visiting churches and consider wearing long pants.

Water is scarce (obviously), so refrain from long soaks in the shower.

SAN PEDRO DE ATACAMA

INFORMATION		
ATM	1	C3
ATM	2	A3
Entel	3	C3
Media Luna	4	C3
Money Exchange	5	C4
Oficina de Información Turística	6	C3
Post Office	7	C3
Posta Médica	8	C3
Valley of the Moon Visitor Center	(see 32)	
Viento Norte	9	C3

SIGHTS & ACTIVITIES		
Atacama Connection	10	C3
Cactus Tour	11	A3
Casa Incaica	12	C3
Cordillera Traveller	13	B3
Cosmo Andino	14	B3
Desert Adventure	15	B3
Iglesia San Pedro	16	B3
Museo Gustavo Le Paige	17	C2
Ruta Tropera	18	C4
Servicios Astronómicos Maury y Compañía	19	A3
Terra Extreme	20	C3
Vulcano	21	C3

SLEEPING		
Camping Los Perales	22	B4
Hostal Edén Atacameño	23	C4
Hostal Sonchek	24	A3
Hosteling International	25	C3
Hotel Kimal	26	A4
Hotel Licancábur	27	C4
Hotel Lickana	28	A3
Hotel Tambillo	29	A3
Hotel Terrantai	30	B3
Hotel Tulor	31	A4
Licanhuasi–Red de Turismo Rural	32	C3
Residencial Vilacoyo	33	B3
Takha Takha Hotel Camping	34	A3

EATING		
Algarrobo	35	C3
Ayllu	36	C3
Café Adobe	37	B3
Café Export	38	B3
Casa Piedra	39	B3
Ckunna	40	B2
Food Stalls	41	B2
La Casona	42	B3
La Estaka	43	B3
Las Delicias de Carmen	44	A2
Quitor	45	A2
Tahira	46	B2
Todo Natural	47	B3

TRANSPORT		
Atacama Connection	(see 10)	
Buses Atacama 2000	48	C2
Buses Frontera	49	B2
Géminis	50	C3
Tur Bus	51	A2

so this octagonal museum is packed with such fascinating finds as well-preserved ceramics and textiles, and an extraordinary collection of shamanic paraphernalia for preparing, ingesting and smoking hallucinogenic plants. The star of the show used to be the Paleo-Indian mummies, but they were recently removed – upon request by the Atacameño people.

Detailed English and Spanish explanations follow the region's evolution through the earliest cultures to the Inka conquest and the Spanish invasion. No opportunity is lost to link information with surrounding archaeological sites, including Pukará de Quitor and Aldea de Tulor.

The credit for this excellent museum goes principally to the Belgian priest and amateur archaeologist after whom it is named. Father Gustavo Le Paige arrived as a priest to San Pedro in 1955, and dedicated the next 35 years of his life to collecting ancient artifacts from the area. His statue now stands outside and a small exhibit is dedicated to him within.

Tours

A bewildering array of tours is on offer. Activities can be as leisurely or hardcore as you please: from nodding off in hot volcanic springs to bombing down steep trails on mountain bikes; from musing over the remains of ancient civilizations to sweating up active volcanoes; and from surfing down giant sand dunes to star-gazing in the cloudless desert nights.

EXCURSION TO UYUNI, BOLIVIA

Colorful altiplano lakes, weird rock playgrounds worthy of Salvador Dali, flamingos, volcanoes and, most famously of all, the blindingly white salt flat of Uyuni: these are some of the rewards for taking an excursion into Bolivia northeast of San Pedro de Atacama. However, be warned that this is no cozy ride in the country, and for every five travelers that gush about Uyuni being the highlight of their trip there is another declaring it a waking nightmare.

The standard trips take three days, crossing the Bolivian border at Portezuelo del Cajón, passing Laguna Colorada and continuing to the Salar de Uyuni before ending in the town of Uyuni. The going rate of CH$52,000 includes transportation in crowded 4WD jeeps, basic and often teeth-chatteringly cold accommodations, plus food; an extra CH$13,000 will get you back to San Pedro on the fourth day (some tour operators drive through the third night). Bring drinks and snacks, warm clothes, and a sleeping bag. Travelers clear Chilean immigration at San Pedro and Bolivian immigration on arrival at Uyuni.

Sadly, none of the agencies offering this trip get consistently glowing reports. **Cordillera Traveler** (☎ 851-966; www.cordilleratravel.cl; Tocopilla s/n) is a small family-run outfit that gets the best feedback from travelers.

Unfortunately, the quality of the tours has become somewhat lax, and travelers complain of operators who cancel abruptly or run unsafe vehicles. Tour leaders are often merely drivers rather than trained guides. Agencies often contract out to independent drivers, many of whom work for different companies, so the quality of your driver can depend on the luck of the draw. That said, don't unfairly dismiss local Spanish-speaking drivers. Many of them are very courteous and knowledgeable, and they can provide a valuable insider's viewpoint.

You may find that the agency you paid is not the same agency that picks you up. Some agencies offer tours in English, German or Dutch, but these tours may require advance notice or extra payment. Competition keeps prices down, and operators come and go.

The tourist information office has a helpful, entertaining and occasionally terrifying book of complaints on various tour agencies; the problem is that nearly every agency is featured and, by the time you read about unlicensed or drunken drivers over the passes to Bolivia, you may decide to do nothing but write postcards from the safety of your hostel, which would be a tragic mistake in such a beautiful area. Nevertheless, when choosing an operator ask lots of questions, talk to other travelers, trust your judgment and try to be flexible.

STANDARD TOURS
Some routinely offered tours follow. Note that entrance fees are not included in the tour prices.

Altiplano lakes (CH$10,000-25,000, entrance fees CH$3000-5000) Leaves San Pedro around 7am to see flamingos at Laguna Chaxa in the Salar de Atacama, the town of Socaire, Lagunas Miñiques and Miscanti, Toconao and the Quebrada de Jere, returning 5pm.

El Tatio geysers (from CH$15,000, entrance fees CH$3500) This hugely popular tour leaves San Pedro at 4am in order to see the geysers at sunrise, returning at noon. Includes thermal baths and breakfast.

Geysers and pueblos (CH$28,000, entrance fees CH$4500) Leaves at 4am for the geysers, then visits Caspana, the Pukará de Lasana and Chiu-Chiu, finishing in Calama, or returning to San Pedro by 6pm.

Uyuni, Bolivia (see boxed text, above) Popular three-day 4WD tour of the remote and beautiful *salar* (salt-lake) region.

Valle de la Luna (CH$5000, entrance fees CH$2000) Leaves San Pedro mid-afternoon to catch the sunset over the valley, returning early evening. Includes visits to the Valle de la Luna, Valle de la Muerte and Tres Marías.

Tulor and Pukara de Quitor (CH$10,000, entrance fees CH$6000) Takes you to these pre-Columbian ruins.

These agencies get the most positive feedback from travelers:

Cactus Tour (☎ 851-534; www.cactustour.cl; Caracoles 163-A) A small outfit, but frequently recommended for its excellent service, polite bilingual guides, comfortable vehicles and above-average food. Prices are marginally higher, but the difference is noticeable.

Cosmo Andino (☎ 851-069; cosmoandino@entelchile .net; Caracoles s/n) Another small operation, which charges a little more than the average but has the most unblemished reputation in town.

Others to try include **Desert Adventure** (☎ 851-067; www.desertadventure.cl; Caracoles s/n) and **Atacama**

Connection (☎ 851-421; www.atacamaconnection.com; cnr Caracoles & Toconao), both of which have bilingual guides. If price is more important to you than blameless service, try **Terra Extreme** (☎ 851-274; terraextreme@gmail.com; Toconao s/n).

TREKKING & ADVENTURE
East of the *salar* rise immense volcanoes, a few of them active, and all begging to be climbed. **Azimut 360** (☎ 851-469; www.azimut360.com; Caracoles 66) Well-established trekking and volcano-climbing specialists. Prices start at around CH$105,000 per person (minimum two people).

Vulcano (☎ 851-023; www.vulcanochile.com; Caracoles 317) Runs enthusiastic trekking tours to several volcanoes and mountains, including Sairecabur (6040m; CH$83,300), Lascar (5600m; CH$83,300) and Toco (5604m; CH$54,200).

HORSEBACK RIDING
Sightseeing from the saddle is available from several places, including **Ruta Tropera** (☎ 099-838-6833; www.rutatropera.cl, in Spanish; Toconao 479). Tours vary from two hours to epic seven-day treks, and day tours cost about CH$4500 per hour.

SAND-BOARDING
Another unique perspective on the altiplano can be had by jumping on a sand-board and sliding down enormous sand dunes. Many agencies (including Atacama Connection, left) can take you to Valle de la Muerte's 150m-high dunes for a half-day session (around CH$15,000). Once you've got the hang of it, you can hire boards directly from Vulcano (left).

Festivals & Events
Fiesta de Nuestra Señora de la Candelaria In early February, San Pedro celebrates with religious dances.
Carnaval Takes place in February or March, depending on the date of Easter.
Fiesta de San Pedro y San Pablo June 29 has the locals celebrating with folk dancing, Mass, a procession of statues, a rodeo and modern dancing that gets rowdy by midnight.
Fiesta de Santa Rosa de Lima On August 30; this is a traditional religious festival.

Sleeping
Most budget places request that solo travelers share a room in the busy summer period. Consider whether it's wise, when half the group is leaving at 4am for a geyser tour.

BUDGET
Takha Takha Hotel Camping (☎ 851-038; Caracoles 101-A; campsites per person CH$4500, with/without bathroom s

DESERT STAR-GAZING
The flats of Chajnantor, 40km east of San Pedro de Atacama, will soon host the most ambitious radio telescope that the world has ever seen. The Atacama Large Milimetre Array (ALMA; meaning 'soul' in Spanish) is slated to be finished in 2011 and will consist of 64 enormous antennae, each around 12m across. Once finished, this field of interstellar 'ears' will simulate a telescope an astonishing 14km in diameter and make it possible to pick up objects as much as 100 times fainter than those currently detected.

This is just the latest of northern Chile's cutting-edge astronomical facilities. Climatic conditions in the Atacama Desert make it an ideal location for star-gazing. This is not only thanks to cloudless desert nights, but also the predictable winds that blow steadily in from the Pacific Ocean, causing minimal turbulence – a crucial requirement for observatories to achieve optimal image quality.

Other major facilities in northern Chile include the European Southern Observatory (ESO) at Cerro Paranal (p228). Norte Chico has Cerro Tololo Interamerican Observatory (p250) and the nearby Cerro El Pachón. Another ESO site is at La Silla, while the Carnegie Institution's Observatorio Las Campanas is just north of La Silla.

If all that whets your appetite for astronomy, consider taking a Tour of the Night Sky from San Pedro. French astronomer Alain Maury ferries travelers into the desert, far from intrusive light contamination, where they can enjoy the stars in all their glory. He owns several chunky telescopes through which visitors can gawk at galaxies, nebulae, planets and more. Shooting stars are guaranteed. Reserve a place at **Servicios Astronómicos Maury y Compañía** (☎ 055-851-935; www.spaceobs.com; Caracoles 166; 2½hr tours CH$12,000). Tours leave nightly at 7:30pm and 10:30pm in winter and 9pm and midnight in summer (except around the full moon), and they alternate between Spanish, English and French. Bring very warm clothes.

CH$29,500/9000, d CH$32,000/17,000; (P) (&) A popular catch-all outfit with decent campsites, plain budget rooms and spotless midrange accommodations set around a sprawling flowery garden. Candles lie around at the ready in case of power cuts.

Residencial Vilacoyo (☎ 851-006; vilacoyo@san pedroatacama.com; Tocopilla 387; per person CH$6000; (P)) A cozy little spot with warm service and a snug gravel patio strategically hung with hammocks. The shared showers only have hot water between 7am and 10pm. There's a kitchen and luggage storage.

Hosteling International (☎ 851-426; hostelsan pedro@hotmail.com; Caracoles 360; incl breakfast members dm/d CH$6000/17,000, nonmembers CH$8000/20,000) This super-friendly HI-affiliated property – guess you could figure that out by the name – offers functional six-bedded dorms and a few private doubles (that still have shared showers). It's kind of like camping, only you get to sleep in a bed. Acrophobes beware: some bunks are nearly 3m up. Services include laundry, lockers, bike rental and sand-boards. Alas, no kitchen.

Hostal Edén Atacameño (☎ 851-154; hostaleden _spa@hotmail.com; Toconao 592; s without bathroom CH$8000, d with/without bathroom CH$25,000/14,000; (P) (💻)) This is a laid-back hostel with rooms spread around a sociable, Alsatian-dotted patio with plentiful seating and a hammock or two. Guests can use the kitchen, and there's a laundry service. The shared bathrooms are immaculately clean – nice! – and you can expect discounts in the low season.

Hostal Sonchek (☎ 851-112; soncheksp@hotmail .com; Gustavo Le Paige 170; s without bathroom CH$9000, d with/without bathroom CH$30,000/14,000; (P)) Thatched roofs and adobe walls characterize the simple rooms at this Slovenian-run hostel, one of the best budget spots in town. It's centered on a small courtyard, and there's a shared kitchen and a few welcoming hammocks strung out back. The common bathrooms are some of the cleanest in town, but you'll need to ask ahead of time to have the hot water turned on. English and French spoken.

Other possibilities:

Camping Buenas Peras (☎ 099-510-9004; Ckilapana 688; campsites per person CH$3000) Sites scattered around a pear orchard 1.5km from town. Gregarious host.

Camping Los Perales (☎ 851-570; campinglos perales@hotmail.com; Tocopilla 481; campsites per person CH$3500) Sprawling site with basic facilities, including kitchen access.

Hotel Licancábur (☎ 851-007; Toconao s/n; with/without bathroom s CH$12,000/8000, d CH$23,000/13,000) Family atmosphere.

MIDRANGE

Exclusively midrange hotels are in short supply at this backpacker's haven, but many hostels in the budget category also have midrange rooms at the ready.

Hostal Quinta Adela (☎ 851-272; Toconao 624; d CH$30,000; (P)) This family-run place, just outside of town, has seven character-filled rooms (each its own individual style) and a sprawling orchard alongside. Large breakfasts cost CH$2000.

Hostal Lickana (☎ 851-940; www.lickanahostal.cl; Caracoles 140; s/d CH$34,000/36,000; (P)) Just off the main drag, this strip hotel has super-clean rooms, but lacks the common-area ambiance of other hostals.

Hotel Tambillo (☎ 851-078; www.hoteltambillo.cl; Gustavo Le Paige 159; d CH$35,000; (P) ✖) Spongy beds and small plain rooms are big drawbacks at this centrally located hotel. The rooms are strung along an inner breezeway and a shady courtyard. While you can probably do better, if everything is full up, you should consider the Tambillo.

TOP END

Top-range hotels have sprouted all around San Pedro, though most are outside the center.

Hotel Kimal (☎ 851-030; www.kimal.cl; Domingo Atienza 452; s/d incl breakfast CH$51,600/62,800; (♨) (💻)) Rustic chic dominates this small but perfectly formed hotel complex; closely knit

---

ESCAPE THE CROWDS

Travelers looking for a glimpse into traditional villages around San Pedro can arrange to stay at remote *refugios* and guesthouses through **Licanhuasi – Red de Turismo Rural** (☎ 851-593; www.licanhuasi.cl; Caracoles 349), which has surprisingly modern properties in such small towns as Socaire, Peine, Machuca and Ollagüe, and beside the Lagunas Miscanti and Miñiques. Prices range from CH$13,000 to CH$15,000 per person. In case you were wondering, *lincan* means house and *huasi* means town in the Kunza language.

one-story buildings are built with simple adobe bricks and topped by cane roofs. Best of all, it fits with the regional character, the rustic decor blending in seamlessly with the surrounding desert. There is also a cute little circular pool with a gurgling Jacuzzi and waterfall.

Hotel Terrantai (☎ 851-045; www.terrantai.com; Tocopilla 411; s/d CH$76,500/98,500; P ⊠ ▢) This is arguably the most intimate of San Pedro's upscale hotels. The key is in the architecture: high, narrow passageways made from smooth rocks from the Loa River lead guests to the simple, elegant rooms. There's a bamboo-shaded sculpture garden out back as well as a delicious (albeit small) dip pool, giving the Terrantai a spa-like feel.

Hotel Tulor (☎ 851-248; www.tulor.cl; Domingo Atienza 253; s/d incl buffet breakfast CH$85,395/102,100; P ⊠) Built and run by a resident archaeologist, using a circular design inspired by the Aldea de Tulor site, the Tulor is a bit more basic than the neighboring Kimal, but has nice tasteful rooms. The pool was dirty when we were there.

Eating

A word of warning: while San Pedro restaurants offer welcome variety, especially for vegetarians, it comes with an elevated price tag. Touristy places have touts offering 10% off or a free drink (make sure you get it).

BUDGET

To best avoid San Pedro's skyrocketing prices, follow the locals out to the town periphery.

Food stalls (empanadas CH$400, set lunch from CH$1000; ☺ breakfast, lunch & dinner) The cheapest eats in town are served in rustic shacks in a parking lot behind the taxi rank on the northern edge of town. Expect simple set lunches of *cazuela*, mains and dessert, and all-day empanadas for snacking.

Quitor (☎ 099-915-9302; cnr Licancábur & Domingo Atienza; set meals CH$2500-4000; mains CH$2000-4000; ☺ lunch & dinner) A large, thatched establishment frequented by locals, Chilean tourists and gringos alike, this small eatery right next to the bus stop has simple but filling meals and an efficient get-it-on-the-table attitude. Save money by going with the smaller set meal.

Tahira (☎ 851-296; Tocopilla 372; CH$2500-3500; ☺ breakfast, lunch & dinner) Another down-to-earth café where the locals outnumber the gringos, Tahira serves up satisfying, no-frills dishes.

MIDRANGE & TOP END

Ayllu (☎ 851-814; Caracoles 330; mains CH$2000-6000; ☺ lunch & dinner) It's pretty much like the other restaurants in town: *fogatas*, open-air dining and a smogasborg of international dishes. But the Ayllu separates itself with warm, friendly service. Seems the waiter's GTI (Gringo Tolerance Indicator) is higher than in most places.

Todo Natural (☎ 851-585; Caracoles 271; mains CH$2800-6000; ☺ breakfast, lunch & dinner; Ⓥ) Healthy offerings include fresh wholemeal sandwiches, a lengthy salad list and numerous vegetarian choices in this cute little café with an open kitchen and small alfresco courtyard. The service is downright bad – guess speedy service just wouldn't be natural – but the food is decent, making it worth a visit.

ourpick La Casona (☎ 851-004; Caracoles 195; mains CH$2800-7000; ☺ breakfast, lunch & dinner) La Casona has been around for a long time. In its current incarnation, this rambling open-air restaurant has tip-top cuisine, focusing on international faves – try the veggie pasta, it's excellent – with speedy service, a wine room up front and occasional live music. And then there's those San Pedro stars blaring their cosmic orchestra overhead – can't get much better than that.

Café Export (cnr Toconao & Caracoles; mains CH$3500-6000; ☺ breakfast, lunch & dinner) This is a funky cavelike spot with an intimate interior: low candlelit tables, roaring fire and prehistoric-style daubing on the walls. Despite off-putting touts hovering on its doorstep, and the loud music, it is hugely popular for strong coffee, homemade pasta and decent pizzas.

Algarrobo (south side of plaza; set lunch CH$5000, mains CH$3500-6500; ☺ breakfast, lunch & dinner) Pretty cheap eats, especially considering its bees-knees location right on the plaza. The Algarrobo has the feel of an older eatery, the kind that dusty miners would have stopped at on their way to the salitre fields. There's a large set menu, but we prefer the pita sandwiches, which are big enough to share.

La Estaka (☎ 851-201; Caracoles s/n; mains CH$3800-6500; ☺ lunch & dinner; Ⓥ) A lively gathering point late into the night, La Estaka is also recommended for its juicy steaks, sinful *dulce de leche* (super-sweet condensed-milk spread) crepes, chicken curries and addictively good vegetarian options. It strives for a trendy, subterranean atmosphere and has a fireplace.

Café Adobe (☎ 851-132; Caracoles s/n; CH$4000-7000; 🕑 lunch & dinner) Ever popular with travelers for its studied rusticity, rock-art decor and smoky fire in the outer dining room, Adobe is a bit pricy for what you get. You may just want to drop by later for a drink.

Las Delicias de Carmen (Calama 370; set lunch & dinner CH$4500; 🕑 lunch & dinner; Ⓥ) Doña Carmen serves up some of the best empanadas in town. Or you can go for the set lunch, which features the town's best salad and a tasty meat or pasta dish. The dining area is less rustic than that of many San Pedro eateries, giving it a bit of a cafeteria feel. Nevertheless, it is clean, honest and, well, good.

CKunna (☎ 851-999; Tocopilla 359; set lunch CH$6000, mains CH$5500-9000; 🕑 breakfast, lunch & dinner) This is an excellent, if touristy, restaurant that gives traditional Atacameño ingredients a contemporary twist. It's housed in a renovated adobe building with a beautiful courtyard to relax in. It also has takeaway service and a welcoming bar.

Entertainment

While San Pedro's small community welcomes tourism, it draws the line at late-night revelers. Establishments that sell only alcohol have been outlawed, no alcohol is sold after 1am, police have cracked down on public drinking *and* local lawmakers recently banned nocturnal dancing in downtown San Pedro. The night is also cut short by travelers with early tours: after all, waking up for a 4am jaunt to El Tatio is enough of a headache *without* a hangover!

However, all is not lost for lovers of nightlife; a very cozy bar-cum-restaurant scene predominates here, with travelers swapping stories around open fires and making the most of abundant happy hours. Especially popular are El Adobe, La Estaka, La Casona and Café Export, with their adobe cave motifs and Euro-ambience music.

Shopping

The shaded Paseo Artesanal, a poker-straight alley squeezing north from the plaza, is the place to hunt down novel *cardón* carvings, llama and alpaca woolens and other curious trinkets. More artisanal outlets are strewn throughout town.

Getting There & Away

Travelers to and from Argentina and Bolivia clear immigration with the Policía Internacional, customs and agricultural inspections, just east of town. **Buses Atacama 2000** (☎ 851-501; Licancábur) has buses to Calama (CH$1800, three daily), Toconao (CH$700) and Peine (CH$2200). **Buses Frontera** (☎ 851-117; Licancábur) serves the same destinations.

Tur Bus (☎ 851-549; Licancábur 294) has buses to Calama (CH$1800, eight daily) and from there onward to Arica (CH$17,000, one daily), Antofagasta (CH$6000, six daily) and Santiago (CH$32,000, three daily, 23 hours).

Géminis (☎ 851-538; Toconao s/n) serves Salta and Jujuy, Argentina, leaving at 11.30am on Tuesday, Friday and Sunday (CH$30,000 to CH$35,000, 12 hours). **Atacama Connection** (☎ 851-421; www.atacamaconnection.com; cnr Caracoles & Toconao) has a Pullman office for trips to Salta.

Getting Around

Mountain bikes are a terrific way to steam around San Pedro. However, to ensure that only calories are burned, be sure to carry water and sunblock.

Vulcano (☎ 851-023; Caracoles 317) rents sturdy mountain bikes (CH$3000/6000 per half/full day). When requested, staff also give out photocopied maps to guide your forays.

Also see p216 for information on trotting around the area on horseback.

AROUND SAN PEDRO DE ATACAMA

Most attractions are beyond walking distance from town, and public transportation is limited. Options include renting a car (in Calama), hiring a bike or taking a tour. Luckily, vigorous competition among numerous operators keeps tours reasonably priced (see p214). Also, consider staying the night in the remote villages and attractions you visit. By spreading the tourist trail, you help create a more sustainable future for the people of the region.

Pukará de Quitor & Catarpe

Dominating a curvy promontory over the Río San Pedro, this crumbling 12th-century **pukará** (adult/student CH$2000/1500; 🕑 8:30am-6:30pm Apr-Dec, 7:30am-7:45pm Jan-Mar) was one of the last bastions against Pedro de Valdivia and the Spanish in northern Chile. The indigenous forces fought bravely but were overcome and many were promptly beheaded. A hundred defensive enclosures hug the slopes here, like big stone bird's nests. The hilltop commands an impressive view of the entire oasis.

The fort is just 3km northwest of San Pedro, and easily accessible on foot, by bike or by vehicle.

Another 3km along the valley is the **Quebrada del Diablo** (Devil's Gorge), a mountain-biking delight with serpentine single tracks going deep into a silent maze. About 2km further north, east of the river, are the ruins of **Catarpe**, a former Inka administrative center.

Aldea de Tulor

Circular adobe structures huddle together like muddy bubble-wrap in the ruins of **Tulor** (admission CH$2000), the oldest excavated village in the region. It's an interesting diversion 11km west of San Pedro; however, you'll have to take a tour, drive along sandy tracks or mountain-bike it.

Termas de Puritama

These idyllic **volcanic hot springs** (admission CH$5000) puddle together in a box canyon 34km north of San Pedro, en route to El Tatio. Maintained by the Explora company, it has changing rooms on site. Few tours stop here because of the hefty admission charged, but taxis will take you from San Pedro for around CH$5000. The springs are a 20-minute walk from the parking lot. The temperature of the springs is about 33°C, and there are several falls and pools. Bring food, water and sunblock.

Pozo 3

You can go swimming at **Pozo 3** (☎ 098-476-7290; admission CH$3000; ☼ 7am-7pm), 3km east of San Pedro off the road to Paso Jama. The swimming pool here is well kept, and there are changing rooms. Gas-heads can rent ATVs, and you can camp for around CH$5000 per person, though you are better off camping in one of the spots closer to town.

RESERVA NACIONAL LOS FLAMENCOS

This sprawling reserve encompasses seven geographically distinct sectors south and east of San Pedro de Atacama, and encloses many of the area's top attractions.

Conaf maintains a **Centro de Información Ambiental** (☼ 10am-1pm & 2:30-4:30pm) at the *ayllu* (small indigenous community) of Solcor, which is located 2km past San Pedro de Atacama's customs and immigration post on the road to Toconao.

Valle de la Luna

Watching the sun set from the exquisite **Valley of the Moon** (☎ 851-574; visitor center in San Pedro 329 Caracoles; adult/student CH$2000/1500; ☼ dawn-dusk) is an unforgettable experience. As you sit atop a giant sand dune, panting from the exertion of climbing it, drinking in spectacular views and watching the sun slip below the horizon, a beautiful transformation occurs: the distant ring of volcanoes, rippling Cordillera de la Sal and surreal lunar landscapes of the valley, are suddenly suffused with intense purples, pinks and golds.

The Valle de la Luna is named after its lunar-like landforms eroded by eons of flood and wind. It's found 15km west of San Pedro de Atacama at the northern end of the Cordillera de la Sal and forms part of Reserva Nacional Los Flamencos.

The valley is San Pedro's most popular and cheapest organized tour; trips typically depart about 4:30pm, leaving good time to explore before sunset. If you want to avoid dozens of tourist vans, all making the same stops, pick an alternative time. Some hardy souls come here at dawn to sidestep the sunset crowds.

Mountain biking is a great way to get here (see p219), but keep to the roads and trails, and make sure you take a flashlight if you're staying for the sunset. If driving, you can leave the highway to explore the dirt roads and box canyons to the north; take care not to get stuck in the sand. Park only on the shoulder or at other designated areas – do not tear up the fragile desert with tire tracks.

Note that camping is not permitted, but occasional underground full-moon parties have been known to occur. The area is now being administrated by the Atacameño people, and these are their ancestral grounds and sacred space, so be considerate: that means cleaning up your trash and foregoing the full-moon debauchery (not to preach).

Laguna Chaxa

The jagged crust of the **Salar de Atacama** looks for all the world like God went crazy with a stippling brush. But in the midst of these rough lifeless crystals is an oasis of activity: the pungent **Laguna Chaxa** (adult CH$2000), about 25km southwest of Toconao and 65km from San Pedro, the reserve's most easily accessible flamingo breeding site. Three of the five known species (James, Chilean and Andean) can be spotted at this salt lake, as well as plovers, coots and ducks: bring zoom lenses and snappy reflexes. Sunrise is feeding time for the birds and is the best time to see them. It's also gorgeous at sunset.

Laguna Miscanti & Miñiques

Shimmery high-altitude lakes dot the altiplano and make for long but worthwhile excursions from San Pedro. From a junction 3km south of Toconao, Ruta 23 heads 46km south toward the village of **Socaire**, which has a pretty colonial church with a cactus-wood ceiling, and a remarkable density of Inkan terraces.

The road then climbs 18km to an eastbound turnoff leading to the glittery-blue sweet-water lakes, **Miñiques** and **Miscanti** (admission to both adult/student CH$2000/1500), watched over by snow-touched volcanoes. The smaller Laguna Miscanti is a high-Andean flamingo breeding site and visitors are kept at bay when the birds are breeding. Rejoining Ruta 23 about 15km south of the turnoff, the road heads eastward past more salt lakes, including **Laguna Tuyajto**, to the Argentine border at Paso de Lago Sico (4079m).

Socaire is 100km from San Pedro, and the lagunas are 120km distant at 4300m.

EL TATIO GEYSERS

Visiting the world-famous El Tatio at dawn is like walking through a gigantic steam bath, ringed by volcanoes and fed by 64 gurgling geysers and a hundred gassy fumaroles. Swirling columns of steam envelop onlookers in a Dantesque vision, and the soundtrack of bubbling, spurting and hissing sounds like a field of merrily boiling kettles. The experience does not *feel* like bathtime, however: unless it's bathtime in the arctic. Most visitors find themselves wishing the geysers would spread their heat more efficiently during the freezing dawn.

At 4300m above sea level, El Tatio is the world's highest geyser field. The sight of its steaming fumaroles in the azure clarity of the altiplano is unforgettable, and the mineral structures formed as the boiling water evaporates are strikingly beautiful. As dawn wears on, shafts of sunlight crown the surrounding volcanoes and illuminate the writhing steam. Plans have been in the works for several years to create a thermo-electric plant here, but, as of press time, the Tatio geysers were still free to shoot their steam skyward.

Information & Sleeping

The geysers are 95km north of San Pedro de Atacama. Administration of the geysers was handed over to indigenous Atacameño people in 2004. You'll need to stop to pay the entrance fee (CH$3500) at the site's administrative kiosk, about 2km before the geysers. You can camp here for CH$2000 per person, but you'll want to bring a warm sleeping bag and many layers of clothing.

Tours, priced from CH$15,000, leave at the forbidding hour of 4am to reach the geysers by 6am, the best time to see them. Almost every tour agency in San Pedro offers this tour, so hundreds of sleepy-eyed tourists stumble from minibuses at the appointed hour. After about 8:30am, the winds disperse the steam, although most tours leave by that time so you can enjoy the large thermal pool in virtual privacy. Watch your step – in some places, visitors have fallen through the thin crust into underlying pools of scalding water and suffered severe burns. Dress in layers: it's toe-numbingly cold at sunbreak but you'll bake in the van on the way back down.

Getting There & Away

Tours from San Pedro (see p214) include breakfast, often with fresh eggs and cartons of milk boiled in geyser pools.

If driving, leave San Pedro no later than 4am to reach the geysers by sunrise. The route north is signed from San Pedro, but some drivers prefer to follow tour minibuses in the dark (the bus drivers do not appreciate this, however). Do not attempt this rough road, which has some difficult stream fords, without a high-clearance pickup or jeep, preferably one with 4WD.

If you rented a vehicle in Calama, consider returning via the picturesque villages of Caspana and Chiu Chiu rather than via San Pedro. Some tours from Calama and San Pedro take this route as well.

TOCONAO
☎ 055 / pop 500

An idyllic oasis of fruit trees, herbs and flowers can be found just outside the traditional Andean village of Toconao, located 38km south of San Pedro. The **Quebrada de Jere** (☎ 852-010; admission CH$1000), sometimes called Quebrada de Jeréz (Sherry Gorge) for its sweet water, nestles in a deep gash in the altiplano.

WORTH THE TRIP: THE UPPER LOA & ITS TRIBUTARIES

A string of typically Andean villages and ancient forts fleck the difficult terrain to the north of San Pedro de Atacama and east of Calama. A few tour operators from San Pedro visit these villages after the early-morning spectacle of watching the El Tatio geysers – taking passes as high as 4800m and jiggling along some tight switchbacks.

From the geysers it's 46km along some switchbacks to highland idyll **Caspana**, as delightful as it is surprising. Nestled in its namesake valley, the 'new' village is built into the rocky escarpment, while the 'old' town teeters on the edge of a high plateau above. It's exactly what an Andean village is supposed to look like – verdant terraces, thatched roofs, the colonial **Iglesia de San Lucas and** an archaeological **museum** (admission CH$500; 10am-1pm & 3-5:30pm). Do not drink the tap water here.

At this point you could head north to **Ayquina**, an agricultural village and the nearby thermal springs **Vegas de Turi**, and then east to tiny **Toconce**.

However, most tours now take the road west from Caspana, taking the turnoff northwest via **Laguna Inca Coya** (also known as Laguna Chiu Chiu), a perfectly round oasis, 80m deep according to an expedition led by Jacques Cousteau. A legend claims it was filled by the tears of the jilted lover of Inka Tupac Yupanqui.

From here the dirt road continues west to a junction, where you can turn north to Chiu Chiu and the 12th-century **Pukará de Lasana** (admission CH$1000), an extensive fortress built into the salmon-pink volcanic rock of the valley. Its husk is pockmarked with bodegas, defensive nooks and occasional petroglyphs. A touristy restaurant sits alongside.

On the trip back to Chiu Chiu, take time to appreciate the enigmatic petroglyphs that smother the valley, some in plain view and some hiding behind hefty boulders.

Chiu Chiu itself is just 33km from Calama via paved Ruta 21. It's difficult to overestimate the significance of its chunky little **Iglesia de San Francisco** (a national monument and thought to be Chile's oldest church, built in 1540). Peek inside at the cactus-wood ceiling and take a stroll around the sandcastle-like whitewashed exterior. The modest **Hotel Tujina** (099-566-4589; Esmeralda s/n; r per person with/without bathroom CH$10,000/5000) accommodates lingering travelers mere paces from the church.

Several companies in San Pedro de Atacama and Calama offer organized tours to this area.

Its cool stream begs visitors to slip off their hot boots and wade awhile, and its trees are heavy with *higera* (fig), *membrillo* (quince), pears and plums (which you're not allowed to eat).

The village itself is also worth exploring for its finely hewn houses, made from a milky-colored volcanic stone called *liparita*. Its **Iglesia de San Lucas**, with a separate bell tower, dates from 1750. A scattering of hole-in-the-wall artesania shops in the town center sell fine llama-wool ponchos, pullovers and gloves, and souvenirs whittled from the pallid volcanic stone.

Toconao has a few inexpensive *residenciales* and restaurants near the plaza. **Residencial y Restaurant Valle de Toconao** (852-009; Calle Lascar 236; r per person CH$7000) has only a handful of rooms but is friendly and serves food.

Buses Frontera and Buses Atacama 2000 have bus services daily to and from San Pedro De Atacama (see p219).

MEJILLONES
 055 / pop 8800

Visitors to this small port town are surprised to bump up against the guano-covered jets and rusty tank-engine trains that scatter its streets. Sixty kilometers north of Antofagasta, Mejillones used to be a key Bolivian port that thrived on the guano, then nitrate, trade. It's now a downmarket beach resort for Antofagasta residents. A huge thermo-electric plant and a new megaport project have recently revived the town at the cost of its tranquility.

Mejillones' main drag is the beachfront Av San Martín. Its historic landmarks include the U-shaped 1866 **Aduana** (customshouse; Francisco Antonio Pinto 110), which now holds the catch-all **Museo de Mejillones** (621-289; adult/child CH$300/free; 10am-2pm & 3-6pm Tue-Fri, 10am-2pm & 3-5pm Sat, 10am-2pm Sun). It displays its scores of miscellaneous exhibits with the guileless enthusiasm of a school project. Quirky footnotes include displays on the *telenovela* (soap opera) *Romané,* which was shot here.

At the foot of Av Manuel Rodríguez, overlooking the Plaza Fuerza Aérea, the 1876 **Capitanía del Puerto** (Port Authority) is a French-style building with a lighthouse tower. The **Iglesia Corazón de María** (cnr Latorre & Almirante Castillo) is a striking wooden building that dates from 1906.

Bus companies and *taxi colectivos* serve Mejillones from Antofagasta.

ANTOFAGASTA
☎ 055 / pop 267,000

Chile's second-largest city is a rough-and-ready jumble of one-way streets, modern mall culture and work-wearied urbanites. As such, this sprawling port city tends not to tickle the fancy of passing travelers, who often choose to leapfrog over Antofagasta en route north to San Pedro de Atacama or south to Copiapó.

However, the city is not all high-rise concrete and gridlocked streets. The old-fashioned plaza is a pleasure to kick back in, and evidence of the golden nitrate era can be found in the wooden-fronted Victorian and Georgian buildings of the coastal Barrio Histórico. Trains still shunt and shake their way along the seafront and ancient spindly *muelles* (piers) molder picturesquely along the grubby guano-stained port.

The port here handles most of the minerals from the Atacama, especially the copper from Chuquicamata, and is still a major import-export node for Bolivia, which lost the region to Chile during the War of the Pacific.

History
Founded in 1870, Antofagasta earned its salt by offering the easiest route to the nitrate mines of the interior. After the turn of the century, when Antofagasta's port proved to be inadequate for the expanded nitrate trade, the nearby harbor of Mejillones took up much of the slack. Later, however, infrastructural improvements restored Antofagasta's preeminence, and it came to handle the highest tonnage of any South American Pacific port.

Orientation
Antofagasta drapes itself over a wide terrace below the coastal range, some 1350km north of Santiago. The Panamericana passes inland, about 15km east of the city.

Downtown's western boundary is north-south Av Balmaceda, immediately east of the modern port; Balmaceda veers northeast at Uribe and eventually becomes Aníbal Pinto; to the south it becomes Av Grecia. Central landmarks include the beautiful Plaza Colón and a scalpel-shaped park squeezed between Av JM Carrera and Av Bernardo O'Higgins. The heart of the city is the recently laid pedestrian mall, which extends from Plaza Colón up to Matta on Arturo Prat, then heads over two blocks on Matta to Maipú.

Information
Numerous ATMs are located downtown. Internet cafés south of Plaza Colón offer access for less than CH$500 per hour.

Cambio Ancla Inn (Baquedano 508)
Conaf (☎ 383-320; Av Argentina 2510; ◷ 8:30am-5:30pm Mon-Thu, 8:30am-4:30pm Fri) For information on the region's natural attractions.
Hospital Regional (☎ 269-009; Av Argentina 1962)
Paris Lavaseco (☎ 222-199; Condell 2455; ◷ 9am-9pm Mon-Sat) Charges CH$7000 for up to 4kg of wash.
Post office (Washington 2623; ◷ 9am-7:30pm Mon-Fri, 9am-12:30pm Sat) Opposite Plaza Colón.
Sernatur (☎ 451-818; infoantofagasta@sernatur.cl; Arturo Prat 384; ◷ 8:30am-5:30pm Mon-Fri) The city tourist office, conveniently located by the plaza.

Sights
The British community left a visible imprint on Antofagasta's 19th-century Plaza Colón, which sports rushing fountains amid its palms, mimosas and bougainvilleas. The cute **Torre Reloj** is a replica of London's Big Ben; its chimes even have a baby Big Ben ring to them, and tiled British and Chilean flags intertwine on its trunk. Pigeons provide amusement by slipping into the shallow fountains with comical regularity.

British influence is also palpable in the 19th-century Barrio Histórico, between the plaza and the old port, where handsome Victorian and Georgian buildings still stand.

On Bolívar, the bottle green–colored **train station** (1887) is the restored terminus of the Antofagasta–La Paz railway, where you'll still see freight trains shuttling their heavy load. It's closed to the public but you can see several old engines and British-style telephone boxes through the western railings.

Across the street, the former Aduana (customshouse) was originally erected in Mejillones in 1869; it was dismantled and

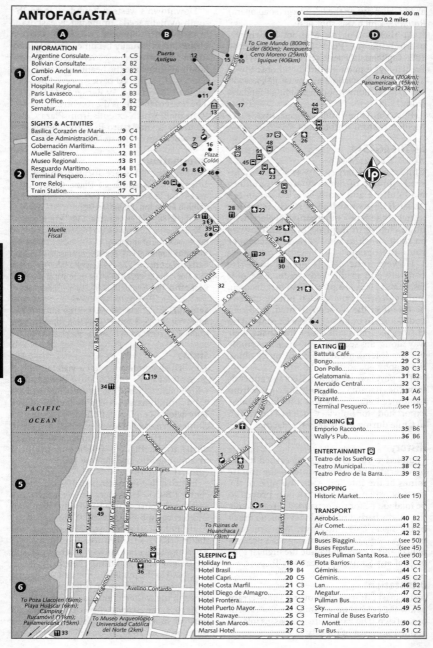

ANTOFAGASTA

0 — 400 m
0 — 0.2 miles

INFORMATION
Argentine Consulate.................1 C5
Bolivian Consulate....................2 B2
Cambio Ancla Inn.....................3 B2
Conaf..4 C3
Hospital Regional.....................5 C5
Paris Lavaseco..........................6 B3
Post Office................................7 B2
Sernatur....................................8 B2

SIGHTS & ACTIVITIES
Basílica Corazón de María.........9 C4
Casa de Administración...........10 C1
Gobernación Marítima.............11 B1
Muelle Salitrero......................12 B1
Museo Regional......................13 B1
Resguardo Marítimo................14 B1
Terminal Pesquero..................15 C1
Torre Reloj..............................16 B2
Train Station...........................17 C1

EATING 🍴
Battuta Café............................28 C2
Bongo.....................................29 C3
Don Pollo................................30 C3
Gelatomania...........................31 B2
Mercado Central.....................32 C3
Picadillo.................................33 A6
Pizzanté.................................34 A4
Terminal Pesquero..............(see 15)

DRINKING 🍷
Emporio Racconto...................35 B6
Wally's Pub............................36 B6

ENTERTAINMENT 🎭
Teatro de los Sueños 37 C2
Teatro Municipal.....................38 C2
Teatro Pedro de la Barra.........39 B3

SHOPPING
Historic Market....................(see 15)

TRANSPORT
Aerobús..................................40 B2
Air Comet...............................41 B2
Avis..42 B2
Buses Biaggini.....................(see 50)
Buses Fepstur......................(see 45)
Buses Pullman Santa Rosa....(see 50)
Flota Barrios...........................43 C2
Géminis...................................44 C1
Géminis...................................45 C2
Lan...46 B2
Megatur..................................47 C3
Pullman Bus............................48 C2
Sky...49 A5
Terminal de Buses Evaristo
  Montt....................................50 C2
Tur Bus...................................51 C2

SLEEPING 🏠
Holiday Inn.............................18 A6
Hotel Brasil.............................19 B4
Hotel Capri.............................20 C5
Hotel Costa Marfil..................21 C3
Hotel Diego de Almagro.........22 C2
Hotel Frontera........................23 C2
Hotel Puerto Mayor................24 C3
Hotel Rawaye.........................25 C3
Hotel San Marcos...................26 C2
Marsal Hotel...........................27 C3

Puerto Antiguo

Muelle Fiscal

PACIFIC OCEAN

Plaza Colón

To Cine Mundo (800m);
Líder (800m); Aeropuerto
Cerro Moreno (25km);
Iquique (406km)

To Arica (700km);
Panamericana (15km);
Calama (212km)

To Poza Llacolen (6km);
Playa Huáscar (6km);
Camping
Rucamóvil (11km);
Panamericana (15km)

To Ruinas de
Huanchaca
(3km)

To Museo Arqueológico
Universidad Católica
del Norte (2km)

transported here piece by piece in 1888. It now houses the **Museo Regional** (Regional Museum; ☎ 227-016; Av Balmaceda & Bolívar; adult/child CH$800/300; ☾ 9am-5pm Tue-Fri, 11am-2pm Sat & Sun), which contains simplistic displays on natural history, and prehistoric and cultural development. Artifacts include mummified babies, a deformed skull, early colonial tidbits and paraphernalia from the nitrate era, including toys fashioned from tin cans.

At the foot of Av Bolívar is the decrepit **Muelle Salitrero** (Nitrate Pier), where locals defy danger signs and fish for crabs. At the entrance to the pier is the former **Resguardo Marítimo** (Coast Guard; ☾ 8:30am-1pm Mon-Fri), a handsome chocolate-colored building with wooden balustrades, built in 1910. A wrought-iron passageway links it to the former **Gobernación Marítima** (Port Authority; cnr Av Balmaceda & Bolívar).

A few blubbery male sea lions, snorting loudly and occasionally snapping at unwary pelicans, circle hopefully below Antofagasta's busy **Terminal Pesquero** (Fish Market), just north of the Port Authority.

Across the street is the old **Casa de Administración** (Administrative Office) of the Sociedad Química de Chile (Soquimich), once the Lautaro Nitrate Company and then the Anglo Lautaro Nitrate Company, until its nationalization in 1968.

If you are in the mood for a walk, head south from the city center to the **Basílica Corazón de Maria** (cnr Lord Cochrane & 21 de Mayo), a lovely Byzantine-style church built in 1913.

MUSEO ARQUEOLÓGICO UNIVERSIDAD CATÓLICA DEL NORTE

At the southern extension of Av Bernardo O'Higgins, the Catholic University's **archaeological museum** (☎ 255-090; Av Angamos 0610; admission free; ☾ 9am-noon & 3-6pm Mon-Fri) focuses on the Norte Grande.

RUINAS DE HUANCHACA (MINAS DE PLATA)

Hovering over the city, at the south end of Av Argentina, the imposing hillside foundations of a 19th-century British-Bolivian silver-refining plant offer some of the best panoramas of the city. From downtown take *colectivo* 3 and ask for Minas de Plata (silver mines).

Festivals & Events

Locals let their hair down on February 14, for the anniversary of the founding of the city.

Expect fireworks at the Balneario Municipal at the south end of Av Grecia.

Sleeping

BUDGET

Antofagasta's cheapie hostels are no great shakes.

You can camp for free in the somewhat ugly patch of beach called **Poza Llacolen** (☎ 247-763), 6km south of town on the coast road. There's no water or showers, but a little kiosk sells food. Plus, it's on the beach! Alternatively, **Camping Rucamóvil** (☎ 262-358; Km11; campsite per person CH$12,000), also south of town on the same road, is a fairly well-equipped site with patchy shade and an ocean view from its terrace. Family cabins (CH$18,000, up to four people) are also available. *Micro* number 2 from Mercado Central goes south to the camping grounds.

Hotel Rawaye (☎ 225-399; Sucre 762; s/d without bathroom from CH$5000/8000) With cheap digs in an oh-so-aquamarine environment, this hotel is a good option for cent-counters. You'll have to share the somewhat dingy bathrooms.

Hotel Capri (☎ 263-703; Copiapó 1208; incl breakfast s without bathroom CH$7000, d CH$15,000; ℗) A satisfactory choice near the university – a relaxed and safe neighborhood a bit from the center – with cleanish rooms, armchairs, a tacky faux coat of arms and kind staff. The Capri is popular with traveling miners. Wi-fi – yippy!

Hotel Brasil (☎ 267-268; JS Ossa 1978; with/without bathroom s CH$14,000/7000, d CH$13,000/19,3000; ℗) It's a bit away from the downtown action, but this hotel is the cleanest in the category (a big plus in Antofagasta, which seems to have a bleach shortage). Andean bedspreads add a bit of flair.

Hotel Frontera (☎ 281-219; Bolívar 558; with/without bathroom s CH$13,000/8000, d CH$18,000/13,000; ℗) Right by the bus station, this place is courteous and clean. It's a bit more expensive than the cheapest of the cheap, but it's also a bit nicer with clean shared baths, sturdy beds and cable TV in every room. A decent breakfast costs CH$1200.

MIDRANGE

Hotel Puerto Mayor (☎ 410-066; JS Ossa 2643; s/d CH$15,000/20,000; ℗) Another anonymous down-to-business hotel with scant personality but relative comfort, the Puerto Mayor is well kept, clean and ever so slightly soulless. Rooms facing the street are noisy.

Hotel Costa Marfil (☎ 283-590; www.hotelcosta marfil.cl; Arturo Prat 950; s/d incl breakfast from CH$16,000/21,000; P 🖳) The blazing neon light might get to you, but the pink or green rooms in this large hotel block are pretty clean. For a little extra you can upgrade to an executive room, which comes with a fridge, bigger bed and bigger TV. Alas, no flat screens.

Hotel San Marcos (☎ 226-303; hsanmarcos@terra .cl; Latorre 2946; s/d incl breakfast CH$16,000/22,000; P) This matriarchal guesthouse exudes a feeling of security and a soothingly slow pace but also slight stuffiness. Everything comes straight from the boilerplate: TV (check), small bathrooms (check), clean titled entryway and slightly stained carpets in the rooms (check, check and check again). The hotel has a restaurant and is family-friendly.

Marsal Hotel (☎ 268-063; www.marsalhotel.cl, in Spanish; Arturo Prat 867; s/d/tr incl breakfast CH$26,000/29,000/40,000; P 🖳) This stony-faced establishment has spacious spotless rooms – though they are a bit smoky – decorated in soothing pinks and greens; expect contemporary furnishings, cable TV, fridge, portable fans and large mirrored wardrobes to unleash your inner 'bom-chicka-bom-bom.'

TOP END

Hotel Diego de Almagro (☎ 268-331; www.dahoteles .com; Condell 2624; s/d incl breakfast CH$33,600/40,700; 🖳) It may seem kitsch, but this chain hotel's liberal use of faux armor, coats of arms and black ironwork succeeds in making it Antofagasta's most character-filled hotel (although that's not saying much). The central location is a blessing and a curse: street-facing rooms get ringside seats over the enthusiastic buskers below. The hotel also has a more upscale offering south of town; check online for specials.

Holiday Inn (☎ 228-888; www.holidayinn.cl; Av Grecia 1490; d incl buffet breakfast CH$56,000; P ⊠ 🖳 🐾) We don't normally review these chain hotels, but the Holiday Inn is better than the local upscale options. You know the deal: mega-chain down by the water with all the amenities.

Eating & Drinking

Perched on the north end of the old port, **Terminal Pesquero** is host to around 24 stalls that peddle tasty fresh shellfish (and other pungent offerings); get there by early afternoon, before all the fish are sold. More fish, as well as meat, vegetables and fruity fare, is available at the attractive old **Mercado Central**

(JS Ossa), which is between Maipú and Uribe. **Lider** (Antofagasta Shopping, Zentero 21; ⏰ 8am-10pm) is a huge supermarket perfect for self-caterers: it's north of the center.

There are several cafés on the Prat pedestrian mall. They make a perfect spot for people watching.

Don Pollo (☎ 263-361; JS Ossa 2594; chicken from CH$1100; ⏰ lunch & dinner) Cheap, cheerful and usually crowded, Don Pollo has plastic tables huddled around a grass-hut patio. The chicken is so succulent it's almost sinful.

Bongo (☎ 263-697; Baquedano 743; set menu CH$2450, mains CH$1300-2400; ⏰ lunch & dinner) Bubbly young eatery and bar with thick-cushioned booths and a tidy mezzanine above, and a good 'n' greasy menu for those times when only a draft beer and burger will do – prepare those arteries.

Gelatomania (☎ 251535; cnr Baquedano & Latorre; snacks CH$1500-3500; ⏰ breakfast, lunch & dinner; V) Satisfies ice-cream cravings with more than two dozen flavors to fight over, fresh juices, tasty cakes, burgers and vegetarian-friendly salads.

Battuta Café (Condell 2573 Local 1-2-3; pie & coffee CH$1800; ⏰ breakfast, lunch & dinner) There's a 'Clockwork Orange Milk Bar' feel to this modern café. Luckily, you won't have to resort to a bit of old ultraviolence to order an excellent pie and coffee, the house specialty.

Pizzanté (☎ 223-344; www.pizzante.cl; Av JM Carrera 1857; pizzas CH$2800-6300; ⏰ lunch & dinner) Antofagasta's top pizzeria throws together imaginative toppings for its tasty pizza menu, as well as a healthier pasta, sandwich and salads selection (vegetarians catered for, but only just). It's a favorite with families and students.

Picadillo (☎ 247-503; Av Grecia 1000; mains CH$4500-8300; ⏰ lunch & dinner) One of Antofagasta's best, this highly recommended restaurant has great service, an eclectic menu featuring steak and seafood, and although it's a bit of a splurge, it's well worth it. The only drawback is its location on busy Av Grecia; this said, the warm dark-wood interior invites you to stay awhile, and enjoy that fancy dinner you were talking about.

Wally's Pub (☎ 223-697; www.wallys.cl, in Spanish; Antonino Toro 982; mains CH$4500-9000; ⏰ from 6pm Mon-Sat) This is a cozy European-style bar with patio seating and a pool table; it serves exotic food, with everything from Thai curries to ostrich meat.

Emporio Racconto (☎ 773-565; Antonino Toro 995; cover Thu-Sat CH$2000; ⏰ from 6pm Tue-Sat) Occasional live music and a homey 'pub-tatmosphere' make this nightspot popular with Antofagasta's bold and beautiful set.

Entertainment

Most of Antofagasta's nightlife is south of the center. Dancing venues cluster around Playa Huáscar, 7km south of town.

Cine Mundo (☎ 490-449; Antofagasta Shopping, Zentero 21, Local 202; admission CH$2500) is a cinema 800m north of the train station showing recent movies.

For performing arts, check **Teatro Pedro de la Barra** (☎ 263-400; Condell 2495) or **Teatro Municipal** (☎ 264-919; Sucre 433).

For a peek inside Antofagasta's underground art scene, visit the funky art cooperative **Teatro de los Sueños** (☎ 286-668; teatronorte@hotmail.com; Serrano 456), which has occasional live shows and does 'art actions' to protest everything from feminocide (a real problem in Chile) to littering (another real problem). The dream train at the end of the alley leads the way.

Shopping

There's a piecemeal market for historical goodies from nitrate *oficinas* at the foot of the Terminal Pesquero.

Getting There & Away

AIR

Lan (☎ 600-526-2000, www.lanchile.com; Arturo Prat 445) has seven to 12 daily flights to Santiago (CH$85,000 to CH$93,000, two hours), as well as direct daily flights to Iquique (CH$50,000 to CH$58,000, 50 minutes), Calama (CH$37,000 to CH$45,000, 35 minutes), and La Serena (CH$70,000 to CH$78,000, 1½ hours).

Sky (☎ 459-090; www.skyairline.cl; General Velasquez 890, Local 3) also flies to Iquique (CH$35,200, two daily), Arica (CH$56,200, two daily), Copiapó (CH$47,200, two daily), and Santiago (CH$92,200, two to four daily), with connections to the south.

Air Comet (☎ 900-995-499; www.aircomet.com; Washington 2548) has economical flights to Santiago and other locations in South America.

BUS

Most of the bus companies operate out of their own terminals near downtown. A few long-distance and most locally based companies use the **Terminal de Buses Evaristo Montt** (Riquelme 513), also known as the Terminal de Buses Rurales.

Nearly all northbound services now use coastal Ruta 1, via Tocopilla, en route to Iquique and Arica.

Buses Pullman Santa Rosa (☎ 282-763; Terminal de Buses Evaristo Montt)

Flota Barrios (☎ 494-115; www.flotabarrios.cl; Condell 2764)

Géminis (☎ 263-968; Latorre 3055)

Pullman Bus (☎ 268-838; Latorre 2805)

Tur Bus (☎ 264-487; Latorre 2751)

Destination	Cost (CH$)	Duration (hr)
Arica	16,000	11
Calama	4000	3
Copiapó	16,000	7
Iquique	14,000	6
La Serena	20,000	12
Santiago	28,000	19

Megatur (☎ 450-819; Latorre) has *micros* to Mejillones every half-hour (CH$1300, one hour). **Buses Fepstur** (☎ 251-176; Latorre 2715) and **Buses Biaggini** (☎ 623-451; Terminal de Buses Evaristo Montt) provide a slightly cheaper bus service to Mejillones.

Géminis goes to Salta and Jujuy, Argentina, on Tuesday, Friday and Sunday at 9am (CH$22,000, 14 hours).

Getting Around

TO/FROM THE AIRPORT

Antofagasta's Aeropuerto Cerro Moreno is 25km north of the city. Taxis cost CH$9000. **Aerobús** (☎ 262-669; Baquedano 328) door-to-door minibus transfer has a stand at the airport; it costs CH$3000 to the airport.

CAR

Avis (☎ 600-601-9966 or 254-674; www.avischile.cl; Baquedano 364)

Budget (☎ 283-667; Aeropuerto Cerro Moreno)

AROUND ANTOFAGASTA

The desolate Antofagasta area is short on sights, except for the small forgotten seaside port towns and the eerie ghost towns that line the highways north, which are all easily appreciated from inside a speeding air-conditioned bus.

Monumento Natural La Portada

This enormous offshore arch is the centerpiece of a 31-hectare protected area. Topped by marine sediments and supported by a sturdy volcanic base, the stack has been eroded into a natural arch by the stormy Pacific. Plans are in the works to create a massive visitor center here, courtesy of the Escondida Mine. (Those miners are so environmentally minded!)

It's situated 25km north of Antofagasta, on a short westbound lateral off the highway; there are picnic tables, a restaurant and clifftop views over surrounding beaches. Take *micro* 15 from Antofagasta's Terminal Pesquero to the junction at La Portada, then walk 3km west. If driving, leave belongings in the trunk and lock your car; break-ins have occurred at the lot.

Juan López & Bolsico

At the south end of Península Mejillones, just north of La Portada, a paved road leads west to the beach villages of Juan López (take the left fork at Km11) and Bolsico (take the right-fork gravel road). The latter route passes offshore Isla Santa María, a site with several impressive ocean blowholes.

SOUTH OF ANTOFAGASTA

The Panamericana south of Antofagasta continues its trip through the dry Atacama Desert, where water, people and tourist attractions are scarce.

Mano del Desierto

A towering **granite hand**, its oddly tapering fingers outstretched in a mock salute, breaks through the desert crust about 45km south of the junction of the Panamericana and Ruta 28. This curious *mano del desierto* was built in 1992 by sculptor Mario Irarrázaval. Bus travelers should look to the west side of the highway.

Observatorio Cerro Paranal

In the world of high-powered telescopes, where rival institutes jostle to claim the 'biggest,' 'most powerful' or 'most technologically advanced' specimens, Paranal is right up there with the big boys. This groundbreaking observatory has a Very Large Telescope (VLT) consisting of an array of four 8.2m telescopes – for a time at least, the most powerful optical array in the world. The **Cerro Paranal observatory** (☎ 55-435-335; www.eso.org) is run by the European Southern Observatory (ESO), and is so futuristic-looking that portions of the James

Bond flick, *Quantum of Solace*, were filmed here. It's situated on Cerro Paranal at 2664m above sea level, 120km south of Antofagasta; an ill-marked lateral leaves the Panamericana just south of the Mano del Desierto.

Free visits are allowed on the last two weekends of every month, except in December, beginning at 2pm and ending at 4pm. You'll need to schedule months in advance, and you'll also need your own vehicle to get there. Call or check the observatory's website for details and updates.

From Paranal it's possible to continue another 120km south to **Tatal**, via a decent dirt road and a rougher descent through the Quebrada de Despoblado and past the coastal fish camp of **Paposo**.

Taltal

☎ 055 / pop 12,852

The only settlement of any size on the long thirsty haul from Chañaral to Antofagasta, the fishing port of Taltal is a surprisingly neat little community. For such a small place, it has a palpable pride in its heritage with elegantly manicured plazas and lovely period architecture from its nitrate export heyday (when its population was 20,000). The town shrank as the *oficinas* closed (between 1940 and 1960), but is growing again as copper miners set up residence here.

From an intersection on the Panamericana, a paved lateral heads northwest to Taltal. The main commercial street of Arturo Prat leads to the central Plaza Arturo Prat. **CTC Mundo** (Prat 635), next to the Tur Bus office, is your place to make calls and to access the internet.

SIGHTS

Fountains trickle and children play among the thick trees on **Plaza Arturo Prat**, the town's heart; it's said that the plaza's layout was designed in subtle mimicry of the British flag on account of the many Brits who worked here. Around the plaza are several photogenic monuments to the nitrate era, including the dapper peach-colored **Teatro Alhambra** (1921). The town's main church, **Iglesia San Francisco Javier** (1897), burnt down in 2007, but plans are in the works to rebuild it.

During the nitrate era, Taltal was the headquarters of the Taltal Railway Company; its restored narrow-gauge **Locomotora No 59** plus carriages sit on the east side of O'Higgins,

---

EXPLORE MORE, VISITING CIFUNCHO & LAS TÓRTOLAS

Midway between Taltal and the Panamericana, a gravel lateral heads southwest to **Cifuncho**, a tiny fishing camp that's also one of the most popular beaches in the area. En route to Cifuncho, a track suitable only for 4WD vehicles heads northwest to isolated **Las Tórtolas**, an even more attractive area. But there are many lost beaches along the endless coastline of Norte Grande. Leave the guidebook behind for a day and see where the dusty road takes you.

between Esmeralda and Prat. Clamber into the cab and note the missing coal box: unusually, this engine was powered by oil. Take great care if you decide to pick your way along the decaying old **Muelle Salitrero** (Nitrate Pier), just north of the locomotive.

At the other end of town, the well-done **Museo de Taltal** (Prat 5; admission free; 9:30am-1pm & 3-5:30pm Mon-Sat) is located in an old government office in a lovely two-story building, three blocks south of the plaza. The museum's exhibits take you from pre-Columbian times to the salitre era. The collection of Andean ceramics is especially impressive.

SLEEPING & EATING

Like most of Norte Grande, Taltal has become popular with visiting miners, so you should call ahead to book lodging.

Hostería Taltal (611-173; btay_u@hotmail.com; Esmeralda 671; with/without bathroom incl breakfast s CH$18,500/11,900, d CH$19,800/14,500; P) Nice gardens out front and ocean views make this one of the better buys in town. But the bathrooms are kind of nasty.

Hotel San Martín (611-088; Martínez 279; s/d CH$12,000/$20,000) Offering up basic digs, this is one of the cheapest lodging options in town, but isn't as nice as the *hostería*.

Hotel Mi Tampi (613-605; www.hotelmitampi.cl, in Spanish; O'Higgins 138; s/d incl breakfast CH$25,500/31,500) One of the more contemporary spots, this cheerful little guesthouse is situated a short stroll from the waterfront and opposite the locomotive. It has wi-fi.

Club Social Taltal (Torreblanca 162; set lunch CH$2500) Just a half block west of the plaza, this is the old British social club, offering great seasonal seafood and friendly service.

GETTING THERE & AWAY

Several companies provide bus services north to Antofagasta (CH$5000), south to Chañaral (CH$3500) and beyond on the Panamericana, including **Tur Bus** (611-426; Prat 631).

NORTE GRANDE

Norte Chico

Caught between the ocean and the Andes, Chile's Norte Chico, or Little North, is unique unto itself. Gone are the vast open spaces of the desolate Atacama Desert to the north, and the lush valleys and mountains of the south are still but a whispered fantasy. This is a land in transition. Heading down from Norte Grande, the harsh desert landscape begins to yield signs of life: a cactus here, a scrub brush there. Then finally, you hit one of the many chartreuse river valleys, a welcome sight in a land rough-hewn in browns and grays. And while Norte Chico may hold less attraction than the big sights to the south, there's a lilting air of blue-skied desert mysticism that keeps your attention.

La Serena, a coastal colonial capital, is the largest city in the region and a must-see for anybody visiting. From there is the Elqui Valley, home to Chile's pisco production, new-age communes and cutting-edge observatories. And further north are some amazing national parks, muscle-bound mining towns, and mile upon mile of uncharted coastline just waiting for you to set up camp or charge out for an afternoon surf. Wildlife lovers won't want to miss the playful penguins of Reserva Nacional Pingüino de Humboldt and Parque Nacional Pan de Azúcar. And high in the Andes, the seldom-visited Parque Nacional Nevado Tres Cruces is a great place to spot vicuña and flamingos. It would seem that despite its diminutive moniker, the little north is just a bit bigger, and just a bit badder, than most people thought.

HIGHLIGHTS

- Bop through the colonial center of **La Serena** (p244), then head to the beach for surf, sun and sand

- Learn just how potent the little pisco grape can be as you hop from village to village in the ever-so-groovy **Elqui Valley** (p252), stopping for nighttime stargazing at the **Observatorio Comunal Cerro Mamalluca** (p255)

- Get lost on your way to the high-Andean lagoons of **Parque Nacional Nevado Tres Cruces** (p240)

- Bounce your way out to the penguin colonies at **Reserva Nacional Pingüino de Humboldt** (p243) on a tiny skiff, passing dolphins, sea lions and otters

- Find your own way as you pioneer camp-sites and surf spots in the beachfront **Parque Nacional Pan de Azúcar** (p233)

Parque Nacional Pan de Azúcar ★

★ Parque Nacional Nevado Tres Cruces

Reserva Nacional Pingüino de Humboldt ★

La Serena ★

★ Observatorio Comunal Cerro Mamalluca

★ Elqui Valley

■ POPULATION: 888,803	■ AREA: 115,755 SQ KM	■ ELEVATION: 0–6893M

NORTE CHICO

History

While later civilizations would find the harsh mountains and semidesert of Norte Chico difficult to tame, pre-Columbian peoples, like the coastal Chango fisherfolk, thrived here. Sedentary Diaguita farmers, who crossed the Andes from what is now Argentina, also found a fruitful niche, raising crops in fertile river valleys and even parts of the barren uplands. Shortly before the conquistadores limped onto the Chilean scene, the Inka empire also began to spread its tentacles south.

The Europeans found forays into Chile infinitely harder. Diego de Almagro's first fateful expedition crossed the freezing Paso San Francisco from Salta (now Argentina) in 1535. Surviving phenomenal hardship, a member of Almagro's party left a graphic, gruesome account of the group's miserable 800km march over the Puna de Atacama, reporting that men and horses froze to death and that members of later expeditions, finding the undecomposed horses, 'were glad to eat them.'

Food and water were available in the lowlands, but Almagro soon scurried back to present-day Peru via Norte Grande. A few years later Pedro de Valdivia's party followed Almagro's return route south to found Santiago, but they met stiff resistance from indigenous warriors at Copiapó; of one party of 30 that Valdivia had ordered back to Cuzco, only two officers survived.

Valdivia founded Copiapó in 1540 and La Serena in 1541. Copiapó lagged behind until its 18th-century gold rush. And when gold failed, silver took its place and Copiapó boomed, tripling its population to 12,000 after a bonanza strike at Chañarcillo in 1832.

Silver mining declined by the late 19th century, but copper soon replaced it. The area around La Serena and Bahía Inglesa subsequently underwent tourist booms, and the Copiapó, Huasco and Elqui Valleys boosted Chile's upsurge in fruit exports and pisco production, but mining continues to be the dominant breadwinner.

Climate

South of the Atacama Desert, Norte Chico is a semiarid transition zone to the central valley's Mediterranean-like climate. Though the region sees only infrequent rain, especially in the northern reaches, its coastline is often cloaked with a moisture-rich ocean fog, known locally as *camanchaca*. For climate charts, see p464.

Getting There & Away

The Panamericana wiggles its way along Norte Chico's coastline, making it easy to reach by car or bus. There are also busy domestic airports near La Serena and Copiapó.

Getting Around

Turning off the Panamericana can quickly feel like venturing into the outback as gravel and dirt roads deteriorate rapidly and public transportation quickly dwindles. As a result, getting to many out-of-the-way national parks and attractions can be tricky without taking a tour or having your own wheels, and in some cases only high-clearance pickup trucks or 4WDs will do.

CHAÑARAL

☎ 052 / pop 14,978

Woebegone Chañaral is a cheerless mining and fishing port set among the rugged headlands of the Sierra de las Animas. Its principal appeal to travelers is as a jumping-off point to the popular coastal Parque Nacional Pan de Azúcar, which straddles the border between Regiones II and III.

Chañaral dates from 1833, after Diego de Almeyda discovered copper reserves nearby; the town's livelihood still depends on copper – now from the enormous El Salvador mine in the interior. El Salvador has been a mixed blessing to Chañaral, however, befouling it with toxic waste. Chile's Environmental Health Service even considered moving the entire town to escape the arsenic-contaminated beach and polluted air. A vigorous clean-up has somewhat ameliorated the situation; expresident Ricardo Lagos even took a swim here in 2003, but environmentalists still raise an eyebrow over the beach's safety. There's a public pool right in front of the beach for those not wanting to have three-legged babies.

Orientation & Information

About 165km northwest of Copiapó, Chañaral has two distinct sections: the industrial port sprawling along the shoreline and the Panamericana, and a residential zone scaling the hills. Merino Jarpa is the main commercial drag.

Centro de Llamadas (Merino Jarpa 505; ⊗ 9am-10pm) Long-distance telephone office and internet.

Post office (Comercio s/n; ⊗ 8:30am-6pm Mon-Fri) Located at the west end of town.

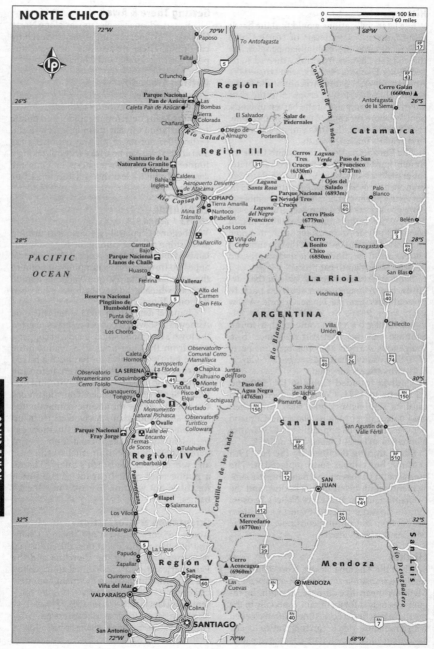

NORTE CHICO

0 —————— 100 km
0 —————— 60 miles

Souvenir Destino Norte (☎ 099-329-3265; cnr Diego de Almeyda & Los Baños; ☯ 9am-7:30pm) Has a tour office directly opposite the Pullman station. Come here to arrange trips to Pan de Azúcar and get tourist info.

Sleeping & Eating

Hotel Jimenez (☎ 480-328; Merino Jarpa 561; r CH$10,000) This cent-saving choice has clean rooms and an obstreperous owner.

Hotel Aqua Luna (☎ 523-868; Merino Jarpa 521; s/d/ tr CH$14,000/20,000/25,000; P) A pleasant down-to-business hotel in the center of town, the Aqua Luna is the best buy around with an atriumlike common area and clean (slightly soulless) rooms with big, thick mattresses. It also has wi-fi.

Restaurant R Porteño (☎ 480-071; Merino Jarpa 567; mains CH$2600-4800; ☯ breakfast, lunch & dinner) Popular with locals, this little joint offers everything from *pollo* (chicken) to *paila* in an open, family-friendly setting.

Getting There & Around

Tur Bus (☎ 481-012; Merina Jarpa 1187) has an office on the outskirts of town. Other bus companies with offices in town are **Flota Barrios** (☎ 480-894; Merino Jarpa 567) and **Pullman Bus** (☎ 800-320-320; www.pullman.cl; cnr Diego de Almeyda & Los Baños). Destinations include Santiago (CH$20,000 to CH$28,000, 15 hours), Copiapó (CH$4000, 2½ hours) and Antofagasta (CH$10,000, six hours).

Chango Turismo (☎ 099-648-6880; Panamericana Norte s/n; ☯ 9am-7:30pm) has 9am departures to Parque Nacional Pan de Azúcar from opposite the Pullman Bus station for CH$12,000. Minibuses also depart from opposite the Pullman station (one-way CH$2000, roundtrip CH$3000, 25 minutes). A taxi to Pan de Azúcar will run around CH$20,000 roundtrip.

PARQUE NACIONAL PAN DE AZÚCAR

An abundance of white sandy beaches – perfect for guerrilla camping or surf-break pioneering – sheltered coves and stony headlands line the desert coastline north of Chañaral. However, it's the wildlife that brings most international travelers to this national park, because the cool Humboldt Current supports a variety of marine life. Star of the show is the endangered Humboldt penguin, which nests on an offshore island. Here you'll also spot slippery marine otters and rowdy sea lions, as well as scores of pelicans and cormorants.

At higher elevations, moisture from the *camanchaca* nurtures a unique collection of more than 20 species of cacti and succulents. Further inland, guanacos are a common sight and wild foxes will approach you in hope of scraps.

The park comprises 437 sq km and its altitude ranges from sea level to 900m. There are excellent coastal campsites, which get busy in summer.

Information

The **Caleta Pan de Azúcar** is the main departure point for trips to Sugarloaf Island. There are restaurants and campsites here, too. Conaf's **Centro de Información Ambiental** (Playa Piqueros; ☯ 8:30am-12:30pm & 2-6pm) has exhibits on the park's flora and fauna and a cactarium, 1km south of Caleta Pan de Azúcar. There is a **Conaf checkpoint** at Km15 on the southern entrance road from Chañaral. Park rangers only charge visitors planning to camp in the interior of the park (CH$3500). Other than that, there's no fee to visit the park.

Sights & Activities

'Sugarloaf' Island, or **Isla Pan de Azúcar**, lies a tantalizingly short distance offshore, its base often shrouded by *camanchaca* at twilight. It's home to about 2000 Humboldt penguins, as well as other birds, otters and sea lions. The island is a restricted area, but local fishermen approach the 100-hectare island by boat for up-close-and-personal views.

Launches charge CH$4000 per person for a minimum of six people from Caleta Pan de Azúcar; in the low season, when there are few visitors, you could end up forking out as much as CH$40,000. Round trips take 1½ hours, and run from 9am to 7pm in the summer and 9am to 6pm in winter.

Sleeping & Eating

Camping (CH$3500 per person) is available at Playa Piqueros, Playa El Soldado and Caleta Pan de Azúcar. Facilities include toilets, water, picnic tables and cold showers. Make camping reservations with **Gran Atacama** (www.granatacama .cl). There are plans to add an ecolodge in the area. You can also guerrilla camp on a lovely arching spit of white sand called El Refugio, 14km north of Chañaral.

A small market at Caleta Pan de Azúcar has limited supplies and fresh fish, but it's better value to stock up in Chañaral.

NORTE CHICO

EXPLORE MORE: VISIT THE LOST BEACHES OF NORTE CHICO

There's a ton of unexplored beaches in the region. North of Caldera are several great spots, including **Playas Pulpo** and **Ramada**, and 56km south of town is **Playa La Virgen** (www.playalavirgen.cl, in Spanish), a little-known beach town popular with vacationing Chileans. But these are just the starting point. Put the guidebook (and your inhibitions) aside for a day or week, and find your own little sliver of sandy paradise.

Getting There & Away

Pan de Azúcar is 30km north of Chañaral by a well-maintained paved road. For public transport and taxis, see p233.

If you are driving from the north, there are also two poorly marked park entrances between Sierro Colorada and Las Bombas, around Km1018, about 45km north of Chañaral on the Panamericana.

CALDERA

☎ 052 / pop 21,132

Year-round sun, some great area beaches and abundant seafood make Caldera – once the second biggest port during the 19th-century mining boom – and its sister resort at nearby Bahía Inglesa (opposite), Región III's most popular seaside retreats. While Caldera is hugely popular with vacationing Chileans, most foreign visitors will find neighboring Bahía Inglesa to be more welcoming – though it's cheaper to stay in Caldera by night and spend your days on Bahía's beach.

Orientation

Caldera is on the south shore of the Bahía de Caldera, 75km west of Copiapó and just west of the Panamericana. Av Diego de Almeyda continues south as Av Carvallo to Bahía Inglesa. The action centers around the large plaza, and the pedestrian mall on Gana leads you down to the brown-sand beach.

Information

Centro Telefónica (Cousiño 329; ⏰ 9am-10pm) For international calling.
Oficina de Turismo (☎ 316-076; west side of Plaza de Armas; ⏰ 9am-2pm & 4-6pm Mon-Sat, 10am-2pm Sun) The tourist office; it's not always staffed.

Post office (Edwards 325; ⏰ 9am-1pm & 3-6:30pm Mon-Fri, 9am-1pm Sat)

Sights

At the eastern approach to Caldera, the **Cementerio Laico** (Av Diego de Almeyda s/n) was Chile's first non-Catholic cemetery, and houses fancy tombs belonging to English, Welsh, Scottish, German and even a few Chinese immigrants.

In the town center there's a pretty plaza-cum-playground, with kamikaze kids on swings and the chocolate-and-cream 19th-century **Iglesia San Vicente** (1862) and its gothic tower.

Down by the seafront, the colorful **Muelle Pesquero** (Fishing Jetty) teems with hungry pelicans, colorful little boats and knife-wielding *señoras* busily gutting and frying the catch. The distinctive **Estación de Ferrocarril** (admission free; ⏰ 10am-midnight Tue-Sun, 2pm-midnight Mon, 10am-1pm & 5-9pm in winter) is on the north side of the jetty. Built in 1850, this was the terminus for South America's first railroad. Inside the free museum you will find changing exhibits. There's also a **paleontology museum** (CH$500) here. Nearby neoclassical **Ex Aduana** (cnr Gana & Wheelwright), once the customshouse, now houses the Centro de Desarrollo Cultural and has exhibitions on the area.

Activities

The town's beach is slightly contaminated with gasoline from the nearby dock. You are better off taking a short day-trip to Bahía Inglesa. There's a bike trail from Caldera to Bahía Inglesa.

Sleeping

Residencial Millaray (☎ 315-528; Cousiño 331; s/d without bathroom CH$10,000/14,000; P) A ramshackle but friendly family home opposite Caldera's plaza, this hotel has a handful of simple rooms with a shared bathroom. Bring your own towel.

Hotel Terrasol (☎ 319-885; hotelterrasol@yahoo.com; Gallo 370; d with/without bathroom incl breakfast CH$22,000/15,000; P) This is a clean, modern option with a laid-back holiday atmosphere. There's a sweet Brady Bunch–style common area complete with AstroTurf.

Hotel Montecarlo (☎ 315-388; www.hotel-montecarlo.cl, in Spanish; Av Carvallo 627; s/d incl breakfast CH$24,500/26,500; P 🖳) Despite being quite a modern hotel block, Montecarlo strives for a twee environment with strategic positioning of cartwheels, vines and trickling fountains. It has warm, familiar service and spotless rooms.

Eating & Entertainment

For international offerings, head over to Bahía Inglesa. There are a number of discos on the road to Bahía Inglesa.

Miramar (☎ 315-381; Gana 090; mains CH$2500-6000; ☽ lunch & dinner) A posh pink restaurant on the seafront in Caldera with lots of windows to maximize the position overlooking both the beach and the busy pier.

Getting There & Around

The **Pullman** (☎ 315-227; cnr Gallo & Cousiño) and **Tur Bus** (☎ 316-832; cnr Ossa Varas & José Santos Cifuentes) terminals, about five blocks southeast of the plaza, offer services to Copiapó (CH$2000, one hour) and Antofagasta (CH$13,000, seven hours). Buses and *taxi colectivos* (shared taxis) run between Caldera and Bahía Inglesa for CH$600. Private taxis to Aeropuerto Desierto de Atacama cost CH$7000.

AROUND CALDERA

Weird rock formations like something from a science-fiction film stud the desert landscape north of Caldera. About 12km up the Panamericana, the **Santuario de la Naturaleza Granito Orbicular** encompasses a number of these oddly shaped mineral conglomerates. There are axle-breaking tracks along the coastline, but it's just as rewarding to stop on the Panamericana at a roadside shrine to **Santa Gemita**, by a lay-by and strewn with colorful offerings. Look behind the shrine for a selection of statuesque stone waves, distorted skulls and writhing rock ghosts.

BAHÍA INGLESA
☎ 052

A short distance south of Caldera is the beautiful seaside resort of Bahía Inglesa. With rocky outcrops scudding out of the crystal waters, this is the place to stay if you are in the area. There's a nice beachfront walking area peppered with shops and restaurants and a cool Mediterranean feel. Bahía Inglesa takes its name from the British privateers who took refuge here in colonial times, and the appeal is obvious.

Activities

Windsurfing is a popular pastime in Bahía Inglesa, though equipment is not available for hire. **Cataban** (☎ 098-929-1984; www.bahiainglesa .com; Av El Morro), next to Domo Chango, arranges snorkeling, kayaking and kitesurfing trips.

Sleeping & Eating

Camping Bahía Inglesa (☎ 315-424; Playa Las Machas; campsites up to 6 people CH$18,000, cabañas CH$24,400-40,300) A big exposed campsite on sandy land overlooking Bahía Inglesa, this is a good camping spot, but is overpriced during high season. Enter from the road to Ruta 5 south of town.

Domo Chango Chile (☎ 316-168; www.changochile.cl; Av El Morro 610; d CH$30,000; ℗ 💻) This is a weird collection of plastic domes resembling enormous golf balls, including a couple of mini tentlike domes for lodgers.

Hotel Rocas de Bahía (☎ 316-005; www.rocas debahia.cl, in Spanish; El Morro 888; s/d incl breakfast CH$67,400/73,100; ℗ 💻) The town's best hotel, Rocas is a five-floor maze shooting up the cliff overlooking the bay. All the modern rooms have ocean views and wonderful balconies.

El Plateao (☎ 099-826-0007; Av El Morro 756; mains CH$4500-8000; ☽ 11am-late) Beachfront views and a funky bohemian vibe are trademarks at this bar and restaurant, which serves a welcome mix of international favorites with everything from Thai to Italian on offer.

Getting There & Away

Transit is out of neighboring Caldera (opposite). You can get there by *colectivo* for CH$600.

COPIAPÓ
☎ 052 / pop 132,934

Powerful hirsute men wrangle through the bars and strip halls of this not-ready-for-TV mining town. But like most places on the frontier, there's a certain atavistic, visceral attraction to it all. And with a pleasant climate and many historic buildings, you may find yourself oddly comfortable amidst the milling miners and down-to-business pace of Copiapó. This said, it's not really worth stopping here unless you want to make a foray into the remote mountains near the Argentine border, especially the breathtaking Parque Nacional Nevado Tres Cruces, Laguna Verde and Ojos del Salado, the highest active volcano in the world.

The town does earn some kudos for being the site of several historical firsts: South America's first railroad (completed in 1852) ran from here to Caldera; here, too, appeared the nation's first telegraph and telephone lines, and Chile's first gas works. All of these firsts came on the back of the 18th-century gold boom and the rush to cash in on silver discovered at neighboring Chañarcillo in 1832. Today, it's copper that keeps the miners and beer-hall gals in the green.

Orientation

Copiapó nestles in the narrow valley floor on the north bank of Río Copiapó. Three blocks north of Av Copayapu (the Panamericana), Plaza Prat marks the city's historical center.

Information

Internet cafés charge around CH$400 and can be found in the Mall Plaza Real, right on Plaza Prat.

LAUNDRY

Lavandería Añañucas (☎ 231-858; Chañarcillo; ☒ 8:30am-9pm Mon-Fri, 10am-9pm Sat) Near Chacabuco; offers drop-off laundry service at CH$2000 per kilo.

MEDICAL SERVICES

Hospital San José (☎ 212-023, 218-833; cnr Los Carrera & Vicuña; ☒ 24hr) Medical care, eight blocks east of Plaza Prat.

MONEY

Numerous ATMs are located at banks around the plaza.
Cambio Fides (☎ 210-550; Mall Plaza Real, Colipí 484, Office B 123, 1st fl; ☒ 9:30am-1:45pm & 4-8pm Mon-Fri, 11am-2pm Sat) Change money here.

POST

Post office (Intendencia Regional, Los Carrera 691; ☒ 9am-7pm Mon-Fri, 9:30am-1pm Sat) Behind the Sernatur office.

TELEPHONE

Entel (Mall Plaza Real, Colipí 484; ☒ 9am-10pm) Telephone center.

TOURIST INFORMATION

Conaf (☎ 213-404; Juan Martínez 55; ☒ 8:30am-5:30pm Mon-Thu, 8:30am-4:30pm Fri) Has limited information on regional parks.
Sernatur (☎ 212-838; infoatacama@sernatur.cl; Los Carrera 691; ☒ 8:30am-5:30pm Mon-Fri Mar-Dec,

8:30am-8pm Mon-Fri, 10am-2pm & 4-8pm Sat Jan & Feb) Well-informed tourist office in a bunkerlike building.

TRAVEL AGENCIES

Turismo Atacama (☎ 214-767; viajes_atacama@ entelchile.net; Los Carrera 716) Useful travel agency.

Sights

Copiapó's mining heyday is evident throughout its town center. Shaded by century-old pepper trees, Plaza Prat is graced by several buildings from the early mining era, not least the elegant **Iglesia Catedral**, with its three-tiered tower, and the musty old municipal **Casa de la Cultura**. Watch out for the roving fortune-tellers; once they get started you'll have a hard time getting away.

Railroad buffs will want to see the **Estación Ferrocarril** (cnr Juan Martínez & Batallón Atacama), the starting point for the very first railroad on the continent. It's now a neglected picture of peeling paint flanked by two graffiti-marred engines (both British-made). However, there's another treat for enthusiasts in the grounds of the historic **Escuela de Minas** (School of Mines; Av Copayapu), now the Universidad de Atacama, just west of town; on its grounds is the beautiful yellow-and-black Locomotora Copiapó (1850), the Norris Brothers locomotive thought to be the first to operate on the Caldera–Copiapó railway line (and hence the first to operate in South America). Attached are 1st-, 2nd- and 3rd-class carriages.

Walking back a few blocks west, you'll pass mining-magnate Apolinario Soto's **Palacete Viña de Cristo** (Av Copayapu; admission free; ☒ 8am-7pm Mon-Fri). Built in 1860 from European materials, and mixing a jumble of oriental and classical styles, this was the town's most elegant mansion. It belongs to the Universidad de Atacama.

Other buildings reminiscent of Copiapó's early boomtown era include the stuffy national monument **Asociación Minera Copiapó** (Atacama) between Avs Vallejos and Colipí.

The must-see **Museo Mineralógico** (☎ 206-606; cnr Colipí & Manuel Rodríguez; adult/child CH$500/200; ☒ 10am-1pm & 3:30-7pm Mon-Fri, 10am-1pm Sat) literally dazzles. This tribute to the raw materials to which the city owes its existence displays a kaleidoscopic collection of more than 2300 samples, some as delicate as coral, others bright as neon under fluorescent light. The museum was founded in 1857 and supported

COPIAPÓ

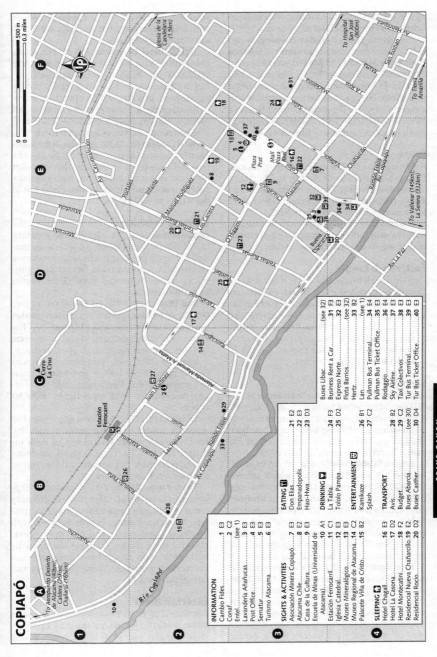

INFORMATION
Cambio Fides.................................1 E3
Conaf..2 C2
Entel..(see 1)
Lavandería Añañucas..................3 E3
Post Office....................................4 E3
Sernatur..5 E3
Turismo Atacama.........................6 B3

SIGHTS & ACTIVITIES
Asociación Minera Copiapó........7 E3
Atacama Chile...............................8 E2
Casa de la Cultura.........................9 E3
Escuela de Minas (Universidad de
  Atacama)...................................10 A1
Estación Ferrocarril....................11 C1
Iglesia Catedral...........................12 E3
Museo Mineralógico..................13 E3
Museo Regional de Atacama.....14 C2
Palacete Viña de Cristo..............15 B2

SLEEPING
Hotel Chagall..............................16 E3
Hotel La Casona.........................17 D2
Hotel Montecatini......................18 F2
Residencial Nueva Chañarcillo..19 E2
Residencial Rocío.......................20 D2

EATING
Don Elías.....................................21 E2
Empanadópolis............................22 E3
Hao-Hwa.....................................23 D3

DRINKING
La Tabla.......................................24 F3
Tololo Pampa..............................25 D2

ENTERTAINMENT
Kamikaze.....................................26 B1
Splash..27 C2

TRANSPORT
Avis..28 B2
Budget...29 C2
Buses Abarcia..............................30 D4
Buses Casther........................(see 30)
Buses Libac............................(see 32)
Business Rent a Car....................31 F3
Expreso Norte.............................32 E3
Flota Barrios...........................(see 32)
Hertz.......................................(see 32)
Lan... (see 1)
Pullman Bus Terminal.................34 E4
Pullman Bus Ticket Office..........35 E4
Rodaggio.....................................36 E4
Sky Airline..................................37 E3
Taxi Colectivos...........................38 E3
Tur Bus Terminal........................39 E3
Tur Bus Ticket Office.................40 E3

NORTE CHICO

by the Universidad de Atacama (successor to Copiapó's famous School of Mines).

Built in the 1840s by industrial moguls and radical politicians, the Matta family, the **Museo Regional de Atacama** (☎ 212-313; Atacama 98; adult/child CH$600/300, Sun admission free; ☉ 2-5:45pm Mon, 9am-5:45pm Tue-Fri, 10am-2:40pm & 3-5:45pm Sat, 10am-12:45pm Sun & holidays; ⛨) is a national monument worth a snoop simply for the architecture. It houses a piecemeal museum with indigenous artifacts and a mock mine made of fiberglass.

Tours

Agencies run tours of the city, Bahía Inglesa, Parque Nacional Pan de Azúcar and highland destinations, such as Parque Nacional Nevado Tres Cruces and Ojos del Salado. There are a few agencies in the Mall Plaza Real.

Atacama Chile (☎ 211-191; www.atacamachile.com; Maipú 580, Local C) offers standard trips and mountaineering in the eastern mountains.

Festivals & Events

Copiapó celebrates its own creation on December 8, while the first Sunday of February sees the **Fiesta de la Candelaria**, celebrated at the Iglesia de la Candelaria at Los Carrera and Figueroa, 2km east of Plaza Prat. The Virgin of the Candelaria is said to protect miners – hence her celebrity in the region. August 10 is **Día del Minero** (Miner's Day).

Sleeping

Residencial Rocío (☎ 215-360; Yerbas Buenas 581; s/d CH$12,000/24,000, without bathroom CH$5000/10,000; P) Expect youthful owners and scampering dogs at this plain guesthouse with a cool bamboo-shaded walkway. Rooms are basic but fair value. Breakfast is available (CH$900).

Residencial Nueva Chañarcillo (☎ 212-368; Manuel Rodríguez 540; s/d CH$11,900/16,600, without bathroom CH$5950/11,900) Obvious pride plays throughout this simple, disarming guesthouse-cum-family home with kitsch kitten posters, faded armchairs and plastic floral posies on every available surface, making it the best budget buy. The only down side: the scent of cigarette smoke still hangs in the rooms.

Hotel Montecatini (☎ 211-363; hotelmontecatini@123.cl; Infante 766; s/d incl breakfast standard CH$15,000/21,000, superior CH$21,000/27,000; P ⛨) It's hard to find this crisply maintained, adobe-fronted hotel as there's no sign. But if you can find it, you'll discover a tranquil courtyard, a pool (which may or may not have water), and a garden

studded with fruit trees. Superior rooms, which are large, carpeted and have cable TV, are worth the extra price.

ourpick **Hotel La Casona** (☎ 217-277; www.lacasonahotel.cl; O'Higgins 150; s/d incl breakfast from CH$26,000/31,500; P ⛶) There's a definite lightness and airiness to this wonderfully homey guesthouse, boasting a hotchpotch of international crafts, a grassy garden and bilingual owners. Rooms have a country-casual feel. The restaurant serves exceptional food.

Hotel Chagall (☎ 352-900; www.chagall.cl; O'Higgins 760; s/d incl breakfast CH$46,900/56,900; P ☒ ⛶) The best business hotel in the city, this four-star high-rise is just off Plaza Prat, with a swanky spotlit lobby and plush rooms. Plans are in the works to build a pool.

Eating & Drinking

Empanadopolis (☎ 216-320; Colipí 320; empanadas CH$450-950; ☉ lunch & dinner) This hole-in-the-wall is hugely popular for its mouthwatering empanadas with unusual flavors and gimmicky names borrowed from Greek heroes and philosophers.

Don Elias (☎ 364-146; Los Carrera 421; set meal CH$2000; ☉ breakfast, lunch & dinner) A downmarket diner with small tables and a blaring TV, 'The Don' churns out excellent-value *almuerzos* (set lunches) and particularly good seafood.

Hao-Hwa (☎ 215-484; Yerbas Buenas 334; set menu CH$6500, mains CH$2500-6300; ☉ lunch & dinner) Enter the dragon at this Cantonese *chifa* (restaurant) decked out with neon lights. Takeout is possible.

La Tabla (☎ 233-029; Los Carrera 895; ☉ 8pm-late) A mock-adobe bar with mellow lighting, studied rustic decor and plenty of dark intimate corners, La Tabla is good for those wanting to share bar snacks and jam out to the hard-rock soundtrack.

Tololo Pampa (Atacama 291; ☉ 8pm-late) A happening *tablas* joint. The hottest culinary trend to hit Chile since adding mayo to mussels, *tablas* are cutting boards adorned with anything from meats and cheeses to ceviche and sushi. Enjoy them on the open-air back patio with rough-hewn furniture and an outdoor fireplace. Come for drinks and late-night snacks.

Entertainment

Kamikaze (☎ 235-890; www.kamikaze.cl, in Spanish; Rómulo Peña 215; ☉ 11pm-late Thu-Sat) Copiapó's most popular pub-club has a grisly WWII

DAY TRIPPER: EXPLORE THE LOST MINES & VILLAGES AROUND COPIAPÓ

A necklace of interesting spots winds up the valley of the Río Copiapó, all easily accessible by public transportation (see below). At nearby Tierra Amarilla, the caramel-and-frosting **Iglesia Nuestra Señora de Loreto** (1898) is the work of Spanish architect José Miguel Retornano, though it looks more a gingerbread house.

About 23km from Copiapó, flood-prone **Nantoco** is the site of a colonial church, a 19th-century silver and copper smelter, and the 1870 former hacienda of Apolinario Soto. At Km34, stop for a quick look at the outside of the **Hacienda Jotabeche**, which belonged to the notable Chilean essayist José Joaquín Vallejo – better known by his pseudonym, Jotabeche.

Los Loros, 64km from Copiapó, is a picturesque agricultural village that yields appetizing grapes, watermelons, citrus and other fruits. After a further 11km or so, a dusty sidetrack leads to **Viña del Cerro** and the restored remains of a 15th-century Diaguita-Inka copper foundry, complete with administration buildings, a ceremonial platform and several dozen circular ovens.

Forget gold fever. It was silver fever that triggered the population explosion in the city of Copiapó – silver found at **Chañarcillo** in 1832. To reach what remains of the mining town's rapidly dissolving ruins – only worth the trip if you are really into history – take the Panamericana south to Km59, where a dusty lateral runs east.

---

theme with a plane nose-diving into the roof. It has live music and serves bar snacks, fajitas and pizza to keep energy levels up.

Splash (Juan Martínez 46; ☯ 11pm-late Thu-Sat) A long-running youth-driven club that will have you living *la vida loca*.

Getting There & Away

AIR

The Aeropuerto Desierto de Atacama is about 40km northwest of Copiapó.

Lan (☎ 600-526-2000; Mall Plaza Real, Colipí 484, Local A-102; ☯ 9am-1:30pm & 3-7:30pm Mon-Fri, 9:30am-1:30pm Sat) flies direct to Antofagasta on Friday only (CH$254,600, one hour), and daily to La Serena (CH$184,000, 45 minutes) and Santiago (CH$123,900, 1½ hours).

Sky Airline (☎ 600-600-2828; www.skyairline.cl; Colipí 526) flies daily to Antofagasta (CH$52,000, one hour) and Santiago (CH$84,300, 1½ hours).

BUS & TAXI COLECTIVO

Bus companies are scattered through Copiapó's southern quarter. Virtually all north–south buses stop here, as do many bound for the interior. **Pullman Bus** (☎ 212-629; cnr Colipí & Av Ramón Freire) has a large terminal and a central **ticket office** (cnr Chacabuco & Chañarcillo). **Tur Bus** (☎ 239-546; Chañarcillo 680) also has a terminal and a **ticket office** (Colipí 510) downtown. Other companies include **Expreso Norte** (☎ 231-176), **Buses Libac** (☎ 212-237) and **Flota Barrios** (☎ 213-645), all located in a common terminal on Chañarcillo. **Buses Abarcia** (☎ 212-483; Chacabuco 122) has service to towns along the Río Copiapó, including

Los Loros (CH$1400, one hour), as do **Buses Casther** (☎ 218-889; Buena Esperanza 557). Note that many buses to northern desert destinations leave at night.

Standard destinations and common fares are shown in the following table:

Destination	Cost (CH$)	Duration (hr)
Antofagasta	16,400-28,000	8
Arica	24,400-36,400	18
Calama	19,800-33,200	10
Iquique	20,700-31,700	13
La Serena	8700-14,200	5
Santiago	20,100-34,400	12
Vallenar	4500-6300	2

Nippy **taxi colectivos** (☎ 243-829; Chacabuco 170A) also shuttle passengers to Caldera (CH$2000, one hour) and Bahía Inglesa (CH$2500, one hour), from the terminal on Chacabuco. Buses Casther will also take you to Caldera for CH$1500.

Getting Around

TO/FROM THE AIRPORT

Private taxis to the new Aeropuerto Desierto de Atacama, 40km west of Copiapó, cost CH$16,000; try **Radio Taxi San Francisco** (☎ 218-788). There's also a **transfer bus** (☎ 218-889) that ferries new arrivals to town (CH$5000, 25 minutes). Buses (CH$3500) and *taxi colectivos* (CH$2500) ploughing between Copiapó and Caldera may also agree to drop you at the junction (CH$2000, 30 minutes), from where it's a straightforward 300m walk to the airport.

CAR

Copiapó's car-hire agencies include **Hertz** (☎ 213-522; Av Copayapu 173), **Avis** (☎ 213-966; copiapo@ avischile.cl; Rómulo Peña 102) and **Budget** (☎ 216-272; Ramón Freire 050); all three can also be found at the airport. Other Chilean options are **Rodaggio** (☎ 212-153; www.rodaggio.cl, in Spanish; Colipí 127) and **Business Rent a Car** (☎ 214-427; Los Carrera 955). Rodaggio has the cheapest unlimited mileage rates, starting at CH$21,400 per day plus 19% *impuesto de valor agregado* (IVA; the value-added tax, or VAT) for a small car. But pickup trucks and 4WDs suitable for exploring the backcountry cost at least CH$55,100 per day.

PARQUE NACIONAL NEVADO TRES CRUCES

Hard-to-reach **Parque Nacional Nevado Tres Cruces** (admission free) has all the rugged beauty and a fraction of the tourists of more famous high-altitude parks further north. Quite apart from pristine peaks and first-rate climbing challenges, the park shields some wonderful wildlife: flamingos spend the summer season here; large herds of vicuñas and guanacos roam the slopes; the lakes are home to giant and horned coots, Andean geese and gulls; and even the occasional condor and puma is spotted.

The park is separated into two sectors of the high Andes along the international highway to Argentina via Paso de San Francisco. The larger **Sector Laguna Santa Rosa** comprises 490 sq km surrounding its namesake lake at 3700m, and includes the dirty-white salt-flat Salar de Maricunga to the north. The smaller **Sector Laguna del Negro Francisco** consists of 120 sq km surrounding a lake of the same name. While flamingos do not nest here, the shallow waters are ideal for the 8000 birds that summer here. About 56% are Andean flamingos, 40% are Chilean flamingos and the remaining 4% are rare James flamingos. The highest quantity of birds is present from December through February.

Outside the park boundaries, 6893m **Ojos del Salado** is Chile's highest peak (just 69m below South America's highest peak, Aconcagua in Argentina) and the highest active volcano in the world; its most recent eruptions were in 1937 and 1956. At the 5100m level the Universidad de Atacama maintains the rustic Refugio UDA that can shelter four to six climbers; at 5700m

Refugio César Tejos has a capacity for 12. The mountain can be climbed between October and April; allow seven days. The climb only becomes technical in the last 50m or so.

Because Ojos del Salado straddles the border, climbers must obtain authorization from Chile's **Dirección de Fronteras y Límites** (Difrol; see p71), which oversees border-area activities. Permission can be granted without fuss through its website.

Another attraction outside the park boundaries, about 65km beyond Laguna Santa Rosa, is the spectacular turquoise lake **Laguna Verde** (elevation 4325m), which glows like liquid kryptonite – brighter even than the intense blue of the sky. There's a frigid campsite beside the lake, as well as shallow thermal baths in which to heat frozen toes.

For more information on visiting the park, stop by the Conaf (p236), Atacama Chile (p238) or Sernatur (p236) offices in Copiapó.

Sleeping

Laguna Santa Rosa (free) has a small *refugio* (rustic shelter) on the south side of the lake. There's a key at the door.

Refugio Laguna del Negro Francisco (dm CH$5000), run by Conaf, is cozy with beds, cooking facilities, electricity, flush toilets and hot showers. Bring your own bed linen, drinking water and cooking gas.

Getting There & Away

It's easy to get lost on your way to the national park, so you should seriously consider taking a tour from Copiapó. By car, a high-clearance 4WD is recommended, though you can make it in a regular car if you are willing to take a few dings and blast out your suspension.

Sector Laguna Santa Rosa is 146km east of Copiapó via Ruta 31 and another (nameless) road up the scenic Quebrada de Paipote. Sector Laguna del Negro Francisco is another 85km south via a ramblin road that drops into the valley of the Río Astaburuaga to arrive at the lake. Note that the road directly west from the Conaf *refugio* to Mina Aldabarán and Quebrada San Miguel is not passable.

There is no public transportation here. For tours, see p238.

NORTE CHICO

HUASCO VALLEY

A lush thumb of greenery snaking its way down from the Andes, the fertile valley of the Río Huasco, roughly midway between Copiapó and La Serena, is famous for its plump olives, pisco and a deliciously sweet wine known as *parajete*. However, the region's other claim to fame – mining – may in time threaten this agricultural oasis.

The threat comes from high up in the Andes, where Canadian mining conglomerate Barrick Gold won approval in 2006 to move forward with a mining operation along the Argentinean border to exploit the Pascua Lama deposits, which are thought to be the world's largest untapped source of gold.

The project has long been disputed by local farmers. After all, the company originally proposed moving three glaciers (totaling a 20-hectare surface) to make room for the mine. Chilean environmental authorities from the Regional Environment Commission (COREMA) approved the mine, but told the company that they could not move the glaciers (guess even the so-called environmental authorities have their limit). Nevertheless, local farmers are still concerned that chemicals like cyanide and mercury will leak from the mine and pollute the valley below.

Vallenar

☎ 051 / pop 53,604

The valley's principal town, Vallenar, is a tidy, bucolic settlement that runs at a soothingly slow pace. Strange as it seems, its name is a corruption of Ballinagh – an Irish town and home to the region's colonial governor, Ambrosio O'Higgins. After serious earthquake damage in 1922, Vallenar was rebuilt with wood instead of adobe, but the city's buildings still rest on unconsolidated sediments.

Though there is little to do in town other than stroll around the central plaza, it's a good jumping-off point for visits to Parque Nacional Llanos de Challe and other sights in the Huasco Valley.

ORIENTATION

Motorists often bypass Vallenar because Puente Huasco (Huasco Bridge), which spans the valley, does not drop into the town itself. At the bridge's southern end, the Vallenar–Huasco Hwy leads east then branches across the river.

Semipedestrian Prat has a wide sidewalk with a single automobile lane, east of Plaza O'Higgins. Everything is within walking distance from here.

INFORMATION

Banks, a post office and long-distance telephone offices are all available around the plaza. The **Centro Computacional Plaza Internet** (Prat at Vallejo; per hr CH$600; ✆ 10am-midnight) offers internet access.

SIGHTS

Teenage daredevils perform skateboarding tricks on Plaza O'Higgins, also home to Vallenar's **Iglesia Parroquial**, which has a shiny copper dome on its wooden tower. A short wander east is the **Museo del Huasco** (☎ 611-320; cnr Ramírez & Brasil; adult/student CH$450/200; ✆ 9am-1pm & 3-6pm Mon-Fri), which shelters diverse bits and bobs on local history.

SLEEPING & EATING

Residencial Oriental (☎ 613-889; Serrano 720; d with/ without bathroom CH$15,000/10,000) One block south of the plaza, the Oriental has dark and rather nasty rooms. But the linen is clean, making this the best choice for budget travelers.

Hostal Quillahue (☎ 619-992; pedroprokurica@ yahoo.com; Prat 70; s/d incl breakfast CH$14,000/20,000; P) Located right on the plaza, this is one of the best midrange buys in town. The rather blah rooms have comfy beds and are clean. The chambers looking onto the street are more airy, but are also more noisy. Be sure to ask the *señora* to turn on the *calefón* (water heater) before you shower.

Hotel Takio (☎ 613-819; hotel_takio@yahoo.es; Prat 600; d incl breakfast CH$27,000; P) Somebody really loves pink in this pleasant business-style hotel one block west of the plaza. The large rooms are bathed in 18 shades of Molly Ringwald, and there are large balconies looking down to the road below.

Hotel Puerto de Vega (☎ 613-870; www.puerto devega.cl, in Spanish; Ramírez 201; s/d incl breakfast from CH$38,500/46,000; P 🖳 🕿) Just one block north of the bus station, this gorgeous European-style villa has a clutch of beautifully kept rooms, personable service, and a kitchen stocked high with tasty treats and self-service drinks. It's the best hotel in town, and the new fancy-pants rooms with cool hardwoods, modern lines and leather headboards are well worth the extra money.

Mercado Municipal (cnr Serrano & Santiago) A huddle of speedy *cocinerías* (greasy spoons) can be found in the municipal market, as can fresh supplies for self-caterers.

our pick Nativo (☎ 611-879; Prat 1193; mains CH$2000-4500; ☽ 10pm-3am; **V**) Occupying the 2nd story of a corner building, this bar and restaurant has wide windows opening onto the anachronistic streets of Vallenar, and occasional live music. While there's an extensive menu in this studiedly bohemian locale, just go for the calzone pizza, the best in northern Chile.

Il Bocatto (☎ 614-609; Prat 750; mains CH$2400-6300; ☽ lunch & dinner Sun-Thu, lunch Fri & Sat) This neon-lit Italian restaurant beside the church and the plaza serves small but good pizzas and snacks.

GETTING THERE & AWAY

Vallenar's **Terminal de Buses** (cnr Prat & Av Matta) is at the west end of town. The **Pullman Station** (☎ 619-587; cnr Atacama & Prat) is 500m west of the Plaza de Armas. **Tur Bus** (☎ 611-738) is opposite the main bus terminal, and has extensive north- and southbound routes. Destinations include Santiago (CH$14,000, 10 hours), La Serena (CH$5000, three hours), Copiapó (CH$4000, two hours) and Antofagasta (CH$16,000, 10 hours).

Huasco

☎ 051 / pop 4312

The picturesque fishing port of Huasco, an hour west of Vallenar by paved highway, has a beautiful seafront studded with squat palms, sculpture, shady benches and a scarlet lighthouse. There's also a good beach that sprawls as far as the eye can see. En route to Huasco,

the village of Freirina is worth a stop to see its sugar-and-peach **Iglesia Santa Rosa de Lima** (1869), a wooden church with an impressive bell tower.

Oddly out of place overlooking a desert shoreline, the alpine-style **Hostal San Fernando** (☎ 531-726; www.hostalsanfernando.dk; Pedro de Valdivia 176; s/d incl breakfast CH$15,000/18,000, r per person without bathroom CH$7000; **P**) has great ocean views from every room. Ask for a new room.

Closer to Huasco's center, **Hostería Huasco** (☎ 531-026; rossanabergamasco@hotmail.com; Ignacio Carrera Pinto 110; s/d incl breakfast from CH$32,000/38,000; **P** 🛍) is slightly aging, but still retains its place as Huasco's best hotel. Work is underway to resuscitate the pool out back and there's wi-fi.

Just below the lighthouse, **El Faro** (☎ 532-785; Av Costanera s/n at Playa Grande; mains CH$2500-5800; ☽ lunch & dinner) offers the best views in town and an eclectic menu featuring everything from tacos to ceviche.

Buses to Huasco depart from the Vallenar bus terminal, and cost CH$1000. To return to Vallenar just flag down a bus from Huasco's main plaza. They pass every 15 minutes or so.

PARQUE NACIONAL LLANOS DE CHALLE

This isolated **national park** (☎ 51-611-555; admission CH$2000) hugs the desert coastline 50km north of Huasco. It generally sees little through-traffic, except in those years when the *desierto florido* (see the boxed text, below) bursts into bloom. There is also an interesting selection of cacti, flighty guanacos and canny foxes.

The park is accessible only by private vehicle. It consists of a coastal sector south of Carrizal Bajo around Punta Los Pozos, where

---

THE FLOWERING DESERT

In some years a brief but astonishing transformation takes place in Norte Chico's barren desert. If there has been sufficiently heavy rainfall, the parched land erupts into a multicolored carpet of wildflowers – turning a would-be backdrop from *Lawrence of Arabia* into something better resembling a meadow scene from *Bambi*.

This exquisite but ephemeral phenomenon is appropriately dubbed the *desierto florido*, the 'flowering desert.' It occurs between late July and September in wetter years when dormant wildflower seeds can be coaxed into sprouting. Many of the flowers are endangered species, most notably the endemic *garra de león* (lion's claw, one of Chile's rarest and most beautiful flowers). Even driving along the Panamericana near Vallenar you may spot clumps of the delicate white or purple *suspiro de campo* (sigh of the field), mauve, purple or white *pata de Guanaco* (Guanaco's hoof), and yellow *corona de fraile* (monk's crown) coloring the roadside.

Llanos de Challe is one of the best places to see this phenomenon, although the region's erratic rainfall patterns make it difficult to predict the best sites in any given year.

there is a **campground** (campsites per person CH$3000, showers CH$600), and an inland sector along the Quebrada Carrizal, 15km southeast of Carrizal Bajo. Campers should bring plenty of water, as there is none onsite, and warm clothes during the winter. You can also try to guerrilla camp at Playa Blanca near the park's entrance for free. There are good beach breaks along the coast here: good news for surfers, bad news for swimmers.

From Huasco, take the decaying asphalt road along the coast north from the nearby farming village of Huasco Bajo. Alternatively, a reasonable dirt road leaves the Panamericana 15km north of Vallenar.

RESERVA NACIONAL PINGÜINO DE HUMBOLDT

Pods of bottle-nosed dolphins play in the waters of this **national reserve** (admission CH$1600; ☺ boat excursions 9am-4pm), while slinky sea otters slide off boulders and penguins waddle along the rocky shoreline – keeping their distance from sprawling sea-lion colonies. The 860-hectare reserve embraces several offshore islands on the border between Regiónes III and IV, and makes one of the best excursions in Norte Chico. The reserve takes its name from the Humboldt penguin, which nests on rocky Isla Choros.

Humboldt penguins breed along the Peruvian and Chilean coasts. The International Union for the Conservation of Nature and Natural Resources lists these little guys as a 'vulnerable species,' with an estimated total population of around 12,000 breeding pairs. Over-fishing and the exploitation of guano were the primary causes for the penguin's decline, and experts say that if new conservation measures are not put in place the species could well become extinct in the next few decades. Visit www.penguins.cl to learn more about the penguin's plight.

At Punta de Choros it's possible to hire a launch to Isla Damas and around Isla Choros (where landing is not permitted). Isla Chañaral, the largest and most northerly of the three islands comprising the reserve, is less easily accessible, but its wildlife is similar to Isla Choros.

Bad weather and high waves can occasionally prevent boat trips: call the **Conaf station** (☎ 099-544-3052; www.conaf.gov.cl, in Spanish; 500m north of the main road, next to Caleta San Augustin; ☺ 8:30am-5:30pm Sat-Thu) to check conditions before leaving.

From a turnoff on the Panamericana, about 78km north of La Serena, a rough gravel road passes through Los Choros, an oasis of olive trees that was one of Spain's earliest (1605) settlements in the area, and continues to Punta de Choros (123km from La Serena).

Sights & Activities

Hired launches from the dock at Punta de Choros (up to 14 people CH$45,000) carry

ECOSYSTEM AT RISK! THE PROS & CONS OF VISITING THE PARK

The Reserva Nacional Pingüino de Humboldt is overrun with tourists, which brings up the very real and very important question of whether you should even visit the park at all. It's a tough question, and one you'll need to make on your own, based on your own sensibilities and the facts at hand.

While noise and pollution from boats visiting the area is affecting local marine life, including the penguins, dolphins and sea lions, it is really Isla Damas – the only place where boats can land – that is suffering the most. Local biologists are reporting that the number of birds that call the island home has significantly dropped in recent years. The island was originally supposed to have a maximum visitation of 60 people per day. But these days, it seems that hundreds of tourists are flocking to the island daily. If you do decide to visit the park, you may consider skipping an excursion to Isla Damas altogether. If you do visit the island, you should definitely keep to the established paths. But this may not necessarily solve the dilemma of over visitation.

It really is a problem of balance. Local fishermen gave up fishing much of the year to create this national reserve with the idea that they could supplement their income by taking tourists on boat excursions. So by not visiting the park, you are affecting the livelihoods of the local fishermen. On the other hand, if you decide to come, you may be playing a small role in changing the ecology of the area forever. It's a tough call. But whatever you decide, it's best to heed that age-old credo of 'leave no trace behind.'

passengers along the east coast of the 320-hectare **Isla Choros**, which has it all – pods of bottle-nosed dolphins that splash alongside the boat, a large sea-lion colony, groups of otters and Humboldt penguins, and massive rookeries of cormorants, gulls and boobies.

Isla Damas, a 60-hectare metamorphic outcrop capped by a low granite summit, is visited on the way back. It has two snowy-white beaches with crystal-clear water: **Playa La Poza**, where boats land, and the fine-sand **Playa Tijeras**, a 1km walk away. Visitors are required to pay the CH$1600 visitor fee at a Conaf stand located at the Isla Damas dock. Be sure to bring along a snack, water and warm clothes for the trip.

Diving and kayaking trips can be arranged through **Explora Sub** (☎ 099-402-4947; www.explora sub.cl; 200m north of the Punta de Choros dock; 1-tank dive with rental CH$30,000).

Sleeping & Eating

There are numerous homes offering both camping (around CH$1500 per person) and *cabañas* (beginning at CH$15,000) along the main road.

Conaf offers **camping** (☎ 099-544-3052; www .conaf.gov.cl, in Spanish; per person CH$12,000) by Playa La Poza on Isla Damas. There are toilets but no potable water, so bring water and food. It's crowded over summer and on weekends but deserted at other times. Bring bags for trash. Request advance permission to camp from Conaf. There's a three-day maximum stay, and you should make arrangements for your return before you head out.

If you want to get away from the crowds, you can hire a launch from the Punta de Choros dock and camp on **Isla Gaviotas**, an uninhabited island less than 1km out to sea from town. The launch costs around CH$10,000 for up to four people, and camping is free.

Explora Sub (☎ 099-402-4947; www.explorasub .cl; 200m north of the Punta de Choros dock; d CH$30,000, each additional person CH$5000; P ♿) is a super-cute group of cabins looking out onto the sea. Each cabin has a double room, bunk-bed room (perfect for the rugrats) and a kitchen and living area. They also offer free kayak rentals and have a CMAS-certified dive center.

Bar y Restaurante Eneyde (Punta de Choros plaza; mains CH$2300-5000; ☽ breakfast, lunch & dinner) is the requisite post-trip lunch spot. Pleasant outdoor seating looks onto the town's main 'plaza.' Try the crispy shrimp empanadas or locally caught seafood.

Getting There & Away

The park is best reached from La Serena. **Profetur** (☎ 51-255-199) offers bus service to and from La Serena (CH$3500, 1½ hours). Buses depart from Almacén Don Oriel, on the town's main road, at 9am and 3pm. La Serena-based travel agencies also offer tours (see p246). Unfortunately, the one-way 123km distance means transit time is long.

LA SERENA

☎ 051 / pop 149,640

Chile's second-oldest city and the thriving capital of Región IV, La Serena is doubly blessed with some beautiful architecture and a long golden shoreline, making it a kind of thinking-man's beach resort. The city absorbs hoards of Chilean holidaymakers in January and February, though it is fairly peaceful outside the summer rush. Sauntering through downtown La Serena reveals dignified stone churches, tree-shaded avenues and some pretty plazas. Some of the city's architecture is from the colonial era, but most of it is actually neocolonial – the product of Serena-born president Gabriel González Videla's 'Plan Serena' of the late 1940s.

La Serena also has numerous attractions in the surrounding countryside, with charming villages and pisco vineyards aplenty, as well as international astronomical observatories that take advantage of the region's exceptional atmospheric conditions and clear skies.

History

Encomendero Juan Bohón, the lieutenant of Pedro de Valdivia, founded La Serena in 1544, but the town was promptly destroyed and Bohón killed in a Diaguita uprising. His successor, Francisco de Aguirre, refounded the city in 1549, but a century later poor old La Serena was razed once more, this time by British pirate Sharpe in 1680. Following Chilean independence, the city grew fat on silver and copper, supported by agriculture in the Elqui Valley. Silver discoveries were so significant that the government created an independent mint in the city.

Orientation

La Serena lies on the south bank of the Río Elqui, 2km above its outlet to the Pacific. The Panamericana, known as Av Juan Bohón, skirts the town's western edge. Centered on the Plaza de Armas, the city's regular grid pattern makes orientation easy.

Information

BOOKSTORES

Librería Andrés Bello (☎ 227-310; Matta 510; ⏲ 10am-2pm & 4:30-8pm Mon-Fri, 10am-1pm Sat) Good selection of Spanish-language books.

INTERNET ACCESS

There are numerous internet joints in town, and most hotels offer wi-fi.

Infernet (☎ 470-004; Balmaceda 417; per hr CH$600; ⏲ 10am-midnight; ⊠) Psychedelic cyber café with private booths, webcams and rock music.

LAUNDRY

Lavaseco (☎ 225-195; Balmaceda 851; per kilo CH$1350; ☎ 9am-1pm & 3-7pm Mon-Fri, 9am-2pm Sat)

MEDICAL SERVICES

Hospital Juan de Diós (☎ 200-500; Balmaceda 916; ⏲ 24hr) The emergency entrance is at the corner of Larraín Alcalde and Anfión Muñóz.

MONEY

Banks with ATMs are readily available in the blocks around Plaza de Armas.

POST

Post office (cnr Matta & Prat; ⏲ 8:30am-6pm Mon-Fri, 9:30am-1pm Sat)

TELEPHONE

Entel (Prat 571; ⏲ 10am-6pm Mon-Fri) Long-distance telephony and money transfers.

TOURIST INFORMATION

In summer there is an information kiosk, Cámara de Turismo, by Iglesia La Merced. There's also a city tourist office in the bus station.

Conaf (☎ 272-798; coquimbo@conaf.cl; Cordovez 281; ⏲ 8:30am-2pm Mon-Fri) For information on Región IV's national parks and reserves.

Sernatur (☎ 225-199; www.regionestrella.cl; Matta 405; ⏲ 8:30am-10pm Mon-Fri, 9am-10pm Sat & Sun) Excellent tourist office by Plaza de Armas.

TRAVEL AGENCIES

Ovitravel (☎ 340-540; www.ovitravel.cl; Prat 475)

Viajes Torremolinos (☎ 228-061; torremolinos@entelchile.net; Prat 464)

Dangers & Annoyances

Women traveling alone should be wary of taxi drivers in La Serena; sexual assaults have been reported. Only take company cabs.

Sights

PLAZA DE ARMAS

La Serena has 29 churches to its credit, many beautiful stone creations in neoclassical or eclectic styles, and a bunch of the prettiest can be found on or near the Plaza de Armas. On the east side, the handsome neoclassical **Iglesia Catedral** (⏲ 10am-1pm & 4-8pm) dates from 1844; it also has a sobering museum of religious art. Just to its north are the bluff facades of the **Municipalidad** – pop your head inside to check out photos of the city's past – and **Tribunales** (Law Courts; cnr Prat & Los Carrera), built as a result of González Videla's Plan Serena.

The dainty-looking bell tower of nearby **Iglesia Santo Domingo** (Cordovez) looks as though it should have a twirling ballerina inside. The tower is a later addition, only a century old, though the attractive limestone church dates back to 1755.

However, the granddaddy of all La Serena's churches is colonial **Iglesia San Francisco** (Balmaceda 640), two blocks southeast of the plaza, and built in the early 1600s. It's a squat stone construction, with a chunky tower and fancy baroque facade.

Three blocks east of the plaza, the august limestone **Iglesia San Agustín** (cnr Cienfuegos & Cantournet) was built by the Jesuits in 1755, then passed to the Augustinians after the Jesuits' expulsion. It has undergone serious modifications.

MUSEO HISTÓRICO CASA GABRIEL GONZÁLEZ VIDELA

Although richly stocked with general historical artifacts, this two-storey **museum** (☎ 215-082; Matta 495; adult/child CH$600/300; ⏲ 10am-6pm Mon-Fri, 10am-1pm Sat) concentrates on one of La Serena's best-known – and most controversial – sons. González Videla was Chile's president from 1946 to 1952. Ever the cunning politician, he took power with communist support but then promptly outlawed the party, driving poet Pablo Neruda out of the Senate and into exile.

As you might expect, the reverent exhibits omit such episodes. But do pop upstairs for a look at the general historical displays and changing modern-art exhibits.

MUSEO ARQUEOLÓGICO
The crescent-shaped **archaeological museum** (☎ 224-492; cnr Cordovez & Cienfuegos; adult/child CH$600/300, Sun admission free; ☼ 9:30am-5:50pm Tue-Fri, 10am-1pm & 4-7pm Sat, 10am-1pm Sun) makes an ambitious attempt to corral Chile's pre-Columbian past. Its highlights include Atacameña mummies, a hefty 2.5m-high *moai* (large anthropomorphic statues) from Easter Island and interesting Diaguita artifacts that include a dinghy made from sea-lion hide.

The González Videla and Museo Arqueológico share admission – entry to one is valid for the other.

KOKORO NO NIWA
With its trickling brooks, drifting swans and neatly manicured rock gardens, this **Japanese garden** (☎ 217-013; adult/child CH$600/300; ☼ 10am-6pm) makes a good escape from the city. It is at the southern end of Parque Pedro de Valdivia.

Activities
A swath of wide sandy **beaches** stretches from La Serena's nonfunctional lighthouse right to Coquimbo: there are so many that you could visit a different beach every day for a two-week vacation. Unfortunately, strong rip currents make some unsuitable for swimming – but good for surfing. Safe swimming beaches generally start south of Cuatro Esquinas and include most beaches around Coquimbo. Those between the west end of Av Francisco de Aguirre and Cuatro Esquinas (ie closer to town) are friskier and generally dangerous for bathers. Look for the signs 'Playa Apta' (meaning beach safe for swimming) and 'Playa No Apta' (meaning beach not safe for swimming).

A bike path now runs all the way to Coquimbo. For quick beach access, take either bus Liserco or *colectivos* running between La Serena and Coquimbo, and get off at Peñuelas and Cuatro Esquinas, a block from the beach. During January and February direct buses head down Av Francisco de Aguirre to Playa El Faro. There is no direct service for the remainder of the year and it's a 3km walk to the lighthouse from town.

Other popular activities include **sailing** (buddy up to a yacht-club member), **surfing** (hit Playa El Faro with local bodyboarders) and **windsurfing** (keep an eye on swimmers within 200m of the beach or you'll run afoul of the Gobernación Marítima). Playa Totoralillo, south of Coquimbo, is rated highly for its surf breaks and windsurfing potential. **Maui Girl** (Av del Mar s/n) is located smack-dab in the middle of Playa El Faro, about 3km south of the lighthouse, and rents a board-wetsuit combo for CH$5000 per day.

Courses
Colectivo de Arte Consciente (☎ 224-289; Lautaro 841) Conversions are possible – but not mandatory – at this Hare Krishna art collective. Classes range from spirituality lectures to vegetarian cooking courses.

La Serena School (☎ 211-487; www.laserena school.cl; Prat 560) Offers Spanish courses (CH$22,000 for 2½ hours of instruction with a minimum of five classes), and homestays (CH$12,000 with breakfast and dinner).

Tours
Agencies offer a wealth of excursions, from national park visits to nighttime astronomical trips, pisco-tasting tours to New Age jaunts in UFO central, Cochiguaz. Traditional excursions include half-day city tours (CH$11,000), full-day trips through the Elqui Valley (CH$12,000 to CH$14,000), Andacollo (CH$11,000), Parque Nacional Fray Jorge and Valle del Encanto (CH$23,000), and Parque Nacional Pingüino de Humboldt (CH$23,000). Agencies also provide transportation to observatories, including Observatorio Comunal Cerro Mamalluca (CH$12,000). The minimum number of passengers ranges from two to six.

City Tour (☎ 099-782-8059; Plaza la Recova) Sign up for a cheap hour-long city tour (CH$3000) at Plaza la Recova. Tours leave at 11am and 2pm.

Ingservtur (☎ 220-165; www.ingservtur.cl; Matta 611) A well-established company with friendly English-speaking staff; it can provide English- or German-speaking guides for about 20% more than the standard prices. Special prices are available for students.

Inti Mahina (☎ 224-350; www.intimahinatravel.cl, in Spanish; Prat 214) A youth-oriented agency offering all the standard tours as well as useful advice on independent travel.

Ovitravel (☎ 340-540; www.ovitravel.cl; Prat 475) Has trips to all the major destinations.

LA SERENA

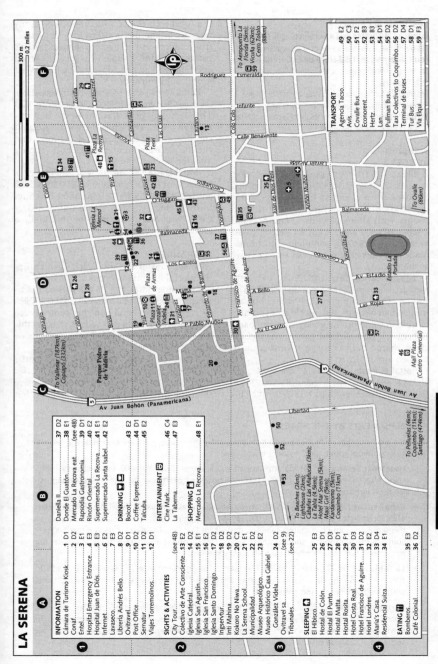

Av Juan Bohón (Panamericana)

To Aeropuerto La
Florida (5km);
Vicuña (62km);
Cerro Tololo
(88km)

To Ovalle
(86km)

To Peñuelas (4km);
Coquimbo (11km);
Santiago (474km)

To Beaches (2km);
Lighthouse (2km);
Cabañas Las Añañucas (3km);
La Tahona (4km);
Hotel Mar Serena (5km);
Maui Girl (5km);
Kardamomo (5km);
Coquimbo (11km)

INFORMATION

Cámara de Turismo Kiosk	1	D1
Conaf	2	D2
Entel	3	E1
Hospital Emergency Entrance	4	E3
Hospital Juan de Diós	5	E2
Infernet	6	E2
Lavaseco	7	E3
Librería Andrés Bello	8	D2
Ovitravel	9	D1
Post Office	10	D2
Sernatur	11	D2
Viajes Torremolinos	12	D2

SIGHTS & ACTIVITIES

City Tour	(see 48)	
Colectivo de Arte Consciente	13	E2
Iglesia Catedral	14	D2
Iglesia San Agustín	15	E1
Iglesia San Francisco	16	E2
Iglesia Santo Domingo	17	D2
Ingsevtur	18	D2
Inti Mahina	19	D2
Kokoro No Niwa	20	C2
La Serena School	21	E1
Municipalidad	22	D2
Museo Arqueológico	23	E2
Museo Histórico Casa Gabriel		
González Videla	24	D2
Ovitravel sa	(see 9)	
Tribunales	(see 22)	

SLEEPING

El Hibisco	25	E3
Hostal de Colón	26	D1
Hostal El Punto	27	D3
Hostal Matta	28	D1
Hostal Rosita	29	F1
Hotel Costa Real	30	D3
Hotel Francisco de Aguirre	31	E2
Hotel Londres	32	E2
María's Casa	33	D4
Residencial Suiza	34	E1

EATING

Bomberos	35	E3
Café Colonial	36	D2
Daniella II	37	D2
Donde El Guatón	38	E1
Mercado La Recova eat	(see 48)	
Rapsodia Gastronomía	39	D1
Rincón Oriental	40	E2
Supermercado La Recova	41	E1
Supermercado Santa Isabel	42	E2

DRINKING

Boicot	43	E2
Coffee Express	44	D1
Talcuba	45	E2

ENTERTAINMENT

Cine Mark	46	C4
La Taberna	47	E3

SHOPPING

Mercado La Recova	48	E1

TRANSPORT

Agencia Tacso	49	E2
Avis	50	C3
Covalle Bus	51	F2
Econoren	52	B3
Hertz	53	B3
Lan	54	D1
Pullman Bus	55	D2
Taxi Colectivos to Coquimbo	56	D2
Terminal de Buses	57	D4
Tur Bus	58	D1
Vía Elqui	59	F3

NORTE CHICO

Festivals & Events

Jornadas Musicales de La Serena In early January this traditional festival sees a series of musical events.

Feria Internacional del Libro de La Serena Brings prominent Chilean authors to the historical museum in early February.

Festival de La Serena This festival attracts big-name Chilean musicians and comedians in early February.

Artisan's fair In the second fortnight of February this fair is held in the historical museum.

Sleeping

BUDGET

El Hibisco (☎ 211-407; mauricioberrios2002@yahoo.es; Juan de Dios Peni 636; s/d CH$5000/10,000; **P**) Familial atmosphere prevails at this simple guesthouse. It offers a dozen wooden-floored rooms with shared facilities, laundry and kitchen access, and serves La Serena's best breakfast (CH$1000) complete with homemade jam (jars of which guests often receive as mementos).

ourpick Maria's Casa (☎ 229-282; www.hostalmariacasa.cl; Las Rojas 18; r per person CH$7000; 🖥) The rooms are as simple as they come, but are immaculately clean. Ask nicely and you may be able to camp on the grassy lawn out back. Other backpacker-friendly amenities include clean shared bathrooms, a quaint country kitchen and internet.

Hostal El Punto (☎ 228-474; www.hostalelpunto.cl; Andres Bello 979; s/d incl breakfast CH$15,000/24,000, dm/s/d without bathroom CH$6500/9000/13,000; **P**) This

is a top-notch choice with a bunch of sunny terraces, bright mosaics, flower gardens, tree-trunk tables and a home-cooked breakfast. It's run by a friendly couple who speak German and English, and provide traveling tips. What more could you ask for?

Hostal Rosita (☎ 213-954; hostalrosita@hotmail.com; Cantournet 976; dm/s/d CH$6500/8000/15,000; **P** 🖥) This rambling place has one of the best terraces in town. And while the rooms are a bit run down, they are clean and the folks that run the place are immensely friendly. There's a shared kitchen and wi-fi.

Hostal Matta (☎ 210-014; www.hostalmatta.cl, in Spanish; Matta 234; r without bathroom CH$12,000, s/d with bathroom CH$16,000/18,000; 🖥) One of the best buys in this category, the Matta is immaculately clean, with bright rooms, a big full kitchen and friendly owners.

MIDRANGE

Also see Hostal El Punto (left), which has wonderful midrange rooms.

Residencial Suiza (☎ 216-092; residencial.suiza@terra.cl; Cienfuegos 250; s/d incl breakfast CH$18,000/22,000; **P**) The cheery rooms in this centrally located hotel are bathed in yellow, making this a good bet for the price. Prices dip outside summer months.

Hostal de Colón (☎ 224-656; www.hostaldecolonlaserena.cl, in Spanish; Colón 311; s/d incl breakfast CH$22,800/27,800; **P**) It's a little more expensive than the other entries in this category, but

---

SLEEPS & EATS BY THE BEACH

There are a number of higher-priced hotels down by the beach. Here are two of our faves, along with a couple of great spots to dine beachside.

- **Hotel Mar Serena** (☎ 241-855; www.marserena.cl, in Spanish; Av del Mar 4900, 3km south of the lighthouse; d/apt CH$45,500/85,500; **P** 🏊) This little hotel has pretty decent prices considering its location right on the beach.

- **Cabañas Las Añañucas** (☎ 215-881; www.cabanasananucas.cl, in Spanish; Av del Mar 970 & Av del Mar 4100; apt for up to 6 people CH$50,000-90,000; **P** 🏊) This mini-chain has two locations. Both have the same price and big shared cabañas, perfect for families. The first location is just 500m south of the lighthouse, and has ocean views. The second is about 1km down, is quieter and has a pool, but doesn't offer beach views like the first.

- **La Tabla** (☎ 212-722; Av del Mar 3200, 2.5km south of the lighthouse; mains CH$3000-8000; 🕐 lunch & dinner) Right on the beach, this fine restaurant offers a bit of everything, from corvina stuffed with shellfish to pizza and empanadas.

- **Kardamomo** (☎ 216-060; Av del Mar 4000, 3km south of the lighthouse; mains CH$3500-7800; 🕐 lunch & dinner) A 'Kool Moe Dee' seafront lounge and restaurant, Kardamomo has the best service in town. And they serve up a much-welcomed international menu with sushi, falafel salads and some great seafood dishes.

the crisp sheets, new beds, plush comforters and clean bathrooms make the Colón worth the price.

Hotel Londres (☎ 219-066; www.hotellondres.cl, in Spanish; Cordovez 550; s/d incl breakfast CH$22,000/30,000; ℗) Besides having the three 'Ls' – location, location, location – this little business-style hotel also has very clean rooms with plush white bedcovers and sparkling bathrooms. There's a nice breakfast area where you can check your emails with the free wi-fi.

TOP END

Hotel Francisco de Aguirre (☎ 222-991; www.diegode almagrohoteles.cl, in Spanish; Cordovez 210; s/d incl breakfast CH$48,000/56,000; ℗ ▦ ▧) This large hotel's imposing neocolonial frontage faces Iglesia Santo Domingo, the bells of which often wake late risers. It has a modern interior and uniformly plush rooms.

Hotel Costa Real (☎ 221-010; www.costareal.cl, in Spanish; Av Francisco de Aguirre 170; s/d incl breakfast from CH$55,800/65,100; ℗ ▦ ▧) For the best comforts central La Serena can offer, head to this flashy five-star hotel, with a conical turret, a gourmet international restaurant, sizable rooms and a lovely swimming pool.

Eating
BUDGET

For those wanting to self cater, there are several markets in town. Some have great food stalls, others have good options to make your own picnic lunch. Supermercado La Recova on Zorilla is also a good place to pick up the fixings for a picnic lunch.

Bomberos (☎ 225-047; cnr Av Francisco de Aguirre & Balmaceda; set meal CH$1190; ☽ lunch) Join the local fire brigade for a no-frills set lunch on the upper floor of the fire station. Note the British-made 1874 Merryweather engine downstairs, and browse firemen mugshots upstairs.

Daniella II (☎ 227-537; Av Francisco de Aguirre; snacks CH$1000, mains CH$2500-4000; ☽ breakfast, lunch & dinner) Numero Dos is a plain-faced local favorite serving hearty portions of Chilean comfort food. The fresh seafood is especially tasty.

Mercado La Recova (cnr Cienfuegos & Cantournet; ☽ 9am-6pm) Upstairs from the market are lots of cheap restaurants serving fresh seafood and *cazuela* (stew usually made with chicken).

Supermercado Santa Isabel (Cienfuegos 545; ☽ 9am-10pm Mon-Sat, 9am-9pm Sun) Large supermarket to satisfy all self-catering needs.

MIDRANGE & TOP END

Café Colonial (☎ 543-158; Balmaceda 475; breakfast from CH$2000, set lunch CH$2500, mains CH$2000-5800; ☽ 9am-late, closed Sun) If you're missing stiff espressos, banana pancakes and burgers, get your fix in this attractive tourist-friendly restaurant. It's used to accommodating kids, vegetarians and non-Spanish speakers. There's live music on weekends.

Donde El Guatón (☎ 211-519; Brasil 750; mains CH$2600-5200; ☽ lunch & dinner) El Guatón prepares sizzling *parrilladas* (grilled meats) right before your hungry eyes. The characterful dining area is hung with flowers and chandeliers made from old bicycle wheels.

Rincón Oriental (☎ 225-553; O'Higgins 570; mains CH$2900-5500; ☽ 11:30am-4pm & 7:30pm-1am) A serene *chifa* in which to escape the busy streets and enjoy excellent noodles, amid oriental screens and fish tanks.

our pick Rapsodia Gastronomía (☎ 543-016; Prat 470; mains CH$3000-5200; ☽ breakfast, lunch & dinner, closed Sun) With several side rooms looking onto the interior courtyard, this old *casona* (mansion) is home to one of La Serena's best restaurants. Come for afternoon drinks or later on for occasional live music, tasty salads and sandwiches.

Drinking

Coffee Express (☎ 221-673; cnr Prat & Balmaceda; ☽ 9am-9pm Mon-Fri, 10am-9pm Sat) Oversized glass-and-plastic coated coffee shop serving some of La Serena's best java.

Talcuba (Eduardo de la Barra 589; ☽ 5:30pm-late Mon-Fri, 7:30pm-late Sat & Sun) Rub shoulders with the university crowd in this darkly lit small tavern that plays contemporary rock and pop.

Boicot (cnr Eduardo de la Barra & O'Higgins; ☽ noon-3am) Stay out late drinking on the interior patio, or head over at midday for a cheap fixed lunch (CH$1500) at this popular student bar.

Entertainment

Nightclubs sparkle along the seafront, past the lighthouse and all the way to Barrio Inglés Coquimbo; they're especially hot during summer.

La Taberna (☎ 229-344; Balmaceda 824) This seedy-looking bar in a 130-year-old house hosts regular acts, including Chilean folk music on weekend nights from midnight.

Cine Mark (☎ 212-144; www.cinemark.cl, in Spanish; Mall Plaza, Av Albert Solari 1490; admission CH$2500) Screens big-name movies.

Shopping

Mercado La Recova (cnr Cienfuegos & Cantournet) Head here for a feast of dried fruits, multicolored jams and other sugary concoctions from the Elqui Valley. There are also plenty of woolens, soapstone ashtrays and musical instruments on offer.

Getting There & Away

AIR

La Serena's **Aeropuerto La Florida** (Ruta 41) is located 5km east of downtown. **Lan** (☎ 600-526-2000; Balmaceda 406; ⏰ 9am-2pm & 3:30-7pm Mon-Fri, 9:30am-2pm Sat) flies three times daily to Santiago (CH$66,800, 50 minutes), once daily to Copiapó (CH$184,000, 45 minutes) and twice daily to Antofagasta (CH$70,000 to CH$78,000). There's another Lan office with longer hours in Mall Plaza.

BUS

La Serena's **Terminal de Buses** (☎ 224-573; cnr Amunátegui & Av El Santo) has dozens of carriers plying the Panamericana from Santiago north to Arica, including **Tur Bus** (☎ 215-953; www.turbus .com, in Spanish; Balmaceda 437), **Pullman Bus** (☎ 218-252, 225-284; Eduardo de la barra 435) and **Pullman Carmelita** (☎ 543-160).

Typical destinations and fares:

Destination	Cost (CH$)	Duration (hr)
Antofagasta	22,000-34,000	13
Arica	34,000-38,000	23
Calama	24,000-39,000	16
Copiapó	13,000-18,000	5
Iquique	24,000-37,000	19
Los Vilos	5000	4
Santiago	14,000-23,000	7
Vallenar	9000	3

To get to Vicuña (CH$1200, one hour) look for Buses Serenamar, Pullman Carmelita and Elqui Bus in the Terminal de Buses, or you can try **Via Elqui** (☎ 312- 422; cnr Juan de Dios Peñi & Esmeralda). For Ovalle (CH$1800, 1¾ hours) give Tur Bus, Elqui Bus or Buses Serenamar a try.

Via Elqui has frequent departures to Pisco Elqui (CH$1800, two hours) and Monte Grande (CH$1800, two hours) between 7am and 10:30pm. In the Terminal de Buses, **Buses Serenamar** (☎ 323-422; terminal de buses) runs several buses a day to Guanaqueros (CH$1200, 50 minutes) and Tongoy (CH$1300, one hour).

For Argentine destinations, **Covalle Bus** (☎ 213-127; Infante 538) travels to Mendoza (CH$25,000, 12 hours) and San Juan (CH$25,000, 14 hours) via the Libertadores pass every Tuesday, Thursday, and Sunday. It leaves at 11pm.

TAXI COLECTIVO

A large number of regional destinations are more frequently and rapidly served by *taxi colectivo. Colectivos* to Coquimbo (CH$600, 15 minutes) leave from Av Francisco de Aguirre between Balmaceda and Los Carrera. **Agencia Tacso** (☎ 227-379; Domeyko 589) goes to Ovalle (CH$2300), Vicuña and Andacollo (CH$2000). There is also the option of hiring a *colectivo* for a day tour to Elqui Valley for approximately CH$25,000.

Getting Around

Private taxis to Aeropuerto La Florida, 5km east of downtown on Ruta 41, cost CH$5000. Alternatively, **She Transfer** (☎ 295-058) provides door-to-door minibus transfer for CH$1500.

For car hire, try **Avis** (☎ 227-171; laserena@ avischile.cl; Av Francisco de Aguirre 063), also at the airport, **Hertz** (☎ 226-171; Av Francisco de Aguirre 0225) or **Econorent** (☎ 220-113; Av Francisco de Aguirre 0135).

AROUND LA SERENA

Observatorio Interamericano Cerro Tololo

Probing the mysteries of stars billions of miles into the past is all in a night's work at this futuristic observatory, which sits at 2200m atop its hill like a huge shiny pimple. And while visitors can't stargaze through its monstrous telescopes (even the astronomers don't do that as the telescopes first feed data into computer monitors), a daytime tour of the facilities is still an enlightening experience.

Operated by the Tucson-based Association of Universities for Research in Astronomy (AURA; a group of about 25 institutions, including the Universidad de Chile), Observatorio Interamericano Cerro Tololo has an enormous 4m telescope, once the southern hemisphere's largest, but since superseded by 8m giants at Cerro Paranal (p228) and the Gemini South telescope on nearby Cerro Pachón (www.gemini.edu).

Free bilingual tours take place on Saturday only. Make advance reservations through **Aura** (☎ 205-200; www.ctio.noao.edu, ctiorecp@noao .edu); the observatory suggests booking one month ahead in high season. Two-hour tours are held at 9am and 1pm. There is no public transportation so rent a car or taxi, or arrange to come with a tour operator (even then you *still* must make your own reservations with the observatory). The well-marked, gated turnoff to Tololo is 52km east of La Serena via Ruta 41; visitors then ascend 36km up a smooth but winding gravel road in a caravan of vehicles.

If you'd rather scan the nighttime skies through telescopes, visit Mamalluca (p255) or Observatorio Turístico Collowara.

Observatorio Turístico Collowara

Like Mamalluca, this shiny new **observatory** (☎ 432-2964; www.collowara.cl; adult/child/senior CH$3500/1500/2500; ♿) is built for tourists; no serious interstellar research is conducted here. Two-hour tours run in summer at 9:15pm, 10:15pm and 11:30pm; in winter they run at 7:30pm, 8:15pm, 9:30pm and 10:30pm. The facility boasts three viewing platforms and a 40cm telescope – slightly larger than that at Mamalluca. There are also three smaller telescopes available, so you won't have to wait for long. Book at the **ticket office** (☎ 051-432-964; 599 Urmeneta St) in nearby Andacollo, and inquire there about transportation to the hilltop observatory.

There is plenty of accommodation in Andacollo, 54km from La Serena and connected by bus (CH$600, 1½ hours) and *taxi colectivo* (CH$1500, one hour); see opposite. Tours from La Serena can also be organized (p246).

COQUIMBO

☎ 051 / pop 159,471

The rough-and-tumble port of Coquimbo has been undergoing something of a revolution in recent years. Clinging to the rocky hills of Península Coquimbo, the town was long written off as La Serena's ugly cousin, but it has blossomed into the area's most up-and-coming spot for nightlife and restaurants – it even hosted the female World Cup of Soccer in late 2008. Outside the beautifully restored 19th-century Barrio Inglés (English Quarter), however, Coquimbo remains a gritty working port.

Information

The **Casa de la Cultura y Turismo** (☎ 313-204; cnr Freire & Av Costanera; ☀ 8:30am-5:30pm) houses a small exhibition hall and the town library. You may be able to get some tourist information here. In summer information is also provided at Museo de Sitio.

Sights & Activities

The modest **Museo de Sitio** (Calle Aldunate; admission free; ☀ 9am-10:30pm Tue-Sat, 10am-6pm Sun) is housed beneath a clear dome in the Plaza Gabriela Mistral, just north of the Plaza de Armas. It is the site of a pre-Columbian graveyard discovered serendipitously when expanding the Plaza de Armas. It dates from Las Animas culture, AD 900 to AD 1100.

You won't get to heaven on this ticket, but you will get a good dizzying view of the bay from atop the **Cruz del Tercer Milenio** (Cross of the Third Millennium; ☎ 327-935; www.cruzdeltercermilenio .cl, in Spanish; Cerro El Vigía; adult/child CH$1500/1000; ☀ 8:30am-10pm; P), reaching for the sky above Coquimbo. A cross between a holy pilgrimage site and theme park, this whopping 93m-high concrete cross can be clearly seen from La Serena's beaches. The cross contains a museum (largely devoted to the late Pope John Paul II), praying rooms and an elevator ride to the top. Mass is held every Sunday. The first level is free.

The town's other iconic landmark is the hilltop mosque **Centro Mohammed VI** (☎ 310-440; Los Granados 500, Cerro Dominante; admission free; ☀ 9:30am-12:30pm & 2:30-5pm Mon-Wed, 2:30-5pm Thu, 9:30am-12:30pm & 2:30-4pm Fri, 11am-1pm &1:30-4pm Sat & Sun; P). The first phase of construction of this massive clifftop spire was finished in 2007. Funded in part by the king of Morocco, the center is intended as a symbol of the cultural cooperation between the two nations. Eventually, it will host an art museum (with artwork from the Islamic world) and a library. For now, visitors can step inside the small mosque – remember to take off your shoes – to revel at the intricate tile work.

Coquimbo's surprisingly pretty **Plaza de Armas** is littered with modern sculpture and hosts a spinning fountain and some preposterously tall palm trees.

Rocky outcrops surround the **Fuerte Coquimbo**, a War of the Pacific–era fort just west of the town's center. There's a nice paved walkway that leads you out to the ocean, and it's free. To get there, take the Costanera west to Regimento Coquimbo.

Hour-long **boat tours** (CH$1000; ☀ 10am-9pm) of the harbor depart regularly from Av Costanera in January and February, weekends only during other months. Popular **beaches** string the

Bahía Herradura de Guayacán, reached from Coquimbo or La Serena. You can arrange **sportfishing trips** for around CH$3000. Boats leave from the dock on the corner of Bilbao and Costanera.

There's good rock-climbing and soccer fields near **La Pampilla**, on the western coast of town.

Sleeping & Eating

<u>our pick</u> **Hostal Nomades** (☎ 315-665; www.hostal nomades.cl; Regimiento Coquimbo 5; campsites per person CH$3000, dm incl breakfast CH$7000; s/d without bathroom CH$11,000/18,000; 🖵) Once the French Consulate, Nomades is now one of the area's best hostels. The building, built in 1850, houses several living rooms complete with odds and ends from the 19th century, a full kitchen, onsite bar, ping-pong table, large garden area and, of course, dorm rooms. It earns bonus points for only putting four people in each dorm.

Hotel Bilbao (☎ 315-767; Bilbao 471; s/d incl breakfast CH$8000/15,000) An aging townhouse just a block from Coquimbo's plaza, this place has high ceilings, squeaky wood floors and an attractive old three-storey atrium, making it feel more like a pirate ship than a hotel. The rooms facing the road are quite noisy, but they have balconies.

Restaurant Coquimbo (cnr Bilbao & Varela; mains CH$2000-6500; ☽ lunch & dinner) The excellent bay views from the upstairs patio make this seafood restaurant a good bet. There's live music on weekends.

The Terminal Pesquero (Fish Market), located along the bay, offers cheaper fish options. Marisquería El Porteño is one of the most popular stalls, with breaded fish, ceviche and more.

Entertainment

Coquimbo now boasts a long list of bars and restaurants. Most of the action is on Aldunate, heading northwest from the Plaza in the Barrio Inglés.

Club de Jazz (☎ 288-784; Aldunate 739; cover CH$2500) An ever-fashionable club that has live music on weekends from 10:30pm.

El Rincón Habanero (Malgarijo 707; ☽ 9am-late) This dance hall and restaurant give the feeling of old Havana. It has live salsa music Tuesday through Saturday. There are good Caribbean eats and a cheap set lunch (CH$1500).

Getting There & Away

Coquimbo's **Terminal de Buses** (Varela) is between Borgoño and Alcalde. Long-distance services are similar to those to and from La Serena. Many local buses and *taxi colectivos* also link the two cities (bus CH$400, *colectivo* CH$750, private taxi from CH$6000).

GUANAQUEROS & TONGOY

Petite Guanaqueros' long white beach makes it one of the area's most popular bucket-and-spade destinations. Situated 30km south of Coquimbo and 5km west of the Panamericana, it's suitable for a day trip, although cabin complexes dot the entrance road.

Just 18km beyond Guanaqueros is another lively little beach resort called Tongoy, which is the perfect place to savor fresh seafood, sink a few chilled *copas* (glasses) and be serenaded by full-throated buskers (in whichever language is most likely to draw tips); you'll find the *marisquerías* (seafood restaurants) alongside Playa Grande. Playa Socos, on the north side of the peninsula, is a much more sheltered spot for a dip.

Hotel Aqua Marina (☎ 391-870; Av Fundicion Sur 192; s/d incl breakfast CH$15,000/30,000), right off the plaza on the main road in Tongoy, is the best budget hotel in town. It's just a few blocks to the beach, and the clean rooms, with their key-lime color scheme, are bright and cheery.

From La Serena's Terminal de Buses, Buses Serenamar runs regular buses to Guanaqueros (CH$1200, 50 minutes), Tongoy (CH$1300) and on to Ovalle (CH$2700). By car, you'll need to pay a toll (CH$500) to enter the towns.

ELQUI VALLEY

The heart of Chilean pisco production, the Elqui Valley is carpeted with a broad cover of striated green. Famous for its futuristic observatories, seekers of cosmic energies, frequent UFO sightings, poet Gabriela Mistral and quaint villages, this is a truly engrossing area, and one of the must-visit places in Norte Chico.

Vicuña

☎ 051 / pop 22,687

The spirit of Gabriela Mistral's somnambulist poetry seeps from every pore of snoozy little Vicuña. Just 62km east of La Serena, this is the easiest base from which to delve deeper into the Elqui Valley. The town itself, with its low-key plaza, lyrical air and

---

SOUR RELATIONS OVER PISCO

Chileans celebrate the ubiquitous pisco sour – a tangy cocktail made from a type of grape brandy called pisco – as their national tipple. But mention this to a Peruvian and you risk having your drink thrown in your face. The trouble is, the Peruvians also claim pisco as their national beverage, and the bitter row over the liquor's rightful origin has been intensifying for decades.

Local legend tells how back in the 1930s the former Chilean president Gabriel González Videla personally changed La Unión's original name to Pisco Elqui to undermine Peruvian claims of having originated the beverage. Meanwhile, Peru points to its own colonial port named Pisco in a grape-growing valley of the same name. The Peruvians have a strong historical case for appellation, if only because it was there that the Spaniards first introduced vineyards, and historical records demonstrate that the drink was consumed in Peru as early as 1613.

But Chileans argue that pisco has also been produced in Chile for centuries and claim that its pisco is of superior quality. They also point out that Chile produces, imbibes and exports vastly more pisco than Peru, and thus claim to have popularized the drink.

After years of acrimony Peru scored a partial victory in 2005 when it received a favorable enactment by World Intellectual Property Organization (WIPO). But the legal wranglings look set to continue for some time yet.

---

compact dwellings, is worth a day visit before you head out into the countryside to indulge in the fresh avocados, papayas and other fruits grown in the region – not to mention the famous grapes that are distilled into Chile's potent grape-brandy pisco.

ORIENTATION

On the north bank of the Río Elqui, across a narrow bridge from Ruta 41, Vicuña has a geometric town plan centered on the wooded Plaza de Armas.

INFORMATION

Banks and universal ATMs are in short supply; it's better to change money in La Serena. There are several internet cafés near the central plaza.

Entel (Av Gabriela Mistral 351; 🕘 9am-10pm) Long-distance telephone office.

Hospital San Juan de Dios (☎ 411-263; cnr Independencia & Prat; 🕘 24hr) Located a few blocks north of Plaza de Armas.

Oficina de Información Turística (☎ 209-125; Torre Bauer, Plaza de Armas; 🕘 8:30am-9pm Jan & Feb, 8:30am-5:30pm Mar-Dec) The Municipalidad's tourist office, where you can gather a bit of info on the town's past.

Post office (cnr Av Gabriela Mistral & San Martín) Located in the Municipalidad.

Telefónica CTC (Prat 331; 🕘 9am-1pm & 3:30-6pm Mon-Fri, 9am-1pm Sat) Long-distance telephone office.

SIGHTS & ACTIVITIES

The town's landmark **Museo Gabriela Mistral** (☎ 411-223; Av Gabriela Mistral 759; adult/child & senior

CH$600/300; 🕘 10am-7pm Mon-Sat, 10am-6pm Sun Jan & Feb, 10am-5:45pm Mon-Fri, 10am-6pm Sat, 10am-1pm Sun Mar-Dec), between Riquelme and Baquedano, is a tangible eulogy to one of Chile's most famous literary figures. Gabriela Mistral was born Lucila Godoy Alcayaga in 1889 in Monte Grande. The museum charts her life, from a replica of her adobe birthplace to her Nobel Prize, and has a clutch of busts making her seem a particularly strict schoolmarm. Her family tree indicates Spanish, indigenous and African ancestry. Like Pablo Neruda she served in the Chilean diplomatic corps.

A sinister portrait of Gabriela Mistral gazes blankly up at the sky from a watery pit in the center of Vicuña's Plaza de Armas; its macabre presence doesn't dissuade kids from breakdancing and playing around its edges, though. Just off the plaza's western edge, the eccentric **Torre Bauer** (1905) is a rusty-colored clock tower resembling a lanky toy castle; it was built by a former German mayor. Nearby **Iglesia de la Inmaculada Concepción** (1909) has a few ceiling paintings and an image of the Virgen del Carmen carried by Chilean troops during the War of the Pacific.

Crawling with color, antennae and pincers, the small **Museo Entomológico y de Historia Natural** (Chacabuco 334; adult/child CH$600/300; 🕘 10:30am-4pm) specializes in insects and kaleidoscopic butterflies, but also has fossils, stuffed birds and invertebrates.

Dating from 1875, and looking good for it, the adobe mansion **Casa Solar de los Madariaga** (☎ 411-220; Av Gabriela Mistral 683; adult/child

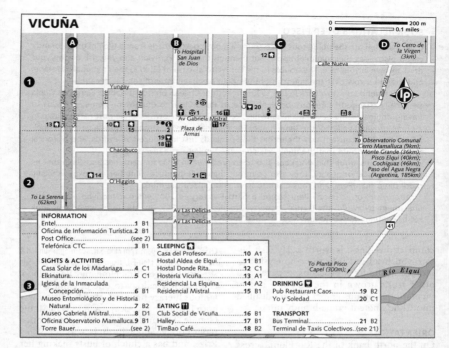

VICUÑA

INFORMATION
Entel...1 B1
Oficina de Información Turística.2 B1
Post Office..............................(see 2)
Telefónica CTC.............................3 B1

SIGHTS & ACTIVITIES
Casa Solar de los Madariaga......4 C1
Elkinatura....................................5 C1
Iglesia de la Inmaculada
    Concepción.............................6 B1
Museo Entomológico y de Historia
    Natural...................................7 B2
Museo Gabriela Mistral................8 D1
Oficina Observatorio Mamalluca.9 B1
Torre Bauer..............................(see 2)

SLEEPING
Casa del Profesor......................10 A1
Hostal Aldea de Elqui................11 B1
Hostal Donde Rita......................12 C1
Hostería Vicuña.........................13 A1
Residencial La Elquina...............14 A2
Residencial Mistral....................15 B1

EATING
Club Social de Vicuña................16 B1
Halley.......................................17 B1
TimBao Café.............................18 B2

DRINKING
Pub Restaurant Caos.................19 B2
Yo y Soledad............................20 C1

TRANSPORT
Bus Terminal.............................21 B2
Terminal de Taxis Colectivos..(see 21)

CH$500/free; ☺ 10am-7pm Jan-Mar, 11am-2pm & 3-6pm Apr-Dec) contains furnishings and artifacts from an influential family who made its money exporting chinchilla.

The dusty hike up **Cerro de la Virgen**, just north of town, offers vast panoramas of the entire Elqui Valley, but it's hot and exposed – bring water. The summit is less than an hour's walk from the Plaza de Armas.

For those seeking some action, **Elkinatura** (☎ 412-070; Gabriela Mistral 549) rents bikes (CH$1500 per hour) and offers tours, horseback rides, rappeling excursions and more.

Two of Vicuña's big attractions, Planta Capel (opposite) and Observatorio Comunal Cerro Mamalluca (opposite), are just outside town.

FESTIVALS & EVENTS
Vicuña holds its annual grape harvest festival, **Festival de la Vendimia**, in February; it ends February 22, the anniversary of the city's founding.

SLEEPING
Residencial La Elquina (☎ 411-317; anamorainostroza @terra.cl; O'Higgins 65; camping per person CH$3000, s/d incl

breakfast CH$8500/17,000, without bathroom CH$5000/12,000; P ⌨) A veil of flowering vines and citrus trees welcome visitors to this humble but attractive *residencial*. The rooms are well worn, and some cramped, but the sheets are clean, so you're all good.

Residencial Mistral (☎ 411-278; Av Gabriela Mistral 180; s/d without bathroom CH$3500/7000) A quirky mix of bric-a-brac, from hubcaps to an enormous vulture figure, fills the concrete courtyard at this down-to-basics guesthouse and restaurant. There are 15 rustic (that's PR-speak for dirty) rooms with a shared bathroom and mountain views from the decrepit wooden balcony. Breakfast is available (CH$1000).

Casa del Professor (☎ 412-026; Av Gabriela Mistral 152; s/d incl breakfast CH$5000/10,000) You wouldn't know it's a hostel from the front, but knock on the door and come on in to this handsome older building with an extension housing tourist accommodations in the backyard. There's a shared kitchen and pretty, chilledout garden area.

Hostal Donde Rita (☎ 419-611; www.hostaldonde rita.com; Condell 443; s/d without bathroom incl breakfast CH$10,000/20,000; P ⌨) A private home with three cozy guest rooms, a surprise pool and a motherly German-speaking hostess – you guessed it, her name is Rita. This little B&B includes a terrific breakfast with home-made jam and fresh coffee, and wi-fi and a shared kitchen.

Hostal Aldea de Elqui (☎ 543-069; Av Gabriela Mistral 192; s/d incl breakfast CH$28,000/30,000; **P**) An old adobe *casona* that was recently converted into a hotel, the Aldea has a tranquil patio, clean rooms and fluffier-than-Felix bedspreads. While it lacks the finishing touches, this may one day be one of the better hotels in town. Plans are underway to make a pool out back, and they have wi-fi for the laptop set.

Hostería Vicuña (☎ 411-301; www.hosteriavicuna .cl, in Spanish; Sargento Aldea 101; s/d/tr incl breakfast CH$40,000/54,000/69,000; **P** **R** **占**) Its 15 floral rooms leave a bit to be desired for the price, but have cable TV, minibar and pristine bathrooms. The gardens outside have warm vine-touched patios, a big pool area (available to nonguests for around CH$4000 per day) and sentinel palm trees.

EATING
TimBao Café (San Martín 203; sandwiches CH$400-2300; ☾ lunch & dinner) This little café with seating looking onto the plaza is a nice place for people watching.

Halley (☎ 411-225; Av Gabriela Mistral 404; mains CH$2100-5900; ☾ lunch & dinner) A spacious colonial-style restaurant with a thatched ceiling and scattered handicrafts, this mainstay is recommended for typical Chilean food, including roast *cabrito* (goat), *conejo* (rabbit) and plentiful salads.

Club Social de Vicuña (☎ 412-742; Av Gabriela Mistral 445; set lunch CH$2500, mains H$3000-6000; ☾ lunch & dinner) Enthusiastic waiters usher passing travelers into this upmarket courtyard restaurant, or into its posh linen-and-candlestick laden side rooms. The food is well prepared, though rather bland, and you should expect Chilean specialties.

DRINKING & ENTERTAINMENT
Yo y Soledad (Carrera s/n; ☾ 9pm to late) Fight off those lonely bugs at the town's most happening spot. This sprawling pub gets going late.

Pub Restaurant Caos (☎ 412-629; San Martín 205; ☾ 9pm to late) This long thin pub, with '80s music videos blaring, is one of your better nightlife spots. It sometimes has live music on the weekends.

GETTING THERE & AWAY
From Vicuña, eastbound Ruta 41 leads over the Andes to Argentina. A rugged, dusty and bumpy (though passable in a regular car) secondary road leads south to Hurtado and back down to Ovalle.

The **bus terminal** (cnr Prat & O'Higgins) has frequent buses that travel to La Serena (CH$1200, one hour), Coquimbo (CH$1200, 1¼ hours), Pisco Elqui (CH$1000, 50 minutes) and Monte Grande (CH$1000, 40 minutes). Some companies have a daily service to Santiago (CH$10,000 to CH$12,000, 7½ hours), including **Pullman** (☎ 411-466). There's a wider choice of destinations in La Serena.

Inside the bus terminal complex is the **Terminal de Taxis Colectivos** (cnr Prat & O'Higgins), which has fast *colectivos* to La Serena (CH$1700, 50 minutes) and Pisco Elqui (CH$2000, 50 minutes).

Around Vicuña
PLANTA PISCO CAPEL
A 20-minute walk from town is the vigorously marketed **Planta Pisco Capel** (☎ 411-251; www.pisco capel.com, in Spanish; admission free; ☾ 10am-6pm Jan & Feb, 10am-12:30pm & 2.30-6pm Mar-Dec), where you can get a swift 20-minute tour and a few skimpy samples, then get herded into the sales room. Capel distils pisco at this facility, and has its only bottling plant here, with 36 million bottles per year shipped to addicts across Chile and abroad.

Tours are bilingual (Spanish and English), and there is no minimum attendance required. In addition to pisco, the sales room offers *parajete*, the region's lip-smacking dessert wine.

To get here, head southeast of town and across the bridge, then turn left.

OBSERVATORIO COMUNAL CERRO MAMALLUCA
This purpose-built observatory, 9km northeast of Vicuña, gives tourists the chance to goggle at distant galaxies, star clusters and nebulae through a 30cm telescope. While puny compared to the elephantine specimens at Chile's world-class observatories, Mamalluca's telescope still magnifies selected stars up to 140 times.

Bilingual guided tours take place nightly at 8:30pm, 10:30pm, 12:30am and 2:30am September through April, and at 6:30pm, 8:30pm and 10:30pm May through August.

Alternatively, the Cosmo Visión Andina tour includes presentations and music, but no access to the telescopes, and is held daily at 9pm, 11pm, 1am and 3am September through April, and at 7pm, 9pm and 11pm May through August. Tours spend two hours at the observatory. The weather is usually almost cloudless, but moonless nights are best for observing distant stars. Just bring a warm sweater!

Make reservations through the **Oficina Observatorio Mamalluca** (☎ 411-352; www.mamalluca.org; Av Gabriela Mistral 260, Vicuña; tour adult/child CH$3500/1500), which recommends bookings be made a month in advance September through April, and one week in advance May through August, although you can often still get a reservation on the same day. The Vicuña tourist office (p253) can also help with reservations.

There is no public transportation, but a minivan is on hand to take a few visitors from the Oficina Observatorio Mamalluca in Vicuña (reserve in advance; per person CH$1500). Some La Serena tour agencies arrange trips (see p246), or you can hire a taxi in Vicuña. Vehicles go by convoy to the site, which is otherwise difficult to find.

Monte Grande
☎ 051

This skinny roadside village is the birthplace of the internationally renowned poet Gabriela Mistral (p48), who is a Nobel Prize winner and national icon. Her burial site, found on a nearby hillside, is the destination of many Chilean and literary pilgrims. Mistral received her primary schooling at the Casa Escuela y Correo, where there is a humble **museum** (admission CH$300; 🕙 10am-8pm Sep-Apr, 10am-1pm & 3-6pm Tue-Sun May-Aug) dedicated to her with a reconstructed schoolroom and dorm.

There's a short **trail** leading down to the river just north of the Hotel Las Pleyadea. It makes for a nice afternoon excursion – be sure to bring a swimsuit.

Set in an old adobe *casona*, **Hotel Las Pleyadea** (☎ 451-107; Monte Grande s/n; d CH$40,000; P 🖭) is a boutique hotel offering nice touches like cane roofs and an outdoor plunge pool.

Monte Grande's restaurant **Mesón del Fraile** (☎ 451-232; 🕙 lunch & dinner), opposite the Casa Escuela y Correo, is worth stopping at for *churrasco* (grilled beef), pizza, sandwiches or fresh juice.

Local buses provide regular service from Vicuña (CH$700, 40 minutes).

Cochiguaz
☎ 051

New Age capital of northern Chile, the secluded valley of Cochiguaz is accredited with an extraordinary concentration of cosmic vibes, much-publicized UFO sightings and formidable healing powers. But you needn't be a believer to enjoy the beautiful valley, which is also the starting point for hikes and horseback rides in the backcountry. It sometimes snows here in the winter, so bring warm clothes. They are building a small **observatory** right in town, but work is proceeding at a hippie pace.

There is no public transit to Cochiguaz, so you'll need to 'hitch-it' from Monte Grande or take your own car.

Camping Cochiguaz (☎ 451-154, 099-884-4122; cabanaschanarblanco@gmail.com; campsites per person CH$4000) has some labyrinthine camping grounds down by the river. It's located 17km from Monte Grande at the end of a tortuous dirt track. They also offer horseback riding trips.

Hummingbirds flit around the lush gardens of **Casa del Agua** (☎ 321-371; www.casadelagua@gmail.com; 2-/4-person cabins CH$50,500/58,500;

EN-ROUTE TO MONTE GRANDE

There are two worthwhile stops on the road to Monte Grande. At the entrance of the Elqui Valley is the small pastoral village of **Paihuano**. While there isn't much to do, it's a worthwhile stop en-route. And you can stay at the **Cabañas el Encanto** (☎ 412-388; www.elencanto.cl, in Spanish; Tres Cruces s/n; d/tr CH$33,000/36,000; 🖭 🚷), which has a nice collection of little yellow *cabañas* down by the Río Claro.

At Km14.5 is the **Cavas del Valle winery** (☎ 541-352; www.cavasdelvalle.cl, in Spanish). Started in 2003, this little boutique bucks the trend by serving actual wine, rather than pisco. The *cosecha otoñal* dessert wine alone is worth the stop. And tastings are free.

NORTE CHICO

P ⚡), a pretty cabin complex 13km north of Monte Grande, perched delicately along the banks of the Río Cochiguaz. There's a bar, restaurant, mountain-bike hire and walking paths. It also offers tours.

Or for hippie kitsch there's always **El Alma Zen** (☎ 099-047-3861; Km11; campsites per person CH$3000, d/tr CH$25,000/40,000), its liberal use of Buddhist and Hindu imagery stretching to an enormous Buddha over the swimming pool. Staff can organize spa therapies here. Nonguests can enjoy the grounds for CH$1500 per day – Buddha would be so proud!

Pisco Elqui
☎ 051

Renamed to publicize the area's most famous product, the former village of La Unión is a placid community in the upper drainage area of the Río Claro, a tributary of the Elqui. It's become the area's most popular backpacker draw in recent years, and while it's a bit overcrowded, it's well worth a day or two. The architecture is rustic, but there remains a bucolic elegance to it, harkening to a Tuscan village.

The star attraction is the **Distelería Mistral** (☎ 451-358; www.piscomistral.cl; tours CH$4000; ☉ 11am-7pm, tours 1-6pm), which produces the premium Mistral brand of pisco. You can tour the grounds for free, and there's a tasty set lunch for CH$3000. The hour-long 'museum' tour gives you glimpses at the distillation process and includes a free tasting.

Horseback rides around the valley are also available – look for horses near the plaza. **Mundo Elqui** (☎ 551-290; www.mundoelqui.cl, in Spanish; O'Higgins s/n, just north of the Plaza de Armas) offers five-hour mountain-bike excursions (CH$8000) and horseback trips complete with a picnic (CH$17,000).

Frequent buses go to Pisco Elqui (CH$700, 50 minutes) from Vicuña.

SLEEPING & EATING
Refugio del Angel (☎ 451-292; refugiodelangel@gmail .com; campsites per person CH$3500, day-use CH$1500) To join the love in, head down to Angel's, an idyllic spot by the river complete with swimming holes, bathrooms, a little shop and, of course, drum circles. The turnoff is 200m south of the plaza on Manuel Rodriguez.

Hostal San Pedro (☎ 451-061; www.mundoelqui.cl; Prat s/n; r per person without bathroom CH$5000) The rooms at this groovy-groupie hostel are small and sim-

---

> **EXPLORE MORE OF THE ELQUI VALLEY**
>
> Heading up the valley from Pisco Elqui, you'll find a series of small pastoral villages: **Los Nichos**, **Horcón** and **Alcohuaz**. It'd be easy enough to hike or bike to each of these from Pisco Elqui – it's only about 14km to the upper-most village of Alcohuaz. Each town has a small lodge and many have restaurants.

ple, but they get the job done. But it's really the view of the entire valley arching down below like a velvet cape that seals the deal.

Hotel Elqui (☎ 451-130; habiles@gmail.com; O'Higgins s/n; s/d without bathroom incl breakfast CH$8000/16,000; ⚡) A good bet for solo travelers, this artless venue has simple shared bathrooms, a big thatched restaurant and creaky wooden floors. There are three pools, and the set lunch (CH$2900) is good value.

El Tesoro de Elqui (☎ 451-069; www.tesoro-elqui .cl; Prat s/n; dm CH$8500, d without bathroom incl breakfast CH$30,000, cabañas CH$40,000; P ⚡) Up the hill from the center plaza, this is Elqui's most romantic spot – a tranquil oasis dotted with lemon trees, lush gardens and flowering vines. There is a great restaurant, too. There are only three beds in the dorm, so book ahead.

DRINKING & ENTERTAINMENT
There are a number of bars and good-vibe night spots on Prat.

La Escuela (Cnr Arturo Prat & Callejón Baquedano; sandwiches CH$2000-3000; ☉ noon-late) Sandwich shop by day, hip hangout by night, La Escuela has a great open-air back patio.

Mi Elqui (Manuel Rodriguez s/n; ☉ 7pm-late) This restaurant and bar serves up homemade chocolates and fresh juices. At night, it has fires, live music and good vibes. It's half a block south of the plaza. Neighboring Kakán is also recommended.

Paso del Agua Negra
A spectacular roller coaster of a road crosses the mountains into Argentina, 185km east of Vicuña. At an ear-popping 4765m above sea level, it's one of the highest Andean passes between Chile and Argentina. It's also one of the best areas to see the frozen snow formations known as *penitentes,* so called because they resemble lines of monks garbed in tunics.

There are also accessible glaciers on both the Chilean and Argentinean sides.

From Vicuña, Ruta 41 climbs the Valle de Turbio to the Chilean customs and immigration post at Juntas del Toro. It continues south along the Río de La Laguna before switchbacking steeply northeast to Agua Negra. The road leads to the hot-springs resort of Termas de Pismanta in Argentina, and to the provincial capital San Juan.

Once mined by the Argentine military during tensions over the Beagle Channel in 1978, the route is usually open to vehicular traffic from mid-November to mid-March or April, and cyclists enjoy the challenge of this steep, difficult route. The road is passable for any passenger vehicle in good condition.

OVALLE

☎ 053 / pop 101,320

This unassuming market town is more famous for its surrounding attractions than its own modest charms, which include an artifact-heavy museum and an animated plaza where men huddle over chess games and stalls peddle colorful trinkets. Founded as a satellite of La Serena in early republican times, Ovalle is the capital of the prosperous agricultural province of Limarí; so it's unsurprising that it also has the liveliest market, Ferio Modelo de Ovalle, in the region. A walk up the hill north of town is worthwhile.

Orientation

Ovalle sits on the north bank of the Río Limarí, 86km south of La Serena and 30km east of the Panamericana. Everything of interest is within walking distance of the Plaza de Armas. At the time of research work was underway to create a pedestrian mall from the main plaza along Vicuña Mackenna. Ferio Modelo de Ovalle is east of town in the former repair facilities of the railroad.

Information

There are ATMs around the plaza.

Entel (Vicuña Mackenna 115; ☼ 9am-10pm) For long-distance calls.

Hospital Dr Antonio Tirado (☎ 620-042; cnr Ariztía Poniente & Socos; ☼ 24hr)

Post office (Vicuña Mackenna; ☼ 8:30am-6pm Mon-Fri, 9am-12:30pm Sat)

Punto.net (☎ 623-432; Vicuña Mackenna 153; per hr CH$500; ☼ 10am-midnight) Has internet access and telephones.

Tourist kiosk (Benavente) In Parque Alameda; offers minimal information.

Tres Valles Turismo (☎ 620-649; cnr Carmen & Libertad; ☼ 9am-2pm & 4-7:30pm) It's better to change money in a larger town, but try here for exchanging US dollars in cash.

Sights

Housed in the right flank of the grand old train station building, the sparsely labeled **Museo del Limarí** (☎ 433-680; museolimari@adsl.tie.cl; cnr Covarrubias & Antofagasta; adult/child CH$600/300; ☼ 9am-6pm Tue-Fri, 10am-1pm Sat & Sun) houses a beautiful selection of ceramics, the majority of which are Diaguita, dating from around AD 1000 to AD 1500, and changing modern-art exhibits. There are also pieces from the earlier Huentelauquén and El Molle cultures.

Sleeping & Eating

Hotel Roxy (☎ 620-080; Libertad 155; s/d/tr CH$7000/9300/11,700, without bathroom CH$5600/7500/8400) Has checkered floors, a serene sun-drenched patio and gardens dotted with lemon trees. However, hygiene can be a bit patchy and bathrooms are pokey: not so foxy, Mr Roxy.

Gran Hotel (☎ 621-084; www.granhotelovalle.cl, in Spanish; Vicuña Mackenna 210; s/d incl breakfast buffet from CH$16,900/26,900; P ⬛) Offering the best bang for your buck, the Gran has an art deco facade, an eager-to-please staff and clean rooms with thick down comforters. Nice touches like wall murals (some of which are quite sexy) and a scrumptious breakfast buffet add to the value.

Hotel Plaza Turismo (☎ 623-258; www.plazaturismo.cl, in Spanish; Vicuña Mackenna 295; s/d incl breakfast buffet from CH$35,700/45,220; P ✸) The recently renovated Plaza is Ovalle's nicest hotel, with classically styled rooms, wi-fi and a big breakfast buffet.

Club Social Arabe (☎ 620-015; Arauco 255; mains CH$3000-4000; ☼ 10am-midnight Mon-Sat, noon-4pm Sun) This delightfully airy neocolonial restaurant with a lofty atrium and deferential waiters serves excellent Middle Eastern dishes – stuffed grape leaves, summer squash or red peppers and baklava – and equally good Chilean specialties.

Feria Modelo de Ovalle (Av Benavente; ☼ 8am-4pm Mon, Wed, Fri & Sat) The town's enormous market is a hive of activity bursting with scores of different fruit and veggies.

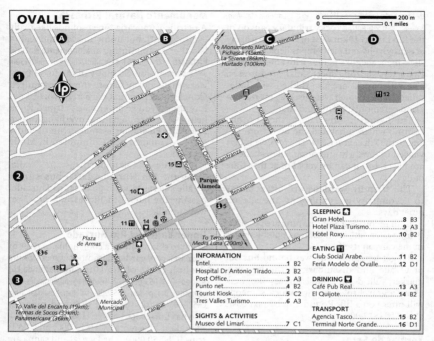

OVALLE

To Monumento Natural
Pichasca (45km);
La Serena (86km);
Hurtado (100km)

To Terminal
Media Luna (200m)

Plaza
de Armas

To Valle del Encanto (19km);
Termas de Socos (39km);
Panamericana (36km)

Mercado
Municipal

INFORMATION	
Entel.................................**1** B2
Hospital Dr Antonio Tirado......**2** B2
Post Office.........................**3** A3
Punto net..........................**4** B2
Tourist Kiosk.....................**5** C2
Tres Valles Turismo..............**6** A3

SIGHTS & ACTIVITIES	
Museo del Limarí..................**7** C1

SLEEPING	
Gran Hotel.........................**8** B3
Hotel Plaza Turismo..............**9** A3
Hotel Roxy.........................**10** B2

EATING	
Club Social Arabe.................**11** B2
Feria Modelo de Ovalle..........**12** D1

DRINKING	
Café Pub Real.....................**13** A3
El Quijote.........................**14** B2

TRANSPORT	
Agencia Tasco.....................**15** B2
Terminal Norte Grande...........**16** D1

Drinking

El Quijote (☎ 098-510-8546; Arauco 295; mains CH$2500-4500; ⏰ 9:30am-1am) This musty, character-rich bar has its walls smothered with pictures of Latin American literary and leftist heroes. Also serves up OK meals.

Café Pub Real (☎ 623-926; Vicuña MacKenna 419; ⏰ 9am-2:30am Mon-Sat) In cosmopolitan Ovalle, this cheery venue is where the cool young things knock back espressos, cold Cristal or cakes and take their turns on the pool table. Occasionally hosts live music.

Getting There & Away

Although Ovalle is 30km east of the Panamericana, many north–south buses pass through here. There are two major stations in town. The biggest is the **Terminal Media Luna** (☎ 626-612; Ariztía Oriente s/n), with service to most northern destinations and Santiago (CH$7000, five hours). **Terminal Norte Grande** (Maestranza 443) services northern destinations, including La Serena (CH$1800, 1¾ hours), Arica (CH$30,000, 25 hours), Iquique (CH$25,000, 22 hours) and Antofagasta (CH$20,000, 14

hours). Regional companies provide service to more out-of-the-way places. To get to Hurtado, look for buses at the Feria Modelo between noon and 4pm.

Faster *taxi colectivos* to La Serena (CH$2300, 1¼ hours) go with **Agencia Tacso** (Ariztía Pontiente 159; ⏰ 7am-8pm).

AROUND OVALLE

If you have your own transportation you can make a loop from La Serena to Vicuña, Hurtado and Ovalle. The 43km gravel road from Vicuña to Hurtado is usually manageable in a regular car, but a 4WD or high-clearance vehicle would be less hair-raising. The drive is through beautiful, sometimes steep, desert scenery with cacti, multicolored rocks and views of hilltop observatories. Public transportation from Ovalle goes as far as Hurtado, but there is no direct connection to Vicuña.

Valle del Encanto

An intriguing gallery of pre-Colombian rock art can be found at **Monumento Arqueológico Valle** del Encanto (admission CH$300; ☼ 8:15am-6pm May-Aug, 8am-8:30pm Sep-Apr), a rocky tributary canyon of the Río Limarí 19km west of Ovalle. An array of petroglyphs and pictographs depict dancing stick-men, alienlike figures with antennae and characters sporting spectacular headdresses. The valley rocks are also riddled with holes called *tacitas*, which were used as mortars to grind ceremonial plants and food.

The figures mostly date to the El Molle culture, which inhabited the area from the 2nd to the 7th century AD. The rock art is best viewed in the early afternoon when shadows are fewer, but it can be very hot at that time of day.

The friendly wardens are often happy to accompany guests around the site on quiet days.

Both picnicking and camping are possible. Bring water, although there is potable water in the canyon itself.

To get here, take any westbound bus out of Ovalle and disembark at the highway marker; Valle del Encanto is an easy 5km walk along a gravel road, but with luck someone will offer you a lift. Round-trip by taxi costs about CH$12,000.

Termas de Socos

After a grueling day in the desert it's blissful to sink into the steamy thermal baths or a refreshingly cool swimming pool at Termas de Socos, a tiny spring hidden 2km off the Panamericana at Km370. To really pull out the stops you can indulge in saunas, Jacuzzis and massages. Private tubs cost CH$3900 for a half-hour soak; access to the public pool also costs CH$3900 for nonguests. Spring water is bottled on site.

The high-class **Hotel Termas Socos** (☎ 053-198-2505; www.termasocos.cl, in Spanish; s/d incl breakfast & thermal bath from CH$33,300/66,800; P 🔊) is an unexpected delight. It is guarded by tall eucalyptus, surrounded by lush foliage and isolated amid arid hills. Its room rates include a piping-hot private bath.

Camping Termas de Socos (☎ 053-361-490; campsites per person CH$4000, cabins per person CH$6500; 🔊 🚿) is a pleasant gravel-and-sand campsite with its own pool and baths, though they are less swanky than those in the neighboring hotel. There's only partial shade but it has a good games room and playground. Nonguests can use the pool or take a bath for CH$3000, and bikes are available for CH$1200 per hour.

Monumento Natural Pichasca

A petrified araucaria forest sounds like really exciting stuff, but unfortunately the reality is rather disappointing at **Monumento Natural Pichasca** (☎ 051-261-410; adult/child CH$1600/1500; ☼ 8:30am-4:30pm). So many of the fossil trees were carted away before the area acquired Conaf protection that it's barely worth a detour unless you've never seen petrified wood before. Also here, a natural overhang known as **Casa de Piedra** has a smattering of badly smoke-damaged pre-Columbian El Molle rock art.

The site is 45km northeast of Ovalle, along the Río Hurtado. Local buses from Ovalle's Feria Modelo go as far as Hurtado, passing the lateral to Pichasca, a hot 3km walk uphill.

Upper Valle del Río Hurtado

Want to skinny dip in a cool highland river or doze in a cool garden hammock? Overlooking the lush banks of Río Hurtado, **Hacienda Los Andes** (☎ 053-691-822; www.haciendalosandes.com; campsites per person CH$3000, s/d incl breakfast from CH$27,000/39,400) offers all that and more. It also has horseback trips (CH$60,000 per day), mountain-bike rental (CH$14,000) and 4WD trips (CH$50,000). The Jacuzzi and sauna are available for guests only – but even campers get to use the facilities.

To get here, take one of the afternoon buses from Ovalle to Hurtado (CH$1500, between noon and 4pm); return buses leave early morning only (around 7am). The hacienda is 6km before Hurtado, just before the bridge. It can provide a pick-up service from Ovalle and Vicuña (per person CH$23,000) or La Serena (CH$40,000). The hacienda is 46km from Vicuña via a gravel mountain road, and 97km from Ovalle (the road is paved as far as Samo Alto).

In nearby Hurtado, shady **Restaurant Rio del Sol** (☎ 053-691-841; set lunch CH$1800, mains CH$2000-3000; ☼ breakfast, lunch & dinner Mon-Sat) is a cheap, friendly place, with freshly prepared *comida típica* (typical meals) and a cute terrace overhung with greenery.

There are scant but cheaper accommodation options in Hurtado. Try **Tambo del Limarí** (☎ contact Orieta Gonzalez 053-691-854; Caupolicán 027; s/d without bathroom incl breakfast CH$6000/18,000), which has a handful of immaculate rooms decorated with iron bedstands and light comforters above the *dueña's* (female owner's) home.

PARQUE NACIONAL FRAY JORGE

The last thing you'd expect to stumble across in a cactus-riddled semidesert would be lush cloud forest of the type found around Valdivia, 1205km south. But that's exactly what you'll find at **Parque Nacional Fray Jorge** (adult/child CH$1600/600; 9am-5pm, day-use only), a smear of green squeezed between the ocean and the desert.

The puzzle of how this pocket of verdant Valdivian cloud forest comes to exist in this parched environment is answered by the daily blanket of moist *camanchaca* that rolls in from the Pacific Ocean. Come around noon and you'll witness this white cushion of clouds cloaking the sea and progressively swallowing the forest's base, giving the impression that you could be on top of the world – when you're only really 600m above the sea. That said, the best time to appreciate the forest's ecology is early morning, when condensation from the fog leaves the plants dripping with moisture.

Patches of green inland suggest that the forest was once far more extensive. Of Fray Jorge's 100 sq km, there remain only 400 hectares of its truly unique vegetation – enough, though, to make it a Unesco World Biosphere Reserve. Some scientists believe this relict vegetation is evidence of dramatic climate change, but others argue that humans are responsible for the forest's destruction, using it for fuel, farming and timber.

The park is named after the first recorded European visitor, a Franciscan priest named Fray Jorge, in 1672.

Wildlife

The effect of the ocean fog is most pronounced at elevations above 450m; here there are cool stands of olivillo (*Aetoxicon punctatum*), arrayán (myrtle; *Myrceugenia correaeifolia*) and canelo (*Drimys winteri*), plus countless other shrubs and epiphytes.

Scant mammals include skunks and sea otters, as well as two species of fox (*Dusicyon culpaeus* and *D griseus*), the larger of which can often be spotted in the park's picnic area waiting to snaffle stray sandwiches. There are also some 80 bird species; small hawks sit atop the cacti while eagles wheel high above in search of prey.

Information

Fray Jorge's gated road may be locked outside opening hours. The Centro de Información has piecemeal displays about 1km past the entrance; admission is paid here. The park is only open for day use.

Activities

In late afternoon the rising *camanchaca* moistens the dense vegetation at **Sendero El Bosque**, a 1km trail that runs along the ridge above the ocean. The trail is at the end of the road from the Panamericana, 7km from El Arrayancito campground. The last segment of the road is very steep, rough and dusty.

With prior permission from Conaf in La Serena (p245), it's possible to walk down the fire trail from the ridge to the coast. Three kilometers from the Centro de Información is the park Administración, a historic building that was once the *casco* (big house) for a local hacienda. From there it's possible to walk 15km to a beach *refugio*, again with prior permission from Conaf in La Serena.

Getting There & Away

Take a westward lateral off the Panamericana, about 20km north of the Ovalle junction. There's no public transportation but several agencies in La Serena and Ovalle offer tours.

LOS VILOS

☎ 053 / pop 19,513

Touristy restaurants rub shoulders with ramshackle cabins in the blue-collar beach resort of Los Vilos, which sits midway between Santiago and La Serena. In the peak summer season up to 20,000 visitors jam the town. The focal point for all the action is the grayish-brown beach.

Orientation

The main road, Av Costanera, leads to the beach and is more of a focus of activity than the Plaza de Armas. You will find most hotels and restaurants along Av Caupolicán, which links the town with the Panamericana.

Information

Change money in Santiago or La Serena. Internet cafés are plentiful along Av Caupolicán. There is a tourist info booth on the east side of the beach.

Sights & Activities

Santuario de la Naturaleza Laguna Conchalí (☎ 02-798-3000; admission free), 3km north of Los Vilos and near the Puerto Punta Chungo, is a protected stretch of coastal wetland and sand dunes rich in birdlife.

For a peek at the Los Vilos art scene, check out the **Bodegón Cultural** (☎ 542-581; Calle Elicura 135; admission free; 🕑 10am-2pm & 5-7pm Tue-Sat, 10am-2pm Sun), which has changing exhibitions housed in a beautifully restored customshouse, and supports arts initiatives throughout the town.

In summer local launches ferry travelers from the dock to seabird colonies on Isla de Huevos (CH$1500 per person, 25-minute roundtrip) and the 1400-strong sea-lion colony of Isla de Lobos (around CH$5000 per person, two hours, available only December through March).

Festivals & Events

The town's best annual knees-up, **Semana Vileña** (Vilos Week), is held in the second week of February.

Sleeping

Hostal El Conquistador (☎ 541-663; joaquin.vidal@gmail .com; Av Caupolicán 210; s/d/tr/q incl breakfast CH$15,000/ 25,000/30,000/48,000) This cheerful B&B is just a short hop from the dock and the picturesquely decaying old pier. The rooms are spacious bungalows spread around a flowery patio. Laundry and heating are available.

Lord Willow (☎ 541-037; www.turlosvilos.com; Calle Hostería 1444; s/d/tr CH$18,000/24,000/25,000; 🖭) According to local legend, the name Los Vilos is a corruption of Lord Willow, a British privateer that shipwrecked nearby. This one-storey hotel continues its nautical theme with a chunky anchor and swashbuckling swords. It overlooks the sea from a hillside and has an attached restaurant and bar.

Eating

Sunday mornings see the lively Caleta San Pedro fish market selling live crab and other scrumptious seafood. Beachfront restaurants close to the beach are also cheap and good.

Módulos Gastronómicas (Food Huts; Av Costanera) These huts line the tip of the headland a short stroll west of the center. The multitasking *señoras* somehow manage to dash in and out to wave down passing cars, dish up tasty fresh fish and attend to customers simultaneously.

La Bodeguita (☎ 098-297-5292; Av Caupolicán 200; 🕑 10am-10pm, sometimes closes during the winter) This is the place to go in high season, when the outdoor patio brims with life and most nights an old movie is played. The Italian eats are also recommended.

Getting There & Away

Turbus has a terminal at Av Caupolicán 898, and just down the street is the Pullman office Av Caupolicán 1111. Both offer services to most major cities, including Santiago (CH$6000, three hours) and La Serena (CH$5700, four hours).

Sur Chico

Whether you're arriving from the south, the north or even Argentina, the commencement of the Chilean south, here in the regions of La Araucanía, Los Ríos and the Lakes District, will jar you with its menacing ice-topped volcanoes; its glacial lakes that look like melted Chinese jade; and the roaring rivers running through old-growth forests and villages inhabited by the indomitable Mapuche people. Though not as rugged or as challenging as Patagonia – call it Patagonia Lite – it is home to seven of Chile's stunning national parks. The region's one of the safest places to travel in Latin America. Though petty crime is increasing in the cities, you're more likely to damage yourself partaking in the near-endless outdoor challenges that beckon the adventurous spirit here – be it hiking, skiing, kayaking, horseback riding, rafting, canyoning and canopying – than fall victim to tourist scams or pickpockets. To recover, there are luxurious lakeside retreats, hot springs, beaches and the region's excellent artisanal beers to quaff.

Growing workhorse cities like Temuco, Valdivia, Osorno and Puerto Montt aren't much to look at, and are mainly transportation hubs that sprawl outwards in a mesh of haphazard concrete architecture. The true beauty of the region is in the hamlets that line the lakes and mountains and in the assorted national parks and nature reserves such as Parque Nacional Vicente Pérez Rosales, where the perfect conical Volcán Osorno stands sentinel over the entire area, a true sign that one has arrived in the south. Despite tourism's firm grip on the area, there are still wonderfully unexplored areas like the Río Puelo Valley and Cochamo that have yet to be tapped by the masses and still offer an authentic local experience.

HIGHLIGHTS

- Hike the otherworldly ash-shroud desert-scape around Crater Navidad in **Reserva Nacional Malalcahuello-Nalcas** (p274)

- Immerse yourself in Mapuche culture on an *etnoturismo* jaunt in **Melipeuco** (p275) or **Curarrehue** (p287)

- Push your adrenaline to the limits every day of the week in **Pucón** (p278)

- Glaciate down **Volcán Villarrica** (p284) after conquering the summit and peering down into its fiery crater

- Jump, ride and slide through spectacular cut gorges on the Río Blanco on a canyoning excursion near **Puerto Varas** (p302)

★ Reserva Nacional Malalcahuello - Nalces

Melipeuco ★

Pucón ★
Volcán ★ ★ Curarrehue
Villarrica

★ Valdivia

Puerto ★
Varas

- POPULATION: 900,797 ■ AREA: 42.108 SQ KM ■ ELEVATION: 0-3000 M

SUR CHICO

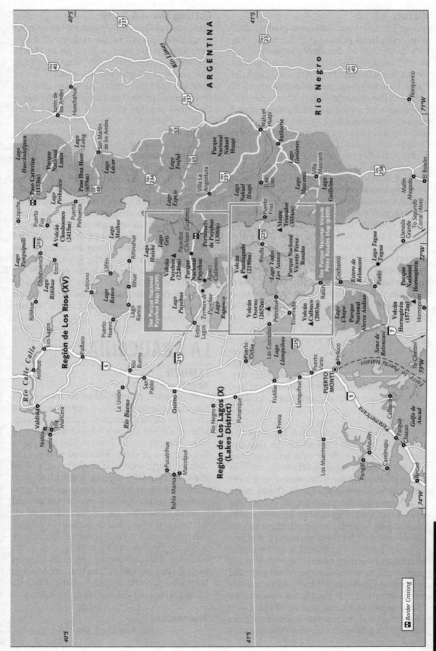

History

As the Spanish conquistadores pushed their way south from present-day Santiago, they were motivated by stories of precious metals and the possibility of a large, docile indigenous workforce. The land of La Araucanía and the Lakes District would be the ideal territory to continue the imperial dream. Or maybe not. The Mapuche waged one of the fiercest and most successful defenses against the European invaders anywhere in the Americas, and the Spanish were not able to settle south of the Río Biobío until the mid to late 19th century.

Germans were recruited to settle the Lakes District, leaving their mark on architecture, food, manufacturing and dairy farming. Today, millions of national and international tourists, plus wealthy Santiago refugees looking for country homes, are doing more than anybody to continue to tame and colonize the once wild lands. Real-estate prices are skyrocketing and the several hundred thousand remaining Mapuche are being pushed further and further into the countryside. Tourism, logging and salmon farming (and more salmon farming still) are driving the future of this beautiful region.

In 2007, the Lakes District was subdivided and Chile's 14th region, Los Ríos, was created with Valdivia as its capital, returning to the city the power it had held up until 1974, when the military junta deemed it second-class during a regional restructuring and stripped it of its designation as an administrative capital.

Climate

Pablo Neruda once wrote that his native La Araucanía was 'the land where the rain was born' where 'threads of rain fell, like long needles of glass snapping off on the roofs or coming up against the windows in transparent waves.' It is here that the Pacific Ocean storm clouds get backed up against the Andes and drop their watery cargo for days or sometimes weeks on end. Fortunately these storms do subside and let forth periods of glorious sunlight. January and February are by far the clearest and warmest months (though you still may need long pants at night), while June and July are the wettest, coldest and frequently windiest months. It does get a touch more chilly in the southern section of the Lakes District, but it makes newspaper headlines when Puerto Montt or Puerto Varas get even one inch of snow.

Getting There & Away

Most visitors enter this region by bus or train from Santiago. All of the major cities also have airports. By the time you get to Puerto Montt you are pretty far from Santiago and the short flight will save you a lot of time on the bus. Puerto Montt is also the ferry terminus for the Patagonian ferries – the most popular of which takes travelers back and forth to Puerto Natales (see boxed text, p319).

Getting Around

La Araucanía, Los Ríos and the Lakes District has an excellent network of buses: big buses, minibuses, vans, minivans and pretty much anything else that you can imagine. Bus transportation is the easiest and most low-maintenance way to get around. To get to some of the smaller and more remote towns, it may be necessary to backtrack to the closest city in order to find the correct bus. The roads are generally accessible for rental cars. There are taxis and occasionally *colectivos* (shared taxis) within all of the larger towns that cannot be covered on foot.

LA ARAUCANÍA

TEMUCO

☎ 045 / pop 259,102

With its leafy, palm-filled plaza, its pleasant Mercado Municipal and its intrinsic link to Mapuche culture, Temuco is the most palatable of all Sur Chico's blue-collar cities to visit. The city is the former home of Pablo Neruda, one of most influential poets of the 20th century, who once called it the Wild West. It is also the regional transit hub, with steady transportation to Santiago and connections to everywhere in Sur Chico and beyond. Temuco does not have a lot of attractions in itself, but it does have affordable prices and gives a sense of the culture in the region that can't always be seen in the sanitized-for-your-protection tourist towns such as Pucón. Often, you'll stumble upon Mapuche protests in front of the city hall, adding a dose of defiant color to the city.

Orientation

On the north bank of the Río Cautín, Temuco is 675km south of Santiago via the

Panamericana. To the north of town, historic Cerro Ñielol overlooks the city and the river. Residential west Temuco is a more relaxed area of the city with upscale restaurants.

Information

ATMs and exchange houses are plentiful all around Plaza de Armas Aníbal Pinto.

Conaf (☎ 298-100; Bilbao 931, 2nd fl) Mainly administrative offices, but has maps of the regional parks in the adjacent building (Pasilla D, 2nd floor).

Hospital Hernán Henríquez Aravena (☎ 212-525; Manuel Montt 115; ☯ 24hr) Six blocks west and one block north of Plaza de Armas Aníbal Pinto.

Lavasec Center (☎ 234-436; Manuel Montt 250; per load CH$2500; ☯ 9am-7:30pm Mon-Sat)

PC Montt (cnr Lynch & Manuel Montt; per hr CH$400; ☯ 24hr) Internet access.

Post office (cnr Diego Portales & Prat)

Sernatur (☎ 312-857; cnr Claro Solar & Bulnes; ☯ 8:30am-8:30pm Mon-Sat, 10am-2pm Sat Dec-Feb, 9am-2pm & 3-5:30pm Mon-Thu, 9am-2pm & 3-4:30pm Fri Mar-Nov) Facing the Plaza de Armas Aníbal Pinto.

Tourist kiosk (☎ 216-360; Mercado Municipal; ☯ 8am-7pm Tue-Sat, 8:30am-4pm Sun Mar-Nov, 8am-8pm Tue-Sat, 8:30am-4pm Sun Dec-Feb) A second Sernatur branch.

Dangers & Annoyances

Petty thievery is more of a problem in Temuco than in other towns, so keep an eye out, particularly for pickpockets at the Mercado Municipal, Feria Libre – anywhere in the center, really. There have been reports of light crime such as snatch-and-grab thievery on the hike up to Cerro Ñielol. While this shouldn't discourage you from taking the hike, it is always smart to go with at least one other person.

Sights

MONUMENTO NATURAL CERRO ÑIELOL

Cerro Ñielol (☎ 298-222; Calle Prat; adult/child CH$1000/500; ☯ 8:30am-10:30pm) is a hill that sits among some 90 hectares of native forest – a little forested oasis in the city. Chile's national flower, the copihue (Lapageria rosea), grows here in abundance, flowering from March to July. Cerro Ñielol is also of historical importance, since it was here in 1881, at the tree-shaded site known as La Patagua, that Mapuche leaders ceded land to the colonists to found Temuco. Whether or not the actual papers were signed on the hill is up for debate. The park has picnic sites, a small lagoon, footpaths and an environmental information center. Take bus 1 from the centro to get to the entrance.

MUSEO REGIONAL DE LA ARAUCANÍA

Housed in a handsome frontier-style building dating from 1924, this regional **museum** (☎ 747-948; Av Alemania 084; ☯ 10am-5:30pm Mon-Fri, 11am-5pm Sat, 11am-2pm Sun) normally has permanent exhibits recounting the history of the Araucanían peoples before, during and since the Spanish invasion, but the majority of the exhibits save the Mapuche pottery have been closed for renovations for several years. It's due to re-open in late 2008; look out for the massive Mapuche canoe, said to run the length of the entire museum.

Buses 1, 9 and 7 run along Av Alemania, but the route is also reasonable walking distance from the centro.

Sleeping

Temuco is not fundamentally a tourist town, and therefore it can be a bit tricky to find a good place to sleep. Budget options around the train station and Feria Libre are inexpensive and downright dirty. The neighborhood between the Plaza de Armas and the university has higher-quality budget options and is more secure at night for women. Budget places rarely include breakfast in the price. Midrange and top-end hotels usually cater to Chilean business people and are more functional than inviting.

BUDGET & MIDRANGE

Hospedaje Tribu Piren (☎ 985-711; www.tribupiren.cl, in Spanish; Prat 69; r per person CH$7000; ℗ ✗ 🖳) The young English-speaking owner at this newer hospedaje (budget accommodation) makes this a great choice for foreigners. Everything is clean, and rooms, some which open out onto a small terrace, offer wi-fi and cable TV. Alvaro, the owner, also guides snowsport tours in the winter. This was also the only budget option in the entirety of Sur Chico from which we didn't have to pry a bath towel.

Hospedaje Klickmann (☎ 748-292; claudiz_7@hotmail.com; Claro Solar 647; r per person with/without bathroom CH$13,000/9800; ℗) This clean and friendly hospedaje is barely a hiccup from several bus companies. Rooms, some holding up to five people, are colorful and well lit, as is the sky-lit terrace on the second floor.

Hostal Austria (☎ 247-169; www.hostalaustria.cl; Hochstetter 599; s/d CH$15,400/23,500, without bathroom

SUR CHICO

TEMUCO

INFORMATION			
Conaf		1	E1
Hospital Hernán Henríquez			
Aravena		2	C2
Lavasec Center		3	C3
PC Montt		4	D3
Post Office		5	E3
Sernatur		6	E3
Tourist kiosk		7	E2

SIGHTS & ACTIVITIES			
Monumento Natural Cerro			
Ñielol		8	D1
Museo Regional de la Araucanía		9	C2

SLEEPING			
Hospedaje Klickmann		10	D3
Hospedaje Tribu Piren		11	E2
Hostal Austria		12	A2
Hotel Don Eduardo		13	D3
Hotel Panamericana Temuco		14	E1

EATING			
Cassis		15	A2
Gohan Sushi		16	D3
Las Tranqueras		17	A2
Luna China		18	B2
Pizería Madonna		19	A2
Tradiciones Zuny		20	F1

SHOPPING			
Feria Libre		21	F2
Mercado Municipal		22	E3

TRANSPORT			
Air Comet		23	E3
Avis		24	D4
Budget		25	D2
Buses Biobío		26	E2
Buses JAC		27	E2
Cruz del Sur		28	D3
Cruz del Sur Office		29	C3
Igi Llaima		(see 31)	
Lan		30	E3
Nar-Bus		31	E2
Nar-Bus		32	F2
Pullman Bus		33	D3
Sky Airlines		34	E3
Terminal de Buses Rurales		35	F2
Tur-Bus		36	D3

To Terminal Rodoviario (400m);
Santiago (677km)

To Aeropuerto
Maquehue (6km);
Fundación Chol-Chol (16km);
Valdivia (762km)

To Adela y Helmut (48km);
Melipeuco (92km);
Parque Nacional
Conguillío (104km)

Cerro Ñielol

Cemetery

Universidad Católica

Plaza de Armas

Plaza Teniente Dagoberto Godoy

Plaza Manuel Recabarren

0 500 m
0 0.3 miles

CH$10,500/13,000; ✕) In a quaint wooden house near some of Temuco's best restaurants, this hostel is a step above the average and is full of homey touches like myriad antique rugs and old-time furniture.

Adela y Helmut (☎ 582-230; www.adelayhelmut .cl; Faja 16,000 Km5 N; dm CH$5050, s/d from CH$16,800/ 21,850; **P**) If a gritty, working-class city isn't your thing, but you're stuck in the area, make your way out to this backpacker favorite on a small farm 48km out of town on the road to Parque Nacional Conguillío. Solar-heated water, small kitchens in every room and outstanding views to still-smoldering Volcán Llaima are highlights, as are the Suabian treats from the kitchen such as *Hefezopf* sweetbread. They also rent bikes and offer horseback riding.

TOP END

Hotel Don Eduardo (☎ 214-133; www.hoteldoneduardo .cl, in Spanish; Andrés Bello 755; r from CH$43,000; **P** 🖳) The equestrian-themed Don Eduardo is a solid choice in reasonable shape offering clean rooms, attentive service and springy mattresses. They also offer day-use rooms for CH$25,000 (7am to 6pm).

Hotel Panamericana Temuco (☎ 239-999; www.panamericanahoteles.cl; Prat 220; s/d CH$71,000/ 75,000; **P** 🖳 🐾) Temuco's swankiest – that's used lightly – hotel suffers from a bad case of poor location complicated by Chain Hotel Syndrome. There's simply nothing remarkable about it. Rooms are cheerier than the lobby, with flat-screen TVs and bright bedspreads, and all the services are here, but it's startlingly unmemorable.

Eating

Most of the choice restaurants and bars are along Av Alemania on Temuco's west side.

Cassis (☎ 210-902; Mall Portal Temuco, 2nd fl; ☾ lunch & dinner) It's worth hitting the mall for the Temuco installment of this Pucón mainstay that offers decadent chocolate and excellent coffee, served here in Patagonian ceramics.

Tradiciones Zuny (Tucapel 1374; meals CH$2000; ☾ lunch Mon-Sat) Temuco's best-kept secret is an underground local's haunt specializing in the fresh, simple food of the countryside served out of an indigenous-themed home. There's no menu – a typical meal here might include salad, beef *cazuela* (stew), pumpkin and quinoa, plus whole-wheat *sopaipillas* (traditional fried dough),

bread and avocado juice (try it!), all for around CH$2000. You're welcome.

Gohan Sushi (☎ 731-110; Av Vicuña MacKenna 530; rolls CH$2300-3600; ☾ lunch & dinner) This trendy sushi spot offers some innovative rolls (shrimp *pil-pil*, avocado and onions) and a soundtrack to get your hips shaking. The two Happy Hour pisco sours for CH$1700 make for a nice chaser. If you stay within these walls, Temuco suddenly starts to feel a little *Temucool*. Prices are discounted at lunch.

Luna China (☎ 273-177; Av Alemania 304; mains CH$2800-7000; ☾ lunch & dinner) This bi-level 'Cantonese' restaurant in an elegant residence on Alemania does a shockingly good Mongolian beef (not Cantonese) and other Chinese specialties such as Peking Duck (not Cantonese) amid Bruce Lee lookalike statuettes and typically beige decor. Someone actually returned to ask how everything was a few minutes after delivering the starter – a miracle in Sur Chico.

Las Tranqueras (☎ 385-046; Alemania 888; mains CH$3200-8000; ☾ lunch & dinner Mon-Sat, lunch Sun) This somewhat exotic, white-tableclothed steakhouse serves goat, wild boar and rabbit, but nothing outsells the perfectly seasoned rib eye, a real treat. There's a loaded wine list as well.

Pizzería Madonna (☎ 329-393; Av Alemania 660; pizzas CH$3800-8500, pasta CH$5200-5600; ☾ noon-4pm & 7pm-midnight) Temuco's top choice for pizza and pasta is a bustling (especially on Sunday) checker-tableclothed spot full of character and classy waitresses. The specialty is Tricotta (ravioli three ways) and there's a to-die-for tiramisu. Grab a pizza to go for a 20% discount.

The cheapest eats can be had at the dynamic Feria Libre, where vendors churn out *cazuelas*, *sopaipillas con queso*, empanadas, seafood stews and other tasty dishes. This cultural slice and dice shouldn't cost more than CH$2000.

Shopping

Temuco is good spot to shop for Mapuche woolen goods (ponchos, blankets and pullovers), pottery and musical instruments, such as *zampoñas* (panpipes) or drums. The Mercado Municipal has the most items in one place, along with a fair amount of kitschy tourist goods and other junk.

Fundación Chol-Chol (☎ 614-007; Camino Temuco a Imperial Km16; ☾ 9am-6pm Mon-Fri) Unfortunately, the best and most responsible spot to buy

A WAR FOR LIFE

Chile's largest indigenous group, the Mapuche (che meaning 'people' and mapu meaning 'of the land'), is unique in the Americas as the first and only indigenous nation on the continent whose sovereignty and independence was legally recognized, but they have exhausted generations in fighting to keep it that way.

The Mapuche, born of modern-day La Araucanía, first successfully fought off the marauding Inka empire, only to take on a sustained 300-year attack by the Spanish empire and, to this day, the Chilean state. The Mapuche used the Río Biobío as a natural frontier against the intruders and resisted colonization until the 19th century. It was the longest and hardest-fought indigenous defense in the Americas. By its end, the nation's once vast territory of 100,000 sq km was reduced to a mere 5000 sq km of communal reducciones (settlements).

Despite signing the Treaty of Killin with the colonizing Spaniards in 1641 (the document solidified the territorial autonomy of the Mapuche and 28 others over two centuries of diplomatic relations), the Mapuche remained, and still remain, under threat of physical and cultural extinction. In the late 1800s, 100,000 Mapuche were massacred by the Chilean and Argentine military.

From 1965 to 1973 land reform improved the situation for the Mapuche, but the military coup of 1973 reversed many of these gains. Between the restoration of democracy in 1989 and 2009, the Mapuche people made limited progress in their continuing fight for reparations and the return of their lands although most of the court rulings granting them land were effectively overturned by powerful business interests.

These days, due to overcrowding and population growth of the dominant Chilean society, the majority of the Mapuche now live in large urban centers. Those that have steadfastly remained in their historical ancestral territory (known as Wallmapu) are organized into four geographical regions (Meli wixan-mapu). Each wixan-mapu is made up of aylla rewe (eight districts), which, in turn, are made up of communities known as lof.

Various human rights organizations, as well as the Special Rapporteur of the UN, have widely reported the imposition of assimilation policies and protests in Temuco are nearly a daily affair. Even tourists, filmmakers and foreign journalists aren't immune: it's not uncommon for people to be harassed by police after being seen among Mapuche communities where there exist ongoing land-dispute conflicts, and two French filmmakers were arrested in March 2008 for talking to a Mapuche leader.

Deprived of most of their ancestral lands, the Mapuche now earn a precarious livelihood from agriculture and handicrafts. Still, they soldier on, managing to preserve their traditional language (Mapudungun, the 'language of the land'), their religion and their socio-political structure. Whether they will win the ongoing war of freedom and independence from the greater country at large remains the question.

Mapuche gear is 16km out of town. This nonprofit, Fair Trade organization works with 600 rural Mapuche women to offer top-quality weavings and textiles made entirely by hand. Throw rugs, wall hangings, bags, shawls – nothing is cheap, everything is simply gorgeous. To get here, take any bus towards the towns of Nueva Imperial, Carahue or Puerto Saavedra from the rural bus terminal and ask to be let off at the Fundación. If you can't make it, a few of their wares are available at the gift shop in the museum.

Mercado Municipal (☎ 973-345; ☽ 8am-7pm Mon-Sat, 8:30am-4pm Sun Mar-Nov, 8am-8pm Mon-Sat, 8:30am-4pm Sun Dec-Feb) Temuco's excellent market caters mainly to tourists looking to dine and shop in touristy comfort, away from the street chaos. The quality of the artisanship varies quite substantially, but there are still some excellent items to be found among the stalls. For woolens, try No 88; for jewelry No 97; and for musical instruments, No 40.

Feria Libre (Barros Arana; ☽ 8am-5pm) is a colorful Mapuche produce market taking up several blocks along Barros Arana. Along the streets more practical wares are sold, while in the Feria itself vendors hawk everything from apples and artisan cheeses to honey and bags of merquén pepper. There is also a fair amount of vibrant hot peppers, though it's unclear who buys them, as the cuisine in Chile is far from spicy.

Getting There & Away

AIR

Aeropuerto Maquehue is located 6km south of town, just west off the Panamericana. **Lan** (☎ 600-526-2000; www.lan.com; Bulnes 687; ☼ 9am-1:30pm & 3-6:30pm) flies to Santiago (from CH$139,900) and has on-again, off-again Saturday flights to Puerto Montt. **Sky Airlines** (☎ 747-300; www.skyairline.cl; Bulnes 677; ☼ 9am-2pm & 3-7:30pm Mon-Fri, 9:30am-1:30pm Sat) flies for considerably less one way to Santiago (from CH$33,300) and Concepción (from CH$14,000). **Air Comet** (☎ 405-000; www.air comet.com; Bulnes 667; ☼ 9am-1:30pm & 3-6:30pm Mon-Fri, 10am-1:30pm Sat) flies daily to Concepción (CH$12,200) with connections to the rest of Chile.

BUS

Temuco is a major bus hub. Long-haul buses run from the **Terminal Rodoviario** (☎ 225-005; Pérez Rosales 1609), at the northern approach to town. Companies have ticket offices around downtown. Times and frequencies vary throughout the year, with fewer buses in winter.

Bus lines serving main cities along the Panamericana include **Tur-Bus** (☎ 278-161; cnr Lagos & Manuel Montt) and **Pullman Bus** (☎ 212-137; Claro Solar 611), both of which offer frequent services to Santiago; **Cruz del Sur** (☎ 730-320; Claro Solar 599, Manuel Montt 290), which also serves the island of Chiloé and Bariloche via Osorno; and **Igi Llaima/Nar-Bus** (☎ 407-777; Miraflores 1535), which also heads over to Argentina. The **Terminal de Buses Rurales** (☎ 210-494; Av Aníbal Pinto 32) serves local and regional destinations. Huincabus goes to Chol Chol every hour (CH$550, 45 minutes), while Nar-Bus goes to Melipeuco (CH$1300, two hours) six times daily and Victoria every 30 minutes, though the latter runs from its station, which is situated on Balmaceda.

Buses JAC (☎ 465-465; cnr Av Balmaceda & Aldunate), with its own terminal, offers the most frequent service to Villarrica and Pucón, plus services to Santiago, Lican Ray and Coñaripe.

Buses Biobío (☎ 465-351; Lautaro 854) operates frequent services to Angol, Los Angeles, Concepción, Curacautín, as well as Lonquimay.

Sample travel times and costs are as follows (prices fluctuate with the quality of the bus):

Destination	Cost (CH$)	Duration (hr)
Angol	CH$3000	1
Chillán	CH$5500	4
Coñaripe	CH$2300	2½
Concepción	CH$4000	5
Curacautín	CH$2400	2
Osorno	CH$3500	4
Pucón	CH$2000	2
Puerto Montt	CH$4500	5
Santiago	CH$11,000	9
Valdivia	CH$2500	3
Valparaíso/Viña del Mar	CH$10,000	10
Villarrica	CH$1500	1½
Zapala & Neuquén (Ar)	CH$14,000	10
San Martín de Los Andes (Ar)	CH$10,000	7

TRAIN

Chile's rail system has unraveled into quite the mess. Temuco, once the end of the line of a beautiful train from Santiago, hasn't seen arrivals from the capital in over two years. During research, the only route available was Temuco–Victoria, of little interest to tourists. That's not to say the trains won't start up again – after all, the tracks are here – but for now, all that remains is the modern but, for the most part, currently useless **Estación de Ferrocarril** (☎ 233-416; www.efe.cl, in Spanish; Av Barros Arana 191), eight blocks east of Plaza de Armas Aníbal Pinto.

Getting Around

Colectivo 11P goes from downtown (Claro Solar) to the bus terminal. Taxis leaving from the east side of the Plaza de Armas Aníbal Pinto take passengers for CH$2000. For those who want to go straight to the airport, many long-haul buses coming into town can drop you at the Cruce del Aeropuerto, from where you can catch a taxi for CH$4000. Car rental is from **Budget** (☎ 232-715; cnr Diego Portales & Vicuña MacKenna) and **Avis** (☎ 237-575; San Martín 755). Both also have branches at the airport.

PARQUE NACIONAL TOLHUACA

As the early-morning mist burns off from the surrounding hill country, gaggles of parrots can sometimes be spotted lingering on the dusty road that leads to the 64-sq-km **Parque Nacional Tolhuaca** (admission adult/child CH$3000/1500) – a clear indication you're on the road less traveled. One of the park system's best-kept secrets, mainly because it's harder to get to than nearby Conguillío, Tolhuaca is located northeast of Temuco, on the north bank of the Río Malleco. The park offers trekking over elevations changes from 850m around Laguna Malleco to 1830m on the summit of Cerro Colomahuida; the 2806m Volcán Tolhuaca is beyond the park's southeast boundaries.

The park's best trip goes to **Laguna Verde** (one way two hours, 4km), reached via a trailhead about 5km east of Laguna Malleco on the road to Termas de Tolhuaca; it's named for its greenish waters and verdant circumference flanked by lush araucaria and lenga trees. The trail crosses the Río Malleco and passes several waterfalls. A shorter trip is to **Salto de Melleco** (one way one hour, 1.7km), a 49m waterfall.

Easily accessed from the eastern sector of the park and 35km north of Curacautín, the rustic **Termas de Tolhuaca** (☎ 463-921; www.termas detolhuaca.cl; Curacautín office at Manuel Rodríguez 560, Curacautín; day use adult/child CH$8000/6000) has some steaming baths in natural outdoor settings, but isn't rumored to be the cleanest termas around. Rooms at **Hotel Termas de Tolhuaca** (r CH$39,700) include full board.

You can stay at **Camping Inalaufquén** (campsites CH$5000), on the southeastern shore of Laguna Malleco. It has secluded woodsy sites, including running water, firepits, picnic tables and toilets with cold showers that could use a little elbow grease. For more information on the park or camping, contact Conaf in Temuco (p267).

Getting There & Away
There is no direct public transportation from Temuco to the park. From Victoria, buses leave every weekday for San Gregorio, from where it's a 19km walk to the campground at Laguna Malleco. The other option is a taxi from Curacautín for CH$18,000. Beyond San Gregorio the road narrows rapidly and deadfalls may be a problem after storms, but any carefully driven passenger car can pass in good weather. This would be an ideal mountain-bike route as it climbs gradually into the precordillera (foothills).

PARQUE NACIONAL CONGUILLÍO
Llaima means 'Blood Veins' in Mapudungun and that's just what tourists visiting **Parque Nacional Conguillío** (www.parquenacionalconguillio.cl, in Spanish; admission adult/child CH$4000/2000), and its towering Volcán Llaima (3125m), got on New Year's Day 2008. As the centerpiece of this Unesco Biosphere Reserve, it is one of Chile's

most active volcanoes. Since 1640, Llaima has experienced 35 violent eruptions. A recent eruption spewed fiery lava 300m into the air and created a 20km-long plume of billowing smoke that forced Chile's National Forestry Corporation (Conaf) to evacuate 43 trapped tourists and 11 of its own employees from the park. Yet another eruption in July 2008 resulted in an evacuation of an additional 40 people. In other words, this monster likes to cough up blood.

Despite the firespitting, this wonderful park, created in 1950 primarily to preserve the araucaria (monkey puzzle tree) and 608 sq km of alpine lakes, deep canyons and native forests, has reopened. The grey-brown magma that has accumulated over the years is to blame for the dramatic landscape and eerie lunarscape atmosphere.

You can access Parque Nacional Conguillío from three directions. The first, and shortest (80km), is directly east of Temuco via Vilcún and Cherquenco; this accesses the ski resorts at Sector Los Paraguas, but doesn't access (by road, anyway) the campgrounds, main visitor center and trailheads. All of those are best reached by taking the more northern route from Temuco via Curacautín (120km). The park's southern entrance, also 120km from Temuco, is accessed via Melipeuco. From here a road heads north through the park to the northern entrance, also accessing the trailheads and campgrounds.

Information
Conaf's **Centro de Información Ambiental** (Laguna Conguillío; ☾ 9am-1pm & 2:30-8:30pm) offers a variety of programs mainly in the summer (January and February), including slideshows and ecology talks, hikes to the Sierra Nevada and outings for children. Good trail maps with basic topographic information and trail descriptions are available here, as are climbing permits.

Activities
HIKING
The 2008 eruption coughed up lava to the southeast into Sector Cherquenco, sparing all of the park's designated trails. One of Chile's finest short hikes, the **Sierra Nevada trail** (one way three hours, 7km) to the base of the Sierra Nevada, leaves from the small parking lot at Playa Linda, at the east end of Laguna Conguillío. Climbing steadily northeast through dense coigüe forests, the trail

passes a pair of lake overlooks; from the second and more scenic, you can see solid stands of araucarias beginning to supplant coigües on the ridge top.

Conaf discourages all but the most experienced, well-prepared hikers from going north on the **Travesía Río Blanco** (one way five hours, 5km), an excursion detailed in Lonely Planet's *Trekking in the Patagonian Andes*.

Near the visitor's center, the **Sendero Araucarias** (45 minutes, 0.8km) meanders through a verdant rainforest. At Laguna Verde, a short trail goes to La Ensenada, a peaceful beach area. The **Cañadon Truful-Truful trail** (30 minutes, 0.8km) passes through the canyon, where the colorful strata, exposed by the rushing waters of Río Truful-Truful, are a record of Llaima's numerous eruptions. The nearby **Los Vertientes trail** (30 minutes, 0.8km) leads to an opening among rushing springs.

CLIMBING

Experienced climbers can tackle Volcán Llaima from **Sector Los Paraguas** on the west side of the park, where there is a *refugio* (rustic shelter) on the road from Cherquenco, or from Captrén on the north side – though, at the time of research, all climbing had been suspended indefinitely due to the eruption. If and when restrictions are lifted, you'll need to obtain permission from Conaf at Centro de Información Ambiental.

SKIING

The **Centro de Ski Las Araucarias** (☎ 562-313; www .skiaraucarias.cl, in Spanish; Temuco; half-/full-day lift tickets CH$12,000/15,000) at Sector Los Paraguas has just three ski runs, but is a tranquil and scenic area to enjoy a day on the slopes. Ski and snowboard rental costs CH$12,000 per day. In winter, the center has an annex office in Hotel Panamericana Temuco.

Sleeping

Conaf operates **campgrounds** (campsites CH$15,000) inside the park around the south shore of Lago Conguillío and northwest shore of Laguna Captrén.

Cabañas Conguillío (☎ 298-213; 3-/6-person cabañas CH$45,000/55,000), on the southwest end of the lake, has a restaurant and a small store (open from mid-December to early March).

La Baita (☎ 581-253; www.labaitaconguillio.cl; s/d half board CH$42,400/63,600, 4-8 person cabins per person half board CH$31,800), spaced amid pristine forest, is

an ecotourism project just outside the park's southern boundary. It's home to six attractive cabins with slow-burning furnaces, limited electricity and hot water; and an extremely cozy new lodge and restaurant with six new rooms complete with granite showers and design-forward sinks. In high season, meals, excursions and a small store are available. La Baita is 15km from Melipeuco and 60km from Curacautín.

Centro de Ski Las Araucarias has three options right on the mountain: **Apart Hotel Llaima** (q apt CH$52,700), **Refugio Pehuén** (dm CH$7695, d with/without bathroom CH$21,900/17,800) and **Refugio Los Paraguas** (dm CH$7700, ste CH$48,600). If you are here to ski take your pick from one of the three. If you are staying in the dorms, you may need to provide your own sleeping bag. Contact the ski center (left) for bookings.

Getting There & Away

To reach Sector Los Paraguas, **Vogabus** (☎ 910-134), at Temuco's Terminal de Buses Rurales, runs hourly to Cherquenco (CH$1300, one hour) from 8am to 6:30pm Monday to Saturday, from where it's a 17km walk or hitchhike to the ski lodge at Los Paraguas.

For the northern entrance at Laguna Captrén, **Buses Flota Erbuc** (☎ 272-204) has regular service to Curacautín (CH$1200, 1½ hours), from where a shuttle (CH$900) runs to the park border at Guardería Captrén in summer on Monday and Friday *only* (6am, 5pm). In winter, the bus will go as far as conditions allow. The only other option is a taxi for CH$15,000.

For the southern entrance at Truful-Truful, **Nar-Bus** (☎ 211-611) in Temuco runs six buses daily to Melipeuco (CH$1300, two hours), where the tourism office can help arrange transport to the park. Travelers who can afford to rent a car can combine these two routes in a loop trip from Temuco.

CURACAUTÍN

☎ 045 / pop 16,995

Curacautín is the northern gateway to Parque Nacional Conguillío. Although there are more services here than in Melipeuco, accommodations leave something to be desired – you'll be happier if you base yourself along the road to Lonquimay, a more central location for the area's three parks. The **tourist office** (☎ 464-858; Plaza de Armas; ⊙ 8am-6:30pm Mon-Fri, 9am-4:30pm Sat) has brochures and information on the park and accommodations in town.

If you do sleep here, **Hostal Rayén** (☎ 099-001-4421; Manuel Rodríguez 104; r without bathroom per person CH$8000) isn't the nicest or the quietest, but hospitality speaks volumes. If you want to waste a few extra pesos on nothing special, **Hotel Cordilleras del Sur** (☎ 882-242; hotelcordillerasdelsur@ yahoo.es; Yungay 315; s/d CH$11,800/20,200; P ✗) is the nicest digs in town, though it's a nightmare in winter without central heating.

The **bus terminal** (cnr Arica & Manuel Rodríguez) is directly on the highway to Lonquimay. **Buses Bío Bío** (☎ 881-123) heads to Temuco via Victoria (CH$2400, seven daily Monday to Saturday), and four times daily via Lautaro (CH$1600, Monday to Friday). **Buses Curacautín Express** (☎ 258-125) goes to Temuco all day long via Lautaro. For transportation details to Parque Nacional Conguillío, see p273. **Tur-Bus** (☎ 881-596; Serrano 101) has four direct buses per day to Santiago in summer and two in winter (CH$18,100).

RESERVA NACIONAL MALALCAHUELLO-NALCAS

The jewel of northern Araucanía's national parks, **Reserva Nacional Malalcahuello-Nalcas** (admission adult/child CH$3000/1500) is a combined reserve of 303 sq km just north of the town of Malalcahuello, en route to Lonquimay, and extends almost to the border of Parque Nacional Tolhuaca. Though off the main park circuit, Malalcahuello-Nalcas offers one of the most dramatic landscapes in all of Sur Chico, a charcoal desertscape of ash and sand that looks like the Sahara with a nicotine addiction. Though not an ambitious hike, the trek to **Cráter Navidad** (two hours, 1.5km), which last blew on Christmas Day 1988, takes in this otherworldly atmosphere – not unlike Mars with its desolate red hues reflecting off the spoils of magma and ash – and the magnificent backdrop of Volcán Lonquimay, Volcán Tolhuaca and Volcán Callaqui off in the distance. Be sure to charge up your camera batteries before coming here.

The most easily accessible trail is **Piedra Santa** (five hours, 7.5km), which is the beginning stretch of the longer Laguna Blanca trail. From Piedra Santa, **El Raleo** (two hours, 3.5km) branches off and leads through coigüe forest and introduced pine. The trail starts near the small Conaf **information center** (☎ 02-196-8514; Camino Internacional Km82) near the road to the hamlet of Malalcahuello along the highway

to Lonquimay. Wild camping is permissible along the trails.

Nalcas' western boundary abuts Volcán Tolhuaca, while Volcán Longuimay marks the division between the two reserves. In Nalcas, **Sendero Tolhuaca** (one way 24 hours, 40km) is accessible only from **Sendero Laguna Blanca** (one way two days, 40km), which traverses the western flank of Volcán Lonquimay and ends in a spectacular aquamarine lake at the foot of Volcán Tolhuaca outside the park's western boundary. Here is a great view of both volcanoes. An old logging road connects the trail west to Termas de Tolhuaca and Laguna Verde in Parque Nacional Tolhuaca (the trails may be hard to find; guides are recommended).

Malalcahuello-Nalcas is best accessed on a tour or by taxi from Curacautín (CH$10,000). The road through the parks requires a 4WD.

Just 3km south of Malalcahuello, the cleanest and most sophisticated hot springs in the area, **Termas de Malalcahuello** (☎ 197-3550; www .malalcahuello.cl, in Spanish; Ruta Biooceánica 181-CH, Km2, Malalcahuello; day use adult/child CH$10,000/6000, r from CH$108,150), has spa services and one large hot springs (in bad need of a refinishing) behind large bay windows with views to Volcán Lonquimay.

There are two great sleeping options for travelers, both on the road to Lonquimay. The Bavarian-styled **Andenrose** (☎ 099-869-1700; www.andenrose.com; Camino Internacional Km68.5; s/d CH$20,200/26,900, without bathroom CH$16,000/22,700; P ✗), on the rushing and kayakable Río Cautín, is built from organic woods and is full of exposed brick and Southern German hospitality (the enthusiastic owner is quite the firecracker). There's wonderful three-course meals (don't miss the veal goulash/spätzle pairing) and a rich breakfast. They also arrange excellent horseback riding, jeep tours and excursions in the area. The slightly more upscale **Suizandina** (☎ 197-3725; www.suizandina.com; Camino Internacional Km83; campsite per person CH$5050, dm CH$10,100, s/d from CH$21,600/28,400; P), which was founded by a young Swiss family who originally came through the area on a bicycle trip. It's spick-and-span and all rooms feature extra cozy comforters. The bathrooms for campers, located in the main house, are surely the nicest in Sur Chico. It's well stocked with wine and mini-küchens to go and the menu features Swiss specialties such as fondue. All prices include a hearty breakfast and treks in the area are organized.

Heading east of Malalcahuello the road passes through the narrow, one-way 4527m Túnel Las Raíces, a converted railway tunnel from 1930 that emerges into the drainage of the upper Biobío and has sealed its place in history as the longest tunnel in South America. The road eventually reaches 1884m Paso Pino Hachado, a border crossing that leads to the Argentine cities of Zapala and Neuquén.

MELIPEUCO

☎ 045 / pop 4980

Melipeuco, the southern gateway to Parque Nacional Conguillío, is 90km east of Temuco via Cunco. It has a helpful **tourist office** (Pedro Aguirre Cerda s/n; ☻ 9:30am-6pm Mon-Fri) and a few restaurants. If you're looking to base yourself nearer the park than Temuco, this is a good spot for day trips, though you're better off going all the way to truly absorb the otherworldly atmosphere of Conguillío.

Hospedaje Icalma (☎ 099-280-8210; Pedro Aguirre Cerda 729; s/d CH$7000/14,000; Ⓟ ✖) is a decent choice with a few basic rooms. **Hostería Huetelén** (☎ 581-203; Pedro Aguirre Cerda 1; s CH$5000, s/d incl breakfast CH$10,000/20,000; Ⓟ ✖) has reasonable accommodations with private bathrooms and heating in a modern home with a roaring fireplace. Try to avoid the older rooms in the adjacent house.

If you want to dig deeper into the indigenous cultures here, **Trafkura Expediciones** (☎ 099-9036-1013; www.trafkuraexpediciones.cl, in Spanish; Caupolicán 334; campsites incl breakfast per person CH$3000, tent with mattress per person CH$7000) offers three-day sustainable tourism immersion trips deep into Pewenche Indian land in Icalma, where you can sleep in an indigenous home. The base is a rustic *refugio* on the slope of Los Cheñes mountain (20km from Melipeuco near Puente Mapocho and just 2km from the Reserva Nacional China Muerta) with a hippie Chilean-kibbutz vibe, compostable toilets and an organic farm that accepts volunteers. Great vegetarian meals are served, including fire stews and bread cooked in the ashes of the *fogón* (campfire), which are worth the trip alone. They also organize treks to the caldera and glacier at Sollipulli. If it's up and running, their small hostel in Melipeuco has wonderful wooden bunk beds – it's above and beyond other options in town.

From Temuco's Terminal de Buses Rurales, Nar-Bus has six buses daily to Melipeuco. A taxi from Melipeuco to Parque Nacional Conguillío costs around CH$35,000 roundtrip, but the tourist office can set you up with a *flete*, a sort of makeshift local taxi, for as low as CH$4000.

VILLARRICA

☎ 045 / pop 39,727

When all the folks in Pucón collectively exhale after they reach maximum adrenaline overload, a torrent of air whips across Lago Villarrica to windswept Villarrica, otherwise known as, 'that town that we passed through on the way from Temuco to Pucón.' But Villarrica is not without some appeal of its own. It is bigger and a bit more chaotic than its touristy neighbor Pucón, but has a down-to-earth feel, more reasonable prices and a faded-resort glory that attracts travelers of a certain lax disposition. It also has more local character than Pucón, which gets packed with vacationing Santiaguinos and foreigners. If you are here in the summer and wish to spend time at the lake you will find superior beaches down the road in Pucón.

Information

Banks with ATMs are plentiful, especially near the corner of Pedro Montt and Av Pedro de Valdivia.

Banco de Chile (cnr Pedro Montt & Av Pedro de Valdivia)
Cámara de Turismo (☎ 414-174; cnr General Urrutia & Andrés Bello; ☻ 9am-8pm Mon-Sat, 10am-4pm Sun) Lists *hospedajes* and activities in the area.
Cyber Mundo (Bilbao 573; per hr CH$500; ☻ 9am-1pm & 3-7pm Mon-Fri, 9am-2pm Sun) Internet. **Hospital Villarrica** (☎ 411-169; San Martín 460; ☻ 24hr)
Oficina de Turismo (☎ 206-619; Av Pedro de Valdivia 1070; ☻ 9am-1pm & 2:30-6pm Mon-Fri) Municipal office that has helpful staff and provides many brochures.
Post office (Anfión Muñoz 315)
Todo Lavado (☎ 414-452; General Urrutia 699; per load CH$3800; ☻ 9:30am-1:30pm & 3-7pm Mon-Sat) Laundry services.

Sights & Activities

Mapuche artifacts – including jewelry, musical instruments and roughly hewn wooden masks – are the focus of the **Museo Histórico y Arqueológico** (☎ 415-706; Av Pedro de Valdivia 1050; admission free; ☻ 9am-1pm & 3-7:30pm Mon-Fri), alongside the tourist office. Gracing the grounds is a Mapuche *ruka*, oblong-shaped with thatched walls and roof, traditionally built by four men in four days under a reciprocal labor system known as *minga*. Reeds from the lake provide the thatch, which is so skillfully intertwined that water cannot penetrate even in this very damp climate.

Many of the same tours organized in Pucón can also be arranged here. Most of the local agencies are just as qualified as any in Pucón; try **Politur** (☎ 414-547; Anfión Muñoz 647; ☼ 8:30am-1:30pm & 4-9pm Mon-Sat, 8:30am-1:30pm Sun).

Festivals & Events

The annual **Muestra Cultural Mapuche**, in January and February, has exhibits of local artisans, indigenous music and ritual dance.

Sleeping

More than half a dozen campgrounds dot the road between Villarrica and Pucón.

La Torre Suiza (☎ 411-213; www.torresuiza .com; Bilbao 969; dm CH$6000, d with/without CH$24,000/14,000; P ☐) Though this Swiss-owned perennial Villarrica favorite is a hot spot for European travelers, it's not without its downsides. The woman in charge seems to be

over dealing with travelers, third-floor show-erheads toss water around like a hurricane and email response is nonexistent. Still, the charming wooden chalet – though too dark in the second floor – offers a fully equipped kitchen, laundry, multilingual book exchange, mountain-bike rental (the owners cycled all over the world) and lots of area information.

Hostal Don Juan (☎ 411-833; www.hostaldonjuan.cl, in Spanish; General Körner 770; s/d CH$10,950/16,800, without bathroom CH$7600/12,600, 2-/4-person cabin CH$23,550/29,450; P ☐) Don Juan wins travelers over with its numerous distractions: Foosball, table tennis, a beautiful *fogón* designed by the owner, a multi-use room that includes a kitchen and shower – it's all here. Some of the towels appear to have been 'mislaid' from the Sheraton and there are fab volcano views from some rooms on the second floor.

Hostería Hue-quimey (☎ 411-462; hue-quemay@ yahoo.com; Valentin Letelier 1030; s/d CH$15,000/20,000; P ☐) Hue-quimey is rife with char-acter, calling upon sailing and indigenous Peruvian motifs to liven up the place. Ask for an upstairs room, where you can see the views that put Villarrica on the map. The

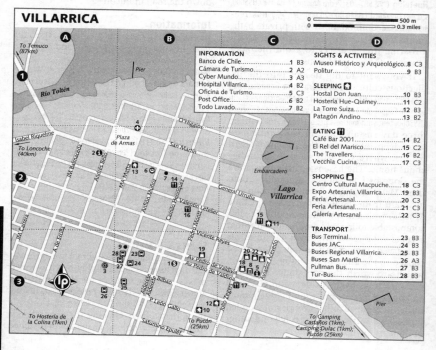

VILLARRICA

0 ____ 500 m
0 ____ 0.3 miles

INFORMATION
Banco de Chile..................1 B3
Cámara de Turismo............2 A2
Cyber Mundo.....................3 A3
Hospital Villarrica..............4 B2
Oficina de Turismo............5 C3
Post Office........................6 B2
Todo Lavado......................7 B2

SIGHTS & ACTIVITIES
Museo Histórico y Arqueológico..8 C3
Politur.............................9 B3

SLEEPING 🛏
Hostal Don Juan................10 B3
Hostería Hue-Quimey..........11 C2
La Torre Suiza...................12 B3
Patagón Andino.................13 B2

EATING 🍴
Café Bar 2001....................14 B2
El Rel del Marisco...............15 C2
The Travellers....................16 B2
Vecchia Cucina...................17 C3

SHOPPING 🛍
Centro Cultural Macpuche.....18 C3
Expo Artesania Villarrica.......19 B3
Feria Artesanal...................20 C3
Feria Artesanal...................21 C3
Galería Artesanal................22 C3

TRANSPORT
Bus Terminal.....................23 B3
Buses JAC.........................24 B3
Buses Regional Villarrica......25 B3
Buses San Martín................26 A3
Pullman Bus......................27 B3
Tur-Bus............................28 B3

To Temuco (87km)
Pier
Río Toltén
To Loncoche (40km)
Isabel Riquelme
Plaza de Armas
O'Higgins
San Martín
General Urrutia
Embarcadero
Lago Villarrica
Anfión Muñoz
Camilo Henríquez
Valentin Letelier
Pedro Montt
Pedro Vicente Reyes
Av Pedro de Valdivia
Av Pedro de Valdivia
Alvaro Acevedo
Alderete Bilbao
Alderete Bilbao
P León Gallo
Tillo Zegers
Saturnino Epuler
To Hostería de la Colina (1km)
To Pucón (25km)
To Camping Castaños (1km); Camping Dulac (1km); Pucón (25km)
Pier

bay windows on the lower floor and the large upstairs windows illuminate the rooms on sunny days.

Patagón Andino (☎ 419-978; www.patagonandino .cl, in Spanish; MA Matta 320; s/d CH$23,600/25,200; ✕ ⌨) This newer lodge is a good midrange option and can hook you up with fly-fishing, trekking and mountain-biking excursions. It sits on the plaza and is steps from the lake. For breakfast, the *calzones rojos*, a sort of sweet *sopaipilla*, is a nice change of pace from bread and marmalade.

Hostería de la Colina (☎ 414-978; www.hosteriade lacolina.com; Las Colinas 115; s/d from CH$30,000/40,000, independent ste from CH$50,000; P ✕ ⌨) This smart *hostería* and restaurant is set on meticulously manicured and lush grounds on a hill with stupendous views just southwest of town. The US-expat owners are some of the few in the area who understand true hospitality (and gardening). Rooms in the main house are classically inclined while the two independent suites offer more privacy and contemporary decor. To get there, take Presidente JA Ríos southeast of town and follow the signs up the hill.

Eating

Café Bar 2001 (☎ 411-470; Camilo Henríquez 379; sandwiches CH$1600-3400; ✆ breakfast, lunch & dinner) The breakfast special here for CH$2000 nabs you küchen, toast, juice and coffee, though they don't open until 9am. There is also a decent selection of rarer microbrews.

El Rey del Marisco (☎ 412-093; Valentin Letelier 1030; mains CH$2200-6800; ✆ lunch & dinner Mon-Sat, lunch Sun) There's a perfect balance of whimsical aquatic art and colorful tablecloths at this don't-miss seafooder. There are 29 types of fish and the chef has worked all over Chile. Start with the near-perfect pisco sours and shellfish empanadas, move on to congrio, salmon, trout, lenguado or corvina prepared numerous ways.

The Travellers (☎ 413-617; Valentin Letelier 753; mains CH$2950-5500; ✆ breakfast, lunch & dinner-late) Chinese, Mexican, Thai, Indian, Italian – it's a passport for your palette at this resto-bar that is Ground Zero for foreigners. The walls are lined with classic B+W pop culture pinups and postcards from *amigos* the world over, and the music is equally all over the map (Shania Twain to Tom Jones?). German and English traveler advice is available, and so are half-priced drinks at the lengthy Happy Hour (6:30pm to 9:30pm). These guys know their stuff – they knew we wrote for a guidebook within seconds.

Vecchia Cucina (Av Pedro de Valdivia 1011; pasta CH$3900-6200, pizza CH$3400-7800; ✆ lunch & dinner) You'll want to genuflect when they bring out the Italian flatbread instead of ubiquitous tortillas at this, 'the old kitchen,' which specializes in antiquated northern Italian recipes. All the ample pasta options are made in-house. Whoever cleans the wine glasses should be fired, though.

Hostería de la Colina (☎ 414-978; Las Colinas 115; mains US$3600-5000; ✆ lunch & dinner) There are actual *green* vegetables at this excellent restaurant worth trying even if you're not staying at the *hostería*. Chilean and international comfort food dominate the limited seasonal menu, with standouts like Aztec soup, a mean veggie lasagna and homemade ice cream (try the ginger) doing their part to set right your culinary deprivations.

Shopping

Surrounding the tourist office, there is a high concentration of *artesanias*. The **Feria Artesanal** (Julio Zegers 570; ✆ 10:30am-8pm), **Galería Artesanal** (✆ 11am-8pm Jan-Mar) and the **Centro Cultural Mapuche** (✆ 10am-midnight) have all the typical tourist wares, the most interesting of which are the Mapuche figures carved from *laurel* wood and *raulí* wood bowls. You can also try the **Expo Artesania Villarrica** (✆ 10am-11pm Jan-Mar) in summer; it's a co-op between the women's association (knit bikinis!) and the woodworker's association (more bowls!).

Getting There & Around

Villarrica has a main **bus terminal** (Av Pedro de Valdivia 621), though a few companies have separate offices nearby. Long-distance fares are similar to those from Temuco (an hour away), which has more choices for southbound travel.

Buses JAC (☎ 467-777; Bilbao 610) goes to Pucón (CH$600) every 10 minutes, Temuco (CH$1500, one hour) every 20 minutes and Lican Ray (CH$600, 40 minutes) and Coñaripe (CH$900) every 30 minutes. From the main terminal, **Buses Vipu-Ray** (☎ 413-449) goes to Pucón every 20 minutes Monday to Saturday (CH$600). **Buses Regional Villarrica** (☎ 411-804; Anfión Muñoz 796) also has frequent buses to Pucón.

Buses leaving the main bus terminal, as well as Buses JAC, provide daily service to Santiago. **Tur-Bus** (☎ 413-652; Anfión Muñoz 657) and **Pullman Bus** (☎ 414-217; cnr Anfión Muñoz & Bilbao) also go to other destinations such as Valdivia (CH$2300), Los

Ángeles (CH$5200), Concepción (CH$7500) and Puerto Montt (CH$5600, six hours).

For Argentine destinations, **Igi Llaima** (☎ 412-733), in the main terminal, leaves at 6:45am Monday, Wednesday, Friday and Saturday at 8:55am for San Martín de los Andes (CH$10,000), Zapala and Neuquén (CH$15,000, 12 hours), via Paso Mamuil Malal. **Buses San Martín** (☎ 411-584; Pedro León Gallo 599) does the same route Tuesday to Sunday at 10am (CH$10,000, six hours).

PUCÓN

☎ 045 / pop 16,970

Often referred to as the Queenstown of South America, Pucón has indeed arrived on the global map as a mecca for adventure sports. If you can hike it, jump off of it, ride it or climb it, you can do it in Pucón; its setting on beautiful Lago Villarrica under the smoldering eye of the volcano of the same name has sealed its fate as a world-class destination for adrenaline junkies.

Once a summer playground for the rich, Pucón is becoming a year-round adventure machine catering to all incomes, especially in February (a time to avoid, if possible), when it is absolutely overrun. The town receives alternating floods of package tourists, Santiago holidaymakers, novice Brazilian snowboarders, adventure-seeking backpackers and New Age spiritualists (in summer, the beautiful black-sand beach here is so packed with bronzed hardbodies, it can rival Miami Beach).

While the popularity and international feel can be off-putting for some (people tend to love it or hate it), Pucón boasts the best small-town tourism infrastructure south of Costa Rica. That means quality accommodations, efficient tourism agencies, hundreds of activities and excursions, vegetarian restaurants, Mexican food, falafel, a chic new casino (re-built after the old one burnt down under questionable circumstances) – you name it.

Like every other place in the region, the crowds do trickle in winter and skiing and snowboarding become the focus. No matter when you go, don't forget: if you hear the Volcano Risks Alert System begin to wail, run!

Orientation

Pucón is 25km from Villarrica at the east end of Lago Villarrica, between the estuary of the Río Pucón to the north and Volcán Villarrica to the south. Structured along a conventional grid system, the main streets in this town are the commercial strip of Av O'Higgins and the upscale Fresia, which runs through Av O'Higgins to the iconic Gran Hotel Pucón. The town is expanding out past the bus station, but is still easily navigated on foot.

Information

INTERNET ACCESS

Ciber-Unid@d G (☎ 444-918; Av O'Higgins 415, Local 2; per hr CH$700; ⊙ 9:30am-11pm Mon-Fri, 10am-11pm Sat, 11am-10pm Sun)

INTERNET RESOURCES

Chile Pucón (www.chile-pucon.com) Complete coverage, non advertising-generated.

LAUNDRY

Lavandería Araucanias (General Basilio Urrutia 108; per load CH$3900)
Lavandería Elena (☎ 444-370; General Basilio Urrutia 520; per load CH$3000)

MEDICAL SERVICES

Hospital San Francisco (☎ 441-177; Uruguay 325; ⊙ 24hr)

MONEY

You can expect a better exchange rate on cash in Temuco. There are several banks with ATMs up and down Av O'Higgins.
Supermercado Eltit (Av O'Higgins 336; ⊙ 7am-9pm) Changes US cash and has an ATM.

POST

Post office (Fresia 183)

TOURIST INFORMATION

Cámara de Turismo (☎ 441-671; cnr Brasil & Caupolicán; ⊙ 9am-1:30pm & 3:30-7pm) Just as you enter town from Villarrica.
Conaf (☎ 443-781; Lincoyán 336) The best-equipped Conaf in the region.
Oficina de Turismo (☎ 293-002; cnr Av O'Higgins & Palguín; ⊙ 8:30am-10pm Dec-Feb, to 7pm Jun-Aug) Has stacks of brochures and usually an English speaker on staff.

Dangers & Annoyances

Petty theft is on the rise in Pucón, especially around the beach. Bikes and backpacks are the biggest targets.

Activities

It's easy to overdose on adrenaline before actually doing any activity in Pucón – the wealth

PUCÓN

Lago Villarrica		
Playa Grande		
0	300 m	
0	0.2 miles	

INFORMATION
Cámara de Turismo.................................1 B3
Ciber-Unid@d G.....................................2 C2
Conaf...3 B2
Hospital San Francisco............................4 C3
Lavandaría Araucanias.............................5 B2
Lavandaría Elena.....................................6 C2
Oficina de Turismo..................................7 C2
Post Office..8 B2
Supermercado Eltit..................................9 C2

SIGHTS & ACTIVITIES
Aguaventura...10 C2
Kayak Pucón..11 B2
Ski Pucón Office.............................(see 18)
Sol y Nieve..12 B2
Termas de Huife Office...................(see 29)
Trancura..13 C2
Trancura..14 C2
Trancura..15 C2

SLEEPING 🛏 🏠
Camping Parque La Poza.......................16 B3
Donde German.....................................17 D2
Gran Hotel Pucón.................................18 B1
Hospedaje Victor..................................19 C2
Hostal El Refugio.................................20 C2
Hostal Gerónimo..................................21 C1
Hotel Huincahue...................................22 B1
La Tetera..23 C2
The Tree House.....................................24 C2
¡école!...25 C2

EATING 🍴
Arabian Café..26 B2
Cassis...27 B2
La Maga...28 B2
Latitude 39°...29 B2
Pizza Cala.....................................(see 12)
Trawen...30 C2
Viva Perú...31 C2

DRINKING 🍷
El Bosque...32 C2
Entre 3...33 C2
Mama's & Tapas...................................34 C2

ENTERTAINMENT 🎭
Enjoy Pucón..35 C1

TRANSPORT
Buses Caburgua...............................(see 42)
Buses JAC..36 D3
Buses San Martín..................................37 D2
Igi Llaima..38 C3
Kilometro Libre.....................................39 C2
Minibuses Vipu Ray..............................40 C3
Pucón Rent a Car..................................41 D2
Pullman Bus...42 C2
Sky Airlines..43 B2
Trans Curarrehue.............................(see 41)
Tur-Bus..44 D2
Tur-Bus Office......................................45 C2

To Antilco (15km); Hot Springs (19km); Huepilmalal Centro Ecuestre (27km); El Cañi (28km); Parque Nacional Huerquehue (37km)

To Hotel Antumalal (2km); Parque Nacional Villarrica (15km); Villarrica (25km)

of adventure operators lining Av O'Higgins and the bounty of activities on offer in and around Pucón can easily overwhelm. For a list of recommended agencies, see p280. Sorting out what to do, when to do it and with whom is all part of the experience. The standards, climbing Villarrica and rafting Río Trancura, are offered by many, but consider some of the other activities – those that allow you to appreciate the area away from the masses, such as horseback riding, renting a bike, snowshoeing or exploring some of the smaller nature reserves on foot.

CANOPY & ZIPLINE

There are seven canopy circuits around Pucón, including the longest canopy tour in South America – some 3400m – that sits 26km from Pucón near the Trancura hot springs. You'll reach heights of 120m and speeds between 30km and 70km per hour. On a clear day, there are views to four volcanoes (Lanín, Quetrupillán, El Colmillo del Diablo and Villarrica) and three lagoons (Ancapulli, León and San Luis). Trips run around CH$10,000. But, in general, be slightly wary of canopy operations. Safety is a loose term in this sport in Chile and you don't even need to be strapped in yet – in 2008 a girl died when a truck carrying participants flipped over in Las Cascadas. The driver did not have a license. We won't name names, but the complaint book at the tourist office does.

HORSEBACK RIDING

There are a few spectacular options for horse treks in this region. Most rides take in various environments and may include stopovers so riders can meet with local *huasos* (cowboys) or Mapuche communities. Half- and full-day rides hover around CH$20,000 to CH$40,000 depending on the grade of difficulty and number of people going. Recommended agencies all offer excursions for first-time riders too; see right.

MOUNTAIN BIKING

Mountain bikes can be rented all over town. Daily rental prices are negotiable but shouldn't be more than CH$6500 unless it is a brand-new bike with full suspension.

The most popular route is the Ojos de Caburgua Loop. Take the turnoff to the airfield about 4km east of town and across Río Trancura. It's a dustbowl in summer, though, and tends to irritate all but the most hardcore riders. Extensions off the same route include the Lago Caburga to Río Liucura Loop and the full Río Trancura Loop.

Two other popular trails that are close to town are Correntoso and Alto Palguín Chinay (to the Palguín hot springs). Any bike-rental agencies will be able to give you more details and should provide a decent trail map.

RAFTING & KAYAKING

Pucón is known for both its river sports and the quality of the rafting and kayaking infrastructure. Most of the larger travel agencies run rafting trips. For recommended agencies see right. The rivers near Pucón and their corresponding rapids classifications are: the Lower Trancura (III), the Upper Trancura (IV), Liucura (II–III), The Puesco Run (V) and Maichín (IV–V). When negotiating a rafting or kayaking trip, recognize that the stated trip durations often include transportation, not just the time spent on the water. Prices can range from CH$12,000 to CH$28,000 depending on the season, the number of people per raft or kayaking trip, the company and the level of challenge. Many of the rivers are swollen in the winter and closed for most sports, although it is still possible to raft or kayak in some. If you have a half-day to kill before a bus ride, consider the No-Carbon paddling experience dreamed up by Aguaventura (right) and ¡école! (p282) to help save the Trancura River Delta from a proposed development.

ROCK CLIMBING

Cerduo, at the foot of Volcán Villarrica, offers 10 different climbing routes ranging from 5.8 to 5.11d for those looking for more serious climbing. There's sport climbing as well as traditional and you will be surrounded by native forest. For more intense and physically demanding climbing, head to pristine Las Peinetas near the Argentine border, where climbs consist of five to six pitches and can last up to 12 hours. It is a three-hour hike in to where the climbing commences. For an experienced guide, call **Claudio Retamal** (☎ 099-277-5074; claudioreta@gmail.com), a former Chilean climbing champion, who can also take you up the other volcanoes: Lanín, Llaima and Lonquimay.

Tours

Most of the tour operators are on Av O'Higgins or within a half block. Prices are similar throughout, but quality of service can vary. In summer seasonal operators pop up on all corners, but are not as established as those listed below. Many *hospedajes* also run their own operations.

Aguaventura (☎ 444-246; www.aguaventura.com; Palguín 336; ☽ 8:30am-9pm) This friendly French-owned agency offers highly skilled guides for the volcano (beer after!); and also specializes in kayaking, rappelling, canyoning and snow sports.

Antilco (☎ 099-713-9758; www.antilco.com; 15km east of Pucón on Río Liucura) This outfitter runs half- to six-day horse treks in Liucura Valley, Parque Nacional Huerquehue and Mapuche reservations, and half-day and two-day kayaking trips, designed for both beginners and experts, with English-speaking guides.

Huepilmalal Centro Ecuestre (☎ 099-643-2673; www.huepilmalal.cl; Km27 Camino Pucón-Huife) This reputable equestrian center uses pure Chilean bred *caballos* (horses) for its half-day to multiday treks in the Cāni cordillera. It's run by a charming couple with over 40 years experience in Europe and South America.

Kayak Pucón (☎ 099-716-2347; www.kayakpucon.net; Av O'Higgins 211; ☽ 9am-9pm Nov-Mar) This well-regarded kayak operator with a clever slogan ('Run the Shit') offers a three-day kayak tour that will get you on five sections of river in the area, as well as a kayak school and longer expeditions.

Patragon (☎ 444-606; www.patragon.net) On the cutting-edge of *etnoturismo*, this excellent agency gets you closer to the Mapuche with cooking classes, pottery workshops and a fascinating cultural immersion tour in the Mapuche enclave of Curarrehue.

DON'T BLOW YOUR TOP

It may seem shocking that so many people live and go about their daily chores in the shadow of the smoking and rumbling Volcán Villarrica. The 2847m-high cone is a basaltic volcano with an open crater and a violent history that includes at least four fatal eruptions. Carbon dating has determined that Villarrica had a massive eruption around 1810 BC. The first historically recorded eruption was in AD 1558, and since then the volcano has had small to medium eruptions on well over 50 occasions. The largest modern erupti ons were in 1640, 1948 and 1971.

That 1971 eruption opened a 4km-wide fissure, spurting out some 30 million cubic meters of lava and displacing several rivers. One flow, down the Río Challupén, was 14km long, 200m wide and 5m high. However, no one is known to have been killed by lava from an eruption. It was mud flows that caused the losses of life in all of the fatal eruptions. The 1971 eruption melted glacial ice, which mixed with earth and sent waves of mud down the mountain. The last minor eruption was in 1984.

Villarrica continues to spew lava, ash and plenty of smoke – on a daily basis. Check out the **Villarrica Volcano Visual Observation Project** (www.povi.cl) for detailed up-to-the-minute activity. It is unnerving for some; others rarely think about it. But there is an undeniable energy that can be felt from living in close proximity to something so powerful.

Sol y Nieve (☎ 463-860; www.solynievepucon.cl; Lincoyán 361 B; ☺ 9am-midnight Jan-Feb, 11am-7pm Mar-Dec) This dependable agency is well regarded for anything to do with the volcano as well as rafting.

Trancura (☎ 443-446; www.trancura.com, in Spanish; Av O'Higgins 211; ☺ 9am-10pm) With three locations in Pucón (also at the corner of Avs O'Higgins and Palguín, and at Av O'Higgins 575) and two more in Villarrica, Trancura is a tourism machine with a rollercoaster reputation. Sheer volume allows them to undercut the prices of most other agencies, but commitment to safety here has been called into question more than once (see the tourism office's complaint book). Think twice.

Sleeping

While Pucón has plenty of places to stay, prices are higher than in other cities (even for the budget options). In the low season, rates are about 20% less. Reservations are necessary in January and February, but aren't a problem in the winter.

BUDGET

Budget accommodations tend to have a few more comfortable and pricier choices. Note that due to the nature of early-rise tourism here, breakfast is often not included. When Pucón fills to capacity in the summer these rooms can become more of a necessity than a choice. Look for the sign *hospedaje* in front of the houses.

Camping Parque La Poza (☎ 444-982; camping lapoza@hotmail.com; Costanera Roberto Geis 769; campsite per person CH$3000) Has about 82 sites on shady grounds, and a fair amount of noise from the busy road. It's a car camping facility with a place to cook, lockers to store your stuff and hot water.

Hostal El Refugio (☎ 441-596; www.hostalelrefugio.cl, in Spanish; Palguín 540; dm CH$6500, d CH$14,600; P X 🖳) Chill and cheap, this casual, multilingual hostel is right across from the Pullman Bus station. True to its name, it feels like you've rented a cabin with your friends.

Hospedaje Victor (☎ 443-525; www.pucon.com /victor; Palguín 705; dm with/without TV CH$9000/8000, r CH$20,000; 🖳 X) Victor stands out for cleanliness and a warm atmosphere, ensured by several wood-burning stoves. It offers kitchen access, big TVs and large, newly renovated bathrooms.

The Tree House (☎ 444-679; www.treehousechile .cl; General Basilio Urrutia 660; dm CH$8000-10,000, d CH$24,000; P X) The new kid on the block is a British-Chilean tag team run by tour leaders for English-based outfitter Journey Latin America. Orthopedic mattresses, individual lockers, British fire alarms and yes, a tree house, give it a leg up in the hostel market, as does opportunities to snuggle with Cortito, the resident puppy dog, in the hammocks.

Donde German (☎ 442-444; www.dondegerman .cl; Brasil 640; dm CH$8000, d CH$25,000, without bathroom CH$18,000; P X 🖳) Donde German had torn down its termite-infested former hostel at time of research and was building the new, improved Donde German in the same location set to open by late 2008. The new spot is sunnier and more stylish, with river and

SUR CHICO

volcanic stone walls and even a swimming pool. It also has an attached tour agency.

our pick **¡école!** (☎ 441-615; www.ecole.cl; General Basilio Urrutia 592; dm with/without bedding CH$7600/5500, d incl breakfast CH$22,700, s/d without bathroom CH$13,000/15,200; P ☐) The eco-conscious ¡école! is a travel experience in itself. It's a meeting point for conscientious travelers and a tranquil and artsy hangout where you can plan excursions, get a massage or learn a something or two about conservation. Rooms are small, clean and comfortable but the walls are thin and voices carry, so it's not a wild party hostel. Don't miss the excellent vegetarian restaurant (which means no picnicking outside your room). The staff are adorable. They even encourage co-showering. Need we say more?

MIDRANGE & TOP END

Many of the midrange places in town also have a few less expensive rooms or dorm options for budget travelers.

La Tetera (☎ 441-462; www.tetera.cl; General Basilio Urrutia 580; s/d CH$18,700/27,600, without bathroom CH$13,800/21,100; P ☒ ☐) As Villarrica is to Pucón, La Tetera lives in the shadow of its famous neighbor ¡école!. This German-Austrian effort has a lot to offer, though, with a small range of cozy and well-heated rooms with indigenous touches such as Mapuche throws on all the beds. There is a garden out back, but it's a little rundown – watch out for the blind cat! Prices include breakfast, which is one of the best in town.

Hostal Gerónimo (☎ 443-762; Gerónimo de Alderete 665; s/d from CH$21,000/26,900; ☐ P ☒) If the vanilla-scented Gerónimo is a hostel, we're the King James Bible! It's actually a quaint B&B with chintzy – but appreciated – touches like potpourri in the bathrooms. Rooms feature tapestries on bright stucco walls, reliable gas heat and private terracotta tile bathrooms, and some balconies face Villarrica's fuming crater.

Hotel Huincahue (☎ 443-540; www.hotelhuincahue.com, in Spanish; Pedro de Valdivia 375; r from CH$79,900; P ☒ ☐) Almost everything is pleasant about this vaguely Spanish-styled boutique hotel with a countryside chic aesthetic fused with local elements like volcanic stone – except the manager, who is so fussy about his beds that he might get upset if you sleep in them. You can hit the casino with a poker chip from here, so it's a bad choice for recovering gambling addicts.

Gran Hotel Pucón (☎ 913-300; www.granhotelpucon.com; Clemente Holzapfel 190; s/d from CH$89,900/112,900; P ☐ ☐) You can just picture Pucón's gorgeous black-sand beach teeming with ladies bathing in caps and skirts at this aged 1936 relic – the whole things looks like an unearthed B&W photo from the '20s. Unfortunately, the hotel has lost much of its heyday charm, and with the destruction of Hotel Del Lago by fire, it now lacks incentive to improve.

Hotel Antumalal (☎ 441-011; www.antumalal.com; Km2; r from CH$134,500; P ☒ ☐ ☐) This testament to Bauhaus architecture on the road to Villarrica is built into a cliffside above the lake. From its tree-bark lamps to volcanic stone floors and countertops, it instills a sense of location while all the while being wildly and wonderfully out of place. Its huge slanting windows give unbeatable views of Lago Villarrica from the swanky common areas and all the minimalist rooms offer fireplaces and some have fern- and moss-covered raw rock for the internal walls. Antumalal offers one of the most luxurious and personalized stays in the Lakes District. You might kill time here doing reiki or throwing yourself under the small waterfall in the parking lot, but you won't want to leave.

Eating

Pucón is the undisputable king of culinary variety in southern Chile. Fresia is the town's Restaurant Row.

Latitude 39° (☎ 099-7430-0016; Gerónimo de Alderete 324-2; mains CH$1800-4200; ☺ breakfast, lunch & dinner) The California transplant owners here are filling a gringo niche – juicy American-style burgers, fat breakfast burritos, veggie tacos, BLTs, chili – that should stay your gastronomic homesickness for another day.

Cassís (☎ 444-715; Fresia 223; sandwiches CH$2000-4500; ☺ breakfast, lunch & dinner; V) This sleek café is swamped for breakfast and *onces* (afternoon tea), but it also does multigrain sandwiches, chocolate fondue, pizza, an endless array of coffees and an entirely too tempting cornucopia of deserts (it's also a *chocolatería*). If you don't eat here, stop by for the decadent Crepe Cassís, a milk caramel crepe buried under scoops of chocolate and *dulce de leche* ice cream and a caramel brownie.

Trawen (☎ 442-024; Av O'Higgins 311; mains CH$2600-6800; ☺ breakfast, lunch & dinner) Like everywhere else in town, there's an outfitter element to this innovative and wonderfully casual deli that churns out some of Pucón's most interesting flavor combinations: ravioli with Roquefort and roasted apples, Antarctic krill empanadas. It's kind of a writer hangout, too.

Pizza Cala (☎ 463-024; Lincoyán 361; pizza CH$2700-9900; ☾ lunch & dinner) The best pizza in town is spit from a massive 1300-brick oven by an Argentine-American pizzamaker who grows his own fresh basil. In winter, it's the only warm restaurant in town.

¡école! (☎ 441-675; General Basilio Urrutia 592; mains CH$2800-5000; ☾ breakfast, lunch & dinner; ✓) As famous as the hostel itself, the ¡école! restaurant is one of the best vegetarian (fish included) restaurants in Chile – a culinary orgasm even for carnivores. From the homemade granola and yogurt breakfasts to the spicy salmon Bengal curry or robust vegetarian lasagna, you'll never be disappointed.

Arabian Café (☎ 443-469; Fresia 354; mains CH$3800-5900; ☾ lunch & dinner; ✓) It's not Jerusalem but considering the distance, you'll be surprised at the job they do here with falafel and hummus at this legit Arab restaurant that considers *lomo a lo pobre* an 'alternative dish.'

Viva Perú (☎ 444-025; Lincoyán 372; mains CH$3900-9700; ☾ lunch & dinner Sep-Jun, lunch & dinner Thu-Sat Jul-Aug) Start with the *yuquitos* (fried mandioca) and move on to the falling-off-the-bone, cilantro-heavy lamb stew at this smart Peruvian that serves slushy pisco sours made with Peruvian pisco. *Chilenos* can't handle the *aji rocoto* salsa served here, but it should satiate your spice-neglected taste buds.

La Maga (☎ 444-277; Fresia 125; steak 350g CH$5900; ☾ lunch & dinner, closed Mon Mar-Dec) There is a *parrilla* for every budget on Fresia between Gerónimo de Alderete and the plaza, but this Uruguayan steakhouse stands out for its *bife de chorizo* and house-cut fries. It's not the cheapest, but there's a consensus it's the best with bang-on service to boot.

Drinking

El Bosque (☎ 443-226; Av O'Higgins 524; ☾ 7pm-late) This chic bar-restaurant is Pucón's most stylish address for a cocktail. There's a sultry vibe, both in its design (hanging cylindrical rust-hued luminaries, artsy B&W volcano photos) and the music (Faithless, Massive Attack – you get the idea). Mixed drinks easily approach CH$5000 here, but when have you ever known cool to come cheap?

Mama's & Tapas (☎ 449-002; Av O'Higgins 597; ☾ 6pm-late) Known simply as 'Mama's,' this is the most popular place to go out in Pucón. It is less stylish than El Bosque, but the bar has an impressive lineup of draft beers, including Kunstmann Bock, which fuels an interesting dilemma when two drunks try to navigate the swiveling bathroom door at the same time. The Mexican food here is worth a try and is discounted 30% before 9pm.

Entre 3 (☎ 441-645; Arauco 302; ☾ 9:30am-late Tue-Sun) If you want to see if your guide is plastered the night before he takes you up the volcano, grab a pitcher of suds here. It's the divier choice, but its new rooftop patio nets views with brews not otherwise available on Av O'Higgins.

Entertainment

Enjoy Pucón (☎ 550-000; Ansorena 121; admission CH$500; ☾ 24hr Jan-Feb, 11am-4pm Sun-Thu, 11am-6am Fri & Sat Mar-Nov) Pucón's sleek new US$12.5 million casino boasts 488 hi-tech slots and a swanky restaurant and bar, the latter, called Üin, means 'fire' in Mapudungun but is pronounced 'Win.' Get it?

Getting There & Away

Bus transportation to and from Santiago (from CH$10,000) is with **Tur-Bus** (☎ 443-934; Av O'Higgins 910) east of town and **Pullman Bus** (☎ 443-331; Palguín 555) in the center.

Buses JAC (☎ 443-326; cnr Uruguay & Palguín) goes to Puerto Montt (CH$5900, five hours). For Temuco, Buses JAC goes every 20 minutes (CH$2000, one hour). For Valdivia, JAC has seven daily buses (CH$2700, three hours). From the same station, **Minibuses Vipu-Ray** and **Trans Curarrehue** (Palguín 550) has continuous services to Villarrica and Curarrehue. Buses JAC and **Buses Caburgua** (☎ 099-838-9047; Palguín 555) have service to Caburgua and Parque Nacional Huerquehue (CH$1000, 45 minutes). For San Martín de los Andes, Argentina, **Buses San Martín** (☎ 443-595; Av Colo Colo 612) offers departures Tuesday to Sunday at 10:35am (CH$10,000, five hours) stopping in Junín on the way. **Igi Llaima** (☎ 444-762; cnr Palguín & Uruguay) goes Monday, Wednesday, Friday and Saturday at 9:25am. In summer only, both **Lan** (☎ in Chile 600-526-2000; www.lan.com; CH$74,900) and **Sky Airlines** (☎ in Chile 600-600-2828; Gerónimo de Alderete 203) offers flights to and from Pucón twice per week.

Getting Around

A number of travel agencies rent cars and prices can be competitive, especially in the low season; though prices tend to climb on weekends. **Pucón Rent a Car** (☎ 443-052; www .puconrentacar.cl, in Spanish; Av Colo Colo 340; per weekday CH$25,000-55,000) is recommended. If you want to dump the car in Puerto Montt, **Kilometro Libre** (☎ 099-218-7307; Gerónimo de Alderete 480) is one of the few that will let you.

Although you can get around town on foot, there are several *colectivos* that run up and down Av O'Higgins and taxis that will negotiate prices to outlying areas, such as the hot springs.

PARQUE NACIONAL VILLARRICA

Parque Nacional Villarrica (adult/child CH$3000/1500) is one of the most popular parks in the country because of its glorious mix of volcanoes and lakes. Its proximity to Pucón, with all of the town's tourism infrastructure, also makes Villarrica an unusually accessible park for everyone from bus trippers to climbers, skiers and hardcore hikers.

The highlights of the park are the three volcanoes: 2847m Villarrica, 2360m Quetrupillán and, along the Argentine border, a section of 3747m Lanín. (The rest of Lanín is protected in an equally impressive park in Argentina, from where it may be climbed.) The park's 630 sq km are officially divided into three sections called Rucapillán, Quetrupillán and Puesco and are crisscrossed with an array of hikes from quick day jaunts to long multiday traverses.

Activities

CLIMBING

The hike up to the smoking, sometimes lava-spitting crater of Volcán Villarrica is a popular full-day excursion (around CH$38,000 to CH$50,000 not including the chairlift fee of CH$5000), leaving Pucón around 7am. You do not need prior mountaineering experience, but it's no Sunday stroll. Crampons and ice axes are required on the snow and it can be treacherous and not unfrightening at times (we witnessed a tourist tumble 30m down the snow, only to be stopped by rocks). Conditions are most difficult in fall when snow levels have depleted. It is important to use reliable equipment and chose an outfitter whose guides are properly trained. Note that bad weather may delay organized ascents for days. Climbs are sometimes cancelled altogether or may be required to turn back part way. Check cancellation policies carefully, but know that less reputable operators may take you part way up on days when they know the weather won't hold, just so they don't have to return the money as per your agreement. Fundamentally you will get what you pay for and it is worth spending CH$5000 to CH$10,000 more to not be treated like part of a cattle drive to the top.

Experienced mountaineers may prefer to take a taxi or bus to the ski area and tackle the volcano without a tour. Most folks ride the ski lift to the top of Chair 5 and start from there. Ascents without a tour group are officially discouraged and should only be done by two or more experienced hikers under clear conditions. Solo climbers must have a mountaineering license and obtain permission from Conaf in Pucón before setting out for the park. Gear rental runs around CH$8000 if you don't have your own.

HIKING

The most accessible sector of the park, Rucapillán, is directly south of Pucón along a well-maintained road and takes in the most popular hikes up and around Volcán Villarrica.

The trail **Challupen Chinay** (23km, 12 hours) rounds the volcano's southern side, crossing through a variety of scenery to end at the entrance to the Quetrupillán sector. This sector is easily accessed via the road that goes to Termas de Palguín. However, if you plan to continue through to Coñaripe, the road south through the park requires a high-clearance 4WD even in good weather. A 32km combination of hikes, with a couple of camping areas, links to the Puesco sector, near the Argentine border, where there is public transportation back to Curarrehue and Pucón (or you can make connections to carry on to Argentina).

SKIING

Ski Pucón (☎ 441-901; www.skipucon.cl in Spanish; Pucón office at Gran Hotel Pucón, Clemente Holzapfel 190, Pucón; full-day lift ticket adult/child CH18,000/13,000; ☼ Jul-Oct) is not on a par with Valle Nevado, Termas de Chillán, Portillo or the other resorts to the north, but it is the most developed ski area in La Araucanía and the Lakes District. Plus, where else do you get to ski on a live, smoking volcano? The views from the mid-

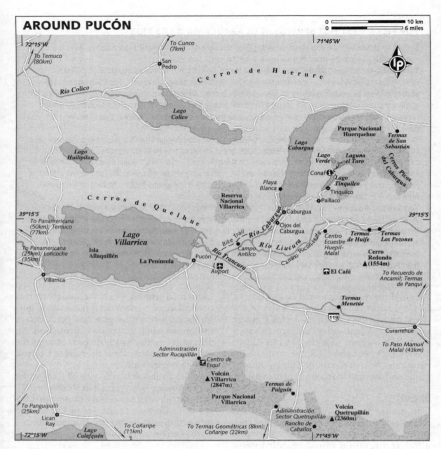

AROUND PUCÓN

mountain lodge almost single-handedly make the lift ticket worth the price. It can get alternately windy or cloudy and shuts down with some frequency.

The ski area is mainly for beginners, with a bit of steeper terrain for intermediates. However, skiing out of bounds just to the left or right of the lifts offers a range of more challenging options for experienced skiers and snowboarders. The lava chutes have created a veritable network of interconnected natural half-pipes and ridges that make for some serious fun.

The weather at the ski area tends to be different from the town of Pucón. Look at how the smoke from the crater is blowing to gauge how windy it will be. Rentals are available on

the mountain, but are less expensive (and often better quality) in town. Almost every agency and a number of hotels send minivans (around CH$6000) up to the base lodge.

Getting There & Away

Taxis, your own car or a tour are the only ways to get to the park (although fit mountain bikers can make it too).

RÍO LIUCURA VALLEY

Heading east out of Pucón, the wishbone road splits into two valleys – 24km to the north you'll find Lago Caburgua and its wonderful Playa Blanca, as well as the waterfall-heavy Ojos del Caburgua, as highlights of the Río Caburgua Valley; to the northeast, the Camino

---

TOP PICKS: BEST HOT SPRINGS IN LA ARAUCANÍA & LOS RÍOS

To get to these *termas* you must arrange group transportation through an agency, taxi or hostel. You can also drive yourself if you have a rental car.

Termas Geométricas (☎ 099-442-5420; www.termasgeometricas.cl; admission adult/child CH$14,000/6000; ☷ 10am-10pm Jan-Feb, 11am-8pm Mar-Dec) For couples and design aficionados, this Asian-inspired, red-planked maze of 17 beautiful slate hot springs set upon a verdant canyon over a rushing stream is the top choice. It's simply gorgeous. There are two waterfalls and three cold plunge pools to cool off and a *fogón*-heated café stocked with natural chicken soup and real coffee. If it weren't for the Spanish, you'd think this was Kyoto. Located 15km north of Coñaripe.

Termas de Panqui (☎ 442-039; panquihotsprings@hotmail.com; day use CH$6000; campsites per person CH$8100, cabins per person CH$12,150) Panqui, 58km east of Pucón, caters to a New Agey crowd and can get overrun in the summer, but these numerous baths are still quite good and are in a tranquil mountainous location. The place promotes itself as an ecological retreat and has a vegetarian restaurant. Come slide into the one of the four pools and soak away the stresses of a long day of enjoying yourself in and around Pucón – bathing suits have even been known to slip off here.

Termas Los Pozones (☎ 197-2350; Km37; day use adult/child CH$3500/1500, night use adult/child CH$4500/2500; ☷ 11am-6am) The most popular *termas* to visit from Pucón has six natural stone pools with a variety of temperatures spaced along the rushing Liucura river. It's open nearly 24 hours but gets crowded so come during nighttime hours (8pm to 6am). It can be a fun spot – people drink alcohol in the pools – so don't count on a place to meditate. A few changing rooms are built overtop the main pool with ladders right into the water. Transportation from Pucón ($10,000) is included the admission price. Keep an eye on your valuables.

Pucón-Huife road leads to myriad hot springs, El Cañi nature sanctuary and views of the silver-ribbon Río Liucura that cuts through this richly verdant valley. Both roads eventually link back up with the road to Parque Nacional Huerquehue. Kilometer markings mentioned below refer to the Camino Pucón-Huife and are well marked along the road.

El Cañi

The nature sanctuary **El Cañi** (Km21; entrance with/without guide CH$6000/3000) is proof that concerned citizens can make a difference and affect conservation of old-growth forests. When logging interests threatened the area in 1991, Fundación Lahuen, a small cluster of concerned folks with start-up funding from Ancient Forests International, formed to purchase the land and develop a drop-dead-gorgeous park with an emphasis on education and scientific research. This success story is now a reserve that protects some 500 hectares of ancient araucaria forest, all of which has been turned over and now successfully maintained by a local guide association, **Cañe Guides Group** (☎ 09/837-3928; santuariocani@chile.com).

A **hiking trail** (9km, three hours) ascends the steep terrain (the first 3km very steep) of lenga and araucaria to arrive at Laguna Negra. On clear days the lookout – another 40 minutes – allows for spectacular views of the area's vol-

canoes. In winter, when the underbrush is covered in snow, the area is particularly gorgeous. All hikers must go with a guide except in summer when the trail is easier to find. An alternative route, which detours around the steepest part, starts along the road to Coilaco; a guide is required.

Make arrangements to visit El Cañi at the park entrance or at ¡école! in Pucón (p282). If you are driving your own car, note that the roads heading northeast out of Pucón turn into parking lots during peak summer hours – traffic can be snarled for hours.

PARQUE NACIONAL HUERQUEHUE

Startling aquamarine lakes surrounded by verdant old-growth forests ensure wonderful **Parque Nacional Huerquehue** (www.parquehuerquehue.cl; adult/child CH$4000/2000) is one of the shining stars of the south and a standout in the Chilean chain of national parks. The 125-sq-km preserve, founded in 1912, is awash with rivers and waterfalls, alpine lakes and araucaria forests, and a long list of interesting creatures, including the *pudú* (the world's smallest deer) and *Arañas Pollitos*, tarantula-like spiders that come out in the fall. The trails here are well marked and maintained and warrant multiple days of exploration, but a day trip from Pucón, about 35km to the southeast, is a must for those in a bigger hurry. Stop off at Conaf's **Centro de Informaciones Ambientales** (8am-8pm Jan-Mar) at the entrance for hiking maps and park info.

The **Los Lagos trail** (round trip four hours, 7km) switchbacks from 700m to 1300m through dense lenga forests with rushing waterfalls, then enters solid stands of araucaria surrounding a cluster of pristine and placid lakes. Most hikers turn back at Lago Verde and Laguna el Toro, the largest of the cluster, but continuing on to the lookout at **Mirador Renahue** will give hikers their just rewards with a spectacular view into the canyon. At Laguna Huerquehue, the trail **Los Huerquenes** (two days) continues north then east to cross the park and access **Termas de San Sebastián** (045-381-272; www .termassansebastian.cl, in Spanish; Río Blanco; campsites per person CH$5000, cabins for 6 CH$40,000), just east of the park boundary. You'll need to call ahead all months outside summer so they know to buy food. From there a gravel road connects to the north end of Lago Caburgua and Cunco.

our pick **Refugio Tinquilco** (02-777-7673 in Santiago; www.tinquilco.cl; campsites CH$5700, dm with/ without bedding CH$6500/5700, d with/without bathroom CH$20,200/16,200; **P**), on private property at the Lago Verde trailhead 2km past the park entrance, is a luxe two-story wood lodge offering a quiet place to get away from it all designed by an architect, a writer, an engineer and a documentary film producer. After hiking, be sure to hit the addictive forest sauna and plunge pool, or curl up with a choice pick from the extensive library or vinyl collection. The kitchen turns out hearty home-style Chilean with welcome touches, such as French-press coffee. They should win an award for the Best Refugio Winelist as well. They also produce an invaluable field guide to the park that is leaps and bounds beyond anything published by Conaf. You could lose yourself for a month here. Breakfast costs CH$1600 to CH$3200, lunch or dinner CH$4500 or there's a kitchen to cook your own.

Camping accommodations are at the Conaf-managed 23-site **Lago Tinquilco** (campsites CH$10,000) and at **Renahue** (campsites CH$10,000) on the Los Huerquenes trail.

Getting There & Away

Buses Caburgua (099-838-9047; Palguín 555, Pucón) has regular service to and from Pucón three times a day (CH$1000, one hour); buy tickets in advance in the summer. Most agencies and outfitters offer organized excursions.

CURARREHUE

 045 / pop 5615

The Mapuche stronghold of Curarrehue, 40km west of the Argentine border, isn't much to look at but it has begun a slow rise to fame for its excellent museum and wealth of *etnoturismo* opportunities. The small pueblo counts 80% of the population as Mapuche and is the last town of note before the border with Argentina. There is a small **tourism office** (197-1587; 9:30am-8:30pm Dec 15-Mar 15) with helpful brochures, but where you'll want to go is straight to **Aldea Intercultural Trawupeyüm** (197-1574; Héroes de la Concepcíon 21; adult/child CH$500/200; 10am-8pm Dec-Mar, 10am-6pm Apr-Nov), a sparse but excellent museum of Mapuche culture housed in a modern interpretation of a mountain *ruka*, a traditional circular Mapuche dwelling oriented to the east. In addition to the museum, this cultural center is also home to **Cocinería La Ñaña**, where Mapuche chef Anita Epulef churns an unforgettable Mapuche tasting menu for CH$3000. You can sample such indigenous delicacies as *Mullokin* (bean puree rolled in *quinoa*), sautéed *Piñones*, the fruit of the araucaria tree, and roasted corn bread with an array of salsas – all excellent.

Patragon (444-606; www.patragon.net) offers fascinating tours in the area that include Mapuche cooking classes and lunch in a traditional *ruka*.

LICAN RAY

 045 / pop 2600

Of all the towns in the municipality, (meaning 'flower among the stones' in Mapudungun) is the prettiest for its location on the lovely north shore of island-studded Lago Calafquén. Just 30km south of Villarrica, this bathing resort is home to a long black-sand beach, ash-strewn roads and grandiose gardens spilling over with bright flowers. The town itself is tiny and organized around its only paved street, Av General Urrutia, which has most of the cabins, restaurants, cafés and artisan markets. In the low season Lican Ray all but closes down.

The **Oficina de Turismo** (431-516; General Urrutia 310; 9am-11pm Dec-Feb), directly on the Plaza de Armas, distributes maps and brochures and has a list of accommodations.

Sleeping & Eating

Within 5km on either side of Lican Ray are lakeside campgrounds charging around

CH$10,000 per site, for up to six people. The camping and a number of the hotels shut down in winter.

Refugio Inaltulafquén (☎ 431-115; Puñulef 510; d incl breakfast CH$10,000; **P** **X**) Right on Playa Grande, this creaky old wooden *refugio* is a great deal with its clean and cozy rooms, well-regarded restaurant, substantial book exchange and outgoing service and traveler's assistance. Some English is even spoken.

Hostal Hofmann (☎ 431-109; www.carmenhof mann@gmail.com; Camino Coñaripe 100; d incl breakfast CH$30,000; **P** **X** **⌨**) This attractive wooden home offers down comforters, strong hot showers and a filling breakfast, including excellent *küchen*. It's also well-known for its *onces*. Go for the upstairs room, which has bigger bathrooms and feels a little more woodsy. English and German are spoken.

Los Ñaños (☎ 431-026; Av General Urrutia 105; mains CH$3000-6300; ☽ lunch & dinner) A popular spot with a great outdoor patio and deck, serving local staples such as steaming-hot *cazuela* and, on weekends, memorable baked empanadas.

Getting There & Away

Buses JAC (☎ 431-616; Marichanquín 240) travels every 15 minutes to Villarrica and Coñaripe. There is also one bus to Santiago daily.

Panguipulli (CH$300, two hours) is serviced six times per day by local minibus.

LOS RÍOS

COÑARIPE
☎ 063 / pop 1416

When Villarrica blows its top, the lava heads straight for town. Living in the shadow of one of Chile's most active volcanoes certainly defines living on the edge – something, unfortunately, those investing in development aren't too fond of, so Coñaripe, despite being in a gorgeous part of the world, hasn't seen the same kind of investment as it neighbors.

Twenty-two kilometers east of Lican Ray, its black-sand beaches and easy access to a number of the smaller hot springs – 14 in all – attract the summer crowds and it's a far more pleasant spot to stay than Liquiñe if you're looking to sooth your aching muscles in a little *agua caliente*. At the east end of town the main drag, Av Guido Beck Ramberga, intersects Ruta 201, the international highway to Junín

de los Andes in Argentina; the westbound fork leads to Panguipulli and the southeast to Termas de Coñaripe, Termas Geométricas (the area's finest), Liquiñe and the border crossing at Paso Carirriñe. The road heading north of town leads to a number of rustic hot springs and the southern boundary of Parque Nacional Villarrica. A small **tourist kiosk** (☎ 317-378; Plaza de Armas; ☽ 9am-11pm Dec-Feb, 10am-1pm & 2-6pm Mar-Nov) is helpful and friendly.

Turismo Aventura Chumay (☎ 317-355; www.lago calafquen.com; Las Tepas 201; ☽ 8am-8pm Mon-Sat, 8am-5pm Sun) organizes glacial trekking and transportation to hot springs, among other adventures in the area. It also rents mountain bikes.

Sleeping & Eating

Campgrounds line the northeast side of the lake all the way to Lican Ray.

Hospedaje Calafquen (☎ 317-301; Beck Ramberga 761; r per person CH$5000; **P**) This dirt-cheap flea-bag has one saving grace: a well-lit courtyard in its restaurant that is absolutely crammed with plants. We ate at the Elizabeth, so we can't speak for the food, but it's a very inviting spot to hang out and have a beer while you're on the road. Don't drink too much – the bathrooms are terrible.

Hotel Elizabeth (☎ 317-279; www.hotelelizabeth .cl, in Spanish; Beck de Ramberga 496; s/d CH$10,900/ 16,800; **P** **X**) Some of the upstairs showers at the Elizabeth are a bit too narrow, but it's the nicest spot in town and has a well-regarded restaurant. Down the road, they also have a bakery and *chocolatería*. It turns out nice *alfajores*.

Hostal Chumay (☎ 317-355; Las Tepas 201; d CH$15,000; **P** **⌨**) Behind the plaza, this is a great deal, not just for the lodgings (which come with breakfast), but for the restaurant and convenience to the adventurer outfitter here.

Getting There & Away

Buses JAC (☎ 317-241; Beck Ramberga) has several buses daily from Villarrica to Coñaripe via Lican Ray (see p277). There is also one bus to Santiago daily. A block away at the main terminal, there are several daily departures to Villarrica, Liquiñe and Panguipulli (all CH$300).

LAGO PANGUIPULLI
☎ 063 / pop 30,123

At the northwest end of Lago Panguipulli, the town of **Panguipulli** is a quiet spot with awkward beach access, a lively main street and a totally odd Swiss-style church founded by Capuchin monks. You won't starve here – there are also a surprising number of restaurants. Most travelers come here just to make transportation connections. The **tourist office** (☎ 310-435; ☼ 9am-11pm Dec-Feb, 9am-1pm & 2:30-6pm Mar-Nov), across from Plaza Arturo Prat, has lots of listings for the area and helpful staff. The regular assortment of traveler services can be found up and down the main road, Martínez de Rozsa, leading toward the lake.

Little more than two streets at the east end of Lago Panguipulli, the cute hamlet **Choshuenco** has a sweeping beach with views that are a study in serenity, with crystal waters and rolling hills of green. It's a relaxing base for hikes, or a good place to rest before or after the Lago Pirihueico crossing between here and Argentina.

Sleeping & Eating

Playa Chauquén, south of town, is a beach area that allows a variety of camping. All of the following sleeping options are located in Panguipulli.

Camping El Bosque (☎ 311-489; campsites per person CH$2000), 200m north of Plaza Prat, has 15 tent sites in a small wooded area (no drive-in sites) and hot but very dingy showers.

Hostal Genesis (☎ 312-737; www.ze.cl/hostalgenesis, in Spanish; Diego Portales 84; s/d CH$12,000/20,000, without bathroom CH$8000/16,000; Ⓟ ⊠ ⌨) is a well-done *hospedaje* that offers very nice beds, a clean atmosphere and even scrambled eggs for breakfast. It's all very homey and a good value.

Of the plethora of restaurants on the main strip in Panguipulli, **Gardylafquen** (☎ 310-922; Martínez de Rozas 722; mains CH$2800-4900; ☼ breakfast, lunch & dinner) stands out, specializing in trout and more exotic dishes (for southern Chile) including stuffed avocados. For pizza, the well-designed **Pizzeria Italiana** (☎ 311-279; O'Higgins 437; pizza CH$4300-7800; ☼ lunch & dinner) has hit-or-miss pizza and pasta in an upscale treehouse atmosphere.

Getting There & Away

Panguipulli's main **Terminal de Buses** (☎ 311-055; Gabriela Mistral 100), at the corner of Diego Portales, has regular departures from Monday to Saturday to Liquiñe, Coñaripe and Lican Ray; to Choshuenco, Neltume and Puerto Fuy; and to Valdivia and Temuco. Buses from Panguipulli to Puerto Fuy (two hours)

pass through Choshuenco and return to Panguipulli early the following morning.

LAGO PIRIHUEICO

The road to Puerto Fuy on Lago Pirihueico parallels Río Huilo Huilo, which tumbles and falls through awe-inspiring scenery. **Huilo-Huilo Reserva Natural Biosfera** (☎ 02-334-4565; www.huilohuilo.cl, in Spanish; admission CH$3000-25,000), encompassing 1000 sq km of private land, has developed the area for low-impact ecotourism and runs two spectacularly insane hotels: **La Montaña Mágica** (d incl lunch or dinner from CH$95,000; Ⓟ ⊠ ⌨), a Frodo-approved spire with a fountain spewing from the top and full of kitschy furniture and supernatural design touches; and the new **Hotel Baobob** (d incl lunch or dinner from CH$116,200; Ⓟ ⊠ ⌨), a Gaudi-inspired inverted cone suspended in the treetops with a restaurant serving international cuisine with Mapuche touches. The reserve offers numerous outdoor adventures (trekking, climbing, mountain biking, horseback riding and ice trekking) but you need a guide to enter everywhere but the 37m **Salto de Huilo Huilo**. The two interconnected hotels can provide guides for nonguests.

From Puerto Fuy, the ferry **Hua-Hum** (☎ 063-197-1585) carries passengers and vehicles to and from Puerto Pirihueico (1½ hours) year-round once daily in each direction. Automobiles pay CH$12,000 to CH$15,000, pedestrians pay CH$1000 and bicycles CH$2000. The *Hua-Hum* can fit 24 vehicles, so make reservations.

VALDIVIA

☎ 063 / pop 139,505

Valdivia is the recently crowned capital of Region XIV (Los Ríos), Chile's newest region, inaugurated in 2007 after years of defection talk surrounding its inclusion in Lakes District despite its geographical, historical and cultural differences. It is the most important university town in southern Chile (the Universidad Austral de Chile is here) and as such, offers a strong emphasis on the arts, student prices at many hostels, restaurants and bars, and a dose of youthful energy that would brighten any foggy riverside town. If you're here in March, you'll see hazed new students slathered in goop and begging for money.

With its German effervescence and subtle café culture, Valdivia is the most attractive city in the region due to its scenic location at the confluence of the Calle Calle, Cau Cau and Cruces rivers. Make sure to visit the Feria Fluvial waterfront where sea lions have discovered the Promised Land – a place where they can float around all day and let tourists and fishmongers throw them scraps from the daily catch.

Orientation

Valdivia, 160km southwest of Temuco and 45km west of the Panamericana, sits on the south bank of the Río Calle Calle where it becomes Río Valdivia. Av Costanera Arturo Prat (known simply as Prat) is a major focus of activity, but the most important public buildings are on Plaza de la República. To the west, the Puente Pedro de Valdivia crosses the river to Isla Teja, a leafy suburb that is the site of the Universidad Austral.

Information

BOOKSTORES
La Librería de Valdivia (☎ 271-818; Lautaro 177; ☒ 10am-1:30pm & 3:30-8pm Mon-Fri, 10am-2pm Sat) Large bookstore, small English section.

EMERGENCY
Police (☎ 241-429; Beauchef 1025)

INTERNET ACCESS
Café Phonet (☎ 341-054; Libertad 127; per hr CH$500; ☒ 9am-9pm) Surly service, lots of internet stations.

LAUNDRY
Lavandería Lavamatica (☎ 211-015; Walter Schmidt 305; per load CH$4000; ☒ 9:30am-1pm & 3-7:30pm Mon-Fri, 9am-4pm Sat) Discounts for students.

MEDICAL SERVICES
Hospital Regional (☎ 297-000; Simpson 850; ☒ 24hr)

MONEY
Downtown ATMs are abundant.
Banco de Chile (Libertad & Henriquez)

POST
Post office (☎ 212-167; O'Higgins 575)

TOURIST INFORMATION
Información Turística (☎ 220-498; ☒ 8am-10pm) At the bus terminal.
Sernatur (☎ 239-060; Costanera Arturo Prat 555; ☒ 8:30am-5:30pm) On the riverfront.

Sights & Activities

Museo Histórico y Antropológico (☎ 212-872; Los Laureles 47; admission CH$1300; ☒ 10am-8pm Dec 15-Mar 15, 10am-6pm Mar 16-Dec 14), housed in a fine riverfront mansion on Isla Teja, is one of Chile's finest. It features a large, well-labeled collection from pre-Columbian times to the present, with particularly fine displays of Mapuche Indian artifacts and household items from early German settlements. Take the bridge across the Río Valdivia, turn left at the first intersection and walk about 200m; the entrance is on the left (east) side.

Museo de Arte Contemporáneo (☎ 221-968; Los Laureles; admission CH$1200; ☒ 10am-2pm & 4-8pm Tue-Sun summer, 10am-1pm & 3-7pm Tue-Sun winter) Valdivia's modern art museum sits alongside the archaeological museum and is built atop the foundations of the former Cervecería Anwandter, the one-time brewery that tumbled during the 1960 earthquake. The museum has fine views across the river to the city.

The **Feria Fluvial** (Av Costanera Arturo Prat s/n; ☒ 8am-3pm) is the lively riverside market south of the Valdivia bridge, where vendors sell fresh fish, meat and produce. Sea lions come right up to the side and beg for handouts – Sea World–style. To get closer to the sea lions, walk up the Costanera another 200m.

Parque Saval on Isla Teja has a riverside beach and a pleasant trail that follows the shoreline of Laguna de los Lotos, covered with lily pads. It's a good place for bird watching.

A couple of turrets can be seen around town: east of the bus terminal, the **Torreón del Barro** (Av Costanera Arturo Prat s/n) is from a Spanish fort built in 1774, while the **Torreón de los Canelos** (cnr Yerbas Buenas & General Lagos) dates from the 17th century.

Tours

Valdivia's main and traditional tourist attraction is the boat cruises (CH$12,000, 6½ hours) that ply the rivers to visit the different forts (for descriptions, see p294). Each tour says it's different, but most take the same route, stopping at Corral and Isla Mancera for 45 minutes to one hour each, and all include lunch and *onces*. Outfitters include the **Reina Sofia** (☎ 207-120), which departs from Puerto Fluvial at the base of Calle Arauco once per day at 1:30pm.

If the large boats aren't intimate enough for you, **Góndolas Valdivianas** (☎ 527-278; www .gondolasvaldivianas.cl, in Spanish; cnr Av Costanera

VALDIVIA

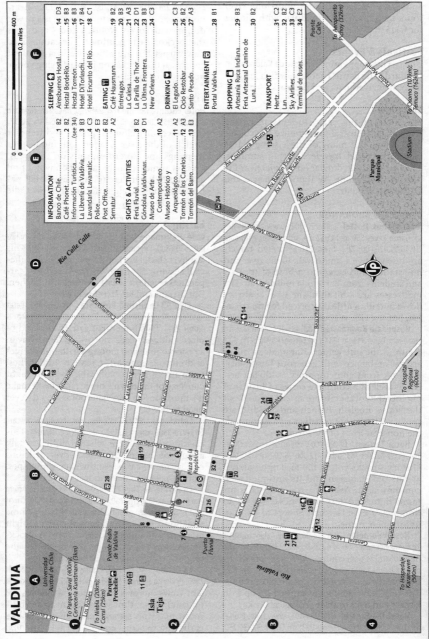

INFORMATION
Banco de Chile.....................1 B2
Café Phonet.........................2 B2
Información Turística............(see 34)
La Librería de Valdivia...........3 B3
Lavandería Lavamatic............4 C3
Police.................................5 E3
Post Office..........................6 B2
Sernatur.............................7 A2

SIGHTS & ACTIVITIES
Feria Fluvial........................8 B2
Góndolas Valdivianas............9 D1
Museo de Arte
  Contemporáneo.................10 A2
Museo Histórico y
  Arqueológico.....................11 A2
Torreón de los Canelos.........12 A3
Torreón del Barro................13 E3

SLEEPING
Airesbuenos Hostal..............14 D3
Hostal BordeRío...................15 B3
Hostal Torreón....................16 B3
Hotel DiTorlaschi.................17 B4
Hotel Encanto del Río...........18 C1

EATING
Café Hausmann....................19 B2
Entrelagos.........................20 B3
La Calesa..........................21 A3
La Parilla de Thor................22 D1
La Última Frontera...............23 B3
New Orleans.......................24 C3

DRINKING
El Legado..........................25 C3
Ocio Restobar.....................26 B2
Santo Pecado......................27 A3

ENTERTAINMENT
Portal Valdivia....................28 B1

SHOPPING
Artesanía Ruca Indiana..........29 B3
Feria Artesanal Camino de
  Luna...............................30 B2

TRANSPORT
Hertz................................31 C2
Lan..................................32 B2
Sky Airlines.......................33 C3
Terminal de Buses...............34 E2

SUR CHICO

Arturo Prat & Carampangue) does hour-long river tours in Italian-style gondolas with dinner for CH$16,000.

Festivals & Events

The largest happening is **Noche de Valdivia**, on the third Saturday in February, which features decorated riverboats and fireworks.

Sleeping

For most of the year students from the Universidad Austral monopolize the cheapest lodging, but many of these same places vigorously court travelers during summer. They are cheaper, dingier *hospedajes* near the bus terminal along Av Ramón Picarte and Carlos Anwandter.

BUDGET & MIDRANGE

Airesbuenos Hostel (☎ 222-202; www.airesbuenos .cl; Garcia Reyes 550; dm CH$7500, s/d without bathroom CH$16,000/20,000; ☐) This HI-affiliated traveler's hub is a five-minute walk to the river and bus station and caters to a host of tourists and students from Barcelona to Belgrade. The mattresses are a bit thin, the wi-fi is always down and it's a little overpriced for this market, but the vibe is cool.

Hospedaje Karamawen (☎ 433-104; karamawen@ gmail.com; General Lagos 1334; r per person CH$9000; P ☐) South of the city center, Karamawen mixes artistic ambience with generous hospitality. Artwork from contemporary Valdivian artists as well as a complete series of historical photographs of the city are spread throughout the house. English, French and Swedish are spoken. There's not usually a sign up, but it's the house in front of the mechanic.

Hostal Torreón (☎ 099-100-0688; hctorreon@entelchile .net; Pérez Rosales 783; s/d CH$12,500/25,000; P ☒ ☐) History smacks you in the face upon arrival at this old mansion and its antique-laden common area. Ask for a room upstairs for more light and less dampness. Say hi to Rommel, a cute German Sheppard with an unfortunate name.

Hostal BordeRío (☎ 214-069; www.valdiviacabanas .cl; CamiloHenriquez 746; s/d CH$18,000/23,000; P) This new hostel is well equipped for travelers with a sunny breakfast nook, large bathrooms, colorful bedspreads and even loveseats in most rooms. They also have cabins and can set you up with kayaks and trips to their ecological park.

Hotel DiTorlaschi (☎ 224-103; www.hotelditorlas chi.cl, in Spanish; Yerbas Buenas 283; s/d CH$26,900/30,250,

cabins for 2/4 CH$33,600/43,700; P ☐) This near-boutique hotel in a restored home is a newer option with lovely wooden doors and beds that beckon early bedtimes. The cabins need new carpet but are otherwise in a pleasant courtyard that tricks you into believing you're no longer in the city.

TOP END

Hotel Encanto del Río (☎ 225-740; Av Costanera Arturo Prat; s/d CH$37,800/45,400; P ☒) Opened in 2007, this newcomer along a quieter and trendier stretch of the river is laden with indigenous weavings and Botero reprints on the walls, given it some extra character you won't find elsewhere. Riverview rooms have small patios that look straight across the Río Calle Calle…to a factory.

Eating

Café Hausmann (☎ 213-878; O'Higgins 394; mains CH$1350-6800; ☺ breakfast, lunch & dinner Mon-Sat) This Valdivia classic is a family-owned hole-in-the-wall serving up the town's top *cruditos* (carpaccio served on toast), strudel and küchen. But instant coffee? *Here*? Jesus.

our pick La Última Frontera (☎ 235-363; Pérez Rosales 787; sandwiches CH$2500-4000; ☺ lunch & dinner; V) This bohemian café is the kind of place Valdivia needs more of, hidden away in a restored mansion among a battalion of trees and cutting-edge art. Creative sandwiches, fresh juices and a chill vibe day and night courtesy of the town's hip artistic front make it a must-stop. If they had rooms, you'd never need to leave.

Entrelagos (☎ 218-333; Pérez Rosales 640; sandwiches CH$1920-3500, cake CH$1900; ☺ lunch & dinner) This classic *salón de Té* is where Valdivians talk about you behind your back over delicious *café cortados*, cakes, sandwiches and crepes. The *chocolatería* next door is also a must.

La Parilla de Thor (☎ 270-767; Av Costanera Arturo Prat 653; steak 400g CH$5850; ☺ lunch & dinner) A waft of cedar and *asado* greets diners at this Argentine steakhouse on the Costanera. A *porteño* might argue, but the *bife de chorizo* here is shockingly close to what you get in Argentina – the only thing missing is the Malbec.

La Calesa (☎ 225-467; Yungay 735; mains CH$5100-7900; ☺ lunch & dinner Mon-Fri, diner Sat) With excellent views out over the water (two tables are outside), this intimate restaurant in a multiroom mansion serves Peruvian staples like garlic-roasted chicken and an excellent *lomo*

SUR CHICO

saltado. The pisco sours are memorable as is the *suspiro*, a Peruvian desert made from *manjar* and meringue and laced with *pisco*.

New Orleans (☎ 218-771; Esmeralda 682; mains CH$5200-8100; 🕑 lunch & dinner Mon-Sat) The seafood gumbo at this speakeasy-style restaurant ain't winning any Louisiana cook-offs, but it's a nice change of culinary pace on the otherwise Chilean-international menu. That said, it's an expensive spot and, worse, an all-smoking restaurant.

For inexpensive seafood visit any of the several restaurants at the **Mercado Central**. Specialties include *choritos al ajillo* (mussels in garlic and chilies).

Drinking

The main concentration of nightlife is on Esmeralda – take your pick.

El Legado (☎ 207-546; Esmeralda 657) A sultry jazz bar featuring live jazz fusion, acid jazz and soul on weekends.

Ocio Restobar (☎ 214-203; Calle Arauco 102; pizza CH$5500; 🕑 7pm-late Mon-Thu, 8pm-late Fri & Sat) This orange-glowing lounge has an array of two-for-one cocktails during its extensive *Hora Feliz* (Happy Hour) and a DJ spins everything from house to hip-hop nightly. There's also pizza and tapas when you get the munchies.

Santo Pecado (☎ 239-122; Yungay 745; mains CH$3200-5600; 🕑 lunch & dinner Mon-Sat) Funky lounge chairs and banquets and *Jetsons*-style lights insure the environment in this lounge-restaurant is uber-trendy. The innovative menu features such missing-in-action culinary flavors as curry, pesto and goat cheese.

Entertainment

Portal Valdivia (cnr Yungay & Carampangue) When it opens in 2010, this striking, twin-towered casino, hotel and shopping complex – Valdivia's most architecturally-interesting building – will house US$72 million worth of entertainment options for visitors and locals alike.

Shopping

Feria Artesanal Camino de Luna (Mercado Municipal) is a good spot to pick up wooden handicrafts or woolen goods. For Mapuche crafts, try **Artesanía Ruca Indiana** (Camilo Henríquez 772).

Getting There & Away
AIR
Aeropuerto Pichoy (☎ 272-295) is 32km from Valdivia on Ruta 5. **Lan** (☎ 246-494; www.lan

.com; Maipú 271) flies to Santiago twice per day from CH$104,100. **Sky Airlines** (☎ 226-280; www .skyairline.cl; Walter Schmidt 303) goes once per day each to Santiago (from CH$32,000) and Concepción (from CH$19,000).

BUS
Valdivia's **Terminal de Buses** (☎ 212-188; Anfión Muñoz 360) has frequent buses to destinations on or near the Panamericana between Puerto Montt and Santiago. Companies include **Tur-Bus** (☎ 226-010) **Tas Choapa** (☎ 213-124), **Andesmar** (☎ 224-665), **Bus Norte** (☎ 212-806), **Igi Llaima** (☎ 213-542), **Pullman** (☎ 278-576), **Pirihueico** (☎ 218-609), **Vía Tur** (☎ 219-016), **San Martín** (☎ 251-062), and **Cruz del Sur** (☎ 213-840), which services the island of Chiloé and elsewhere.

Regional bus carriers include Pirihueico to Panguipulli; **Bus Futrono** (☎ 257-644) to Futrono; **Buses JAC** (☎ 212-925) to Villarrica, Pucón and Temuco; and **Buses Cordillera Sur** (☎ 229-533) to other interior Lakes District destinations. Ruta 5 goes to Lago Ranco. For Niebla, bus 20 leaves every 10 minutes.

Tas Choapa and Andesmar both go to Bariloche, Argentina daily at 8:45am. San Martín goes to San Martín de los Andes and Neuquén Wednesday, Friday and Sunday at 7:30am.

Destination	Cost (CH$)	Duration (hr)
Bariloche (Ar)	CH$13,000	7
Castro	CH$8000	7
Futrono	CH$1500	2
Lago Ranco	CH$1200	2
Neuquén (Ar)	CH$15,000	12
Osorno	CH$2200	1¾
Panguipulli	CH$2200	2¼
Pucón	CH$2700	3
Puerto Montt	CH$3200	3½
San Martín de los Andes (Ar)	CH$10,000	8
Santiago	From CH$14,500	11
Temuco	CH$3000	2½
Villarrica	CH$2300	2¼

Getting Around

From the bus terminal, any bus marked 'Plaza' will take you to Plaza de la República. There are also *colectivos* around town.

To and from the airport, **Transfer Aeropuerto Valdivia** (☎ 225-533) provides an on-demand minibus service (CH$3000). A taxi costs

CH$12,000. For car rental, try **Hertz** (☎ 218-316; Av Ramón Picarte 640).

AROUND VALDIVIA

At **Cervecería Kunstmann** (☎ 292-969; www.lacerveceria .cl, in Spanish; Ruta T-350 950; pitchers CH$4700-4900, mains CH$4950-6900; ⊙ noon-midnight), on Isla Teja at Km5 on the road to Niebla, you'll find the South's best brewery. Call ahead if you're interested in a free tour, but we know you're really just here for the suds. Make sure to try the unfiltered versions of the Toro Bayo and lager at this large brewpub and beer museum – they aren't available anywhere else. In the evening, the hearty German fare includes lots of pork chops, späetzle, sauerkraut, and apple sauce, which – let's be frank – is only good if your name is Rolf and you suffer from a debilitating case of homesickness. bus 20 from Carampague to Isla Teja (CH$300) can drop you off.

The 81-hectare **Parque Punta Curiñanco**, 35km northwest of Valdivia in Curiñanco, is a unique piece of Valdivian rainforest featuring four types of subforest within its boundaries. It's great for hiking and there are spectacular ocean views and a long, beautiful beach. Keep an eye out for the Darwin's Frogs; they look conspicuously like an autumn leaf. To get here from Valdivia, grab a bus marked Curiñanco to the left of the bridge to Isla Teja (on the Valdivia side). The entrance to the park is hidden behind two private properties. The second is a little house where a man will open the gate to the park.

Southwest of Valdivia, where the Río Valdivia and the Río Tornagaleones join the Pacific, lie the 17th-century Spanish fortifications at **Corral**, **Niebla** and **Isla Mancera**. Largest and most intact is the **Castillo de Corral**, consisting of the Castillo San Sebastián de la Cruz (1645), the gun emplacements of the Batería de la Argolla (1764) and the Batería de la Cortina (1767). **Fuerte Castillo de Amargos**, a half-hour walk north of Corral, lurks on a crag above a small fishing village.

On the north side of the river, **Fuerte Niebla** (1645) allowed Spanish forces to catch potential invaders in a crossfire. The broken ramparts of **Castillo de la Pura y Limpia Concepción de Monfort de Lemus** (1671) are the oldest remaining ruins. Isla Mancera's **Castillo San Pedro de Alcántara** (1645) guarded the confluence of the Valdivia and the Tornagaleones rivers; later it became the residence of the military governor.

Niebla itself makes for a fine day trip – the coastal town emits a northern California beach-town vibe and is an easy escape from Valdivia.

The tours that leave from the Puerto Fluvial in Valdivia would like you to believe they are the only way to get to the fortifications, but there's a much more economic alternative: *colectivos* (leaving from the corner of Chacabuco and Yungay; CH$600) or bus 20 (CH$300). From Niebla, ferries go back and forth between Corral and Isla Mancera every 20 minutes. The ferries run between 8am and 8:40pm, and each leg is CH$700.

LAGO RANCO
☎ 063

When it comes to southern Chilean lakes, Lago Ranco, 124km from Valdivia, is a true sleeper: though not heavily visited or well-known outside Chile, it's a glistening sapphire hideaway bound by lush mountains and peppered with verdant islands. For whatever reason, tourism hasn't dug in its heels here yet, so it's great if you want to escape the crowds and get away with your best friend's spouse or hunker down to finish that screenplay, but bad if you want to eat or sleep well while you're doing it. In one circuit around this cerulean lake you can enjoy majestic views of the Andes, simple working towns, high-end fishing resorts and Mapuche communities. This section takes you clockwise from Futrono to the town of in Lago Ranco, the two most accessible towns on the lake.

Futrono
☎ 063 / pop 16,756

On the north shore of Lago Ranco, 102km from Valdivia via Paillaco, Futrono is a dusty old town with a frontier feel. As it's the main service center for the lake and the Mapuche community on Isla Huapi, there's way more action here than in Lago Ranco, but that's not saying much.

The **Oficina de Turismo** (☎ 482-636; www.turismo futrono.cl, in Spanish; O'Higgins & Balmaceda; ⊙ 8:30am-9pm Mon-Fri, 10am-9pm Sat & Sun Dec-Feb) is at the western approach to town and can help arrange boat passage to Isla Huapi and to hot springs, *agroturismo* and community stays at Lago Maihue and horse treks, among other excursions. They are very eager to help.

At **Hospedaje Futronhué** (☎ 481-265; hospedaje futronhue@gmail.com; Balmaceda 90; r per person without bathroom CH$5000, d with bathroom CH$6000), the only thing more startling than the bright-orange exterior is the aqua interior at this simple but clean and fairly priced *hospedaje*. Breakfast costs CH$1000.

Magnificent views are tableside at **Don Floro** (☎ 481-271; Balmaceda 114; mains CH$3500-6200; ✆ lunch Apr-Oct, lunch & dinner Nov-Mar), the most coveted restaurant on the lake. Even Santiaguinos rave about the *cazuela* and the *lomo de lo pobre* (steak and fries topped with fried egg).

Boats leave from Puerto Futrono at the end of Av Sanfuentes for Isla Huapi on Monday, Wednesday and Friday at 5pm; returns are the same days at 7:30am, so you need to stay two nights. The only lodging option is with a Mapuche family at **Cabañas Wuichikülen** (☎ 099-115-373; campsites per person CH$4000, r per person without bathroom CH$5000). Breakfast is included and other meals cost CH$2500.

Buses to Valdivia leave every half hour from the parking lot next to Supermercado Big on Balmaceda. For Lago Ranco, Buses Lago Ranco via Riñinahue also leave from here.

Lago Ranco
☎ 063 / pop 11,538

On the south shore, modest and tranquil Lago Ranco is a terraced town leading down to a long and rocky beach. At the time of research, its waterfront was getting a makeover, with a newly paved road and spruced-up plaza. A road continues west and north, crossing over Río Bueno and accessing beaches and anglers' lodges; eventually it joins up with the main road, which leads west to Paillaco and Ruta 5 and east to Futrono. The **tourist office** (☎ 491-212; cnr Av Concepción & Linares; ✆ 11am-8m Dec-Feb) and the municipality distribute area information.

Two adorable cocker spaniels greet travelers at the friendly **Hospedaje Los Pinos** (☎ 491-329; Valparaiso 537; r per person CH$8000; ⓅⓍ▣), which has a lovely owner and good meals for an extra CH$3000. There's also a cabin that sleeps five for CH$30,000.

Hostería Phoenix (☎ 491-226; www.hosteriaphoenix.cl, in Spanish; Viña del Mar 359; r per person CH$10,000; ⓅⓍ▣) A delightful spot despite a couple of leaky faucets, the Phoenix has rooms with a bit of a lake view and rates that include an ample breakfast. The restaurant serves meticulously prepared and served dishes and there's a small bar and laundry, too.

There is regular bus service daily to both Futrono and Lago Ranco from Valdivia

(CH$1500 and CH$1200, 2½ hours) and to Lago Ranco from Osorno (CH$1500, two hours), but you could also catch a bus to the town of Río Bueno and transfer there. From Lago Ranco's rural bus station on La Serena, buses go to Llifén at 12:30pm and 9pm, continuing to Futrono. From the Tur-Bus station on Temuco, you can catch buses for Santiago once per day at 7pm as well as Valdivia and Rio Bueno daily. Only the western edge of the lake is currently not accessible by bus. The crossing at Puerto Lapi is a manually operated barge, run on demand.

THE LAKES DISTRICT

OSORNO
☎ 064 / pop 149,443

Osorno (the city, not the volcano) is a bustling place and the commercial engine for the surrounding agricultural zone. But if anyone tells you they like it, they're lying. In fact, nobody ever has anything particularly positive to say about Osorno, other than that it's a good place to work, but that's a little hard to believe as well. After all, this is a town that has allowed its oldest surviving Germanic structure to be turned into a bar and café (though a good one) and whose central plaza looks converted from a municipal swimming pool. Though it's an important transportation hub on the route between Puerto Montt and Santiago, most visitors spend little time here.

Information
There are plenty of banks and exchange houses around the plaza.

Ciber Café del Patio (Patio Freire; per hr CH$400; ✆ 9:30am-11:30pm Mon-Sat, 3pm-10pm Sun) Internet access at Osorno's swankiest address, Patio Freire. There are also several nice restaurants here.

Conaf (☎ 234-393; Martínez de Rosas) Has details on Parque Nacional Puyehue.

Hospital Base (☎ 235-571; Av Bühler 1765; ✆ 24hr) On the southward extension of Arturo Prat.

Post office (O'Higgins 645)

Sernatur (☎ 237-575; O'Higgins 667; ✆ 8:30am-6:30pm daily Dec-Feb, 8:30am-1pm & 2-5pm Mon-Fri Mar-Nov) On the west side of the Plaza de Armas.

Tourist kiosk (Plaza de Armas; ✆ 8:30am-7pm Mon-Fri, 11am-5pm Sat & Sun Jan-Feb) Offers info on Osorno,

SUR CHICO

OSORNO

INFORMATION	
Ciber C@fé del Patio...........1	D2
Conaf..............................2	B1
Post Office.......................3	C2
Sernatur..........................4	C2
Tourist Kiosk....................5	C2

SIGHTS & ACTIVITIES	
Club Andino Osorno Office...(see 7)	
Museo Histórico Municipal...6	C3
Ski Antillanca Office...........7	C4

SLEEPING	
Hospedaje Sánchez.............8	F2
Hostal Bilbao Express..........9	D3
Hostal Reyenco..................10	D1
Hotel Villa Eduviges...........11	F3

EATING	
BouleBar..........................12	D3
Clube de Artesanos............13	B2
Del Piero.........................14	D4
La Parilla de Pepe..............15	D3

TRANSPORT	
Buses Barria.....................16	E2
Expresso Lago Puyehue.......17	E2
Full Travel.......................18	D3
Lan................................19	C2
Main Bus Terminal..............20	F2
Sky Airlines.....................21	D2
Terminal Mercado Municipal..22	E2

the surrounding areas here and select parts of Chile. In low season, hours are scaled back.

Sights

Osorno's well-arranged **Museo Histórico Municipal** (☎ 238-615; Av Matta 809; admission free; ⏰ 9:30am-6pm Mon-Fri, 2pm-7pm Sat Jan-Feb, 9:30am-5pm Mon-Fri, 2pm-6pm Sat Mar-Dec) includes exhibits on Mapuche culture, the city's shaky colonial origins, German colonization and 19th-century development, all in an impressive neocolonial building dating from 1929.

The block of Mackenna, between Cochrane and Freire, has a row of early Germanic houses. From 1876, the former Casa Mohr Pérez, now BouleBar (right), is Osorno's oldest surviving Germanic construction.

Sleeping

BUDGET

There are some bottom-of-the-barrel *hospedajes* around the bus station, though these are less than ideal.

Hospedaje Sánchez (☎ 422-140; Los Carrera 1595; r per person CH$5000; **P**) It's quite dingy from the outside and not much better from the inside, but this is the best budget option, run by a nice older couple who mean well. There's cable TV in all the rooms and a whole lot of caged birds in the kitchen.

Hostal Reyenco (☎ 236-285; reyenco@surnet.cl; Freire 309; s without bathroom CH$12,000, d 16,000; **P**) For a few extra *pesos* over the budget options, you'll be much more comfortable here, with a nice living room and breakfast area (remember eggs?). Most rooms have a private bathroom.

MIDRANGE & TOP END

Hostal Bilbao Express (☎ 262-200; www.hotelbilbao.cl, in Spanish; Francisco Bilbao 1019; s/d CH$14,300/20,200; **P**) It's totally middle of the road, but the location is good and you can get all the amenities of their more expensive sister hotel here for less money, including free wi-fi. Breakfast is laughable, though.

Hostal Trucaya (☎ 249-829; www.turismotruyaca.cl; Av Alcalde Fuchslocher 1420; s/d CH$14,300/20,200; **P** ✕ **□**) If you're stuck here for a night, it's worth the 10-minute taxi ride out to this working farm on Ruta 215. The motel-style rooms are more comfortable and newer than anything in town at this price, and the setting is far more agreeable. But use of the word 'dorm' in their pamplets (of which there aren't any) is irritatingly misleading.

Hotel Villa Eduviges (☎ 235-023; www.hoteleduviges .cl, in Spanish; Eduviges 856; s/d CH$15,450/25,750; **P** **□**) Eduviges is one of the few hotels in Region X that allows singles to sleep in a room with a double bed without paying for a double. The relaxed setting in a residential area south of the bus terminal sets it apart from other options in town, with spacious rooms, private bathrooms, tranquil gardens and kind management.

Eating

Café Central (☎ 257-711; O'Higgins 610; mains CH$1250-6100; ⏰ breakfast, lunch & dinner) This bi-level spot on the plaza gets crowded for its coffee, Kunstmann draft, colossal burgers and breakfast. There's also a counter for solo travelers.

Clube de Artesanos (☎ 230-307; Juan Mackenna 634; mains CH$2600-5200; ⏰ lunch & dinner Mon-Sat, lunch Sun) A union house that's been converted into the most alluring place to put away a pint or *pastel del choclo*. The bar, brimming with personality, is also one of few places that serve local homebrew Märzen – don't miss it.

Del Piero (☎ 256-767; Manuel Rodriguez 1081; mains CH$2000-7800; ⏰ lunch & dinner Mon-Sat) You're craving Italian, aren't you? There's a sexy vibe at this upscale eatery decked out in dark woods and reds. There's a wealth of signature seafood dishes as well as mix-and-match pastas. Try the creamy crab-stuffed calamari.

La Parilla de Pepe (☎ 249-653; cnr Juan Mackenna & Freire; mains CH$3800-6000; ⏰ lunch & dinner Mon-Sat, lunch Sun) Pepe runs a one-man show on the grill at this locals' haunt for cheap steaks. The aged exterior is intriguing, the interior far more respectful. They are a bit skimpy on the fries, but the steaks are cooked to perfection. Reservations are recommended, especially at weekends.

BouleBar (☎ 232-370; Juan Mackenna 949; ⏰ breakfast, lunch & dinner Mon-Fri) One of Osorno's few hip spots, though not quite as cool as its sister bar in Puerto Montt. Still, pickings are slim, so drinks here are obligatory, if for no other reason then to toast to its former history as the town's oldest surviving Germanic structure. *Probst!*

Getting There & Away

AIR

Osorno's Aeropuerto Carlos Hott Siebert (also known as Cañal Bajo) is 7km east of downtown, across the Panamericana via Av Buschmann. **Lan** (☎ 600-526-2000; Eleuterio

Ramírez 802) flies twice daily to Santiago (from CH$141,000). **Sky Airlines** (☎ 230-186; Galeria Centroosorno, Cochrane) flies to Santiago (from CH$32,000), Temuco (from CH$14,000) and Concepción (from CH$30,000).

BUS

Long-distance and Argentine-bound buses use the **main bus terminal** (☎ 234-149; Errázuriz 1400), near Angulo.

Bus companies include **Andesmar** (☎ 233-050), **Pullman Bus** (☎ 318-529), **Tas Choapa** (☎ 233-933), **JAC** (☎ 553-300), **Tur-Bus** (☎ 201-526), **Tal Norte** (☎ 236-076), **Inter** (☎ 324-160), **Igi Llaima** (☎ 234-371), **Bus Norte** (☎ 233-933), **Queilen Bus** (☎ 250-026), **Turibús** (☎ 232-777) and **Cruz del Sur** (☎ 232-777).

Most services going north on the Panamericana start in Puerto Montt, departing about every hour, with mainly overnight service to Santiago. Buses to destinations in Argentina and Chilean Patagonia, such as Coyhaique, Punta Arenas and Puerto Natales, go via Ruta 215 and Paso Cardenal Antonio Samoré.

Try Quellen Bus for Coyhaique and Pullman or Cruz del Sur for Punta Arenas. Igi Llaima goes to Zapala and Neuquén on weekdays via Temuco, while Cruz del Sur, Andesmar and Tas Choapa have daily service to Bariloche. **Ruta 5** (☎ 317-040) goes to Lago Ranco. Many but not all of these services also originate in Puerto Montt; for more details, see p317.

Sample travel times and fares follow:

Destination	Cost (CH$)	Duration (hr)
Ancud	CH$4500	4
Bariloche (Ar)	CH$12,000	5
Concepción	CH$12,000	9
Coyhaique	CH$30,000	20
Puerto Montt	CH$1500	1½
Punta Arenas	CH$40,000	27
Santiago	from CH$1800	12
Temuco	CH$4000	4½
Valdivia	CH$2000	1¾
Valparaíso/Viña del Mar	CH$18,900	14
Zapala-Neuquén (Ar)	CH$14,000	17

Also from the main bus terminal is a service to Río Bueno, with connections to Lago Ranco and to Panguipulli (via Valdivia), and many trips daily to places around Lago Llanquihue at the foot of Volcán Osorno. Other local and regional destinations leave from the **Terminal**

Mercado Municipal (☎ 201-237; cnr Errázuriz & Arturio Prat) behind the Mercado Municipal. **Buses Barria** (☎ 201-306) goes to Entre Lagos from behind the northwest corner of the market, while **Expreso Lago Puyehue** (☎ 243-919) goes to Termas Puyehue/Aguas Calientes (CH$1700) and Anticura (CH$4000) from behind the northeast corner.

To get to the Mapuche communities of San Juan de la Costa – Bahía Mansa, Pucatrihue and Maicolpué – cross the Río Ráhue to the bus stops at **Feria Libre Ráhue** (☎ 269-704; cnr Chillán & Temuco). *Colectivos* head off there from the corner of Tarapaca and Republica.

Getting Around

Osorno is not particularly difficult to get around. An airport cab costs about CH$4100. **Full Travel** (☎ 235-579; Av Francisco Bilbao 1011) rents cars from CH$20,000 per day.

ENTRE LAGOS
☎ 064 / pop 3,358

Entre Lagos is a slow-paced lakeside town 50km east of Osorno on Ruta 215, on the southwest shore of Lago Puyehue. It's a good alternative to Osorno, especially if you're on your way to Parque Nacional Puyehue or embarking on the Puyehue traverse from El Caulle. It's also the first town of significance after crossing the border on the road from Bariloche. The town is split into two; the western entrance is more commercial (with the post office, ATM and gas station), and the eastern entrance leads to lodging choices and the beach.

Camping No Me Olvides (☎ 371-633; campsite per person CH$4000; cabins 2/6 people CH$36,000/62,000), 6km east of town on Ruta 215, is a top-notch campground with large garden sites divided by pruned hedges under plum and apple trees. It offers abundant firewood, excellent showers and a kiosk selling breads and cakes in the summer.

Hospedaje Panorama (☎ 371-398; General Lagos 687; r per person CH$12,000; **P**) was under a complete renovation during research, though we got a taste of the new rooms with private bathrooms – a steal at these prices, though it would be nice if the curtains weren't sheer and you didn't have to ask for hot water to be fired up. The numerous dogs are friendlier than the family (at least when the owner is away in Argentina), but the pillow-top beds are snug and there's excellent breakfasts.

Buses between Osorno and Aguas Calientes (CH$1700) stop in town in a parking lot next to the Casa de Deportes on O'Higgins every half-hour. There is also continuous service to and from Osorno (CH$1000).

TERMAS DE PUYEHUE

Alcohol problem? Can't shake cigarettes? Battling a time-consuming porn habit? There's no cure here for those, but the therapeutic waters at **Termas de Puyehue** (☎ 02-293-6000; www .puyehue.cl; day use from CH$30,000, s CH$124,200-138,000, d CH$172,800-192,000; P 🖳 🏊) are said to cure just about everything else. This baronial destination resort, set on an elegant 36 sq km just off Ruta 215, 76km east of Osorno, bills itself as Chile's first five-star, all-inclusive resort. It is indeed impressive: colossal stone archways, never-ending staircases, heated hallways, three thermal pools, a full-blown spa and three restaurants. The waters aren't in as good a shape as the resort itself (the outdoor option with views is preferred), but if it eases your arthritis and rheumatism, who cares, right? Rooms are sensibly furnished, but numbers 250-469 have more comfortable beds and partial lake views.

From the resort the north fork of Ruta 215 goes to Anticura and to the Argentine border, while the southern lateral leads to Aguas Calientes and Antillanca in Parque Nacional Puyehue.

PARQUE NACIONAL PUYEHUE

Volcán Puyehue, 2240m tall, blew its top the day after the earthquake in 1960, turning a large chunk of dense, humid evergreen forest into a stark landscape of sand dunes and lava rivers. Today, **Parque Nacional Puyehue** (www.parquepuyehue.cl, in Spanish) protects 1070 sq km of this contrasting environment, and it is one of the more 'developed' of the country's national parks, with a ski resort and several hot-spring resorts within its boundaries. There are also several hikes that explore more pristine areas of the national park. Aguas Calientes is the main sector of the park, with the hot-springs resort and Conaf's **Centro de Información Ambiental** (Aguas Calientes; 🕘 9am-7pm Jan-Feb, 9am-1pm & 2-6pm Mar-Dec), which houses an informative display on Puyehue's natural history and geomorphology.

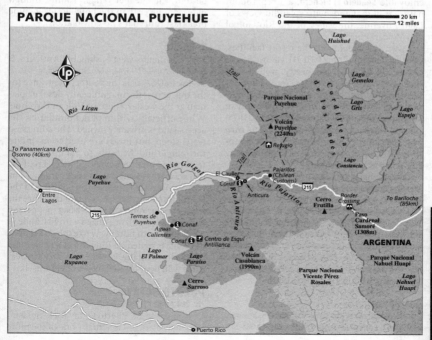

PARQUE NACIONAL PUYEHUE

The park's western border is about 75km east of Osorno via the paved Ruta 215, which continues through the park, following the course of the Río Golgol to the Argentine border.

Buses and *colectivos* from Osorno's Mercado Municipal go to Termas de Puyehue, Aguas Calientes, Anticura and Chilean customs and immigration at Pajaritos. Any bus heading to Anticura can drop off trekkers at El Caulle. In winter, there may be a shuttle to the ski lodge at Antillanca; contact the Club Andino Osorno. Otherwise, you'll need to arrange your own transportation.

Aguas Calientes

An unassuming **hot-springs resort** (day use CH$3500-7000), Aguas Calientes is overrun with Chilean families and gets crowded in the summer months. On offer are typical spa services, individual tubs, a very hot indoor pool and a large shallow cement pool by the side of the river. However, you can access the free **Pocitos Termas** 80m across the Colgante bridge from the Conaf parking lot. Another way to get your heart rate up is to hike the enjoyable **Sendero El Pionero**, a steep 1800m nature trail that ends with splendid views of Lago Puyehue, the valley of the Río Golgol and Volcán Puyehue.

Down the street from the resort facilities, **Camping Chanleufú** (☎ 064-331-711 in Osorno; 4-person campsites CH$10,000; ☒) has pretty, well-spaced sites, some near the river. It doesn't have hot showers, but fees entitle you to use the outside pool and facilities. Nearby, open only in summer, **Camping Los Derrumbes** (☎ 064-331-711 in Osorno; 4-person campsites CH$10,000) heats its own water. In January and February, both campsites fill to maximum capacity, obstructing any sense of natural serenity.

Cabañas Aguas Calientes (☎ 064-236-988; www.termasaguascalientes.com, in Spanish; office at O'Higgins 784, Osorno, cabins at Ruta 215, Km 4 Camino Antillanca; 4-10 person cabins CH$58,823-109,243; ℗ ☒) is the only lodging option. Its A-frame cabins are stacked up along the hillside like a miniature well-planned village, and they are remarkably comfortable, with plush beds, full kitchens, hot showers and wood stoves. Rates include spa facilities and a filling breakfast.

Antillanca

On the southwest slope of Volcán Casablanca (1990m), **Centro de Esquí Antillanca** (☎ 064-235-114; www.skiantillanca.com, in Spanish; office at O'Higgins 1073, Osorno) is a popular beginner/intermediate ski resort – just 18km from Aguas Calientes. It has a friendly small-resort ambiance, but is not challenging for the more advanced skier. The road up to the resort twists and turns through scenic areas and past glassy lakes. During the no-snow months, Antillanca is rather drab and unattractive, and the resort's appeal rests with its trails, especially the walk or drive (per vehicle CH$2500) to the crater lookout, where you can drink in a spectacular view of the surrounding mountain range. The ski season runs from early June to late October; full-day lift tickets cost CH$17,600, and rentals CH$16,000. The ski area has five surface lifts and 460m of vertical drop. For details on ski packages contact the **Club Andino Osorno** (☎ 064-235-114; O'Higgins 1073, Osorno).

Hotel Antillanca (☎ 064-235-114; s/d in refugio CH$39,750/53,600, in hotel CH$53,200/73,600; ℗ ☐ ☒) is outrageously overpriced, but its typical ski-resort trimmings (gym, sauna, disco, boutique and shops) are the only option unless you're going to ski down to Aguas Calientes. Truth be told, the cheaper *refugio* rooms, though older, are nicer than the hotel. Rates include breakfast (but that's no consolation).

El Caulle

Two kilometers west of skipable Anticura, **El Caulle** (☎ 099-924-3244; www.elcaulle.com, in Spanish; one-time fee CH$7000) is the southern entrance for the trek across the magnificently desolate plateau at the western base of Volcán Puyehue. While officially within park boundaries, the access land is privately owned. The admission fee is steep, but funds are used to maintain the *refugio* and the trails, to put up signs and to provide emergency assistance. Trekkers can stash any extra gear at the entrance. The **Puyehue Traverse** (three to four days) and the **Ruta de los Americanos** (six to eight days) are the most popular routes. **Horse trekking** (per person daily CH$25,000), organized with El Caulle, is a fun and much faster way to explore the area. El Caulle is signed on Ruta 215 as a restaurant, which, incidentally, is extremely cozy and features wild boar hunted by the chef himself.

PUERTO OCTAY
☎ 064 / pop 11,540
Cute and quaint, Puerto Octay (ock-tie) isn't heavily visited, but is actually one of the more

charming towns on Lake Llanquihue and a good escape from more touristy towns to the south. The tranquil streets, perched on a hillside above the lake, yield interesting 1800s German settler architectural treasures around every turn, making for a nice tour of historic homes and buildings and giving the town a supremely sedate and picturesque colonial air. Prior to the establishment of the road around the perimeter of the lake, Puerto Octay was an important harbor for water transportation and was the main connection to the markets in the city of Osorno and is the oldest town on the lake settled by Germans.

Puerto Octay's **tourist office** (☎ 391-750; Esperanza 555; ☼ 8:30am-8pm Nov-Feb) is on the east side of the Plaza de Armas. Ask for the map of the town's historic houses.

The hospitable Chilean-Swiss owners make **Zapato Amarillo** (☎ 310-787; www.zapatoamarillo.cl; dm CH$7000; s/d CH$26,000/30,000, without bathroom CH$15,000/20,000; P ✗ 🖵) a favorite with all age groups. Nestled on a small farm, approximately 2km north of town toward Osorno, you'll find an octagonal dorm house with two impeccably clean bathrooms as well as three separate buildings housing farmhand-chic rooms. Lunch or dinner are CH$5000, and the kitchen results are miraculous – you won't eat better than this for CH$5000 (beg for the smoked pork *cazuela*).

Hotel Centinela (☎ 391-326; www.hotelcentinela.cl; Peninsula de Centinela; r with lake/forest view CH$77,300/ 64,700, cabins 2/6 people CH$59,650/82,350; P 🐾 🖵) is a lovely restored 1913 German chalet, situated at the end of a quiet and secluded peninsula. The disappointing and sparse rooms aren't as inviting as the handsome dark *alerce* wood structure itself, but the plush beds ensure getting up to explore this romantic option won't be easy. The new chef has upped the ante in the restaurant, which now features such southern Chile rarities as Japanese Wagyu beef. There is a new outdoor pool and hot tub, just in case you do manage to get out of bed.

Rancho Espantapájaros (☎ 330-049; buffet CH$9000; ☼ lunch & dinner Dec-Mar, lunch Apr-Nov), the most famous restaurant on the lake, is 7km outside Puerto Octay on the road to Frutillar, and packs in the crowds for the main attraction, succulent *jabalí* (wild boar) cooked on 3.5m spits across a giant *fogón* at the front entrance. It's an expensive buffet, but everything is excellent. Popular with families.

Puerto Octay's **bus terminal** (cnr Balmaceda & Esperanza) has regular service to Osorno (CH$1000), Frutillar (CH$700), Puerto Varas (CH$1300), Puerto Montt (CH$1500) and Cruce de Rupanco (CH$800), from where you can grab a bus to Las Cascadas, another of the lake's less touristy towns.

FRUTILLAR
☎ 065 / pop 14,551

Frutillar is an enchanting lakeside retreat right up the coastline of Lago Llanquihue from Puerto Varas. There is an attractive pier, a long, drawn-out lakeside beach, and, above all, quaint German architecture and küchen aplenty. Though the Germanness of this town can sometimes feel forced compared to Puerto Octay, for instance, it remains a serene spot that makes for a pleasant alternative to staying in more chaotic Puerto Varas. As budget accommodation is scarce unless you're camping, Frutillar is a better option for mature travelers who are looking for relaxation and a premium view than the relatively sporty Puerto Varas to the south.

The town's **tourist kiosk** (☎ 421-198; Av Phi-lippi; ☼ 10am-9pm) is open December to March.

Sights

The **Museo Histórico Colonial Alemán** (☎ 421-142; cnr Pérez Rosales & Prat; admission CH$1800; ☼ 10am-2pm & 3-6pm) was built with assistance from Germany and is managed by the Universidad Austral. It features nearly perfect reconstructions of a water-powered mill, a smithy and a mansion set among manicured gardens. It is considered the best museum on German colonialism in the region.

The impressive **Teatro del Lago** (☎ 422-900; www.teatrodellago.cl; Av Philippi 1000) is still a work in progress, but this new waterfront cultural performing arts center houses a 1200-seat concert hall, 200-seat amphitheatre (with views of four volcanoes) and a wonderful café. It currently hosts a wealth of cultural events, including the music festival, and is due for final completion by 2010.

Festivals & Events

For 10 days from late January to early February (usually January 27 through February 4) the **Semana Musical de Frutillar** showcases a variety of musical styles, from chamber music to jazz, with informal daytime shows and more formal evening performances from 8pm to 10pm.

Sleeping & Eating

Camping Los Ciruelillos (☎ 420-163; Km1; 6-person campsite CH$10,000, 6-person cabin CH$30,000) On a small peninsula at the south end of Frutillar Bajo on the road to Punta Larga, this is a tourist complex with a restaurant, boat dock and hotel. The 50 campsites are well distributed with enough dividing bushes. It's got all the amenities: hot showers, electricity, laundry and firepits.

Hotel Kaffee Bauerhaus (☎ 420-003; Av Philippi 663; s/d CH$37,800/42,000; P ☒ ▯) This restored 1918 colonial home is a classic choice with its tearoom decor and historic feel, right on the water.

Hotel Ayacara (☎ 421-550; www.hotelayacara.cl; Av Philippi 1215; r from CH$57,150; P ☒ ▯) Streams of light flow through the inviting living areas, and upstairs front-facing rooms get a spectacular volcano view in this remodeled 1910 house turned boutique hotel.

Café CapPuccini (☎ 099-208-7691; Av Philippi 1000; sandwiches CH$1300-1700; ☽ lunch & dinner) Inside the Teatro del Lago, this modern café serves great coffee, küchen and sandwiches.

Getting There & Around

All transportation leaves from Frutillar Alto. **Cruz del Sur** (☎ 451-552; Alessandri 51) has the most frequent services to Osorno or Puerto Montt, plus four daily departures to Chiloé and one per day to Bariloche. **Tur-Bus** (☎ 421-390; Christiana y Misonera) and its affiliates go to Santiago, Pucón and Valdivia. At the Alessandri terminal, Thaebus goes to Puerto Octay, Puerto Varas, Puerto Montt and Osorno.

PUERTO VARAS
☎ 065 / pop 32,216

Two menacing, snow-capped volcanoes, Osorno and Calbuco, stand sentinel over picturesque Puerto Varas and its scenic Lake Llanquihue like soldiers of adventure, allowing only those on a high-octane quest to pass. Just 23km from Puerto Montt but world's apart in charm, scenery and options for the traveler, Puerto Varas has been touted in the past as the 'next Pucón,' but unlike its kindred spirit to the north, Puerto Varas been able to better manage its rise as a go-to destination for outdoor adventure sports, and, as a result, avoids some of the tourist-package onslaught that besieges Pucón.

There is great access to water sports here – kayaking and canyoning in particular – as well as climbing, fishing, hiking and even skiing. While Puerto Varas gets packed in the summer, it receives many more independent travelers than Pucón. It basically shuts down in the winter except for a few hearty skiers and mountaineers.

But Puerto Varas offers much more than just outdoor sports. It's a friendly town with some decent bars, restaurants and accommodations. With all of the conveniences of Puerto Montt just a short trip away, Puerto Varas is a top choice for an extended stay and also makes a good base for exploring the region. The scenary is changing here, though – ground has broken on two new five-star hotels – so the verdict is still out on whether the quaint town can maintain its interesting juxtaposition of German heritage and contemporary Chilean adrenaline.

Information

Banco de Chile (cnr Del Salvador & Santa Rosa)
Centro Médico Puerto Varas (☎ 232-792; Walker Martínez 576; ☽ 24hr)
CTS (☎ 237-330; www.ctsturismo.cl; Santa Rosa 560; ☽ 9am-6:30pm Mon-Fri, 9am-12:30pm Sat) This Chilean mega-agency owns the Volcán Osorno ski area. It can arrange transportation to the mountain for clients who purchase packages, book plane tickets and car rental and also arranges tours throughout Chile.
La Comarca (☎ 099-799-1920; www.pueloadventure .cl; San Pedro 311; ☽ 8:30am-8:30pm) This eco-sensitive collective marries smaller outfitters specializing in dramatic and custom-tailored adventure trips to less explored areas of the Rio Puelo Valley and Chiloé with independent travelers looking for an experience beyond the norm. Groups are never more than 10-strong and options include half-day bike trips to Volcán Osorno (CH$30,000) and full-day treks to Volcán Calbuco (CH$30,000). They rent bikes as well.
Parque Pumalín office (☎ 250-079; www.puma linpark.org; Klenner 299; ☽ 8:30am-6:30pm Mon-Fri, 9am-1pm Sat) Though the park is found in Northern Patagonia, this is the official tourism office for Parque Pumalín (p345).
Tourist office (☎ 232-437; San Francisco 431; ☽ 9am-9pm Dec-Feb, 10am-2pm & 4-6pm Mar-Nov) Has basic brochures and free maps of the area.
Tourist office (☎ 232-437; San Francisco 431; ☽ 9am-9pm Dec-Feb, 10am-2pm & 4-6pm Mar-Nov) Has basic brochures and free maps of the area.

Sights

Puerto Varas' well-maintained German colonial architecture gives the town a dis-

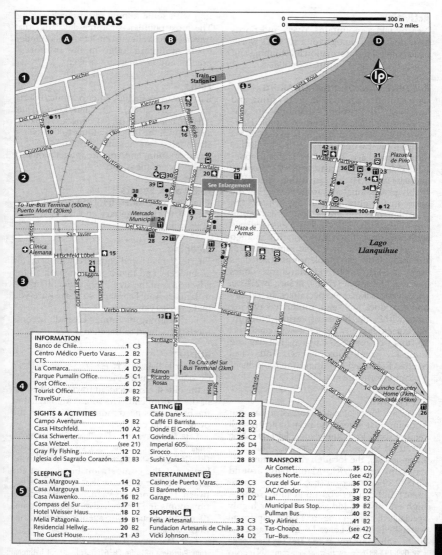

PUERTO VARAS

INFORMATION
Banco de Chile.....................1 C3
Centro Médico Puerto Varas.....2 B2
CTS.................................3 C3
La Comarca.........................4 D2
Parque Pumalín Office..............5 C1
Post Office.........................6 D2
Tourist Office.....................7 B2
TravelSur..........................8 B2

SIGHTS & ACTIVITIES
Campo Aventura.....................9 B2
Casa Hitschfeld...................10 A2
Casa Schwerter....................11 A1
Casa Wetzel.................(see 21)
Gray Fly Fishing..................12 D2
Iglesia del Sagrado Corazón.......13 B3

SLEEPING
Casa Margouya.....................14 D2
Casa Margouya II..................15 A3
Casa Mawenko......................16 B2
Compass del Sur...................17 B1
Hotel Weisser Haus................18 D2
Melia Patagonia...................19 B1
Residencial Hellwig...............20 B2
The Guest House...................21 A3

EATING
Café Dane's.......................22 B3
Caffé El Barrista.................23 D2
Donde El Gordito..................24 B2
Govinda...........................25 C2
Imperial 605......................26 D4
Sirocco...........................27 B3
Sushi Varas.......................28 B3

ENTERTAINMENT
Casino de Puerto Varas............29 C3
El Barómetro......................30 B2
Garage............................31 D2

SHOPPING
Feria Artesanal...................32 C3
Fundación Artesanís de Chile......33 C3
Vicki Johnson.....................34 D2

TRANSPORT
Air Comet.........................35 D2
Buses Norte.................(see 42)
Cruz del Sur......................36 D2
JAC/Condor........................37 D2
Lan...............................38 B2
Municipal Bus Stop................39 B2
Pullman Bus.......................40 B2
Sky Airlines......................41 B2
Tas-Choapa.................(see 42)
Tur-Bus...........................42 C2

tinctive middle-European ambience. The imposing and colorful 1915 **Iglesia del Sagrado Corazón** (cnr San Francisco & Verbo Divino), overlooking downtown from a promontory, is based on the Marienkirche of the Black Forest, Germany.

Other notable constructions are private houses from the early 20th century. Ask at the tourist offices for the brochure *Paseo Patrimonial,* which suggests a walking tour of 10 different houses, or the brochure *Monumentos Nacionales.* Several of these houses serve as *hospedajes,* including the 1941–42 **Casa Schwerter** (Del Carmen 873), the 1930 **Casa Hitschfeld** (Arturo Prat 107) and the 1930 **Casa Wetzel** (O'Higgins 608).

Activities

Nearby lakes, mountains, rivers and fjords provide variety enough for a season's worth of activities. For information on climbing and skiing on Volcán Osorno, see p308.

RAFTING, CANYONING & KAYAKING

Opportunities abound for great rafting and kayaking. Río Petrohué's diamond-blue waters churn up Class III and IV rapids. Half-day rafting trips run around CH$25,000 (5½ hours total, two hours river time). All-day kayaking on Lago Todos Los Santos is about CH$55,000. **Pachamagua** (☎ 099-208-3660; www .pachamagua.com) is the canyoning specialist, highly professional and truly pioneering the sport in the area. Its half-day trip on the Río Blanco is the area's don't-miss if you are fit and unafraid – it ends spectacularly with a rappel down the 34m Río Blanco waterfall followed by a final jump through the falls. You can book tours (half-days start at CH$29,000) via Margouya Tours at Casa Margouya (right). **Al Sur** (☎ 232-300; www.alsurexpeditions.com) specializes in rafting and also does high-end, multiday kayaking trips within the fjords of Parque Pumalín. **Yak Expediciones** (☎ 234-409; www.yakexpediciones .cl) runs well-regarded half-day, full-day and multiday kayak trips on Lago Todas Los Santos, Reloncavi Fjord and the foothills of Volcán Osorno from CH$34,775.

FLY-FISHING

There are loads of places to cast a line, but knowing just where the best spots are will require some local knowledge. **Gray Fly Fishing** (☎ 232-136; San José 192; ☷ 9:30am-1pm, 3-7pm Mon-Fri, 9:30am-1pm Sat), the local Orvis rep, runs half-day trips on the Río Maullin for around CH$39,805 per person (not including equipment) and can set you up at more remote, high-end fishing lodges as well. For highly specialized, custom one- to 14-day trips to all watersheds in the Lakes District as far as La Junta, call John Joy at the **Tres Los Ríos Lodge** (☎ 099-792-8376; www.tresrioslodge.com). Niccolo Cantaruti at **Rios Araucanos** (☎ 8136-8745; bigtrout@ surnet.cl) is also well regarded around town.

HORSE TREKKING

The best spot for a horse trek is the Cochamó Valley. **Campo Aventura** (☎ 232-910; www .campo-aventura.com; San Bernardo 318) offers single-day to multiday treks, often in conjunc-tion with some hiking, rafting or kayaking. The most popular is a three-day jaunt that traverses the valley from its riverside lodge to its mountain lodge in the rainforest. English and German are spoken.

Tours

Easy day tours include Puerto Montt/Puerto Varas (CH$8000), Frutillar/Llanquihue (CH$10,000), Saltos del Petrohué (CH$15,000) and around the lake. Day tours to Chiloé are also offered, but most of your tour is spent in transportation, and you do not get a quality experience of the island.

Festivals & Events

The city celebrates its 1854 founding in the last week of January and the first week of February.

Sleeping

Puerto Varas is well equipped with beds for all budgets, and many can also book all the adventures in the area. *Hospedajes* fill up fast in January and February, so make sure you make a reservation.

For camping or calmer lakeside accom-modations, head to Ensenada.

BUDGET

Residencial Hellwig (☎ 232-472; San Pedro 210; s/d CH$6000/15,000) In a 1915 German house, this is the oldest *residencial* in town and the best of the bottom end. The rooms are large, but the bathrooms need more attention and the owner is a bit crotchety.

Casa Margouya (☎ 237-640; www.margouya.com; Santa Rosa 318; dm CH$6100-6500, s/d without bathroom CH$9720/12,960; ▣) This French-owned hostel beats out the competition because of the friendly communal vibe that it cultivates be-tween its visitors (it's vaguely hippie) and its tidy rooms and comfy bedspreads. It also has its own in-house tour agency for activities in the area.

Casa Margouya II (☎ 237-695; www.margouya .com; Purrisima 681; dm CH$6100, s/d without bathroom CH$9700/12,950, d with bathroom CH$17,800; ✕ ▣) Margouya is creating a hostel empire in Puerto Varas with this, its second location in a large historic 1932 home on the town's list of Patrimonial Heritage sites. It's quieter and offers much larger rooms and bath-rooms for the same price as the more central Casa Margouya.

Casa Mawenko (☎ 232-673; casamawenco@gmail.com; Pasaje Ricke 224; dm/s/d CH$7500/10,000/20,000; P 🖳) This quiet female-run hostel is almost too chill – it's difficult to find help – but it's clean for the most part (there was that Escudo under the bed) and has very cozy new beds and comforters. There are some cramped architectural flaws, but sophisticated design touches all over the house help you forget, as will the breakfast (miraculous at these prices). It's a similar vibe to Margouya (due to a few irresistible permanent residents) but less clutter per square centimeter and more incense.

MIDRANGE & TOP END

Compass del Sur (☎ 652-320; www.compassdelsur.cl; Klenner 467; dm/s/d CH$9000/17,000/21,000; P ✕ 🖳) This charming colonial house with Scandinavian touches sits above the main area of town near the park and is accessed by a staired walking street. It has comfortable beds and extra-strength showers that outperform its price point (there's even turndown service). Basic breakfast is included but travelers can spring for muesli with yogurt or eggs for CH$500 extra.

Hotel Weisser Haus (☎ 346-479; www.weisserhaus.cl, in Spanish; San Pedro 252; s/d CH$29,400/37,800; P 🖳) This new 10-room hotel built in German style is well designed with large bathrooms, light hardwoods and soft colors, burlap lampshades and Rosen beds (one of Chile's best). It's family run and small touches such as pillows along the stairwell and house-made küchen and jams for breakfast make it a likable midrange choice.

our pick The Guest House (☎ 231-521; www.vicki-johnson.com/guesthouse; O'Higgins 608; s/d CH$37,800/43,400; P ✕ 🖳) In the historic Casa Wetzel, this Art Nouveau–era home caters to baby boomers with backpacks: it's simply but tastefully decorated with antiques, snug beds, and beautifully resorted Alerce doors. Breakfast here is legendary (rightfully so, the owner is the town's gourmand) and there's a lush garden and patio area to enjoy a glass of wine and light meals in the evening.

Melia Patagonia (☎ 201-000; www.solmelia.com; Klenner 349; r CH$100,840-273,109; P ✕ 🖳) Blame the Chilean architect for the exterior, but the Argentine-designed interior of this newcomer is a work of art transforming harsh Patagonian landscapes into a minimalist haven for the senses – llama pillows, burlap slip covers, oak-tree tables and the lambskin front desk – and

are all designed to bring the look and feel of Patagonia into a warm boutique hotel. The bar, with its massive open fire, is the town's chicest. There are two restaurants and a spa as well.

Quincho Country Home (☎ 330-737; www.quinchocountryhome.cl; Ruta 225, Km10; 3 nights all-inclusive s CH$1,030,000-1,190,000, d CH$12,600,000-14,600,000; P ✕ 🖳) Luxurious seclusion is the calling of this exquisite Chilean-German pine-log home offering serenity, pampering and exclusivity (maximum eight guests). Guests are profiled Israeli security–style before tailor-made meals, excursions and ultimate pampering commences. Guests can cook with the chef, take a helicopter ride around Osorno or just sit around the massive volcanic fireplace in the beyond comfortable living room and wallow in their own good fortune.

Eating

The dining scene here is picking up, with a couple of notable offerings as well as a good variety of international flavors and a heralded local seafood spot, La Olla, 2km from town along the beach.

Café Dane's (☎ 232-371; Del Salvador 441; mains CH$950-5500; ☾ breakfast, lunch & dinner) This local favorite sums up the hybrid history of the region within its walls: küchen and empanadas, Alpen architecture and Spanish menus, *apfelstrudel* (apple strudel) and conger eel. It's one of the few open early on Sunday. Try the *empanada de horno* (beef, egg, onions and olives), the town's best (CH$1400).

Caffé El Barrista (☎ 233-130; Walker Martínez 211; sandwiches CH$2200-3100; ☾ breakfast, lunch & dinner) The smart Italian coffeehouse has the best brew in this chapter. There's a small selection of sandwiches as well.

Sushi Varas (☎ 310-822; Del Salvador 537; meals CH$4000-8000; ☾ lunch & dinner) If you don't like cream cheese, speak up when you order; otherwise the sushi here will fulfill your cravings for raw fish but OD you on the Philadelphia. Your wallet will appreciate the CH$3900 lunch special.

Sirocco (☎ 232-372; San Pedro 537; mains CH$4200-9500; ☾ lunch & dinner) Divine contemporary Patagonian specialties such as Magellanic lamb and native rabbit are worth forking over the *pesos* for a special night out at this high-end haute restaurant in a large house accented with local art. The *puré rustico* are the best mashed potatoes this side of grandma's house.

Donde El Gordito (☎ 233-425; San Bernardo 560; mains CH$4500-6000; ☯ lunch & dinner, closed Jun) From the same family that owns the more famous La Olla, this smaller and cheaper (and some say better) seafood spot in the Mercado Municipal does wonderful things with crab sauce. It's rich, but excellent.

Govinda (☎ 233-080; Santa Rosa 218; mains CH$7400-10,700; ☯ lunch & dinner; Ⓥ) Though this intimate restaurant owned by a Spanish expatriate suffers from perpetual identity crises (first Italian, this Chilean-Spanish fusion with Indian accents, now changing to straight-up Spanish *tapas* and downsizing the prices), there remains one constant worth visiting for: the roasted eggplant in a house-made ricotta, tomato and yogurt sauce, an innovative dish that sends your palette dancing after *mucho* travel in southern Chile. The artisanal homebrew is also excellent.

our pick **Imperial 605** (☎ 233-105; Imperial 605; mains CH$9000; ☯ lunch & dinner) This historic house above the *costanera* is dressed in sexy reds, saucy blacks and hardwood ceilings, upping the style ante in town. The food follows suit – lentil burgers with curry and grilled goat cheese, pork medallions in red wine reduction with mushroom and fava bean risotto – taking Puerto Varas to new culinary heights without sacrificing flavor for fashion.

Entertainment
Nightlife here has two warring factions: Salmon industry vs everyone else.

El Barómetro (☎ 346-100; Walker Martínez 584; ☯ 7pm-late) This place got too cool for its own good, expanding into a larger space housing lacquered Alerce tables, mismatched leather couches and polka-dot curtains, but with a crowd that has become a tad too rife with *cuicos* (Chilean yuppies) from the salmon industry. There are DJs Thursday to Saturday and an eclectic bar menu that includes hummus and tilapia, but the see-and-be-seen cachet has worn somewhat thin. That said, everyone still goes.

Garage (☎ 232-856; Walker Martínez 220; ☯ 6:30pm-late Mon-Sat) As the name suggests, Garage, attached to the Copec station, caters to a more artsy, less fishy crowd, staying up later than it should and hosting everything from impromptu jazz sessions to all-out Colombian *Cumbia* shakedowns. The crowds start gathering here around 11pm before shifting to Barómetro in the wee hours.

Casino de Puerto Varas (☎ 492-000; Del Salvador 21; ☯ 11am-late Mon) As far as Chilean casinos go, this could be filed under 'boutique' with its dark hardwood skin and industrial-chic shell, but it's still home to a corny knot of slot machines, desperate retirees and wannabe high rollers. It was adding a new five-star hotel during research. If you go, Puerto Varas legend says that you will have better luck if you enter through the doors that face the lake.

Shopping
Fundacíon Artesanías de Chile (☎ 346-332; Del Salvador 109; ☯ 9am-9pm Nov-Mar) A not-for-profit foundation offering beautiful Mapuche textiles as well as high-quality jewelry and ceramics from all over southern Chile.

Vicki Johnson (☎ 232-240; Santa Rosa 318; ☯ 9am-9pm summer) Anyone who tries the ginger chocolate here would be hard-pressed to argue against this being Chile's best artisanal chocolate. There is also a wealth of high-end *rauli*-wood kitchen utensils, jewelry, chutneys, olive oils and other tasty take-home treats.

Getting There & Around
Most long-distance bus services from Puerto Varas originate in Puerto Montt; for fares and duration information see p318. Buses leave from the new terminal, with the exception of Cruz del Sur, and sell tickets through their individual offices around downtown. For Osorno (CH$1400), Valdivia (CH$3500) and Temuco (CH$5000), **Cruz del Sur** (Walker Martínez 230) has nine departures daily from the terminal at San Francisco 1317; it also goes to Chiloé (CH$5000) several times per day and Punta Arenas (CH$43,000) on Tuesday, Wednesday, Thursday and Saturday. Also check out **Tur-Bus/Tas-Choapa** (☎ 234-163; San Pedro 210), which leave from a new terminal at Del Salvador s/n, and **Pullman Bus** (☎ 234-612; Portales 18). For Santiago, Tur-Bus, Pullman Bus, **Buses Norte** (☎ 234-298; San Pedro 210) **JAC/Condor** (☎ 383-800; Walker Martínez 227) have several daily departures. The latter also goes to Temuco and three times daily to Pucón (CH$5900, 5½ hours).

For Bariloche (Argentina), Tas-Choapa departs daily at 8:40am and 2pm (CH$12,000); Cruz del Sur goes once daily at 8:50am (CH$13,000). For information on the popular bus-boat combination to Bariloche, see the boxed text, p308.

Minibuses to and from Ensenada (CH$1000), Petrohué (CH$2000), Puerto Montt (CH$700), Puelo (CH$3000), Frutillar (CH$700), Ralún (CH$1300) and Cochamó (CH$1500) all leave from a small stop near the corner of Walker Martínez and San Bernardo. From the Puerto Montt airport, taxis cost approximately CH$15,000.

Lan (☎ 600-526-2000; Av Gramado 560; ☽ 9am-1pm & 3-6:30pm Mon-Fri, 9:30am-1:30pm Sat), **Sky Airlines** (☎ 231-030; San Bernardo 430; ☽ 9am-1pm & 3-7pm Mon-Fri, 9am-1pm Sat) and **Air Comet** (☎ 234-244; Walker Martinez 227; ☽ 9am-1:30pm & 3:30-7pm Mon-Fri, 9am-1pm Sat) keep offices in town but fly from Puerto Montt.

ENSENADA
☎ 065 / pop 1250

Rustic Ensenada, 45km along a picturesque shore-hugging road from Puerto Varas, is really nothing more than a few restaurants, *hospedajes* and adventure outfitters, but for those looking for more outdoors, less hardwood floors, it's a nice natural setting in full view of three majestic beasts: Volcán Osorno, Volcán Calbuco and Volcán Puntiagudo. Staying here over Puerto Varas has a few advantages for those looking for their adventures a little beyond the beaten track: if you plan to climb or ski Osorno, you can save an hour of sleep by overnighting here (and if the weather turns, you won't have come quite as far for nothing). Volcán Calbuco is also within striking distance – just to the south of Ensenada. And between them is the breathtaking Parque Nacional Vicente Pérez Rosales, the entrance of which sits just outside town.

It is recommended that you have a car if you stay in these parts although buses do come through with some frequency and most Puerto Varas–based travel agencies will pick you up in Ensenada.

Activities
Highly regarded Puerto Varas rafting and kayak outfitter **Ko'Kayak** (☎ 481-171; www.kokayak .com; Ruta 225, Km40) has moved its entire operation to Ensenada. A full day of sea kayaking runs about CH$60,000 while half-day rafting trips go for CH$27,000 with two departures daily. There are also several folks along the road offering horseback riding, canopy and the like.

Sleeping & Eating
Escala II (☎ 075-931; Ruta 225, Km40; r per person CH$5000) This friendly spot has nice new

mattresses and bedspreads in rooms that are all positioned to have one volcanic view or another. Rates include breakfast and dinner and the four-course lunch runs an extra CH$4000. We tried the trout – it's the best deal in Ensenada.

Casa Ko' (☎ 584-8171; www.kokayak.com/casa; r with/without bathroom CH$14,000/12,000; P ⊠ ▣) Ko'Kayak's newish 'hostel' is actually the owner's house, ofering a bang-up view of Osorno 3km up a dirt road from the highway. Rooms are simple but well appointed and most have private bathrooms. It's all very homey and upscale for this price range. Kayakers and rafters get a free ride home, others need a car. The location may have changed by the time you read this, so check ahead.

Hospedaje Ensenada (☎ 098-828-2876; www.hospe dajeensenada.blogspot.cl; Ruta 225, Km43; r per person CH$12,000; P ⊠) An impossibly relaxed and immaculately clean option, this welcoming big house has an inviting patio and huge yard, and is close to the beach. It's only open December to late April/early May.

Yankee Way Lodge (☎ 212-030; www.southern chilexp.com; Ruta 225, Km42; r CH$100,000; P ▣ ☎) This North American–owned lodge caters largely to wealthy fly-fishers. It has a gorgeous lakeside setting, but the rooms skew slightly more Holiday Inn than the lovely, forest-hued structure itself does. You don't have to tie a fly at all, however, to eat at Latitude 42° (mains CH$5700-9700), which took home best regional restaurant honors from Santiago's *El Mercurio* newspaper in 2006 and 2007. Salmon is the highlight, either the in-house smoked version marinated in Cognac, or poached in Chardonnay.

Don Salmón (☎ 202-108; Ruta 225, Km42; mains CH$6000-9000; ☽ breakfast, lunch & dinner) This new spot emits the wonderful smell of freshly cut cypress, from which it was entirely made by the owner. The adorable chef is Brazilian (where the food is far superior to that found in Chile) and she does some wonderful things with salmon. Try it off menu with caper sauce or the stuffed *congrio* in white wine sauce. There's even French toast for breakfast.

Getting There & Away
Minibuses frequently shuttle between Ensenada and Puerto Montt (CH$2.50, one hour) or Puerto Varas (CH$1, 50 minutes). There is no public transportation between

---

THROUGH THE ANDES

Why plod through a line at a boring bureaucratic border crossing when you can make your way from Puerto Montt or Puerto Varas through the majestic lakes and mountains of the Pérez Rosales Pass to Bariloche, Argentina? The trip is a series of buses and boat trips from one breathtaking view to the next including the Saltos del Petrohué (waterfalls), Lago Todos Los Santos and Volcán Osorno.

Although you can make the trip section by section and spend time in the small scenic towns of Petrohué or Peulla, most travelers do it in a straight shot. **Cruce de Lagos** (www.crucedelagos.cl) runs the trip and can be contacted via its agency arm, Andina del Sud, in Puerto Montt (p315). Reservations for the whole excursion must be made two days in advance; however, if you're only going as far as Peulla, tickets may be purchased at the Petrohué dock. The total fare is approximately CH$78,200 although there are seasonal discounts and pricing for students and seniors. It's also worth nothing that this is largely dominated by the package-tour crowd.

There are daily departures throughout the year, but the 12-hour trip requires a mandatory overnight in Peulla in winter (May to August). Bring your own food for the first part of the trip, since meals aboard the catamaran to Peulla and in Peulla are expensive and dull.

Section	Transportation	Duration (hr)
Puerto Montt – Puerto Varas – Petrohué	bus	2
Petrohué – Peulla	boat	1¾
Peulla – Puerto Frías	bus	2
Puerto Frías – Puerto Alegre	boat	½
Puerto Alegre – Puerto Blest	bus	¼
Puerto Blest – Puerto Pañuelo	boat	1
Puerto Pañuelo – Bariloche	bus	½

Ensenada and Las Cascadas, a distance of 22km on the road to Puerto Octay. Pedestrians and cyclists should beware that this is a hot, exposed route infested with *tábanos* (large biting horseflies) from December to the end of February.

PARQUE NACIONAL VICENTE PÉREZ ROSALES

In this park of celestial lakes and soaring volcanoes, Lago Todos Los Santos and Volcán Osorno may be the standouts but they're actually just part of a crowd. One lake leads to the next and volcanoes dominate the skyline on all sides of this storied pass through the Andes range. The needlepoint of Volcán Puntiagudo (2493m) lurks to the north and craggy Monte Tronador (3491m) marks the Argentine border to the east. From the higher levels you can see where lava flows pinched off rivers and lakes, detouring them into new bodies of water.

Established in 1926, the 2510-sq-km Pérez Rosales was Chile's first national park, but its history goes back much further. In pre-Columbian times Mapuche traveled the 'Camino de Vuriloche,' a major trans-Andean route they managed to conceal from the Spaniards for more than a century after the 1599 uprising. Jesuit missionaries traveled from Chiloé, continuing up the Estuario de Reloncaví and crossing the pass south of Tronador to Lago Nahuel Huapi, avoiding the riskiest crossings of the region's lakes and rivers.

The park is open year-round, depending on weather conditions. There is a Conaf **Visitor Center** (9am-1pm, 2-6pm) at the entrance to the park, with basic info.

Volcán Osorno

Volcán Osorno, only to be rivaled by Volcán Villarrica, is a perfect conical peak towering above azure glacial lakes. It retains its idyllic shape due to the 40 craters around its base – it's there that the volcano's eruptions have taken place, never at the top. You can spend a day trekking under its nose for around CH$35,000 from Puerto Varas, but if you want to summit the volcano, plan on CH$200,000 for solo climbers and CH$125,000 per person for two people (including snow and ice-climbing gear) and a full day starting at 5am. The trip is technical and not for the unfit. If the weather turns and the trip is aborted before leaving, agencies will refund the cost. Once

PARQUE NACIONAL VICENTE PÉREZ ROZALES

you reach the snow, there is no refund regardless of weather cancellation. Trips up Volcán Calbuco (2003m), the region's most active volcano, cost CH$90,000 per person for two people. All the outfitters more or less hire the same guides. Contact Puerto Montt–based **Trekka Patagonia** (☎ 65-256-760; www.trekka.cl).

Independent climbers must obtain Conaf permission, providing detailed personal qualifications as well as lists of equipment and intended routes.

Centro de Ski y Montaña Volcán Osorno (☎ 233-445; info@volcanosorno.com; Santa Rosa 560, Puerto Varas; lift ticket CH$6500-8000) has two lifts for skiing and sightseeing and has recently undergone an expansion of its restaurant and rental shop. It has ski and snowboard rentals and food services on the mountain year-round. In summer, you can take the ski lift up for impossibly scenic views for CH$6500.

Just downhill from the ski slopes, the rustic **Teski El Refugio** (☎ 099-7000-370; dm CH$11,500; ☺ year-round) offers unparalleled access to the mountain. It's under new ownership and has gotten the requisite touch-ups. Beds are still small (bring a sleeping bag for extra warmth) but

the lodge has outstanding views of Lago Llanquihue, especially from the two mountainside hot tubs they rent for CH$16,000, and two-for-one Happy Hour drinks at sunset.

To get to the ski area and the *refugio*, take the Ensenada-Puerto Octay road to a signpost about 3km from Ensenada and continue driving 10km up the lateral. It's well worth your money renting a car and driving up the newly paved road, taking in spectacular views flanked by Osorno on one side, Calbuco on the other and Lake Llanquihue down below. There are no transportation services to or from the slopes for anyone except for package-tour buyers. Contact CTS in Puerto Varas (p302) for details.

Petrohué

People may come for the ferry cruise to Peulla, but Petrohué's majestic lakeside setting and serenity tend to convince visitors to stay a little longer. It's only 20 minutes from Ensenada down a reasonable dirt road, so it has similar advantages in an infinitesimally prettier locale (but there's little for lodging).

Expediciones Petrohué (☎ 212-025; www.petro hue.com; ⏰ 9am-6pm Nov-Mar) arranges climbing, rafting and canyoning excursions and has kayaks right on the lake for CH$3500 per hour. Trips to **Isla Margarita**, a wooded island with a small interior lagoon, cost CH$35,000 for up to four in a small fishing boat or CH$4500 each with Andina del Sud (p315) from December to March only.

From the woodsy **Conaf campground** (campsites 1-5 persons CH$7000) just beyond the parking area, a dirt track leads to **Playa Larga**, a long black-sand beach much better than the one near the hotel. From the beach, **Sendero Los Alerces** heads west to meet up with **Sendero La Picada**, which climbs past Paso Desolación and continues on to Refugio La Picada on the volcano's north side. Alternatively, follow Los Alerces back to the hotel. Six kilometers southwest of Petrohué, the **Saltos del Petrohué** (admission CH$1200) is a rushing, frothing waterfall raging through a narrow volcanic rock canyon carved by lava. Anyone wondering why the rafting trips don't start from the lake will find the answer here, although experienced kayakers have been known to take it on (though we'd like to see the canyoners try it).

If coming for a day trip, consider bringing food from Puerto Varas.

SLEEPING & EATING

Hospedaje Küschel (campsite/r per person CH$4000/8000) You're in the thick of it with the pigs and the chickens at this rundown farmhouse across the lake (reached by boat at the dock for CH$500), but the old woman here is good-hearted, you are situated right on the lake (from where your startlingly good home-smoked trout dinner comes), and the only alternative if you're not camping is 17 times the price! Rightfully so, as some rooms feature rudely constructed particleboard ceilings and walls, and hot water is scarce. Breakfast is included but dinner or lunch runs at CH$4000.

Petrohué Hotel & Cabañas (☎ 212-025; petro hue.com; s/d CH$67,200/92,450; cabins for 4 CH$88,250; P ✕ 🐾) In a gorgeous stone and wood-gabled building replete with a tower, this high-end adventure lodge deserves a visit. Its abundant skylights and roaring fires in the lounge make it a romantic place to relax, read a book or conceive. The rooms, rich in wood, have beds piled high with blankets and are

scattered with candles. The restaurant is open to the general public and packages with excursions are offered. The equally luxe cabañas sit on the lakeshore.

Peulla

After the stunning catamaran ride across emerald Lago Todas Los Santos from Petrohué, you'll find puny Peulla tucked into a gorgeous valley rife with tall, grassy *junquillo* (a grassy weed that sure does pretty up the place). The town has been on the tourist map since 1907 but nearly its entire infrastructure was built by one family, also owners of Andina del Sud (p315), the travel agency that controls it, and both hotels. The whole area is best appreciated after the boat and buses of Bariloche-bound tourists leave.

Cascada de los Novios is a waterfall just a few minutes' walk along an easy footpath from upscale Hotel Peulla. For a longer excursion, take the 8km **Sendero Laguna Margarita**, a rewarding climb. If you are not heading on to Bariloche, daytrippers have the option of canopy or horseback riding and overnighters can do a serene kayak trip on the Río Negro (no need to book in advance; you can pay onboard).

Lodging options, however, are limited. **Hotel Peulla** (☎ 560-481; www.hotelpeulla.cl; s/d CH$56,700/65,600; mains CH$5000-9600), 800m from the dock, is dated and overpriced – why haven't they used some of that money to buy new carpet? – but the rooms are large and will do for those that can't spring for the newer, nicer **Hotel Natura** (☎ 560-483; www.hotelnatura.cl; s/d CH$93,350/104,450; 🖥). Similar to the Petrohué Hotel, this cozy lodge birthed from masculine hardwoods and granite stones offers chic rooms with small patios and sink-into beds. Relaxing spa music is piped into the common areas and restaurant (mains CH$3600 to CH$8400), which make solid use of the view with large bay windows looking over the valley. The food is a *little* more cutting-edge here (beef *Bourgogne* with Patagonian rice, Thai salmon), but we're not sure why they serve soda in wine glasses. Grab a cocktail mixed at the fab bar, carved directly from a chunk of *Coigüe* tree.

In summer, shuttles from Puerto Montt and Puerto Varas to Petrohué are frequent, but limited to twice daily the rest of the year. For details on the boat trip across the lake to Peulla, see the boxed text, p308.

COCHAMÓ

☎ 065 / pop 4366

The Chilote-style, Alerce-shingled **Iglesia Parroquial María Inmaculada** stands picturesque and proud against a backdrop of milky-blue water along the road to Cochamó, forming one of the most stunning spots throughout the region and the gateway to the upper Río Cochamó Valley.

The municipal office in town provides a very useful Cochamó hiking map and brochure. Within town are **Hospedaje Edicar** (☎ 216-256; cnr Av Prat & Sargento Aldea; r per person CH$7000), right on the Costanera with lovely views and a little balcony, but less friendly than newly renovated **Hospedaje Maura** (☎ 098-243-9937; J Molina 12; r per person CH$8000), with charming owners, good beds and very low ceilings. The best bet for meals is with the *hospedajes*, or try **Restaurant Relocavi** (Av Cathedral; mains CH$2400-2900), just up from the church, which has salmon and merluza (hake).

Campo Aventura (☎ 232-910; www.campo-aventura .com; office at San Bernardo 318, Puerto Varas; campsite per person CH$2950; r per person incl breakfast CH$14,950; r per person full board CH$25,200; ✗) runs three splendid shared cabins, a kitchen and indoor and outdoor dining areas at its riverside camp at Cochamó. Here you'll find lovely meals (breakfast CH$2000 to CH$4000, lunch CH$4000, dinner CH$8200), a beautiful camping area at the river's edge and candlelight showers. At its 80-hectare La Junta backcountry camp it has three bedrooms – one with five bunks (comfortable but cramped) and the other two with double beds – wood-fired showers and a dining room with a central woodstove. Nice touches like wine, homemade bread and local artisan teas are available. They also arrange trekking, kayaking and boat trips.

Guides in town can also lead you up on horseback, but be wary – at least one shifty character has been known to suddenly increase the agreed-upon price after arrival in the valley.

Getting There & Away

There are three daily bus departures to and from Puerto Montt (CH$3500), stopping in Puerto Varas and Ensenada. Most buses continue to Río Puelo.

RÍO COCHAMÓ VALLEY

With its impressive granite domes rising above the verdant rainforest and colossal Alerce trees dominating the forest, the spectacular Río Cochamó Valley is being touted by some as the Chilean Yosemite. It's near here where the glacial waters of the Lakes District give way to the saltwaters of the 80km Reloncaví Fjord, forming the gateway to Northern Patagonia. The region is growing fast, especially with the rock climbers – each year new climbing routes and trails open with more adrenalists clambering around the valley to reach them. The area is indeed a beautiful spot worthy of multiple days and tourism has not yet overwhelmed the area, so go now before it *does* turn into Yosemite.

To reach the valley, the route follows a 19th-century log road built for oxcarts, which carried seafood to Argentina and beef back to Chile. You can trek in, or hire horses. The road to the trailhead begins just before the bridge to Campo Aventura, but most folks grab a taxi or drive themselves this first 8km to the trailhead (you can park at the last house on the right for CH$500). From there, it's a splendid 12km trek through the deep Valdivian rainforest along the Río Cochamó to La Junta, an impressive valley under the watch of massive granite domes jutting from the top of the surrounding mountains. Unless they build a road here, it should remain a gorgeous and serene spot. Here you'll find the impressive **Refugio Cochamó** (☎ 099-771-9990; www.cochamo .com; campsites per person CH$1500, dm per person CH$7000, d without bathroom CH$17,000), a fantastic gringo-Argentine climber-run cabin with wood-fired showers, water straight from the Trinadad waterfall, homemade pizza (CH$6000) and its very own homebrew, *Tábano* Pale Ale! It's open from November to April. To reach it, you must cross the river via a rudimentary but effective pulley system. In January, the *tábanos* are relentless.

Beyond La Junta the route continues to Lago Vidal Gormaz, passing El Arco, where there's a rustic *refugio*. For those who take the trail, be prepared for rain and mud, and allot extra time should some of the rivers be too high to cross.

Campo Aventura (p304) is the most established outfitter in this area, organizing horseback-riding trips from its camp at 5km south of the Cochamó to its camp at mountain camp at La Junta and through the Andes. Horse treks last from one to 10 days (and cost from CH$41,000 to CH$911,000), with meals and lodging included. Treks often include meeting locals. If you are interested in getting higher up into the surrounding peaks, **Mira Lejos** (☎ 099-361-1003; www.miralejos.cl), part of the La Comarca collective (p302), runs three- to 10-day treks (CH$193,000 to CH$516,000 per person including meals, lodging and load horses). They can take you up to the 900m viewpoint at Arco Iris through three types of native forest, with wine and cheese to boot.

PUELO

The road from Cochamó continues along the Reloncavi Fjord another 31km through to Puelo, a little hamlet that's bound for growth as a new land-lake route into Argentina develops. Under the watchful eye of Volcán Yates and the jade-hued Río Puelo, it's a serene and photogenic spot that makes for a great base for exploration further afield into the Río Puelo Valley. Head to the **tourist office** (www.cochamo.cl; ⊙ 9am-9pm Jan-Feb, 11am-5pm Mar-May; plaza) for options on local treks, rustic family lodgings and guides. If nobody is in, ask around for Spanish-speaking **Azucena Calderón** (☎ 099-949-4425), she can also be helpful with making plans.

SLEEPING & EATING

Most decent accommodations are in Puelo Alto, 2km east of the center.

Camping Río Peulo (☎ 098-479-2700; Puelo Alto; campsites per person CH$4000; P) The bathrooms are makeshift but nice on the inside at this basic campground with lovely Andes views. Breakfast (CH$2500) and lunch (CH$3000) are extra.

La Casona (☎ 099-514-8638; Puelo Bajo; r per person CH$12,500) This poor man's fishing lodge isn't homey at all, but it's nicer than it looks and is actually the cheapest bed in town. Meals are extra. It's in Peulo Bajo near the police station.

Domo Camp (☎ 099-138-2310; www.andespatagonia .cl; Puelo Alto; r 2/4 people CH$25,200/42,000; P) These geodesic domes connected by planks through native forest are one of the most interesting places to stay in Region X. Each has its own fireplace for warmth and cozy mattresses and sleeping bags are provided. The only downside is that it's a long and uncomfortable haul to the showers – robes and headlamps are provided, but slippers are not, so your feet take a beating. The owner also offers reliable mountain-guide services (hikes from CH$45,000) in the valley.

Andes Lodge (☎ 234-454; www.andeslodge.com; s/d full board CH$67,200/100,850; P ✕ ▢) This newish high-end fishing lodge 14km from Peulo sits on a pristine piece of real estate right on the Reloncavi Fjord. The lodge, forged from Oregon pine, offers fishing excursions on the Ríos Blanco and Llaguepa as well as the Laguna Sin Nombre and the fjord from CH$95,000 for two per day. Gourmet meals are served.

Restaurant Tique (☎ 099-549-1069; Puelo Alto; meals CH$5600; ⊙ breakfast, lunch and dinner) Located at the Domo Camp, this is the best spot to eat in town. Coca runs a rustic kitchen but the meals are home prepared and leave you feeling like you've eaten at your aunt's house, the one that always overfeeds you.

Buses Fierro has five daily departures to and from Puerto Montt (four hours, CH$3500), stopping in Puerto Varas, Ensenada and Cochamó. From the village, the road continues inland to Los Canelos on Lago Tagua-Tagua, where a ferry service (cars CH$7000, pedestrians CH$500) crosses the lake to the road's extension, which parallels the river to Llanada Grande.

RÍO PUELO VALLEY

☎ 065 / pop 500

Like a country lass of modest origins, the Río Puelo Valley remains unfazed by that massive industry called tourism, offering a few homespun adventures. It has become a hotbed of ecotourism of late, mainly due to the proposed dam at El Portón near Llanada Grande, which is threatening the beauty and integrity of the area, and would flood most of the valley, see the boxed text, p359. Locals are turning to tourism as a means of halting the plans. Fishing, trekking and horseback riding are king here and each offers days of satiating adventures in the area. Go now, or forever hold your peace.

Llanada Grande & Beyond

After the lake crossing at Tagua-Tagua, the gravel road continues by mountainsides peppered with patches of dead *coigüe* trees (killed by fire but tragically pretty) and lands still traversed by *gaucho* families on horseback. This is Llanada Grande – you are now off the grid. A system of pioneer homes and rustic B&Bs is in place for travelers here (inquire at Hospedaje El Salto), making your treks and horseback rides feel a little less touristy, a little more like visiting long-lost family. A new road connecting Lago Tagua-Tagua to Lago Blanco, just beyond Llanada Grande, has just been finished and plans are in place to carry it on to Argentina. Most treks start in Llanada Grande and take different routes along the valley, including unforgettable jaunts to Lago Azul and Argentina. Hard-core hikers should seek out the amicable services of **Lolo Escobar** for an extraordinary five-day round-trip to the Ventisquero Glacier near Segundo Corral, the last Chilean settlement in the valley. If you fancy fishing, call on **Reiner Grellich**, a reputable fishing guide who also has cabins on Lago Verde (Blanca from Hospedaje El Salto can radio both, but call with advance notice).

Good options for overnighting include **Camping Oro Verde** (campsites per person CH$5000; Nov-Apr), located on the soft sands of the Southern shore of glassy Lago Totoral. An invaluable choice is **Hospedaje El Salto** (02-196-9212; agroturelsalto@gmail.com; r per person without bathroom CH$21,000; P), in an impeccably clean and sensibly furnished log home owned by Blanca Eggers, who can set up accommodations in pioneer homes and B&Bs all the way to Lago Puelo in Argentina. Breakfast and dinner (and wine!) is included and often involves traditional lamb or wild boar *asado*. The postcard setting in front of the 1200m El Salto waterfall is a destination in itself. **Martín Pescador** (099-884-7108; www.ecotravel.cl; s/d CH$25,200/29,400) is a two-room B&B-style fishing and birdwatching lodge with hearty food and what is perhaps the most idyllic dining table in the region – over the water on Lake Totoral. Lunch and dinner is CH$10,000 extra.

The same bus to Puelo continues on to the ferry at Los Canelos on the north side of Lago Tagua-Tagua, where boats leave twice a day (9am, 11:30pm). At Puerto Maldonado on the south side, a minibus will be waiting to carry you on to Llanada Grande (CH$3000). To return, ferries leave Puerto Maldonado twice a day (11:30am, 4:30pm).

PUERTO MONTT
065 / pop 168,242

Say what you will about Puerto Montt (locals certainly don't hold back, with *Muerto Montt*, meaning, 'Dead Montt,' topping the list), but if you choose to visit southern Chile's ominous volcanoes, its celestial glacial lakes, its mountainous national parks, you will have the unfortunate honor bestowed upon you of visiting the capital of Los Lagos and the region's commercial and transportation hub.

For the pessimist, Puerto Montt can be seedier than a botanist's backyard; optimists see it as one massive dive bar. Either way, it's a grimy transport hub, whose most redeeming quality of which is the plethora of exit points: be it by plane, ferry, bus or rental car, you can make a quick and virtually painless getaway to a near-endless inventory of memorable locales, some no further than the 20km hop north to Puerto Varas (where you should be sleeping, anyway).

All is not lost in Puerto Montt, however. The city can be a welcome change of pace, and one of the region's most beautiful hotels is here. If you do end up killing time here, head straight for the quirky port area, Angelmó, which is full of tiny seafood restaurants and crafts shops, or Plaza de Armas, which can get quite lively with indigenous musical groups.

Orientation
Puerto Montt is 1020km south of Santiago via the Panamericana, which skirts the northern edge of the city as it continues on to Chiloé.

The city center occupies a narrow terrace, partly on landfill, behind which hills rise steeply. The waterfront Av Diego Portales turns into Av Angelmó as it heads west to the small fishing and ferry port of Angelmó. To the east, Av Soler Manfredini continues to the bathing resort of Pelluco, connecting with the Carretera Austral.

Information
BOOKSTORES
Sotavento Libros (256-650; Av Diego Portales 570) Has a good selection of books on local history and literature and a few English-language mystery novels.

CONSULATES
Argentine Consulate (253-996; Pedro Montt 160, 6th fl; 9am-noon & 3-5pm Mon-Fri)

INTERNET ACCESS
Lots of internet places line Av Angelmó and encircle the plaza.
Latin Star (278-318; Av Angelmó 1672; per hr CH$500; 9am-10pm Mon-Sat, 10am-8pm Sun) Also has a call center and book exchange.

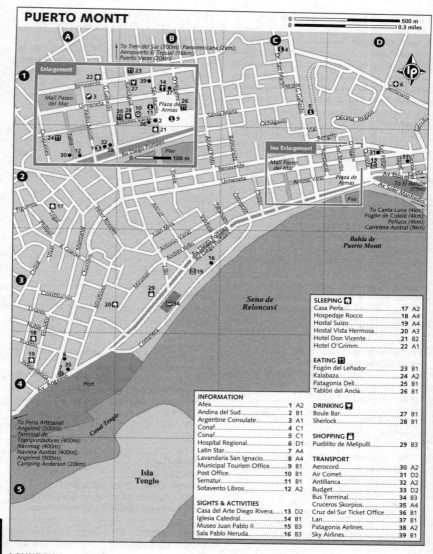

PUERTO MONTT

INFORMATION

Afex......................................**1** A2	
Andina del Sud.....................**2** B1	
Argentine Consulate............**3** A1	
Conaf..................................**4** C1	
Conaf..................................**5** C1	
Hospital Regional................**6** D1	
Latin Star............................**7** A4	
Lavandaria San Ignacio.......**8** A4	
Municipal Tourism Office.....**9** B1	
Post Office..........................**10** B1	
Sernatur..............................**11** B1	
Sotavento Libros.................**12** A2	

SIGHTS & ACTIVITIES

Casa del Arte Diego Rivera....**13** D2	
Iglesia Catedral....................**14** B1	
Museo Juan Pablo II.............**15** B3	
Sala Pablo Neruda................**16** B3	

SLEEPING

Casa Perla..........................**17** A2	
Hospedaje Rocco.................**18** A4	
Hostal Suizo.......................**19** A4	
Hostal Vista Hermosa..........**20** A3	
Hotel Don Vicente...............**21** B2	
Hotel O'Grimm....................**22** A1	

EATING

Fogón del Leñador..............**23** B1	
Kalabaza............................**24** A2	
Patagonia Deli....................**25** B1	
Tablón del Ancla.................**26** B1	

DRINKING

Boule Bar...........................**27** B1	
Sherlock.............................**28** B1	

SHOPPING

Pueblito de Melipulli............**29** B3	

TRANSPORT

Aerocord............................**30** A2	
Air Comet...........................**31** D2	
Antillanca..........................**32** A2	
Budget...............................**33** D2	
Bus Terminal......................**34** B3	
Cruceros Skorpios...............**35** A4	
Cruz del Sur Ticket Office....**36** B1	
Lan.....................................**37** B1	
Patagonia Airlines...............**38** A2	
Sky Airlines........................**39** B1	

LAUNDRY
Lavandaria San Ignacio (☎ 343-737; Chorillos 1585; per kilo CH$1000; ☻ 9:30am-7pm Mon-Sat)

MEDICAL SERVICES
Hospital Regional (☎ 261-100; Seminario s/n; ☻ 24hr) Near the intersection with Décima Región.

MONEY
There are more banks along Antonio Varas near Plaza de Armas than there are in Switzerland.
Afex (Av Diego Portales 516) Money exchange.

POST
Post office (Rancagua 126) One block west of the plaza.

TOURIST INFORMATION
Conaf (☎ 486-130; Ochagavía 458) Can provide details on nearby national parks. You can also try the second office on Dr San Martin 566.

Municipal tourism office (☎ 261-823; Antonio Varas 415; ☻ 9am-9pm) More eager to help than Sernatur, with plenty of national park info. It's on the plaza.

Sernatur (☎ 256-999; ☻ 8:30am-1pm & 2:30-5pm Mon-Fri) On the west side of Plaza de Armas.

TRAVEL AGENCIES
Andina del Sud (☎ 437-115; www.andinadelsud.com, in Spanish; Antonio Varas 437; ☻ 8:30am-7pm Mon-Fri, 9am-1pm Sat) The agency wing of the Cruce de Lagos bus-ferry combo trip to Argentina, but they can also arrange excursions throughout the region.

Dangers & Annoyances
The areas around Puerto Montt's bus station as well as the more southwest end of Antonio Varas have seen an increase in pickpocketing and petty theft. Watch your back.

Sights
Built entirely of Alerce in 1856, the **Iglesia Catedral** (Urmeneta s/n), located on the Plaza de Armas, is the town's oldest building, and its only attractive one. The upstairs Sala Hardy Wistuba at the **Casa del Arte Diego Rivera** (☎ 261-836; Quillota 116; admission free; ☻ 9am-8pm Mon-Fri, 11am-6pm Sat & Sun), a joint Mexican-Chilean project finished in 1964, displays work by local and foreign artists and photographers. It was getting a makeover during research. Expect an elevator and a new exhibition space, café and boutique by 2009.

Puerto Montt's waterfront **Museo Juan Pablo II** (☎ 261-700; Av Diego Portales 997, 2nd fl; admission CH$500; ☻ 9am-6pm Mon-Fri) has displays on natural history, archaeology, the island of Chiloé, maritime history and weapons, religious iconography, German colonization and local urbanism. Check out the gaudy bracelets from singer and ballerina, Tilda Tibau, and the prehistoric radio by Telefunken – our next band name. Next door to the museum, **Sala Pablo Neruda** (Costanera s/n; ☻ 10am-6pm Mon-Sat) hosts exhibitions by some of the region's best artists and is definitely worth a peek.

Along busy, diesel-fume-laden Av Angelmó is a dizzying mix of streetside stalls (selling artifacts, heaps of smoked mussels, *cochayuyo* – edible sea plant – and mysterious trinkets), crafts markets and touristy seafood restaurants with croaking waiters beckoning you to a table. Enjoy the frenzy, but keep on going. The best-quality crafts and food are found at the end of

---

FISHY BUSINESS

Salmon was first imported to Chile about a century ago. It wasn't until the mid-1980s that salmon farming in submerged cages was developed on a massive scale. It is now one of Chile's top five exports, making the country the world's second-largest producer of salmon, right on the tail of Norway. Much of the product goes to the voracious US and Japanese markets, with Russia, Brazil, China and Mexico not far behind. Puerto Montt is the epicenter of the farming and exportation industry, which directly employs some 60,000 people and is estimated to indirectly employ another 30,000 Chileans. Billions of dollars in investment are pushing the farming operations further south into Patagonia as far as the Strait of Magellan and the industry is expected to double in size and growth in the next decade, overtaking Norway.

Unfortunately not all of the news is good. There is poor distribution of the profits and veritable mountains of organic waste from extra food and salmon feces. This has led to substantial contamination and depletion of other types of fish. Moreover, it takes even 4kg of other kinds of fish to make 1kg of the fish meal that is fed to salmon, to produce roughly 1kg of salmon. Additionally, a vicious disease called Infectious Salmon Anemia, detected in 2007, wiped out over US$118 million in profits for Marine Harvest, the world's largest salmon-farming company.

Environmentalists, including the Chilean environmental organization **Oceana** (http://americadelsur .oceana.org in Spanish) and Doug Tompkins (owner of Parque Pumalín; p345), have expressed their concerns about the negative effects of the salmon industry directly to the Chilean government. **Fundación Terram** (www.terram.cl), which closely monitors the industry, have published very critical reports over a range of topics from working conditions to environmental damage.

Book your stay at lonelyplanet.com/hotels

the road at the picturesque fishing port of Angelmó, about 3km west of downtown. It is easily reached by frequent local buses and *colectivos*.

Offshore Isla Tenglo, reached by inexpensive launches from the docks at Angelmó, is a favorite local beach spot.

Sleeping

Puerto Montt is more of a business town and port than travelers' destination and so it does not have a lot of good budget and midrange accommodations. Many of the fancier options are drab business hotels. Therefore, most travelers decide to stay down the road in the more hospitable Puerto Varas.

BUDGET

Most of the budget places (except campgrounds) are within a few blocks of the bus station – particularly along Av Juan Mira. If arriving at night, stay alert while walking; petty thievery is on the rise.

Camping Anderson (☎ 099-517-7222; www.chipsites .com/camping/; Panitao, Km20, road to Calbuco; campsites per person CH$3000) This ecologically minded campground on the shores of the shimmering Bahía de Huequillahue is a bit outside of town, but is worth the short trip. Those on a budget can work for their lodging. Fresh food provisions are available on site. Buses Bohle makes the 20km trip from Puerto Montt's bus terminal to Panitao (nine times daily, CH$750)

Casa Perla (☎ 262-104; www.casaperla.com; Trigal 312; campsites per person CH$5000, dm & r per person CH$7000; ✗ ⛿) It's an extra 10-minute walk, but this family home is as welcoming as can be, with plenty of art and bric-a-brac on the walls and a fresh coat of paint and new mattresses. Perla and her family will have you feeling like a sibling. English and German are spoken (well) and you can take Spanish lessons, too. They offer sea kayaking in summer.

Hostal Vista Hermosa (☎ 319-600; www.hostal vistahermosa.cl, in Spanish; Miramar 1486; r per person CH$7000; ⓟ ✗ ⛿) A quick but uphill walk from the bus terminal, Vista Hermosa is run by a sweet woman and has plush (by budget standards) rooms. Beds are comfortable and rooms have cable TV. If you can snag No 1, you'll get fantastic views of the sea and Volcán Calbuco – it'd be perfect if it weren't for the office building that went up.

Hostal Suizo (☎ 262-640; roelckers@yahoo.es; Independencia 231; s/d CH$12,600/19,350, without bathroom CH$7150/12,600; ⓟ ✗) This gated home oozes junkyard charm and is laced with paintings by the owner. You don't get the English and warm family atmosphere of Perla, or the breakfast of Rocco, but it's shockingly more comfortable at this price. Breakfast is extra.

Hospedaje Rocco (☎ 272-897; www.hospedajerocco .cl; Pudeto 233; dm/s/d CH$8000/10,000/20,000; ⛿) You'll be greeted with open arms at this traveler's mainstay five blocks from the Navimag. It has a large sunny kitchen full of travel info and warm wooden walls and floors. Home-cooked breakfasts of sweet crepes with *manjar* (Chilean milk caramel) are a standout. The showers, though, spontaneously and drastically change temperature and there's nowhere to run!

MIDRANGE & TOP END

ourpick Tren del Sur (☎ 343-939; www.trendelsur.cl; Santa Teresa 643; s/d from CH$21,800/29,900; ⓟ ✗ ⛿) This stunning boutique hotel – by far Puerto Montt's best – in the old neighborhood of Modelo is full of furniture (headboards, wardrobes) fashioned from rescued railway trestles. It's high style and cozy, adheres to feng shui, and has 16 wonderful rooms with private bath, central heating, and wi-fi, entered from a sky-lit hallway. Guests are referred to as 'passengers,' but you won't want to go anywhere.

Hotel O'Grimm (☎ 252-845; www.ogrimm.com; Gallardo 211; s/d CH$37,800/43,700; ⓟ ⛿) The O'Grimm is a classic, though it's a little ...well, *grim* in places (the carpet is hurting), but there's little competition in this price range in the center and it's centrally located with a helpful staff. Wi-fi's available.

Hotel Don Vicente (☎ 432-900; www.granhoteldon vicente.cl, in Spanish; Av Diego Portales 450; s CH$39,500-52,100, d CH$42,000-54,600; ⓟ ✗ ⛿) This contemporary hotel is the top dog in *centro*. The large, hardwood-floored lobby features lots of inviting couches, a grand piano and a massive fireplace with half of a boat sticking out of it. It's on the sea, but if you want a sea view, you'll need to spring for the spacious superior rooms.

Eating

Kalabaza (☎ 262-020; Antonia Varas 629; mains CH$1900-2700) A burger-and-pitcher kind of place, but with a touch more style than the ubiquitous trash found up and down Antonio Vargas. They serve the kind of burger that's great when you're drunk at 2am, but not necessarily the one you'd want for lunch at noon.

Tablón del Ancla (☎ 367-554; Antono Varas 350; mains CH$1900-5900; ☾ lunch & dinner) This soccer-fueled, caricature-walled bar-restaurant on prime Plaza de Armas real estate has a great bunless hamburger *de lo pobre* (hold the eggs), but insanity surrounds the *parilla mixta,* a mountain of mixed grilled meats served in a flame-contained bucket that feeds you, four friends and your unborn child for CH$18,500. They throw in pisco sours, too, just in case you need something to wash it all down.

El Balcón (☎ 714-059; Egaña 156; mains CH$2900-4200; ☾ lunch & dinner; **V**) This stylish, all-wood urban café is a little too hip for Muerto Montt. Chilax tunes stream overhead as contemporary spins on classic dishes like *humitas del mar* (corn cooked in tusks with king crab and shrimp) and revolutionary *sopaipillas* (fried batter bread) with spicy *ají* and eggless mayonnaise delight the palettes of the artistic and culturally inclined crowd that gathers here.

Patagonia Deli (☎ 482-898; Antonio Varas 486; mains CH$3900-6900; ☾ lunch & dinner Mon-Sat; **V**) This spot packs 'em in at lunch, when its set menu featuring an appetizer, main, a drink and an espresso is a steal at CH$3600. There are also sandwiches, pasta and a few veggie choices.

our pick Fogón del Leñador (☎ 489-299; Rancagua 245; mains CH$6000-9500; ☾ lunch & dinner) The menu at the other best steak in town states that all meat takes a minimum of 40 minutes to cook. That says it all, really, and they aren't exaggerating. *Sopaipillas* are served with four house-made sauces, all of which are just as tasty on the superior filet.

Fogón de Cotelé (☎ 278-000; Balneario Pelluco; steak per kilo CH$15,000; ☾ lunch & dinner) Reviews are mixed as to whether it's still the best steak in town, but the experience at this intimate *quincho*-designed steakhouse with just seven tables surrounding an open hearth is priceless. Watching the owner methodically slow-cook your chosen weight of *bife chorizo* evokes Picasso in his prime. Just down the road in Pelluco, it can easily be reached by *colectivo* or buses from the terminal marked Chamiza (CH$300). Reservations are a good idea, especially Thursday through Sunday.

You can also head to Angelmó's plethora of hole-in-the-wall lunch counters and renovated *palafito* restaurants, some of which can't be discounted for great fresh fish. This is as much of a cultural experience as a culinary one – though it can be tour-bus hell in high season.

Drinking

There are several low-rent spots for a drink around the plaza, and a good selection around the corner of Benavente and Rancagua. Those seeking to stumble from bar to bar should head to Pelluco.

Boule Bar (☎ 348-973; Benavente 435; ☾ 6pm-late) Old *Rolling Stone* covers and other musical propaganda dot this multi-roomed bar lit with candles and featuring several tables and a bar rack made from tree bark. The perfect-volume music jumps from, 'Hit the Road, Jack' to hip-hop. It's a good spot to carry on late into the evening with a crowd that appreciates a smart soundtrack.

Sherlock (☎ 288-888; Antonio Varas 452; mains CH$2500-5500; ☾ 9am-late) It doesn't take much investigation to find out that Sherlock is one of the better places to hang out in town. Based on the fact that Detective Holmes was supposed to have paid a visit to Puerto Montt, this bar-restaurant has a touch more style than the cookie-cutter competition. It has nearly the full gamut of Kunstmann and Austral beers, and downstairs sees live music most nights of the week.

Canta Luna (☎ 843-454; Soler Manfredini 1860, Pelluco; ☾ 4pm-late Wed-Sat) Pelluco's most diverse option, with a *Salsateca* in the cavernous downstairs and live music upstairs. Apaché, down the road, skews younger and has a full-blown discotheque; Taytao, next door, wins the award for decor, but this newly renovated spot is the classiest.

Shopping

This being a regular stopover for tourists and cruise ships, the **Feira Artesanal Angelmó** is wall-to-wall with souvenir stands along Av Angelmó selling crafts from throughout the country and an amazing amount of stuff (some junk, some decent) from more northerly countries. Also try the labyrinthine waterfront market **Pueblito de Melipulli**, opposite the bus terminal.

Getting There & Away
AIR
Lan (☎ 600-526-2000; O'Higgins 167, Local 1-B) flies twice daily (once on Thursday) to Punta

Arenas (from CH$105,350), twice daily to Balmaceda/Coyhaique (from CH$62,100) and up to three times daily to Santiago (from CH$108,100).

Sky Airlines (☎ 437-555; www.skyairline.cl, in Spanish; cnr San Martin & Benavente; ☺9am-6:45pm Mon-Fri, 10am-1pm Sat) flies to Punta Arenas twice daily (from CH$51,300) and four times to Santiago (from CH$32,300) with considerably cheaper fares than Lan. If they're sold out, try **Air Comet** (☎ 319-434; www.aircometchile.cl, in Spanish; Urmeneta 290; ☺9am-7pm Mon-Fri, 10am-1pm Sat), a budget start-up.

Aerocord (☎ 262-300; www.aerocord.cl; Talca 81; ☺8:30am-6:30pm Mon-Fri, 9am-2pm Sat) flies Beechcraft and Twin Otters to Chaitán twice daily Monday to Saturday and once on Sunday (CH$40,000). **Patagonia Airlines** (☎ 544-440; www.patagoniaairlines.cl, in Spanish; Av Diego Portales 504; ☺8:30am-6pm Mon-Thu, 8:30am-5pm Fri, 8:30-11:30am Sat) flies twice daily to Chaitán (CH$49,000). All include transfer to the airport.

BUS – REGIONAL
Puerto Montt's waterfront **bus terminal** (☎ 253- 143; cnr Av Diego Portales & Lillo) is the main transportation hub for the region, and it gets busy and chaotic – watch your belongings or leave them with the *custodia* while sorting out travel plans. In summer, trips to Punta Arenas and Bariloche can sell out, so book in advance.

Minibuses to Puerto Varas (CH$700, 25 minutes), Frutillar (CH$1000, one hour) and Puerto Octay (CH$1400, two hours) leave frequently from the eastern side of the terminal. Buses leave for the villages of Ralún (CH$1500, two hours) and Cochamó (CH$2000, 2½ hours) five times daily, two of which carry on to Río Puelo.

BUS – LONG DISTANCE
Bus companies, all with offices at the bus terminal, include **Cruz del Sur** (☎ 252-872), with frequent services to Chiloé; **Tur-Bus/Tas-Choapa** (☎ 259-320), with daily service to Valparaíso/ Viña del Mar; **Igi Llaima** (☎ 254-519); and **Pullman Bus** (☎ 254-399). All of these services go to Santiago, stopping at various cities along the way; **Buses Fierro** (☎ 289-024) has an 8:15pm 'direct' service that only stops in Frutillar and Osorno. For long-haul trips to Coyhaique and Punta Arenas via Argentina, try Cruz del Sur, **Queilen Bus** (☎ 253-468) or

Pullman Bus, all of which go a few times per week.

For Bariloche, Argentina, Tur-Bus/Tas-Choapa, **Río de La Plata** (☎ 253-841) and **Andesmar** (☎ 312-123) go daily via the Cardenal Samoré pass east of Osorno. Cruz del Sur goes on Thursday and Sunday only. For information on the popular bus-boat combination trip to Bariloche, see the boxed text, p308.

Some sample travel times and costs are as follows:

Destination	Cost (CH$)	Duration (hr)
Ancud	3300	2½
Bariloche (Ar)	13,000	6
Castro	4700	3½
Concepción	14,000	9
Coyhaique	30,000	24
Osorno	1500	1¾
Pucón	5900	6
Punta Arenas	35,000	30
Quellón	6200	5½
Santiago	20,900	12
Temuco	8000	5½
Valdivia	3000	3¼
Valparaíso/Viña del Mar	25,800	14
Villarrica	5600	5½

BOAT
Puerto Montt is the main departure port for Patagonia. At the **Terminal de Transbordadores** (Av Angelmó 2187) you can find ticket offices and waiting lounges for both **Navimag** (☎ 432-360; www.navimag.com) and **Naviera Austral** (☎ 270-430; www.navieraustral.cl, in Spanish). Both companies are primarily commercial transporters, so don't expect thread counts and Dom Pérignon.

The most popular trip is Navimag's Ferry *Evangelistas*, which sails on Monday to Puerto Natales (and back on Friday, though boarding takes place Thursday night). It is a popular three-night journey through Chile's fjords; book passage at Navimag's Santiago office (opposite) in Puerto Montt or via the website.

High season is from November to March and low season is April to October. Prices for the trip include full board (vegetarian meals can be requested). Per-person fares, which vary according to the view and whether it is a private or shared bathroom (ranging from the upper-deck AAA room with an en suite bathroom to the least-attractive C class, where only every four berths have windows though some share levels with the higher classes), are as listed in the table on p320 (prices converted at time of publication; exchange rates may vary).

Cars are CH$250,000 extra. Bicycles and motorcycles can also be carried along for an additional cost. Travelers prone to seasickness should consider taking medication prior to the 12-hour crossing of Golfo de Penas, which is exposed to rolling Pacific swells – particularly in winter. The southern route now includes passage by the glacier Pio XI, the largest in South America (it's as big as Santiago).

THE NAVIMAG EXPERIENCE: THE GOOD, THE BAD & THE UGLY

Back in the prehistoric Patagonian travel days of the 1980s and early '90s, travelers had to beg and swindle just to stow away on the rusty cargo freighters that plied the waters between Puerto Montt and Puerto Natales. No regular passenger ferries were installed as tourism to the region increased, but the Navimag shipping company caught on and decided to dedicate a section of their boats to passenger transportation. So, these days, you can have that same experience of stowing away on a freighter – packed with 18-wheelers, drunken truck drivers and cattle – but you can make a reservation online and they will charge you hundreds of dollars for your bunk.

The Navimag is not a cruise. If you are looking for a cruise, check out Skorpios (p320) and ready your credit card. The Navimag is a quirky travel experience that comes with the good, the bad and the ugly. If you like to have different experiences and are adventurous it just might be the highlight of your trip.

The Good

The boat takes you through days of uninhabited fjords, close encounters with glaciers and views of surreal orange sunsets over the Pacific. It passes through Aisén's maze of narrow channels, navigates the Angostura Inglesa (a passage so confined that the ship seems to graze the shoreline on both sides) and stops at the impossibly remote Puerto Edén, a small fishing port and the last outpost of the region's Qawashqar Indians. To the south, the channels become narrower, the snowy peaks get closer and hundreds of waterfalls tumble from glacial valleys to the water's edge.

Beyond the stellar scenery, the trip has become a unique bonding experience for independently minded travelers. Strangers become tight friends after numerous bottles of wine, round after round of pointless card games, sympathizing about queasy stomachs, deck-top soccer matches, late-night dance parties and plans to meet up in Torres del Paine. Even though the ship's common spaces are bare and not particularly comfortable, the crew does a yeoman's job of trying to entertain with games, slide shows, music and a respectable selection of English-language movies.

The Bad

If the weather is poor, your views are limited and you will spend much of your time watching movies or drinking in the dining area. If the weather is worse, you can spend a day or so pitching back and forth on rough seas and fighting to hold down your lunch. If the weather is worse than that your trip can be delayed (for days) prior to departure and you can even be delayed en route if the Golfo de Penas (on the open Pacific) is too rough to cross.

In the winter the boat can have less than a dozen passengers, which can be fine or can really detract from the social experience. In the heart of summer, it is often so full that people are packed on top of each other and must dine in shifts. A very crowded boat can make the cramped downstairs dorm rooms seem less bearable.

The Ugly

During the winter, when there are fewer passengers and more cargo, hundreds of head of cattle are kept on the top and middle decks in open-top trucks. They are packed together so tightly that not all animals can keep their feet on the ground and after a day or two the stench of 300 cattle can be tough on your nose – especially if you are already seasick.

However, as you should know by now, no valuable travel experience comes without a dose of hardship. If you have the time, trips on the Navimag will not only change the way that you see and understand Chilean Patagonia, it will also add depth to your entire trip.

SUR CHICO

FERRY COSTS & SEASONS

Class	AAA (CH$)	AA (CH$)	A (CH$)	C (CH$)
(Nov–March)				
Single	1,284,400	1,232,400	1,092,000	-
Double	650,000	626,000	572,000	-
Triple	-	455,000	390,000	-
Quad	-	358,800	317,200	265,200
(Apr–Oct)				
Single	847,600	759,200	624,000	-
Double	452,400	400,400	327,600	-
Triple	-	286,000	239,200	-
Quad	-	226,200	208,000	202,800

Navimag also sails the Ferry *Puerto Eden* to Puerto Chacabuco on Wednesdays in high season. Prices range from CH$143,000 for the AA single to CH$38,000 for the C berth. The company also heads to Laguna San Rafael on most Saturdays from September to April, with a stop in Chacubuco. Round-trip prices from Puerto Montt range from CH$865,000 for an AA single to CH$250,000 for C berth. In low season, the *Evangelistas* sails to Chacubuco while the *Puerto Eden* heads to Puerto Natales.

Naveira Austral leaves several times a week to Chaitén. The trip takes 10 hours and usually runs overnight and is less than comfortable. Service is scaled back in the winter and is limited in the low season. Prices are CH$18,900 per seat and CH$76,000 for vehicles.

Cruceros Skorpios (☎ 252-619; www.skorpios.cl; Av Angelmó 1660) calls itself 'semi-elegant.' It's a legitimate cruise, sailing the Skorpios II to Laguna San Rafael and the Chilean fjords with departures on Saturdays from Puerto Montt all year except June and July. The seven-day round-trip cruise stops at its exclusive hot-springs resort, Quitralco, and at towns in the Chiloé archipelago. Double occupancy rates, which include abundant buffets, open bar and hotel-class rooms, range seasonally from CH$1150,000 to CH$1525,000.

Cruz del Sur operates auto-passenger ferries from Pargua, 60km southwest of Puerto Montt, to Chacao, on the northern tip of Chiloé. Fares are CH$600 for passengers (included in bus fares to Chiloé) or CH$8500 per car, no matter how many passengers.

Getting Around

ETM shuttles go to **Aeropuerto El Tepual** (☎ 252-019), 16km west of town, from the bus terminal (CH$1500). Catch the bus 1½ hours before your flight's departure. They also offer door-to-door service from the airport (CH$4000). Taxis between the airport and downtown cost CH$8000.

Car-rental agencies **Budget** (☎ 286-277; Antonia Varas 162) and **Antillanca** (☎ 258-060; Av Diego Portales 514) can help get the permission certificate (CH$58,000) to take rental vehicles into Argentina with two days' notice. Rates hover around CH$35,000 per day for unlimited mileage in an economy car.

SUR CHICO

Chiloé

When the imposing, early morning fog shrouds misty-eyed and misunderstood Chiloé, it's immediately apparent something different this way comes. People say that once you're south of Puerto Montt, you're on the frontier, and this verdant archipelago was long the dividing line between the supposed cultural homogeneity of Chile and a fiercely independent, sea-faring people who developed culturally and historically in defiance of Santiago.

At about 180km long but only 50km wide, the Isla Grande de Chiloé is the second-largest island in South America. It remained isolated and off the commercial route until nearby Puerto Montt was founded in the mid-19th century, but it wasn't until a massive earthquake in 1960 leveled Ancud that the fiercely ethnocentric Chilote people yielded to both Chilean and international influence. Even so, Chiloé today staunchly upholds its regional distinction, one forged by harsh rainy weather and a deeply intimate marriage with the sea. On the surface you will see changes in architecture and cuisine: *tejuelas*, the famous Chilote wood shingles; *palafitos* (houses mounted on stilts along the water's edge); more than 150 iconic wooden churches (16 of which are Unesco World Heritage sites); and the renowned meat, potato and seafood stew, *curanto*. A closer look reveals a rich spiritual culture that is based on a distinctive mythology of witchcraft, ghost ships and forest gnomes. Easily accessed by a short ferry ride, the main island is lush with undulating hills dotted with farms to the north, and blanketed in dense forest to the south and west near Parque Nacional Chiloé. Nearly 40 smaller islands strewn throughout the gulf are even more remote, isolated and traditional.

HIGHLIGHTS

- Kayak at dawn on the misty and undis-covered Río Puntra in **Chepu** (p327)
- Tear into a bowl of *curanto*, Chiloé's most traditional dish, in local restaurants such as Kuranton in **Ancud** (p326) and El Chejo in **Quemchi** (p328)
- Visit the island's astounding wooden churches, including the Unesco-listed gems in **Tenaún** (p328) and **Castro** (p332)
- Hike along the raging and wild west coast in **Parque Nacional Chiloé** (p337)
- Wander the picturesque unpaved roads of **Isla Mechuque** (p328), an idyllic microcosm of Chiloé on a stunning little island

| POPULATION: 158,692 | AREA: 9181.5 SQ KM | ELEVATION: 0–1000M |

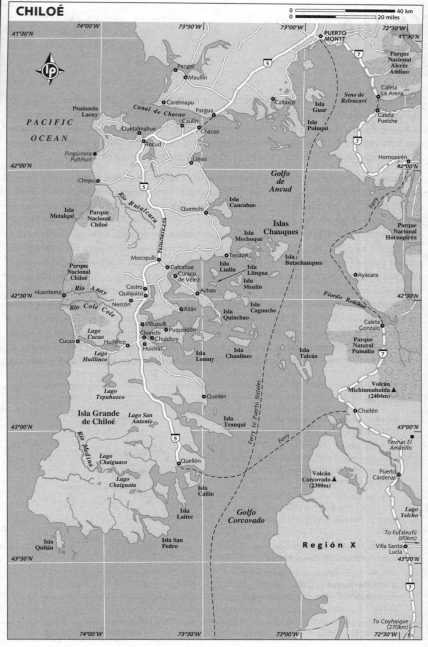

History

The islands were first populated by the Chono people, who were pushed towards the Archipelago de Aisén as the Mapuche invaded from the north. The Spaniards took full possession of Chiloé in 1567, some five years after a smallpox epidemic killed much of the indigenous population. A measles epidemic in 1580 further weakened the native influence.

During the wars of independence, Chiloé was a Spanish stronghold; the Spanish resisted criollo attacks in 1820 and 1824 from heavily fortified Ancud, until their final defeat in 1826. In 1843, the schooner *Ancud* left the shores of Chiloé full of islanders, who stuck out four months of sailing to lay Chilean claim to Magallanes at Fuerte Bulnes. The later wool and ranching booms in Magallanes were built on the backs of migrant Chilote labor. Their cultural influence is still felt in the far southern regions.

Chiloé itself stayed off the radar until the 1850s when its proximity to the new Puerto Montt gave the islands increasing commercial importance. It took another century to establish a road running the length of the main island. Fishing was and is the main industry, but is now heavily steeped in salmon and shellfish farming. Tourism has increased significantly during the last two decades.

Climate

When it is not misting or raining, it tends to be sprinkling or drizzling. The rain here is not to be feared or loathed but understood as an essential characteristic of this enchanting land – that which gives Chiloé its unforgettable deep-green coloring. The weather can change rapidly and the sun will peek through even in the heart of winter in June and July. Summer, especially January and February, is your best bet for clear skies.

Dangers & Annoyances

Much of the fun in Chiloé centers on eating the island's fresh shellfish, but before you indulge in anything raw here, check if there have been any recent cases of *Marea Roja* (Red Tide), a vicious disease resulting from bloomed algae absorbed by oysters, clams and mussels, and sparked by unusually high sea temperatures (thus the risk is higher in the mid to late summer months). If you down the toxic shellfish, symptoms range from diarrhoea and vomiting to asphyxiation, paraly-sis, seizures and even death from cardiac and respiratory failure – no doubt not the desired effect you were looking for from your dozen on the half shell. It's rare, but there were documented cases around Dalcahue, Castro, and Quellón in early 2008. Check with the captain of the port, who is in charge of monitoring instances of the disease, or just order cooked shellfish and seduce your target with pisco sours like the rest of us.

Getting There & Away

Nearly all traffic reaches and leaves Isla Grande de Chiloé by ferry between Pargua, on the mainland 56km southwest of Puerto Montt, and Chacao, a small town of little interest at the northeast corner of the island. Bus fares to/from the mainland include the half-hour ferry crossing; pedestrians pay CH$600, cars CH$8500. For details on ferries from Quellón to Chaitén, see p340. For bus details from Puerto Montt, see p318. There are no regular flights to Chiloé.

Getting Around

The easiest way to get around Chiloé is the bus. Buses connect every major destination on the main island with some frequency and link up with ferries to smaller islands. It is also easy to explore with a car, which allows you to visit some of the more remote parts of this remote land. You can rent a car in Ancud or Castro, or bring one over from the mainland on the ferry.

ANCUD

☎ 065 / pop 49,551

Ancud was once a rather wealthy place with gracious buildings, *palafitos* and a railway line. But the earthquake of 1960 decimated the town and now the sprawling city is built primarily of boxy concrete structures and is not particularly attractive, save the spectacular waterfront, which glistens throughout the better part of each summer day. There's a quality museum, some rugged beaches and sea-kayaking spots, and one of Latin America's most interesting town plazas – full of Foosball tables. Go on, challenge a local.

Information

Banco de Chile (Libertad 621) ATM.

BancoEstado (Ramirez 229) ATM.

Clean Center (☎ 623-838; Pudeto 45; per kg CH$900; ☺ 10am-4pm Mon-Sat) Laundry service.

Hospital de Ancud (☎ 622-355; Almirante Latorre 301; ☼ 24hr) At the corner of Pedro Montt.

Post office (cnr Pudeto & Blanco Encalada; ☼ 9am-1:30pm & 3-6pm Mon-Fri, 10am-12:30pm Sat)

Sernatur (☎ 622-800; Libertad 665; ☼ 8:30am-8pm Mon-Fri, 9am-8pm Sat & Sun Dec-Feb, 8:30am-5pm Mon-Fri Mar-Nov) On the Plaza de Armas, this is the only formal national tourist office on the island. It has very helpful staff, brochures, town maps and lists of accommodations for the archipelago.

Zona Net (Pudeto 276; per hr CH$600; ☼ 9am-midnight Mon-Sat, 2-11pm-Sun) Internet access.

Sights

The **Museo Regional Aurelio Bórquez Canobra** (☎ 622-413; Libertad 370; adult/child CH$600/300; ☼ 9:30am-7:30pm Mon-Fri, 10am-7:30pm Sat & Sun Jan-Feb, 10am-5pm Mon-Fri, 10am-2pm Sat & Sun Mar-Dec), casually referred to as Museo Chilote, makes Ancud a worthwhile stop in itself. Looking more like a fortress than a museum, it has fantastic displays tracking the history of the island and a full-sized replica of the *Ancud*, which sailed the treacherous fjords of the Strait of Magellan to claim Chile's southernmost territories.

During the wars of independence, **Fuerte San Antonio** (cnr Lord Cochrane & Baquedano; admission free; ☼ 8:30am-9pm Mon-Fri, 9am-8pm Sat & Sun) was Spain's last Chilean outpost. At the northwest corner of town, late-colonial cannon emplacements look down on the harbor from the early-19th-century remains of the fortress. There's not much left but a well-preserved wall, but the views and historical significance are impressive. There's a somewhat secluded beach, Playa Gruesa, behind the north wall.

Tours

Austral Adventures (☎ 625-977; www.austral-adventures.com; Av Costanera 904) Once recommended as your one-stop shop for English-speaking tours of the archipelago, Austral Adventures has shifted its focus to two- to three-day private tours arranged in advance, icing out the independent walk-ins. It still does good work, just to a smaller, more exclusive public.

La Red de Agroturismo (www.viajesrurales.cl, in Spanish) Chiloé's agrotourism association organizes excursions to farming and fishing communities and private homes that offer meals and lodging in several small towns that don't make most maps. Arrangements must be made through the website, or by ringing up the president of the association, Luisa Maldonado (☎ 643-7046).

Patagón Chiloé (☎ 622-128; www.patagonchiloe.cl, in Spanish; Bellavista 491; ☼ 8am-7pm Mon-Sat) This agency

is a better bet for independent travelers and walk-ups. They do excursions all over Chiloé, but you're more likely to use them to visit the penguin colonies. They offer three trips out per day for CH$20,000 per person with discounts for groups.

Festivals & Events

During the second week in January, Ancud observes the **Semana Ancuditana** (Ancudian Week), when everyone gets all fired up over the island's music, dance and cuisine.

Sleeping
BUDGET

Camping Arena Gruesa (☎ 623-428; arenagruesa@yahoo.com; Av Costanera Norte 290; campsites per person CH$3000, s/d CH$20,000/22,000) Located atop a bluff on the north side of town, city campsites don't get much better views than this. The area is grassy and well maintained with electricity, hot water and a *refugio* (rustic shelter) for rainy nights (unfortunately, the strong ocean winds whip through with little remorse). It's also a minute's walk to the beach (it ain't Malibu, but still). A warning: the Rottweiler bites the French (and maybe you, too).

Hostal Mundo Nuevo (☎ 628-383; www.newworld.cl; Costanera 748; dm CH$8000, s/d CH$20,000/30,000, without bathroom CH$16,000/20,000; P ☒ ☐) This Swiss-owned hostel is just a quick walk down the hill and around the corner from the new bus station and boasts postcard-perfect sunset views over the Bay of Ancud from a big, comfortable bench on its front porch. All rooms come complete with a sea view and decent breakfast, including homemade multigrain bread.

Cabañas y Hospedaje Vista al Mar (☎ 622-617; www.vistaalmar.cl; Costanera 918; dm CH$8500, s/d CH$18,000/24,000, cabins 6-8 people CH$55,000; P ☒ ☐) If you are traveling in a group of three to eight people, this is the place in town to get a shared cabin. There's also a spiffy dorm room, decent kitchen and larger-than-average shared bathrooms. It is open year-round, has sea views and is only a few minutes from the Plaza de Armas.

MIDRANGE & TOP END

Hostal Lluhay (☎ 622-656; www.hostal-lluhay.cl, in Spanish; Lord Cochrane 458; s/d CH$10,100/20,200; P ☐) Lluhay wins over visitors with its very welcoming owners. Don't be surprised if they start feeding you homemade küchen, pouring you cocktails by the fireplace or knocking out a few bars on the piano.

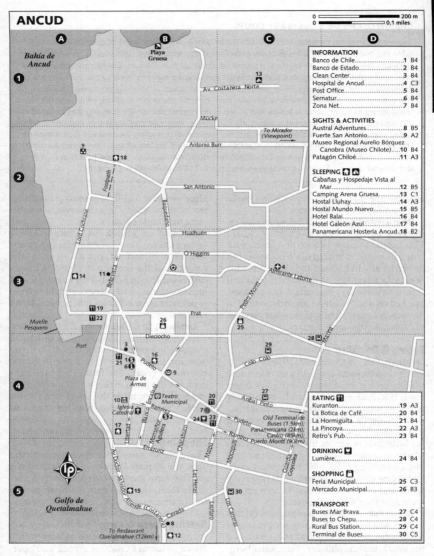

ANCUD

Bahía de Ancud

Playa Gruesa

Av Costanera Norte

Mücke

To Mirador (Viewpoint)

Antonio Burr

San Antonio

Hualhuén

O'Higgins

Almirante Latorre

Prat

Diéciocho

Pedro Montt

Colo-Colo

Anibal Pinto

Pudeto

Old Terminal de Buses (1.5km); Panamericana (2km); Castro (85km); Puerto Montt (90km)

Muelle Pesquero

Port

Plaza de Armas

Teatro Municipal

Iglesia Catedral

Ramírez

Golfo de Quetalmahue

To Restaurant Quelalmahue (12km)

Baquedano

Lord Cochrane

Footpath

Bellavista

Pudeto

Errázuriz

Blanco

Eleuterio

Monseñor Aguilera

Chacabuco

Maipú

Mocopulli

Guardia Goycolea

Las Heras

Lártaro

Los Carrera

Cavada

N Doctor S Ignacio Allende (Costanera)

Matta

INFORMATION	
Banco de Chile	1 B4
Banco de Estado	2 B4
Clean Center	3 B4
Hospital de Ancud	4 C3
Post Office	5 B4
Sernatur	6 B4
Zona Net	7 B4

SIGHTS & ACTIVITIES	
Austral Adventures	8 B5
Fuerte San Antonio	9 A2
Museo Regional Aurelio Bórquez Canobra (Museo Chilote)	10 B4
Patagón Chiloé	11 A3

SLEEPING	
Cabañas y Hospedaje Vista al Mar	12 B5
Camping Arena Gruesa	13 C1
Hostal Lluhay	14 A3
Hostal Mundo Nuevo	15 B5
Hotel Balai	16 B4
Hotel Galeón Azul	17 B4
Panamericana Hostería Ancud	18 B2

EATING	
Kuranton	19 A3
La Botica de Café	20 B4
La Hormiguita	21 B4
La Pincoya	22 A3
Retro's Pub	23 B4

DRINKING	
Lumière	24 B4

SHOPPING	
Feria Municipal	25 C3
Mercado Municipal	26 B3

TRANSPORT	
Buses Mar Brava	27 C4
Buses to Chepu	28 C4
Rural Bus Station	29 C4
Terminal de Buses	30 C5

Hotel Balai (☎ 622-541; www.hotelbalai.cl; in Spanish; Pudeto 169; s/d CH$16,800/20,200; ℗ ☒ ▣) This homey, 12-room spot right on the Plaza de Armas is an affordable midrange option stuffed with handicrafts, art and trinkets. The place can seem a little cluttered and worse for wear, but is full of character and has a friendly staff.

Panamericana Hostería Ancud (☎ 622-340; www .panamericanahoteles.cl; San Antonio 30; s/d CH$36,500/ 40,000; ℗ ☒ ▣) Though not the priciest, this is the nicest hotel in town. The cozy, cabinlike rooms are not outrageously more comfortable than the cheaper spots, though. Book a room in the north wing for glistening sea views. Everything about the restaurant is forgettable

CHILOÉ

CURANTO: CHILOÉ'S CULINARY COUP

No words can quite prepare you for the first moment a piping hot bowl of *curanto* lands on the table in front of you, but 'What did I get myself into?' comes to mind. Rest assured, however, your slack-jaw will come in handy when it's time to shove all that food in. Chiloé's most traditional dish is of unknown origins, but historically its preparation harkens back to the earth ovens of Polynesian culinary ancestry. Traditionally *curanto* was made by heating up stones in a hole in the ground and waiting until they crackle, then directly piling on shellfish, pork and chicken, followed by nalca or pangue leaves and damp cloths before the whole shebang was covered in dirt and grass and left to simmer for nearly two hours. They still prepare it this traditional way, called *curanto al hoyo*, in a few places around the island, including **Restaurant Quetalmahue** (☎ 099-8791-9410; ⊗ lunch & dinner) in Quetalmahue, a small fishing village 12km from Ancud. If you can't make it there (a taxi runs CH$10,000 roundtrip from Ancud), the next best thing – minus the pit and dirt – is Kuranton (below) in Ancud and El Chejo (p328) in Quemchi.

save the appalling decor – you won't shake that memory for a while.

Hotel Galeón Azul (☎ 622-567; www.hotelgaleonazul .cl, in Spanish; Libertad 751; s/d CH$38,900/62,500; **P** ⊠ ⌨) This brilliant-yellow beacon of a hotel, with blue trimmings, is in need of a renovation, but its bright, sky-lit hallway and abundant windows take advantage of the natural light and expansive views over the harbor. The grounds, perched on a hill where an old fortress used to be, includes a garden of antique stone carvings of Chiloé mythological figures.

Eating & Drinking

La Botica de Café (☎ 629-650; Pudeto 277; desserts CH$750-1500; ⊗ breakfast, lunch & dinner) A cute coffeehouse serving up the most elusive thing in Chiloé: real coffee (read: not instant) and a ridiculously tempting selection of international desserts.

La Hormiguita (☎ 626-999; Pudeto 44; sandwiches CH$1000-5000; ⊗ lunch & dinner; **V**) This delightful little bakery serves massive sandwiches (damn near impossible to eat without looking like a bumbling fool), pies, fruit juices and a few veggie choices. It alternates days serving lunch and dinner, so it's best to turn up and see where they're at in the cycle.

Retro's Pub (☎ 626-410; Maipú 615; mains CH$2500-9500; ⊗ 10am-late; **V**) This cozy spot rides the fence between restaurant and pub, serving up the usual suspects plus Tex–Mex, killer burgers and a small veggie menu (though we're not sure what the chicken Caesar salad is doing there). As far as bars go, this is the town classic for an atmospheric drink, a pretty perfect spot in light of the weather.

La Pincoya (☎ 622-511; Prat 61; mains CH$3000-6500; ⊗ lunch & dinner) La Pincoya is a two-story, formal (but not stuffy) affair. The view is the place's greatest highlight as most of the dishes are local standards. It is, however, a reliable place to sample *curanto*.

Kuranton (☎ 623-090; Prat 94; curanto CH$5000; ⊗ lunch & dinner) This institution has an extensive menu of seafood, but it's all about the *curanto* (see the boxed text, above), Chiloé's gastronomic bombshell. This hearty stew of mussels, clams, chicken, pork and three types of potatoes is a meal fit for hibernation. Don't miss it.

Lumière (☎ 621-980; Ramirez 278; ⊗ 12pm-late) This restaurant/bar skews *slightly* older and cheaper, offering an extensive cocktail and beer list under the watchful eye of classic cinematic scenes. The four-sided bar in the center of the room makes a nice spot to plant yourself. They serve the usual fare (mains CH$2500 to CH$5500), plus popcorn, just like the movies.

Shopping

There are an abundance of craft markets in both the **Mercado Municipal** (Dieciocho) and the nearby **Feria Municipal** (cnr Pedro Montt & Prat). Both locations also contain a municipal tourist office.

Getting There & Away

Ancud's colorful new **Terminal de Buses** (☎ 622-249; cnr Los Carreras & Cavada) is owned and operated by **Cruz del Sur** (☎ 621-777) and its affiliates, which offer the most departures to Chiloé's more southerly towns, with departures about every hour, and to cities on the Panamericana to the north (including six daily departures to Santiago in high season). It's a five-minute walk from the waterfront and downtown. A taxi to/from the terminal to Av Costanera in downtown costs CH$1500. **Queilen Bus** (☎ 621-140) still operates out of the nearly abandoned old bus terminal 1.5km from the center. Buses go to Punta Arenas every Monday, Wednesday, Friday and Saturday at 7:45am in high season. However, travelers bound to most southerly regions beyond Chiloé and to Bariloche, Argentina, will do better to take buses from Puerto Montt.

Sample fares and times are as follows:

Destination	Cost (CH$)	Duration (hr)
Castro	1500	1½
Concepción	17,000	12
Osorno	5000	4
Puerto Montt	3300	2
Punta Arenas	43,000	32
Quellón	3500	4
Quemchi	1000	1¼
Santiago	24,000	17
Temuco	8500	8
Valdivia	7000	6

Chiloé's more rural destinations to the east, as well as late buses to Chepu, the gateway to the northern end of Parque Nacional Chiloé, are serviced by buses that leave from a small rural bus station on Colo Colo above the FullFresh grocery store. The schedule is posted near the bathroom – simply buy tickets on the bus. **Buses Mar Brava** (☎ 622-312), departing from a residential area of Aníbal Pinto, heads to rural destinations to the northwest, including Pingüinera Puñihuil.

PINGÜINERA PUÑIHUIL

Three islands off the coast of Puñihuil, on the Pacific Ocean, are breeding grounds for Magellanic and the near-extinct Humboldt penguins. These islands are monitored by **Fundación Otway** (☎ 065-278-500; www.fundacion otway.cl), the nonprofit organization managed by German volunteers that for years had protected the penguins north of Punta Arenas. The best time of year to go is when the penguins are breeding, from September to March. Several travel agencies in Ancud organize excursions to the site, or you can grab a Mar Brava bus from central Ancud on your own (except Sunday). No matter how you arrive, your transportation will drive right out onto a magnificent rugged beach. Local fisherman take tourists out for a closer (but quick) look at the penguins for CH$4000 per person. All-weather gear is provided. If the

rickety rural buses leave too early for you (6:45am), but the organized tours are too pricey, a good midrange option is **Taxi Tour** (☎ 622-135). Owner Luis Cárdenas is bang on time – a miracle in Latin America – and will take up to four people out to the penguins and back for CH$20,000, including the boat and tour. Always check ahead with a travel agency or two to make sure that the penguins are in fact in the region.

If you want to make a night of it, **Pinguinland Cabañas** (☎ 099-373-7511; www.pinguinland.net; cabins for 4/6 persons CH$29,400/42,200; **P**) offers fantastic cabins with large kitchens, good towels – even bathtubs! – all on top of a bluff with spectacular views of the islet. If you have binoculars or a telescope, you can observe the penguins and, if you're lucky, see whales with your naked eye from here as well. There are a few decent restaurants on the beach, but avoid eating loco, a regional mollusk similar to abalone, which is fished relentlessly and irresponsibly in direct ignorance of local hunting restrictions.

CHEPU

Previously difficult to access and lacking infrastructure, Chepu, the northern sector of Parque Nacional Chiloé (p337), 38km southwest from Ancud, remains Chiloé's undiscovered sanctuary of pristine beauty. Arriving here gives one an elusive sense of discovery. You'll find stunning coastline, gorgeous rivers and 128 species of birds here, totally untapped by mass tourism thus far. **El Mirador de Chepu** is a breathtaking spot overlooking the confluence of three rivers and 140 sq km of sunken forest, a surreal phenomena created by the 1960 quake, which sunk the ground some 2m, allowing salt water to enter the area and kill the trees. **Chepu Adventures** (☎ 099-379-2481; www.chepuadventures.com; campsites for 2 CH$6000, dm per person CH$2000; **P** 🖳) runs a spectacular eco-campground here with infrared solar showers and electricity, and construction from wood alternative recycled fiber. It offers a mystical self-guided kayak trip at dawn on the Río Puntra, and treks to the nearby penguin colony at Ahueco, which, at low tide, you can walk right onto. And life-changing barbeques. For non-campers, there are also five Argentine-style *dormis* (mini sleeping rooms) or try **Hospedaje Yosara** (☎ 099-8869-0000; full board without bathroom CH$14,000; **P**) for better food or **Hospedaje Perez-Diaz** (☎ 099-8523-6960; full board with/without bathroom CH$18,000/14,000; **P**), part of the Agroturismo

Network, for extra comfort and fine artisanal cheeses made on premises.

Access to the park from here involves a 30-minute boat ride and a three-hour coastal trek. This is the most untouched part of Parque Nacional Chiloé. There is a small *refugio* for camping near the entrance. Go now – this secret is out.

Buses Yañez has two buses daily from Ancud to Chepu Monday to Friday. The 6:30am bus leaves from the Esso gas station on the corner of Prat and Marina while the second, at 4pm, leaves from the rural bus station. Buses return to Ancud at 5pm (CH$1200). On Saturday, there is only one bus each way, at 2pm to Chepu and 5pm to Ancud.

QUEMCHI

☎ 065 / pop 9102

On a clear summer day, the snow-capped mountains of southern Chile loom in the distance over misty Quemchi, topping off an already impressive view from the sea wall of this sleepy little town. Quemchi's waterfront is an ideal place to lose yourself for a day, strolling along the bay and passing the hours in one of Chiloé's best restaurants – El Chejo. It has the highest change in tides (7m) on the island, which makes for a surreal scene of beached fishing boats while the water's out.

Rural buses make the trip to Ancud and Castro (CH$1000, 1½ hours to either destination) every few hours throughout the day, less on Sunday. Check at the library and adjacent supermarket for schedules.

Sleeping & Eating

Hospedaje Costanera (☎ 691-230; Diego Bahamonde 141; s/d CH$12,000/16,000, without bathroom CH$6000/8000; P) Stubborn service, no hot water, and no (instant) coffee until 9am – monopoly on the soulless has its privileges. It isn't the only game in town, but it boasts the best sea views (though some are obstructed by electrical wires) and prime location 50m from El Chejo. Ask for one of the front rooms to get a glimpse, but avoid No 3 as there is no room for luggage!

El Chejo (☎ 691-490; Diego Bahamonde 251; mains CH$3000-5000; ✹ lunch & dinner) A family-run treasure. El Chejo is the kind of restaurant one travels to but rarely finds, not only for its great food and warm Chilote hospitality, but for personality as well. There's no menu – you get what's good that day. That could

mean starting with the excellent *empanada de centolla* (a fried pastry filled with king crab) followed by a choice of several locally caught fish, all washed down with a sampling of Chilote fruit liqueurs (try the *murtado*, a medicinal berry). When it's not too full, Jessica will fawn over you as well as invite you back into the kitchen. *Curanto* is served once a week or by calling ahead. If you are on death row in Chiloé, this is your last meal.

TENAÚN

☎ 065 / pop 574

Tiny Tenaún is rural – 37km northeast along a gravel road from Dalcahue (opposite) – but there are two very compelling reasons to visit. The magnificent **Nuestra Señora del Patrocinio church** (1837), for which the town is named (Tenaún means 'three mounts'), one of Chiloé's Unesco gems. Its three magnificent blue towers, in stark contrast to almost any other church you will ever see, appear to be reflecting the cerulean blue sea that sits right across the street on orders from God himself. Its distinctive stars and trimmings add to the surreal architecture.

our pick **Hospedaje Mirella** (☎ 099-647-6750; meals CH$3500), located next to the church and part of the Agroturismo Network, makes it worth staying in Tenaún (room CH$7000). The indomitable Mirella is an exceptional cook and is serious about making sure her guests enjoy the multicourse meals she prepares. She does *curanto al hoyo* or whatever fresh catch her son, Javier, grabs that day. Try to call ahead. On a clear day, you can see Volcán Corcovado across the Gulf of Ancud from her front porch.

Buses run between Castro and Tenaún approximately four times daily (CH$1200, 1½ hours). All of them stop in Dalcahue (CH$1000).

ISLA MECHUQUE

☎ 065 / pop 500

The further you venture into Chiloé's smaller islands, the more it feels as if you've traveled back in time. Isla Mechuque is only 45 minutes by boat from Tenaún, but feels like it's caught in a bygone era. A part of the Islas Chauques – considered Chiloé's most beautiful island chain – Mechuque is small but stunning. With its **museum** (✹ 8am-8pm summer), *tejuela*-shingled homes, splendid viewpoint, picturesque bridge, famous *curanto al hoyo*

MYTHOLOGICAL CREATURES OF CHILOÉ

For centuries Chiloé's distinctive mythology swirled through the foggy towns, blew from one island to the next and gave form to the culture and lives of the intriguing Chilote people. Outside of the commercial centers, these traditional beliefs are still very much alive today. The beliefs, syncretic with the island's Catholicism, weave together a story of the creation of the island, tales of destruction on the stormy seas and warnings about straying from the 'clean' way of life.

Brujos (broo-hos) The center of Chiloé's mythology, brujos are warlocks with black-magic powers, bent on corrupting and harming normal Chilote folks. They are based in a secret location (most likely a cave) near Quicavi.

Cai-Cai Vilú (kai-kai-vee-loo) The Serpent God of the Water who waged a battle against Ten-Ten Vilú (Serpent God of the Earth) for supremacy over the domain. Cai-Cai Vilú eventually lost but was successful in covering enough territory with water that Chiloé stayed separated from the mainland.

El Caleuche (el-ka-le-oo-che) A glowing pirate ship piloted by singing, dancing brujos. Their melodious songs draw commercial vessels into El Caleuche's trap. It is capable of sailing into the wind and navigating under the water's surface.

Fiura (fee-oo-ra) A short, forest-dwelling hag with a ravenous sexual appetite and breath that causes sciatica in humans and is enough to kill smaller animals.

Invunche (een-voon-che) The grotesque guardian of the cave of the brujos. Invunche was born human, but the brujos disfigured him as he grew: turning his head 180 degrees, attaching one leg to his spine and sewing one of his arms under his skin. He eats human flesh and cat's milk, and is extremely dangerous.

Pincoya (peen-koi-a) A naked woman of legendary beauty who personifies the fertility of the coasts of Chiloé and its richness of marine life. On the rocky shores she dances to her husband's music. The way that she faces determines the abundance of the sea harvest.

Ten-Ten Vilú (ten-ten-vee-loo) Serpent God of the Earth (see Cai-Cai Vilú).

Trauco (trow-ko) A repugnant, yet powerful, forest gnome who can kill with a look and can fell any tree with his tiny stone hatchet. He is simply irresistible to young virgins, giving them impure erotic dreams and sometimes even a 'mysterious' child out of wedlock.

Viuda (vee-oo-da) Meaning 'the widow,' Viuda is a tall, shadowy woman dressed in black with milk-white bare feet. She appears in solitary places and seduces lonely men. The next day she abandons them where she pleases.

La Voladora (la-vo-la-do-ra) A witch messenger, who vomits out her intestines at night so that she is light enough to fly and deliver messages for the brujos. By the next morning, she swallows her intestines and reassumes human female form.

---

and *palafitos*, it's like a mini Chiloé offering all of the larger archipelago's attractions condensed down into an area that makes for an easy and memorable day trip.

Boats leave for Isla Mechuque from Dalcahue's fishing dock Monday, Thursday, Friday and Saturday at 1pm (CH$3000). Returns are available Monday, Wednesday, Thursday and Friday departing Mechuque at 7:30am, though lodging is scarce on Mechuque. You're much better off hopping on an organized day tour in Castro. Try Turismo Pehuén (p334).

DALCAHUE

☎ 065 / pop 8000

Dalcahue, in Huilliche, means 'Dalca's Place' and is named after the boats, called *dalcas*, constructed by the first inhabitants of Chiloé. It's a feisty little town facing the inner sea of the island and is best known as the departure dock for Isla Quinchao, one of archipelagic Chile's more accessible and interesting islands (and home to attractive Curaco de Vélez and Achao, and for its Doric-columned, silver-hued **Nuestra Señora de Los Dolores church**. Founded in 1849, the church is another one of the island's 16 Unesco World Heritage sites (take special note of the painting behind the entrance door; the juxtaposition of Jesus with Chiloé's mythological characters was used as Jesuit propaganda to convert the indigenous inhabitants). The town, a short 20km jaunt from Castro, is best visited on Sunday, when its **crafts fair** (7am-5pm) expands to include the surrounding streets. You'll find the island's most authentic arts and crafts here, dominated by sweaters, socks, and hats woven from *oveja* (wool) and dyed with natural pigments made from roots, leaves and iron-rich mud. All the surrounding islands participate. It's not worth the trip in itself, but it shakes things up a bit.

There's a semi-helpful **tourism office** (9am-7pm Mon-Fri, 10am-6:30pm Sat & Sun) at the corner of Freire and the ferry dock.

Sleeping & Eating

Residencial Playa (099-822-9123; Rodríguez 09; s/d without bathroom CH$4000/8000) The walls are paper thin, the beds squeak and the whole place shudders like an aftershock from the '60s quake every time someone so much as lifts a finger, but still, this ain't a bad budget option. Rooms are clean and comfortable – though the padlocked doors are quite shady – and reached via a deadly staircase above the restaurant of the same name (watch it after a few Escudos).

Onde Nacho (641-201; www.ondenachoturismo .blogspot.com; Freire 490; s without bathroom CH$8000, s/d CH$12,000/17,000; P X □) A comfortable midrange *pension* in a well-appointed home across the street from one of the bus stops to/from Castro. There's wi-fi and the homeowners are quite friendly. It's a five-minute walk to the church and crafts fair.

Hotel La Isla (641-241; Av Mocopulli 113; s/d CH$21,000/26,000; P X) The best hotel in town is inside a cute red-and-blue trimmed cabin-like building a few minutes' walk from the church. The bright rooms are spacious and offer soft beds and showers big enough for two – a miracle in Chiloé.

La Cocinera (mains CH$2000-6000; 8am-9pm) Tucked behind the crafts market, this is the place to go for a true taste of local color. It's a collection of several kitchenette stalls manned by stout grandmotherly types dishing up *curanto,* pounding out *milcao* (potato bread), and dosing out Chilota sweets. Plop yourself down at the counter that looks best to you and take it all in. The food doesn't move mountains, but the atmosphere is priceless.

Dalca (641-222; mains CH$1800-6000; lunch & dinner Mon-Sat, lunch Sun) Just when you thought you were sick of shellfish, the *caldillo de mariscos* (shellfish stew, CH$2400) at this highly regarded seafood restaurant located above the fishing dock shows up at your table and restores your faith in *culimanity* in one bite. It's worth the trip here alone. Get there before 6pm on Sunday.

Getting There & Away

There is no bus terminal in Dalcahue. Dalcahue Expreso runs buses to Castro (CH$300, 30 minutes) every 15 minutes from a stop on Freire in front of Supermercado Otimarc be-

tween Henriquez and Eugenin. You can also catch buses at various points up and down the main street of Freire. **Cruz del Sur** (641-050; San Martín 102; 8:30am-1pm & 2:30-7pm) has two buses per day to Ancud and Puerto Montt leaving at 9:10am and 3:15pm. Buses depart from the office on San Martín right next to the church. There are also two buses per day to Tenaún (Buses Ojeda, CH$1000). Catch them along the main street.

Ferries for Isla Quinchao leave continuously between 7am and midnight. Pedestrians go free, but try and time it so you cross with an Achao-bound bus as you'll need to be on it once you get to the other side. Cars cost CH$5000 (round trip). Boats also leave here for Isla Mechuque several days per week (see p329).

ISLA QUINCHAO

065 / pop 9203

The elongated island of Quinchao, easily accessed via a short ferry crossing from Dalcahue, is a hilly patchwork of pasturelands punctuated by small villages. A good road runs the length of the island and carries you through the island's most popular destinations, Curaco de Vélez and Achao.

Curaco de Vélez

An unexpected treasure lies in wait in the form of lovely Curaco de Vélez, the first town you come to along the main road from the ferry dock on Isla Quinchao. A superbly tranquil town, it's well worth spending an afternoon strolling the streets here, taking in the fascinating two- and three-story ornately shingled wooden homes (kind of like Chilote log cabins, if you will) and eight traditional water mills for which the town is known. On the town square there is also an interesting church and a new cultural center and museum. Don't miss the underground crypt of War of the Pacific hero Galvarino Riveros Cardenas – he's buried right in the square!

In the summer, head straight for **Ostras Los Troncos** (lunch & dinner), an open-air restaurant across the street from the beach. You'll find the wooden trunk tables and chairs packed in like sardines with patrons slurping down buckets of fresh oysters (CH$300 to CH$400 each) awash in lemon and salt, chased with *cerveza* (beer). From the main square, follow Calle Francisco Bohle down and to the right.

The buses that run frequently between Achao and Dalcahue stop in Curaco.

Achao

When the early morning fog rolls into the village of Achao, 22km southeast of Dalcahue, it can be an eerie sight, leaving no doubt you are in a remote Chilote seaside town. Though it lacks some of the indisputable charm and stillness of Curaco, Achao, too, is a worthwhile stop for its landmark church and outstanding architecture. People from nearby islands come to Achao to sell their wares and produce, creating quite a buzz of activity along its small jetty and adjacent Feria Artisanal.

SIGHTS

Achao's 18th-century Jesuit church, **Iglesia Santa María de Loreto**, on the south side of the Plaza de Armas, is Chiloé's oldest (1740) and also a Unesco World Heritage site. Crowned by a 25m tower, it is sided with alerce shingles and held together by wooden pegs rather than nails. The church has been slowly restored, with new wood juxtaposing the old, but its restoration has remained faithful to the original design. Its hours are erratic – knock on the door and see if anyone is around.

Museo de Achao (cnr Delicias & Amunátegui; admission CH$300; ☉ 10am-1pm & 2-6pm Dec-Feb) highlights aspects of the Chono people of Achao and other indigenous groups in Chiloé. Wood products, weavings, stones and plants used for tinting materials are all elegantly presented with informative material (in Spanish).

The **Grupo Artesanal Llingua** (cnr Serrano & Ricardo Jara), artisans from the nearby Isla Llingua, have a well-stocked market of their crafts behind the now-abandoned tourist kiosk.

Highlights of their basket-weaving wares includes coffee cups (absolutely useless for actually holding liquids), handbags for the ladies, and breadbaskets. It's only open on days when the ferry comes over from Isla Llingua on Monday, Wednesday and Friday.

FESTIVALS & EVENTS

Encuentro Folklórico de las Islas del Archipiélago, held in the first week of February, attracts musical groups from throughout the archipelago.

SLEEPING & EATING

In the busy summer season everything can get booked up and most places close down during the winter.

Hospedaje São Paulo (☎ 661-245; Serrano 52; r per person without bathroom CH$5000) This requisite budget option is tired and woefully lacks appropriately high ceilings, but it serves its purpose. The rooms aren't horrible and the shared bathrooms are actually quite big. Anyone taller than 175cm or aching for a tad more comfort will want to spring for an upgrade in the adjacent wing (CH$7500 per person).

Hostal Plaza (☎ 661-283; Amunátegui 20; s/d CH$6000/12,000, without bathroom CH$5000/10,000) A super-friendly family home that is right on the plaza above the post office. It's kinda like staying at grandma's house. There's a big kitchen with an old-timey wood-burning stove and the owner can wash a few clothes for you as well.

Hospedaje Sol y Lluvias (☎ 661-383; Ricardo Jara 9; s incl breakfast without bathroom CH$9520, r incl breakfast CH$28,650; P ✗) The top choice in town sits in a wonderful rust-orange house on the corner of Ricardo Jara and Serrano. It offers all the makings of a well-run home, right down to the substantial breakfasts.

LICOR DE ORO

Every fine food is accompanied by an equally fine beverage. To match Chiloé's distinguished cuisine is an endless list of unique island liqueurs. The multi-colored drinks are concocted by soaking different herbs, grasses, flowers, fruits or berries in alcohol. Nothing is off-limits, from sticks and leaves to chicken eggs. The most famous is *licor de oro* (gold liquor), which looks a bit like a cheap tequila or you-know-what. The basic recipe is 1L of milk, 1L of alcohol, 1.5kg of sugar, eight cloves, two sliced lemons, a teaspoon of saffron, two to three bitter almonds, two pods of vanilla and an optional dose of cinnamon. The liqueur is then made by a slow process of soaking the ingredients together and painstakingly filtering out the liquid, drop by drop, to remove the cloudiness from the milk. The resulting beverage is supposed to confuse and excite the palate with its chimera of ingredients. It tastes like liquid Christmas with a sweet little Mediterranean twitch thrown in. Some like it, some don't, but you are unlikely to have tried anything like it before.

Mar y Velas (☎ 661-375; Serrano 2; mains CH$2900-5800; ☺ 10am-late) Overlooking the bustling jetty (and usually a thick blanket of intimidating fog) is this recommended seafood restaurant with an extensive menu and flirtatious servers. Try the house-style fish smothered in cheese, sausage and mussels. La Nave next door is also good.

GETTING THERE & AWAY

The **bus terminal** (cnr Miraflores & Zañartu) is a block south of the church. Buses run daily to Dalcahue and Castro every 15 to 30 minutes (CH$1400). Queilen Bus also goes to Puerto Montt (CH$4500) Monday to Saturday at 6:20am and 1pm Sunday.

Boats for Isla Llingua, also home to an interesting church, leave Monday, Wednesday and Friday at 3pm.

CASTRO

☎ 065 / pop 34,537

If there is one town that sums up all the idiosyncrasies and attractions of Chiloé, it is beautiful Castro. At times loud and boisterous like some working class towns in Mexico, the capital of the archipelago somehow retains its local Chilote character side by side with a dash of modern development and comfortable tourism infrastructure. Just 85km south of Ancud, it's located in the dead center of the island, making it the main transportation hub and a perfect base for exploring attractions further afield.

The 1960 earthquake destroyed the port, the railway, the town hall, and some *palafitos*, but Castro rebounded and turned itself into a charming destination that's easily navigable on foot. Perhaps the greatest single attraction is simply walking down the streets and around the central plaza, soaking up all of Castro's curious energy. The town sits on a bluff above its sheltered estuary lined with distinctive *palafitos* houses. If you only have time to visit one town in Chiloé, come to Castro.

Information

BOOKSTORES

Anay Libros (☎ 630-158; anaylibros@tutopia.com; Serrano 437; ☺ 9:30am-2pm & 3-8pm Mon-Fri, 10am-8pm Sat) Has a few English titles.

El Tren Libros (☎ 633-936; alibroseltren@hotmail.com; Thompson 229; ☺ 10am-1:30pm & 3:30-9pm Mon-Sat) Specializes in cultural books and has a very limited English section.

INTERNET ACCESS

Ciber Café (☎ 632-466; Latorre 267; per hr CH$500; ☺ 9:30am-11:30pm Mon-Sat, 2-10pm Sun)

LAUNDRY

Clean Center (☎ 633-132; Balmaceda 220; per kg CH$1100; ☺ 9:30am-1pm & 3-7pm Mon-Sat) Laundry service.

MEDICAL SERVICES

Hospital de Castro (☎ 632-212; Freire 852)

MONEY

ATMs can be found at the numerous banks on or around the Plaza de Armas.

POLICE

(☎ 765-366; Portales 457)

POST

Post office (O'Higgins 388; ☺ 9am-1:30pm & 3-6pm Mon-Fri, 10am-12:30pm Sat) On the west side of Plaza de Armas.

TOURIST INFORMATION

Conaf (☎ 532-503; Gamboa 424; ☺ 8:45am-1pm & 2-5:45pm Mon-Thu, 8:45am-1pm & 2-5:45pm Fri) The official Chilean parks department. The office has a limited amount of information in Spanish on Parque Nacional Chiloé.

Tourist kiosk (Plaza de Armas; ☺ 10am-8pm) A large kiosk featuring scale models of Chiloé's churches. It also stocks some helpful brochures and maps, though we're not entirely sure why they must guard them behind the counter.

Sights

PALAFITOS

Castro is the best place to see the *palafitos*, shingled houses built up on stilts along the dark estuaries and lagoons. From the street, they resemble any other house in town, but the backsides jut over the water and, at high tide, serve as piers with boats tethered to the stilts. This truly singular architecture, now protected as a national historic monument, can be seen along six areas in town. The postcard view from land is the **Puente Gamboa Mirador** just west of centro.

IGLESIA SAN FRANCISCO DE CASTRO

Italian Eduardo Provasoli chose a marriage of neo-Gothic and Classical architecture in his design for the elaborate **Iglesia San Francisco** (San Martín), finished in 1912 to replace an earlier

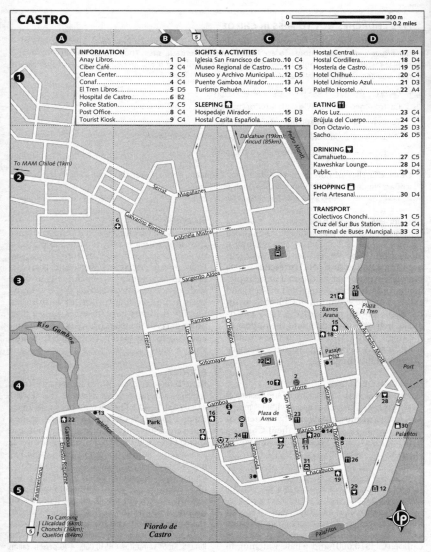

CASTRO

0	300 m
0	0.2 miles

INFORMATION
Anay Libros.............................**1** D4
Ciber Café..............................**2** C4
Clean Center..........................**3** C5
Conaf....................................**4** C4
El Tren Libros.........................**5** D5
Hospital de Castro...................**6** B2
Police Station.........................**7** C5
Post Office.............................**8** C4
Tourist Kiosk..........................**9** C4

SIGHTS & ACTIVITIES
Iglesia San Francisco de Castro..**10** C4
Museo Regional de Castro......**11** C5
Museo y Archivo Municipal.....**12** D5
Puente Gamboa Mirador........**13** A4
Turismo Pehuén.....................**14** D4

SLEEPING 🛏
Hospedaje Mirador.................**15** D3
Hostal Casita Española...........**16** B4

Hostal Central........................**17** B4
Hostal Cordillera.....................**18** D4
Hostería de Castro..................**19** D5
Hotel Chilhué.........................**20** C4
Hotel Unicornio Azul...............**21** D3
Palafito Hostel........................**22** A4

EATING 🍴
Años Luz...............................**23** C4
Brújula del Cuerpo..................**24** C4
Don Octavio...........................**25** D3
Sacho...................................**26** D5

DRINKING 🍸
Camahueto.............................**27** C5
Kaweshkar Lounge..................**28** D4
Public...................................**29** D5

SHOPPING 🛍
Feria Artesanal......................**30** D4

TRANSPORT
Colectivos Chonchi.................**31** C5
Cruz del Sur Bus Station..........**32** C4
Terminal de Buses Muncipal....**33** C3

To MAM Chiloé (1km)

Dalcahue (19km);
Ancud (85km)

Río Gamboa

Fiordo de
Castro

To Camping
Llicaldad (6km);
Chonchi (36km);
Quellón (84km)

Serrat

Magallanes

Galvarino Riveros

Gabriela Mistral

Sargento Aldea

Ramirez

Los Carrera

O'Higgins

Freire

Sotomayor

Gamboa

Palafitos

Panamericana

Ernesto Riquelme

Pedro Montt

Costanera Av Pedro Montt

Barros
Arana

Plaza
El Tren

Pasaje
Díaz

Latorre

San Martín

Serrano

Port

Plaza de
Armas

Blanco Encalada

Thompson

Esmeralda

Chacabuco

Lillo

Palafitos

Palafitos

Park

Portales

Balmaceda

---

church that burned down (which had replaced an even earlier church that had burned down). One of Chiloé's Unesco gems, the church once assaulted the vision with its exterior paint job – salmon with violet trim – but it's in bad need of a touch up these days. Inside, the varnished-wood interior is stunning. It is best to visit on a sunny day – if you are lucky enough – as the interior is more charming illuminated by the rows of stained-glass windows.

MUSEO REGIONAL DE CASTRO

Eternally in the process of moving to a surprisingly post-modern, cutting-edge hunk of architecture along the waterfront (on which construction has stalled due to lack of funds),

---

FIVE CHURCHES NOT TO MISS IN CHILOÉ

Chiloé boasts more than 150 gorgeous wooden *iglesias* (churches) and *capillas* (chapels), one of the region's main attractions; 16 are Unesco World Heritage sites. They are almost all built in a similar fashion with a single tower in the front, slanted side roofs, arched entrances and attractive wooden shingles. Five standouts:

- Achao – the oldest of Chiloé's churches (1740)
- Castro – neo-Gothic style with interior built entirely of native wood
- Tenaún – for its dramatic blue-starred exterior
- Villupulli – the church with the most delicate and slender tower
- Quinchao – the largest of the island's churches

Other churches of note include Aldachildo, Caguach, Chelín, Chonchi, Colo, Dalcahue, Detif, Ichuac, Nercón, Quehui, Quetalco, San Juan and Rilán.

---

this **museum** (Esmeralda; admission free; 9:30am-7pm Mon-Sat, 10:30am-1pm Sun Jan-Feb, 9:30am-1pm & 3-6:30pm Mon-Sat, 10:30am-1pm Sun Mar-Dec), half a block from Plaza de Armas, houses a well-organized collection of Huilliche relics, musical instruments, traditional farm implements and Chilota wooden boat models, and exhibits on the evolution of Chiloé's towns. Its B&W photographs of the 1960 earthquake help you to understand the impact of the tragic event. The museum's new waterfront home will be in the Museo y Archivo Municipal building.

MAM CHILOÉ

Castro's spacious **MAM** (Museo de Arte Moderno de Chiloé; 635-454; Parque Municipal; 10am-8pm summer), features innovative works by contemporary Chilean artists, many of them Chilotes. It's a fair hike from town, but worth it if you're an art buff.

Tours

Turismo Pehuén (675-254; www.turismopehuen.cl, in Spanish; Blanco Encalada 208; 9am-1:30pm & 3-6:30pm Mon-Fri, 10am-1pm Sat) is a highly regarded agency that organizes tours to nearby islands such as Mechuque (CH$20,000), Parque Nacional Chiloé (CH$10,000) and whale-watching in March and April (CH$60,000). It was said to be opening an outlet in Ancud as well. There is also a Lan office here.

Festivals & Events

Castro celebrates **Festival Costumbrista** in mid-February. It's a week-long party with folk music and dance, and traditional foods.

Sleeping

Castro is well set up for budget and midrange travelers, with a variety of affordable places, mostly along San Martín and O'Higgins, their immediate side streets, and the eastern end of Sotomayor, which turns into the wide concrete staircase called Barros Arana with a high concentration of *hospedajes*. Quality is higher here for your money than other parts of the island. Unless it is summer and rooms are scarce, take your time and shop around.

BUDGET

Hostal Cordillera (532-247; hcordillera@hotmail.com; cnr Serrano & Sotomayor; r per person without bathroom CH$8000, d CH$22,000;) The owner speaks no more English than, 'Do you need a room?' but she's still a crack-up and makes you feel at home at this traveler's hub, which features some sea views, large bathrooms, comfy beds, cable TV, and wi-fi (though some travelers have complained it's chilly in winter). The kitchen could be kept more spiffy and some general touch-ups are needed, but you should be hanging out on the pleasant little deck out back taking in the water views over a few drinks.

Camping Llicaldad (632-380; Panamericana Ruta 5 Km6; campsites CH$10,000, 4-/6-person cabins CH$25,000/30,000) The best campground in relation to distance from the city. Sites here have beautiful views overlooking the Fiordo de Castro and have small shelters from the rain. Some say it's overpriced, however.

Hostal Central (637-026; hostalcentralpm@hotmail.com; Los Carrera 316; s/d CH$13,400/21,800, without bathroom CH$8400/15,500;) The nicest of the traditional budget options in town. It features large, colorful bathrooms and rooms with cable TV, wi-fi and even mirrors – an obscurity in Chiloé's budget lodgings. The breakfast room rivals any on the island.

Hospedaje Mirador (☎ 633-795; maboly@yahoo.com; Barros Arana 127; s/d without bathroom CH$9000/18,000, r CH$25,000; ☒ ▢) One of the better Barros Arana choices, Mirador has some seaside views, fantastic bathrooms (by Chiloé standards), hearty breakfasts, wi-fi and a welcoming atmosphere.

Palafito Hostel (☎ 531-008; Ernesto Riquelme 1210; dm CH$8000-12,000, d CH$25,000; ▢) A brand new hostel sitting on Palafitos Gamboa with spiritual views over the Fiordo de Castro. It's a five-minute walk from centro.

MIDRANGE & TOP END

Hotel Chilhué (☎ 632-596; hotelchilhue@yahoo.com; Blanco Encalada 278; s/d CH$16,000/18,500; ℙ ▢ ☒) Almost as good as the location, just a clam's throw from Plaza de Armas, are the newly renovated 3rd-floor rooms, which have been made over with new carpet, bedspreads and more room than the rest of the hotel.

Hostal Casita Española (☎ 635-186; casitaespanola@telsur.cl; Los Carrera 359; s/d CH$16,700/23,600; ℙ ▢) This homey spot has hit middle age, but the lush garden gives it an edge over the competition, as does the hospitable and outgoing owner. It's a nicely appointed home one block from the plaza.

Hotel Unicornio Azul (☎ 632-808; Costanera Av Pedro Montt 228; www.hotelunicornioazul.cl, in Spanish; s/d CH$32,700/38,800) In a land raised on mythology it is only fitting that one of the fanciest hotels in town is named the 'Blue Unicorn' and decorated from head to toe with the legendary beasts. This sister hotel of Ancud's Galeón Azul has a pretty wacky color scheme, too (pink exterior, pink doors). Rooms are a little more rundown than the common areas, but there are exceptional views.

Hostería de Castro (☎ 625-688; www.hosteria decastro.cl, in Spanish; Chacabuco 202; s/d CH$33,500/ 41,100; ℙ ▢ ☎) Forget the tattered old rooms at this vaguely churchlike guesthouse, the newly added wing – a completely different hotel in reality – offers 49 ultra modern, urban cool rooms and suites that wouldn't be out of place in Los Angeles or London, but are certainly fishes out of water here. Large bay windows offer startling sea views and there's a pool and a nice restaurant as well.

Eating & Drinking

Brújula del Cuerpo (☎ 633-225; O'Higgins 308; mains CH$1310-5990; ☒ breakfast, lunch & dinner) A godsend for those tired of seafood, this Chilota-style diner does pizza, fajitas, American-style breakfast and other *comida rapida*. The burger, fries and drink combo meal (CH$1590) is pretty much heaven after days of mussels and clams.

Don Octavio (☎ 632-855; Costanera Av Pedro Montt 261; mains CH$2500-9500; ☒ lunch & dinner) You can practically dine on top of the fishing boats at this atmospheric *palafito* restaurant. There's way too much mayonnaise on the menu, but in addition to the usual suspects, there's also king crab and octopus. The curious signature dish, featuring your choice of fish, smothered in a sauce of onions, tomatoes, green peppers and sausage, then buried under a bound of thinly cut fried potatoes, is excellent.

our pick Años Luz (☎ 532-700; San Martín 309; mains CH$2600-9500; ☒ lunch & dinner Mon-Sat) For a country that doesn't exactly bowl foodies over with its culinary arts, this sophisticated refuge built around a centerpiece bar made out of an old fishing boat is an exception. Stylistically and gastronomically, it's worth all the pesos in your wallet. The salmon ceviche is gorgeous; the filet *del pueblo* (filet with onions, bacon and a fried egg) is perfectly cooked; the house pisco sour (with honey and a cinnamon rim) is a welcomed twist on a classic; and the ice-cold Kunstmann drafts are served in proper beer mugs. Service isn't exactly swift, but you'll soon forget. As long as the naysayers claim it's 'not Chilota enough,' there'll be more for the rest of us.

Sacho (☎ 632-079; Thompson 213; mains CH$3300-5500; ☒ lunch & dinner) The languages flying through the air at this well-regarded seafood spot evoke the breakroom at the UN, but the food is all Chilota, served in a semi-refined atmosphere (whimsical tablecloths, linen napkins). The specialty is *pulmay*, a *curanto*-like shellfish dish featuring clams and mussels, but a little less meat and potatoes.

Drinking

There are a few places on the plaza that get going as the evening progresses. Just walk around and take your pick – anything with Kunstmann on draft must have some semblance of class.

Kaweshkar Lounge (www.kaweshkarlounge.cl; Blanco Encalada 31; mains CH$2000-3400; ☒ 12pm-late Mon-Sat; ♥) This newcomer prides itself on

CHILOÉ

indie cool: the retro furniture and industrial vogue vibe would be right at home in New York's East Village. Music is one-part Blur, one part Velvet Underground (DJs visit from Santiago in summer). There's food, too. The menu features several vegetarian choices and some edgy entrees for Chiloé (salmon crepes with béchamel!).

Camahueto (☎ 534-943; Blanco Encalada 350; 11am-late) If you'd rather get sauced with Chilotes than *turistas*, your hangover will be the same, but your journey starts here. The live music on weekends is worth a good laugh.

Public (Thompson; cover men/women CH$6000/ 5000; midnight-late Fri & Sat) The top nightclub in town only opens on weekends, so you can imagine locals and tourists alike are clamoring to get in. Show up around 1am.

Shopping

Castro's waterfront **Feria Artesanal** is by far the island's biggest, but be wary here – much of the merchandise is secretly imported from China, India, Peru and Equador. That said, you'll find venders hawking a fine selection of woolen ponchos and sweaters (ones you'd *actually* be caught dead in), caps, gloves, basketry and liquors.

Getting There & Around

Centrally located Castro is the major hub for bus traffic on Chiloé. There are two main bus terminals. The rural station, **Terminal de Buses Municipal** (San Martín), has the most services to smaller destinations around the island and some long-distance services. Buses to Dalcahue and Isla Quinchao leave from here. **Queilen Bus** (☎ 632-173) and an office representing Cruz del Sur, Transchiloé, Turibús and others also operates out of here to most destinations of importance, including Punta Arenas and Bariloche. **Buses Ojeda** (☎ 573-488) and **Inter Lagos** (☎ 635-312) also depart from here for Cucao and Parque Nacional Chiloé on the west coast around five times per day (CH$1400 to CH$1600). Sit on the right side for most outstanding views of Lago Cucao.

The second terminal, the main depot of **Cruz del Sur** (☎ 632-389; San Martín 486), also houses Transchiloé and Turibús, and focuses on transportation to the main Chilote cities, Quellón and Ancud, and long-distance services.

Destination	Cost (CH$)	Duration (hr)
Ancud	1000	1½
Concepción	18,000	14
Puerto Montt	4300	4
Quellón	1200	½
Quemchi	1000	1½
Santiago	23,000	16
Temuco	9500	10
Valdivia	8000	7½
Punta Arenas	40,000	36

For Chonchi, *colectivos* are a faster alternative. **Colectivos Chonchi** leave from Chacabuco near Esmeralda (CH$700).

Occasional summer ferries to/from Chaitén (p350) were grounded at the time of writing, but these schedules tend to change frequently. Check with **Naviera Austral** (☎ 65-270-430; www .navieraustral.cl, in Spanish; Angelmó 2187, Puerto Montt) and **Navimag** (☎ 65-432-360; www.navimag.com; Angelmó 2187, Puerto Montt).

CHONCHI
☎ 065 / pop 12,236

Chonchi must have won the lottery – the regional government is dumping money into this small seaside town-cum-departure-point to the national park, just 23km south of Castro. There is a beautiful new CH$4 million Mercado Municipal, with a delightful space for artisans, small art expositions and a restaurant jutting out over the Bahiá de Chonchi; the town's Plaza de Armas is currently getting a CH$2.6 million makeover; and there's a fancy new school being built as well.

The town was once a pirate's delight and a port for the export of cypress. These days it makes for a pleasant stopover on your way to/ from the park, but keep it brief. The sad beach is in dire need of a cleanup, and the town itself is less interesting than other Chilote options of similar size, though folks do dig the tranquility here.

Most tourist services can be found along Centenario, including a **tourist office** (cnr Sargento Candelaria & Centenario; 9am-7pm Dec-Feb). Chonchi's landmark church, the pastel-hued **Iglesia San Carlos de Borroneo**, with multiple arches, dates from the mid-19th century. **El Museo Viviente de las Tradiciones Chonchinas** (☎ 671-214; Centenario 116; admission CH$500; 9am-1pm & 2-6pm Mon-Fri, 9am-1pm Sat) smartly displays exhibits to give a sense of a traditional Chilote household, including an original-style kitchen, bedroom and cooking hearth.

Sleeping & Eating

Esmeralda by the Sea (☎ 671-328; www.esmeralda bythesea.cl; Irarrázaval 267; dm & r per person without bathroom CH$5000, d CH$20,000; P X 💻) On the beachfront, this *hospedaje* has a helpful expat owner, Carlos, who, being nicely Canadian and all, sometimes upgrades guests and is generally entertaining and helpful with stories of Chonchi lore and national park info. He rents bikes and organize hikes to a nearby Jesuit church or blackberry fields – if you're bored, he'll find you something to do. It should be noted, though, that opinions of travelers have been very mixed. Two-day minimum.

Posada El Antiguo Chalet (☎ 671-221; Irarrázaval s/n; s/d CH$30,000/35,000, without bathroom CH$20,000/ 25,000; P) This 73-year-old wooden house, tucked away in a quiet location above the marina, teems with character and antiques, but it was nearly deserted on our visit (guests *and* staff). Still, its cozy attic rooms covered in woolen rugs are Chonchi's most atmospheric and comfortable, and the house-made *licor de oro* is otherwise worth stopping in for.

El Trébol (☎ 671-203; Irarrázaval 187; mains CH$1500-4500; 🕙 lunch & dinner Mon-Sat) Consistently the best restaurant in Chonchi. You can't go wrong ordering anything they do with *congrio* (conger eel).

Getting There & Away

Opposite the Plaza de Armas, **Cruz del Sur** (☎ 671-218) and Transchiloé run several buses daily to Castro (CH$600), Quellón (CH$1200) and destinations further afield such as Puerto Varas (CH$5800) and Valdivia (CH$8500). *Taxi colectivos* to Castro (CH$700) cruise the town regularly looking for patrons.

There is an hourly bus service in summer to Cucao (CH$1200) and Parque Nacional Chiloé (CH$1400, 1½ hours). Buses Interlagos departs from the small lot next to Cruz del Sur twice daily at 9:30am and 3pm, though these buses often fill up in Castro. Buses Arroyo and Ojeda fill in the other hourly spaces between 8:30am and 4:30pm (all subject to spontaneous Chilote changes, of course). The latter leave from the intersection of Sargento Candelaria and Centenario (at the tourist kiosk) and do not come through town. All year long, Inter Lagos departs the entrance of the park for Cucao and Castro at 10:45am and 3:45pm.

There are free launches from the port of Huichas on Isla Lemuy. The ferry leaves every half-hour between 8am and 8pm Monday to Saturday from Puerto Huichas, 5km to the south; on Sunday and in the off-season the service is hourly. The ferry lands at Chulchuy, with connections to Puqueldón.

PARQUE NACIONAL CHILOÉ

Running back from the pounding Pacific coastline, and over extensive stands of native evergreen forest, the 430-sq-km **Parque Nacional Chiloé** (adult/child CH$1000/free) is only 30km west of Chonchi and 54km west of Castro. The park teems with Chilote wildlife, from 110 different types of bird, to foxes and the reclusive pudú (the world's smallest deer), which inhabits the shadowy forests of the contorted tepú tree. Within the park and along the eastern perimeter is a number of Huilliche indigenous communities, some of which are involved with the management of campsites within the park.

The park comprises three sections. The northern sector is called **Chepu** (p327) and includes Isla Metalqui (and its sea-lion colony) and is best accessed from Ancud. In addition, Metalqui is highly restricted because of ecological concerns and can only be visited with special arrangements from the parks service. The middle sector, **Abtao**, is restricted by Conaf and accessible only by an 18km hike from the Pichihué property. The more accessible southern sector, **Chanquín**, contains the majority of the eight official hikes in the park, ranging from quick jaunts to 25km slogs.

Visitors are at the mercy of Pacific storms, so expect lots of rain. The mean annual rainfall at Cucao is 2200mm, and anyone planning more than an hour-long walk should have water-resistant footwear, woolen socks and a decent rain jacket. Insect repellent is not a bad idea, either. There is a **Conaf visitor center** (🕙 9am-8pm Jan-Feb, 9am-1pm & 2-7pm Mar-Dec) 1km past the bridge from Cucao, but apparently they spend more money on cute little green sweaters for their rangers than on practical information for tourists (like trail maps, for instance). The center does cover flora and fauna extensively and it also houses a small museum. Once inside the park, there is little infrastructure or well-marked trails.

Cucao is your last chance to pick up supplies, although you will find better prices and wider selections back in Chonchi or Castro.

Sights & Activities

The raw beauty of this national park is best appreciated on foot, and there are several hikes that can easily hold your attention for a day or two. The **Sendero Interpretivo El Tepual**, a short 1km nature trail built with tree trunks, branches and short footbridges, loops through dense, gloomy forest. The **Sendero Dunas de Cucao** starts from the visitor center and heads 2km through a remnant of coastal forest to a series of dunes behind a long white sandy beach.

Day hikers can follow the coast north on a 3km trail to **Lago Huelde** or a shorter 1.5km trek to **Playa Cucao**, a roaring Pacific beach. The most popular route is the **Sendero Chanquín-Cole Cole**, a 25km hike (about five hours one-way) along the coast, past Lago Huelde to Río Cole Cole. Lots of people set out to make this hike and back in one day, but nobody usually makes it further than the indigenous settlement at Huentemó, where there are basic camping facilities for CH$1500 per person (no kitchen) and a new *hospedaje*. The hike extends another 8km north to **Río Anay**, passing through a stand of arrayán to arrive at another rustic *refugio* in reasonable shape. Keep in mind, you take the gravel highway about 6km past the visitors center before it dead ends on the beach (near the end of this highway, you'll find your last chance for food: El Arco de Noé Café).

Several of the camping sites within the park have been shut down, but you are allowed to camp anywhere you want. At the time of writing a new camping project was in the works for the 2009 season at Cole Cole.

Sleeping & Eating

Most accommodations and restaurants are in Sector Chanquín, just past the bridge from Cucao.

Hospedaje El Paraíso (☎ 099-296-5465; Laura Vera, Cucao; campsites per person CH$1000, r without bathroom CH$7000; P ⊠) This is the basic budget option in Cucao, well run by a lovely woman, inside a pink house just before the bridge. It offers a fantastic river view.

Camping Sector Chanquín (☎ 532-503; campsites per person CH$2000, cabins up to 7 people CH$25,000) This Conaf-maintained camping and cabin complex lies about 200m beyond the visitors center and into the park. The sites have privacy, running water, firewood, hot showers and toilets. The cabins are spacious and fully equipped and were set for a renovation during off-season 2008. There is a small administration building on the site that handles reception.

El Fógon de Cucao (☎ 099-946-5685; Sector Chanquín; campsites per person CH$3000, s/d without bathroom CH$10,000/20,000; P) Your one-stop shop if you aren't pinching *pesos:* the hostel here is an upscale rustic gem and the most luxurious on the edge of the park; the campsites sit on the shore of Lago Cucao, and the restaurant (open for lunch and dinner; meals CH$4500) across the street does a set fish menu over lake views. It can also arrange excursions on horseback to Lago Huelde (CH$15,000, two hours) or Río Cole Cole (CH$40,000, three hours), and kayaks on Lago Cucao (CH$2500 per hour).

Hospedaje Chucao (☎ 099-787-7319; r per person CH$5000) A new option at Huentemó for those attempting Sendero Chanquín-Cole Cole.

Parador Darwin (☎ 099-799-9923; www.cucao.cl; Sector Chanquín; r per person CH$10,000; ☿ closed May-Oct; P ⊠) Full of character and charm, this colorful German-owned wooden house surrounded by massive nalca plants is a fantastic midrange choice. The restaurant (open lunch and dinner, mains CH$3000 to CH$4900) does *nueva* Chilota cuisine, which includes memorable smoked salmon and Hungarian goulash, and German küchen with chocolate and seaweed. The almost frozen, shot-sized pisco sours are lethally good.

El Arrayán (☎ 099-219-3565; Sector Chanquín; mains CH$2500-3500; ☿ breakfast, lunch & dinner) A small café just before the park entrance and a good choice for basic local fare done well and cheaply. The set breakfasts are a must if you are hitting the park for a full day.

Getting There & Away

Cucao is 54km from Castro and 34km west of Chonchi via a bumpy gravel road, passable in all but the most inclement weather. There is regular bus transportation between Castro and Cucao. Schedules vary, but there are usually four to five buses daily (CH$1400 to CH$1600); see p336 for details of the bus companies. Service from Chonchi is hourly in summer, but slims down considerably other parts of the year; see p337 for more information.

QUELLÓN

☎ 065 / pop 23,161

Fancy making the Great Transamerican Road Trip? If you high-tail it out of Fairbanks, Alaska, on the Panamericana Hwy heading south, stop for tamales in Mexico City, and can figure out a way to get through the Darien Gap in Colombia, your journey ends in Quellón, the southern terminus for one of the world's great highways, also known as Hwy 5. Salmon farming, most of which is exported to the US and Japan, pays the bills here – the town has seen quite a growth spurt in the last decade (and the subsequent upsurge in crime) and is now home to a sophisticated hotel and a lot of new money. But unless you're looking to get into that lucrative industry, there's no reason to linger.

If you come in on the ferry from Chaitén and have had enough traveling for a day, there is enough here to keep you happy for one night, including one of the island's best restaurants and the chance of spotting endangered blue whales in the Golfo de Corcovado or south around Isla de Melinka. Several outfitters in town offer whale-watching excursions from November to March.

Information

BancoEstado (cnr Ladrilleros & Freire) Has an ATM.

Cyber Zoán (Ladrilleros 540B, 2nd fl; per hr CH$550; ☽ 10:30am-midnight) Internet access.

Hospital de Quellón (☎ 681-443; Dr Ahués 305; ☽ 24hr)

Lavandaria Lim Blanc (☎ 681-400; J Carrera Pinto 75; per kg CH$700; ☽ 9am-7pm Mon-Fri, 9am-2pm Sat) Laundry services.

Post office (22 de Mayo; 9am-1:30pm & 3-6pm Mon-Fri, 10am-12:30pm Sat) Between Ladrilleros and Santos Vargas.

Tourist kiosk (cnr Gómez García & Santos Vargas; ☽ 9am-7pm Mon-Fri, 9am-noon Sat Jan-Feb) Offers information on boats that go to the nearby islands and whale-watching excursions from January 14 to February 28.

Sleeping & Eating

Camping Paico's (☎ 099-103-6939; Estero Quellón; campsites per person CH$5000) The closest of the campsites situated in Punta de Lapa, the spit of land southwest of downtown. There are city views and it's walkable to town. New bathrooms were scheduled for summer 2009 at the time of writing.

Hotel Playa (☎ 681-278; Costanera Pedro Montt 427; r per person without bathroom CH$5000) The logical

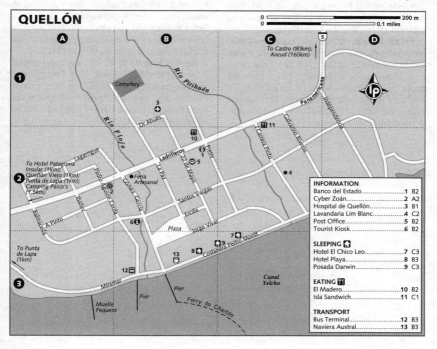

QUELLÓN

0 ────── 200 m
0 ────── 0.1 miles

To Castro (80km);
Ancud (160km)

Río Pitihuén

Cemetery

Río Flojo

Dr Ahués

Ladrilleros

Lagartigue

Pedro Aguirre Cerda

Gómez García

Feria Artesanal

Santos Vargas

Ercilla

Calvuco Bueras

Carrera Pinto

Freire

22 de Mayo

Jorge Vivar

Plaza

Miramar

Canal Yelcho

Muelle Pequeño

Pier

Pier

Ferry to Chaitén

Costanera Pedro Montt

Panamericana

Independencia

To Hotel Patagonia Insular (1km);
Quellón Viejo (1km);
Punta de Lapa (1km);
Camping Paico's (1.5km)

To Punta de Lapa (1km)

Ramírez

Balmaceda

A Pinto

INFORMATION	
Banco del Estado	**1** B2
Cyber Zoán	**2** A2
Hospital de Quellón	**3** B1
Lavandaria Lim Blanc	**4** C2
Post Office	**5** B2
Tourist Kiosk	**6** B2

SLEEPING	
Hotel El Chico Leo	**7** C3
Hotel Playa	**8** B3
Posada Darwin	**9** C3

EATING	
El Madero	**10** B2
Isla Sandwich	**11** C1

TRANSPORT	
Bus Terminal	**12** B3
Naviera Austral	**13** B3

budget choice right across the street from the ferry dock to Chaitén. The simple rooms here are actually more spacious than nearly all of the pricier options.

Hotel El Chico Leo (☎ 681-567; irma1.0@hotmail.com; Costanera Pedro Montt 325; r per person without bathroom CH$7000, d CH$25,000; P ✗ 🖳) Known for its clean, bright rooms, attentive staff and quality beds, El Chico Leo is a comfortable choice, though the low-ceilinged bathrooms could pose a challenge for taller travelers. The justifiably popular restaurant (mains CH$1800 to CH$6300) is known for its seafood. You can also stop in to shoot a game of pool and unwind after a few days on the road.

Posada Darwin (☎ 681-064; posadadarwin@gmail .com; Costanera Pedro Montt 355; s CH$12,600, d with/ without bathroom CH$18,500/15,000; 🖳) This newcomer along the waterfront has a little bit more character than some of the more worn and torn spots, with *mimbre* (wicker) baskets lining the walls and a great wooden staircase. A good midrange choice.

Hotel Patagonia Insular (☎ 681-610; www .hotelpatagoniainsular.cl; Ladrilleros 1737; s/d CH$37,800/ 41,200; P 🖳) If there's one piece of evidence of Quellón's steady climb up the social status chart, it's this sleek, citrus-toned boutique hotel sitting on a small hilltop just outside centro. It has all the comforts of a four-star hotel, including a wonderful circular bar under massive bay windows with views to the sea.

Isla Sandwich (☎ 680-683; Ladrilleros 190; sandwiches CH$2500-4000; ⌚ 11am-11pm Mon-Sat) This stylish café does 36 different kinds of upscale sandwiches, perfect for taking away to the ferry.

El Madero (☎ 681-330; Freire 430; mains CH$2500-5500; ⌚ 10am-midnight Mon-Sat) Like Años Luz in Castro, this great restaurant, tucked away in a residential home, is outclassing the town. The refreshingly presented dishes (mashed potatoes served in a hollowed-out squash) are unexpectedly sophisticated, and the grilled salmon here is far and away the island's best. Pop in for an evening drink, too.

Getting There & Away

Buses to Castro (CH$1200, two hours) are frequent with Cruz del Sur and Transchiloé, which leave from the **bus terminal** (cnr Pedro Aguirre Cerda & Miramar). The last bus leaves for Castro at 7:30pm. There are also services to Puerto Montt (CH$6200) and Temuco (CH$11,000).

Naviera Austral (☎ 682-207; www.navieraustral.cl, in Spanish; Pedro Montt 457) sails the *Pincoya* and the *Alejandrina* to Chaitén on Wednesday (12pm) and Sunday (3pm) throughout the year. Passengers cost CH$17,300 and vehicles CH$70,600.

Northern Patagonia

In this remote region separated by ferries, ox trails and roads that wash out in the blink of a storm, old folks still call a ferry ride to Puerto Montt 'going to Chile'. And it isn't hard to see why. For a century, Northern Patagonia has been the most rugged and remote part of continental Chile, where scant pioneers quietly set forth a Wild West existence. While life here may be tough for its residents, it doesn't lack for scenery. Exuberant rainforest, scrubby steppe and unclimbed peaks crowd the horizon, but the essence of this place is water, from the clear cascading rivers to the turquoise lakes, massive glaciers and labyrinthine fjords. Southbound visitors often bypass Northern Patagonia on a sprint to Torres del Paine, but its backcountry treasures are pay dirt to the adventurous traveler.

An oft-neglected provincial backwater, Northern Patagonia has retained its pristine state only to face an onslaught of industrialization. Chile's high-stakes salmon farming industry is looking to expand here. But the biggest threat to the region, which even environmentalists and the salmon industry can agree on, are proposals for a dozen hydroelectric dams on major waterways, including Río Baker, Chile's highest flowing river. Developing the projects would require creating the longest transmission lines in the world. On one hand, Chile sees itself in an energy crunch without the dams. But the proposals herald sad tidings for the great Patagonian wilderness. It may be wise to see Northern Patagonia while you can. With a few ferry interruptions, the gravel Carretera Austral rumbles from Puerto Montt to Villa O'Higgins, some 1200km south. This section runs north to south, from Hornopirén to Villa O'Higgins.

HIGHLIGHTS

- Plonk into pristine hot springs after a hard day's paddle in the misty fjords of **Parque Pumalín** (p345)

- Giddy up into **pioneer Patagonia** (p353) on remote Andean trails

- Face a whirl of white water, rafting the world-class rapids of **Río Futaleufú** (p351)

- Forget what day it is and stop caring as you dally in **Caleta Tortel** (p370), a seaside village set on boardwalks

- Scout for cave paintings and spy on flamingos in the little-known **Reserva Nacional Jeinemeni** (p366)

★ Parque Pumalín

★ Río Futaleufú

★ Reserva Nacional Jeinemeni

★ Caleta Tortel

■ POPULATION: 105,000　　■ AREA: 121,012 SQ KM　　■ ELEVATION: 0–2500M

lonelyplanet.com

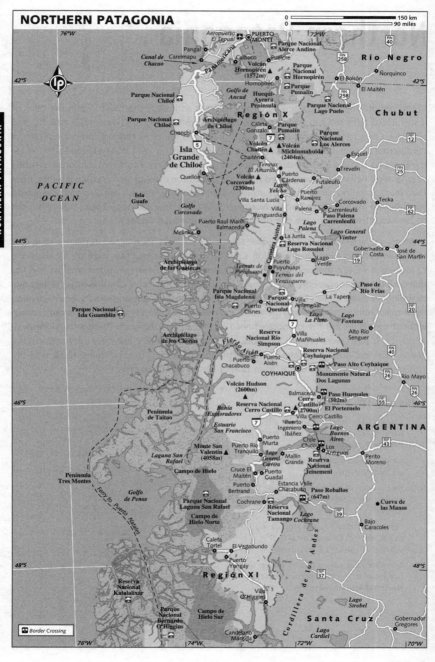

History

Long isolated and still remote, Northern Patagonia is the youngest area of the Chilean nation and the last to integrate. Chile only started promoting colonization in the early 20th century and many of the towns are barely 50 years old.

For thousands of years, the Chonos and Alacalufes people inhabited the intricate canals and islands, while Tehuelches lived on the mainland steppes. Aisén's rugged geography deterred European settlement for centuries, though fortune seekers believed the legendary 'City of the Caesars' to be in Trapananda, as Aisén was first known. A great many expeditions (including Captain Robert Fitzroy's British expedition, for which Darwin served as a naturalist) visited the area in the late 18th and early 19th centuries, some in search of a protected passage to the Atlantic.

In the early 1900s the government granted nearly 10,000 sq km in and around Coyhaique to the Valparaíso-based Sociedad Industrial Aisén as a long-term lease for exploitation of livestock and lumber. The company dominated the regional economy, and colonists trickled into the region to claim remote lands for farming. Encouraged by a Chilean law that rewarded clearance with land titles, the Sociedad and colonists burned nearly 30,000 sq km of forest and destroyed many of Aisén's native southern beech in a series of fires that raged for nearly a decade in the 1940s. Some of the planned fires raged out of control and the scorched trunks of downed trees still litter hillsides from Villa Mañihuales to Puerto Ingeniero Ibáñez.

Since the 1960s agrarian reform the influence of the Sociedad and other large landowners has declined. The region is sparsely populated, most notably south of Coyhaique, an area that was devastated by the 1991 eruption of Volcán Hudson. The eruption dumped tons of ash over thousands of square kilometers in both Chile and Argentina, ruining cropland and killing livestock by burying pasture grasses.

Salmon farming is a major industry and Patagonia's cold waters provide optimal farming conditions. The industry continues its exponential growth, creeping south since the practice has contaminated some Lakes District waters past sustainability, with waste from farms causing serious ecological disruption. The lobby for salmon farming is still quite strong and effective, given that there are few other jobs in the region.

A number of controversial hydroelectric projects (see p359) and other industrial plans define the continual push and pull between development and conservation in this region.

Climate

Northern Patagonia effectively closes down in winter, when temperatures plummet, pipes freeze and transportation slows to a trickle. For hard-nosed travelers winter is an interesting time to explore the region, as long as you have a flexible schedule and cold-weather gear. Summer, loosely from December to February or early March, gets relatively warm and sunny during the day, but you'll still need some layers for chilly evenings. *Tábano* (black horsefly) season is in January – avoid wearing dark colors that attract them. Though they are mainly a nuisance, they can make treks and horse riding unpleasant. Wear sunscreen as the UV rays can be strong.

Getting There & Away

Most travelers opt to take a ferry from Puerto Montt or Chiloé to Chaitén or Puerto Chacabuco; fly to Chaitén or Coyhaique; or go overland via Argentina, accessing the region through Futaleufú. For those who choose to drive the length of the Carretera Austral, there are three ferry crossings: Caleta Arena, Caleta Gonzalo (both mandatory if motoring south on the Carretera Austral) and Puerto Chacabuco; the ferry to Caleta Gonzalo (p344) only runs in January and February.

Getting Around

If not in your own vehicle, there is a solid network of buses between the major towns and a reasonably frequent flight schedule between the more major destinations. Some high-end lodges arrange transportation for visitors. There are also a number of ferries connecting points of interest along the water. Hitchhiking, not recommended by Lonely Planet, is possible along the Carretera Austral, but difficult for groups or travelers with big packs.

HORNOPIRÉN

☎ 065 / pop 2500

While this salmon-farming hub is not much to look at, you'll find its surroundings stunning. Many end up spending more time here than originally planned – not because of Hornopirén's subtle charms, but because the ferry is often full. Carretera Austral–bound cars queue up here to ferry around the roadless northern section of Parque Pumalín to Caleta Gonzalo, where the road continues south. The town is also the closest entrance to Parque Nacional Hornopirén (see right).

A **tourist kiosk** (☎ 217-222; hualaihue@hotmail.com; ⊙ 9am-7pm Dec-Feb), Conaf office, call center and supermarket can all be found around the main plaza.

Sights

Hot-springs resort **Isla Llancahué**, a 45-minute boat ride away, includes hotel **Termas de Llancahue** (☎ 099-642-4857; www.termasdellancahue.cl, in Spanish; d with/without bathroom incl full pension CH$30,000/25,000) and indoor and outdoor thermal pools (admission CH$10,000). While the pools are artificial, it's an attractive spot with warm water spilling into the ocean. Hotel guests have free use of the 50°C hot springs. A water shuttle leaves Hornopirén at 3pm daily in high season, returning at 7pm (CH$5000 round-trip). Fishermen at the ferry dock can also provide transportation (approximately CH$25,000 for up to four people); this allows you some prime soaking time before the shuttle rush arrives.

Sleeping & Eating

Campgrounds flank the road to Parque Nacional Hornopirén, including a large site at the Hornopirén bridge. Otherwise, there's wilderness camping in Parque Nacional Hornopirén itself.

Camping Vista Hermosa (campsites/r per person without bathroom CH$3500/5000) These basic campsites and no-frills farmhouse rooms have a cool and unusual backyard accessory – a waterfall. The proprietor sells baked goods and homemade cheese. A waterfall visit (what, you thought it was free?) costs CH$500.

Hotel Hornopirén (☎ 217-256; Carrera Pinto 388; r per person without bathroom CH$8000) Patagonian character pervades this somewhat cavernous hotel with low ceilings and rambling hallways. Take some time to relax on the outdoor patios and enjoy the views of the water.

Cabañas Rehbein (☎ 217-350, 099-132-6050; Av Ingenieros Militares s/n; 5-person cabins CH$25,000; ⬚) These comfortable two-story cabins are

fully equipped with kitchens and attended by their kindly owner, Señora Myriam.

Getting There & Away

Buses Fierro (Plaza de Armas) has buses daily to and from Puerto Montt (CH$3500, three hours) at 5:30am, 6:30am and 1:45pm. The bus ticket includes the fee for the ferry across the narrow Estuario de Reloncaví. The **Transmarchilay** (☎ 065-270-000; www.transmarchilay.cl, in Spanish; Angelmó 2187, Puerto Montt) ferry *Tehuelche* makes the 30-minute crossing from Caleta La Arena to Puelche. There are nine to 11 sailings daily between 7am and 8pm with extended hours in summer. Ordinary cars cost CH$8000 and pickup trucks CH$9000, with no additional passenger charge.

Between Hornopirén and Parque Pumalín, **Naviera Austral** (☎ 065-270-430; www.navieraustral.cl, in Spanish; Angelmó 2187, Puerto Montt) makes the five-hour trip to Caleta Gonzalo daily at 3pm in summer only, from the first week of January to the end of February. Summer is busy, so reserve ahead by arranging a direct deposit to the Naviera Austral bank account. Passengers pay CH$10,000, cars and pickups CH$64,000.

PARQUE NACIONAL HORNOPIRÉN

Relatively unknown and not often accessed, **Parque Nacional Hornopirén** (admission free) protects a lush wilderness of alpine terrain. It remains obscure mainly because there's no public transportation to it and you can't drive right up to any park entrance. Trails to and in the park are marked but at times hard to follow. Still, it offers great scenery and backcountry escapes. If planning on making an overnight hike, check in with Conaf before departing town.

About 6km south of Hornopirén, the road forks. The right fork eventually leads to the end of the road at Pichanco; the left fork is a rugged dirt road (for high-clearance vehicles only) leading to Fundo Chaqueihua Alto, a privately owned reserve. Continue walking another 8km from here along a faintly marked trail to the park's entrance. Three kilometers from here is **Lago General Pinto Concha**, with a pristine beach where wild camping is possible. From there a poorly marked trail meanders north toward the town of Puelo (two to three days), from where bus connections to Puerto Montt can be made.

ROAD TRIP!

Ranking among the world's ultimate road trips, the **Carretera Austral** runs 1240 mostly unpaved kilometers alongside ancient forests, glaciers, pioneer farmsteads, turquoise rivers and the crashing Pacific. Completed in 1996, it cost an initial investment of US$300 million, took more than 20 years to build and cost 11 workers their lives. Pinochet's quest to cut a road through Aisén was not based on common sense or a pragmatic plan, it arguably had more to do with the symbolism of a highway that tied together the disparate regions of the country.

Highway may be a glorified name for it – part of the adventure is simply navigating sections of gargantuan ruts and potholes. Yet travelers are drawn here in part because the route is not lined with Subway, Shell stations and Starbucks. Don't skimp on planning and a good dose of prudence.

To the north of the Carretera Austral, ferry service is inadequate for the amount of traffic and only runs regularly during summer – so don't even bother outside summer. The harsh climate can make maintenance a nightmare, with rock slides common and landslides closing sections of the road for days. In the south, the road sits barely 1m above the flood-prone Río Baker, the mightiest of any Chilean river.

While the majority of the traffic is long-distance commercial trucks that rumble up and down the highway, an increasing number of SUVs and pickups ply the roads carrying determined anglers, outdoor adventurers and old-fashioned road-trippers. More and more courageous cyclists and motorcyclists brave the highway during summer too.

In preparation, we suggest the following:

- Get your vehicle checked out prior to departure.
- When possible, reserve ferry crossings in advance.
- Drive during the day, as curves are not marked with reflectors.
- Carry extra food, water and even gas, as a breakdown or empty tank can leave you marooned. It is smart to top up your tank whenever you see a gas station as it may be a long, long time before you find another one.
- Always carry a spare tire (*neumático*) and make sure the vehicle has a car jack (*una gata*).
- High-speed turns on loose gravel roads are a recipe for disaster, so take your time and enjoy the scenery.
- Stop if someone looks like they might need help.
- Give trucks a wide berth and don't tail anyone too closely as much of the road is made of gravel – broken windshields on the Carretera Austral are as common as parking tickets in Manhattan.

If planning to cross into Argentina, start your trip with all papers in order, permission to take the vehicle out of the country (if it isn't yours) and the required insurance. Extra fuel, produce and dairy products can't cross borders. All of the larger towns listed in this chapter have some sort of gas station.

PARQUE PUMALÍN

☎ 065

Verdant and pristine, this 2889-sq-km park encompasses vast extensions of temperate rainforest, clear rivers, seascapes and farmland. A remarkable forest-conservation effort, Parque Pumalín attracts 10,000 visitors yearly (no small number, considering that tourist season is a three-month period) to explore these tracts of forest stretching from near Hornopirén to Chaitén. Owned by American Doug Tompkins (p347), it is Chile's largest private park and one of the largest private parks in the world. For Chile it's a model park, with well-maintained roads and trails, extensive infrastructure and minimal impact. Concessions are minimal to give local businesses a boost.

Agricultural use goes on alongside forest preservation in a park model that's 'unique in the world,' according to Dagoberto Guzmán,

ALERCE

Waterproof and nearly indestructible, the valuable alerce shingle once served as currency for the German colonists in the south. Known as lahuan in Mapuche, *Fitzroya cupressoides* ranks among the oldest and largest tree species in the world, with specimens reaching almost 4000 years old. This 40m to 60m jolly evergreen giant plays a key role in temperate rainforests, though its prime value as a hardwood (and surefire shelter in a rainy climate) means it was logged to near-extinction. It is no longer legal to harvest live trees, but you can see alerce shingles on Chilote houses and the real deal deep in Lakes Region and Northern Patagonian forests.

park manager. Staff participate in projects that range from bee-keeping and organic farming to animal husbandry and ecotourism. Private *fundos* (small farms) within the park boundaries continue to operate but with an emphasis on sustainable living. The park maintains a free *refugio* (rustic shelter) for the local workers, and it doesn't charge admission. Tompkins' goal is to allow visitors to immerse themselves in pristine nature and come out with a deeper appreciation for the natural environment.

With spiked ferry costs, most people get to the park from Chaitén in the south. The 'center' of the park, where you'll find the visitors center, café and cabins, is at the small cove called Caleta Gonzalo, the landing for the ferry from Hornopirén.

Fires are prohibited in the park.

At the time of writing, due to the activity of the Chaiten volcano, all cabins and campgrounds were set to be closed for the 2008–2009 summer season. Contact the Centro de Visitantes for the latest details.

Information

The **Centro de Visitantes** (www.pumalinpark.org; Caleta Gonzalo; ☽ 9am-7pm Mon-Sat, 10am-4pm Sun) has park brochures, photographs and environmental information as well as regional artisan goods for sale. If it's locked, ask someone at the café to open it for you. For more details before arriving, contact a Pumalín information center in **Puerto Varas** (☎ 065-250-079; Klenner 299; ☽ 9am-5pm Mon-Fri), **Chaitén** (☎ 065-731-341;

O'Higgins 62; ☽ 9am-1:30pm & 3-7pm Mon-Sat, 10am-4pm Sun) or the **USA** (☎ 415-229-9339; Bldg 1062, Fort Cronkhite, Sausalito, CA 94965). The website has updated information.

Activities

HIKING

Check with an information center before assuming your hiking plans as conditions are changeable and new trails continue to be developed.

Near the café at Caleta Gonzalo, the **Sendero Cascadas** (three hours round-trip) is an undulating climb through dense forest that ends at a large waterfall. The river crossing about an hour into the hike can be dangerous at high water.

About 12km south of Caleta Gonzalo, the marked route to **Laguna Tronador** is not so much a trail as it is, often literally, a staircase. Beginning as a boardwalk, it crosses a rushing stream on a *pasarela* (hanging bridge) before ascending a series of wooden stepladders where the soil is too steep and friable for anything else. After about an hour's climb, at the saddle, there's a mirador (platform) with fine views of Volcán Michinmahuida above the forest to the south. The trail then drops toward the lake, where there's a two-site campground with sturdy picnic tables (one set on a deck) and a latrine.

One kilometer further south, only a few minutes off the highway to Chaitén, **Sendero los Alerces** crosses the river to a substantial grove of alerce trees, where interpretive signs along the way explain the importance of conserving these ancients. At **Cascadas Escondidas**, 14km south of Caleta Gonzalo, a one-hour trail leads from the campground to a series of waterfalls.

At **Michinmahuida**, 33km south of Caleta Gonzalo, a 12km trail leads to the base of the volcano. **Sendero Mirador**, another 12km trail between the campgrounds at Leptepú and Pillán, is also being built. The trailhead is near the concrete bridge but is hard to find – ask for directions.

In the newly inaugurated sector south of Chaitén, a flat, open 10km trek to **Ventisquero Amarillo** starts at the Ventisquero campground toward the base of the Michinmahuida Glacier; cross the river at its widest point, closer to the campground.

THE TOMPKINS LEGACY

Ecobarons – the wealthy philanthropists recycling their greenbacks into green causes – have stamped an indelible presence into Southern Cone conservation and none more so than US entrepreneur Douglas Tompkins. The founder of Esprit clothing and the North Face, along with his wife Kris Tompkins (a former CEO of Patagonia-brand clothing), started by creating Parque Pumalín, a Rhode Island–sized conservation project cobbled together from small Patagonian farms abutting ancient forest.

Today the couple's holdings include 5180 sq km in Chile and 2924 sq km across the border in Argentina. They have inspired copycat contributions, like former Chilean presidential candidate Sebastian Piñera's Parque Tantauco in Chiloé. And it just keeps going. Tompkins also donated two smaller national parks, Corcovado and Tic Toc, to the state, but remains steadfast in his protection of Pumalín (where he lives for much of the year). Donated to Fundación Pumalín in 2005, it will eventually become a national park.

Having dedicated the rest of his life to his Patagonian conservation, Tompkins can be found fighting off one attempt after another to retake the land, build dams near it or extend highways thorough it. At present, there's a tussle with the Chilean government over the best route to build a road alternative to the Hornopirén–Caleta Gonzalo ferry: the government is pushing for a direct route through the heart of Pumalín, while Tompkins proposes a less-costly coastal route that would more closely follow the settlement pattern.

Tompkins' interventionist style has stirred up some regional resentment, although much of the initial criticism has died down and many Chileans have found the parks to be a worthwhile contribution. Is Tompkins an environmental visionary or just another foreigner with designs on Patagonia? One thing is for sure: it's not easy being green.

Tours

Currently, the only way to access some of the isolated northern reaches of the park is by boat. A few operators organize boating and kayaking trips through the fjords and to otherwise inaccessible hot springs.

Al Sur Expeditiones (☎ 065-232-300; www.alsur expeditions.com; Del Salvador 100, Puerto Varas) Specializes in multiday trips sea kayaking, trekking and visiting the remote Cahuelmo Hot Springs.

Austral Adventures (☎ /fax 065-625-977; www .austral-adventures.com; Lord Cochrane 432, Ancud, Chiloé) All-inclusive trips on the *Cahuella*, a 15m Chilote-style wooden motor cruiser, sailing around Chiloé's islands and through Pumalín's fjords. Prices from CH$420,000 to CH$800,000 per person.

Yak expeditions (www.yakexpediciones.cl) Kayaking tours.

Sleeping & Eating

Information centers and the park website have details on all of the campgrounds, some of which are at trailheads.

NORTH PARQUE PUMALÍN

Camping Cahuelmo (☎ 232-300; reservasalsur@ surnet.cl; North Pumalín; campsites per person CH$1500) Cahuelmo has hot springs (CH$2500) and six good tent spaces at the southeast corner of the Cahuelmo Fjord, accessed by boat via Hornopirén or Leptepu.

PENÍNSULA HUEQUI-AYCARA

Avellano Lodge (☎ 264-419; www.elavellano-lodge .com; Aycara; d with/without bathroom CH$38,000/28,000; 🖳) Just outside of the park on the peninsula, this gorgeous hardwood lodge offers an unbeatable combination of access to the park, service and comfort. Hiking, fly-fishing and sea-kayaking tours with all-inclusive packages, including transfer from Puerto Montt, are available.

SOUTH PARQUE PUMALÍN

The following camping options are listed from the north to the south in the south section of Parque Pumalín. There is also basic camping on a farm in Huinay (the zone between the north and south sections of the park). Caleta Gonzalo is the terminus of the ferry trip from Hornopirén, with connections to the Carretera Austral. It has the most established tourism facilities of the greater Pumalín area. Vodudahue has free camping on a small organic farm, but no facilities.

Visitors can eat at Cafe Caleta Gonzalo or arrange *asados* in advance (through reservation) with spit-fire roasted lamb and fresh farm veggies; for a group of seven it's CH$10,000 per person.

Camping Pillan (campsites per person CH$1500) A private farm on Reñihué Fjord with camping on an open field: ask farm administration where to pitch your tent. It's accessed by boat from Caleta Gonzalo or by road via Fiordo Largo or Leptepu.

Camping Río Gonzalo (reservasalsur@surnet.cl; Caleta Gonzalo; campsites with fire pit CH$5000) On the shores of Reñihué Fjord, this walk-in campground has a shelter for cooking and bathrooms with cold showers.

Caleta Gonzalo Cabañas (☎ 232-300; s/d CH$25,000/35,000, extra person CH$5000) Cozy cabins (without kitchen facilities) that overlook the fjord.

Café Caleta Gonzalo (lunch CH$7500; ☺ breakfast, lunch & dinner) The park's only restaurant is this attractive café with a huge fireplace. Fresh bread, local honey and organic vegetables put it a notch above average. Homemade oatmeal cookies, honey or picnic boxes (CH$5000) are available to go.

Camping Tronador (campsites free) Free campsites at the basin of the stunning amphitheater lake on Tronador trail, 1½ hours from the trailhead.

Fundo del Río Cabañas (☎ 232-300; s/d CH$25,000/35,000, extra person CH$5000) Tucked into farmland, these ultraprivate cabins with kitchen facilities have sea or valley views. A nearby kiosk sells supplies and food.

Cascadas Escondidas (covered campsites CH$5000) Features platform sites with roof at the trailhead to Cascadas Escondidas.

Lago Negro (campsites per person CH$1500, covered campsites CH$5000) Large camping area close to the lake.

Lago Punta (campsites per person CH$1500, covered campsites CH$5000) Room for numerous tents near the lake.

Lago Blanco (covered campsites CH$5000) Twenty kilometers south of Caleta Gonzalo and 36km north of Chaitén, Lago Blanco has a few covered sites and great views of the lake. Make sure you hike the short distance to the mirador for a better view. There is excellent fishing in the lake, but you'll need to get a permit from a ranger station.

Michinmahuida (campsites per person CH$1500) Sites have no bathroom but there's water nearby and a fire pit. It is at the start of the 12km Volcán Michinmahuida volcano hike.

Camping El Volcán (campsites per person CH$1500, covered campsites CH$5000) At the southern end of the park, 2.5km before the southern entrance ranger station, this big camping zone has car camping and a kiosk open year-round with supplies, information and food.

Amarillo (campsites free) This newest sector south of Chaitén occupies former farmland beyond the Termas El Amarillo, with great views and flat, open sites. It is a couple of days' hiking from other areas or accessible by car.

Getting There & Away

The summer-only **Naviera Austral** (☎ 065-270-430) ferry sails daily from Caleta Gonzalo to Hornopirén (five to six hours) at 9am. For fares and full details, see p344. For transportation to and from Chaitén, see p350.

CHAITÉN

☎ 065 / pop 4000

An emerald enclave on the rainy bay, Chaitén is little more than a six by eight grid of wide streets. Developed as a port and supply center for settlers, it has rapidly grown as the southern gateway to Parque Pumalín. Rugged hills encircle the town, and when the rain finally pauses there are spectacular views of 2404m Volcán Michinmahuida to the northeast and 2300m Volcán Corcovado to the southwest. It is also a major transport stop for the ultrarural Carretera Austral. If you arrive by ferry the port is a 10-minute walk northwest of town. Chaitén is 56km south of Caleta Gonzalo and 45km northwest of Puerto Cárdenas.

The sudden 2008 eruption of Volcán Chaitén devastated the town. It was evacuated and residents were relocated as heavy ash fell and floods later engulfed houses. While the volcano remains active, the ongoing status of Chaitén is undecided (see opposite).

Information

BancoEstado (cnr Libertad & O'Higgins) Has an ATM and poor exchange rates on cash.

Entel (Plaza de Armas) On the east side of the plaza.

Hospital de Chaitén (☎ 731-244; Av Ignacio Carrera Pinto; ☺ 24hr) Emergency is open 24 hours.

Lavandería Stihl (☎ 731-566; Costanera s/n; per kilo CH$1800) This laundry service also happens to sell chainsaws – yep, only in Patagonia.

Post office (cnr Almirante Riveros & O'Higgins)

Pumalín Information Center (☎ 731-341; www.pumalinpark.org; O'Higgins 62; ☺ 9am-1:30pm & 3-7pm)

VOLCÁN CHAITÉN WAKES UP

No one even considered it a volcano, but that changed quickly. On May 2, 2008, Volcán Chaitén, 10km northeast of its namesake town, began a month-long eruption. The rampage caused flooding and severe damage to homes, roads and bridges, decimated thousands of livestock and spewed ash as far as Buenos Aires. Chaitén's 4000 inhabitants were hastily evacuated but the government remains uneasy about Mother Nature's future plans for the area. Four months post-eruption, locals remained displaced as volcanic activity continued. While locals hope to rebuild on the old site, there are proposals to relocate some or all of Chaitén to a more secure location further north.

This chapter was updated pre-eruption; please check the current status of Chaitén and its lodgings and services before you go. At the time this book went to press, flights were still suspended but ferry services had resumed. Parque Pumalín will be closed through March 09 but hopes to reopen for the following summer season. The road is closed to Caleta Gonzalo until bridge repairs may be made. Ferry service to and from Caleta Gonzalo may also be suspended for a time.

In support of local businesses, we are listing those we updated below, but some may have changed addresses, delayed opening or suspended service. For updates on the situation and changes to area lodgings and services, see the Chile page on **Lonely Planet's website** (www .lonelyplanet.com/chile), or check directly with Parque Pumalín or local municipal offices. Also, check out Lonely Planet's **Thorn Tree** (www.lonelyplanet.com/thorntree) travel forum for updates from fellow travelers – or post one yourself if you're in the area.

Mon-Sat, 10am-4pm Sun) Has information to help you plan what to do in the park.

Telefónica del Sur (Costanera)

Tourist kiosk (cnr Costanera & O'Higgins; ☉ 9am-9pm Jan-Feb) Has a handful of leaflets and a list of *hospedajes* (budget accommodations).

Tours

The best source of information in town, English-speaking Nicholas at **Chaitur** (☎ 731-429; www.chaitur.com; O'Higgins 67) dispatches most of the buses and arranges trips with bilingual guides to Pumalín, the Yelcho glacier, Termas El Amarillo and beaches with sea-lion colonies. Chaitur also rents bikes (CH$6000 per day).

Sleeping

Camping Los Arrayanes (☎ 731-136; campsites per person CH$2500) The nearest campground, 4km north of Chaitén, with beachfront sites, hot showers and *quincho* (barbecue house).

our pick **Casa Hexagon** (☎ 098-286-2950; www .casahexagon.com; Calle Río Blanco 36; s/d without bathroom CH$7000/14,000; 🖳) This gorgeous hexagonal home is the pet project of German artist and musician Stefan. Decorated with textiles and fantastic pen-and-ink drawings, it draws the active crowd into communal living and napping (hence the living-room hammock). Rooms are cozy nooks, some with river views.

Hospedaje Don Carlos (☎ 731-287; turismochaiten@ surnet.cl; Almirante Riveros 53; d CH$20,000, s/d without bathroom CH$7000/14,000; Ⓟ 🖳) Cozy and clean, this affordable *hospedaje* has small upstairs rooms with firm beds and fluffed down bedding. If you have an early departure, note that the breakfast service is slow.

Hospedaje Llanos (☎ 731-332; Corcovado 378; s/d CH$11,000/22,000, without bathroom CH$8000/15,000) The simple seafront rooms are worn but impeccably clean, run by a dear hostess.

Hotel Mi Casa (☎ 731-285; www.hotelmicasa.cl; Av Norte 206; s/d CH$24,000/34,000; 🖳) Situated on a hill overlooking town, this old-style hotel features long hallways with rocking chairs and great bay views. Rooms are smart and minimally adorned while perks include TV, internet, gym and sauna. The dining room uses fine china and local products (meals CH$5000). If you are hungry between meals, check out the filling *onces* (tea service; CH$3000), whether lodging here or not.

Hostería Puma Verde (☎ 731-184; www.parquepumalin.cl; O'Higgins 54; s/d CH$25,000/40,000) This gorgeous Pumalín-managed guesthouse is comfortable and intimate; guests slip around in socks and gather around the big table in the beautiful copper-clad kitchen. Whole-wheat breads and homemade jams make the breakfast a standout. Book ahead.

Hostería Los Coihues (☎ 731-461; www.tierranativa .cl; Pedro Aguirre Cerda 398; s/d/tr CH$25,000/48,000/60,000; 🖳) This warm wooden lodge has stylish furniture, modern heating and quiet rooms. More formal than other local lodgings, it also has the perks of crisp linens, abundant towels and sizable continental breakfasts.

Eating

Melys Café (Libertad 641; snacks CH$1000; ☺ breakfast & lunch) Stop in for excellent pies, cakes and *pastel de choclo* (maize casserole); it is run by an endearing radio aficionado.

Campo Base Pizzería (Almirante Riveros 479; pizzas CH$2000-3500; ☺ lunch & dinner) Ready your appetite for the real deal: crispy, thin-crust pizza. And you thought it didn't exist in Patagonia! With an inviting atmosphere and good Chilean microbrews, this shoebox restaurant does a thriving business. Try the *rustica* with sausage and olives. Homemade pastas and salads are also served.

Café Ventisquero Yelcho (☎ 099-057-5131; Almirante Riveros 278; mains CH$2500; ☺ breakfast, lunch & dinner; Ⓥ) Catering a bit to vegetarians with grilled cheese and tomato sandwiches and salads, this casual café is also good for an espresso.

our pick Cocinerías Costumbristas (Portales 258; meals CH$3000; ☺ breakfast, lunch & dinner) It started out as a microbusiness for local women, but this warehouse of slim kitchens with picnic-table service became a huge local hit. Apron-clad señoras serve up piping-hot seafood empanadas, fish platters and fresh shellfish concoctions.

Mercado Municipal (Costanera s/n; meals CH$4000; ☺ breakfast, lunch & dinner) Modeled after the Cocinerías Costumbristas, this new municipal market has six dining rooms with great ocean views, but lacks the chaotic, friendly vibe of its counterpart. Still, it's perfect if you want atmosphere with your seafood. There's also an attached fish market open mornings.

Shopping

Both Hostería Puma Verde (p349) and the waterfront **Feria Artesanal** (Costanera s/n) inside the Mercado Municipal have quality locally made handicrafts, especially woolen hats, mittens and socks, wood carvings, homemade jams and honey.

Getting There & Away

AIR

At the time of writing, Chaitén's airstrips were covered in ash and out of commission. Check with the following airlines for resumed services. **Aerotaxis del Sur** (ATS; ☎ 731-228; cnr Av Ignacio

Carrera Pinto & Almirante Riveros) has an air-taxi to Puerto Montt (CH$38,000, 45 minutes), as do the slightly more expensive **Aerocord** (☎ in Puerto Montt 262-300; www.aerocord.cl; Costanera s/n) and **Patagonia Airlines** (☎ 731-571; www.patagoniaairlines.cl, in Spanish; cnr Av Padre & Almirante Riveros); the latter two fly into Puerto Montt's regional airport La Paloma.

BOAT

Ferry schedules change, so confirm them before making plans.

Catamaranes del Sur (☎ 731-199; Juan Todesco 118) runs passenger-only ferries to Puerto Montt and Castro thrice weekly in summer.

The **Naviera Austral** (☎ 731-272; www.navieraustral.cl, in Spanish; Corcovado 266) auto-passenger ferry *Pincoya* or new ferry *Don Baldo* sails to Puerto Montt (CH$19,000, 12 hours) three times a week. In summer, a ferry goes to Quellón (CH$17,000, six hours), Chiloé, two times a week and daily from Caleta Gonzalo in Parque Pumalín to Hornopirén (CH$10,000), where buses depart for Puerto Montt.

BUS

Transportation details for the Carretera Austral change seasonally. Unless otherwise indicated, departures are from the main **bus terminal** (☎ 731-429; O'Higgins 67). **Chaitur** (☎ 731-429; www.chaitur.com) runs a bus to Caleta Gonzalo (CH$5000) for the ferry at 7am with reservations; to Futaleufú (CH$6000, four hours) at 3pm daily except Sunday. **Buses Palena** (O'Higgins 67) goes to Palena (CH$6000, 4½ hours) on Monday, Wednesday and Friday from the terminal.

Buses Norte (☎ 731-390; O'Higgins 67) goes to Coyhaique (CH$15,000, 12 hours) daily except Wednesday, stopping in La Junta (CH$7000, four hours) and Puyuhuapi (CH$8000, 5½ hours).

TERMAS EL AMARILLO

About 25km southeast of Chaitén, on a spur north off the Carretera Austral, **Termas El Amarillo** (admission CH$3000) has simple hot springs in one large cement pool and two smaller, hotter tubs overlooking Río Michinmahuida. During the day it's bursting with day-trippers and families but peace reigns when the gate closes at 9pm and campers (campsites CH$4500) can savor a starlight soak.

About 5km away, in the town of El Amarillo, **Residencial Marcela** (☎ 065-264-422; r per person CH$6000) is a simple lodging renovating for improved installations. If you call in advance, all-day horse treks (CH$30,000 per person with meals and transfer) can be arranged to Volcán Michinmahuida.

LAGO YELCHO

A brilliant blue under glacial peaks, and fed by the raging Río Futaleufú, the 110 sq km Lago Yelcho is adored by anglers. The small port of **Puerto Cárdenas** has modest lodging choices, all open in summer only. By the phone booth, **Hostal Lago Yelcho** (☎ 065-264-429; Carretera Austral Km46; r with/without bathroom CH$15,000/9000; ☯ Dec-Feb) is a worn rambler surrounded by gladiolus. Anglers like it for the big breakfasts and clean rooms; those in the back have direct sun and a lovely view.

Only 15km south of Puerto Cárdenas, **Puente Ventisquero** (Glacier Bridge) is the starting point for a hike to **Ventisquero Yelcho**, a large hanging glacier. Camping is possible near the parking lot, where there is also a *quincho* and bathrooms. Just five minutes from the parking lot is a lookout of the glacier, but continue on about 50m for a better view. The trail continues 2½ hours along the riverbanks toward the glacier, but just one hour into the trail gives those short on time a good spot to stop and admire the view.

VILLA SANTA LUCÍA

The road to Futaleufú and Palena begins 78km south of Chaitén at the village of Villa Santa Lucía, site of a large military compound and transfer point for buses. **El Encuentro** (Calle Los Cypresses s/n; r per person CH$6000) has simple doubles in a family home; good in a pinch.

Where the road splits to Futaleufú (to the northeast) and to Palena (southeast) is **Puerto Ramírez** at the southeast corner of Lago Yelcho. **Hostería Verónica** (☎ 264-431; s incl breakfast CH$8000) also offers camping.

FUTALEUFÚ

☎ 065 / pop 1800

The Futaleufú's wild, frosty-mint waters have made this modest mountain town famous. Not just a mecca for kayaking and rafting, it also boasts fly-fishing, hiking and horse riding. Improved roads and growing numbers of package-tour visitors mean it isn't off the map anymore. Just note the ratio of Teva sandals to woolen *mantas*; that said, it's still a fun place to be.

The town of Futaleufú, a small 20-block grid of pastel-painted houses 155km southeast of Chaitén, is mainly a service center to the Argentine border, only 8km away, and a bedroom community for boaters. For those not planning to run the river or continue on to the nearby Argentine towns of Trevelín and Esquel, and to Argentina's Parque Nacional Los Alerces, there's little here but a fine landscape to explore.

Strong local activism may have kicked a longtime proposal for river dams, but gold mining may be imminent. US and Canadian mining groups are looking to establish an open pit mine near the Lago Espolón, which could result in significant effects on the region's drinking water, as well as the aquatic health of pristine lakes and rivers, and tourism.

Information

BancoEstado (cnr O'Higgins & Manuel Rodríguez) Bring all the money you'll need; this the only choice for changing money.

Post office (Manuel Rodríguez)

Tourist office (O'Higgins 536) The municipal office is on the south side of the Plaza de Armas.

Activities

WHITE-WATER RAFTING & KAYAKING

Rafting trips on the Class III Río Espolón cost about CH$12,000 for the five-hour trip. Novice kayakers can try this river or head to Lago Espolón for a float trip. The Futa or Fu, as it's known, is a much more technical, demanding river, with some sections only appropriate for experienced rafters. Depending on the outfitter you choose and the services included, rafting the Futaleufú starts at CH$40,000 per person for a halfday section known as Bridge to Bridge with Class IV and IV+ rapids. A full day trip for experienced rafters only goes from Bridge to Macul, adding two Class V rapids, starting at CH$60,000.

Tours

Austral Excursions (☎ 721-239; Hermanos Carrera 500) A locally owned outfitter with river descents as well as trekking and canyoning excursions.

Bio Bio Expeditions (☎ 800-246-7238; www.bbxrafting.com) A pioneer in the region, this ecologically minded group offers river descents, horse treks and more. It is well established but may take walk-ins.

Expediciones Chile (☎ 721-386; www.exchile.com; Mistral 296) A secure rafting operator with loads of experience. Specializes in week-long packages but offers kayaking, mountain biking and horse riding as well.

H2O Patagonia (☎ in USA 888-426-7238; www .h2opatagonia.com) A US-based adventure company that can coordinate your entire trip, including luxurious accommodations on its ranch.

Sleeping

Cara del Indio (☎ 02-196-4239; www.caradelindio.cl; campsites per person CH$3000, 9-person cabins CH$55,000) With a spectacular riverfront setting, this adventure base camp is 15km from Puerto Ramiréz and 35km from the Carretera Austral. Run by Luis Toro and his family, the camp boasts 10km of riverfront. Sites have access to hot showers, an outdoor kitchen and a wood-burning sauna. Guests can purchase homemade bread, cheese and beer from the family's house. December and March, on either end of the two-month summer rush, are more peaceful times to be here.

Camping Puerto Espolón (☎ 696-5324; puertoes polon@latinmail.com; campsites per person CH$5000; ☺ Jan & Feb) A gorgeous setting on a sandy riverbank flanked by mountains, just before the entrance to town.

Las Natalias (shagrinmack@hotmail.com; d/tr CH$17,000/ 25,000, dm/d without bathroom CH$6000/15,000) Named for four generations of Natalias, this welcoming newcomer is a great deal for backpackers. Brand new and fully decked out, it has plenty of shared bathrooms, a large communal area, mountain views and kitchen for guest use. It's a 10-minute walk from the center. Follow Cerda and the signs for the northeast sector out of town; it's on the right after the hill climb.

Adolfo's B&B (☎ 721-256; O'Higgins 302; r per person with/without bathroom CH$8000/6000; ☐) The best bargain digs in town are in this warm wood-finish home with wi-fi and computer connection. Run by a hospitable family, breakfast includes eggs, homemade bread and coffee cake.

Madreselva (☎ 721-220; Cerda 393; d CH$15,000, s/d without bathroom CH$6000/10,000; ☐) Rooms are small and a little run-down, but a quiet bar scene is right downstairs with guitars ready for strumming.

Posada Ely (☎ 721-205; Balmaceda 409; s/d without bathroom CH$10,000/20,000) These well-kept rooms sit under the sure guardianship of Betty, who makes a mean rosehip jam, served with a breakfast of fresh bread, eggs, juice, tea and more.

Hostería Río Grande (☎ 721-320; O'Higgins 397; s/d CH$30,000/50,000; ℗ ☐) This comfortable shingled lodge caters to sporty gringos who, between raft trips, can pump iron in the attached weight room. Expect bright, carpeted rooms with portable heaters and low-slung beds in deep frames.

Hotel El Barranco (☎ 721-314; www.elbarrancochile .cl; O'Higgins 172; s/d CH$70,000/80,000; ☐ ☻) At this elegant lodge on the edge of the grid of town, rooms are snug with carved woodwork, colonial accents and big beds. Service could be more attentive, but it is the most ambient option in town. There's also a swimming pool and outdoor excursions.

Eating

Since most supplies have to be trucked in from afar, fresh vegetables can be in short supply.

SurAndes (☎ 721-405; www.surandes.com; Cerda 308; mains CH$2500; ☺ breakfast, lunch & dinner; ☐) Real coffee and fresh juices perk up tired travelers who bask in this lovely atmospheric café serving fresh omelettes, custom burgers and veggie plates. There are also local crafts for sale and an attractive five-person apartment (CH$14,000 per person) for rent upstairs.

El Encuentro (☎ 721-247; O'Higgins 653; meals CH$6000) Don't think about the plastic-covered lace tablecloths, this place oozes friendly ambience. A pisco sour starts you off right; meat comes from regional ranches, or there's salmon or chicken à la crema.

Martín Pescador (☎ 721-279; Balmaceda 603; mains CH$6000; ☺ dinner) Serving regional delicacies such as chicken with morel mushrooms, salmon carpaccio or baked crab dishes, this exclusive eatery with a roaring log fire is perfect for a special dinner.

Getting There & Away

Transportes Altamirano (☎ 721-360; cnr Balmaceda & Prat) goes to Chaitén (CH$6000, four hours) at 7am Monday through Friday, Villa Santa Lucía (where you can transfer south to Coyhaique), Puerto Cárdenas and Termas El Amarillo. To Coyhaique (CH$17,000, 10 to 12 hours) a bus goes at 7am on Saturday. To Puerto Montt (CH$23,000 with lunch, 10 to 12 hours) a bus goes at 8:30am Monday and Friday.

The **Futaleufú border post** (☺ 8am-8pm) is far quicker and more efficient than the crossing at Palena, opposite the Argentine border town of Carrenleufú.

DETOUR TO PIONEER PATAGONIA

When winds roar sidelong and rains persist, take refuge by the woodstove, drink a round of *mates* and *echar la talla* (pass the time) with the locals. Rural Patagonia offers a rare and privileged glimpse of a fading way of life. To jump-start their slack rural economy, government and nonprofit initiatives have created local guide and homestay associations.

These family enterprises range from comfortable roadside *hospedajes* and farm stays to wild country multiday treks and horseback-riding trips through wonderland terrain. Prices are reasonable – starting from CH$8000 per day for lodging and CH$12,000 per day for guide services – although extras include horses and only Spanish is spoken.

Travelers can link with rural home stays and guide services through **Casa del Turismo Rural** (www.casaturismorural.cl) in Coyhaique (see p360) or the **Municipalidad de Cochamó** (www.cochamo.cl) in Puelo (see p312). Some of the best opportunities are around Palena, Cerro Castillo and Llanada Grande (in Sur Chico). It's best to book a week in advance or more, as intermediaries will have to make radio contact with the most remote hosts. That's right – no phones, no electricity, no worries.

There's no gas station in Futaleufú. The grocery store on Sargento Aldea sells fuel by the jug; it's cheaper in Argentina, if you make it.

PALENA

☎ 065 / pop 1500

The road less traveled will take you through Palena, a quiet mountain town with a cowboy edge. With only a few family lodgings and no restaurants (lodgers eat in), tourism here has been slow to mosey. But one big draw is exploring the valleys beyond the ultraturquoise Río Palena on foot or horseback, where you'll find remnants of pioneer lifestyle and down-home hospitality. Just 8km west of the border, Palena is a low-traffic crossing point into Argentina.

The **Rodeo de Palena** is held on the last weekend in January. The **Semana Palena**, a week of dance and cowboy festivities, is celebrated in late February.

Information

A log **tourism office** (www.palenaonline.cl, in Spanish; Cacique Blanco s/n) with brochures sits next to the municipal building on the square. Visitors can arrange horse packing, rafting and fishing trips with local guides. Allow some lead time before your trip, since some rural outfitters must be reached by radio.

Telefónica del Sur (Pedro Montt 856; per hr CH$800) has internet.

Sleeping

Adventuras Cordilleranas (☎ 319-111, 741-388; www.rutatranspatagonia.cl; El Malito bridge; s incl breakfast CH$8000) Mireya pampers guests like part of the brood at this cozy place. The family also offers riverfront cabin accommodations and rides to rural El Tranquilo. If arriving from the west, have the bus drop you off 22km before Palena.

Residencial La Chilenita (☎ 731-212; Pudeto 681; r per person without bathroom CH$8000) In town, the friendly La Chilenita has adequate rooms though it is sometimes full with itinerant workers.

Rincón de la Nieve (☎ 741-269; Valle Azul; s/d CH$6000/12,000) Adventurers can ride or hike to the wonderful Casanova family farm in Valle Azul. Meals are CH$2500 extra. Chill there or continue on a truly incredible five-day round-trip ride to remote Lago Palena (see boxed text, above); arrange in advance.

Getting There & Away

Buses Palena (Plaza de Armas) goes to Chaitén (CH$5000, 4½ hours) at 6:45am Monday, Wednesday and Friday. From Chaitén, the bus departs at 3:30pm each Wednesday and Friday.

LA JUNTA

With the slow feel of a Rocky Mountain backwater, La Junta is a former *estancia* that formed a crossroads for ranchers headed to market. Unmistakable with its centerpiece monument to Pinochet, it now serves as a major fuel stop for travelers, replete with old-fashioned hardware stores and a rocky butte bookending town. Lately, rock climbers and fly-fishers are hitting the hidden attractions around town. Brown, rainbow and

Chinook trout abound at Reserva Nacional Lago Rosselot and Lago Verde.

An important transfer point for north–south connections, La Junta is just south of the boundary between Regións X and XI, at the confluence of the Río Palena and Río Figueroa.

The **tourist kiosk** (Varas s/n; 9am-9pm Mon-Fri, 10:30am-7:30pm Sat & Sun), on the plaza, has information about lodgings, activities and campgrounds. Visitors can take float trips on Río Palena, go fly-fishing or hike in area reserves. Contact can be made by radio only.

Private hot springs **Termas del Sauce** (Camino a Raul Marin Balmaceda Km12; CH$1000) offers pleasant but rustic pools on a brook 12km out of town. A full-service camping area is also in the works. Contact is be radio only – visitors can radio from the Copec station, where you can also get directions. **Conaf** (314-128; cnr Patricio Lynch & Manuel Montt) has details on the nearby parks and reserves.

There is no bus terminal here; ask locals the schedules and catch a bus passing by.

Sleeping & Eating

Hostería Mirador del Río (Camino a Raul Marin Balmaceda Km6; r per person incl breakfast CH$8000) For a welcome retreat from the dusty Carretera Austral, get outside of town to this charming farmhouse. The family is lovely and breakfast satisfies with homemade jam and bread hot out of the woodstove. Guests can also do *catanoa* (double canoe) trips (two people CH$22,000) down the mellow Río Palena. Contact via the radio at the Copec station or the tourist kiosk.

Pension Hospedaje Tía Lety (314-106; Varas 596; r per person incl breakfast CH$9000) A friendly family setting in town, with bulky beds in well-kept rooms. Breakfast is filling.

Hostería Valdera (314-105; cnr Varas & Cinco de Abril; d with/without bathroom incl breakfast CH$15,000/13,000) Surrounded by rose bushes, the Valdera offers tidy pink rooms and a bathroom heated by wood-burning stove. Other meals can be requested.

Espacio y Tiempo (314-141; espacio@patagonia chile.cl; Carretera Austral s/n; s/d/tr CH$32,500/47,000/60,500;) This well-heeled and comfortable lodge relaxes visiting anglers and travelers with classical music, sprawling green gardens and a well-stocked bar. Further perks include private porches and an abundant buffet breakfast with real coffee. Dinner (mains CH$5000) can be provided upon request; specialties in-

clude local elk. The hosts happily arrange local excursions or you can just visit the llamas out back.

PUERTO PUYUHUAPI
 067

Tucked into the Jurassic scenery of overgrown ferns and nalca plants, this quaint seaside village is the gateway to Parque Nacional Queulat and Termas de Puyuhuapi, a prestigious hot-springs resort. In 1935 four German immigrants settled here, inspired by explorer Hans Steffen's adventures. The town sits at the northern end of the Seno Ventisquero, a scenic fjord that's part of the larger Canal Puyuhuapi.

The agricultural colony grew with Chilote textile workers whose skills fed the success of the 1947 German **Fábrica de Alfombras** (325-131; www.puyuhuapi.com; Calle Aysén s/n; tours per group CH$5000), still weaving high-end carpets. Visitors can stop by the **tourist office** (Otto Uebel s/n; 10am-2pm & 4-7:30pm Mon-Sat) in front of the park for comprehensive information on lodgings, hot springs and restaurants. Ask here for a map to the town walking circuit.

Just outside of town, Termas del Ventisquero (opposite) offers affordable hot-springs soaking.

Sleeping & Eating

Day visitors to the hot springs often lodge in town since there are good midrange options, but reserve ahead in summer.

Camping La Sirena (325-100; Costanera 148; campsites per person CH$2500) Sites are cramped but there are tent shelters, bathrooms and hot showers. Enter via the road passing the playground to the water.

Hospedaje Ventisquero (325-130; O'Higgins s/n; r per person CH$5000) This rambling white house with a bus terminal on the 1st floor lets out affordable but bleak rooms without breakfast.

our pick Casa Ludwig (325-220; www.casaludwig .cl; Otto Uebel s/n; s/d CH$20,000/35,000; without bathroom CH$12,000/20,000) A historic landmark, this classic home is elegant and snug, with roaring fires in the sprawling living room and big breakfasts at the communal table. Room prices can vary according to room size. The English- and German-speaking owners can help with tour arrangements.

Cabañas & Café Aonikenk (325-208; aonikenk turismo@yahoo.com; Hamburgo 16; d CH$20,000, 2-6-person cabins CH$30,000-48,000) Hosted by the amicable Veronica, these new all-wood cabins have paraffin stoves, snug white bedding and small balconies. The more economical double is usually reserved. A cute café (meals CH$4000) with upstairs sofas and lounge space is the perfect place to snag refuge on a rainy day. Laundry service and bike rentals (CH$10,000 per day) are also offered.

Hostería Alemana (☎ 325-118; www.hosteria alemana.cl; Otto Uebel 450; s/d/tr incl breakfast CH$20,000/27,000/35,000) Sturdy and cozy, this meticulous German guesthouse has rooms with bay views or fireplaces. Calico seats, plaids and handsome wood paneling highlight the old-fashioned charms.

Cocinería Real (☎ 525-613; Gabriela Mistral 8; mains CH$4500) With fast and friendly service, Señora Raquel serves heaping plates of fresh fish with side salads and cold cans of beer. It's low-key and local, with fishermen bringing in the daily catch.

Getting There & Away

Buses that run between Coyhaique and Chaitén will drop passengers in Puerto Puyuhuapi. Buy your return ticket as far ahead as possible, as demand exceeds availability in summer. **Buses Norte** (☎ 232-167; Gral Parra 337) and Transportes Emanuel buses leave for Chaitén (CH$8000, 5½ hours) and Coyhaique (CH$7000, six hours) between 3pm and 5pm from the store next to the police station.

TERMAS DEL VENTISQUERO

If you don't have the time or resources to boat out to the other hot springs, **Termas del Ventisquero** (☎ 067-325-228; admission CH$10,000; ☼ 9am-11pm Dec-Feb & some winter weekends) is an excellent alternative. Located roadside on the Carretera Austral, 6km south of Puyuhuapi, this new miniresort has one big pool and three small pools facing the sound, surrounded by umbrellas and lounge chairs. The water is 36–40°C and there are adequate changing rooms with showers and lockers. Food is not allowed but you can grab a bite at the acclaimed restaurant (mains CH$5000) that serves home-made pasta, fish and quiche, in addition to English teas, espresso and pisco sours.

TERMAS DE PUYUHUAPI

Chile's leading hot-springs resort, the luxurious **Termas de Puyuhuapi Hotel & Spa** (☎ 067-325-103/117; 3-night package d CH$560,000) sits in a lush forest on the western shore of the Seno Ventisquero. The only access is by boat. Buildings combine the rustic look of Chilote *palafitos* (houses on stilts) with Bavarian influences, but their interiors could be updated. Currently, guests on package vacations make up most of the clientele. Independent travelers may have a hard time booking a one-night reservation.

Food is served at the hotel restaurant and a cheaper café near the changing rooms for day guests. Meals are expensive by local standards but there is a good range of dishes and flavors.

Three outdoor baths, including a fern-shaded hot mud lagoon, sit right by the water, allowing visitors to soak and steam away then jump into the cool sound. The indoor spa is more elaborate but less ambient. Families frequent its cold-water pools, Jacuzzis and one large pool with different jets. Boat transfer and day use of the outdoor pools is available (adult/child CH$15,000/7500). To include the indoor pools and spa access guests pay CH$25,000 (CH$12,500 for children). Spa treatments and massages cost extra.

Termas de Puyuhuapi is accessed via boat trips that run from the Bahía Dorita mainland dock, 13km south of Puerto Puyuhuapi. Launches leave the dock at 10am, 1pm, 3:30pm and 7pm, returning at 9:30am, 12:30pm, 3pm and 6pm, but there are often unscheduled crossings as well. Contact **Patagonia Connection** (☎ in Santiago 02-225-6489; www.patagonia-connection .com) for information on package excursions.

PARQUE NACIONAL QUEULAT

The 1540-sq-km **Parque Nacional Queulat** (admission CH$3000) is a wild realm of rivers winding through forests thick with ferns and southern beech. When the sun is out it's simply stunning, with steep-sided fjords flanked by creeping glaciers and 2000m volcanic peaks. The park straddles the Carretera Austral for 70km, midway between Chaitén and Coyhaique.

Created in 1983, the park is extremely popular but its far-flung location keeps it within reach of the select few willing to venture this far. Visitors are also challenged by the almost constant rain (up to 4000mm per year) and impenetrable foliage. Despite its impressive size, hiking trails are few. Conaf has struggled to maintain trailhead signs, most of which are either hidden by the aggressive growth or missing.

The **Centro de Información Ambiental** (🕑 9am-6pm), 22km south of Puerto Puyuhuapi and 2.5km from the road, at the parking lot for the Ventisquero Colgante, is the main center to the park and where admission fees are collected. It has well-organized, informative displays of plants and glacial activity, and rangers can help with hiking ideas.

Activities

Near the information center, there's a quick walk to a lookout of the **Ventisquero Colgante**, the park's most popular attraction. You can also take the bridge across Río Ventisquero and follow a 3.2km trail along the crest of a moraine on the river's north bank for great views of the glacier and the crash of ice onto the rocks below. At **Laguna de Los Tempanos**, boat cruises (CH$3000, summer only) take you from the boat launch across the lake to view the glacier.

North of the southern entrance, at Km170, a damp trail climbs the valley of the **Río de las Cascadas** through a dense forest of delicate ferns, copihue vines, tree-size fuchsias, podocarpus and lenga. The heavy rainfall never directly hits the ground but seems to percolate through the multistoried canopy. After about half an hour, the trail emerges at an impressive granite bowl, where half a dozen waterfalls drop from hanging glaciers.

Twenty kilometers south of the information center, on the left – there's barely space to pull over – is **Sendero Padre García**, a 100m staircase that drops to an overlook of an impressive waterfall and its transparent pool. Padre García was a Jesuit priest who trekked through Queulat in search of the mythical Ciudad de Los Césares. Continuing on, the road begins to zigzag treacherously up the Portezuelo de Queulat between Km175 and Km178, from where the view of the Queulat Valley is outstanding.

Top-notch fishing can be found at the larger streams, such as the Río Cisnes, and the glacial fingers of Lago Rosselot, Lago Verde and Lago Risopatrón.

Sleeping

Camping Ventisquero (campsites CH$5000) Near the Ventisquero Colgante, this has 10 attractive, private sites with covered barbecues and picnic tables. Beware: the bathrooms have glacial showers. The sites themselves are a bit rocky for pitching multiple tents. Firewood is available.

Camping Angostura (Lago Risopatrón; campsites CH$5000) In a sopping rainforest, 15km north of Puerto Puyuhuapi, but the facilities are good (cold showers only).

Getting There & Away

Buses connecting Chaitén and Coyhaique will drop passengers at Puerto Puyuhuapi or other points along the western boundary of the park. See p350 for details. Make seat reservations on the next bus you plan to take, and be prepared to wait.

AROUND PARQUE NACIONAL QUEULAT

At the southern approach to Parque Nacional Queulat, **Villa Amengual** is a pioneer village with a Chilote-style shingled chapel and basic services. It's at the foot of 2760m Cerro Alto Nevado. Family-run **Residencial El Encanto** (☎ 171-2-196-4516; Francisca Castro 33-A; r per person CH$4000) and the slightly more comfortable **Hospedaje Michay** (☎ 02-196-4578; Carmen Arias 14; r per person CH$6500) offer lodgings with breakfast.

Another 55km south, **Villa Mañihuales** was founded in 1962. It has a couple of *hospedajes*, including **Residencial Mañihuales** (☎ 067-431-403; E Ibar 280; r per person CH$8000), and some simple cafés.

A further 13km south, the Carretera Austral splits. The highway southwest to Puerto Aisén and Puerto Chacabuco is completely paved. Access to Coyhaique takes an incredibly scenic route crossing the western-sloping Andes through primary forest thick with ferns and lianas. The southern route is currently in the process of being paved.

PUERTO CISNES
☎ 067 / pop 2500

An isolated offshoot in the Puyuhuapi Sound, Puerto Cisnes is prototypically quaint, a drowsy town of painted fishing boats and munching horses that keep the cemetery lawn trim. Its easy pace and indifference to the world make it an attractive detour, although with little organized touring visitors will have to make their own adventure. The town sits 35km west of the Carretera Austral. at the mouth of its namesake river. As industrial salmon farming overtakes traditional fishing, big changes are afoot. Local boat captains may arrange trips around the area (CH$20,000 to CH$30,000 per day).

West of Puerto Cisnes, **Parque Nacional Isla Magdalena** (not to be confused with the penguin colony near Punta Arenas) is an island sanctuary with hot springs and trails. For adventurous types it makes an engaging trip but there is little infrastructure from Conaf and travel options are expensive. Ask around locally to organize a trip. Travelers can approach other visitors to split boat costs, which run around CH$100,000 for groups of 10.

Information on the area can be found at **La Municipalidad de Cisnes** (www.cisnes.org, in Spanish).

Sleeping & Eating

Camping El Salmon (☎ 099-674-334; per tent CH$5000) On family property 5km from Puerto Cisnes, these flat spots on a soccer field have picnic tables and access to a *quincho*. Bathrooms are tidy with hot showers.

Hospedaje Bellavista (☎ 346-408; www.tourbellavista.cl, in Spanish; Séptimo de Línea 112; s/d without bathroom CH$8000/14,000) Bright and modern, Bellavista has well-appointed rooms with Berber carpet and a spacious dining room. The only downside is having bathrooms downstairs. The family also organizes excursions to Isla Magdalena.

Cabañas Brisas del Sur (☎ 346-587; Arturo Prat 51; 5-person cabins CH$35,000) A row of wooden cabins facing the bay, these clean, ample and fully equipped cabins have comfortable beds, large bathrooms and TV. Expect little privacy, as it's along the main road. The owner is a good resource for fishing enthusiasts.

El Guairao Restaurant & Cabañas (☎ 346-473; Costanera s/n; d/tr/q cabins CH$25,000/30,000/35,000) These nice two-story cabins feature firm beds and balconies, but no kitchen. The attached restaurant (mains CH$4000, open for lunch and dinner) is the best bet in town, with 25 years in business. Options include wild salmon and local favorite *puyes al pilpil* (anguila in garlic oil), as well as pastas and grilled meats.

Getting There & Away

Perhaps the biggest perk of Puerto Cisnes are the bus services which will pick you up from your lodgings. Reserve in advance. **Buses Alegría** (☎ 346-434; Piloto Pardo), at the stadium, services leave for Coyhaique (CH$6000, four hours) at 6am Monday to Saturday and at 2pm on Sundays. **Transporte Terraustral** (☎ 346-757; Piloto Pardo) travels to Coyhaique (CH$6000) at 6am and 8am Monday to Saturday and at 2pm on Sundays. Buses also go to La Junta

(CH$5000, three hours) at 4pm Monday to Saturday. **Entreverdes** (☎ 099-103-196; Gabriela Mistral s/n) goes to La Junta (CH$5000) at 4pm on Monday and Friday.

COYHAIQUE
☎ 067 / pop 44,900

The cow town that kept growing, Coyhaique is the regional hub of rural Aisén, urbane enough to house the latest techie trends, kids in Goth styles and discos. All this is plopped in the middle of an undulating range, with rocky humpback peaks and snowy ranges in the backdrop. For the visitor, it's the launch pad for far-flung adventures, be it fly-fishing, trekking the ice cap or rambling the Carretera Austral to its end at Villa O'Higgins. For those fresh from the rainforest wilderness of northern Aisén, it can be a jarring relapse into the world of semitrucks and subdivisions.

Industry is braced to pounce here, with a number of regional hydroelectric projects in the works and a recently defeated aluminum plant. Rural workers come to join the timber or salmon industries and add to the growing urban mass.

Orientation

At the confluence of the Río Simpson and Río Coyhaique, the sprawling city center has its plaza at the heart of a disorienting pentagonal plan. A paved highway links the city to Puerto Chacabuco to the west, and partly paved roads lead to Puerto Ingeniero Ibáñez to the south and Chaitén to the north. It's also accessible from Argentine Patagonia to the east.

Av General Baquedano, which skirts the northeast side of town, eventually connects with the paved highway to Puerto Chacabuco and a gravel road east to the Argentine border at Paso Alto Coyhaique. Av Ogana heads south to Balmaceda, Puerto Ingeniero Ibáñez and other southerly points on the Carretera Austral.

Information
EMERGENCY
Police (☎ 215-105; Baquedano 534)

INTERNET ACCESS
Entel (Arturo Prat 340) Also with telephone and fax.
Visual.com (☎ 236-300; 12 de Octubre 485-B; per hr CH$400) Nonsmoking internet café.

COYHAIQUE

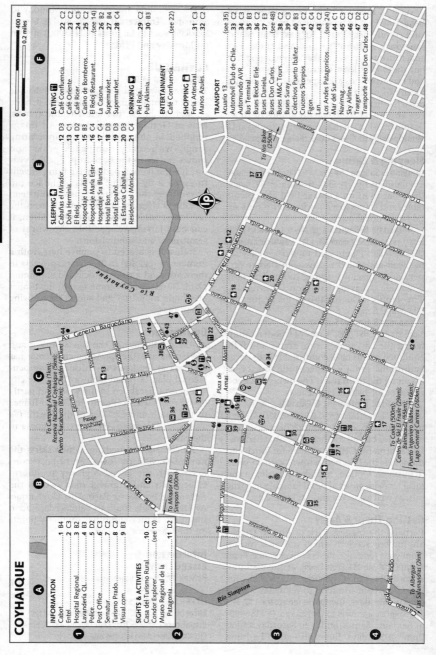

INFORMATION
Cabot......................................	**1** B4
Entel.......................................	**2** C3
Hospital Regional...................	**3** B2
Lavandería Ql.........................	**4** B3
Police.....................................	**5** D2
Post Office.............................	**6** C3
Sematur..................................	**7** C2
Turismo Prado........................	**8** C2
Visual.com.............................	**9** B3

SIGHTS & ACTIVITIES
Casa del Turismo Rural...........	**10** C2
Condor Explorer.....................	(see 10)
Museo Regional de la Patagonia..............................	**11** D2

SLEEPING
Cabañas el Mirador..................	**12** D3
Doña Hermina..........................	**13** C1
El Reloj...................................	**14** D2
Hospedaje Lautaro...................	**15** B3
Hospedaje María Ester.............	**16** C4
Hospedaje Sra Blanca...............	**17** C4
Hostal Bon..............................	**18** D3
Hostal Español........................	**19** D3
La Estancia Cabañas................	**20** D3
Residencial Mónica..................	**21** C4

EATING
Café Confluencia.....................	**22** C2
Café Oriente............................	**23** C3
Café Ricer...............................	**24** C2
Casino de Bomberos................	**25** B3
El Reloj Restaurant..................	(see 14)
La Casona...............................	**26** B2
Supermarket............................	**27** B4
Supermarket............................	**28** C4

DRINKING
Piel Roja.................................	**29** C2
Pub Alkimia............................	**30** B3

ENTERTAINMENT
Café Confluencia.....................	(see 22)

SHOPPING
Feria Artesanal........................	**31** C3
Manos Azules..........................	**32** C2

TRANSPORT
Acuario 13..............................	(see 35)
Automóvil Club de Chile..........	**33** C2
Automundo AVR......................	**34** C3
Bus Terminal...........................	**35** B3
Buses Becker Eirle...................	**36** C2
Buses Daniela..........................	**37** E3
Buses Don Carlos....................	(see 48)
Buses M&C Tours....................	**38** C2
Buses Suray............................	**39** C3
Colectivos Puerto Ibáñez.........	**40** B3
Cruceros Skorpios....................	**41** C2
Figon......................................	**42** C4
Lan..	**43** C2
Los Andes Patagonicos............	(see 24)
Mar del Sur.............................	**44** C1
Navimag..................................	**45** C3
Sky Airline..............................	**46** C3
Traeger...................................	**47** D2
Transporte Aéreo Don Carlos...	**48** C3

LAUNDRY
Lavandería QL (☎ 232-266; Bilbao 160; per load CH$3000; ⊙ 9am-8pm Mon-Fri, 10am-6pm Sat & Sun) Prompt and efficient service.

MEDICAL SERVICES
Hospital Regional (☎ 219-100; Ibar 68; ⊙ 24hr) Emergency is open 24 hours.

MONEY
Along Condell, between the plaza and Av Baquedano, are a number of banks with ATMs.
Turismo Prado (☎ 231-271; 21 de Mayo 417; ⊙ 9am-6pm) Changes currency.

POST
Post office (Lord Cochrane 202) Near Plaza de Armas.

TOURIST INFORMATION
A tourism office is slated to be added to the plaza, with information about fishing and daily outings from town.

Conaf (☎ 212-125; Av Ogana 1060; ⊙ 9am-8pm Mon-Sat, 10am-6pm Sun) Provides information on area parks and reserves.
Sernatur (☎ 233-949; sernatur_coyhaiq@entelchile .net; Bulnes 35; ⊙ 8:30am-8pm Mon-Fri, 10am-6pm Sat & Sun summer) A helpful office with lists of activity, lodging and transportation options and costs. Regional information is also available.

TRAVEL AGENCIES
Cabot (☎ 230-101; Lautaro 331) A general service travel agency.

Sights & Activities
Prime river vistas can be gained at **Mirador Río Simpson**, reached by walking west on JM Carrera. Hikers can tread trails in **Reserva Nacional Coyhaique** (admission CH$2000), 5km from town: take Baquedano north across the bridge and go right at the gravel road; from the entrance it's 3km to Laguna Verde.

Anglers can hook brown and rainbow trout from November to May, with some restrictions.

PATAGONIA'S RIVER DEBATE

Patagonia boasts one of the world's great water reserves, with deep glacial lakes, two of the planet's largest non-polar ice fields and powerful, pristine rivers rushing from the Andes to the Pacific. It's a dream if you're a salmon, a nature lover or kayaker. Or a hydroelectric company.

Energy is a hot topic in Chile, where natural resources are few. Spurred by fears of a pending national energy crisis Spanish–Italian multinational Endesa and Chile-based conglomerate HydroAysén are laying plans for large-scale dams throughout Patagonia. By some estimates, 12 Patagonian rivers, including the Baker, Pascua, Futaleufú, Manso and Puelo, are threatened. A study by the University of Chile found that tourism, the region's second-largest industry, would take a severe hit if the dams are built. While the dams would provide a short-term energy solution, in the long term they would transform one of the greatest wildernesses on earth into an industrial engine.

Popular views construe the project as necessary to protect the nation's energy reserves, but in fact the public sector uses only a third of Chile's energy – over half is consumed by the mining industry. Pristine ecosystems and rural farms are at stake, but an even greater issue is building the world's longest transmission lines. Thousands of high-voltage towers would run 2415km to bring power to Santiago and mining operations in the north.

'As a planet we are in a freshwater crisis and global warming will make it worse,' assures Aaron Sanger of International Rivers. 'These rivers are immensely valuable. We should safeguard our remaining sources of freshwater.'

In the Puelo Valley, the flood zone would put the farm and family burial ground of third-generation subsistence farmer Segundo Cardenas underwater. A century ago, the government gave citizens incentives to populate this remote region. In a reversal, it's now asking Patagonians to give up their waterways and in some cases their livelihood. Some feel that the country is pillaging its resource-rich south to feed the energy-hungry north.

'It doesn't make sense,' Cardenas wondered. 'When you build a house, would you take a board from one wall to patch another? That's what Chile's doing.'

For more information, contact **Patagonia Sin Represas** (Patagonia Without Dams; www.patagonias inrepresas.cl) or the US-based **NRDC** (National Resources Defense Council; www.nrdc.org). For information about dams and development, check out the website at World Commission on Dams (www.dams.org).

From June to September, skiers can make turns at the **Centro de Ski El Fraile** (☎ 231-690), only 29km south of Coyhaique. A T-bar and pommel lift access 800m of vertical terrain. Experts can hike past the lifts to some bowls with heavy, wet snow and lovely tree-skiing. Rental equipment is available.

In town, **Museo Regional de la Patagonia** (☎ 213-175; cnr Baquedano & Eusebio Lillo; admission CH$500; ☺ 9am-6pm Dec-Feb, limited hr rest of year) catalogues pioneer artifacts and Jesuit regalia. It also houses a fine collection of labeled photographs on regional history, including the construction of part of the Carretera Austral.

Tours

Casa del Turismo Rural (☎ 214-031; www.casaturismorural.cl; Dussen 357-B) Networks visitors to rural home stays & local guide services for a grass-roots approach to trekking, fishing and horseback riding.

Condor Explorer (☎ 670-349; www.condorexplorer.com; Dussen 357) Gear shop with topo maps and top outdoor brands also has a good guide service doing logistical support for expeditions. Day trips to rock climb or trek go for CH$25,000.

Sleeping

The following lodgings include breakfast unless otherwise noted.

BUDGET

Hospedaje Lautaro (☎ 238-116; Lautaro 269; campsites per person/dm without bathroom CH$2000/5000; ☺ summer only) Frayed but kept clean, this budget lodging offers OK rooms, classic leather couches and cooking privileges, though the appeal of camping on the front lawn is minimal. Try to avoid the dreary interior rooms.

Camping Alborada (☎ 238-868; campsites per person CH$2500) Besides camping options at nearby Reserva Nacional Coyhaique, this place, only 1km from the city, has exceptionally clean and sheltered sites (with roofs), lots of bathrooms and individual sinks, hot showers, fire pits and electricity.

Doña Herminia (☎ 231-579; 21 de Mayo 60; r per person without bathroom CH$6000) Surrounded by thick hedges, this ship-shape home gleams from Doña Herminia's mother-hen attention. Guests dig its little extras like reading lamps and big fresh towels.

Residencial Mónica (☎ 234-302; Eusebio Lillo 664; r per person with/without bathroom CH$9000/6000) Well-attended and warm, this prim '60s-style home is always full.

Albergue Las Salamandras (☎ 211-865; www.salamandras.cl; Teniente Vidal Km1.5; dm/d/cabin CH$7000/19,000/32,000; ☐) On a wooded bank of Río Simpson, this rustic guesthouse offers ample common spaces, two kitchens, and dorm beds weighted in blankets. It's 2km south of town. Also arranges trips, including some off-the-beaten-track adventures.

Hospedaje María Ester (☎ 233-023; Lautaro 544; s/d CH$12,000/18,000, s without bathroom CH$6000) Think cramped but inviting, with bright petite rooms, each with a window. Singles are limited.

Hospedaje Sra Blanca (☎ 232-158; Almirante Simpson 459; s/d CH$12,000/16,000) Quaint and homey, Blanca's rooms are spotless, some country-style and others just kitsch. The rose garden is a cheerful centerpiece. Reserve ahead; rooms with bath go for the same price.

MIDRANGE & TOP END

Cabañas el Mirador (☎ 233-191; Baquedano 848; s CH$18,000, d CH$28,000-38,000; ☐) Small and family run, these shingled cabin rooms sport new fixtures and impeccable kitchenettes. The grounds are precious, with wildflower gardens and mountain views.

Hostal Bon (☎ 231-189; Ignacio Serrano 91; s/d CH$18,000/28,000) With new midrange competition, Bon feels a bit overpriced but its winning attitude and heart-shaped pillows just might win you over. Rooms have private baths, TVs and phones. Breakfast fanatics will perk up with the fresh coffee, homemade jam, eggs and bacon cooked on request.

La Estancia Cabañas (☎ 250-193; cabanaslaestancia@latinmail.com; Colón 166; cabins per person CH$20,000) These rustic, well-spaced cabins fill a quiet orchard of apple trees. Two-story cabins have tile floors, wood stoves and kitchenettes. It's a great deal for small groups.

Hostal Español (☎ 242-580; www.hostalcoyhaique.cl; Sargento Aldea 343; s/d CH$25,000/35,000; ℗ ☐) Tasteful and modern, this ample wooden house has 10 rooms with fresh quilted bedding, claret carpets and a personal touch. Service is great and there's a comfortable living room to put your feet up by the crackling fire. A frigobar, central heating and wi-fi are other perks.

El Reloj (☎ 231-108; www.elrelojhotel.cl; Baquedano 828; s/d CH$38,000/56,000; ☐) Comfortably upscale, this lovely lodging is actually a renovated warehouse. Old rustic remnants blend with a smart, clean design. Think cypress walls, colonial furniture and a cozy stone fireplace. Rooms are quiet, with those upstairs boasting better light and views. Use cash to avoid the room tax, technically not necessary for foreigners.

Eating

Café Oriente (☎ 231-622; Condell 201; sandwiches CH$3000; ☽ lunch & dinner; ▦) Chandeliers and mirrors overstate this modest sandwich stop serving satisfying *ave paltas* (chicken and avocado sandwiches) on warm bread, ice cream and coffee.

Casino de Bomberos (☎ 231-437; General Parra 365; fixed-price lunch CH$3500; ☽ lunch) Call it a cultural experience, this classic but windowless eatery packs with locals downing seafood plates or steak and eggs. The one thing they're short of is fresh air, with empanadas and French fries sizzling up the griddle.

our pick **Café Confluencia** (☎ 245-080; 25 de Mayo 548; mains CH$3000-5000; ☽ breakfast, lunch & dinner) The town's best new find, this chic eatery serves heaping bowls of greens and themed dinner nights that bring fresh tacos way south. Mint pisco sours are standouts but teapots and fresh juices are good daytime fixes.

La Casona (☎ 238-894; Obispo Vielmo 77; mains CH$5000; ☽ lunch & dinner) Considered the best restaurant in town, with an intimate family atmosphere and a dose of white-linen formality. The menu features grilled lamb, seafood options and steaks. Palta Victoria, an avocado stuffed with crab, makes a great start.

Café Ricer (☎ 232-920; Horn 48; mains CH$5000-7500; ☽ 9:30am-midnight; ▼) Best described as a gringo zoo, this high-priced café occupies soft sheepskin seats and a choice spot on the plaza. Offerings are many, from a selection of ice creams to cakes and pies or salmon on a bed of greens. Vegetarians have OK options here.

El Reloj Restaurant (☎ 231-108; www.elrelojhotel .cl; Baquedano 828; mains CH$7000) Part of an elegant, intimate hotel, this small restaurant offers a finer touch with sumptuous meals made with regional products, such as crab and austral hake. Check out the wine selection and homemade desserts. If the weather's good, reserve a table in the apple grove.

The two large supermarkets side by side on Lautaro are ideal for self-caterers.

Drinking & Entertainment

Coyhaique has a surprisingly active nightlife in the summer months.

Pub Alkimia (Arturo Prat s/n) Behind the plush black curtains there's a club scene trussed up for a younger crowd and well-heeled 30-somethings alike, with upstairs-downstairs lounges.

Piel Roja (☎ 237-832; Moraleda 495; ☽ 6pm-5am) Rumbling with late-night life, this bar swarms with local youths and the occasional adventure guide. The circular bar downstairs is the best place for wallflowers to hide; upstairs becomes a romping dance floor in the wee hours.

Café Confluencia (☎ 245-080; 25 de Mayo 548) Two-for-one drink specials and live music weekends featuring a range of rock 'n' roll and Latin acts turn this cool café into a crowded nightspot.

Shopping

Several crafts outlets sell woolens, leather goods and wood carvings. The **Feria Artesanal** (Plaza de Armas) and **Manos Azules** (Riquelme 435) are worth a look.

Getting There & Away

AIR

Lan (☎ 231-188; General Parra 402) has several daily flights (most leaving in the morning) to Puerto Montt (CH$94,000) and Santiago (CH$125,000 round-trip) from the Balmaceda airport.

Sky Airline (☎ 240-827; www.skyairline.cl; Arturo Prat 203) flights from Santiago stop at Balmaceda on the way to Punta Arenas.

Transporte Aéreo Don Carlos (☎ 231-981; www .doncarlos.cl; Cruz 63) flies small craft to Villa O'Higgins (CH$35,000) on Monday and Thursday. Charter flights are available to Parque Nacional Laguna San Rafael, Chile Chico, Caleta Tortel and Cochrane.

For information on scheduled flights to Parque Nacional Laguna San Rafael, see p364.

BOAT

Ferries and cruises to Puerto Montt, Chiloé and Parque Nacional Laguna San Rafael leave from Puerto Chacabuco, two hours west of Coyhaique by bus, but the closest regional offices are in Coyhaique.

Navimag (☎ 223-306; www.navimag.com; Paseo Horn 47-D) sails from Puerto Chacabuco to Puerto Montt (high season CH$38,000 to CH$143,000, 18 hours) several times per week; see the website for current departure days and times. **Cruceros Skorpios** (☎ 213-755;

www.skorpios.cl; General Parra 21) runs luxury trips to Parque Nacional Laguna San Rafael. For fares, see p320.

Travelers to Chile Chico can buy ferry tickets in town at **Mar del Sur** (☎ 231-255; Baquedano 146-A), whose ferry *Pilchero* crosses Lago General Carrera between Puerto Ingeniero Ibáñez and Chile Chico. If you're driving, make reservations early.

BUS

Buses operate from the **bus terminal** (☎ 258-203; cnr Lautaro & Magallanes) and separate offices. Schedules change continuously; check with **Sernatur** (☎ 233-949; Bulnes 35) for the latest information. Busing in and out of Coyhaique is just about as confusing as getting around the plaza. Service along the Carretera Austral is improving in frequency and quality, but it still has a long way to go. Companies and departures vary on demand, and unless noted leave from the terminal.

Companies serving destinations north:

Bus Transaustral (☎ 232-067; bus terminal) Osorno and south to Comodoro Rivadavia, Argentina, for connections to Punta Arenas.

Buses Becker Eirle (☎ 335-050; Ibáñez 358) Pullman service twice weekly to Puyuhuapi, La Junta, Villa Santa Lucía and Chaitén.

Buses Daniela (☎ 231-701, 099-512-3500; Baquedano 1122) Four times a week to Puyuhuapi, La Junta, Villa Santa Lucía and Chaitén.

Buses Don Carlos (☎ 231-981; Cruz 63) Hourly to Puerto Chacabuco.

Buses M&C Tours (☎ 242-626; General Parra 329) Three times a week to Puyuhuapi, La Junta, Villa Santa Lucía and Chaitén.

Buses Suray (☎ 238-387; Arturo Prat 265) Hourly to Puerto Chacabuco.

Queilen Bus (☎ 240-760; bus terminal) Osorno, Puerto Montt and Chiloé via Argentina.

Companies serving destinations south:

Acuario 13 (☎ 240-990) Cochrane.

Buses Don Carlos (☎ 231-981; Cruz 63) Villa Cerro Castillo, Puerto Murta, Puerto Río Tranquilo, Puerto Bertrand and Cochrane.

Buses Interlagos (☎ 240-840; www.turismointerlagos.cl, in Spanish; bus terminal) Cochrane and Chile Chico.

Colectivos Puerto Ibáñez (cnr Arturo Prat & Errázuriz) Door-to-door shuttle to Puerto Ingeniero Ibáñez (CH$3500, 1½ hours).

Transporte Bellavista (☎ 244-855) Puerto Río Tranquilo (CH$7500, five hours) with connections to Chile Chico (CH$6000). Picks up passengers from lodgings.

Destination	Cost (CH$)	Duration (hr)
Osorno	28,000	20
Puerto Montt	30,000	24
Chaitén	15,000	12
La Junta	8000	7-10
Puyuhuapi	8000	6
Chile Chico	13,500	12
Cochrane	10,000	7-10

Getting Around

TO/FROM THE AIRPORT

Door-to-door shuttle service (CH$3000) to Balmaceda airport, 50km southeast of town, leaves two hours before flight departure. Call **Transfer Coyhaique** (☎ 210-495, 099-838-5070) or **Transfer Aisén Tour** (☎ 217-070, 099-489-4760).

CAR & BICYCLE

Car rental is expensive and availability limited in summer. However, it's a popular option since public transportation is infrequent, sometimes inconvenient and focused on major destinations. Shop around for the best price and, if possible, reserve ahead. Try **Traeger** (☎ 231-648; fax 231-264; Baquedano 457), **Automundo AVR** (☎ 231-621; fax 231-794; Francisco Bilbao 510) or **Los Andes Patagónicos** (☎ 232-920; Horn 48). The **Automóvil Club de Chile** (☎ 231-847; JM Carrera 333) is exceptionally friendly and helpful; staff meet clients at the airport and pick up the cars there as well.

Figon (☎ 234-616; Almirante Simpson 888; per day CH$5000-14,000) rents and repairs bicycles.

RESERVA NACIONAL COYHAIQUE

Draped in lenga, ñirre and coigue, the 21.5 sq km **Reserva Nacional Coyhaique** (admission CH$2000) has small lakes and the 1361m Cerro Cinchao. The park is 5km from Coyhaique (about 1½ hours), a good day hike, offering excellent views of the town and Cerro Macay's enormous basalt columns in the distance. Take Baquedano north, across the bridge, then go right at the gravel road, a steep climb best accessed by 4WD. Condor Explorer (p360) runs hiking and winter ski trips in the park.

From the park entrance, it's 2.5km to the **Casa Bruja** sector, with five campsites (CH$4500 per site) with fire pits, hot water, showers and bathrooms. You can also hike 4km through coigue and lenga forests to Laguna Verde, where there are picnic sites and camping with basic facilities. Hiking trails also lead to Laguna Los Sapos and Laguna Venus.

RESERVA NACIONAL RÍO SIMPSON

Rocky elephant buttes flank the lazy curves of Río Simpson in a broad valley 37km west of Coyhaique. Straddling the highway to Puerto Chacabuco, the 410-sq-km Reserva Nacional Río Simpson is an easily accessed scenic area that is popular with anglers and summer soakers. Conaf's **Centro de Visitantes** (10am-4pm Mon-Sat, 11am-2pm Sun), on the Coyhaique–Puerto Aisén road, has a small natural history museum and botanical garden. A short walk leads to **Cascada de la Virgen**, a shimmering waterfall on the north side of the highway.

Five kilometers east of the Centro de Visitantes, **Camping San Sebastián** (per tent CH$4500) has sheltered sites and hot showers. Near the confluence of the Río Simpson and Río Correntoso, 24km west of Coyhaique, **Camping Río Correntoso** (067-232-005; per tent CH$4500) has 50 spacious riverside sites in a bucolic setting. The showers are rustic, but hot.

To get there, take any of the frequent buses between Coyhaique and Puerto Aisén; for details, see opposite.

MONUMENTO NATURAL DOS LAGUNAS

On the road to Paso Alto Coyhaique on the Argentine border, this 181-hectare **wetland reserve** (admission CH$1000) hosts diverse bird life, including black swans, coots and grebes; the area is an ecological transition zone from southern beech forest to semi-arid steppe. Orchids abound. A short hiking trail goes to Laguna El Toro while a longer loop flanks the northern edge of Laguna Escondida. Near the reserve's entrance, Conaf maintains a self-guided nature trail (1km), a **campground** (per tent CH$3500) and a picnic area. While the park lacks regular public transportation, Coyhaique's branch of Conaf (p359) may be able to offer suggestions for getting there.

PUERTO CHACABUCO

☎ 067 / pop 20,000

Tourism wasn't exactly a priority when Puerto Chacabuco put in the fish-meal processing plants. With a peculiar, pungent air, this port town is a hodgepodge mix of high-end glacier tourism from Parque Nacional Laguna San Rafael and run-down remainders for everybody else. At the east end of a narrow fjord, Chacabuco is a frequent port of entry to Aisén for ferries from Puerto Montt or from Chiloé's

Quellón. A smooth paved highway connects it to Coyhaique, 82km away.

Catamaranes del Sur (see p364) owns and runs the 300-hectare private nature reserve **Parque Aikén del Sur** (admission CH$32,500), located 5km from town. Package-tour clients and guests at Hotel Loberías del Sur are the primary visitors to this exclusive park. However, it could be an interesting stop for independent travelers with the means to afford it. Hikers travel with mandatory English-speaking guides who do an impressive job of teaching about the native forest and regional ecosystem. Past the guarded gate, there are three easy hiking trails (ranging from three to five hours) that wind through native forests. Guided catch and release fishing is also allowed.

Unless you are too tired to travel on or have money to spend at Hotel Loberías del Sur, it is recommended that you don't spend too much time in Puerto Chacabuco.

Sleeping & Eating

Residencial el Puerto (☎ 351-147; juojve_59@hotmail.com; O'Higgins 80; r per person incl breakfast CH$7000) A crash pad with adequate rooms and hot showers, this *residencial* is a fair deal considering inflated local prices.

Hotel Moraleda (☎ 351-155; O'Higgins 82; r per person incl breakfast CH$6500, 5-person cabin CH$35,000) Convenient for late arrivals on the ferries, Moraleda sits just outside the harbor compound. Groups should try for the fully equipped cabin. Check for low-season discounts.

Hotel Loberías del Sur (☎ 351-115; www.catamaranesdelsur.cl; JM Carrera 50; two-night package CH$540,000; 🖳) Four-star luxury means soft sheets and spa treatments, not to mention unnecessary air-conditioning, in a remote Patagonian port. Geared mostly toward cruisers, this large-scale hotel is elegant but somewhat generic. The Chucao (CH$20,000) is a worthwhile splurge for squid, foil-baked salmon or the trusty buffet.

Getting There & Away

Buses from Coyhaique schedule departures to meet arriving and departing ferries, which go to and from Puerto Montt, Puerto Natales and Parque Nacional Laguna San Rafael. **Navimag** (☎ 351-111; www.navimag.com) sails from Puerto Chacabuco to Puerto Montt; see p361 for full bus and ferry details.

NORTHERN PATAGONIA

PARQUE NACIONAL LAGUNA SAN RAFAEL

This awesome and remote **national park** (admission CH$3000) brings visitors face to face with calving icebergs shaving off the chalky face of San Valentín ice field. The glacier dates back 30,000 years. Established in 1959, the 12,000 sq km Unesco Biosphere Reserve is the region's most impressive and popular attraction, despite the difficulty and expense of getting here. Scientific interest has been drawn to the extreme fluctuation in water level of the glacier-fed lagoon. The park encompasses peaty wetlands, pristine temperate rainforest of southern beech and epiphytes, and 4058m Monte San Valentín, the southern Andes' highest peak.

Most visitors arrive by sea, shifting to smaller craft and rubber rafts to approach the glacier's 60m face. The disadvantage of this approach is you only get a few hours at the glacier and don't set foot on land. Those who fly get to hike to the glacier, but with limited time as well. Well-equipped travelers in top physical condition and with the funds to organize transportation can stay to hike or climb around the area. A new road from Puerto Río Tranquilo to Bahía Exploradores on the Estuario San Francisco may improve access to the park in the near future, but this is still some distance from the glacier.

Camping Laguna Caiquenes (6-person campsites CH$3500), near the Conaf office by the airstrip, has five rustic campsites with water and bathrooms. Fires are not allowed and no food is available at the park.

Tours

The following ships sail from Puerto Chacabuco and Puerto Montt.

Catamaranes del Sur (☎ 067-351-112; www.catamaranesdelsur.cl; JM Carrera 50, Puerto Chacabuco) Runs a 12-hour day trip from Puerto Chacabuco on the *Catamaran Chaitén* and the smaller *Iceberg Expedition*, leaving at 8am, thereby ensuring you get to see the fjords to the glacier during the day, but with less time at the glacier face. Package trips that include lodging at its hotel, Loberías del Sur (p363), are available. Trip rates start at CH$147,100 per person, including meals.

Cruceros Skorpios (in Santiago ☎ 02-477-1900; www.skorpios.cl) The *Skorpios II* sails from Puerto Montt on Saturdays between September and March, with more limited trips until the end of May. Accommodations are very comfortable, with touches of luxury and excellent food. The ship spends all of the third day at the glacier and visits the island of Chiloé on its return. A highlight is the stop at Quitralco, Skorpios' private hot-springs resort. Seven-day trips start at US$2700 per person.

Navimag (☎ 067-233-306; fax 067-233-386; www.navimag.com; Paseo Horn 47-D, Coyhaique) *Puerto Eden* sails from Puerto Montt (high season singles/doubles from CH$680,000/820,000) every Saturday, twice-monthly in low season. From Puerto Chacabuco (from CH$615,000/740,000), it departs every Sunday. High season is December to March. The trip takes two days, sailing to the glacier at night. Students (with ID) can get a 10% discount, senior travelers over 60 get 15% off.

RESERVA NACIONAL CERRO CASTILLO

Cerro Castillo's basalt spires are the crowning centerpiece of **Reserva Nacional Cerro Castillo** (admission CH$1000), a sprawling 1800-sq-km mountain reserve of southern beech forest, 75km south of Coyhaique. The park boasts fine fishing and hiking, along with little foot traffic. Its namesake, the 2700m triple-tier Cerro Castillo, is flanked by three major glaciers on its southern slopes. Hikers can complete a segment of Sendero de Chile with the 16km trail to Campamento Neozelandés. Another recommended four-day trek (described in Lonely Planet's *Trekking in the Patagonian Andes*) leaves from Km75, at the north end of the reserve, and goes to Villa Cerro Castillo at the south end via a high route passing glaciers, rivers and lakes.

Conaf operates a sheltered **campground** (tent CH$3500) at Laguna Chaguay, 67km south of Coyhaique. It has bathrooms and hot showers. Backcountry camping is also possible. Before going into the backcountry, check in with the ranger to avoid seasonal hazards.

Upon request, public buses will stop to leave passengers at the ranger station and campground.

VILLA CERRO CASTILLO

Under the sparkly five-carat face of Cerro Castillo, pioneer town Villa Cerro Castillo has a congenial dusty-heeled feel. It's a good base to explore the reserve and a short distance from the Carretera Austral, 10km west of the Puerto Ingeniero Ibáñez junction. The town's **Festival Costumbrista**, usually held in February, offers an authentic take on Patagonian rodeo and draws artists and artisans from all over Chile and Argentina. The **tourist office** (Los Antiguos 208; ✆ 10am-8pm Jan-Feb) is helpful with general information.

The clean and comfortable **Cabañas Don Niba** (☎ public phone 067-419-200; Los Pioneros 872; r per person CH$7000) family lodging dishes out whopping breakfasts and the company of Don Niba, guide, storyteller and grandson of pioneers. He also offers horseback treks and hikes.

Rooms are on the dark side at **La Querencia** (☎ 067-411-610; O'Higgins 460; s/d without bathroom CH$5000/10,000) but they're well kept and there is a large shared bathroom. Lunch in María's quirky restaurant is a good deal.

Don Carlos buses shuttle daily to and from Coyhaique and twice weekly to Puerto Murta and Puerto Río Tranquilo (for details, see p362).

PUERTO INGENIERO IBÁÑEZ

☎ 067 / pop 3000

On the north shore of Lago General Carrera, sleepy Puerto Ingeniero Ibáñez serves as a transit station for ferry goers and little else. Clobbered in Volcán Hudson's 1991 eruption, it has since unearthed and repaired, but when the sky darkens with ashy dust storms, townspeople go scurrying inside.

Ferries to Chile Chico, on the lake's south shore, leave from here. If local handicrafts interest you, ask around for pottery artist Señora Marta Aguila or weaver and herbal remedy specialist Señora Juana Vega. It's that informal. Locals can also point you to cave paintings or the Río Ibañez falls, 8km away.

Around 1.5km before town, **La Casona** (☎ 423-365; r per person CH$8000) offers friendly farmhouse lodgings, ideal for cyclists or hikers. Camping may also be available. **Residencial Ibáñez** (☎ 423-227; Dickson 31; s CH$8000), opposite the ferry dock, has surprisingly good beds stocked with extra blankets. Meals (CH$4000) are available. Campers will find friendly faces at countryside **Maitenal Camping** (☎ 098-532-7680; Camino a Levican Km12; campsites per person CH$1000), whose host Lillian is also certified to guide local treks.

For road transportation from Coyhaique to Puerto Ingeniero Ibáñez, see p362. Ferry schedules seem to change from year to year and season to season. **Mar del Sur** (☎ 231-255, 411-864; Baquedano 146-A) ferries cars and passengers on *Pilchero* to Chile Chico (2½ hours) almost daily. For rates see p366.

CHILE CHICO

☎ 067 / pop 4000

Bordering Argentina, this pint-sized orchard town occupies the windy southern shore of Lago General Carrera. A sunny microclimate makes it a pleasant oasis on the steppe. It is linked to Chile by ferry or a roller-coaster road dotted with gold and silver mines. Locals traditionally earned their living from raising livestock and farming but have turned to mining in numbers.

Hikers shouldn't miss the Reserva Nacional Jeinemeni, 60km away, with solitary treks in an arid wonderland of flamingo-filled turquoise mountain lagoons. Travelers tend to zip through town, but there are worthwhile side trips and connections to Los Antiguos and Ruta 40 leading to southern Argentine Patagonia.

Traveling the abrupt curves of Paso Las Llaves, west from Chile Chico to the junction with the Carretera Austral, is one of the region's highlights. Scary and stunning, it hits blind corners and steep inclines on loose gravel high above the lake with no guardrails. If driving, proceed very slowly; in some places the roadway is barely wide enough for a single vehicle.

Information

BancoEstado (González 112; ⊗ 9am-2pm Mon-Fri) Changes US cash only and has reasonable rates, but collects a commission on all traveler's checks.
Conaf (☎ 411-325; Blest Gana 121; ⊗ 10am-6pm Mon-Fri, 11am-4pm Sat) For information on Reserva Nacional Jeinemeni.
Entel (O'Higgins; per hr CH$800) Phone center with internet access.
Oficina de Información Turística (☎ 411-123; cnr O'Higgins & Lautaro; ⊗ 8:30am-1pm & 2-5pm Mon-Fri) For area information.
Post office (Manuel Rodríguez 121)

Sights & Activities

Chile Chico's museum and cultural center, **Casa de la Cultura** (☎ 411-355; cnr O'Higgins & Lautaro; admission CH$500), features a ground-floor collection of works by regional artists and a 2nd-floor assemblage of local artifacts, including minerals and fossils. Outside is the restored *El Andes*, which was built in Glasgow, Scotland, to navigate the Thames, but was brought here to carry passengers and freight around the lake.

Antonio Rodríguez (☎ 411-209; Pedro González 253) rents horses (CH$5000 for half a day, CH$10,000 for a full day) and arranges excursions to Laguna Jeinimeni, Cueva de las Manos (Argentina) and other nearby sites.

Sleeping & Eating

Camping Chile Chico (☎ 411-598; Pedro Burgos 6; campsites per person CH$2500) A row of poplars block the cutting winds at this quiet little campground. There are hot showers, and the kind owners sell firewood, share the bounty of local produce and organize the occasional *asado* or salmon bake.

Hospedaje No Me Olvides (☎ 099-8330-8006; Sector Chacras; campsites/s without bathroom CH$3000/7500) Rooms are snuggly and ample at this country farmhouse, 200m from town. Attention is quite friendly and guests can use the kitchen. Campers bed down in the orchard.

Hospedaje Brisas del Lago (☎ 411-204; Manuel Rodríguez 443; s/d without bathroom CH$7500/15,000) There are a number of good-sized rooms, both clean and comfortable, but service lacks a spark.

Kon Aiken (☎ 411-598; Pedro Burgos 6; s/d without bathroom CH$6500/12,000, 6-person cabin CH$30,000) With a family atmosphere, this handy lodging offers good rates. The range of services (including camping) sometimes give it a busy atmosphere but the friendly hosts are warm and welcoming.

Hostería de la Patagonia (☎ 411-337; hdelapatagonia@gmail.com; Camino Internacional s/n; camping per person CH$1500, d with/without bathroom CH$25,000/20,000) Descendants of Belgian colonists run this sweet farmhouse with gardens and horses. Rooms have private bathrooms. Look for the yellow roof, leaving town toward Argentina.

Café Elizabeth y Loly (☎ 411-451; Pedro González 25; mains CH$2500-5000; ✆ lunch & dinner) Considering this is Chile Chico, this quirky stop is a café-culture hotspot, serving strong coffee and authentic baklava, opposite the plaza.

Getting There & Away

AIR

Transportes Aéreos Don Carlos (☎ 411-490; www.doncarlos.cl; O'Higgins 264) has charter flights to Coyhaique. The airfield is just outside town, on the road to the Argentine border.

BOAT

Mar del Sur (☎ 231-255, 411-864; Baquedano 146-A) ferries *Pilchero* between Chile Chico and Puerto Ingeniero Ibáñez (2½ hours) almost daily.

Departure days and times change often: check at the Entel office on O'Higgins in Chile Chico for the latest posting. Rates are: passengers CH$4000, bicycles CH$1900, motorcycles CH$4700 and vehicles CH$24,000. Arrive one hour before departure time. Vehicle reservations are highly recommended.

BUS

A number of shuttle buses cross the border to Los Antiguos, Argentina (CH$2000, 20 minutes), just 9km east. Shuttles, which coordinate with buses that run directly to El Chaltén, leave from O'Higgins 420.

From Los Antiguos, travelers can make connections in Argentina to Perito Moreno, Caleta Olivia, El Chaltén and southern Argentine Patagonia.

Transportes Ale (☎ 411-739; Rosa Amelia 800) goes to Puerto Río Tranquilo (CH$12,000, five hours), stopping in Puerto Guadal (CH$6000, 2½ hours) at 1:30pm on Tuesday and Thursday. A southbound bus goes to Cochrane (CH$12,000, six hours) at 1:30pm on Wednesday and Saturday, stopping at Puerto Guadal and Cruce Maitén (CH$7000, three hours).

RESERVA NACIONAL JEINEMENI

Turquoise lakes and the rusted hues of the steppe mark the rarely visited **Reserva Nacional Jeinemeni** (admission CH$1000), 52km southwest of Chile Chico. Its unusual wonders range from cave paintings to foxes and flamingos. In the transition zone to the Patagonian steppe, it covers 1610 sq km. Through-hikers can link to Valle Chacabuco via a two-day mountain traverse on **Sendero La Leona**; for information contact Estancia Valle Chacabuco (p369).

Three private **camping areas** (per tent CH$3500) are on the banks of the startlingly blue Lago Jeinemeni, about 400m from the Conaf office. **Sendero Lago Verde** takes visitors on a three-hour, 10km-round-trip hike to a gemstone lake. The road into the park is passable only by 4WD vehicles because Río Jeinemeni cuts across the road, causing flooding conditions mid-afternoon. Day-trippers should leave early enough to cross on the way back before 4pm.

En route to the reserve, about 25km south of Chile Chico, an access road leads to **Cueva de las Manos**, Tehuelche cave paintings. Reaching the cave requires a steep uphill climb (unmarked) and is best done with a guide.

A few locals with minivans arrange tours for groups, including **Jaime Berrocal** (☎ 067-411-461), who also arranges fishing trips.

PUERTO RÍO TRANQUILO

The largest settlement between Coyhaique and Cochrane, humble Puerto Río Tranquilo flanks the western shores of Lago General Carrera. For most travelers it amounts to a pee break, but its outstanding access to lake kayaking, glaciers and cool marble caves mean all that is missing is a little infrastructure.

An east–west road under construction from here to Bahía Exploradores will eventually reach Laguna San Rafael. Gorgeous but rough, part of it is already accessible for driving and biking. Boat tours visit **Capilla de Mármol** (marble chapel), an intriguing geological formation, when the water's calm on General Carrera.

Sleeping

El Puesto (☎ satellite 02-196-4555; www.elpuesto .cl; Pedro Lagos 258; s/d CH$45,000/55,000) Guests are pampered in this modern wood home, with woolen slippers, hand-woven throws and rockers. English-speaking owners Francisco and Tamara also have a reputable professional guide service offering ice trekking on Glacier Exploradores and other services.

Hostería Costanera (☎ 067-411-537; Pedro Lagos 9; d CH$25,000, s without bathroom CH$8000) Worn but well-cared-for rooms upstairs from the roadside restaurant.

Residencial Darka (☎ 067-419-500; Arrayanes 330; r per person CH$6000) Has a few decent rooms and a friendly owner.

Camping Pudu (☎ 067-573-003, 098-920-5085; aliciaconce@gmail.com; campsites per person CH$3000; ☙ Dec-March) offers beach camping with hot showers and laundry service, 1km south of Puert Río Tranquilo. Guided fishing and hikes are also available.

Getting There & Away

Regular buses between Coyhaique and Cochrane will drop off and pick up passengers here. **Transportes Ale** (☎ 067-411-739; Rosa Amelia 880) goes to Chile Chico (CH$12,000, five hours) several times a week.

CRUCE EL MAITÉN

Cruce el Maitén is little more than a fork in the road. To the west, the Carretera Austral begins to wind its way to Puerto Bertrand,

Cochrane and beyond. To the east is the beginning of the road, alongside Lago General Carrera, to Chile Chico. A number of high-end fishing lodges have sprung up in the area. Most offer a variety of activities, such as horse trekking, trips to Capilla de Marmól as well as catch-and-release fishing. Relatively remote, these lodgings usually need advance notice in order to have guides at the ready or produce for meals. Accommodations are usually in individual cabins overlooking the lake. Expect quality service, either a Jacuzzi or sauna, and excellent food. Some of these include the dude-ranch-styled **Pasarela 2 Lodge** (☎ 067-411-425; www.lapasarela.cl; Km265; s/d CH$35,000/60,000), specializing in fishing, or the elegant and airy boutique hotel **Hacienda Tres Lagos** (☎ 067-411-323; www.haciendatreslagos.com; Km274; d CH$143,000), right at the junction, with excursions.

PUERTO GUADAL

Windy and forlorn, but damn postcard beautiful, Puerto Guadal sits at the southwest end of Lago General Carrera on the highway to Chile Chico. The location, 13km east of the junction with the Carretera Austral, was once ideal for shipping lines; now it is a quiet petrol stop. Chilotes settled the area, evidenced in the shingled houses and the hard-won hospitality. It makes a good stop for budget travelers, since lodgings further out are midrange to high end.

Near the beachfront at the eastern edge of town there's camping, though finding a windbreak among the rocky sites proves challenging. **Riconada** (☎ 067-431-224; Las Camelias 157; 5-person cabins CH$30,0005) provides a good alternative for small groups. The well-weathered **Hostería Huemules** (☎ 067-431-212; Las Magnolias 382; r per person CH$4500) feels saggy and strange, but that won't stop you being charmed by its next-door host Don Kemel. No less than legend, he regales visitors with tales of navy days or his youth in Beirut.

Anglers and mountaineers hunker down at **Terra Luna** (☎ 067-431-263; www.terra-luna.cl; 2-person huts CH$30,000, d/tr/q incl breakfast CH$80,000/90,000/110,000), 1.5km from Chile Chico, where there are attractive cabins and a hot tub tucked into the woods. Budget travelers should check out the rustic Conejera huts with kitchen.

Transportes Ale (☎ 067-411-739; Rosa Amelia 800) has shuttles to Chile Chico (CH$12,000) and south to Cochrane (CH$12,000) several times a week. Call or enquire in Coyhaique about the most recent schedules, as they change frequently.

PUERTO BERTRAND

☎ 067 / pop 1500

Banking the ultramarine blue Lago Bertrand below the snow-covered San Valentín and Campo de Hielo Norte, Puerto Bertrand is a show of contrasts. Weathered shingle homes overgrown with rose blossoms and high-end fishing lodges share the space of this humble, dusty stop. Bertrand occupies the southeast shore of the lake, 11km south of Cruce El Maitén. It is also the base for mountaineering expeditions to the northern ice field and rafting trips on Río Baker, Chile's most voluminous river.

About 40km south of Puerto Bertrand and 17km north of Cochrane, at the scenic confluence of the Río Baker and Río Nef, a decent gravel road climbs eastward up the valley of Río Chacabuco to the Argentine border at Paso Roballos.

Patagonia Adventure Expeditions (☎ 411-330; www.adventurepatagonia.com) offers floating on the Río Baker (eight days, all inclusive CH$675,000), but its staple adventures are 10-day hikes on the Aysén Glacier trail. Focusing on 'cultural geography,' bilingual guides take groups (maximum six people) on journeys involving horse trekking through glacially carved valleys and old lenga forests, forging streams, climbing to Ventisquero Soler, ice climbing and meeting up with gauchos for an *asado*. The price includes transfers to and from Coyhaique. Longer and custom trips are also arranged.

Sleeping & Eating

Most places, except for the fishing lodges, take messages from the **public phone** (☎ 419-900).
Lunch or dinner is usually a reasonable extra fee but make arrangements in advance.

Camping Municipal (per person CH$2500) These sites on the riverside are small but appealing.

Hospedaje Doña Ester (☎ 411-099; Esparza 8; dm CH$7000) Simple yet well scrubbed, this precious family home offers hospitable lodgings in town and homemade lunch for a little extra (CH$3500). The owners also help guests find out about area activities.

Hostería Puerto Bertrand (☎ 419-900; Costanera s/n; d with/without bathroom CH$18,000/8000) Above the general store, this rickety wood home has a cozy atmosphere of soft armchairs and lace-covered tables. Shop around for a room with ventilation.

La Casa del Río Konaiken (www.konaiken.blog.com; 2-person cabins CH$40,000) These stylish cabins on the forested shores of the Baker River, 6km south of Puerto Bertrand, dish out relaxation in the form of tranquility. The owners are also local conservation advocates. There's plenty of personalized attention if you want it, including reiki and massage, as well as treats like woodstove fires, wholegrain pies and homemade jams.

Patagonia Baker Lodge (☎ 411-903; www.pbl.cl; d incl breakfast CH$80,000) Pampering anglers, the Baker Lodge is 3km south of Puerto Bertrand. Upscale but friendly, it sports six rooms, each with two double beds, large bathrooms and river views. The main lodge has an enormous sundeck with splendid views and a fly-tying loft. All-inclusive packages (including fly-fishing, activities, lodging, meals and transfers) start at CH$390,000 per day. The food is excellent.

COCHRANE

☎ 067 / pop 3000

An old ranching outpost, Cochrane may be the southern hub of the Carretera Austral, but that isn't saying much. The streets are so quiet you'd think that there's a showdown set for noon; it's definitely a sleeper, not a thriller. Yet Cochrane finds itself at a decisive moment – poised to become a company town if proposals for nearby hydroelectric dams succeed. At present, neighbors are divided over progress that might mean a mini-economic boom but would double the population with itinerant workers and definitively change the landscape.

Eclipsing other regional attractions, the park-in-progress Estancia Valle Chacabuco (see opposite) is worth driving through, though there are no services available to the public just yet. It is not hard to glimpse guanaco herds, fox and flamingos in a stunning setting of arid, undulating steppe. Visitors should take advantage of other activities a spring step away – fishing on Lago Cochrane, horse treks and hiking. Cochrane has the last gas station and is the best place for information along this lonely stretch of road.

Information

Call center (cnr San Valentín & Las Golondrinas; ◷ 9am-7pm Mon-Sat, 11am-6pm Sun)

EXPLORE MORE: VALLE CHACABUCO

Twenty miles north of Cochrane, a former *estancia* is home to flamingo, guanaco huemul (endangered Andean deer), viscacha and fox. Dubbed as the Serengeti of the Southern Cone, the 690 sq km Valle Chacabuco – a national park in the making – features Patagonian steppe, forests, mountains, lakes and lagoons. While it isn't yet fully open to the public, visitors are welcome to drive through and take in the beauty or help restore it by taking part in an extensive volunteer program.

Kris Tompkins (see p347) purchased the run-down ranch through nonprofit Conservacion Patagonica with one grand plan: creating Parque Nacional Patagonia. Combining this valley with Reserva Nacional Jeinimeni to the north and Reserva Nacional Tamango to the south will eventually result in a 2400 sq km park worthy of one day rivaling the uber-popular Torres del Paine.

Major rehabilitation is reinstating the ranch as an important wildlife corridor but re-creating a home on the range was never so hard won. So far 644km of fencing has been removed so native guanaco and huemul may return. The invasive plant species that proliferated with cattle have to be ripped out by hand. Sound like a good time? We've heard a few rave reviews. If you'd like to help, contact English-speaking volunteer coordinator Paula Herrera at **Conservacion Patagonica** (pherrera@conservacionpatagonica.cl; www.conservacionpatagonica.org).

Ciber Cochrane (cnr Dr Steffan & Las Golondrinas; per hr CH$600; ☺ 9:30am-2pm & 4pm-midnight Mon-Sat, 6pm-midnight Sun) Internet access.

Conaf (☎ 522-164; Río Nef 417; ☺ 10am-6pm Mon-Sat)

Hospital (☎ 522-131; O'Higgins 755; ☺ 24hr) Emergency is open 24 hours.

Museo de Cochrane (San Valentín 555; ☺ 9am-5:45pm Mon-Fri) Features archeological displays and pioneer artifacts, and sells local crafts.

Post office (Esmeralda 199; ☺ 9am-3pm Mon-Fri, 11am-2pm Sat)

Tourist kiosk (☎ 522-326; turismo@cochranepata gonia.cl; Plaza de Armas; ☺ 10am-1pm & 2-9pm Jan-Feb) Open only in summer.

Sleeping & Eating

Residencial Cero a Cero (☎ 522-158; Lago Brown 464; s/d CH$12,000/20,000, r per person without bathroom CH$7000) A log home with ample space, Cero a Cero is a comfortable option with good beds, plenty of windows and a warm, cozy interior.

Latitude 47 (☎ 522-280; Lago Brown 564; r per person without bathroom CH$8000) With warm hospitality, this big white house has a selection of narrow upstairs rooms with single beds. Mattresses are on the saggy side and carpets thin. Front rooms are superior to their windowless counterparts on the interior side.

Hospedaje Rubio (☎ 522-173; Sargente Marino 871; s/d CH$14,000/24,000) Immaculate and prim, this frilly B&B has comfortable, well-furnished doubles. A wood fire keeps the house toasty warm and the last-stop location means plenty of quiet.

El Fogon (☎ 522-240; San Valentín 653; set menu CH$3800; ☺ lunch & dinner) Behind a white picket fence, this welcoming and attentive spot serves hearty set menus of chicken or meat with rice, a soup starter and dessert.

Café Restaurant Ñirrantal (☎ 522-760; Av O'Higgins 650; mains CH$5000; ☺ lunch & dinner) Salmon and mashed potatoes or meat are served up in a proper restaurant atmosphere, but service lags and food doesn't necessarily come to order. Try the redeeming homemade cherry compote.

Getting There & Away

Buses to Coyhaique (CH$10,000, seven to 10 hours) go with **Buses Don Carlos** (☎ 522-550; Prat 334) at 9:30am on Tuesday, Thursday and Saturday or **Buses Acuario 13** (☎ 522-143; Río Baker 349) at 8am from Tuesday through Saturday. **Buses Interlagos** (☎ 522-606; San Valentín 599) goes at 9:30am on Monday, Wednesday, Friday and Saturday.

For Caleta Tortel (CH$5000), check out **Buses Aldea** (☎ 522-143; Río Baker 349), going at 9am on Monday, Tuesday, Thursday and Sunday.

For Villa O'Higgins (CH$12,000, six hours), **Buses Los Ñadis** (☎ 522-448; Los Helechos 490) departs at 2:30pm on Monday and Thursday. Don Carlos buses also go twice weekly.

Chile Chico (CH$12,000, six hours) is served by **Transportes Ale** (☎ 522-448; Las Golondrinas 399) at 10am on Sunday and Thursday, with stops in Puerto Bertrand and Puerto Guadal.

RESERVA NACIONAL TAMANGO

Boasting Chile's largest population of endangered huemul deer, **Reserva Nacional Tamango** (admission CH$3000) protects a 70 sq km transition zone to the Patagonian steppe. Huemul are notoriously shy, but chances of sighting one are better here than anywhere. At the entrance, trails (1.5km to 7km in length) lead to Laguna Elefantina, Laguna Tamanguito and 1722m Cerro Tamango. **Camping Las Correntadas** (Embarcadero, Playa Paleta; 6-person campsites CH$8000, 4-person cabins CH$25,000) provides large campsites (ask about individual rates) with potable water, wash basins and toilets. Cabins have bathrooms but not showers. The reserve is 6km northeast of Cochrane; there is no public transportation to the entrance. At the corner of Colonia and San Valentín, hikers can take Pasaje No 1 north and then east to access trails to the entrance. Cochrane's Conaf (p369) may have trail maps.

CALETA TORTEL
☎ 067 / pop 550

A network of creaky boardwalks tracing the milky waters of the glacier-fed sound, Caleta Tortel feels fabled. Dedicated as a national monument, this fishing village cobbled around a steep escarpment is certainly unique. Seated between two ice fields at the mouth of Río Baker, it was first home to canoe-traveling Alacalufes (Qawashqar); colonists didn't arrive until 1955. The village has island isolation, with no newspaper and local phone lines that connect with the dialing of an extension. More outwardly social than other Patagonians, locals live off tourism and cypress wood extraction and eat king crab in winter and salmon in summer.

The road stops at the edge of town, near the El Rincon sector. Boardwalks and staircases lead to the center and past, to the sector of Playa Ancha, a wide beach. In the municipal building, the **tourism office** (☎ 211-876; www .municipalidaddetortel.cl; ☙ 8:30am-5:30pm Mon-Fri) can be very helpful, with some English-speaking staff. **Patagonia Austral** (☎ local line 140) arranges excursions and has radio contact with remote outfitters. The town's public phone at **Telefónica** (☎ 234-815; ☙ 10am-1pm & 3-8pm Mon-Sat) can take messages. For internet, the **Biblioteca** (library; ☙ 10am-7pm Mon-Fri) offers free half-hour access.

All-day **glacier visits** with combination boat and hiking or horseback riding go to Ventisqueros Montt (Campo de Hielo Sur) and Steffens (Campo de Hielo Norte). Motorized boat trips for eight to 10 persons cost between CH$150,000 and CH$200,000. Individuals

can try to join existing groups. The boat *Santa Fe* offers good service. Otherwise, ask around at the docks or with a tour office. Also, boat trips can be geared toward shipwreck visits. Above the Rincon sector of Tortel, **hiking trails** to Junquillo offer views of the Baker estuary and canals. Depending on the distance you go, the trip lasts one to three hours.

Sleeping & Eating
Playa Ancha Camping (Playa Ancha; campsites free) Camping is free but primitive with a stunning river-mouth setting; campers can use shower facilities (CH$1500) across the street at Brisas del Sur.

Residencial Estilo (☎ local line 143; r per person CH$8000-12,000) Javier Pinella's well-kept wooden house has newish doubles in wood finish.

Brisas del Sur (☎ 411-099; Playa Ancha sector; d CH$20,000, r per person without bathroom CH$8000) Señora Valería puts guests at ease in snug rooms by the waterfront, with smells of good cooking wafting up the stairs.

Sabores Locales (mains CH$3000-6000; ☙ 1pm-1am) Maritza cooks up a storm of tasty soups, smoked salmon and ceviche dishes in this cute café with plenty of vegetarian options.

Getting There & Away
All buses depart from a stop next to the tourist information center in the upper entrance to the village since there is no motorized access to town. To Cochrane (CH$5000, three hours) try **Buses Acuario 13** (☎ 522-143), with trips Tuesday through Thursday, or **Buses Aldea** with a 2:30pm trip on Tuesday, Thursday, Friday and Sunday.

El Mosco goes to Villa O'Higgins (CH$10,000, four hours) at 4:30pm on Sundays. **Buses Los Ñadis** (☎ 522-196) drives to El Vagabundo, 20km north of Puerto Yungay, at 10am on Sunday.

Charging per trip, not per person, boat taxis leave from the Rincon sector to the center (CH$2000), Playa Ancha (CH$3000) and Isla de los Muertos (CH$35,000); they also do tours of the bay (CH$5000).

SOUTH TO VILLA O'HIGGINS
Wild stretches of rushing rivers and virgin forest flank the curvy road south of El Vagabundo and the access road to Caleta Tortel. Here the Carretera Austral demands constant attention with sectors of washboard road and potential slides. You will be happy if you are traveling in a high-clearance vehicle.

At **Puerto Yungay**, a government ferry hauls passengers and four cars to the east end of Fiordo Mitchell at Río Bravo, usually four times a day at 9am, noon, 3pm and 6pm (free, one hour). Space is limited, so if you are driving arrive early and expect to wait, passing the time with a scrumptious empanada from the next-door kiosk.

VILLA O'HIGGINS
☎ 067 / pop 500

The last stop on the Carretera Austral, the isolated **Villa O'Higgins** boasts mythic status. First settled by the English (1914–16), the outpost attracted a few Chilean colonists but wasn't officially founded until 1966. The road didn't reach here until 1999. Alluring in its isolation, O'Higgins provides spectacular country to explore on horseback or foot, and it has world-class fishing. Its popularity has also grown due to increasingly easy (but still arduous and complicated) transportation to El Chaltén and Parque Nacional Los Glaciares in Argentina (see below).

After Mitchell Fjord, another 100km of rugged road leads to the north end of a narrow arm of Lago O'Higgins (known as Lago San Martín on the Argentine side). Almost no one uses addresses in town but locals are happy to point you in the right direction.

Information
A tourist office on Plaza Cívica is planned for the future.

Biblioredes (Plaza Cívica; ☒ 8:30am-5:30pm; ▣) Public library with free internet.

Centro de Llamadas Lulu (☎ 431-818; Lago O'Higgins & Río Mosco; ☒ 9:30am-2pm & 3-11pm) Call center.

Tours
Adventure and travel outfitter **Hielo Sur** (☎ 431-821/822; www.villaohiggins.com; ☒ 9am-1pm & 3-7pm Mon-Sat) has the inside scoop on almost everything; check out the website for information about town. Guided horseback riding or trekking trips are available with advance booking. Bike rentals (CH$900 per hour) are also available.

Hielo Sur runs catamaran tours from Bahía Bahamondes to Candelario Mansilla (CH$20,000), where you can go on to El Chaltén in Argentina, and Glacier O'Higgins (one way/round-trip CH$33,000/40,000). The trip leaves at 8:30am on Wednesday and Saturday in summer, with some extra dates.

NORTHERN PATAGONIA

EXPLORE MORE: ARGENTINA VIA BACK DOOR

Gonzo travelers can skirt the Southern Ice Field to get from Villa O'Higgins to Argentina's Parque Nacional Los Glaciares and El Chaltén (p405). The one- to three-day trip can be completed between November and March. Bring all provisions, plus your passport and rain gear. The trip goes as follows:

- Take the 8am bus from Villa O'Higgins to Puerto Bahamondez (CH$1500).

- Take the Hielo Sur catamaran (CH$20,000, four hours) from Villa O'Higgins to Candelario Mansilla on the south edge of Lago O'Higgins. It goes one to three times a week, most often on Saturdays with some Monday or Wednesday departures. Candelario Mansilla has lodging, guided treks and horse rental (riding/pack horse CH$15,000/15,000 per day). Pass through Chilean customs and immigration here.

- Trek or ride to Laguna Redonda (two hours). Camping is not allowed.

- Trek or ride to Laguna Larga (1½ hours). Camping is not allowed.

- Trek or ride to the north shore of Lago del Desierto (1½ hours). Camping is allowed. Pass through Argentine customs and immigration here.

- Take the ferry from the north to the south shores of Lago del Desierto (AR$50 or CH$8000, 4½ hours). Another option is to hike the coast (15km, five hours). Camping is allowed. Check current ferry schedules with Argentine customs.

- Grab the shuttle bus to El Chaltén, 37km away (AR$50 or CH$8000, one hour).

For more information, consult **Hielo Sur** (☎ 067-431-821/822; www.villaohiggins.com; ☒ 9am-1pm & 3-7pm Mon-Sat) in O'Higgins or **Rancho Grande Hostel** (☎ 54-2962-493-092; www.hostelspatagonia .com; San Martín 724, El Chaltén) on the Argentine side.

Bernardino Vera (☎ 431-871; horse & guide daily rate CH$24,000) can take visitors riding; the most notable multiday route is the Ruta de los Pioneros, which traces the pioneer route to Cochrane.

Sleeping & Eating

Camping & Albergue El Mosco (☎ 431-837; patagonia elmosco@yahoo.es; Carretera Austral Km1240; camping/dm CH$2500/6000) Friendly and full-service, this new hostel has kitchen and bathroom privileges for campers, hosted by friendly Spaniard Jorge.

Hospedaje Rural (☎ 431-805; r per person without bathroom CH$6000) If you're reaching for the final, final frontier, check out this lodging in the southernmost sector of Candelario Mansilla. It must be reached by Hielo Sur catamaran (p371) and contacted via the municipal office. Host Don Ricardo can help you explore area trails to glaciers, lakes and rivers.

Hospedaje Cascada (☎ 431-833; Pasaje Lago & Río Mosco; r per person without bathroom CH$7000) Six plain rooms with twin beds, all nonsmoking, are on offer. The shared kitchen is immaculate and the bakery smells from downstairs are divine.

Hospedaje Patagonia (☎ 431-818; Río Pascua & Lago Christie; d without bathroom CH$13,000) Clean and well-cared for, with a selection of simple doubles

in a rambling green house. Meal or tea service may be possible.

Hostal Runin (☎ 431-870; Av Carretera Austral s/n; s/d CH$18,000/28,000, without bathroom CH$14,000/22,000) Chilote hospitality infuses this woodsy and well-equipped lodging with comfortable beds and a greenhouse out back. Coming into town, it's 400m before the village, on the right.

Entre Patagones (☎ 431-810; Av Carretera Austral s/n; mains CH$4000) This faux-rustic log restaurant and bar serves up tasty and abundant meals of salmon and salad or barbecue specialties. It's in front of Hostal Runin.

Getting There & Away

Transporte Aéreo Don Carlos (☎ in Coyhaique 231-981; www.doncarlos.cl) flies from Coyhaique (CH$35,000, 1½ hours) on Monday and Thursday. **Buses Los Ñadis** (☎ 522-196) goes to Cochrane (CH$12,000, six hours) at 10am on Tuesday and Friday; buy your return ticket in advance. **El Mosco** bus, leaving from the Carretera Austral, goes to Tortel (CH$10,000, four hours) at 8:30am on Sunday.

For information on connecting to Argentina by catamaran, see p371. If driving, keep the headlights on, stop for huemules and carry a spare tire.

Southern Patagonia

Pounding westerlies, barren seascapes and the ragged spires of Torres del Paine define the rugged provinces of Magallanes and Última Esperanza. For many, these landscapes represent the distilled essence of Patagonia, matched only in frontier appeal by the deep Amazon and a few stretches of Alaska. Southern Patagonia is ideal for adventure and travelers will find plenty while taking in the cool panoramas of national parks, islands colonized by penguins, and the remote ranches with hard-livin' gauchos.

Throughout the region, the lines are blurred between Argentina and Chile (although the border guards don't think so). Here there's much more Argentine-Chilean bonhomie than in the north; it's the only place in the country where you might spy a Chilean rooting for the Argentine national soccer team (not against Chile, of course). Like many locals, you will probably skip back and forth between the two countries. With that in mind, this chapter also contains Argentine points of interest.

Southern Patagonia's main destination is Chile's Parque Nacional Torres del Paine and the seemingly obligatory 'W' trek. This primo park attracts hundreds of thousands of visitors every year, even some towing wheeled luggage (we don't recommend it). Yet there is plenty more here to explore. Don't miss the towering glaciers, windy sea passages and sprawling *estancias* (grazing ranches). Long before humans set foot on the continent, glaciers chiseled and carved these fine landscapes. And their power still resonates.

SOUTHERN PATAGONIA

HIGHLIGHTS

- Wander a fairy-tale forest to Valle Francés' stunning rock amphitheater in **Parque Nacional Torres del Paine** (p395)
- Join the march of the penguins among the population of thousands at **Isla Magdalena** (p384)
- Clomp through the cool blue contours of 15-story **Glaciar Perito Moreno** (p404) on an ice trek
- Get why ancient Tehuelches dubbed the gnarled volcanic steppe **Parque Nacional Pali Aike** (p385) Devil's Country
- Ride the range and trade fireside yarns at a working *estancia* on **Seno Skyring** (p384)

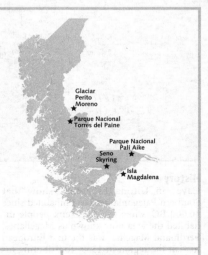

| POPULATION: 155,000 | AREA: 132,297 SQ KM | ELEVATION: 0–3600M |

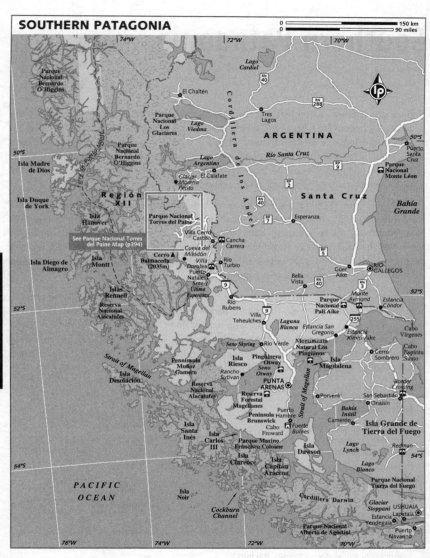

SOUTHERN PATAGONIA

See Parque Nacional Torres del Paine Map (p394)

History

Caves in Última Esperanza show that Southern Patagonia has been inhabited since 10,000 BC, when the Aonikenk people inhabited the area now known as Magellanes. Ferdinand Magellan was the first European to visit the region in 1520, contributing his name but not much else.

It was to be a land of adventurers. Chilean writer Francisco Coloane described those who ventured here as 'courageous men whose hearts were no more than another closed fist.' Missionaries and fortune seekers lived in hardship and isolation. The area finally started to develop when the California gold rush brought trade via the ships that sailed the straits on journeys between Europe and California and Australia.

In the late 19th century the formation of *estancias* and the regional wool boom that followed had massive, reverberating effects for both Chilean and Argentine Patagonia. Great wealth for a few was gained at the cost of native populations, who were all but wiped out by disease and warfare.

The opening of the Panama Canal in 1914 reduced traffic around Cabo de Hornos and the area's international importance diminished.

Today fisheries, silviculture, small oil reserves and methanol production, in addition to a fast-growing tourism industry, keep the region relatively prosperous compared to other regions of Chile.

Climate

Be prepared for harsh weather – and that does not just mean cold. Wind and strong sun are also issues, and the weather can go through a full four seasons in the course of a day. The ozone hole over Antarctica means that the UV levels are stronger here (particularly in the spring, October and November) and you should take precautions to prevent sunburn. Temperature ranges fluctuate throughout the region, throughout the season and throughout the day. While most of the city areas receive little snow, they can get quite cold in the winter (though temperatures rarely drop below 0°C). January and February are the height of summer, while July and August are the heart of winter.

Getting There & Away

The easiest way to get to Southern Patagonia is to fly from Santiago or Puerto Montt to Punta Arenas. There are multiple flights daily and less frequent flights from a few other major Chilean cities. Other transportation options include the Navimag ferry from Puerto Montt to Puerto Natales (see p319), or a long bus trip from Puerto Montt that tucks into Argentina and then pops back over to Punta Arenas.

Getting Around

Unlike most of Patagonia, the roads around Punta Arenas are paved and smooth – a pleasure after all those bumpy bus rides. Buses to major destinations are frequent but should be booked ahead in summer. A new gravel road from outside Puerto Natales into Parque Nacional Torres del Paine cuts down travel time considerably. Travelers must fly or take a ferry to get to Porvenir or Puerto Williams, but be aware that schedules change frequently.

CROSSING INTO ARGENTINA

Transportation between Argentina and Chile is frequent and easy, with crossing the border a normal daily occurrence for locals, on par with a trip to the bank. This chapter includes the most-visited Argentine spots for Chilean travelers. The Chilean entry fee (US$132 for residents of USA and Canada, US$56 for Australian residents) does not have to be paid again upon re-entry as it is valid for the life of the passport. There is no Argentine consulate between Puerto Montt and Punta Arenas, so if you need a visa before you reach either of these towns get one at the Argentine consulate in Santiago.

Do not cross the border where there are no officials to stamp you through or you will risk expulsion. The most-used border crossings are at Cancha Carrera, between Torres del Paine and El Calafate, and Monte Aymond, between Punta Arenas and Río Gallegos.

Frequent buses link Puerto Natales with the Argentine towns El Calafate and El Chaltén, and Punta Arenas with Ushuaia; in fact, many travelers fly into Ushuaia as the starting point for southern explorations. If you travel from Ushuaia to Chile's Isla Navarino by boat, make sure to visit customs at the airport.

For expanded coverage of the Argentine destinations, see Lonely Planet's *Argentina*.

MAGALLANES

It is hard to believe that this rugged, weather-battered land has actually been inhabited for hundreds, if not thousands, of years. While its modern inhabitants have little in common with natives who once paddled the channels in canoes and hunted guanacos, they still remain cut off from the rest of the continent by formidable mountains and chilly waters. A supreme sense of isolation (and hospitality) is what attracts most visitors to Magallanes. The only way to get here from the rest of Chile is by air or sea, or by road through Argentine Patagonia.

While the capital, Punta Arenas, offers all of the conveniences of a major Chilean city, its surroundings are desolate, raw and often bleak. Here visitors will find the pioneering end-of-the-world feeling recent and real.

Magallanes' modern economy depends on commerce, petroleum development and fisheries. Prosperity means it has some of the highest levels of employment and school attendance, and some of the best quality housing and public services in Chile.

PUNTA ARENAS
☎ 061 / pop 130,136

A sprawling metropolis on the edge of the Strait of Magellan, Punta Arenas defies easy definition. It's a strange combination of the ruddy and the grand, witnessed in the elaborate wool-boom mansions and port renovations contrasted with windblown streams of litter and urban sprawl. Set at the bottom of the Americas, it is downright stingy with good weather – the sun shines through sidelong rain.

Magellanic hospitality still pervades local culture, undeterred (or perhaps nurtured by) nature's inhospitality. The city is remarkably relaxed and friendly. Recent prosperity, fed by a petrochemical industry boom and growing population, has sanded down the city's former roughneck reputation. It would be nice if it were all about restoration but duty-free shopping and mega malls on the city outskirts are the order of the future.

Easy connections to Tierra del Fuego and Torres del Paine and Argentina, and good traveler's services make Punta Arenas a convenient base for traveling. A growing volume of cruise-ship passengers and trekkers have effectively replaced yesteryear's explorers, sealers and sailors.

History

Little more than 150 years old, Punta Arenas was originally a military garrison and penal settlement conveniently situated for ships headed to California during the gold rush in later years. Compared to the initial Chilean settlement at Fuerte Bulnes, 60km south, the town had a better, more protected harbor, and superior access to wood and water. English maritime charts dubbed the site Sandy Point, and thus it became known as its Spanish equivalent.

In its early years Punta Arenas lived off natural resources, including sealskins, guanaco hides and feathers, as well as mineral products (including coal and gold), guano, timber and firewood. The economy didn't take off until the last quarter of the 19th century, after the territorial governor authorized the purchase of 300 purebred sheep from the Falkland Islands. This successful experiment encouraged others to invest in sheep, and by the turn of the century nearly two million animals grazed the territory.

The area's commercial and pastoral empires were built on the backs of international immigrant labor, including English, Irish, Scots, Croats, French, Germans, Spaniards, Italians and others. Many locals trace their family origins to these diverse settlers. Today evidence of this mass migration can be seen in the street names throughout town and on headstones in the cemetery. Church services are still held in English, while the many mansions created by the wealthy are now hotels, banks and museums.

Orientation

Punta Arenas' regular grid street plan, with wide streets and sidewalks, makes it easy to navigate. Plaza Muñoz Gamero, also known as the Plaza de Armas, is the center of town. Street names change on either side of the plaza, but street addresses fronting the plaza bear the name Muñoz Gamero. Most landmarks and accommodations are within a few blocks of here.

Av Costanera parallels the rocky coast, which is predominantly industrial. The avenue continues south of town toward Fuerte Bulnes. Both Av España and Av Bulnes are main thoroughfares to the north of the city (the latter accesses the large duty-free shopping area known as the Zona Franca). Both roads head to the airport and to Ruta 9, which goes to Puerto Natales.

MAPS

The Sernatur tourist office (opposite), hotels and other touristy establishments have city brochures with useful maps of Punta Arenas.

Information
BOOKSTORES

World's End (☎ 213-117; Plaza Gamero 1011) Maps, photo books, souvenirs and Lonely Planet guides in English and Spanish.

EMERGENCY
Police (☎ 241-714; Errázuriz 977)

INTERNET ACCESS
Lodgings, cafés and telephone call centers also have internet access.
Chill-e (Colón 782; ☒ 9:30am-12:30am Mon-Fri, 11-12:30am Sat, 3-11pm Sun) A comfy art deco space with long hours and wi-fi connections.

INTERNET RESOURCES
Punta Arenas (www.puntaarenas.cl, in Spanish) The municipality's website.

LAUNDRY
Hostels do laundry for a bit less.
Lavasol (☎ 243-067; O'Higgins 969; per load CH$3000; ☒ 7am-7pm)

MEDICAL SERVICES
Sernatur has a list of recommended doctors.
Hospital Regional (☎ 205-000; Angamos 180; ☒ 24hr)

MONEY
Travel agencies in the center along Roca and Lautaro Navarro change cash and traveler's checks. All are open weekdays and Saturday, with a few open on Sunday morning. Banks with ATMs dot the city center.

POST
Post office (Bories 911) Located one block north of Plaza Muñoz Gamero.

TELEPHONE
Telefónica (Nogueira 1116)

TOURIST INFORMATION
Conaf (☎ 230-681; Bulnes 0309) Has details on the nearby parks.
Information kiosk (☎ 200-610; www.puntaarenas.cl, in Spanish; Plaza Muñoz Gamero; ☒ 8am-7pm Mon-Sat, 9am-7pm Sun) South side of the plaza.
Sernatur (☎ 241-330; www.sernatur.cl; infoma gallanes@sernatur.cl; Lautaro Navarro 999; ☒ 8:15am-8pm Mon-Fri Dec-Feb, 8:15am-6pm Mon-Thu, 8:15am-5pm Fri rest of year) With friendly, well-informed, multilingual staff and lists of accommodations and transportation.

Sights
PLAZA MUÑOZ GAMERO
Magnificent conifers line this central plaza in the heart of Punta Arenas, surrounded by opulent mansions, including the former Sara Braun mansion, open for visits. The monument commemorating the 400th anniversary of Magellan's voyage was donated by wool baron José Menéndez in 1920. Within the Sara Braun mansion is the **Club de la Unión** (☎ 241-489; admission CH$1000; ☒ 10:30am-1pm & 5-8:30pm Tue-Fri, 10:30am-1pm & 8-10pm Sat, 11am-2pm Sun). Just east is the former Sociedad Menéndez Behety, which now houses Turismo Comapa (p379). The **cathedral** sits west.

RESERVA FORESTAL MAGALLANES
This **reserve** (admission free; ☒ daylight hr), 8km from town, offers great hiking and mountain biking through dense lenga and coigue. A steady slog takes you to the top of Mt Fenton, where views are spectacular and winds impressively strong.

MUSEO REGIONAL BRAUN-MENÉNDEZ
Also known as the Palacio Mauricio Braun, this opulent mansion testifies to the wealth and power of pioneer sheep farmers in the late 19th century. One of Mauricio Braun's sons donated the house to the state against other family members' wishes. The well-maintained interior is divided into one part regional historical museum (booklets with English descriptions are available) and the other half displays the original exquisite French art nouveau family furnishings, from the intricate wooden inlay floors to Chinese vases.

The **museum** (☎ 244-216; Magallanes 949; admission CH$1000, Sun free; ☒ 10:30am-5pm Mon-Sat, 10:30am-2pm Sun in summer, to 2pm daily in winter) is most easily accessed from Magallanes. There's a café downstairs in what used to be the servants' quarters.

CEMENTERIO MUNICIPAL
Among South America's most fascinating cemeteries, **Cementerio Municipal** (Av Bulnes 949; ☒ 7:30am-8pm) contains a mix of humble immigrant graves and extravagant tombs under topiary cypresses. In death as in life, Punta Arenas' first families flaunted their wealth – wool baron José Menéndez's extravagant tomb is, according to Bruce Chatwin, a scale replica of Rome's Vittorio Emanuele monument. But the headstones also tell the stories of Anglo, German, Scandinavian and Yugoslav immigrants. There's also a monument to the Selk'nam (Onas) and a map posted inside the main entrance gate.

PUNTA ARENAS

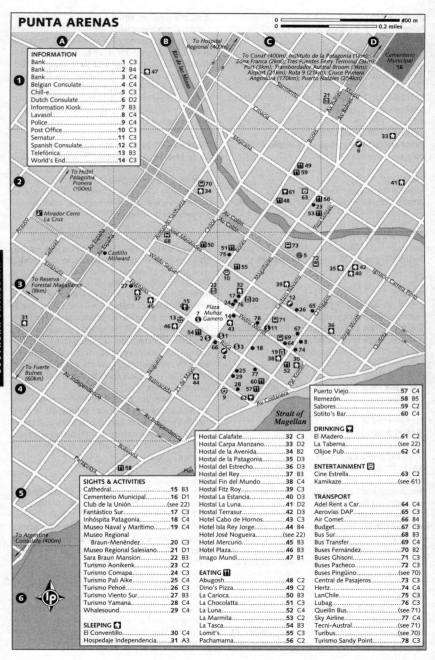

0		400 m
0		0.2 miles

INFORMATION
Bank	1 C3
Bank	2 B4
Bank	3 C4
Belgian Consulate	4 C4
Chill-e	5 C3
Dutch Consulate	6 D2
Information Kiosk	7 B3
Lavasol	8 C4
Police	9 C4
Post Office	10 C3
Sernatur	11 C3
Spanish Consulate	12 C3
Telefónica	13 B3
World's End	14 C3

To Hospital Regional (400m)

To Conar (400m); Instituto de la Patagonia (1km); Zona Franca (2km); Tres Puentes Ferry Terminal (3km); Port (3km); Transbordador Austral Broom (3km); Airport (21km); Ruta 9 (21km); Cruce Primera Angostura (170km); Puerto Natales (254km)

Cementerio Municipal

To Hotel Patagonia Pionera (100m)

Mirador Cerro La Cruz

To Reserva Forestal Magallanes (8km)

Castillo Milward

Plaza Muñoz Gamero

To Fuerte Bulnes (60km)

Strait of Magellan

To Argentine Consulate (400m)

SIGHTS & ACTIVITIES
Cathedral	15 B3
Cementerio Municipal	16 D1
Club de la Unión	(see 22)
Fantástico Sur	17 C3
Inhóspita Patagonia	18 C4
Museo Naval y Marítimo	19 C4
Museo Regional Braun-Menéndez	20 C3
Museo Regional Salesiano	21 D1
Sara Braun Mansion	22 B3
Turismo Aonikenk	23 C2
Turismo Comapa	24 C3
Turismo Pali Aike	25 C4
Turismo Pehoé	26 C3
Turismo Viento Sur	27 B3
Turismo Yamana	28 C4
Whalesound	29 C4

SLEEPING
El Conventillo	30 C4
Hospedaje Independencia	31 A3

EATING
Abugosh	48 C2
Dino's Pizza	49 C2
La Carioca	50 B3
La Chocolatta	51 C3
La Luna	52 C4
La Marmita	53 C2
La Tasca	54 B3
Lomit's	55 C3
Pachamama	56 C2

Hostal Calafate	32 C3
Hostal Carpa Manzano	33 D2
Hostal de la Avenida	34 B2
Hostal de la Patagonia	35 D3
Hostal del Estrecho	36 D3
Hostal del Rey	37 B3
Hostal Fin del Mundo	38 C3
Hostal Fitz Roy	39 C3
Hostal La Estancia	40 D3
Hostal La Luna	41 D2
Hostal Terrasur	42 D3
Hotel Cabo de Hornos	43 C3
Hotel Isla Rey Jorge	44 B4
Hotel José Nogueira	(see 22)
Hotel Mercurio	45 B3
Hotel Plaza	46 B3
Imago Mundi	47 B1

Puerto Viejo	57 C4
Remezón	58 B5
Sabores	59 C2
Sotito's Bar	60 C4

DRINKING
El Madero	61 C2
La Taberna	(see 22)
Olijoe Pub	62 C4

ENTERTAINMENT
Cine Estrella	63 C2
Kamikaze	(see 61)

TRANSPORT
Adel Rent a Car	64 C4
Aerovías DAP	65 C3
Air Comet	66 B4
Budget	67 C4
Bus Sur	68 B3
Bus Transfer	69 C4
Buses Fernández	70 B2
Buses Ghisoni	71 C3
Buses Pacheco	72 C3
Buses Pingüino	(see 70)
Central de Pasajeros	73 C3
Hertz	74 C4
LanChile	75 C3
Lubag	76 C3
Queilin Bus	(see 71)
Sky Airline	77 C4
Tecni-Austral	(see 71)
Turibus	(see 70)
Turismo Sandy Point	78 C3

SOUTHERN PATAGONIA

The main entrance to the cemetery is on Bulnes, an easy 15-minute stroll northeast of the plaza, or catch any *taxi colectivo* (shared cab with specific route) from in front of the Museo Regional Braun-Menéndez on Magallanes.

MUSEO NAVAL Y MARÍTIMO

Punta Arenas' naval and maritime **museum** (☎ 205-479; Pedro Montt 981; adult/child CH$1500/800; ◷ 9:30am-12:30pm & 3-6pm Tue-Sat) has varied exhibits on model ships, naval history, the unprecedented visit of 27 US warships to Punta Arenas in 1908 and a fine account of the Chilean mission that rescued British explorer Sir Ernest Shackleton's crew from Antarctica. The most imaginative display is a ship's replica, complete with bridge, maps, charts and radio room.

MUSEO REGIONAL SALESIANO

Especially influential in settling the region, the Salesian order collected outstanding ethnographic artifacts, but their **museum** (☎ 221-001; Av Bulnes 336; admission CH$1500; ◷ 10am-12:30pm & 3-6pm Tue-Sun) touts their role as peacemakers between Indians and settlers. The best materials are on indigenous groups and the mountaineer priest Alberto de Agostini.

INSTITUTO DE LA PATAGONIA

Pioneer days are made real again at the Patagonian Institute's **Museo del Recuerdo** (☎ 207-056; www.umag.cl, in Spanish; Av Bulnes 01890; admission CH$1000; ◷ 8:30am-11am & 2:30-6pm Mon-Fri), part of the Universidad de Magallanes. On display are a collection of antique farm and industrial machinery, a typical pioneer house and shearing shed, and a wooden-wheeled shepherds' trailer. The library has historical maps and a series of historical and scientific publications. Any *taxi colectivo* to the Zona Franca (duty-free zone) will drop you across the street.

Tours

Worthwhile day trips include tours to the **Seno Otway Pingüinera** (penguin colony; ◷ Oct-March), located 65km north. Tours (CH$15,000) leave at 4pm daily; see p384. Visits to the town's first settlements at **Fuerte Bulnes** and **Puerto Hambre** (historical site admission CH$1000) leave at 10am. Both tours can be done in one day; by sharing a rental car and visiting the sites in reverse order, you can avoid the strings of tour

groups. Most lodgings either help to arrange tours or run their own operations.

If you have the time, a more atmospheric alternative to Seno Otway is **Isla Magdalena** (adult/child CH$15,000/7500) and its thriving Magellanic penguin colonies. Five-hour tours on the *Melinka* ferry land for an hour at the island and depart the port on Tuesday, Thursday and Saturday from December through February. Confirm times in advance. Book tickets through **Turismo Comapa** (☎ 200-200; www.comapa .com; Magallanes 990) and bring a picnic.

Tours to Parque Nacional Torres del Paine are abundant from Punta Arenas, but the distance makes for a very long day; it's best to head to Puerto Natales (p388) and organize transport from there.

Recommended agencies:

Fantástico Sur (☎ 710-050; www.lostorres.com; Magallanes 960)

Inhóspita Patagonia (☎ 224-510; Lautaro Navarro 1013) Does trekking trips to Cabo Froward, the southernmost point on mainland South America.

Turismo Aonikenk (☎ 228-332; www.aonikenk.com; Magallanes 619) English-, German- and French-speaking guides.

Turismo Pali Aike (☎ 223-301; www.turismopaliaike .com; Lautaro Navarro 1129)

Turismo Pehoé (☎ 244-506; www.pehoe.com; José Menéndez 918)

Turismo Viento Sur (☎ 226-930; www.vientosur.com; Fagnano 565)

Turismo Yamana (☎ 221-130, www.yamana.cl; Errazurriz 972) Kayaking trips on Magellan Strait.

Whalesound (☎ 221-076; www.whalesound.com; Lautaro Navarro 1163, 2nd fl) Supports science with study-based sailing and kayak trips to the remote Coloane Marine Park. Humpback whale-watching trips are available from December to May.

Festivals & Events

Winter solstice The longest night of the year is celebrated on June 21.

Carnaval de Invierno (Winter Carnival) This two-day carnival, held in the last week of July, is a big party that kicks off the beginning of the winter season with fireworks, floats and all of the standard carnival fanfare.

Sleeping

Almost all lodgings include a breakfast of tea or instant coffee, rolls and jam.

BUDGET

Hospedaje Independencia (☎ 227-572; Av Independencia 374; camping CH$1500, dm CH$4500)

Shoestring travelers pack this cheaper than cheap lodging, run by a young couple. Despite the chaos, rooms are reasonably clean and guests get kitchen use and bike rentals.

Hostal La Estancia (☎ 249-130; www.backpackers chile.com/en/hostel-estancia.php; O'Higgins 765; dm/d without bathroom CH$6500/20,000; 🖥) This slightly rickety residence has big rooms with vaulted ceilings and tidy shared bathrooms. Alex and Carmen are attentive hosts, generous with insider tips. It is nearly always booked, even in off-season, so reserve ahead.

Hostal Fitz Roy (☎ 240-430; www.hostalfitzroy .com; Lautaro Navarro 850; dm/s/d/tr without bathroom CH$7000/12,000/20,000/25,000; 🅿 🖥) A country house in the city, Fitz Roy offers rambling, good-value rooms and an inviting old-fashioned living room to pore over books or sea charts. Rooms have phones, TV and wi-fi connections. Accepts credit cards.

ourpick Imago Mundi (☎ 613-115; www.imago mundipatagonia.cl; Mejicana 252; dm with/without bathroom CH$10,000/8000; 🖥) A young brother-sister duo channeled their wanderlust into these cool digs with just eight snug bunks, electric colors and cozy spaces. The onsite café serves homemade treats, savory *pascualinas* (pies), sandwiches and natural juice. It's all environmentally conscious – the hostel has crafted tables out of old doors, recycles and composts organic waste. Look for a cultural center with arthouse movies and a climbing gym in the works.

El Conventillo (☎ 242-311; www.hostalconventillo .com; Pje. Korner 1034; dm CH$8000; 🖥) In the reviving waterfront district, this appealing brick hostel has remodeled, carpeted dorms and clean row showers. Bright colors mask the fact that rooms are windowless and teensy. But breakfast includes yogurt and cereal and there's 24-hour reception, laundry and a library of cool Chilean flicks.

Hostal La Luna (☎ 221-764; hostalluna@hotmail.com; O'Higgins 424; s/d without bathroom CH$8000/12,000; 🖥) Goose-down comforters and a scruffy tabby spell home at this friendly family lodging. Six tidy rooms have shared bath and guests get kitchen and laundry privileges.

Hostal del Rey (☎ 223-924; www.chileaustral .com/hdelrey; Fagnano 589; d CH$20,000, s/d/tr without bathroom CH$8000/16,000/24,000, 2-person apt CH$24,000; 🅿) Amid a haphazard decor of indigenous portraits, lace and kitsch, this cramped home features decent rooms with down-comforter beds. Apartments have full kitchens, hot water and TV.

Hostal Fin del Mundo (☎ 710-185; www.alfin delmundo.cl; O'Higgins 1026; s/d/tr without bathroom CH$10,000/20,000/24,000) On the 2nd and 3rd floors of a creaky downtown building, these cheerful rooms share bathrooms with hot showers and a large kitchen, but the shared space is rather dull.

MIDRANGE

Rates at midrange establishments include breakfast but don't reflect the additional 18% IVA charge, which foreigners in Chile aren't required to pay if paying with US cash, traveler's checks or credit card. Off-season (mid-April to mid-October) rates can drop by up to 40%.

Hostal Calafate (☎ 241-281; www.calafate.cl, in Spanish; Magallanes 922; s/d CH$27,000/38,500, without bathroom CH$17,500/27,000; 🅿 🖥) This downtown hub bustles with traffic. Guests can choose from a selection of plain but good rooms not quite insulated from the street noise below. Perks include phones, TV and central heating. A continental breakfast is included and there's a popular internet café in the lobby.

Hostal de la Avenida (☎ 710-744; Av Colón 534; s/d CH$28,000/37,000; 🅿) Chintzy but cozy, this mustard-yellow home has plants sprouting from a claw tub and other funky installations, the staff are pleasant and there's cable TV and central heating.

Hostal Terrasur (☎ 247-114; www.hostalterrasur.cl; O'Higgins 123; s/d CH$28,500/38,500; 🖥) The slightly upscale Terrasur nurtures a secret garden atmosphere, from its rooms with flowing curtains and flower patterns to the miniature green courtyard. There's also friendly desk service.

Hostal Carpa Manzano (☎ 710-744; www.hotelcarpa manzano.com; Lautaro Navarro 336; s/d CH$30,000/35,000; 🅿) These snappy colored rooms feature private bathroom, carpet and cable TV. A comfortable house, though it's run more like a hotel, with uniformed staff and formal airs.

Hostal de la Patagonia (☎ 249-970; www.ecotour patagonia.com; O'Higgins 730; s/d CH$30,000/35,000; 🅿) This unmistakable turquoise lodging offers eight sunny rooms with light wood accents and a decent buffet breakfast. Tour bookings and car hire are available.

Hotel Mercurio (☎ 242-300; www.chileaustral.com /mercurio; Fagano 595; s/d/tr incl breakfast CH$45,000/ 53,000/62,000) Well kept and proper, this corner hotel boasts wide staircases that lead to slightly dated stucco rooms. The staff are bilingual and very accommodating.

Hotel Plaza (☎ 241-300; www.hotelplaza.cl; Nogueira 1116; s/d CH$50,000/62,000; 🖥) This converted mansion just off the plaza boasts vaulted ceilings, plaza views and historical photos lining the hall. Inconsistent with such grandeur, the country decor is unfortunate. But service is genteel and the location unbeatable.

Hotel Patagonia Pionera (☎ 222-045; www.hotelpatagoniapionera.cl; Arauco 786; d CH$55,200) While a little bland to be boutique, this immaculate restored brick mansion does provide an elegant and more intimate alternative to the big downtown hotels. Do expect crisp white duvets, tangerine accents and super-shiny hardwood floors. It's in a well-heeled residential neighborhood.

TOP END

Hotel Isla Rey Jorge (☎ 248-220; www.hotelislareyjorge.com; 21 de Mayo 1243; s/d/ste CH$60,000/74,000/100,000; 🅿 🖥) Elegant and relaxed, this 1918 house exudes character; we just wonder about the cannon on the lawn. Traditional British style is flaunted with 25 attractive rooms and a sun room for reading.

Hotel José Nogueira (☎ 248-840; www.hotelnogueira.com; Bories 959; s/d incl breakfast CH$80,000/95,000; 🅿 🖥) This high-end hotel in the Sara Braun mansion lacks the original grandeur, but staff ghost sightings and the beautiful atrium dining room (mains CH$6500) rescue some of the romance. Modern amenities combine with period furnishings in rooms and the lobby is wired for wi-fi.

Hotel Cabo de Hornos (☎ 242-134; www.hoteles-australis.com; Plaza Muñoz Gamero 1025; s/d CH$90,000/100,000; 🅿 ✕ 🖥) This smart business hotel begins with a cool interior of slate and sharp angles, but rooms are more relaxed, with bright color accents and top-notch views. The well-heeled bar just beckons you to have a scotch.

Eating

The port's seasonal seafood is an exquisite treat. *Centolla* (king crab) comes in season between July and November. For *erizos* (sea urchins) try between November and July. If heading to Torres del Paine, get groceries here beforehand.

BUDGET

Abugosh (Bories 647) A large, well-stocked supermarket.

Pachamama (☎ 226-171; Magallanes 619-A) A natural market with bulk trail-mix munchies and organic products.

La Chocolatta (☎ 248-150; Bories 852; coffee drinks CH$1200; 🕑 9:30am-8:30pm Mon-Sat, 11am-8pm Sun; 🖥) Serving bite-sized chocolates, tea and coffee, this granny-style café stays bustling with families and laptop addicts.

La Carioca (☎ 224-809; José Menéndez 600; sandwiches CH$2500) Cold lager and sandwiches are the mainstay at this downtown institution that overflows when there's a televised soccer match.

Dino's Pizza (☎ 247-434; Bories 557; mains CH$2500; 🕑 11am-11pm Wed-Mon) Dark but lively, this is the place for pizza pie; like most Chilean versions it's a little heavy on the cheese but popular with the local student crowd.

Lomit's (☎ 243-399; José Menéndez 722; mains CH$3000; 🕑 10am-2:30am) Chile's answer to the sidecar diner is this atmospheric café where cooks flip dripping made-to-order burgers at a center-stage griddle. Portions are generous but the service sure dallies.

Sabores (☎ 227-369; Mejicana 702, 2nd fl; mains CH$3500) Think grilled salmon, seafood stews and pasta. Low on pretense, this cozy spot serves up abundant Chilean fare at a price we like.

MIDRANGE

La Luna (☎ 228-555; O'Higgins 974; mains CH$4000-7000; 🕑 lunch & dinner) Serving tasty seafood concoctions and pastas, the lively Luna caters to an international crowd with prices that show it. Though overpriced, La Luna compensates with consistent quality and a friendly welcome.

La Tasca (☎ 242-807; Plaza Muñoz Gamero 771; mains CH$4000-8000) For great views, hit this local favorite in the stylish Casa España. Locals take advantage of the midweek lunch specials featuring fresh seafood.

La Marmita (☎ 222-056; Plaza Sampaio 678; mains CH$5000-8000) Unbeatable for ambiance, Marmita prepares fresh salads and hearty, home-cooked creations. It's certainly cozy – with bright colors, a crackling woodstove and the chef-owners circulating among guests. For a light entrée, try Pablo Neruda's *caldillo de congrio* (conger eel soup).

Puerto Viejo (☎ 225-103; O'Higgins 1176; mains CH$5000-8000) With curved walls like a ship's hull and raw wood details, this chic eatery sets sail with fresh options such as hake in

SOUTHERN PATAGONIA

cider and warm abalone salad. New ownership means the attention may not be quite as fussy.

TOP END

Remezón (☎ 241-029; 21 de Mayo 1469; mains CH$10,000) Take a cue from locals and start with a tart pisco sour. Then dive into the chef's game and seafood innovations: oysters and clams au gratin in their shells or salmon smoked with black tea, to name a few. Service is unpretentious and welcoming.

Sotito's Bar (☎ 243-565; O'Higgins 1138; mains CH$5000-12,000; ☽ lunch only Sun) When locals celebrate a special event, you'll find them here. Sotito's is a city classic, a long-lasting formal affair with top-notch seafood. Fresh crab and salmon smothered in seafood sauce are good picks.

Drinking

La Taberna (☎ 241-317; Sara Braun Mansion; ☽ 7pm-2am, to 3am weekends) A magnet for travelers, this dark and elegant pub is a classic old-boys club, with no old boys in sight. Ambiance is tops, but the mixed drinks could be better.

Olijoe Pub (☎ 223-728; Errázuriz 970; ☽ 6pm-2am) Leather booths and mosaic tabletops lend pretension but this is your usual pub with good beer and bad service. Mix it up with the house special, Glaciar: a mix of pisco, *horchata* (spiced rice milk), milk and curaçao.

El Madero (Bories 655) A warm-up spot for clubbers, Madero bustles with crowds sipping stiff drinks.

Entertainment

Kamikaze (☎ 248-744; Bories 655; cover CH$3000 with a free drink) Tiki-torches warm up this most southerly dance club and, if you're lucky, the occasional live rock band. It is upstairs from El Madero.

Cine Estrella (Mejicana 777) Shows first-run movies.

Shopping

Zona Franca (Zofri; ☽ closed Sun) The duty-free zone is a large, polished conglomeration of shops that is worth checking out if you're looking for electronics, outdoor gear, computer accessories or camera equipment. *Colectivos* shuttle back and forth from downtown along Av Bulnes throughout the day.

Getting There & Away

The tourist offices distribute a useful brochure which details all forms of transport available.

AIR

Book ahead online for the best **LanChile** (☎ 241-100, toll free 600-526-2000; www.lan.com; Bories 884) deals on national flights. Lan flies several times daily to Santiago (CH$194,000) with a stop in Puerto Montt (CH$124,000), and Saturdays to the Falkland Islands/Islas Malvinas (CH$250,000 round-trip). A new service goes direct three times a week to Ushuaia (CH$107,500).

Smaller **Air Comet** (☎ 227-766; toll free 600-625-000; www.aircometchile.cl; Roca 809, Local 2) offers direct, nonstop flights twice daily between Santiago and Punta Arenas, with an initial published advance-purchase fare of CH$73,000. **Sky Airline** (☎ 710-645; www.skyairline.cl; Roca 935) flies daily between Santiago and Punta Arenas, with a stop either in Puerto Montt or Concepción.

From November to March **Aerovías DAP** (☎ 223-340, airport 213776; www.dap.cl; O'Higgins 891) flies to Porvenir (CH$19,000) Monday through Saturday; to Puerto Williams (CH$52,000) Wednesday through Saturday and Monday. Luggage is limited to 10kg per person.

DAP also offers charter flights over Cabo de Hornos (seven-passenger plane CH$1,825,000) and to other Patagonian destinations, including Ushuaia and Calafate. Charters to Chile's Teniente Marsh air base in Antarctica tour Base Frei (one/two days CH$1,250,000/1,750,000); weather depending, the schedule permits one night in Antarctica before returning to Punta Arenas.

DAP also provides shuttle service (CH$2000) to the airport.

BOAT

Car ferry *Melinka*, operated by **Transbordador Austral Broom** (☎ 218-100; www.tabsa.cl, in Spanish; Av Bulnes 05075), sails to Porvenir, Tierra del Fuego (CH$4600, 2½ to four hours) from the Tres Puentes ferry terminal north of town; catch *taxi colectivos* in front of Museo Regional Braun-Menéndez. Boats usually depart in the early morning and return in the late afternoon six days a week in high season. Schedules and travel time depend on the mercurial weather. Make reservations to ferry your vehicle (CH$29,000) by calling the office.

A faster way to get to Tierra del Fuego (CH$1500, 20 minutes) is the Punta Delgada–Bahía Azul ('Cruce Primera Angostura') crossing, northeast of Punta Arenas. Broom ferries sail every 90 minutes between 8:30am and 10pm. Call ahead for vehicle reservations (CH$12,000).

Broom is also the agent for ferries from Tres Puentes to Puerto Williams (p415), on Isla Navarino. Ferries sail three or four times per month, Wednesday only, returning Saturday, both at 7pm (reclining seat/bunk CH$65,250/78,000 including meals, 38 hours) – trust us, the extra cost of a bunk is worthwhile.

September through May, **Cruceros Australis** (☎ in Santiago 02-442-3110; www.australis.com) runs breathtakingly scenic four- to seven-day luxury cruises aboard the 130-passenger MV *Mare Australis* and brand-new MV *Via Australis,* from Punta Arenas through the Cordillera Darwin, Parque Nacional Alberto de Agostini, the Beagle Channel, Puerto Williams and Ushuaia (Argentina), and back. Rates for three nights start from CH$495,000 per person, double occupancy in low season (September–October and mid-March–April) and reach CH$1,100,000 for a high-season single. Most passengers only sail one leg. Departures from Ushuaia include a possibility of disembarking at Cape Horn. Turismo Comapa (p387) handles local bookings.

BUS

A central terminal is perennially promised; in the meanwhile, depart from company offices, most within a block or two of Av Colón. Buy tickets at least a couple of hours (if not a day or two during summer) in advance. The **Central de Pasajeros** (☎ 245-811; cnr Magallanes & Av Colón) is the closest thing to a central booking office.

For Ushuaia, Buses Ghisoni continues direct, but travelers report Buses Pacheco stops too long in Río Grande. In Río Grande minivans (Lider or Transportes Montiel) go to Ushuaia throughout the day and may cost slightly less (depending on exchange rates) than a through ticket.

Companies and daily destinations:

Buses Fernández/Pingüino (☎ 221-429/812; www .busesfernandez.com; Armando Sanhueza 745) Puerto Natales, Torres del Paine and Río Gallegos.

Buses Ghisoni/Queilen Bus (☎ 222-714; Lautaro Navarro 975) Río Gallegos, Río Grande, Ushuaia and Puerto Montt.

Buses Pacheco (☎ 225-527; www.busespacheco.com; Av Colón 900) Puerto Natales, Puerto Montt, Río Grande, Río Gallegos and Ushuaia.

Bus Sur (☎ 614-224; www.bus-sur.cl) José Menéndez 552) El Calafate, Puerto Natales, Río Gallegos, Río Turbio, Ushuaia and Puerto Montt.

Bus Transfer (☎ 229-613; Pedro Montt 966) Puerto Natales and airport transfers.

Tecni-Austral (☎ 222-078; Lautaro Navarro 975) Río Grande.

Turíbus (☎ 227-970; www.busescruzdelsur.cl, in Spanish; Armando Sanhueza 745) Puerto Montt, Osorno and Chiloé.

Destination	Cost (CH$)	Duration (hr)
Puerto Montt	35,000	36
Puerto Natales	4000	3
Río Gallegos	7000	5-8
Río Grande	15,000	8
Ushuaia	24,000	10

Getting Around
TO/FROM THE AIRPORT

The door-to-door shuttle service operated by **Turismo Sandy Point** (☎ 222-241; Pedro Montt 840; CH$3000) runs to/from town to coincide with flights. Bus Fernandez does regular airport transfers (CH$2500).

To get to Puerto Natales, there's no need to go into Punta Arenas since buses depart directly from the airport, 21km north of town.

BUS & COLECTIVO

Taxi colectivos, with numbered routes, are only slightly more expensive than buses (about CH$450, a bit more late at night and on Sundays), far more comfortable and much quicker.

CAR

Cars are a good option for exploring Torres del Paine but renting one in Chile to cross the border into Argentina becomes prohibitively expensive due to international insurance requirements. If heading for El Calafate, it's best to rent in Argentina. Purchasing a car to explore Patagonia has its drawbacks. Chilean Patagonia has no through roads that link Northern and Southern Patagonia, so travel is largely dependent on Argentine roads or expensive ferry travel.

Punta Arenas has Chilean Patagonia's most economical rental rates, and locally owned agencies tend to provide better service. Recommended **Adel Rent a Car** (☎ 235-471/2,

099-882-7569; www.adelrentacar.cl; Pedro Montt 962) provides attentive service, competitive rates, airport pickup and good travel tips. Other choices include **Budget** (☎ 202-720; O'Higgins 964), **Hertz** (☎ 248-742; O'Higgins 987) and **Lubag** (☎ 242-023; Magallanes 970).

AROUND PUNTA ARENAS
Penguin Colonies
There are two substantial Magellanic penguin colonies near Punta Arenas: easier to reach is **Seno Otway** (Otway Sound) with about 6000 breeding pairs, about an hour northwest of the city, while the larger (50,000 breeding pairs) and more interesting **Monumento Natural Los Pingüinos** is accessible only by boat to Isla Magdalena in the Strait of Magellan (p379). Neither is as impressive as the larger penguin colonies in Argentina or the Falkland Islands. Tours to Seno Otway usually leave in the afternoon; however, visiting in the morning is best for photography because the birds are mostly backlit in the afternoon.

Since there is no scheduled public transport to either site, it's necessary to rent a car or join a tour. Admission to Seno Otway is CH\$2000, while admission to Isla Magdalena is included in the tour. Of the two options, the trip to Isla Magdalena is more often recommended.

Puerto Hambre & Fuerte Bulnes
Founded in 1584 by Pedro Sarmiento de Gamboa, 'Ciudad del Rey don Felipe' was one of Spain's most inauspicious and short-lived South American outposts. Its inhabitants struggled against the elements and starved to death at what is now known as Puerto Hambre (Port Hunger).

In May 1843 Chilean president Manuel Bulnes sent the schooner *Ancud,* manned by Chilotes and captained by John Williams, a former English officer, to Magallanes to occupy this southern area, then only sparsely populated by indigenous peoples. Four months later on September 21, when the *Ancud* arrived at Puerto Hambre, Williams declared the area Chilean territory and began to establish camp on a hilltop, dubbed Fuerte Bulnes. The exposed site, lack of potable water, rocky soil and inferior pasture soon made him abandon the site and move northward to a more sheltered area, originally called Punta Arenosa.

A decent gravel road runs 60km south from Punta Arenas to the restored wooden fort,

where a fence of sharpened stakes surrounds the blockhouse, barracks and chapel. There isn't any scheduled public transportation but several tour companies make half-day excursions to Fuerte Bulnes and Puerto Hambre; for details, see p379.

Cabo Froward
The most southerly point on the continent, Cabo Froward (Cape Froward) is 90km south of Punta Arenas and accessible by a two-day hike along wind-whipped cliffs. At the cape, a 365m hill leads to an enormous cross, originally erected by Señor Fagnano in 1913 but the latest one was erected in 1987 for Pope John Paul II's visit. Camping is possible along the trail; ask about guided hikes at any of the tour companies in Punta Arenas (p379) or Puerto Natales–based Erratic Rock (p388).

Faro San Isidro, about 15km before Cabo Froward, is a lighthouse near the base of Monte Tarn (830m). This rugged area is home to prolific bird life and some good hiking. It's also a launch point for humpback whale-watching trips to Isla Carlos III in **Parque Marino Francisco Coloane**, Chile's first marine park. Humpbacks and Minke whales feed seasonally here between December and May. Package stays are available at **Hostería Faro San Isidro** (☎ 061-221-076; www.whalesound.com; Punta Arenas; 2-day packages CH\$180,000 per person), which also offers kayaking, hiking and whale watching through Whalesound (p379).

Río Verde
☎ 61 / pop 300
About 50km north of Punta Arenas, a graveled lateral leads northwest toward Seno Skyring (Skyring Sound), passing this former *estancia* before rejoining Ruta 9 at Villa Tehuelches at Km100. Only visitors with a car should consider this interesting detour to one of the region's best-maintained assemblages of Magellanic architecture.

Ranch life spills from the pores of **Estancia Río Verde** (☎ 311-131/123; www.estanciarioverde.cl; Ruta Y50 Km97; d incl breakfast CH\$57,000), a working sheep ranch and horse-breeding farm on the shores of Skyring Sound. Its gracious English-speaking host Josefina keeps a relaxed atmosphere while Sergio runs the ranch hands-on; or maybe it's the other way around. Regardless, a ride around the property affords an interesting close-up of operations. Rodeos are held at the *medialuna* (a traditional half-moon stadium)

SOUTHERN PATAGONIA

WANTED: THE ULTIMATE ADVENTURE

Considered the most savage of adventure races, February's annual **Patagonia Expedition Race** (www.patagoniaexpedition race.com) is a grueling 600km slog through roadless mountains, wind-whipped oceans and squelchy peat bogs. Amateurs can get a taste too now. Organizer Nomads (www .nomads.cl) customizes VIP expedition-style adventure trips for nonpros. You'll hardly get a break – the trailless terrain is just as rugged – but vacationers don't have to beat the clock. Just themselves.

in the summer; there are also sailing, fishing and sightseeing trips on offer. Guests stay in a beautiful restored *casco* (the main house of the *estancia*) with 14 elegant rooms.

The kitchen churns out regional delicacies, including Patagonian lamb, with fresh bread, garden vegetables and plenty of wine. Passersby can stop for lunch (CH$5000) and check out the small museum. It's 43km north of Punta Arenas via Route 9; follow gravel road Y50 to Km97.

Isla Riesco

Just across the sound from Río Verde is Isla Riesco, whose western half is protected as the **Reserva Nacional Alacalufes**, an area that's close to impossible to access. Nearby, however, is the 270 sq km *estancia*-cum-private-park Monte León. Preferring preservation to logging, the owner of Monte León sold it to conservation group **Fundación Yendegaia** (☎ 02-204-1914; fax 02-209-2527; yendegaia@patagonia.com). A number of trails allow for multiday hikes in the area, but note that rain is a constant feature. Evergreen forests are found in the higher elevations, while near the ocean trees are wind-battered into unnatural contortions. Condors soar overhead and the elusive huemul makes an occasional showing. Boats across the sound can be expensive. For information on the park, contact the conservation group.

Visitors can get way off the beaten track at **Rancho Sutivan** (☎ 061-615-390; www.ranchosutivan .cl; r per person with all meals & activities CH$90,000) for a dose of the real rural Magellanes. Guests go hiking and horseback riding in pristine areas. A cottage which holds up to eight is ideal for family or groups of friends. Contact Margarita Jutronich.

Río Rubens

Roughly midway between Villa Tehuelches and Puerto Natales on blustery, paved Ruta 9, Río Rubens is a fine trout-fishing area and, for travelers with their own transport, an ideal spot to break the 250km journey from Punta Arenas.

An old-style country inn, **Hotel Río Rubens** (☎ 099-640-1583; www.hotelriorubens.cl, in Spanish; Km 183; r per person incl breakfast CH$8000; **P**) has more than a few tales told in its worn wooden floors and simple, ample rooms. It's worth a stop for a steak sandwich (CH$3000) and fries at the downstairs restaurant.

Parque Nacional Pali Aike

Rugged volcanic steppe pocked with craters, caves and twisted formations, Pali Aike translated from the Tehuelche language means 'devil's country.' This dry and desolate landscape is a 50 sq km park along the Argentine border, west of the Monte Aymond border crossing to Río Gallegos. It is a complete contrast from the terrain of Torres del Paine. Lava rocks can be red, yellow or green-grey, depending on their mineral content. Fauna includes abundant guanaco, ñandu, grey fox, armadillo and bats. In the 1930s Junius Bird's excavations at 17m-deep **Pali Aike Cave** yielded the first Paleo-Indian artifacts associated with extinct New World fauna such as the milodon and the native horse *Onohippidium*.

The **park** (admission CH$1000) has several hiking trails, including a 1700m path through the rugged lava beds of the **Escorial del Diablo** to the impressive **Crater Morada del Diablo**; wear sturdy shoes or your feet could be shredded. There are hundreds of craters, some as high as a four-story building. There's also a 9km trail from Cueva Pali Aike to **Laguna Ana**, where there's another shorter trail to a site on the main road, 5km from the park entrance.

The *portería* (entrance gate) has a basic *refugio* (CH$6000) that holds four guests. Parque Nacional Pali Aike is 200km northeast of Punta Arenas via Ruta 9, Ch 25 and a graveled secondary road from Cooperativa Villa O'Higgins, 11km north of Estancia Kimiri Aike. There's also an access road from the Chilean border post at Monte Aymond. There is no public transport but Punta Arenas travel agencies (see p379) offer full-day tours from CH$38,000.

ÚLTIMA ESPERANZA

With a name that translates to last hope, the once-remote Última Esperanza fills the imagination with foreboding. Storms wrestle the vast expanse and the landscape falls nothing short of grand; after all, Parque Nacional Torres del Paine and part of the Southern Patagonian Ice Field are in the back yard. Often lumped together with neighboring Magallanes, Última Esperanza is a separate southern province. While it can still be a challenging place to travel in winter, it is no longer so far off the beaten path. In fact, the tourism boom has transformed parts of it from rustic to outright decadent; still, there's something for everyone here.

PUERTO NATALES

☎ 061 / pop 18,000

A formerly modest fishing port on Seno Última Esperanza, Puerto Natales has blossomed into a Gore-Tex mecca. The gateway to Parque Nacional Torres del Paine, this town is reaping the benefits of its business savvy: boutique beers and wine tastings are overtaking tea time and gear shops have already replaced the yarn sellers. The town now feeds off tourism, and it's an all-you-can-eat feast with unwavering demand. While some sectors cater to international tastes, there's appeal in Natales' corrugated tin houses strung shoulder to shoulder and cozy granny-style lodgings. Most notably, in spite of a near-constant swarm of summer visitors, the town still maintains the glacial pace of living endemic to Patagonia.

Puerto Natales sits on the shores of Seno Última Esperanza, 250km northwest of Punta Arenas via Ruta 9, and has some striking views out over the mountains. It is the capital of the province of Última Esperanza and the southern terminus of the ferry trip through the Chilean fjords.

Orientation & Information

A compact town on the sound, Puerto Natales is an easy place to cover on foot – even in the dead of winter. Most services are found within a triangle delimited by Bernado Phillipi to the north, Costanera Puerto Montt to the west and Manuel Bulnes to the south. The Plaza de Armas is a large open spot, around which are found the municipal buildings, the church, some pubs and restaurants, and a bank. Six blocks southeast of this plaza, along

Baquedano, is the smaller Plaza O'Higgins between Miraflores and Yungay, an area with more budget lodgings. The Costanera (coastal road) provides a pleasant walk along the sound, but it is blocked off to the south by the main pier where the Navimag ferry arrives.

A great source of local information is the free English-language newspaper the *Black Sheep* (www.theblacksheep.com), easily found in cafés around town. To glimpse Puerto Natales' current weather, check out **Patagonia Webcam** (www.patagoniawebcam.com).

MAPS

There are maps of Puerto Natales in tourist brochures and pamphlets found in hostels, hotels and restaurants throughout the town.

Information

BOOKSTORES

World's End (☎ 414-725; Blanco Encalada 226-A; ☽ 9am-8pm) Tip-of-the-world souvenirs, books, guidebooks and Torres trekking maps.

LAUNDRY

Servilaundry (☎ 412-869; Bulnes 513) Most hostels also offer service.

MEDICAL SERVICES

Hospital Puerto Natales (☎ 411-583; cnr O'Higgins & Ignacio Carrera Pinto)

MONEY

Most banks in town have ATMs.

Casa de Cambios (Bulnes 692; ☽ 10am-1pm & 3-7pm Mon-Fri, 10am-1pm & 3:30-7pm Sat) Best rates on cash and traveler's checks.

POST

Post office (Eberhard 429)

TELEPHONE & INTERNET ACCESS

Internet is widespread but slow throughout town.

Entel (Baquedano 270)

TOURIST INFORMATION

The best bilingual portal for the region is **Torres del Paine** (www.torresdelpaine.cl).

Conaf (☎ 411-438; O'Higgins 584) National parks service administrative office.

Municipal tourist office (☎ 411-263; Bulnes 285; ☽ 8:30am-12:30pm & 2:30-6pm Tue-Sun) In Museo Histórico, with attentive staff and region-wide lodgings listings.

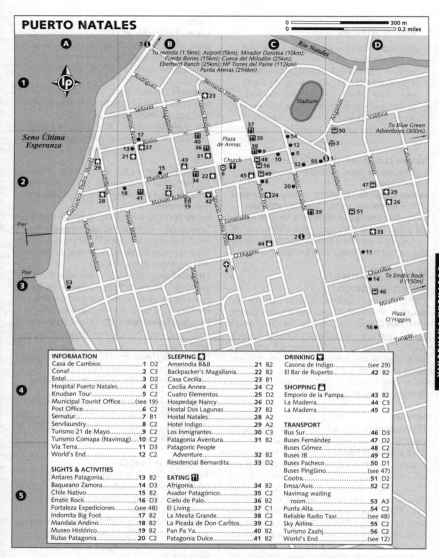

PUERTO NATALES

INFORMATION
Casa de Cambios................1 D2
Conaf................2 C3
Entel................3 D2
Hospital Puerto Natales................4 C3
Knudsen Tour................5 C2
Municipal Tourist Office......(see 19)
Post Office................6 C2
Sernatur................7 B1
Servilaundry................8 C2
Turismo 21 de Mayo................9 C2
Turismo Comapa (Navimag)....10 C2
Via Terra................11 D3
World's End................12 C2

SIGHTS & ACTIVITIES
Antares Patagonia................13 B2
Baqueano Zamora................14 D3
Chile Nativo................15 B2
Erratic Rock................16 D3
Fortaleza Expediciones......(see 48)
Indomita Big Foot................17 B2
Mandala Andino................18 B2
Museo Histórico................19 B2
Rutas Patagonia................20 C2

SLEEPING
Amerindia B&B................21 B2
Backpacker's Magallania........22 B2
Casa Cecilia................23 B1
Cecilia Annex................24 C2
Cuatro Elementos................25 D2
Hospedaje Nancy................26 D2
Hostal Dos Lagunas................27 B2
Hostal Natales................28 A2
Hotel Indigo................29 A2
Los Inmigrantes................30 C3
Patagonia Aventura................31 B2
Patagonic People
  Adventure................32 B2
Residencial Bernardita................33 D2

EATING
Afrigonia................34 B2
Asador Patagónico................35 C2
Cielo de Palo................36 B2
El Living................37 C1
La Mesita Grande................38 B2
La Picada de Don Carlitos....39 C2
Pan Pa Ya................40 B2
Patagonia Dulce................41 B2

DRINKING
Casona de Indigo................(see 29)
El Bar de Ruperto................42 B2

SHOPPING
Emporio de la Pampa................43 B2
La Maderra................44 C3
La Maderra................45 C2

TRANSPORT
Bus Sur................46 D3
Buses Fernández................47 D2
Buses Gómez................48 C2
Buses JB................49 C2
Buses Pacheco................50 D1
Buses Pingüino................(see 47)
Cootra................51 D2
Emsa/Avis................52 C2
Navimag waiting
  room................53 A3
Punta Alta................54 C1
Reliable Radio Taxi................(see 48)
Sky Airline................55 C2
Turismo Zaahj................56 C2
World's End................(see 12)

Sernatur (☎ 412-125; infonatales@sernatur.cl; Costanera Pedro Montt 19; ☼ 9am-7pm) Not as helpful as the municipal tourist office.

TRAVEL AGENCIES
Most travel agencies ply similar services: park tours, maps and equipment rental. The following have some bilingual staff:

Knudsen Tour (☎ 414-747; knudsentour@yahoo.com; Blanco Encalada 284) Well regarded, with trips to Calafate, Torres del Paine and alternative routes along Seno Último Esperanza.

Turismo Comapa (☎ 414-300; www.comapa.com; Eberhard 555; ☼ 9am-1pm & 3-7pm Mon-Fri, 10am-2pm Sat) Agency that takes Navimag ferry and airline bookings.

URBAN SOAKING

You don't need a gold card to get a little pampering here. With mini-spa **Mandala Andino** (☎ 414-143; mandalaandino@yahoo .com; Eberhard 161; per person per hr CH$10,000) hikers fresh off the trail need not stay sore. Three large wooden tubs, one in a covered dome, are heated to a toasty temperature and massages are also available.

Turismo 21 de Mayo (☎ 411-978; Eberhard 554) Organizes day-trip cruises and treks to Balmaceda and Serrano glaciers.

Vertice Patagonia (☎ 412-742; www.verticepatagonia .cl) Runs *refugios* and campsites Mountain Lodge Paine Grande, Lago Grey, Dickson and Perros in Torres del Paine.

Via Terra (☎ 410-775; www.viaterra.cl; Baquedano 558) For now, the only service to the park using the new, faster route but as a tour it doesn't arrive any faster.

Sights & Activities

MUSEO HISTÓRICO

OK for a crash course in local history, the **museum** (☎ 411-263; Manuel Bulnes 285; admission free; ☽ 8:30am-12:30pm & 2:30-6pm Tue-Sun) is a quick visit. There are natural history items (mostly stuffed animals), archaeological artifacts, such as stone and whalebone arrowheads and spear points, plus a Yaghan canoe, Tehuelche bolas and historical photographs of Puerto Natales' development.

HIKING

If you want to take a break from organizing your trip to the park, get in a good warm-up hike at **Mirador Dorotea**, less than 10km from Natales. Dorotea is the large rocky outcrop just off Ruta 9. There is a big sign that identifies the hike to the lookout at lot 14 just off the road. The hike (two hours round-trip; entrance fee including snack on return US$6) takes you through a lenga forest and up to a splendid view back over Puerto Natales, the glacial valley and the surrounding mountains.

Surrounded by tranquil fjords and looming mountains, the original homestead and *estancia* in the region, **Eberhard Ranch**, is impossibly scenic and gives a taste of the area beyond the outdoor-sports mecca of Puerto Natales. Here you can see gauchos at work. It's not a tourist show, but real work, including the slaughter of sheep – so it's not for the faint of heart. To arrange a visit contact Estancia Travel (right).

Tours

Antares Patagonia (☎ 414-611; www.antarespata gonia.com; Barros Arana 111) Specializes in trekking in El Calafate, El Chaltén and Torres del Paine. Can facilitate climbing permits, science expeditions and made-to-order trips.

Baqueano Zamora (☎ 613-531; www.baqueano zamora.com, in Spanish; Baquedano 534) Runs horseback-riding trips and Posada Río Serrano.

Blue Green Adventures (☎ 410-009; www.bluegreen adventures.com; 1200 Bulnes) A quality outfitter offering *estancia* horseback-riding trips in and out of Torres del Paine.

Chile Nativo (☎ 411-835; www.chilenativo.cl; Eberhard 230, 2nd fl) Links visitors with local gauchos, organizes photo safaris and can competently plan your tailor-made dream adventures.

Erratic Rock (☎ 410-355; Baquedano 719) Aims to keep Torres del Paine sustainable with good visitor advice, alternative options, informative talks and gear rentals. Guide service specializes in treks to Cabo Froward, Isla Navarino and lesser-known destinations.

Estancia Travel (☎ 412-221; www.estanciatravel .com; Bories 13-B, Puerto Bories) Run by a former Chilean equestrian champion, this professional outfit facilitates horseback-riding trips in and out of Torres del Paine.

Fortaleza Expediciones (☎ 410-595; www.fortaleza patagonia.cl; Arturo Prat 234) Knowledgeable; rents camping gear.

Indomita Big Foot (☎ 414-525; www.indomitapata gonia.com; Bories 206) Popular kayaking, trekking and mountaineering trips, plus ice- and rock-climbing seminars.

Rutas Patagonia (☎ 061-613-874; www.rutaspata gonia.com; Blanco Encalada 353; ☽ 9am-1pm & 3-10pm) Glaciar Grey ice trekking and ice climbing (CH$90,000), as well as kayaking on Lago Grey and Río Grey.

Festivals & Events

Festival de Cine de la Patagonia This newly inaugurated week-long festival features movies and the Banff Mountain Film Festival, shown in the Cueva del Milodon (p392) in mid-February.

Big Rock Festival A rockin' long weekend of live bands, beach clean-up and athletic contests in mid-April.

Sleeping

For a small town, Puerto Natales brims with lodging. Most places include a basic breakfast. Prices at nonbudget establishments don't reflect the additional 19% IVA, which foreigners are not required to pay if paying with US dollars or credit cards. In the off-season, many places drop prices by as much as 40%. Reserve ahead if you are arriving on the ferry.

BUDGET

Many budget accommodations are in quirky family homes. Hostels often rent equipment and help arrange transport.

Hospedaje Nancy (☎ 410-022; www.nateslodge.cl; Ramírez 540; r per person without bathroom CH$5000; 🖳) Oft-praised for its adoptable hostess, Nancy, this two-story home offers lived-in rooms with kitchen privileges and internet access. It's a family environment with twin or double beds available with shared bath.

Backpacker's Magallania (☎ 414-950; Tomás Rodgers 255; dm CH$6000) A sleeping bag is handy for these bargain bunks. The owner is well disposed and the decor is quirky but dorms fill up fast. Guests get kitchen privileges.

Los Inmigrantes (☎ 413-482; Ignacio Carrera Pinto 480; r per person without bathroom CH$7000) This *residencial* (budget accommodation) and rental center makes a smart choice for dedicated hikers seeking the inside scoop on trails. Kitchen privileges are available.

Patagonia Aventura (☎ 411-028; Tomás Rogers 179; dm/d without bathroom CH$7500/18,000) On the plaza, this comfortable full-service hostel has small, ambient rooms, an attached gear shop and good café with creative fare. Guest breakfasts include fresh homemade bread.

Hostal Dos Lagunas (☎ 415-733; Barros Arana 104; dm/s/d without bathroom CH$8000/10,000/20,000) Natales natives Alejandro and Andrea are attentive hosts, spoiling guests with filling breakfasts, steady water pressure and travel tips. The rooms are ample and warm; singles occupying a double pay CH$5000 extra.

Hostal Natales (☎ 410-081; www.hostelnatales.cl; Ladrilleros 209; dm/d/tr CH$9000/25,000/33,000; 🖳) This tranquil green inn boasts tasteful and toasty rooms, decked in neutrals, all with private bath. It doesn't have the energy of a hostel but dorms are good value. Guests can use the internet terminals in the lobby.

Residencial Bernardita (☎ 411-162; O'Higgins 765; s/d without bathroom CH$9000/18,000) Guests highly recommend Bernardita's quiet rooms and good service. There's also kitchen use and breakfast. Choose between rooms in the main house or more private ones in the back annex.

MIDRANGE

Amerindia B&B (☎ 411-945; www.hostelamerindia .com; Barros Arana 135; d CH$30,000, s/d/tr without bathroom CH$15,000/20,000/30,000; 🖳) With hand weavings, an earthy palette and retro touches, this guesthouse is a stylish retreat. Don't expect a hov-

ering host, the atmosphere is chill. Breakfast includes homemade bread and fruit. Guests can use the backyard grill, there's laundry service and renovations under way to give all rooms private bathrooms.

Casa Cecilia (☎ 613-560; www.casaceciliahostal.com; Tomás Rogers 60; d with/without bathroom CH$30,000/20,000; ✗) Well kept and central, Cecilia is a reliable mainstay with good showers, helpful service and homemade wheat toast for breakfast. The only drawbacks are a small kitchen and cramped rooms. Its multilingual owners can provide good tips and there's quality camping gear for hire.

Erratic Rock II (☎ 412-317; www.erraticrock2.com; Benjamin Zamora 732; d CH$25,000; 🖳) Ideal for couples, this snuggly home offers spacious doubles decked in soft neutrals with throw pillows and tidy new bathrooms. Breakfasts in the bright dining room are abundant and guests can prepare coffee or tea on a whim.

Cuatro Elementos (☎ 415-751; www.4elementos.cl, Esmeralda 813; s/d/tr CH$20,000/25,000/37,000) Eccentric-central, this eco-friendly house with a few spare rooms is coolly crafted with recycled zinc, driftwood and old woodstoves. Guests are drawn by the near-religious recycling and guided trips with an ecological bent to Torres del Paine and other trekking destinations. There's no sign: sniff out the smells of wholegrain bread baking.

Patagonic People Adventure (☎ 412-014; www .patagonicpeopleadventure.com; Bulnes 280; dm/d/tr CH$30,000/40,000/50,000; 🖳) Simple but stylin', this lodging feels like a yuppy home away from home. It's spotless, with hardwood floors, crisp linens and hand-woven blankets. Guests can use the kitchen or get dinner service. Perks include free wi-fi and coffee and tea. Breakfast includes homemade bread, cheese, eggs, juice and yogurt.

TOP END

Hotel Indigo (☎ 418-718; www.indigopatagonia.com; Ladrilleros 105; d/std/ste CH$97,500/110,000/132,500; ✗ 🖳) A pampered finale to your trip, hikers head first to Indigo's rooftop Jacuzzis and spa, but restful spaces abound, from the dark hallways dotted with hammocks to plush rooms with down duvets and candles lit for your return. Materials like eucalyptus, slate and iron overlap the modern with the natural for an interesting effect. The standard corner rooms are slightly more spacious than doubles, with two window views. Service passes muster, but the main star here is the fjord in front of you, which even captures your gaze in the shower.

remota (☎ 414-040, bookings 02-387-1500; www .remota.cl; 3 nights s/d CH$840,000/1,160,000; P ☐ ☒) Unlike most hotels, the exclusive remota draws your awareness to what's outside: silence broadcasts the gusty winds, irregular window patterns imitate old stock fences and a crooked passageway pays tribute to *estancia* sheep corridors. This vast post-modern addition to Puerto Natales offers sumptuous but spare comfort. Though rooms are cozy, you'll probably want to spend all your time at 'the beach,' a glass-walled barn room with lounge futons to gape at the wild surroundings.

Eating

Pan Pa Ya (☎ 415-474; Bories 349; ☽ 9am-8pm) For bread rolls or whole-wheat loaves to take on the trail, check out this bakery with ultrafresh products.

Patagonia Dulce (☎ 415-285; www.patagoniadulce.cl, in Spanish; Barros Arana 233; drinks CH$1500; ☽ 9am-8pm) Coffee and chocolate shop, Patagonia Dulce also serves fresh baked goods, homemade ice creams and velvety hot chocolate.

La Picada de Don Carlitos (☎ 414-232; Blanco Encalada 444; menú del día CH$2000) Abundant, hearty Chilean fare, like chicken stew and mashed potatoes, is served at this down-home eatery. Greasy spoon it may be, but it's bursting with locals at lunchtime.

El Living (www.el-living.com; Arturo Prat 156; mains CH$3500; ☽ 11am-11pm Nov–mid-Apr; Ⓥ) Indulge in the London lounge feel of this chill café with proper vegetarian fare, stacks of European glossies and a stream of eclectic tunes. In addition to real coffee, tea and fresh juice, organic salads, burritos and soups are served. Wine and local beer are also at the ready. Choose a comfy chair or check out the new garden space.

our pick **Afrigonia** (☎ 412-232; Eberhard 343; mains CH$4200) Don't doubt it – even though the Afro-Patagonian wave has yet to hit mainstream, this romantic restaurant is easily the best in town. Diners delight in the innovation and attention to detail. Combine *Papas tsavo* (crisp fried new potatoes in herb sauce) with *kayapas* (curried chicken stuffed with spinach and mashed peanuts). Or try mint roasted lamb. There is no way to lose. It's run by a friendly Zambian-Chilean couple.

La Mesita Grande (Prat 196; pizzas CH$5000; ☽ lunch & dinner) Happy diners share one long worn table that is not unlike a post-trek feeding trough. But it's kind of gourmet. The thin-crust pizzas are outstanding, with toppings like arugula and prosciutto or lemon-spiked salmon. Plus there are quality pastas and organic salads from a local greenhouse. Look for local Baguales beer, available on tap.

Casona de Indigo (☎ 418-718; Ladrilleros 105; mains CH$6500; ☽ lunch & dinner; Ⓥ) Located in the Indigo hotel, this cozy upstairs restaurant warmed with chimney fires serves vegetarian fare, including quiche and soups, and local specialties including king crab. The first floor serves as a lounge and casual dining area.

Cielo de Palo (Tomás Rogers 179; mains CH$6500; ☽ lunch & dinner) Served in a ceramic bowl bubbling over with cheese, the king crab lasagne at this small café could easily serve two. Lighter fare includes pumpkin soup and falafel plates. It's a little pricey but portions do satisfy.

Asador Patagónico (☎ 413-553; Arturo Prat 158; mains CH$8000) If trekking left you with a mastodon appetite, splurge at this upscale Argentine-style grill. Flame-seared lamb, steak and salads, as well as sweetbreads, are served as you wish alongside quality wines.

Drinking

El Bar de Ruperto (☎ 410-863; cnr Bulnes & Magallanes; ☐) Ideal for a rainy day, this typical bar entertains you with board games, Foosball and chess. Guinness and other imports help you forget you're so far from home.

Casona de Indigo (Ladrilleros 105; ☽ 10am-11pm; ☐) For sunset cocktails, hit this stylish bar in the Indigo complex.

Shopping

Emporio de la Pampa (☎ 413-279; Eberhard 302; ☽ 9am-10:30pm Sep-Apr; ☐) Attached to a Northface boutique, this wine and cheese shop has goodies galore for the trail. Treats include fresh coffee, hearty brown bread and regional goat cheese. A tasting (CH$10,000) will help you get your bearings.

La Madddera (413-318, 24hr emergency 099-418-4100; Prat 297; www.lamadderaoutdoor.com; ☽ 8am-11:30pm; ☐) You'll find camping gear galore at this friendly shop; also fixes damaged gear and does guided excursions. Also at Prat 499.

Getting There & Away

AIR

Commercial flights to Puerto Natales became available recently, in spite of protests from nearby Punta Arenas. Airport transfers by **Sonia** (☎ 410-546; per person CH$2000) provide a cheaper alternative to taking a taxi.

Aerovías DAP (www.dap.cl) offers charter flights to El Calafate, Argentina, from the small airfield (PNT), a few kilometers north of town on the road to Torres del Paine. The closest LanChile office is in Punta Arenas (p382).

Sky Airline (☎ 410-646; www.skyairline.cl; Bulnes 692, Local 4) has a new service from Santiago to Puerto Natales (round-trip CH$43,000) with a stop in Puerto Montt (round-trip CH 77,000) that is oddly more expensive.

Air Comet (☎ toll free 600-625-000; www.aircometchile .cl) flies Santiago–Natales (round-trip CH$100,000) on Saturdays and Sundays from October through March. Bookings can be made at **Punta Alta** (☎ 410-115; Blanco Encalada 244; ☷ 10am-1pm & 2:30-8pm Mon-Sat) travel agency.

BOAT

For many travelers, a journey through Chile's spectacular fjords aboard Navimag's car and passenger ferry becomes a highlight of their trip. This four-day and three-night northbound voyage has become so popular it should be booked well in advance.

You can also try your luck. To confirm when the ferries are due, contact **Turismo Comapa** (p379) a couple of days before the estimated arrival date. The *Magallanes* leaves Natales early Friday and stops in Puerto Edén (or the advancing Glaciar Pía XI on southbound sailings) en route to Puerto Montt. Boats usually arrive in Puerto Natales the morning of the same day and depart either later that day or on the following day, but schedules vary according to weather conditions and tides. Disembarking passengers must stay on board while cargo is transported; those embarking have to spend the night on board.

High season is November to March, midseason is October and April, and low season is May to September. Most folks end up in dorm-style, 22-bed berths but often wish they had sprung for a private cabin. Fares, which vary according to view, cabin size and private or shared bathroom, include all meals (including vegetarian options if requested while booking, but bring water, snacks and drinks anyway) and interpretive talks.

Per-person fares range from CH$170,000 for a bunk berth in low season to CH$975,000 for a triple-A cabin in high season; students/

seniors receive a 10% to 15% discount. Check online (www.navimag.com) for current schedules and rates.

BUS

Puerto Natales has no central bus terminal, though several companies stop at the junction of Valdivia and Baquedano. Book at least a day ahead, especially for early-morning departures, in high season. Services are greatly reduced in the off-season.

A new road has been opened to Torres del Paine that, although gravel, is much more direct. For now the only transportation service using it is Via Terra, but look for others to follow soon. This alternative entrance goes alongside Lago del Toro to administración.

Otherwise, to Torres del Paine, most buses leave two to three times daily at around 7am, 8am and 2:30pm. If you are headed to Mountain Lodge Paine Grande in the offseason, take the morning bus (CH$8000) to meet the catamaran (CH$11,000 one way, two hours). Be aware that the upcoming addition of a new road into the park will provide shorter travel times and more drop-off options. These schedules are in constant flux, so double-check them before heading out.

Buses to Río Gallegos, Argentina, leave on Tuesday and Thursday with Bus Sur, Pingüino goes at 11am Wednesday and Sunday.

To El Calafate, Argentina (CH$11,000), Turismo Zaahj, Cootra and Bus Sur have the most services.

Companies and destinations include:

Bus Sur (☎ 614-221; www.bus-sur.cl, in Spanish; Baquedano 658) Punta Arenas, Torres del Paine, Puerto Montt, El Calafate, Río Turbio and Ushuaia.

Buses Fernández/Pingüino (☎ 411-111; www .busesfernandez.com; cnr Esmeralda & Ramirez) Torres del Paine and Punta Arenas.

Buses Gómez (☎ 411-971; www.busesgomez.com, in Spanish; Arturo Prat 234) Torres del Paine.

Buses JB (☎ 412-824; busesjb@hotmail.com; Arturo Prat 258) Torres del Paine.

Buses Pacheco (☎ 414-513; www.busespacheco.com; Baquedano 244) To Punta Arenas, Río Grande and Ushuaia.

Cootra (☎ 412-785; Baquedano 456) Goes to El Calafate daily at 7:30am.

Turismo Zaahj (☎ 412-260/355; www.turismozaahj .co.cl, in Spanish; Arturo Prat 236/70) Torres del Paine and El Calafate.

Via Terra (☎ 410-775; www.viaterra.cl; Baquedano 558) Daily park tour (round-trip CH$21,500) departing 7:30am arrives at administración at 11:30am, returns to Natales at 7:30pm; can do drop-offs.

Destination	Cost (CH$)	Duration (hr)
El Calafate	11,000	5
Punta Arenas	4000	3
Torres del Paine	8000	2
Ushuaia	28,000	12

Getting Around

Car rental is expensive and availability is limited; you'll get better rates in Punta Arenas or Argentina. Try **Emsa/Avis** (☎ 241-182; Bulnes 632). **World's End** (Blanco Encalada 226-A) rents bikes.

Reliable Radio Taxi (☎ 412-805; cnr Prat & Bulnes) can even be counted on for after-hours deliveries.

CUEVA DEL MILODÓN

In the 1890s German pioneer Hermann Eberhard discovered the partial remains of an enormous ground sloth in a cave 25km northwest of Puerto Natales. The slow-moving, herbivorous *milodón*, which stood nearly 4m tall, was supposedly the motivating factor behind Bruce Chatwin's book *In Patagonia* (see boxed text, below*)*. The 30m-high **Cueva del Milodón** (admission CH$4000) pays homage to its former inhabitant with a life-size plastic replica of the animal. It's not exactly tasteful, but still worth a stop, whether to appreciate the grand setting and ruminate over its wild past or to take an easy walk up to a lookout point. Camping (no fires) and picnicking are possible. In February the cave hosts a cinema festival (see p388).

Torres del Paine buses pass the entrance, which is 8km from the cave proper. There are infrequent tours from Puerto Natales; alternatively, you can hitch or share a *taxi colectivo* (CH$15,000). Outside of high season, bus services are infrequent.

PARQUE NACIONAL BERNARDO O'HIGGINS

Virtually inaccessible, O'Higgins remains the elusive and exclusive home of glaciers and waterfowl. The national park can only be entered by boat.

ENIGMATIC PATAGONIA: CHATWIN'S MASTERPIECE

In 1977 the late English writer Bruce Chatwin penned *In Patagonia*, far and away the most famous book on the region and an iconic touchstone in the field of travel writing. Three decades after its original publication the book continues to inspire people to travel to such far-flung places as Ushuaia, Punta Arenas and Puerto Natales. And it further inspires travelers to try their hand at writing.

According to the story, Chatwin was fascinated by Patagonia since early childhood, when he coveted a scrap of giant sloth skin kept in a 'glass-fronted cabinet' in his grandmother's house in England. The skin, covered in orange hair, had been sent as a gift from his eccentric seafaring relative Charley Milward, who resided in Punta Arenas. Chatwin was also intrigued by the seemingly out-of-place immigrant communities, such as the Patagonian Welsh, and colorful, free-spirited characters like Robert Leroy Parker and Harry Longabaugh (aka Butch Cassidy and the Sundance Kid). A six-month journey through Patagonia resulted in Chatwin's masterpiece at the age of 37. It recounts his journey and personal encounters while heading south from Buenos Aires to his final destination, Cueva del Milodón – the one-time home of the prehistoric sloth.

While Chatwin mixed fluid storytelling, intriguing regional history, personal portraits and old-fashioned travel memoir, he tossed one last ingredient into the pot: fiction. This was, and continues to be, controversial because there was no acknowledgement that any of the stories were fabricated. *In Patagonia* reads primarily as a nonfiction travel memoir. However, after the publication of the book, a number of Patagonian residents came forward to challenge and contradict the events that were depicted in the book. Many of the conversations and characters that Chatwin reported as true were just figments of the writer's imagination.

It is worth considering that Patagonia is a land of mystery and legend: a place that the first European explorers described as being populated by giants. Perhaps the story fits with this fringe of the world that is known as Patagonia; a land with its own pace of time, history and reality. No, it wouldn't hold up to a fact-checking department, but *In Patagonia* vividly depicts the many layers of this enigmatic land and is an indispensable companion for the Patagonian traveler.

Chatwin died of AIDS in 1989. He claimed to the end that he was ill due to the bite of a Chinese bat and a tropical fungal infection.

Full-day boat excursions (CH$45,000 without lunch) to the base of Glaciar Serrano are run by **Turismo 21 de Mayo** (☎ 061-411 978; www.turismo21demayo.cl, in Spanish; Eberhard 560, Puerto Natales). You can also access Torres del Paine via boat to Glaciar Serrano with **Turismo 21 de Mayo** (☎ 061-411-978; Eberhard 554, Puerto Natales; CH$75,000). Passengers transfer to a Zodiac (a rubber boat with a motor), stop for lunch at Estancia Balmaceda (CH$12,000) and continue up Río Serrano, arriving at the southern border of the park by 5pm. The trip offers great views of the Southern Ice Field and native forest. The same tour can be done leaving the park, but may require camping near Río Serrano to catch the Zodiac at 9am.

PARQUE NACIONAL TORRES DEL PAINE

Soaring almost vertically more than 2000m above the Patagonian steppe, the granite pillars of Torres del Paine (Towers of Paine) dominate the landscape of what may be South America's finest **national park** (www.pntp.cl; admission high/low season CH$15,000/5000). Before its creation in 1959, the park was part of a large sheep *estancia*, and it's still recovering from nearly a century of overexploitation of its pastures, forests and wildlife.

Most people visit the park for its one greatest hit but, once here, realize that there are other (less-crowded) attractions with equal wow power. We're talking about azure lakes, trails that meander through emerald forests, roaring rivers you'll cross on rickety bridges and one big, radiant blue glacier. Variety spans from the vast openness of the steppe to rugged mountain terrain topped by looming peaks.

Part of Unesco's Biosphere Reserve system since 1978, the park is home to flocks of ostrich-like rhea (known locally as the *ñandú*), Andean condor, flamingo and many other bird species. Its star success in conservation success is undoubtedly the guanaco (*Lama guanicoe*), which grazes the open steppes where pumas cannot approach undetected. After more than a decade of effective protection from poachers, these large and growing herds don't even flinch when humans or vehicles approach.

When the weather is clear panoramas are everywhere. However, unpredictable weather systems can sheath the peaks in clouds for hours or days. Some say you get four seasons in a day here, with sudden rainstorms and knock-down gusts part of the hearty initia-

tion. Bring high-quality foul-weather gear, a synthetic sleeping bag and, if you're camping, a good tent. It is always wise to plan a few extra days to make sure that your trip isn't torpedoed by a spot of bad weather.

However, the crowning attraction of this 1810-sq-km park is its highly developed infrastructure, which makes it possible to do the whole 'W' hike (p395) while sleeping in beds, eating hot meals, taking showers and even drinking the random cocktail. Make reservations ahead of time (for contact details see p397).

Plan a minimum of three to seven days to enjoy the hiking and other activities. Guided day trips on minibuses from Puerto Natales are possible, but permit only a glimpse of what the park has to offer.

In 2005 a hiker burned down 10% of the park using a portable stove in windy conditions. Sloppy camping has consequences. Be conscientious and tread lightly – you are one of 120,000 yearly guests.

Orientation & Information

Parque Nacional Torres del Paine is 112km north of Puerto Natales via a decent but sometimes bumpy gravel road. A new road from Puerto Natales to the Administración provides a shorter, more direct southern approach to the park.

At Cerro Castillo there is a seasonal border crossing into Argentina at Cancha Carrera. The road continues 40km north and west to **Portería Sarmiento**, the main entrance where user fees are collected. It's another 37km to the Administración (park headquarters) and the **Conaf Centro de Visitantes** (☼ 9am-8pm in summer), with good information on park ecology and trail status.

Be sure to make reservations! Arriving at the park without them, especially in the high season, enslaves you to make camp in the few free options. Travel agencies offer reservations, but it's best to go directly through the concessions.

The park is open year-round, subject to your ability to get there. Transportation connections are less frequent in the low season and winter weather adds additional challenges to hiking. Visitor flow is edging toward regulation. Shoulder seasons of November and March are some of the best times for trekking, with fewer crowds and windy conditions usually abating in March.

SOUTHERN PATAGONIA

Internet resources include **Torres del Paine** (www.torresdelpaine.com) and **Erratic Rock** (www.erraticrock.com), with a good backpacker equipment list. Park administration distributes a detailed map to all visitors and the same map is available as a download on the official park website. The best trekking maps, by JLM and Luis Bertea Rojas, are easily found in Puerto Natales.

CLIMBING PERMITS

Climbers must obtain a climbing permit (CH$60,000) at park headquarters. The application requires climbers to submit a climbing résumé, emergency contact numbers and authorization from their consulate.

Climbers must also get permission from the **Dirección de Fronteras y Límites** (Difrol; Map pp84-5; ☎ 02-671-4110; www.difrol.cl, in Spanish; Bandera 52, 4th fl, Santiago), which takes about an hour to get if in Santiago and up to five days if requested from Puerto Natales. Ask for plenty of time for the permission to avoid paying a separate fee each time you enter the park. Avoid delays by arranging the permissions with a climbing outfitter, such as **Antares Patagonia** (☎ 061-414-611; www.antarespatagonia.com; Barros Arana 111, Puerto Natales) in Puerto Natales, before arrival in the country.

Dangers & Annoyances

Black widow spiders have been spotted in the Laguna Amarga sector. The spiders are

TREKKING LIGHTLY

Some 200,000 tourists visit Torres del Paine each year and with the park headlining life adventure lists everywhere, its popularity will only grow. And there is sure to be an impact. Already, in the high season of January and February, trails have traffic jams and campgrounds resemble Woodstock. In that peace-and-love spirit, we've come up with some trip tips:

- Don't drink bottled water, since the bottles become a recycling nightmare (trash is taken out on pack horses, if you can imagine). Instead opt to bring a purifier or use tablets.

- Pack out all garbage, as little scavengers, mainly mice, love to make merry in campgrounds.

- Respect the official camp zones and hike only in designated areas.

- Be extremely mindful of fire from cigarettes, camp stoves, lighters, lamps etc. In early 2005 a hiker used a campstove in windy conditions and burned down nearly 10% of the park. Nobody wants to get famous that way.

- Stay friendly. Park regulars have noted that as traffic increases the community feeling diminishes. But it doesn't have to be that way. So say hi to your fellow hikers and let the fleet-footed ones pass.

Want to lend a hand to preserve the park? You can volunteer for trail maintenance, biological studies or an animal census with nonprofits **AMA Torres del Paine** (www.amatorresdelpaine.org) or Wyoming-based student exchange **Global Community Project** (www.globalcommunityproject.blogspot .com), but be sure to make contact well in advance of your trip.

hourglass shape and females have a red dot. Avoid encounters by shaking off clothing before putting it on and being careful when handling firewood. If bitten, stay calm but seek medical care immediately.

Activities

HIKING

Torres del Paine's 2800m granite spires inspire hikers around the world in mass pilgrimage. Most go for the circuit or the 'W' to soak up these classic panoramas, leaving other incredible routes deserted. Doing the circuit (the 'W' plus the backside of the peaks) requires seven to nine days, while the 'W' (named for the rough approximation to the letter that it traces out on the map) takes four to five days. Add another day or two for transportation connections.

Most trekkers start either route from Laguna Amarga and head west. You can also hike from the Administración or take the catamaran from Pudeto to Lago Pehoé and start from there; hiking roughly southwest to northeast along the 'W' presents more views of the black-striped sedimentary peaks known as Los Cuernos (2200–2600m). Trekking alone, especially on the backside of the circuit, is inadvisable and restricted by Conaf.

The 'W'

Most people trek the 'W' from right to left (east to west), starting at Laguna Amarga, but hiking west to east – especially in the section from Lago Pehoé to Valle Francés – provides superior views of the Cuernos (which are otherwise to your back in that segment).

Refugio Las Torres to Mirador Las Torres Four hours one way. A moderate hike up Río Ascencio to a treeless tarn beneath the eastern face of the Torres del Paine proper. This is the closest view you will get of the towers. The last hour is a knee-popping scramble up boulders (covered with knee- and waist-high snow in winter). There are camping and *refugios* at Las Torres and Chileno, with basic camping at Camping Torres. In summer stay at Camping Torres and head up at sunrise to beat the crowds.

Refugio Las Torres to Los Cuernos Seven hours one way. Hikers should keep to the lower trail (many get lost on the upper trail, unmarked on maps). There's camping and a *refugio*. Summer winds can be fierce.

To Valle Frances Five hours one way from Cuernos or Lago Pehoé. In clear weather, this hike is the most beautiful stretch between 3050m Paine Grande to the west and the lower but still spectacular Torres del Paine and Los Cuernos to the east, with glaciers hugging the trail. Camp at Italiano and at Británico, right in the heart of the valley.

Mountain Lodge Paine Grande to Refugio Lago Grey Four hours one way from Lago Pehoé. This hike follows a relatively easy trail with a few challenging

THE 'W'

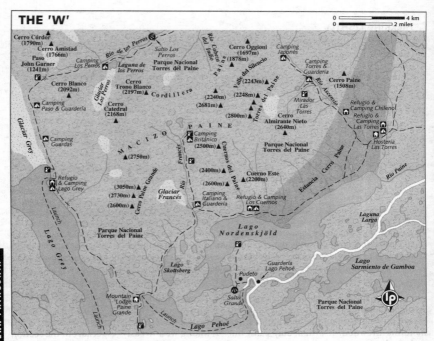

downhill scampers. The glacier lookout is another half-hour's hike away. There are camping and *refugios* at both ends.

Mountain Lodge Paine Grande to the Administración Five hours. Up and around the side of Lago Pehoé, then through extensive grassland along Río Grey. This is not technically part of the 'W,' but after completion of the hike you can cut out to the Administración from here and avoid backtracking to Laguna Amarga. Mountain Lodge Paine Grande can radio in and make sure that you can catch a bus from the Administración back to Puerto Natales. You can also enter the 'W' this way to hike it west to east.

The Circuit

For solitude, stellar views and bragging rights over your compadres doing the 'W,' this longer trek is the way to go. The Circuit is comprised of the 'W,' as described previously, plus the backside between Refugio Lago Grey and Refugio Las Torres. There is only one *refugio* along this stretch (renovating at the time of writing) and camping is basic. You'll need foul-weather camping and trekking gear, as mud (sometimes knee-deep), snow and wind are inevitable. While the popularity of the 'W' means you'll see lots of people along the way, that's not the case along the backside. Trekking alone is inadvisable (and restricted by Conaf). Make friends with others before heading out. The Circuit is closed during winter.

Refugio Lago Grey to Camping Paso Four hours from Refugio Grey to Paso, about two hours going the opposite way; hikers might want to go left to right (west to east), which means ascending the pass rather than slipping downhill.

Camping Paso to Los Perros Approximately four hours. This route has plenty of mud and sometimes snow. Don't be confused by what appears to be a campsite right after crossing the pass. Keep on going until you see a shack.

Camping Los Perros to Dickson Around 4½ hours. A relatively easy but windy stretch.

Camping Dickson to Serón Six hours, as the trail wraps around Lago Paine, winds can get fierce and the trails vague; stay along the trail furthest away from lake. It's possible to break the trek at Camping Coirón, although it is currently recovering from the fire in 2005.

Camping Serón to Laguna Amarga Four to five hours. You can end the trek with a chill-out night and a decent meal at Refugio Las Torres.

Other Hikes

From Guardería Lago Grey, a four-hour trail follows Río Pingo to Conaf's Camping Zapata, from where hikes (about another 1½ to two hours) continue to a lookout with impressive views of **Glaciar Zapata** and **Lago Pingo**. Many people who have already done the 'W' hike to Pingo on their second visit to the park (as do a lot of the guides when they aren't working). It is less trafficked and gives a chance to view glaciers.

From Guardería Laguna Amarga a four-hour hike leads to **Laguna Azul**, where there camping is possible on the northeastern shore. This area was burnt by the fire in 2005 and was temporarily closed, so check with Conaf about the state of recuperation before heading out there. After another two-hour hike north the trail reaches **Lago Paine**. Accessibility to meet up with the Circuit trail near the other side of the lake is made impossible by the river.

From the Administración, the three-hour hike to Hostería Pehoé is an easy, mainly flat trail with great views. For more solitude, a four-hour hike branches east after crossing Río Paine, zigzags up the skirt of the Sierra del Toro to access a string of lakes, ending with **Laguna Verde**. There is no camping along this route, but those inclined could splurge for a night at Hostería Mirador del Payne. This is a hike mainly for bird-watching.

AVOID THE MULITITUDES

- Most hikers go up to the Torres around 8am and down at 4pm. With full summer light, you can go against traffic by starting a couple of hours earlier or later (inquire about the times of sunset/sunrise at your *refugio* or *guardaparques*)

- Hike on less crowded routes like Glaciar Zapata or the Full Circuit

- Try joining a multiday trip kayaking Río Serrano or horseback riding; you'll get a completely different perspective and incredible views

- Hike in the shoulder season, when the weather is still warm enough but the crowds are gone: March is an excellent time in the park; for the hearty, winter can be too

---

Day Hikes

Walk from Guardería Lago Pehoé, on the main park highway, to **Salto Grande**, a powerful waterfall between Lago Nordenskjöld and Lago Pehoé. Another easy hours' walk leads to **Mirador Nordenskjöld**, an overlook with superb views of the lake and mountains.

For a more challenging day hike, try the four-hour trek leading to **Lago Paine**, whose northern shore is accessible only from Laguna Azul. The route offers tranquility and gorgeous scenery.

KAYAKING

Paddle your way to pristine corners of the park on multiday trips with **Indomita Big Foot** (☎ 061-414-525; www.indomitapatagonia.com; Bories 206, Puerto Natales). Few see the sights around Río Serrano, and these trips aren't budget travel but they can be a lot of fun. It's a great way to get up close to glaciers. **Rutas Patagonia** (☎ 061-613-874; www.rutaspatagonia.com; Blanco Encalada 353, Puerto Natales) takes paddlers on Lago Grey and Río Grey (half-day CH$40,000).

HORSEBACK RIDING

The park is certainly a beautiful place to ride. Due to property divisions within the park, horses cannot cross between the western sections (Lagos Grey and Pehoé, Río Serrano) and the eastern part managed by Hotel Las Torres (Refugio Los Cuernos is the approximate cut-off).

Baqueano Zamora (☎ 061-613-531; www.baqueano zamora.com; Baquedano 534, Puerto Natales) runs excursions to Lagos Pingo, Paine and Azul, and Laguna Amarga (half-day CH$27,500, lunch included). Hotel Las Torres (p399) controls the eastern area of the park and charges CH$35,000 (snack included) for full-day trips around Lago Nordenskjöld and beyond.

ICE TREKKING

There's probably no better way to get to know a glacier than trekking or climbing it. Contact **Rutas Patagonia** (above; ice trek CH$70,000), the sole company with a park concession for ice treks on Glaciar Grey, available from October to May.

Sleeping & Eating

Make reservations! Arriving without them, especially in high season, limits you to camp in the few free options. Travel agencies offer reservations, but it's best to go directly through the concessions. **Vertice Patagonia** (☎ 061-412-742;

INDECENT EXPOSURE *Jocelyn Turnbull Phd*

In the mid-1980s British scientists at Halley Station in Antarctica noticed that their ozone measuring instrument seemed to have gone wrong – ozone levels were vastly lower than had ever been recorded before. Unfortunately, it was not their instrument that had gone wrong, but the ozone itself – ozone levels over Antarctica in springtime were dropping to a fraction of the regular amount.

Soon after, they were able to isolate the culprit: chlorofluorocarbons (CFCs), which are manmade gases used in aerosols, refrigeration, air-conditioning, industrial solvents, asthma inhalers and fire control. Most of the time these gases are innocuous, but in the Antarctic springtime the combination of very cold temperatures and the return of sunshine to the polar region allow the CFCs to rapidly gobble up the stratospheric ozone, resulting in the famed ozone hole. Once the Antarctic temperatures start to warm as spring progresses, the ozone begins to recover, only to be depleted again when the next spring arrives.

Ozone protects the Earth's surface from UV radiation, the stuff that causes sunburn, among other things. Without it, sunburn and skin cancer become very serious concerns. The ozone hole has impacted Southern Patagonia more than any other inhabited area on earth. It is particularly bad during the spring, when its UV rays are most powerful. Visitors should wear brimmed hats and sunglasses, slather on the sunscreen and be particularly mindful of children.

The adoption and strengthening of the 1987 Montreal Protocol has cut the quantity of CFCs out there and Antarctic ozone levels are beginning to recover, but it's a slow process and it will take another 50 years or so to get back to normal ozone levels.

Sound like the barely believable plot of a sci-fi flick? Unfortunately, it's reality, so wear your sunscreen and make sure you dispose of that old fridge in an environmentally friendly way.

---

www.verticepatagonia.cl) owns Mountain Lodge Paine Grande and also manages *refugios* and campgrounds Lago Grey, Dickson and Perros. **Fantastico Sur** (☎ 061-710-050; www.fantastico sur.com; Magallanes 960, Punta Arenas; ✆ 9am-5pm Mon-Fri, 10:30am-1:30pm & 3-5pm Sat & Sun) owns Torres, Chileno and Los Cuernos, and their associated campgrounds.

Some *refugios* may require photo ID (ie a passport) upon check-in. Photocopy your tourist card and passport for all lodgings in advance to expedite check-in. Staff can radio ahead to confirm your next reservation. Given the huge volume of trekkers, snags are inevitable, so practice your Zen composure.

CAMPING

Camping at the *refugios* costs CH$4000 per site, hot showers included. *Refugios* rent decent equipment – tent (CH$7000 per night), sleeping bag (CH$4500) and mat (CH$1500) – but potential shortages in high season make it prudent to pack your own gear. Small kiosks sell expensive pasta, soup packets and butane gas.

Sites administered by Conaf are free and very basic (rain shelters and pit toilets). Many campers have reported wildlife (in rodent form) lurking around campsites; don't leave food in packs or in tents; hang it from a tree instead. Campsites at Británico are pretty deep into Valle Francés, but on a clear night, with a view of the mountains on three sides, it is a superb place to stay.

REFUGIOS

Refugio rooms have four to eight bunk beds each, kitchen privileges (for lodgers and during specific hours only), hot showers and meals. A bed costs CH$12,500 to CH$17,500, sleeping-bag rental CH$4500 and meals CH$4000 to CH$7500. Should the *refugio* be overbooked, staff provide all necessary camping equipment. Most *refugios* close by the end of April. Mountain Lodge Paine Grande is the only one that stays open year-round, but it has very limited operations.

HOTELS & HOSTERÍAS

Many of the park hotels are heading toward all-inclusive multiday packages that provide a range of activities for guests. The following have high-season prices listed.

Posada Río Serrano (☎ 02-193-0338, 061-613-531 in Puerto Natales; www.baqueanozamora.com; dm CH$15,000-18,000, d with/without bathroom CH$66,000/48,000; **P**) This rustic 19th-century ranch house is a boon to bargain hunters. While fixtures are dated, the 13 rooms with central heating are pretty cozy. The restaurant offers set meals (CH$8400) and the family-style living room gathers guests around the fireplace. It's popular with horseback riders (arranged through the same company that owns the posada) and fishing groups.

Mountain Lodge Paine Grande (☎ 061-412-742; www.verticepatagonia.cl; camping per person CH$3500, dm CH$20,000, full board CH$36,000, 2-person dome CH$20,000; ☺ year-round; 🖥) Sometimes referred to as Pehoé (its predecessor), this boxy dormitory reveals a smart interior made to give sublime Cuernos views to all rooms. The lodge has received criticism for its unsustainable scale, but plans to hush critics by adding recycling and a hydroelectric turbine – check on these developments. Between Lago Grey and Valle Francés, it is a perfect day hike from either and is conveniently located at the Lago Pehoé ferry dock. It also offers camping and deluxe camping accommodations in domes.

Hostería Mirador del Payne (☎ 061-226-930; www.miradordelpayne.com; Fagnano 585, Punta Arenas; s/d/tr CH$80,000/97,500/108,000; 🅿) On the Estancia El Lazo in the seldom-seen Laguna Verde sector, this comfortable inn is known for its serenity, proximity to spectacular viewpoints and top-rate service – but not for easy park access. Activities include bird-watching, horseback riding and sport fishing. Call to arrange a ride from the road junction.

Hotel Las Torres (☎ 061-710-050; www.lastorres.com; Magallanes 960, Punta Arenas; s/d CH$76,000/87,000, superior CH$117,000/139,000; ☺ closed Jun; 🅿) A hospitable and well-run hotel with international standards and good guided excursions. Most noteworthy, the hotel recycles and donates a portion of package fees to the nonprofit park-based enviromental group AMA (Agrupación Medio Ambiental Torres del Paine). The restaurant's hearty buffet (CH$15,000)

serves mostly organic vegetables from the hotel greenhouse and organic meat raised on nearby ranches. The spa has a sauna and Jacuzzi, and offers massages and revitalizing treatments. It's just 7km west of Guardería Laguna Amarga.

Hostería Lago Grey (☎ 061-712-100; www.lagogrey.cl; s/d/tr incl breakfast CH$131,000/151,250/173,030; 🅿 🖥) Open year-round, this tasteful hotel has 30 rooms. Snug and elegant, clusters of white cottages are linked by raised boardwalks. Rooms have forest views but the snug bar, living and dining rooms sport great glacier views. Zodiac boat tours (three hours, CH$40,000) are available on the lake, but not to the glacier.

Hostería Pehoé (☎ 061-244-506, 061-248-888; www.pehoe.com; d CH$152,000; 🅿) On the far side of Lake Pehoé towards explora, the hostería is linked to the mainland by a long footbridge. The park's first hotel, it nabbed a five-star location with views of Los Cuernos and Paine Grande. However, it's poor value, with dated rooms that bring to mind a roadside motel. The restaurant is open to the public.

explora (☎ 02-206-6060 in Santiago; www.explora.com; 4 nights d per person US$2724; 🅿 🖥 🛥) With otherworldly luxury, this elite retreat spoils sophisticated travelers taking a stab at adventure. You'll find baskets of trekking poles, not umbrellas, in the lobby, spa treatments and ivy-league handsome guides poised to lead you down the trail. Ultramodern architecture draws attention to the dramatic panoramic views, which you can also soak in from an open-air Jacuzzi. Rates include airport transfers, full gourmet meals and a wide variety of excursions led by bilingual guides.

Pueblito Río Serrano

Heralded as the future of Torres del Paine development, this new 'village' sector sits

SOUTHERN PATAGONIA

GREEN TORRES

It seems ironic, but parks are among the places where you are least likely to see an ecological approach, either because they are remote, lack the infrastructure or cannot afford the costs. But we're happy to see private-run outfits in Torres del Paine buck that trend. As of 2008, Refugio Chileno treats its sewage with a biofilter – yes, that would be worms – and has plans to use a wind turbine and solar panels to supply 100% of its energy (staff are excited about getting a washing machine). Refugio Cuernos powers up via water turbine and Refugio Las Torres uses solar panels. Not to be outdone, Mountain Lodge Paine Grande hopes to recycle in 2009 and set up a turbine for hydro-power. If you have news on who is going green, contact us at www.lonelyplanet.com/contact.

just outside the park on the new road from Puerto Natales. It occupies a choice spot banked on the s-curves of Río Serrano, with stunning views of the entire Paine massif. It's too bad that there isn't any zoning. Development so far has been fast-paced and rather hodgepodge. It seems rather sad to see a grey fox trotting around a golf course.

Hostería Lago del Toro (☎ 061-223-351; d/tr incl breakfast CH$67,500/83,250, superior d CH$83,250; 🖳) Sandwiched between two behemoth hotels, this more intimate charmer has fresh carpeted rooms and a warm fire to greet guests. The house, with a corrugated-iron face, resembles an old-fashioned inn, with macrame lace decor and dense wood furniture.

Hotel Cabañas del Paine (☎ 061-220-174; www .cabanasdelpaine.cl; d incl breakfast CH$112,500; 🖳) These cabin-style rooms stand apart as tasteful and well integrated into the landscape. Rooms are modern and smart, with down comforters, hardwood floors and great views.

Getting There & Away
For details of transportation to the park, see p391. Going to El Calafate from the park on the same day requires joining a tour or careful advance planning, since there is no direct service. Your best bet is to return to Puerto Natales.

Getting Around
Buses drop off and pick up passengers at Laguna Amarga, the Hielos Patagónicos catamaran launch at Pudeto and at park headquarters. A new, more direct road to Puerto Natales has opened but is not yet in use by most bus services; for more information, see p391.

The catamaran leaves Pudeto for Mountain Lodge Paine Grande (one way/roundtrip per person CH$11,000/17,000) at 9:30am, noon and 6pm December to mid-March, noon and 6pm in late March and November, and at noon only in September, October and April. Another launch travels Lago Grey between Hostería Lago Grey and Refugio Lago Grey (CH$70,000 roundtrip, 1½ to two hours) a couple of times daily; contact the *hostería* for the current schedule.

ARGENTINE PATAGONIA

Patagonia die-hards won't want to miss the Argentine side, and why not? With easy access to wilderness and a well-developed tourism infrastructure, it combines well with a trip to Chilean Patagonia. In contrast to the Chilean side, here the mountains are surrounded by vast tracts of steppe and plains. Personality-wise it also provides contrast: Argentines are notably more gregarious, a trait that even carries over to competition among tour operators, dining habits and nightlife.

EL CALAFATE
☎ 02902 / pop 15,000

Named for the berry that, once eaten, guarantees your return to Patagonia, El Calafate hooks you with another irresistible attraction: Glaciar Perito Moreno, 80km away in Parque Nacional Los Glaciares. The glacier is a magnificent must-see but its massive popularity has encouraged tumorous growth and rapid upscaling in the once-quaint Calafate. At the same time, it's a fun place to be, with a range of traveler services. The town's strategic location between El Chaltén and Torres del Paine (Chile) make it an inevitable stop for those in transit.

The main strip, Av Libertador, is dotted with cutesy knotted-pine constructions of souvenir shops, chocolate shops, restaurants and tour offices. Beyond, main-street pretensions melt away quickly; muddy roads lead to ad-hoc developments and open pastures.

January and February are the most popular and costly months to visit, but as shoulder-season visits are growing steadily, both availability and prices remain a challenge.

Information
LAUNDRY
El Lavadero (☎ 492-182; 25 de Mayo 43; per load AR$15; ☺ 8am-8pm)

MEDICAL SERVICES
Hospital Municipal Dr José Formenti (☎ 491-001; Av Roca 1487; ☺ 24hrs)

MONEY
Withdraw your cash before the weekend rush – it isn't uncommon for ATMs to run out on Sundays.
Banco Santa Cruz (Av Libertador 1285) Changes traveler's checks and has ATM.

EL CALAFATE

INFORMATION
ACA...1 B2
Banco Santa Cruz (ATM)..................2 B2
Cal Tur.......................................3 B2
Cooperativa Telefónica (CTC).........4 C2
Cooperativa Telefónica (CTC).........5 C1
El Lavadero..............................(see 9)
Hospital Municipal Dr José Formenti.6 A2
Parques Nacional Los Glaciares
    Office....................................7 B2
Post Office.................................8 B2
Thaler Cambio.........................(see 21)
Tiempo Libre..............................9 B2

SIGHTS & ACTIVITIES
Hielo y Aventura.......................10 C2
Museo de El Calafate.................11 D2
René Fernandez Campbell..........12 C2

SLEEPING
America del Sur.........................13 D1
Camping El Ovejero....................14 C2
Hospedaje Familiar Las Cabañitas..15 A2
Hostel del Glaciar Libertador.......16 D2
Hotel La Loma..........................17 C2
Marco Polo Inn.........................18 D1
Newenkelen.............................19 D1

EATING
Casimiro & Casimiro Biguá...........20 C2
el b'ar.....................................21 B2
La Cocina.................................22 B2
La Tablita.................................23 D2
Viva la Pepa.............................24 C2

DRINKING
The Grouse...............................25 D3

TRANSPORT
Aerolíneas Argentinas..............(see 21)
Bus Terminal...........................26 B2
Chalten Travel.........................27 B2
LADE....................................(see 26)
Localiza.................................28 D2

Thaler Cambio (9 de Julio s/n; 10am-1pm Mon-Fri, 5:30-7:30pm Sat & Sun) Usurious rates for traveler's checks, but open weekends.

POST
Post office (Av Libertador 1133)

TELEPHONE & INTERNET ACCESS
Cooperativa Telefónica (CTC; cnr Espora & Moyano) Also on Av Libertador near Perito Moreno.
Cyberpoint (Libertador 1070; 24hr) All-night internet.

TOURIST INFORMATION
ACA (Automóvil Club Argentino; 491-004; cnr 1 de Mayo & Av Roca; 9am-9pm) Argentina's auto club; good source for provincial road maps.
Municipal tourist office (491-090/466; www

.elcalafate.gov.ar, in Spanish; 8am-10pm) At the bus terminal; some English-speaking staff.
Parque Nacional Los Glaciares office (491-005/755; Av Libertador 1302; 8am-7pm Mon-Fri, 10am-8pm Sat & Sun) Better to get info here than at the park. Offers brochures and a decent map of Parque Nacional Los Glaciares.

TRAVEL AGENCIES
Most agents deal exclusively with nearby excursions and are unhelpful for other areas.
Tiempo Libre (491-207; tiempolibre@cotecal.com.ar; 25 de Mayo 43) Books flights.

Sights & Activities
North of town, **Laguna Nimez** (admission AR$3; 9am-9pm) is prime avian habitat but watching

birds from Calafate's shoreline on Lago Argentino can be just as good. Hiking up **Cerro Calafate** (850m) is possible but the route passes through marginal neighborhoods. While they are not considered dangerous, it is not exactly the ideal setting for hiking. To avoid them, ask a taxi to take you part way.

Anglers can take to the lakes with **Calafate Fishing** (☎ 493-311; Av Libertador 1826; ⊗ 10am-7pm Mon-Sat), offering fun fly-fishing trips to Lago Roca (full day AR$450) and Lago Strobbel, where you can test rumors that the biggest rainbow trout in the world lives here.

Biking is an excellent way to get a feel for the area and cruise the dirt roads by the lake. Tour operators (see below) offer 4WD trips to fossil beds as well as stays at regional *estancias*, where you can hike, ride horses or relax.

Tours

Some 40 travel agencies arrange excursions to the glacier and other local attractions. Tour prices (around AR$90 per person) for Glaciar Perito Moreno don't include the park entrance fee. Ask agents and other travelers about added benefits, like extra stops, boat trips, binoculars or multilingual guides.

Cal Tur (☎ 491-368; Av Libertador 1080) Specializes in El Chaltén tours and lodging packages.

Chaltén Travel (☎ 492-212/480; www.chaltentravel .com, in Spanish; Av Libertador 1174) Recommended tours to the glacier, stopping for wildlife viewing; binoculars provided; also specializes in RN 40 trips.

Hielo y Aventura (☎ 492-094/205; www.hieloyaven tura.com; Av Libertador 935) Glaciar Perito Moreno catamaran and trekking tours.

Overland Patagonia (☎ 491-243, 492-243; www .glaciar.com) Operates out of Hostel del Glaciar Libertador (right) and organizes recommended 'alternative' and full-moon trips to the glacier and guided trekking, camping and ice-hiking combos in El Chaltén.

René Fernandez Campbell (☎ 492-340; www.fernan dezcampbell.com; Libertador 867) Operates hourly passenger boats to the glacier.

Sleeping

Rates and availability fluctuate widely by season; high season is January and February, but it can extend from early November to April. In general, rates are relatively poor value compared to the rest of Argentina.

BUDGET

Most hostels offer pickup from the bus terminal.

Hostel de las Manos (☎ 492-996; www.hosteldelas manos.com.ar; Feruglio 59; d AR$150, dm without bathroom AR$30) Immaculate and personable, this hostel alternative is across the footbridge from 9 de Julio. Dorms are small but doubles have white wood paneling, bright bedspreads and new fixtures.

Hostel del Glaciar Libertador (☎ 491-792; www .glaciar.com; Av Libertador 587; dm/s/d HI members AR$31/183/200, nonmembers AR$37/220/241; ⊠ 🖵) At this complex with the Victorian facade the best deals are dorm bunks with thick covers. Modern facilities include a top-floor kitchen and a spacious common area with a plasma TV glued to sports channels. The staff seem overtaxed and inquiries take patience.

Marco Polo Inn (☎ 493-899; www.marcopoloinn calafate.com; Calle 405, No 82; HI members dm/d/tr AR$38/200/250, nonmembers AR$40/220/270; Ⓟ 🖵) A new addition with attentive service and spacious dorms featuring quilted bedspreads and wood-finished bunks.

our pick America del Sur (☎ 493-525; www.america hostel.com.ar; Puerto Deseado 151; dm/d AR$40/140; 🖵) This backpacker favorite boasts top-tier service and a stylish lodge setting with views. One thing you won't find here is solitude – it's bustling at every hour. All-you-can-eat barbecues are put on nightly (AR$35) to the rave review of guests. Reserve ahead.

MIDRANGE & TOP END

The tourist office has a complete list of *cabañas* and apartment-hotels, which are the best deals for groups and families.

Los Grillos (☎ 491-160; Los Condores 1215; d with/ without bathroom AR$140/110, 4-person cabin AR$180; Ⓟ) A quiet B&B with fresh rooms, soft beds and attentive service. Guests can serve themselves coffee, tea and spring water in the dining nook. The backyard cabin offers shaggy bedspreads and all new installations.

Hotel La Loma (☎ 491-016; www.lalomahotel.com; Av Roca 849; s/d AR$140/170, superior AR$175/265; Ⓟ 🐾) Antiques fill the creaky hallways and the reception boasts an open fire and plenty of books. While its exterior is nondescript, superior rooms are spacious and bright. Breakfast includes homemade bread and guests can take dips in the only indoor pool in town.

Hospedaje Familiar Las Cabañitas (☎ 491-118; lascabanitas@cotecal.com.ar; Valentin Feilberg 218; d/tr/q AR$160/210/240) Run by the endearing Giordano family, these storybook A-frames are somewhat dated but snug, with spiral

SOUTHERN PATAGONIA

staircases leading to loft beds. Sweet touches include English lavender and a sheltered dining patio brimming with plants. There's hot beverage service, kitchen use and meals upon request.

Newenkelen (☎ 493-943; www.newenkelen.com.ar; Puerto Deseado 223; d incl breakfast AR$180; **P**) Perched on a hill above town, this intimate option features a handful of immaculate brick rooms with tasteful bedding and mountain views. The Porteña owner can be convinced to give tango lessons in low-season.

Eating

el ba'r (9 de Julio s/n; snacks AR$8-17) The hotspot for you and your sweater-clad puppy to order espresso, *submarinos* (hot milk with melted chocolate bar), green tea or sandwiches is this trendy patio café.

Viva la Pepa (☎ 491-880; Amado 833; mains AR$21-40; ☯ 10am-midnight Thu-Tue) Decked in children's drawings, this cheerful café specializes in crepes but also offers great sandwiches (try the chicken with apples and blue cheese) with homemade bread, fresh juice and gourds of *maté*.

La Cocina (☎ 491-758; Av Libertador 1245; mains AR$20-30) This classic pasta factory makes satisfying noodles with savory sauces and serves up a whopping *lomo a la pobre* (steak and eggs) for the carb-adverse.

La Tablita (☎ 491-065; Coronel Rosales 24; mains AR$30-50) Steak and spit-roasted lamb are the stars at this satisfying *parrilla*, popular beyond measure. For average appetites even a half steak will do, rounded out with a good Malbec, fresh salads or garlic fries. Reserve ahead.

Pura Vida (☎ 493-356; Libertador 1876; mains AR$32-49; ☯ dinner Thu-Tue; **V**) Whole grains and abundant vegetarian dishes make this ambient eatery a traveler's treat. The tables are candlelit and the kitchen serves healthy food in huge portions. Try the gnocchi with saffron, rabbit with cream or pumpkin stew served in an enormous gourd. It's a 10-minute walk west of center.

Casimiro & Casimiro Bigua (☎ 492-590; Libertador 963; mains AR$35) With warm copper accents and a hustling staff, this chic eatery and *vinoteca* (wine bar) stocks 180 different Argentine wines. The chef creates wonderful homemade pastas, risotto, lamb stew and grilled trout, but the star feature is the grill.

Drinking

Grouse (☎ 491-281; Av Libertador 351; drinks AR$4-12) This Celtic pub-slash-karaoke hub aims to appeal to all whims. Look for live acts in summer, generous mixed drinks and draft cans of Guinness.

Shackleton Lounge (☎ 493-516; Libertador 3287) This laid-back lounge, 3km from the center, pleases crowds with good music and strong daiquiris.

Getting There & Away

AIR

The modern **Aeropuerto El Calafate** (ECA; ☎ 491-220/30) is 23km east of town off RP 11; the departure tax is US$18.

Aerolíneas Argentinas (☎ 492-814/16; 9 de Julio 57) flies every day to Bariloche (AR$879), Ushuaia (AR$35), Trelew (AR$820) and both Aeroparque and Ezeiza in Buenos Aires (AR$380 to AR$675).

LADE (☎ 491-262), at the bus terminal, flies a few times a week to Río Gallegos (AR$118), Comodoro Rivadavia (AR$203), Ushuaia (AR$280), Esquel (AR$412), Puerto Madryn (AR$335), Buenos Aires (AR$336) and other smaller regional airports.

BUS

Calafate's hilltop **bus terminal** (Av Roca s/n) is easily reached by a pedestrian staircase from the corner of Av Libertador and 9 de Julio. Book ahead in high season, as outbound seats can be in short supply. All of the following services depart from the bus terminal.

For El Chaltén (AR$55, 3½ hours), several companies share passengers and leave daily at 7:30am, 8am and 6:30pm, stopping midway at Estancia La Leona for coffee and tasty pies.

For Puerto Natales (AR$50, five hours), **Cootra** (☎ 491-444) departs daily at 8:30am, crossing the border at Cerro Castillo, where it may be possible to connect to Torres del Paine.

For Río Gallegos (AR$20 to AR$40, four hours), buses go daily at 3am, 4am, noon, 12:30pm and 2:30pm. **Freddy** (☎ 452-671) and Interlagos offer connections to Bariloche and Ushuaia that require leaving in the middle of the night and a change of buses in Río Gallegos.

From mid-October to April, **Chaltén Travel** (☎ 492-212; www.chaltentravel.com; Av Libertador 1174) goes to El Chaltén (AR$100 round-trip, three hours) daily at 8am and 6:30pm. Shuttles also

SOUTHERN PATAGONIA

run north along RN 40 to Perito Moreno and Los Antiguos (AR$215, 12 hours), departing on even-numbered days at 8am, to connect with onward service to Bariloche (AR$395, two days from Calafate) the next morning. The same service leaves from El Chaltén.

Getting Around

Call airport shuttle **Ves Patagonia** (☎ 494-355) for door-to-door service (one way/round-trip AR$15/25). There are several car rental agencies at the airport. **Localiza** (☎ 491-398, 02902-15-622-565; www.localiza.com.ar) offers car rentals for AR$186 daily with 200km.

PERITO MORENO & PARQUE NACIONAL LOS GLACIARES (SOUTH)

Among the Earth's most dynamic and accessible ice fields, **Glaciar Perito Moreno** is the stunning centerpiece of the southern sector of **Parque Nacional Los Glaciares** (admission AR$30). The glacier measures 30km long, 5km wide and 60m high, but what makes it exceptional in the world of ice is its constant advance – up to 2m per day, causing building-sized icebergs to calve from its face. In some ways, watching the glacier is a very sedentary park experience but it manages to nonetheless be thrilling.

The glacier formed as a low gap in the Andes allowed moisture-laden Pacific storms to drop their loads east of the divide, where they accumulated as snow. Over millennia, under tremendous weight, this snow has recrystallized into ice and flowed slowly eastward. The 1600 sq km trough of Lago Argentino, the country's largest single body of water, is unmistakable evidence that glaciers were once far more extensive than today.

Visiting the Moreno Glacier is no less an auditory than visual experience, as huge icebergs on the glacier's face calve and collapse into the **Canal de los Témpanos** (Iceberg Channel). From a series of catwalks and vantage points on the Península de Magallanes, visitors can see, hear and photograph the glacier safely as these enormous chunks crash into the water. The glacier changes appearance as the day progresses (the sun hits the face of the glacier in the morning).

Sights & Activities

Boat trips allow one to sense the enormity of the glacier, even though the boats keep a distance. **Hielo y Aventura** (☎ 02902-492-094/205; www.hieloyaventura.com; Av Libertador 935, El Calafate) runs

Safari Nautico (AR$35), a one-hour tour of Brazo Rico, Lago Argentino and the south side of Canal de los Témpanos. Catamarans crammed with up to 130 passengers leave hourly between 11:30am and 3:30pm from Puerto Bajo de las Sombras.

To see the glacier's main north face, **René Fernandez Campbell** (☎ 02902-492-340; www.fernandezcampbell.com; Libertador 867, El Calafate) operates 320-passenger boats (AR$38) from below the UTVM restaurant near the main lookout, hourly between 10:30am and 2:30pm.

Hielo y Aventura also offers **minitrekking** (AR$275) on the Moreno Glacier, a five-hour trek for groups of up to 20, involving a quick boat ride from Puerto Bajo de las Sombras, a walk through lenga forests, a quick chat on glaciology and then a 1½-hour ice walk using crampons. The more extensive **big ice** (AR$375) offers a worthwhile four-hour ice trek. Children under eight are not allowed; reserve ahead and bring your own food.

Sleeping & Eating

Unfortunately, camping at Bahía Escondida has been closed for recovery, since unattended campfires were threatening the area. Inquire about changes at the park. At the time of writing, a hotel and new confitería were being built near the glacier lookout. At the lookout, the year-round **UTVM** (☎ 02902-499-400; snacks AR$9-16, mains AR$20; ☼ 10am-6pm) restaurant offers sandwiches, coffee and desserts, and a set lunch for which reservations are advised.

Hostería Estancia Helsingfors (in Buenos Aires ☎ 011-4315-1222; www.helsingfors.com.ar; s/d AR$1068/1727; ☼ Oct-Apr) The simply stunning location oogling Mt Fitz Roy from Lago Viedma makes for lots of love-at-first-sight impressions. Intimate and welcoming, this former Finnish pioneer ranch is a highly regarded luxury destination, though it cultivates a relaxed, unpretentious ambiance. Guests pass the time on scenic but demanding mountain treks, rides and visits to Glaciar Viedma. Vintage wines accompany gourmet meals made with fresh garden produce. Rates represent a two-day, one-night stay, with transfers, an excursion and meals. It's on Lago Viedma's southern shore, 170km from El Chaltén and 180km from El Calafate.

Getting There & Away

The Moreno Glacier is 80km west of El Calafate via paved RP 11, passing through the

THE ERASURE OF GLACIERS

Ribbons of ice, stretched flat in sheets or sculpted by weather and fissured by pressure, glaciers' raw magnificence is boggling to behold. Some of the best places to see, hike or climb these massive conglomerations of ice, snow and rock are here in Patagonia.

During the ice age nearly a third of the planet was under glaciers, now they only cover about 10%. Yet hundreds dot the Patagonian landscape. The most accessible can be found in Argentina's Parque Nacional Los Glaciares (home of the famous Perito Moreno glacier), Chile's Torres del Paine and Bernardo O'Higgins National Parks, along the Beagle Channel and Chile's Patagonian fjords.

Glaciers are much more complex than simple mounds of frozen water. These rivers of ice flow downslope due to gravity, which deforms their layers as they move. Melted ice mixes with rock and soil on the bottom, grinding it into a lubricant that allows the glacier to slide along its bed. At the same time, debris from the bed is forced to the sides of the glacier, creating features called moraines. Movement also causes cracks and deformities called crevasses. As snow falls on the accumulation area, it compacts to ice. The ablation area is where all the winter snow melts revealing bare ice in the summer. When accumulation outpaces melting, the glacier advances; but when there's more melting or evaporation than accumulation, the glacier recedes. Since 1980, global warming has contributed greatly to widespread glacial retreat. Currently, all the world's small ice caps and glaciers, such as those in Chile and Argentine, contribute about 60% of the sea level rise caused by global ice mass loss.

While the Perito Moreno glacier is advancing, it is an anomaly among the rest of Patagonia's glaciers. Most northern Patagonian glaciers are thinning at a rate of 2m per year; over the past decade some have been retreating hundreds of meters per year. Scientists believe the change is both a product of rising temperatures and a drier climate overall.

Glaciers will play a crucial role in the future of our world. Changes to the atmosphere affect the health of glaciers and changes to glaciers, in turn, affect the health of the atmosphere. The melting of glaciers around the world will affect significant changes to the sea level. Also, as we head into a period of increasing scarcity of potable water, we should remember that 75% of the world's fresh water is contained in glaciers.

Carolyn McCarthy with contributions by Ursula Rick

breathtaking scenery around Lago Argentino. Bus tours are frequent in summer; see p402, or simply stroll down Av Libertador. Buses to the glacier leave El Calafate (AR$90 round-trip) in the early morning and afternoon, returning around noon and 7pm.

EL CHALTÉN & PARQUE NACIONAL LOS GLACIARES (NORTH)
☎ 02962 / pop 600

The Fitz Roy Range, with its rugged wilderness and shark-tooth summits, is the de-facto mountaineering mecca of Argentina. Occupying the northern half of Parque Nacional Los Glaciares, this sector offers numerous, well-marked trails for trekking and jaw-dropping scenery – that is, when the clouds clear. The town effectively closes down in winter and services are few during the muddy shoulder seasons.

At the entrance to the northern sector, the ragtag village of **El Chaltén** serves the thousands of visitors who make summer pilgrimages to explore the range. This is a frontier town: it was slapped together in 1985 to beat Chile to the land claim. As Argentina's youngest town, it still has to sort out details like banks (there are no ATMs), roads and zoning. Hiker services continue to evolve rapidly; the recent paving of RP 23 may improve them, even as it makes way for large-scale tourism.

Information
Newspapers, cell phones and money exchange have yet to hit El Chaltén, but there's now mercurial satellite internet, a gas station, long-distance call centers – and land set aside for an ATM, bus terminal and mobile phone antennae.

Chaltén Travel (☎ 493-005/92; cnr Güemes & Lago del Desierto) Books airline tickets and offers weather-dependent internet service for AR$12 per hour.

Municipal tourist office (☎ 493-270; comfomel chalten@yahoo.com.ar; Güemes 21; ⊗ 8am-8pm) Friendly and extremely helpful, with lodging lists and good information on town and tours. English is spoken.

Park ranger office (☎ 493-004/24; admission free, but donations welcome; ☺ 8am-7pm) Daytime buses all stop for a short bilingual orientation at this new visitor center, just before the bridge over the Río Fitz Roy. Park rangers distribute a map and town directory and do a good job of explaining the park's ecological issues. Climbing documentaries are shown at 3pm daily – great for rainy days. Rangers can answer questions about the area's hikes, and issue climbing permits. They also post a lodging list.

Puesto Sanitario (☎ 493-033; Agostini btwn McLeod & Güemes) Provides basic health services.

Viento Oeste (☎ 493-021/200; San Martín 898) En route to Campamento Madsen, this shop sells books, maps and souvenirs and rents a wide range of camping equipment, as do several other sundries shops around town.

Zafarrancho Behind Rancho Grande Hostel, this bar-café has internet and screens movies.

Activities

Most travelers come to El Chaltén for the hiking, but don't discount other outdoor opportunities. You can trade dirt for ice with guided ice trekking or ice climbing, rock climb or give your gams a rest by horseback riding, kayaking or canoeing.

Casa de Guias (☎ 493-118; Av San Martín s/n; www.casadeguias.com.ar) Friendly, with AAGM (Argentine Association of Mountain Guides) certified guides who speak English. Offerings include mountain traverses, mountain ascents for the very fit and rock-climbing classes.

El Relincho (☎ 493-007, in El Calafate 02902-491961; San Martín 505, El Chaltén) Guided horseback riding to the pretty valley of Río de las Vueltas (AR$110, three hours).

Fitzroy Expediciones (☎ 493-017; www.fitzroyexpediciones.com.ar; Lionel Terray 145, El Chaltén) Mountaineering and watersport-oriented, with glacier-trekking excursions and guided kayaking trips on the Río de las Vueltas (half-day) and Río La Leona (two days). Daily trips go to Lago del Desierto for three-hour canoe and kayak excursions.

Patagonia Aventura (☎ 493-110; www.patagoniaaventura.com.ar, in Spanish) Offers trekking (AR$230) and ice climbing ($270) on Glaciar Viedma.

Sleeping

Reservations should be made at least one month in advance for the January–February high season – demand here is that great. Or, bring a tent since campgrounds are a sure bet.

CAMPING

Campamento Confluencia (El Chaltén; campsites free) A free, zero-amenity campground across from the park ranger office and visitor center.

Campamento Madsen (El Chaltén; campsites free) Near the start of the Fitz Roy hike, this windy and exposed campground sits on the banks of Río de las Vueltas. Showers (AR$4) and laundry service (AR$20) are available for all campers at Rancho Grande Hostel (see below).

Camping El Refugio (☎ 493-221; San Martín s/n; camping per person AR$15, dm AR$35) In front of Rancho Grande, this private campground is attached to a basic hostel with hot showers included in the fee. Sites are exposed and there is some sparse firewood (fires are OK).

El Relincho (☎ 493-007; San Martín 505; campsites per person AR$16) Another private campground, similarly wind-whipped.

HOTELS & HOSTERÍAS

Rancho Grande Hostel (☎ 493-092; www.hostelspatagonia.com; San Martín 724; dm/d/tr/q AR$35/180/195/230; P X 🖳) Serving as Chaltén's Grand Central Station (Chaltén Travel buses stop here), this bustling backpacker factory has a little something for everyone: from bus reservations to internet (AR$12 per hour) and café service. Clean four-bed rooms are stacked with blankets and bathrooms have shower stalls. The shared kitchen is tiny, and the common dining area (meals AR$13 to AR$30) bright, but both are often crowded with nonguests. HI discounts.

Albergue Patagonia (☎ 493-019; patagoniahostel@yahoo.com.ar; San Martín 493; d AR$180, dm/d without bathroom AR$40/100; ☺ Sep-May; P X) This welcoming wooden farmhouse has a dormitory building with spacious, modern dorms and common areas. Services are good and the atmosphere is humming. Credit cards and travelers checks are accepted. HI discounts.

Condor de Los Andes (☎ 493-101; www.condordelosandes.com; cnr Río las Vueltas & Halvorsen; dm/d AR$40/180; ☺ Oct-April) This homey hostel has the feel of a ski lodge, with worn bunks, toasty rooms and a roaring fire. Service is good, the guest kitchen is immaculate and there are comfortable lounge spaces. Extras include breakfast (AR$7), lunch boxes (AR$22) and laundry (AR$15).

Hospedaje La Base (☎ 493-031; labase@elchaltenpatagonia.com.ar; cnr Lago del Desierto & Hensen; d incl breakfast AR$150) These spacious, good-value rooms also offer kitchen access. The reception area has a popular video loft with a multilingual collection.

our pick Nothofagus B&B (☎ 493-087; www.elchalten.com/nothofagus; cnr Hensen & Riquelme; s/d/tr

incl breakfast AR$170/180/220; 🕑 Sep-Apr; 🅿 ⊠)
Attentive and adorable, this chalet-style inn
offers a great green retreat. It is one of few
Patagonian lodgings to separate organic
waste and replaces towels only when asked.
Wooden-beam rooms have carpet and some
views but most have bathrooms shared with
one other room. Owners Eva and Gerardo,
former guides, offer top service.

Hostería El Puma (☎ 493-095; www.hosteria
elpuma.com.ar; Lionnel Terray 212; s/d/tr incl breakfast
AR$330/420/460; 🅿) This luxury lodge with 12
comfortable rooms offers intimacy without
pretension. The rock climbing and summit
photographs and maps lining the hall may
inspire your next expedition but lounging by
the fireplace is the most savory way to end the
day. There's attentive service, a good breakfast
and gourmet eating at El Terray on site.

Eating & Drinking

Groceries, especially anything fresh, are limited and expensive, so bring what you can
from El Calafate.

La Chocolatería (☎ 493-008; Lago del Desierto 104;
snacks AR$6-15) This irresistible chocolate factory
makes an intimate evening out, with options
ranging from spirit-spiked hot cocoa to wine
and fondue.

El Bodegón Cervecería (☎ 493-109; San Martín
s/n; snacks AR$12) That aprés-hike pint usually
evolves into a night out in this humming
pub with *simpatico* staff and a feisty female
beer-master. Savor a stein of unfiltered blond
pilsner or turbid bock with a bowl of popcorn.
Pizza, pastas and *locro* (stew typical to the
north) are available.

Fuegia Bistro (☎ 493-019; San Martín 493; mains
AR$18-34; ⊠ Ⓥ) Favored for its warm ambi-
ance and savory entrees, this upscale eatery
boasts good veggie options and a reasonable
wine list. Try the lamb in ginger sauce or trout
with sage butter. It's also open for breakfast.

Patagonicus (☎ 493-025; cnr Güemes & Madsen;
pizzas AR$21) The best pizza in town, with
20 kinds of pie, salads and wine served at
sturdy wood tables. Cakes and coffee are also
worth trying.

Estepa (☎ 493-069; cnr Cerro Solo & Antonio Rojo; mains
AR$22-35) Local favorite Estepa cooks up con-
sistent, flavorful dishes like lamb with calafate
berry sauce, trout ravioli or spinach crepes.
Pizza is popular and hikers can also order
lunch boxes.

Getting There & Away

El Chaltén is 220km from El Calafate via
newly paved roads.

For El Calafate (AR$60, 3½ hours), **Chaltén
Travel** (☎ 493-092; www.chaltentravel.com; Av Güemes &
Lago Desierto) departs daily in summer at 6:30am,
7am, 1pm and 6pm from Rancho Grande. **Cal-
tur** (☎ 493-079; San Martín 520) and **Taqsa** (☎ 493-068;
Av Antonio Rojo 88) also make the trip, but none of
these companies will take advance reservations. Service is less frequent off-season.

Tierra del Fuego

'In those far-away places,' writes pioneer Lucas Bridges about Tierra del Fuego, 'a patient was either dead or better by the time the doctor arrives.' That was 1947. Fast-forward to today and this hooked isle punctuating Patagonia's tail is no longer so desperately secluded, yet it sustains its end-of-the-world allure. Virgin it was. Less than a century after its original peoples perished, petroleum has been discovered, resorts and fishing lodges have appeared and the eastern seaboard has been paved. But the immense Fuegian wilderness, with its slate-gray seascapes, murky crimson bogs and wind-worn forests, endures as awesome and irritable as it had been in the days of Bridges.

Split down the middle between Chile and Argentina, the remote Chilean side consists of hardscrabble outposts, lonely sheep ranches, and a roadless expanse of woods, lakes and nameless mountains. Porvenir, a former gold mining post, is the provincial capital. In contrast, the Argentine half buzzes with tourism and industry. Adventure hub Ushuaia sits within arm's reach of ski resorts and the daunting Darwin Range. The Beagle Channel separates Tierra del Fuego from Chile's Isla Navarino and uninhabited groups of islands that peter out at Cabo de Hornos, the southern terminus of the Americas.

And if Tierra del Fuego is not remote enough, Antarctica remains just a flight away.

HIGHLIGHTS

- Skirt the scenic cliffs of Bahía Inútil while exploring the empty back roads around **Porvenir** (p410)
- Steal alongside sea lions while kayaking the chop of the **Beagle Channel** (p420)
- Whiz through the frozen valleys above **Ushuaia** (p420) while mushing a team of huskies
- Engulf yourself in austral wilderness trekking around Isla Navarino's jagged peaks on the five-day **Circuito Dientes de Navarino** (p414)
- Put yourself where two great oceans meet by circumnavigating the legendary **Cabo de Hornos** (p414) in a sailboat

■ POPULATION: 47,992 SQ KM ■ AREA: 47,992 SQ KM

TIERRA DEL FUEGO

History

In 1520, when Magellan passed through the strait that now bears his name, neither he nor any other European explorer had any immediate interest in the land and its people. Seeking a passage to the Spice Islands of Asia, early navigators feared and detested the stiff westerlies, hazardous currents and violent seas that impeded their progress. Consequently, the Selk'nam, Haush, Yaghan and Alacaluf peoples who populated the area faced no immediate competition for their lands and resources.

These groups were hunters and gatherers. The Selk'nam, also known as Ona, and the Haush subsisted primarily on hunting guanaco and dressing in its skins, while the Yaghan and Alacalufes, known collectively as 'Canoe Indians,' lived on fish, shellfish and marine mammals. The Yaghan (also known as the Yamaná) consumed the 'Indian bread' fungus that feeds off the ñire, a species of southern beech. Despite frequently inclement weather, they wore little clothing, but constant fires kept them warm. European sailors dubbed the region 'Land of Fire' for the Yaghan campfires they spotted along the shoreline.

As Spain's control of its American empire dwindled, the area slowly opened to settlement by other Europeans, ensuring the rapid demise of the indigenous Fuegians, whom Europeans struggled to understand. Darwin, visiting the area in 1834, wrote that the difference between the Fuegians ('among the most abject and miserable creatures I ever saw') and Europeans was greater than that between wild and domestic animals. On an earlier voyage, though, Captain Robert Fitzroy of the *Beagle* had abducted a few Yaghan, whom he returned after several years of missionary education in England.

No European power took any real interest in settling the region until Britain occupied the Falkland Islands (Islas Malvinas) in the 1770s. However, the successor governments of Chile and Argentina felt differently. The Chilean presence on the Strait of Magellan beginning in 1843, along with increasing British evangelism, spurred Argentina to formalize its authority at Ushuaia in 1884. In 1978 Chile and Argentina nearly went to war over claims

TIERRA DEL FUEGO

to three small disputed islands in the Beagle Channel. International border issues in the area were not resolved until 1984 and are still the subject of some discussion.

Climate

Unrelenting winds sweep the relatively arid northern plains of Isla Grande while high rainfall supports dense deciduous and evergreen forests in the mountainous southern half. The maritime climate is surprisingly mild, even in winter, but its unpredictability makes foul-weather gear essential year-round. Weather is typically wet around the storm-battered bogs characteristic of the archipelago's remote southern and western zones.

Getting There & Away

The most common route from Patagonia to Tierra del Fuego is via the Chilean ferry crossing at Punta Delgada (p382). Roads within Chilean Tierra del Fuego are largely rough and unpaved. If you are taking a vehicle past Porvenir, it should be 4WD or at least have good clearance and a spare tire. Those renting a car will need special documents and extra insurance to cross into Argentina; most rental agencies can arrange this paperwork given advance notice.

Visitors can hop a short flight from Punta Arenas to Porvenir. It is also possible to enter the region from Ushuaia (Argentina), a major transportation hub with planes, ferries and buses that access many of southern Patagonia's destinations. Frequent buses link Punta Arenas with Ushuaia; in fact, many travelers fly into Ushuaia as the starting point for southern explorations. If you travel from Ushuaia to Chile's Isla Navarino by boat make sure to visit customs at the airport.

For expanded coverage of the Argentine places mentioned in this guide and for information on destinations further into Argentina, see Lonely Planet's *Argentina*.

Getting Around

Half the island is Argentine; have your passport ready for border crossings. It's necessary to take a car-passenger ferry to Tierra del Fuego, either from Punta Arenas on the *Melinka* or via the shorter crossing at Punta Delgada (p382). Those traveling by bus can make connections through Punta Arenas (p383) or cities in southern Argentina.

CHILEAN TIERRA DEL FUEGO

Foggy, windy and wet, Chile's slice of Tierra del Fuego includes half of the main island of Isla Grande, the far-flung Isla Navarino and a group of smaller islands, many of them uninhabited. Only home to 7000 Chileans, this is the least populated region in Chile. Porvenir is considered the main city, though even that status could be considered an overstatement. These parts can't help but exude a rough and rugged charm and those willing to venture this far can relish its end-of-the-world emptiness. Increasingly, anglers are lured to the little-known inland lakes and adventurers to the wild backcountry of Estancia Yendegaia. Tourism should ramp up as the road from Estancia Vicuña to Estancia Yendegaia nears completion and a public airport is added.

PORVENIR

☎ 061 / pop 5465

For a slice of home-baked Fuegian life, this is it. Most visitors come on a quick daytrip from Punta Arenas often tainted by a touch of sea-sickness from the crossing. But spending a night in this rusted village of metal-clad Victorians affords you an opportunity to explore the nearby bays and countryside and absorb a little laid-back local life. As one Chilean said of it, 'There's nothing to see – but that's the point!'

Porvenir has a peculiar heritage. When gold was discovered in 1879, waves of immigrants arrived, many from Croatia, and most did not strike it rich. When sheep *estancias* (grazing ranches) began to spring up, the immigrants found more reliable work. Chilotes (from the Chilean island of Chiloé) appeared in droves for the fishing and *estancia* work, and the chance of a better life. Today's population is a unique combination of the two.

The gravel road east, along scenic stretches of Bahía Inútil to the Argentine border at San Sebastián, is in good shape. From San Sebastián (where there's gas and a motel), northbound motorists should avoid the heavily traveled and rutted truck route directly north and instead take the equally good route from Onaisín to the petroleum company town

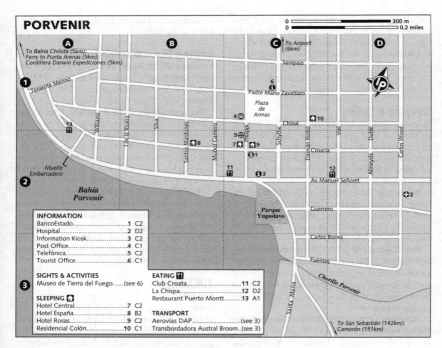

PORVENIR

INFORMATION
BancoEstado.............................1 C2
Hospital...................................2 D2
Information Kiosk......................3 C2
Post Office...............................4 C1
Telefónica................................5 C2
Tourist Office...........................6 C1

SIGHTS & ACTIVITIES
Museo de Tierra del Fuego......(see 6)

SLEEPING
Hotel Central...........................7 C2
Hotel España............................8 B2
Hotel Rosas..............................9 C2
Residencial Colón....................10 C1

EATING
Club Croata.............................11 C2
La Chispa................................12 D2
Restaurant Puerto Montt.........13 A1

TRANSPORT
Aerovías DAP........................(see 3)
Transbordadora Austral Broom..(see 3)

of Cerro Sombrero en route to the crossing of the Strait of Magellan at Punta Delgada–Puerto Espora.

Information

BancoEstado (cnr Philippi & Croacia; Mon-Fri 9am-2pm) Has a 24-hour ATM.

Hospital (580-034; Carlos Wood, btwn Av Manuel Señoret & Guerrero)

Post office (Phillipi 176; 9am-1pm & 3-6pm Mon-Fri, 10am-12:30pm Sat) Faces the verdant plaza.

Telefónica (Philippi 277)

Tourist office (580-094/8; Padre Mario Zavattaro 402; 9am-5pm Mon-Fri, 11am-5pm Sat & Sun) Information is also available at the handicrafts shop on the *costanera* (seaside road) between Philippi and Schythe.

Sights

On the plaza, the intriguing **Museo de Tierra del Fuego** (580-094/8; Padre Mario Zavattaro 402; admission CH$500; 8am-5pm Mon-Thu, 8am-4pm Fri) has some unexpected materials, including Selk'nam skulls and mummies, musical instruments used by the mission Indians on Isla Dawson and an exhibit on early Chilean cinematography.

Tours

Gold-panning, horseback riding and 4WD tours can be arranged through the tourist office. Outfitter **Cordillera Darwin Expediciones** (580-167, 099-888-6380; www.cordilleradarwin.com; Bahía Chilota s/n at Ferry) organizes cool outings to view Peale's dolphins around Bahía Chilote in a traditional Chilote-style fishing boat (CH$15,000, including meals). Well-recommended, longer camping and horseback-riding trips include visits to Río Condor (three days/two nights CH$150,000) and an intense, week-long adventure that includes

---

BEST ENEMIES

The excellent Chilean film *Mi Mejor Enemigo* (2005) takes viewers inside Chile's 1970's border dispute with neighboring Argentina from the soldiers' point of view. In the story, a lost Chilean troop meets up with an Argentine patrol in the middle of nowhere. Precarious relations ensue since neither group knows which country they are technically in.

TIERRA DEL FUEGO

kayaking, centolla- (king crab) and fly-fishing, and riding to Glaciar Marinelli (groups of seven or more, November to May). Trips leave only with a minimum number of participants. The office is located in front of the ferry landing in a restaurant; ask for the friendly Pechuga.

Sleeping & Eating

Sleeping options in Porvenir are slim, owing to the fact that long-term workers season-ally occupy hotels. Travelers shouldn't have a problem finding something, but reserve in advance in the off-chance that there's a min-ing convention in town.

Residencial Colón (☎ 581-157; Damián Riobó 198; r per person without bathroom CH$8000; P) Often filled with fisheries employees, this rickety pension offers the cheapest digs in town. Cheap meals can also be arranged.

Hotel Central (☎ 580-077; Philippi 298; s/d incl break-fast CH$12,000/20,000) Facing Hotel Rosas, this un-assuming option brims with matronly charm on the inside. Snug rooms have hardwood floors and good beds. There is a comfortable sitting area as well.

Hotel Rosas (☎ 580-088; hotelrosas@chile.com; Philippi 296; s/d CH$14,000/20,000) Eleven clean and pleasant rooms offer heating and cable TV. Alberto, the owner, knows heaps about the region and ar-ranges tours to Circuito del Loro, a historical mining site. The restaurant gets crowded for meals (plato del día CH$3500), serving fresh seafood and more.

Hotel España (☎ 580-160; Croacia 698; s/d/t incl break-fast AR$15,000/25,000/36,000; P) This ambling hotel has spacious, impeccably kept rooms with views of the bay. Rooms have Berber carpets, TV and central heating. There is a downstairs café and parking in the back.

La Chispa Restauant (☎ 580-054; Av Manuel Señoret 202; plato del día CH$3000; 🕑 noon-3.30pm & 8pm-1am) In an aquamarine century-old fire house, El Chispa packs with locals for salmon dinners, lamb and mashed potatoes and other home-cooked fare. The lodgings (single/double CH$7000/12,000) are several basic rooms upstairs, often filled with workers. It's a cou-ple of blocks uphill from the water.

Club Croata (☎ 580-053; Av Manuel Señoret 542; mains CH$3000-5000; 🕑 11am-4pm, 7-10:30pm Tue-Sun) Formal to the verge of stuffy, this traditional restaurant nonetheless puts together good sea-food meals at reasonable prices, in addition to Croat specialties like pork chops with chucrut

(sauerkraut). The polished pub section stays open until 3am.

Getting There & Around

Aerovías DAP (☎ 580-089; www.dap.cl; Av Manuel Señoret near Philippi) flies to Punta Arenas (CH$19,000) Monday to Saturday from November to March, with fewer flights in low season.

Transbordadora Austral Broom (☎ 580-089; www.tabsa.cl; Av Manuel Señoret) operates the car-passenger ferry Melinka to Punta Arenas (CH$4300/CH$28,000 per person/vehicle, 2½ to four hours), which usually leaves at 9am but has some afternoon departures; check the current online schedule.

The bus to the ferry terminal (CH$500), 5km away, departs from the waterfront kiosk on Av Manuel Señoret an hour before the ferry departure. Tickets are purchased on-board.

For the airport, 6km north of town, DAP runs a door-to-door shuttle (CH$1500) and taxis charge CH$3000.

TIMAUKEL

pop 420

South of Bahía Inútil (the Useless Bay), the region of Timaukel occupies the southern section of Chilean Tierra del Fuego. It is ea-gerly trying to reinvent itself as an ecotourism destination – a far rosier option than being logged by US-based Trillium Corporation, which was the plan some years back. Few roads lead into this region, with even less public transportation. On the southern shore of the bay, **Camerón** is a large estancia owing its name to a pioneer sheep-farming family from New Zealand. Here, the municipal tourist office may have information on latest developments. To the south, the cherished fly-fishing getaway **Lago Blanco** is accessible only by car, and the only accommodations on offer are the nearby exclusive fishing lodges. A controversial new road leads south of Lago Blanco to access Lago Fagnano (a new park currently administered by Fundación Yendegaia), Estancia Yendegaia and the Beagle Channel.

ESTANCIA YENDEGAIA

Serene glacier-rimmed bays and native Fuegian forest comprise Estancia Yendegaia, a 400-sq-km park pending donation to Parques Nacionales. Located in the Cordillera Darwin, it is a strategic conservation link be-tween Argentina's Parque Nacional Tierra del Fuego and Chile's Parque Nacional Alberto de Agostini. A one-time *estancia*, this private park is in the process of removing livestock and rehabilitating trails. Its transformation should be large-scale, with an airport in the works and a road soon open to the public. Trails are planned to Glaciar Stoppani and through Valle Lapataia to Paso de Las Lagunas, although the many river crossings make horseback trekking a more viable option. For now only wild camping (without toilets or services) is possible.

Unfortunately, access is difficult and expensive. Transbordadora Austral Broom's ferry between Punta Arenas and Puerto Williams will drop passengers off if given advance notice; for details see p382. From Puerto Williams, the trip takes seven hours. The once-weekly naval boats from Punta Arenas to Puerto Williams will drop passengers at the southern approach.

The park will soon be donated to Chile and run by Parques Nacionales, but for now, visitor information can be obtained through **Fundación Yendegaia** (☎ /fax 02-204-1914; fax 209-2527; yendegaia@patagonia.com).

ISLA NAVARINO
☎ 061 / pop 2200
For authentic end-of-the-earth ambiance, this remote outpost wins the contest without even campaigning. Isla Navarino is a rugged backpacker's paradise. Located south across the Beagle Channel from Ushuaia, its mostly uninhabited wilderness hosts a rugged terrain of peat bogs, southern beech forest and jagged, toothy spires known as Dientes del Navarino, also a famed trekking route. By a quirk, the island is considered by Santiago to be part of Chilean Antarctica, not Chilean Tierra del Fuego or Magallanes. The naval settlement of Puerto Williams is the only town on the island, the official port of entry for vessels en route to Cabo de Hornos and Antarctica, and home to the last living Yaghan speaker.

A permanent European presence was established on the island by mid-19th-century missionaries who were followed by fortune-seekers during the 1890s gold rush. Current inhabitants include the Chilean navy, municipal employees and octopus and crab fishermen. The remaining mixed-race descendants of the Yaghan people live in the small coastal village of Villa Ukika.

Some 40,000 beavers (see the boxed text, p416) introduced from Canada in the 1940s now plague the island. You can do your part to eradicate this invader by choosing to have it for dinner, if you can find an open restaurant.

Puerto Williams
☎ 061 / pop 2500
Those stationed here might feel marooned, but for travelers Puerto Williams smarts of great adventure. Not much happens. In town, action means the wind hurtling debris while oblivious cows graze on the plaza and yards are stacked roof-deep with firewood. With transportation expensive and irregular, Williams feels cut off, but complaints that it's a forgotten burg are far more common from locals than its few tourists, who recognize buried treasure when they see it.

The village centers around a green roundabout and a concrete slab plaza called the Centro Comercial. Walk a few minutes from town and you will be in moss-draped lenga forest, climbing steeply above treeline. The island's 150km of trails could easily rival those of Torres del Paine, but there are no *refugios* here and certainly no cold brewskis on the hoof. If hiking, take a companion, get directions from locals before heading out and register with the *carabineros* (police), as trail markings may be worn and maps hard to come by.

INFORMATION
Near the main roundabout, the Centro Comercial has the post office, internet, DAP airline and a couple of call centers. There is no money exchange but Banco de Chile has an ATM machine.

Good general information is available online at www.ecoturismocabodehornos.cl. **Turismo SIM** (☎ 621-150/227; www.simltd.com; santa maria@simltd.com; Margaño 168) is a good source of local information. The **municipalidad** (☎ 621-011; www.municipalidadcabodehornos.cl, in Spanish; O'Higgins 165) has some tourist information.

SIGHTS
The original bow of the *Yelcho*, which rescued Ernest Shackleton's Antarctic expedition from Elephant Island in 1916, sits near the entrance to the military quarters.

Newly remodeled, the **Museo Martín Gusinde** (☎ 621-043; cnr Araguay & Gusinde; donation requested; ❤ 9am-1pm & 2:30-7pm Mon-Fri, 2:30-6:30pm Sat & Sun) explores the history of Yaghan settlement with displays of key objects (many from the Guisinde collection and on loan) and descriptive information panels (soon to be translated into English). There is a beautiful authentic bark canoe near the entrance. The museum honors the German priest and ethnographer who worked among the Yaghans from 1918 to 1923. Volunteers with some Spanish are welcome. At the time of writing, a stylish café was in the works, as well as an internet center.

A 15-minute walk east of town along the waterfront leads to the settlement of Villa Ukika. Its modest crafts shop **Kipa-Akar** (House of Woman) sells language books, jewelry and whale-bone knives. Ask a villager for help if it's closed.

Latin America's southernmost ethnobotanical park, **Omora** (www.omora.org) has trails with plant names marked in Yaghan, Latin and Spanish. Take the road to the right of the Virgin altar 4km (one hour) toward Puerto Navarino.

ACTIVITIES
Within minutes of Puerto Williams, you can be in some of the Southern Cone's most breathtaking scenery, Dientes de Navarino (Teeth of Navarino). Beginning at the Virgin altar just outside of town, the five-day, 53.5km **Circuito Dientes de Navarino** (Navarino Circuit) winds around the jagged mountainous spires, taking you through a spectacular wilderness of exposed rock and secluded lakes. This circuit is normally done in a clockwise direction over a five-day period, but can be extended with numerous possible side trips, including the Mirador de los Dientes, Laguna Chevallay, Laguna Alta or even the remote Lago Windhond. Fit hikers can knock out the trek in four days in the (relatively) dry summer months. Be aware that markings have faded on the hike: GPS, used in conjunction with marked maps, is a handy navigational tool. Winter hikes are only recommended for the most experienced and prepared trekkers.

Another alternative is the four-day **Lago Windhond** trek, with decent markings and more sheltered hiking through forest and peat bogs, making it a better alternative if the weather is particularly windy. For more details on trekking possibilities, refer to Lonely Planet's *Trekking in the Patagonian Andes*.

If you aren't a hardnosed hiker, there is a superb lookout point (three to four hours

round-trip), **Cerro Bandera**, which can be reached via the beginning of the Navarino circuit. The trail ascends steeply through the wind-sculpted ñire forests draped with old man's beard to blustery stone-littered hilltops with stunning vistas of the Beagle Channel, Tierra del Fuego and the Dientes.

For maps, contact Turismo Shila (below) or Fuegia & Co (below).

TOURS
Many local lodgings can arrange tours of the island with negotiable prices. For guided fishing and hiking, contact local guide Luis Tiznado at **Turismo Shila** (☎ 621-745; www.turismo shila.cl; Plaza de Ancla s/n; ☽ 9am-1pm, 3pm-7pm). The small kiosk stocks basic hiking maps and gas for camp stoves. You can also rent camping gear and bikes (CH$5000 per day) here.

For guided trekking or logistical support, Denis Chevallay at **Fuegia & Co** (☎ 621-251; fuegia@ usa.net; Patrullero Ortiz 049) offers professional guiding for two people or more (four-day hiking trip CH$325,000 per person). He speaks French, German and English and has a wealth of botanical and historical knowledge. Guiding includes porter support and a satellite emergency phone. Day trips to archaeological sites are also available.

For yacht tours, contact **Turismo SIM** (☎ 621-150/062; www.simltd.com; Margaño 168), whose warm German and Venezuelan owners Wolf and Jeanette run reputable sailing trips on the Beagle Channel, Cabo de Hornos and the Antarctic Peninsula. Flying under the Chilean flag, their boats enjoy better access than foreign vessels. They also arrange trekking, horseback riding and expeditions, including Dientes de Navarino, Cordillera Darwin, the far-flung lakes of Isla Navarino and the South Georgia Islands.

Fishing trips and tailor-made nautical excursions are available through **Lancha Patriota** (☎ 621-367; 6-person boat US$300/day) with captain Edwin Olivares.

SLEEPING
Refugio El Padrino (☎ 621-136; ceciliamancillao@yahoo .com.ar; Costanera 267; dm CH$10,000; ☒) Guests get to feel right at home at this cheery, clean space that's all self-serve (including check in). Your best bet for budget views, it sits right on the channel, with an outdoor deck to watch the sunset from. If you get here on foot, note that the houses do not go in numerical order.

Hostal Coirón (☎ 621-227; www.simltd.com; Maragano 168; dm/d CH$10,000/25,000; 🖳) Settle yourself into the loungy atmosphere of strummers strumming and backpackers repacking for the woods. Run by friendly Argentine Martin, this basic hostel fosters unkempt cool, with free laundry, internet and cooking privileges. It's also the place to book boat transfers to Ushuaia.

our pick **Residencial Pusaki** (☎ 621-118; patty pusaki@yahoo.es; Piloto Pardo 260; s/d CH$10,500/21,000) With legendary warmth, Patty welcomes travelers into this cozy home with comfortable, carpeted rooms, some with bathrooms (at no extra cost – first come, first served). Mirthful outbreaks and social sprees make it the place to meet people and make friends, but it isn't always ideal for getting those forty winks.

Hostal Lajuwa (☎ 621-267; Villa Ukika; dm incl breakfast CH$12,000) These clean dorm-style rooms in the Yaghan community are a bit isolated but make for an interesting cultural exchange.

Lakutaia (☎ 621-733; www.lakutaia.cl; d CH$125,000) Think of it as an elegant retreat, starting with a sprawling great room offering Beagle Channel panoramas. Given how slow tourism is on the island, guests might find this high-style lodge on the quiet side for now. Local history books, botanical guides and maps make the library worth a rainy-day visit, but get outside if you can. Lakutaia's multiday programs take you sailing a schooner around glaciers or following in Darwin's route. There's also guided treks and horseback riding. It's near the airport, three kilometers east of town.

EATING & DRINKING

Of the few supermarkets, Simon & Simon is the best, with fresher vegetables, fast food and great pastries.

Club de Yates Micalvi (☎ 621-042; sandwiches CH$3000, drinks CH$2500; ☙ open late, closed Jun–Aug) As watering holes go, this may be like no other. A grounded German cargo boat, the *Milcalvi* was declared a regional naval museum in 1976 but found infinitely better use as a floating bar, frequented by navy men and yachties. Drinks don't come cheap, but if you're lucky you'll see an earring ceremony, where a young sailor gets a golden hoop rammed through his earlobe in old pirate fashion. You've never seen someone bleeding appear so happy.

Los Nonos Pizzeria (☎ 621-144; Presidente Ibañez 147; personal pizza CH$3000; ☙ lunch & dinner) Don't expect the typical – thick slices of cheese and fresh seafood top these Fuegian pizzas. The new hot spot for locals, it's just a few benches and tables, replete with Austral beer.

Dientes de Navarino (☎ 621-074; Centro Comercial; mains CH$3000; ☙ lunch & dinner) This hole-in-the-wall dining hall serves a few well-prepared selections that may include seafood platters, *combinados* (pisco and colas) and box wine.

Residencial Pusaki (☎ 621-020; Piloto Pardo 242; dinner from CH$4000) This ultra-friendly *residencial* also serves dinner family-style for a menagerie of travelers, visiting workers and whomever else makes a reservation. Don't miss Patty's spicy shellfish and centolla concoction known as Caldillo Pusaki. The jovial environment is more easily appreciated if you speak at least some Spanish.

GETTING THERE & AWAY

Aerovías DAP (☎ 621-051; www.dap.cl; Plaza de Ancla s/n) flies to Punta Arenas (one-way CH$52,000) Wednesday through Saturday and Monday from November to March, with fewer winter options. Often passengers are wait-listed until the company has enough bookings to run a flight; the practice can be frustrating for visitors with little extra time to spare. Note luggage restrictions when you purchase your ticket. DAP flights to Antarctica may make a brief stopover here.

The **Transbordadora Austral Broom** (www.tabsa .cl) ferry *Patagonia* sails from Puerto Williams to Punta Arenas two or three times a month on Fridays (reclining seat/bunk CH$72,500/ CH$87,500 including meals, 38 hours). Travelers rave about the trip: good weather means great deck views and the possibility of spotting dolphins or whales. Booking a bunk is worth the extra dollars since passenger berths are small and the reclining Pullman seats leave much to be desired on such a long trip.

Ushuaia Boating (☎ 061-621-227; Maragano 168; one-way CH$60,000) runs zodiac boats that head to Ushuaia at 9:30am and 4pm daily from September to March with limited winter service. The boat trip takes 30 minutes but a transfer bus (included) must first take passengers from Puerto Williams to Puerto Navarino (1½ hours). The service is run out of Hostal Coirón. Private yachts making the trip can sometimes be found at the Club de Yates Micalvi.

TIERRA DEL FUEGO

CABO DE HORNOS & SURROUNDING ISLANDS

If you've made it to Isla Navarino or Ushuaia you may as well push on to the absolute end of the Americas at Cabo de Hornos (Cape Horn). This small group of uninhabited Chilean islands has long been synonymous with adventure and the romance of the old days of sail (although sailors usually dreaded the rough and brutally cold trip). The cape was 'discovered' in January 1616 by Dutchmen Jakob Le Maire and Willem Schouten aboard the *Unity*. They named the cape for their ship *Hoorn*, which had accidentally burned at Puerto Deseado on the Argentine Patagonian coast. Horn Island, of which the famous cape forms the southernmost headland, is just 8km long. The cape itself rises to 424m, with striking black cliffs on its upper parts. Aerovías DAP has charter flights above Cabo de Hornos that don't land. Potential visitors can also charter a sailboat trip with Turismo SIM (p414).

The South Shetland Islands at the northern end of the Antarctic Peninsula are one of the continent's most visited areas, thanks to the spectacular scenery, abundant wildlife and proximity to Tierra del Fuego, which lies 1000km to the north across the Drake Passage. The largest of the South Shetlands, King George Island, has eight national winter stations crowded onto it. Chile established Presidente Eduardo Frei Montalva station in 1969. Ten years later Chile built Teniente Rodolfo Marsh Martin station less than 1km across the Fildes Peninsula from Frei Base. The human population fluctuates between 10 and 20, while the estimated penguin population is around two to three million.

As part of Chile's policy of trying to incorporate its claimed Territorio Chileno Antártico into the rest of the country as much as possible, the government has encouraged families to settle at Frei station, and the first of several children was born there in 1984. Today the station accommodates a population of about 80 summer personnel in sterile, weatherproofed houses.

LEAVE IT TO BEAVERS

Forget guns, germs and steel, Canadian beavers *(Castor canadensis)* have colonized Tierra del Fuego and Isla Navarino using only buck teeth and broad tails.

It all goes back to the 1940s, when Argentina's hapless military government imported 25 pairs of beavers from Canada, hoping they would multiply and, in turn, generate a lucrative fur industry in this largely undeveloped area. Without natural predators, the beavers did multiply, but in turn, felted beaver hats became about as fashionable as whalebone corsets and the nascent fur industry foundered.

These days there are some 250,000 beavers on Tierra del Fuego and the surrounding islands, where they are officially considered a plague. Beavers' damaging effects are many. Flooding from beaver dams destroys roads and meadows, ruining infrastructure and creating havoc for livestock. Loggers, competing with the rodents for the best wood, fear losing their livelihoods. A sole beaver couple has the chewing power to create their own lake, felling hundreds of trees. Beavers also pass giardia into the lakes, which can get into water supplies and work its black magic on human intestines.

The Chilean government has proposed control with a nearly US$1-million-dollar program to fight the invader species by offering bounties (US$5 per tail) to trappers with 'humanitarian' traps from Canada and by encouraging exports to foreign markets. In the past, the beaver debate has pitted ecologists and loggers against animal-rights activists, and has turned government officials against each other. Somewhere in the middle are tourism companies, who are trying to make beaver-spotting a popular side excursion, but are also worried about devastation to the countryside.

On a positive note, since beavers need to live in water, they can only spread so far across the land and they don't reproduce as wildly as rabbits or other rodents. However, there are concerns that beavers will make their way across the Strait of Magellan, spreading the beaver plague to the rest of the South American continent.

If you're eager to do your part, look for beaver meat on Fuegian menus.

Getting There & Away

All transportation is weather-dependent, although ships are more likely to do the trip in rough conditions than the small airplanes. Plan for the possibility of delays and if you can't wait, don't plan on a refund.

Aerovías DAP (☎ 061-223-340; fax 061-221-693; www.dap.cl) has one- and two-day programs from Punta Arenas to Frei Base on King George Island, involving tours to Villa Las Estrellas, sea-lion and penguin colonies and other investigation stations on the island. The one-day program costs US$2950 and the two-day program costs US$3950 and requires a minimum of eight passengers. Departures run from November through March. Note that the flight to Frei Base takes about three hours. Flights to Cabo de Hornos can also be chartered. Check the Aerovías DAP website for updated departure dates and prices, which are constantly changing.

AntarcticaXXI (☎ Punta Arenas 56-61-614-100; www.antarcticaxxi.com; 7 days/6 nights from US$7600) runs the only air-cruise combo, flying from Punta Arenas to Chile's Frei station on King George Island, then with a transfer to the 46-passenger ship *Grigoriy Mikheev* for several days of cruising the South Shetlands and peninsula region. IAATO member, a body that mandates strict guidelines for responsible travel to Antarctica.

ARGENTINE TIERRA DEL FUEGO

In contrast to its Chilean counterpart, this side of the island is bustling, modern and industrial. Argentina's half of the Fuegian pie boasts a paved highway and two major cities with growing economies. That doesn't mean that nature isn't grand here. There are historical *estancias*, excellent Atlantic Coast fly-fishing, and Antarctic access via Ushuaia. The toothy Cordillera Darwin rises 2500m above Ushuaia, flush with trails and excellent skiing in winter. Dog sledding and sailing outings offer an alternative to the usual Patagonian fare of trekking and toasting to a hard-day's walk. The island is home to Parque Nacional Tierra del Fuego (p425), Argentina's first shoreline national park.

USHUAIA

☎ 02901 / pop 58,000

Days are long gone since this former missionary outpost and penal colony had to woo or shackle its occupants to stay put. Now a bustling port and adventure hub, Ushuaia draws hundreds of thousands of willing visitors yearly. The city occupies a narrow escarpment between the Beagle Channel and the snowcapped Martial Range. Though remote, it is plugged into modern commerce with a critical mass of shops, cafés and restaurants. While not quite the southernmost city in the world, Ushuaia is the southernmost city of size.

The city caters well to visitors with its dazzling outdoor options that include hiking, sailing, skiing, dog mushing, kayaking and even scuba diving close to town. After a hard day of play, you can tip back a pint of the world's southernmost microbrew in a city pub. The spectacular Parque Nacional Tierra del Fuego, with thick stands of native lenga, is a must-see.

Tierra del Fuego's comparatively high wages draw Argentines from all over to resettle here. Some locals lament the loss of the small town culture that until recently existed. Meanwhile, expansion means a jumble of housing developments advancing in the few directions the mad geography allows.

Orientation

Paralleling the Beagle Channel, Maipú becomes Malvinas Argentinas west of the cemetery, then turns into RN 3, continuing 12km to Parque Nacional Tierra del Fuego. To the east, public access ends at Yaganes, which heads north to meet RN 3 going north toward Lago Fagnano. Most visitor services are on or within a couple blocks of San Martín, a block inland from the waterfront.

Information

BOOKSTORES

Boutique del Libro (☎ 432-117; 25 de Mayo 62; ◷ 9am-8pm Mon-Sat) Comprehensive, multilingual selection of literature, guidebooks and pictorials.

IMMIGRATION

Immigration (☎ 422-334; Beauvoir 1536; ◷ 9am-noon Mon-Fri)

MEDICAL SERVICES

Hospital Regional (☎ 107, 423-200; cnr Malvinas Argentinas & 12 de Octubre)

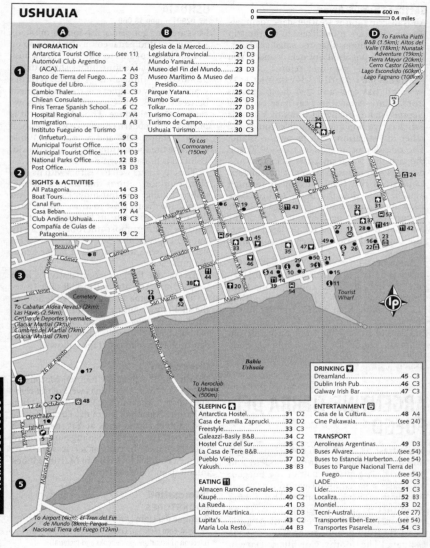

USHUAIA

INFORMATION
Antarctica Tourist Office ......(see 11)
Automóvil Club Argentino
(ACA)...................................**1** A4
Banco de Tierra del Fuego....**2** D3
Boutique del Libro..................**3** C3
Cambio Thaler.........................**4** C3
Chilean Consulate...................**5** A5
Finis Terrae Spanish School...**6** C2
Hospital Regional....................**7** A4
Immigration............................**8** A3
Instituto Fueguino de Turismo
(Infuetur)...........................**9** C3
Municipal Tourist Office........**10** D3
Municipal Tourist Office........**11** D3
National Parks Office.............**12** B3
Post Office.............................**13** D3

Iglesia de la Merced................**20** C3
Legislatura Provincial..............**21** D3
Mundo Yamaná.......................**22** D3
Museo del Fin del Mundo.......**23** D3
Museo Marítimo & Museo del
Presidio.............................**24** D2
Parque Yatana.........................**25** C2
Rumbo Sur..............................**26** D3
Tolkar....................................**27** D3
Turismo Comapa....................**28** D3
Turismo de Campo.................**29** C3
Ushuaia Turismo....................**30** C3

SIGHTS & ACTIVITIES
All Patagonia.........................**14** C3
Boat Tours.............................**15** D3
Canal Fun..............................**16** D3
Casa Beban............................**17** A4
Club Andino Ushuaia.............**18** C3
Compañía de Guías de
Patagonia...........................**19** C2

To Familia Piatti
B&B (1.5km); Altos del
Valle (18km); Nunatak
Adventure (19km);
Tierra Mayor (20km);
Cerro Castor (26km);
Lago Escondido (60km);
Lago Fagnano (100km)

To Los
Cormoranes
(150m)

Beauvoir

To Cabañas Aldea Nevada (2km);
Las Hayas (2.5km);
Centro de Deportes Invernales
Glaciar Martial (7km);
Cumbres del Martial (7km);
Glaciar Martial (7km)

Cemetery

Bahía
Ushuaia

To Aeroclub
Ushuaia
(500m)

Tourist
Wharf

To Airport (4km); El Tren del Fin
de Mundo (8km); Parque
Nacional Tierra del Fuego (12km)

SLEEPING
Antarctica Hostel...................**31** D2
Casa de Familia Zaprucki.......**32** D2
Freestyle................................**33** C3
Galeazzi-Basily B&B..............**34** C2
Hostel Cruz del Sur...............**35** C3
La Casa de Tere B&B.............**36** D2
Pueblo Viejo..........................**37** D2
Yakush..................................**38** B3

EATING
Almacen Ramos Generales.....**39** C3
Kaupé....................................**40** C2
La Rueda................................**41** D3
Lomitos Martinica..................**42** D3
Lupita's..................................**43** C2
María Lola Restó.....................**44** B3

DRINKING
Dreamland..............................**45** C3
Dublin Irish Pub.....................**46** C3
Galway Irish Bar.....................**47** C3

ENTERTAINMENT
Casa de la Cultura..................**48** A4
Cine Pakawaia.....................(see 24)

TRANSPORT
Aerolíneas Argentinas.............**49** D3
Buses Alvarez.......................(see 54)
Buses to Estancia Harberton...(see 54)
Buses to Parque Nacional Tierra del
Fuego................................(see 54)
LADE....................................**50** C3
Líder.....................................**51** C3
Localiza................................**52** B3
Montiel.................................**53** D2
Tecni-Austral......................(see 27)
Transportes Eben-Ezer.........(see 54)
Transportes Pasarela..............**54** C3

0 .... 600 m
0 .... 0.4 miles

MONEY

Several banks on Maipú and San Martín have ATMs.

Banco de Tierra del Fuego (San Martín 396; ⏰ 10am-3pm Mon-Fri) Best rates for traveler's checks.

Cambio Thaler (San Martín 778; ⏰ 10am-1pm & 5-8pm Mon-Sat, 5-8pm Sun) Convenience equals slightly poorer exchange rates.

POST

Post office (cnr San Martín & Godoy; ⏰ 9am-5pm Mon-Fri, 9am-1pm Sat)

TELEPHONE & INTERNET ACCESS

Internet access (around AR$3 per hour) is available at call centers along San Martín.

TOURIST INFORMATION

Automóvil Club Argentino (ACA; ☎ 421-121; cnr Malvinas Argentinas & Onachaga) Argentina's auto club; good source for provincial road maps.

Instituto Fueguino de Turismo (Infuetur; ☎ 421-423; www.tierradelfuego.org.ar; Maipú 505; ☯ 8am-9pm Mon-Fri, 9am-8pm Sat & Sun) On ground floor of Hotel Albatros.

Municipal tourist office (☎ 432-000, airport 423-970, on Tierra del Fuego 0800-333-1476; www.e-ushuaia .com, in Spanish; San Martín 674; ☯ 8am-9pm Mon-Fri, 9am-8pm Sat & Sun) Very helpful, with a message board and multilingual brochures, as well as good lodging, activities and transport info and English- and French-speaking staff. Also at the airport and pier.

National Parks office (Administración de Parques Nacionales; ☎ 421-315; San Martín 1395; ☯ 9am-4pm Mon-Fri)

Sights

MUSEO MARÍTIMO & MUSEO DEL PRESIDIO

When convicts were moved from Staten Island (Isla de los Estados) to Ushuaia in 1906 they began building the national prison, which was finished in 1920. The spoke-like halls of single cells were designed to house 380, but in the prison's most active period held up to 800. It closed as a jail in 1947 and now houses the **Museo Marítimo & Museo del Presidio** (☎ 437-481; www.ushuaia.org; cnr Yaganes & Gobernador Paz; admission adults/students AR\$35/20; ☯ 9am-8pm). It's a fine port of call on a blustery day. Halls showing penal life are intriguing, but mainly because of the informative plaques, which are only in Spanish. Two of the more illustrious inmates were author Ricardo Rojas and Russian anarchist Simón Radowitzky.

Other displays include models of famous ships, a display on Antarctic exploration and the remains of the world's narrowest gauge freight train, which transported prisoners between town and work stations.

MUNDO YAMANÁ

More an experience than museum, the modest **Mundo Yamaná** (☎ 422-874; Rivadavia 56; admission adult/child AR\$8/5; ☯ 10am-8pm) explores Fueguinos' attempts to bring the Yaghan (Yamaná) culture to life. Some of the expertly detailed dioramas (details in English and Spanish) are based on accessible bays and inlets of the national park; coming here before hiking in the park will give you new bearings.

MUSEO DEL FIN DEL MUNDO

Built in 1903 for the territorial governor Manuel Fernández Valdés, this building was a branch of the Banco de la Nación up until 1978 when it was transformed into the **Museo del Fin del Mundo** (☎ 421-863; cnr Maipú & Rivadavia; admission AR\$10; ☯ 9am-8pm). Exhibits on Fuegian natural history, stuffed bird life, aboriginal life and the early penal colonies, and replicas of an early general store and bank, are of moderate interest.

PARQUE YATANA

Part art project, part urban refuge, **Parque Yatana** (Fundación Cultiva; ☎ 425-212; cnr Magallanes & 25 de Mayo; admission free; ☯ 2:30-8pm Tue-Sat) is a city block of lenga forest preserved from the encroaching development by one determined family.

HISTORIC BUILDINGS

The tourist office distributes a free city-tour map with information on many of the historic houses around town. At Maipú 465, **Legislatura Provincial** (Provincial Legislature; 1894) was the governor's official residence. The century-old **Iglesia de la Merced** (San Martín & Don Bosco), was built with convict labor. **Casa Beban** (cnr Malvinas Argentinas & Pluschow; admission free; ☯ 10am-8pm Mon-Fri, 4-8pm Sat & Sun) was built in 1911 using parts ordered from Sweden. The house sometimes hosts local art exhibits.

Activities

HIKING & CANOPY TOURS

Hiking possibilities should not be limited to Parque Nacional Tierra del Fuego; the entire mountain range behind Ushuaia, with its lakes and rivers, is a hiker's high. However, many trails are poorly marked or not marked at all; some hikers who have easily scurried uphill have gotten lost trying to find the trail back down.

The **Club Andino Ushuaia** (☎ 422-335; Juana Fadul 50; ☯ 10am-12:30pm & 2-9:30pm Mon-Fri, 10am-2pm Sat) sells a map and bilingual trekking, mountaineering and mountain-biking guidebook with rough maps and plenty of trail description. The club occasionally organizes hikes and can recommend hiking guides. Unguided trekkers are strongly encouraged to register with the club or the tourist office (left) before heading out – and check in after a safe return. In an emergency, contact the **Civil Guard** (☎ 103, 22108).

Compañía de Guías de Patagonia (opposite) organizes treks and is often recommended as a reliable information source.

Cerro Martial & Glaciar Martial

A hearty hike from downtown leads up to Glaciar Martial, with fantastic panoramas of Ushuaia and the Beagle Channel; in fact, the views are possibly more impressive than the actual glacier. Catch a taxi up the hill for under AR$20, or if you're up for an all-day hike, follow San Martín west and keep ascending as it zigzags (there are many hiker shortcuts) to the ski run 7km northwest of town. At this point either take the **aerosilla** (AR$20; ☺ 10am-4pm) chairlift or walk another two hours to make a full day of it. The cozy **Refugio de Montaña** (snacks AR$7; ☺ 10am-5:30pm Oct-Jun) offers coffee, desserts and beer at the chairlift base. The weather is changeable so take warm, dry clothing and sturdy footwear. Minivans leave from the corner of Maipú and Juana Fadul every half-hour from 8:30am to 6:30pm (AR$15 round-trip).

New **canopy tours** (Refugio de Montaña; escuela@ iterradelfuego.org.ar; AR$80; ☺ 10am-5:30pm Oct-Jun) run from the base of the chairlift, offering an hour-long blast through the forest, with 11 zip-line cables and two hanging bridges. The highest cable is 8m.

BOATING

Navigating the Beagle's steely waters pocked with rocky isles offers a fresh perspective and decent wildlife watching. On the wharf a string of operators sell similar offerings: four-hour morning or afternoon excursions (AR$95 to AR$120) that visit the sea-lion colony at Isla de los Lobos and the extensive cormorant colonies at Isla de los Pájaros. An alternative tour takes hikers to the park and they return via private transfer after hiking. Quality may vary: ask about the number of passengers, whether food is served and which sights are visited. A highlight is an island stop to hike and look at *conchales*, shell mounds left by the native Yaghan. The tourist pier is on Maipú between Lasserre and Roca.

Patagonia Adventure Explorer (☎ 02901-15-465-842; www.patagoniaadvent.com.ar; Tourist Wharf) has comfortable boats and trips include snacks and a short hike on Isla Bridges. For extra adventure, set sail in the 18ft sailboat. Full-day sails with wine and gourmet snacks or multidays are also available.

Resembling a bathtub toy, the sturdy but small vessel operated by **Tres Marías Excursions** (☎ 421-897; www.tresmariasweb.com; Tourist Wharf) takes a maximum of 8 passengers. It is the only outfitter with permission to land on Isla 'H' in the Isla Bridges natural reserve, which has shell mounds and a rock-cormorant colony.

Alternatively, try a more expensive catamaran trip or the historic 70-passenger **Barracuda** (☎ 437-606), which chugs to the Faro Les Eclaireurs lighthouse, Isla de los Lobos and Isla de los Pájaros (AR$115, three hours).

KAYAKING

Professional guide **Daniel Urriza** (☎ 433613, 02901-15-618777; danyurriza@hotmail.com; day trip per person AR$450) has plenty of experience; rounding Cape Horn in a kayak might be the most noteworthy. Excursions can be tailor-made, but expect to explore the channel and see penguins or head to Lago Escondido. Kayaking is also a component of many tours to Parque Nacional Tierra del Fuego; see the Nunatak Adventure and Canal Fun listings under Tours (opposite).

DOG MUSHING

Outfitter **Nunatak Adventure** (☎ 437-454; www.nuna takadventure.com; RN 3, Km 3018; guided ride AR$50) takes dog sleds bumping across the valley floor on 2km and 6km rides. Meet at Tierra Mayor.

Ski area **Altos del Valle** (☎ 02901-15-616-383; www.gatocuruchet.com.ar) teaches mushing and also is the primary sponsor to popular annual sled dog races at the end of August where kids also compete. Owner Gato Cruchet was the first South American to participate in the Iditarod.

SKIING

With the surrounding peaks loaded with powder, winter visitors should jump at the chance to explore the local ski resorts. Accessed from RN 3, resorts offer both downhill and cross-country options. The season runs from June to September, with July (during schools' winter vacation) is the busiest month. Ushuaia's biggest ski event is the annual **Marcha Blanca**, a symbolic re-creation of San Martín's historic August 17 crossing of the Andes.

The largest resort is **Cerro Castor** (☎ 02901-15-605-604/6; www.cerrocastor.com, in Spanish; full-day lift tickets adult/child AR$110/75), 27km from Ushuaia, with 15 slopes spanning 400 hectares. Rentals are available for skis, boards, blades and cross-country skis. There's a good restaurant at the base and a summit lodge conducive to afternoon coffee breaks.

The closest ski area to Ushuaia, **Altos del Valle** (☎ 02901-15-616-383; www.gatocuruchet.com.ar) also has good cross-country and snowshoeing areas, equipment rentals and full-moon trips. Extreme skiers can check out the snowcat skiing.

For a quick run near town, Club Andino (p419) runs cross-country and downhill slopes only 3km and 5km away. The family-oriented **Centro de Deportes Invernales Glaciar Martial** (☎ 421-423, 423-340), 7km northwest of town, has downhill runs well suited for beginners; it also rents equipment.

Transportes Pasarela and Buses Alvarez run shuttles (AR$25) from the corner of Juana Fadul and Maipú to the ski centers along RN 3 hourly from 9am to 2pm daily. Each resort also provides its own transportation from downtown Ushuaia.

Tours

Many travel agencies sell tours around the region; you can go horseback riding, visit Lagos Escondido and Fagnano, stay at an *estancia*, spy on birds and beavers, and even get pulled by husky-dog sleds (winter only).

All Patagonia (☎ 433-622; www.allpatagonia.com; Juana Fadul 60) Amex rep offering more conventional and luxurious trips.

Canal Fun (☎ 437-395; www.canalfun.com; Rivadavia 82) Hip outfitter with hiking and kayaking in the park (AR$220), off-roading around Lago Fagnano (AR$280) and a multisport outing around Estancia Harberton (AR$390) which includes kayaking and a visit to the penguin colony.

Compañía de Guías de Patagonia (☎ 437-753, 02901-15-618-426; www.companiadeguias.com.ar; Campos 795) Full-day treks with climbing and ice-hiking on Glaciar Vinciguerra (AR$175) and two-day high-mountain treks to Cerro Alvear (AR$520) with glacier camping.

Nunatak Adventure (☎ 430-329; www.nunatakadventure.com) Offers competitively priced adventure tours and has its own mountain base.

Rumbo Sur (☎ 422-275; www.rumbosur.com.ar; San Martín 350) Ushuaia's longest-running agency, offering conventional activities.

Tolkar (☎ 431-408/12; www.tolkarturismo.com.ar; Roca 157) Helpful all-round agency affiliated with Tecni-Austral buses.

Turismo de Campo (☎ 437-451; www.turismodecampo.com, in Spanish; 25 de Mayo 64) Organizes light trekking, Beagle Channel sailing trips and *estancia* visits. Also sells a wide variety of nine- to 12-night Antarctica passages.

Turismo Comapa (☎ 430-727; www.comapa.com; San Martín 245) Confirm Navimag and Cruceros Australis passages here.

Ushuaia Turismo (☎ 436-003; ushuaiaturismo@speedy.com.ar; Gobernador Paz 865) Offers last-minute Antarctica cruise bookings.

A number of private yachts also charter trips to Cabo de Hornos, Antarctica and, less often, South Georgia Island. These trips must be organized well in advance; the most popular weeklong charter, rounding Cabo de Hornos, costs upwards of AR$5400 per person. A recommended option is **Mago del Sur** (☎ 02901-15-5148-646; charter per person per day AR$750), captained by Alejandro Damilano, whose lifetime of sailing ensures skill and safety at the helm. Individuals can join scheduled trips (check online) to Islas Malvinas (Falkland Islands), Antarctica, Cabo de Hornos, Puerto Natales and beyond.

From September through May, Cruceros Australis (p383) runs luxurious four-day (per person low/high season from AR$3109/3925) and five-day sightseeing cruises to Punta Arenas and back, catering mostly to mature travelers. Saturday departures from Ushuaia include the possibility of disembarking at Cabo de Hornos. Low season is considered to be September to October and mid-March to April. The cruise visits many otherwise inaccessible glaciers, but time alone or hiking opportunities are limited; focus is more on nature talks and group excursions. Turismo Comapa (above) handles local bookings.

Courses

Study Spanish at **Finis Terrae Spanish School** (☎ 433-871; www.spanishpatagonia.com; cnr Triunvirato & Magallanes; 1-week lodging & 20 hrs of classes AR$1177). Courses last from one to six weeks and private classes are available as well. They can also arrange home stays.

Sleeping

Lodging is scarce in the January and February high season and during early March's Fin del Mundo Marathon, so reserve ahead. Most lodgings offer free transfers in. The municipal tourist office has lists of B&Bs and *cabañas* and also posts a list of available lodgings outside after closing time. Most hotels offer laundry service.

ANTARCTICA: THE ICE

If the absolute end of the Americas isn't enough for you, there is always Antarctica. Once this mass of ice was barely touched by humans; now Antarctica is firmly established (for better or for worse) as a trendy travel destination. Despite its high price tag, it is much more than just a continent to tick off your list. You will witness both land and ice shelves piled with hundreds of meters of undulating, untouched snow. Glaciers drop from mountainsides and icebergs form sculptures as tall as buildings. The wildlife, from thousands of curious penguins to a wide variety of flying birds, seals and whales, is nothing short of thrilling.

Antarctic tourism comes not without its costs. On November 23, 2007, the MS *Explorer* was holed by ice but evacuated successfully before sinking. The circumstances were highly unusual, although the incident will likely provoke more safety measures. We can only hope that careful management will assure that this glorious continent remains intact. In 2007, around 33,000 tourists cruised the ice from Ushuaia – a stunning contrast to the continent's summer and overwintering populations of 5000 and 1200 scientists and staff.

So long as you've got two or three weeks to spare, hopping on board a cruise ship is not out of the question. Some voyages take in the Islas Malvinas (Falkland Islands) and South Georgia (human population 10 to 20, estimated penguin population two to three million!); others go just to the Antarctic Peninsula, while others focus on retracing historic expeditions.

A small but growing handful of visitors reach Antarctica aboard private vessels. All are sailboats (although equipped with auxiliary engines), and some have even wintered in sheltered anchorages, such as Yankee Harbor at Greenwich Island or near Palmer station on the Antarctic Peninsula.

The season runs from mid-October to mid-March, depending on ice conditions. It used to be that peak season voyages sold out, but now most do. When shopping around, ask how many days you will actually spend in Antarctica, as crossing the Southern Ocean takes up to two days each way. And how many landings will there be? The smaller the ship, the more landings there are per passenger (always depending on the weather, of course). Tour companies charge anywhere from US$7000 to US$70,000, although some ships allow walk-ons, which can cost as little as US$5000.

Due to Ushuaia's proximity to the Antarctic Peninsula, most cruises leave from here. Last-minute bookings can be made through **Ushuaia Turismo** (☎ 436-003; ushuaiaturismo@speedy.com.ar; Gobernador Paz 865). Other travel agencies offering packages include **Rumbo Sur** (☎ 422-275; www.rumbosur .com.ar; San Martín 350), **All Patagonia** (☎ 433-622; www.allpatagonia.com; Juana Fadul 60) and **Canal Fun** (☎ 437-395; www.canalfun.com; Rivadavia 82), though there are many more.

If you are interested in a sailing trip, check out **Turismo Sim** (p414) in Puerto Williams.

The following companies are members of **IAATO** (www.iaato.org), which mandates strict guidelines for responsible travel to Antarctica.

Abercrombie & Kent (www.abercrombiekent.com) Charters *Minerva*, an ice-reinforced vessel carrying 199 passengers.

Aurora Expeditions (www.auroraexpeditions.com.au) Operates the 56-passenger *Polar Pioneer* and the 100-passenger *Marina Svetaeva,* which carries two helicopters. Aurora also offers scuba diving, kayaking, mountain climbing and camping.

Heritage Expeditions (www.heritage-expeditions.com) Award-winning New Zealand company that also goes to Ross Sea and East Antarctica regions.

Lindblad Expeditions (www.expeditions.com) Operates the 110-passenger *National Geographic Endeavour* and the 148-passenger *National Geographic Explorer* and offers kayaking.

Quark Expeditions (www.quarkexpeditions.com) Three kinds of ships, from an icebreaker to a 48-passenger small ship for close-knit groups.

WildWings/WildOceans Travel (www.wildwings.co.uk) Operates bird- and wildlife-focused tours to Antarctica.

For more information see Lonely Planet's *Antarctica* guidebook. Online, check out www.70south .com for up-to-date information and articles. In Ushuaia, consult the very helpful **Antarctica tourist office** (☎ 421-423; infoantartida@tierradelfuego.org.ar) at the pier. And one last thing: bring more film and/or extra memory cards than you think you'll need. You'll thank us later.

BUDGET

Ushuaia hostels breed like Canadian beaver. All have kitchens and most offer internet access. Rates typically drop 25% in the low season (April to October).

Yakush (☎ 435-807; www.hostelyakush.com.ar; Piedrabuena 118; dm/d AR$35/150) Exuding warmth, this artsy hostel is a prime choice: it is friendly, dorms have fresh sheets and good beds, and social spaces include an ample upstairs lounge with futons. Breakfast includes *medialunas* (croissants), coffee and *maté*, with leftovers left out for nibbling.

Hostel Cruz del Sur (☎ 423-110; www.xdelsur.com .ar; Deloquí 636; dm AR$35; 🖳) Cramped but cozy, this popular hostel features four- to six-bed dorms with heaters and thin mattresses and bedding, plus some rooms come with a view. Rooms can get loud, and bathrooms taxed to the max. But the welcoming hosts do a fine job of rounding up groups to explore nearby areas. Kitchens are well stocked, there's a pleasant library and hot drinks are always available.

Antarctica Hostel (☎ 435-774; www.antarcticahostel .com; Antártida Argentina 270; dm/d/t AR$40/150/180; 🖳) An open floor plan and beer on tap makes this trendy backpacker hub conducive to making friends. The cement rooms are the biggest drawback: though ample in size, some smell of insecticide. Doubles share bathroom but there are plenty of showers (check the fluctuating temperature before climbing in).

Freestyle (☎ 432-874; www.ushuaiafreestyle.com; Gobernador Paz 866; dm/d/apt AR$40/180/220; 🖳) This five-star hostel boasts immaculate dorms with cozy fleece blankets, a sleek cooking area and a sprawling, sunny living room with views. If it's howling outside, cue up a billiards game or lounge in a comfy bean-bag chair. Doubles are a bit cramped and darker.

MIDRANGE

La Casa de Tere B&B (☎ 422-312, 435-913; www.lacasa detere.com.ar; Rivadavia 620; d with/without bathroom AR$150/120; 🅿) Tere showers her guests with attention in this beautiful modern home with great views. Its three tidy rooms fill up fast. Guests can cook, there's also cable TV and a fireplace in the living room. It's a short but steep walk uphill from the center.

Galeazzi-Basily B&B (☎ 423-213; www.avesdelsur .com.ar; Valdéz 323; tw AR$120, 5-person cabin AR$180; 🅿 🖳) Peaceful and elegant, the best feature of this wooded residence is its warm and hospitable family. Rooms are small but offer a personal touch. Some share a bathroom. Since beds are twin-sized, couples may prefer one of the modern cabins out back. It's a peaceful spot, and where else can you practice your English, French, Italian and Portuguese? Book ahead.

Pueblo Viejo (☎ 432-098; www.puebloviejo.info; Deloquí 242; d without bathroom AR$150; 🅿 🖳) Great value, this snug and relaxed eight-room lodging has tasteful rooms with firm mattresses and central heating. Freddy gives guests the local lowdown. Cars can also be rented here and guests get discount rates.

Familia Piatti B&B (☎ 437-104, 02901-15-613-485; www.interpatagonia.com/familiapiatti, in Spanish; Bahía Paraíso 812, Bosque del Faldeo; s/d/tr AR$155/215/275; 🅿 🖳) If idling in the forest sounds good, head for this friendly B&B with warm down duvets and native lenga wood furniture. Hiking trails nearby lead up the mountains. The friendly owners are multilingual (English, Italian and Portuguese) and can arrange transport and guided excursions. Extras include massage and babysitting service.

Casa de Familia Zaprucki (☎ 421-316; Deloquí 271; 2-person apt incl breakfast AR$180; ✗) Well-crafted and tenderly cared for, these garden apartments surrounded by zinnias and rose bushes are a delight and a find. Guests get a warm reception. Kitchens are well equipped and cabins have nice wood details and area rugs.

TOP END

Cabañas Aldea Nevada (☎ 422-851/68; www.aldea nevada.com.ar; Martial 1430; d AR$250, 3-night minimum; 🅿) Any minute you expect the elves to come: this beautiful patch of lenga forest is discreetly dotted with 13 log cabins with outdoor grills and rough-hewn benches contemplatively placed by the ponds. Interiors are rustic but modern, with functional kitchens, wood stoves to fire up and hardwood details. Internet is extra.

our pick **Cumbres del Martial** (☎ 424-779; www .cumbresdelmartial.com.ar, in Spanish; Martial, Km 5; r/ste AR$550/848; 🅿 🖳) A getaway that you may not ever want to leave, these stylish lodgings sit at the base of the Martial glacier. Standard rooms have a touch of the English cottage while the two-story wooden cabins are simply stunners, with stone fireplaces, Jacuzzis and dazzling vaulted windows. Lush robes, optional massages (extra) and your country's newspaper delivered to your mailbox are some of the delicious details. To top it all off, the breakfast treats are homemade.

Las Hayas (☎ 430-710/8; www.lashayas.com.ar; Martial 1650; d ARS863, ste ARS1105-1633; P □ ☎) Serving the likes of Nelson Mandela and Mercosur presidents, Ushuaia's only five-star resort is dramatically perched 3km above town. Its elegant, traditional rooms have fine monochrome patterns, some canopy beds and delicious bay views. If you can swing the upgrade, suites offer Jacuzzi tubs and linen towels.

Eating

Almacen Ramos Generales (☎ 427-317; Maipú 749; snacks ARS7) The real draw of this rustic general store and museum are the baked goods: the French pastry chef bakes crusty baguettes, croissants and desserts. There is also grain coffee and a wine bar.

Lomitos Martinica (San Martín 68; mains ARS9-13; ☺ 11:30am-3pm & 8:30pm-12am) Dive dining at its best, this cheap *parrillada* with grillside seating serves enormous *milanesa* sandwiches and offers an economical lunch special.

Lupita's (☎ 437-675; 25 de Mayo 323; pizzas ARS25; ☺ lunch & dinner) This sliver-sized pizza shop delivers crisp thin-crust pizzas hot out of a brick oven. Consider it the perfect takeaway.

María Lola Restó (☎ 421-185; Deloquí 1048; mains ARS35; 12pm-12am Mon-Sat) Satisfying defines the experience of this creative café-style restaurant overlooking the channel. Locals pack this silver house for homemade pasta with seafood or strip steak in rich mushroom sauce. Service is good and portions tend toward humungous: desserts can easily be split.

La Rueda (☎ 436-540; San Martín 193; buffet ARS36; ☺ lunch & dinner) Good *tenedor libre* (all-you-can-eat buffet) offers a variety of salads alongside tasty *parrillada* grilled over coals in the window. Ordering a drink is mandatory with the buffet, which includes dessert.

Kaupé (☎ 422-704; Roca 470; mains ARS40; ☺ lunch & dinner) For an out-of-body seafood experience, head to this candlelit house. Chef Ernesto Vivian employs the freshest of everything and service is nothing less than impeccable. We can't leak our faves, since the chef protests that readers always repeat the order! Service is attentive, the wine list extensive and the views of the bay, well, we doubt you'll bother to notice them. Reservations advised.

Drinking

Geographically competitive drinkers should note that the southernmost bar in the world is not here but on a Ukrainian research station in Antarctica.

Dreamland (☎ 421-246; www.dreamlandushuaia.com.ar; cnr 9 de Julio & Deloquí; drinks ARS9; ☺ 11am-late; □) The bar du jour, this ambient house mixes it up with DJs, free tango nights and happy hours. During the day it's a quiet café with lunch specials and wi-fi access.

Dublin Irish Pub (cnr 9 de Julio & Deloquí; ☺ 8pm-late) Dublin doesn't feel so far with the lively banter and Guinness at this dimly lit foreigners' favorite. Look out for the occasional live music. There are a couple of other Irish bars around town, including the Galway.

Galway Irish Bar (Lasserre 108; ☺ 8pm-late) This big bar affords less ambiance but recovers favor with its dart board and Beagle beer (Ushuaia's beer) on tap.

Entertainment

Cine Pakawaia (☎ 436-500; cnr Yaganes & Gobernador Paz; tickets ARS6) First-run movies are shown at Presidio's fully restored hangar-style theater.

Casa de la Cultura (☎ 422-417; cnr Malvinas Argentinas & 12 de Octubre) Hidden behind a gym, this center hosts occasional live-music shows.

Getting There & Away

AIR

The airport departure tax is ARS24. **Aerolíneas Argentinas** (☎ 421-218; Roca 116) jets several times daily to Buenos Aires (ARS703), sometimes stopping in Río Gallegos (ARS266) or El Calafate (ARS506). **LADE** (☎ 421-123; San Martín 542) flies to Buenos Aires (ARS363), Comodoro Rivadavia (ARS280), El Calafate (ARS280) and Río Gallegos (ARS163).

Chilean airline **Aerovías DAP** (www.dap.cl) offers charter-only flights to destinations in Patagonia, as well as overflights of Cabo de Hornos and trips to Chile's Frei base in Antarctica.

Aeroclub Ushuaia (☎ 421-717, 421-892; www.aeroclubushuaia.org.ar) offers scenic flightseeing tours (ARS150 to ARS300 per person).

BOAT

Charter boats anchored in Ushuaia's harbor may take passengers to Puerto Williams (ARS377) the next time they are heading out. See the Tours section (p421) for chartered

See the Tours section (p421)

tours to Cabo de Hornos, Antarctica and South Georgia Island.

BUS

Ushuaia has no bus terminal. Book outgoing bus tickets with as much anticipation as possible; many readers have complained about getting stuck here in high season. Depending on your luck, long waits at border crossings can be expected.

Tecni-Austral (☎ 431-408/12; Roca 157) buses for Río Grande (AR$25, four hours) leave from the travel agency Tolkar daily except Sunday at 5:30am, stopping in Tolhuin. There's an onward connecting service on Monday, Wednesday and Friday to Punta Arenas (AR$125, 12 hours) and weekdays to Río Gallegos (AR$125, 12 hours).

Lider (☎ 436-421; Gobernador Paz 921) and **Montiel** (☎ 421-366; Deloquí 110) run door-to-door minivans to Tolhuin (AR$20, 2½ hours) and Río Grande (AR$40, four hours) six to eight times daily, with less frequent departures on Sunday.

At the corner of Maipú and Juana Fadul, **Transportes Pasarela** (☎ 433-712) runs round-trip shuttles to Lago Esmeralda (AR$25), Lago Escondido (AR$80) and Lago Fagnano (AR$80), leaving around 10am and returning at 2pm and 6:30pm. If planning to stay overnight, ask to pay just one way (more likely if there are many people traveling) and arrange for pick up. Transportes Eben-Ezer offers similar service and leaves from nearby.

For transportation to Parque Nacional Tierra del Fuego, see p426.

Getting Around

Taxis to/from the modern airport (USH), 4km southwest of downtown on the peninsula across from the waterfront, cost AR$18, plus there's a local bus service along Maipú. Taxis can be chartered for around AR$60 per hour.

Rental rates for compact cars (including insurance) start around AR$150. Try **Pueblo Viejo** (p423) and **Localiza** (☎ 430-739; San Martín 1222). Some agencies may not charge for drop off in other parts of Argentine Tierra del Fuego.

PARQUE NACIONAL TIERRA DEL FUEGO

Banked against the channel, the hush, fragrant southern forests of Tierra del Fuego, are a stunning setting to explore. West of Ushuaia by 12km, **Parque Nacional Tierra del Fuego** (via RN 3; admission AR$20), Argentina's first coastal national park, extends 630 sq km from the Beagle Channel in the south to beyond Lago Fagnano (also known as Lago Kami) in the north. However, only a couple of thousand hectares along the southern edge of the park are open to the public, with a miniscule system of short, easy trails that are designed more for day-tripping families than backpacking trekkers. The rest of the park is protected as a *reserva estricta* (strictly off-limits zone). Despite this, a few scenic hikes along the bays and rivers, or through dense native forests of evergreen coihue, canelo and deciduous lenga, are worthwhile. For truly spectacular color, come in the fall when hillsides of ñire burst out in red.

Birdlife is prolific, especially along the coastal zone. Keep an eye out for condors, albatross, cormorants, gulls, terns, oystercatchers, grebes, kelp geese and the comical, flightless, orange-billed steamer ducks. Common invasive species include the European rabbit and the North American beaver, both of which are wreaking ecological havoc in spite of their cuteness. Gray and red foxes, enjoying the abundance of rabbits, may also be seen.

Hiking

Just 3km from the entrance gate, the **Senda Pampa Alta** (5km) heads up a hill with impressive views from the top. A quick 300m further leads to a *senda* (trail) paralleling the Río Pipo and some waterfalls. A more popular saunter is along the **Senda Costera** (6.5km), accessed from the end of the Bahía Ensenada road. This trail meanders along the bay, once home to Yaghan people. Keep an eye out for shell middens, now covered in grass. The trail ends at the road, which leads 1.2km further to the **Senda Hito XXIV** (5km), a level trail through lenga forest along the northern shore of Lago Roca; this trail terminates at an unimposing Argentine–Chilean border marker. **Senda Cerro Guanaco** (8km) starts at the same trailhead, but climbs up a 970m hill to reach a great viewpoint.

After running 3242km from Buenos Aires, RN 3 takes its southern bow at gorgeous Bahía Lapataia. **Mirador Lapataia** (1km), connecting with **Senda Del Turbal** (2km), winds through lenga forest to access this highway terminus. Other walks in this section include the self-guided nature trail **Senda Laguna Negra** (950m), through peat bogs, and the **Senda Castorera** (800m), along which beaver dams, and possibly beavers themselves, can be spotted in the ponds.

Getting There & Away

Buses leave from the corner of Maipú and Juana Fadul in Ushuaia several times daily from 9am to 6pm, returning approximately every hour between 8am to 8pm. Depending on your destination, a round-trip fare runs AR$30 to AR$40, and you need not return the same day. Private tour buses go for AR$90 round-trip. Taxi fares shared between groups can be the same price as bus tickets.

The most touristy and, beyond jogging, the slowest way to the park, **El Tren del Fin de Mundo** (☎ 431-600; www.trendelfindemundo.com.ar; one way/round-trip plus park entrance AR$65/70) originally carted prisoners to work camps. It departs (*sans* convicts) from the Estación del Fin del Mundo, 8km west of Ushuaia (taxis AR$25 one way), three or four times daily in summer and once or twice in winter. The one-hour, scenic, narrow-gauge train ride comes with historical explanations in English and Spanish. Reserve in January and February, when cruise-ship tours take over. If you are not a train fanatic, take it one way and return via minibus.

Hitching to the park is feasible, but many cars will already be full.

ESTANCIA HARBERTON

Historic **Estancia Harberton** (☎ in Ushuaia 01901-422-742, Aves del Sur 01901-423-213; www.estanciaharberton.com; tour AR$20; ☉ 10am-7pm Oct 15-Apr 15) was founded in 1886 by missionary Thomas Bridges and family. As Tierra del Fuego's first *estancia* it contains the island's oldest house still in use. The location earned fame from a stirring memoir Bridges' son Lucas wrote, titled *Uttermost Part of the Earth*. The *estancia* is now owned and run by the Goodalls, direct descendents of the Bridges.

Harberton is a working station, although only a handful of sheep and 1000 cattle remain on 200 sq km. The location is splendid and the history alluring. A one-hour **guided tour** (at 11am, 1:30pm, 3pm and 5pm) takes in the family cemetery and a garden where foliage names are given in Yaghan, Selk'nam and Spanish. There's also an abundant farmhouse tea service (AR$20), complete lunch (AR$45), optional excursions to the Reserva

Yecapasela penguin colony and a replica of a Yaghan dwelling. It's also a popular destination for birders. In the summer, Acawaya Parillada, a new grill house, plans to open, though it is owned and run separately from the *estancia*.

Worth the trip is the impressive **Museo Acatushún** (www.acatushun.com; admission AR$10), created by Natalie Prosser Goodall, a North American biologist who married into the family. Emphasizing the region's marine mammals, the museum has thousands of mammal and bird specimens inventoried; among the rarest specimens is a Hector's beaked whale. Much of this vast inventory was found at Bahía San Sebastián, north of Río Grande, where an up to 11km difference between high and low tide leaves animals stranded.

Volunteers and interns are taken to work as tour guides and research assistants (for the museum), mostly advanced university students studying tourism or biology. Volunteers stay one month and get food and lodging and the occasional possibility to be in the field. Competition is fierce and positions are filled with preference to Argentines.

Harberton has no phones on site so make reservations well in advance. With advance permission, free primitive camping is allowed at Río Lasifashaj, Río Varela and Río Cambaceres. Lodging is offered in the 1950 Shepherds' house (AR$300 per person) and remodeled 1901 Cook house (AR$180 to AR$240 per person, shared bath), with an extra AR$90 for full board.

Harberton is 85km east of Ushuaia via RN 3 and rough RC-j, a 1½ to 2-hour drive one way. Shuttles leave from the base of 25 de Mayo at Av Maipú in Ushuaia at 9am, returning around 3pm (AR$100 round-trip); or take a taxi (AR$300 round-trip). Daylong catamaran tours are organized by agencies in Ushuaia.

TOLHUIN
☎ 02901 / pop 2000

Named for the Selk'nam word meaning 'like a heart,' Tolhuin is a lake town nestled in the center of Tierra del Fuego, 132km south of Río Grande and 104km northeast of Ushuaia via smooth pavement. This fast-growing frontier town of small plazas and sheltering evergreens fronts the eastern shore of Lago Fagnano, also known as Lago Kami. Most travelers tend to skip right over it, but

---

A PIONEER'S GUIDE TO TIERRA DEL FUEGO

It was a childhood too fabulous for fiction. E Lucas Bridges grew up with the Beagle Channel as his backyard, helped his dad rescue shipwrecked sailors and learned survival from the native Yaghan and Selk'nam (Ona) people. His memoir *Uttermost Part of the Earth* fed Bruce Chatwin's boyhood obsession with Patagonia. Now, after decades out of print, this 1947 classic has been rereleased in English.

Bridges' tale starts with his British father establishing an Anglican mission in untamed Ushuaia. Little house on the prairie it wasn't. After the family trades the missionary life for pioneering on an *estancia*, Bridges' father dies. As a young adult, Bridges tries adventuring with the Selk'nam, which meant surviving on lean guanaco meat, crossing icy rivers and negotiating peace between quarreling factions.

Measles epidemics and sparring with hostile colonists wreaked havoc on Tierra del Fuego's native peoples. By the time the book was first published, their population had nosedived to less than 150. *Uttermost Part of the Earth* captures the last days of these hardy civilizations and one island's transformation from virgin wilderness to a frontier molded by fortune seekers, missionaries and sheep ranchers.

---

if you are looking for a unique and tranquil spot, Tolhuin is well worth checking out.

A local highlight – and usually a stop on buses headed towards Ushuaia, **Panadería La Unión** (☎ 492-202; www.panaderialaunion.com.ar, in Spanish; Jeujepen 450; ☎ 24hr) serves first-rate pastries and some decent empanadas. The best spot for basic lodgings and camping is **Camping Hain** (☎ 02901-15-603-606; www.campinghain .com.ar; Lago Fagano; camping per person AR$10, 8-person refugios AR$130), with grassy, sheltered sites, hot-water showers, a huge barbecue pit and *fogon* (sheltered fire pit and kitchen area). Roberto, the conscientious owner, can recommend local excursions and guides.

RÍO GRANDE

☎ 02964 / pop 68,776

The island's petroleum service center has an industrial feel and an addiction to urban sprawl, egged on by its duty-free status. But look further and you will find some of the world's best trout fishing and exclusive lodges that cater to serious anglers. If you didn't come with rod in hand, the longest that you will likely stay in windswept Río Grande is a scant hour to change buses to Ushuaia, 230km southwest.

Eating & Sleeping

Catering towards suits and anglers, lodging tends to be overpriced, not to mention sparse. High-end places discount 10% for cash.

our pick **Hostel Argentino** (☎ 422-546; www.inter patagonia.com; San Martín 64; dm AR$40, d with shared/private

bath & breakfast AR$80/110; ☐) Locals and travelers kick back in this friendly hostel hosted by the effervescent Graciela. Guests get hot showers, a shared kitchen, breakfast and luggage storage. A new wing of small, neat doubles have twin beds and fresh paint. Long-distance cyclists even have a spot to store their bikes inside.

Hotel Ibarra (☎ 430-071, 430-883; www.federico ibarrahotel.com.ar, in Spanish; Rosales 357; s/d/tr incl break-fast AR$163/198/230; ☐) Aimed at the business crowd, this plaza-front hotel has carpeted, well-kept rooms. The *confitería* (café) is ideal for coffee or a light meal.

Posada de los Sauces (☎ 432-895; www.posadadelos sauces.com.ar; Elcano 839; s/d/tr AR$195/235/290; P ☐) Catering mostly to high-end anglers, this warm and professional hotel fosters a lodge atmosphere. Deluxe rooms have Jacuzzi. The upstairs bar-restaurant, decked in dark wood and forest green, is just waiting for stogies and tall tales to fill the air.

La Nueva Colonial (☎ 425-353; cnr Lasserre & Belgrano; mains AR$18-30) Enough reason to delay your departure, chef Cesar's outstanding pastas (we recommend the *sorrentinos* with pesto) are divine creations, served up with fresh foccacia bread and a bottle of red. And if you don't like it, it's free (but a hard argument to make). He also prepares massive pepper steaks, salads and generous-sized desserts.

El Rincón de Julio (☎ 02964-15-604-261; Elcano 805; all-you-can-eat AR$35) Dive into this ambient wood shack with seven tables for the best *parilla* in town. It's in front of the YPF service station.

Getting There & Around

The **airport** (RGA; ☎ 420-699) is off RN 3, a short cab ride from town. **Aerolíneas Argentinas** (☎ 424-467; San Martín 607) flies direct daily to Buenos Aires (AR$568). **LADE** (☎ 422-968; Lasserre 445) flies a couple of times weekly to Río Gallegos (AR$174), and El Calafate (AR$280).

At the time of writing, there was no central bus terminal, but plans for one were in the works. **Tecni-Austral** (☎ 432-885, 430-610; Moyano 516) goes to Ushuaia (AR$25, four hours) daily from 6am to 8pm, with a stop in Tolhuin

(AR$40, 1½ hours); to Río Gallegos (AR$85, eight hours) and to Punta Arenas (AR$85, eight hours) at 10am on Monday, Wednesday and Friday. **Buses Pacheco** (☎ 425-611; 25 de Mayo 712) goes to Punta Arenas (AR$80) several times a week.

Lider (☎ 420-003, 424-2000; Moreno 1056) and **Transportes Montiel** (☎ 427-225; 25 de Mayo 712) offer door-to-door minivan service to Ushuaia (AR$40) and Tolhuin (AR$20) several times daily. Call to reserve a seat; tickets must be paid for in person.

Archipiélago Juan Fernández

This craggy Pacific outpost is where castaway Alexander Selkirk whittled away lost years scampering after goats and scanning the cobalt horizon for ships. A chain of small volcanic islands 667km east of Valparaíso, Archipiélago Juan Fernández once served as an anonymous waypoint for pirates, sealers and war ships, but in modern times it has slid into relative anonymity…save for the occasional multi-million-dollar treasure hunt. Strange, because the islands' jagged landscape and clear waters fall nothing short of spectacular.

A national park since 1935 and a Unesco Biosphere Reserve, the islands are starting to gain attention as a destination for world-class diving. But they are really a paradise for outdoors lovers, who can hike staircase-steep trails, visit fur seal colonies or search for the elusive Juan Fernández hummingbird. Visitors trickle in during summer (December to March) and the rest of the year sees precious few foreigners or mainlanders.

The main island is named Robinson Crusoe, in honor of the fictional Daniel Defoe character inspired by Selkirk. The archipelago also includes the ultraremote Isla Alejandro Selkirk and the uninhabited Isla Santa Clara.

HIGHLIGHTS

- Climb the breathless pitch up **Mirador de Selkirk** (p437) to see the sun rise
- Reel in lobster traps on a working **fishing boat** (p435), or just find out what it's like
- Play with the fur seals while **snorkeling** or **scuba diving** (p435) the island's clear Pacific waters
- Trek through steep and stunning panoramas on the cross-island trail to **La Punta de Isla** (p437)
- Search **Parque Nacional Juan Fernández** (p436) for the scarlet whirr of the super-rare Juan Fernández hummingbird

- **POPULATION: 650**
- **AREA: 95 SQ KM**
- **ELEVATION: 0–1650M**

History

In November 1574, Portuguese mariner Juan Fernández veered off course between Peru and Valparaíso and discovered these islands that now bear his name. He first dubbed them Masatierra (meaning closer to land), Masafuera (further away) and Santa Clara (unchanged). In following centuries the islands proved a popular stop-off for ships skirting around the Humboldt Current. Pirates sought refuge in the few bays – hunting feral goats and planting gardens to stock future visits. Traffic increased with sealers, who would nearly hunt to extinction the endemic Juan Fernández fur seal.

But the archipelago's claim to fame is Scotsman Alexander Selkirk, who spent four years and four months marooned on Masatierra after requesting to be put ashore. He had had a dispute with the captain of the privateer *Cinque Ports* in 1704 over the seaworthiness of the vessel (the ship was rotting). Abandonment was tantamount to a death sentence for most castaways, who soon starved or shot themselves, but Selkirk adapted to his new home and endured, despite his desperate isolation.

Although the Spaniards vigorously opposed privateers in their domains, their foresight made Selkirk's survival possible. Unlike many small islands, Masatierra had abundant water and goats, thanks to the Spaniards. Disdaining fish, Selkirk tracked these feral animals, devoured their meat and dressed himself in their skins. He crippled and tamed some for their company and easy hunting. Sea lions, feral cats and rats – the latter two European introductions – were among his other companions.

Selkirk would often climb to a lookout above Bahía Cumberland (Cumberland Bay) in hope of spotting a vessel on the horizon, but not until 1708 did his savior, Commander Woodes Rogers of the British privateers *Duke* and *Duchess*, arrive with famed privateer William Dampier as his pilot. Rogers recalled his first meeting with Selkirk when the ship's men returned from shore:

> Immediately our Pinnace return'd from the shore, and brought abundance of Craw-fish, with a man Cloth'd in Goat-Skins, who look'd wilder than the first Owners of them.

After signing on with Rogers and returning to Scotland, Selkirk became a celebrity.

After Selkirk's departure, privateers (personae non grata on the South American mainland) frequented the islands to rest and hunt seals. In response, Spain re-established a presence at Bahía Cumberland in 1750, founding the village of San Juan Bautista, but it was only sporadically occupied.

After the turn of the 18th century, Masatierra played a notorious role in Chile's independence struggle, as Spanish authorities exiled 42 criollo patriots to damp caves above San Juan Bautista after the disastrous Battle of Rancagua in 1814. The patriots in exile

---

SELKIRK IN PRINT

The inspiration for a rag-tag army of reality shows, theme park rides and great literature alike, Scotsman Alexander Selkirk is the quintessential castaway. It makes good sense to dip into Daniel Defoe's classic *Robinson Crusoe* while visiting the namesake island, but there are other accounts worthy of exploration. Laudable reads include Captain Woodes Rogers' *A Cruising Voyage Round the World*, by Selkirk's actual rescuer, *Robinson Crusoe's Island* (1969) by Ralph Lee Woodward and Nobel Prize winner JM Coetzee's revisionist novel *Foe* (1986).

Traditional biography was cast away when British writer Diane Souhami made a portrait of the man through the place. Her take, *Selkirk's Island*, won the 2001 Whitbread Biography Award. While there researching, Souhami became intrigued with the way the island pared down modern life, leaving what was essential. There was the absence of choice: if there was fish, you ate fish. When the supply ship came, there were oranges. 'The island was dictating things,' she observed, 'just as it had for Selkirk.'

Solitude becomes a metaphor for identity, according to Souhami. That's the whole island attraction. Souhami noted how Selkirk's relationship to the island he once cursed changed post-rescue. 'He started calling it "my beautiful island,"' said Souhami. 'It became the major relationship in his life.'

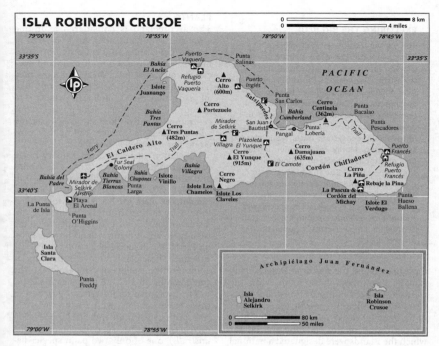

ISLA ROBINSON CRUSOE

included Juan Egaña and Manuel de Salas, figures from the Chilean elite who would not quickly forget their cave-dwelling days.

Chile established a permanent settlement in 1877. For many years the island remained a nearly escape-proof political prison for the newly independent country. Later during WWI it again played a memorable historic role, as the British naval vessels *Glasgow* and *Orama* confronted the German cruiser *Dresden* at Bahía Cumberland; the German crew scuttled their vessel before it could be sunk.

The last half century has been marked by the slow development of fishing and small-scale tourism, with a bit of treasure hunting to keep the memory of Juan Fernández's pirate days vibrant.

Geography & Climate

Adrift in the open Pacific Ocean, the Juan Fernández archipelago consists of Isla Robinson Crusoe; tiny Isla Santa Clara (known to early privateers as Goat Island), just 3km off the main island's southern tip; and Isla Alejandro Selkirk, another 170km away from the continent.

The islands' land areas are very small, but their topography is extraordinarily rugged; geologically, the entire archipelago is a group of emergent peaks of the submarine mountain range known as the Juan Fernández Ridge, which goes east–west for more than 400km at the southern end of the Chile Basin. Isla Robinson Crusoe comprises only 93 sq km, with a maximum length of 22km and a maximum width of 7.3km.

The archipelago is far enough from the continent for subtropical water masses to moderate the chilly sub-Antarctic waters of the Humboldt Current, which flows northward along the Chilean coast. The climate is distinctly Mediterranean, with clearly defined warm, dry summers and cooler, wet winters.

Because of the islands' irregular topography, rainfall varies greatly over short distances. In particular, the Cordón Chifladores (of which Cerro El Yunque is the highest point) intercepts most of the rainfall, which causes a pronounced rain shadow to form on the southeastern portion of Isla Robinson Crusoe – creating a difference as great as that between

ARCHIPIÉLAGO JUAN FERNÁNDEZ

EXPLORING THE BIG BLUE

Pull on your flippers and plunge in – diving around Robinson Crusoe is like slipping into a great abyss. On all sides of the island, the seafloor drops abruptly to over 4000m below sea level, leaving little continental shelf to support marine fauna and flora. Marine life is concentrated incredibly close to the island's edge. This idiosyncratic ecosystem hosts world-class scuba diving. Moray eel, flounder, lobster and enormous schools of yellowtail troll the clear waters. But the biggest attraction is the playful Juan Fernández fur seal (*Arctocephalus philippii*), once the easy target of 17th-century sealers. The species was thought to be extinct up until the mid-20th century, but now boasts a population of around 40,000.

---

the Amazon and the Atacama Desert. Daily rainfall is common above 500m, while the western slope of Robinson Crusoe and Santa Clara are quite dry. By contrast, the area north of the range is dense rainforest, with a high concentration of the endemic species for which the islands were designated a national park and biosphere reserve.

Wildlife

ANIMALS

The only native mammal, the Juan Fernández fur seal inhabits the seas and shores of Isla Robinson Crusoe and Isla Santa Clara. The southern elephant seal *Mirounga leonina*, hunted for its blubber, no longer survives here. Of 11 endemic bird species, the most eye-catching is the Juan Fernández hummingbird (*Sephanoides fernandensis*). The male is conspicuous because of its bright red color; the female is a more subdued green with a white tail. Only about 700 hummingbirds survive, feeding off the striking Juan Fernández cabbage that grows in many parts of San Juan Bautista, but the birds do best in native forest.

Introduced rodents and feral cats endanger nesting marine birds, such as Cook's petrel (*Pterodroma cookii defilippiana*), by preying on their eggs or young. Another mammal that has proliferated since its introduction in the 1930s is the South American coatimundi (coatí in Spanish).

PLANTS

The archipelago is considered a unique ecoregion with plants that slowly evolved in isolation, adapting to local environmental niches. The introduction of mainland species is causing a great shakeup. Goats may have helped to keep Selkirk alive but, like all goats, they have a stubborn penchant to devour all before them. The greatest concentration of native flora survives in sectors where these agile invaders can neither penetrate nor completely dominate.

Vegetation spans an extraordinary range of geographic affinities, from the Andes and sub-Antarctic Magallanes to Hawaii and New Zealand. In its oceanic isolation, though, the plant life has evolved into something very distinct from its continental and insular origins. Of 87 genera of plants on the islands, 16 are endemic, found nowhere else on earth; of 140 native plant species, 101 are endemic. These plants survive in three major communities: the evergreen rainforest, the evergreen heath and the herbaceous steppe.

The evergreen rainforest is the richest of these environments, with a wide variety of tree species, such as the endemic luma (*Nothomyrcia fernandeziana*) and the chonta (*Juania australis*), one of only two palm species native to Chile. Perhaps the most striking vegetation, however, is the dense understory of climbing vines and the towering endemic tree ferns *Dicksonia berteroana* and *Thyrsopteris elegans*.

Evergreen heath replaces rainforest on the thinner soils of the highest peaks and exceptionally steep slopes. Characteristic species are the tree fern *Blechnum cyadifolium* and various tree species of the endemic genus *Robinsonia*. The steppe, which is largely confined to the arid eastern sector of Isla Robinson Crusoe and to Isla Santa Clara, consists of perennial bunch grasses, such as *Stipa fernandeziana*.

Exotic mainland species have provided unfortunate competition for native flora. At lower elevations, the wild blackberry (*Rubus ulmifolius*) and the shrub maqui (*Aristotelia chilensis*) have proven to be aggressive colonizers, despite efforts to control them (incidentally, lobster catchers use branches from the maqui for their traps). Visiting ships seeking fresh provisions not only collected edible wild species, such as cabbage, but they even planted gardens that they, and others, later harvested.

Getting There & Away

AIR

From Santiago, flights to Juan Fernández leave almost daily between September and April, but depart weekly the rest of the year. The 2¼-hour flight takes 10 to 20 passengers and accepts 10kg of luggage per person. Foul weather on the island can provoke last-minute departure changes.

Flights depart from Santiago's Aeródromo Tobalaba in the eastern residential neighborhood of La Reina. To get there take the metro to Principe de Gales and hail a taxi (CH$2500) to the nearby hangar. Upon arrival to the island, passengers take a one-hour boat taxi (usually included in the airfare) to the pier of San Juan Bautista. Return flights require a minimum number of passengers to depart, so keep travel arrangements flexible enough to allow for a few extra days on the island.

Lassa (☎ 02-273-4354; lassa@entelchile.net; Larraín Alcalde s/n) has a 19-seat Twin Otter (round trip CH$340,000) that usually departs at 9:30am. Flight payments can be made directly at Aeródromo Tobalaba upon departure.

ATA (☎ 02-234-3389; www.aerolineasata.cl; Larraín Alcalde s/n) flies out of Aeródromo Tobalaba, but has fewer low-season departures (round trip CH$340,000) and smaller planes than Lassa.

SEA

At the time of writing, the concession for island boat transport was in flux. For updates, see www.comunajuanfernandez.cl (in Spanish) or consult any island lodging.

Naval supply ships sail to the island about six times annually. A no-frills trip costs CH$8500 per day. To apply, passengers must write a letter to the navy, **Armada de Chile: Comando de Transporte** (☎ 032-2506-354; Primera Zona Naval, Prat 620, Valparaíso), one month in advance. Call for details. This is no cruise ship – guests share one enormous bunkroom, bathrooms are few and the food is basic. Take a sleeping bag, motion-sickness tablets and extra snacks.

Getting Around

With only a few kilometers of roads in San Juan Bautista and steep peaks that bookend the valleys, boating is the best way to get around. To arrange a water taxi, ask around at the Municipalidad across from the plaza.

A water taxi to Puerto Inglés, for example, costs approximately CH$30,000 round trip for up to five passengers. A thrifty alternative is to accompany lobster catchers to their grounds.

The island boasts a number of trails, none flat, with some crossing fragile terrain that requires professional guiding. To walk to the airstrip from San Juan Bautista, or in reverse, see walking details from Villagra to La Punta de Isla, p437.

SAN JUAN BAUTISTA

☎ 032 / pop 600

The sole town on Isla Robinson Crusoe, San Juan Bautista (St John the Baptist) is the proverbial sleepy fishing village, down to the lobster catchers in knitted caps, and dusty stores that run out of cheese and beer before the provisions ship arrives. But when the ship docks the ambiance cranks into Kathmandu – with the whole village crowding the pier with wheelbarrows to sort sacks of flour, boxes of provisions and propane tanks.

The village's steep hills are strewn with lush gardens and modest cottages with paths leading into horse pastures and wooded hiking trails. Despite rumors of a major airline starting service to the island, tourism remains very small-scale. Few islanders visit the mainland, known as 'el conti,' but neighbors greet each person who passes on the mud-puddled streets.

Lobster fishing drives the island's economy and the European slow food movement has embraced San Juan's traditional industry. Open skiffs leave at first light and return in the evening, when you can pick up fresh lobster on the dock before it journeys to the linen-clad tables of Paris or Madrid.

Orientation

San Juan Bautista occupies a snug east-facing site on Bahía Cumberland. The surrounding forests of exotic conifers and eucalyptus were planted to stem erosion. The jetty leads into the main street of Larraín Alcalde, which leads into Costanera El Palillo a few hundred meters south. Other streets and staircase passages climb steeply away from shore. The mouth of Estero Lord Anson serves as San Juan Bautista's beach, but swimming and diving are preferable off the rocks at El Palillo, at the southern end of the *costanera* (coastal road).

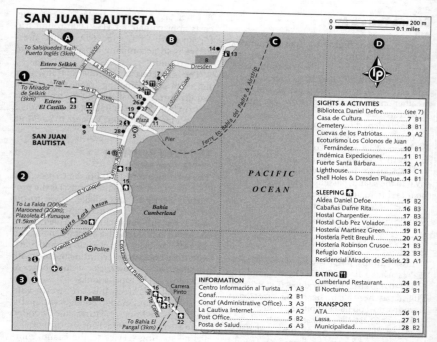

Information

There are no banks or money changers on the island, so bring all the pesos you need, preferably in small bills. Credit cards are rarely accepted, though some tour operators or hotels will take US dollars or euros at poor rates.

Several kiosks have public telephones, although international rates are prohibitively expensive.

Centro Información al Turista (Vicente González; ⏰ 8am-12:30pm & 2-6pm Mon-Fri, 8am-12:30pm & 2-4:30pm Sat & Sun) At the top of Vicente González, this large open hall has photo displays, a meeting room, and detailed information on the park and the history of the islands, all with decent English translations.

Conaf (Larraín Alcalde; ⏰ 8am-6pm Mon-Fri, 9am-6pm Sat & Sun) This small kiosk near the plaza collects park admission and distributes leaflets with decent maps. For information on visiting any part of the park outside the immediate environs of San Juan Bautista, it's advisable to contact Conaf in advance.

Conaf administrative office (☎ 275-1004, 275-1022; Vicente González) Located next door to Centro Información al Turista. Ask for a tour of the next door plant nursery, where more than 40 endemic species are

cultivated and the saplings later replanted in the park and given to locals to plant around the town.

La Cautiva Internet (Larraín Alcalde s/n; per hr CH$1000; ⏰ 9:30am-1pm, 3:30-6pm & 8:30-11pm Mon-Fri, 7-11pm Sat & Sun)

Post office (⏰ 9am-6pm Mon-Fri, 9am-12pm Sat) On the south side of the plaza.

Posta de Salud (☎ 275-1067; Vicente González) A government medical clinic, just below the entrance to Conaf's grounds.

Sights

San Juan is the organizational and departure point for all of the islands' main activities, including fishing, hiking, boat tours of the islands, diving and tours of the local sights. For fishing, boat and diving tours, see the list of recommended agencies (opposite).

CEMETERY & LIGHTHOUSE

San Juan's cemetery, at the northern end of Bahía Cumberland near the lighthouse, has a polyglot assortment of Spanish, French and German surnames – the latter survivors of the sinking of the *Dresden*.

Just beyond the cemetery, fur seals frolic offshore beneath a spot where, after missing the German cruiser *Dresden*, shells from British ships lodged in the volcanic cliffs.

FUERTE SANTA BÁRBARA
Built in 1749 to discourage incursions by pirates, these Spanish fortifications were reconstructed in 1974. To get there, follow the path from Cuevas de los Patriotas, or climb directly from the plaza via Subida El Castillo. The track continues to Mirador de Selkirk (p437).

CUEVAS DE LOS PATRIOTAS
Up a short footpath from Larraín Alcalde and illuminated at night, these damp caverns sheltered Juan Egaña, Manuel de Salas and 40 other patriots exiled for several years during Chile's independence movement after their defeat in the Battle of Rancagua in 1814.

CASA DE CULTURA & BIBLIOTECA DANIEL DEFOE
The uninspired **museum** (Larraín Alcalde s/n; admission free; 8:30am-1pm & 3:30-5pm Mon-Fri, 11am-1pm & 5-8pm Sat) and combined library exhibits historic photos, a few plates from the *Dresden* and relics from colonial days. Guests can reserve a free half-hour of internet use in the library.

Tours
The Conaf kiosk on the plaza has a list of registered guides and tour schedules.
Ecoturismo Los Colonos de Juan Fernández (275-1216; www.colonosdejuanfernandez.cl, in Spanish; Larraín Alcalde s/n) Offers all of the island's main activities, including diving and fishing. One popular option is the guided boat trip to Puerto Inglés (CH$40,000).
Endémica Expediciones (032-275-1003; www.endemica.com; Larraín Alcalde 399b) Multilingual and cutting-edge, this excellent agency offers scuba diving, hiking, kayaking, fishing and snorkeling trips. Recommended are day trips to lobstering grounds with artisan fisherfolk. Single dives per person cost CH$38,000 to CH$43,000 depending on the number of overall divers. Snorkeling with fur seals costs from CH$65,000. Serious divers (six or more) can do a five-day all-inclusive dive and accommodations package for CH$625,000 per person.
Marooned (032-275-1030; lactorisfernandeziana@hotmail.com) A small, personalized operation offering guided hikes in Parque Nacional Juan Fernández. Staff speaks English and can tailor trips for those with interests in history, botany or bird-watching.

Festivals & Events
Rodeo de Villagra Held at the end of January or early February, this is an island-wide rodeo festival with more cattle than you can possibly imagine live out here.
Fiesta de San Pedro The patron saint of fishermen is honored on June 29 with decorated boats making a procession at sea.
Fiesta de Aniversario On Día de la Isla, held on November 22, a celebration commemorates the day Portuguese sailor Juan Fernández discovered the archipelago in 1574. Festivities include a regatta and a 13km foot race from Punta de Isla to Bahía Cumberland.

Sleeping & Eating
Since restaurants are few, most guests take half-board (dinner and breakfast); lodging rates quoted here include half-board. Typical extras include laundry service (CH$4000) or lunch (around CH$5000). Reserve ahead

---

THE CATCH WITH LOBSTER

Succulent and in somewhat short supply, the Juan Fernández lobster (*Jasus frontalis*, really a crayfish) is the real treasure of this isolated Pacific island chain. Here, where three-quarters of families fish grounds that have been handed down through the generations, lobster is culture. Islanders harvest about 50,000 of these poppy-colored crustaceans annually. But could this be too much of a good thing?

Enter **Slow Food** (www.slowfood.com), an international movement to preserve biodiversity and sustainable small-scale production. Linking local fishing families to the haute cuisine markets in Spain, France and Italy, it has come to play an essential role in preserving traditional lobstering – practiced without nets in small wooden boats.

Some still question the sustainability of a product that is literally shrinking; towards the end of the trapping season, few lobsters meet the regulation size of 11.5cm. One solution is to focus more on the healthy bounty of amberjack, silver snapper and grouper. Yet anyone who has been invited to share a roiling pot of *perol* – lobster stew spiced with fresh vegetables, squash and the lobster's own innards – would rally to keep this native pleasure alive.

when dining out, especially for groups or when requesting a specific dish.

Residencial Mirador de Selkirk (☎ 275-1028; Pasaje del Castillo 251; r per person without bathroom CH$15,000) High on the hillside, this family home has three snug rooms and a sprawling deck overlooking the bay (where you recover your breath from the hike up). Señora Julia serves up fantastic meals (CH$5000). Foodies shouldn't miss her lobster empanadas or seafood *parol* (stew).

Hostería Martínez Green (☎ 275-1039; Subida El Castillo 116; r per person CH$15,000) Opposite the plaza, this sprawling complex of rooms is basic but comfortable, and it's the only lodging in town with kitchen facilities for guests. Terraces are plentiful and an adjoining teahouse serves appetizing snacks.

Hostería Petit Breulh (☎ 275-1121; Vicente González 80; r per person CH$22,500) Bedside minibars, dark leather, massage showers and cable TV nurture a haven for would-be playboys that relish a few pelts on the wall (think 1980s). Yet, meals (CH$6000) are showstoppers – think ceviche with capers and zucchini stuffed with fresh fish and baked under bubbling cheese. Nonguests should make reservations.

Cabañas Dafne Rita (☎ 275-1042; ritachamorro_g@ yahoo.com; Carrera Pinto 198; cabins CH$24,000) Value-minded guests will like these clean, no-frills wood-shingled cabins, set just above the water. Request the larger cabin; both are doubles. Service is attentive but meals must be taken elsewhere.

Hostería Robinson Crusoe (☎ 275-1123; www.hosteria robinsoncrusoe.cl, in Spanish; Carrera Pinto 222; r per person CH$30,000; 🖳) Before you know it you'll be playing poker with hosts Homero and Lorraine and sampling their chestnut liqueur. Warmth infuses this rustic waterfront refuge. There is one combined living/dining area, so it's the ideal place to make friends but not for privacy. Low season (April to November) discounts are ample.

Hostal Charpentier (☎ 275-1020; www.hostalchar pentier.cl; Carrera Pinto 256; 3-person cabins CH$30,000) Set on a sprawling green lawn, this small, ocean-view cabin is ideal for families. There's big picture windows and a kitchenette.

Aldea Daniel Defoe (☎ 275-1223; www.robinson crusoeisland.cl; Larraín Alcalde 449; 2-3 person cabins with half-board CH$35,000; 🖳) This iconic bar-restaurant (mains CH$6000) with tucked-away terrace rooms are the baby of Maria Eugenia, source supreme of island lore. The sprawling hibiscus gardens and owner-made paintings foster a relaxed, homespun feel. While the older lodgings lack sparkle, new cabins feature canopy beds and massage-jet showers replete with radio.

Hostal Club Pez Volador (☎ 275-1227; fabianapersia@ endemica.com; Larraín Alcalde 399b; s/d CH$35,000/70,000; 🖳) Modern and chic, this new addition overflows with happy vibes, thanks to its great hosts. A playful spirit even infuses the architecture, which echoes a seafaring vessel with porthole windows and curved wooden walls. Bright colors punctuate ample, spiffy rooms but best of all, its clubhouse atmosphere makes it a fun base camp, right on the water.

Refugio Náutico (☎ 275-1077; www.islarobinson crusoe.cl, in Spanish; Carrera Pinto 280; s/d CH$40,000/60,000; 🖳) This waterfront refuge is stylin' with kitchen competence and all the comforts of home. Its bright terraced rooms are plenty private but the real treat is the living area brimming with books, DVDs and music – perfect for that rainy day, or for your post-meal coma. Kayak rentals, hiking and dive trips are available through the onsite PADI-certified dive center. Credit cards are accepted.

Cumberland Restaurant (☎ 275-1030; Larraín Alcalde s/n; mains CH$4000; 🕑 lunch & dinner, closed Mon) Tasty fish sandwiches, grilled snapper and steak and salad are staples at this popular, family-friendly spot. Check out the weekend happy hour with two-for-one drinks.

El Nocturno (☎ 275-1113; Larraín Alcalde 66; mains CH$4000) The Nocturno serves empanadas and large portions of local seafood in a no-frills sports bar.

PARQUE NACIONAL JUAN FERNÁNDEZ

This **national park** (admission for 7 days CH$3000) covers the entire archipelago, a total of 93 sq km, though the township of San Juan Bautista and the airstrip are de-facto exclusions. In an effort to control access to the most fragile areas of the park, Conaf requires many of the hikes to be organized and led by local registered guides. A list of the guides with pricing information is posted at the kiosk near the plaza, where you should register before taking any self-guided hike. Day hikes for a group of six people cost CH$15,000 to CH$25,000. Still, a number of areas are accessible without guides. Another way to see the park is by boat. Local tour operators (p435) can arrange trips to see fur seal colonies at different points around the island. Camping is possible only in organized campsites, each with a one-night limit.

Self-guided Hiking Trails
MIRADOR DE SELKIRK
Perhaps the most rewarding and stunning hike on the island is to Selkirk's mirador (lookout) above San Juan Bautista, where he would look for ships appearing on the horizon. The 3km walk, gaining 565m in elevation, takes about 1½ hours of steady walking but rewards the climber with views of both sides of the island. Start early and take at least a light cotton shirt, since the overlook, exposed to wind and weather, can be much cooler than at sea level. If it's been raining, the trail can be muddy and slippery.

On the saddle two metal plaques commemorate Selkirk's exile on the island, one placed by officials of the Royal Navy (1868) and the other by a Scottish relative (1983). The trail to the mirador begins at the south end of the plaza of San Juan Bautista, climbs the Subida El Castillo, and follows the north side of Estero El Castillo before zigzagging up Cerro Portezuelo to Selkirk's lookout. Fill your water bottle before continuing up the hillside through thickets of edible maqui, murtilla and blackberry, which gradually give way to native ferns and trees. Conaf's inexpensive brochure (Spanish only) entitled *Sendero Interpretativo Mirador Alejandro Selkirk* describes the environment in detail.

VILLAGRA TO LA PUNTA DE ISLA
Beyond Selkirk's overlook, the trail continues on the south side, taking one hour to reach **Villagra** (4.8km), where there are campsites. From here the wide trail skirts the south-

ern cliffs to **La Punta de Isla** (13km, approximately four hours) and the airstrip, where there is also camping available. En route is **Bahía Tierras Blancas**, the island's main breeding colony of Juan Fernández fur seals. This scenic and reasonably challenging hike takes in a significant part of the island and is an excellent way to take in its serenity.

It is possible to walk to the airstrip to catch your flight or to walk from here to San Juan Bautista, but make prior arrangements to stash your pack on the airport boat. Definitely confirm the actual date and time of your flight in advance of walking. Allow five hours to walk from San Juan Bautista to the airstrip.

PLAZOLETA EL YUNQUE
Plazoleta El Yunque is a tranquil forest clearing with bathrooms, water and picnic areas at the base of the 915m-high Cerro El Yunque (The Anvil). It is a half-hour walk from San Juan Bautista via a road that becomes a footpath. You will pass the crumbled foundation of the home of a German survivor of the *Dresden* who once homesteaded here. He was known as the 'German Robinson.'

The easiest access to native forest without a guide is a 1200m interpretive trail that starts at Plazoleta El Yunque.

CENTINELA
Cerro Centinela (362m) holds the ruins of the first radio station on the island, which was established in 1909. The 3km hike is accessed from Pangal. Hiking from San Juan Bautista to Pangal via jeep road takes about 45 minutes, but sometimes road gates are closed; inquire about the road status at your lodgings before trying it.

MY MAN FRIDAY
Decades before Alexander Selkirk was cast away, a Miskito from Nicaragua had spent three solitary years on the island. Known as Will, he survived with a resourcefulness that Selkirk would have envied, only to get cast as Crusoe's native sidekick, Friday, in Daniel Defoe's famed retelling. Will had been inadvertently left ashore when Spanish forces surprised William Dampier's 1681 expedition at Bahía Cumberland. For three years he evaded Spanish detection. His deft survival skills meant he could afford to be selective in his diet, eschewing seal entirely, which he deemed 'very ordinary meat.' The term 'Man Friday' has come to mean an assistant or devoted helper in the English language. In truth, had they inhabited the island at the same time, Selkirk would have been a dependent of Will.

TREASURE ISLAND

It's taking heaps of conviction, dough and cigarettes, but American millionaire Bernard Keiser has dedicated nearly a decade to trawling for an elusive treasure on Robinson Crusoe. An avid amateur historian, Keiser believes that General Juan de Ubilla y Echeverría buried loot from a Spanish galleon around 1713. Oh, just some 800 sacks of gold, barrels of gems and jewelry, and a trunk full of emeralds, gold and silver. Digging is based in Puerto Inglés but so far the only encouragement has been the 2007 discovery of some very old silver coins stamped with a Maltese cross. The search has been frustrating, long and, ironically, resource-depleting for Keiser.

But while locals and Chileans first derided this *gringo loco,* he has come to represent an important island sentiment. 'The treasure in itself isn't important,' says resident Pedro Niada, 'What is important is having a man behind a dream. It's a luxury few can persue. But he's doing it.'

SALSIPUEDES

At the top of La Pólvora, a trail zigzags through eucalyptus groves, then endemic ferns, then thickets of murtilla to reach the ridge Salsipuedes, which translates to 'Leave if you can.' With great views of Bahía Cumberland, the ridge is also home to a wind-energy research project.

Guided Hiking Trails

To arrange a guided hike, contact any of the island's travel agencies (see p435).

PUERTO INGLÉS & PUERTO VAQUERÍA

The 2.3km trail to Puerto Inglés starts at Salsipuedes and continues down a very precarious ridge to the beach area, where there is a reconstruction of Selkirk's shelter. Puerto Inglés is the site of US researcher Bernard Keiser's search for millions of dollars worth of buried gold (see above). Puerto Inglés has eight campsites with water and a bathroom.

A 4.3km continuation goes to Puerto Vaquería on the north side of the island, where there is a colony of about 100 seals. Conaf has two campsites and a *refugio* here with water and a bathroom.

VILLAGRA TO CERRO NEGRO

From Villagra guided hikes go to the base of Cerro El Yunque and Cerro Negro (3.5km).

PUERTO FRANCÉS

Located on the eastern shore of the island, Puerto Francés was a haven for French privateers, whose presence motivated Spain to erect a series of fortifications in 1779, the ruins of which are all but gone. From Cerro Centinela a 6.4km trail reaches the port where there are five campsites, a *refugio,* running water and a bathroom. From there guided treks continue 7.6km to Rebaje La Piña (a well-preserved area of native forest), La Pascua and Cordón del Michay on the southern side.

ISLA ALEJANDRO SELKIRK

If Robinson Crusoe falls short of castaway ambiance, search out Isla Alejandro Selkirk. Hard to reach and rarely visited by foreigners, the island lies 181km west of Robinson Crusoe. It's a seasonal lobstering base for 25 families from Crusoe who, when not fishing, can be found playing soccer, fixing boats or on Crusoe-esque hunts for feral goats. More mountainous than Crusoe, Selkirk's highest point in the archipelago is 1650m Cerro Los Inocentes.

Currently Conaf is working out a formal plan to initiate responsible tourism. Diving, hiking and hunting tours can be booked through Endemica Expediciones (p435). Otherwise, transportation is sporadic and sometimes limited to the needs of the fishing community. Contact the **Municipalidad** (☎ 032-275-1001, 275-1046; im_juanfernandez@entelchile.net; Larraín Alcalde 320, San Juan Bautista) for information. During lobster season a Conaf ranger stays on the island. Islanders are welcoming to respectful visitors, but you should plan to camp and bring provisions. Make sure that you settle your return trip in advance, or you may be putting in some time as an island exile.

Easter Island (Rapa Nui)

Easter Island (Rapa Nui to its native Polynesian inhabitants) is like nowhere else on earth. Historically intriguing, culturally compelling and scenically magical, this tiny speck of land looks like it's fallen off another planet. In this blissfully isolated, unpolished gem it's hard to feel connected even to Chile, over 3700km to the east, let alone the wider world. Just you, the indigo depths and the strikingly enigmatic *moai* (giant statues) scattered amid an eerie landscape.

When the *moai* have finished working their magic on you, there are dead volcanoes to climb, *motus* (islets) to dive or snorkel along, and waves to surf. And there's no better eco-friendly way to experience the island's savage beauty than on horseback or from a bicycle saddle. Once you've had your fill of hiking and clambering, gawking and gasping, a couple of expanses of silky sand beckon (with not a jet ski in sight).

Easter Island is refreshingly void of bling and large-scale development. It's all about eco-travel, and this is why it's gaining in popularity. With the exception of one recently built ritzy resort, tourism infrastructure is limited to a flurry of family-run ventures, which ensures your money goes straight into local pockets.

If your visit is in February, try to make it coincide with the hugely popular Tapati Rapa Nui festival, featuring a vibrant program of music, dance and traditional cultural events.

One thing is sure, you'll have a lump in your throat the day you leave.

HIGHLIGHTS

- Clip-clop on the flanks of the extinct volcano **Maunga Terevaka** (p455) and feast your eyes on the mesmerizing 360-degree views

- Hike across the ruggedly beautiful **Península Poike** (p457) and seek out the ghosts of virgins at Ana O Keke

- Ogle the stunning limpid blue waters of Motu Nui on a **snorkeling** or **diving** (p446) trip

- Take a lesson in history at **Rano Raraku** (p456), the 'nursery' of the *moai*, and at the spellbinding **Orongo ceremonial village** (p455), perched on the edge of **Rano Kau** (p455), a lake-filled crater

- Watch the sun rise at the row of enigmatic statues at **Ahu Tongariki** (p456) while enjoying breakfast

- **Maunga Terevaka**
- **Península Poike** ★
- **Rano Raraku** ★ ★ **Ahu Tongariki**
- **Orongo Ceremonial Village** ★ **Rano Kau**
- **Motu Nui**

■ POPULATION: 4400   ■ AREA: 117 SQ KM   ■ ELEVATION: 507M

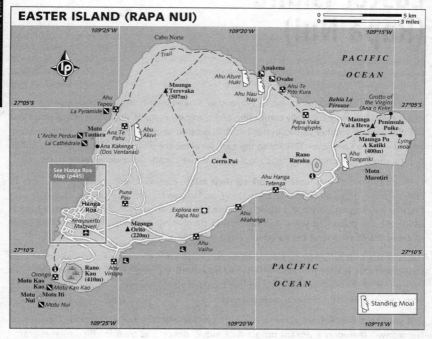

EASTER ISLAND (RAPA NUI)

Getting Started

WHEN TO GO

The weather is pleasant on Rapa Nui year-round. The peak tourist season runs from January to March. Prices are highest and accommodations scarcest during this period, especially during February's Tapati Rapa Nui festival (see p449). The rest of the year is quiet and at times you'll have the whole island to yourself. July and August might be a bit chilly for some tastes but they're ideal for hiking.

CLIMATE

Winds and ocean currents strongly influence Rapa Nui's subtropical climate. The hottest months are January and February, and the coolest are July and August. The average maximum summer temperature is 28°C and the average minimum 15°C, but these figures understate what can be a fierce sun and formidable heat. The average winter maximum is 22°C and the minimum 14°C, but it can seem much cooler when Antarctic winds lash the island with rain. Light showers are the most frequent form of precipitation. May is the wettest month, but tropical downpours can occur during any season.

MAPS

Tourist maps, which are distributed freely at Sernatur information office and tour agencies, show the most important archaeological sites. Ask for the *Rapa Nui National Park – Free Visitors Guide,* a good aerial map that helps explain the geography of the island. Other maps are available at local shops.

MONEY

US dollars are the best foreign currency to carry, followed by euros. A number of businesses on Rapa Nui, especially *residenciales,* hotels and rental agencies, quote their prices in US dollars and accept US cash (and euros, albeit at a pinch), but the weak dollar has made this practice less common over the last few years, and Chilean pesos are now commonly used. Note that exchange rates on Easter Island are lower than those offered in mainland Chile. Travelers from Tahiti must bring US cash (or euros) and not Tahitian currency. Many *residenciales,* hotels, restaurants and tour agencies accept credit cards but they usually charge an additional 5% to 10% commission.

Easter Island has only two ATMs. They only accept MasterCard. Don't rely solely on your credit card and make sure you keep some cash in reserve.

History

How did such a tiny island become inhabited? While Thor Heyerdahl's *Kon Tiki* expedition theorized that the island was settled from South America, the most accepted answer is that the first islanders arrived either from the Marquesas, the Mangarevas, the Cook Islands or Pitcairn Island around the 8th century.

According to legend, the initial settlers were led by King Hotu Matua *(matua* is a Polynesian word for 'ancestor' and means 'father' on Rapa Nui), who came from the east and landed at Anakena on the island's north coast. Some experts estimate that Hotu Matua arrived around AD 450, though the earliest archaeological evidence of people dates from around 800.

In 2007, José Miguel Ramirez Aliaga, an archaeologist from the University of Valparaíso, put forth the hypothesis that Polynesians, by sailing eastwards, might have continued on to central or southern Chile after discovering Rapa Nui. He based his assumption on the fact that Polynesians and various South American Indian groups, including the Mapuche, share several cultural traits.

CLAN WARFARE

Although islanders were few after Hotu Matua first landed at Anakena, their numbers grew over the centuries, first slowly and then rapidly. However, there were limits to this development and sheer numbers eventually threatened the available resources. Conflict over land and resources erupted in warfare by the late 17th century, only shortly before the

WHAT'S IN A NAME?

A Chilean territory since 1888, Rapa Nui is officially known by its Spanish name, Isla de Pascua. The island was named after it was discovered by the Dutch admiral Jacob Roggeveen on Easter Sunday 1722. Easter Island is the English translation, and Rapa Nui (Big Rapa) is the Polynesian name.

European arrival, and the population started to decline. Population estimates for the early 19th century range from 4000 to 20,000.

Dissension between different clans led to bloody wars and cannibalism, and many *moai* were toppled from their *ahu* (ceremonial platforms). Natural disasters – earthquakes and tsunamis – may also have contributed to the damage. The only *moai* standing today have been restored during the last century.

CONTACT WITH EUROPEANS

On Easter Sunday, 1722, a Dutch expedition under admiral Jacob Roggeveen brought the first Europeans to set foot on Rapa Nui.

Not until 1770 did Europeans again visit Rapa Nui, when a Spanish party from Peru under Don Felipe González de Haedo claimed the island for Spain. At the time, most islanders inhabited caves, while others lived in elliptical boat-shaped houses. The absence of goods and metal implements suggested no commerce with the outside world.

In 1774 the celebrated Englishman Captain James Cook led the next European expedition to land on Rapa Nui. Cook, familiar with the people of the Society Islands, Tonga and New Zealand, concluded that the inhabitants of Rapa Nui belonged to the same general lineage. His account is the first to mention that, although some *moai* still stood and carried their topknots, others had fallen and their *ahu* were damaged.

Only one other 18th-century European, the French explorer and naval officer Comte de La Pérouse, visited Rapa Nui in 1786, coming from Chile. In 1804 a Russian visitor reported more than 20 *moai* still standing. Existing accounts from ensuing years suggest another period of destruction, so that perhaps only a handful of *moai* stood a decade later.

EUROPEAN COLONIZATION

Whether or not the people of Rapa Nui experienced a period of self-inflicted havoc, their discovery by the outside world nearly resulted in their annihilation. By the late 18th century European and North American entrepreneurs saw the Pacific as an unexploited 'resource frontier.' First came the whalers, followed by planters who set out to satisfy an increasing European demand for tropical commodities such as rubber, sugar and coffee.

Then came slavers who either kidnapped Polynesians or induced them to sign contracts to work in mines and plantations in lands as remote as Australia and Peru. The worst example of this occurred in 1862, when Peruvian slavers made a ruthless raid on Rapa Nui and took about a thousand islanders – including the king – to work the guano deposits on Peru's Chincha Islands. After Bishop Jaussen of Tahiti protested to the French representative at Lima, Peruvian authorities ordered the return of the islanders to their homeland, but disease and hard labor had already killed about 90% of them. On the return voyage, smallpox killed most of the rest, and the handful who survived brought back an epidemic that decimated the remaining inhabitants of the island, leaving only a few hundred traumatized survivors. The knowledge and culture lost has never been fully regained.

In the mid-1860s Catholic missionaries converted the few remaining islanders, suppressing and degrading local customs and practices.

Commercial exploitation of the island began in 1870 when the French adventurer Jean-Baptiste Dutroux-Bornier introduced the wool trade to Rapa Nui. Importing sheep, he intended to transform the entire island into a ranch and expel the islanders to the plantations of Tahiti. He raided the missionary settlements and forced the missionaries, who opposed his claims of sovereignty over the island, to evacuate. Most reluctantly accepted transportation to Tahiti and Mangareva, leaving about a hundred people on the island. Dutroux-Bornier ruled until the remaining islanders killed him in 1877.

ANNEXATION BY CHILE

Chile officially annexed the island in 1888 during a period of expansion that included the acquisition of territory from Peru and Bolivia after the War of the Pacific (1879–84).

By 1897 Rapa Nui had fallen under the control of a single wool company, which became the island's de facto government, continuing the wool trade until the middle of the 20th century.

In 1953 the government took charge of the island, continuing the imperial rule to which islanders had been subject for nearly a century.

Rapa Nui remained under military rule until the mid-1960s, followed by a brief period of civilian government until the military coup of 1973 once again brought direct military control. However, 1967 was a turning point; the establishment of a regular commercial air link between Santiago and Tahiti, with Rapa Nui as a refueling stop, opened up the island to the world and brought many benefits to the Rapa Nui people.

RAPA NUI TODAY

In 2008 Easter Island was granted a special status. It is now a *territoria especial* (special territory) within Chile, which means greater autonomy for the islanders. But independence is not the order of the day – ongoing economic reliance on mainland Chile renders this option unlikely in the foreseeable future.

The main claim is for the return of native lands, and the new status should help settle these matters in the forthcoming years. Indigenous Rapanui control almost no land outside Hanga Roa. A national park (designated in 1935) comprises more than a third of the island, and nearly all the remainder belongs to Chile. Native groups have asked the Chilean government and the UN to return the park to aboriginal hands.

The Rapanui are also concerned about the development and control of the tourism industry. Mass tourism it ain't, but the rising number of visitors – approximately 50,000 tourists each year – has an impact on the environment, and signs are that the upward trend looks set to continue (there has been a 10% increase each year over the last few years). New measures and regulations will probably be introduced to better protect the heritage sites.

Culture

Rapa Nui people are generally very easygoing and there are very few pitfalls for unwary visitors. Nonetheless, it's worth keeping in mind that it's a fairly conservative society and that family life, marriage and children still play a central role in everyday life, as does religion.

A third of the population is from the mainland or Europe. The most striking feature is the intriguing blend of Polynesian and Chilean customs – you'll hear a '*ia ora na*' being followed by a stream of Spanish, or an '*ola*' being followed by Rapanui. Although they will never admit it overtly, the people of Rapa Nui have one foot in South America and one foot in Polynesia. This constant sway between two cultures can be disconcerting.

Although Rapa Nui has largely adapted to a modern Westernized lifestyle, the people are fiercely proud of their unique history and culture, and they keep their traditions alive. Treat the archaeological sites with respect.

LANGUAGE

Islanders speak Rapanui, an eastern Polynesian dialect related to Cook Islands Maori, but they also speak Spanish, the official language. Many people in the tourist business speak English.

Environment

THE LAND

Rapa Nui, just south of the tropic of Capricorn, is a tiny volcanic island formed where lava from three separate cones of different ages coalesced in a single triangular landmass. Its maximum length is just 24km. At its widest point the island is only 12km.

All three of its major volcanoes are now extinct. Terevaka, the largest, rises 507m above sea level in the northern part of the island, Pu A Katiki (about 400m) forms the eastern headland of the Poike peninsula, and Rano Kau (about 410m) dominates the southwest corner. Rano Kau and Rano Raraku both contain freshwater lakes.

For the most part, Rapa Nui's volcanic slopes are gentle and grassy, except where wave erosion has produced nearly vertical cliffs. In contrast, rugged lava fields cover much of the island's interior.

Although some coral occurs in shallow waters, Rapa Nui does not have coral reefs. In the absence of reefs, the ocean has battered the huge cliffs, some of which rise to 300m. Anakena on the north coast has the only broad sandy beach.

Erosion, exacerbated by overgrazing and deforestation, is the island's most serious problem. In the most dramatic cases, the ground has slumped, leaving eroded landslides of brownish soil (it's particularly striking on Península Poike). To counteract the effects of erosion, a small-scale replanting program is currently underway on Península Poike and at Ovahe. Only plants native to Oceania, such as albizzia, purau (Hibiscus tiliaceus) or aito (ironwood), have been introduced.

WILDLIFE

You'll probably be struck by the barren landscapes of the island. Vegetation was once more luxuriant on Rapa Nui – including forests with palms, conifers and other species that are now extinct – but islanders cut the forests long ago. Most of today's trees, such as the eucalyptus, were planted only within the past century. Like other remote islands, Rapa Nui is particularly lacking in native fauna; even seabirds are relatively few. Some plants are endemic, most notably the tree species toromiro (Sophora toromiro) and several genera of ferns.

Horses and sheep were brought by Europeans in the 19th century.

Getting There & Away

Lan (☎ 210-0920; Av Atamu Tekena s/n; ✆ 9am-4:30pm Mon-Fri, 9am-12:30pm Sat), near Av Pont, is the only airline serving Rapa Nui. It has four to seven flights per week to/from Santiago depending on season and two per week to/from Papeete (Tahiti). A standard economy round-trip fare from Santiago can range from US$600 to US$900. Flights are often overbooked, so it is essential to reconfirm your ticket two days before departure. It's not uncommon for your luggage to arrive one day late.

For travelers coming from Asia or Australia, a cheaper alternative is to stop here en route to (or from) South America, via Auckland, New Zealand. There you'll need to join an Air New Zealand flight to Papeete and connect with Lan's Papeete–Easter Island–Santiago service (see p476).

Getting Around

Outside Hanga Roa, nearly the entire east coast road and the road to Anakena are paved. Other roads are not paved, but are in decent enough condition.

If you walk, ride a mountain bike or motorcycle around the island, carry extra food and water, since neither is easily available outside Hanga Roa.

The airport is just on the outskirts of Hanga Roa. Hotel and residencial owners wait at the airport and will shuttle you for free to your accommodation.

BICYCLE

Mountain bikes can be rented in Hanga Roa for about CH$10,000 per day. Enquire at your residencial or hotel. **Makemake Rentabike** (☎ 210-0580; www.makemakerapanui.com; Av Atamu Tekena s/n; ✆ 9am-1pm & 4-8pm) has the best bikes available.

CAR & MOTORCYCLE

Some hotels and agencies rent 4WDs for CH$25,000 to CH$45,000 per eight-hour day, and CH$30,000 to CH$60,000 for 24 hours depending on the vehicle. A word of warning: insurance is not available, so you're not covered should the vehicle get any damage. Drive safely! Don't leave valuables in your car – thefts are not uncommon.

Scooters and motorcycles are rented for about CH$25,000 to CH$30,000 a day.

Gasoline costs less than it does on the continent, so it's not a major expense for the island's relatively short distances.

You can contact the following outfits.

Oceanic Rapa Nui Rent a Car (☎ 210-0985; Av Atamu Tekena s/n)

Rent a Car Insular (☎ 210-0480; Av Atamu Tekena s/n)

Rent-a-Car Moira (☎ 210-0718; Av Te Pito o Te Henua s/n)

TAXI

Taxis cost a flat CH$1500 for most trips around town. Longer trips around the island can be negotiated, but don't expect any guidance on the archaeological sites.

HANGA ROA

☎ 032 / pop 4400

Hanga Roa is the island's sole town. Upbeat it ain't, but with most attractions almost on its doorstep and nearly all the island's hotels, restaurants, shops and services lying within its boundaries, it's the obvious place to anchor oneself. It features a picturesque fishing harbor, a couple of modest beaches and surf spots, as well as a scattering of archaeological sites, including a few *moai*. Oh, and it also offers the island's best sunsets.

Although it's a bit touristy in January and February, Hanga Roa has so far managed to keep a languid pace of life and a bemusing atmosphere. Where else in the world can you see young lads who go bar- or club-hopping on horseback, leaving their horses tethered beneath the trees while they tear it up on the dance floor?

Orientation

Despite Hanga Roa being a fairly sprawling village, your chances of getting lost here are virtually nonexistent. The main road is north–south Av Atamu Tekena, with a number of shops, a supermarket, an artisans' market and several eateries. Another drag is east–west Av Te Pito

o Te Henua, which connects Caleta Hanga Roa, the town's small bay and fishing port, and the church. Av Policarpo Toro extends along the waterfront. Tahai is a quiet neighborhood to the north where there are several places to stay and the museum. The airport is on the southern edge of Hanga Roa.

The Sernatur information office has a basic map of Hanga Roa.

Information

For international calls and calls to mainland Chile, head to any internet café – they all double as call centers.

BancoEstado (☎ 210-0221; Av Pont s/n; ☻ 8am-1pm Mon-Fri) Changes US dollars and euros. Charges a CH$1500 commission on traveler's checks. There's also an ATM but it only accepts MasterCard. Visa holders can get cash advances at the counter during opening hours (bring your passport); the bank charges a US$2 fee for the service.

Farmacia Cruz Verde (☎ 255-1540; Av Atamu Tekena; ☻ 9am-7:30pm Mon-Sat) Large and well-stocked pharmacy. Sells sunscreen lotions.

Hare Taui Moni (☎ 210-0265; Av Atamu Tekena s/n; ☻ 9am-3pm Mon-Fri, 9am-1pm Sat) The exchange office charges a 15% commission on MasterCard or Visa cash advances and a US$8 commission on traveler's checks (in dollars only). Its opening hours are a bit erratic.

Hospital Hanga Roa (☎ 210-0215; Av Simon Paoa s/n)

Lavandería Tea Nui (Av Atamu Tekena s/n; per kg CH$2500; ☻ 9am-4pm Mon-Sat) Laundry service.

Omotohi Cybercafé (Av Te Pito o Te Henua s/n; per hr CH$1500; ☻ 9am-10pm) Internet access and call center. Fast and reliable.

Police (☎ 133)

Post office (Av Te Pito o Te Henua s/n; ☻ 9am-1pm & 2:30-6pm Mon-Fri, 9am-12:30pm Sat)

Puna Vai (Av Hotu Matua; ☻ 8:30am-1pm & 3-9pm Mon-Sat, 9am-2pm Sun) This petrol station also doubles as an exchange office. Much more convenient than the bank (no queues, better rates, longer opening hours, no commission on traveler's checks). There's an ATM inside (MasterCard only).

Sernatur (☎ 210-0255; ipascua@sernatur.cl; Tu'u Maheke s/n; ☻ 8:30am-5:30pm Mon-Fri) Has various brochures and maps of the island. Staff speak some English and can recommend official guides. It also has a small counter at the airport, open to meet arriving flights.

Taim@net (Av Atamu Tekena s/n; per hr CH$1500; ☻ 10am-10pm) Internet café and call center. Good connections.

Sights

For a town this size, Hanga Roa is pretty well endowed with sights, such as the museum,

HANGA ROA

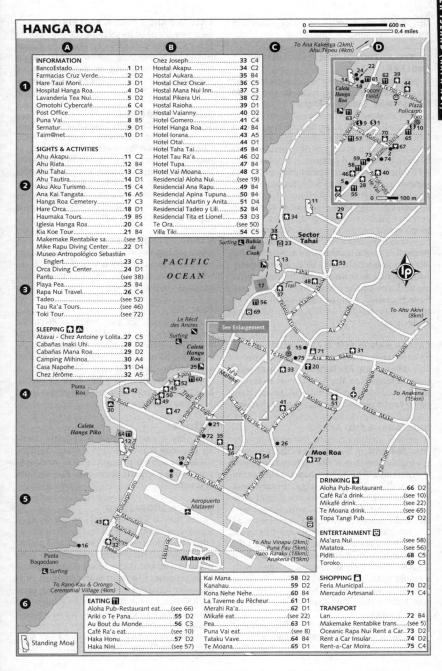

INFORMATION
BancoEstado...1 D1
Farmacias Cruz Verde...2 D2
Hare Taui Moni...3 D1
Hospital Hanga Roa...4 D4
Lavandería Tea Nui...5 D2
Omotohi Cybercafé...6 C4
Post Office...7 D1
Puna Vai...8 B5
Sernatur...9 D1
Taim@net...10 D1

SIGHTS & ACTIVITIES
Ahu Akapu...11 C2
Ahu Riata...12 B4
Ahu Tahai...13 C3
Ahu Tautira...14 D1
Aku Aku Turismo...15 D1
Ana Kai Tangata...16 A5
Hanga Roa Cemetery...17 C3
Hare Orca...18 D1
Haumaka Tours...19 B5
Iglesia Hanga Roa...20 C4
Kia Koe Tour...21 B4
Makemake Rentabike sa...(see 5)
Mike Rapu Diving Center...22 D1
Museo Antropológico Sebastián Englert...23 C3
Orca Diving Center...24 D1
Pantu...(see 38)
Playa Pea...25 B4
Rapa Nui Travel...26 C4
Tadeo...(see 52)
Tau Ra'a Tours...(see 46)
Toki Tour...(see 72)

SLEEPING
Atavai - Chez Antoine y Lolita...27 C5
Cabañas Inaki Uhi...28 D2
Cabañas Mana Roa...29 D2
Camping Mihinoa...30 A4
Casa Napohe...31 D4
Chez Jérôme...32 A5

Chez Joseph...33 C4
Hostal Akapu...34 C2
Hostal Aukara...35 B4
Hostal Chez Oscar...36 C5
Hostal Mana Nui Inn...37 C3
Hostal Pikera Uri...38 C2
Hostal Raioha...39 D1
Hostal Vaianny...40 D2
Hotel Gomero...41 C4
Hotel Hanga Roa...42 B4
Hotel Iorana...43 A5
Hotel Otai...44 D1
Hotel Taha Tai...45 B4
Hotel Tau Ra'a...46 D2
Hotel Tupa...47 B4
Hotel Vai Moana...48 C3
Residencial Aloha Nui...(see 19)
Residencial Ana Rapu...49 B4
Residencial Apina Tupuna...50 B4
Residencial Martin y Anita...51 D4
Residencial Tadeo y Lili...52 B4
Residencial Tita et Lionel...53 D3
Te Ora...(see 50)
Villa Tiki...54 C5

EATING
Aloha Pub-Restaurant eat...(see 66)
Ariki o Te Pana...55 D2
Au Bout du Monde...56 C3
Café Ra'a eat...(see 10)
Haka Honu...57 D2
Haka Nini...(see 57)
Kai Mana...58 D2
Kanahau...59 D2
Kona Nehe Nehe...60 B4
La Taverne du Pêcheur...61 D1
Merahi Ra'a...62 D1
Mikafé eat...(see 22)
Pea...63 D1
Puna Vai eat...(see 8)
Tataku Vave...64 B4
Te Moana...65 D1

DRINKING
Aloha Pub-Restaurant...66 D2
Café Ra'a drink...(see 10)
Mikafé drink...(see 22)
Te Moana drink...(see 65)
Topa Tangi Pub...67 D2

ENTERTAINMENT
Ma'ara Nui...(see 58)
Matatoa...(see 56)
Piditi...68 C5
Toroko...69 C3

SHOPPING
Feria Municipal...70 D2
Mercado Artesanal...71 C4

TRANSPORT
Lan...72 B4
Makemake Rentabike trans...(see 5)
Oceanic Rapa Nui Rent a Car...73 D2
Rent a Car Insular...74 D2
Rent-a-Car Moira...75 C4

Standing Moai

the church and a couple of *moai* thrown in for good measure.

MUSEO ANTROPOLÓGICO SEBASTIÁN ENGLERT

If you want to know your *ahu* from your *moai* and your *pukau*, head to the **Museo Antropológico Sebastián Englert** (☎ 255-1020; www.museorapanui.cl; Sector Tahai; admission CH$1000; ☒ 9:30am-12:30pm & 2-5:30pm Tue-Fri, 9:30am-12:30pm Sat & Sun), north of town. This well-organized museum does a good job of explaining the island's history and culture. It displays basalt fishhooks, obsidian spearheads and other weapons, a *moai* head with reconstructed fragments of its eyes, sketches of elliptical houses, circular beehive-shaped huts and the ceremonial houses at Orongo. It also features replica Rongo-Rongo tablets, covered in tiny rows of symbols resembling hieroglyphs. According to oral tradition, these wooden tablets were brought here by Hotu Matua, along with learned men who knew the art of writing and reciting the inscriptions. Researchers have proposed various theories on the nature of the script, but it's still an enigma to decipher.

CALETA HANGA ROA & AHU TAUTIRA

Your first encounter with the *moai* will probably take place at **Ahu Tautira**, which overlooks Caleta Hanga Roa, the fishing port in Hanga Roa at the foot of Av Te Pito o Te Henua. Here you'll find a platform with two superb *moai*.

AHU TAHAI & AHU AKAPU

A perfect introduction to the more remote sites, **Ahu Tahai**, in the vicinity of the museum, is a highly photogenic site that contains three restored *ahu*. Ahu Tahai proper is the *ahu* in the middle, supporting a large, solitary *moai* with no topknot. On the north side of Ahu Tahai is Ahu Ko Te Riku, with a topknotted and eyeballed *moai*. On the other side is Ahu Vai Uri, which supports five *moai* of varying sizes and shapes. Along the hills are foundations of *hare paenga* (traditional houses resembling an upturned canoe, with a single narrow doorway). Be sure to come here at dusk and watch the big yellow ball sink behind the silhouetted statues – a truly ethereal sight.

Continue further north along the coast and you'll soon come across **Ahu Akapu**, with its solitary *moai*.

CALETA HANGA PIKO & AHU RIATA

Easily overlooked by visitors, the little Caleta Hanga Piko is used by local fishermen. Come in the early morning, when freshly caught fish is landed and sold on the quay. Facing the *caleta*, the restored **Ahu Riata** supports a solitary *moai*.

IGLESIA HANGA ROA

The unmissable **Iglesia Hanga Roa** (Av Tu'u Koihu s/n), the island's Catholic church, is well worth a visit for its spectacular wood carvings, which integrate Christian doctrine with Rapanui tradition. It also makes a colorful scene on Sunday morning, when it is bursting at the seams with a devout congregation neatly dressed and belting out rousing *himene* (hymns). Visitors are welcome.

HANGA ROA CEMETERY

Overlooking the sea near Ahu Tahai, Hanga Roa's colorful **cemetery** is full of tombstones with Polynesian names, and it is also the site of ritual visits at Easter.

BEACHES

For a little dip, the tiny beach at **Playa Pea**, on the south side of Caleta Hanga Roa, fits the bill. There's another postage stamp-sized beach near Pea restaurant, as well as a pebbly beach beside Ahu Tahai. All in all, nothing thrilling in the beach department; beachy types will head to picture-postcard Anakena (p459).

Activities

Not only is Easter Island a fantastic open-air museum that appeals to culture vultures, it's also a superb playground for outdoorsy types, with a superfluity of activities on land and sea.

DIVING & SNORKELING

Oh to have a few more days in the week to squeeze in more dives in such gin-clear waters! The lack of pollution, runoff and plankton guarantees maximum water clarity – 40m is the norm, but it can reach a phenomenal 60m. Another highlight is the dramatic underwater terrain, lending most sites an eerie atmosphere. And there are absolutely no crowds. The weak point is marine life, which is noticeable only in its scarcity.

Rapa Nui is diveable year-round, but keep in mind that Rapa Nui waters are devoid of any protective barrier reef, so expect difficult conditions to get to the sites sometimes, especially from June to September. When the sea is too choppy, diving trips are cancelled. Water temperatures vary from as low as 21°C in winter to almost 27°C in summer. You don't need to be a strong diver – there are sites for all levels.

Most sites are scattered along the west coast. A few favorites:

La Cathédrale (The Cathedral; maximum depth 15m) Features an underwater lava tube broken up by numerous faults.

La Pyramide (The Pyramid; maximum depth 28m) A lava seamount festooned with corals and broken up by arches. Very scenic.

L'Arche Perdue (The Lost Arch; maximum depth 35m) A charismatic site, with a huge arch in 35m.

Le Récif des Ancres (Anchors' Reef; maximum depth 22m) A relaxing dive in Hanga Roa Bay, with corals, anchors and even a *moai* to round out the fun.

Motu Kao Kao (maximum depth 28m) A bijou site. Looks like a giant *moai* rising from the sea bed at 55m. The typical dive plan consists of swimming around the structure, starting at about 25m. Shoals of sea chubs are common.

Motu Nui (maximum depth 28m) Rapa Nui's signature site. Bottom depth is about 80m. A truly magical drop-off, wreathed with corals.

If the idea of total immersion doesn't appeal to you, you can ogle the coral and translucent water on a snorkeling trip to Motu Nui.

Orca Diving Center (☎ 255-0375; www.seemorca.cl; Caleta Hanga Roa s/n; 🕑 Mon-Sat) is a state-of-the-art diving center. Almost next door, you'll find **Mike Rapu Diving Center** (☎ 255-1055; www.mikerapu.cl; Caleta Hanga Roa s/n; 🕑 Mon-Sat). Prices start at CH$30,000 for a single dive. Both outfits offer snorkeling trips to Motu Nui (CH$15,000 per person, minimum four).

SURFING

Calling all surfers! Rapa Nui is hit with powerful swells from all points of the compass throughout the year, offering irresistible lefts and rights – mostly lava reef breaks – that are perfect for both beginners and experienced surfers. The most popular spots are scattered along the west coast. For beginners, there are a couple of good waves off Caleta Hanga Roa. Seasoned surfies will take to Mataveri, to the southwest, or Tahai, to the northwest, where the waves are more challenging. What makes surfing here so unique is the lack of crowds – utter bliss if you come from the mainland. In general, the best conditions are from September to March.

A handful of seasonal (usually from December to March) outfits based near Pea restaurant offer *clases de surf* (surfing courses) for about CH$9000 (two hours) and also rent surfboards. You can also arrange lessons with **Alicia Acuña Ika**, a famous local surfer. She can be reached through the tourist office.

The shop **Hare Orca** (☎ 255-0375; Caleta Hanga Roa s/n), next to the Orca Diving Center, rents body boards and surfboards (CH$10,000 for a half day).

HORSEBACK RIDING

Seeing Easter Island from the saddle of a horse is a typical Rapanui experience and an ecofriendly way to experience the visual appeal of the island. A network of trails leading to some of the most beautiful sites can be explored on horseback. Good news: you don't need to be an experienced rider. Some reliable operators include **Piti Pont** (☎ 210-0664) – just ask someone to call him and he will come to you, **Pantu** (☎ 210-0577; www.pantupikerauri.cl; Sector Tahai s/n) and **Tadeo** (☎ 210-0422; Av Apina s/n). Expect to pay about CH$25,000 for a half-day tour and CH$30,000 to CH$40,000 for a full-day tour with a guide. They offer guided trips that take in some of the sites near Hanga Roa or more remote places, such as Orongo, Anakena, Rano Raraku or the north coast. The ultimate is an excursion that takes in the eerie landscape around Terevaka or Península Poike – highly recommended. Two- to three-day excursions can also be organized.

HIKING

You can take some fantastic trails through the island. A memorable (but taxing) walk is the way-marked Ruta Patrimonial, which runs from the museum up to Orongo Ceremonial Village (about four hours, 7km). Other recommended walks are the climb to Terevaka from near Ahu Akivi (about three hours) and the walk around Península Poike (one day). You can also follow the path along the northern coastline from Ahu Tahai to Anakena Beach, then hitch back (should take about seven hours).

You can't get lost, but bring water and food and have a detailed map at hand. Keep in mind that there's no shade.

BIKING

With its spectacular scenery, awesome viewpoints and quiet, scenic roads, Easter Island is a top two-wheel playground. Hire a mountain bike in Hanga Roa and follow the roads and tracks at your leisure, but keep in mind that roads around the southern part of the island are steep and winding. Oh, and there's no shade.

Makemake Rentabike (☎ 210-0580, 255-2030; www .makemakerapanui.com; Av Atamu Tekena; ☺ 9am-1pm & 4-8pm) rents mountain bikes in top condition with helmet, repair kit and map. It also advises on circuits ranging from 7.5km to 42km, depending on your level of fitness. An easy loop is from Hanga Roa up to Ahu Tepeu, then east to Ahu Akivi and back to Hanga Roa (about 17km). The dirt track from Hanga Roa to Orongo Ceremonial Village is another stunner.

Tours

We recommend joining an organized tour since you get the benefit of an English-speaking guide who can explain the cultural significance of the archaeological sites. After your guided tour, you can explore at your leisure, either riding a bike or horse, or on foot.

Plenty of operators do tours of the sites, typically charging CH$20,000 to CH$25,000 for a full day and CH$15,000 for a half day. Entrance fees to Parque Nacional Rapa Nui (CH$5000) aren't included.

The tourist office has a list of official guides. The following are a few outfits, based in Hanga Roa, that we believe offer a reliable service and English-speaking guides. Ask about the party size (opt for smaller groups) and avoid multilingual tours.

Aku Aku Turismo (☎ 210-0770; www.akuakuturismo .cl; Av Tu'u Koihu s/n)

Haumaka Tours (☎ 210-0274; www.haumakatours .com; cnr Avs Atamu Tekena & Hotu Matua) Offers customized tours.

Kia Koe Tour (☎ 210-0852; www.kiakoetour.cl; Av Atamu Tekena s/n)

Rapa Nui Travel (☎ 210-0548; www.rapanuitravel .com; Av Tu'u Koihu) Run by a Rapanui-German couple.

Tau Ra'a Tours (☎ 210-0463; www.tauraahotel.cl; Av Atamu Tekena s/n) At Hotel Tau Ra'a.

Toki Tour (☎ 255-1026; www.tokitour.cl; Av Atamu Tekena s/n)

Festivals & Events

Tapati Rapa Nui Incredibly colorful, fortnight-long celebration with music, dance and traditional cultural events (opposite). Held in February.

Easter Given the island's links to Christianity through the date of its European discovery, Easter has a special resonance. Sunday morning mass is a particular attraction.

Día de la Lengua Rapanui A cultural festival celebrating the local language, held in late November.

Sleeping

If you come here from mainland Chile, be prepared for a shock. Accommodation on Easter Island is fairly pricey for what you get. Note that prices are listed in pesos but a number of establishments still quote their prices in US$. We've placed accommodation costing less than CH$30,000 a night for a double in the budget category, CH$30,000 to CH$60,000 in the midrange category and more than CH$60,000 in the top end.

Unless otherwise stated, most places come equipped with private bathroom, and breakfast is included. Air-con is still scarce but fans are provided in the hottest months.

Upon arrival at the airport, you'll find *residencial* proprietors waiting there. Transfers are included.

BUDGET

Camping Mihinoa (☎ 255-1593; www.mihinoa.com; Av Pont s/n; campsites per person CH$4000, dm CH$7000, d without bathroom CH$8000, d CH$18,000-20,000; 🖳) The relaxed, family atmosphere in a green location (but no shade to speak of) and the proximity of the seashore make this the kind of place where you quickly lose track of the days. Pitch your tent on the grassy plot, within earshot of the crashing waves, or choose one of the rooms in the main house; they feel a tad compact but are well scrubbed. The five-bed dorm is claustrophobic but fits the bill for budgeteers. Precious perks include a kitchen for guests' use, bike, car and tent hire (CH$1000), wi-fi access and laundry service.

Residencial Apina Tupuna (☎ 210-0763; www.apina tupuna.com; Av Apina s/n; campsites per person CH$10,000, s/d without bathroom CH$6000/12,000, d CH$30,000-35,000) The six drab-yet-tidy rooms arranged around a large communal area are a cast-iron bargain for budget travelers, but if purse strings are a bit more relaxed, the three bungalows at the entrance to the property are well worth bookmarking. They come with paintings, knickknacks and a cheerful mix of wood and volcanic stones, which create a warmly authentic atmosphere. Campers can pitch their tent on the grassy lawn.

TAPATI RAPA NUI: WHEN THE ISLAND GOES WILD

Colorful, spectacular, engaging – words do little justice to Rapa Nui's premier festival, which lasts about two weeks in the first half of February. It's so impressive that it's almost worth timing your trip around it (contact the tourist office for exact dates and events program).

The Tapati Rapa Nui revolves around a series of music, dance, cultural and sport contests between two clans that put up two candidates who stand for the title of Queen of the Festival. After each event, the winning individuals or groups are allocated points and at the end of the festival the candidate whose group has garnered the most points is crowned queen. On the last day the parade throughout Hanga Roa is the culmination of the festival, with floats and costumed figures.

Most events take place in or around Hanga Roa. They include traditional Rapa Nui meal preparations, canoe races, arts and crafts displays, fishing, *moai* carving contests, body painting contests, singing contests… In the evening the dancing contests take place on a purpose-built stage in a vast field by the seashore in Tahai.

The pinnacle of the festival is certainly the spectacle of Haka Pei, which takes place on the grassy flanks of Cerro Pui, an extinct volcano in the middle of the island. A dozen male contestants, wearing nothing but body paint and an oh-so-sexy breechcloth, run downhill on a makeshift sled (feet first, like on a luge) made of banana tree logs tied together, at a speed that can reach 70km/h. It's fairly scary – there's an ambulance waiting at the base of the hill.

No less awesome are the horse races, along a coastal track in Vaihu. The bareback riders tear along the racetrack several times with a speed and motivation that makes your hair stand on end.

Equally heart-pumping (and our favorite) is the Taua Rapa Nui. This triathlon unfolds in the magical setting of the Rano Raraku crater. The first stage consists of paddling across the lake on a reed *totora* boat. Then the contestants race around the lake carrying banana bunches on their shoulders. The last leg consists of swimming across the lake using a reed *totora* raft as a board.

The Tapati is your best chance to immerse yourself in traditional Rapanui culture. All islanders take it very seriously. As one organizer told us, '*la esencia se ha mantenido y no se ha perdido el espíritu*' (we've kept the essence of the festival and its spirit has not been lost). And it's free (though there is talk of introducing entrance tickets). Based on our experience, it's not necessary to book your lodgings well ahead of your arrival time – you can turn up and find a room. But it's wise to book your Lan flight a few months in advance. Note that all events are weather-permitting.

Whatever your experience, you'll quickly fill up your memory card with all the photo ops – show us your blog!

Residencial Ana Rapu (☎ 210-0540; www.anarapu .cl; Av Apina s/n; s/d without bathroom CH$8000/15,000, s/d CH$15,000/20,000, cabañas CH$50,000-60,000; ☐) This unabashed cheapie is set back slightly from the ocean front. The rooms with shared bathroom are spartan, dark and scarcely large enough to swing a flannel in. Alternatively, hunker down in a room with a private bathroom or, better still, opt for a *cabaña*, blessed with plenty of natural light and *vistas al mar* (sea views). Perks include horseback riding and snorkeling excursions, laundry, a kitchen for guests' use and internet service.

Hostal Vaianny (☎ 210-0650; www.vaianny.com; Av Tuki Haka He Vari; s/d CH$10,000/20,000) It's good budget-hotel fodder here. Teresa Araki, your affable host, certainly likes your life to be colorful: 'I change the paint every six months,' she says proudly. It was lime green and turquoise when we dropped by. Rooms are cramped but tidy, and at these rates nobody's complaining.

Hostal Chez Oscar (☎ 255-1261; chezoscar@123mail .cl; Av Pont s/n; s/d CH$15,000/30,000) This place does the basics well. Secure and well-scrubbed: yes. Shady veranda: present. Friendly hosts: definitely. Just forget about anything more fancy in this modest house, with four boxy rooms that are arranged around a communal lounge.

Hostal Raioha (☎ 210-0851; raioha@123mail.cl; Av Te Pito o Te Henua s/n; d CH$30,000) In this recent venture, the three rooms won't knock your socks off but they are well appointed and open onto a grassy property. They're also within hollering distance from the town's restaurants and shops. No breakfast is served but there's a communal kitchen.

Cabañas Inaki Uhi (☎ 255-1160; www.inaki-uhi.cl; Av Atamu Tekena; s/d CH$15,000/30,000) 'Exudes a surgical level of cleanliness; ideally located; yawn-inducing décor' – this is what came to our mind when visiting this place. Indeed, the 16 rooms that occupy two rows of low-slung buildings feel sterile and functional, with white walls and tiles (note to management: borrow some paint from the owner of Hostal Vaianny), but it's spotless and there are five shared *cocinas* (kitchens) and wi-fi access.

Hostal Aukara (☎ 210-0539; aukara@entelchile.net; Av Pont s/n; s/d CH$20,000/35,000) No frills but plenty of heart and a few artistic touches (there's an art gallery featuring paintings and woodcarvings by the proprietor) characterize this quaint *hostal* in a tranquil neighborhood. Angle for the two rooms in a separate building, which are bigger and more appealing than the three crude and seriously tight rooms in the main house. You can also do some minor food prep here, as there's a small kitchen, and unwind in the shade of a stately tulip tree in the lovely garden.

Casa Napohe (☎ 255-1169; www.napohe.com; Ara Roa Rakei s/n; s/d CH$23,000/30,000) A chilled-out universe is created here by a lazy-day garden overflowing with blossoming tropical plants and a clutch of quirky bungalows embellished with *pareos* (Polynesian sarongs), carved posts, friezes sporting traditional patterns and brick walls. Flake out in the serene setting or chatter with Napoleon, the friendly owner (and a local character).

MIDRANGE

Atavai – Chez Antoine y Lolita (☎ 210-0145; antoine rapanui@entelchile.net; Sector Moe Roa; s/d CH$24,000/32,000, without bathroom CH$15,000/30,000) Run by a Rapanui-French (well, Corsican) family, this venture offers a soothing collection of white bungalows (nine rooms in total). Quarters are a bit cramped, but otherwise it's extremely well run and serviceable, and there are cooking facilities (add CH$1000 per person). Lovers of fine food should try Antoine's French-inspired evening meals (CH$11,000). The newly planted, colorful garden will hopefully grow to add a little shade. The only downside: its location near the airport is not *that* exceptional, though it's a 10-minute walk to the church via a shortcut (you'll need a torch at night).

Residencial Tita et Lionel (☎ 255-1279; www .ifrance.fr/titaetlionel, in French; Av Atamu Tekena s/n; s/d CH$25,000/35,000) The quirkiest bungalows in town can be yours at this low-key spot. The two adjoining units imitate two *hare paenga* and come equipped with bathrooms decorated with small colorful tiles (sadly, the partition wall between the bathroom and the bedroom doesn't make it to the ceiling). There are also two ordinary rooms in a separate building. It's perched on a small hill in Tahai, a flick out of the action, but the pervading tranquility is worth it – not to mention the wraparound views from the terrace and Tita's hearty home cooking.

Residencial Aloha Nui (☎ 210-0274; haumaka@ entelchile.net; Ave Atamu Tekena s/n; s CH$30,000-40,000, d CH$30,000-45,000; ▣) In this agreeable B&B set amid a manicured garden, the six rooms exemplify functional simplicity with no knick-knacks to clutter things up, just wood-paneled or painted walls as well as back-friendly beds and a vast, shared living room. But the real reason you're staying here is to discuss Rapa Nui archaeology in flawless English with Josefina Nahoe Mulloy – a more knowledgeable person you'd be hard-pressed to find.

Chez Jérôme (☎ 210-0590; www.chezjerome.net; Sector Mataveri s/n; s/d CH$30,000/45,000) Monsieur is French, la Señora is Rapa Nui, and you'll get the best of both worlds. The five rooms are meticulously maintained, the bathrooms are in good nick, and the atmosphere is chilled-out to the max. The garden with fruit trees and flowers blossoming will tempt you to mooch around. It also helps that everyone usually has a full belly; Jérôme employs a chef who can cook up some seriously gourmet (and copious) dinners (CH$12,500). There's no sea view and it's a bit far from the action, but within spitting distance from the rock pool at Ana Kai Tangata. Wi-fi access is available.

Hostal Mana Nui Inn (☎ 210-0811; www.rapanui web.com/mananui; Sector Tahai; s/d CH$30,000/45,000) The Mana Nui follows the standard recipe for success: offer clean, light-filled, affordable accommodation with prim bathrooms in a chilled-out setting. The knock-out ocean views from the terrace make a sundowner all the sweeter. There are eight rooms in total, occupying several small cottages. One downer: there's no shade on the property.

Villa Tiki (☎ 210-0327; tiki@entelchile.net; Av Pont s/n; s/d CH$30,000/45,000) There's not much in the way of a view here as this establishment is located well inland, but there's nothing to disturb your dreams in this peaceful neck of the woods. The six unadorned rooms hardly fuel the imagination but you probably won't be inside much – mellow out in the tropical garden or loll in the hammock out the back.

Hostal Akapu (☎ 210-0954; www.hostalakapurapa nui.cl; Sector Tahai s/n; s CH$25,000-30,000, d CH$40,000-60,000) A good choice if you're looking for a relaxed setting, within earshot of the sea. Hint: aim for one of the three detached bungalows. Although they are on the small side and packed rather close together, they are sunny and comfortable enough and open onto (partial) sea views. The six *dormitorios* (rooms) are darker and miniscule. Guests can use the kitchen in the *comedor* (dining room).

our pick Te Ora (☎ 255-1038; www.rapanuiteora .com; Av Apina s/n; r CH$35,000-55,000) The perfect soft landing onto Easter Island. Small, offbeat and atmospherically ramshackle, this little cracker seduces those seeking character and authenticity, with three cocoonlike rooms that ingeniously blend hardwoods and volcanic stones. They are not spacious but they open onto a flourishing courtyard. We recommend booking the Teora Roa, which offers cracking views of the ocean. Your Canadian host, Sharon, will give you the lowdown on all that's worth seeing on the island – in perfect English, of course. No breakfast is served, but there's a communal kitchen and wi-fi access.

Chez Joseph (☎ 210-0373; www.rapanuihotel.cl.tc; Av Avareipua s/n; s/d CH$35,000/60,000; ▣) An excellent first impression is made by the contemporary stone carvings scattered in the garden. The rooms are a bit less endearing, despite some walls built from volcanic stones, but it all feels very proper and immaculate, and staff are attentive and the location is ace.

Hotel Vai Moana (☎ 210-0626; www.vai-moana.cl; Av Atamu Tekena s/n; s CH$35,000-45,000, d CH$45,000-65,000; ▣) The rooms here are fairly unremarkable (especially the 'standards'; the 'superior' rooms are better equipped) and rates somewhat inflated, but visitors usually forgive these shortcomings for the manicured garden, the ocean views, the onsite restaurant (full meals CH$10,000) and the decorative touches that enliven the communal areas.

Hostal Pikera Uri (☎ 210-0577; www.pantupikerauri .cl; Sector Tahai s/n; s CH$40,000-46,000, d CH$51,000-60,000) Entering this property, you feel as if you've stumbled onto the set of *Little House on the Prairie*. In the role of Charles Ingalls features

Pantu, who organizes horseback-riding excursions. Digs are in bungalows dotted on a grassy plot. Aside from the boxy (and rather sombre) unit adjoining the dining room, they are commodious and beautifully attired, and most offer superb ocean panoramas. Hopefully the two new bungalows that were being built at the time of research won't make the place feel too built-up.

Residencial Martin y Anita (☎ 210-0593; hmanita@ entelchile.net; Av Simon Paoa s/n; s/d CH$45,000/60,000; ✂) A bit further up from the church, this is a solid choice with an ample dose of hospitality awaiting guests, although the rooms are none too inspiring (but they do have air-con). The ambience of the leafy courtyard makes it an excellent place to retreat to after a day's *moai*-seeing. Martin speaks good English.

Residencial Tadeo y Lili (☎ 210-0422; www.tadeo lili.com; Av Apina s/n; s/d CH$45,000/60,000) This champ of a B&B run by a Rapanui-French couple prides itself on cleanliness, friendliness and real coffee at breakfast, and as a reward has earned favorable word of mouth. The well-designed bungalows boast a terrace that delivers full frontal bay views, and there are traditional stone carvings scattered in the garden for added appeal. Tadeo organizes horseback-riding excursions while well-informed Lili runs reputable tours of the island.

Hotel Gomero (☎ 210-0313; www.hotelgomero.com; Av Tu'u Koihu s/n; s CH$45,000-55,000, d CH$55,000-65,000; ✂ ✇) A safe bet in the midrange category, the Gomero does its best to put on a welcoming face, with superbly carved posts outside the reception, lush gardens, an on-site restaurant, zealously looked after rooms and a pool that's ideal to dunk your cares away. Angle for the superior rooms in the new wing (Nos 20 to 23), which are more modern, or for the 'standards' Nos 7, 8, 12 or 15, which are more recent (the other rooms look tired).

our pick Cabañas Mana Ora (☎ 210-0769; www .manaora.cl; Sector Tahai; cabañas CH$60,000) A spiffing location plus stylish touches make this hidden treasure one of Hanga Roa's best retreats. Mana Ora is a cute-as-a-button cottage perched scenically on a gentle slope overlooking the ocean. Cocooned in a wonderfully private setting, it consists of a kitchen, sitting room, bedroom, bathroom and terrace – perfect for couples looking for an escape. You'll need your own wheels (or a bike), as it's on the outskirts of town – but you wanted a love nest, right? The proprietor has plans to build two more bungalows any time soon.

TOP END

Recommended luxurious accommodation options are scarce in Hanga Roa, and most existing top-end options are in need of a touch-up. If you want full-on luxury, stay at the Explora en Rapa Nui (p456).

Hotel Otai (☎ 210-0250; www.hotelotai.com; Av Te Pito o Te Henua s/n; s CH$45,000-55,000; d CH$60,000-75,000; ✖ ▢ ☎) The Otai has a split personality. The mundane 'standard' rooms could use some TLC while the 'superior' rooms (especially Nos 138, 139 and 140, in a more recent wing) are much more comfortable and come equipped with modern fixtures. The pool, nestled in the lush garden, is a bonus, although the water looked stagnant when we visited.

Hotel Tau Ra'a (☎ 210-0463; www.tauraahotel.cl; Av Atamu Tekena s/n; s/d CH$70,000/80,000; ▢) What makes this place worth considering is how well it's maintained – Bill, the Aussie owner, and his wife Edith, do care and it is reflected in the 10 spotless rooms, equipped with blue-tiled bathrooms, solid amenities and quality mattresses. They get plenty of natural light (each room has two windows) but there's no sea view. The substantial breakfast is another plus. Bill is well clued-up and can organize tours in English.

Hotel Taha Tai (☎ 255-1192; www.hoteltahatai.cl; Av Apina s/n; s/d CH$70,000/85,000; ✖ ☎) The L-shaped Taha Tai is an old-timer that's holding on strong, though the sterile rooms and communal areas have about as much personality as a dentist's waiting room. Be sure to snag a room with a sea view – it won't cost you any more. There's a swimming-pool (yeah!) but no shade (boo!).

Hotel Iorana (☎ 210-0312; www.ioranahotel.cl; Av Policarpo Toro s/n; s/d CH$105,000/120,000; ✖ ☎) What the Iorana lacks in atmosphere and character it makes up for with a sensational clifftop location. The motel-ish decor leaves some guests kvetching about the prices, but if you score an oceanside room, you'll be too distracted by the swoony coastal views to care. Try to bargain the rates down if it's quiet.

Hotel Hanga Roa (☎ 210-0299; www.hotelhangaroa .cl; Av Pont s/n; d CH$120,000; ✖ ▢) As we speak, the people behind the sprawling Hanga Roa are jackhammering away for what promises to be a pretty serious makeover. The whole process is expected to be completed by 2010. The new

Hanga Roa will feature a spa and 75 luxurious rooms (see the website). Meanwhile 18 renovated rooms are available for guests.

Hotel Tupa (☎ 210-0225; www.tupahotel.com; Hetereki s/n; d CH$180,000; ✖ ▢) This ecoresort was under construction when we dropped by. It should be completed by 2010. Check out the website.

Eating

The culinary scene is not exactly enthralling but there are enough options to please most palates and suit every wallet.

Ariki o Te Pana (☎ 210-0171; Av Atamu Tekena s/n; mains CH$1200-8000; ☼ lunch & dinner Mon-Sat) Adored by locals and travelers alike, this no-frills hole-in-the-wall serves melt-in-your-mouth empanadas. Oh dear, the belt-bustingly good *queso y atún* (cheese and tuna) continues to torment us.

our pick Mikafé (☎ 255-1059; Caleta Hanga Roa s/n; ice creams CH$1500-2500, sandwiches & cakes CH$1800-3000; ☼ 9am-8pm) This snazzy café is famous for its dangerously addictive *helados artesanales* (homemade ice creams) and also turns out sandwiches and cakes (the banana cake will make you weep) just as well. Stop! We're nearly licking the page.

Café Ra'a (☎ 255-1530; Av Atamu Tekena; mains CH$4000-10,000; ☼ 9am-10pm) This light-as-a-feather café on the main drag serves delicately presented salads, fish and meat dishes. Generous sandwiches too.

Tataku Vave (☎ 255-1544; Caleta Hanga Piko; mains CH$6000-8000; ☼ lunch & dinner Mon-Sat) Local ingredients and freshly caught seafood are the staples of the simple menu. Nab a seat on the terrace and drink in the views of the harbor below. The only drawback is the out-of-the-way location.

Haka Nini (☎ 210-0918; Av Policarpo Toro s/n; mains CH$6000-8000; ☼ lunch & dinner Mon-Sat) A carbon copy of Haka Honu: same location, same family, same dishes and same views. Meat dishes are disappointing, but the ceviche is tasty.

Aloha Pub-Restaurant (☎ 255-1383; Av Atamu Tekena; mains CH$6000-11,000; ☼ dinner Tue-Sun) The moodily lit interior fits the bill for that special evening with your significant other. The menu runs the gamut from seafood to meat dishes and salads to tacos. The *ceviche aloha* (ceviche with prawns) is superb.

Kona Nehe Nehe (☎ 255-1677; Av Apina s/n; mains CH$6500-9000; ☼ lunch & dinner; Ⓥ) Kona Nehe Nehe is your spot for pasta, lasagna, voluminous salads, beef and *pescados de la isla* (local fish). The open-air terrace is perfect for enjoying the cool, ocean breezes.

Merahi Ra'a (☎ 255-1125; Av Te Pito o Te Henua s/n; mains CH$7000-9000; ◷ lunch & dinner) Fish lovers, you'll find nirvana here: the Merahi Ra'a has a wide assortment of fish delivered daily from the harbor, including tuna and *mahi mahi* (dorado). Order it grilled, raw, sashimi- or carpaccio-style. The spiffing balcony on the 1st floor (three tables only) is a good place to soak up the atmosphere of the seafront.

Haka Honu (Av Policarpo Toro s/n; mains CH$8000-12,000; ◷ lunch & dinner Tue-Sun) Fish dishes, steaks, pasta and salads round out the menu at this buzzy eatery. The outside terrace catches every wisp of breeze and is perfect for watching the world surf by.

Te Moana (☎ 255-1578; Av Atamu Tekena; CH$9000-15,000; ◷ lunch & dinner Mon-Sat) Buzzy café-bar on the main drag. Its satisfying burgers will get the cholesterol oozing through your veins, or you can devour salads, fish and meat dishes. The Te Moana Delight (fish fillet with vegetables, coconut milk, pineapple and mashed taro roots) is particularly flavorsome.

our pick Au Bout du Monde (☎ 255-2060; Av Policarpo Toro s/n; mains CH$9000-15,000; ◷ lunch & dinner Wed-Mon) Watch your back La Taverne du Pêcheur: local gourmands have started calling Au Bout du Monde the best restaurant in town. With sturdy wooden tables and walls built from volcanic stone, the dining room resembles a ski chalet. The windowed walls bathe the place in amber at sunset, or you can enjoy the rooftop terrace in summer. Duck foie gras, smoked salmon, tuna in vanilla sauce and prawns in ginger are some of the ambitious dishes on offer. Leave room for the amazingly decadent Belgian chocolate mousse.

La Taverne du Pêcheur (☎ 210-0619; Av Te Pito o Te Henua s/n; mains CH$10,000-47,000; ◷ lunch & dinner Mon-Sat) Whether you're a shoestringer or you're dropping pesos like they were going out of style, everyone needs a slap-up meal once in a while and there's no better place than this French institution right by the harbor. Our verdict: *très bon* (very good), judging from the *entrecôte d'Argentine sauce roquefort* (beefsteak from Argentina with a Roquefort sauce) and the killer crème brûlée. Seafood also features prominently. Management can be grumpy, but that's part of the experience.

For self-caterers, there are a couple of supermarkets on Av Atama Tekena. The market has

excellent fresh fruit and veggies. Hot tip: the **Puna Vai petrol station** (Av Hotu Matua; ◷ 8:30am-1pm & 3-9pm Mon-Sat, 3-9pm Sun) has the best selection of wines on the island.

Other options:

Pea (☎ 210-0382; Av Policarpo Toro s/n; mains CH$6000-8000; ◷ lunch & dinner Thu-Tue) The Pea boasts a vast veranda jutting out onto the ocean. Fish and beef dishes.

Kanahau (☎ 255-1923; Av Atamu Tekena s/n; mains CH$6000-9000; ◷ lunch & dinner Mon-Sat) Excellent steaks and noodles.

Kai Mana (☎ 255-1740; Av Atamu Tekena s/n; mains CH$6000-19,000; ◷ lunch & dinner Mon-Sat) Nice rustic setting, but we waited 45 minutes for our grilled fish to be served, and it tasted bland. Enough said.

Drinking

After a long day's *moai*-seeing or hiking under the fierce sun, a slew of drinking holes bring a bit of excitement. Av Atamu Tekena is the main hot spot, with a smattering of pleasant bars featuring live music most evenings, including **Te Moana** (Av Atamu Tekena s/n; ◷ Mon-Sat 11am-late) and **Topa Tangi Pub** (Av Atamu Tekena s/n; ◷ Wed-Sat 6pm-late). Further south, **Aloha Pub-Restaurant** (Av Atamu Tekena s/n; ◷ Mon-Sat 6pm-late) is another hangout of choice, with a loungey feel, excellent piscos and tapas.

With an appealing terrace overlooking Caleta Hanga Roa, **Mikafé** (☎ 255-1059; Caleta Hanga Roa s/n; ◷ 9am-8pm) is pure nirvana for its delicious cups of espresso (a rarity on the island) and its freshly squeezed juices. **Café Ra'a** (☎ 255-1530; Av Atamu Tekena s/n; ◷ 9am-10pm) is great for a beer or a fruit juice any time of the day, and its sidewalk terrace offers great people-watching opportunities.

Entertainment

If there's one thing you absolutely *have* to check out while you're on Easter Island it's a traditional dance show. The elaborately costumed troupe Kari Kari performs four times a week at a venue called **Ma'ara Nui** (Av Atamu Tekena s/n; shows CH$10,000). Another well-regarded group, **Matatoa** (☎ 255-1755; www.matatoa.com; shows CH$10,000), ignites the scene three times a week at Au Bout du Monde restaurant. Check with your hotel or Sernatur information office for current schedules.

If all you need is to let off steam, head to **Toroko** (Av Policarpo Toro s/n; cover charge CH$1500; ◷ 11pm-4am Thu-Sat) or **Piditi** (Av Hotu Matua s/n; cover charge CH$1500; ◷ 11pm-4am Thu-Sat), both with a mix of modern tunes and island pop.

Shopping

Hanga Roa has numerous souvenir shops, mostly on Av Atamu Tekena and on Av Te Pito o Te Henua, leading up to the church. The best prices are at the open-air **Feria Municipal** (cnr Avs Atamu Tekena & Tu'u Maheke; ☙ Mon-Sat). The **Mercado Artesanal** (cnr Avs Tu'u Koihu & Ara Roa Rakei; ☙ Mon-Sat), across from the church, has more choices. Both are open mornings and late afternoon. Look for small stone or carved wooden replicas of standard *moai* and *moai kavakava* (literally 'statues of ribs'), replicas and cloth rubbings of Rongo-Rongo tablets, and fragments of obsidian.

Discourage reef destruction by not purchasing any coral products.

PARQUE NACIONAL RAPA NUI

Since 1935, much of Rapa Nui's land and all of the archaeological sites have been a **national park** (admission non-Chileans CH$5000) administered by **Conaf** (☎ 210-0236; www.conaf.cl), which charges admission at Orongo that is valid for the whole park for the length of one's stay. The park teems with caves, *ahu*, fallen *moai*, village structures and petroglyphs galore. Spending the extra cash on a guided tour or an islander who can explain what you are seeing is a very worthy investment.

There are ranger information stations at Orongo, Anakena and Rano Raraku.

For information on the activities on offer throughout the park, such as diving, snorkeling, surfing, horseback riding, kayaking, biking and hiking, see p446.

Northern Route

WEST COAST

North of Ahu Tahai, the road is rough but passable if you drive slowly. Your best bet is to explore the area on foot, on horseback or riding a mountain bike, but there were no signs marking the sites at the time of writing.

About 2km north of Tahai is **Ana Kakenga**, or Dos Ventanas. This site comprises two caves opening onto the ocean (bring a flashlight). Continue about 2km north and you'll come across **Ahu Tepeu**. The seaward side of the *ahu* is its most interesting feature, with a wall about 3m high near the center composed of large, vertically placed stone slabs. A number of *moai* once stood on the *ahu*, but all have fallen. Immediately east is an extensive village site with foundations of several large *hare paenga* and the walls of several round houses, consisting of loosely piled stones. To the west, the Pacific Ocean breaks against rugged cliffs up to 50m high.

ANA TE PAHU

After visiting the *moai* along the coast, you can follow the faint, rough but passable track to Ana Te Pahu, a site of former cave dwellings whose entrance is via a garden planted with sweet potatoes, taro, bananas and other plants from the Polynesian horticultural complex. The caves here are lava tubes, created when rock solidified around a flowing stream of molten lava.

AHU AKIVI

This enigmatic *ahu* sporting seven *moai* will give you plenty to ponder. Why is it the sole *ahu* that was erected inland? And why, unlike most others, which face inland, do these statues look out to sea? And there's a third oddity (which is probably connected to the two previous ones): at the equinoxes, the seven statues look directly at the setting

---

SUSTAINABLE TOURISM

Easter Island is a superb open-air museum. To preserve it, it's essential to respect the archaeological sites. As Enrique Tucki, director of Parque Nacional Rapa Nui, told us, 'it's vital to follow a few rules. We have only a few rangers in the park, so it's crucial that visitors behave properly. Visitors mustn't walk on the *ahu*, as they are revered by locals as burial sites. It's also illegal to remove or relocate rocks from any of the archaeological structures. Visitors should also resist the temptation to touch petroglyphs, as they're very fragile, and should stay on designated paths to limit erosion. Remember that motor vehicles are not allowed on Península Poike or Terevaka and that camping is forbidden in the park. And please, carry out all litter!' Not following these simple rules could result in restricted access to certain sites in the forthcoming years. The case of a Finnish tourist, who was caught red-handed breaking off the ear of a *moai* to take home as a souvenir in March 2008, makes this issue all the more sensitive.

sun, which means that the site has had an astronomical significance.

Ahu Akivi was restored in 1960 by a group headed by Mulloy and Chilean archaeologist Gonzalo Figueroa. In raising the *moai,* Mulloy and Figueroa used methods similar to those used at Ahu Ature Huki (p459) and steadily improved their speed and technique.

Mulloy calculated that 30 men working eight hours a day for a year could have carved the *moai* and topknot at Ahu Te Pito Kura, and 90 men could have transported it from the quarry over a previously prepared road in two months and raised it in about three months.

PUNA PAU
The small volcanic crater at Puna Pau has a relatively soft, easily worked reddish scoria from which the *pukao* (cylindrical topknots) were made. Some 60 of these were transported to sites around the island, and another 25 remain in or near the quarry.

MAUNGA TEREVAKA
Maunga Terevaka is the island's highest point (507m). This barren hill is only accessible on foot or on horseback (see p447) and is definitely worth the effort as it offers panoramic views that will have you gasping in awe.

Southwestern Route
ANA KAI TANGATA
Past the Hotel Iorana in Hanga Roa, a sign points the way to Ana Kai Tangata (Map p445), a vast cave carved into black cliffs, which sports beautiful rock paintings (don't enter the cave, though, as there's a risk of falling rocks). Nearby is a small purpose-built rock pool where you can cool off to the sounds of seawater crashing up through a blowhole beside the pool.

RANO KAU & ORONGO CEREMONIAL VILLAGE
Arriving at this site, you'll pinch yourself to see if it's real. Partly covered in a bog of floating *totora* reeds and filled with opalescent waters, the crater lake of the dead volcano Rano Kau looks like a giant witch's cauldron. Perched 400m above, on the edge of the crater wall on one side and abutting a vertical drop plunging down to the cobalt-blue ocean on the other side, **Orongo ceremonial village** (admission CH$5000) boasts a phenomenal setting. It overlooks several small *motu* (offshore is-

lands), including Motu Nui, Motu Iti and Motu Kao Kao.

Partly restored, this ancient village is built into the side of the slope. The houses have walls made of horizontally overlapping stone slabs, with an earth-covered arched roof of similar materials, giving the appearance of being partly subterranean. Since the walls have to be thick enough to support the roof's weight, the doorway is a low narrow tunnel. At the edge of the crater is a cluster of boulders carved with numerous birdman petroglyphs with long beaks and hands clutching eggs.

Orongo was the focus of an islandwide bird cult linked to the god Makemake in the 18th and 19th centuries. The climax of the cult's ceremonies was a competition to obtain the first egg of the sooty tern *(Sterna fuscata),* which bred on the tiny islets of Motu Nui, Motu Iti and Motu Kao Kao. Each contestant or his stand-in would descend the cliff face from Orongo and, with the aid of a small reed raft, swim out to the islands. He who found the first egg became birdman for the ensuing year and won great status in the community. The last ceremonies took place at Orongo in 1866 or 1867.

Despite its ceremonial significance, it's a much later construction than the great *moai* and *ahu.* It is also demonstrably fragile, and visitors should keep to beaten paths.

From the winding dirt road that climbs from Hanga Roa to Orongo, there are spectacular views of the entire island.

The admission charge to the Orongo ceremonial village is collected by rangers at the site. These fees are valid for the length of your stay.

Rano Kau and Orongo Ceremonial Village are best enjoyed midafternoon – preferably on a sunny day – when it's virtually deserted.

AHU VINAPU
For Ahu Vinapu, follow the road from Mataveri Airport to the end of the runway, then follow the road south between the airstrip and some large oil tanks to an opening in a stone wall. A sign points to nearby Ahu Vinapu, where there are two major *ahu.*

One of them features neatly hewn, mortarless blocks akin to those found in Inka ruins – a startling vision. Both once supported *moai* that are now broken and lying face down. Accounts by 18th- and early-19th-century visitors suggest that the *moai* were not overturned simultaneously but were all tipped over by the mid-19th century.

One striking find is a long brick-red stone, shaped rather like a four-sided column, standing in front of one of the *ahu*. Closer inspection reveals a headless *moai* with short legs, unlike the mostly legless *moai* elsewhere, resembling pre-Inka column statues in the Andes. Originally, this was a two-headed *moai* between whose heads ran a wooden platform on which islanders placed corpses that, when desiccated, were finally interred.

SLEEPING & EATING

our pick **Explora en Rapa Nui** (☎ in Santiago 395-2703; www.explora.com; 3-night all-inclusive packages from s US$3350, d US$4560; ☒ ⬜ ☎) Chile's most exciting new property is also one of its greenest: Pedro Ibáñez' remote hotel concept – also present in Patagonia and Atacama – blends unobtrusively into a small forested patch of volcanic-singed countryside. Rooms, all overlooking the roaring Pacific and fiery sunsets, are abundant with indigenous materials (local rauli wood, volcanic stone) that instill a sense of place and ease environmental impact. Prices include excursions. One downside: it feels a bit cut off from the rest of the island (it's about 6km away from Hanga Roa).

Northeastern Route

This loop takes in the three finest sites on the island. It's good to go counterclockwise, because Rano Raraku is a magnificent highlight in the late afternoon.

SOUTH COAST

On the south coast, east of Ahu Vinapu, enormous ruined *ahu* and their fallen *moai* testify to the impact of warfare. **Ahu Vaihu** has eight large *moai* that have been toppled and now lie face down, their topknots scattered nearby. **Ahu Akahanga** is a large *ahu* with fallen *moai*, and across the bay is a second *ahu* with several more. On the hill are the remains of a village, including foundations of several boat-shaped houses and ruins of several round houses.

Also on the coast, the almost completely ruined **Ahu Hanga Tetenga** has two *moai*, both toppled and broken into fragments.

RANO RARAKU

For poignancy and eeriness, this site is hard to beat. Known as 'the nursery,' the (extinct) volcano Rano Raraku is the quarry for the hard tuff from which the *moai* were cut. Approaching these stony faces with their mad, staring eyes, you can't help but feel surrounded by petrified aliens who, according to legend, might start walking at any time.

You can wander among *moai*, in all stages of progress, studded on the southern slopes of the volcano. Most *moai* on the south slope are upright but buried up to their shoulders or necks in the earth, so that only their heads gaze across the grassy slopes. Ask your guide to show you the 21m giant *moai* – the largest *moai* ever carved. Follow the trail to the right to several other large *moai* still attached to the rock, or turn left along the trail that leads over the rim and into the crater. At the top the 360-degree view is truly ecstatic.

Within the crater is a small, glistening lake and about 20 standing *moai*, plus a number of fallen ones and others only partly finished – about 80 in all. Note also the great holes at the crater rim that were used to maneuver the statues down the crater rim.

It's estimated that, when work stopped, some 320 *moai* had been completed but not yet erected on *ahu*, or were being worked on.

A unique discovery at Rano Raraku is the kneeling *moai* Tukuturi, which was almost totally buried when it was found. Slightly less than 4m high, it now sits on the southeastern slope of the mountain. Placing it upright required a Jeep, tackle, poles, ropes, chains and 20 workers. It has a fairly natural rounded head, a goatee, short ears, and a full body squatting on its heels, with its forearms and hands resting on its thighs.

AHU TONGARIKI

East of Rano Raraku, this awesome *ahu* sports 15 *moai* that were re-erected by a Japanese company between 1992 and 1995. It's the largest *ahu* ever built. A 1960 tsunami, produced by an earthquake between Rapa Nui and the South American mainland, had flattened the statues and scattered several topknots far inland. Only one topknot has been returned to its place atop a *moai*.

Be sure to look at the petroglyphs that lie near the bend of the road some distance from the *moai*. They include various figures, including those of a turtle with a human face, a tuna fish, a birdman motif as well as Rongo-Rongo figures.

A LOWDOWN ON RAPA NUI ARCHAEOLOGICAL SITES

Although the giant *moai* are the most pervasive image of Rapa Nui, islanders created several other types of stonework, most notably the large *ahu* (ceremonial platform) on which the *moai* were erected, burial cairns (large piles of rock where bodies were entombed) and the foundations of the unusual *hare paenga* (boat-shaped thatched houses).

Ahu

About 350 *ahu* form a line along the coast. They tend to be sited at sheltered coves and areas favorable for human habitation, but only a few were built inland.

Of several varieties of *ahu*, built at different times for different reasons, the most impressive are the *ahu moai* that support the massive statues. Each is a mass of loose stones held together by retaining walls and paved on the upper surface with more or less flat stones, with a vertical wall on the seaward side and at each end.

Usually a gently sloping ramp comprises the landward side of the platform. Next to the ramp is a large plaza.

Researchers have learned little about the ceremonies connected with these *ahu* complexes. One theory is that the *moai* represented clan ancestors and that the ceremonies were part of an ancestor cult. *Ahu* were also burial sites, and some of the bodies were cremated.

Moai

Although all *moai* look similar, few are identical. The standard *moai* at Rano Raraku has its base at about where the statue's hip would be. Generally, the statues' arms hang stiffly, and the hands, with long slender fingers, extend across a protruding abdomen. The heads are elongated and rectangular with heavy brows and prominent noses, small mouths with thin lips, prominent chins and elongated earlobes, which are often carved for inserted ear ornaments. Hands, breasts, navels and facial features are clear. *Moai* mostly depict males, but several specimens have carvings that clearly represent breasts and vulva.

Moai vary greatly in size; some are as short as 2m, and the tallest is just under 21m. The usual length is from 5.5m to 7m.

Since the quarry at Rano Raraku contains *moai* at all stages of construction (the carvings abandoned as work gradually ceased), it's easy to visualize the creation process. Most *moai* were carved face up, in a horizontal or slightly reclining position. Workers dug a channel large enough for the carvers around and under each *moai*, leaving the statue attached to the rock only along its back. The *moai* was then detached and somehow transported down the slope. At the base of the cliff at Rano Raraku, workers raised the *moai* into a standing position in trenches, where sculptors carved the finer details. Basalt *toki*, thousands of which once littered the quarry site, were the carving tools.

When carving was finished, *moai* were moved to their coastal *ahu*. In total, islanders placed 300 *moai* on *ahu* or left them along the old roads on various parts of the island.

Topknots

Archaeologists believe that the reddish cylindrical topknots (*pukao*) on many *moai* reflect a male hairstyle once common on Rapa Nui. Quarried from the small crater at Puna Pau, the volcanic scoria from which the topknots are made is relatively soft and easily worked.

Since only about 60 *moai* had topknots, and another 25 remain in or near the quarry, they appear to have been a late development. Carved like the *moai*, the topknots may have been simple embellishments, which were rolled to their final destination and then, despite weighing about as much as two elephants, somehow placed on top of the *moai*.

Top tip: come here at sunrise. When the sun peeps over the horizon, the silhouetted statues are washed in a deep, warm, golden light.

PENÍNSULA POIKE

And now, Península Poike, Rapa Nui's forgotten corner. At the eastern end of the island, this high plateau crowned by the extinct volcano

---

MOAI ON THE MOVE

What techniques did the islanders employ to move and raise the colossal *moai*? Legend says that priests moved the *moai* using the power of *mana*, an ability to make a *moai* walk a short distance every day until eventually it reached its destination. Most experts believe they were dragged on a kind of wooden sledge, or pushed on top of rollers. Some of the wackiest interpretations even claim that *moai* are the work of extra-terrestrials!

In late 2005, Sergio Rapu, one of the island's most respected archaeologists, conducted various experiments and measurements in the field and came to the conclusion that the *moai* were not dragged horizontally but moved in a vertical position, with the base of the statue specially carved in a subtle convex shape so as to lower the center of gravity and allow gentle pivoting and swiveling movements. This theory would tally with oral history, which says that the *moai* 'walked' to their *ahu*. We asked Sergio Rapu about his latest works. 'I have recently found that the *moai* had a small "tail" at the back of the base, which would ensure more stability on the platform. And thus, the statues could look over the village, like guardians.'

Sergio Rapu also debunks the widely accepted theory of the toppling of the *moai*, suggesting that they were not toppled by enemies but instead by the owners of the *moai* (the chiefs, or the priests), who simply wanted to replace them – it was a way to keep the population under control by providing work.

As you'll soon realize, it's a never-ending debate, which adds to the sense of mystery and makes this island so fascinating.

Maunga Pu A Katiki (400m) and bounded in by steep cliffs remains largely overlooked by visitors (which is reason enough to go there). Here the land feels even wilder, without roads, tracks or houses, and you'll feel like the last person on earth. The landscape is stark, with huge fields of grass, free-roaming horses and intimidating cows. Access by 4WD is prohibited to prevent erosion. The best way to soak up the primordial rawness of Península Poike is to take a two-day horseback-riding excursion from Hanga Roa, or a day hike from the main road (leave your car at the farm, at the base of the volcano). It's best to hire a guide because the sights are hard to find.

From the farm, it's a strenuous one-hour climb to the summit of the volcano. From the summit you can walk down the eastern slope of the volcano to a series of small *moai* that lie face down, hidden amid the grass. Only three of them are in a good state of preservation. The other ones are broken up. From there, your guide will lead you to the **Grotto of the Virgins** (Ana O Keke), carved into the cliffs. Legend has it that this cave was used to confine virgins so that their skin would remain as pale as possible. It's definitely worth crawling inside if you don't feel dizzy (there's a little path that leads to it, on a ledge, with the unbroken sweep of the Pacific below) to admire a series of petroglyphs. On the way back to the farm, you'll pass three small volcanic domes, called *maunga*, including **Maunga Vai a Heva**, which sports a huge mask carved into the rock featuring the god of rain. It looks like a giant gargoyle – a stunning sight.

PAPA VAKA PETROGLYPHS
About 100m off the coastal road (look for the sign): you'll find a massive basaltic slab decorated with prolific carvings. There are clearly visible representations of tuna, sharks, turtles and hooks.

AHU TE PITO KURA
On the north coast, overlooking a fishing cove at Bahía La Pérouse, is the largest *moai* ever moved from Rano Raraku and erected on an *ahu*. Nearly 10m long, the *moai* lies facedown on the inland slope of the platform. Its ears alone are more than 2m long. A topknot – oval rather than round as at Vinapu – lies nearby.

The *ahu*'s name comes from a stone that was found nearby called *te pito kura*, which presumably means 'navel of light.' The legend claims that Hotu Matua himself brought this stone here, symbolizing the navel of the world. The stone is magnetic and lies about 40m to the left of the fallen *moai*.

OVAHE
Another unspoilt delight, Ovahe, between La Perouse and Anakena, is a gorgeous place to work your tan. At the foot of a volcanic

cliff, this small beach is less frequented than Anakena but is considered dangerous because of falling rocks.

ANAKENA

For those who love nothing better than splashing in lapis lazuli–colored waters or strolling across powder-soft beaches, **Anakena Beach** is the perfect answer. This white-sand beach backed by a lovely coconut grove is deservedly popular at weekends. From December to March there are a couple of shacks selling refreshments, pastries (banana cakes!) and snacks.

Anakena also has a highly symbolic significance. It is the storied landing place of Hotu Matua. One of the several caves along the beach is said to have been Hotu Matua's dwelling as he waited for completion of his *hare paenga*.

Anakena must be the only beach in the world that is blessed with two major archaeological sites. On the hillside above Anakena Beach stands **Ahu Ature Huki** and its enigmatic lone *moai,* re-erected by Thor Heyerdahl with the help of a dozen islanders. They raised this giant onto its *ahu* with wooden poles and stones, the logs being levered with ropes when the men could no longer reach them. It took them almost 20 days.

It's also home to the grandiose **Ahu Nau Nau**. During the excavation and restoration of this site in 1979, researchers learned that the *moai* were not 'blind' but actually had inlaid coral and rock eyes, some of which were reconstructed from fragments at the site. Of the seven *moai* at Ahu Nau Nau, four have topknots, while only the torsos remain of two others. Fragments of torsos and heads lie in front of the *ahu*.

Directory

CONTENTS

Accommodations	460
Activities	462
Addresses	463
Business Hours	463
Children	463
Climate Charts	464
Courses	464
Customs	465
Dangers & Annoyances	465
Discount Cards	466
Embassies & Consulates	466
Festivals & Events	467
Food	467
Gay & Lesbian Travelers	467
Holidays	468
Insurance	468
Internet Access	468
Legal Matters	468
Maps	469
Money	469
Photography & Video	470
Post	470
Senior Travelers	470
Shopping	470
Solo Travelers	471
Telephone & Fax	471
Time	472
Toilets	472
Tourist Information	472
Travelers with Disabilities	473
Visas	472
Volunteering	473
Women Travelers	473
Work	474

ACCOMMODATIONS

Chile has accommodations to suit every budget – from chic hotels to family homes with chickens in the backyard. We've organized regional accommodations listings in ascending order of price and, where appropriate, split into budget (double occupancy – either dorm or double room – up to CH$18,000), midrange (CH$18,000 to CH$40,000) and top end (CH$40,000 and above) categories; these price ranges differ in a few particularly expensive destinations, especially Easter Island.

PRACTICALITIES

- Catch up with Chilean news in English through the *Santiago Times* (www .santiagotimes.cl).

- Keep a finger on the pulse by reading *El Mercurio* (www.elmercurio.cl, in Spanish) – a conservative, dry but hugely respected newspaper. The alternative *The Clinic* provides cutting-edge editorials and satire on politics and society.

- Cable TV is common; most hotels and *hospedajes* have a hookup.

- A recommended radio news station is Radio Cooperativa (103.1FM).

- The electricity current operates on 220V, 50 cycles.

- Plug gadgets into two-pronged outlets that accept round (European) plugs.

- Use the metric system except for tire pressure, which is measured in pounds per square inch.

Price ranges for destinations in Argentina are divided into budget (up to AR$60), midrange (AR$60 to AR$180) and top end (AR$180 and above). All prices listed are high-season rates for rooms that include a private bathroom, unless otherwise specified.

Budget accommodations have a wide variation of quality but most have hot showers (usually but not always shared). Midrange rooms almost always have private showers. Air-con is not as frequent as you might think, but rooms often have cable TV, mini-fridge and telephone. Top-end hotels and resorts have international standards, with direct-dial phones, hairdryers, alarm radios, room service and internet access.

Be aware that, in tourist hot spots, prices can double during the high season in late December to mid-March; outside high season prices slip and you can wield more bargaining power, especially in lower-range accommodations or when you're staying for more than one night. Try asking very politely for a discount, '*¿Me podría hacer precio?*'

At many midrange and top-end hotels, payment in US dollars (either cash or credit) legally sidesteps the crippling 19% IVA (*impuesto de valor agregado*, value-added tax). If there is any question as to whether IVA is included in the rates, clarify before paying. A few places that get only a handful of foreign visitors can't be bothered with the extra paperwork, but most find it advantageous to be able to offer the discount.

Cabins

Excellent value for small groups or families, Chile's *cabañas* are common in resort towns and national park areas, and integrated into some campsites. Most come with a private bathroom and fully equipped kitchen. Resort areas cram *cabañas* into urban properties, so if you're looking for privacy, check on the details when booking.

Camping

Chile has a developed camping culture, though it's more of a sleepless, boozy sing-along atmosphere than a back-to-nature escape. Most organized campgrounds are family-oriented with large sites, full bathrooms and laundry, fire pits, a restaurant or snack bar and grill for the essential *asado* (barbecue). Many are costly because they charge a five-person minimum. Try asking for per person rates. If you cannot arrange a discount, a basic *hospedaje* may be cheaper. Remote areas have free camping, often without potable water or sanitary facilities.

For camping, your best resource is Turistel's *Rutero Camping* guide, accompanied by handy maps and distances. Santiago's **Sernatur** (www.sernatur.cl) has a free pamphlet listing campsites throughout Chile.

Camping equipment is widely available in Chile but high-quality international brands have a significant markup. In rainy regions like Patagonia, a synthetic sleeping bag is preferable over down since it will dry much more quickly. White gas (*bencina blanca*) for camp

stoves can be hard to find but butane cartridges are common in the outdoors section of big department stores or small hardware stores (*ferreterías*). Bring mosquito repellent, since many campsites are near rivers or lakes.

Casas de Familia & Rural Homestays

There is no better way to steep yourself in Chilean culture than staying at a *casa de familia*. Especially in the south, it's common for families to rent rooms to visitors, allowing you to converse with and get to know typically shy Chileans. Guests do not always have kitchen privileges but usually can pay modest prices for abundant meals or laundry service. Tourist offices maintain lists of such accommodations.

Even families in rural and indigenous communities are increasingly taking in tourists as part of a bid to diversify their income, providing camping, homestays and/or helping out on farms. This is a great way to get off the gringo trail and enjoy rural hospitality.

There are many organized networks in the south, most notably in Chiloé, Lago Ranco, around Pucón and Patagonia. For options in Patagonia, check out Coyhaique's **Casa de Turismo Rural** (www.casaturismorural.cl). For countrywide options, visit **Viajes Rurales** (www.viajesrurales.cl) or inquire at tourist offices.

Hospedajes & Residenciales

The difference between a *hospedaje* and *residencial* is vague, moreover, most *residenciales* are changing their name to the more fashionable *hospedaje*. Both offer homey, simple accommodations, usually with foam-mattress beds, hard pillows, clean sheets and blankets. Never hesitate to ask to see a room before making a decision.

Especially in high season, room rates may be the same for single or double occupancy, but singles can try to negotiate, especially if staying several days. Bathrooms and shower facilities are usually shared, but a few will have rooms with a private bathroom, usually with a *matrimonial* double bed for couples. Mostly in the north, but not exclusively, you may have to ask staff to turn on the *calefón* (hot-water heater) before taking a shower.

Breakfast is usually included in the price. If you grow weary of Nescafé and white bread, you may be able to negotiate a slightly lower rate and skip the breakfast. Sernatur and most municipal tourist offices have lists of licensed budget lodgings.

Hostels

Hostels have a broad definition in Chile, ranging from bare bones to downright swank, community-oriented lodgings. But a new generation of stylish and savvy hostels has dramatically improved options in Chile. These dorm-style lodgings usually set aside a few well-heeled doubles for couples who want a social atmosphere but greater creature comforts.

Independent backpackers hostels are increasingly joining forces to advertise their existence. Look for pamphlets for **Backpackers Chile** (www.backpackerschile.com), which has many European-run listings, or **Backpacker's Best of Chile** (www.backpackersbest.cl).

Most places don't insist on a Hostelling International (HI) card, but charge a bit more for nonmembers. The local affiliate of HI is **Asociación Chilena de Albergues Turísticos Juveniles** (Map pp90-1; ☎ 02-411-2050; www.hostelling.cl; Hernando de Aguirre 201, Oficina 602, Providencia, Santiago). One-year membership cards are available at the head office or at Santiago's Hostelling International Hostel (p97) for CH$14,000/16,000 for under/over 30s.

The national sports institute **Chiledeportes** (☎ 02-754-0200; www.chiledeportes.cl, in Spanish; Fidel Oteíza 1956, 5th fl, Providencia) organizes cheap temporary summer *albergues juveniles*, catering mainly to schoolchildren and students, at sports stadiums, schools or churches. Local tourist offices should be able to refer you to them.

Hotels

From one-star austerity to five-star luxury, Chile has a wide range of hotels. However, correlation between these categories and their standards is less than perfect; many midrange options seem to be better value than their high-end brethren. Most hotels provide a room with private bathroom, a telephone, wi-fi or computer access and cable or satellite TV. Breakfast is often, but not always, included in the price.

Reservations are usually necessary if you'll be arriving at an awkward hour, during the summer high season or over a holiday weekend.

In some areas, motels are what North Americans and Europeans expect: roadside accommodations with convenient parking. However, the term 'motel' can also be a euphemism for a 'love hotel,' catering to couples with no other alternative for privacy. The external decor usually gives the game away. With safe parking and economical rates, these love shacks can make decent, if not entertaining, options for those with their own wheels. Within cities, the counterpart is known as a *hotel parejero*.

Refugios

Within some national parks, **Conaf** (Corporación Nacional Forestal; Map pp84-5; ☎ 02-663-0000; www.conaf.cl, in Spanish; Av Bulnes 285, Centro; ☽ 9:30am-5:30pm Mon-Thu, 9:30am-4:30pm Fri) maintains rustic shelters (*refugios*) for hikers and trekkers, which unfortunately lack upkeep due to Conaf's limited budget. In some of the more popular parks, most notably Torres del Paine, private concessions manage comfortable and well-appointed *refugios* with bunks, mattresses, showers and even restaurants. Private reserves sometimes have *refugios* set up along their trails.

Rental Accommodations

For long-term rentals in Santiago, check listings in Sunday's **El Mercurio** (www.elmercurio.cl, in Spanish), **Santiago Craigslist** (santiago.craigslist.org) or the weekly classified listing **El Rastro** (www.elrastro.cl, in Spanish). In vacation areas such as Viña del Mar, La Serena, Villarrica or Puerto Varas, travelers could consider renting an apartment together to keep costs down. In towns such as Valdivia and La Serena, people line the highway approaches in summer to offer houses and apartments. You can also check the tourist offices, bulletin boards outside grocery stores or local papers.

ACTIVITIES

Squeezed between the Andes to the east and a long strip of Pacific surf to the west, Chile is paradise for the active. The activities on offer are incredibly diverse, including horseback riding, hiking, mountain biking, mountaineering, white-water rafting, sea kayaking, skiing and snowboarding, sand-boarding and surfing. The Outdoors chapter (p70) offers details of all these activities and more.

If that all sounds like too much work, there is plenty of mellow, even hedonistic recreation on offer. Excellent wildlife watching (see p63) is found throughout Chile. Archaeological sites with petroglyphs, forts and ancient mummies can all be found in Norte Grande and Norte Chico. Sunbathers can pick a spot on Chile's never-ending coastline, with high-lights being seaside resorts such as Viña del Mar, La Serena, Caldera, Arica and Iquique. Meanwhile, with a pipeline of volcanic activity running down its spine, Chile has an abundance of hot springs for soaking; try Puritama outside San Pedro de Atacama or various pools by Pucón or Puyehue. Chile's famous reds also make wine tasting at vineyards worth a dedicated detour in Middle Chile and around Santiago.

ADDRESSES

Names of streets, plazas and other features are often unwieldy, and usually appear abbreviated on maps. So Avenida Libertador General Bernardo O'Higgins might appear on a map as Avenida B O'Higgins, just O'Higgins or even by a colloquial alternative (Alameda). The common address *costanera* denotes a coastal road.

Some addresses include the expression *local* (locale) followed by a number. *Local* means it's one of several offices at the same street address. Street numbers may begin with a zero, eg Bosque Norte 084. This confusing practice usually happens when an older street is extended in the opposite direction, beyond the original number 1.

The abbreviation 's/n' following a street address stands for *sin número* (without number) and indicates that the address has no specific street number.

BUSINESS HOURS

Shops in Chile open by 10am, but some close at about 1pm for two to three hours for lunch then reopen until about 8pm. Government offices and businesses open from 9am to 6pm. Banks are open 9am to 2pm weekdays. Tourist offices stay open long hours daily in summer, but have abbreviated hours in the off-season. In many provincial cities and towns restaurants and services are closed on Sunday. Museums are often closed Monday. Restaurant hours vary widely, but most places are open from noon till 11pm. Many restaurants do not open for breakfast and quite a few close for the lull between lunch and dinner.

CHILDREN

Children and *guaguas* (babies) are adored in Chile and bringing them here will do much to break down cultural barriers. The country is also quite child-friendly in terms of safety, health and family-oriented activities.

People are helpful on public transportation; often someone will give up a seat for parent and child. Expecting mothers get special parking spaces and shorter grocery store lines. In terms of food and health there are no special concerns in most of the country, but bottled water is a good idea for delicate stomachs. While special kids' meals are not offered in restaurants, most offer a wide variety of dishes suitable for children, and Chilean cuisine is generally bland despite the occasional hot sauce. It is perfectly acceptable to order a meal to split between two children or an adult and a child; most portions are abundant. Just ask for additional cutlery. High chairs are rarely available.

One thing to be aware of: children sometimes come off the worse for encounters with dogs. If you are visiting someone check to see if their pet is child-friendly.

In general, public toilets are poorly maintained; always carry toilet paper, which is almost nonexistent. While a woman may take a young boy into the ladies' room, it would be socially unacceptable for a man to take a girl into the men's room.

For general information on the subject, look for Lonely Planet's *Travel with Children,* by Cathy Lanigan and Lonely Planet cofounder Maureen Wheeler.

Practicalities

Childcare is not particularly easy to find in Chile, and babysitting services or children's activity clubs tend to be limited to upmarket hotels and ski resorts – where they exist at all. However, formula and disposable diapers are easy to find and many top-end hotels can produce a cot on request.

Sights & Activities

While it's possible to take your kids anywhere in Chile, certain areas are easier than others. Santiago has family-oriented attractions, including a theme park, zoo, cable car, swimming pools, and interactive museum (see p94 for more information). A short jaunt outside Santiago, nature reserve Cascada de las Animas (p118) has ample space and a working horse ranch that kids often love.

In the north, seaside resorts at La Serena, Caldera, and Arica among others provide beach fun. In the northern altiplano San Pedro de Atacama has child-friendly hotels and excursions.

Pucón and Puerto Varas are probably the best family options in the south. These lake towns are well set up for family package tours of Santiaguinos and Brazilians; ski resorts here and closer to Santiago are also frequently equipped with easy terrain, beginner's classes and more. Taking children to adventurous locations such as Torres del Paine may prove frustrating for those with young children as the emphasis here is on more challenging activities.

Adult international movies are subtitled for Chile's Spanish-speaking audience, but unfortunately most movies for children are dubbed entirely into Spanish; consult newspapers such as *El Mercurio* for listings.

CLIMATE CHARTS

As you'd expect, Chile is host to a stark range of climates from the windy southern reaches to the rainy Lakes District and the dry desert north. The following climate charts reflect that diversity; for more specific advice on when to visit different regions see p21.

COURSES
Arts, Cooking & Culture

In Pucón, **Patragon** (☎ 45-444-606; www.patragon.net) offers Mapuche cooking classes, pottery workshops and a fascinating cultural immersion tour in the Mapuche enclave of Curarrehue. La Serena's Hare Krishna–run **Colectivo de Arte Consciente** (☎ 51-224-289) has classes ranging from spirituality lectures to vegetarian cooking (p246). Valparaíso chefs who offer cooking courses (p129) include **Gonzalo Lara** (☎ 32-223-0665; gonzalolarachef@yahoo.es) and **Aventura Local** (☎ 259-3918; www.aventuralocal.cl).

Language

Spanish-language courses can be found in major cities and resort areas. For details of

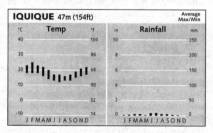

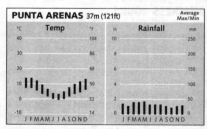

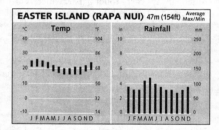

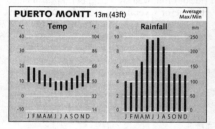

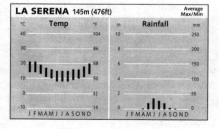

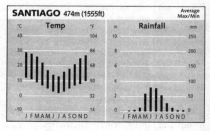

schools and programs, see the listings in Santiago (p94), Arica (p181), Iquique (p198), La Serena (p246), Valparaíso (p129). Lonely Planet's *Latin American Spanish Phrasebook* is helpful for beginners.

Outdoor Activities

With Chilean headquarters at Coyhaique, the **National Outdoor Leadership School** (NOLS; ☎ 1-800-710-6657; www.nols.edu; 284 Lincoln St, Lander, WY 82520, USA) offers a 75-day 'Semester in Patagonia,' teaching mountain wilderness skills, sea kayaking and natural history for university credit. **Abtao** (Map pp80-1; ☎ 02-211-5021; www.abtao.cl; El Director 5660, Las Condes, Santiago) organizes selective courses on Chilean ecosystems and wildlife.

Wine Tasting

Santiago's **Vinoteca** (Map pp90-1; ☎ 02-269-5659; www.lavinoteca.cl, in Spanish; Manuel Montt 1452, Providencia) organizes short wine courses for groups of up to 10 people on a regular basis as well as on request; see p111 for more information.

CUSTOMS

Check the website for **Chilean customs** (www.aduana.cl) if you're concerned about what and how much you can take in and out of the country.

There are no restrictions on import and export of local and foreign currency. Duty-free allowances include purchases of up to US$500. Travelers should consult the Chilean Customs website information for foreigners at www.aduana.cl/prontus_aduana_eng/site/edic/base/port/foreign_travelers.html (in English) for information on allowances.

Inspections are usually routine, although some travelers have had to put up with more thorough examinations because of drug smuggling from Peru and Bolivia. Travelers from Regions I and XII, both of which enjoy *zona franca* (duty-free) status, are subject to internal customs inspections when leaving those regions.

At international borders, officials of the SAG (Servicio Agrícola-Ganadero; Agriculture and Livestock Service) rigorously check luggage for fruit, dairy and organic products, the importation of which is strictly controlled to prevent the spread of diseases and pests that might threaten Chile's booming fruit exports.

Customs officials sometimes put baggage through X-ray machines at major international border crossings such as Los Libertadores (the crossing from Mendoza, Argentina) and Pajaritos (the crossing from Bariloche, Argentina).

DANGERS & ANNOYANCES

Compared with other South American countries, Chile is remarkably safe. Petty thievery is a problem in larger cities, bus terminals and at beach resorts in summertime, so always keep a close eye on all belongings. Photographing military installations is strictly prohibited.

Dogs & Bugs

Chile's stray canines are a growing problem. These are usually not your emaciated, mongrel variety, but well-fed purebreds – especially Labradors and German shepherds. Chile doesn't have much of a spaying or neutering program (most Chileans think it immoral to chop the *cojones* off any beast) and, in more rural areas, locals may purchase the dogs and coddle them as puppies but then let them fend for themselves later on. Nonprofit **Albergando un Amigo** (www.albergandounamigo.cl) is an advocacy group for stray animals.

In tourist towns, dogs sniff out the foreigners and follow them everywhere, but are usually harmless: they know who'll pet them and feed them half an empanada. Scabies can be common in street dogs; don't pet those that have bad skin problems, it's highly contagious. Dog attacks are more probable with aggressive guard dogs than their street cousins – check with their owners before finding out the hard way. If driving, be prepared for dogs barking and running after the bumper.

Summertime in the south brings about the pesty tábano, a large biting horsefly that is more an annoyance than a health risk. Bring along insect repellent and wear light-colored clothing.

Natural Hazards

Earthquakes are a fact of life for most Chileans. Local construction often does not meet seismic safety standards; adobe buildings tend to be especially vulnerable. The unpredictability of quakes means there is little that a traveler can do to prepare.

Active volcanoes are less likely to threaten safety, since they usually give some warning. Nevertheless, the unexpected eruptions of Volcán Chaitén and Volcán Llaima in 2008 have the country monitoring more closely than ever.

DIRECTORY

Many of Chile's finest beaches have dangerous offshore rip currents, so ask before diving in and make sure someone on shore knows your whereabouts. Many beaches post signs that say *apto para bañar* (swimming OK) and *no apto para bañar* (swimming not OK) or *peligroso* (dangerous).

In the winter, the smog in Santiago can become a health risk. The city declares 'preemergency' or 'emergency' states when the level of smog is dangerously high and takes measures to limit emissions. Children, senior citizens and people with respiratory problems should avoid trips to downtown Santiago at these times.

Personal Security & Theft

Santiago's central plazas, Barrio Brasil, markets and bus terminals are prone to pickpockets and petty thievery – as are its buses and metro. Keep an eye on all belongings, and take advantage of the secure left-luggage services at bus terminals and hotels. Violent crime is still fairly unusual in Santiago; men or women can travel in most parts of the city at any time of day or night without excessive apprehension. In Valparaíso, some of the nontouristy neighborhoods are best avoided (see p125).

Those staying in cabins should close and lock windows before heading out, particularly in popular resort towns where thefts soar in summer. In summer, beach resorts are prime territory for thievery. When at the beach, be alert for pickpockets and avoid leaving valuables on the beach while you go for a swim. Never leave an unattended car unlocked and keep all valuables in the trunk.

Don't fall for distractions, such as someone tapping you on the shoulder, spitting or spilling something on you, since these 'accidents' are often part of a team effort to relieve you of your backpack or other valuables. Grip your bag or purse firmly, carry your wallet in a front pocket and avoid conspicuous displays of expensive jewelry. Valuables such as passports and air tickets can be carried in money belts or neck pouches; alternatively an elastic leg pouch is less cumbersome but can get very sweaty in hot weather.

Baggage insurance is a good idea. Since the doors to rooms in many budget hotels have only token locks, do not leave valuables such as cash or cameras in your room. You may want to bring your own lock. Upmarket hotels often have secure strongboxes in each room.

DISCOUNT CARDS

An ISIC international student card or youth card will grant you varying discounts at some museums and tourist sites, though most national parks do not offer reductions. Some bus companies offer 25% discounts to students. Senior discount cards are not generally used.

EMBASSIES & CONSULATES

Argentina Antofagasta (☎ 055-220-440; Blanco Encalada 1933); Puerto Montt (☎ 065-253-996; Pedro Montt N 160, Piso 6, Oficina 50 B); Punta Arenas (☎ 061-261-912; 21 de Mayo 1878); Santiago (Map pp84-5; ☎ 02-582-2606; www.embargentina.cl; Vicuña Mackenna 41, Centro)

Australia (Map p99; ☎ 02-500-3500; consular .santiago@dfat.gov.au; Isidora Goyenechea 3621, 12th fl, Las Condes)

Belgium (Map p378; ☎ 241-472; Roca 817, Oficina 61, Punta Arenas)

Bolivia Antofagasta (☎ 055-259-008; Jorge Washington 2675); Arica (☎ 058-231-030; www.rree.gov.bo; Patricio Lynch 298); Calama (☎ 055-341-976; Latorre 1395); Iquique (☎ 057-421-777; Gorostiaga 215, Dept E, Iquique); Santiago (Map pp80-1; ☎ 02-232-8180; cgbolivia@manquehue.net; Av Santa María 2796, Las Condes)

Brazil Santiago (☎ 02-698-2486; www.embajadade brasil.cl; Alonso Ovalle 1665, Centro)

Canada (Map p99; ☎ 02-362-9660; enqserv@dfait -maeci.gc.ca; Tajamar 481, 12th fl, Las Condes)

France (Map pp90-1; ☎ 02-470-8000; www.france.cl; Av Condell 65, Providencia)

Germany Arica (☎ 058-231-657; Arturo Prat 391, 10th fl, Oficina 101); Santiago (off Map pp80-1; ☎ 02-463-2500; www.embajadadealemania.cl; Las Hualtatas 5677, Vitacura)

Ireland (☎ 02-696-0278; Huérfanos 1294, 3rd fl, Santiago)

Israel (Map p99; ☎ 02-750-0500; San Sebastián 2812, 5th fl, Las Condes)

Netherlands Punta Arenas (Map p378; ☎ 061-248-100; Sarmiento 780); Santiago (Map p99; ☎ 02-756-9200; www.holanda-paisesbajos.cl; Av Apoquindo 3500, piso 13, Las Condes)

New Zealand (Map p99; ☎ 02-290-9802; embajada@ nzembassy.cl; El Golf 99, Oficina 703, Las Condes)

Peru Arica (☎ 058-231-020; 18 de Septiembre 1554); Iquique (☎ 057-411-466; Zegers 570, 2nd fl, Iquique); Santiago (Map pp80-1; ☎ 02-235-4600; conpersantiago@ adsl.tie.cl; Padre Mariano 10, Oficina 309, Providencia)

Spain (Map p378; ☎ 061-243-566; Jose Menéndez 910, Punta Arenas)

UK Punta Arenas (☎ 061-244-727; Cataratas del Niagara 01325); Santiago (Map p99; ☎ 02-370-4100; consular .santiago@fco.gov.uk; Av El Bosque Norte 0125, 3rd fl, Las Condes)

USA (Map p99; ☎ 02-232-2600; santiago.usembassy
.gov; Av Andrés Bello 2800, Las Condes)

FESTIVALS & EVENTS

In January and February every Chilean town
and city puts on some sort of show with live
music, special feasts and fireworks. Tourist
offices have exact dates. Religious holidays
and the mid-September Fiestas Patrias mark
other festivities. See p23 for a list of the
top 10 festivals in Chile and the Festivals &
Events sections of destination chapters for
more information.

JANUARY
Semana Ancuditana Chiloé, and Ancud in particular,
makes merry over the second week in January in a series
of celebrations across the island, highlighting its unique
culture, music, dance and cuisine.
Brotes de Chile A folk-song festival attracting talent
from across Chile with plenty of dancing, food and crafts to
boot. Held in Angol in the second week in January.
Jornadas Musicales de Pucón Another popular musical
festival held in Pucón in mid-January.
Festival de Huaso Chilote Castro, in Chiloé, celebrates
the local *huasos* (cowboys) in late January.
Semana Musical (p301) Headlines a variety of music,
from chamber music to jazz. Held in Frutillar from late
January to February.

FEBRUARY
Fiesta de la Candelaria (p238) A religious festival
in early February, most fervently celebrated in Copiapó,
where thousands of pilgrims and dancers converge.
Encuentro Folklórico de Chiloé A delightful festival
promoting Chiloé's typical music, dance and cuisine, held
on the first week of February.
Festival Internacional de la Canción (p135) A series
of concerts showcasing top names in Latin American pop,
held in Viña del Mar.
Festival Costumbrista (p364) An opportunity to
witness an authentic Patagonian rodeo in Villa Cerro
Castillo.
Carnaval (p188) Highland merriment and flour bombs,
ending with the burning of the *momo* – a figure symbolizing
the frivolity of Carnaval. Held in Putre.
Festival Costumbrista Yet another chance to enjoy
Chiloé's distinctive folk music and dance, plus traditional
foods. Held mid-February in Castro.
Carnaval Ginga (p181) Held in Arica, in mid-February,
this festival features the traditional dancing and musical
skills of regional *comparsa* groups.
Noche de Valdivia Valdivia's annual knees-up, held on
the third Saturday in February, enlivened with decorated
riverboats and fireworks.

MARCH–DECEMBER
Campeonato Nacional de Rodeo (National Rodeo
Championship; p145) Feasting, *cueca* dancing and, most
importantly, Chilean cowboys showing off their fancy horse
skills. Held in Rancagua in late March.
Fiesta de San Pedro y San Pablo A religious festival
held in San Pedro de Atacama on June 29, celebrated with
folk-dancing groups, a rodeo and solemn processions.
Festival de la Virgen del Carmen (p203) Some 40,000
pilgrims pay homage to Chile's virgin with lots of street
dancing, curly-horned devil masks with flashing eyes and
spangly cloaks. Held in La Tirana in mid-July.
Carnaval de Invierno Southerly fireworks and parades
to cheer up the winter are held in Punta Arenas in late July.
New Year's Eve One of the biggest parties of the year,
with spectacular fireworks displays and all-night dancing.

FOOD

For descriptions of Chilean cuisine to get your
taste buds tingling, turn to p53. Throughout
the book restaurant listings are in ascending
budget order and have been split into price
ranges when necessary: budget (mains up to
CH3500), midrange (CH3500 to CH$8000)
and top end (CH$8000 and up).

GAY & LESBIAN TRAVELERS

Chile is still a conservative, Catholic-minded
country and many frown upon homosexuality here; however, younger generations are far
more tolerant. Provincial areas are definitively
far behind in attitudes towards gays. Chilean
males are often more physically demonstra-
tive than their counterparts in Europe or
North America, so behaviors like a vigorous
embrace will seem innocuous. Santiago's gay
scene (and general tolerance) has improved in
leaps and bounds during recent years. Perhaps
because it was underground for so long, the
gay scene has awoken with particular vigor.
Most gay bars and nightclubs can be found
in Barrio Bellavista. For more information
see p109.

Gay Chile (www.gaychile.com) has the low-down
on all things gay, including current events,
Santiago nightlife, lodging recommendations,
legal and medical advice and personals. While
in Santiago, keep an eye out for Chile's first
magazine oriented toward gays and other socially disenfranchised groups, **Opus Gay** (www
.opusgay.cl, in Spanish), teasingly named after the
conservative Catholic Opus Dei group.

Chile's main gay-rights organization is
Movimiento Unificado de Minorías Sexuales (MUMS;
www.orgullogay.cl, in Spanish).

DIRECTORY

HOLIDAYS

National holidays, when government offices and businesses are closed, are listed below. There is pressure to reduce these or to eliminate so-called sandwich holidays, which many Chileans take between an actual holiday and the weekend, by moving some to the nearest Monday.

Año Nuevo (New Year) January 1
Semana Santa (Easter Week) March or April
Día del Trabajo (Labor Day) May 1
Glorias Navales Commemorating the naval Battle of Iquique; May 21
Corpus Christi May/June; dates vary
Día de San Pedro y San Pablo (St Peter & St Paul's Day) June 29
Asunción de la Virgen (Assumption) August 15
Día de Unidad Nacional (Day of National Unity) First Monday of September
Día de la Independencia Nacional (National Independence Day) September 18
Día del Ejército (Armed Forces Day) September 19
Día de la Raza (Columbus Day) October 12
Todo los Santos (All Saints' Day) November 1
Inmaculada Concepción (Immaculate Conception) December 8
Navidad (Christmas Day) December 25

INSURANCE

In general, signing up for a travel-insurance policy is a good idea. For Chile, a basic theft/loss and medical policy is recommended. Read the fine print carefully as some companies exclude dangerous activities from coverage, which can include scuba diving, motorcycling, and even trekking. You may prefer a policy that pays doctors or hospitals directly rather than you having to pay on the spot and make a claim later.

Make copies of all insurance information in the event that the original is lost. For information on health insurance, turn to p488 and for car insurance, see p485.

INTERNET ACCESS

Most regions have excellent internet connections and reasonable prices; it is typical for hotels and hostels to have wi-fi or computer terminals. Family guesthouses, particularly outside urban areas, lag behind in this area. Internet cafés can be found pretty well everywhere, even in villages where they provide the only Friday-night entertainment for youth. Rates range from CH$400 to CH$2000 per hour, with very high rates only in remote areas.

Throughout this book, the internet icon is used to show wireless access or computer terminals.

LEGAL MATTERS

Chile's *carabineros* (police) have a reputation for being professional and polite; they cherish the slogan *'siempre un amigo'* (always a friend), although this usually brings a wry smile to the face of motorists. Penalties for common offences are similar to those given in much of Europe and North America. However, the possession, use or trafficking of drugs – including soft drugs such as cannabis – is treated very seriously and results in severe fines and imprisonment.

Police can demand identification at any time, so carry your passport. Throughout the country, the toll-free emergency telephone number for the police is ☎ 133.

Chileans often refer to police as *pacos,* a disrespectful (though not obscene) term that should *never* be used to a police officer's face.

Members of the military take themselves seriously, so avoid photographing military installations.

If you are involved in any automobile accident, your license (usually your international permit) will be confiscated until the case is resolved, although local officials will usually issue a temporary driving permit within a few days. A blood-alcohol test is obligatory; purchase a sterile syringe at the hospital or clinic pharmacy when the police take you there. After this, you will be taken to the station to make a statement and then, under most circumstances, released. Ordinarily you cannot leave Chile until the matter is resolved; consult your consulate, insurance carrier and a lawyer at home.

Police do not harass drivers for minor equipment violations but they can be uptight about parking violations. Don't *ever* make the error of attempting to bribe the police, whose reputation for institutional integrity is high.

MAPS

In Santiago, the **Instituto Geográfico Militar** (IGM; Map pp84-5; ☎ 02-460-6800; www.igm.cl, in Spanish; Dieciocho 369, Centro; 9am-5:30pm Mon-Fri), just south of the Alameda, produces excellent maps, which can be ordered through the website or bought directly. Their *Guía Caminera* is a good highway map, with scales ranging from 1:500,000 to 1:1,500,000. They also produce an easy-to-navigate city street-finder of Santiago, *Guia de Calles de Santiago*, and a map that charts the entire length of the Carretera Austral at a scale of 1:1,000,000. The IGM's 1:50,000 topographic series is valuable for trekkers, although the maps are out of date and those of sensitive border areas (where most national parks are) may not be available.

JLM Mapas publishes maps for all major regions and trekking areas at scales ranging from 1:50,000 to 1:500,000. The maps are widely distributed, easy to use and provide decent information, but they don't claim to be perfectly accurate.

Drivers in particular will appreciate the popular Turistel guidebook series, which contains detailed highway maps and excellent plans of Chilean cities, towns and even many villages, though many maps lack scales. The guides are annually updated but published in Spanish only, with separate volumes on the north, center and south of the country, plus an additional volume on camping. Turistel guides also provide thorough background information and mark tourist amenities. They cost around CH$5000 from any large bookstore.

In most major Chilean cities the Automóvil Club de Chile (Acchi) has an office that sells highway maps, although not all of them are equally well stocked.

Online maps vary in quality: **Plano Digital de Publiguías** (www.planos.cl, in Spanish) has online city maps but it is a frustrating website to navigate. Santiago maps are available on **Map City** (www.mapcity.cl, in Spanish). Some local government websites have interactive maps that allow you to search for a street address in major cities.

MONEY

The Chilean unit of currency is the peso (CH$). Bank notes come in denominations of 500, 1000, 2000, 5000, 10,000 and 20,000 pesos. Coin values are 1, 5, 10, 50, 100 and 500 pesos, although one-peso coins are fast disappearing, and even fives and tens are un-

common. Carry small bills with you; it can be difficult to change bills larger than CH$1000 in rural areas. Gas stations and liquor stores are usually able to, just make an apologetic face and ask, '¿Tiene suelto?'.

Exchange rates are usually best in Santiago, where there is also a ready market for European currencies. Chile's currency has been pretty stable in recent years. The value of the dollar seems to decline during peak tourist season and shoot back up again come March. Paying a bill with US cash is sometimes acceptable, especially at tour agencies (check their exchange rate carefully). Many top-end hotels publish rates in US dollars with a lower exchange rate than the daily one. It's best to pay all transactions in pesos.

Money transferred by cable should arrive in a few days; Chilean banks can give you money in US dollars on request. Western Union offices can be found throughout Chile, usually adjacent to the post office.

ATMs

Chile's many ATM machines, known as *redbanc,* are the easiest and most convenient way to access funds. Your bank will likely charge a small fee for each transaction. Most ATMs have instructions in Spanish and English. Choose the option 'foreign card' (*tarjeta extranjera)* before starting the transaction. You *cannot* rely on ATMs in San Pedro de Atacama (the one ATM breaks down), Easter Island (Rapa Nui) or in small Patagonian towns.

Cash

A few banks will exchange cash (usually US dollars only); *casas de cambio* (exchange houses) in Santiago and more tourist-oriented destinations will also exchange. However, they also charge some commission or have less agreeable rates. More costly purchases, such as tours and hotel bills, can sometimes be paid in US cash.

Credit Cards

If you've got plastic in your pocket (especially Amex, Visa and MasterCard) you'll be welcome in most established businesses; however, it's best not to depend on credit. Many businesses will charge up to 6% extra to cover the charge they have to pay for the transaction. Credit cards can also be useful to show 'sufficient funds' before entering another South American country.

DIRECTORY

Tipping

It's customary to cough up an extra 10% of the bill as a tip in restaurants, except in family-run places, which rarely expect a tip. In general, waiters and waitresses are poorly paid, so if you can afford to eat out, you can afford to tip, and even a small *propina* will be appreciated. Taxi drivers do not require tips, although you may round off the fare for convenience.

Traveler's Checks

Traveler's checks are the least convenient way to go. Hardly anyone wants to exchange traveler's checks, and those who do offer poor rates. Carrying a combination of monetary forms is wise (traveler's checks are a more secure back-up), but depositing funds into a debit account before going will be most useful.

PHOTOGRAPHY & VIDEO

The larger internet cafés usually have the capability to download photos and video from your camera and some sell storage CDs. Kodak has stores throughout Chile, some with automatic photo printing, although the cost of developing prints (CH$400 each) might encourage you to wait until you get home.

At high altitudes, especially in northern Chile, the bright light can wash out photographs; a polarizing filter is recommended. Photographers should be circumspect about indigenous peoples, who often resent the intrusion. When in doubt, ask permission to photograph a stranger.

Lonely Planet's *Travel Photography* book has a wealth of tips and information to help secure those perfect snaps.

POST

Correos de Chile (☎ 800-267-736; www.correos.cl, in Spanish), Chile's national postal service, has reasonably dependable but sometimes rather slow postal services. Within Chile, it costs around CH$120 to send a letter.

Receiving Mail

You can receive mail via *lista de correos*, or poste restante (equivalent to general delivery), at any Chilean post office. Some consulates will also hold correspondence for their citizens. To collect your mail from a post office or embassy, you need your passport as proof of identity. Instruct correspondents to address letters clearly and to precede your name with either Señora or Señor, as post offices divide lists of correspondence by gender. There is usually a small charge, about CH$200 per item. Mail is held for one month.

Sending Mail

Chilean post offices are generally open 9am to 6pm Monday to Friday and 9am to noon Saturday. Send important overseas mail *certificado* (registered) to ensure its arrival; this costs around CH$500. Airmail takes around a week to both Europe and the US.

Sending parcels is straightforward, although a customs official may have to inspect your package before a postal clerk will accept it. Vendors in or near the post office will wrap parcels upon request. International courier services are readily available in Santiago, less so outside the capital.

To send packages within Chile, sending via *encomienda* (the bus system) is much more reliable. Simply take the package to a bus company that goes to the destination. Label the package clearly with the destination and the name of the person who will pick it up, either on arrival or from the company's office.

SENIOR TRAVELERS

Senior travelers should encounter no particular difficulties traveling in Chile, where older citizens typically enjoy a great deal of respect. On crowded buses, for instance, most Chileans will readily offer their seat to an older person.

Folks over 50 may want to check out tour operators that cater to them. Two of the most established are **Elderhostel** (☎ 800-454-5768; www.elderhostel.org; Boston, MA) and **Eldertreks** (☎ 800-741-7956; www.eldertreks.com; Ontario).

SHOPPING

Chile is one of only two countries in the world where the semiprecious stone lapiz lazuli is found. It is a deep navy-blue color and makes sophisticated jewelry that can be bought in most Chilean jewelers and a few *ferias* (artisans' markets). However, this unique stone can empty your wallet in a flash: expect a pair of good-quality earrings to cost around CH$20,000. Check the quality of the setting and silver used – they are often only silver plated and very soft.

Craft markets can be found throughout the country. In the north, artisans put shaggy llama and alpaca wool to good use by making thick jumpers, scarves, and other garments to take the bite off the frigid highland nights. Many of these goods are similar to those in Bolivia and Peru. You'll also see crafts made with cactus wood, and painstakingly crafted leather goods in Norte Chico.

In Chiloé and Patagonia, hand-knit woolens such as bulky fishermen's sweaters and blankets are reasonably priced and useful in winter. In the Araucanía, look for jewelry based on Mapuche designs, which are unique to Chile. They also produce quality weavings and basketry. In the Lakes District and Patagonia, artisans carve wooden plates and bowls out of the (sustainable) hardwood raulí.

Wine lovers will not want for Chilean wines to choose from: stick to the boutique wineries with wines that you can't find in your own country, or pick up bottles of the powerful grape-brandy pisco, which is difficult to find outside of Chile. Other artisanal edibles include *miel de ulmo*, a very aromatic and tasty honey special to Patagonia, and *mermelada de murtilla*, a jam made of a tart red berry. As long as such goods are still sealed, there shouldn't be a problem getting through international customs.

Many cities have good antiques markets, most notably Santiago's Mercado Franklin and Valparaíso's Plaza O'Higgins. Flea markets are commonly known as *Ferias Persas* (Persian Fairs).

For a preview, check out the website of **Fundación Artesanías de Chile** (Chilean Craft Foundation; www.artesaniasdechile.cl) to see a selection of local artesanía.

Bargaining

Buying items in a crafts market is the only acceptable time to bargain. Transport and accommodation rates are generally fixed and prominently displayed, but during a slow summer or in the off-season, ask politely for a discount, '*¿Me podría hacer precio?*'.

SOLO TRAVELERS

Solo travelers will have no trouble avoiding or hooking up with companions as the mood strikes them. Chileans are generally more reserved than other Latin Americans but they are friendly and eager to help if you strike up a conversation. Inexpensive hostels with communal kitchens encourage social exchange, while a large number of language schools,

tours and volunteer organizations will provide every traveler with an opportunity to meet others. However, it isn't recommended to undertake long treks in the wilderness by yourself. Women travelers, see p473.

TELEPHONE & FAX

The two largest telephone companies, Entel and Telefónica, have call centers from which you call directly from private cabins; most close by 10pm. Some call centers will place the call for you then tell you in which *cabina* your call is transferred. International rates are reasonable.

Each telephone carrier installs its own public phones, which take only their calling cards or coins. Kiosks sell calling cards *(tarjetas telefónicas)*. A local call costs about CH$100 per minute, and less outside peak hours (8am to 8pm weekdays, 8am to 2pm Saturday).

In rural areas, it's common to have one public pay phone for the town; while these are OK for calls out, it's difficult to get the person you want on the line. Remote tour operators and lodges have satellite phones with a Santiago prefix.

Cell Phones

Cell-phone numbers have seven digits, prefixed by ☎ 099 or ☎ 098. Drop the 09/08 prefix when calling cell-to-cell. If calling cell-to-landline, add the landline's area code. Cell phones sell for as little as CH$12,000 and can be charged up by prepaid phone cards. Cell

---

CALLING ARGENTINE CELL PHONES

Cellular phone numbers in Argentina are always preceded by '15.' After that simple fact, it gets confusing. Usually you just dial the regional code corresponding to the location, regardless of where the phone was purchased, but sometimes the regional code corresponds to where the person bought the cellular phone. First, try using the regional code followed by '15,' then the number. If you're calling a cell phone from within the same regional code, you don't have to dial the regional code. When calling an Argentine cellular phone from abroad, first you dial Argentina's country code (54), then '9' (instead of '15'), then the regional code, followed by the telephone number itself.

phones have a 'caller-pays' format. Calls between cell and landlines are expensive and quickly eat up prepaid card amounts.

Short-term visitors can also rent a cell phone. **Rent A Phone** (☎ 02-633-7600; www.chile cellrent.com; Miraflores 537, Santiago) is one of several companies offering this service: it charges US$7 for delivery and a further US$7 when you drop the phone off. Daily rental fee is US$1.90. All incoming calls are free of charge for the user, but outgoing national calls cost around US$0.90 per minute. Outgoing international calls vary from US$1.90 per minute to US$2.50 per minute.

Do your homework if you want to bring your own cell phone: you'll need a SIM-unlocked GSM-compatible phone that operates on a frequency of 1900 MHz (commonly used in the US). If you have such a phone you can buy a new SIM card from a Chilean operator such as Entel or Telefónica.

You'll get reception in most inhabited areas but reception is scarce in the middle of the Atacama Desert or from many parts of Patagonia.

Phone Codes

Chile's country code is ☎ 56. All telephone numbers in Santiago and the Metropolitan Region have seven digits; all other telephone numbers have six digits except for certain toll-free and emergency numbers. The toll-free number for the police is ☎ 133, ambulance is ☎ 131. You'll reach directory assistance at ☎ 103.

Long-distance calls are based on a carrier system: to place a call, precede the number with the telephone company's code: **Entel** (☎ 123), **Telefónica** (☎ 188), for example. To make a collect call, dial ☎ 182 to get an operator.

TIME

For most of the year, Chile is four hours behind GMT, but from mid-December to late March, because of daylight-saving time (summer time), the difference is three hours. The exact date of the changeover varies from year to year. Because of Chile's great latitudinal range, the summer sunrise in the desert tropics of Arica, where the durations of day and night are roughly equal throughout the year, occurs after 8am. Easter Island is two hours behind the mainland. Chileans commonly use the 24-hour clock.

TOILETS

Pipes and sewer systems in older buildings are quite fragile: used toilet paper should be discarded in wastebaskets. Cheaper accommodations and public toilets rarely provide toilet paper, so carry your own wherever you go. Better restaurants and cafés are good alternatives to public toilets, which are often dirty.

TOURIST INFORMATION

Every regional capital and some other cities have a local representative of **Sernatur** (☎ 600-737-62887; www.sernatur.cl), the national tourist service. Offices vary in usefulness – some have astonishingly knowledgeable multilingual staff, but others bury visitors in dusty brochures and leaflets instead of actually answering their questions.

Many municipalities also have their own tourist office, usually on the main plaza or at the bus terminal. In some areas, these offices may be open during the summer only.

Some official international representatives for Chilean tourism can be found abroad. Consulates in major cities may have a tourist representative, but more accessible and comprehensive information can be found through specialized travel agencies and on the internet.

Chile has a few general travel agencies that work with affiliates around the world. **Chilean Travel Service** (Map pp90-1; CTS; ☎ 02-251-0400; www .ctsturismo.cl; Antonio Bellet 77, Providencia, Santiago) has well-informed multilingual staff and can organize accommodations and tours all over Chile through your local travel agency.

TRAVELERS WITH DISABILITIES

Travel within Chile is still a robust challenge for those with disabilities, though patient planning can open a lot of doors. Even top-end hotels and resorts cannot be relied upon to have ramps or rooms adapted for those with impaired mobility; an estimated 10% of hotels in Santiago cater to wheelchairs. Lifts are more common in large hotels and the law now requires new public buildings to provide disabled access.

Santiago's **Metro** (www.metrosantiago.cl, in Spanish) is in the process of making subway lines more accessible. At present, Línea 5 and Línea 4 have been refitted, as well as the extensions of Líneas 2 and 5, the Línea to Maipú and the extension of Línea 1 to plaza Los Dominicos. Public bus company **Transantiago** (www.transan

tiago.cl, in Spanish) has access ramps and spaces for wheelchairs on new buses. Some street lights have noise-indicated crossings for the blind. Those in wheelchairs will find Chile's narrow and poorly maintained sidewalks awkward to negotiate. Crossing streets is also tricky, but most Chilean drivers are remarkably courteous toward pedestrians – especially those with obvious handicaps.

Santiago's **Tixi Service** (☎ toll-free 800-372-300, 02-481-3235; www.tixi.cl, in Spanish) caters to disabled individuals and has hydraulic elevators to accommodate wheelchairs. Trips within the capital generally cost around CH$7500. American organization **Accessible Journeys** (☎ in USA 800-846-4537; www.disabilitytravel.com) organizes independent travel to Chile for folks with disabilities.

There are some benefits to visiting Chile as a disabled person: national parks are often discounted – sometimes free – for disabled visitors (check ahead with Conaf). Cruises or ferries such as Navimag will sometimes give free upgrades to disabled travelers, and some of the ski resorts near Santiago have outrigger poles for disabled skiers.

VISAS

Nationals of the US, Canada, Australia and the EU do not need a visa to visit Chile. Passports are obligatory and are essential for cashing traveler's checks, checking into hotels and other routine activities.

The Chilean government collects a US$132/56/132 'reciprocity' fee from arriving US/Australian/Canadian citizens in response to these governments imposing a similar fee on Chilean citizens applying for visas. The payment applies only to tourists arriving by air in Santiago and is valid for the life of the passport. Payment must be made in cash; exact change necessary.

It is advisable to carry your passport: Chile's police can demand identification at any moment, and many hotels require you to show it upon check-in.

If your passport is lost or stolen, notify the police, ask them for a police statement, and notify your consulate as soon as possible.

TOURIST CARDS

On arrival, you'll be handed a 90-day tourist card. Don't lose it! If you do, go to the **Policía Internacional** (Map pp80-1; ☎ 02-737-1292; Gral Borgoño 1052, Santiago; 🕑 8:30am-5pm Mon-Fri) or the nearest police station. You will be asked for it upon leaving the country.

It costs US$100 to renew a tourist card for 90 more days at the **Departamento de Extranjería** (Map pp84-5; ☎ 02-550-2484; www.extranjeria.gob.cl; Agustinas 1235, 2nd fl, Santiago; 🕑 8:30am-2pm Mon-Fri). Take with you photocopies of your passport and tourist card. You can also visit the Departamento de Extranjería in any of Chile's regional capitals. Many visitors prefer a quick dash across the Argentine border and back.

VOLUNTEERING

Experienced outdoor guides may be able to exchange labor for accommodations during the busy high season, if you can stick out the entire season. **Experiment Chile** (www.experiment.cl) organizes 14-week language-learning/volunteer programs. Language schools often place students in volunteer work as well. Nonprofit **Un Techo Para Chile** (www.untechoparachile.cl, in Spanish) builds homes for low-income families throughout the country, with contact information on the website.

If you want to dig deeper into the indigenous cultures, **Trafkura Expediciones** (☎ 099-9036-1013; www.trafkuraexpediciones.cl) in Melipeuco offers sustainable-tourism immersion trips deep into Pewenche Indian land in Icalma, where their organic farm accepts volunteers.

At Parque Nacional Torres del Paine, volunteers can help with trail maintenance, biological studies or an animal census. Spanish-language skills are always a plus. In the park, **AMA Torres del Paine** (www.amatorresdelpaine.org) works with a limited number of volunteers. The USA-based **Global Community Project** (www.globalcommunityproject.blogspot.com) takes student-exchange volunteers with advance notice.

The annual *Directorio de Organizaciones Miembros* published by **Renace** (Red Nacional de Acción Ecológica; www.renace.cl, in Spanish) lists environmental organizations.

WOMEN TRAVELERS

Compared with their hot-blooded neighbors, Chilean men are often shy and downright circumspect. For lone female travelers, it is safer to travel here than most other Latin American countries, the US and many areas of Europe. The sight of women traveling, be it in a group or alone, is not met with much surprise although the very family-bound, group-oriented Chilean has a hard time imagining anyone enjoying solo travel. For a woman, the biggest bother is being constantly asked how old you are and if you're married. Take it with a sense of humor.

Women may meet up with antiquated attitudes about female roles and capability, yet this is a country that elected a woman president. Ports and mining towns tend to have the most aggressive courters; if this isn't your game, these places are less fun to travel solo. In the north or central regions guys may be quick with *piropos* (come-ons), but these hormonal outbursts evaporate upon utterance – don't dwell on them. Ignoring them is the best way to curb interest. Flirting back, however, may be interpreted as a green light to be chatted up.

Many Chilenas are intimidated by their foreign counterparts and they can be difficult to befriend at first. A traveler might notice that men and women tend to socialize separately or go to a party in groups but socialize by gender.

In smaller towns, tampons are hard to come by.

WORK

It's increasingly difficult to obtain residence and work permits for Chile. Consequently, many foreigners do not bother to do so, but the most reputable employers will insist on the proper visa. If you need one, go to the **Departamento de Extranjería** (Map pp84-5; ☎ 02-550-2484; Agustinas 1235, Santiago; ☽ 8:30am-2pm Mon-Fri).

It is not unusual for visiting travelers to work as English-language instructors in Santiago. Industries with an international trading focus, such as salmon farming and fishmeal processing, have a growing need for English-language instruction around Puerto Montt. In general, wages aren't very good and full-time employment is hard to come by without a commitment to stay for some time.

Transportation

CONTENTS

Getting There & Away	**475**
Entering the Country	475
Air	475
Land	478
Getting Around	**480**
Air	480
Bicycle	481
Boat	482
Bus	483
Car & Motorcycle	484
Hitchhiking	486
Local Transportation	486
Tours	486
Train	487

GETTING THERE & AWAY

ENTERING THE COUNTRY

Most short-term travelers touch down in Santiago, while those on a South American odyssey are more likely to sidle in at their leisure – via bus from Peru, boat or bus from Argentina, or a bouncy bus or 4WD trip from Bolivia. Entry is generally straightforward so long as your passport is valid for at least six months beyond your arrival date. For general information on visas and tourist tickets, see p473.

Onward Tickets

Theoretically, Chile requires a return or onward ticket for arriving travelers, and occasionally officials may ask for evidence of an onward ticket if the date of your return ticket is beyond the initial 90-day tourist-card limit. Although this is rare, not having an onward ticket can pose a problem at the flight counter in your departure country. If the agent is a stickler, they can refuse to board you. The solution is to either purchase a refundable return air ticket or get the cheapest possible onward bus ticket from a bus company that offers online sales.

AIR

Chile has direct connections with North America, the UK, Europe, Australia and New Zealand. You can also fly to one of Chile's neighboring countries, such as Argentina, Bolivia or Peru, and continue to Chile by air or land. International flights within South America tend to be fairly expensive unless they are purchased as part of intercontinental travel, but there are bargain round-trip fares between Buenos Aires and Santiago.

Airports & Airlines

Most long-distance flights to Chile arrive at Santiago, landing at **Aeropuerto Internacional Arturo Merino Benítez** (☎ 02-690-1752; www.aeropuertosantiago.cl) in the suburb of Pudahuel. There are also flights from neighboring countries to regional airports such as Arica, Iquique, Temuco and Punta Arenas.

Many major national and international airlines have offices or representatives in Santiago.

Aerolíneas Argentinas (airline code AR; ☎ 800-610-200; www.aerolineas.com.ar)

Air Canada (airline code AC; ☎ 02-337-0022; www.aircanada.com)

Air France (airline code AF; ☎ 02-290-9300; www.airfrance.com)

Alitalia (airline code AZ; ☎ 02-378-8230; www.alitalia.com)

American Airlines (airline code AA; ☎ 02-679-0000; www.aa.com)

Avianca (airline code AV; ☎ 02-270-6600; www.avianca.com)

British Airways (airline code BA; ☎ 02-330-8600; www.britishairways.com)

Copa (airline code CM; ☎ 02-200-2100; www.copaair.com)

THINGS CHANGE...

The information in this chapter is particularly vulnerable to change. Check directly with the airline or a travel agent to make sure you understand how a fare (and ticket you may buy) works and be aware of the security requirements for international travel. Shop carefully. The details given in this chapter should be regarded as pointers and are not a substitute for your own careful, up-to-date research.

TRANSPORTATION

TRANSPORTATION

Delta (airline code DL; ☎ 800-202-020; www.delta.com)
Iberia (airline code IB; ☎ 02-870-1070; www.iberia.com)
KLM (airline code KL; ☎ 02-233-0991; www.klm.com)
Lan (airline code LA; ☎ 600-526-2000; www.lan.com) See p481 for addresses.
Lloyd Aéreo Boliviano (LAB; airline code LB; ☎ 02-688-8680; www.labairlines.com)
Lufthansa (airline code LH; ☎ 02-630-1655; www.lufthansa.com)
Qantas (airline code QF; ☎ 02-232-9562; www.qantas.com)
Swiss International Airlines (airline code LX; ☎ 02-940-2900; www.swiss.com)
Taca (airline code TA; ☎ 800-461-133; www.taca.com)
United Airlines (airline code UA; ☎ 02-337-0000; www.united.com)
Varig (airline code RG; ☎ 02-707-8001; www.varig.com)

Tickets

To cut steep costs in getting to South America take advantage of seasonal discounts and try to avoid peak times such as Christmas, New Year's or Easter. Advance purchase will normally provide the best, but not necessarily most flexible, deal. Discount ticketing is rare in Latin America.

If buying on the web, shop around as prices vary. Tickets for midweek flights are cheaper than weekends. The following internet sites are reliable, but there are scores more you can choose from. Check travel magazines and the weekend travel sections of newspapers for some more ideas. Also see the suggestions given under specific countries.
Ebookers (www.ebookers.com)
Expedia (www.expedia.com)
Flight Centre (www.flightcentre.com)
Flights.com (www.eltexpress.com)
Kayak (www.kayak.com)
STA (www.statravel.com)
Travelocity (www.travelocity.com)

COURIER FLIGHTS

If you're flexible with dates, don't mind traveling solo and are prepared to travel with only carry-on luggage, you may be able to fly to Santiago cheaply as a courier. This is only practical if you're flying from major US-based gateways or London. For more information:
Air Courier Association (☎ 800-383-6814; www.aircourier.org)
International Association of Air Travel Couriers (www.courier.org, www.iaatc.com)

INTERCONTINENTAL (RTW) TICKETS

Most intercontinental airlines traveling to Chile also offer round-the-world (RTW) tickets in conjunction with their alliances. Other companies, such as **Airtreks** (☎ North America 415-977-7100, toll-free 877-247-8735; www.airtreks.com), offer more flexible, customized RTW tickets that don't tie you into airline affiliates. Similar 'Circle Pacific' fares allow excursions between Australasia and Chile, often with a stop at Easter Island. These types of tickets are certain to have restrictions, so check the fine print carefully. The following websites advertise RTW tickets:
Airfare (www.airfare.com.au)
Ebookers (www.ebookers.com)
Flight Centre (www.flightcentre.com)
STA (www.statravel.com)
Trailfinders (www.trailfinders.co.uk)
Travel Bag (www.travelbag.co.uk)

Australia & New Zealand

Lan and Qantas share a flight from Sydney to Santiago, stopping in Auckland. A round-trip ticket from Australia to Santiago averages around US$2000. **Lan** (☎ 1300-361-400; 64 York St, Sydney) also has an office in Australia.

Canada

Canadians will have to take connecting flights through a US city. Air Canada, American Airlines and Delta offer connections to Santiago from Toronto.

Continental Europe

There are regular direct flights from Madrid to Santiago with Lan and Iberia, and several airlines have flights from major European cities via Argentina or Brazil, including Lufthansa and Varig. Fares from Western Europe start from around €650, and usually a few more hundred euros for most other destinations. **STA Travel** (www.statravel.com) has offices in Austria, Denmark, Finland, Sweden, Switzerland and Germany.

South America

Many airlines fly daily between Santiago and Buenos Aires, Argentina, for a standard fare of about US$290 for the round-trip. However, European airlines that pick up and discharge most of their passengers in Buenos Aires sometimes try to fill empty seats by selling cheap round-trips between the Argentine and Chilean capitals.

There are Lan flights from Santiago to Mendoza (round-trip US$188, twice daily), and to Córdoba (round-trip US$248, twice daily), but discount round-trips are also frequent on these routes. In Patagonia from November through mid-March, **Aerovías DAP** (☎ 061-213-776; www.dap.cl) flies from Punta Arenas to Ushuaia (CH$19,000, 15 minutes) in Tierra del Fuego, and offers charter service from Puerto Natales to El Calafate.

Lan and Taca have numerous daily flights from Lima, Peru, to Santiago for about US$344 (round-trip), and many discount fares pop up on this route. Lan also flies from Lima to the southern city of Tacna, only 50km from the Chilean border city of Arica, for CH$112,000 one way. Crossing overland from Tacna and flying from Arica to Santiago (one way CH$187,000) is slightly cheaper than flying nonstop from Lima to Santiago.

Lan flies daily from Santiago to La Paz (round-trip US$700) via Iquique and Arica. LAB flies from La Paz to Santiago regularly via Santa Cruz.

Taca and Avianca link Santiago with Bogotá, Colombia, daily (round-trip US$879), either nonstop or via Buenos Aires. Lan flies to Montevideo, the Uruguayan capital (round-trip US$232). Varig and TAM fly to Brazilian and Paraguayan destinations.

Recommended agencies:

ASATEJ (☎ 011-4114-7544; www.asatej.com) In Argentina.

Student Travel Bureau (☎ 011-3038-1555; www.stb .com.br) In Brazil.

UK & Ireland

At the time of writing there were no direct flights between London and Santiago. Connections from the UK go through Madrid, Buenos Aires and the US. Prices

---

CLIMATE CHANGE & TRAVEL

Climate change is a serious threat to the ecosystems that humans rely upon, and air travel is the fastest-growing contributor to the problem. Lonely Planet regards travel, overall, as a global benefit, but believes we all have a responsibility to limit our personal impact on global warming.

Flying & Climate Change

Pretty much every form of motor travel generates CO_2 (the main cause of human-induced climate change) but planes are far and away the worst offenders, not just because of the sheer distances they allow us to travel, but because they release greenhouse gases high into the atmosphere. The statistics are frightening: two people taking a return flight between Europe and the US will contribute as much to climate change as an average household's gas and electricity consumption over a whole year.

Carbon Offset Schemes

Climatecare.org and other websites use 'carbon calculators' that allow jetsetters to offset the greenhouse gases they are responsible for with contributions to energy-saving projects and other climate-friendly initiatives in the developing world – including projects in India, Honduras, Kazakhstan and Uganda.

Lonely Planet, together with Rough Guides and other concerned partners in the travel industry, supports the carbon offset scheme run by climatecare.org. Lonely Planet offsets all of its staff and author travel.

For more information check out our website: lonelyplanet.com.

average between £760 and £900, depending on the time of year.

Journey Latin America (☎ 020-8747-3108; www .journeylatinamerica.co.uk) is a reputable agency.

USA

From the USA, the principal gateways to South America are Miami, New York, Los Angeles, Atlanta and Dallas. One alternative to landing in Santiago is to fly to Lima, Peru, and on to the Peruvian border city of Tacna, or to Arica (in northern Chile). For visitors to the Atacama Desert, this would save a long trip north from Santiago.

Exito (www.exitotravel.com) is recommended for online bookings.

LAND
Border Crossings

Chile's northern border touches Peru and Bolivia, while its vast eastern boundary hugs Argentina. Of the numerous border crossings with Argentina, only a few are served by public transportation. Chile's Ministerio de Obras Públicas (MOP; Public Works Ministry) is working to improve border crossings, especially those to Argentina. At major land borders – such as the Los Libertadores complex between Santiago and Mendoza, and the Pajaritos crossing between Osorno and Bariloche – Chilean customs officials X-ray the baggage of arriving bus passengers (photographers may want to separate their film). Most international buses depart from Terminal de Buses Santiago.

Bus

There are buses to almost every country on the continent, but only masochists are likely to attempt the 4½- to 10-day marathons to destinations like Quito, Ecuador and Caracas, Venezuela. Common destinations are served by the following bus companies, all located in the Terminal de Buses Santiago:

Argentina
Andesmar (☎ 02-779-6839)
Buses Ahumada (☎ 02-778-2703)
Cata (☎ 02-779-3660; busescatachile@terra.cl)
Crucero del Norte (☎ 02-776-2416) Also goes to Brazil and Paraguay.
El Rápido (☎ 02-776-0049; www.elrapidoint.com.ar, in Spanish) Also goes to Uruguay.
Fenix Pullman Norte Internacional (☎ 02-776-1727; fenixpullman@amarillas.cl)

Pullman del Sur (☎ 02-776-2424; www.pdelsur.cl, in Spanish)
TAC (☎ 02-779-6920)
Tur Bus (☎ 02-779-5624; www.turbus.com, in Spanish)
Turismo Nevada (☎ 02-776-4116)

Brazil
Chilebus Internacional (☎ 02-776-5557)
Pluma (☎ 02-779-6054)

Peru
Ormeño (☎ 02-779-3443; www.ormenochile.cl)
Tas Choapa (☎ 02-779-4925) Also goes to Argentina.

Sample costs and trip times:

Destination	Cost (CH$)	Duration (hr)
Asunción, Paraguay	$32,000	30
Bariloche, Argentina	$25,000	28
Buenos Aires, Argentina	$28,000	22
Córdoba, Argentina	$20,000	17
Lima, Peru	$53,000	48
Mendoza, Argentina	$9000	8
Montevideo, Uruguay	$36,000	25
Río de Janeiro, Brazil	$70,000	72
São Paulo, Brazil	$63,000	55

From Terminal Santiago, travelers can also ask about less frequent *taxi colectivos* to Mendoza (CH$14,000) with **Chi-Ar** (☎ 02-776-0048). Drivers may stop on request for photo opportunities on the spectacular Andean crossing.

Car & Motorcycle

There can be additional charges and confusing paperwork if you're taking a hired car out of Chile; ask the rental agency to talk you through it. See p484 for road rules and further information about fuel and insurance.

From Argentina

Unless you're crossing from Chile's extreme south there's no way to avoid the Andes. Spectacular scenery and popping ears are guaranteed but there is public transportation on only a few of the crossings to Argentina, and many passes are closed in winter.

NORTHERN ROUTES

Calama to Jujuy & Salta A popular route over the Andes via San Pedro de Atacama, Ruta 27 goes over the Paso de Jama. It has a regular bus service (advance booking is highly advisable); it's a good road as far as the border and is open all year. Slightly further south, on Ruta 23, motorists will find the 4079m Paso de Lago Sico a rougher but passable summer alternative. Chilean customs are at San Pedro de Atacama.

Iquique to Oruro A few scattered bus services run along a paved road from Iquique past the Parque Nacional Volcán Isluga to the Paso Colchane; you can catch a truck or bus on to Oruru from here (on an unpaved road).

Copiapó to Catamarca & La Rioja There is no public transportation over the 4726m Paso de San Francisco; it's a dirt road that should only be driven in a vehicle with high clearance, but rewards with spectacular scenery – including the luminous Laguna Verde.

La Serena to San Juan Dynamited by the Argentine military during the Beagle Channel dispute of 1978–79, the 4779m Paso del Agua Negra is a beautiful route, but the road is unpaved beyond Guanta and buses eschew it. It is a good bicycle route and tours run to hot springs on the Argentine side.

MIDDLE CHILE

Santiago or Valparaíso to Mendoza & Buenos Aires A dozen or more bus companies service this beautiful and vital lifeline to Argentina, along Ruta 60 through the Los Libertadores tunnel. Winter snow sometimes closes the route, but rarely for long.

Talca to Malargüe & San Rafael There's no public transportation through Ruta 115 to cross the 2553m Paso Pehuenche, southeast of Talca. Another crossing from Curicó over the 2502m Paso Vergara is being developed but is still hard to access.

SOUTHERN MAINLAND ROUTES

Several scenic crossings squeeze through to Argentina from Temuco south to Puerto Montt, some involving bus-boat shuttles that are popular in summer (book ahead).

Temuco to Zapala & Neuquén A good road crosses the Andes over the 1884m Paso de Pino Hachado, directly east of Temuco along the upper Río Biobío. A secondary unpaved route just south of here is the 1298m Paso de Icalma. There may be occasional bus traffic in summer.

Temuco to San Martín de los Andes The most popular route from Temuco passes Lago Villarrica, Pucón and Curarrehue en route to the Paso de Mamuil Malal (known to Argentines as Paso Tromen). On the Argentine side, the road skirts the northern slopes of Volcán Lanín. There is a regular summer bus service, but the pass is sometimes closed due to snow in winter.

Valdivia to San Martín de los Andes This mix-and-match route starts with a bus from Valdivia to Panguipulli, Choshuenco and Puerto Fuy, followed by a ferry across Lago Pirihueico to the village of Pirihueico. From Pirihueico a local bus goes to Argentine customs at 659m Paso Huahum, where travelers can catch a bus to San Martín.

Osorno to Bariloche via Paso Cardenal Samoré This crossing, commonly known as Pajaritos, is the quickest land route in the southern Lakes District, passing through Parque Nacional Puyehue on the Chilean side and Parque Nacional Nahuel Huapi on the Argentine side. It has a frequent bus service all year.

Puerto Montt & Puerto Varas to Bariloche Very popular in summer but open all year, this bus-ferry combination via Parque Nacional Vicente Pérez Rosales starts in Puerto Montt or Puerto Varas. A ferry goes from Petrohué, at the western end of Lago Todos Los Santos, to Peulla, and a bus crosses 1022m Paso de Pérez Rosales to Argentine immigration at Puerto Frías. After crossing Lago Frías by launch, there's a short bus hop to Puerto Blest on Lago Nahuel Huapi and another ferry to Puerto Pañuelo (Llao Llao). From Llao Llao there is a frequent bus service to Bariloche.

SOUTHERN PATAGONIAN ROUTES

Puerto Ramírez to Esquel There are two options here. From the village of Villa Santa Lucía, on the Camino Austral, there is a good lateral road that forks at Puerto Ramírez, at the southeastern end of Lago Yelcho. The north fork goes to Futaleufú, where a bridge crosses the river to the Argentine side where you can catch colectivos to Esquel. The south fork goes to Palena and Argentine customs at Carrenleufú, which has bus services to Corcovado, Trevelin and Esquel. Customs and immigration are much more efficient at Futaleufú.

Coyhaique to Comodoro Rivadavia There are several buses per week, often heavily booked, from Coyhaique to Comodoro Rivadavia via Río Mayo. For private vehicles, there is an alternative route from Balmaceda to Perito Moreno via the 502m Paso Huemules.

Chile Chico to Los Antiguos From Puerto Ibáñez take the ferry to Chile Chico on the southern shore of Lago Carrera and a shuttle bus to Los Antiguos, which has connections to the Patagonian coastal town of Caleta Olivia or south to El Chaltén or El Calafate. There is also a narrow mountain road with a regular bus service to Chile Chico from Cruce El Maitén at the southwestern end of Lago General Carrera.

Cochrane to Bajo Caracoles Perhaps the most desolate crossing in the Aisén region, 647m Paso Roballos links the hamlet of Cochrane with a flyspeck outpost in Argentina's Santa Cruz province.

Puerto Natales to Río Turbio & El Calafate Frequent buses connect Puerto Natales to the Argentine coal town of Río Turbio; and from Río Turbio to Río Gallegos and El Calafate. All year, but far more frequently in summer, there are buses from Puerto Natales to El Calafate, the gateway to Argentina's Parque Nacional Los Glaciares, via Paso Río don Guillermo.

Punta Arenas to Río Gallegos Many buses travel the highway between Punta Arenas and Río Gallegos. It's a five- to eight-hour trip because of slow customs checks and a rough segment of Argentine Ruta Nacional (RN) 3.

Punta Arenas to Tierra del Fuego From Punta Arenas a 2½-hour ferry trip or a 10-minute flight takes you to Porvenir, on Chilean Tierra del Fuego, where there are sporadic bus services to the Argentine city of Río Grande, which has connections to Ushuaia (it's also possible to hitchhike). Direct buses travel from Punta Arenas to Ushuaia via the more northerly, more frequent and shorter ferry crossing at Primera Angostura.

Puerto Williams to Ushuaia The passenger boat service from Puerto Williams, on Isla Navarino (reached by plane or boat from Punta Arenas), to the Argentine city of Ushuaia can be sporadic, and the journey nearly impossible without a chartered boat or flight in the winter.

From Bolivia

Road connections between Bolivia and Chile have improved dramatically, with an excellent paved highway running from Arica to La Paz. The route from Iquique to Colchane is also paved – although the road beyond to Oruro is not. There are bus services on both routes, but more on the former.

It's possible to travel from Uyuni, Bolivia, to San Pedro de Atacama via the Portezuelo del Cajón but no regularly scheduled public transportation exists in this area. See p215 for details on organized trips to Uyuni.

From Peru

Getting from Chile to Peru is a piece of cake. Tacna to Arica is the only overland crossing and there is a choice of bus, *colectivo,* taxi or train. For details, see p184.

GETTING AROUND

Traveling from head to tail in Chile is child's play, with a constant procession of flights and buses connecting cities up and down the country. What is less convenient is the service widthwise and south of Puerto Montt, where the country turns into a labyrinth of fjords, glaciers and mountains. However, a few choice routes *are* being improved, new roads built (some contentious) and the railways revamped.

AIR

With fresh competition, flights have become more affordable in Chile and are sometimes cheaper than a comfortable long-distance bus. A flight will save visitors tiresome and time-consuming backtracking up and down

DOMESTIC AIR ROUTES

the country's spindly length. For instance, a flight from Arica to Santiago takes a few short hours, compared to a crippling 28 hours on board a bus. Other than taking leisurely ferries, flights are often the only option to guarantee you reach isolated regions of the south in a timely manner. Always ask the difference between round-trip fares and one-way trips, because you'll often find the former is even cheaper than the latter.

Airlines in Chile
There are three principal domestic airlines within Chile.

Air Comet (Map p99; ☎ 600-625-0000; Roger de Flor 2915, Las Condes) Formerly Aerolíneas del Sur.

Lan (☎ 600-526-2000; www.lan.com) Centro (Map p84-5; Paseo Huérfanos 926-B); Las Condes (Map p99; Av El Bosque Norte 0194); Providencia (Map pp90-1; Providencia 2006) The biggest and longest-established national carrier, with the most extensive system of connecting cities both north and south of Santiago; Lan also flies to Easter Island.

Sky Airline (Map pp80-1; ☎ 600-600-2828; www.skyair line.cl, in Spanish; Andrés de Fuenzalida 55, Providencia) Lan's main competitor, also with an impressive list of routes.

A handful of regional airlines and air-taxi services also operate, especially connecting isolated regions in the south and shuttling to the Juan Fernández archipelago. You'll find details in the relevant chapters.

Most Chilean cities are within striking distance of domestic airports with commercial air service. Santiago's Aeropuerto Internacional Arturo Merino Benítez has a separate domestic terminal; Santiago also has smaller airfields for air-taxi services to the Juan Fernández archipelago.

See p480 for an idea of which cities receive passenger flights. For domestic flights, there is a departure tax of about CH$11,000 to CH$14,000, usually included in the ticket price.

Air Passes
The best rates with **Lan** (www.lan.com) are found on its website, where weekly specials give cut-rate deals with as much as 40% off, especially on well-traveled routes such as Puerto Montt to Punta Arenas. Rates with Lan can vary dramatically according to how far in advance you book – reserving a flight three weeks in advance could save you as much as 30%. Round-trips are usually cheaper than one-way fares; especially when purchased on the internet.

The prices quoted online to Easter Island are also substantially lower than the regular rate. The internet has had its glitches though, and the agents in Lan offices are instructed not to help with any internet purchases or customer-service issues. You can ask for the telephone number for the internet service and call to confirm your purchase.

The other way to cut costs is signing up with Lan's generous frequent fliers package, called the LanPass. Lan is a member of the One World alliance, with partners such as American Airlines, British Airways, Iberia and Qantas.

Destination	Cost (round-trip, CH$)
Antofagasta	101,000
Arica	133,000
Calama	90,000
Concepción	57,000
Copiapó	59,000
Coyhaique	90,000
Iquique	130,000
La Serena	44,000
Puerto Montt	68,000
Punta Arenas	121,000
Temuco	53,000

BICYCLE
Who's afraid of a little saddle soreness? Certainly not the growing number of cyclists peddling their way through Chile. If you're thinking of joining them, a *todo terreno* (mountain bike) or touring bike with beefy tires is essential. The climate can be a real challenge: from Temuco south, it is changeable and you must be prepared for rain and occasional snow; from Santiago north, especially in the vast expanses of the Atacama Desert, water sources are infrequent and towns are separated by alarmingly long distances. In some areas the wind can slow your progress to a crawl; north to south is generally easier than south to north, but some readers report strong headwinds southbound in summer. Roads leading into the mountains are predictably challenging even for a vehicle. Chilean motorists are usually courteous, but on narrow, two-lane highways without shoulders, passing cars can be a real hazard.

Car ferries in Patagonia often charge a fee to carry a bike on, but not if it's in the back of someone's pickup; ask kindly if you see an empty back. Throughout Chile, towns have bike-repair shops.

Long-distance bus companies are usually amenable to stashing a bike in the luggage hold, although they become less sympathetic around Christmas when holds are packed with parcels. Bikes are allowed on domestic airlines and account for the one allotted piece of checked luggage if disassembled and boxed. If assembled, they are considered 1½ pieces of luggage. If you have something else to check, the bike will be considered extra luggage and will be charged by weight.

Hire

Hiring your own two wheels is easy as pie in many of Chile's more touristy towns, although the quality of rental bikes varies wildly. There are relatively few bike-rental shops, but *hospedajes* and tour agencies often have a few handy. Expect to pay between CH$5000 and CH$10,000 per day. A quality mountain bike with front suspension and decent brakes can cost CH$15,000 per day or more, but you're only likely to find them in outdoor activity destinations such as the Lakes District and San Pedro de Atacama.

It's common to leave some form of deposit or guarantee: a copy of your passport will often suffice.

Purchase

Bikes are not especially cheap in Chile. A decent mountain bike with suspension sells for CH$100,000 and up. If you're looking to sell your wheels at the end of your trip, try approaching tour agencies that rent bikes.

BOAT

Chile's preposterously long coastline is strung with a necklace of ports and harbors, but opportunities for travelers to get about by boat are concentrated in the south.

Ferry

Navigating southern Chile's jigsaw-puzzle coast by ferry is about more than just getting from A to B – it's an essential part of the travel experience. From Puerto Montt south, Chilean Patagonia and Tierra del Fuego is accessed by a web of ferry lines through an intricate maze of islands and fjords. So, while bus services south between Puerto Montt and Coyhaique must pass through Argentina, the ferries sidle down past spectacular coastal scenery.

It's important to note, however, that the end of the high season also marks limited ferry service.

Navimag's ferry service from Puerto Montt to Puerto Natales (see p319) is one of the continent's great travel experiences. The following information lists only the principal passenger ferry services. Also on offer are a few exclusive tour operators that run their own cruises; see p486. More details on the routes below are given under the respective destinations.

Catamaranes del Sur (Map pp90-1; ☎ 02-231-1902; www.catamaranesdelsur.cl; Av Pedro de Valdivia Norte 0210, Providencia)

Mar del Sur (☎ 067-231-255; Baquedano 146-A, Coyhaique)

Naviera Austral (☎ 065-270-430; www.navieraustral .cl, in Spanish; Angelmó 2187, Puerto Montt)

Navimag (Map p99; ☎ 02-442-3120; www.navimag .com; Av El Bosque Norte 0440, 11th fl, Las Condes)

Transbordador Austral Broom (☎ 061-218-100; www.tabsa.cl; Av Bulnes 05075, Punta Arenas)

Transmarchilay (☎ 065-270-000; www.transmar chilay.cl, in Spanish; Angelmó 2187, Puerto Montt)

Common routes include:

Chiloé to Chaitén Transmarchilay, Naviera Austral and Navimag run between Quellón, on Chiloé, and Chaitén in summer. There are also summer services from Castro to Chaitén.

Hornopirén to Caleta Gonzalo In the summer, Naviera Austral ferries loop around from one side of Parque Pumalín to the other at Caleta Gonzalo, about 60km north of Chaitén.

La Arena to Puelche Ferries shuttle back and forth across the gap, about 45km southeast of Puerto Montt, to connect two northerly segments of the Carretera Austral.

Mainland to Chiloé Regular ferries plug the gap between Pargua and Chacao, at the northern tip of Chiloé.

Puerto Ibáñez to Chile Chico Mar del Sur operates automobile/passenger ferries across Lago General Carrera, south of Coyhaique. There are shuttles from Chile Chico to the Argentine town of Los Antiguos.

Puerto Montt to Chaitén Naviera Austral runs carpassenger ferries from Puerto Montt to Chaitén.

Puerto Montt to Laguna San Rafael Expensive cruises with Catamaranes del Sur and Cruceros Skorpios (see p486) go direct to take a twirl about the stunning Laguna San Rafael.

Puerto Montt to Puerto Chacabuco Navimag goes from Puerto Montt to Puerto Chacabuco, with bus service continuing on to Coyhaique and Parque Nacional Laguna San Rafael.

Puerto Montt to Puerto Natales Navimag departs Puerto Montt weekly, taking about four days to puddle-

TRANSPORTATION

jump to Puerto Natales. Erratic Patagonian weather can play havoc with schedules.

Puerto Williams to Ushuaia This most necessary connection still has no regular ferry but does have regular motorboat service.

Punta Arenas to Tierra del Fuego Transbordador Austral Broom runs ferries from Punta Arenas' ferry terminal Tres Puentes to Porvenir; from Punta Delgada, east of Punta Arenas, to Bahía Azul; and from Tres Puentes to Puerto Williams, on Isla Navarino.

BUS

Long-distance buses in Chile have an enviable reputation for punctuality, efficiency and comfort, although prices and classes vary significantly between companies. Most Chilean cities have a central bus terminal but in some the companies have separate offices, usually within a few blocks of each other. The bus stations are well organized with destinations, schedules and fares prominently displayed. Major highways and some others are paved (except for large parts of the Carretera Austral south of Puerto Montt), but many secondary roads are gravel or dirt. Long-distance buses generally have toilet facilities and often serve coffee, tea and even meals on board; if not, they make regular stops. By European or North American standards, fares are a bargain. On Chile's back roads transportation is slower and buses (micros) are less frequent, older and more basic.

The nerve center of the country, Santiago, has four main bus terminals, from which buses leave to northern, central and southern destinations.

Chile's biggest bus company is **Tur Bus** (Map pp80–1; ☎ 600-660-6600; www.turbus.cl, in Spanish), with an all-embracing network of services around the country. It is known for being extremely punctual. Discounts are given for tickets purchased online (you then have to retrieve your ticket at the counter). The Tur Bus club card provides a 10% discount on one-way fares, and a point collection system that adds up to free trips. You can join at any Tur Bus office.

Its main competitor is **Pullman** (Map pp80–1; ☎ 600-320-3200; www.pullman.cl, in Spanish), which also has extensive routes throughout the country. The Pullman Pass loyalty card offers much the same benefits as that of Tur Bus.

Specifically aimed at backpackers, **Pacha-mama by Bus** (☎ 02-688-8018; www.pachamamabybus .com; Agustinas 2113, Barrio Brasil) is a hop-on hop-off service with two long routes exploring the

north and south respectively. It's not cheap (for example, it costs CH$106,000/134,000 for a seven-day pass in the south/north of Chile), but it takes you straight to many out-of-the-way national parks and other attractions not accessible by public transport. It also offers pick-up and drop-off at your chosen hostel, and camping equipment at isolated overnight stops.

Argentina's **Chalten Travel** (www.chaltentravel.com) provides transportation between El Calafate and Torres del Paine and on Argentina's Ruta 40. Services are planned to expand throughout Chilean Patagonia – check the website for information.

Classes

An array of bewildering names denotes the different levels of comfort on long-distance buses. For a classic experience, *clásico* or *pullman* has around 46 ordinary seats that barely recline, two on each side of the aisle. Don't expect great bathrooms. The next step up is *executivo* and then comes *semi-cama*, both usually mean around 38 seats, providing extra legroom and calf rests. *Semi-cama* has plusher seats that recline more fully and buses are sometimes double-decker. The pinnacle of luxury, *salón cama* sleepers seat only 24 passengers, with only three seats per row that almost fully recline. Superexclusive infrequent *premium* services enjoy seats that flatten with fold-down leg rests to resemble a flat bed. Note that movie quality does not improve with comfort level. On overnighters breakfast is usually included but you can save a few bucks by not ordering dinner and bringing a deli picnic. If you have any doubt about the type of service offered, ask for a seating diagram.

Normally departing at night, the *salón cama* and *premium* bus services cost upwards of 50% more than ordinary buses, but you'll be thankful on long-haul trips. Regular buses are also comfortable, especially in comparison to the chicken buses of neighboring Peru and Bolivia. Smoking is prohibited on all buses.

Costs

Fares vary dramatically among companies and classes, so shop around. Promotions (*ofertas*) outside the high summer season can reduce normal fares by half and student fares by 25%.

Reservations

Except during the holiday season (Christmas, January, February, Easter and mid-September's patriotic holidays), it is rarely necessary to book more than a few hours in advance. On very long trips, like Arica to Santiago, or rural routes with limited services (along the Carretera Austral, for instance), advance booking is a good idea.

CAR & MOTORCYCLE

Having your own wheels is not only liberating but often necessary to get to remote national parks and most places off the beaten track. This is especially true in areas such as the Atacama Desert and the Carretera Austral. Hiring a car is easily the best way to scoot around on Easter Island. Security problems are minor, but always lock your vehicle and leave valuables out of sight. Note that, because of smog problems, there are frequent restrictions on private vehicle use in Santiago and the surrounding region (see opposite).

The annual Turistel guides (p469) are a great source of recent changes, particularly with regard to newly paved roads, as well as maps of most significant cities, towns and even villages.

Automobile Associations

The **Automóvil Club de Chile** (Acchi; Map pp90-1; ☎ 600-464-4040, 02-431-1000; www.automovilclub.cl, in Spanish; Andres Bello 1863, Santiago) has offices in most major Chilean cities, provides useful information, sells highway maps and rents cars. It also offers member services and grants discounts to members of its foreign counterparts, such as the American Automobile Association (AAA) in the USA or the Automobile Association (AA) in the UK. Membership includes free towing and other roadside services within 25km of an Automóvil Club office.

Bring Your Own Vehicle

Given its openness toward foreign trade and tourism, Chile is one of the best countries on the continent to ship an overseas vehicle to. Check your local phone directory under Automobile Transporters, and when shipping do not leave anything of value in the vehicle.

Permits for temporarily imported tourist vehicles may be extended beyond the initial 90-day period, but it can be easier to cross the border into Argentina and return with new paperwork.

For shipping a car from Chile back to your home country, try the consolidator **Ultramar** (☎ 02-630-1000; www.ultramar.cl).

Driver's License

Bring along an International Driving Permit as well as the license from your home country. Some rental-car agencies don't require an IDP, but others do, so it's best to have one on hand. Police at highway checkpoints or on the road are generally firm but courteous and fair, with a much higher reputation for personal integrity than most Latin American police. *Never* attempt to bribe them.

Fuel & Spare Parts

The price of *bencina* (gasoline) starts from about CH$800 per liter, depending on the grade, while *gas-oil* (diesel fuel) costs less. The 93-octane *común* is available in both unleaded *(sin plomo)* and leaded *(con plomo)*, while 95- and 97-octane grades are invariably unleaded.

Even the smallest of hamlets always seem to have at least one competent and resourceful mechanic.

Hire

Major international rental agencies like **Hertz** (☎ 02-601-0477; www.hertz.com), **Avis** (☎ 600-368-2000; www.avischile.cl) and **Budget** (☎ 02-598-3200; www.budget.cl) have offices in Santiago (see p114 for more information), as well as in major cities and tourist areas. The Automóvil Club de Chile also rents cars at some locations. To rent a car you must have a valid international driver's license, be at least 25 years of age (some younger readers have managed to rent cars, however) and have either a major credit card (such as MasterCard or Visa) or a large cash deposit. Travelers from the USA, Canada, Germany and Australia are not required to have an international driver's license to rent a car but, to avoid confusion, it is best to carry one.

Even at smaller agencies, rental charges are high, with the smallest vehicles going for about US$38 to US$103 per day with 150km to 200km included, or sometimes with unlimited mileage. Adding the cost of any extra insurance, petrol and the crippling 19% IVA *(impuesto de valor agregado)*, the value-added tax (VAT), it becomes very pricey to operate a rental vehicle. Weekend or weekly rates, with unlimited mileage, are a better bargain.

One-way rentals can be awkward or impossible to arrange. Some companies will arrange such rentals but with a substantial drop-off charge (the long-distance average is US$209). With smaller local agencies this is next to impossible. Some smaller agencies will, however, usually arrange paperwork for taking cars into Argentina, so long as the car is returned to the original office. There may be a substantial charge for taking a car into Argentina and extra insurance must be acquired.

When traveling in remote areas, where fuel may not be readily available, carry extra fuel. Rental agencies often provide a spare *bidón* (fuel container) for this purpose.

Insurance

All vehicles must carry *seguro obligatorio* (minimum insurance) and additional liability insurance is highly desirable. Car-hire companies offer the necessary insurance. Check if there are any limitations to your policy. Traveling on a dirt road is usually fine (indeed necessary in many parts of the country), but off-roading is strictly off limits. Check before renting to see if your credit card includes some sort of car-rental insurance.

Purchase

For a trip of several months, purchasing a car merits consideration; reselling the car afterwards can potentially save you a packet on rentals. However, any used car is a risk, especially on Chile's axle-breaking back roads. Imported vehicles (the vast majority in Chile) also tend to cost more than in Europe or the USA.

Once purchased, you must change the vehicle's title within 30 days or risk a hefty fine; you can do this through any notary by requesting a *compraventa* for about CH$5000. You'll need a RUT (Rol Unico Tributario) tax identification number, available through **Impuestos Internos** (www.sii.cl, in Spanish), the Chilean tax office; issuance takes about 10 days. In order to go into Argentina, special insurance is required (try any insurance agency; the cost is about CH$10,000 for 10 days). If you buy a car in Chile you are not allowed to sell it abroad.

Note that, while many inexpensive vehicles are for sale in the duty-free zones of Regionés I and XII (Tarapacá and Magallanes), only legal permanent residents of those regions may take a vehicle outside of those regions, for a maximum of 90 days per calendar year.

Road Conditions

The Panamericana has undergone substantial improvements, especially in central Chile, but it comes at a cost: toll booths *(peajes)* now chop the highway into paying sections. There are two types: tolls you pay to use a distance of the highway (CH$400 to CH$1500), and the tolls you pay to get off the highway to access a lateral to a town or city (CH$500). Paying the former sometimes voids the need to pay the latter.

Costs rise the closer you get to Santiago. For example, the journey from Santiago to La Serena (474km) costs around CH$10,000 in tolls, yet there are no tolls from La Serena to Arica (1588km). You'll find a list of tolls (in Spanish) on www.turistel.cl.

You'll notice distance markers every 5km along Chile's two major roads, the Panamericana and the Carretera Austral, and you may be given directions that refer to these kilometer markers.

Road Hazards

Stray dogs wander around on the roads – even highways – with alarming regularity, and visitors from European and North American countries are frequently disconcerted by how pedestrians use the motorway as a sidewalk.

Road Rules

Chilean drivers are restrained in comparison to the horn-happy racers of many South American countries; they are especially courteous to pedestrians. However, city drivers have a reputation for jumping red lights and failing to signal, so keep your wits about you. Driving after dark is not recommended, especially in rural areas in southern Chile, where pedestrians, domestic animals and wooden carts are difficult to see on or near the highways. If you are involved in an automobile accident, see p468. Chile's police enforce speed limits with CH$35,000 fines; bribing them is not an option.

There are additional rules for those intending to drive in Santiago. When the smog is really bad, cars are subject to *restricción vehicular* (vehicular restrictions). The system works according to the last digits on a vehicle's license plates: the chosen numbers are announced in the news on the day before those vehicles will be subject to restrictions. You'll receive fines for driving a car in Santiago if you ignore the restrictions. There are more details and current restrictions on www.uoct.cl (in Spanish).

HITCHHIKING

Thumbing a ride is common practice in Chile, and this is one of the safest countries in Latin America to do it. However, a major drawback is that Chilean vehicles are often packed with families, and a wait for a lift can be long. Some backpackers try to solicit rides at *servicentros* (service centers) on the outskirts of Chilean cities on the Panamericana, where truckers gas up their vehicles. That said, hitchhiking is never entirely safe, and Lonely Planet does not recommend it. People who do choose to risk hitchhiking will be safer if they travel in pairs and let someone know of their plans.

In Patagonia, where distances are great and vehicles few, hitchhikers should expect long waits and carry warm, windproof clothing. In the Atacama you may wait for some time, but almost every ride will be a long one. It's also a good idea to carry some snack food and plenty of water, especially in the desert north.

LOCAL TRANSPORTATION

Bus

Even small towns usually have a chaotic jumble of bus routes that can be intimidating to the novice rider. Prices are extremely cheap (around CH$250 for a short trip). Buses (*micros*) are clearly numbered and usually carry a placard indicating their final destination. Since many identically numbered buses serve slightly different routes, pay attention to these placards. On boarding, mention your final destination and the driver will tell you the fare and give you a ticket. Do not lose this ticket, which may be checked en route. Buses are often crammed with jostling people, so keep an eye on your pockets and bags.

Santiago's reformed bus system, **Transantiago** (www.transantiagoinforma.cl), has brand-new buses with automatic fare machines although passengers now complain about the long wait between buses. You can map your route online. For details see p114.

Colectivo

Nearly all Chilean cities have handy *taxi colectivos*, which resemble normal taxis but run on fixed routes much like buses: you'll see a roof sign or placard in the window indicating the destination. They are fast, comfortable and not a great deal more expensive than buses (usually CH$300 to CH$500 within a city).

Commuter Rail

Both Santiago and Valparaíso have commuter rail networks. The former is the modern *metrotren* line running from San Fernando through Rancagua, capital of Región VI, to Estación Central, on the Alameda in Santiago; while the latter runs between Viña del Mar and Valparaíso. For details, see the respective city entries.

Metro

Santiago is blessed with a superefficient subway, the Metro. It is clean, cheap and fast expanding. For details, see p114.

Taxi

Most Chilean cabs are metered, but fares vary. In Santiago it costs CH$200 to *bajar la bandera* ('lower the flag'), plus CH$80 per 200m. Each cab carries a placard indicating its authorized fare.

In some towns, such as Viña del Mar, cabs may cost twice as much. In others, such as Coquimbo, meters are less common, so it is wise to agree upon a fare in advance. Taxis may charge more late at night. Tipping is not necessary, but you may tell the driver to keep small change.

TOURS

Adventure tour operators have mushroomed throughout Chile; most have offices in Santiago and seasonal offices in the location of their trips. There are many more listed in regional chapters throughout the book.

Altué Active Travel (☎ 02-235-1519; www.altue.com) One of Chile's pioneer adventure tourism agencies: it covers almost any outdoor activity but specialties include sea kayaking and cultural trips in Chiloé.

Austral Adventures (☎ 065-625-977; www.austral -adventures.com) Specializes in cruises around the Pumalín fjords, fishing, kayaking and customized cultural trips around Chiloé.

Azimut 360 (☎ 02-235-1519; www.azimut.cl) Offers volcano climbing, mountain biking and sightseeing in the northern altiplano, as well as multiactivity trips in Patagonia.

Cruceros Australis (☎ 02-442-3110; www.australis .com) Runs large luxury cruises between Punta Arenas and Ushuaia – a trip that lasts five days.

Cruceros Skorpios (☎ 065-252-996; www.skorpios cruises.com; Av Angelmó 1660, Puerto Montt) Arranges slick luxury cruises from Puerto Montt and Puerto Chacabuco to Laguna San Rafael, stopping in its own private reserve with hot springs. More southerly cruises include Puerto Natales.

Explora (☎ 02-206-6060; www.explora.com) Exclusive resorts in Parque Nacional Torres del Paine, Easter Island and San Pedro de Atacama, with all-inclusive packages with swish accommodations and excursions.

Opentravel (☎ 065-260-524; www.opentravel.cl) Offers excellent trekking trips and horseback-riding adventures to remote areas in Northern Patagonia and across the Andes to Argentina.

Pared Sur (☎ 02-207-3525; www.paredsur.cl) This is all about mountain biking, with a wide variety of challenges throughout Chile.

Patagonia Connection (☎ 02-225-6489; www .patagonia-connection.com) Sells luxury spa packages in Northern Patagonia and trips along the Carretera Austral or to Laguna San Rafael via catamaran.

Trails of Chile (☎ 065-330-737; www.trailsofchile.cl) Specializes in top-shelf, professional tours and adventure travel with excellent service.

Yak Expediciones (☎ 02-227-0427; www.yakexpedi ciones.cl) Takes small groups sea kayaking and white-water rafting.

TRAIN

Chile's railroads blossomed in the late 19th century courtesy of the country's rich mines. In the early 20th century thousands of hectares of native forest were felled to make way for lines running from Santiago to Puerto Montt. Yet, despite the early investment and sacrifices, Chile's train system went into decline for a century and most tracks now lie neglected or abandoned.

The promised railway renovations south of Santiago haven't made it past Chillán. There is service throughout Middle Chile, however, and a *metrotren* service goes from Santiago as far as San Fernando (see opposite).

Train travel has fewer departures and is slower and more expensive than bus travel. See p113 for details and prices or check the website of **Empresa de Ferrocarriles del Estado** (EFE; ☎ 600-585-5000; www.efe.cl, in Spanish).

There are no long-distance passenger services north of Santiago. It's difficult but not impossible to travel by freight from Baquedano (on the Panamericana northeast of Antofagasta) to the border town of Socompa, and on to Salta, in Argentina.

TRANSPORTATION

Health Dr David Goldberg

CONTENTS

Before You Go 488
Insurance 488
Internet Resources 488
Recommended Immunizations 489
Further Reading 489
In Transit 489
Deep Vein Thrombosis 489
Jet Lag & Motion Sickness 489
In Chile 490
Availability & Cost of Health Care 490
Infectious Diseases 490
Travelers' Diarrhea 492
Environmental Hazards 492
Traveling with Children 494
Traveling while Pregnant 494

HEALTH

Prevention is the key to staying healthy while traveling abroad. Travelers who receive the recommended vaccines and follow the basic, commonsense precautions usually come away with nothing more than a little diarrhea.

Medically speaking there are two South Americas: tropical South America, which includes most of the continent except for the southernmost portion, and temperate South America, which includes Chile, Uruguay, southern Argentina, as well as the Falkland Islands. In the temperate South America zone, most infections are related to the consumption of contaminated food and beverages. Mosquito-borne illnesses such as malaria, yellow fever and dengue fever are generally not a problem in this region.

BEFORE YOU GO

Bring medications in their original containers, clearly labeled. A signed, dated letter from your physician describing all medical conditions and medications, including generic names, is also a good idea. If carrying syringes or needles be sure to have a physician's letter documenting their medical necessity.

INSURANCE

If your health insurance does not cover you for medical expenses abroad, consider supplemental insurance (check Bookings & Services on www.lonelyplanet.com for more information). Find out in advance if your insurance plan will make payments directly to providers or reimburse you later for overseas health expenditures.

INTERNET RESOURCES

There is a wealth of travel health advice on the internet. For further information, the **Lonely Planet website** (www.lonelyplanet.com) is a good place to start. The **World Health Organization** (WHO; www.who.int/ith/) publishes a superb book called *International Travel*

MEDICAL CHECKLIST

- Antibiotics
- Antidiarrhea drugs (eg loperamide)
- Acetaminophen (Tylenol) or aspirin
- Anti-inflammatory drugs (eg ibuprofen)
- Antihistamines (for hay fever and allergic reactions)
- Antibacterial ointment (eg Bactroban) for cuts and abrasions
- Steroid cream or cortisone (for poison ivy and other allergic rashes)
- Bandages, gauze, gauze rolls
- Adhesive or paper tape
- Scissors, safety pins, tweezers
- Thermometer
- Pocket knife
- DEET-containing insect repellent for the skin
- Permethrin-containing insect spray for clothing, tents and bed nets
- Sunblock
- Oral rehydration salts
- Iodine tablets (for water purification)
- Syringes and sterile needles

Vaccine	Recommended for	Dosage	Side effects
chickenpox	travelers who've never had chickenpox	2 doses 1 month apart	fever; mild case of chickenpox
hepatitis A	all travelers	1 dose before trip; booster 6-12 months later	soreness at injection site; headaches; body aches
hepatitis B	long-term travelers in close contact with the local population	3 doses over 6-month period	soreness at injection site; low-grade fever
measles	travelers who have never had measles or completed a vaccination course	1 dose	fever; rash; joint pains; allergic reactions
rabies	travelers who may have contact with animals and may not have access to medical care	3 doses over 3- to 4-week period	soreness at injection site; headaches; body aches
tetanus-diphtheria	all travelers who haven't had booster within 10 years	1 dose lasts 10 years	soreness at injection site
typhoid	all travelers	4 capsules by mouth, 1 taken every other day	abdominal pain; nausea; rash

and Health, which is revised annually and is available online at no cost. Another website of general interest is **MD Travel Health** (www.mdtravelhealth.com), which provides complete travel health recommendations for every country, updated daily, also at no cost.

It's usually a good idea to consult your government's travel health website before departure, if one is available.
Australia (www.dfat.gov.au/travel/)
Canada (www.travelhealth.gc.ca)
UK (www.nhs.uk/Healthcareabroad/Pages/Healthcareabroad.aspx)
United States (www.cdc.gov/travel/)

RECOMMENDED IMMUNIZATIONS

Since most vaccines don't produce immunity until at least two weeks after they're given, visit a physician four to eight weeks before departure. Ask your doctor for an International Certificate of Vaccination (otherwise known as the yellow booklet), which will list all the vaccinations you've received. This is mandatory for countries that require proof of yellow fever vaccination upon entry, but it's a good idea to carry it wherever you travel.

No vaccines are required for Chile, but several are recommended.

FURTHER READING

For further information see *Healthy Travel Central & South America*, also from Lonely Planet. If you're traveling with children,

Lonely Planet's *Travel with Children* may be useful. The *ABC of Healthy Travel,* by E Walker et al, is another valuable resource.

IN TRANSIT

DEEP VEIN THROMBOSIS

Blood clots may form in the legs (deep vein thrombosis) during plane flights, chiefly because of prolonged immobility. The longer the flight, the greater the risk. Though most blood clots are reabsorbed uneventfully, some may break off and travel through the blood vessels to the lungs, where they could cause life-threatening complications.

The chief symptom of deep vein thrombosis is swelling or pain of the foot, ankle or calf, usually but not always on just one side. When a blood clot travels to the lungs it may cause chest pain and difficulty breathing. Travelers with any of these symptoms should immediately seek medical attention.

To prevent the development of deep vein thrombosis on long flights you should walk about the cabin, perform isometric compressions of the leg muscles (ie contract the leg muscles while sitting), drink plenty of fluids, and avoid alcohol and tobacco.

JET LAG & MOTION SICKNESS

Jet lag is common when crossing more than five time zones, resulting in insomnia, fatigue,

HEALTH

malaise or nausea. To avoid jet lag try drinking plenty of fluids (nonalcoholic) and eating light meals. Upon arrival, get exposure to natural sunlight and readjust your schedule (for meals, sleep etc) as soon as possible.

Antihistamines such as dimenhydrinate (Dramamine) and meclizine (Antivert, Bonine) are usually the first choice for treating motion sickness. Their main side-effect is drowsiness. A herbal alternative is ginger, which works like a charm for some people.

IN CHILE

AVAILABILITY & COST OF HEALTH CARE

There are two modern facilities in Santiago that offer 24-hour walk-in service for urgent problems, as well as specialty care (by appointment) and inpatient services: **Clínica Las Condes** (☎ 210-4000; Lo Fontecilla 441, Las Condes) and **Clínica Alemana** (☎ 212-9700; Av Vitacura 5951, Vitacura). For a list of additional physicians, dentists and laboratories in Santiago, go to the **US Embassy website** (http://santiago.usembassy.gov).

The medical care in Santiago and Valparaiso is generally good, but it may be difficult to find assistance in remote areas. Most doctors and hospitals expect payment in cash, regardless of whether you have travel health insurance.

If you develop a life-threatening medical problem you'll probably want to be evacuated to a country with state-of-the-art medical care. Since this may cost tens of thousands of dollars, be sure you have insurance to cover this before you depart. You can find a list of medical evacuation and travel insurance companies on the US State Department website at http://travel.state.gov.

Most pharmacies in Chile are well stocked and the pharmacists are fully trained. The quality of medications is generally comparable to that found in industrialized countries. Many drugs that require a prescription elsewhere are available over the counter in Chile. If you're taking any medication on a regular basis be sure you know its generic (scientific) name since many pharmaceuticals go under different names in Chile.

Medical care on Easter Island is extremely limited. There is a hospital but the quality of care is unreliable and supplies are often inadequate. Serious medical problems require evacuation to the mainland.

INFECTIOUS DISEASES

Hepatitis A

Hepatitis A is the second most common travel-related infection (after travelers' diarrhea). It's a viral infection of the liver that is usually acquired by ingestion of contaminated water, food or ice, though it may also be acquired by direct contact with infected persons. The illness occurs throughout the world, but the incidence is higher in developing nations. Symptoms may include fever, malaise, jaundice, nausea, vomiting and abdominal pain. Most cases resolve without complications, though hepatitis A occasionally causes severe liver damage. There is no treatment.

The vaccine for hepatitis A is extremely safe and highly effective. If you get a booster six to 12 months after your first, it lasts for at least 10 years. You really should get it before you go to Chile or any other developing nation. Because the safety of the hepatitis A vaccine has not been established for pregnant women or children under the age of two, they should instead be given a gammaglobulin injection.

Hepatitis B

Like hepatitis A, hepatitis B is a liver infection that occurs worldwide but is more common in developing nations. Unlike hepatitis A, the disease is usually acquired by sexual contact or by exposure to infected blood, generally through blood transfusions or contaminated needles. The vaccine is recommended only for long-term travelers (on the road more than six months) who expect to live in rural areas or have close physical contact with the local population. Additionally, the vaccine is recommended for anyone who anticipates sexual contact with the local inhabitants or a possible need for medical, dental or other treatments while abroad, especially if a need for transfusions or injections is expected.

Hepatitis B vaccine is safe and highly effective. However, a total of three injections is necessary to establish full immunity. Several countries added hepatitis B vaccine to the list of routine childhood immunizations in the 1980s, so many young adults are already protected.

Typhoid Fever

Typhoid fever is caused by ingestion of food or water contaminated by a species of *Salmonella* known as *Salmonella typhi*. Fever occurs in virtually all cases. Other symptoms may include headache, malaise, muscle aches, dizziness, loss of appetite, nausea and abdominal pain. Either diarrhea or constipation may occur. Possible complications include intestinal perforation, intestinal bleeding, confusion, delirium or (rarely) coma.

Unless you expect to take all your meals in major hotels and restaurants, a typhoid vaccine is a good idea. It's usually given orally, but is also available as an injection. Neither vaccine is approved for use in children under two years of age.

The drug of choice for typhoid fever is usually a quinolone antibiotic such as ciprofloxacin (Cipro) or levofloxacin (Levaquin), which many travelers carry for treatment of travelers' diarrhea. However, if you self-treat for typhoid fever you may also need to self-treat for malaria, since the symptoms of the two diseases can be indistinguishable.

Rabies

Rabies is a viral infection of the brain and spinal cord that is almost always fatal. The rabies virus is carried in the saliva of infected animals and is typically transmitted through an animal bite, though contamination of any break in the skin with infected saliva may result in rabies. Rabies occurs in all South American countries.

The rabies vaccine is safe, but a full series requires three injections and is quite expensive. Those at high risk for rabies, such as animal handlers and spelunkers (cave explorers), should certainly get the vaccine. In addition, those at lower risk for animal bites should consider asking for the vaccine if they might be traveling to remote areas and might not have access to appropriate medical care if needed. The treatment for a possibly rabid bite consists of the rabies vaccine with rabies immune globulin. It's effective, but must be given promptly. Most travelers don't need the rabies vaccine.

All animal bites and scratches must be promptly and thoroughly cleansed with large amounts of soap and water and local health authorities contacted to determine whether or not further treatment is necessary (see p493).

Other Infections
ANTHRAX
Anthrax is an occupational hazard among those working with farm animals. The infec-

tion begins as a small raised area on the skin that ulcerates and turns black. (The name anthrax is derived from the Greek word for coal.) When untreated the illness may be complicated by high fevers, swelling of the area around the ulcer and enlargement of nearby lymph nodes. Anthrax usually responds well to treatment with either doxycycline or ciprofloxacin (Cipro).

BARTONELLOSIS (OROYA FEVER)
This is carried by sandflies in the arid river valleys on the western slopes of the Andes, between altitudes of 800m and 3000m. (Curiously, it's not found anywhere else in the world.) The chief symptoms are fever and severe body pains. Complications may include marked anemia, enlargement of the liver and spleen, and sometimes death. The drug of choice is chloramphenicol, though doxycycline is also effective.

BRUCELLOSIS
An infection of domestic and wild animals that may be transmitted to humans through direct animal contact or by consumption of unpasteurized dairy products from infected animals. Symptoms may include fever, malaise, depression, loss of appetite, headache, muscle aches and back pain. Complications may include arthritis, hepatitis, meningitis and endocarditis (heart-valve infection).

CHOLERA
Cholera is extremely rare in Chile. An outbreak occurred in the northern part of the country in January 1998, but no cases have been reported since that time. The cholera vaccine is not recommended.

DENGUE FEVER
This fever was reported for the first time in March 2002 from Easter Island, but has not been observed in the years since then. Dengue is a flulike illness that is sometimes complicated by hemorrhage or shock. The disease is transmitted by Aedes mosquitoes, which bite primarily in the daytime and favor densely populated areas, though they also inhabit rural environments. There is no treatment for dengue except to take analgesics such as acetaminophen/paracetamol (Tylenol) and drink plenty of fluids. Severe cases may require hospitalization for intravenous fluids and supportive care. There is no vaccine. The

cornerstone of prevention is insect protection measures (opposite).

ECHINOCOCCUS
Echinococcus is a parasite that infects the liver, usually in people who work with sheep.

FASCIOLIASIS
Fascioliasis is a parasitic infection that is typically acquired by eating contaminated watercress grown in sheep-raising areas. Early symptoms may include fever, nausea, vomiting and painful enlargement of the liver.

HANTAVIRUS PULMONARY SYNDROME
A rapidly progressive, life-threatening infection acquired through exposure to the excretion of wild rodents. An outbreak was reported from rural areas in the southern and central parts of Chile in late 2001. Sporadic cases have been reported since that time. The disease occurs in those who live in close association with rodents.

It is unlikely to affect most travelers, though those staying in forest areas may be at risk. Backpackers should never camp in an abandoned *refugio* (cabin or hut), where there may be a risk of exposure to infected excretion. Pitching a tent is the safer option. If backpacking in an area with hanta virus, campers can get more information from ranger stations.

HIV/AIDS
HIV/AIDS has been reported from all South American countries. Be sure to use condoms for all sexual encounters.

LOUSE-BORNE TYPHUS
This infection occurs in mountain areas.

MAREA ROJA
For information on Marea Roja (Red Tide), a disease that results from bloomed algae being absorbed by shellfish, see p323.

TRAVELERS' DIARRHEA
To prevent diarrhea, avoid tap water unless it has been boiled, filtered, or chemically disinfected (iodine tablets); only eat fresh fruits or vegetables if cooked or peeled; be wary of dairy products that might contain unpasteurized milk; and be highly selective when eating food from street vendors.

If you develop diarrhea, be sure to drink plenty of fluids, preferably an oral rehydration solution containing lots of salt and sugar. A few loose stools don't require treatment but if you start having more than four or five stools a day you should start taking an antibiotic (usually a quinolone drug) and an antidiarrhea agent (such as loperamide). If diarrhea is bloody or persists for more than 72 hours or is accompanied by fever, shaking chills or severe abdominal pain you should seek medical attention.

ENVIRONMENTAL HAZARDS
Altitude Sickness
Altitude sickness may develop in those who ascend rapidly to altitudes greater than 2500m. Being physically fit offers no protection. Those who have experienced altitude sickness in the past are prone to future episodes. The risk increases with faster ascents, higher altitudes and greater exertion. Symptoms may include headaches, nausea, vomiting, dizziness, malaise, insomnia and loss of appetite. Severe cases may be complicated by fluid in the lungs (high-altitude pulmonary edema) or swelling of the brain (high-altitude cerebral edema).

The best treatment for altitude sickness is descent. If you are exhibiting symptoms, do not ascend. If symptoms are severe or persistent, descend immediately.

One option for prevention of altitude sickness is to take acetazolamide (Diamox). The recommended dosage ranges from 125mg (twice daily) to 250mg (three times daily). It should be taken 24 hours before ascent and continued for 48 hours after arrival at altitude.

Possible side effects include increased urinary volume, numbness, tingling, nausea, drowsiness, myopia and temporary impotence. Acetazolamide should not be given to pregnant women or anyone with a history of sulfa allergy. For those who cannot tolerate acetazolamide, the next best option is 4mg dexamethasone taken four times daily. Unlike acetazolamide, dexamethasone must be tapered gradually upon arrival at altitude, since there is a risk that altitude sickness will occur as the dosage is reduced. Dexamethasone is a steroid, so it should not be given to diabetics or anyone for whom steroids are contraindicated. A natural alternative is gingko, which some people find quite helpful.

When traveling to high altitudes, it's also important to avoid overexertion, eat light meals and abstain from alcohol.

If your symptoms are more than mild or don't resolve promptly, see a doctor. Altitude sickness should be taken seriously; it can be life threatening when severe.

Animal Bites

Do not attempt to pet, handle or feed any animal, with the exception of domestic animals known to be free of any infectious disease. Most animal injuries are directly related to a person's attempt to touch or feed the animal.

Any bite or scratch by a mammal, including bats, should be promptly and thoroughly cleansed with large amounts of soap and water, followed by application of an antiseptic such as iodine or alcohol. The local health authorities should be contacted immediately for possible postexposure rabies treatment, whether or not you've been immunized against rabies. It may also be advisable to start an antibiotic, since wounds caused by animal bites and scratches frequently become infected. One of the newer quinolones, such as levofloxacin (Levaquin), which many travelers carry in case of diarrhea, would be an appropriate choice.

Chilean Recluse Spider

The Chilean recluse spider (*Loxosceles laeta*) is found throughout the country. Although they are generally not aggressive, these spiders often hide in clothes or bedding and bite the unsuspecting person who disturbs them. Their venom is very dangerous: reactions can include lesions, renal failure and even death. Chilean recluse spiders are 8mm to 30mm long (including their legs) and can be identified by their brown color, violinlike markings and unusual six eyes (most spiders have eight), though if you're close enough to count their eyes you're probably too close. Always check your clothes before putting them on, your bed before getting in, and don't leave your clothes on the floor. If bitten, put ice on the bite and get immediate medical attention.

Cold Exposure

Cold exposure may be a significant problem in the Andes, particularly at night. Be sure to dress warmly, stay dry, keep active, consume plenty of food and water, get enough rest, and avoid alcohol, caffeine and tobacco. Watch out for the 'umbles' – stumbles, mumbles, fumbles, and grumbles – which are important signs of impending hypothermia.

Mosquito Bites

To prevent mosquito bites, wear long sleeves, long pants, hats and shoes (rather than sandals). Bring along a good insect repellent, preferably one containing DEET, which should be applied to exposed skin and clothing, but not to eyes, mouth, cuts, wounds or irritated skin. Products containing lower concentrations of DEET are as effective, but for shorter periods of time. In general, adults and children over 12 should use preparations containing 25% to 35% DEET, which usually lasts about six hours. Children between two and 12 years of age should use preparations containing no more than 10% DEET, applied sparingly, which will usually last about three hours. Neurologic toxicity has been reported from DEET, especially in children, but appears to be extremely uncommon and generally related to overuse. DEET-containing compounds should not be used on children under the age of two.

Insect repellents containing certain botanical products, including oil of eucalyptus and soybean oil, are effective but last only 1½ to two hours. DEET-containing repellents are preferable for areas where there is a high risk of malaria or yellow fever. Products based on citronella are not effective.

For additional protection you can apply permethrin to clothing, shoes, tents, and bed nets. Permethrin treatments are safe and remain effective for at least two weeks, even when items are laundered. Permethrin should not be applied directly to skin.

Don't sleep with the window open unless there is a screen. If sleeping outdoors or in accommodations that allow entry of mosquitoes, use a bed net, preferably treated with permethrin, with edges tucked in under the mattress. The mesh size should be less than 1.5mm. If the sleeping area is not otherwise protected, use a mosquito coil, which will fill the room with insecticide through the night. Repellent-impregnated wristbands are not effective.

Snake Bites

Snakes and leeches are a hazard in some parts of South America. In the event of a venomous snake bite, place the victim at rest, keep

HEALTH

TRADITIONAL REMEDIES	
Problem	**Treatment**
altitude sickness	gingko
jet lag	melatonin
motion sickness	ginger
mosquito-bite prevention	oil of eucalyptus; soybean oil

the bitten area immobilized, and move the victim immediately to the nearest medical facility. Avoid tourniquets, which are no longer recommended. There are no snakes on Easter Island.

Sun

To protect yourself from excessive sun exposure, try to stay out of the midday sun, wear sunglasses and a wide-brimmed sun hat, and apply sunscreen with SPF 15 or higher, with both UVA and UVB protection. Sunscreen should be generously applied to all exposed parts of the body approximately 30 minutes before sun exposure and should be reapplied after swimming or vigorous activity. Travelers should also drink plenty of fluids and avoid strenuous exercise when the temperature is high.

Water

The tap water in Chile's cities is generally safe but has a high mineral content that can cause stomach upsets; bottled water is a good idea for delicate stomachs and in rural areas.

Vigorous boiling for one minute is the most effective means of water purification. At altitudes greater than 2000m, boil for three minutes.

Another option is to disinfect water with iodine pills. Instructions are usually enclosed and should be carefully followed. Or you can add 2% tincture of iodine to one quart or liter of water (five drops to clear water, 10 drops to cloudy water) and let it stand for 30 minutes. If the water is cold, longer times may

be required. The taste of iodinated water may be improved by adding vitamin C (ascorbic acid). Iodinated water should not be consumed for more than a few weeks. Pregnant women, people with a history of thyroid disease and those allergic to iodine should not drink iodinated water.

A number of water filters are on the market. Those with smaller pores (reverse osmosis filters) provide the broadest protection, but they are relatively large and are readily plugged by debris. Those with somewhat larger pores (microstrainer filters) are ineffective against viruses, although they remove other organisms. Manufacturers' instructions must be carefully followed.

The Steripen, a new product on the market, purifies water with a laser pen. While it isn't cheap, it is light and convenient. Campers can find it at outdoor stores.

TRAVELING WITH CHILDREN

When traveling with young children, be particularly careful about what you allow them to eat and drink, because diarrhea can be especially dangerous in this age group and because the vaccines for hepatitis A and typhoid fever are not approved for use in children under the age of two. It's sometimes appropriate to give children some of their routine vaccines a little early before visiting a developing nation. You should discuss this with your pediatrician.

TRAVELING WHILE PREGNANT

Travel to Chile is generally safe during pregnancy, but pregnant travelers should be sure to avoid any questionable food or beverages. Before departure check the **US Embassy website** (http://santiago.usembassy.gov) to find the name of one or two English-speaking obstetricians, just in case. However, medical facilities will probably not be comparable to those in your home country. In general, it's safer to avoid travel to Chile late in pregnancy, so you don't have to deliver there.

Language

CONTENTS

Chilean Spanish 495
Phrasebooks & Dictionaries 495
Pronunciation 496
Gender & Plurals 497
Accommodations 497
Conversation & Essentials 498
Directions 498
Emergencies 499
Health 499
Language Difficulties 499
Numbers 499
Shopping & Services 500
Time & Dates 500
Transportation 501
Travel with Children 502

Every visitor to Chile should attempt to learn some Spanish, whose basic elements are easily acquired. If possible, take a short course before you go or during your travels (see p464). Even if you can't do so, Chileans are gracious hosts and will encourage your Spanish, so there is no need to feel self-conscious about vocabulary or pronunciation. There are many similar sounding English words, so if you're stuck, try Hispanicizing an English word – it is unlikely you'll make a truly embarrassing error. Do not, however, admit to being *embarazada* (which sounds like 'embarrassed') unless you are in fact pregnant!

Note that in Latin American Spanish, the plural of the familiar *tu* is *ustedes* rather than *vosotros*, as in Spain. Chileans and other Latin Americans have no trouble understanding Castilian Spanish, but may find it either quaint or pretentious.

CHILEAN SPANISH

Chile is not known for having 'standard' Spanish. Even travelers fluent in Spanish as a second language will be stumped by the volume of slang that Chileans use and their often different pronunciation. Chilean speakers relax word-final consonants (and even some internal ones) to the point of

total disappearance, so that it can be difficult to distinguish plural from singular. For example, *las islas* (the islands) may sound more like 'la ila' to someone unfamiliar with the local language. Chileans tend to speak rather more rapidly than other South Americans – the conventional *¿quieres?* (Do you want?) sounds more like 'querí' on the tongue of a Chilean.

Other Chilean peculiarities include pronunciation of the second person informal of 'ar' verbs as 'ai' rather than 'as.' So *¿Adónde vas?* (Where are you going?) will sound more like '¿Adónde vai?' In the south particularly, speakers shorten the common interjection *pués* (meaning 'well' or 'certainly') to 'pue' or 'po,' and add it as filler in sentences or at the end of words to give emphasis, such as *sí po* or *no po*. Other vernacular terms include: *¿Cachai?/Te cacho* (Do you get it/understand?/I get it), *fome* (boring, drab), *luca* (a thousand pesos) and *pasarlo chancho* (to have a great time). The most used slang term is *huevón,* which has been diluted from its literal meaning of 'big balls' to mean 'dude' or used as a verb, as in *No me hueves,* or in shortened form, *No me hue* (Don't fuck with me/Don't put me on). *Así con la hueva pu huevón* means, well, nothing really; ask a Chileno to explain it to you.

Latin Lingo

There are many differences in vocabulary between Castilian and Latin American Spanish. There are also considerable regional differences within these countries that aren't attributable to accent alone. In Chilean speech, for instance, many words have been adopted from Mapuche, while the residents of Santiago sometimes use *coa,* a working-class slang.

Chileans and other South Americans normally refer to the Spanish language as *castellano* rather than *español.*

PHRASEBOOKS & DICTIONARIES

Lonely Planet's compact and comprehensive *Latin American Spanish Phrasebook* is definitely a worthwhile addition to your backpack. Another very useful resource is

RAPA NUI LANGUAGE

Although the Rapa Nui of Easter Island speak Spanish, among themselves many of them still use the island's indigenous language (also called Rapa Nui). Due to the island's isolation, the Rapa Nui language developed relatively untouched but retains similarities to other Polynesian languages, such as Hawaiian, Tahitian and Maori. These days the language also increasingly bears the influence of English and Spanish. The hieroglyph-like Rongorongo script, developed by the Islanders some time after the Spanish first arrived in 1770 and in use until the 1860s, is believed to have been the earliest written form of Rapa Nui. The written Rapa Nui used today was developed in the 19th century by missionaries, who transliterated the sounds of the language into the Roman alphabet. Sadly, while most understand Rapa Nui, few of the younger Islanders speak it fluently, though work is being done to keep this endangered language, and the culture it carries, alive.

Rapa Nui pronunciation is fairly straightforward, with short and long vowels pronounced as they would be in Spanish or Italian. There are only ten consonants, plus a glottal stop ('), which is pronounced like the pause in the word 'uh-oh.' Any attempt at a few basic Rapa Nui greetings and phrases will be greatly appreciated by the locals, whatever your level of mastery. For more extensive Rapa Nui coverage, pick up a copy of Lonely Planet's *South Pacific Phrasebook*. To learn more, and to read about efforts to preserve the local culture, check out the Easter Island Foundation website www.islandheritage.org.

Hello.	*'Iorana.*	My name's ...	*To'oku ingoa ko ...*
Goodbye.	*'Iorana.*	What?	*Aha?*
How are you?	*Pehē koe/kōrua? (sg/pl)*	Which?	*Hē aha?*
Fine.	*Rivariva.*	Who?	*Ko āi?*
Thank you.	*Maururu.*	How much is this?	*'Ehia moni o te me'e nei?*
What's your name?	*Ko āi to'ou ingoa?*	To your health!	*Manuia paka-paka.*

the University of Chicago *Spanish-English, English-Spanish Dictionary*. Its small size, light weight and thorough entries make it ideal for travel.

Visitors confident of their Spanish (and judgment) can tackle John Brennan's and Alvaro Taboada's *How to Survive in the Chilean Jungle* (1996), jointly published by Dolmen Ediciones and the Instituto Chileno Norteamericano, an enormously popular book that has gone through nine editions explaining Chilean slang to the newcomer.

PRONUNCIATION

Pronunciation of Spanish is not difficult. Many Spanish sounds are similar to their English counterparts, and the relationship between pronunciation and spelling is clear and consistent. Unless otherwise indicated, the English examples used below reflect standard American pronunciation.

Vowels & Diphthongs

a	as in 'father'
e	as in 'met'
i	as the 'i' in 'police'
o	as in British English 'hot'
u	as the 'u' in 'rude'
ai	as in 'aisle'
au	as the 'ow' in 'how'
ei	as in 'vein'
ia	as the 'ya' in 'yard'
ie	as the 'ye' in 'yes'
oi	as in 'coin'
ua	as the 'wa' in 'wash'
ue	as the 'we' in 'well'

Consonants

Spanish consonants are generally the same as in English, with the exception of those listed below.

The consonants **ch**, **ll** and **ñ** are generally considered distinct letters, but in dictionaries **ch** and **ll** are now often listed alphabetically under **c** and **l** respectively. The letter **ñ** still has a separate entry after **n** in alphabetical listings.

b	similar to English 'b,' but softer; referred to as 'b larga'
c	as in 'celery' before **e** and **i**; elsewhere as the 'k' in 'king'
ch	as in 'choose'

d	as in 'dog'; between vowels and after **l** or **n**, it's closer to the 'th' in 'this'
g	as the 'ch' in Scottish *loch* before **e** and **i** ('kh' in our pronunciation guides); elsewhere, as in 'go'
h	invariably silent
j	as the 'ch' in Scottish *loch* ('kh' in our pronunciation guides)
ll	as the 'y' in 'yellow'
ñ	as the 'ni' in 'onion'
r	as in 'run,' but strongly rolled
rr	very strongly rolled
v	similar to English 'b,' but softer; referred to as 'b corta'
x	usually pronounced as **j** above; as in 'taxi' in other instances
z	as the 's' in 'sun'

Word Stress

In general, words ending in vowels or the letters **n** or **s** are stressed on the second-last syllable, while those with other endings have stress on the last syllable. Thus *vaca* (cow) and *caballos* (horses) are both stressed on the next-to-last syllable, while *ciudad* (city) and *infeliz* (unhappy) are stressed on the last syllable.

Written accents generally indicate words that don't follow the rules above, eg *sótano* (basement), *América* and *porción* (portion).

GENDER & PLURALS

In Spanish, nouns are either masculine or feminine, and there are rules to help determine gender (with exceptions, of course). Feminine nouns generally end with -**a** or with the groups -**ción**, -**sión** or -**dad**. Other endings typically signify a masculine noun. Endings for adjectives also change to agree with the gender of the noun they modify (masculine/feminine singular -**o**/-**a**). Where both masculine and feminine forms are included in this language guide, they are separated by a slash, with the masculine form first, eg *perdido/a* (lost).

If a noun or adjective ends in a vowel, the plural is formed by adding **s** to the end. If it ends in a consonant, the plural is formed by adding **es** to the end.

ACCOMMODATIONS

I'm looking for ...
Estoy buscando ...   e·*stoy* boos·*kan*·do ...
Where is ...?
¿Dónde hay ...?   *don*·de ai ...

a boarding house/hostel
una pensión/un hostal   oo·na pen·*syon*/oon o·*stal*
budget lodgings
un hospedaje   oon o·spe·*da*·khe
a cabin
una cabaña   oo·na ka·*ba*·nya
a hotel
un hotel/una residencia   oon o·*tel*/oo·na re·see·*den*·sya
a guesthouse/inn
una hostería   oo·na o·ste·*ree*·a
a youth hostel
un albergue juvenil   oon al·*ber*·ge khoo·ve·*neel*

MAKING A RESERVATION

(for phone or written requests)

To ...	*A ...*
From ...	*De ...*
Date	*Fecha*

I'd like to book ...	*Quisiera reservar ...* (see the list under 'Accommodations' for bed and room options)
in the name of ...	*en nombre de ...*
for the nights of ...	*para las noches del ...*
credit card ...	*tarjeta de crédito ...*
number	*número*
expiry date	*fecha de vencimiento*
Please confirm ...	*Puede confirmar ...*
availability	*la disponibilidad*
price	*el precio*

Are there any rooms available?
¿Hay habitaciones libres?
ay a·bee·ta·*syon*·es *lee*·bres
Can you give me a cheap deal?
¿Me puede hacer precio?
me *pwe*·de a·ser pre·*see*·yo

I'd like a ... room.	*Quisiera una habitación ...*	kee·*sye*·ra oo·na a·bee·ta·*syon* ...
double	*doble*	*do*·ble
single	*individual*	een·dee·bee·*dwal*
twin	*con dos camas*	kon dos *ka*·mas

How much is it per ...?	*¿Cuánto cuesta por ...?*	*kwan*·to *kwes*·ta por ...
night	*noche*	*no*·che
person	*persona*	per·*so*·na
week	*semana*	se·*ma*·na

private/shared bathroom	*baño privado/ compartido*	*ba*·nyo pree·*va*·do/ kom·par·*tee*·do

full board	pensión	pen·*syon*
	completa	kom·*ple*·ta
too expensive	demasiado caro	de·ma·*sya*·do *ka*·ro
cheaper	más económico	mas e·ko·*no*·mee·ko
discount	descuento	des·*kwen*·to

Does it include breakfast?
  ¿Incluye el desayuno?   een·*kloo*·ye el de·sa·*yoo*·no
May I see the room?
  ¿Puedo ver la   *pwe*·do ver la
  habitación?   a·bee·ta·*syon*
I don't like it.
  No me gusta.   no me *goos*·ta
It's fine. I'll take it.
  OK. La alquilo.   o·*kay* la al·*kee*·lo
I'm leaving now.
  Me voy ahora.   me voy a·*o*·ra

CONVERSATION & ESSENTIALS

In their public behavior, Chileans are exceptionally polite and expect others to reciprocate. Never approach a stranger for information without extending a greeting like *buenos días* or *buenas tardes*. Most young people use the informal *tú* and its associated verb forms among themselves, but if in doubt, you should use the more formal *usted* and its forms.

Hello.	Hola.	o·la
Good morning.	Buenos días.	bwe·nos dee·as
Good afternoon.	Buenas tardes.	bwe·nas *tar*·des
Good evening/	Buenas noches.	bwe·nas *no*·ches
night.		
Bye/See you soon.	Hasta luego.	as·ta *lwe*·go
Yes.	Sí.	see
No.	No.	no
Please.	Por favor.	por fa·*vor*
Thank you.	Gracias.	*gra*·syas
Many thanks.	Muchas gracias.	moo·chas *gra*·syas
You're welcome.	De nada.	de *na*·da
Pardon me.	Perdón.	per·*don*
Excuse me.	Permiso.	per·*mee*·so
(used when asking permission)		
Forgive me.	Disculpe.	dees·*kool*·pe
(used when apologizing)		

How are things?
  ¿Qué tal?   ke tal
What's your name?
  ¿Cómo se llama? (pol)   *ko*·mo se *ya*·ma
  ¿Cómo te llamas? (inf)   *ko*·mo te *ya*·mas
My name is ...
  Me llamo ...   me *ya*·mo ...

It's a pleasure to meet you.
  Mucho gusto.   *moo*·cho *goos*·to
The pleasure is mine.
  El gusto es mío.   el *goos*·to es *mee*·o
Where are you from?
  ¿De dónde es? (pol)   de *don*·de es
  ¿De dónde eres? (inf)   de *don*·de *er*·es
I'm from ...
  Soy de ...   soy de ...
Where are you staying?
  ¿Dónde está alojado/a? (pol)   *don*·de es·ta a·lo·*kha*·do/a
  ¿Dónde estás alojado/a? (inf)   *don*·de es·*tas* a·lo·*kha*·do/a
May I take a photo?
  ¿Puedo sacar una foto?   *pwe*·do sa·*kar* oo·na *fo*·to

DIRECTIONS

How do I get to ...?
  ¿Cómo puedo llegar a ...?   *ko*·mo *pwe*·do ye·*gar* a ...
Is it far?
  ¿Está lejos?   es·ta *le*·khos

SIGNS	
Entrada	Entrance
Salida	Exit
Información	Information
Abierto	Open
Cerrado	Closed
Prohibido	Prohibited
Comisaria	Police Station
Servicios/Baños	Toilets
Hombres/Varones	Men
Mujeres/Damas	Women

Go straight ahead.
  Siga derecho.   see·ga de·*re*·cho
Turn left.
  Voltée a la izquierda.   vol·*te*·e a la ees·*kyer*·da
Turn right.
  Voltée a la derecha.   vol·*te*·e a la de·*re*·cha
Can you show me (on the map)?
  ¿Me lo podría indicar   me lo po·*dree*·a een·dee·*kar*
  (en el mapa)?   (en el *ma*·pa)

north	norte	*nor*·te
south	sur	soor
east	este	*es*·te
west	oeste	o·*es*·te

here	aquí	a·*kee*
there	allí	a·*yee*
avenue	avenida	a·ve·*nee*·da
block	cuadra	*kwa*·dra
street	calle	*ka*·ye

Geographical Expressions

These are among the most common you will encounter in this book and in maps.

bay	*bahía*
bridge	*puente*
farm	*fundo, hacienda*
glacier	*glaciar, ventisquero*
highway	*carretera, camino, ruta*
hill	*cerro*
lake	*lago*
marsh, estuary	*estero*
mount	*cerro*
mountain range	*cordillera*
national park	*parque nacional*
pass	*paso*
ranch	*estancia*
river	*río*
sound	*seno*
waterfall	*cascada, salto*

EMERGENCIES

Help!	*¡Socorro!*	so·*ko*·ro
Fire!	*¡Incendio!*	een·*sen*·dyo
I've been robbed.	*Me robaron.*	me ro·*ba*·ron
Go away!	*¡Déjeme!*	*de*·khe·me
Get lost!	*¡Váyase!*	va·ya·se
Call ...!	*¡Llame a ...!*	*ya*·me a
an ambulance	*una ambulancia*	oo·na am·boo·*lan*·sya
a doctor	*un médico*	oon *me*·dee·ko
the police	*la policía*	la po·lee·*see*·a

It's an emergency.
Es una emergencia.   es oo·na e·mer·*khen*·sya
Could you help me, please?
¿Me puede ayudar,   me *pwe*·de a·yoo·*dar*
    por favor?   por fa·*vor*
I'm lost.
Estoy perdido/a. (m/f)   es·*toy* per·*dee*·do/a
Where are the toilets?
¿Dónde están los baños?   don·de es·*tan* los *ba*·nyos

HEALTH

I'm sick.
Estoy enfermo/a.   es·*toy* en·*fer*·mo/a
I need a doctor.
Necesito un médico.   ne·se·*see*·to oon *me*·dee·ko
Where's the hospital?
¿Dónde está el hospital?   don·de es·*ta* el os·pee·*tal*

I'm pregnant.
Estoy embarazada.   es·*toy* em·ba·ra·*sa*·da
I've been vaccinated.
Estoy vacunado/a.   es·*toy* va·koo·*na*·do/a

I'm allergic to ...	*Soy alérgico/a a ...*	soy a·*ler*·khee·ko/a a ...
antibiotics	*los antibióticos*	los an·tee·*byo*·tee·kos
peanuts	*las nueces*	las *nwe*·ses
penicillin	*la penicilina*	la pe·nee·see·*lee*·na

I'm ...	*Soy ...*	soy ...
asthmatic	*asmático/a*	as·*ma*·tee·ko/a
diabetic	*diabético/a*	dee·ya·*be*·tee·ko/a
epileptic	*epiléptico/a*	e·pee·*lep*·tee·ko/a

I have ...	*Tengo ...*	*ten*·go ...
a cough	*tos*	tos
diarrhea	*diarrea*	dya·*re*·a
a headache	*un dolor de cabeza*	oon do·*lor* de ka·*be*·sa
nausea	*náusea*	*now*·se·a

LANGUAGE DIFFICULTIES

Do you speak (English)?
¿Habla/Hablas (inglés)?   a·bla/a·blas (een·*gles*) (pol/inf)
Does anyone here speak English?
¿Hay alguien que hable   ai al·*gyen* ke a·ble
    inglés?   een·*gles*
I (don't) understand.
(No) Entiendo.   (no) en·*tyen*·do
How do you say ...?
¿Cómo se dice ...?   *ko*·mo se *dee*·se ...
What does ... mean?
¿Qué quiere decir ...?   ke *kye*·re de·*seer* ...

Could you please ...?	*¿Puede ..., por favor?*	*pwe*·de ... por fa·vor
repeat that	*repetirlo*	re·pe·*teer*·lo
speak more slowly	*hablar más despacio*	a·*blar* mas des·*pa*·syo
write it down	*escribirlo*	es·kree·*beer*·lo

NUMBERS

0	*cero*	*ce*·ro
1	*uno/a*	*oo*·no/a
2	*dos*	dos
3	*tres*	tres
4	*cuatro*	*kwa*·tro
5	*cinco*	*seen*·ko
6	*seis*	seys
7	*siete*	*sye*·te
8	*ocho*	*o*·cho
9	*nueve*	*nwe*·ve

LANGUAGE

10	diez	dyes
11	once	on·se
12	doce	do·se
13	trece	tre·se
14	catorce	ka·tor·se
15	quince	keen·se
16	dieciséis	dye·see·seys
17	diecisiete	dye·see·sye·te
18	dieciocho	dye·see·o·cho
19	diecinueve	dye·see·nwe·ve
20	veinte	vayn·te
21	veintiuno	vayn·tee·oo·no
30	treinta	trayn·ta
31	treinta y uno	trayn·tai oo·no
40	cuarenta	kwa·ren·ta
50	cincuenta	seen·kwen·ta
60	sesenta	se·sen·ta
70	setenta	se·ten·ta
80	ochenta	o·chen·ta
90	noventa	no·ven·ta
100	cien	syen
101	ciento uno	syen·to oo·no
200	doscientos	do·syen·tos
1000	mil	meel

SHOPPING & SERVICES

I'm looking for (the) ...
Estoy buscando ...   es·toy boos·kan·do

ATM
el cajero automático   el ka·khe·ro ow·to·ma·tee·ko
bank
el banco   el ban·ko
bookstore
la librería   la lee·bre·ree·a
internet café
un cibercafé   oon see·ber·ka·fe
embassy
la embajada   la em·ba·kha·da
exchange office
la casa de cambio   la ka·sa de kam·byo
general store
la tienda   la tyen·da
laundry
la lavandería   la la·van·de·ree·a
market
el mercado   el mer·ka·do
pharmacy
la farmacia/la droguería   la far·ma·sya/la dro·ge·ree·a
post office
los correos   los ko·re·os
supermarket
el supermercado   el soo·permer·ka·do
tourist office
la oficina de turismo   la o·fee·see·na de too·rees·mo

I'd like to buy ...
Quisiera comprar ...   kee·sye·ra kom·prar ...
I'm just looking.
Sólo estoy mirando.   so·lo es·toy mee·ran·do
May I look at it?
¿Puedo mirarlo?   pwe·do mee·rar·lo
How much is it?
¿Cuánto cuesta?   kwan·to kwes·ta
That's too expensive for me.
Es demasiado caro   es de·ma·sya·do ka·ro
para mí.   pa·ra mee
Could you lower the price?
¿Podría bajar un poco   po·dree·a ba·khar oon po·ko
el precio?   el pre·syo
I don't like it.
No me gusta.   no me goos·ta
I'll take it.
Lo llevo.   lo ye·vo

Do you accept ...? ¿Aceptan ...?   a·sep·tan ...
credit cards   tarjetas de   tar·khe·tas de
crédito   kre·dee·to
traveler's   cheques de   che·kes de
checks   viajero   vya·khe·ro

less/more   menos/más   me·nos/mas
large/small   grande/pequeño   gran·de/pe·ke·nyo

What time does it open/close?
¿A qué hora abre/cierra?   a ke o·ra a·bre/sye·ra
I want to change some money/traveler's checks.
Quiero cambiar dinero/cheques de viajero.   kye·ro kam·byar dee·ne·ro/che·kes de vya·khe·ro
What's the exchange rate?
¿Cuál es el tipo de cambio?   kwal es el tee·po de kam·byo
I want to call ...
Quiero llamar a ...   kye·ro ya·mar a ...
I'd like to get internet access.
Quisiera usa el internet.   kee·sye·ra oo·sar el een·ter·net

airmail   correo aéreo   ko·re·o a·e·re·o
fax   fax   faks
letter   carta   kar·ta
registered mail   certificado   ser·tee·fee·ka·do
stamps   estampillas   es·tam·pee·yas

TIME & DATES
What time is it?   ¿Qué hora es?   ke o·ra es
It's (one) o'clock.   Es la (una).   es la (oo·na)
It's (seven)   Son las (siete).   son las (sye·te)
o'clock.

midnight	medianoche	me·dya·*no*·che
noon	mediodía	me·dyo·*dee*·a
half past two	dos y media	dos ee *me*·dya
now	ahora	a·*o*·ra
today	hoy	oy
tonight	esta noche	es·ta *no*·che
tomorrow	mañana	ma·*nya*·na

Monday	lunes	*loo*·nes
Tuesday	martes	*mar*·tes
Wednesday	miércoles	*myer*·ko·les
Thursday	jueves	*khwe*·ves
Friday	viernes	*vyer*·nes
Saturday	sábado	*sa*·ba·do
Sunday	domingo	do·*meen*·go

January	enero	e·*ne*·ro
February	febrero	fe·*bre*·ro
March	marzo	*mar*·so
April	abril	a·*breel*
May	mayo	*ma*·yo
June	junio	*khoo*·nyo
July	julio	*khoo*·lyo
August	agosto	a·*gos*·to
September	septiembre	sep·*tyem*·bre
October	octubre	ok·*too*·bre
November	noviembre	no·*vyem*·bre
December	diciembre	dee·*syem*·bre

TRANSPORTATION
Public Transportation
What time does ... leave/arrive?
¿A qué hora sale/llega ...?
a ke *o*·ra *sa*·le/*ye*·ga ...
the bus
el autobus/bus   el ow·to·*boos*/boos
the plane
el avión   el a·*vyon*
the ship
el barco   el *boo*·ke
the small bus
el colectivo/micro   el ko·lek·*tee*·vo/*mee*·kro

airport
el aeropuerto
el a·e·ro·*pwer*·to
bus station/terminal
la estación/terminal de buses
la es·ta·*syon*/ter·mee·*nal* de *boo*·ses
bus stop
la parada de buses
la pa·*ra*·da de *boo*·ses
bus
la terminal de buses
la ter·mee·*nal* de *boo*·ses

train station
la estación de ferrocarril
la es·ta·*syon* de fe·ro·ka·*reel*
luggage check room
guardería/equipaje
gwar·de·*ree*·a/e·*kee*·pa·khe
ticket office
la boletería
la bo·le·te·*ree*·a
I'd like a ticket to ...
Quiero un boleto a ...
kye·ro oon bo·*le*·to a ...
What's the fare to ...?
¿Cuánto cuesta hasta ...?
kwan·to *kwes*·ta *a*·sta ...

student's (fare)	de estudiante	de es·too·*dyan*·te
1st class	primera clase	pree·me·ra *kla*·se
2nd class	segunda clase	se·*goon*·da *kla*·se
one-way	ida	*ee*·da
round trip	ida y vuelta	*ee*·da ee *vwel*·ta
taxi	taxi	*tak*·see

Private Transportation
pickup (truck)	camioneta	ka·myo·*ne*·ta
truck	camión	ka·*myon*
hitchhike	hacer dedo	a·ser *de*·do

I'd like to hire a/an ...
Quisiera alquilar ...
kee·*sye*·ra al·kee·*lar* ...
bicycle
una bicicleta   oo·na bee·see·*kle*·ta
car
un auto   oon *ow*·to
4WD
un todo terreno   oon *to*·do te·*re*·no
motorbike
una moto   oo·na *mo*·to

Is this the road to ...?
¿Se va a ... por esta carretera?
se va a ... por es·ta ka·re·*te*·ra
Where's a gas/petrol station?
¿Dónde hay una gasolinera?
don·de ai oo·na ga·so·lee·*ne*·ra
Please fill it up.
Lleno, por favor.
ye·no por fa·*vor*
I'd like (20) liters.
Quiero (veinte) litros.
kye·ro (*vayn*·te) *lee*·tros

| diesel | diesel | *dee*·sel |
| gas/petrol | gasolina | ga·so·*lee*·na |

LANGUAGE

ROAD SIGNS

Acceso	Entrance
Aparcamiento	Parking
Ceda el Paso	Give Way
Despacio	Slow
Dirección Única	One-Way
Mantenga Su Derecha	Keep to the Right
No Adelantar/	No Passing
No Rebase	
Peligro	Danger
Prohibido Aparcar/	No Parking
No Estacionar	
Prohibido el Paso	No Entry
Pare	Stop
Salida de Autopista	Exit Freeway

(How long) Can I park here?
¿(Por cuánto tiempo) Puedo aparcar aquí?
(por *kwan*·to tyem·po) pwe·do a·par·*kar* a·*kee*
Where do I pay?
¿Dónde se paga?
don·de se *pa*·ga
I need a mechanic.
Necesito un mecánico.
ne·se·*see*·to oon me·*ka*·nee·ko
The car has broken down in ...
El carro se ha averiado en ...
el *ka*·ro se a a·ve·*rya*·do en ...
The motorbike won't start.
No arranca la moto.
no a·*ran*·ka la *mo*·to
I have a flat tyre.
Tengo un pinchazo.
ten·go oon peen·*cha*·so
I've run out of gas/petrol.
Me quedé sin gasolina.
me ke·*de* seen ga·so·*lee*·na
I've had an accident.
Tuve un accidente.
too·ve oon ak·see·*den*·te

TRAVEL WITH CHILDREN

I need ...
Necesito ...   ne·se·*see*·to ...
Do you have ...?
¿Hay ...?   ai ...
   a car baby seat
   un asiento de seguridad para bebés
   oon a·*syen*·to de se·goo·ree·*da* pa·ra be·*bes*
   a child-minding service
   un servicio de cuidado de niños
   oon ser·*vee*·syo de kwee·*da*·do de *nee*·nyos
   a children's menu
   una carta infantil
   oo·na *kar*·ta een·fan·*teel*
   a creche
   una guardería
   oo·na gwar·de·*ree*·a
   (disposable) diapers/nappies
   pañales (de usar y tirar)
   pa·*nya*·les de oo·*sar* ee tee·*rar*
   an (English-speaking) babysitter
   una niñera (de habla inglesa)
   oo·na nee·*nye*·ra (de *a*·bla een·*gle*·sa)
   infant formula (milk)
   leche en polvo para bebés
   le·che en *pol*·vo pa·ra be·*bes*
   a highchair
   una trona
   oo·na *tro*·na
   a potty
   una pelela
   oo·na pe·*le*·la
   a stroller
   un cochecito
   oon ko·che·*see*·to

Do you mind if I breast-feed here?
¿Le molesta que dé de pecho aquí?
le mo·*les*·ta ke de de *pe*·cho a·*kee*
Are children allowed?
¿Se admiten niños?
se ad·*mee*·ten *nee*·nyos

Also available from Lonely Planet:
Latin American Spanish Phrasebook

Glossary

See p60 for useful words and phrases dealing with food and dining. Also see p495 for other useful words and phrases. RN indicates that a term is a Rapa Nui (Easter Island) usage.

ahu (RN) – stone platform for *moai* (statues)
alameda – avenue/boulevard lined with trees
albergue juvenil – youth hostel
alpaca – wool-bearing domestic camelid, related to llama
altiplano – high plains of northern Chile, Bolivia, southern Peru and northwestern Argentina
anexo – telephone extension
apunamiento – altitude sickness
Araucaníans – groups of indigenous peoples, including Mapuche, Picunche and Pehuenche
arroyo – watercourse
asado – barbecue
ascensor – funicular (cable car)
Ayllu – indigenous community of Norte Grande
Aymara – indigenous inhabitants of Andean altiplano of Peru, Bolivia and northern Chile

bahía – bay
balneario – bathing resort or beach
barrio – neighborhood
bencina – petrol or gasoline
bencina blanca – white gas for camping stoves
bidón – spare fuel container
bodega – cellar or storage area for wine
bofedal – swampy alluvial pasture in altiplano

cabañas – cabins
cacique – Indian chieftain
calefón – hot-water heater
caleta – small cove
callampas – shantytowns, literally 'mushrooms'
cama – bed; also sleeper-class seat
camanchaca – ocean fog along coastal desert
camarote – sleeper class on ship
carabineros – police
caracoles – winding roads; literally 'snails'
carretera – highway
casa de cambio – money exchange
casa de familia – modest family accommodation
cerro – hill
chachacoma – native Andean plant; said to relieve altitude sickness
Chilote – inhabitant of Chiloé; sometimes connotes 'bumpkin'

ciervo – deer
ciudad – city
cobro revertido – collect (reverse-charge) phone call
cocinerías – greasy-spoon cafés/kitchens
Codelco – Corporación del Cobre, state-owned enterprise overseeing copper mining
colectivo – shared taxi, also called *taxi colectivo*
comparsa – group of musicians or dancers
comuna – local governmental unit
congregación – colonial-era concentration of diverse native populations in a town, see also *reducción*
cordillera – chain of mountains
costanera – coastal road; also along river or lakeshore
criollo – colonial term for American-born Spaniard

desierto florido – rare and ephemeral desert wildflower display in Norte Chico
DINA – National Intelligence Directorate; feared agency created after 1973 coup to oversee police and military intelligence

elaboración artesanal – small-scale production, often by family
empanada – a turnover with a sweet or savory filling
encomienda – colonial labor system in which indigenous communities worked for Spanish *encomenderos*
esquí en marcha – cross-country skiing
estancia – extensive cattle- or sheep-grazing establishment with resident labor force
estero – estuary

feria – artisans' market
Frontera – region of pioneer settlement, between Río Biobío and Río Toltén, dominated by Araucanían indigenous groups until late 19th century
fuerte – fort
fundo – hacienda, smaller irrigated unit in central heartland

garúa – coastal desert fog
geoglyph – large pre-Columbian figures or designs on desert hillsides
golfo – gulf
golpe de estado – coup d'état
guanaco – wild camelid related to llama; also police water cannon

hacienda – large rural landholding, with dependent resident labor force
hare paenga (RN) – elliptical (boat-shaped) house

hospedaje – budget accommodation, usually family home with shared bathroom
hostal – hotel, hostel
hostería – inn or guesthouse that serves meals
hotel parejero – short-stay 'love motels' aimed at couples needing privacy
huaso – horseman, a kind of Chilean gaucho or cowboy

IGM – Instituto Geográfico Militar; mapping organization
intendencia – Spanish colonial administrative unit
invierno boliviano – 'Bolivian winter'; summer rainy season in Chilean altiplano
isla – island
islote – small island, islet
istmo – isthmus
IVA – *impuesto de valor agregado,* value-added tax (VAT)

küchen – sweet, German-style cakes

lago – lake
laguna – lagoon
latifundio – large landholding, such as *fundo, hacienda* or *estancia*
lista de correos – poste restante
llareta – dense shrub in Chilean altiplano with deceptive, cushionlike appearance
local – part of address indicating office number where there are several in the same building
lomas – coastal desert hills

maori (RN) – learned men, reportedly able to read Rongo-Rongo tablets
Mapuche – indigenous inhabitants of the area south of Río Biobío
marisquería – seafood restaurant
matrimonial – double bed
matua (RN) – ancestor, father; associated with leader of first Polynesian immigrants
media pensión – half board in hotel
mestizo – person of mixed Indian and Spanish descent
micro – small bus
minga – reciprocal Mapuche Indian labor system
mirador – lookout point
moai (RN) – large anthropomorphic statues
moai kavakava (RN) – carved wooden 'statues of ribs'
motu (RN) – small offshore islet
municipalidad – city hall
museo – museum

ñandú – rhea; large flightless bird similar to ostrich
nevado – snowcapped mountain peak

oferta – promotional fare, often seasonal, for plane or bus travel

oficina – 19th- and early 20th-century nitrate mining enterprise
onces – 'elevenses'; Chilean afternoon tea

palafitos – rows of houses built on stilts over water in Chiloé
pampa – vast desert expanse
parada – bus stop
parrillada – a mix of grilled meats
peatonal – pedestrian mall
peña folclórica – folk music and cultural club
penquista – inhabitant of Concepción
pensión – family home offering short-term accommodations
pensión completa – full board in hotel
picada – informal family restaurant
pingüinera – penguin colony
playa – beach
Porteño – native or resident of Valparaíso
portezuelo – mountain pass
posta – clinic or first-aid station
precordillera – foothills
propina – tip
puente – bridge
puerto – port
pukao (RN) – topknot on head of a *moai*
pukará – pre-Columbian hilltop fortress
puna – Andean highlands, usually above 3000m
punta – point

quebrada – ravine
quinoa – native Andean grain grown in northern *precordillera*

Rapa Nui – Polynesian name for Easter Island
reducción – colonial-era concentration of indigenous peoples in towns for purposes of political control or religious instruction, see also *congregación*
refugio – rustic shelter in national park or remote area
residencial – budget accommodations
rhea – flightless bird similar to ostrich; *ñandú* in Spanish
río – river
rodeo – annual cattle roundup on *estancia* or *hacienda*
Rongo-Rongo (RN) – indecipherable script on wooden tablets
ruka – traditional thatched Mapuche house
ruta – route, highway

salar – salt lake, salt marsh or salt pan
salón de cama – bus with reclining seats
salón de té – literally 'teahouse,' but more upscale café
Santiaguino – native or resident of Santiago
seno – sound, fjord
sierra – mountain range
s/n – 'sin número'; street address without number
soroche – altitude sickness

tábano – horsefly
tabla – shared plate of appetizers
tejuelas – shingles, typical of Chiloé architecture
teleférico – gondola cable car
termas – hot springs
todo terreno – mountain bike
toki (RN) – basalt carving tool
toqui – Mapuche Indian chief
torres – towers
totora (RN) – type of reed used for making rafts

Unidad Popular – leftist coalition that supported
Salvador Allende in 1970 presidential election

ventisquero – glacier
vicuña – wild relative of llama, found at high altitudes
in the north
villa – village, small town
viscacha – wild Andean relative of chinchilla
volcán – volcano

Yaghans – indigenous inhabitants of Tierra del Fuego
archipelago

zampoña – panpipe
zona franca – duty-free zone

The Authors

CAROLYN McCARTHY
Coordinating Author, Northern Patagonia, Southern Patagonia, Tierra del Fuego, Archipiélago Juan Fernández

Author and journalist Carolyn McCarthy first met Chile as a tourist, returned seasonally as a trekking guide and moved there in 2003 on a Fulbright grant to document pioneer Patagonia. She now proudly calls Chile's magnificent south home. Her work has appeared in *National Geographic,* the *Boston Globe, Salt Lake Tribune* and other publications. For Lonely Planet, she has co-authored guides to Argentina, Central and South America, and Yellowstone and Grand Teton National Parks. You can visit her blog at www.carolynswildblueyonder.blogspot .com. For this edition, Carolyn also wrote the front- and endmatter chapters.

GREG BENCHWICK
Norte Grande, Norte Chico

A former commissioning editor at Lonely Planet, Greg turned down a life of high-walled cubicle insanity to get back to his writing and rambling roots. He's rumbled in the jungles of Peru and Costa Rica, walked across Spain on the Camino de Santiago and challenged the peaks of Alaska and his native Colorado. He specializes in Latin American travel, sustainable travel and new media, and has written more than a dozen guidebooks on travel in Latin America. This was his fourth time traveling through Norte Chico and Norte Grande. When he's not on the road, he develops his new-media company www.monjomedia.com. Some day he dreams of visiting Chile's south, but for now, he'll always have Arica.

JEAN-BERNARD CARILLET
Easter Island (Rapa Nui)

A Paris-based journalist and photographer, Jean-Bernard is a die-hard Polynesia lover, a diving instructor and a Polynesian dance aficionado. For this edition he made his trip coincide with the Tapati Rapa Nui, the island's big festival, and immersed himself in traditional Rapa Nui culture. Between the dance and sport contests, he dived off Motu Nui, hiked around Poike Peninsula, climbed Maunga Terevaka on horseback, discussed the wackiest theories about the history of the island with archaeologists and wandered amid more *moai* than he cares to remember. Jean-Bernard is also an expert on French Polynesia, Easter Island's western neighbor, about which he has written numerous articles and guides.

LONELY PLANET AUTHORS

Why is our travel information the best in the world? It's simple: our authors are passionate, dedicated travellers. They don't take freebies in exchange for positive coverage so you can be sure the advice you're given is impartial. They travel widely to all the popular spots, and off the beaten track. They don't research using just the internet or phone. They discover new places not included in any other guidebook. They personally visit thousands of hotels, restaurants, palaces, trails, galleries, temples and more. They speak with dozens of locals every day to make sure you get the kind of insider knowledge only a local could tell you. They take pride in getting all the details right, and in telling it how it is. Think you can do it? Find out how at **lonelyplanet.com**.

VICTORIA PATIENCE   Santiago, Middle Chile

Since her first chicken-bus ride from Lima to Buenos Aires in 1999, Latin American roadtripping has had Victoria Patience hooked. Two of Chile's most intoxicating products, literature and wine, proved equally addictive at university. Thankfully, her degree in Hispanic Studies was a good excuse to indulge. She settled in Argentina in 2000, and an impulsive bout of hitchhiking first took her over the Andes soon after. Victoria has spent the last few years in Buenos Aires weathering political turmoil and writing guidebooks, but traded in steak for seafood and Malbec for Carmenere for six weeks on the road researching Santiago and Middle Chile.

KEVIN RAUB   Sur Chico, Chiloé

Kevin Raub grew up in Atlanta and started his career as a music journalist in New York City, working for *Men's Journal* and *Rolling Stone* magazines. The rock-'n'-roll lifestyle took its toll, so he needed an extended vacation and took up travel writing. He has previously co-authored Lonely Planet guides to Mexico and Brazil (where he currently lives), and has been traveling extensively in Chile since climbing the 5604m El Toco volcano in the Atacama Desert in 2003. He pounds the world's pavements with one goal in mind: membership of the Travelers' Century Club before the age of 40. His country count currently stands at 60.

CONTRIBUTING AUTHORS

Dr David Goldberg MD wrote the Health chapter. Dr Goldberg completed his training in internal medicine and infectious diseases at Columbia-Presbyterian Medical Center in New York City, where he has also served as voluntary faculty. At present he is an infectious diseases specialist in Scarsdale, NY, and the editor-in-chief of the website MDTravelHealth.com.

Grant Phelps wrote the special section on Chilean wine (p56). Born and raised in New Zealand, Grant completed a masters degree in enology before embarking on a 13-year career as an international 'flying winemaker,' working in such diverse climes as Australia, USA, France, Hungary, Chile and New Zealand. In between winemaking gigs he has dedicated his intellectual processes to the study of the Spanish language in Cuba, Colombia and Guatemala. For the past six years Grant has been Chief Winemaker of Viña Viu Manent, located in the picturesque Colchagua Valley of Chile.

Behind the Scenes

THIS BOOK

This is the 8th edition of *Chile & Easter Island*. Carolyn McCarthy served as coordinating author, writing the front and back chapters as well as the Northern Patagonia, Southern Patagonia, Tierra del Fuego and Archipiélago Juan Fernández chapters. Greg Benchwick covered Norte Grande and Norte Chico. Jean-Bernard Carillet covered Easter Island (Rapa Nui). Victoria Patience covered Santiago and Middle Chile and Kevin Raub wrote Sur Chico and Chiloé. Grant Phelps contributed the feature on Chilean wine, and Dr David Goldberg MD wrote the Health chapter. The 7th edition was written by Charlotte Beech, Jolyon Attwooll, Jean-Bernard Carillet and Thomas Kohnstamm. The 6th edition was written by Carolyn Hubbard, Bridgitte Barta and Jeff Davis. The 5th edition was written by Wayne Bernhardson. This guidebook was commissioned in Lonely Planet's Oakland office, and produced by the following:

Commissioning Editors Jay Cooke, Catherine Craddock, Jennye Garibaldi, Kathleen Munnelly
Coordinating Editor Rosie Nicholson
Coordinating Cartographer Owen Eszeki
Coordinating Layout Designer Margaret Jung
Managing Editor Bruce Evans
Managing Cartographers Shahara Ahmed, Alison Lyall
Managing Layout Designer Laura Jane
Assisting Editors Janet Austin, Charlotte Harrison, Margedd Heliosz, Kate James
Assisting Cartographer Ross Butler
Cover Designer Pepi Bluck
Project Manager Ruth Cosgrove
Language Content Coordinator Quentin Frayne

Thanks to Jessica Boland, Jennifer Garrett, Debra Herrmann, Rachel Imeson, Lisa Knights, Raphael Richards, Amanda Sierp, Sarah Sloane, Andrew Smith, Celia Wood

THANKS
CAROLYN MCCARTHY

Many Chileans were wonderful hosts along the way. Big thanks to Pedro and Fabiana in San Juan Bautista, Joaquina in Futaleufú, Mirella in Palena and Trauko in Puerto Natales. Alan Grundy proved valiant – thanks for pushing the truck. In Chaitén, Nicolas La Penna and Pumalín's Dagoberto Guzmán shared their time and enthusiasm. My best wishes go out to the community of Chaitén as it rebuilds. On the home front, my appreciation goes to editors Kathleen Munnelly, who conceived this project, Jay Cooke, who slam-dunked it to completion and the indefatigable team Chile. Last and not least, thanks to Joe.

THE LONELY PLANET STORY

Fresh from an epic journey across Europe, Asia and Australia in 1972, Tony and Maureen Wheeler sat at their kitchen table stapling together notes. The first Lonely Planet guidebook, *Across Asia on the Cheap,* was born.

Travelers snapped up the guides. Inspired by their success, the Wheelers began publishing books to Southeast Asia, India and beyond. Demand was prodigious, and the Wheelers expanded the business rapidly to keep up. Over the years, Lonely Planet extended its coverage to every country and into the virtual world via lonelyplanet.com and the Thorn Tree message board.

As Lonely Planet became a globally loved brand, Tony and Maureen received several offers for the company. But it wasn't until 2007 that they found a partner whom they trusted to remain true to the company's principles of traveling widely, treading lightly and giving sustainably. In October of that year, BBC Worldwide acquired a 75% share in the company, pledging to uphold Lonely Planet's commitment to independent travel, trustworthy advice and editorial independence.

Today, Lonely Planet has offices in Melbourne, London and Oakland, with over 500 staff members and 300 authors. Tony and Maureen are still actively involved with Lonely Planet. They're traveling more often than ever, and they're devoting their spare time to charitable projects. And the company is still driven by the philosophy of *Across Asia on the Cheap*: 'All you've got to do is decide to go and the hardest part is over. So go!'

GREG BENCHWICK

Big love to my traveling companion, partner and constant teacher Alejandra Castañeda. I'd also like to thank the amazing 'big thinkers' at Lonely Planet. A special *gracias* goes to the people of Norte Chico and Norte Grande, especially Patricio Polanco and Guillermo Morales.

And I'd like to thank Brian Kluepfel and Calum Crozier, who accompanied me on my first journey through Chile's north. The days of 'Grandpa, the Decrepit Octogenarian from Alabama' will live on in my warmest memories for the rest of my life.

Last but not least, I'd like to thank my family. I love you so much.

JEAN-BERNARD CARILLET

A huge *mauruuru roa* to everyone who helped out and made this trip an enlightenment, including Sergio Rapu, Enrique Tucki, Lionel, Jérôme, Antoine and Sabrina. Carolyn, coordinating author extraordinaire, deserves huge thanks for her support and efficient liaising – not to mention an *apéro* in Buttes-aux-Cailles in Paris – as do all the people behind the scenes at Lonely Planet. I'm also grateful to Kathleen for her trust.

At home, a phenomenal *gros bisou* to my daughter Eva, who gives direction to my otherwise gypsy life.

VICTORIA PATIENCE

Miles de gracias to Carolyn McCarthy, who tirelessly solved my dilemmas and doubts. Kevin Raub was a dangerous drinking partner, as was wine-god Grant Phelps, whose hospitality was humbling: thank you both. I owe one to Juan de Diós Ortúzar for answering a thousand questions and to the inimitable Lara brothers, Allan, Gonzalo and Iván, for fab food and mad missions. Nicole Heyman was the best partner-in-wine-crime ever. I'm grateful for support on the road from Rodrigo Pinto, Noel and Melissa Hutchings, Simon Shalders, Kate Farrell, Cameron Wright, and Jan Rihak, and online from Jay Cooke and Kathleen Munnelly. To Diego González, my all-time favorite travel companion: *gracias por todo, amor*.

KEVIN RAUB

Un beso grande to my wife, Adriana Schmidt, who is actually Brazilian, but we won't hold that against her here. At Lonely Planet, Kathleen Munnelly and Carolyn McCarthy. And along the way: Ana Claudia Domingues, Kristina Schreck, Martin Sicher, Jorge Vlloa, Renato Arancibia, Carlos Grady, Fernando Claude, La Comarca, Marcelo Brevis, Alan Coar, Tracy Katelman, Emily Gosche, Vincent Baudin and Alvaro Saez.

OUR READERS

Many thanks to the travelers who used the last edition and wrote to us with helpful hints, useful advice and interesting anecdotes:

A Nelleke Aben, Helmut Adelay, Kate Adlam, Beverley Aldrich, Trudy Aldridge, Simone Alin, Marcelo Amelunxen, Bud Anderson, Jane Anderson, Sidsel Angelo-Pérez, Mary Ann Appleton, Pete Appleyard, Anne Appoldt, Gill Armstrong, Claude Auger, Reto Augsburger, Eduardo Avalos **B** Jacob De Baar, Elisa Baier, Ian Baker, Amanda Baltazar, Tina Barrett, Helene Barrette, Bruce Bartrug, Yves Baumgartner, Linda Bayless, Blum Beat, Anja Beckmann, Lina Behrens, Christian Belviso, Rameen Beroukhim, Maria Beskow, Cynthia Blackburn, Jane Blackmore, Carl Blackstone, Joaquín Bode, Thomas Bohne, James Boles, Jos Borghuis, Paul Bossenmaier, Jaap Bouwer, John Bowen, Mikowhy Boyd, Nadine Brauns, Dave Breemans, Lori Bridenstine, Aviet Brigitte, Peter Britz, Russ Brompton, Sarah Brooks, Lionel Brossi, Heleen Brouwer, Louise Brown, Tim Brown, Rolf Burgermeister, Nathanael Burgess, Mara Büter **C** Lynette Cardoch, Jacqueline Perez Caro, Fabian Castro, Doris Cavegn, Ken & Barbara Cerotsky, Tanguy Ceulemans, Fiona Clark, Steven Cline, Julienne Coffey, Philip Coletto, Andrea Confalonieri, Dorothee Conrad, John Cooper, Ellen Cornelissen, Sergio Cortez, Hester Costerus, Bonnie Craven-Francis, Nathan Crooks **D** Maria Trinidad De Smet D'Olbecke, Paul Dalebout, Luz Dall'Orso, Thomas Daly, Paul Davy, Richard Dedeyan, Flor Diaz, Phillip Docken, Margaret Doherty, Ingrid Donnelly, Chris Droege, James Dunn **E** Chris Edmunds, Patrick Edwards, Christian Eichenlaub, Alexander Elbert, John Elliott, Roger Emanuels, Amanda Essenmacher, Karen Etheridge, Robert Evans **F** Gabrielle Faget, Heidi Farber, Liliana Fernandez, Nancy Fingerhood, Caroline Fink, Charlotte Finlay, Frauke Finster, Silvia Forsthuber, Robert-Jan Friele, Anja Funke, Barbara Fusco **G** Gerry Garbulsky, Maria Elena Garcia, Rebecca Gasser, Sebastian Geissler, Helmut Genkinger, Dave Gerard, Enzo Giacchero, John Gillespie, Jolanta Glabek, Amit Gnessin, Neville Gorman, Anne Grabinsky, April Graves, Duncan Gray, Caroline Greene, Silvia Groner, Alain Guay, Kathryn Del Guercio, Renato Guimaraes, Ernesto Guiraldes **H** Karl Hafner, Margreet Hagreis, Pat Halcro, Bashar Hamarneh, Rainer Hamet, Marie Hamilton-Smith, Ulf Hampel, Eich Hanspeter, Ania & Josh Hargrove, Kristin Harms, Kara Hartshorne, Vinny Hayes, Jim Head, Laura Heckman, Yvonne Heierle, Katrien Heirman, Nienke Hensbroek, Sarah Hilding, Vikki Hoare, Marieke Hobrink, Henning Hoffmann, Kalle Holmqvist, Naoko Holnagel, Becky Holt, Mark Hommerson, Alexandra Horner, Christina Horsten, Helen Humphreys, Ian Humphreys, Jadrino Huot, Stefanie Hägele **I** Luz Maria Ibanez, Ricardo Imaeda **J** Philipp Jackel, Victoria Jadot, Miroslava Jadrievic, Joachim N Jensen, Bjørn Fossli Johansen, Vicki Johnson, Sharon Jones, Teresa Chin Jones, Johan Jonk, Vincent F Biondo Jr **K** Ingvill Kaasin, Patrick Kabouw, Barry Kaiser, Tracy Katelman, Erin Nelson Keegan, Matthew W Kelley, Jill Kent, Robin King, Julie Kiser, Mariana Kistler, John Klenota, Kelley Koehler, Edward Kommers, Sally Kondziolka, Jaap Koomen, Charlotte De Kort, Doris Kramm, Sarai Krappmann, Andreas Kubach, Nils Kuhlmann, Sarah Kunz, Michele Könnecke **L** Pilar Lagos, Nicole Landset, Allan Lara, Ronald Larsen, Mick Larson, Anthony & Felicia Lau, Philippe Lefroid,

Rougemont Leonore, Silvia Leto, Gregg Lewis, Angela Liesner, Graham Lines, Loretta Llorente, Marina Loeffler, Chris Louie **M** Pete Macdonald, Mandy Macgregor, Bev Mackenzie, Kathy Mackenzie, Simon Major, Rebecca Mansell, Joseph Marolles, Emmanuel Martins, Greta Mathews, Omer Ben Matityahu, Xavier Matteucci, Sam Mcclure, Maeve Mcdonagh, Shawn Mclaughlin, Jennifer McManus, Mary Medicus, Harald Merz, Sophie Mesmacque, Elke Messner-Küttner, Carlos Meza, Sebastien Mierzwa, Kevin Mininger, Ko Moelker, Truus Moelker, Stephan Morf, Susan Muller **N** Edith & Doug Naegele, Christiane Nahrendorf, Edward Naritomi, Jeannette Nelissen, Ilka Neugebauer, Pia S Nielsen, Aart Nierop, Charlotte Noll, Barbara Nowak **O** Marion Opdam, Barak Ori, Juan De Dios Ortuzar, Emily Owen **P** Margit Pabst, Nicholas Pachrysostomou, Ernesto Palm, Charles Pankow, Katerina Peiros, Montse Pejuan, Sandra Pendelin, Ricardo Pereira, Rutger Pieko, Michael Poesen, Norman Prentice, Eileen Prince, Luka Caric Pujadas **Q** Angelica De Queiroz **R** Nyoka Rajah, Magie Ramirez, Jette Ramshøj, Rebecca Rathjen, Nicholas Read, Ursula Reischl, Christopher Restivo, Pablo Retamal, Andre Ribeiro, André Ribeiro, Ralph Rieck, Alberto Rocha, Cristián Rodríguez, Julie Rogers, Lorraine Ruffing, Mirta Ruiz, Maria & Berthold Rumpel, Malcolm Rushan, Nicole Rähle **S** Jorge Salgado, Tanja Sanchez, Gina Sanders, Katie Sands, Mariella Sarestoniemi, Iska Schewe, Sabine Schiedermair, Juergen Schlossbauer, Sarah Schmeer, Vera Schmidt-Gregory, Jort Scholten, Rafael Secemski, Caroline Seuren, Stephen Shaw, Richard Sheets, Mar Sheffield, Christie Smith, David John Solano Smith, Ross Smith, Diego Sogorb, Beatriz Souza, Daan Steijnen, Nadine Steiner, Leslie Storozuk, Clem Strain, Edrienne Su, Helga Svendsen, Claudia Szabo, Monika Szyszlowska **T** Amy Tate, Philip Tervit, Mirko Thiessen, Jan Thomas, Ben Thompson, Linda Thomson, Alex Thornton, Roberto Tilio, Jonathan Tjader, Thalita Tomazetti, Tom Tressel **V** Mattia Vaccari, Miguel Garcia Valenzuela, Mark van Breemen, Karen van Burkleo, Marieke der van Eerden, Essa van Gray-Schopfer, Anabel van Hove, Hester van Santen, Martijn de van Ven, Judith van den Hengel, Astrid Vandenbosch, Loreto Vasquez, Patrica Veerman, Johan Velema, Sigurjon Vilhjalmsson, Tim Vincent, Gerald Vlach, Bill Volk **W** Meredith Wade, Claire Wagstaff, Susan Waldock, Emily Walker, Emma Wall, Mike Wallace, Kaegan Walsh, Liz Walton, Margott Weinberg, Peter Weinberg, Madeleine Weiss, Marcus Wenzel, Amanda Wildeman, Christopher Willans, Henning Wilmes, Krista Wishart, Frank Wollenweber, Edric Wong, Sherra Wong, Guy Woodhouse, Glynn & Mel Wright **Y** Alma Young **Z** Laurence Zhang

SEND US YOUR FEEDBACK

We love to hear from travelers – your comments keep us on our toes and help make our books better. Our well-traveled team reads every word on what you loved or loathed about this book. Although we cannot reply individually to postal submissions, we always guarantee that your feedback goes straight to the appropriate authors, in time for the next edition. Each person who sends us information is thanked in the next edition – and the most useful submissions are rewarded with a free book.

To send us your updates – and find out about Lonely Planet events, newsletters and travel news – visit our award-winning website: **lonelyplanet.com/contact**.

Note: we may edit, reproduce and incorporate your comments in Lonely Planet products such as guidebooks, websites and digital products, so let us know if you don't want your comments reproduced or your name acknowledged. For a copy of our privacy policy visit lonelyplanet.com/privacy.

ACKNOWLEDGMENTS
Many thanks to the following for the use of their content:

Globe on title page ©Mountain High Maps 1993 Digital Wisdom, Inc.

Internal photographs p13 (#2) Mark Titterton / Alamy. All other images by Lonely Planet Images, p9 (#3), Chrisina Aslund; p12, Chris Bell; p16 (#1), Jean-Bernard Carllet; p10 (#2), Tom Cockrem; p16 (#2), Lee Foster; p9 (#2), Roberto Gerometta; p6 (#1), p8 (#1, #2), p11 (#4), Paul Kennedy; p13 (#3), p15 (#4) Carolyn McCarthy; p5, Garet Cormack; p7 (#3), Olivre Strewe; p15 (#3), Wes Walker; p11 (#3) Woods Wheatcroft; p10 (#1), p14 (#1, #2), Brent Winebrenner.

512

Index

ABBREVIATIONS

Arg Argentina
Bol Bolivia

4WD tours
    Iquique 198
    Porvenir 411-12
    Uyuni (Bol) 215

A
accommodations 460-2, *see also
    individual locations*
    language 497-8
Achao 331-2
activities 23, 70-5, 462-3, *see also
    individual activities*
addresses 463
Aguas Calientes 300
ahu 457
Ahu Akahanga 456
Ahu Akapu 446
Ahu Akivi 454-5
Ahu Ature Huki 459
Ahu Hanga Tetenga 456
Ahu Nau Nau 459
Ahu Riata 446
Ahu Tahai 446
Ahu Tautira 446
Ahu Te Pito Kura 458
Ahu Tepeu 454
Ahu Tongariki 456-7, 16
Ahu Vaihu 456
Ahu Vinapu 455-6
air travel
    air passes 481
    airlines 475-6, 481
    airports 475-6
    carbon offset 477
    deep vein thrombosis (DVT) 489
    departure tax 476
    internet resources 476
    to/from Chile 475-8
    within Chile 480-1, **480**
Alacaluf peoples 343, 370, 409
Alcohuaz 257

000 Map pages
000 Photograph pages

Aldea de Tulor 220
alerce 65, 346
Allende, Salvador 36, 37-8, 92
alpacas 64
Altiplano lakes 215
Ana Kai Tangata 455
Ana Te Pahu 454
Ancud 323-7, **325**
Angol 171-2
animals 63-4, 432, *see also individual
    species*
Antarctica 421, 422
Antillanca 300
Antofagasta 223-7, **224**
aquaculture 69, 315
araucaria 65, 260, 272, 286
archaeological sites, *see* geoglyphs,
    petroglyphs
Archipiélago Juan Fernández 429-
    38, **431**
architecture 51
area codes 472, *see also inside front
    cover*
Arica 177-85, **179**
art galleries & art museums
    Bodegón Cultural 262
    Casa del Arte Diego Rivera 315
    Centro Cultural Matucana 91
    Centro Cultural Palacio La
        Moneda 83
    Centro de Cultura (Iquique) 195
    Estación Mapocho 83
    La Casa del Arte 164
    MAM Chiloé 334
    Museo a Cielo Abierto 125
    Museo Arqueológico de
        Santiago 87
    Museo Chileno de Arte
        Precolombino 83
    Museo de Arte Contemporáneo
        (Santiago) 87
    Museo de Arte Contemporáneo
        (Valdivia) 290
    Museo de Arte Contemporáneo
        Espacio Quinta Normal 91
    Museo de Artes Visuales 87
    Museo de la Moda 92
    Museo de la Solidaridad Salvador
        Allende 92
    Museo Lukas 125

Museo Municipal de Bellas Artes
    (Viña del Mar) 135
Museo Nacional de Bellas Artes
    (Santiago) 87
arts 47-52
Atacama Desert 21, 62, 207, 216
Atacameño peoples 31, 46, 175, 220
Atoca 185
ATMs 469
Ayquina 222
Aymara peoples 31, 45, 46, 181, 187,
    190, 191

B
Bachelet, Michelle 42, 43
Bahía Inglesa 235
Bahía Tierras Blancas 437
Baños Morales 119
Baquedano 207
bargaining 471
bars 54
bathrooms 472
beaches
    Arica 180
    Bahía Inglesa 235
    Concón 139
    Coquimbo 251-2
    Easter Island 446, 458-9, 459
    Guanaqueros 252
    Horcón 139
    Iquique 197
    La Serena 246
    Maintencillo 139
    Norte Chico 234
    Papudo 140
    Quintay 140
    Reñaca 139
    Ritoque 138
    safety 466
    Tongoy 252
    Zapallar 140
Beagle Channel 383, 420, 421, 15
beavers 68, 416
beer 55, *see also* breweries
Belén 188
bicycle travel, *see* cycling & mountain
    biking
bird watching
    books 64
    El Calafate (Arg) 401

Isla de Huevos 262
Isla de los Pájaros 420
Laguna Chaxa 220-1
Laguna Cotacotani 190
Laguna Miñiques 221
Laguna Miscanti 221
Monumento Natural dos Lagunas 363
Monumento Natural Salar de Surire 192-3
Parque Nacional Lauca 191
Parque Nacional Nevado Tres Cruces 240
Parque Nacional Tierra del Fuego (Arg) 425
Parque Nacional Torres del Paine 393
Reserva Nacional Jeinemeni 366-7
Santuario de la Naturaleza Laguna Conchalí 261-2
Valdivia 290
Valle Chacabuco 369
birds 64
black widow spiders 394-5
boat tours
    Antarctica 421, 422
    Archipiélago Juan Fernández 435
    Beagle Channel 383, 420, 421, 15
    Cabo de Hornos 421
    Caleta Tortel 370
    Coquimbo 251-2
    Cordillera Darwin 383
    Iquique 197
    Isla Navarino 414
    Navimag 319
    Parque Nacional Alberto de Agostini 383
    Parque Nacional Bernardo O'Higgins 392-3
    Parque Nacional Queulat 356
    Parque Pumalín 347
    Pérez Rosales Pass 308
    Puerto Montt 320
    South Georgia Island 421
    Valdivia 290-2
boat travel 482-3, *see also* boat tours, kayaking
Bolsico 228
books 22-4, *see also* literature
    bird watching 64
    climbing 71
    culture 48, 52
    cycling 72
    environment 65, 66, 68
    food 54, 58
    health 489

hiking 70
history 32, 33, 36, 39, 40
    language 44, 495-6
    wine 55
border crossings 478
    Argentina 308, 371, 375, 478-80
    Bolivia 480
    Peru 480
breweries
    Cervecería Kunstmann 294
    HBH Brewery 107
Bridges, Lucas 426, 427
Bucalemu 150
Buchupureo 163
Buque Huáscar 167
bus travel
    to/from Chile 478
    within Chile 483-4, 486
bushwalking, *see* hiking
business hours 463

C
cabañas 461
cabins 461
Cabo de Hornos 416-17, 421
Cabo Froward 384
cabs 486
Cachagua 139
cacti 64
café con piernas 105
Cajón de Mapocho 119-20
Cajón del Maipo 116-19
Calama 206-10, **208**
Caldera 234-5
Caleta Tortel 370
camanchaca 177
Camerón 412
camping 461
Cañete 168
canopying 74
    Glaciar Martial (Arg) 420
    Peulla 310
    Pucón 279
    Ushuaia (Arg) 420
canyoning 74
    Futaleufú 351
    Parque Nacional Vicente Pérez Rosales 310
    Puerto Varas 304
car travel
    driver's licenses 484
    insurance 485
    legal matters 468
    rental 484-5
    road rules 485-6

to/from Chile 478
    within Chile 484-6
carbon offset 477
Carretera Austral 345
casa de familia 461
Casablanca Valley 141
Caspana 222
Castillo de Corral 294
Castillo de la Pura y Limpia Concepción de Monfort de Lemus 294
Castillo San Pedro de Alcántara 294
Castro 332-6, **333**
Catarpe 219-20
cathedrals, *see* churches & cathedrals
cell phones 471-2
cemeteries
    Cementerio Municipal (Punta Arenas) 377-9
    Hanga Roa cemetery 446
    Pisagua 193
Cerro Azul 157
Cerro Centinela 437
Cerro El Roble 141
Cerro Guane Guane 191
Cerro La Campana 141
Cerro Martial (Arg) 420
Cerro Sagrado 185
Cerro Unita 198
Chacabuco 207
Chaitén 348-50
Chañaral 231-3
Chañarcillo 239
Chapa Verde 146
Chatwin, Bruce 392
chemists 490
Chepu 327-8
children, travel with 463-4
    food 59
    health 494
    language 502
    Santiago 94
Chile Chico 365-6
Chilean recluse spider 493
Chillán 158-61, **159**
Chiloé 321-40, **322**
Chiloé mythology 329
Chinchorro peoples 186
chirimoya 53
Chiu Chiu 222
Chonchi 336-7
Choshuenco 289
Chuquicamata 210-12
churches & cathedrals 334
    Catedral de Chillán 158
    Catedral Metropolitana 82

churches & cathedrals *continued*
Iglesia Catedral 245
Iglesia de Nuestra Señora del
Rosario 203
Iglesia de Putre 188
Iglesia de San Andrés 205
Iglesia de San Antonio 205
Iglesia de San Francisco (Chiu
Chiu) 222
Iglesia de San Francisco
(Santiago) 83
Iglesia de San Gerónimo 186
Iglesia Hanga Roa 446
Iglesia Nuestra Señora de Loreto 239
Iglesia Parroquial María Inmaculada
311
Iglesia San Agustín 245
Iglesia San Francisco (La Serena)
245
Iglesia San Francisco (Valparaíso)
128
Iglesia San Francisco de Castro 332-3
Iglesia San Marcos 180
Iglesia San Pedro 213
Iglesia Santa María de Loreto 331
Iglesia Santo Domingo 245
Nuestra Señora de Los Dolores
church 329
Nuestra Señora del Patrocinio
church 328
Parinacota church 190
Villupulli church 334
Cifuncho 229
cinema 49-50
climate 21, 464
internet resources 75
climate change 69, 405, 477
climbing 71-2
books 71
Huilo-Huilo Reserva Natural
Biosfera 289
Parque Nacional Villarrica 284
Parque Nacional Vicente Pérez
Rosales 308-9
Parque Nacional Torres del Paine
394
Pucón 280
Puerto Natales 388
Volcán Calbuco 309
Volcán Llaima 273
Volcán Osorno 308-9

Cobija 206
Cobquecura 162-3
Cochamó 311
Cochiguaz 256-7, 246
Cochrane 368-9
colectivos 486
Colchagua Valley 148
Coñaripe 288
Concepción 163-7, **165**
Concón 139
conservation, *see* environmental
issues
consulates 466-7
Copiapó 235-40, **237**
Coquimbo 251-2
costs 21
accommodations 460
food 467
courses 464-5
cooking 129, 246
culture 181, 246
language 94, 181, 198, 246, 421
Coyhaique 357-62, **358**
credit cards 469
Cruce el Maitén 367
Crusoe, Robinson 430
Cueva del Milodón 392
Cuevas de los Patriotas 435
cultural centers
Casa de la Cultura (Chile Chico) 365
Centro Cultural Kespikala 203
Centro Cultural La Sebastiana 128
Centro Cultural Matucana 100 91
Centro Cultural Palacio La Moneda
83
Centro de Cultura (Iquique) 195
Estación Mapocho 83
culture 44-52
books 48, 52
courses 181, 246
internet resources 46, 47
Curacautín 273-4
Curaco de Vélez 330
curanto 326
Curarrehue 287
Curicó 151-2
customs 46, 59
customs regulations 465
cycling & mountain biking 72-3,
481-2
books 72
Easter Island 448
Huilo-Huilo Reserva Natural
Biosfera 289
internet resources 72

Pisco Elqui 257
Pucón 280
Santiago 93

D
Dalcahue 329-30
dance 52
dangers, *see* safe travel
deep vein thrombosis (DVT) 489
dengue fever 491-2
departure tax 476
desierto florido 242
Dientes de Navarino 414
digital photography 470
disabilities, travelers with 472-3
diving & snorkeling 74
Archipiélago Juan Fernández
432, 435
Easter Island 446-7
Quintay 140
Reserva Nacional Pingüino de
Humboldt 244
dog mushing 420
dogs 465
dolphins 63
Porvenir 411-12
Reserva Nacional Pingüino de
Humboldt 243, 244
drinks 55-8, *see also* beer, wine
driver's licenses 484
driving, *see* car travel
drugstores 490
duty-free zones 205

E
earthquakes 465
Easter Island 439-59, **440**, 16
accommodations 448-52
activities 446-8
attractions 444-6
climate 440
culture 442-3
drinking 453
entertainment 453
environment 443
food 452-3
history 441-2
internet resources 51
language 496
shopping 454
tours 448
travel to/from 443
travel within 443-4
economy 42, 43, 45
education 43

El Calafate (Arg) 400-4, **401**
El Cañi 286
El Caulle 300
El Chaltén (Arg) 405-7
El Colorado 120
El Gigante de Atacama 202
El Tatio geysers 221, 10
electricity 460
elephant seals 432
Elqui Valley 246, 252-8
embassies 466-7
emergencies, *see also inside front cover*
　language 499
Enquelga 202
Ensenada 307-8
Entre Lagos 298-9
environment 62-9
　books 65, 66, 68
environmental issues 67-9
　aquaculture 69, 315
　beavers 416
　carbon offset 477
　glaciers retreating 69, 405
　hydroelectricity 68, 359
　mining 68
　ozone layer 398
environmental organizations 69, 385
estancias
　Eberhard Ranch 388
　Estancia Harberton (Arg) 426
　Estancia Río Verde 384-5
　Estancia Yendegaia 412-13
exchange rates, *see inside front cover*

F
Farellones 120
ferries, *see* boat travel
festivals & events 23, 467
　Artisan's fair (La Serena) 248
　Big Rock Festival 388
　Brotes de Chile 171
　Campeonato Nacional de Rodeo
　　145
　Carnaval (Putre) 188
　Carnaval (San Pedro de Atacama)
　　216
　Carnaval de Invierno 379
　Carnaval Ginga 181
　Concurso Nacional de Cueca 181
　Día de la Lengua Rapanui 448
　Día del Minero 238
　Encuentro Folklórico de Chiloé 467
　Encuentro Folklórico de las Islas
　　del Archipiélago 331
　Feria Internacional de Artesanía 95

Feria Internacional del Aire y del
　Espacio 95
Feria Internacional del Libro 95
Feria Internacional del Libro de La
　Serena 248
Feria Regional (Putre) 188
Festival Costumbrista (Castro) 334
Festival Costumbrista (Villa Cerro
　Castillo) 364
Festival de Cine de la Patagonia 388
Festival de Huaso Chilote 467
Festival de Jazz de Ñuñoa 95
Festival de La Serena 248
Festival de la Vendimia 151, 254
Festival de la Virgen del Carmen 467
Festival del Barrio Brasil 95
Festival Internacional de la Canción
　135
Festival Nacional del Folklore 95
Fiesta de Aniversario 435
Fiesta de la Candelaria 238
Fiesta de la Vendimia 147-8
Fiesta de Nuestra Señora de la
　Candelaria 216
Fiesta de San Andrés 205
Fiesta de San Pedro 435
Fiesta de San Pedro y San Pablo
　216
Fiesta de Santa Rosa de Lima 216
Jornadas Musicales de La Serena 248
Jornadas Musicales de Pucón 467
Marcha Blanca 420
Muestra Cultural Mapuche 276
Noche de Valdivia 292
Patagonia Expedition Race 385
Rodeo de Palena 353
Rodeo de Villagra 435
rodeo season (Santiago) 95
Santiago a Mil 95
Santiago Festival Internacional de
　Cine 95
Semana Ancuditana 324
Semana Ariqueña 181
Semana Musical de Frutillar 301
Semana Palena 353
Semana Vileña 262
Tapati Rapa Nui 448, 449, 16
Virgin of Carmen festival 203
Winter solstice 379
fishing 75
　Archipiélago Juan Fernández 435
　Coquimbo 252
　Coyhaique 359-60
　Cruce el Maitén 367
　El Calafate (Arg) 402

Isla Navarino 414
La Junta 354
Parque Nacional Queulat 356
Porvenir 411-12
Puerto Varas 304
Reserva Nacional Cerro Castillo 364
Reserva Nacional Jeinemeni 366-7
Reserva Nacional Río Simpson 363
flamingos 64
　Laguna Chaxa 220
　Laguna Miñiques 221
　Laguna Miscanti 221
　Monumento Natural Salar de
　　Surire 192
　Parque Nacional Lauca 191
　Parque Nacional Nevado Tres
　　Cruces 240
　Parque Nacional Torres del Paine
　　393
　Reserva Nacional Jeinemeni 366-7
　Valle Chacabuco 369
flowering desert 242
food 53-61, 58, 467
　books 54, 58
　courses 129, 246
football 46, 110
Frutillar 301-2
Fuerte Bulnes 384
Fuerte Castillo de Amargos 294
Fuerte Niebla 294
Fuerte San Antonio 324
Fuerte Santa Bárbara 435
fur seals 63, 432, 435
Futaleufú 351-3
fútbol 46
Futrono 294-5

G
Gatico 206
gay travelers 467
　Santiago 109
geoglyphs 185, 186
　Atoca 185
　Cerro Sagrado 185
　El Gigante de Atacama 202
　Geoglifos Chug Chug 212
　Lluta geoglyphs 186
　Pintados 198, 204
　Pukará San Lorenzo 185
geology 62-3
ghost towns 201
　Chacabuco 207
　Chañarcillo 239
　Humberstone 201-2
　Sewell 146

Gigantes de Lluta 186
Glaciar Martial (Arg) 420
Glaciar Perito Moreno (Arg) 402, 404
Glaciar Zapata 397
glacier trekking
  Coñaripe 288
  El Chaltén (Arg) 406
  Huilo-Huilo Reserva Natural
    Biosfera 289
  Parque Nacional Los Glaciares
    (South) (Arg) 404
  Parque Nacional Torres del Paine
    397
  Puerto Natales 388
  Steffens 370
  Ushuaia (Arg) 421
  Ventisqueros Montt 370
glaciers 69, 405
golf 92
Grotto of the Virgins 458
Guallatire 192
guanacos 64
  Parque Nacional Llanos de Challe
    242
  Parque Nacional Nevado Tres
    Cruces 240
  Parque Nacional Pali Aike 385
  Parque Nacional Pan de Azúcar 233
  Parque Nacional Torres del Paine
    393
  Reserva Nacional Río de los
    Cipreses 147
  Valle Chacabuco 369, 15
Guanaqueros 252
Guevara, Che 29, 210

H
handicrafts
  Arica 184
  Chillán 160
  Mamiña 203
  Puerto Varas 306
  Santiago 110-11
  Temuco 269-71
  Villarrica 277
Hanga Roa 444-54, **445**
hantavirus pulmonary syndrome 492
Haush peoples 409
health 488-94
  books 489
  insurance 488

internet resources 488-9
language 499
hepatitis A 490
hepatitis B 490
hiking 70-1
  Archipiélago Juan Fernández 435
  books 70
  Cerro Martial (Arg) 420
  Circuito Dientes de Navarino 414
  Easter Island 447
  El Cañi 286
  Futaleufú 351
  Glaciar Martial (Arg) 420
  Huilo-Huilo Reserva Natural
    Biosfera 289
  Isla Navarino 414
  Lago Windhond 414
  Monumento Natural El Morado 119
  Ojos del Salado 240
  Parque Nacional Chiloé 338, 13
  Parque Nacional Conguillío 66,
    272-3, 12
  Parque Nacional Fray Jorge 261
  Parque Nacional Huerquehue 287
  Parque Nacional Isla Magdalena 357
  Parque Nacional Juan Fernández
    436-8
  Parque Nacional La Campana 142
  Parque Nacional Laguna del
    Laja 169
  Parque Nacional Lauca 191, 11
  Parque Nacional Nahuelbuta 172-3
  Parque Nacional Nevado Tres
    Cruces 240
  Parque Nacional Pali Aike 385
  Parque Nacional Puyehue 300
  Parque Nacional Queulat 356
  Parque Nacional Tierra del Fuego
    (Arg) 425-6
  Parque Nacional Tolhuaca 272
  Parque Nacional Torres del Paine
    395-7
  Parque Nacional Vicente Pérez
    Rosales 308-9
  Parque Nacional Villarrica 284
  Parque Pumalín 346, 347, 14
  Parque Tantauco 340
  Peulla 310
  Puerto Natales 388
  Reserva Nacional Alacalufes 385
  Reserva Nacional Altos de Lircay
    156-7
  Reserva Nacional Cerro Castillo 364
  Reserva Nacional Coyhaique 359,
    362

Reserva Nacional Jeinemeni 366-7
Reserva Nacional Malalcahuello-
  Nalcas 274-5
Reserva Nacional Río Clarillo 116
Reserva Nacional Río de los
  Cipreses 147
responsible hiking 71
Río Puelo Valley 313
Salto Grande 397
San Pedro de Atacama, around 216
Sanctuario de la Naturaleza
  Cascada de las Animas 118
Santiago 93
Sendero Bicentenario 129
Sendero de Chile 72
Ushuaia (Arg) 419-20
Valparaíso 129
Ventisquero Yelcho 351
Villa O'Higgins 371
Volcán Calbuco 309
Volcán Osorno 308-9
'W', the 395-6, **396**
historic buildings
  Casa Colorada 82-3
  Casa Solar de los Madariaga 253-4
  Edificio de la Aduana 197
  Ex-Aduana de Arica 180
  La Chascona 87
  Palacete Viña de Cristo 236
  Palacio Cousiño 92
  Palacio de la Moneda 83
history 30-43
  Allende administration 37-8
  Bachelet administration 42, 43
  books 32, 33, 36, 39, 40
  colonization 31-3
  early cultures 30-1
  independence 33-4
  internet resources 33
  Pinochet regime 38-41
  Santiago 77
hitchhiking 486
holidays 468
home stays 353, 461
Horcón (Middle Chile) 139
Horcón (Norte Chico) 257
Hornopirén 343-4
horse racing 110
horseback riding 73
  Easter Island 447
  El Chaltén (Arg) 406
  Futaleufú 351
  Huilo-Huilo Reserva Natural
    Biosfera 289
  Isla Navarino 414

INDEX

Pisco Elqui 257
Parque Nacional Torres del Paine 397
Porvenir 411-12
Pucón 280
Puerto Natales 388
Puerto Varas 304
Reserva Nacional Altos de Lircay 157
Río Puelo Valley 313
Ritoque 138
Santuario de la Naturaleza Cascada de las Animas 118
San Pedro de Atacama, around 216
Villa O'Higgins 371-2
horseflies 465
hospedaje 461
hostels 462
hotels 462
Huasco 242
Huasco Valley 241-2
huemul deer 65, 369-70
Humberstone 201-2
hydroelectricity 68, 359

I
indigenous peoples 32, *see also* Mapuche
    Alacaluf peoples 343, 370, 409
    Atacameño peoples 31, 46, 175, 220
    Aymara peoples 31, 45, 46, 181, 187, 190, 191
    Chinchorro peoples 186
    Haush peoples 409
    Selk'nam (Ona) peoples 33, 409, 427
    Yaghan (Yamaná) peoples 409, 413, 414, 419
insurance
    health 488
    travel 468
    vehicle 485
internet access 468
internet resources 24
    air tickets 476
    culture 46, 47
    cycling 72
    Easter Island 51
    health 488-9
    history 33
    maps 69
    Mapuche 45
    music 51
    national parks & other nature reserves 67

skiing & snowboarding 72
weather 75
white-water rafting 73
wine 55
Iquique 194-201, **196**, 11
Isla Alejandro Selkirk 438
Isla de Huevos 262
Isla de Lobos 262
Isla de los Pajaros 420
Isla Magdalena 379
Isla Mechuque 328-9, 13
Isla Navarino 413-15
Isla Negra 141
Isla Pan de Azúcar 233
Isla Quinchao 330-2
Isla Riesco 385
itineraries 25-9
    Che Guevara route 29
    Chile circuit 25, 26
    northern desert 28
    Patagonia 27
    Santiago 78
    wineries 29

J
Juan Fernández hummingbirds 432
Juan López 228

K
kayaking 73, 280
    Archipiélago Juan Fernández 435
    Beagle Channel 420
    El Chaltén (Arg) 406
    Ensenada 307
    Futaleufú 351
    Magellan Strait 379
    Parque Nacional Chiloé 327
    Parque Pumalín 347
    Porvenir 411-12
    Puerto Natales 388
    Puerto Varas 304
    Parque Nacional Torres del Paine 397
    Reserva Nacional Pingüino de Humboldt 244
    Ritoque 138
    Ushuaia (Arg) 421
King George Island 416
kitesurfing 73-4, 235

L
La Junta 353-4
La Parva 120
La Punta de Isla 437

La Serena 244-50, **247**
La Tirana 203-4
Lago Chungará 191
Lago General Pinto Concha 344
Lago Paine 397
Lago Panguipulli 288-9
Lago Pingo 397
Lago Pirihueico 289
Lago Ranco 294-8
Lago Ranco (village) 295
Lago Yelcho 351
Laguna Azul 397
Laguna Chaxa 220-1
Laguna Cotacotani 190
Laguna del Alto 157
Laguna Inca Coya 222
Laguna Miñiques 221
Laguna Miscanti 221
Laguna Verde (Parque Nacional Nevado Tres Cruces) 240
Laguna Verde (Parque Nacional Torres del Paine) 397
Lagunillas 119
landsailing 74
language 60, 495-502
    books 44, 495-6
    courses 94, 181, 198, 246, 421
Las Tórtolas 229
legal matters 468
lesbian travelers 467
    Santiago 109
Lican Ray 287-8
Licor de Oro 331
literature 48-9, *see also* books
llamas 64
Llanada Grande 312-13
Llico 150
Lluta geoglyphs 186
lobsters 435
Lolol 149
Los Andes 142-3
Los Angeles 170-1
Los Loros 239
Los Nichos 257
Los Vilos 261-2
Lota 167-8
Lucas 426
Lupica 188

M
Maintencillo 139
Maipo Valley 118
Mamiña 203
Mano del Desierto 228
maps 69, 77, 469

Mapuche 270, *see also* indigenous
peoples
communities 280, 287, 298
festivals 276
history 31, 32, 33, 34, 43, 45, 77,
123, 168, 270
internet resources 45
museums 168, 170, 267, 275-6,
287, 290, 297
Marea Roja (Red Tide) 323
María Elena 206
markets
Arica 183
Castro 336
Chillán 159
Dalcahue 329
Santiago 83, 89, 111
Temuco 270
Valdivia 290
Valparaíso 129
Maule Valley 157
Maunga Pu A Katiki 458
Maunga Terevaka 455
Maunga Vai a Heva 458
measures 460
medical services 490
Mejillones 222-3
Melipeuco 275
metric conversions, *see inside front
cover*
Mina Chiflón del Diablo 167
mining 43, 68, 167, 195, 210-12, 241,
see also ghost towns
Mirador de Selkirk 437
Mistral, Gabriela 48, 253, 256
moai 457, 458
mobile phones 471-2
money 21, 466, *see also inside front
cover*
Monte Grande 256
Monumento Arqueológico Valle del
Encanto 259-60
Monumento Natural Cerro Ñielol 267
Monumento Natural dos Lagunas 363
Monumento Natural El Morado 119
Monumento Natural La Portada 227-8
Monumento Natural Los Pingüinos 384
Monumento Natural Pichasca 260
Monumento Natural Salar de Surire
192-3
mosques 251

mosquitos 493
motorcycle travel 484-6
driver's license 484
insurance 485
legal matters 468
road rules 485-6
to/from Chile 478
within Chile 484-6
mountain biking, *see* cycling &
mountain biking
mountaineering, *see* climbing
museums, *see also* art galleries & art
museums
Asociación Minera Copiapó 236
Buque Huáscar 167
Casa de la Cultura (Chile Chico) 365
El Museo Viviente de las Tradiciones
Chonchinas 336
Galería de la Historia (Concepción)
164
Isla Negra 141
La Chascona 87
La Sebastiana 125-8
Mundo Yamaná (Arg) 419
Museo Acatushún 426
Museo Antiguo Monasterio del
Espíritu Santo 143
Museo Antropológico Sebastián
Englert 446
Museo Arqueológico (La Serena) 246
Museo Arqueológico (Los
Andes)143
Museo Arqueológico San Miguel
de Azapa 185
Museo Arqueológico Universidad
Católica del Norte 225
Museo Arqueológico y Etnológico
207
Museo Artequín 94
Museo Colonial de San Francisco 83
Museo de Achao 331
Museo de Arqueología e Historia
Francisco Fonck 135
Museo de Colchagua 147
Museo de Historia Natural
(Valparaíso) 128
Museo de Historia Natural y
Cultural del Desierto 207
Museo de la Alta Frontera 170
Museo de la Solidaridad Salvador
Allende 92
Museo de Santiago 83
Museo de Sitio 251
Museo de Taltal 229
Museo de Tierra del Fuego 411

Museo del Fin del Mundo (Arg)
419
Museo del Limarí 258
Museo del Presidio (Arg) 419
Museo del Recuerdo 379
Museo Dillman Bullock 171
Museo Entomológico y de Historia
Natural 253
Museo Gabriela Mistral 253
Museo Gustavo Le Paige 213-14
Museo Histórico (Puerto Natales)
388
Museo Histórico Casa Gabriel
González Videla 245-6
Museo Histórico Colonial Alemán
301
Museo Histórico Militar (Iquique)
197
Museo Histórico Municipal
(Osorno) 297
Museo Histórico Nacional 82
Museo Histórico y Antropológico
(Valdivia) 290
Museo Histórico y Arqueológico
(Villarrica) 275-6
Museo Histórico y de Armas 180
Museo Interactivo Mirador 94
Museo La Merced 83
Museo Mapuche de Cañete 168
Museo Marítimo (Arg) 419
Museo Martín Gusinde 413-14
Museo Nacional de Historia
Natural 94
Museo Naval (Iquique) 197
Museo Naval y Marítimo (Punta
Arenas) 379
Museo Naval y Marítimo
(Valparaíso) 128
Museo Regional (Antofagasta)
225
Museo Regional (Iquique) 195
Museo Regional Aurelio Bórquez
Canobra 324
Museo Regional Braun-Menéndez
377
Museo Regional de Atacama 238
Museo Regional de Castro 333-4
Museo Regional de la Araucanía 267
Museo Regional de la Patagonia
360
Museo Regional de Rancagua 145
Museo Regional Salesiano 379
Palacio Cousiño 92
Villa Cultural Huilquilemu 156
music 50-1

N
ñandú 191, 192
Nantoco 239
national parks & other nature reserves 23, 65-7
El Cañi 286
Estancia Yendegaia 412-13
Huilo-Huilo Reserva Natural Biosfera 289
internet resources 67
Monumento Natural Cerro Ñielol 267
Monumento Natural dos Lagunas 363
Monumento Natural El Morado 119
Monumento Natural La Portada 227-8
Monumento Natural Los Pingüinos 384
Monumento Natural Pichasca 260
Monumento Natural Salar de Surire 192-3
Parque Marino Francisco Coloane 384
Parque Nacional Alerce Andino 66
Parque Nacional Bernado O'Higgins 66, 392-3
Parque Nacional Chiloé 66, 327, 334, 337-8, 13
Parque Nacional Conguillío 66, 272-3, 12
Parque Nacional Fray Jorge 66, 261
Parque Nacional Hornopirén 344
Parque Nacional Huerquehue 66, 286-7
Parque Nacional Isla Magdalena 357
Parque Nacional Juan Fernández 66, 436-8
Parque Nacional La Campana 66, 141-2
Parque Nacional Laguna del Laja 66, 169-70
Parque Nacional Laguna San Rafael 66, 364
Parque Nacional Lauca 66, 189-92, 11
Parque Nacional Llanos de Challe 66, 242-3
Parque Nacional Los Glaciares (North) (Arg) 405-7
Parque Nacional Los Glaciares (South) (Arg) 404-5
Parque Nacional Nahuelbuta 66, 172-3, **172**
Parque Nacional Nevado Tres Cruces 66, 240

Parque Nacional Pali Aike 385
Parque Nacional Pan de Azúcar 67, 233-4
Parque Nacional Puyehue 67, 299-300, **299**
Parque Nacional Queulat 355-6
Parque Nacional Rapa Nui 67, 454-9
Parque Nacional Tierra del Fuego (Arg) 425-6
Parque Nacional Tolhuaca 271-2
Parque Nacional Torres del Paine 67, 393-400, **394**, **5**, **14**
Parque Nacional Vicente Pérez Rosales 67, 308-10, **309**
Parque Nacional Villarrica 67, 284-5
Parque Nacional Volcán Isluga 67, 202-3
Parque Pumalín 345-8, 349, 14
Parque Tantauco 340
Reserva Forestal Magallanes 377
Reserva Nacional Alacalufes 385
Reserva Nacional Altos de Lircay 67, 156-8
Reserva Nacional Cerro Castillo 364
Reserva Nacional Coyhaique 359, 362
Reserva Nacional Jeinemeni 366-7
Reserva Nacional Las Vicuñas 192, 198
Reserva Nacional Los Flamencos 67, 220-1
Reserva Nacional Malalcahuello-Nalcas 274-5
Reserva Nacional Pampa del Tamarugal 204
Reserva Nacional Pingüino de Humboldt 67, 243-4
Reserva Nacional Radal Siete Tazas 67, 152-3
Reserva Nacional Río Clarillo 116
Reserva Nacional Río de los Cipreses 146-7
Reserva Nacional Río Simpson 363
Reserva Nacional Tamango 67, 369-70
Santuario de la Naturaleza Cascada de las Animas 118
Santuario de la Naturaleza Laguna Conchalí 261-2
Navimag 319
Neruda, Pablo 48, 49, 87, 125-8, 141
newspapers 460

O
observatories 216
Atacama Large Milimetre Array 216
Observatorio Cerro Paranal 228
Observatorio Comunal Cerro Mamalluca 255-6
Observatorio Interamericano Cerro Tololo 250-1
Observatorio Turístico Collowara 251
Ojos del Salado 240
Ona (Selk'nam) peoples 33, 409, 427
opening hours 463
Orongo ceremonial village 455
Osorno 295-8, **296**
Ovalle 258-9, **259**

P
Paihuano 256
painting 52
palafitos 332
Palena 353
Panguipulli 288-9
Papa Vaka 458
Papudo 140
paragliding 74, 197-8
Parinacota 190
parks & gardens
Cerro San Cristóbal 87-9, **6**
Cerro Santa Lucía 86
Jardín Botánico Mapulemu 88-9
Jardín Botánico Nacional 135
Jardín Japonés 89
Kokoro No Niwa 246
Omora 414
Parque Botánico Isidora Cousiño 167
Parque de las Esculturas 92
Parque Forestal 87
Parque Metropolitano 87-9, 94, **6**
Parque por la Paz 92
Parque Punta Curiñanco 294
Parque Quinta Normal 91
Parque Quinta Vergara 135
Parque Yatana (Arg) 419
Parque Marino Francisco Coloane 384
Parque Nacional Alerce Andino 66
Parque Nacional Bernardo O'Higgins 66, 392-3
Parque Nacional Chiloé 66, 327, 334, 337-8, **13**
Parque Nacional Conguillío 66, 272-3, **12**
Parque Nacional Fray Jorge 66, 261
Parque Nacional Hornopirén 344
Parque Nacional Huerquehue 66, 286-7

Parque Nacional Isla Magdalena 357
Parque Nacional Juan Fernández 66, 436-8
Parque Nacional La Campana 66, 141-2
Parque Nacional Laguna del Laja 66, 169-70
Parque Nacional Laguna San Rafael 66, 364
Parque Nacional Lauca 66, 189-92, 11
Parque Nacional Llanos de Challe 66, 242-3
Parque Nacional Los Glaciares (North) (Arg) 405-7
Parque Nacional Los Glaciares (Arg) (South) 404-5
Parque Nacional Nahuelbuta 66, 172-3, **172**
Parque Nacional Nevado Tres Cruces 66, 240
Parque Nacional Pali Aike 385
Parque Nacional Pan de Azúcar 67, 233-4
Parque Nacional Puyehue 67, 299-300, **299**
Parque Nacional Queulat 355-6
Parque Nacional Rapa Nui 67, 454-9
Parque Nacional Tierra del Fuego (Arg) 425-6
Parque Nacional Tolhuaca 271-2
Parque Nacional Torres del Paine 67, 393-400, **394**, 5, 14
Parque Nacional Vicente Pérez Rosales 67, 308-10, **309**
Parque Nacional Villarrica 67, 284-5
Parque Nacional Volcán Isluga 67, 188, 202-3
Parque Pumalín 345-8, 349, 14
Parque Tantauco 340
passports 475
penguins 64
    Isla Magdalena 379
    Monumento Nacional Isla de Cachagua 139
    Monumento Natural Los Pingüinos 384
    Parque Nacional Pan de Azúcar 233
    Pingüinera Puñihuil 327
    Reserva Nacional Pingüino de Humboldt 243-4
    Seno Otway 379, 384
    Ushuaia (Arg) 421

Península Poike 457-8
petroglyphs, *see also* geoglyphs
    Monumento Arqueológico Valle del Encanto 259-60
    Papa Vaka 458
Petrohué 309-10
Peulla 310
pharmacies 490
phone codes 472
photography 470
Pica 204-5
Pichilemu 149-51, 8
Pingüinera Puñihuil 327
Pinochet, Augusto 38-41
Pintados 198, 204
Pirque 116
Pisagua 193-4, 198
pisco 55, 253
pisco distilleries
    Distelería Mistral 257
    Planta Pisco Capel 255
Pisco Elqui 257, 10
planning 21-4, 466, 488, 489, *see also* costs, itineraries
plants 64-6, 242, 432, *see also* individual species
Poconchile 186
poetry 48-9
Pokemones 44
Pomaire 115-16
population 46
Portillo 143-4
Porvenir 410-12, **411**
postal services 470
potatoes 30
public holidays 468
Pucón 278-84, **279**
pudú 63, 337
Puelo 312
Puente Ventisquero 351
Puerto Bertrand 368
Puerto Chacabuco 363
Puerto Cisnes 356-7
Puerto Francés 438
Puerto Guadal 367-8
Puerto Hambre 384
Puerto Ingeniero Ibáñez 365
Puerto Inglés 438
Puerto Montt 313-20, **314**
Puerto Natales 386-92, **387**
Puerto Octay 300-1
Puerto Puyuhuapi 354-5
Puerto Río Tranquilo 367
Puerto Vaquería 438
Puerto Varas 302-7, **303**

Puerto Williams 413-16
Pukará de Lasana 222
Pukará de Quitor 219-20
Pukará San Lorenzo 185
Puna Pau 455
Punta Arenas 376-84, **378**
Putre 187-9

Q
Quellón 339-40, **339**
Quemchi 328
Quillagua 205
Quintay 140

R
rabies 491
radio 460
Rancagua 144-6, **145**
Rano Kau 455
Rano Raraku 456
Rapa Nui, *see* Easter Island
Rapa Nui language 496
refugios 462
religion 47
Reñaca 139
Reserva Nacional Alacalufes 385
Reserva Nacional Altos de Lircay 67, 156-8
Reserva Nacional Cerro Castillo 364
Reserva Nacional Coyhaique 359, 362
Reserva Nacional Jeinemeni 366-7
Reserva Nacional Las Vicuñas 192, 198
Reserva Nacional Los Flamencos 67, 220-1
Reserva Nacional Malalcahuello-Nalcas 274-5
Reserva Nacional Pampa del Tamarugal 204
Reserva Nacional Pingüino de Humboldt 67, 243-4
Reserva Nacional Radal Siete Tazas 67, 152-3
Reserva Nacional Río Clarillo 116
Reserva Nacional Río de los Cipreses 146-7
Reserva Nacional Río Simpson 363
Reserva Nacional Tamango 67, 369-70
residenciales 461
responsible travel 21-2, *see also* GreenDex
    Easter Island 454
    hiking 71, 395
rhea 63
Río Cochamó Valley 311-12

INDEX

Río Grande (Arg) 427-8
Río Liucura Valley 285-6
Río Puelo Valley 312-13
Río Rubens 385
Río Verde 384-5
Ritoque 138
road rules 485-6
Robinson Crusoe 430
rock art, *see* petroglyphs
rock climbing, *see* climbing
Roman Catholicism 47

S

safe travel, *see also* emergencies
   beaches 466
   dogs 465
   hitchhiking 486
   water 494
Salar de Surire 188
salmon farming 69, 315
Salto del Laja 168-9
San Alfonso 118-19
San Juan Bautista 433-6, **434**
San Pedro de Atacama 212-19, **214**
sand-boarding 74
   Iquique 197
   San Pedro de Atacama, around
      216
Santa Cruz 147-9
Santa Laura 201-2
Santiago 76-120, **80-1**
   accommodations 95-8
   activities 92-3
   attractions 82-92
   Barrio Bellas Artes 86-7, 96, 100-1,
      105-6
   Barrio Bellavista 87-9, 96, 101-2,
      106, **88**
   Barrio Brasil 89-91, 96-7, 102,
      106, **89**
   Barrio Lastarria 86-7, 96, 100-1,
      105-6, **7**
   Centro 82-7, 95-6, 98-100, 105,
      84-5
   courses 94
   dangers 82
   drinking 104-7
   emergency services 78
   entertainment 107-10
   festivals & events 95
   food 98-104
   for children 94
   gay & lesbian travelers 109
   itineraries 78
   Las Condes 98, 103-4, 106, **99**

Ñuñoa 104, 107, **104**
   Providencia 91-2, 97-8, 102-3,
      106, **90-1**
   shopping 110-11
   tourist information 79, 82
   tours 94-5
   travel to/from 112-13
   travel within 113-15, **115**
   Vitacura 92
   walking tour 93-4, **93**
Santuario de la Naturaleza Granito
   Orbicular 235
Santuario de la Naturaleza Laguna
   Conchalí 261-2
Saxamar 188
sculpture 52
sea-kayaking, *see* kayaking
sea lions 63
   Cobquecura 162
   Isla de Lobos 262
   Isla de los Lobos 420
   Pisagua 193
   Valdivia 290
Selkirk, Alexander 430, 437, 438
Selk'nam (Ona) peoples 33, 409, 427
Sendero de Chile 72
senior travelers 470
Seno Otway 379, 384
Sewell 146
shopping 470-1, *see also* handicrafts
   duty-free zones 205
   language 500
skiing & snowboarding 72
   Antillanca 300
   Chapa Verde 146
   Coyhaique 360
   El Colorado 120
   Farellones 120
   internet resources 72
   La Parva 120
   Lagunillas 119
   Nevados de Chillán 161, **9**
   Parque Nacional Conguillío 273
   Parque Nacional Laguna del
      Laja 169
   Parque Nacional Vicente Pérez
      Rosales 309
   Parque Nacional Villarrica 284-5
   Portillo 143-4
   Tres Valles 119-20
   Ushuaia (Arg) 420
   Valle Nevado 120
   Volcán Osorno 309
smog 466
snorkeling, *see* diving & snorkeling

snowboarding, *see* skiing &
   snowboarding
Socaire 221
soccer 46, 110
Socoroma 187
solo travelers 471
South Shetland Islands 416
Spanish 495-502
spiders 394-5, 493
sports 46
surfing 73-4
   Arica 180-1
   Buchupureo 163
   Cobquecura 162
   Easter Island 447
   Iquique 197
   La Serena 246
   Pichilemu 149-50, **8**
   Ritoque 138
sustainable travel 21-2, 477, *see also*
   GreenDex

T

tábano 465
Talca 153-6, **154**
Taltal 228-9
Tapati Rapa Nui 448, 449, **16**
Tarapacá 202, 205
taxis 486
telephone services 471
Temuco 266-71, **268**
Tenaún 328
tennis 92-3
Termas de Chillán 161-2
Termas de Puyehue 299
theater 52
theft 466
theme parks 94
thermal springs
   Aguas Calientes 300
   Coñaripe 286
   Curarrehue 286
   Isla Llancahué 344
   Mamiña 203
   Parque Nacional Huerquehue 287
   Parque Nacional Isla Magdalena 357
   Parque Nacional Lauca 189-90
   Parque Nacional Tolhuaca 272
   Parque Pumalín 347
   Reserva Nacional Malalcahuello-
      Nalcas 274
   Termas del Ventisquero 355
   Termas de Puritama 220
   Termas de Puyehue 299
   Termas de Puyuhuapi 355

thermal springs *continued*
  Termas de Socos 260
  Termas El Amarillo 349, 350-1
  Termas Valle de Colina 119
  Valle de Liucara 286
  Valle Hermoso 161
  Vegas de Turi 222
Tierra del Fuego 408-28, **409**
Tignamar Viejo 188
Timaukel 412
time 472
tipping 470
Toconao 221-2
Toconce 222
Tocopilla 205-6
toilets 472
Tolhuin (Arg) 426-7
Tompkins, Douglas 66-7, 347
Tongoy 252
tourist information 472
tours 486-7, *see also* boat tours
  Altiplano lakes 215
  Andacollo 246
  Antarctica 421, 422
  Archipiélago Juan Fernández 435
  Arica 181
  Atacama Desert 207
  Aysén Glacier 368
  Azapa Valley 181
  Bahía Inglesa 238
  Beagle Channel 383, 420, 421, **15**
  Cabo Froward 388
  Cerro Unita 198
  Chiloé 324
  Chuquicamata 212
  Cochiguaz 246
  Copiapó 238
  Cueva de las Manos (Arg) 366
  Easter Island 448
  El Gigante de Atacama 198
  El Tatio geysers 215, **10**
  Elqui Valley 246
  Estancia Harberton (Arg) 421
  Frutillar 304
  Glaciar Perito Moreno (Arg) 402
  Humberstone 198
  Isla Magdalena 379
  Isla Mechuque 334, **13**
  Isla Navarino 388, 414
  Lago Fagnano 421
  Lago Grey 388

Lago Llanquihue 304
Laguna Jeinimeni 366
Mapuche communities 280
Monumento Nacional Salar de
  Surire 198
observatories 246
Ojos del Salado 238
Parque Nacional Fray Jorge 246
Parque Nacional Laguna San Rafael
  364
Parque Nacional Lauca 181, 188,
  191, 198, **11**
Parque Nacional Los Glaciares
  (South) (Arg) 404
Parque Nacional Nevado Tres
  Cruces 238
Parque Nacional Pan de Azúcar
  233, 238
Parque Nacional Torres del Paine
  379, 388, **14**
Parque Nacional Volcán Isluga 198
Parque Pumalín 347, 349, **14**
Pewenche indigenous land
  (Icalma) 275
Pintados 198
Pisagua 198
pisco tasting 246
Punta Arenas 379
Pukara de Quitor 215
Putre 188
Reserva Nacional Altos de Lircay 157
Reserva Nacional Las Vicuñas 198
Reserva Nacional Pingüino de
  Humboldt 246
Río Baker 368
Santiago 94-5
Seno Otway 379
star gazing 216
Termas El Amarillo 349
Tulor 215
Uyuni (Bol) 215
Valle de la Luna 215
Valle del Encanto 246
Valparaíso 129
Yelcho Glacier 349
train travel 486, 487
trains
  El Tren del Fin de Mundo 426
  Locomotora No 59 228-9
  Tren del Vino 147
tramping, *see* hiking
traveler's checks 470
travel to/from Chile 475-80
travel within Chile 480-7
trekking, *see* hiking

Tres Valles 119-20
TV 460
typhoid fever 490-1

U
Unesco sites 62, 334
  Cabo de Hornos 416-17
  Chiloé churches 334
  Humberstone 201-2
  Iglesia San Francisco de Castro 332-3
  Iglesia Santa María de Loreto 331
  Nuestra Señora de Los Dolores
    church 329
  Nuestra Señora del Patrocinio
    church 328
  Parque Nacional Conguillío 66,
    272-3, **12**
  Parque Nacional Juan Fernández
    66, 436-8
  Parque Nacional Fray Jorge 66, 261
  Parque Nacional La Campana 66,
    141-2
  Parque Nacional Laguna San
    Rafael 66, 364
  Parque Nacional Lauca 66,
    189-92, **11**
  Parque Nacional Rapa Nui 67,
    454-9
  Parque Nacional Torres del Paine
    67, 393-400, **394**, **5**, **14**
  Santa Laura 201-2
  Valparaíso 123-34, **126-7**, **8**, **9**
  Villupulli church 334
Ushuaia (Arg) 417-25, **418**
Uyuni (Bol) 215

V
vacations 468
vaccinations 489
Valdivia 289-94, **291**
Valdivia, Pedro de 31, 32
Valle Chacabuco 369, **15**
Valle de Aconcagua 142-4
Valle de la Luna 215, 220
Valle del Encanto 246, 259-60
Valle del Río Hurtado 260
Valle Las Trancas 161-2
Valle Nevado 120
Vallenar 241-2
Valparaíso 123-34, **126-7**, **8**, **9**
  accommodations 129-31
  attractions 125-9
  courses 129
  drinking 132
  entertainment 132-3

food 131-2
shopping 133
tours 129
travel to/from 133
travel to within 134
vegetarian travelers 59
Ventisquero Yelcho 351
Vicuña 252-5, **254**
vicuñas 63, 64, 190, 191, 192, 240
Villa Amengual 356
Villa Cerro Castillo 364-5
Villa Mañihuales 356
Villa O'Higgins 371-2
Villa Santa Lucía 351
Villagra 437
Villarrica 275-8, **276**
Viña del Mar 134-8, **136-7**
vineyards 29
  Casa Apostolle Clos Apalta Winery
    148
  Casa Donoso 157
  Catrala 141
  Cavas del Valle 256
  Emiliana 148
  Estampa 148
  Montes 148
  MontGras 148
  Viña Almaviva 118
  Viña Aquitania 118
  Viña Balduzzi 157
  Viña Bisquertt 148
  Viña Casa Silva 148
  Viña Casas del Bosque 141
  Viña Concha y Toro 118
  Viña Cousiño Macul 118
  Viña de Martino 118
  Viña Gillmore 157
  Viña Hugo Casanova 157
  Viña Indómita 141
  Viña Mar 141
  Viña Matetic 141
  Viña Santa Carolina 118
  Viña Santa Laura 148
  Viña Santa Rita 118
  Viña Undurraga 118
  Viña Veramonte 141

Viñedos Orgánicos Emiliana 141
Viu Manent 148
William Cole 141
visas 473, *see also* passports
viscachas
  Parque Nacional Lauca 190, 191
  Valle Chacabuco 369
Volcán Antuco 169
Volcán Calbuco 309
Volcán Chaitén 348, 349
Volcán Descabezado 157
Volcán El Palomo 146
Volcán Isluga 202
Volcán Llaima 272
Volcán Osorno 308-9
Volcán Villarrica 281
volcanoes 465
volunteering 426, 473

W
walking, *see* hiking
water 494
waterfalls
  Chilcas 169
  Salto del Laja 168-9
  Salto del Torbellino 169
  Salto la Leona 152
  Saltos del Petrohué 310
  Santuario de la Naturaleza Cascada
    de las Animas 118
  Siete Tazas 152
  Velo de la Novia 152
water sports
  Bahía Inglesa 235
  La Serena 246
weather 21, 464
  internet resources 75
websites, *see* internet resources
whale watching
  Castro 334
  Parque Marino Francisco Coloane
    379, 384
whales 68
white-water rafting 73
  Ensenada 307
  Futaleufú 351

internet resources 73
Parque Nacional Vicente Pérez
  Rosales 310
Pucón 280
Puerto Varas 304
wildlife reserves, *see* national parks &
  other nature reserves
wildlife watching
  Parque Nacional Lauca 189-90,
    191
  Parque Nacional Nevado Tres
    Cruces 240
  Parque Nacional Torres del Paine
    393
  Parque Tantauco 340
  Reserva Nacional Las Vicuñas 192
  Reserva Nacional Pingüino de
    Humboldt 243-4
  Reserva Nacional Río de los
    Cipreses 147
  Santuario de la Naturaleza Cascada
    de las Animas 118
  Valle Chacabuco 369
windsurfing 235
wine 29, 56-7
  books 55
  internet resources 55
  shopping 111, 471
wine regions 56-7
  Casablanca Valley 141
  Colchagua Valley 148
  Maipo Valley 118
  Maule Valley 157
wineries, *see* vineyards
women in Chile 47
women travelers 473-4
  health 494
work 474
World Heritage sites, *see* Unesco sites

Y
Yaghan (Yamaná) peoples 409, 413,
  414, 419

Z
Zapallar 140

GreenDex

GOING GREEN

The following listings have been selected by Lonely Planet authors because they demonstrate a commitment to sustainability. GreenDex eating selections support local producers or their devotion to the 'slow food' cause – so they might serve seasonal, locally sourced produce or meat on their menus. Accommodations may be considered environmentally friendly because of responsible water use, a commitment to recycling or energy conservation. Attractions listed are involved in conservation or environmental education. We also include local, grass-roots organizations and services worth supporting.

For more tips about traveling sustainably in Chile, turn to the Getting Started chapter (p21).

We want to keep developing our sustainable-travel content. If you think we've omitted a listing, or if you disagree with our choices, contact us at www.lonelyplanet.com/contact and set us straight for next time. For more information about sustainable tourism and Lonely Planet, see www.lonelyplanet.com/responsibletravel.

ARCHIPIÉLAGO JUAN FERNÁNDEZ
activities
Endémica Expediciones 435
attractions
Parque Nacional Juan Fernández 436

CHILOÉ
accommodations
Chepu Adventures 327
activities
Chepu Adventures 327
attractions
Parque Nacional Chiloé 337
Parque Tantauco 340

EASTER ISLAND
accommodations
Cabañas Mana Ora 451
Explora en Rapa Nui 456
Residencial Tita et Lionel 450
Te Ora 451
activities
Haumaka Tours 448
attractions
Parque Nacional Rapa Nui 67

MIDDLE CHILE
accommodations
Biota Maule 158
Ecobox Andino 162
attractions
Parque Nacional La Campana 141

Parque Nacional Laguna del Laja 169
Parque Nacional Nahuelbuta 172
Reserva Nacional Altos de Lircay 156
Reserva Nacional Radal Siete Tazas 152
Reserva Nacional Río de los Cipreses 146

NORTE CHICO
attractions
Parque Nacional Fray Jorge 261
Parque Nacional Llanos de Challe 242
Parque Nacional Nevado Tres Cruces 240
Parque Nacional Pan de Azúcar 233
Reserva Nacional Pingüino de Humboldt 243

NORTE GRANDE
accommodations
Posada Pueblo Taki 187
Eco-Truly 186
activities
Raices Andinas 181
attractions
Parque Nacional Lauca 189
Parque Nacional Volcán Isluga 202
Reserva Nacional Las Vicuñas 192

Reserva Nacional Los Flamencos 220
Reserva Nacional Pampa del Tamarugal 204
Valle de la Luna 220
eating
Eco-Truly 186

NORTHERN PATAGONIA
accommodations
Hostería Puma Verde 349
Hostería Mirador del Río 354
La Casa del Río Konaiken 368
Pioneer Patagonia 353
Rincón de la Nieve 353
activities
Casa del Turismo Rural 360
Festival Costumbrista 364
Patagonia Adventure Expeditions 368
attractions
Caleta Tortel 370
Parque Nacional Hornopirén 344
Parque Nacional Isla Magdalena 357
Parque Nacional Laguna San Rafael 364
Parque Nacional Queulat 355
Parque Pumalín 345
Reserva Nacional Cerro Castillo 364
Reserva Nacional Coyhaique 362

Reserva Nacional Jeinemeni 366
Reserva Nacional Río Simpson
363
Reserva Nacional Tamango 369
eating
Café Caleta Gonzalo 348

SANTIAGO

attractions
Reserva Nacional Río Clarillo 116
shopping
Artesanías de Chile 110
Centro de Exposición de Arte
Indígena 110
Ona 110

SOUTHERN PATAGONIA

accommodations
Cuatro Elementos
389
Hotel Las Torres 399

Imago Mundi 380
Nothofagus B&B 406
activities
Erratic Rock 388
attractions
Parque Marino Francisco Coloane
384
Parque Nacional Bernardo
O'Higgins 392
Parque Nacional Pali Aike 385
Parque Nacional Torres del Paine 393
eating
El Living 390
La Mesita Grande 390

SUR CHICO

accommodations
¡école! 282
Campo Aventura 311
activities
Patragon 280
Trafkura Expediciones 275

attractions
El Cañi 286
Huilo-Huilo Reserva Natural
Biosfera 289
Parque Nacional Conguillío 272
Parque Nacional Huerquehue
286
Parque Nacional Puyehue 299
Parque Nacional Tolhuaca 271
Parque Nacional Vicente Pérez
Rosales 308
Parque Nacional Villarrica 284
Parque Punta Curiñanco 294
Reserva Nacional Malalcahuello-
Nalcas 274-5
shopping
Fundación Chol-Chol 269

TIERRA DEL FUEGO

attractions
Estancia Yendegaia 412
Parque Yatana 419